Century 21 Accounting

10e Advanced

Wraparound Teacher's Edition

Claudia Bienias Gilbertson, CPA, PhD
Retired
North Hennepin Community College
Brooklyn Park, Minnesota

Mark W. Lehman, CPA, CFE, PhD
Associate Professor Emeritus
Richard C. Adkerson School of Accountancy
Mississippi State University
Starkville, Mississippi

Dan Passalacqua, MA
Retired
Oak Grove High School
San Jose, California

SOUTH-WESTERN
CENGAGE Learning

Australia • Brazil • Japan • Korea • Mexico • Singapore • Spain • United Kingdom • United States

SOUTH-WESTERN
CENGAGE Learning

Century 21 Accounting Advanced, Tenth Edition, Wraparound Teacher's Edition

Claudia Bienias Gilbertson, CPA, PhD
Mark W. Lehman, CPA, CFE, PhD
Dan Passalacqua, MA

Consulting Author: Debra Harmon Gentene

SVP Global Product Development—Research, School & Professional: Frank Menchaca

Executive Director of Marketing: Carolyn Pestritto

General Manager, K-12 School Group: CarolAnn Shindelar

Acquisitions Editor: Jeff Werle

Sr. Development Editor: Diane Bowdler

Sr. Content Project Manager: Martha Conway

Consulting Editor: Kenneth Martin

Media Developer: Lysa Kosins

Sr. Digital Content Operations Analyst: Ed Stubenrauch

Product Marketing Manager: Kelsey Hagan

Manufacturing Planner: Kevin Kluck

Production Service: Cenveo

Sr. Art Director: Michelle Kunkler

Cover and Internal Designer: Ke Design

Cover Image: © iStockphoto.com/Christopher Futcher

End of Lesson Image: © iStockphoto.com/urbanglimpses

Lesson Opener Images: © Robert Kneschke/Shutterstock.com; © iStockphoto.com/svetikd; © Lucky Business/Shutterstock.com; © Mike Flippo/Shutterstock.com

Intellectual Property Project Manager: Lisa Brown

Photo Researcher: Darren Wright

Text Permissions Researcher: PreMedia Global

© 2015, 2012 Cengage Learning

WCN: 01-100-101

ALL RIGHTS RESERVED. No part of this work covered by the copyright herein may be reproduced, transmitted, stored or used in any form or by any means graphic, electronic, or mechanical, including but not limited to photocopying, recording, scanning, digitizing, taping, Web distribution, information networks, or information storage and retrieval systems, except as permitted under Section 107 or 108 of the 1976 United States Copyright Act, without the prior written permission of the publisher.

For product information and technology assistance, contact us at **Cengage Learning Customer & Sales Support, 1-800-354-9706**

For permission to use material from this text or product, submit all requests online at **www.cengage.com/permissions**
Further permissions questions can be emailed to **permissionrequest@cengage.com**

Student Edition ISBN 13: 978-1-111-99064-0
Student Edition ISBN 10: 1-111-99064-6
Instructor's Edition ISBN 13: 978-1-133-10366-0
Instructor's Edition ISBN 10: 1-133-10366-9

Cengage Learning
200 First Stamford Place, 4th Floor
Stamford, CT 06902
USA

Microsoft Office Excel is a registered trademark of Microsoft Corporation.

Intuit and QuickBooks are registered trademarks of Intuit, Inc.

© 2013 Sage Software, Inc. All rights reserved. Sage, the Sage logos, and the Sage product and service names mentioned herein are the registered trademarks of Sage Software, Inc.

Cengage Learning is a leading provider of customized learning solutions with office locations around the globe, including Singapore, the United Kingdom, Australia, Mexico, Brazil, and Japan. Locate your local office at: **www.cengage.com/global**

Cengage Learning products are represented in Canada by Nelson Education, Ltd.

For your course and learning solutions, visit **www.cengage.com/school**
Visit our company website at **www.cengage.com**

The Career Clusters icons are being used with permission of the States' Career Clusters Initiative, 2010, **www.careerclusters.org**

All illustrations, tables, and graphs are © Cengage Learning.

Printed in the United States of America
2 3 4 5 6 7 20 19 18 17 16

Instructional Strategies Table of Contents

INSTRUCTIONAL STRATEGIES

MORE THAN A CENTURY OF INNOVATION

Featuring time-tested elements and ground-breaking innovations that set the standard, *Century 21 Accounting* has guided countless students to accounting success. In the 10th edition, the trusted approach and comprehensive support that have defined this market-leading text are even stronger. You will find a wealth of enhancements and updates, such as greater emphasis on conceptual understanding and financial statement analysis; new features and real-world examples that encourage learning; emphasis on critical thinking and technology use identified as core skills needed for 21st Century workers; and integrated commercial technology coverage to keep students involved, connected, and a step ahead of today's changing business times.

A Reorganized, Clear Approach

Using the proven teaching techniques that have been trusted for years, *Century 21 Accounting Advanced, 10e* continues to extend coverage from the first-year course. Students begin the Advanced course by reviewing some of the topics learned in the first-year course. The remaining parts of the text explore various aspects of accounting, including accounting control systems, accounting adjustments, management and cost accounting, and not-for-profit accounting.

Knowing that performance indicators are essential in today's classroom, learning objectives are now labeled in each chapter and tied to main headings and end-of-chapter problems, making measurement and reteaching easier and more effective.

Short, Accessible Lessons

Each chapter is divided into 2-4 short, accessible lessons that cover one or two concepts each, for maximum understanding. Corresponding assessment activities, which include application problems, allow for immediate feedback. You can use these end-of-lesson pages to make sure that students fully understand all concepts and procedures before moving on to the next lesson. This Wraparound Teacher's Edition contains comprehensive lesson plans for each lesson, which allows you to plan your instructional time with greater efficiency.

Problems, Problems, Problems

Century 21 Accounting 10E gives students numerous short problems. Many of the end-of-chapter problems can be completed using Automated Accounting Online, Sage 50, QuickBooks, and/or Microsoft Excel software.

INNOVATIONS THAT REACH TODAY'S STUDENTS

The *Century 21 Accounting* 10E package offers a wealth of materials that feature both time-tested methods and ground-breaking innovations.

Integrated Technology Tools

Century 21 Accounting 10E offers a perfect blend of cutting-edge technology to engage and assist students.

- *Online Working Papers* takes the work out of homework—boosting students' grades while reducing instructors' course preparation time and effort. Students can enhance their skills with practice problems, receive immediate feedback, and complete assigned homework, all from the convenience of their computers.
- The *MindTap Reader eBook* contains digital material that offers the same rich visuals and illustrations as the printed text.
- *Automated Accounting Online* is integrated into every chapter of the textbook and combines the functionality of commercial software with proven educational features to make teaching and learning easier.
- A Sage 50 Accounting symbol in the textbook denotes end-of-chapter problems that can be worked with Sage 50.
- A QuickBooks symbol in the textbook denotes end-of-chapter problems that can be worked with QuickBooks.
- An Excel symbol in the textbook denotes end-of-chapter problems and feature activities that can be worked with Microsoft Excel.
- The *Accounting website* offers a variety of resources and provides opportunities for enrichment and assessment.

Special Features and Activities

Exciting special features and activities in the textbook enhance the accounting instruction to add interest to the course.

These extended learning features and activities present numerous opportunities to implement Common Core Standards through interdisciplinary studies. Practice is provided in the common core areas of English Language Arts & Literacy and Mathematical Practice. Many of these activities require short, critical-thinking and decision-making responses that apply reading, writing, speaking, listening, language, media and technology, and mathematical skills.

- *Accounting in the Real World* describes a real company and provides students with a big-picture introduction to each chapter. It contains critical-thinking questions that are linked to the chapter content, and students are asked to consider them while reading the chapter.
- *Think Like an Accountant* presents challenging problems related to chapter concepts that correspond to higher level skills based on the criteria established in Bloom's Taxonomy. It asks students the following questions: Once an accountant accurately records and analyzes data, what does he or she do with the information? How does the analysis inform or determine best practices? Students will use Excel template files to complete their analysis to see how decisions affect the company's bottom line.
- *Ethics in Action* recognizes ethical dilemmas, both real and fictitious, in the workplace. It asks students to consider the actions one might take in a variety of situations and determine their consequences or possible outcomes. Students learn to understand complicated concepts in the business world such as integrity and confidentiality.
- *Global Awareness* merges two features from the previous edition (Cultural Diversity and Global Perspectives) into one feature. It presents the role of accounting in a global environment and the

cultural implications that occur as a result of the trans-migratory nature of the marketplace.

- *Financial Literacy* will guide your students in exploring financial literacy topics that meet national guidelines created by the National Endowment for Financial Education (NEFE) and Jump$tart Coalition. Financial literacy topics such as credit, savings, insurance, investments, take-home pay, taxes, and budgets, integrated with 21st century skills, will provide students with a foundation on which to make sound financial decisions for a lifetime.
- *Forensic Accounting* is a new feature that provides fictitious fraud scenarios emulating real world possibilities.
- *Careers in Accounting* promotes accounting as a profession. It introduces students to fictitious people working as accountants or in careers where accounting knowledge is valuable. Topics include entry-level job requirements, career paths, and projected trends for future employment.
- *Why Accounting?* This feature provides examples of how accounting skills are applicable in a variety of business situations. It demonstrates how accounting knowledge transfers into the workplace and validates accounting's importance in the marketplace.
- *A Look at Accounting Software* shows windows/screens from a fictional accounting software program. The objective is to help students understand that what they are learning to do manually still applies when computers are used.
- End-of-lesson activities and problems provide reinforcement. *Terms Review* lists new accounting terms introduced in the lesson. *Audit Your Understanding* questions provide an informal review of comprehension. *Work Together* problems offer the opportunity for the instructor and the students to work as a group to complete a problem based on the lesson before proceeding to independent work. *On Your Own* problems provide the student's first opportunity to work a short problem, based on the content covered in the lesson. On Your Own is designed to mirror the concepts and procedures covered in Work Together.
- End-of-chapter problems are linked to the content of the lessons. *Application Problems* are provided so that students can apply their learning to extended problems. *Mastery Problems* integrate the learning from all the lessons into one problem and demonstrate mastery of the chapter content. *Challenge Problems* stretch students to apply their learning to slightly different applications.
- *Using Source Documents* and *Auditing for Errors* provide students with specific situations in which they can analyze and investigate accounting tools.
- *Analyzing Home Depot's Financial Statements* allows students to examine a real business's annual report and financial documents and put their knowledge to work.
- *21st Century Skills* provides activities that cultivate mastery of essential skills and helps students develop personal characteristics that are linked to success in life and work, as established by the Partnership for 21st Century Skills.

STUDENT SUPPORT MATERIALS

Major student supplements aid student understanding and reinforcement of skills.

Working Papers

Using the Working Papers is the most efficient method of assuring that students complete problems accurately and in the least time necessary. Each workbook provides sufficient ruled paper for completing the Work Together problems, On Your Own problems, Source Documents Problems, Application Problems, Mastery Problems, Challenge Problems, and Reinforcement Activities 1–4. In addition, Study Guides present objective questions and matching exercises for terminology that cover the presentation of each chapter.

All Working Papers volumes have accompanying Teacher's Editions.

Recycling Problem Working Papers

For each chapter, Recycling Problems provide an additional problem for students who need more reinforcement after completing the Application and Mastery Problems. The narrative of the recycling problems is in Appendix C of the student text. The Recycling Problems Working Papers provide ruled paper for completing these problems.

The Recycling Problem Working Papers workbook has an accompanying Teacher's Edition.

Simulations

Manual and automated simulations give students hands-on, real-world experience in accounting practice. The simulations available are as follows:

Organic Aisles, a departmentalized organic grocery store organized as a corporation, is recommended for use after Part 1.

Adventure Gear, a merchandising business organized as a corporation, is recommended for use after Part 3.

All manual simulations have accompanying Teacher's Keys.

ORGANIZATION OF THE TEXT

The student text is organized in a logical manner. Learning progresses from the simple to the complex both within a given Part and across Parts as similar topics are treated in progressively more detail in each succeeding Part.

- The **Part Opener page** lists the chapter titles in the Part.
- The **Chart of Accounts** provides a point of reference for account titles and numbers.
- The **Chapter Opener page** shows a list of the learning objectives and a preview of the terms to be defined.
- **Accounting vocabulary terms** are carefully defined in complete sentences and highlighted in color.
- The chapters feature many **illustrations**, most of which include steps indicated within the illustrations.
- **End-of-Lesson activities** include Terms Review, Audit Your Understanding, Work Together, and On Your Own.
- **End-of-Chapter activities** include Explore Accounting; Application, Mastery, and Challenge Problems; 21st Century Skills, Auditing for Errors; and Analyzing Home Depot's Financial Statements.
- **A Look at Accounting Software**, provided in Chapters 1–10, 15, and 20, describes how accounting activities are automated.
- **Reinforcement Activities** in Parts 1–4 synthesize all learning from the Part. These activities can be used by students to prepare

for success at FBLA and BPA competitive events. The *Winning Edge* logo directs students to the *Winning Edge* website (cengage .com/winningedge) for additional information.

- **Appendices** present Accounting Concepts; Home Depot's Financial Statements; Recycling Problems; and Answers to Audit Your Understanding.
- English and Spanish **Glossaries** list and define the vocabulary terms from the text.
- A detailed **Index** directs the reader to the appropriate pages covered in each entry.
- A **Features Index** guides the reader to specific feature topics throughout the book.

USING SOFTWARE AND TECHNOLOGY

After manual accounting procedures are mastered, computer software may be used as an enrichment activity to facilitate the processing of accounting data and the use of computers in accounting.

Several technology-related products are available to use with *Century 21 Accounting* 10E to augment teacher instruction: Online Working Papers; Automated Accounting Online and its accompanying data files; Sage 50 Accounting and its accompanying data files; QuickBooks and its accompanying data files; Microsoft Excel data files; and the website. Software applicable to individual chapters is noted in lesson plans and interleaf pages. An Automated Accounting Online icon in the student textbook denotes end-of-chapter problems that can be worked with Automated Accounting Online. A Sage 50 Accounting icon denotes problems that can be worked with Sage 50. A QuickBooks icon denotes problems that can be worked with QuickBooks. In addition, a Microsoft Excel icon in the textbook denotes end-of-chapter problems and feature activities that can be worked with Microsoft Excel software.

Online Working Papers

This homework solution helps students to enhance their skills with practice problems and to complete assigned homework while receiving immediate feedback. An integrated gradebook allows you to track students' progress and review their completed assignments online.

Automated Accounting Online

Automated Accounting Online may be used to complete selected end-of-chapter problems, all four Reinforcement Activities, and both simulations.

You may choose to demonstrate the operation of Automated Accounting Online. A good method would be to open a data file provided for the chapter being covered. You can then enter sample transactions from the end-of-chapter problem corresponding to the data file.

Accounting with Sage 50

Various end-of-chapter and Reinforcement Activity problems in *Century 21 Accounting* are marked with a Sage 50 Accounting symbol, which indicates that the problems can be worked with *Sage 50 Accounting.*

Accounting with QuickBooks

Various end-of-chapter and Reinforcement Activity problems in *Century 21 Accounting* are marked with a QuickBooks symbol, which indicates that the problems can be worked with *QuickBooks.*

Microsoft Excel

A Microsoft icon in the textbook denotes end-of-chapter problems and some feature activities that can be worked with Microsoft Excel software already possessed by the school or student. Excel data files are located on the companion website.

Accounting Website

This online learning and study tool offers an interactive learning experience for students, with online opportunities for enrichment and assessment, such as the following:

- Crossword puzzles
- Spanish and English glossaries
- PowerPoint slides
- Sage 50 data files
- QuickBooks data files
- Excel data files
- Lesson plans

USING THE WRAPAROUND TEACHER'S EDITION

The Wraparound Teacher's Edition has margin notes next to reduced student pages that contain lesson plans for each lesson of each chapter; teaching suggestions that address relevant topics; answers to features; and check figures for end-of-chapter problems.

Chapter Interleaf Pages

Preceding each chapter, interleaf pages contain grids to assist you in planning the presentation of the chapter.

Lesson Plans

A complete lesson plan is printed in the margins of the Wraparound Teacher's Edition for each lesson in each chapter. In addition, modified lesson plans are provided for the beginning of each part and chapter, as well as for the end-of-chapter pages. A typical plan for each chapter is as follows:

Introductory Pages

- **Overview.** The opener page for each of the Parts describes the chapter content of all the chapters in that Part, as well as opportunities to integrate accounting software, the simulation, and the reinforcement activity that are appropriate for that Part.
- **Chart of Accounts.** The chart of accounts page has a list of important points about the chart of accounts for that Part.
- **Introduce the Chapter.** The chapter opener sets the stage and helps to guide the students into a receptive frame of mind by generating curiosity and providing a frame of reference for the chapter. The three sections in Introduce the Chapter are: (1) Guiding Questions, (2) Preview Chapter Objectives, and (3) Preview Accounting Terms.
- **Accounting in the Real World.** This feature appears on the second page of each chapter. This section of the teaching suggestions gives suggested answers to the questions asked of the students.

Lesson Plan for Each Lesson

Every lesson in every chapter has its own lesson plan. The following elements are included in each lesson plan:

- **Bridge.** The Bridge section relates previous lessons to the objectives of the new lesson through suggested questions, examples, or group discussion topics and activities. The Teaching Resources list shows the transparency masters, software, and working papers available for the lesson.

- **Engage.** This section suggests ways to connect and engage students in the lesson content, with emphasis on student participation/involvement. A Preview subheading suggests ways to encourage students to preview the lesson using good study habits.
- **Input.** Items detailed are the points that should be emphasized in the presentation of the lesson.
- **Model**. This section describes how to demonstrate accounting procedures. You may wish to vary the order of presentation of the Input and Model sections to fit the needs of the classroom.
- **Formative Assessment.** Ongoing assessment allows you to observe and respond to student questions and practice problems as students apply their learning. A Troubleshooting section describes problems students typically have with the content of the lesson.
- **Check for Understanding.** Terms Review and Audit Your Understanding questions provide a verbal checkpoint before applying the lesson.
- **Guided Practice.** The Work Together problems are the means for providing guided practice. The instructor and students do the suggested guided practice activities together. Your role is to demonstrate, monitor, observe, and answer questions.
- **Independent Practice.** Students perform suggested independent practice activities by themselves. The On Your Own and Application Problems are the means for providing independent practice for the lesson.
- **Reteach.** The Reteach suggestions give specific means of reteaching the lesson.
- **Closure.** Closure suggestions describe ways to review and reinforce the lesson. Essential Questions can be used to end the lesson to create inquiry and conceptional connections for the future.
- **Essential Questions.** Essential Questions probe for deeper meaning and promote inquiry and conceptual connections for future learning.
- **Extended Learning.** Suggestions for feature assignments take students beyond the traditional assignments.

End of Chapter

The end-of-chapter pages also contain a lesson plan. Different activities are suggested for completing the chapter.

- **Closure.** This section suggests a summarizing activity.
- **Independent Practice.** Mastery and Challenge Problems bring together all lessons of the chapter. In addition, this section specifies ancillary products (such as Study Guides, Online Working Papers, and the website) that are appropriate for independent practice.
- **Formative Assessment.** Solutions are reviewed, and reteaching is conducted as needed.
- **Reteach.** Recycling Problems are available for reteaching purposes.
- **Extended Learning.** Included in this section are suggestions for activities to extend the chapter presentation.
- **Summative Evaluation.** Formal assessment instruments (tests) are suggested.

Teaching Suggestions

In addition to the lesson plans, notes in the side and bottom margins of the Wraparound Teacher's Edition describe various teaching strategies or tips.

1. *Teaching Ideas:* These creative tips bring the lessons to life.
2. *Suggestions Related to Differentiated Instruction:* Aligned with instructional objectives, these strategies take into account learner preferences, multiple intelligences, gifted, English as a Second Language (ESL), and Limited English Proficiency (LEP). They can be categorized in the following areas:
    - Visual/Spatial
    - Interpersonal
    - Intrapersonal
    - Tactile/Kinesthetic
    - Auditory/Linguistic
    - Musical
    - Mathematical/Logical
    - ESL/LEP
    - Gifted
3. *Suggestions Related to Student Features:* Many activities present opportunities to implement Common Core Standards in the areas of English Language Arts & Literacy and Mathematical Practice through interdisciplinary studies. These notes highlight special student features and their solutions:
    - Accounting in the Real World
    - Ethics in Action
    - Think Like an Accountant
    - Global Awareness
    - Why Accounting?
    - Financial Literacy
    - Forensic Accounting
    - Careers in Accounting
    - A Look at Accounting Software
    - Explore Accounting
    - 21st Century Skills
    - Analyzing Home Depot's Financial Statements
    - Auditing for Errors

Check Figures

Check figures are given for end-of-chapter activities and reinforcement activities. When student solutions match these check figures, it can be assumed that the student's solutions are significantly correct.

OTHER RESOURCES FOR INSTRUCTORS

In addition to this Wraparound Teacher's Edition, the *Century 21 Accounting* 10E package contains a host of instructor resources for preparation, presentation, and testing—all designed to minimize your time while maximizing your impact within the classroom.

- The *Instructor's Resource CD-ROM* is an all-in-one convenient tool, offering PowerPoint teaching presentations, solutions to working papers and tests, Spanish and English accounting glossaries, and numerous supplemental materials to support you.

- The *Instructor's Resource Kit* contains solutions to Working Papers, Recycling Problems Working Papers, tests, and manual simulations.
- *Teacher's Editions of Working Papers, Recycling Problems,* and *Tests* show all the student editions with answers in place, for easy use by instructors.

STRATEGIES FOR OPTIMIZING INDIVIDUAL LEARNING

The student population not only reflects the cultural diversity in American society as a whole, but it also consists of students with different abilities and styles of learning. Many of these individual student differences require an adjustment in teaching style or presentation. This section describes teaching strategies for students with different learning abilities and styles, and cooperative learning.

Teaching Strategies for Students with Different Learning Abilities

Classrooms typically contain students with a wide variation of ability, intelligence, and motivation. Although the instructor must direct a majority of the instruction to the "average" student, optimal learning will occur only when the curriculum is modified to meet the needs of each individual student.

The first and greatest challenge facing the instructor is identifying the special abilities of each student. Learning disabilities can be very difficult to detect and categorize. Classifying students solely on examination scores and prior classroom performance may be misleading and should be avoided. For example, poor subject examination scores and short attention spans may be the symptoms of either a student with a specific learning disability or a gifted student who is bored.

The correct assessment of students should be a combined effort of the instructor, the school counselor or special education instructor, and the student. Together, this team can design an individualized program that will challenge the student while providing adequate opportunity to achieve attainable goals.

Gifted Students

One objective of programs for gifted students should be the development of leadership skills. Current literature suggests that four skill areas are involved in the development of effective leadership.

1. *Cognition*—The ability to identify, research, and learn factual knowledge.
2. *Problem Solving*—The ability to identify problems and develop creative solutions.
3. *Interpersonal Communication*—The ability to work with other people.
4. *Decision Making*—The ability to develop and implement realistic goals and evaluate performance of the goals.

Different hemispheres of the brain control these functions. Cognition and problem solving are typically associated with left-brain functions; interpersonal communication and decision making are associated with right-brain functions. Therefore, effective leadership training must target development of both hemispheres. Most students will enter the classroom with stronger development in some skill areas than in others. Thus, a student lacking interpersonal communication skills should undertake projects to develop those skills.

The Ethics in Action activities in the student textbook provide opportunities for gifted students to develop these leadership skills. Encourage gifted students to extend these activities by developing related activities.

Gifted students may need to move through the accounting program at an accelerated pace. It may not be appropriate for gifted students to work every problem provided. For example, after a chapter has been reviewed, gifted students may demonstrate mastery by working only the Mastery or Recycling Problem. Others may need to work one or more of the Application Problems. The Challenge Problem should always be assigned to gifted students to provide the "stretch" for exploring alternatives to the chapter content.

Additional activities might include the following:

1. Gifted students should master transaction analysis quickly; therefore, challenge them to identify a special research project that interests them. The students should be encouraged to identify a project that requires interaction with a businessperson. For example, a student could contact a bank loan officer to learn how a proprietor would apply for a loan, research formats for a business plan, and develop a business plan for a hypothetical business. Finally, the student could invite the bank loan officer to class and use role-playing to demonstrate how communication skills can enhance an individual's chance of getting the loan.
2. Using gifted students as tutors for other students can be an effective way of teaching the topics students find most difficult. Allow the gifted student to complete one of these chapters while the class completes the first chapters of a Part. The gifted students can then assist you in presenting the concepts and procedures on their chapter to the class. Encourage the students to use visual aids and develop methods to assess student learning.

Limited English Proficiency Students

Limited English Proficiency (LEP) students are individuals whose native or dominant language is a language other than English. Although these students may be involved in special English-as-a-Second-Language (ESL) classes, the instructor can significantly improve learning by adopting several strategies.

1. Provide students with translations of key terms prior to presenting each chapter. Encourage students to use dictionaries.
2. Create visual instructional methods, such as posters and bulletin boards, that reinforce accounting concepts in both English and the other dominant language(s).
3. At early levels, LEP students have limited comprehension of English and can respond with one- or two-word answers. Assess understanding by having students match, choose, move, draw, or point. Students at this level can respond to directions that require them to name, list, categorize, label, or reply with one or two words.
4. Allow for longer pauses when you ask questions. Non-native speakers need more time to formulate their answers.
5. Speak directly. Avoid negative constructions and passive verbs, such as "Don't forget that Cash is not debited in this transaction." Instead say, "Remember to credit Cash in this transaction."
6. Rather than asking students whether they understand what you have said, ask them to restate what you have said in their own words.

7. Adjust the length of time allotted to complete assignments and tests. Remember that the primary objective is to assess knowledge of accounting rather than the ability to translate and comprehend the question or problem.
8. Be cautious if there are no interruptions or questions. It may mean that very little has been understood.

Additional activities might include the following:

1. Recruit businesspersons willing to act as mentors for LEP students. These mentors should be invited to speak to the class and periodically meet with LEP students to assist with assignments. The instructor should be actively involved in any meetings with LEP students to show support for both the mentor and the students.
2. Although LEP students may feel handicapped in the classroom, their knowledge of two languages provides them with excellent career opportunities in today's international business environment. LEP students should identify what unique career opportunities exist for them in various types of organizations, such as international businesses and government. Students could create a bulletin board to inform other students of these opportunities. Successful bulletin boards could also be used in the classrooms of younger students, or in elementary schools.

Specific Learning Disability (SLD) Students

Instructors need not be reminded that adolescence is a period of turmoil and adjustment. What many instructors often view as adolescent behavior may, however, be caused by a student's specific learning disability (SLD). The correct assessment of SLD students is difficult because some adolescent behavior is similar to the typical characteristics of SLD students.

- Passive Learners. When faced with making a decision, SLD students avoid making a decision in favor of waiting for an instructor to provide specific direction.
- Poor Self-Concept. Years of failure cause SLD students to have low self-esteem, thus reducing their confidence that they can achieve academic success.
- Inept Social Skills. SLD students often have difficulty making and keeping friends.
- Attention Deficits. SLD students often lack the ability to concentrate on one topic for an extended period.
- Lack of Motivation. Years of failure have conditioned SLD students to doubt their abilities and therefore view their efforts as being futile.

Once an SLD student is correctly assessed, the instructor should work with the student to develop an individualized program. The basic objective of the program should be the development of functional (life) skills. The student should be counseled to establish challenging yet attainable goals and provide frequent feedback as to the attainment of these goals. The student's academic success should be measured on the demonstrated ability to learn as much as the mastery of a defined body of knowledge.

Several general instructional strategies are effective in teaching SLD students:

1. When asking questions during class, ask SLD students questions that they can likely answer successfully. Save more difficult or unstructured questions for better students.
2. Rotate instructional materials rather than trying to complete a single text. Supplemental instructional materials may include additional texts, business magazines, government publications, etc.
3. Encourage students to maintain a daily log or journal that describes their academic progress. Students can share this log, if they desire, with you when updating their individual program.
4. When feasible, SLD students should become involved in work-study programs that are consistent with course content. When work-study opportunities are unavailable, simulations can be used to provide a simulated work environment. Field trips are an excellent method to expose students to the business world.

Additional activities might include the following:

1. The popular board game Monopoly is well known as an enjoyable way to practice mathematical skills. The game also provides students the opportunity to analyze and record their transactions. Playing Monopoly enables students to see how transaction analysis and the accounting equation provide information for business decisions.
2. Many students will ultimately work in inventory-related jobs. Simulating the inventory of a business will enable students to actively participate in the accounting for inventory. For example, students could establish a classroom store carrying school supplies, snacks, or other low-cost items. The students would record the purchase and sales transactions and update the perpetual inventory. Students would periodically take inventory and reconcile the periodic and perpetual inventory quantities.

At-Risk Students

Many environmental factors may negatively affect a student's ability and motivation to succeed academically. Any student who is a potential dropout may be classified as an at-risk student. At-risk students typically are deficient in mathematics, reading, and language skills. These students provide a unique challenge to the accounting instructor because the instructor has little, if any, power to correct problems in the home environment.

Effective instructional strategies for at-risk students should be based on the premise that all individuals have a need for achievement and social acceptance. Within the accounting classroom, these needs can be fulfilled by developing a curriculum that promotes academic success and acceptance by the instructor. Techniques for working with at-risk students include the following:

1. Develop a personal profile of the student. Avoid placing too much significance on past academic performance as this may represent a symptom rather than the underlying problem.
2. Together with the student, develop an individualized program that allows the student to attain both short-term and long-term goals. When identifying goals, consider the student's anticipated career goals.
3. Modify presentation strategies to include more visual displays, and supplement explanations with current, realistic examples.
4. Organize field trips and mentor programs to expose students to the business environment.

Additional activities might include the following:

1. Assist students to understand how accounting is a useful skill in careers that interest them. This could be accomplished in many ways. For example, a student who shows interest in auto mechanics could be introduced to the owner of a local auto repair

business. The student could then report his/her observations in oral or written form. If no mentor is available, trade magazines often present articles to assist their readers in managing their businesses.

2. Many at-risk students can become motivated to begin self-improvement only when they recognize that they have a need to improve. One method of promoting self-evaluation is to have students identify the qualities they would require of another individual. Have students imagine that they are partners in a business that is considering hiring employees for both service and office positions. Require the student to prepare a job description that includes both skill and personal characteristics that applicants should possess. This activity should enable students to compare their qualifications with the job descriptions they have developed.

Visually Impaired Students

Students with mild visual impairments are typically mainstreamed and may elect to enroll in accounting. The nature and degree of students' visual impairments will vary. A student's visual impairment may include a difficulty in reading print, an inability to distinguish colors, sensitivity to light, and/or a limited field of vision. The instructor must identify each student's exact impairment and adapt teaching strategies appropriately.

Many sources exist for providing alternative teaching materials. Most states have schools for the blind and rehabilitation service agencies that can enlarge the textbook and working papers. Consult these organizations to identify the latest technologies available for assisting the students.

The instructor and student should develop an individualized program that establishes a time frame for achieving specific learning objectives. The learning objectives should be consistent with the student's anticipated career goals. The time frame should consider the student's impairment and the availability of technical assistance, such as enlarged materials and closed circuit television. The use of software should not be overlooked for visually impaired students, particularly if oversized monitors with larger displays are available.

Additional activities might include the following:

1. It is important for visually impaired students to have confidence in their ability to participate fully within the business world. Require students to prepare an oral or written report that profiles a successful visually impaired business professional.
2. New technologies are continually being developed that help visually impaired students to participate fully in both school and business. Students must be aware of these technologies and know how to continually learn of new technologies. Using government agencies as a resource, assist the students in preparing a report concerning anticipated technologies.

Teaching Strategies for Students with Different Learning Styles

There are many different learning styles. Some people learn best from reading material. Others need to see a demonstration or learn by feeling. Still others may learn best from auditory cues. It is important to remember, however, that no matter what learning style works best for any individual, learning style is not an indicator of intelligence. Two people of similar levels of intelligence may learn best in two different styles of learning. Learning style is also not necessarily a rigid behavior. Many individuals may have a dominant learning style; however, most also have the flexibility to adapt their learning styles to the demands of the material to be learned. Different learning styles include print, visual, auditory, tactile, and kinesthetic learning.

Print Learners

The print learner prefers to see the data in print—preferably printed in words.

1. When introducing the T account, a print learner would prefer to study the illustration in the textbook which shows a T account, labeled with the words *DEBIT* and *CREDIT.*
2. When covering journal entries, you should discuss the entries, using the textbook examples and referring to the textbook. The print learner can later go back and study the entries.
3. When learning how to post, the print learner would prefer to see the process in print. This can be done by distributing a handout that explains the steps in the posting process. Allow the student to study the handout.

Visual Learners

The visual learner needs to *see* the concept. One way for the learner to see the concept is mental visualization. Illustrations and visual aids are important to the visual learner.

1. Ask the student (with eyes closed) to picture a T account. The student should be able to see both sides of the account. Next, the student should visualize the word *DEBIT* on the left side of the account. Finally, the student should visualize the word *CREDIT* on the right side of the account. Once this concept takes on a visual form, the student will be able to access it when needed.
2. When covering journal entries, you should discuss the entries, using a transparency or the chalkboard to record the entry. In addition, the student should be asked to mentally picture each part of the entry before you actually write it on the transparency or chalkboard.
3. To teach posting, you could use a transparency to assist in the lecture. The transparency could be (1) a blank transparency that you complete or (2) a prepared transparency that uses arrows to trace the steps involved in posting.

Auditory Learners

The auditory learner will best learn by hearing. Auditory learners who read a textbook chapter benefit from hearing reinforcement of key concepts spoken out loud.

1. When introducing the T account, have the student say out loud that "the left side is the debit side of the account." Repeating this statement a few times will increase the chances of its being reinforced. Repeat the process with the statement "the right side is the credit side of the account."
2. To reinforce the learning of journal entries, the auditory learner should verbally repeat the analysis of the transaction. The student should also verbally list the steps involved in making the entry.

3. When learning how to post, the auditory learner would prefer to hear the steps involved in posting. This can be done via a live lecture or a taped tutorial. To reinforce learning, the student could recite the posting steps to another student or group of students.

Tactile Learners

The tactile learner learns best by touching or handling objects.

1. Using play money, have the student touch the right side of the desk and place an amount of money on it to reinforce an amount in the right side or credit side of an account. Repeat the process for the left/debit side.
2. Tactile learners may benefit from using the computer to key journal entries and then print reports. The student should be encouraged to place a finger on each account title in the journal entries report and trace it over to the amount in the amount column of the report to check it for accuracy. Tactile learners should also be given the opportunity to journalize transactions from at least one simulation that contains source documents, which must be handled to analyze, journalize, and file.
3. The tactile learner can use a group of index cards to represent the general ledger. Each card should represent an account and should have three vertical lines to distinguish between the debit and credit columns, and balance columns. Have the tactile learner post each example of a journal entry to the appropriate cards (accounts).

Kinesthetic Learners

The kinesthetic learner learns best by taking an active part in the instruction. Motion is an important part of kinesthetic learning.

1. Have the student draw a T account in the air or use a finger to draw a T account on the back of the hand or arm. Next, have the student label the left side with the word *DEBIT* and the right side with the word *CREDIT.*
2. The kinesthetic learner would prefer to participate in the posting process. Use a transparency of the ledger account and have each student complete one or more steps of the posting process at the overhead projector. Other students can be completing the posting process individually on printed ledger accounts.
3. Provide the opportunity to perform the calculations to solve formulas. Calculators or computerized spreadsheet programs may be used.

COOPERATIVE LEARNING

Cooperative learning activities should be an integral part of accounting pedagogical strategies. Cooperative learning involves small heterogeneous groups of students who work together to share the responsibility for learning. Cooperative learning activities should be designed with the following goals in mind:

1. All students should be able to participate.
2. Groups should be heterogeneous.
3. Each student needs to be held accountable for his or her contribution to the group.

Cooperative learning is more successful with heterogeneous rather than homogeneous groups. Research further supports cooperative learning as a teaching strategy to increase students' motivation, achievement, and behavior. You should select team members for a cooperative learning activity. Group composition should include a mixture of gender, ability level, cultural or ethnic background, and learning style. For example, placing a visual learner with an auditory learner enhances and strengthens the group's performance. Group members should be rotated frequently.

The time needed to complete an activity will vary among groups. Therefore, you need to provide additional activities to be completed by groups as they finish. These activities might include, for example, specific questions about the activity. These additional activities are often referred to as debriefing.

Cooperative learning promotes the development of higher-order thinking skills where brighter students explain concepts or principles to slower students. Using higher-order thinking skills to articulate ideas in accounting will normally result in the material being learned more effectively with improved retention rates.

To be successful, each student must be held accountable for his/her contribution to the cooperative learning activity. A variety of evaluation methods may be employed. These methods may include (1) a short quiz taken individually, (2) instructor observation of individual contributions to a group activity, or (3) bonus points assigned to individuals only if all group members do well individually. Performance on cooperative learning activities in accounting should range from no more than 5 to 10 percent of the final grade.

One of the goals of cooperative learning is to have students work out the roles of the group members themselves. Some groups will assign a role to an individual, such as when a representative of the group will need to record results and present them to the class, and sometimes individuals within a group will assume roles within the group without being asked to do so.

Some cooperative learning activities are as follows:

1. *Assign a research project:* Assign students to groups of two. Each group researches the financial statements (through the annual report) of a company in which they are interested, perhaps because they are familiar with the product. Students look for a list of specific items such as what kinds of stock the corporation is authorized to issue, what categories of assets are listed on the balance sheet, the total of current liabilities, whether net income increased/decreased from the previous period, and so on. The group must then plan and deliver a presentation of the data to the entire class. Additional time outside class is needed to complete research and prepare the presentation. Time frame: 45 minutes.
2. *Explain what component percentages measure.* Assign students to groups of three. Each group is to plan, prepare, and deliver a presentation to *non-accountants.* The presentation should explain what component percentages are and how they are used to analyze financial statements. Time frame: 30 minutes over several class periods.
3. *Divide the class into groups of two or three students each.* Have each group discuss and prepare a list of service businesses found in the local community. Each group should appoint a leader who will present the list of businesses and services to the class. Time frame: 20 minutes.

4. *Divide the class into two groups.* Each group stands and faces each other. The instructor or a student moderator states an accounting term. The first student to raise a hand has the opportunity to give the correct definition. The group with the most correctly defined terms is declared the winner. As an alternative to this game, the instructor or moderator may read the definition of a term, such as "anything of value that is owned," while the groups must identify the term. If you wish to imitate a popular television show, the answer should be given in a question format, such as "What is an asset?"
5. *Assign reinforcement activities:* Assign reinforcement activities as homework. Divide the class into groups of two students each. Each pair of students exchange and evaluate each other's work in class. Students are permitted to correct their work, based on their partner's evaluation. Time frame: 15 minutes.
6. *Divide the class into groups of two or three students each.* Each group will discuss and prepare a list of merchandising businesses found in the local community. The group-appointed leader presents to the class the list and merchandise being sold. Time frame: 25 minutes.
7. *Divide the class into auditing groups of three or four students per group.* Each auditing group is responsible for assisting other class members as well as correcting homework assignments. A lead auditor is appointed by the group and is responsible for turning in completed homework assignments for each group member to the instructor.

SUGGESTIONS FOR TEACHING BUSINESS ETHICS

Businesses have recently become aware of the severe implications of unethical behavior on the part of employees. In response, many businesses have begun training their employees to make ethical decisions and establishing company codes of conduct. The message from businesses today is clear—employees must be capable of making ethical decisions to protect the business from legal liability and to maximize long-term profits.

Most students' principles of right and wrong are well established prior to their enrolling in high school accounting. Thus, the presentation of business ethics does not involve the teaching of right and wrong. Instead, students need to learn how to apply their principles of right and wrong to business situations.

Ethics in Action

There are 24 Ethics in Action features in this text to give instructors an opportunity to teach ethics in the accounting class.

Steps for Analyzing Ethical Situations

In Chapter 2, a four-step ethical model is presented to help students analyze the ethics of an action. This approach encourages students to collect pertinent information that will provide a basis for their decision. Ultimately, students' decisions are based on their personal ethics applied to the facts of the situation.

Assessment

Correct solutions are generally obvious if the action is either illegal or violates a business or professional standard. For example, most students will agree that it is unethical to dispose of hazardous waste into the water supply. However, students may challenge compliance with other laws and standards. A class discussion of whether the truck drivers of a business should be required to drive the speed limit and wear safety belts may demonstrate many students' willingness to disregard selected laws.

Many of the situations in the Ethics in Action activities involve circumstances where the line between right and wrong is unclear. As a result, students will likely differ in their decisions as to whether the action is ethical. Assessment of Ethics in Action activities should be based on the students' analysis of the facts and the objective support for their decisions.

You can adopt several strategies to cover an Ethics in Action activity. The activity can be presented initially as a classroom discussion. Alternately, the activity can be assigned as an individual or group project. Whichever method is used, students should be given the opportunity to discuss the case in class. This exchange of ideas enables students to observe how other individuals make and support their decisions. When asking questions and making observations, you should be careful not to reveal your personal bias.

Suggested Solutions for Some Ethics in Action Features

Chapter 2: A Business Lunch Light on Business

This case, by design, contains what some students might consider to be a minor issue. The fact that no business was ultimately discussed at this meeting is an insignificant issue. It is logical to assume that the lunch will be the first step in Samantha's efforts to book the conference. But her misrepresentation of the purpose of the meeting appears to be a clear violation of the code. Thus, Samantha has demonstrated a willingness to overlook the code. This action could have serious implications on her relationship with her manager and, ultimately, her professional career.

Suggested Solution

1. *Recognize that you are facing an ethical dilemma.* Samantha realized that she had an ethical dilemma when she had to pause before entering the purpose of the meeting. She obviously felt uncomfortable about the lack of any business activity that occurred.
2. *Identify the action taken or the proposed action.* Rather than entering the little information she knew, she elected to make up an organization name. Thus, she falsified her expense report.
3. *Analyze the action.*
    a. *Is the action illegal?* Possibly. Claiming the lunch as a business expense may violate income tax laws.
    b. *Does the action violate company or professional standards?* Possibly. Two sentences in the *Accurate Books, Records, and Reports section* of the *Business Corporate Guide* appear to apply.
        - "Ensure that all travel and entertainment expenses are supported by actual receipts and have a valid business purpose."
        - "Do not distort the true nature of any transaction, no matter what the reason and no matter how insignificant the result may be."
    c. *Who is affected, and how, by the action?* See the analysis in the Instructional Strategies section at the front of this book.

Stakeholders	Negative	Positive
Samantha Jones	Her reputation may be damaged by her knowingly violating the code. Her ability to advance to higher management positions may be hindered.	She is able to submit the lunch expense for reimbursement without having to explain the nature of the lunch to her manager.
Samantha's manager	Samantha's actions may cause her manager to question other decisions she makes.	
Other employees	Employees who learn of Samantha's actions may be more willing to submit questionable expense reimbursements.	
Natural Springs Hotel and its stockholders	Samantha's actions may increase the risk of tax issues for Natural Springs Hotel.	

4. *Determine if the action is ethical.* Samantha should have been honest when entering the purpose of the meeting. Her manager would likely understand the circumstances. In addition, there is no way of knowing whether the relationship established will lead to booking the association's conference.

Chapter 3: The Danger of Social Media

Since personal ethics are unique, students' solutions will vary. Some students will conclude that Angela is qualified to assess the ability of her customers to wear the Christiana brand. These students will contend that Angela's opinions are a matter of fact and not opinion, and that there is no ethics violation. Other students may question how Angela's criticism could negatively affect Chandler's relationship with the Christiana brand. Some students may focus on Maggie's reaction to comments indirectly related to her physical size and shape.

Ask students to assume the role of Angela's supervisor. What actions, if any, would they take? In what form (e-mail, private meeting, etc.) should they communicate with Angela?

Suggested Solution:

1. *Recognize that you are facing an ethical dilemma.* Angela should recognize that she should be careful in discussing the quality of merchandise sold at Chandler's Fashions.
2. *Identify the action taken or the proposed action.* Angela criticized the Christiana brand and indirectly communicated to the public that Maggie does not possess a supermodel figure.
3. *Analyze the action.*
   a. *Is the action illegal?* Possibly. Angela is free to express her personal opinions. However, her statements must not reach a level that would be considered to be libelous.
   b. *Does the action violate company or professional standards?* Possibly. In the Communication section, the code states, "We don't tolerate communications that violate Target's policies or that are libelous or obscene." Later in the section, the code states, "If you choose to publish your opinions or post information about Target through social media, you're responsible for that content and for making it clear that your opinions are your own and not Target's." Although Angela does not identify herself as a Chandler's employee, her position with Chandler's is known to Maggie and other regular customers.
   c. *Who is affected, and how, by the action?*

Stakeholders	Negative	Positive
Angela	Possible violation of the code of ethics may damage her reputation with the company's management.	She provided honest advice to a regular customer.
Maggie	Readers of the blog know she does not have a supermodel figure.	Received honest advice from a trusted source.
Christiana brand	Although the Christiana brand may pride itself in fitting those with supermodel figures, it probably would not approve of the tone of Angela's blog.	
Chandler's Fashions	May lose a regular customer if Maggie is offended by Annie's comments. May have damaged relationship with the Christiana brand.	May benefit from Angela providing honest advice to a regular customer.

4. *Determine if the action is ethical.* Answers may vary.

Chapter 4: Insider Trading

Detecting and prosecuting illegal insider trading is a priority for the SEC. Insider trading undermines investor confidence in the securities markets. This activity requires students to analyze whether the action is illegal and violates company policies. By searching the Internet for "SEC insider trading," students will access a page that provides clear guidance on insider trading rules (www.sec.gov/answers/insider.htm). Because the action is considered illegal, students are not required to consult the company code of conduct. However, as an extension of this activity, have students read the insider trading section of Citigroup's *Code of Conduct.*

See a suggested solution for this feature in the Instructional Strategies section at the front of this book.

Suggested Solution:

1. *Recognize that you are facing an ethical dilemma.* As a loan officer, David should be aware of laws relating to insider trading.
2. *Identify the action taken or the proposed action.* David purchased the stock of a customer of his employer. Through his relationship with the customer, he had access to confidential information.
3. *Analyze the action.*
   a. *Is the action illegal?* Yes. The SEC states that employees of banks who were given information while providing services to the corporation whose securities they traded are involved in insider trading.

b. *Does the action violate company or professional standards?* No analysis is required because the action is illegal. However, Citigroup's *Code of Conduct* clearly forbids its employees from using material, nonpublic information to trade securities for a personal account.

c. *Who is affected, and how, by the action?* No analysis is required because the action is illegal.

4. *Determine if the action is ethical.* David's purchase of the stock was both illegal and unethical.

Chapter 5: Is Someone Reading Your E-mail?

Suggested Solution:

1. *Recognize that you are facing an ethical dilemma.* Managers should always evaluate a decision to dismiss an employee.
2. *Identify the action taken or the proposed action.* Sylvia dismissed Janice for sending threatening messages.
3. *Analyze the action.*
   a. *Is the action illegal?* No. It is not illegal to fire an employee for conduct that is inconsistent with corporate policies.
   b. *Does the action violate company or professional standards?* No. The company's code of conduct specifically states that e-mail communication is subject to monitoring. However, the policy does not address whether the company will hold "private" messages confidential.
   c. *Who is affected, and how, by the action?*

Stakeholders	Negative	Positive
Janice Tillman	Lost her job.	
Sylvia Hernandez		Worry about Janice's threats is removed.
Other company employees	Some employees may feel uncomfortable with the reality that their e-mails are being monitored.	Employees have an increased feeling of security, knowing that an employee who has shown some tendency toward violence has been removed from the workplace.
Company	May have to defend itself against a discrimination lawsuit if Janice elects to sue the company.	Increased employee security should yield higher profits.
Stockholders		Increased employee security should yield higher profits.

4. *Determine if the action is ethical.* Sylvia's action appears to be ethical.

Chapter 9: Sharing Nonpublic Information

Encourage students to evaluate each of Juanita's statements. Juanita can discuss the change in grain prices, assuming that this information is available publicly. However, she should not discuss the impact of these costs on the financial results of the company.

This activity illustrates how easily an employee can reveal nonpublic information while participating in casual conversations with friends and family. As an extension of this activity, ask students with part-time jobs to suggest statements they could make regarding the financial performance of their employer that would constitute the sharing of nonpublic information.

Suggested Solution:

1. *Recognize that you are facing an ethical dilemma.* Juanita should realize that any statement she makes containing information obtained in her position as a financial analyst may constitute nonpublic information.
2. *Identify the action or the proposed action.* Juanita's statement contains four distinct statements. The first statement regarding the use of grain for alternative fuel is public information and contains no reference to Natural Stores. However, the next three statements discuss how cost increases are impacting the company.
3. *Analyze the action.*
   a. *Is the action illegal?* Possibly. Securities laws prohibit the sharing of nonpublic information.
   b. *Does the action violate company or professional standards?* Possibly. The code contains guidance on this issue in the form of the following question and answer:

      How do I know whether I am aware of "material" nonpublic information about the company?

      Information is material if it is important to an investor making a decision about buying or selling the company's stock. This information includes financial results, business acquisitions or sales, changes in senior management, government investigations, changes in significant customers, and product recalls. If you are unsure whether you have material information, refrain from trading and consult your manager or the Law Department.

   This guidance specifically includes financial results. Thus, the decision requires an analysis of each of the three statements.

Statement	Evaluation
Our grain costs have skyrocketed.	This statement is a logical conclusion based on the increase in grain prices. Costs can be expected to be increasing for all food manufacturers. Thus, I do not believe this statement constitutes the disclosure of nonpublic information.
We're passing only part of the cost on to the consumer.	This statement discloses a company policy that can be expected to have an impact on its earnings.
People are going to be surprised when we report earnings.	This statement suggests that "people" (a reference to financial professionals that follow Natural Stores' earnings) are expecting higher earnings. Any disclosure that the company expects to miss expectations is clearly the disclosure of nonpublic information.

   c. *Who is affected, and how, by the action?* No analysis is required because the action may be illegal and likely violates the code of conduct.

4. *Determine if the action is ethical.* Answers will vary.

Chapter 11: Exercising Stock Options

Most students will conclude that issuing stock options as part of the CEO's compensation package appears to be ethical. However, excessive management compensation continues to be a controversial issue.

Although the management compensation packages of public corporations can seem excessive, the compensation is warranted if the executive can increase the profitability of the company and the wealth of its stockholders. In too many instances, however, executives have received excessive compensation, even when their corporations were declining.

As an extension of this activity, have students research current business magazines and newspapers for articles relating to excessive management compensation.

Suggested Solution:

1. *Recognize that you are facing an ethical dilemma.* The corporation should recognize that any employee receiving substantially more compensation than other employees may be unethical.
2. *Identify the action or the proposed action.* The corporation issued stock options as part of the CEO's compensation package.
3. *Analyze the action.*
   a. *Is the action illegal?* No. No laws limit the salary that any individual can earn in a private business.
   b. *Does the action violate company or professional standards?* Possibly. The code requires that employee compensation be consistent with that employee's contribution. Did Emily make a contribution to the corporation consistent with her salary? Further analysis is required.
   c. *Who is affected, and how, by the action?*

Stakeholders	Negative	Positive
Emily Tillman		Provides a substantial increase in salary if she can improve the company's profitability
Employees	May resent the high salary provided to the CEO.	Improved profitability results in more and better paying jobs.
Mena Corp.		Provides CEO with incentive to improve profitability.
Stockholders	Additional shares reduce earnings per share, lowering the stock market price.	Increases the wealth of stockholders only if the CEO is successful in increasing profitability.

4. *Determine if the action is ethical.* Answers will vary.

Chapter 14: Bribing Government Officials

Suggested Solution:

The section "Government Business Dealings—International" provides guidance for these situations.

a. It may be permissible for the employee to pay for the lunch. However, the employee should get prior approval from Harley-Davidson's Government Affairs Department or Legal Department.
b. It may be permissible for the employee to give small gifts. However, the employee should get prior approval from Harley-Davidson's Government Affairs Department or Legal Department.
c. It is a violation of the Harley-Davidson code and the Foreign Corrupt Practices Act to give anything of value to a foreign government official. These restrictions also apply to companies working on behalf of Harley-Davidson. The employee should immediately report the gift to Harley-Davidson's Government Affairs Department or Legal Department.
d. It may be permissible for an employee to make this payment. However, the employee should get prior approval from Harley-Davidson's Government Affairs Department or Legal Department.

Chapter 19: The Bad Pizza

Suggested Solution:

1. *Recognize that you are facing an ethical dilemma.* Devon should realize that the information might need to be communicated to the appropriate managers of the company.
2. *Identify the action or the proposed action.* Devon did not communicate the information to any appropriate manager or department of NBD Foods.
3. *Analyze the action.*
   a. *Is the action illegal?* No. No laws require an employee to report on the quality of its product from an unsubstantiated source.
   b. *Does the action violate company or professional standards?* Yes. In the section titled "Monitoring the Safety, Performance and Quality of Our Products," the code contains a Q&A example that closely parallels Devon's situation. The answer states that regardless of how the information was obtained or the severity of the event, the information must be reported within 24 hours.
   c. *Who is affected, and how, by the action?* No analysis of the stakeholders is necessary in this case.
4. *Determine if the action is ethical.* Devon violated the code when he did not report the information to the appropriate manager or department of NBD Foods.

Chapter 23: Evaluating Auditor Independence

Suggested Solution:

1. *Recognize that you are facing an ethical dilemma.* Teresa should be well educated in professional standards related to auditor independence. Any possible independence problem should be thoroughly evaluated.
2. *Identify the action or the proposed action.* Teresa would be auditing a company who employs a member of her family. Further, the family member would be working in an area of the business that would be directly involved in the audit.
3. *Analyze the action.*
   a. *Is the action illegal?* No. No laws govern the relationship between auditors and employees of non-public companies.
   b. *Does the action violate company or professional standards?* Probably not as an intern, but possibly as a full-time employee. ET Section 101.02 states that an immediate family member of the auditor may be employed by an attest (audit) client in a position other than a key position. ET Section 93.13 states that an immediate family is a spouse, spousal equivalent, or dependent (whether or not related). Based on this definition, Robbie would not be considered an immediate family member. ET Section 93.18 states that a key position is one where the individual has primary responsibility or the ability to

influence functions that impact the financial statements. As an intern, Robbie is unlikely to have such a level of responsibility. If Robbie accepts a full-time position, it is likely that he will eventually advance into a position of responsibility.

c. *Who is affected, and how, by the action?*

Stakeholders	Negative	Positive
Teresa	Her relationship with her client may be damaged if Robbie's performance is subpar or if Robbie's full-time employment becomes an independence issue.	
Robbie	Robbie may be unable to obtain permanent employment with RBH Industries; or, if hired by RBH, he may be unable to be promoted into a key position.	Robbie is able to gain professional experience and earn money by completing the internship.
Turner & Avant	The firm's ability to continue as the auditor may become an issue if Robbie becomes a full-time employee in a key position.	
RBH Industries	The company may be forced to choose between continuing its relationship with its auditor or a valued employee.	The company is expecting Robbie will be a positive addition as both an intern and a full-time employee.
Users of the financial statements	Any perception that the auditors lacked independence can damage the user's level of trust in the financial statements.	

4. *Determine if the action is ethical.* Answers will vary.

Chapter 24: Ethics in Government

Most students will conclude that Jacob may accept the invitation if he feels confident he can present the information without bias toward any political party. However, students may question whether Jacob risks the chance that some attendees, and ultimately the media, may view his acceptance as self-serving. Some students may recommend that Jacob accept the speaking invitation but refuse the speaking honorarium.

Suggested Solution:

1. *Recognize that you are facing an ethical dilemma.* Jacob should be sensitive to how the topic and timing of the speech could be perceived as his taking personal advantage of his position.
2. *Identify the action or the proposed action.* Jacob would be paid for giving a speech on a topic closely related to his current position as the chief of staff to the president of the United States.
3. *Analyze the action.*
   a. *Is the action illegal?* Subpart H, Outside Activities, §2635.807(a) provides guidance on whether a government employee may receive compensation for teaching, speaking, and writing. The section states that an employee "shall not receive compensation from any source other than the Government for teaching, speaking or writing that relates to the employee's official duties." In §2635.807(a)(1), the code lists circumstances that indicate whether an action relates to an employee's official duties. None of these provide clear guidance on whether Jacob would be precluded from making the speech. Further analysis is required.
   b. *Does the action violate company or professional standards?* There is no indication that Jacob is subject to any professional standards. Thus, further analysis is required.
4. *Who is affected, and how, by the action?*

Stakeholders	Negative	Positive
Jacob Estrada	If Jacob makes any statements that are perceived to be critical of either party, it may negatively impact his ability to perform his job.	Jacob receives a significant amount of compensation. His presence at the meeting provides exposure to the president's reelection campaign, which increases the chance he will retain his current position.
The president of the United States	Any of Jacob's statements that are viewed negatively by an attendee may have a negative impact on the president's reelection.	Any of Jacob's statements that are viewed positively by an attendee may have a positive impact on the president's reelection.
Attendees at the national meeting	To avoid criticism, Jacob may be hesitant to provide objective statements regarding a political party. Other unbiased speakers might be better candidates to give the speech.	Attendees are able to hear the thoughts of a noted historian who has first-hand knowledge of the political system.
Political parties	The content of the speech may contain information that reflects poorly on a political party.	The content of the speech may contain information that reflects favorably on a political party.
Citizens of the United States	Any time spent preparing and delivering the speech reduces the time Jacob can devote to his position.	

5. *Determine if the action is ethical.* Answers will vary.

SUGGESTED SOLUTIONS FOR SELECTED FEATURES

Below are suggested or expanded solutions for select features in the book.

Chapter 3: Think Like an Accountant

Lesson 3-2: Labor Costs

Sample Solution

1. The Layout 2 design provides the best information. The chart has a clean look because the lines connecting the two charts and slice labels to the chart slices are eliminated. The percent of each slice

assists the user in comparing amounts. The right pie, containing the employer taxes and contributions, is smaller than the left pie. The smaller right pie communicates that the amounts of these items are smaller than those in the left pie.

2. Just over 50% of the total cost of an employee is paid directly to the employee. Approximately 15% of the total cost results from employer taxes and contributions. Health insurance and retirement contributions comprise the majority of these expenses.
3. Changing to a pie chart eliminates many of the lines that caused the pie-of-pie chart to be confusing. Rotating the chart to position the majority of the labels to the right of the chart makes these labels easier to read and shortens the lines connecting the data labels to the related slices.
4. To further reduce the number of slices, the (1) federal and state unemployment taxes and (2) social security and Medicare tax amounts should be combined. This strategy would eliminate two of the smallest slices, yet continue to provide the board with the information needed to make business decisions.

A sample final solution, implementing the changes in the answer to question 4, is shown below.

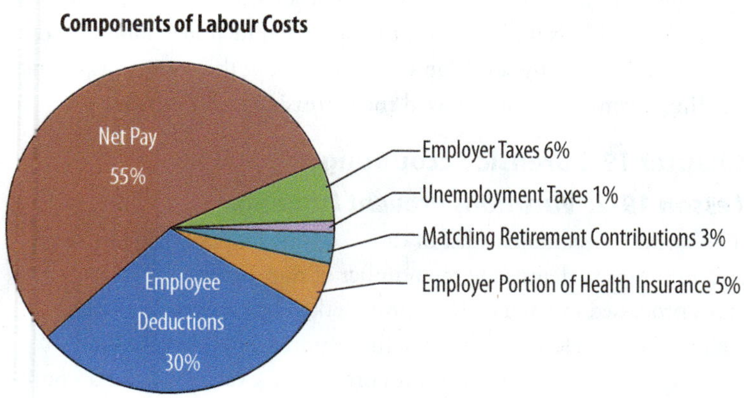

Chapter 4: Think Like an Accountant

Lesson 4-4: Allocating Corporate Expenses

This activity has many acceptable solutions. Encourage students to compare and debate their decisions.

Rounding errors may occur that result in a department's total allocations being $1,000 different from the total in column B. In practice, this rounding error would likely be resolved by adding or subtracting the rounding error from the largest division allocation.

Suggested Solution

The number of owner reservations is directly related to the number of owners and, therefore, the number of units available for sale. Many of the corporate departmental expenses relate more to the number of resorts rather than to the quality or number of units at each resort. As a result, the revised allocation method assigns more expenses to the number of resorts in each division.

The allocation methods for a reasonable solution are presented in the following table:

Department	Allocation Method	Justification
Accounting	Resorts	Regardless of size, most resorts will generate the same number of accounting transactions. The number of resorts measures the level of business activity that is not influenced by the number or quality of the units.
Acquisitions	Resorts	A measure of relative size of each division that does not included the number or quality of units.
Advertising	New contracts	Advertising should influence the number of contracts signed.
Board of Directors	Resorts	A measure of relative size of each division that does not included the size or quality of the individual resorts.
CEO Office	Resorts	A measure of relative size of each division that does not included the size or quality of the individual resorts.
Finance	Units	The financing of resort construction would be related to the size of each resort, as measured by the number of units.
Human Resources	Employees	The efforts of human resources are directly related to the number of employees.
Internal Audit	Resorts	Regardless of size, most resorts will generate the same number of accounting transactions. The number of resorts measures the level of business activity that is not influenced by the number or quality of the units.
Legal	Lawsuits initiated	Both formal complaints and lawsuits initiated are measures of legal activity. The legal staff likely spends more effort with lawsuits than with complaints.
Owner Relations	Units	The number of owners is directly related to the number of units available for sale.
Reservations	Units	The number of owner reservations is directly related to the number of owners and, therefore, the number of units available for sale.
Taxation	Resorts	One tax return is filed for each resort, regardless of the size of the resort.
Technology	Resorts	Tech support is based more on the number of systems than the number of stations for each system. Each resort has the same systems for check-in and scheduling, for example.

ESTIMATED MERCHANDISE INVENTORY SHEET

Gross Profit Method

DEPARTMENT *Douglass Music Store* DATE *9/23/20--*

1	Beginning inventory		*$ 45,750.00*
2	Net purchases to date		*264,890.00*
3	Merchandise available for sale		*$310,640.00*
4	Net sales to date	*$563,180.00*	
5	Less estimated gross profit (Net sales × Estimated gross profit percentage *53.8* %)	*302,990.84*	
6	Estimated cost of merchandise sold		*260,189.16*
7	Estimated ending inventory		*$ 50,450.84*
	Salvaged inventory		*12,625.00*
	Inventory lost in fire		*37,825.84*

Chapter 6: Think Like an Accountant

Lesson 6-2: Charting Sales and Accounts Receivable Trends

This activity requires students to create a chart to show the relationship between sales and the accounts receivable turnover ratio. Charting two sets of amounts having dramatically different scales (one in millions, one less than 15) requires a chart with two axis scales.

Remind students to average accounts receivable to compute each year's ratio. For this reason, no ratio is calculated for 20X1. The formula for the 20X2 ratio is =+C5/((B12+C12)/2). Alternately, this formula could use a function to determine the average accounts receivable balance: =C5/AVERAGE(B12,C12).

Question 3 requires students to consider the impact of bad debts expense on the analysis. Encourage students to create a chart that includes the operating expenses (since no detail of operating expenses is provided). This chart will reveal that the company's increase in sales has not translated to a similar increase in operating income.

Comparison of Sales the Accounts Receivable Turnover Ratio

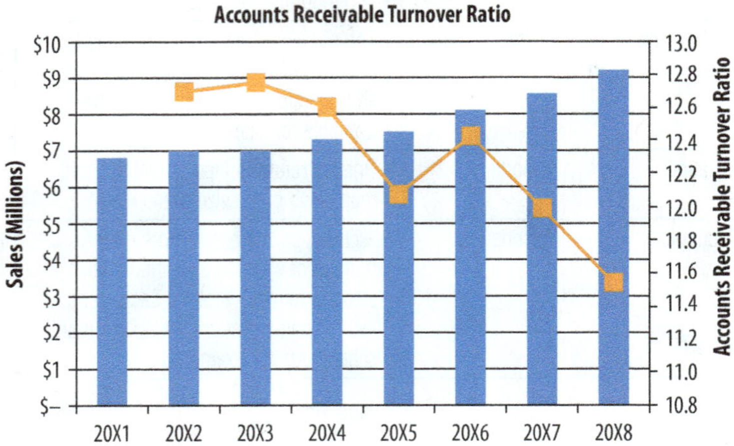

Suggested Solution:

1. The annual increase in sales began accelerating in 20X4.
2. The rate of increase in sales began in 20X4, the same year that the accounts receivable turnover ratio began to decrease. After an increase in 20X6, the turnover ratio has continued to decline.
3. The effectiveness of the new credit policy can only be evaluated by including bad debts expense in the analysis. Although that information is not available, the operating income could be added to the chart. This addition would show that the company's operating income has not followed the increasing trend in sales.

Chapter 19: Forensic Accounting

Lesson 19-2: Vacations Prevent Lapping

The workbook contains a list of cash receipts. Students use functions and formulas to determine the number of days between transactions processed by each cash receipts clerk. The absence of a large gap indicates that a clerk did not take the required extended vacation. Although students may find it humorous that a vacation is an accounting control, today's auditors closely examine the vacation patterns of employees in management and accounting positions.

Solutions

1. Ten rows are identified.
2. A suggested table for this question is shown below.

Date	User ID	Gap in Days	Explanation
7/14/2014	Davis	17	Took an extended vacation from 6/28 to 7/13.
12/29/2014	Davis	6	Took off the day before and after Christmas.
6/30/2014	LaGrange	(183)	The negative number is meaningless—calculation between two clerks.
7/7/2014	LaGrange	4	Time extends over 4th of July holiday (on Friday).
1/3/2014	Stillman	(189)	The negative number is meaningless—calculation between two clerks.
3/17/2014	Stillman	4	Took off on Friday, resulting in a three-day weekend.
6/16/2014	Stillman	4	Took off on Friday, resulting in a three-day weekend.

Date	User ID	Gap in Days	Explanation
7/7/2014	Stillman	4	Took off on Friday, resulting in a three-day weekend.
10/20/2014	Stillman	4	Took off on Friday, resulting in a three-day weekend.
11/3/2014	Stillman	4	Took off on Friday, resulting in a three-day weekend.

3. Amanda Stillman did not take any extended vacation. Instead, she took five three-day weekends. In contrast, Jonas LaGrange worked for two weeks, while Desha Davis took an extended vacation. This evidence indicates the possibility that lapping has occurred.

Chapter 21: Auditing for Errors

Solution

Russell's \$32,000 contribution for one-fourth equity indicates that the partnership is valued at \$158,000 after the contribution ($\$42,000 \times 3 + \$32,000$). Thus, each partner's equity account should reflect one-fourth, or \$39,500 ($\$158,000 \div 4$), interest in the partnership.

After reversing the bookkeeper's entry, the following entries should be recorded.

GENERAL JOURNAL PAGE 7

	DATE		ACCOUNT TITLE	DOC. NO.	POST. REF.	DEBIT	CREDIT	
7		1	*Inventory*	*M23*		32 000 00		7
8			*Kelly Russell, Capital*				32 000 00	8
9		1	*James Mangione, Capital*	*M23*		2 500 00		9
10			*Carl Nelson, Capital*			2 500 00		10
11			*Marris Trevathon, Capital*			2 500 00		11
12			*Kelly Russell, Capital*				7 500 00	12

PLANNING THE YEAR'S WORK

A time schedule for a complete year should be planned before the year begins. Five steps for planning the year's work are given below.

1. Allocate the equivalent of five 50-minute periods for the completion of each chapter, reinforcement activity part, and simulation. Modify the time allotted to each item based on previous experience with the pace of work that students have maintained in past accounting classes.
2. Determine how many business simulations and reinforcement activities are to be used during the current year.
3. Decide how much allowance should be made for interruptions in the school day that occur on short notice.
4. Determine if computers will be used in the class. Learning how to use software may require additional class time. However, if computers are used to complete some problems, reinforcement activities, and simulations (rather than working them manually), time may be saved in the schedule.
5. Prepare a proposed schedule of work to be completed. Inspect the schedule to determine if typical breaks in the school year (vacations, special events, and scheduled reporting periods) come at a logical time.

SPECIAL FEATURES GRID

Century 21 Accounting covers many contemporary special features. The following grid illustrates the features and their chapter locations.

Chapter	Accounting in the Real World	Ethics in Action	Think Like an Accountant	Why Accounting?	Careers in Accounting	Financial Literacy	Global Awareness	Forensic Accounting	A Look at Accounting Software	Explore Accounting
1	Skechers	Researching Codes of Conduct	Analyzing Purchases Discounts	Microcredit			International Terms of Sale	Embezzlement Made Easy	Setting Up Accounts for a Corporation	Accounting Certifications
2	Expedia, Inc.	A Business Lunch Light on Business	Evaluating Departmental Sales	Distribution Impacts a Company's Goals	Owner of CPA Firm	What's the Trade-off? Considering Choices and Costs			Receiving a Payment on Account	Transfer Pricing
3	Automatic Data Processing, Inc.	The Danger of Social Media	Labor Costs	Executive Compensation			International Clubs	Crazy Eddie	Managing Employee Information	Pretax Benefits
4	Whole Planet Foundation	Insider Trading	Allocating Corporate Expenses	Accounting for Engineers	Junior Accountant/Senior Accountant	How Secure Is Social Security?			Modifying a Report	Exception Reports
5	Johnson & Johnson	Is Someone Reading Your E-mail?	Helping a Client Avoid Penalties	Retraining after Workplace Injuries			Work/Holiday Visa	Restatement at Rite Aid Corporation	Setting Prices	Computerized Purchasing Systems
6	Target Corporation	Integrity in Management Accounting	Charting Sales and Accounts Receivable Trends	Cost of Preventing Work-place Injuries	Accounting Advisory Specialist	Avoid Debt Distress			Setting Credit Limits	Credit Scoring Systems
7	Union Pacific	The Land of Opportunity?	Calculating Depreciation Expense	Accounting for Environmental Costs in Agriculture			Applying for a Passport	A Pyramid Scheme at Equity Funding	Applying Depreciation	Tax Laws Encourage Plant Asset Purchases
8	Tanger Outlets	The Boss Made Me Do It	Calculating Accrued Interest	Cost of ADA Implementation	Tax Preparer/ Tax Advisor	Fun with FAFSA			Drawing on a Line of Credit	Impact of Changes in Foreign Exchange Rates on a Note Payable
9	Southwest Airlines Co.	Sharing Nonpublic Information	Creating an Amortization Schedule	Getting What They Want to Sell			Legal Rights in Foreign Countries	A Royal Disaster	Setting Up a Note Receivable	Legal Issues Surrounding Breakage
10	E. I. du Pont de Nemours and Company	Good Investing or Insider Trading?	Charting the Capital Structure	Getting Paid to Communicate	Financial Planner	Making Cents of Dollar- Cost Averaging			Maintaining Shareholder Records	A Delaware Corporation
11	Pandora Media, Inc.	Exercising Stock Options	Evaluating a Stock Buyback Program	How the Bottom Line Can Affect Jail Sentences			Importing and Exporting Goods	Insider Trading		Stock Splits
12	The U.S. Treasury	Reporting Ethics Violations	Financing a Takeover	How Marketing Can Use Accounting Ratios	Tax Examiner/ Collector	Superman and Savings Bonds				Bond Sinking Funds

Chapter	Accounting in the Real World	Ethics in Action	Think Like an Accountant	Why Accounting?	Careers in Accounting	Financial Literacy	Global Awareness	Forensic Accounting	A Look at Accounting Software	Explore Accounting
13	Chipotle Mexican Grill	Client Referrals	Charting Earnings per Share	Uniform System of Accounts for Restaurants			World Trade Organization	Channel Stuffing		EBIT and EBITDA
14	EMC Corporation	Bribing Government Officials	Charting the Statement of Cash Flows	Bottom Line May Affect Theatrical Performance	Financial Analyst	Money Chase				Changing Rules for the Recognition of Revenue
15	Walmart	Sharing Your Knowledge	Charting Financial Ratios	State Parks and Sources of Revenue			Foreign Corrupt Practices Act	Shell Companies	Preparing Budgets Using Open Database Connectivity (ODBC)	Contingent Liabilities
16	Nintendo	Fraud Awareness	Analyzing Relationships to Predict Sales	Computerized Breakeven Analysis	Loan Officer	House Poor				The High-Low Method
17	General Mills	Client Referrals	Measuring Material Variances	Limited Resources			Why Do Foreign Exchange Rates Change?	It Just Doesn't Add Up		ISO 9001 Certification
18	Verizon Communications	It's Just a Day or Two	Evaluating Projects with the Internal Rate of Return	Selling Waste Products for a Profit?	Enterprise Resource Planning Project Manager	Costs of Lost Productivity				The Power of Compounding
19	Wm. Wrigley Jr. Company	The Bad Pizza	Consolidating Corporate Information	College Marketing			Repatriation of Profits Earned Abroad	Vacations Prevent Lapping		Responsibility Centers
20	PetSmart Inc.	Reporting Violations	Documenting Cash Collections	Clergy	Partner in an Accounting Firm	Stash the Cash			Setting User Access Privileges	Preventive and Detective Control Activities
21	Pricewaterhouse Coopers, LLP	Serving as an Expert Witness	Improving Efficiency with Templates	Changing Services to Match the Times			Currency Manipulation	Improper Revenue Recognition		Limited Liability Partnerships
22	PVR Partners, L.P.	The Client Is Not Always Right	Analyzing Partnership Distributions	Should We Buy Another Mill?	Credit Analyst	Signing Away the Future				Determining the Value of a Partnership
23	Amtrak	Evaluating Auditor Independence	Organizational Structure	Charitable Giving Watchdogs			Foreign Currency Exchange Gains or Losses	Single Audits		Accounting Opportunities in Not-for-Profit Organizations
24	City of Tampa	Ethics in Government	Improving Your Efficiency	Campaign Financing	Municipal Treasurer	Domino Effect in Detroit				Components of a Comprehensive Annual Financial Report

SOFTWARE CORRELATION

After manual accounting procedures are mastered, software may be used as an enrichment activity to facilitate the processing of accounting data and experience the use of computers in accounting.

Data files and instructions for several software products are available on the *Century 21 Accounting* 10E website to augment teacher instruction: Automated Accounting Online, Sage 50 Accounting, QuickBooks, and Microsoft Excel. Symbols in the textbook for each software program denote problems that can be worked with the software indicated.

Automated Accounting Online may be used to complete selected end-of-chapter problems, all four Reinforcement Activities, and both simulations.

Sage 50, QuickBooks, Excel, And Automated Accounting Online Problems

Chapter	Sage 50 Accounting	QuickBooks	Excel	AAO
1	**1-3 Application Problem:** Journalizing and posting departmental cash payments **1-M Mastery Problem:** Journalizing departmental purchases and cash payments	**1-3 Application Problem:** Journalizing and posting departmental cash payments **1-M Mastery Problem:** Journalizing departmental purchases and cash payments	**1-3 Application Problem:** Journalizing and posting departmental cash payments **1-M Mastery Problem:** Journalizing departmental purchases and cash payments	**1-3 Application Problem:** Journalizing and posting departmental cash payments **1-M Mastery Problem:** Journalizing departmental purchases and cash payments
2	**2-2 Application Problem:** Journalizing and posting departmental cash receipts **2-M Mastery Problem:** Journalizing departmental sales, sales returns and allowances, and cash receipts	**2-2 Application Problem:** Journalizing and posting departmental cash receipts **2-M Mastery Problem:** Journalizing departmental sales, sales returns and allowances, and cash receipts	**2-2 Application Problem:** Journalizing and posting departmental cash receipts **2-M Mastery Problem:** Journalizing departmental sales, sales returns and allowances, and cash receipts	**2-2 Application Problem:** Journalizing and posting departmental cash receipts **2-M Mastery Problem:** Journalizing departmental sales, sales returns and allowances, and cash receipts
3	**3-M Mastery Problem:** Completing payroll records, journalizing payment of a payroll, and journalizing payroll taxes **3-S Source Documents Problem:** Completing payroll records, journalizing payment of a payroll, and journalizing payroll taxes	**3-M Mastery Problem:** Completing payroll records, journalizing payment of a payroll, and journalizing payroll taxes **3-S Source Documents Problem:** Completing payroll records, journalizing payment of a payroll, and journalizing payroll taxes	**3-M Mastery Problem:** Completing payroll records, journalizing payment of a payroll, and journalizing payroll taxes **3-S Source Documents Problem:** Completing payroll records, journalizing payment of a payroll, and journalizing payroll taxes	
4	**4-4 Application Problem:** Journalizing closing entries **4-M Mastery Problem:** Completing end-of-fiscal-period work for a departmentalized merchandising business	**4-4 Application Problem:** Journalizing closing entries **4-M Mastery Problem:** Completing end-of-fiscal-period work for a departmentalized merchandising business	**4-4 Application Problem:** Journalizing closing entries **4-M Mastery Problem:** Completing end-of-fiscal-period work for a departmentalized merchandising business	**4-1 Application Problem:** Preparing an adjusted trial balance **4-2 Application Problem:** Preparing a departmental margin statement **4-3 Application Problem:** Preparing financial statements **4-M Mastery Problem:** Completing end-of-fiscal-period work for a departmentalized merchandising business
Reinforcement Activity 1	Processing and Reporting Departmentalized Accounting Data	Processing and Reporting Departmentalized Accounting Data	Processing and Reporting Departmentalized Accounting Data	Processing and Reporting Departmentalized Accounting Data
5	**5-2 Application Problem:** Determining inventory cost using FIFO, LIFO, weighted-average, and lower of cost or market	**5-2 Application Problem:** Determining inventory cost using FIFO, LIFO, weighted-average, and lower of cost or market **5-M Mastery Problem:** Costing and financial analysis of merchandise inventory	**5-2 Application Problem:** Determining inventory cost using FIFO, LIFO, weighted-average, and lower of cost or market **5-M Mastery Problem:** Costing and financial analysis of merchandise inventory	**5-1 Application Problem:** Keeping perpetual inventory records **5-2 Application Problem:** Determining inventory cost using FIFO, LIFO, weighted-average, and lower of cost or market

Chapter	Sage 50 Accounting	QuickBooks	Excel	AAO
6	**6-2 Application Problem:** Estimating amount of uncollectible accounts expense; journalizing the adjusting entry **6-M Mastery Problem:** Journalizing entries for uncollectible accounts—allowance method; calculating and journalizing the adjusting entry for uncollectible accounts expense	**6-2 Application Problem:** Estimating amount of uncollectible accounts expense; journalizing the adjusting entry **6-M Mastery Problem:** Journalizing entries for uncollectible accounts—allowance method; calculating and journalizing the adjusting entry for uncollectible accounts expense	**6-2 Application Problem:** Estimating amount of uncollectible accounts expense; journalizing the adjusting entry	**6-1 Application Problem:** Journalizing entries to write off uncollectible accounts—direct write-off method **6-2 Application Problem:** Estimating amount of uncollectible accounts expense; journalizing the adjusting entry **6-M Mastery Problem:** Journalizing entries for uncollectible accounts—allowance method; calculating and journalizing the adjusting entry for uncollectible accounts expense
7	**7-3 Application Problem:** Recording the disposal of plant assets **7-M Mastery Problem:** Recording entries for plant assets	**7-3 Application Problem:** Recording the disposal of plant assets **7-M Mastery Problem:** Recording entries for plant assets	**7-3 Application Problem:** Recording the disposal of plant assets **7-M Mastery Problem:** Recording entries for plant assets	**7-1 Application Problem:** Journalizing asset purchase transactions **7-2 Application Problem:** Calculating and journalizing depreciation **7-3 Application Problem:** Recording the disposal of plant assets **7-M Mastery Problem:** Recording entries for plant assets
8	**8-3 Application Problem:** Journalizing adjusting and reversing entries for accrued expenses **8-M Mastery Problem:** Journalizing notes payable transactions and adjusting and reversing entries	**8-3 Application Problem:** Journalizing adjusting and reversing entries for accrued expenses **8-M Mastery Problem:** Journalizing notes payable transactions and adjusting and reversing entries	**8-3 Application Problem:** Journalizing adjusting and reversing entries for accrued expenses **8-M Mastery Problem:** Journalizing notes payable transactions and adjusting and reversing entries	**8-1 Application Problem:** Journalizing notes payable transactions **8-M Mastery Problem:** Journalizing notes payable transactions and adjusting and reversing entries
9	**9-3 Application Problem:** Journalizing installment notes receivable transactions **9-M Mastery Problem:** Journalizing unearned revenue, accrued revenue, and gift card and installment note receivable transactions	**9-3 Application Problem:** Journalizing installment notes receivable transactions **9-M Mastery Problem:** Journalizing unearned revenue, accrued revenue, and gift card and installment note receivable transactions	**9-3 Application Problem:** Journalizing installment notes receivable transactions **9-M Mastery Problem:** Journalizing unearned revenue, accrued revenue, and gift card and installment note receivable transactions	**9-3 Application Problem:** Journalizing installment notes receivable transactions **9-M Mastery Problem:** Journalizing unearned revenue, accrued revenue, and gift card and installment note receivable transactions
Reinforcement Activity 2	Processing Accounting Data for a Corporation	Processing Accounting Data for a Corporation	Processing Accounting Data for a Corporation	Processing Accounting Data for a Corporation
10	**10-2 Application Problem:** Journalizing preferred stock transactions **10-M Mastery Problem:** Journalizing stock transactions	**10-2 Application Problem:** Journalizing preferred stock transactions **10-M Mastery Problem:** Journalizing stock transactions	**10-2 Application Problem:** Journalizing preferred stock transactions **10-M Mastery Problem:** Journalizing stock transactions	
11	**11-M Mastery Problem:** Journalizing dividend, treasury stock, and investment transactions **11-C Challenge Problem:** Journalizing stock and dividend transactions	**11-M Mastery Problem:** Journalizing dividend, treasury stock, and investment transactions **11-C Challenge Problem:** Journalizing stock and dividend transactions	**11-M Mastery Problem:** Journalizing dividend, treasury stock, and investment transactions **11-C Challenge Problem:** Journalizing stock and dividend transactions	
12	**12-M Mastery Problem:** Journalizing bond transactions **12-C Challenge Problem:** Journalizing bond transactions	**12-M Mastery Problem:** Journalizing bond transactions **12-C Challenge Problem:** Journalizing bond transactions	**12-M Mastery Problem:** Journalizing bond transactions **12-C Challenge Problem:** Journalizing bond transactions	

Chapter	Sage 50 Accounting	QuickBooks	Excel	AAO
13			**13-1 Application Problem:** Analyzing short- and long-term financial strength **13-2 Application Problem:** Calculating profitability measures **13-3 Application Problem:** Calculating and analyzing efficiency measures and market ratios **13-M Mastery Problem:** Analyzing financial statements **13-C Challenge Problem:** Calculating the effect of transactions on the current ratio	
14			**14-1 Application Problem:** Preparing the operating activities section of a statement of cash flows **14-2 Application Problem:** Completing the statement of cash flows **14-M Mastery Problem:** Preparing a statement of cash flows **14-C Challenge Problem:** Preparing a statement of cash flows with amortization expense	
Reinforcement Activity 3	Processing and Analyzing Accounting Data for a Corporation	Processing and Analyzing Accounting Data for a Corporation	Processing and Analyzing Accounting Data for a Corporation	Processing and Analyzing Accounting Data for a Corporation
15			**15-1 Application Problem:** Preparing a sales budget and a purchases budget **15-2 Application Problem:** Preparing budgets for selling expenses, administrative expenses, and other expenses and preparing a budgeted income statement **15-3 Application Problem:** Preparing a cash receipts budget, a cash payments budget, and a cash budget **15-4 Application Problem:** Completing a performance report **15-M Mastery Problem:** Preparing a budgeted income statement and a cash budget with supporting budgets	**15-4 Application Problem:** Completing a performance report
16			**16-1 Application Problem:** Preparing an income statement with contribution margin **16-2 Application Problem:** Calculating breakeven in sales dollars and unit sales and preparing a breakeven income statement **16-3 Application Problem:** Calculating sales, sales mix, and the effect of volume and price changes **16-M Mastery Problem:** Calculating breakeven and the sales required for a desired income	

Chapter	Sage 50 Accounting	QuickBooks	Excel	AAO
17	**17-1.2 Application Problem:** Recording and journalizing materials and labor costs **17-M Mastery Problem:** Preparing cost records and journalizing entries that summarize cost records at the end of a fiscal period	**17-1.2 Application Problem:** Recording and journalizing materials and labor costs **17-M Mastery Problem:** Preparing cost records and journalizing entries that summarize cost records at the end of a fiscal period	**17-1.2 Application Problem:** Recording and journalizing materials and labor costs **17-M Mastery Problem:** Preparing cost records and journalizing entries that summarize cost records at the end of a fiscal period	
18			**18-3 Application Problem:** Using net present value to make business decisions **18-M Mastery Problem:** Calculating net present values	
19	**19-M Mastery Problem:** Calculating equivalent units of production and completing journal entries in process costing	**19-M Mastery Problem:** Calculating equivalent units of production and completing journal entries in process costing	**19-1 Application Problem:** Calculating equivalent units of production and completing journal entries in process costing **19-M Mastery Problem:** Calculating equivalent units of production and completing journal entries in process costing	
Reinforcement Activity 4	Processing and Analyzing Cost Accounting Data for a Manufacturing Business	Processing and Analyzing Cost Accounting Data for a Manufacturing Business	Processing and Analyzing Cost Accounting Data for a Manufacturing Business	Processing and Analyzing Cost Accounting Data for a Manufacturing Business
20	**20-3 Application Problem:** Journalizing transactions in a voucher system **20-M Mastery Problem:** Analyzing a voucher system and journalizing transactions in a voucher system	**20-3 Application Problem:** Journalizing transactions in a voucher system **20-M Mastery Problem:** Analyzing a voucher system and journalizing transactions in a voucher system	**20-3 Application Problem:** Journalizing transactions in a voucher system **20-M Mastery Problem:** Analyzing a voucher system and journalizing transactions in a voucher system	
21	**21-2 Application Problem:** Admitting a partner with no change in total equity **21-M Mastery Problem:** Forming and expanding a partnership **21-C Challenge Problem:** Expanding a partnership	**21-2 Application Problem:** Admitting a partner with no change in total equity **21-M Mastery Problem:** Forming and expanding a partnership **21-C Challenge Problem:** Expanding a partnership	**21-2 Application Problem:** Admitting a partner with no change in total equity **21-M Mastery Problem:** Forming and expanding a partnership **21-C Challenge Problem:** Expanding a partnership	**21-1 Application Problem:** Forming a partnership **21-M Mastery Problem:** Forming and expanding a partnership
22	**22-3 Application Problem:** Liquidating a partnership **22-M Mastery Problem:** Completing end-of-period work for a partnership	**22-3 Application Problem:** Liquidating a partnership **22-M Mastery Problem:** Completing end-of-period work for a partnership	**22-3 Application Problem:** Liquidating a partnership **22-C Challenge Problem:** Completing end-of-period work for a partnership	**22-M Mastery Problem:** Completing end-of-period work for a partnership **22-C Challenge Problem:** Completing end-of-period work for a partnership
23	**23-3 Application Problem:** Journalizing governmental encumbrances, expenditures, and other transactions **23-M Mastery Problem:** Journalizing governmental transactions	**23-3 Application Problem:** Journalizing governmental encumbrances, expenditures, and other transactions **23-M Mastery Problem:** Journalizing governmental transactions	**23-3 Application Problem:** Journalizing governmental encumbrances, expenditures, and other transactions **23-M Mastery Problem:** Journalizing governmental transactions	
24	**24-2 Application Problem:** Preparing financial statements for a governmental organization **24-M Mastery Problem:** Completing the end-of-period work for a governmental organization	**24-2 Application Problem:** Preparing financial statements for a governmental organization **24-M Mastery Problem:** Completing the end-of-period work for a governmental organization	**24-2 Application Problem:** Preparing financial statements for a governmental organization **24-M Mastery Problem:** Completing the end-of-period work for a governmental organization	

LOCATION OF ANSWERS AND SOLUTIONS

Due to the abundance of instructor support material available with this course, the table below is provided to guide you in locating solutions to student activities.

Item	Found In
Accounting in the Real World	Margins of Wraparound Teacher's Edition
Ethics in Action	Margins of Wraparound Teacher's Edition and Instructional Strategies section in Wraparound Teacher's Edition
Careers in Accounting, Think Like an Accountant, Forensic Accounting, Financial Literacy, Global Awareness, Why Accounting? features	Margins of Wraparound Teacher's Edition; some expanded solutions in Instructional Strategies section in Wraparound Teacher's Edition
Terms Review	Glossary in Student Text
Audit Your Understanding	Appendix D in Student Text
Work Together Problems	Teacher's Edition of Working Papers
On Your Own Problems	Teacher's Edition of Working Papers
Explore Accounting	Margins of Wraparound Teacher's Edition
Application Problems	Teacher's Edition of Working Papers
Mastery Problems	Teacher's Edition of Working Papers
Challenge Problems	Teacher's Edition of Working Papers
Auditing for Errors	Margins of Wraparound Teacher's Edition
Source Documents Problems	Teacher's Edition of Working Papers
Analyzing Home Depot's Financial Statements	Margins of Wraparound Teacher's Edition
Reinforcement Activities	Teacher's Edition of Working Papers
Recycling Problems	Teacher's Edition of Recycling Problem Working Papers
Study Guides	Teacher's Edition of Working Papers
Tests	Teacher's Edition of Tests
Manual Simulations	Printed keys for manual simulations; C21 Accounting Website
Automated Simulations	C21 Accounting Website
Sage 50 Problems	C21 Accounting Website
QuickBooks Problems	C21 Accounting Website

Century 21 Accounting

10e Advanced

Century 21 Accounting

10e Advanced

Claudia Bienias Gilbertson, CPA, PhD
Retired
North Hennepin Community College
Brooklyn Park, Minnesota

Mark W. Lehman, CPA, CFE, PhD
Associate Professor Emeritus
Richard C. Adkerson School of Accountancy
Mississippi State University
Starkville, Mississippi

Dan Passalacqua, MA
Retired
Oak Grove High School
San Jose, California

SOUTH-WESTERN
CENGAGE Learning

Australia • Brazil • Japan • Korea • Mexico • Singapore • Spain • United Kingdom • United States

SOUTH-WESTERN
CENGAGE Learning

Century 21 Accounting Advanced, Tenth Edition

Claudia Bienias Gilbertson, CPA, PhD
Mark W. Lehman, CPA, CFE, PhD
Dan Passalacqua, MA

SVP Global Product Development—Research, School & Professional: Frank Menchaca

Executive Director of Marketing: Carolyn Pestritto

General Manager, K-12 School Group: CarolAnn Shindelar

Acquisitions Editor: Jeff Werle

Sr. Development Editor: Diane Bowdler

Sr. Content Project Manager: Martha Conway

Consulting Editor: Kenneth Martin

Media Developer: Lysa Kosins

Sr. Digital Content Operations Analyst: Ed Stubenrauch

Product Marketing Manager: Kelsey Hagan

Manufacturing Planner: Kevin Kluck

Production Service: Cenveo

Sr. Art Director: Michelle Kunkler

Cover and Internal Designer: Ke Design

Cover Image: © iStockphoto.com/Christopher Futcher

End of Lesson Image: © iStockphoto.com/urbanglimpses

Lesson Opener Images: © Robert Kneschke/Shutterstock.com; © iStockphoto.com/svetikd; © Lucky Business/Shutterstock.com; © Mike Flippo/Shutterstock.com

Intellectual Property Project Manager: Lisa Brown

Photo Researcher: Darren Wright

Text Permissions Researcher: PreMedia Global

© 2015, 2012 Cengage Learning

WCN: 01-100-101

ALL RIGHTS RESERVED. No part of this work covered by the copyright herein may be reproduced, transmitted, stored or used in any form or by any means graphic, electronic, or mechanical, including but not limited to photocopying, recording, scanning, digitizing, taping, Web distribution, information networks, or information storage and retrieval systems, except as permitted under Section 107 or 108 of the 1976 United States Copyright Act, without the prior written permission of the publisher.

For product information and technology assistance, contact us at **Cengage Learning Customer & Sales Support, 1-800-354-9706**

For permission to use material from this text or product, submit all requests online at **www.cengage.com/permissions**
Further permissions questions can be emailed to
permissionrequest@cengage.com

ISBN-13: 978-1-111-99064-0
ISBN-10: 1-111-99064-6

Cengage Learning
200 First Stamford Place, 4th Floor
Stamford, CT 06902
USA

Microsoft Office Excel is a registered trademark of Microsoft Corporation.

Intuit and QuickBooks are registered trademarks of Intuit, Inc.

© 2013 Sage Software, Inc. All rights reserved. Sage, the Sage logos, and the Sage product and service names mentioned herein are the registered trademarks of Sage Software, Inc.

Cengage Learning is a leading provider of customized learning solutions with office locations around the globe, including Singapore, the United Kingdom, Australia, Mexico, Brazil, and Japan. Locate your local office at: **www.cengage.com/global**

Cengage Learning products are represented in Canada by Nelson Education, Ltd.

For your course and learning solutions, visit **www.cengage.com/school**
Visit our company website at **www.cengage.com**

The Career Clusters icons are being used with permission of the States' Career Clusters Initiative, 2010, **www.careerclusters.org**

All illustrations, tables, and graphs are © Cengage Learning.

Printed in the United States of America
2 3 4 5 6 7 20 19 18 17 16

Contents

Part 1 Departmentalized Accounting

Part 2 Accounting
Adjustments and Valuation

Part 3 Corporation Accounting

Part 4 Management Accounting

Part 5 Internal Control and Other Organizational Structures

Reviewers

Marilyn Achelpohl
Business Instructor
Galesburg High School
Galesburg, Illinois

Carolyn Holt Balis
Business/Marketing Educator
Valley Forge High School
Parma Heights, Ohio

Keith Brady
Business Teacher
Pequannock Township High School
Pompton Plains, New Jersey

Shelly Christensen
Business Educator
Glen Ullin Public School
Glen Ullin, North Dakota

Dan Doseck
Business Teacher
Alexander High School
Albany, Ohio

Tami A. Evanosky
Career and Technology Education Department Chair
Perry Hall High School
Baltimore, Maryland

Kathryn L. Focht, CPA
Business Educator
Wilson High School
West Lawn, Pennsylvania

Kathleen O'Connor Ford
Business Teacher
Rochester Community Schools
Rochester Hills, Michigan

Josh Freese
Accounting Teacher
Hicksville High School
Hicksville, Ohio

Darlene Gliese
Business Teacher
South River High School
South River, New Jersey

Mary Greydanus
Accounting Teacher
Thompson M-TEC, O.A.I.S.D.
Holland, Michigan

Michael Hackman
Business Teacher
Columbus North High School
Columbus, Indiana

Kathleen Harenza
Business Education Teacher
Mukwonago High School
Mukwonago, Wisconsin

Susan Heaney
Business Teacher
Whitney M. Young Magnet High School
Chicago, Illinois

Dana Hurda
Business Teacher
Evansville High School
Evansville, Wisconsin

Sheryl C. Kirby
Business Education/CTE Teacher
George Washington High School
Philadelphia, Pennsylvania

Mrs. Michelle Kirkland
CTE Business Teacher
Vidor High School
Vidor, Texas

Brenda Knight
Accounting, Business, and Information Technology Teacher
Rouse High School
Leander, Texas

Joseph Kramer
Department of Business & Information Technology Chairperson
Seton-La Salle Catholic High School
Pittsburgh, Pennsylvania

Kerri Largo
Business Education Department Chair
Hoffman Estates High School
Hoffman Estates, Illinois

Jane Melroy
Business Teacher
USD 438, Skyline Schools
Pratt, Kansas

Trish Miller
Business Teacher
Wawasee High School
Syracuse, Indiana

Judy Mitchell
Business Teacher
Thomas More Prep-Marian
Hays, Kansas

Matt Pohlman
Accounting Instructor
CAL-Latimer
Latimer, Iowa

Bart Prosser
Business Teacher
Parkway North High School
St. Louis, Missouri

Patsy J. Sooter
Business Education Teacher
Bentonville High School
Bentonville, Arkansas

Transform Your High School Accounting Course with Century 21 Accounting, from the leader in high school accounting education for 100+ years.

Input from educators, accounting professionals, content experts, and high school accounting students has shaped the 10th Edition of Century 21 Accounting. New critical-thinking activities, real-world applications, and enhanced online learning solutions—including Online Working Papers and Automated Accounting Online computerized accounting software—help you transform your accounting course.

- **Proven pedagogy** using a **renowned instructional design** supports teaching the mechanics of accounting and measuring learning outcomes in the 10th Edition.
- **Greater emphasis on conceptual understanding and financial statement analysis** encourages students to apply accounting concepts to real-world situations and develop higher-level thinking skills to make informed business decisions.
- **Critical thinking and technology use**, as defined by the Partnership for 21st Century Skills, have been expanded throughout with these new features to give students real-world practice and help them master valuable skills:

Forensic Accounting	*Think Like an Accountant*
Financial Literacy	*Why Accounting?*

- **Commercial technology** is integrated throughout the text to equip students to work with Microsoft Excel®, Sage 50®, QuickBooks®, and Automated Accounting Online. Students are given step-by-step instructions and the flexibility to use a variety of popular commercial software.

Sage 50 Accounting   QuickBooks   Automated Accounting ONLINE

- **Unparalleled teaching tools and assessment resources**—in addition to exclusive CourseCare instructor training support—help ensure your success.

CourseCare

Transform Your Course with

The Century 21 Accounting program provides students with a complete learning system designed to keep them on track and helps you measure outcomes.

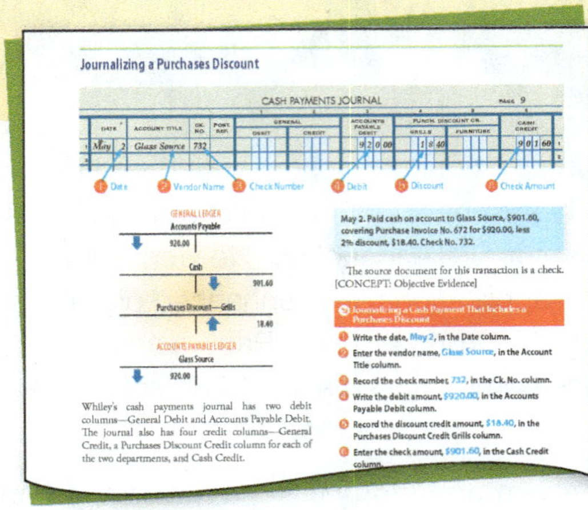

The **organization** ensures clear student understanding. Students start with departmentalized accounting and then learn about corporation and management accounting, before concluding with internal control and other organizational structures.

The **step-by-step instructional approach** clearly reinforces text concepts, while the consistent use of T accounts increases student comprehension of journalizing transactions.

Learning *NEW!* **Objectives** connect the chapter coverage from beginning to end. Learning objectives are identified at point of introduction and in the end-of-chapter problems, making it easier for students to stay on track. By paying attention to the Learning Objectives, students can focus on what is important and you can better measure outcomes.

> *"I believe you have provided us with just what we need to get the objectives introduced, practiced and then mastered."*
>
> Kathleen O'Connor Ford, Rochester Community Schools, Rochester Hills, MI

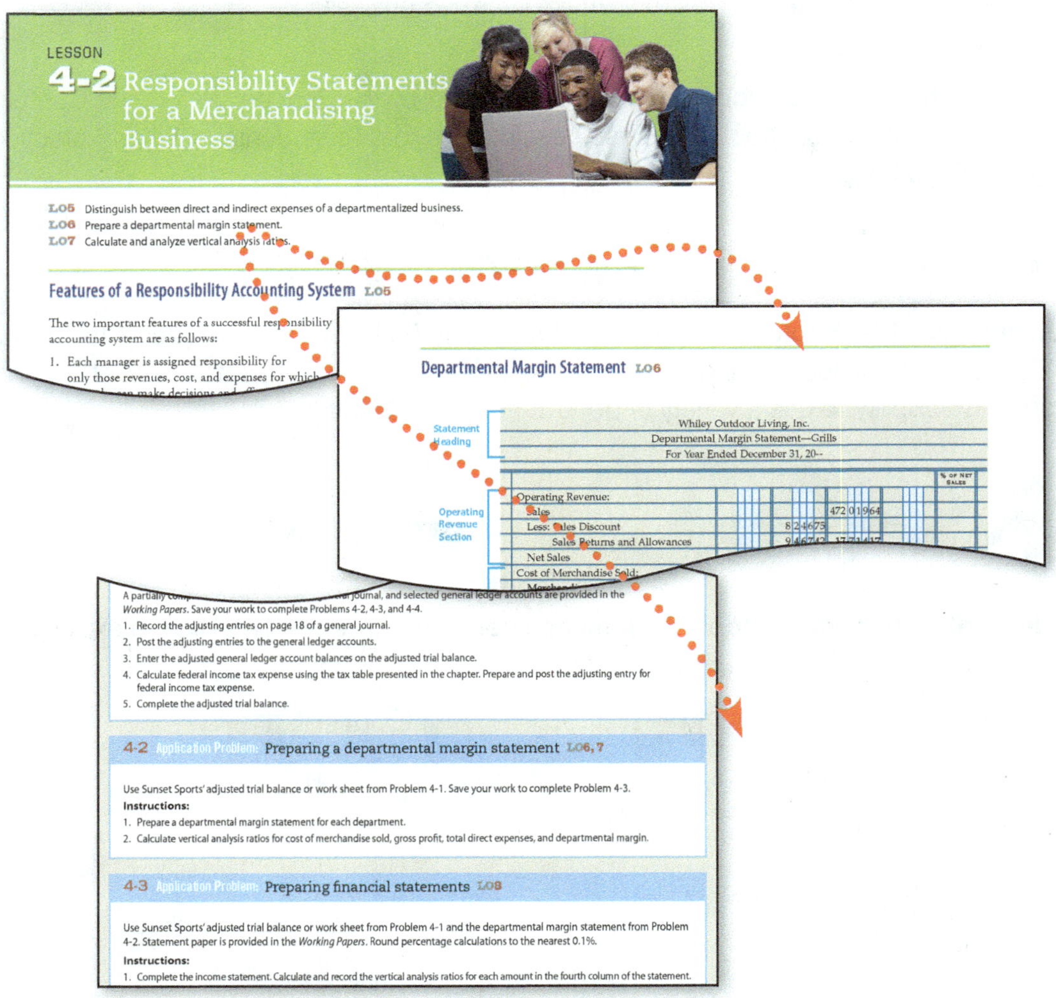

Measurable Outcomes

The **lesson structure** consists of three to five lessons per chapter and corresponding assessment activities. Each end-of-lesson section includes a **Work Together** problem and an **On Your Own** assignment. The Work Together problem allows you to demonstrate the new accounting concept to your class. Students can then check their understanding by completing the On Your Own assignment.

The **end-of-chapter material** includes short application problems to ensure students' understanding before they tackle the longer mastery and challenge problems.

"The activities and problems at the end of the chapter do a great job of providing students with the chance to use their knowledge and skills from the chapter sections."

Kathleen Harenza,
Mukwonago High School,
Mukwonago, WI

End of Lesson Review

LO5 Estimate the cost of merchandise inventory.

LO6 Calculate the inventory turnover ratio and days' sales in inventory.

Terms Review

gross profit method of estimating inventory
retail method of estimating inventory
inventory turnover ratio
days' sales in inventory

Audit your understanding

1. On what assumptions is the gross profit method of estimating inventory based?
2. To use the retail method of estimating inventory, what records must be kept?
3. Explain an inventory turnover ratio of 5.0.
4. Explain a days' sales in inventory of 60.

Work together 5-3

Estimating inventory using the gross profit and retail methods; financial analysis of merchandise inventory

The following information is available for Debbie's Fabrics for the month of October. Estimated merchandise inventory sheets are provided in the *Working Papers*. Your instructor will guide you through the following examples.

	Cost	Retail
Beginning inventory, October 1	$96,850.00	$205,190.00
Net purchases for October	19,480.00	40,750.00
Net sales for October		40,510.00
Gross profit percentage	52.6%	

1. Estimate the ending inventory using the gross profit method.
2. Estimate the ending inventory using the retail method. Round the percentage to the nearest 0.1%.
3. The inventory for Debbie's Fabrics was $92,890.00 on January 1 and $101,700.00 on December 31. The cost of merchandise sold for the year was $496,710.00. Calculate the inventory turnover ratio and the days' sales in inventory. Round the inventory turnover ratio to two decimal places and the days' sales in inventory to the nearest day.

On your own 5-3

Estimating inventory using the gross profit and retail methods; financial analysis of merchandise inventory

The following information is available for Kelly Music for the month of July. Estimated merchandise inventory sheets are provided in the *Working Papers*. Work independently to complete the following problem.

	Cost	Retail
Beginning inventory, July 1	$65,180.00	$159,750.00
Net purchases for July	24,740.00	58,900.00
Net sales for July		62,730.00
Gross profit percentage	58.4%	

1. Estimate the ending inventory using the gross profit method.
2. Estimate the ending inventory using the retail method. Round the percentage to the nearest 0.1%.
3. Kelly Music's inventory was $63,250.00 on January 1 and $70,960.00 on December 31. The cost of merchandise sold for the year was $289,210.00. Calculate the inventory turnover ratio and the days' sales in inventory. Round the inventory turnover ratio to two decimal places and the days' sales in inventory to the nearest day.

162 Chapter 5 Inventory Planning and Valuation

Transform Your Course by **Bringing**

Problem Solving Creativity

Greater emphasis on conceptual understanding and financial statement analysis has been incorporated into the 10th Edition, making it easier to balance coverage of accounting mechanics with how accounting information is used to make business decisions.

NEW! 21ST CENTURY SKILLS

included in the end-of-chapter material, provides activities that cultivate mastery of essential skills such as problem solving, communication, and technology use as defined by the Partnership for 21st Century Learning. Acquisition of the knowledge and skills taught in this feature will prepare students to compete in a workplace that demands creativity and innovation.

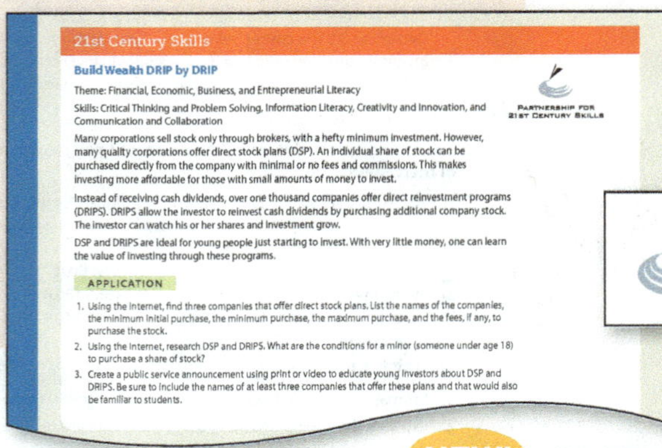

21st Century Skills

Build Wealth DRIP by DRIP

Theme: Financial, Economic, Business, and Entrepreneurial Literacy

Skills: Critical Thinking and Problem Solving, Information Literacy, Creativity and Innovation, and Communication and Collaboration

Partnership for 21st Century Skills

Many corporations sell stock only through brokers, with a hefty minimum investment. However, many quality corporations offer direct stock plans (DSP). An individual share of stock can be purchased directly from the company with minimal or no fees and commissions. This makes investing more affordable for those with small amounts of money to invest.

Instead of receiving cash dividends, over one thousand companies offer direct reinvestment programs (DRIPS). DRIPS allow the investor to reinvest cash dividends by purchasing additional company stock. The investor can watch his or her shares and investment grow.

DSP and DRIPS are ideal for young people just starting to invest. With very little money, one can learn the value of investing through these programs.

APPLICATION

1. Using the Internet, find three companies that offer direct stock plans. List the names of the companies, the minimum initial purchase, the minimum purchase, the maximum purchase, and the fees, if any, to purchase the stock.
2. Using the Internet, research DSP and DRIPS. What are the conditions for a minor (someone under age 18) to purchase a share of stock?
3. Create a public service announcement using print or video to educate young investors about DSP and DRIPS. Be sure to include the names of at least three companies that offer these plans and that would also be familiar to students.

CRITICAL THINKING ACTIVITIES

are infused throughout the text to provide more opportunities for higher-level thinking and analysis, preparing students for college and career readiness.

CRITICAL THINKING

PARTNERSHIP FOR 21ST CENTURY SKILLS

NEW! THINK LIKE AN ACCOUNTANT

presents challenging problems that correspond to higher-level thinking skills based on the criteria established in Bloom's Taxonomy.

Excel templates are provided for students to use as an analysis tool to compare and contrast employer benefit plans and analyze how their decisions affect the company's bottom line.

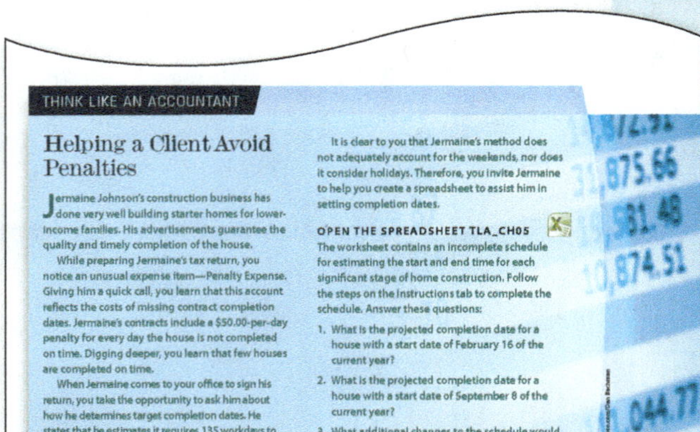

THINK LIKE AN ACCOUNTANT

Helping a Client Avoid Penalties

Jermaine Johnson's construction business has done very well building starter homes for lower-income families. His advertisements guarantee the quality and timely completion of the house.

While preparing Jermaine's tax return, you notice an unusual expense item—Penalty Expense. Giving him a quick call, you learn that this account reflects the costs of missing contract completion dates. Jermaine's contracts include a $50.00-per-day penalty for every day the house is not completed on time. Digging deeper, you learn that few houses are completed on time.

When Jermaine comes to your office to sign his return, you take the opportunity to ask him about how he determines target completion dates. He states that he estimates it requires 135 workdays to

It is clear to you that Jermaine's method does not adequately account for the weekends, nor does it consider holidays. Therefore, you invite Jermaine to help you create a spreadsheet to assist him in setting completion dates.

OPEN THE SPREADSHEET TLA_CH05

The worksheet contains an incomplete schedule for estimating the start and end time for each significant stage of home construction. Follow the steps on the Instructions tab to complete the schedule. Answer these questions:

1. What is the projected completion date for a house with a start date of February 16 of the current year?
2. What is the projected completion date for a house with a start date of September 8 of the current year?
3. What additional changes to the schedule would

Accounting Practices to Life

Forensic Accounting presents criminal investigations involving fraud, providing students the opportunity to apply what they're learning in class to a real-world scenario. Students will examine the fraud scenarios using Excel® to analyze the data and continue the investigation.

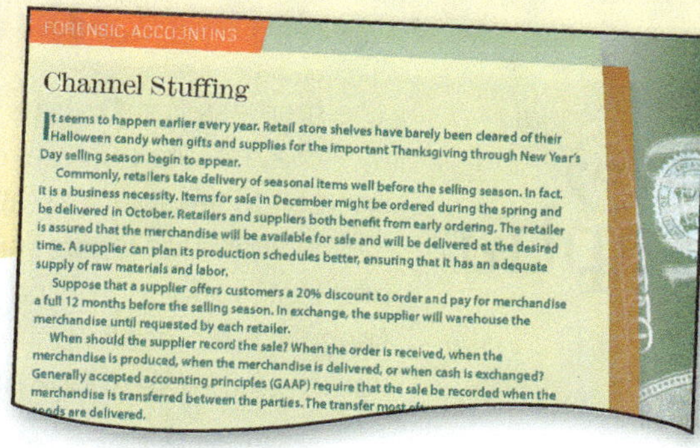

Why Accounting? provides examples of how accounting skills are applicable in a variety of business situations. Tied to the National Career Clusters, this feature illustrates how accounting knowledge transfers into the workplace and validates accounting's importance in the marketplace.

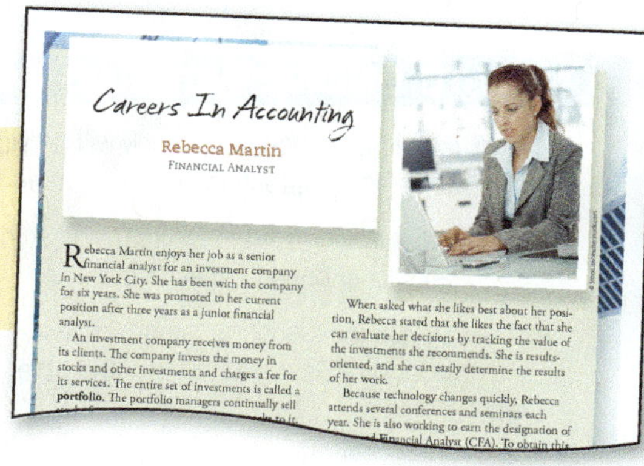

Careers in Accounting, designed to encourage students to think about their future in accounting, features a broad range of careers in the accounting field and promotes accounting as a profession through one-on-one interviews with various accounting professionals.

Bring Accounting Practices to Life with *Relevant Simulations*

Manual and automated simulations give your students hands-on, real-world experience in accounting practice. Automated simulations are completed using Automated Accounting Online, powered by CengageNOW.

Simulation 1: Organic Aisles

Students sell organice produce and grocery items in Organic Aisles, a departmentalized grocery store organized as a corporation. Students complete the simulation after Chapter 4. *Completion time: 10–20 hours.*

Simulation 2: Adventure Gear

Adventure rules as students bring adventure sport gear and accessories into the world of accounting within this merchandising business organized as a corporation. Students complete the simulation after Chapter 14. *Completion time: 10–20 hours.*

Online Working Papers

The market's first **Online Working Papers**, *powered by Aplia*, feature automatic grading for instructors and immediate feedback for students. C21 Accounting Online Working Papers mirror the print working papers and tests including online journals, ledgers, worksheets, financial statements, and other forms students use to complete their textbook problems and tests.

- Mirror the C21 Accounting Print Working Papers
- Immediate Feedback for Students
- Automatically Graded Assignments for Instructors
- Chapter Tests Included

Students who stay engaged with material put more effort into the course. Century 21 Online Working Papers give **students instant feedback**, making sure they are learning from each question while gaining a better understanding of accounting basics.

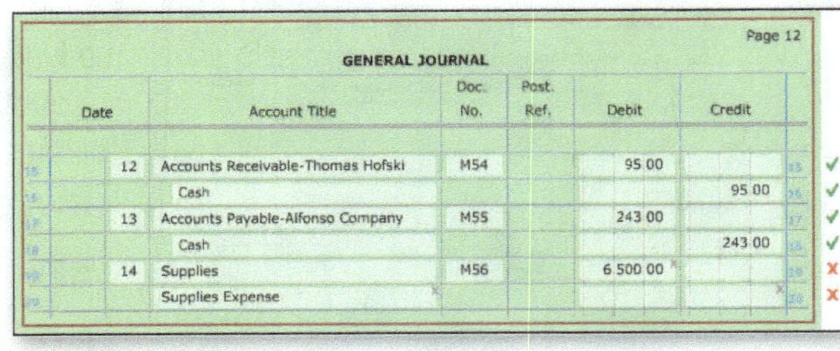

NEW TO ONLINE WORKING PAPERS FOR 10E

- Enhanced student feedback will provide students with additional instruction beyond right and wrong answers
- Algorithmic problems will provide students with additional opportunities to practice
- Device independent, the new online working papers will work on PCs, MACs, iPads, and other devices

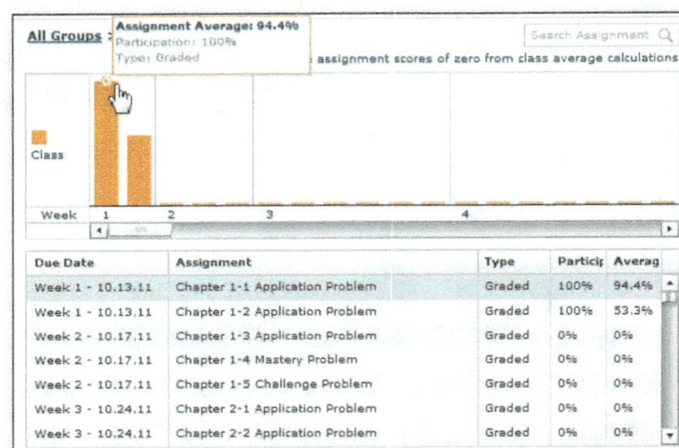

The Online Working Papers **automatically grade assignments**, relieving instructors of the burden of grading homework by hand. As students complete the assignments, the instructor receives a complete assessment of their work and comprehension levels, while their grades are instantly recorded in the instructor's online grade book.

The Online Working Papers keep instructors informed about student participation, progress, and performance through real-time graphical reports. Instructors can easily download, save, manipulate, print, and import student grades into their current grading program.

What Users Are Saying!

- **73%** say that **student performance has improved** in their class since using the Online Working Papers!
- **82%** report that their students are **more engaged** in the Accounting course.
- **75%** say their ability to **monitor student progress** has improved.
- **57%** say that after using Online Working Papers, their students are **more likely to enroll in further study in accounting** and/or other business education courses.

Visit www.cengage.com/school/accounting for a demo!

Accounting Digital Solutions

NEW! Automated Accounting Online is the next generation of the Automated Accounting software program that has successfully introduced students to computerized accounting for many years. Automated Accounting Online provides the functionality of commercial software incorporated with educational features that make teaching and learning computerized accounting easy. The completely redesigned interface is even more realistic and similar to what users see in commercial software programs such as Sage 50® and QuickBooks®.

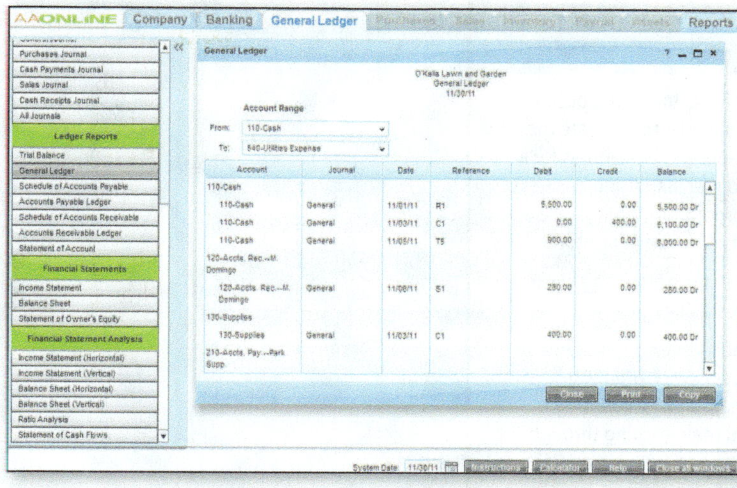

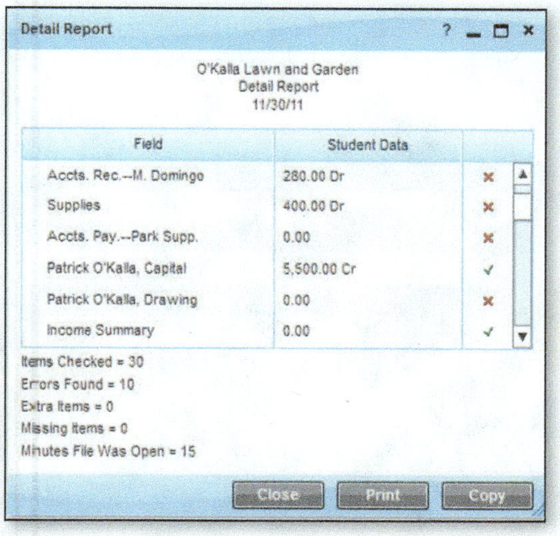

Automated Accounting Online:

- Is integrated into every chapter of Century 21 Accounting
- Provides immediate feedback for students
- Allows automatic grading for instructors
- Is compatible with PCs and MACs
- Is available anywhere with an Internet connection

For a free trial course, contact the CourseCare team at schoolscoursecare@cengage.com.

Student Companion Website extends the learning experience beyond the book with study tools, crossword puzzles, and data files.
www.c21accounting.com

Getting ready to start your class? Need help getting started?

CourseCare

Available exclusively from Cengage Learning, **CourseCare** is a revolutionary program designed to provide you with an unparalleled user experience with your Cengage Learning Digital Solution.

- 24/7 on-demand training resources
- Regularly scheduled professional training
- Dedicated Digital Solutions Coordinator

Please contact the CourseCare team at schoolscoursecare@cengage.com.

To learn more about the live and recorded training sessions available, please visit www.cengage.com/school/coursecare.

Part 1
Departmentalized Accounting

OVERVIEW

Whiley Outdoor Living, Inc., is the business that will be used in Part 1 to illustrate the accounting concepts and procedures for a departmentalized merchandising business organized as a corporation. Whiley has two sales departments: Grills and Furniture.

Part 1 is a review of the accounting cycle for a merchandise business.

Chapter organization and content provide students with a preview of what was presented in a first year of accounting study and expand their learning through applications relevant to a departmental accounting system.

- **Chapter 1** describes purchases and cash payments.
- **Chapter 2** describes sales and cash receipts.
- **Chapter 3** describes departmental payroll.
- **Chapter 4** describes financial reporting for a departmentalized business.

ACCOUNTING SOFTWARE

For those instructors who want to integrate the accounting program fully, A Look at Accounting Software feature is provided at the end of all of the chapters in Part 1. The feature is designed to show how the accounting procedures described in these chapters are handled in commercial accounting software. In addition, problems at the end of each chapter are flagged to show when files are provided for completing a problem using Excel, QuickBooks, or Sage 50 Accounting.

Part 1 Departmentalized Accounting

Reinforcement Activity

Reinforcement Activity 1, Processing and Reporting Departmentalized Accounting Data, may be completed after Chapter 4.

SIMULATION

The simulation *Organic Aisles* may be completed after Chapter 4.

THE BUSINESS—
WHILEY OUTDOOR LIVING, INC.

Whiley Outdoor Living, Inc., is the business that will be used in the chapters in Part 1 to illustrate the accounting concepts and procedures for a departmentalized merchandising business organized as a corporation. Whiley has two sales departments: Grills and Furniture.

© iStockphoto.com/Tim Abramowitz

Chart of Accounts
WHILEY OUTDOOR LIVING, INC.

GENERAL LEDGER

Balance Sheet Accounts

(1000) ASSETS

1100–1400 Current Assets
- 1105 Cash
- 1110 Petty Cash
- 1205 Accounts Receivable
- 1210 Allowance for Uncollectible Accounts
- 1305 Merchandise Inventory—Grills
- 1310 Merchandise Inventory—Furniture
- 1405 Supplies
- 1410 Prepaid Insurance

1500 Plant Assets
- 1505 Office Equipment
- 1510 Accumulated Depreciation—Office Equipment
- 1515 Store Equipment
- 1520 Accumulated Depreciation—Store Equipment

(2000) LIABILITIES

2100–2300 Current Liabilities
- 2105 Accounts Payable
- 2110 Sales Tax Payable
- 2215 Employee Income Tax Payable—Federal
- 2220 Employee Income Tax Payable—State
- 2225 Social Security Tax Payable
- 2230 Medicare Tax Payable
- 2235 Medical Insurance Payable
- 2240 Retirement Plan Payable
- 2245 Unemployment Tax Payable—Federal
- 2250 Unemployment Tax Payable—State
- 2305 Federal Income Tax Payable
- 2310 Dividends Payable

(3000) STOCKHOLDERS' EQUITY
- 3105 Capital Stock
- 3110 Retained Earnings
- 3115 Dividends
- 3205 Income Summary

Income Statement Accounts

(4000) OPERATING REVENUE
- 4105 Sales—Grills
- 4110 Sales Discount—Grills
- 4115 Sales Returns and Allowances—Grills
- 4205 Sales—Furniture
- 4210 Sales Discount—Furniture
- 4215 Sales Returns and Allowances—Furniture

(5000) COST OF MERCHANDISE
- 5105 Purchases—Grills
- 5110 Purchases Discount—Grills
- 5115 Purchases Returns and Allowances—Grills
- 5205 Purchases—Furniture
- 5210 Purchases Discount—Furniture
- 5215 Purchases Returns and Allowances—Furniture

(6000) DIRECT EXPENSES
- 6100 DIRECT EXPENSES—GRILLS
- 6105 Advertising Expense—Grills
- 6110 Payroll Taxes Expense—Grills
- 6115 Salary Expense—Grills
- 6200 DIRECT EXPENSES—FURNITURE
- 6205 Advertising Expense—Furniture
- 6210 Payroll Taxes Expense—Furniture
- 6215 Salary Expense—Furniture

(7000) INDIRECT EXPENSES
- 7105 Credit Card Fee Expense
- 7110 Depreciation Expense—Office Equipment
- 7115 Depreciation Expense—Store Equipment
- 7120 Insurance Expense
- 7125 Miscellaneous Expense
- 7130 Payroll Taxes Expense—Administrative
- 7135 Phone Expense
- 7140 Rent Expense
- 7145 Salary Expense—Administrative
- 7150 Supplies Expense
- 7155 Uncollectible Accounts Expense
- 7160 Utilities Expense

(8000) INCOME TAX
- 8105 Federal Income Tax Expense

The chart of accounts for Whiley Outdoor Living, Inc., is illustrated above for ready reference as you study Part 1 of this textbook.

DIFFERENTIATED INSTRUCTION

Interpersonal learners are people-oriented and learn best when working with cooperative learning groups or with a partner. Working with a group to compare similarities and differences in the chart of accounts is often rewarding for these students.

Chart of Accounts

- Emphasize that students should refer to this chart of accounts throughout the chapters in Part 1.
- Explain that this chart of accounts is used by a merchandising business organized as a corporation.
- Stress that charts of accounts are extremely important to companies because they drive the accounting system. Employees usually cannot even receive reimbursement for expenses without knowing to which account the expense should be charged.
- Emphasize that charts of accounts are used for determining the classification of accounts and show which accounts are temporary and permanent accounts.
- Stress that the chart of accounts is useful for completing automated accounting activities, because account numbers are required for both data entry and file maintenance activities.

TEACHING IDEA **Place students in groups and instruct them to identify similarities and differences between this chart of accounts and the one used for a nondepartmentalized merchandising business organized as a corporation presented in the first-year course.**

- Point out the typical divisions for a merchandising business (and the familiar accounts within divisions):
  - Assets
  - Liabilities
  - Stockholders' Equity
  - Operating Revenue
  - Cost of Merchandise
  - Direct Expenses
  - Indirect Expenses
  - Income Tax
- Departmentalized businesses have many accounts specific to departments. In the Assets section, there is a merchandise inventory account for each department. The Operating Revenue and Cost of Merchandise accounts are all departmentalized.
- The Direct Expenses section is divided into Direct Expenses—Grills and Direct Expenses—Furniture to track expenses chargeable to the operations of a specific department.
- The Indirect Expenses section contains expense accounts required for the overall operations of the business.

Chapter 1

Recording Departmental Purchases and Cash Payments

Scope & Sequence

	New	Review/Enrich
Introduction		
Introduce the Chapter		
Lesson 1-1: Using Accounting Principles and Records		
Financial Reporting for Departments	✓	
Accounting Equation		✓
Accounting Records		✓
General Journal		✓
Normal Balances of Accounts		✓
General and Subsidiary Ledgers		✓
General and Subsidiary Ledger File Maintenance		✓
Lesson 1-2: Journalizing and Posting Purchases and Purchases Returns		
Departmental Accounting System	✓	
Journalizing Purchases on Account	✓	
Posting from a Purchases Journal	✓	
Posting the Totals of a Purchases Journal	✓	
Journalizing Purchases Returns and Allowances	✓	
Lesson 1-3: Journalizing and Posting Cash Payments		
Departmental Cash Payments	✓	
Journalizing a Purchases Discount	✓	
Recording Entries in a Cash Payments Journal	✓	
Cash Payment to Replenish Petty Cash	✓	
Posting from a Cash Payments Journal	✓	
Closure		

Enhancing Instruction

Features	Common Core Standards
• Accounting in the Real World: Skechers	• ELAL—reading
• Ethics in Action: Researching Codes of Conduct • Forensic Accounting: Embezzlement Made Easy	• ELAL—writing • Mathematics
• Global Awareness: International Terms of Sale	• ELAL—media and technology, writing
• Why Accounting: Microcredit • Think Like an Accountant: Analyzing Purchases Discounts	• ELAL—media and technology, writing • Mathematics
• A Look at Accounting Software • Explore Accounting • 21st Century Skills • Source Documents Problem • Auditing for Errors • Analyzing Home Depot's Financial Statements	• ELAL—reading • ELAL—speaking, listening • ELAL—speaking, writing • Mathematics • Mathematics • Mathematics

ELAL = English Language Arts & Literacy

Calculator: © iStockphoto.com/picstodisc Paper: © iStockphoto.com/Qingwa

Technology & Media	Teaching Strategies
	• Interpersonal Learners
• Instructor's Resource CD/Website: PowerPoint Slides Accounting Concepts • Online Working Papers • Transparency Master: General Journal	
• Instructor's Resource CD/Website: PowerPoint Slides Accounting Concepts • Online Working Papers • Transparency Masters: Purchases Journal, Departmental Purchases Journal, General Journal	• Gifted Learners
• Instructor's Resource CD/Website: PowerPoint Slides Accounting Concepts • Online Working Papers • Transparency Master: Departmental Cash Payments Journal	• Mathematical/Logical Learners
• Online Working Papers	• Common Core and Interdisciplinary Studies

Practice and Assessment

Guided Practice	Independent Practice	Reteach/Enrich
• Terms Review • Audit Your Understanding • Work Together 1-1	• On Your Own 1-1 • Application Problem 1-1 • Formative Assessment, p. 11 • Online Working Papers	• Reteach, p. 12
• Terms Review • Audit Your Understanding • Work Together 1-2	• On Your Own 1-2 • Application Problem 1-2 • Formative Assessment, p. 18 • Online Working Papers	• Reteach, p. 19
• Terms Review • Audit Your Understanding • Work Together 1-3	• On Your Own 1-3 • Application Problem 1-3 • Formative Assessment, p. 26 • Online Working Papers	• Reteach, p. 27
	• Mastery Problem 1-M • Study Guide 1 • Chapter 1 Test • Cognero Chapter 1	• Challenge Problem 1-C • Reteach, p. 32 • Recycling Problem 1-R

Introduce the Chapter

SET THE STAGE

GUIDING QUESTIONS

- Ask students to brainstorm familiar businesses in the area. Ask students to name departments that might exist in each of the businesses.
- Why would a manager of an individual department want financial data specific to that department only? Provide an example.

PREVIEW CHAPTER OBJECTIVES

- Explain that a departmentalized merchandising business operates similarly to a nondepartmentalized business. However, a departmentalized business requires information about the performance of each department. Consequently, additional accounts are used to accumulate the departmental data needed.

TEACHING IDEA **Create a visual to display the accounting equation in the classroom or in another permanent location to refer to throughout the course.**

PREVIEW ACCOUNTING TERMS

- Read each term aloud to verify its pronunciation for students.
- Point out terms or parts of terms that should already be familiar to most students.
- Lead an interactive discussion that reviews and explains the terms. Stress that special attention should be directed to all boldfaced words presented in the text.

Chapter 1

Recording Departmental Purchases and Cash Payments

LEARNING OBJECTIVES

After studying Chapter 1, in addition to defining key terms, you will be able to:

LO1 Explain the relationship between the accounting equation and accounting records.

LO2 Explain the relationship between a subsidiary ledger and a controlling account.

LO3 Explain the purpose of a departmental accounting system.

LO4 Journalize departmental purchases of merchandise on account using a purchases journal.

LO5 Post merchandise purchases to an accounts payable ledger and a general ledger.

LO6 Journalize departmental purchases returns and allowances.

LO7 Journalize departmental cash payments using a cash payments journal.

LO8 Post cash payments to an accounts payable ledger and a general ledger.

Calculator: © iStockphoto.com/picstudio; Paper: © iStockphoto.com/Qingwa

© wavebreakmedia/Shutterstock.com

Accounting In The Real World

Skechers

A veteran of the shoe industry, Robert Greenberg founded Skechers USA, Inc., in 1992. The company began as a distributor of shoes and fashions of several existing companies. But Greenberg quickly recognized that no other company was marketing contemporary street shoes for men. In 1993, Greenberg introduced the Skechers brand of shoes that became the foundation of his business.

With over 3,000 brands today, Skechers is best known for its line of toner shoes. These innovative shoes do more than support an athlete's feet. Skechers' line of Shape-up shoes is designed to improve the results of any athletic activity, from a casual walk to strenuous exercise. Skechers claims that its curved sole burns more calories, tones leg muscles, and improves posture.

Skechers now offers a complete line of shoes for women, men, boys, and girls. Shoe styles go well beyond traditional athletic shoes. Skechers incorporates its technology into its boots, casual shoes, dress shoes, sandals, sneakers, and work shoes. These shoes are sold in the United States and internationally throughout Canada, Europe, Asia, and South America.

Inspired by a competitor, Skechers introduced its BOBS footwear in 2010. BOBS stands for Benefitting Others By Shoes. For each pair of BOBS sold, Skechers donates a pair of BOBS shoes to boys and girls in need.

With so many shoes and product lines being sold around the world, how should Skechers' financial statements report its sales? The financial statements Skechers submits to the public report financial information in four divisions: domestic wholesale sales, international wholesale sales, retail sales, and e-commerce sales.

CRITICAL THINKING

1. Managers need more detailed financial information than is reported to the public. Managers in Skechers' e-commerce division need to know which shoes its online consumers are buying. How would you suggest sales in this division be further divided?
2. Would you recommend that Skechers record BOBS sales and expenses as a separate division? Explain.

Source: www.skechers.com; www.fundinguniverse.com.

Background: © iStockphoto.com/Buzz Productions; Real World: Daniel Barry/Bloomberg/Getty Images

Key Terms

- asset
- liability
- equities
- owners' equity
- stockholders' equity
- accounting equation
- source documents
- double-entry accounting
- journal
- special journal
- account
- ledger
- general ledger
- subsidiary ledger
- controlling account
- file maintenance
- departmental accounting system
- merchandising business
- posting
- debit memorandum
- contra account
- cash discount
- purchases discount
- petty cash

Accounting In The Real World

Each chapter introduction spotlights an actual business familiar to students. You may use this feature and the accompanying intriguing questions to demonstrate how the chapter's content applies to real businesses today.

Ask students to share any experience they have had involving a Skechers product. Motivate students by asking them how they became familiar with Skechers (store fronts, print ads, television advertising, websites, etc.). Spark discussion by asking students if they know any of Skechers' competitors who have a line similar to that of BOBS.

Ask students to read the feature or have one or more students read the feature aloud. Remind them to pay close attention to the detail of the business as they read. Give students 5–10 minutes to jot down ideas for answering the Critical Thinking questions. Then discuss the answers in class.

As an alternative, you can organize students into groups of 3 or 4 individuals to generate possible answers to the questions. With this approach, you may also want to record the suggestions and save them for additional discussion after the chapter is completed.

Answers

1. Answers may vary. One method of answering the question would be to follow the structure of Skechers' e-commerce site. Consumers are offered four links into its catalog of products: Women, Men, Girls, and Boys. A consumer can then browse by style, price, size, and color. For example, if Skechers divided a sales division by style, it might look at sales of athletic shoes versus casual shoes versus sandals. Sales could also be divided by country or by domestic region.
2. Answers may vary. It is unlikely that a division consisting solely of BOBS' sales and expenses would be significant relative to the existing divisions. However, the company should maintain detailed accounting records of BOBS' sales and expenses. This information could prove useful in evaluating and publicizing the charitable initiative.

LESSON
1-1

BRIDGE

- Discuss work experiences with students. Ask for examples of tasks that required knowledge of accounting concepts or principles.
- Explain that the accounting concepts and principles previously learned will remain unchanged and will now be applied to a business with multiple departments.
- Emphasize that the first-year accounting course presented the accounting concepts and practices related to recording, summarizing, and reporting the financial information for a merchandising business organized as a corporation. Explain that this lesson will review the accounting equation, the use of special journals and the general journal, the use of general and subsidiary ledgers, and the chart of accounts numbering system and file maintenance.

TEACHING RESOURCES

- **Instructor's Resource CD/Website:**
  PowerPoint Slides
  Accounting Concepts
- **Working Papers:**
  Teacher's Edition of the Working Papers for Lesson 1-1
  Online Working Papers
- **Transparency Master:**
  General Journal

ENGAGE

- Have students read the text. Ask them why a large clothing store with separate men's, women's, and children's departments would be interested in knowing how well each department is doing.
- Ask students what types of information should be collected about each department. Write answers on the board.
- Emphasize that regardless of the accounting procedures used for a departmentalized business, the same accounting concepts and practices are followed.

© Robert Kneschke/Shutterstock.com

LESSON 1-1 Using Accounting Principles and Records

LO1 Explain the relationship between the accounting equation and accounting records.
LO2 Explain the relationship between a subsidiary ledger and a controlling account.

Financial Reporting for Departments LO1

Financial information for a business can be recorded, summarized, and reported in a variety of ways. Accountants design accounting systems to meet the specific needs of the business. The way in which information is kept and reported in the accounting system is determined by the size, type, and complexity of the business. When designing financial records, the business should also consider the types of decisions that will be made, based on the financial statements.

If managers of individual departments want to use financial statements to assist in making decisions, information for each department must be recorded separately. The types of information to be gathered by department include purchases, sales, and expenses. Payroll data may also be identified by department. Gathering information by department requires a somewhat different set of accounting procedures. Regardless of the accounting procedures used, the same accounting concepts and practices are followed.

If a business decides to record information by department, it must establish procedures to ensure that transactions are assigned to the correct department. The chart of accounts must contain departmental accounts for significant types of transactions, such as purchases, sales, and salary expense.

ETHICS IN ACTION

Researching Codes of Conduct

The Sarbanes-Oxley Act of 2002 requires publicly traded companies to have a code of conduct. Most companies make their codes available on the Internet. Companies title and link their codes differently. Accessing these codes on the Internet requires knowledge of common search terms and methods.

Begin your Internet search by visually scanning the available links on the company's home page. *Code of Conduct*, *Code of Ethics*, and *Corporate Governance* are common links. A company whose website is designed primarily to sell its product is unlikely to have an ethics-related link on its home page. In this case, look at the top or bottom of the web page and find a link such as *Investor Relations*.

Most companies provide a search tool. Use the search tool to search for any of these terms: *ethics*, *code of conduct*, *code of ethics*, and *corporate governance*.

INSTRUCTIONS

Access the code of conduct for three publicly traded companies. Prepare a summary of the links and searches you used to access the code for each company.

© iStockphoto.com/LdF

PREVIEW

- Call on students to read the accounting terms and definitions introduced in this lesson: *asset, liability, equities, owners' equity, stockholders' equity, accounting equation, source documents, double-entry accounting, journal, special journal, account, ledger, general ledger, subsidiary ledger, controlling account*, and *file maintenance*.
- Point out the learning objectives for this lesson.
- Direct students to read the headings on each page in this lesson and to examine the illustrations.

ETHICS IN ACTION

Answers will vary.

Throughout this textbook, the ethics features may require students to access the code of conduct of certain companies. This activity helps students access these codes regardless of the code title and how the code is linked on the company's website. You may allow students to select their three companies or assign different companies to each student or group of students.

Accounting Equation

Accounting Equation

Assets	=	Liabilities + Owners' Equity

Accounting Equation

(LEFT side of equation) Assets	=	(RIGHT side of equation) Liabilities + Owners' Equity

Anything of value that is owned is called an **asset**. An amount owed by a business is called a **liability**. Financial rights to the assets of a business are called **equities**. The amount remaining after the value of all liabilities is subtracted from the value of all assets is called **owners' equity**. The owners' equity in a corporation is called **stockholders' equity**.

An equation showing the relationship among assets, liabilities, and owners' equity is called the **accounting equation**. The accounting equation may be stated as assets = equities. More commonly, the equation is stated as assets = liabilities + owners' equity.

The equation is often viewed as forming a "T." In the figure above, assets are listed on the left side of the T account and equities (liabilities and owners' equity) on the right side of the T account. Total assets must always equal total liabilities plus owners' equity.

Accounting Records

Accounting records show changes and the current account balance of each asset, liability, and owners' equity (or stockholders' equity) account. Business transactions are reported in numbers that have common values—that is, using a common unit of measurement. If part of the information in the accounting records is financial and part is nonfinancial, the financial statements will not be clear. In the United States, the amounts are stated in dollars and cents. [CONCEPT: Unit of Measurement]

Accounting concepts are described throughout this textbook. When an application of a concept first occurs, it is explained. When additional applications occur, a concept reference, such as [CONCEPT: Business Entity], is used to indicate an application of a specific accounting concept. A brief description of each accounting concept used in this text is also provided in Appendix A and on the Century 21 Accounting website at www.C21accounting.com.

Business papers from which information is obtained for a journal entry are called **source documents**. Each journal entry must be supported by a source document proving that a transaction occurred. [CONCEPT: Objective Evidence] The source document is the original business paper indicating that the transaction did occur and that the amounts recorded in the accounting records are accurate and true. When accounting information reported on the financial statements needs to be verified, an accountant will first check the accounting record. If the details of an entry need further checking, an accountant will then check the source documents as objective evidence that the transaction did occur.

fyi

The government's first regulation of accounting information occurred in 1917 with the Federal Reserve Board's publication of "Uniform Accounts."

INPUT

- Explain the accounting equation by discussing the relationship among assets, liabilities, and owners' equity, as shown in the illustration.
- Explain that source documents are used as the evidence that a business transaction occurred.
- Explain the Unit of Measurement concept.

MODEL

Accounting equation

- Show the relationship among assets, liabilities, and owners' equity by writing the accounting equation on the board. Remind students that in a corporation, the value of the owners' equity is referred to as stockholders' equity.
- Emphasize the relationship by asking students to name an automobile. Write the approximate value of the auto under "assets" in the accounting equation (e.g., $8,500). Ask students if the owner put $2,000 down, where that amount would be recorded. Write $2,000 under "owners' equity." Ask students to determine the amount owed and write $6,500 under "liabilities."
- Bring several source documents to class. Have students work in groups to create a T account analysis of the business transaction shown on the source documents.

INPUT

- Review the accounting equation and explain how it is the basis for double-entry accounting.
- Review the use of a general journal and explain the relationship of the accounting equation to the amount columns in a general journal.
- Review the use of the four special journals.

MODEL

Review the accounting equation

- Write the accounting equation. Remind students that any time there is a change in a company's assets, liabilities, or owners' equity, it is important to record that change. Point out that the accounting equation helps ensure the accuracy of recording changes, because Assets must always equal Liabilities + Owners' Equity.

Review journals

- Show a general journal transparency. Discuss the use of the general journal as a form for recording transactions in chronological order. Remind students that with each transaction, at least two accounts change, and that debits equal credits.
- Draw a *T* on the transparency over the debit and credit columns to emphasize that the left side of a T account represents the debit column of the general journal and that the right side of a T account represents the credit column.
- Point out to students that "debit" does not necessarily mean increase, nor does "credit" necessarily mean decrease. Reinforce this concept by referring students to the illustration.
- Write the titles of the four special journals. Ask students to identify the one kind of transaction recorded in each journal. Write correct responses next to the appropriate journal title.

General Journal

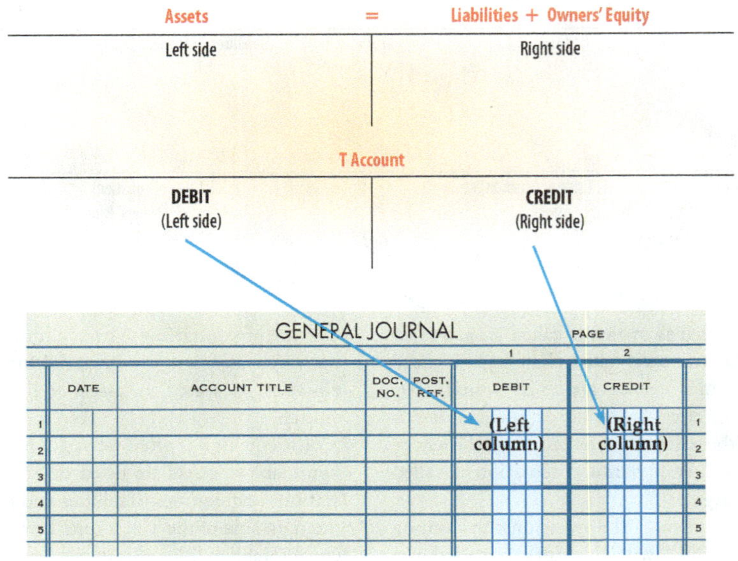

The recording of debit and credit parts of a transaction is called **double-entry accounting**. With every transaction, at least two accounts will change. Two accounting principles are common to double-entry accounting: (1) The total value of things owned by a business (assets) equals the total value of claims of outsiders (liabilities) and claims of owners (owners' equity). (2) Debits equal credits for each business transaction recorded.

A form for recording transactions in chronological order is called a **journal**. A general journal may be used to record all business transactions. A general journal includes amount columns for recording the dollars and cents of a transaction. [CONCEPT: Unit of Measurement] The general journal has two amount columns. The left amount column is labeled *Debit*. The right amount column is labeled *Credit*. An entry recorded in the debit column is known as a *debit*. Likewise, an entry recorded in the credit column is known as a *credit*. The "T" previously described in the accounting equation is also present in a general journal's debit and credit amount columns.

A journal used to record only one kind of transaction is called a **special journal**. A business with many daily transactions may use special journals. Special journals include amount columns used to record debits or credits to specific accounts. For example, a cash payments journal includes a Cash Credit amount column. Whiley uses four special journals along with a general journal to record its transactions:

1. Purchases journal—for all purchases of merchandise on account
2. Cash payments journal—for all cash payments
3. Sales journal—for all sales of merchandise on account
4. Cash receipts journal—for all cash receipts

Whiley uses a general journal to record all other transactions.

remember Total assets must always equal total liabilities plus total owners' equity.

Normal Balances of Accounts

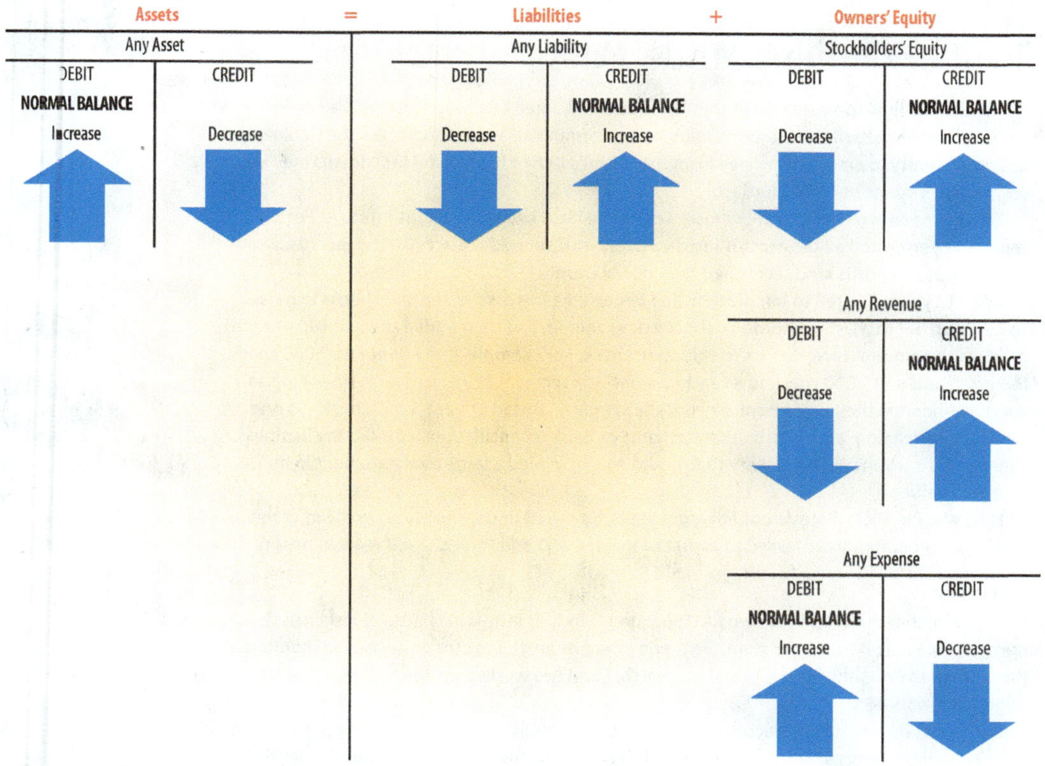

Transactions are journalized in chronological order. Periodically, information is sorted to summarize like kinds of information. A record that summarizes all the transactions pertaining to a single item in the accounting equation is called an **account**.

The amount in an account is known as an *account balance*. Each business transaction causes a change in two or more account balances. Increases in an account balance are recorded in the same column as its normal balance. Decreases in an account balance are recorded in the column opposite its normal balance. The normal balances of different classifications of accounts are shown in the figure above.

Asset account balances are increased by debits and decreased by credits. Liability and owners' equity account balances as well as revenue account balances are increased by credits and decreased by debits. Expense account balances are increased by debits and decreased by credits.

remember

Increases in revenue accounts increase owners' equity. Therefore, the normal credit balance of revenue accounts is the same as the normal balance of owners' equity. Increases in expense accounts decrease owners' equity. Therefore, the normal debit balance of expense accounts is opposite the normal balance of revenues or owners' equity.

INPUT

- Refer students to the illustration and review the rules for increasing and decreasing asset, liability, owners' equity, revenue, and expense accounts.
- Point out to students that transactions are initially journalized in chronological order, but that periodically it is important to summarize information regarding the changes in each account.
- Remind students of the rules and reasoning related to normal balance sides for revenue and expense accounts. For example, increases in revenue accounts increase owners' equity. Therefore, the normal credit balance of revenue accounts is the same as the normal balance of owners' equity. Increases in expense accounts decrease owners' equity. Therefore, the normal debit balance of expense accounts is opposite the normal balance of owners' equity.

MODEL

Review normal account balances

- After having students review the illustration, ask them to close their texts and take out a sheet of paper. Direct students to write the accounting equation on the paper. Instruct them to draw a *T* under the headings Assets, Liabilities, and Owners' Equity. Ask students to put a + on the increase side and a – on the decrease side of each account classification. Discuss answers. Point out that assets are on the left side of the accounting equation and are therefore increased with debits. Point out that liabilities and owners' equity are on the right side of the equation and are therefore increased with credits.
- Ask students to draw two more *T*s under owners' equity. Label one *revenue* and the other *expenses*. Ask students to record a + or – on the appropriate sides. Point out that revenue and expenses represent temporary capital accounts. Remind students that revenue increases owners' equity and is therefore increased with a credit. Explain that expenses decrease owners' equity. Because decreases to owners' equity are recorded on the debit side, the normal balance side for an expense is also on the debit side.

FORENSIC ACCOUNTING

Students create formulas and use the filter tool to identify checks that were processed by the bank but not recorded in the client's computerized accounting system. The VLOOKUP function is used to match a field from the Records worksheet to the checks on the Bank worksheet. Although students are directed to use the Vendor Name column, any column from the Records worksheet could be used.

The results exhibit some common traits of embezzlements. Employee theft typically increases in both amount and frequency over time. These traits provide forensic accountants with trends that can be detected with data analysis.

Suggested Solution

1. Eight checks cleared the bank but are not in the client's accounting records.
2. Three distinct trends are indicated by the checks:
   a. All the checks are written to an even hundred dollars.
   b. The amounts are gradually increasing in value.
   c. The checks are increasing in frequency.

FORENSIC ACCOUNTING

Embezzlement Made Easy

The danger is all too common in small businesses. A small business requires the services of a single bookkeeper. With responsibility for performing all accounting tasks, the bookkeeper has opportunity to embezzle money from the business. Over time, some individuals may be tempted to engage in such fraud.

So was the case of Kay Lemon, who served as the bookkeeper of a lighting store. For 20 years, she performed all the accounting duties. She maintained the accounting records, wrote checks, made deposits, and reconciled the bank account.

After 12 years, Kay fell to temptation. She began stealing cash by writing checks to herself. To cover up her theft, she recorded each check as voided. She then added the amount of each check to the amount recorded for a legitimate check. For example, if she wrote a $5,000 check to herself and a $15,000 check to a vendor, she would record a $20,000 disbursement to the vendor. When the bank statement arrived, she simply disposed of her $5,000 check. No one besides Kay ever looked at the bank statements or bank reconciliations. Nor did the business ever count its inventory, an activity that would have revealed a large overstatement in its recorded value.

How was her theft discovered? For eight years, Kay lived under the pressure of her crime. Finally, she voluntarily confessed to embezzling $416,000 and served three years in prison.

ACTIVITY

Randy Selman and Paul Deeds own R&P Sporting Goods. Randy is in charge of merchandise purchasing. Paul operates the store. Neither owner has much time for or interest in monitoring the work of their bookkeeper, Carol Hainsworth. Carol has worked for the business since it began ten years ago.

Randy has delivered R&P's accounting records to its public accounting firm for preparation of its annual tax returns. At the suggestion of the firm's partner, Randy has agreed to let the firm's forensic accounting staff perform a few basic tests on the data.

The workbook contains two worksheets. One worksheet contains a list of all checks obtained from the computerized accounting system. The second worksheet is a list of all bank transactions downloaded from R&P's online banking system.

1. How many checks cleared the bank but were not recorded in R&P's accounting records?
2. What trends do you detect in the list?

INSTRUCTIONS

Open the spreadsheet FA_CH01 and complete the steps on the Instructions tab.

Source: "Enemies Within," Joseph T. Wells, *Journal of Accountancy*, December 2001.

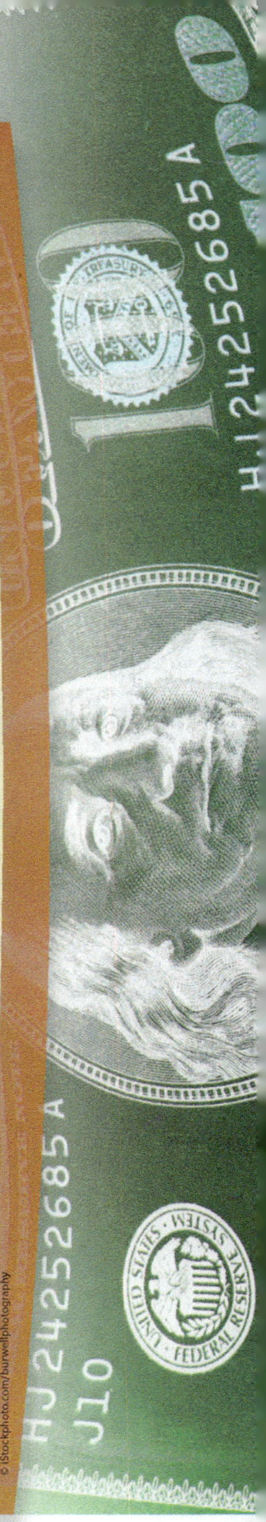

© iStockphoto.com/burwellphotography

General and Subsidiary Ledgers LO2

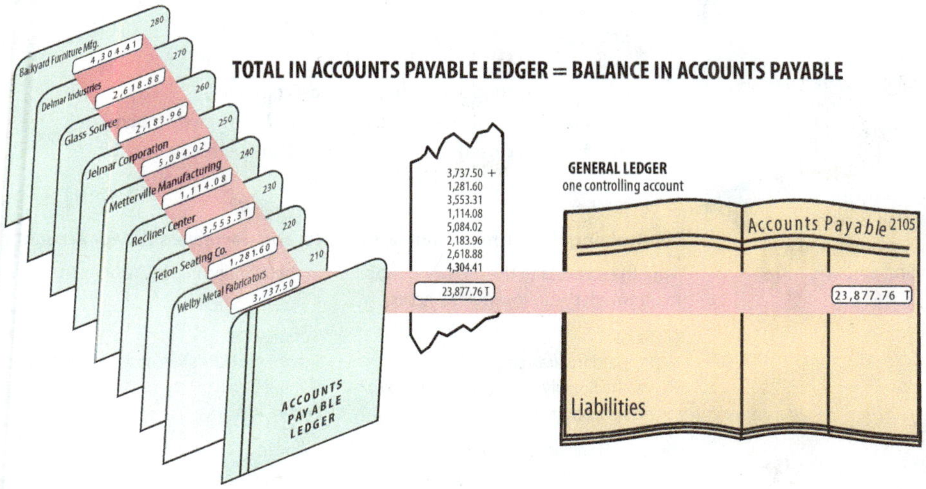

A group of accounts is called a **ledger**. A ledger that contains all accounts needed to prepare financial statements is called a **general ledger**. A ledger that is summarized in a single general ledger account is called a **subsidiary ledger**. An account in a general ledger that summarizes all accounts in a subsidiary ledger is called a **controlling account**.

Two subsidiary ledgers and two general ledger controlling accounts are commonly used:

Subsidiary Ledgers
Accounts Receivable Ledger
Accounts Payable Ledger

Controlling Accounts
Accounts Receivable
Accounts Payable

Accounts for customers who buy merchandise on account are kept in an accounts receivable ledger. The corresponding controlling account is Accounts Receivable. Separate accounts are kept in an accounts payable ledger for vendors to whom money is owed. The corresponding controlling account is Accounts Payable. The total of the subsidiary ledger account balances should equal the balance of the controlling account.

General and Subsidiary Ledger File Maintenance

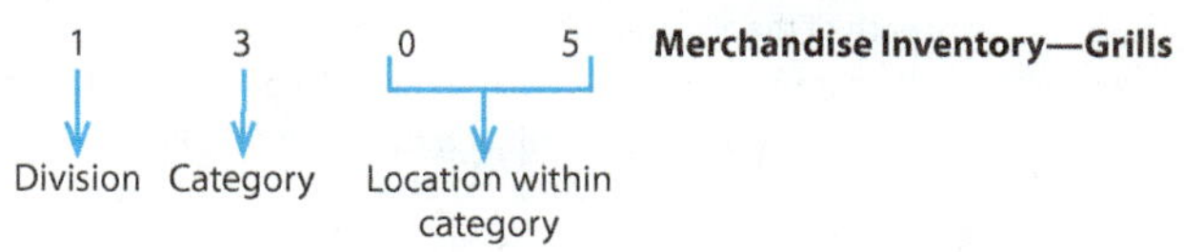

Whiley uses a general ledger account numbering system that meets three needs: (1) A separate numeric listing is provided for each ledger division. (2) A predesigned arrangement of numbers is provided within each ledger division. (3) Account number digits are spaced to allow the addition of new accounts. The procedure for arranging accounts in a general ledger, assigning account numbers, and keeping records current is called **file maintenance**.

The number assigned to Merchandise Inventory—Grills is analyzed above. Whiley's general ledger chart of accounts has eight divisions. The first digit of each four-digit account number shows the general ledger division in which the account is located. For example, asset accounts begin with the number 1.

The accounts in some divisions, such as Assets, are divided into categories. The second digit of the account number shows the category in which the account is located. Whiley assigns the number 3 to all inventory accounts. The categories are not necessarily labeled in the chart of accounts. However, an analysis of the accounts in a category should reveal the nature of a category. For example, all liability accounts in category 2 are related to payroll taxes.

The last two digits show the location of a specific account with respect to other accounts in that division and category.

INPUT

- Review the definitions of *ledger, general ledger, subsidiary ledger,* and *controlling account*.
- Explain how the general ledger controlling account summarizes all accounts in a subsidiary ledger.
- Emphasize that the total of the subsidiary accounts must equal the balance in the appropriate controlling account.
- Explain the difference between accounts receivable and accounts payable.

MODEL

Review subsidiary ledgers

- Use the illustration to show the relationship between accounts payable subsidiary accounts and the controlling account. Emphasize that the individual account totals shown on the calculator tape equal the total in the controlling account.
- Ask students to prepare a similar example to show the relationship between accounts receivable subsidiary accounts and the controlling account. Ask students to write their examples on the board.
- Ask students to explain the difference between accounts payable and accounts receivable. Ask for examples.

INPUT

- Review the definition of *file maintenance*.
- Review the chart of accounts numbering system.

MODEL

File maintenance

- Direct student attention to the chart of accounts presented on page 3. Ask students to explain the purpose of each digit of the numbering system. (*First number indicates the division, second digit indicates the category, and third and fourth digits indicate position in category.*)

TEACHING IDEA **Foam Ball Review Game: Ask students to stand in a circle. Using the chart of accounts, assign an account name to each student, being sure to assign accounts randomly, so that not all classifications are next to each other. Throw the ball to a student. That student must state his or her account name and the first number in his or her account number in the chart of accounts. If students are having difficulty, they may ask the person to their right for help.**

FORMATIVE ASSESSMENT

- This is an ongoing process. Circulate around the classroom or lab, observing which students have problems with the assignments.
- Troubleshooting: Students may have problems identifying account classifications and the rules for increasing and decreasing assets, liabilities, owners' equity, revenue, and expense accounts.
- Assess student understanding by checking solutions to Independent Practice assignments and noting their answers to the Terms and Audit Your Understanding questions.

CHECK FOR UNDERSTANDING

Terms Review

- Call on students to define each term in the Terms Review. Definitions are given in the Glossary.

Audit Your Understanding

- Call on students to answer the Audit Your Understanding questions. Answers are given in Appendix D of the textbook.

GUIDED PRACTICE

Work Together

- Have students write the solution to the Work Together problem as you guide the class through the examples.
- Call on students for solutions.
- Ask a student to provide the rule for increasing and decreasing assets, liabilities, and owners' equity.

INDEPENDENT PRACTICE

On Your Own

- Assign the On Your Own problem to be worked independently.

Application Problem

- Assign Application Problem 1-1.

Online Working Papers

- Students can access the Lesson 1-1 problems using this software.

RETEACH

- Place the accounting equation and a list of accounts on the board. Select accounts from the chart of accounts on page 3. Ask students to classify accounts and assign account numbers. Using T accounts, ask students to indicate the increase and decrease sides of each account.
- Write a list of accounts. Ask students to arrange accounts based on their classifications. Direct students to assign appropriate numbers.
- Ask a student to explain the relationship between a T account and the debit and credit columns of a general journal. Ask another student to illustrate the relationship using a transparency of the general journal.

CLOSURE

- Ask students to name the classifications for accounts. As each classification is announced, ask students the rules for increasing and decreasing an account under that particular classification.

End of Lesson Review

LO1 Explain the relationship between the accounting equation and accounting records.

LO2 Explain the relationship between a subsidiary ledger and a controlling account.

Terms Review

asset
liability
equities
owners' equity
stockholders' equity
accounting equation
source documents
double-entry accounting
journal
special journal
account
ledger
general ledger
subsidiary ledger
controlling account
file maintenance

Audit your understanding

1. How is the accounting equation stated most commonly?
2. What is the normal balance of an asset account? A revenue account?
3. What are the three needs met by Whiley's account numbering system?

Work together 1-1

Determining the normal balance, increase, and decrease sides for accounts

Write the answers to the following problems in the *Working Papers*. Your instructor will guide you through the following examples.

Sales	Supplies
Prepaid Insurance	Trent Associates (an account receivable)
Pacific Supply (an account payable)	Capital Stock
Advertising Expense	Petty Cash

For each of the accounts above, complete the following.

1. Prepare a T account for each account. Enter the title of the account.
2. In parentheses to the right of the account title, identify the account as asset, liability, owners' equity, revenue, or expense.
3. Label the debit and credit sides.
4. Label each side of the T account using the labels *Normal Balance*, *Increase*, or *Decrease*.

On your own 1-1

Determining the normal balance, increase, and decrease sides for accounts

Write the answers to the following problems in the *Working Papers*. Work this problem independently.

Rent Expense	Equipment
Utilities Expense	Mount Air Co. (an account receivable)
Sales	Pace Corp. (an account payable)
Cash	Retained Earnings

For each of the accounts above, complete the following.

1. Prepare a T account for each account. Enter the title of the account.
2. In parentheses to the right of the account title, identify the account as asset, liability, owners' equity, revenue, or expense.
3. Label the debit and credit sides.
4. Label each side of the T account using the labels *Normal Balance*, *Increase*, or *Decrease*.

© iStockphoto.com/urbanglimpses

- Review the illustration on page 9 showing normal balances of accounts.
- Review the figure on page 11 showing ledgers to help students understand the relationship between subsidiary accounts and a controlling account.

Essential Questions

- Why would it be beneficial for my business to have an accounts payable subsidiary ledger? (*Answers might include knowing the account history of each vendor—how much is owed and how much has been paid.*)
- What would be the similarities and differences in the chart of accounts if I started my own landscaping business? (*A landscaping business would likely have different inventory, expenses, and revenue. Revenues might come from landscaping services and products sold.*)

EXTENDED LEARNING

- Assign Accounting in the Real World on page 5.
- Assign Ethics in Action on page 6.
- Assign Forensic Accounting on page 10.

LESSON

1-2 Journalizing and Posting Purchases and Purchases Returns

LO3 Explain the purpose of a departmental accounting system.
LO4 Journalize departmental purchases of merchandise on account using a purchases journal.
LO5 Post merchandise purchases to an accounts payable ledger and a general ledger.
LO6 Journalize departmental purchases returns and allowances.

Departmental Accounting System LO3

Management decisions depend on accounting information about each phase of a business. When a business has two or more departments, accounting information can help management decide whether a department's performance is acceptable or unacceptable. Accounting information can also determine the kinds of merchandise that produce the greatest or the least profit.

An accounting system showing accounting information for two or more departments is called a **departmental accounting system**. In a departmental accounting system, gross profit is calculated for each department. The general ledger, therefore, must include a number of separate departmental accounts. Shoe stores, furniture stores, computer stores, department stores, and sporting goods stores are examples of firms that commonly organize on a departmental basis.

A business that purchases and sells goods is called a **merchandising business**. Whiley sells grills and outdoor furniture. The business is a corporation organized on a departmental basis.

Whiley uses a departmental accounting system. Accounting information is recorded and reported for two departments: (1) Grills and (2) Furniture. The separate departmental accounts for Whiley are in the chart of accounts at the beginning of Part 1. All accounts for the grills department include "Grills" in the account title. All accounts for the outdoor furniture department include "Furniture" in the account title. For example, the grills department's inventory account is titled Merchandise Inventory—Grills and is assigned number 1305. The first digit, 1, indicates that the account is an asset. The second digit, 3, shows the account is in the third category (inventory accounts) of the asset division. The last two digits, 05, show the location of the account with respect to the other accounts in the inventory account category.

All departmental purchases of merchandise on account are recorded in a purchases journal. A business with more than one department records a purchase on account in the same way as a business with a single department, except for two differences: (1) Each purchase invoice has a notation placed on it showing to which department the purchase applies. (2) Each department has a separate Purchases Debit column in the purchases journal. Whiley's purchases journal, shown on the next page, has special Purchases Debit columns for each department—Grills and Furniture. Purchase invoices are used as the source documents for all purchases on account. [CONCEPT: Objective Evidence]

fyi CPAs help small businesses avoid many of the pitfalls of doing business. Business owners rely on CPAs for advice in such areas as taxation, payroll requirements, banking policies, and business planning.

LESSON 1-2

BRIDGE

- Explain that students are already familiar with purchases transactions. However, in this lesson, students will make purchases transactions for a departmental merchandising business organized as a corporation.

TEACHING RESOURCES

- **Instructor's Resource CD/Website:**
  PowerPoint Slides
  Accounting Concepts
- **Working Papers:**
  Teacher's Edition of the Working Papers for Lesson 1-2
  Online Working Papers
- **Transparency Masters:**
  Purchases Journal
  Departmental Purchases Journal
  General Journal

ENGAGE

- Ask students to state examples of businesses that commonly organize on a departmental basis. Write responses on the board. Ask students why these businesses would want to keep separate accounting records for each department. Ask students what types of decisions a firm would make regarding a department.

PREVIEW

- Call on students to read the accounting terms and definitions introduced in this lesson: *departmental accounting system*, *merchandising business*, *posting*, *debit memorandum*, and *contra account*.
- Point out the learning objectives for this lesson.
- Direct students to read the headings in this lesson and to examine the illustrations.

INPUT

- Review the definition of a merchandising business. Lead into a discussion of a departmental accounting system. Present the departmental purchases journal and explain that the journal has a separate Purchases Debit column for each department. Discuss the numbering process used in a chart of accounts for a departmentalized business. Reinforce that source documents serve as the objective evidence for business transactions.

MODEL

- Write the definition of *merchandise*. Ask students for examples of merchandise. Then ask for examples of businesses that sell merchandise.
- Direct students to the chart of accounts on page 3. Ask them to look at the four-digit numbers under Income Statement Accounts. Ask them to explain what the first digit, a 4 or 5, represents and then the second digit, a 1 or a 2. Lead into a discussion of account numbering for a departmentalized business.
- Compare a transparency of a purchases journal and a departmental purchases journal. Ask students what is different.

INPUT

- Describe the source document used for all purchases on account—a purchase invoice.
- Remind students of the single type of transaction recorded in a purchases journal.
- Explain the steps for journalizing a departmental purchase on account.

MODEL

Analyze the transaction

- Direct attention to the illustration. Question students regarding quantity purchases, item no., unit price, terms, total amount, department, etc. Discuss the significance of using source documents in accounting.
- Use T accounts to explain the transaction presented. Ask students how they would record the same transaction if cash were paid. Emphasize that only purchases of merchandise on account are recorded in the purchases journal.
- Use a transparency to illustrate the procedures for journalizing the purchase of merchandise on account in the purchases journal. Emphasize, as with all transactions, that there must be at least one debit part and one credit part and that both parts must be equal.

Journalizing Purchases on Account LO4

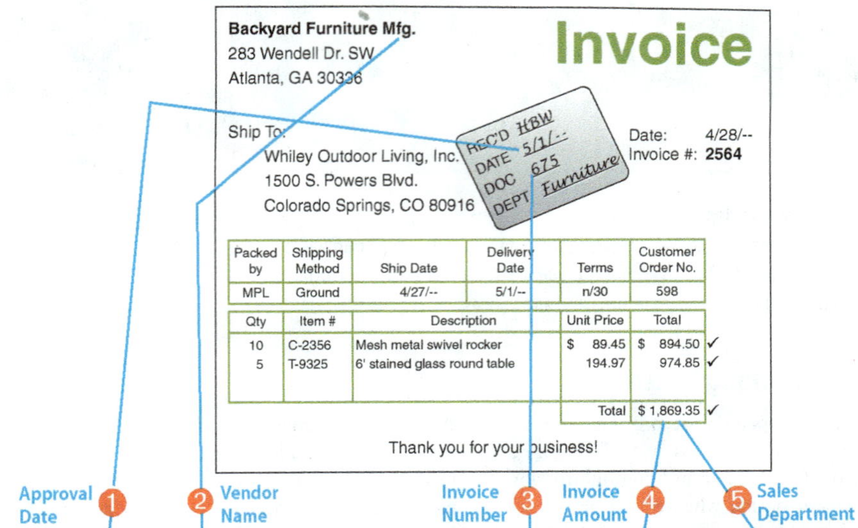

PURCHASES JOURNAL PAGE 5

	DATE		ACCOUNT CREDITED	PURCH. NO.	POST. REF.	1 ACCOUNTS PAYABLE CREDIT	2 PURCHASES DEBIT GRILLS	3 PURCHASES DEBIT FURNITURE	
1	20-- May	1	Backyard Furniture Mfg.	675		1 8 6 9 35		1 8 6 9 35	1
2									2

GENERAL LEDGER

Purchases—Furniture

Debit	Credit
↑ 1,869.35	

Accounts Payable

Debit	Credit
	↑ 1,869.35

ACCOUNTS PAYABLE LEDGER

Backyard Furniture Mfg.

Debit	Credit
	↑ 1,869.35

May 1. Purchased furniture on account from Backyard Furniture Mfg., $1,869.35. Purchase Invoice No. 675.

When a purchase invoice is received, an employee verifies the accuracy of the invoice. A stamp may be used to provide a place to enter his or her initials, the date the invoice is received, the purchase invoice number assigned, and the department.

Journalizing a Purchase on Account

1. Write the date the invoice was received and approved, May 1, in the Date column. Since this is the first entry on page 5, include the current year, 20--.
2. Enter the vendor name, Backyard Furniture Mfg., in the Account Credited column.
3. Record the invoice number, 675, in the Purch. No. column. Since only purchase invoice numbers are recorded in this column, no identifying letter is necessary.
4. Write the credit amount, $1,869.35, in the Accounts Payable Credit column.
5. Record the debit amount, $1,869.35, in the Purchases Debit Furniture column.

Posting from a Purchases Journal LO5

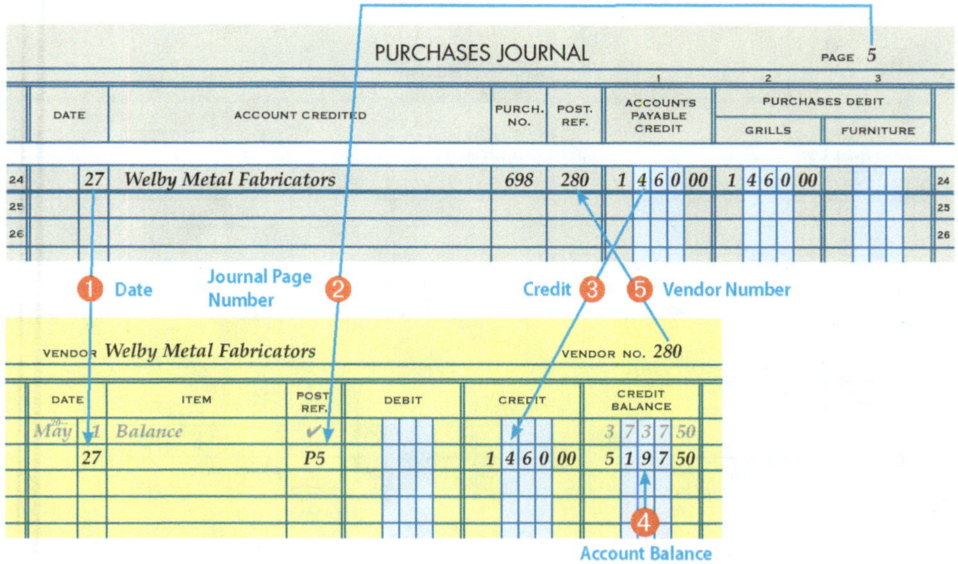

Transferring transaction information from a journal entry to a ledger account is called **posting**. Whiley keeps vendor accounts in an accounts payable ledger. Individual amounts in the Accounts Payable Credit column of the purchases journal are posted often to the appropriate vendor accounts. The purchases journal is abbreviated as *P* in the Post. Ref. column of the ledger accounts. Posting from the Accounts Payable Credit column of the purchases journal to a ledger account is shown above.

© Champion Studio/Shutterstock.com

Posting from the Purchases Journal to the Accounts Payable Ledger

1. **Write the date of the transaction, 27, in the Date column of the ledger account.**
2. **Enter the purchases journal page number, P5, in the Post. Ref. column of the ledger account.**
3. **Record the credit amount, $1,460.00, in the Credit column of the account for Welby Metal Fabricators. All postings from the purchases journal to the ledger accounts will be to the Credit amount column of the ledger.**
4. **Add the amount in the Credit amount column to the previous balance in the Credit Balance column. Write the new account balance, $5,197.50, in the Credit Balance column.**
5. **Record the vendor number, 280, in the Post. Ref. column of the journal. The vendor number shows that the posting for this entry is complete.**

remember

The number recorded on the invoice, *675*, is the unique number Whiley assigned to this invoice. This number should not be confused with the invoice number, *2564*, assigned by the vendor. Each vendor uses a different numbering system. Therefore, vendor invoice numbers would not be recorded in sequence.

INPUT

- Ask a student to explain the term *posting*. Write the definition.
- Direct students to the illustration. Review steps 1–5 for posting from a purchases journal to the accounts payable ledger.
- Remind students that only purchases of merchandise on account are recorded in the purchases journal.

MODEL

Post the transaction

- Refer to the departmental purchases journal and the accounts payable subsidiary ledger account on page 16 to illustrate the five steps for posting from a purchases journal to the accounts payable ledger. Explain the abbreviation *P5* (Purchases Journal, page 5).
- Provide several numerical examples on the board to illustrate how a new balance in the accounts payable ledger is calculated.

DIFFERENTIATED INSTRUCTION

Gifted Learners: Gifted students need additional challenges, such as research, to maintain a high level of motivation. Students should be asked to interview a merchandising manager of a local store to learn how purchases are determined.

INPUT

- Use the illustration to explain how a purchases journal is proved and ruled at the end of each month.
- Review steps 1–5 for posting the total of the Accounts Payable column to the general ledger. Point out that the last day of the month is used when recording column totals for the purchases journal. Remind students that the sum of the debit column totals must equal the credit column total before the amount columns are double-ruled. Emphasize that each amount column total is posted to the general ledger account named in the column heading.
- Ask students to identify the name of the accounts to which column totals are posted.
- Ask students if the column totals will be posted as a debit or a credit to the account title in the column heading.

MODEL

Post the totals of a purchases journal

- Prepare a handout that includes a departmental purchases journal with the information presented in the illustration on this page. However, omit the general ledger account numbers in parentheses on the last line of the purchases journal. The handout should also include three general ledger account forms, one each for Accounts Payable, Purchases—Grills, and Purchases—Furniture. Enter the appropriate account number and a June 1 balance.
- Guide students through the complete posting process of a purchases journal.

Posting the Totals of a Purchases Journal

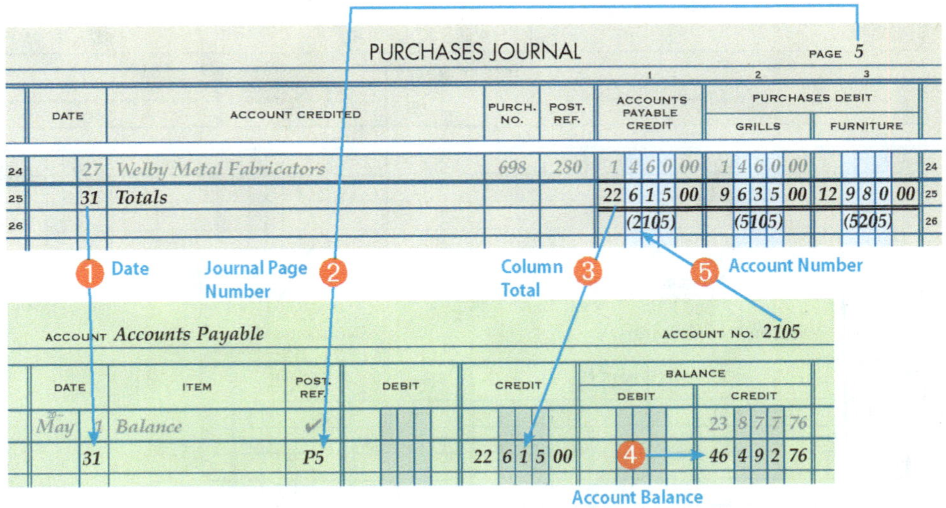

The purchases journal is proved and ruled at the end of each month. A purchases journal is proved by adding each column and then proving that the sum of the debit column totals equals the credit column totals, as shown below.

Credit Column Totals	Debit Column Totals	Credit Column Totals
Accounts Payable Credit		$22,615.00
Purchases Debit—Grills	$ 9,635.00	
Purchases Debit—Furniture	12,980.00	
Totals	$22,615.00	$22,615.00

Double lines are then ruled across the amount columns to show that the totals have been verified as correct. Each amount column total is posted to the general ledger account named in the column heading. The posting of the purchases journal's Accounts Payable Credit column total to the Accounts Payable account in the general ledger is shown above. The same procedure is used to post the totals of the Purchases Debit—Grills and the Purchases Debit—Furniture columns.

Posting the Total of the Accounts Payable Column to the General Ledger

1. Write the date, 31, in the Date column of the account.
2. Write the purchases journal page number, P5, in the Post. Ref. column of the account.
3. Write the Accounts Payable Credit column total, $22,615.00, in the Credit amount column of the Accounts Payable account.
4. Calculate and record the new account balance, $46,492.76, in the Balance Credit column.
5. Write the general ledger account number, 2105, in parentheses below the column total in the purchases journal.

fyi Every special journal is proved by comparing the totals of the debit and credit columns. After any errors are corrected, a double line is drawn to indicate the journal has been proved.

Journalizing Purchases Returns and Allowances LO6

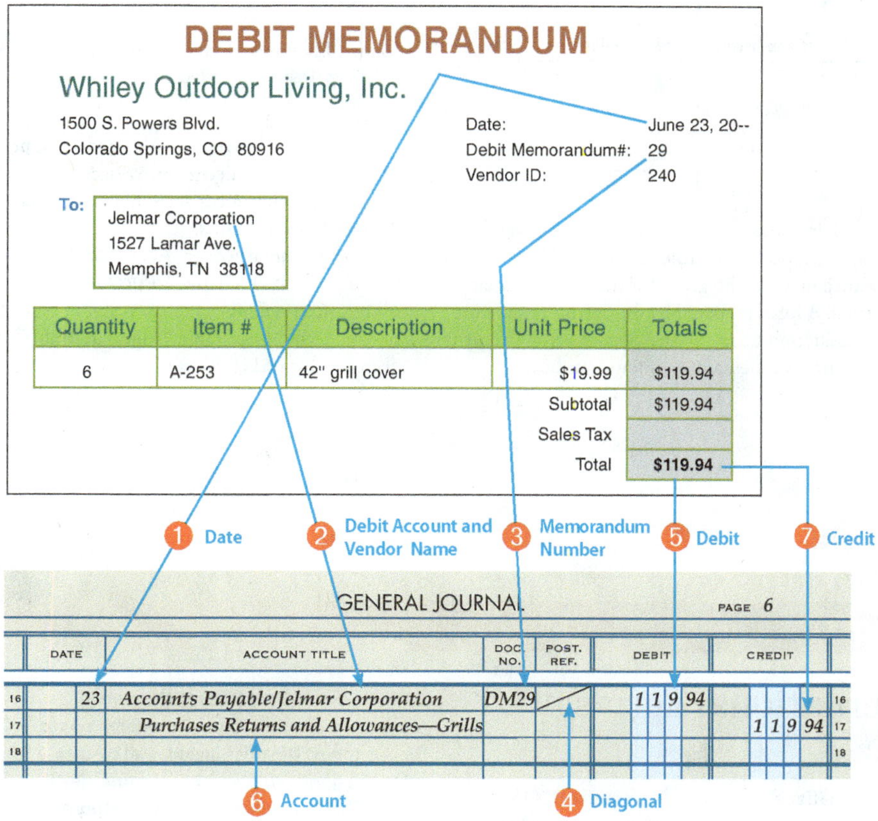

Journalizing a Purchases Return

1. Write the date, 23, in the Date column of the general journal.
2. Write the titles of the accounts to be debited, Accounts Payable/Jelmar Corporation, in the Account Title column.
3. Record the debit memorandum number, DM29, in the Doc. No. column.
4. Draw a diagonal line in the Post. Ref. column to indicate that the single debit amount is posted to two accounts.
5. Write the debit amount, $119.94, in the Debit column.
6. Indent and write the title of the account to be credited, Purchases Returns and Allowances—Grills, in the Account Title column.
7. Record the credit amount, $119.94, in the Credit column.

INPUT

- Direct students to the illustration. Ask students to whom the merchandise was returned, which items were returned, what the date of the return was, and what total value of merchandise was returned.
- Ask students which accounts would be used to indicate that (1) the amount of money owed to a company is less and (2) the amount of grill purchases for the month should be reduced. Continue questioning until students answer Accounts Payable/Jelmar Corporation and Purchases—Grills. Introduce the contra cost account, Purchases Returns and Allowances—Grills. Point out that the contra account allows businesses to see what proportion of the merchandise was returned to vendors.
- Draw the three T accounts (Purchases—Grills, Accounts Payable, and Jelmar Corporation), including the amounts shown on page 17, on the board. Ask students to describe the transaction. (*the purchase of grill merchandise on account from Jelmar Corporation, $119.94*)
- Using only these three accounts, ask students to record the entry for the purchases return. Without a return account, the credit amount would have to be placed under the *Purchases—Grills* account. Discuss with students the disadvantages of doing so. Lead into a discussion of the importance of using a Purchases Returns and Allowances—Grills account so that the business can determine what proportion of the merchandise was returned to vendors. A high percentage of returns may indicate poor manufacturing, shoddy products, damage during shipping, etc.

MODEL

Analyze the transaction

- Direct students to the illustration. Question students regarding quantity returned, item no., unit price, date, total amount, debit memo number, etc. Discuss the significance of using source documents in accounting.
- Use T accounts to explain the transaction presented.
- Using a transparency, illustrate the procedures for journalizing the return of merchandise in the general journal. Follow steps 1–7.

GENERAL LEDGER

Accounts Payable

Debit	Credit
119.94	

Purchases Returns and Allowances—Grills

Debit	Credit
	119.94

ACCOUNTS PAYABLE LEDGER

Jelmar Corporation

Debit	Credit
119.94	

When merchandise is returned to a vendor, the vendor's account and Accounts Payable are reduced by a debit. An allowance may also be given for merchandise that is not returned. A form prepared by the customer showing the price deduction taken by the customer for a return or an allowance is called a **debit memorandum.**

Whiley documents all purchases returns and allowances with a debit memorandum and records the transaction in a general journal.

June 23. Returned six grill covers to Jelmar Corporation, $119.94. Debit Memorandum No. 29.

An account that reduces a related account on a financial statement is called a **contra account**. The purchases returns and allowances accounts are contra accounts to the purchases accounts.

In the general ledger, Accounts Payable decreases by a $119.94 debit. Purchases Returns and Allowances—Grills increases by a $119.94 credit. In the accounts payable ledger, Jelmar Corporation decreases by a $119.94 credit.

GLOBAL AWARENESS

International Terms of Sale

The International Chamber of Commerce (ICC) has developed a set of pre-defined words to be used for international business transactions. These terms are referred to as "Incoterms® Rules." The terms define clearly the responsibilities, costs, and risks of sellers and buyers for the delivery of goods under international sales contracts.

The ICC has updated regularly the first set of terms, established in 1936. The most recent set of terms is Incoterms® 2010, which went into effect January 1, 2011. Selected terms are described below.

CIF (Cost, Insurance, and Freight) to the named port of destination. The seller quotes a price for the goods. The price includes insurance, all transportation, and all miscellaneous charges to bring the goods to the port of destination. Once in port, all costs are the responsibility of the buyer.

DDP (Delivered Duty Paid) to the named place of destination. The seller quotes a price for the goods. The price includes all costs to bring the goods all the way to the final destination. This term places maximum responsibility for costs on the seller.

EXW (Ex Works) to the named place of delivery. This is the opposite of DDP. In EXW, the buyer is responsible for all costs from the named place of delivery, which is usually the seller's factory or warehouse.

CRITICAL THINKING

Other Incoterms® are FCA, CFR, and FAS. Use the Internet to find the rules for these terms. Write a brief summary of the rule for each term.

Source: www.iccwbo.org.

© iStockphoto.com/Lusky

GLOBAL AWARENESS

Answers

FCA: (Free Carrier) to the named place of delivery. The seller must get the goods, cleared for export, into the hands of the first carrier, which is named by the buyer.

CFR: (Cost and Freight) to the named port of destination. This is the same as CIF, except the seller does not need to arrange and pay for insurance. Therefore, the quoted price includes all transportation and miscellaneous charges to bring the goods to the port of destination, except for the cost of insurance. Once in port, all costs are the responsibility of the buyer.

FAS: (Free Alongside Ship) at the named port of shipment. The seller must get the goods, cleared for export, alongside the ship at the named port. This term is typically used for bulk cargo.

FORMATIVE ASSESSMENT

- This is an ongoing process. Circulate around the classroom or lab, observing which students have problems with the assignments.
- Troubleshooting: Diagnose the kinds of problems students have with this lesson. They sometimes become confused about when to post in the subsidiary ledger and when to post to the controlling account.
- Assess student understanding by checking solutions to Independent Practice assignments and noting their answers to the Terms Review and Audit Your Understanding questions.

End of Lesson Review

LO3 Explain the purpose of a departmental accounting system.

LO4 Journalize departmental purchases of merchandise on account using a purchases journal.

LO5 Post merchandise purchases to an accounts payable ledger and a general ledger.

LO6 Journalize departmental purchases returns and allowances.

Terms Review

- departmental accounting system
- merchandising business
- posting
- debit memorandum
- contra account

Audit your understanding

1. When Whiley's grills department purchases merchandise on account, which general ledger accounts are affected, and how?
2. Which general ledger accounts are affected, and how, by a return of furniture department merchandise?

Work together 1-2

Journalizing and posting purchases on account and purchases returns and allowances

Electronic Warehouse has two departments: Audio and Video. A purchases journal, general journal, and partial general and accounts payable ledgers are provided in the *Working Papers*. The balances are recorded as of June 1 of the current year. Post the following transactions when journalized: (1) transactions impacting the accounts payable subsidiary ledger and (2) transactions recorded in the general journal. Source documents are abbreviated as follows: debit memorandum, DM; purchase invoice, P. Your instructor will guide you through the following examples.

1. Journalize the transactions completed during June of the current year. Use page 6 of a purchases journal and page 6 of a general journal. Post the items that are to be posted individually.

   Transactions:

   June 3. Purchased audio equipment on account from Davis Corporation, $1,625.00. P243.
   5. Returned video equipment to TPC Supply, $42.50, from P239. DM38.
   8. Purchased video equipment on account from TPC Supply, $995.00. P244.
   12. Purchased audio equipment on account from National Industries, $1,100.00. P245.
   18. Received an allowance on audio equipment from National Industries, $165.80, from P245. DM39.
   23. Purchased audio equipment on account from Davis Corporation, $820.00. P246.

2. Prove and rule the purchases journal. Post the totals.

On your own 1-2

Journalizing and posting purchases on account and purchases returns and allowances

Ashley's Fashions has two departments: Clothing and Shoes. A purchases journal, general journal, and partial general and accounts payable ledgers are provided in the *Working Papers*. The balances are recorded as of July 1 of the current year. Post the following transactions when journalized: (1) transactions impacting the accounts payable subsidiary ledger and (2) transactions recorded in the general journal. Source documents are abbreviated as follows: debit memorandum, DM; purchase invoice, P. Work this problem independently.

1. Journalize the transactions completed during July of the current year. Use page 7 of a purchases journal and page 7 of a general journal. Post the items that are to be posted individually.

   Transactions:

   July 2. Purchased clothing on account from Keller Corporation, $2,418.00. P366.
   7. Returned clothing to Keller Corporation, $185.90, from P366. DM45.
   9. Purchased clothing on account from Ackerman Supply, $1,680.00. P367.
   13. Received an allowance on shoes from Peters Company, $115.30, from P365. DM46.
   16. Purchased shoes on account from Peters Company, $1,150.00. P368.
   22. Purchased clothing on account from Keller Corporation, $925.00. P369.

2. Prove and rule the purchases journal. Post the totals.

CHECK FOR UNDERSTANDING

Terms Review

- Call on students to define each term in the Terms Review. Definitions are given in the Glossary.

Audit Your Understanding

- Call on students to answer the Audit Your Understanding questions. Answers are given in Appendix D of the textbook.

GUIDED PRACTICE

Work Together

- Have students write the solution to the Work Together problem as you guide the class through the examples.
- Direct students to record each transaction in the proper journal and ledger account as you elicit class participation in determining and calculating each amount.
- Ask students how to total and rule the purchases journal.
- Ask a student to describe the steps for posting journal totals.

INDEPENDENT PRACTICE

On Your Own

- Assign the On Your Own problem to be worked independently.
- Use the Formative Assessment techniques to diagnose student understanding.

Application Problem

- Assign Application Problem 1-2.

Online Working Papers

- Students can access the Lesson 1-2 problems using this software.

RETEACH

- Ask a student to explain the procedure for proving the accuracy of journal totals. (*The sum of debit column totals must equal the sum of credit column totals.*) Use the illustration on page 16. Write calculations on the board.

Essential Question

- Why would a company use the contra account, Purchases Returns and Allowances, rather than credit Purchases to record returns? (*The contra account allows the company to more easily see what proportion of the merchandise was returned to vendor.*)

EXTENDED LEARNING

- Assign Global Awareness on page 18.

CLOSURE

- Use the illustrations on pages 14–17 to review briefly the procedures for journalizing and posting transactions concerning the purchase of merchandise on account.

LESSON
1-3

BRIDGE

- Explain that the cash payments journal presented in this lesson is similar to the cash payments journal presented in the first-year course. However, two new columns have been added to accommodate a departmental business.

TEACHING RESOURCES

- **Instructor's Resource CD/Website:**
  PowerPoint Slides
  Accounting Concepts
- **Working Papers:**
  Teacher's Edition of the Working Papers for Lesson 1-3
  Online Working Papers
- **Transparency Master:**
  Departmental Cash Payments Journal

ENGAGE

- Ask students what business strategy is employed by vendors to encourage prompt payment. Lead into a discussion of cash discounts. Explain the terms *2/10, n/30*. Point out that Whiley is the customer in this case. The cash discount on purchases taken by the customer, Whiley, is referred to as a *purchases discount*.

PREVIEW

- Call on students to read the accounting terms and definitions introduced in this lesson: *cash discount*, *purchases discount*, and *petty cash*.
- Point out the learning objectives for this lesson.
- Direct students to read the headings in this lesson and to examine the illustrations.

INPUT

- Emphasize that checks are an excellent tool for controlling and safeguarding cash.
- Ask a student to explain the terms *2/10, n/30*. Point out that a purchases discount reduces the net amount of cash paid for a purchase.
- Introduce the contra cost account, Purchases Discount. Remind students that an account that reduces a related account is known as a *contra account*.

LESSON
1-3 Journalizing and Posting Cash Payments

LO7 Journalize departmental cash payments using a cash payments journal.
LO8 Post cash payments to an accounts payable ledger and a general ledger.

Departmental Cash Payments LO7

Most of Whiley's cash payments are made by check. Therefore, checks are the source documents for most cash payments. [CONCEPT: Objective Evidence] All cash payments are recorded in the cash payments journal.

CASH PAYMENTS ON ACCOUNT

Purchases on account are expected to be paid within the stated credit period. A seller may encourage early payment by allowing a deduction from the invoice amount. A deduction that a vendor allows on the invoice amount to encourage prompt payment is called a **cash discount**. When a company that has purchased merchandise on account takes a cash discount, this is referred to as a **purchases discount**.

A purchases discount is usually stated as a percentage. For example, the terms of an invoice may be written as 2/10, n/30. The expression 2/10 means that 2% of the invoice amount may be deducted from the amount due if payment is made within 10 days of the invoice date. The expression n/30 means that payment of the total invoice amount must be made within 30 days of the invoice date. No discount can be deducted, however, if payment is made after 10 days from the invoice date. Whiley attempts to take advantage of all discounts allowed by vendors.

A purchases discount reduces the net amount of cash paid for a purchase. The account Purchases Discount—Furniture is in the cost of merchandise division of Whiley's general ledger. Purchases discounts are kept in separate accounts and not deducted directly from the purchases accounts. This procedure helps the business see what proportion of purchases on account were allowed purchases discounts.

WHY ACCOUNTING?

Microcredit

Have you ever pictured yourself as a banker? You could serve in the role of a bank loan manager—making microloans to people in poverty throughout the world.

The idea of microloans began in Bangladesh in 1974 when Muhammad Yunus served as a banker to 42 women who needed the money to support a small business. Muhammad lent the women approximately $27 (U.S.) at a low interest rate.

Today, there are opportunities for you to make loans to people for a variety of projects. Most organizations that handle such loans allow the donor to pick the project to be funded. As a donor, you would play the role of a banker and look at the financial status of the project to determine if it can make enough income to repay the loan.

CRITICAL THINKING

1. Search the Internet for microcredit organizations. List the names of three different organizations.
2. Investigate one organization identified in item (1) above and write a short report that answers the following questions:
   a. Does the organization charge interest on the microloans or make interest-free loans?
   b. What happens to the money when the loan is repaid?
   c. What percentage of loans is actually repaid?

© iStockphoto.com/AleksKo

WHY ACCOUNTING?

Answers

1. Answers will vary. At the time of publication, some organizations were World Vision's Micro program, Global Partnerships, Oikocredit USA, United Nations Millennium Campaign, Opportunity International, and KIVA.
2. Answers will vary. Most organizations charge some interest to cover organizational administration costs. In some organizations, once the loan is repaid, the money is given to another project, chosen by the organization. In at least one organization (KIVA), the money repaid is put back in the donor's account. The donor can withdraw the money or make another loan. The repayment percentage is usually 90% or higher.

Source: National Geographic News, October 13, 2006.

Journalizing a Purchases Discount

CASH PAYMENTS JOURNAL — PAGE 9

	DATE		ACCOUNT TITLE	CK. NO.	POST. REF.	1 GENERAL DEBIT	2 GENERAL CREDIT	3 ACCOUNTS PAYABLE DEBIT	4 PURCH. DISCOUNT CR. GRILLS	5 PURCH. DISCOUNT CR. FURNITURE	6 CASH CREDIT	
1	20-- May	2	Glass Source	732				920 00	18 40		901 60	1
2												2

1 Date 2 Vendor Name 3 Check Number 4 Debit 5 Discount 6 Check Amount

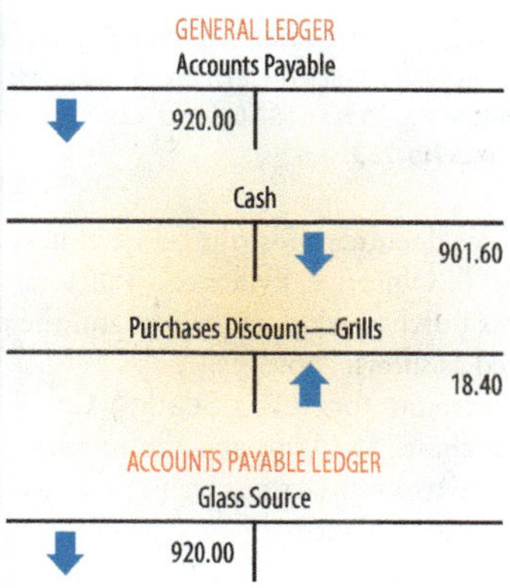

May 2. Paid cash on account to Glass Source, $901.60, covering Purchase Invoice No. 672 for $920.00, less 2% discount, $18.40. Check No. 732.

The source document for this transaction is a check. [CONCEPT: Objective Evidence]

Journalizing a Cash Payment That Includes a Purchases Discount

1. Write the date, May 2, in the Date column.
2. Enter the vendor name, Glass Source, in the Account Title column.
3. Record the check number, 732, in the Ck. No. column.
4. Write the debit amount, $920.00, in the Accounts Payable Debit column.
5. Record the discount credit amount, $18.40, in the Purchases Discount Credit Grills column.
6. Enter the check amount, $901.60, in the Cash Credit column.

Whiley's cash payments journal has two debit columns—General Debit and Accounts Payable Debit. The journal also has four credit columns—General Credit, a Purchases Discount Credit column for each of the two departments, and Cash Credit.

TAKING A DISCOUNT AFTER A PURCHASE RETURN

An additional calculation is necessary when a discount is taken after a purchase return or allowance has been granted. The discount is calculated on the amount owed at the time the invoice is paid. Therefore, the amount of the return or allowance must be deducted from the amount of the original purchase before the discount can be calculated.

Amount owned on invoice:

Original Purchase Invoice Amount (P670)	–	Purchases Return (DM28)	=	Purchase Invoice Amount After Return
$824.00	–	$182.00	=	$642.00

Purchases discount:

Purchase Invoice Amount After Return	×	Purchases Discount	=	Purchases Discount
$642.00	×	2%	=	$12.84

Amount due after purchases discount:

Purchase Invoice Amount After Return	–	Purchases Discount	=	Total Amount Due
$642.00	–	$12.84	=	$629.16

INPUT

- Display a transparency of a departmental cash payments journal. Ask students what is different from the cash payments journal previously used. Point out the Purchases Discount Credit columns for each department.
- Ask students the purpose of designing a journal that includes Purchases Discount Credit columns. (*It is easier to record numerous transactions of a like nature.*)
- Use the illustration to review the steps for journalizing a cash payment that includes a purchases discount.

MODEL

Analyze the transaction

- Show the mathematical process for calculating the 2% discount described in the May 2 transaction. Create other discount problems and ask students to calculate discount amounts to assess comprehension levels.
- Draw a vertical stack of four T accounts and label them as shown on the page. Analyze the May 2 transaction into debit and credit parts. Emphasize that the discount amount, $18.40, is not recorded as a credit to Purchases—Grills to reduce the cost, but rather is placed in a separate contra account, Purchases Discount—Grills.

Journalize the transaction

- Distribute copies of a blank cash payments journal. Use a transparency to explain the process for journalizing a cash payment that includes a purchases discount. Journalize the May 2 transaction using steps 1–6. Reinforce learning by creating other transactions for students to journalize. Ask students to save the cash payments journal for later use.
- Ask students to verify discount amounts through the use of a calculator.

INPUT

- Pose this problem to students: A business purchased $100 of merchandise on account last week and returned $25 of the merchandise due to damage. If the company takes advantage of a 2% discount, how much is its payment? *($73.50)* Emphasize that the company owes $75 at the time the invoice is paid and therefore calculates the discount based on $75 and not $100. The amount of the return is deducted from the original purchase before the discount is calculated.
- Ask a student to read the May 3 transaction on page 22. Use the math box to explain the procedures for calculating the proper amount of payment.
- Use the information shown on line 2 of the cash payments journal presented in the illustration to review steps 1–4.

MODEL

Analyze the transaction

- Show the mathematical calculations for determining the 2% discount after a purchase return as described in the May 3 transaction.
- Show the remaining mathematical calculations for determining the total amount due. Create similar return and discount problems and ask students to solve them.
- Draw a vertical stack of four T accounts and label them as shown on page 22. Analyze the May 3 transaction into debit and credit parts.

Journalize the transaction

- Direct students to retrieve the previously distributed cash payments journal.
- Use a transparency of a cash payments journal to record the transaction.
- Have students calculate the amount due and record each item in the journal, following the four steps shown.
- Reinforce learning by creating other transactions for students to journalize. Ask students to save the cash payments journal for later use.
- Ask students to verify all amounts with a calculator.

CASH PAYMENTS JOURNAL PAGE 9

	DATE		ACCOUNT TITLE	CK. NO.	POST. REF.	1 GENERAL DEBIT	2 GENERAL CREDIT	3 ACCOUNTS PAYABLE DEBIT	4 PURCH. DISCOUNT CR. GRILLS	5 PURCH. DISCOUNT CR. FURNITURE	6 CASH CREDIT	
1	20-- May	2	Glass Source	732				920 00	18 40		901 60	1
2		3	Teton Seating Co.	733				642 00		12 84	629 16	2
3												3

1 Date 2 Vendor Name 3 Check Number 4 Debit 5 Discount 6 Check Amount

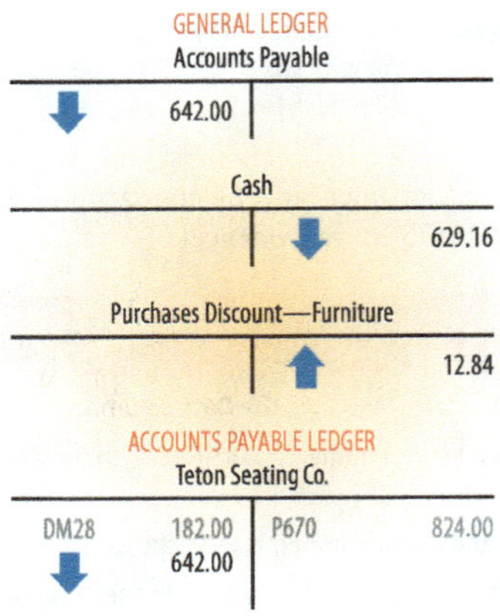

May 3. Paid cash on account to Teton Seating Co., $629.16, covering Purchase Invoice No. 670 for $824.00, less Debit Memorandum No. 28 for $182.00, and less 2% discount, $12.84. Check No. 733.

The source document for this transaction is a check. [CONCEPT: Objective Evidence] The total amount due for this purchase after the return and the discount is calculated as shown above.

The T account for Teton Seating Co. shows the original purchase, $824.00, and the purchases return, $182.00. The two transactions result in a $642.00 outstanding account balance.

This transaction is journalized in the same way as a payment of cash when there is no purchases return or allowance. The only difference is the way in which the amounts are calculated.

Calculating a Discount After a Return or Allowance is Granted and Journalizing the Cash Payment

1. Write the date, 3, in the Date column of the cash payments journal.
2. Enter the vendor name, Teton Seating Co., in the Account Title column.
3. Record the check number, 733, in the Ck. No. column.
4. Write the debit amount, $642.00, in the Accounts Payable Debit column.
5. Record the discount credit amount, $12.84, in the Purchases Discount Credit Furniture column.
6. Enter the check amount, $629.16, in the Cash Credit column.

remember For the first entry in a journal or ledger, include the year in the Date column above the month.

Purchases Discount and Purchases Returns and Allowances are both contra accounts to Purchases. The contra accounts are presented on the income statement, as shown below. Net purchases is determined by deducting the contra accounts from purchases.

Cost of Merchandise Sold:			
Merchandise Inventory, Jan. 1, 20--			
Purchases.		$154,865.35	
Less: Purchases Discount.	$2,614.26		
Purchases Returns and Allowances	5,148.95	7,763.21	
Net Purchases			147,102.14

© iStockphoto.com/Dan Bachman

THINK LIKE AN ACCOUNTANT

Analyzing Purchases Discounts

The accounting procedures manual of Rackley Corporation includes the following statement regarding purchases discounts:

> "The corporation strives to obtain purchase discount agreements with its merchandise vendors. Accounting personnel are responsible for processing cash payments on a timely basis to take advantage of all purchase discounts offered by merchandise vendors. Exceptions to this policy should be approved by an appropriate level of management."

Cheryl Rosario, an internal auditor for Rackley Corporation, is performing a review of the purchasing processes of the company. It's not unusual for Cheryl to notice a couple of instances where purchases discounts were not taken. After all, mistakes do occur. But on this review, she notices more than the typical number of lost discounts.

Cheryl's audit manager directs her to perform a more in-depth analysis of cash payments. Before talking with accounting personnel, she decides to quantify the extent of purchase discounts lost during the current fiscal year.

OPEN THE SPREADSHEET TLA_CH01

The worksheet contains a list of cash payments for merchandise. The list includes the purchase discount percent offered by the vendor, if any, and the amount of discount taken. Follow the steps on the Instructions tab to analyze the cash payments and discounts lost. Use the analysis to answer the following questions:

1. What is the number of discounts taken?
2. What is the average, maximum, and total amount of discounts taken?
3. What is the number of discounts lost?
4. What is the average, maximum, and total amount of discounts lost?
5. Does the information collected suggest any reason for the unusually high number of discounts lost? Support your answer.

THINK LIKE AN ACCOUNTANT

This activity requires students to create a formula and apply a filter. Students use the statistics displayed on the Status Bar to quantify the amount of discounts taken and lost.

The formula for discounts lost calculates the available discount and subtracts the amount of discount taken. A ROUND function is used to round the calculation to the nearest cent. The function created in cell G5 is =ROUND(D5*E5-F5,2). If the *Use table names in formulas* option has been selected in Excel options, the formula will appear as follows:

=ROUND(Table1[[#This Row],[Purchases]]*Table1[[#This Row],[Discount Offered]]–Table1[[#This Row],[Discount Taken]],2)

Answers

1. Number of discounts taken, 167.
2. Average, $88.40; maximum, $177.91; total (sum), $14,763.20.
3. Number of discounts lost, 24.
4. Average, $15.21; maximum, $37.20; total (sum), $364.96.
5. The analysis reveals that 12.6% (24 ÷ [24 + 167]) of the available discounts were lost. However, these discounts were generally small in value relative to the discounts taken. The average discount lost, $15.21, is significantly less than the average of the discounts taken, $88.40. It would appear that Accounting Department personnel, for reasons to be determined, are less likely to follow corporate policies when the amount of the discount is relatively small.

INPUT

- Use this illustration to review the steps for recording a cash payment for supplies, rent, and merchandise (grills). Emphasize to students that the process is the same as the one used in the first year of accounting.
- Distinguish between the payment for merchandise and the payment for supplies.
- Ask students why the General Debit column is used, rather than the Accounts Payable Debit column, to record cash payments for supplies, rent, and merchandise.

MODEL

Analyze the transaction

- Draw two blank T accounts on the board.
- Read the transaction statement regarding the purchases of supplies.
- Ask students to analyze the transaction into debit and credit parts. Complete the T accounts as the information is provided.
- Repeat the above procedure for the rent expense and merchandise inventory transactions.

Journalize the transaction

- Use the transparency of a cash payments journal to illustrate recording each transaction.
- Record each step in the journal, following the five steps shown.
- Students should copy the entries using the previously distributed cash payments journal.

Recording Entries in a Cash Payments Journal

CASH PAYMENTS JOURNAL — PAGE 9

	DATE		ACCOUNT TITLE	CK. NO.	POST. REF.	1 GENERAL DEBIT	2 GENERAL CREDIT	3 ACCOUNTS PAYABLE DEBIT	4 PURCH. DISCOUNT CR. GRILLS	5 PURCH. DISCOUNT CR. FURNITURE	6 CASH CREDIT	
3		4	Supplies	734		214 00					214 00	3
4		5	Rent Expense	735		1 800 00					1 800 00	4
5		7	Merchandise Inventory—Grills	736		152 60					152 60	5

1 Date 2 Account Title 3 Check Number 4 Debit 5 Check Amount

May 4. Paid cash to Jenkins Co. for supplies, $214.00. Check No. 734.

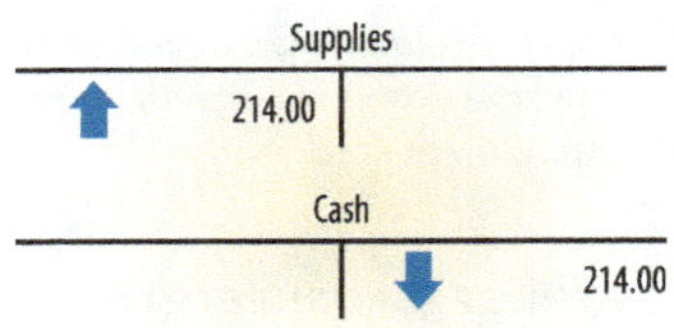

Journalizing Buying Office Supplies for Cash

1. Write the date, 4, in the Date column.
2. Enter the account title, Supplies, in the Account Title column.
3. Record the check number, 734, in the Ck. No. column.
4. Write the debit amount, $214.00, in the General Debit column.
5. Record the credit amount, $214.00, in the Cash Credit column.

May 5. Paid cash to Rackley Properties for rent, $1,800.00. Check No. 735.

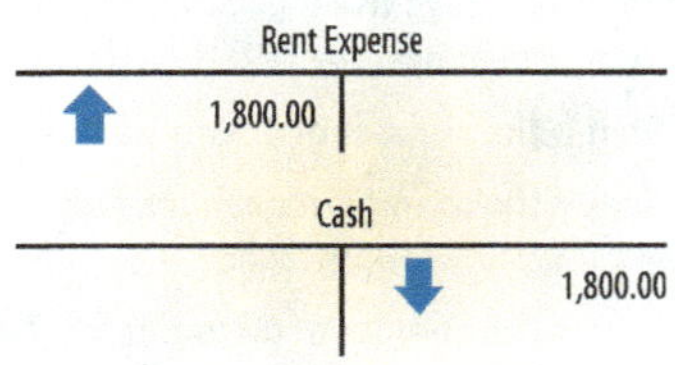

Journalizing the Cash Payment of an Expense

1. Write the date, 5, in the Date column.
2. Enter the account title, Rent Expense, in the Account Title column.
3. Record the check number, 735, in the Ck. No. column.
4. Write the debit amount, $1,800.00, in the General Debit column.
5. Record the credit amount, $1,800.00, in the Cash Credit column.

May 7. Paid cash to GH Patrick Industries for grill accessories, $152.60. Check No. 736.

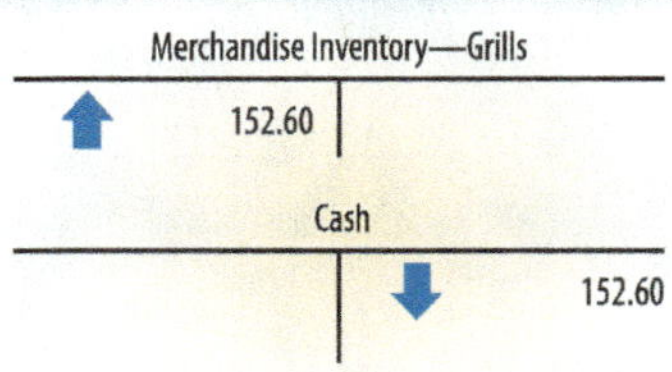

Journalizing the Cash Payment for Merchandise

1. Write the date, 7, in the Date column.
2. Enter the account title, Merchandise Inventory—Grills, in the Account Title column.
3. Record the check number, 736, in the Ck. No. column.
4. Write the debit amount, $152.60, in the General Debit column.
5. Record the credit amount, $152.60, in the Cash Credit column.

Cash Payment to Replenish Petty Cash

CASH PAYMENTS JOURNAL — PAGE 10

	DATE	ACCOUNT TITLE	CK. NO.	POST. REF.	1 GENERAL DEBIT	2 GENERAL CREDIT	3 ACCOUNTS PAYABLE DEBIT	4 PURCH. DISCOUNT CR. GRILLS	5 PURCH. DISCOUNT CR. FURNITURE	6 CASH CREDIT	
15	31	*Supplies*	742		35 75					120 70	15
16		*Advertising Expense—Grills*			50 00						16
17		*Miscellaneous Expense*			34 95						17

1 Date 2 Account Title 3 Check Number 4 Debit 5 Check Amount

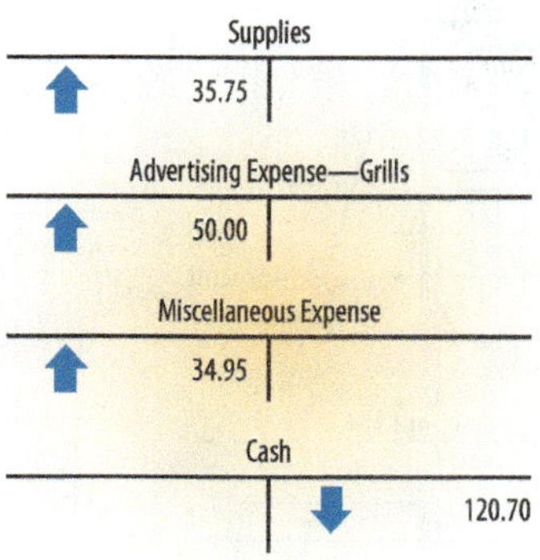

Business activities for an accounting period are summarized in financial statements. To adequately report how a business performed during an accounting period, all revenue earned as a result of business operations must be reported. Likewise, all expenses incurred in producing the revenue during the same accounting period must be reported. [CONCEPT: Matching Expenses with Revenue] The concept of matching expenses with revenue gives a true picture of business operations for an accounting period.

An amount of cash kept on hand and used for making small payments is called **petty cash**. Whiley's petty cash fund is $250.00. It replenishes petty cash whenever the fund drops below $100.00. In addition, the petty cash fund is replenished on the last business day of each fiscal period to ensure that all expenses are recorded during the fiscal period in which they occurred. [CONCEPT: Matching Expenses with Revenue]

May 31. Paid cash to replenish the petty cash fund, $120.70: supplies, $35.75; advertising expense—grills, $50.00; miscellaneous expense, $34.95. Check No. 742.

To replenish petty cash, a check is written for the amount spent from the fund. The check is cashed and the money placed back in the fund.

Journalizing the Cash Payment to Replenish Petty Cash

1. Write the date, 31, in the Date column.
2. Enter the account titles, Supplies, Advertising Expense—Grills, and Miscellaneous Expense, in the Account Title column.
3. Record the check number, 742, in the Ck. No. column on the first line of the entry.
4. Write the debit amounts for the appropriate accounts, $35.75, $50.00, and $34.95, in the General Debit column.
5. Record the check amount, $120.70, in the Cash Credit column on the first line of the entry.

INPUT

- Ask students for the purpose of establishing a petty cash fund. Emphasize that a petty cash fund is used for making small payments for which writing a check is not time- or cost-effective.
- Ask students for the process for replenishing petty cash. Remind them that a check is written for the amount spent from the fund, the check is then cashed, and the money is placed back into the fund.

MODEL

Analyze the transaction

- Draw a stack of four blank T accounts on the board.
- Read the transaction statement regarding the replenishing of petty cash.
- Ask students to analyze the transaction into debit and credit parts. Using the accounts and amounts shown in the illustration, complete the T accounts as the information is provided.

Journalize the transaction

- Use the transparency of a cash payments journal to illustrate recording the transaction to replenish petty cash.
- Students should copy the entries using the previously distributed cash payments journal.

TEACHING IDEA **Select one student to demonstrate how petty cash works. Use the analogy of giving the student $75 to keep in his or her wallet in case of emergencies and call the wallet "petty cash." Draw two T accounts on the board to illustrate decreasing cash to create petty cash. Explain that any monies used from petty cash will be replaced as long as there is documentation of the expenditure (a receipt). Using T accounts, demonstrate replenishing petty cash.**

DIFFERENTIATED INSTRUCTION

Mathematical/Logical learners enjoy solving problems and working with numbers. The wallet/petty cash analogy allows students to apply mathematical and problem-solving skills to demonstrate the accounts used to replenish petty cash.

INPUT

- Explain that amounts recorded in the General Debit and Credit columns are posted frequently to keep accounts in the general ledger up to date.
- Explain that amounts recorded in the Accounts Payable Debit column are posted frequently to the accounts payable ledger to keep vendor accounts up to date.
- Use the illustration to review the process for proving and ruling the cash payments journal. Explain the procedures for posting the totals of special columns.

Posting from a Cash Payments Journal LO8

CASH PAYMENTS JOURNAL PAGE 10

	Date	Account Title	Ck. No.	Post. Ref.	1 General Debit	2 General Credit	3 Accounts Payable Debit	4 Purch. Discount Cr. Grills	5 Purch. Discount Cr. Furniture	6 Cash Credit	
20	31	Delmar Industries	763	220			1,945.00	38.90		1,906.10	20
21	31	Purchases—Furniture	764	5205	687.00					687.00	21
22	31	Totals			8,194.42	1,644.20	28,491.52	124.68	304.84	34,612.22	22
23					(✔)	(✔)	(2105)	(5110)	(5120)	(1105)	23
24											24

VENDOR *Delmar Industries* VENDOR NO. 220

Date		Item	Post. Ref.	Debit	Credit	Credit Balance
May	22		P5		1,945.00	1,945.00
	31		CP10	1,945.00		—

ACCOUNT *Accounts Payable* ACCOUNT NO. 2105

Date		Item	Post. Ref.	Debit	Credit	Balance Debit	Balance Credit
	31		P5		22,615.00		46,492.76
	31		CP10	28,491.52			18,001.24

The accounting procedures for posting from a cash payments journal are the same as those followed for posting from the purchases journal. During the month, Whiley posts from the General Debit and General Credit columns to the general ledger when the transaction is entered in the journal. Whiley also posts from the Accounts Payable Debit column to the accounts payable ledger when the transaction is entered in the journal. This procedure permits Whiley to keep each vendor account balance in the accounts payable ledger up to date.

When the journal page is full or at the end of each month, the cash payments journal is proved and ruled. Totals of the special amount columns are posted to their respective accounts in the general ledger. The general ledger account number is written in parentheses immediately below the total. A check mark is recorded in parentheses below the totals of the General Debit and Credit columns to show that these totals are not posted. Whiley's departmental cash payments journal is shown after all posting has been completed.

Posting from a Cash Payments Journal

1. Post individual amounts from the General Debit and General Credit columns to the appropriate accounts in the general ledger. Post individual vendor amounts from the Accounts Payable Debit column to the appropriate accounts in the accounts payable ledger. Do this when the transaction is journalized.
2. Record the account or vendor number in the Post. Ref. column of the journal. The number shows that the posting for this entry is complete. Do this when the transaction is journalized.
3. Post the total of each special amount column to the account named in the journal's column headings.
4. Write the account number in parentheses under the totals as a posting reference.

FORMATIVE ASSESSMENT

- This is an ongoing process. Circulate around the classroom or lab, observing which students have problems with the assignments.
- Troubleshooting: Students may have trouble (1) calculating purchases discounts, (2) remembering to deduct a return or allowance before determining the discount amount, or (3) journalizing a cash payment that includes a discount after a return or allowance is granted. Students often debit Accounts Payable for the original amount of the invoice, rather than the original amount less the return or allowance.
- Assess student understanding by checking solutions to Independent Practice assignments and noting their answers to the Terms Review and Audit Your Understanding questions.

End of Lesson Review

LO7 Journalize departmental cash payments using a cash payments journal.

LO8 Post cash payments to an accounts payable ledger and a general ledger.

Terms Review

cash discount

purchases discount

petty cash

Audit your understanding

1. Which general ledger accounts are affected, and how, by a cash payment on account for outdoor furniture that includes a purchases discount?
2. Where are cash payments affecting accounts that are not listed in the column headings recorded?
3. Why is a petty cash fund always replenished on the last day of a fiscal period?

Work together 1-3

Journalizing and posting departmental cash payments

Bass Craft Center has two departments: Crafts and Frames. Post the following transactions when journalized: (1) transactions impacting the accounts payable subsidiary ledger and (2) cash payments entered in a general amount column of the cash payments journal. Source documents are abbreviated as follows: check, C; debit memorandum, DM; and purchase invoice, P. Your instructor will guide you through the following examples.

1. Journalize the transactions completed during June of the current year. Use page 6 of a cash payments journal. Post the items that are to be posted individually.

Transactions:

June 3. Paid cash to Peterson Supply for a miscellaneous expense, $164.34. C345.
5. Paid cash on account to Harris Industries for crafts purchased on P342, $2,141.00, less DM23 for $245.00, and less 2% discount. C346.
12. Paid cash to Mason Office Source for supplies, $86.35. C347.
18. Paid cash on account to Fulton Corporation covering P343 for frames, $2,840.00, less 2% discount. C348.
22. Paid cash to Daniel Woodworks for frames, $580.00. C349.
30. Paid cash to replenish the petty cash fund, $102.10: advertising for crafts, $50.00; miscellaneous expense, $32.60; supplies, $19.50. C350.

2. Prove and rule the cash payments journal. Post the totals.

On your own 1-3

Journalizing and posting departmental cash payments

Angela's Designs, Inc., has two departments: Ceramic and Stone. Post the following transactions when journalized: (1) transactions impacting the accounts payable subsidiary ledger and (2) cash payments entered in a general amount column of the cash payments journal. Selected general ledger and accounts payable ledger accounts are provided in the *Working Papers*. Source documents are abbreviated as follows: check, C; debit memorandum, DM; and purchase invoice, P. Work this problem independently.

1. Journalize the transactions completed during July of the current year. Use page 7 of a cash payments journal. Post the items that are to be posted individually.

Transactions:

July 4. Paid cash to Artistic Ceramics for ceramic tiles, $698.00. C422.
8. Paid cash to Peterson Supply for a miscellaneous expense, $297.00. C423.
11. Paid cash on account for ceramic tiles from Marris Ceramics covering P308 for $2,984.00, less 2% purchases discount. C424.
14. Paid cash to Abraham Corporation for supplies, $109.35. C425.
21. Paid cash on account for stone purchased from Overland Stone covering P312 for $2,351.00, less DM53 for $375.00, and less 2% discount. C426.
26. Paid cash to Z&Z Landscaping for stone, $743.00. C427.
31. Paid cash to replenish the petty cash fund, $99.10: advertising for stone, $45.00; miscellaneous expense, $22.90; supplies, $31.20. C428.

2. Prove and rule the cash payments journal. Post the totals.

CHECK FOR UNDERSTANDING

Terms Review

- Call on students to define each term in the Terms Review. Definitions are given in the Glossary.

Audit Your Understanding

- Call on students to answer the Audit Your Understanding questions. Answers are given in Appendix D of the textbook.

GUIDED PRACTICE

Work Together

- Have students write the solution to the Work Together problem as you guide the class through the examples.
- Direct students to record each amount on the proper form as you elicit class participation in determining and calculating each amount.
- Call on students to describe the various steps used to complete each problem.

INDEPENDENT PRACTICE

On Your Own

- Assign the On Your Own problem to be worked independently.

Application Problem

- Assign Application Problem 1-3.

Online Working Papers

- Students can access the Lesson 1-3 problems using this software.

CLOSURE

- Ask students to brainstorm and identify the most difficult concepts, transactions, or principles introduced in this lesson. Write responses on the board.

Essential Questions

- How would I safely control the petty cash account for my business so that I do not end up short on cash? (*Answers could include placing several responsible people in charge of the petty cash fund and creating petty cash slips to maintain records.*)
- If my company had the option of taking a purchases discount of 2/10 or delaying payment for 60 days, which would be the best option? (*Usually, hanging on to cash as long as possible is the better option. However, one should calculate the savings, and if cash flow is not a problem, it may be advantageous to take the purchases discount.*)

RETEACH

- Write on the board several transactions that include purchases discounts and purchases discounts after a return or allowance is granted. Arrange the class into cooperative learning groups of 3 or 4 students. Ask the groups to analyze each transaction by answering which accounts are affected and how each account is classified, whether it is increased or decreased, and whether it is debited or credited. Direct students to journalize transactions in a blank cash payments journal.
- For students who need additional review of posting, lead a class discussion on preparing the detailed five steps for posting to each ledger.

EXTENDED LEARNING

- Assign Why Accounting on page 20.
- Assign Think Like an Accountant on page 23.

A Look at Accounting Software

As stated in this feature, computerized accounting systems offer tremendous advantages over manual systems, which is why virtually every business uses an automated accounting system today. Students will likely believe that when a company purchases and installs an automated accounting system, it comes ready for entering transactions.

It might help students to realize that many hours of planning and effort are required to set up a computerized accounting system for a specific business. Dozens of choices need to be made and many pieces of information need to be entered before the system is ready to receive, process, and organize the financial data that will eventually be keyed in. Then there is the training period during which the users of the system learn what its capabilities and limitations are and how to enter data properly. While the system may come with standard reports already set up, many of them must be customized for the business and others need to be created.

Today, small businesses usually begin with *off-the-shelf* accounting systems such as QuickBooks. As the business grows, managers and accountants eventually realize that a new, more powerful system, such as SAP or Oracle, is required. Transitioning from an existing accounting system to a new one can require even more time and effort than setting one up initially, because data must be re-coded for the new system. In most cases, new hardware is required as well.

It might be interesting for students to become familiar with some of the accounting systems available. An online search on "compare accounting systems" will bring up several sites that provide comparisons and reviews of the many systems available. Bringing in a guest speaker from a company that has recently installed a new accounting system would add a real-life perspective to the process.

A Look at Accounting Software

Setting Up Accounts for a Corporation

When Whiley Outdoor Living, Inc., was first organized, its accountants would have set up a computerized accounting system to record the company's financial transactions. Compared to the manual system you experienced in this chapter, an automated system (a) improves the efficiency of the accounting staff, (b) reduces the likelihood of errors, (c) allows for significantly greater detail in the data, (d) simplifies the search and retrieval of accounting information, and (e) makes the reporting of financial information incredibly fast and flexible.

Prior to setting up the chart of accounts, as illustrated in these windows, accountants would have entered general company information on the first tab. After setting up the accounts, they would proceed to set up the subsidiary ledgers for customers and vendors. Finally, as Whiley began to order inventory and hire employees, the accountants would set up inventory items to manage pricing, sales, and reorders and set up employees to account for salaries, wages, benefits, and payroll taxes.

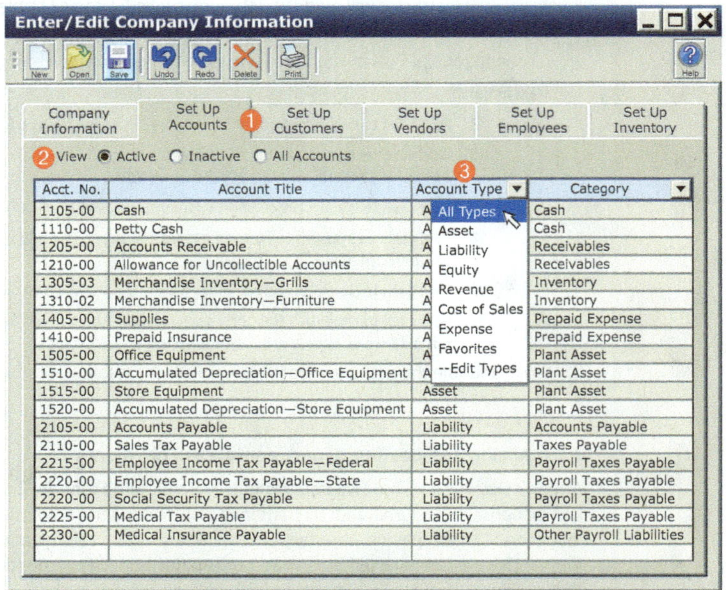

Acct. No.	Account Title	Account Type	Category
1105-00	Cash	A	Cash
1110-00	Petty Cash	A	Cash
1205-00	Accounts Receivable	A	Receivables
1210-00	Allowance for Uncollectible Accounts	A	Receivables
1305-03	Merchandise Inventory—Grills	A	Inventory
1310-02	Merchandise Inventory—Furniture	A	Inventory
1405-00	Supplies	A	Prepaid Expense
1410-00	Prepaid Insurance	A	Prepaid Expense
1505-00	Office Equipment	A	Plant Asset
1510-00	Accumulated Depreciation—Office Equipment	A	Plant Asset
1515-00	Store Equipment	Asset	Plant Asset
1520-00	Accumulated Depreciation—Store Equipment	Asset	Plant Asset
2105-00	Accounts Payable	Liability	Accounts Payable
2110-00	Sales Tax Payable	Liability	Taxes Payable
2215-00	Employee Income Tax Payable—Federal	Liability	Payroll Taxes Payable
2220-00	Employee Income Tax Payable—State	Liability	Payroll Taxes Payable
2220-00	Social Security Tax Payable	Liability	Payroll Taxes Payable
2225-00	Medical Tax Payable	Liability	Payroll Taxes Payable
2230-00	Medical Insurance Payable	Liability	Other Payroll Liabilities

1. The user selects the **Set Up Accounts** tab. The system lists a default set of accounts based upon the type of business chosen on the Company Information window. The user then modifies, adds, or deletes accounts to customize the list for the new business.
2. The system selects the **VIEW Active** button by default to list only active accounts. If the user wanted to view only accounts that had been deactivated, the Inactive button would be selected. The **All Accounts** button would show both active and inactive accounts. When an account is no longer needed, it is made inactive. Accounts are rarely deleted because they contain historical data that may be needed for comparative financial reports.
3. The account type describes where the account appears in the financial statements. Account categories are chosen by the accountant to simplify account search and retrieval and to facilitate the creation of financial reports. Account types and categories are set up or edited using their drop lists.

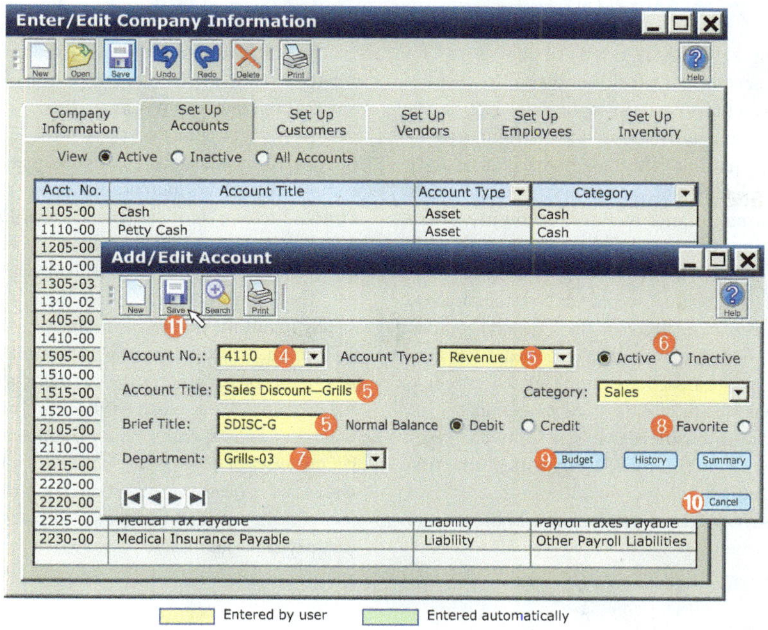

4 To add a new account, the user would click on **New** on the menu bar. The system would open a blank pop-up window. The Add/Edit Account window could also be opened by double-clicking an account number or title in the account list. In that case, the pop-up window would appear with that account's data already entered, allowing it to be modified as needed. In this pop-up window, the accountant has entered a new account.

5 Drop lists are used to select the account type and category. The user continues by entering an account title and brief title. Abbreviations are useful for labeling accounts on financial reports where there isn't room for complete titles. The system applies a default setting for the account's normal balance. In this window, Credit would have been the default setting for Sales Discount because the user categorized it as a Sales account. The user has changed it to Debit because Sales Discount is a contra account to Sales.

6 The system default for a new account is *active*. As a business continues to operate over time, it undergoes changes that can affect the accounts it uses to record transactions. It will sometimes be useful to set accounts to *inactive* so they no longer show up in reports or menu lists.

7 When setting up the type of business on the Company Information tab, the accountant would have selected *Departmental* and set up the departments. The system then sets departmental fields on transaction and report windows. In this window, the user selects the correct department from the drop list.

8 There are certain accounts that the accounting department may wish to give special attention. Perhaps a brief daily report would be used to show managers the status of those accounts. Marking an account as a favorite allows it to be easily selected.

9 To set up or view the budget for this account, or to view the account history or a summary statement of the account, the user would click on the appropriate button.

10 The user can click the **Cancel** button at any time to clear the data from the pop-up window and start over.

11 Clicking on **Save** records the new or edited account. Clicking on **New** clears all fields to enable the user to create another new account.

CLOSURE

- Review the Chapter Summary. Ask students for examples of each summary item. List responses on the board. Refer to illustrations in the text that match students' responses and Chapter Summary items.

Essential Questions

- What would be your options as a small business owner if your petty cash custodian continually came up short in the petty cash account? (*Answers may include offering additional training and having more than one person oversee petty cash to check one another's work.*)
- Would it always be useful for a company to have an accounts payable ledger in addition to the general ledger? Explain your answer. (*yes, to save time and errors*)
- How does a merchandising business predict what to purchase? (*Answers might include studying previous buying history, knowing the buying habits of potential customers, and understanding the nature of retail business and busy seasons.*)

EXTENDED LEARNING

- Review A Look at Accounting Software on pages 28 and 29.
- Assign Explore Accounting on page 30.

EXPLORE ACCOUNTING

Answers

Students may work independently or in groups to complete this activity. Through personal contacts, local chapters of professional organizations, or business directories and Internet searches, students can identify individuals who are certified. Students should be well prepared for the interview before contacting the individual. Require students to prepare a list of questions in advance. The questions should be organized to promote an interview that easily transitions between topics. Consider enlisting the assistance of another instructor or administrator to allow students to perform a mock interview.

During the actual interview, students should record carefully the responses to all questions. Direct students to prepare a brief written or oral report using the information from the interview.

Chapter Summary

The accounting equation is often viewed as a "T" account with assets on the left side and equities (liabilities and owners' equity) on the right side. Debits are recorded on the left and credits on the right side of the accounting equation. The normal balance of asset accounts, on the left side of the accounting equation, is a debit. The normal balance of equity accounts, on the right side of the accounting equation, is a credit.

Accounting transactions are recorded in journals. Four special journals are used to record similar transactions. All other transactions are recorded in a general journal. Transactions impacting an account are posted to its general ledger account. Transactions impacting a controlling account are also posted to subsidiary ledger accounts.

A merchandising business that sells different types of products can benefit from using a departmental accounting system. Sales, merchandise purchases, and selected expense transactions are recorded in the general ledger by department.

The purchase of merchandise on account is efficiently recorded in the special amount columns of the purchases journal. The transaction is immediately posted in the vendor's accounts payable ledger account to update the amount owed to the vendor. The totals of the special columns of a completed purchases journal are posted to the general ledger. Purchase returns and allowances, journalized in a general ledger, reduce the amount owed to the vendor.

All cash payments are recorded in the cash payments journal. The journal contains special amount columns to efficiently record the many cash payments made for purchases on account. To encourage early payment, some vendors offer a cash discount that allows the customer to pay less than the full amount of the purchase invoice. The cash payments journal includes special amount columns for purchase discounts for each department. Cash payments for other purchases and expenses are also recorded in the cash payments journal. The totals of the special columns of a completed cash payments journal are posted to the general ledger.

EXPLORE ACCOUNTING Accounting Certifications

© iStockphoto.com/Makhnach_M

The complexity of modern medicine requires that most physicians develop a specialty. In the same manner, many accountants develop a specialty in one area of accounting. Financial accounting, taxation, managerial accounting, information systems, and forensic accounting are just a few of the disciplines within accounting. Accountants demonstrate their expertise in a discipline by earning a related certification.

The Certified Public Accountant (CPA) is the most widely recognized certification. To become a CPA, an individual must pass a certifying examination and meet the educational and experience requirements of the board of accountancy in the individual's state. A CPA is qualified to perform a variety of accounting functions, including auditing financial statements, preparing tax returns, and providing tax planning. Many CPAs focus in one of these areas.

A partial list of other accounting certifications follows:

Certified Management Accountant: Responsible for the accounting information system; assists managers in using accounting information in decision making; works to provide the company with adequate financial resources to conduct business.

Certified Internal Auditor: Audits the accounting information system and other operational reporting systems.

Certified Information Systems Auditor: Evaluates the operations of an organization's information technology systems.

Certified Fraud Examiner: Investigates alleged fraudulent activities by examining accounting records and interviewing personnel; prepares evidence for admission into court.

Enrolled Agent: Represents taxpayers before the Internal Revenue Service on issues related to collections, audits, and appeals.

Certified Financial Planner: Assists individuals in developing investment strategies to meet future financial needs, such as retirement.

Accredited in Business Valuation (a special CPA designation): Determines the value of businesses involved in acquisitions or dispositions.

INSTRUCTIONS

Identify an individual who has one of the certifications listed above. Ask the individual to describe how the certification has played a role in his or her professional career.

Apply Your Understanding

INSTRUCTIONS: Download problem instructions for Excel, QuickBooks, and Sage 50 from the textbook companion website at www.C21accounting.com.

1-1 Application Problem: Determining the normal balance, increase, and decrease sides for accounts LO3

Write the answers for the following problem in the *Working Papers*.

Prepaid Insurance	Northland Supply (an account payable)
Advertising Expense	Supplies
Capital Stock	Sales—Video
Daniel Miller (an account receivable)	Retained Earnings

1	2	3	4	5	6	7	8
Account Title	Account Classification	Account's Normal Balance		Increase Side		Decrease Side	
		Debit	Credit	Debit	Credit	Debit	Credit
Prepaid Insurance	*Asset*	✔		✔			✔

Instructions:

Do the following steps for each account. The Prepaid Insurance account is given above as an example.

1. Write the account title in Column 1.
2. Write the account classification in Column 2.
3. Place a check mark in either Column 3 or 4 to indicate the normal balance of the account.
4. Place a check mark in either Column 5 or 6 to indicate the increase side of the account.
5. Place a check mark in either Column 7 or 8 to indicate the decrease side of the account.

1-2 Application Problem: Journalizing and posting departmental purchases on account and purchases returns and allowances LO4, 5, 6

Jessie's Landscapes has two departments: Flowers and Gifts. A purchases journal, general journal, and partial general and accounts payable ledgers are provided in the *Working Papers*. The balances are recorded as of August 1 of the current year. Post the following transactions when journalized: (1) transactions impacting the accounts payable subsidiary ledger and (2) transactions recorded on the general journal. Source documents are abbreviated as follows: debit memorandum, DM; purchase invoice, P.

Instructions:

1. Journalize the transactions completed during August of the current year. Use page 8 of a purchases journal and page 8 of a general journal. Post the items that are to be posted individually.
2. Prove and rule the purchases journal. Post the totals.

Transactions:

Aug. 4. Purchased statues on account from Tennessee Crafts, $4,165.00. P392.
5. The order from Tennessee Crafts contained broken statues, $68.45, from P390. DM41.
7. Purchased artwork on account from Glade Arts Center, $2,148.00. P393.
14. Returned dead plants to Marlon Nursery, $318.10, from P388. DM42.
16. Purchased cut flowers from Carson Growers, $3,269.00. P394.
21. Returned broken gifts to Tennessee Crafts, $265.00, from P392. DM43.
22. Took delivery of flowering plants from Marlon Nursery, $450.00. P395.
29. Purchased gifts on account from Glade Arts Center, $1,845.00. P396.

CHECK FIGURES

For complete solutions to Chapter 1 problems, see the Teacher's Edition of the Working Papers.

Application Problem 1-1

Daniel Miller and Supplies are assets with normal debit balances.

Northland Supply is a liability; Capital Stock and Retained Earnings are owners' equity; Sales—Video is a revenue account. These four accounts have normal credit balances.

Advertising Expense is an expense with a normal debit balance.

Application Problem 1-2

Purchases Journal column totals: $11,877.00; $3,719.00; $8,158.00.

General Journal: Three entries dated Aug. 5, 14, and 21.

Application Problem 1-3

Cash Payments Journal column totals: $813.35; N/A; $4,386.60; $48.12; $39.61; $5,112.22.

1-3 Application Problem: Journalizing and posting departmental cash payments LO7, 8

Sage 50 Accounting

1. Journalize and post transactions to the cash disbursements journal.
2. From the menu bar, select Reports & Forms; Accounts Payable.
3. Make the selections to the print the purchase journal and the cash disbursements journal.

QB

1. Journalize and post payments to vendors on account in the Pay Bills window.
2. Journalize and post payments to vendors in the Write Checks window.
3. From the menu bar, select Reports; Banking, Check Detail.
4. From the menu bar, select Reports; Vendors and Payables, Vendor Balance Detail.

X

1. Journalize and post vendor transactions on account to the cash payments journal and accounts payable ledger.
2. Make the selections to print the worksheets.

AAONLINE

1. Go to www.cengage.com/login
2. Click on AA Online to access.
3. Go to the online assignment and follow the instructions.

Step Music has two departments: Guitars and Keyboards. Post the following transactions when journalized: (1) transactions impacting the accounts payable subsidiary ledger and (2) cash payments entered in a general amount column of the cash payments journal. A cash payments journal and partial general and accounts payable ledgers are given in the *Working Papers*. The balances are recorded as of March 1 of the current year. Source documents are abbreviated as follows: check, C; debit memorandum, DM.

Instructions:

1. Journalize the transactions completed during March of the current year. Use page 3 of a cash payments journal. Post the items that are to be posted individually.
2. Prove and rule the cash payments journal. Post the totals.

Transactions:

Mar. 2. Paid cash to Z96 Radio, Inc., for advertising announcing a guitar sale, $350.00. C642.
5. Paid cash on account to Airways Music covering P584 for a keyboard, $1,980.60, less 2% discount. C643.
9. Paid cash to C&C Supplies for office supplies, $145.60. C644.
17. Paid cash on account to Campbell Guitar covering P592 for six bass guitars, $2,774.00, less DM32 for $368.00, less 2% discount. C645.
24. Paid cash to Elon Accessories, Inc., for a keyboard stand, $235.95. C646.
31. Paid cash to replenish the petty cash fund, $81.80: miscellaneous, $26.73; guitar strings (Purchases—Guitars), $12.95; supplies, $42.12. C647.

Mastery Problem 1-M

Purchases Journal column totals: $10,863.00; $6,496.00; $4,367.00.

General Journal: Two entries dated Aug. 4 and 9.

Cash Payments Journal column totals: $3,459.84; N/A; $8,911.00; $92.84; $85.38; $12,192.62.

1-M Mastery Problem: Journalizing departmental purchases and cash payments LO4, 5, 6, 7, 8

Sage 50 Accounting

1. Journalize and post vendor transactions on account to the purchase journal.
2. Journalize and post vendor transactions on account to the cash disbursements journal.
3. From the menu bar, select Reports & Forms; Accounts Payable.
4. Make the selections to the print the purchase journal and the cash disbursements journal.

QB

1. Journalize and post vendor transactions on account in the Enter Bills window.
2. Journalize and post payments to vendors on account in the Pay Bills window.
3. Journalize and post payments to vendors in the Write Checks window.
4. From the menu bar, select Reports; Banking, Check Detail.

Jan's Jewelry has two departments: Costume and Fine. Post the following transactions when journalized: (1) transactions impacting the accounts payable subsidiary ledger, (2) transactions recorded in the general journal, and (3) cash payments entered in a general amount column of the cash payments journal. Journals and partial general and accounts payable ledgers are given in the *Working Papers*. Source documents are abbreviated as follows: check, C; debit memorandum, DM; purchase invoice, P.

Instructions:

1. Journalize the transactions completed during August of the current year. Use page 8 of a purchases journal, page 8 of a general journal, and page 12 of a cash payments journal. Post the items that are to be posted individually.
2. Prove and rule the purchases journal. Post the totals.
3. Prove and rule the cash payments journal. Post the totals.

Transactions:

Aug. 1. Paid cash to Gallup Properties for rent, $2,400.00. C685.
2. Purchased fine jewelry on account from Austin Creations, $4,367.00. P567.
3. Paid cash to Davis Office Source for supplies, $123.14. C686.
4. Returned costume jewelry to Destin Crafters, $109.50, from P562. DM46.
6. Paid cash to Sanders Hardware for paint (miscellaneous expense), $56.34. C687.

INDEPENDENT PRACTICE

- Assign Mastery Problem 1-M for students as a culminating problem that combines all activities from the chapter.
- Assign Source Documents Problem 1-S, utilizing source documents necessary for purchases and cash payments.
- Assign Challenge Problem 1-C to accelerated students who work at a faster pace.
- Assign Study Guide 1.
- Students can access Online Working Papers to work end-of-chapter problems on the computer.
- Direct students to the C21 Accounting companion website for additional practice and review opportunities.

FORMATIVE ASSESSMENT

- Review solutions to the assigned problems in class, diagnosing trouble spots.

RETEACH

- Call on students to describe how they avoid the trouble spots diagnosed.
- Use reteaching suggestions from lesson plans as required.
- Assign Recycling Problem 1-R if needed.

1. Journalize and post vendor transactions on account to the purchases journal.
2. Journalize and post vendor transactions on account to the cash payments journal, general journal and accounts payable ledger.
3. Make the selections to print the worksheets.

AAONLINE

1. Go to www.cengage.com/login
2. Click on AA Online to access.
3. Go to the online assignment and follow the instructions.

9. Returned fine jewelry to Austin Creations, $98.00, from P567. DM47.
10. Paid cash on account to Austin Creations covering P567 for fine jewelry for $4,367.00, less DM47 for $98.00, less 2% discount. C688.
14. Paid cash to Williams Accessories for beads (costume jewelry), $275.00. C689.
16. Purchased costume jewelry on account from Jenkins Designs, $4,642.00. P568.
21. Paid cash to City Electric Department for the utility bill, $512.12. C690.
24. Paid cash on account to Jenkins Designs covering P568 for costume jewelry, $4,642.00, less 2% discount. C691.
25. Purchased costume jewelry on account from Ketler Krafts, $1,854.00. P569.
31. Paid cash to replenish the petty cash fund, $93.24: advertising for fine jewelry, $40.00; miscellaneous, $21.56; supplies, $31.68. C692.

1-C Challenge Problem: Establishing a departmental accounting system LO3

Each business in this chapter has illustrated a two-department accounting system. In real life, a company may elect to have more than two departments. Management must evaluate its operations and determine the information value of having multiple departments. Having too few departments may not provide enough information for making informed decisions. Yet the effort required to record transactions in too many departments may outweigh the value of the information provided to management.

Eupora Music currently uses two departments: Guitars and Other. The manager has asked that you suggest how the company could be divided into more focused departments. To assist in your decision, the manager has provided you with a list of recent inventory purchases.

Quantity	Description	Unit Cost	Sales Price
3	Guitar straps	$ 6.95	$ 12.95
1	5-string banjo	149.00	299.00
15	6-string nylon guitar strings	5.95	12.95
1	Acoustic guitar	1,495.98	2,399.00
50	Sheet music, recent publication mix	3.99	6.99
25	20′ electric guitar cable	8.95	19.99
2	Wireless microphone	325.95	650.00
5	Effects pedal	99.99	209.95
6	Beginner guitar package	89.99	199.99
3	Harmonica with case	159.25	249.99
5	Bass guitar package	129.99	199.99
2	Tom drums with stand	109.95	189.99
6	Digital metronome	59.99	109.95
20	5B drumsticks	4.95	9.99
3	Acoustic electric guitar with gig bag	219.99	379.99
4	12-string nylon guitar strings	5.95	12.95
20	Microphone wind screens	2.99	4.95
4	100′ 8-channel audio snake	129.99	259.99
2	Bass guitar with case	799.99	1,799.99
15	Ear plugs	2.95	5.95
12	5-string bass guitar strings	6.95	15.95
3	Drum set	495.95	795.95

Instructions:

Use the form in the *Working Papers* to determine three- and four-department solutions for Eupora Music. The form includes the current two-department category for each item.

Challenge Problem 1-C

The *Working Papers* contain a suggested solution. Students may identify other ways of categorizing the items into other departments. Encourage students to verbalize the logic they used to determine the departments.

Three departments: Acoustic Guitars, Other String Instruments, Other.

Four departments: Acoustic Guitars, Other String Instruments, Drums, Other.

EXTENDED LEARNING

- Assign 21st Century Skills on page 34.
- Assign Auditing for Errors on page 35.
- Assign Analyzing Home Depot's Financial Statements on page 35.

SUMMATIVE EVALUATION

- Chapter 1 Test
- Cognero for Chapter 1

Source Documents Problem 1-S

Purchases Journal column totals: $11,043.63; $9,726.63; $1,317.00.

Cash Payments Journal column totals: $9,534.18; N/A; $4,011.38; $54.91; $25.31; $13,465.34.

General Journal: Four entries dated May 3, 7, 14, and 31.

21ST CENTURY SKILLS

Answers

1. a. Answers will vary.
   b. The summary should explain the options considered and a final recommendation. The letter should be professionally written, be easy to follow, and include the rationale for the final decision.
2. a. Answers will vary. Visual aids could enhance the presentations if time permits.
   b. Letters should be formatted correctly and be easy to follow and understand.

1-S Source Documents Problem: Journalizing purchase and cash payment transactions LO4, 6, 7

Mike's Discount Golf sells golf and tennis equipment. Journals and source documents related to the purchase and cash payments are provided in the *Working Papers*. Post the following transactions when journalized: (1) transactions impacting the accounts payable subsidiary ledger, (2) transactions recorded in the general journal, and (3) cash payments entered in a general amount column of the cash payments journal. Mike's Discount Golf uses a chart of accounts similar to Whiley Outdoor Living.

Instructions:

1. Journalize the transactions shown in the source documents, by date, using page 5 of a purchases journal, page 5 of a general journal, and page 7 of a cash payments journal. Some transactions may be related to more than one source document.
2. Prove and rule the purchases journal.
3. Prove and rule the cash payments journal.

21st Century Skills

Supplier Savvy

PARTNERSHIP FOR 21ST CENTURY SKILLS

Theme: Financial, Economic, Business, and Entrepreneurial Literacy

Skills: Creativity and Innovation, Critical Thinking and Problem Solving, Communication and Collaboration, ICT Literacy

Suppliers, or vendors, are essential to a merchandising business. Careful selection of suppliers can create a meaningful partnership that allows the business to flourish. Good business partners can help cut costs and improve products and services.

Suppliers can be divided into four categories:

Manufacturing—Some products are sold directly from the manufacturer, or from a sales representative for the manufacturer. This is usually the lowest-cost option; however, shipping can be costly.

Distributors/Wholesalers—A distributor usually buys large quantities from several manufacturers and places the merchandise in a warehouse to sell to retailers. The distributor's cost of merchandise is usually more than a manufacturer's, due to additional markup and selections.

Jobbers/Independent Craftspeople—These individuals usually make daily deliveries to grocery stores or present unique creations at trade shows.

Importer—Products are sent from another country and usually operate much like a domestic wholesaler.

APPLICATION

1. Clemente has decided to sell insulated water bottles in his sporting goods store.
   a. Using the Internet, find five vendors (suppliers) and obtain the following information: product description, price, quantity discounts, additional charges such as art or setup charges, shipping costs, and estimated delivery time. Place this information in a spreadsheet.
   b. Write a letter to Clemente summarizing your findings and making a recommendation for purchase. Be sure to state the reasons for your conclusions.
2. Visit a small merchandising business in your local community or online. Examine the products available for sale. Then, with a partner, brainstorm three new products that you think would be beneficial for this business to sell.
   a. Present your findings to the class.
   b. Compose a letter to the business explaining your assignment and suggestions.

COMMON CORE AND INTERDISCIPLINARY STUDIES

Extended learning features and activities present numerous opportunities to implement Common Core Standards through interdisciplinary studies. Practice is provided in the common core areas of English Language Arts & Literacy and Mathematical Practice. Many of these activities require short, critical-thinking and decision-making responses that apply reading, writing, speaking, listening, language, media and technology, and mathematical skills.

Auditing for errors

A manager at Lambert Industries just prepared the chart below, which lists all the account titles from the company's chart of accounts. For each account, a "+" or "–" was recorded in the appropriate debit and credit column to show the impact of a debit or credit to each account's balance. The last column indicates the normal balance for each account. The intent of creating the chart is to provide an easy reference tool to help new accounting clerks accurately record journal entries and calculate general ledger balances.

Review the manager's chart below. Make a new chart so that the reference tool is accurate.

Account Title	Debit	Credit	Normal Balance
Petty Cash	+	–	Dr.
Accounts Receivable	+	–	Dr.
Allowance for Uncollectible Accounts	+	–	Dr.
Merchandise Inventory	+	–	Dr.
Store Equipment	+	–	Dr.
Accumulated Depreciation—Store Equipment	–	+	Dr.
Accounts Payable	–	+	Cr.
Interest Payable	–	+	Cr.
Capital Stock	–	+	Cr.
Retained Earnings	+	–	Cr.
Dividends	+	–	Cr.
Sales	–	+	Cr.
Sales Returns and Allowances	–	+	Cr.
Purchases	+	–	Dr.
Purchases Discount	+	–	Dr.
Rent Expense	+	–	Dr.
Federal Income Tax Expense	+	–	Dr.

Analyzing Home Depot's financial statements

Selected published financial information for Home Depot, Inc., is reproduced in Appendix B of this textbook. Like many companies, Home Depot rounds dollar amounts when reporting financial data on various financial statements. It is very important when reviewing data in Home Depot's annual report to determine if the amounts presented have been rounded to the nearest million, nearest thousand, or not rounded at all. Look at page B-6 in Appendix B. Under the heading at the top of the page, notice the phrase "amounts in millions, except per share data." This means that all dollar amounts above and including Net Earnings are rounded to the nearest million. For example, the reported fiscal year 2012 Net Sales amount of $74,754 actually represents $74,754,000,000. Actual dollar amounts on this page are calculated by multiplying the amount reported by 1,000,000 ($74,754 × 1,000,000 = $74,754,000,000).

INSTRUCTIONS

Refer to the Consolidated Statements of Earnings in Appendix B on page B-6 to identify the following amounts:

1. List the actual dollar amount of Cost of Sales and Operating Income for fiscal year 2012.
2. List the actual dollar amount of Total Assets for fiscal year 2012.
3. List Home Depot's diluted earnings per share for fiscal year 2012.

AUDITING FOR ERRORS

Answers

Allowance for Uncollectible Accounts: reverse debit/credit, Cr. normal balance.

Accumulated Depreciation—Store Equipment: Cr. normal balance.

Retained Earnings: reverse debit/credit.

Dividends: reverse debit/credit, Dr. normal balance.

Sales Returns and Allowances: reverse debit/credit, Dr. normal balance.

Purchases Discount: reverse debit/credit, Cr. normal balance.

ANALYZING HOME DEPOT'S FINANCIAL STATEMENTS

Answers

1. Cost of Sales, $48,912,000,000; Operating Income, $7,766,000,000.
2. $41,084,000,000.
3. $3.00.

Chapter 2

Recording Departmental Sales and Cash Receipts

Scope & Sequence

	New	Review/Enrich
Introduction		
Introduce the Chapter		
Lesson 2-1: Departmental Sales on Account and Sales Returns and Allowances		
Departmental Sales on Account	✓	
Journalizing Sales on Account		✓
Posting from a Sales Journal to the Accounts Receivable Ledger		✓
Posting from a Sales Journal to a General Ledger Account		✓
Journalizing Sales Returns and Allowances		✓
Posting from a General Journal		✓
Lesson 2-2: Journalizing and Posting Cash Receipts		
Cash Receipts on Account		✓
Journalizing a Cash Receipt with a Sales Discount		✓
Journalizing Cash and Credit Card Sales		✓
Journalizing and Posting a Cash Receipt with a Sales Discount		✓
Posting from a Cash Receipts Journal		✓
Closure		

Enhancing Instruction

Features	Common Core Standards
• Accounting in the Real World: Expedia, Inc	• ELAL—reading, writing
• Ethics in Action: A Business Lunch Light on Business • Financial Literacy: What's the Tradeoff? Considering Choices and Costs	• ELAL—reading • ELAL—media and technology, speaking; Mathematics
• Why Accounting?: Distribution Impacts a Company's Goals • Careers In Accounting: Owner of CPA Firm • Think Like an Accountant: Evaluating Departmental Sales	• ELAL—reading, writing • ELAL—reading • Mathematics
• A Look at Accounting Software • Explore Accounting • 21st Century Skills • Source Documents Problem • Analyzing Home Depot's Financial Statements	• ELAL—reading • ELAL—speaking, listening; Mathematics • ELAL—speaking, media and technology, writing • Mathematics

ELAL = English Language Arts & Literacy

Calculator: © iStockphoto.com/picstodisc; Paper: © iStockphoto.com/Qingwa

Practice and Assessment

Technology & Media	Teaching Strategies	Guided Practice	Independent Practice	Reteach/Enrich
• Instructor's Resource CD/Website: PowerPoint Slides Accounting Concepts • Online Working Papers • Transparency Masters: Departmental Sales Journal, General Journal	• Interpersonal Learners • Tactile/Kinesthetic Learners	• Term Review • Audit Your Understanding • Work Together 2-1	• On Your Own 2-1 • Application Problem 2-1 • Formative Assessment, p. 45 • Online Working Papers	• Reteach, p. 46
• Instructor's Resource CD/Website: PowerPoint Slides Accounting Concepts • Online Working Papers • Transparency Masters: Departmental Cash Receipts Journal, Accounts Receivable Ledger, General Ledger-Accounts Receivable Account	• Gifted Learners	• Terms Review • Audit Your Understanding • Work Together 2-2	• On Your Own 2-2 • Application Problem 2-2 • Formative Assessment, p. 53 • Online Working Papers	• Reteach, p. 54
• Online Working Papers	• Common Core and Interdisciplinary Studies		• Mastery Problem 2-M • Study Guide 2 • Chapter 2 Test • Cognero Chapter 2	• Challenge Problem 2-C • Reteach, p. 59 • Recycling Problem 2-R

Introduce the Chapter

SET THE STAGE

GUIDING QUESTIONS

- Ask students to explain what they learned about discounts and allowances from a buyer's point of view.
- Ask students if any have ever returned merchandise, and if so, why.
- Ask students if they or anyone they know have ever paid a debt early. Ask for their rationale for paying early.

PREVIEW CHAPTER OBJECTIVES

- Point out that in this chapter, sales and cash receipts will be distributed among departments just as purchases and cash payments were in the previous chapter.
- Point out that a company that keeps records of sales and the cost of merchandise by department can determine gross profit from operations for each department.
- Emphasize that gross profit information for a department can help determine if a department is earning an appropriate profit. If it is not, departmental information can help managers determine which items are causing the problem.

PREVIEW ACCOUNTING TERMS

- Read each term aloud to verify its pronunciation for students.
- Point out terms or parts of terms that should already be familiar to most students.

Chapter 2 Recording Departmental Sales and Cash Receipts

LEARNING OBJECTIVES

After studying Chapter 2, in addition to defining key terms, you will be able to:

LO1 Explain the purpose of a departmental accounting system.

LO2 Journalize and post departmental sales on account using a sales journal.

LO3 Journalize and post departmental sales returns and allowances.

LO4 Explain the impact of sales discounts on the collection of accounts receivable.

LO5 Journalize and post departmental cash receipts using a cash receipts journal.

Calculator: © iStockphoto.com/picstudisc; Paper: © iStockphoto.com/Qingwa

© wavebreakmedia/Shutterstock.com

Accounting In The Real World

Expedia, Inc.

It was not that long ago when people needed a travel agent to book a vacation, especially to international locations. Arranging flights, hotels, and rental cars was simply too complex. Travel agents had access to information that would help prevent any unwanted travel surprises. People often expected their travel agents to have personal knowledge of their destinations.

Expedia harnessed the power of the Internet to provide an alternative to using a travel agent. Expedia's customers can book a flight, hotel, rental car, cruise, or any combination of the four. Customers can also access information and links to theme parks, tours, museums, sporting venues, restaurants, and other attractions.

A travel agent's personal knowledge of a destination cannot be replaced. Nevertheless, Expedia strives to deliver the next best thing. For hotels, Expedia uses a four-star rating system. Customers can also read the independent reviews of other hotel guests.

Expedia has seen many changes in its short business life. Microsoft first launched Expedia in 1996. Three years later, Microsoft established Expedia as an independent corporation. Over the next few years, Expedia began to acquire other Internet travel businesses. In 2002, InterActiveCorp purchased Expedia, but established it as an independent corporation again in 2005.

Expedia operates a variety of Internet travel sites, including Hotels.com, Hotwire.com, and TripAdvisor. These sites are often customized to suit the unique needs of international markets. For example, Expedia acquired a majority ownership in eLong.com to serve the China market.

Departmental accounting provides a business with useful information about distinct parts of the business. Generally accepted accounting principles have similar requirements for published financial statements. Corporations must report revenue and expenses for distinct parts of the business. These parts are known as segments. Until 2008, Expedia reported its financial statements in geographic segments: North America and Europe. A company reorganization resulted in a change in the company's reporting segments.

CRITICAL THINKING

1. Access the latest Form 10-K of Expedia. Identify and describe Expedia's segments.
2. Identify a local business, school district, or university. Suggest the segments the organization could use to report its financial activity.

Sources: Expedia.com; eLong.net.

Background: © iStockphoto.com/pagadesign; Real World: © iStockphoto.com/cru photo

Key Terms

- credit memorandum
- sales discount
- point-of-sale (POS) terminal
- terminal summary

Accounting In The Real World

Answers

1. For its 2013 fiscal year, Expedia disclosed its financial activities in two segments:
   - The Leisure segment provides travel and advertising services through brands that include Expedia.com, Hotels.com, and Hotwire.com.
   - The Egencia segment provides travel services to corporate customers in North America, Europe, and the Asia Pacific region.
2. Answers will vary. As an example, students may suggest reporting a school district by academics, sports, and transportation segments.

LESSON
2-1

BRIDGE

- The previous chapter explained why businesses keep purchases and cash payments information by department. This chapter explains why businesses keep sales and cash receipts information by department.
- Explain that students have already learned how to record sales on account and sales returns and allowances in first-year accounting. This chapter will explain recording these transactions for a departmentalized business.

TEACHING RESOURCES

- **Instructor's Resource CD/Website:** PowerPoint Slides
  Accounting Concepts
- **Working Papers:** Teacher's Edition of the Working Papers for Lesson 2-1
  Online Working Papers
- **Transparency Masters:** Departmental Sales Journal
  General Journal

ENGAGE

- Ask students to prepare a list of all businesses in which they have worked that sold merchandise.
- Ask if any of the businesses were departmentalized.
- Ask if any of the businesses that were not departmentalized could have been and what the departments would be.

PREVIEW

- Call on a student to read the accounting term and definition introduced in this lesson: *credit memorandum*.
- Point out the learning objectives for this lesson.
- Direct students to read the headings in this lesson and to examine the illustrations.

INPUT

- Explain that Whiley is required to collect a sales tax of 6.0%.
- Explain that some of Whiley's customers are exempt from sales tax.
- Explain that sales on account are recorded separately for each of the two departments, Grills and Furniture.
- Review the Objective Evidence and Realization of Revenue concepts presented in first-year accounting but reintroduced in this lesson.

© iStockphoto.com/svetikd

LESSON
2-1 Departmental Sales on Account and Sales Returns and Allowances

LO1 Explain the purpose of a departmental accounting system.
LO2 Journalize and post departmental sales on account using a sales journal.
LO3 Journalize and post departmental sales returns and allowances.

Departmental Sales on Account LO1

Managers use departmental data to make decisions relating to business operations. Companies such as Whiley Outdoor Living, Inc., are often organized into departments, based on the different types of products or services they sell. In order to maximize business operations, Whiley identified two departments based on the two categories of merchandise it sells—Grills and Furniture. Whiley's management team uses departmental information to analyze the profitability of each department, set annual goals, evaluate managers, and determine company bonuses.

In order to have comprehensive departmental data, however, a business should record sales and cash receipts data separately for each department. For example, gross profit from operations for each department is one type of valuable information for management decision making. Departmental gross profit from operations helps business managers decide if each department is earning an appropriate profit. If not, departmental information can help managers determine which items are causing the problem. To determine departmental gross profit from operations, the business must keep records of sales and the cost of merchandise sold by department.

Chapter 1 presented how to account for purchases transactions for a departmental merchandising business. To have complete departmental data, Whiley also records all sales transactions by department. Whiley makes sales on account to individuals, business firms, and schools. It sells merchandise in two departments. The grills department sells home and commercial grills. The furniture department sells a variety of outdoor furniture, including chairs, chaise lounges, swings, and tables.

Whiley records all departmental sales on account in a sales journal. The sales journal has one debit column—Accounts Receivable Debit. The journal also has three credit columns—Sales Tax Payable Credit and special Sales Credit columns for Grills and Furniture.

The Sales Tax Payable Credit column is used to record all sales tax amounts that Whiley collects. Most states require vendors to collect sales tax from their customers. The city and state in which Whiley is located have a combined sales tax rate of 6.0%. Some customers are not required to pay a sales tax. Many agencies supported by local and state governments and not-for-profit organizations are exempt from paying a sales tax. For example, Central Community College is a tax-exempt customer of Whiley.

Whiley prepares sales invoices in duplicate for each sale on account. [CONCEPT: Objective Evidence] Each sales invoice shows the amount of merchandise sold by department. The customer receives the original copy of the sales invoice. The duplicate copy is the source document for journalizing the transaction.

Whiley records all departmental sales at the time of sale, regardless of when payment is made. [CONCEPT: Realization of Revenue] The *Realization of Revenue* concept states that revenue is recorded at the time goods or services are sold. A business may sell either goods or services. Cash may be received at the time of sale, or an agreement may be made to receive payment at a later date. Regardless of when the business actually receives cash, it records the sale amount in the accounting records at the time of sale. For example, during November a business sells office furniture on account for $2,000.00. The customer pays its account in January of the next fiscal year. The business records $2,000.00 of revenue in November, at the time of the sale, even though the $2,000.00 is collected later.

TEACHING IDEA

Have students conduct research with officials in the city government or the chamber of commerce to find out how a new business registers with the state government to qualify as an exempt organization for sales tax and what determines the nonprofit/tax-exempt status.

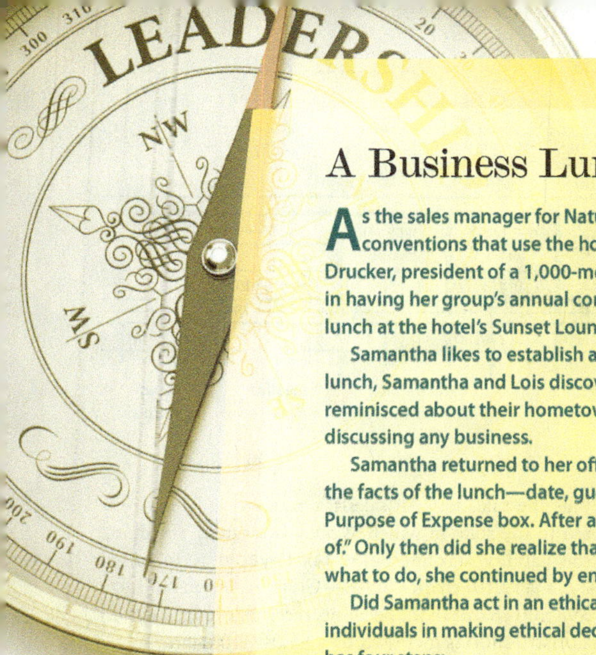

© iStockphoto.com/LdF

ETHICS IN ACTION

A Business Lunch Light on Business

As the sales manager for Natural Springs Hotel, Samantha Jones is responsible for selling conventions that use the hotel's grand ballroom. Samantha received a call from Lois Drucker, president of a 1,000-member national education association. Lois expressed interest in having her group's annual conference at the hotel. Therefore, Samantha invited Lois to lunch at the hotel's Sunset Lounge to sell her on the merits of Natural Springs Hotel.

Samantha likes to establish a relationship with the potential customer. So minutes into the lunch, Samantha and Lois discovered they grew up in the same town. Time flew by as they reminisced about their hometown. Before they knew it, the lunch hour was over without them discussing any business.

Samantha returned to her office and opened her expense report software. She entered all the facts of the lunch—date, guest's name, and amount spent. She paused as she stared at the Purpose of Expense box. After a moment, she entered "Preliminary meeting with president of." Only then did she realize that she never learned the name of Lois's organization. Not sure what to do, she continued by entering "National Association of Educators."

Did Samantha act in an ethical manner? Many models have been promoted to assist individuals in making ethical decisions. The ethical decision-making model used in this textbook has four steps:

1. Recognize you are facing an ethical dilemma.
2. Identify the action taken or the proposed action.
3. Analyze the action.
   a. Is the action illegal?
   b. Does the action violate company or professional standards?
   c. Who is affected, and how, by the action?
4. Determine if the action is ethical.

The first two steps often occur as the situation unfolds. If the action is either illegal or violates company or professional standards, the action should not be taken. However, it is often necessary to analyze the action further by determining the parties affected and whether they are affected in a negative or positive way.

INSTRUCTIONS

Access the *Business Corporate Guide* for Marriott International, Inc. Using this code as a guide, use the ethical model to help determine whether the action by Samantha demonstrates ethical behavior.

ETHICS IN ACTION

This case, by design, contains what some students might consider to be a minor issue. The fact that no business was ultimately discussed at this meeting is an insignificant issue. It is logical to assume that the lunch will be the first step in Samantha's efforts to book the conference. But her misrepresentation of the purpose of the meeting appears to be a clear violation of the code. Thus, Samantha has demonstrated a willingness to overlook the code. This action could have serious implications on her relationship with her manager and, ultimately, her professional career.

Suggested Solution

1. *Recognize you are facing an ethical dilemma.* Samantha realized that she had an ethical dilemma when she had to pause before entering the purpose of the meeting. She obviously felt uncomfortable about the lack of any business activity that occurred.
2. *Identify the action taken or the proposed action.* Rather than entering the little information she knew, she elected to make up an organization name. Thus, she falsified her expense report.
3. *Analyze the action.*
   a. *Is the action illegal?* Possibly. Claiming the lunch as a business expense may violate income tax laws.
   b. *Does the action violate company or professional standards?* Possibly. Two sentences in the *Accurate Books, Records, and Reports* section of the *Business Corporate Guide* appear to apply.
      - "Ensure that all travel and entertainment expenses are supported by actual receipts and have a valid business purpose."
      - "Do not distort the true nature of any transaction, no matter what the reason and no matter how insignificant the result may be."
   c. *Who is affected, and how, by the action?* See the analysis in the Instructional Strategies section at the front of this book.
4. *Determine if the action is ethical.* Samantha should have been honest when entering the purpose of the meeting. Her manager would likely understand the circumstances. In addition, there is no way of knowing whether the relationship established will lead to booking the association's conference.

INPUT

- Use the illustration to explain the columns used for a departmental sale on account. Point out that there is a separate Sales Credit column for each department.
- Remind students that a sales invoice is the source document for a sale on account.
- Remind students that a sale on account always includes an amount in the Accounts Receivable Debit column and that the name of the customer is written in the Account Debited column.
- Point out that the sales tax amount is recorded in the Sales Tax Payable Credit column. Remind students that a sale on account to a tax-exempt customer does not include a sales tax amount.
- Explain to students that any business that is tax-exempt must have a federal tax identification number in order not to pay sales tax.

MODEL

Analyze the transaction

- Draw four blank T accounts on the board.
- Read the transaction statement.
- Ask students to analyze the transaction by answering these questions: Which accounts are affected? Are they increased or decreased? Are they debited or credited? Complete the T accounts as the information is provided.
- Review the effect on the account for Lynch Construction.

Record the transaction

- Use the departmental sales journal transparency to illustrate recording the transaction in the sales journal.
- Record each item in the journal, following the six steps shown.
- Point out that no abbreviation for sales invoice is necessary in the Sale No. column. Sales invoices are the source document for all sales recorded on the sales journal.

Journalizing Sales on Account LO2

SALES JOURNAL PAGE 7

	DATE		ACCOUNT DEBITED	SALE NO.	POST. REF.	1 ACCOUNTS RECEIVABLE DEBIT	2 SALES TAX PAYABLE CREDIT	3 SALES CREDIT GRILLS	4 SALES CREDIT FURNITURE	
1	20-- July	4	Lynch Construction	793		1 044 10	59 10	985 00		1
26		30	Central Community College	818		4 520 00			4 520 00	26

1 Date 2 Customer Name 3 Sales Invoice Number 4 Total Invoice Amount 5 Sales Tax 6 Sales Amount

July 4. Sold a grill on account to Lynch Construction, $985.00, plus sales tax, $59.10; total, $1,044.10. Sales Invoice No. 793.

GENERAL LEDGER

Accounts Receivable	
↑ 1,044.10	

Sales—Grills	
	↑ 985.00

Sales Tax Payable	
	↑ 59.10

ACCOUNTS RECEIVABLE LEDGER

Lynch Construction	
↑ 1,044.10	

This transaction is recorded in the departmental sales journal. The source document for this transaction is a sales invoice. [CONCEPT: Objective Evidence]

In the general ledger, Accounts Receivable is increased by a $1,044.10 debit. The amount that the customer owes represents the price of the merchandise plus the sales tax. All sales tax received is later remitted to the state in which Whiley is located. Therefore, the liability account Sales Tax Payable is increased by a $59.10 credit. Sales—Grills is increased by a $985.00 credit. In the accounts receivable ledger, Lynch Construction is increased by a $1,044.10 debit.

The transaction on line 26 of the sales journal shows a transaction for a tax-exempt customer. Since Central Community College is an educational institution, it is not required by the state to pay sales tax.

Recording Sales on Account in the Sales Journal

1. **Write the date, 20--, July 4, in the Date column.**
2. **Write the customer name, Lynch Construction, in the Account Debited column.**
3. **Record the sales invoice number, 793, in the Sale No. column.**
4. **Enter the total invoice amount, $1,044.10, in the Accounts Receivable Debit column.**
5. **Enter the credit amount, $59.10, in the Sales Tax Payable Credit column.**
6. **Enter the credit amount, $985.00, in the Sales Credit Grills column.**

fyi

All businesses and nonprofit entities that have employees must have a federal tax identification number. This number is used in much the same way that individuals use their social security numbers. The Internal Revenue Service identifies entities that are exempt from federal income tax by their federal identification numbers. States may require vendors to keep a written record of the federal tax identification numbers of their tax-exempt customers.

DIFFERENTIATED INSTRUCTION

Interpersonal learners are people-oriented and learn best with cooperative learning groups or with a partner. Assign students to groups of three. Each group is to explore the credit policies of two businesses in the community. Students should prepare a group presentation explaining the types of individuals who receive credit, the credit terms, and the results if an account is uncollectible at these places of business.

Posting from a Sales Journal to the Accounts Receivable Ledger

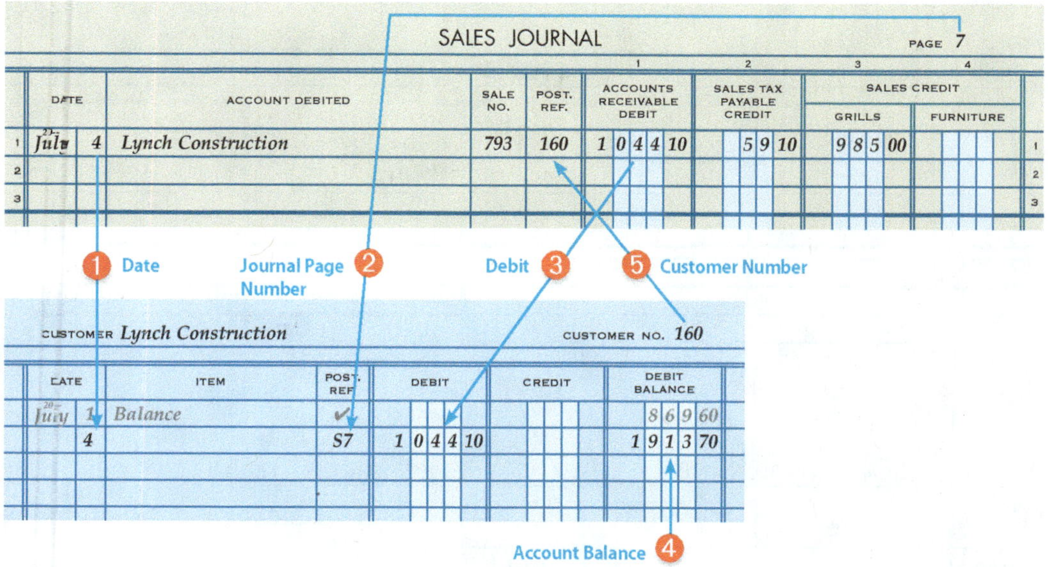

Whiley keeps customer accounts in an accounts receivable ledger. Individual amounts in the Accounts Receivable Debit column are posted when the transaction is recorded in the sales journal. This procedure keeps the customers' accounts up to date. The sales journal is abbreviated as *S* in the Post. Ref. column of the ledger accounts.

© Moon Light PhotoStudio/Shutterstock.com

Posting from the Sales Journal to the Accounts Receivable Ledger

1. Write the date, 4, in the account's Date column.
2. Record S7 in the Post. Ref. column of the subsidiary ledger account to indicate that the posting came from page 7 of the sales journal.
3. Enter the debit amount, $1,044.10, in the account's Debit column. This is the total amount due from the customer. It includes the price of the grill and the sales tax.
4. Add the amount in the debit column, $1,044.10, to the previous balance of $869.60. Write the new account balance, $1,913.70, in the Debit Balance column.
5. Record the customer number, 160, in the Post. Ref. column of the sales journal to show that posting is completed for this line.

fyi Sales taxes collected by businesses must be sent to the appropriate governmental agency. In many states, sales taxes are paid monthly. The payment is accompanied by a form that provides information such as total sales, sales tax collected, and sales exempt from sales tax.

INPUT

- Explain that individual amounts in the Accounts Receivable Debit column are posted frequently from the sales journal to the accounts receivable ledger so that customer accounts are up to date.
- Point out to students that sales tax collected by businesses must be sent to the appropriate government agency. In many states, sales tax is paid monthly.

MODEL

- Direct students to the illustration to explain the posting procedure from a sales journal to an accounts receivable ledger.
- As you read each step, ask students to point to the related arrows in the illustration.
- Remind students that the abbreviation for the sales journal, *S*, and the page number are recorded in the Post. Ref. column of every ledger account affected to furnish an audit trail.
- Remind students that the accounts receivable account number is recorded in the sales journal's Post. Ref. column to indicate that posting has been completed and to furnish an audit trail. This should be the last step of posting.

DIFFERENTIATED INSTRUCTION

Tactile/Kinesthetic learners: These students experience learning best through hands-on activities. Provide index cards for these students to use in representing the general ledger. Each card should represent an account and should have three vertical lines to distinguish between debit and credit columns and balance columns. Have students post each example of a journal entry to the appropriate cards (accounts).

INPUT

- Point out that the steps to rule and prove a sales journal are the same as for other journals.
- Point out that students have already learned how to post the special column totals of other journals to general ledger accounts.
- Note that the total of the Sales Tax Payable column is a credit.
- Point out the last transaction on the sales journal. Explain that some states exempt schools, government agencies, and some not-for-profit organizations from paying sales taxes.

MODEL

Proving a sales journal

- Direct students to the illustration as you describe how to prove and rule a sales journal at the end of a month.
- Remind students that the single rule indicates that a column is to be totaled.
- Remind students that a double rule indicates that the equality of debits and credits has been proved by adding the debit amount totals and comparing the sum to the sum of the credit amount totals.

Posting from a sales journal

- Direct students to the illustration as you read each step for posting from a sales journal to a general ledger account. Ask students to point to the related arrows in the illustration.
- Remind students that the abbreviation for the sales journal, *S*, and the page number are recorded in the Post. Ref. column of every ledger account affected to furnish an audit trail.
- Remind students that the general ledger account number is recorded in parentheses under the column total to show that posting has been completed and to furnish an audit trail.

Posting from a Sales Journal to a General Ledger Account

SALES JOURNAL — PAGE 7

	DATE		ACCOUNT DEBITED	SALE NO.	POST. REF.	1 ACCOUNTS RECEIVABLE DEBIT	2 SALES TAX PAYABLE CREDIT	3 SALES CREDIT GRILLS	4 SALES CREDIT FURNITURE	
1	20-- July	4	Lynch Construction	793	160	1,044.10	59.10	985.00		1
2		6	Wilson Properties	794	195	2,346.84	132.84		2,214.00	2
3		7	Jenkins Landscapes	795	125	1,317.32	74.57	1,242.75		3
27		30	Central Community College	818	125	4,520.00			4,520.00	27
28		31	Totals			30,147.92	1,546.34	12,567.24	16,034.34	28
29						(1205)	(2110)	(4105)	(4205)	29

1 Date

2 Journal Page Number

3 Column Total

5 Account Number

ACCOUNT *Accounts Receivable* — ACCOUNT NO. 1205

DATE		ITEM	POST. REF.	DEBIT	CREDIT	BALANCE DEBIT	BALANCE CREDIT
20-- July	1	Balance	✓			22,491.94	
	31		S7	30,147.92		52,639.86	

4 Account Balance

The sales journal is proved and ruled when the page is filled and always at the end of each month. Each amount column total is posted to the general ledger account named in the column heading.

remember

Proving a journal means verifying that the total debits equal the total credits. To prove a journal:

1. Add each amount column and write the total.
2. Add the column totals for all debit columns.
3. Add the column totals for all credit columns.
4. Verify that total debits and total credits are equal. Once a journal is proved, it should be ruled.

Posting a Column Total from the Sales Journal to the General Ledger

1. Write the date, **31**, in the account's Date column.
2. Write **S7** in the Post. Ref. column of the ledger account to indicate that the posting came from page 7 of the sales journal.
3. Write the column total, **$30,147.92**, in the Debit column of the ledger account.
4. Add the amount in the Debit column, $30,147.92, to the previous debit balance of $22,491.94. Write the new debit balance, **$52,639.86**, in the Balance Debit column.
5. Write the general ledger account number, **1205**, in parentheses immediately below the column total in the sales journal to show that the amount has been posted.

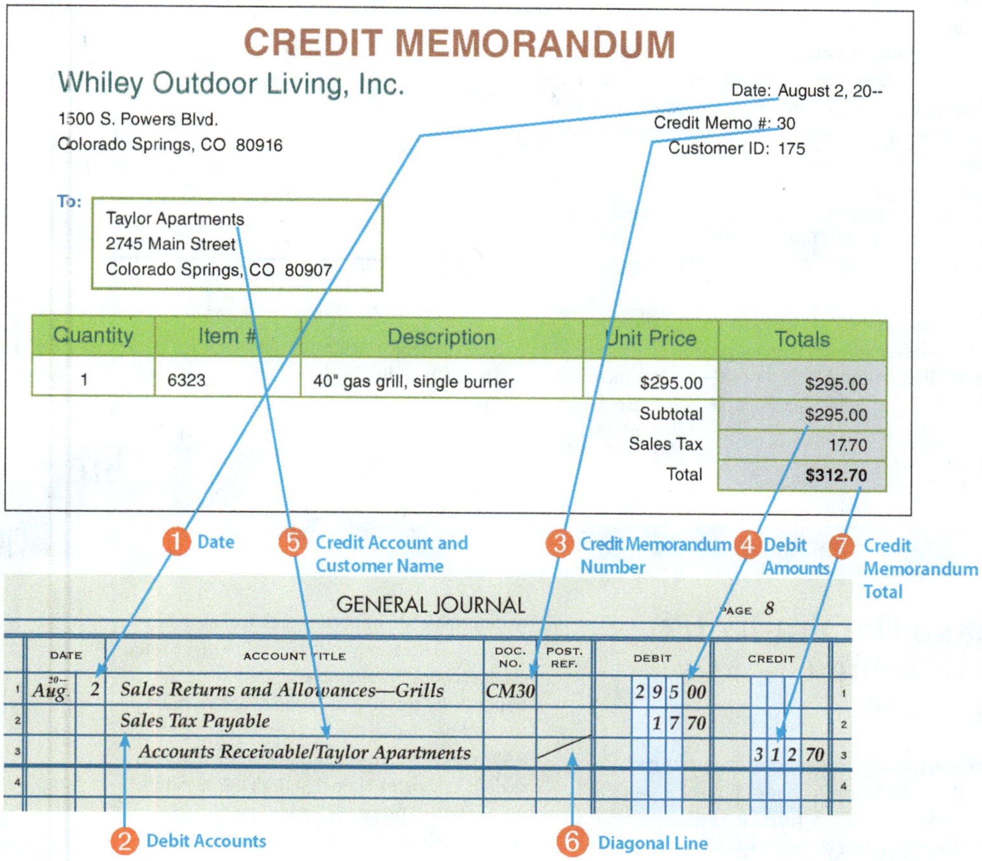

CREDIT MEMORANDUM

Whiley Outdoor Living, Inc.
1500 S. Powers Blvd.
Colorado Springs, CO 80916

Date: August 2, 20--
Credit Memo #: 30
Customer ID: 175

To: Taylor Apartments
2745 Main Street
Colorado Springs, CO 80907

Quantity	Item #	Description	Unit Price	Totals
1	6323	40" gas grill, single burner	$295.00	$295.00
			Subtotal	$295.00
			Sales Tax	17.70
			Total	**$312.70**

GENERAL JOURNAL — PAGE 8

	DATE		ACCOUNT TITLE	DOC. NO.	POST. REF.	DEBIT	CREDIT	
1	20-- Aug.	2	Sales Returns and Allowances—Grills	CM30		295 00		1
2			Sales Tax Payable			17 70		2
3			Accounts Receivable/Taylor Apartments		/		312 70	3
4								4

When merchandise is returned by a customer, the customer's account and Accounts Receivable are reduced by a credit. A form prepared by the vendor showing the amount deducted for returns and allowances is called a **credit memorandum**. [CONCEPT: Objective Evidence] Whiley records all sales returns and allowances in a general journal.

Recording a Sales Return and Allowance in a General Journal

1. Write the date, 20--, Aug. 2, in the Date column.
2. Write the debit accounts, Sales Returns and Allowances—Grills and Sales Tax Payable, in the Account Title column.
3. Record the credit memorandum number, CM30, in the Doc. No. column.
4. Write the debit amounts, $295.00 and $17.70, in the Debit column.
5. Indent and write Accounts Receivable and the customer name, Taylor Apartments, in the Account Title column.
6. Draw a diagonal line in the Post. Ref. column to indicate that the single debit amount is posted to two accounts.
7. Record the total of the credit memorandum, $312.70, in the Credit column.

INPUT

- Explain that a business may grant credit or give a cash refund for returned merchandise.
- Explain that a sales allowance does not involve the return of any merchandise.
- Explain that a vendor prepares a credit memorandum for a sales return or allowance because the return or allowance usually involves a credit to the customer's account receivable.
- Remind students that a credit memorandum is the source document for a sales returns and allowances transaction.
- Point out that sales returns and allowances on account are recorded in the general journal. If a business accepted a return on a cash sale, cash would be paid to the customer and the transaction would be recorded in the cash payments journal.
- Remind students that a sales return or allowance for a sale on account always includes the name of the customer as written in the accounts receivable subsidiary ledger.
- Point out that the sales tax amount is calculated on the amount of the return.
- Remind students that the normal balance for Sales Returns and Allowances is a debit because it is opposite its related account—Sales—which has a normal credit balance.

MODEL

Analyze the transaction

- Draw a stack of four blank T accounts on the board.
- Read the transaction statement.
- Ask students to analyze the transaction by answering these questions: Which accounts are affected? Are they increased or decreased? Are they debited or credited? Complete the T accounts as the information is provided.
- Review the effect on the account for Taylor Apartments in the accounts receivable ledger.

Record the transaction

- Use the general journal transparency to illustrate recording the transaction in the general journal.
- Record each item in the journal, following the seven steps shown.
- Point out that a credit memorandum is the source document for a return sale recorded in the general journal.

INPUT

- Explain that sales returns and allowances are posted frequently to the accounts receivable ledger so that customer accounts are up to date.
- Note that the Sales Tax Payable amount is a debit.
- Point out that a sales return on a sale to an exempt organization does not include a debit to Sales Tax Payable.
- Mention that when a sales return or allowance is granted after the customer has paid for the purchase, the customer account after posting may have a credit balance instead of a normal debit balance. Use T accounts to demonstrate this dilemma.
- Remind students that the Debit and Credit columns of the general journal are never ruled and totaled.

MODEL

Posting from a general journal

- Direct students to the illustration to explain the posting procedure from a general journal to the general ledger.
- As you read each step, ask students to point to the related arrows in the illustration.
- Remind students that the journal page number and the ledger account number are recorded in the Post. Ref. column of the ledger and the journal to furnish an audit trail.

FINANCIAL LITERACY

Answers

1. Answers will vary. Many Roth IRA Savings Calculators are available online. At publication, a Roth IRA Savings Calculator can be found at www.learnvest.com. Search for tools and calculators.
2. If time permits, students can keep a weekly spending diary, which is beneficial for comparing daily spending. Answers will vary based on spending habits.

An account that reduces a related account on a financial statement is known as a *contra account*. An account showing deductions from a sales account is a contra revenue account. Sales Returns and Allowances—Grills is a contra revenue account. Sales returns and allowances are kept in a separate account and not deducted directly from the sales account. This procedure helps the business see what proportion of the merchandise sold was returned by customers.

August 2. Granted credit to Taylor Apartments for the return of a gas grill, $295.00, plus sales tax, $17.70, from Sales Invoice No. 816; total, $312.70. Credit Memorandum No. 30.

When a sales return is accepted or an allowance is granted, the sales tax amount is no longer due. In the general ledger, Sales Returns and Allowances—Grills is increased by a $295.00 debit. Sales Tax Payable is decreased by a $17.70 debit. Accounts Receivable is decreased by a $312.70 credit. In the accounts receivable ledger, Taylor Apartments is decreased by a $312.70 credit.

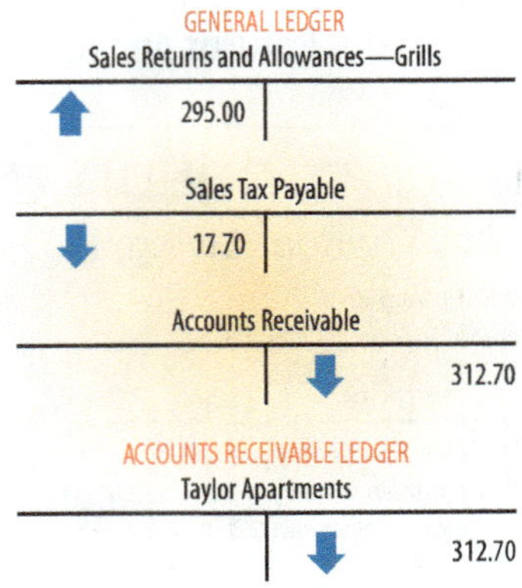

FINANCIAL LITERACY

What's the Tradeoff? Considering Choices and Costs

With every choice comes an opportunity cost. By choosing to use money or time one way, you give up an opportunity to use it a different way. For example, if you decide to go to a movie, you lose the money that you could have spent on a restaurant meal. Or, if you watch your favorite program on TV, you lose the time that you could have spent studying for a test.

People evaluate opportunity costs differently. However, by recording your choices every day, you can decide how to better use your time and resources. A planning tool or a budget can help you make choices about how to use your money and time. Your decisions should be based on long-term as well as immediate effects.

ACTIVITIES

1. Using the Internet, search for a Roth IRA Savings Calculator. Use the following information to determine the opportunity cost of each listed item versus investing this money in a given retirement account. For example, to determine the opportunity cost of a daily cup of coffee, multiply the cost per day by the number of purchases over a 40-year career. Then, plug this figure into your savings calculator. Note that Roth IRA accounts require you to prepay estimated taxes of 25%, which is to be deducted from the savings investment. Also, assume a 6% return over the 40 years.
   a. Daily cup of coffee, $1.50 per day
   b. Weekly lunch at local fast-food restaurant, $8.00
   c. Weekly manicure, $15
   d. Music downloads, $20 per month
   e. Haircut, $35 per month
2. Record your spending for one day (or one week, if time permits). Create a spreadsheet of your spending and explain your opportunity costs. Then, use the Roth IRA Savings Calculator to determine the opportunity cost of the daily expenditure if you invested in a Roth IRA at 6% over a 40-year career.
   Explain your findings to the class.

© iStockphoto.com/Norebbo

Posting from a General Journal

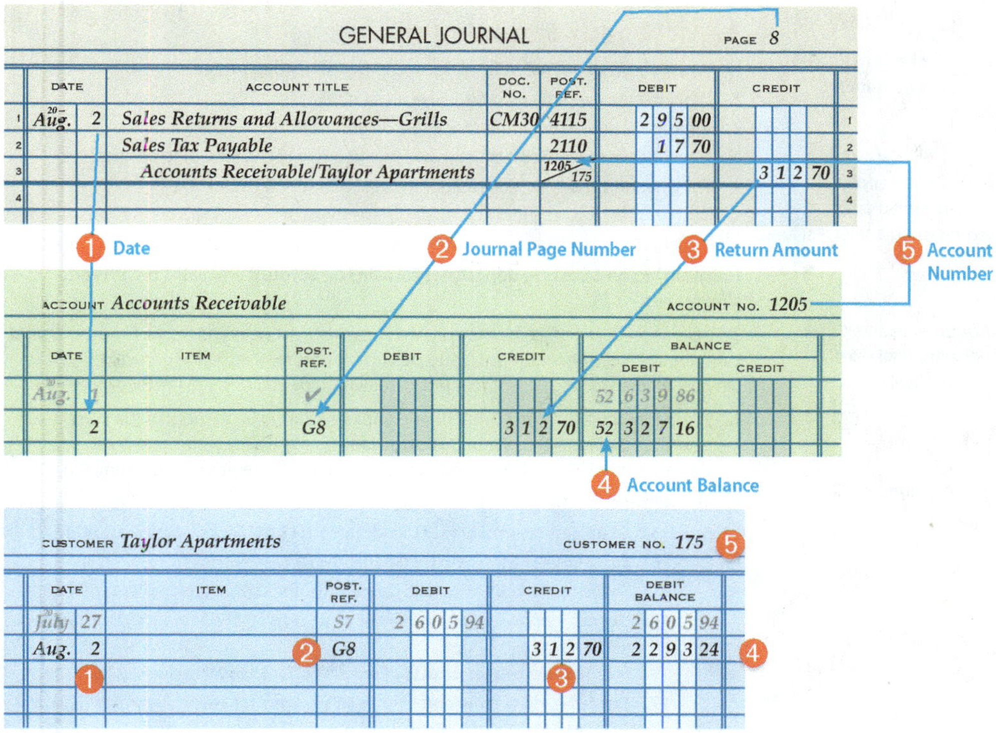

Sales returns and allowances are posted when the transaction is journalized. This procedure keeps an individual customer's account up to date.

When a sales return or allowance is granted after the customer has paid for the purchase, the customer account after posting may have a credit balance instead of a normal debit balance. The credit balance, a contra balance, reduces the amount to be received from a customer for future sales on account. When a three-column account form is used, a contra balance is shown by enclosing the amount in parentheses.

Posting Amounts from a General Journal

1. Write the date, **Aug. 2**, in the Date column.
2. Write **G8** in the Post. Ref. column of the account to indicate that the posting came from page 8 of the general journal.
3. Write the debit or credit amount in the appropriate column of the account.
4. Record the updated account balance.
5. Record the account numbers in the Post. Ref. column of the journal.

FORMATIVE ASSESSMENT

- This is an ongoing process. Circulate around the classroom or lab, observing which students have problems with the assignments.
- Troubleshooting: Students may have difficulty recording transactions involving a tax-exempt organization or make careless mistakes recording amounts in the wrong departmental account.
- Assess student understanding by checking solutions to Independent Practice assignments and noting their answers to the Term Review and Audit Your Understanding questions.

CHECK FOR UNDERSTANDING

Term Review

- Call on a student to define the term in the Term Review. A definition is given in the Glossary.

Audit Your Understanding

- Call on students to answer the Audit Your Understanding questions. Answers are given in Appendix D of the textbook.

GUIDED PRACTICE

Work Together

- Have students write the solution to the Work Together problem as you guide the class through the examples. Direct students to record each transaction in the journals as you elicit class participation in analyzing and recording each transaction.
- Call on students to describe each step in the process for posting separate amounts from the journals to the accounts receivable ledger.
- Ask a student to describe how to total and rule the sales journal.
- Ask another student to describe the steps for posting the journal totals from the sales journal to the general ledger.

INDEPENDENT PRACTICE

On Your Own

- Assign the On Your Own problem to be worked independently.
- Use the Formative Assessment techniques to diagnose student understanding.

Application Problem

- Assign Application Problem 2-1.

Online Working Papers

- Students can access the Lesson 2-1 problems using this software.

RETEACH

- Ask students to make up an original sale on account transaction statement and write it on the board. Ask another student to analyze the transaction using T accounts.
- Ask a student to name each column title in the sales journal and describe what is recorded in it, both generally and specifically for the transaction.
- Repeat for a sales returns and allowances transaction.
- Ask students to describe the effect of recording a sale or a return in the wrong departmental account.

End of Lesson Review

LO1 Explain the purpose of a departmental accounting system.

LO2 Journalize and post departmental sales on account using a sales journal.

LO3 Journalize and post departmental sales returns and allowances.

Term Review

credit memorandum

Audit your understanding

1. What is a benefit of recording sales and expenses by department?
2. What is a tax-exempt customer? Give an example.
3. What is the source document for a sale on account?
4. How does the *Realization of Revenue* concept apply to the recording of sales?
5. For what purpose is a credit memorandum issued?

Work together 2-1

Journalizing and posting departmental sales on account and sales returns and allowances

Back Office sells used office furniture in two departments: Chairs and Desks. Page 3 of a sales journal, page 6 of a general journal, and partial accounts receivable and general ledgers are provided in the *Working Papers*. Your instructor will guide you through the following examples.

1. Journalize the following transactions completed during September of the current year. Post the items that are to be posted individually. The sales tax rate is 8%. Source documents are abbreviated as follows: sales invoice, S; credit memorandum, CM.

   Transactions:

   Sept. 3. Sold a desk on account to LKL Products Co. for $1,415.00, plus sales tax. S422.
   6. Sold a chair on account to United Charities (tax exempt) for $310.00. S423.
   11. Sold three desks on account to Grasson, Inc., for $2,400.00, plus sales tax. S424.
   16. Granted credit to Grasson, Inc., for one of the desks sold on S424, $800.00, plus sales tax. CM45.
   23. Sold 10 chairs on account to LKL Products Co. for $3,650.00, plus sales tax. S425.
   27. Granted credit to Davenport Corp. as an allowance for a defective chair, $75.00, plus sales tax from sales invoice S421. CM46.

2. Prove and rule the sales journal. Post the totals to the general ledger.

On your own 2-1

Journalizing and posting departmental sales on account and sales returns and allowances

Danger Downhill has two departments: Equipment and Accessories. Page 10 of a sales journal, page 15 of a general journal, and partial accounts receivable and general ledgers are provided in the *Working Papers*. Work this problem independently.

1. Journalize the following transactions completed during October of the current year. Post the items that are to be posted individually. The sales tax rate is 8%. Source documents are abbreviated as follows: sales invoice, S; credit memorandum, CM.

   Transactions:

   Oct. 2. Sold ski equipment on account to Mason Dent for $763.00, plus sales tax. S144.
   7. Sold 5 hand warmers on account to Sara Stennis for $35.00, plus sales tax. S145.
   12. Granted credit to Sara Stennis as an allowance for two defective hand warmers, $14.00, plus sales tax from sales invoice S145. CM16.
   18. Sold 10 sets of skis and boots on account to Mountain Pass High School, $4,250.00. No sales tax. S146.
   19. Granted credit to Mason Dent for the return of ski poles, $52.00, plus sales tax from sales invoice S144. CM17.
   27. Sold training videos (accessories) on account to Davis Reese for $375.00, plus sales tax. S147.

2. Prove and rule the sales journal. Post the totals to the general ledger.

CLOSURE

- Ask students to summarize briefly the procedure for journalizing and posting sales on account and sales returns and allowances.

Essential Questions

- What are the implications if my business does not permit sales on account? (*There is a risk of less revenue from customers who cannot afford to pay at the time of the sale or who find it inconvenient.*)
- Can using a sales journal reduce my costs? (*Yes, differentiating transactions involving sales can save time and extra work.*)

EXTENDED LEARNING

- Assign Accounting in the Real World on page 37.
- Assign Ethics in Action on page 39.
- Assign Financial Literacy on page 44.

LESSON

2-2 Journalizing and Posting Cash Receipts

LO4 Explain the impact of sales discounts on the collection of accounts receivable.
LO5 Journalize and post departmental cash receipts using a cash receipts journal.

Cash Receipts on Account LO4

Whiley keeps a record of all cash receipts. The sources of most cash receipts are (1) cash received from customer payments on account and (2) cash and credit card sales.

Each customer is expected to pay the amount due within the agreed credit terms. To encourage early payment, a business may grant a deduction on the invoice amount. A deduction that a vendor allows on the invoice amount to encourage prompt payment is known as a *cash discount*. A cash discount on a sale taken by the customer is called a **sales discount**. Whiley sells on account using 2/10, n/30 terms. The *2/10* means that a 2% sales discount may be deducted if sales on account are paid within 10 days of the invoice date. All sales on account must be paid within 30 days of the invoice date, or *n/30*.

When a sale is made on account, the amount debited to Accounts Receivable reflects the total amount owed by the customer, including sales tax. Sales is credited only for the pretax selling price. An additional credit must be made to Sales Tax Payable for the sales tax liability on the total sales invoice amount. Whiley prepares a receipt as the source document for cash received on account. [CONCEPT: Objective Evidence]

The amount of cash received when payment is made within a discount period is calculated as follows:

Sales Amount	+	6.0% Sales Tax	=	Invoice Amount
$1,400.00	+	$84.00	=	$1,484.00
Invoice Amount	×	**Discount Rate**	=	**Sales Discount**
$1,484.00	×	2%	=	$29.68
Invoice Amount	−	**Sales Discount**	=	**Amount Due**
$1,484.00	−	$29.68	=	$1,454.32

WHY ACCOUNTING?

Distribution Impacts a Company's Goals

Transportation, Distribution & Logistics

A famous ice cream company in New England had the goal of using local suppliers and making all of the ice cream locally. The company also strived to minimize its impact on the environment. These two goals seemed attainable at the start. Local dairies provided the cream. Local residents were hired to make the ice cream, and it was delivered to local shops via fuel-efficient trucks. This strategy worked until the demand for ice cream spread to the west coast.

The company realized that the environmental impact of shipping ice cream across country in refrigerated containers was too high. A decision had to be made: Continue making the product locally and harm the environment during shipping, or expand the production facilities to the west coast. An environmental audit was performed, and the company decided to relax its "make ice cream locally" goal.

Not all companies use the effect on the environment to decide where to locate their production facilities. Oftentimes, the "bottom line" is the determining factor, meaning that the plants will be located where all costs of production are the lowest.

CRITICAL THINKING

1. Besides shipping costs, what other costs could be considered by a company when determining where to locate its production facility?
2. Name three non-accounting factors that must also be considered when deciding where to locate a production facility.

© iStockphoto.com/AlekslIo

WHY ACCOUNTING?

Answers

1. Answers will vary, but may include the following costs: availability of raw materials, shipping raw materials to the plant, labor, workers' compensation insurance, state unemployment tax, and environmental restrictions.
2. Answers will vary, but may include the availability of a trained labor force, the availability of various forms of transportation for bringing raw materials to the facility and shipping finished goods to customers, and the feelings of the residents of the community toward the company and product.

LESSON 2-2

BRIDGE

- Explain that students are already familiar with purchases discounts and cash payments. This lesson will explain cash receipts and how to account for offering sales discounts.

TEACHING RESOURCES

- **Instructor's Resource CD/Website:** PowerPoint Slides; Accounting Concepts
- **Working Papers:** Teacher's Edition of the Working Papers for Lesson 2-2; Online Working Papers
- **Transparency Masters:** Departmental Cash Receipts Journal; Accounts Receivable Ledger; General Ledger—Accounts Receivable Account

ENGAGE

- Point out that many businesses offer discounts to customers who pay their accounts early. Ask students under what circumstances a business might not take advantage of a sales discount. (*Cash is not available to make the early payment.*)

PREVIEW

- Call on students to read the accounting terms and definitions introduced in this lesson: *sales discount, point-of-sale (POS) terminal,* and *terminal summary*.
- Point out the learning objectives for this lesson.
- Direct students to read the headings on each page in this lesson and to examine the illustrations.

INPUT

- Explain that most cash receipts are from customer payments on account or for cash and credit card sales.
- Explain that to encourage early payment, a business may offer a deduction on the invoice amount, called a sales discount.

MODEL

Calculating sales discounts

- Direct students to the math illustration as you demonstrate how to calculate sales discounts and the amount of cash received.
- Demonstrate how to calculate the amount of discount on the total sales invoice amount.
- Demonstrate how to calculate the amount of cash received.
- Call on students to provide additional examples of amounts and percentages and to repeat the calculations.

TEACHING IDEA **Ask students to create three additional examples of amounts and percentages to repeat the calculations. Students should write their examples with the correct answers on the flip side of the paper. Allow students to exchange papers with a partner for additional practice in calculating the amount due with returns and discounts.**

INPUT

- Direct students to the illustration of the departmentalized cash receipts journal.
- Explain that a departmental cash receipts journal has departmental columns for Sales Credit and Sales Discount Debit.
- Ask students which transactions are recorded in this journal. (*cash receipts on account, cash and credit card sales, and any other cash receipts*)

MODEL

Analyzing cash receipts on account with sales discounts

- Draw four blank T accounts on the board.
- Read the transaction statement.
- Ask students to analyze the transaction by answering these questions: Which accounts are affected? Are they increased or decreased? Are they debited or credited? Complete the T accounts as the information is provided.

Journalizing cash receipts on account with sales discounts

- Use a transparency of a departmental cash receipts journal to demonstrate journalizing a cash receipt on account with a sales discount.

Journalizing a Cash Receipt with a Sales Discount LO5

CASH RECEIPTS JOURNAL PAGE *8*

					1	2	3	4	5	6	7	8	9	
	DATE		ACCOUNT TITLE	DOC. NO. / POST. REF.	GENERAL DEBIT	GENERAL CREDIT	ACCOUNTS RECEIVABLE CREDIT	SALES TAX PAYABLE CREDIT	SALES CREDIT GRILLS	SALES CREDIT FURNITURE	SALES DISCOUNT DEBIT GRILLS	SALES DISCOUNT DEBIT FURNITURE	CASH DEBIT	
1	20-- Aug.	1	Wilson Properties	R842			1 4 8 4 00					2 9 68	1 4 5 4 32	1
2														2
3														3

1 Date 2 Customer Name 3 Receipt Number 4 Invoice Amount 5 Sales Discount 6 Cash Received

August 1. Received cash on account from Wilson Properties, $1,454.32, covering Sales Invoice No. 812 for outdoor furniture for $1,484.00 ($1,400.00 plus sales tax, $84.00), less 2% discount, $29.68. Receipt No. 842.

Whiley records all cash receipts in a cash receipts journal. The journal has five credit columns—General Credit, Accounts Receivable Credit, Sales Tax Payable Credit, Sales Credit Grills, and Sales Credit Furniture. The journal also has four debit columns—General Debit, Sales Discount Debit Grills, Sales Discount Debit Furniture, and Cash Debit.

Whiley sold merchandise to Wilson Properties using 2/10, n/30 payment terms. The 2/10 means that a 2% discount may be deducted if a sale on account is paid within 10 days of the invoice date. The sale on account must be paid within 30 days of the invoice date, or n/30.

Cash is increased by a $1,454.32 debit. The contra revenue account, Sales Discount—Furniture, is increased by a $29.68 debit. Using a separate account to record discounts allows the business to determine the proportion of available discounts that customers actually take. Accounts Receivable is decreased by a $1,484.00 credit. In the accounts receivable ledger, Wilson Properties is decreased by a $1,484.00 credit.

GENERAL LEDGER

Cash	
↑ 1,454.32	

Sales Discount—Furniture	
↑ 29.68	

Accounts Receivable	
	↓ 1,484.00

ACCOUNTS RECEIVABLE LEDGER

Wilson Properties	
	↓ 1,484.00

Recording the Receipt of Cash When the Sales Discount is Taken

1. Write the date, **20--, Aug. 1**, in the Date column.
2. Write the customer name, **Wilson Properties**, in the Account Title column.
3. Record the document number, **R842**, in the Doc. No. column.
4. Write the invoice amount, **$1,484.00**, in the Accounts Receivable Credit column.
5. Write the sales discount, **$29.68**, in the Sales Discount Debit Furniture column.
6. Write the amount of cash received, **$1,454.32**, in the Cash Debit column.

© iStockphoto.com/4x6

- Record each item in the cash receipts journal, following the six steps shown in the illustration.
- Emphasize that the customer name is written in the Account Title column whenever there is an amount recorded in the Accounts Receivable Credit column to show to which accounts receivable ledger account the amount will be posted.

Journalizing Cash and Credit Card Sales

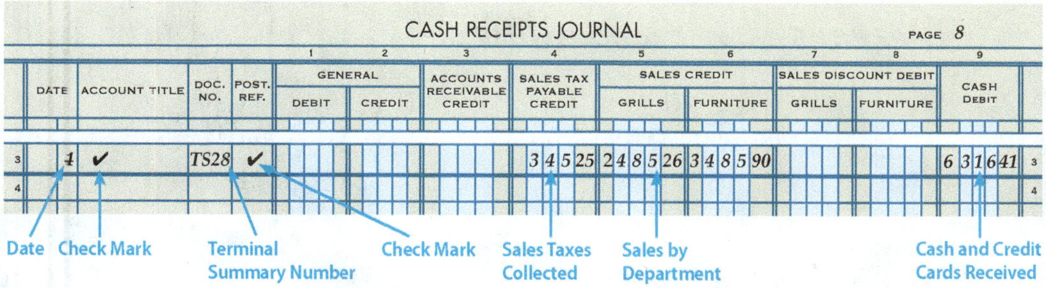

Whiley accepts cash or credit cards from its customers. An independent company or bank hired by Whiley to process credit card sales automatically deposits the daily total of credit card sales in Whiley's bank account. Because credit card sales are usually deposited in Whiley's account within two or three days, credit card sales and cash sales are recorded together in the cash receipts journal.

Both cash and credit card sales are entered into a modern version of a cash register. A specialized computer used to collect, store, and report all the information about a sales transaction is called a **point-of-sale (POS) terminal**. The POS terminal prints a receipt for the customer and internally accumulates data about total departmental sales. At least once a week, Whiley instructs the POS terminal to print a report of all cash and credit card sales. The report that summarizes the cash and credit card sales of a point-of-sale terminal is called a **terminal summary**. The terminal summary is identified with a *TS* and a sequential number. Whiley uses the terminal summary as the source document for cash and credit card sales. [CONCEPT: Objective Evidence] For a departmental business, the POS terminal would be programmed to report departmental sales on the terminal summary.

August 4. Recorded cash and credit card sales: grills, $2,485.26; outdoor furniture, $3,485.90; plus sales tax, $345.25; total, $6,316.41. Terminal Summary No. 28.

Cash increases by a $6,316.41 debit. Sales Tax Payable increases by a $345.25 credit. Sales—Grills increases by a $2,485.26 credit, and Sales—Furniture increases by a $3,485.90 credit.

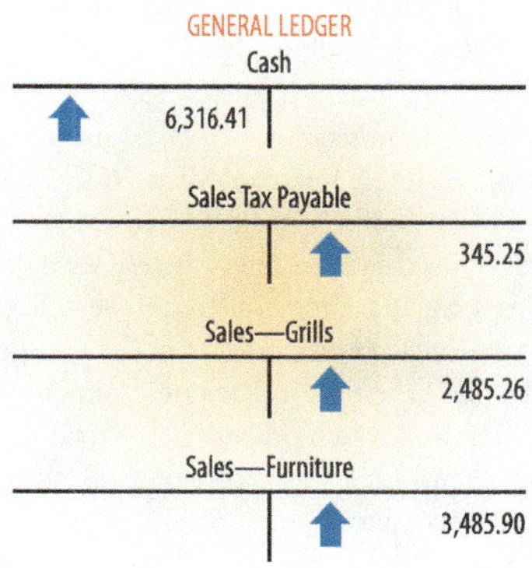

The details of Terminal Summary No. 28 are recorded on line 3 of the cash receipts journal. The steps needed to record this transaction are similar to those required to record other cash receipts transactions. Place a check mark in the Account Title column to show that no account title needs to be written. Place a check mark in the Post. Ref. column to show that amounts on this line are not to be posted individually.

fyi Cash and credit card sales may include sales to tax-exempt organizations. Thus, the sales tax payable amount may not equal total sales multiplied by the sales tax rate.

INPUT

- Explain that credit card sales are recorded with cash sales because credit card sales are automatically deposited to the vendor's bank account.
- Explain that cash and credit card sales are entered into a point-of-sale (POS) terminal that prints a weekly summary, a *terminal summary*, of sales for the week, which is used as the source document for cash and credit card sales transactions.

MODEL

Analyze the transaction

- Draw four blank T accounts on the board.
- Read the transaction statement.
- Ask students to analyze the transaction by answering these questions: Which accounts are affected? Are they increased or decreased? Are they debited or credited? Complete the T accounts as the information is provided.
- Point out the separate credits to the two departmental sales accounts.

Record the transaction

- Use the transparency of a departmental cash receipts journal to illustrate recording the transaction.
- Record each item in the journal, following the seven arrows shown.
- Point out that the check marks are recorded in the Account Title column and the Post. Ref. column to indicate that no amounts on this line need to be posted individually.
- Point out that the abbreviation for *terminal summary*, *TS*, and the day of the month are recorded in the Doc. No. column.
- Point out that the sales tax amount is recorded in the Sales Tax Payable Credit column.

DIFFERENTIATED INSTRUCTION

Gifted learners need additional challenges to maintain a high level of motivation. Ask these learners to contact a local bank and determine the fees associated with accepting credit cards. Students should report the cost per transaction and any monthly equipment/software fees.

Careers In Accounting

Review a career as an owner of a CPA firm.

Careers In Accounting

Ahmed Rucker

OWNER OF CPA FIRM

© Monkey Business Images/Shutterstock.com

Immediately out of college, Ahmed Rucker started working in a large accounting firm. He enjoyed his work, and after a few years, he started thinking that he would like to have his own accounting practice someday. Ahmed started by doing part-time work in the evenings and on weekends for a few small businesses. After about four years, he decided to quit his job with the large accounting firm and go on his own full time.

With the help of a mentor from the Small Business Administration (SBA), Ahmed developed a business plan. He hired an office administrator and rented a small office. At first, he needed to spend much of his daytime hours meeting with prospective new clients. Ahmed offered these new clients a full range of accounting services. For some clients, he did all of their recordkeeping, from recording transactions through preparing financial statements. Many clients hired Ahmed to prepare tax returns and give tax advice.

Some small businesses recorded their own transactions, hiring Ahmed to complete year-end work, such as adjusting entries and preparing financial statements. He found that he sometimes needed to advise and educate these clients on how to follow standard procedures for recording transactions. In the early years of his business, he also did payroll services. However, as he took on more and more accounting clients, he realized he couldn't do it all and gave up his payroll clients. When asked about those early years, Ahmed doesn't like to think about how much he made per hour. He will admit that he worked many hours and had some periods of negative cash flow.

As his business grew, Ahmed needed to spend less time meeting with potential new clients. Most of his new business was acquired by referrals from his current clients. He also found that if he took the time to educate his clients up front, he could spend less time correcting errors and more time focusing on advisory services.

Today, Ahmed has two additional CPAs working for him. These assistants do much of the daily work of the firm. Ahmed focuses on scheduling projects for himself and his staff, meeting with major clients, and overseeing and finalizing the work of his assistants. However, he still has contact with all clients. He feels that this personal contact is very important to each client and a major reason why each client chose to work with a smaller accounting firm.

Looking back over the years, Ahmed feels all the hard work was very worthwhile. He enjoys his relationship with his clients. He feels good when he can give them advice and help them with accounting issues.

Salary Range: The salary range for the owner of a small accounting firm varies greatly, depending on several factors, such as geographic location, specialization of services, and number of employees.

Qualifications: The qualifications for the owner of a small accounting firm vary, based on the services offered. For broad-based services, the designation of CPA is required. Additional education in tax preparation is also required for tax preparers.

Occupational Outlook: The growth for accounting positions is projected to be much higher than average (20% or higher) for the period from 2008 to 2018.

Source: www.onetonline.org.

© iStockphoto.com/Mlenny

Journalizing and Posting a Cash Receipt with a Sales Discount

CASH RECEIPTS JOURNAL PAGE *8*

	DATE	ACCOUNT TITLE	DOC. NO.	POST. REF.	GENERAL DEBIT	GENERAL CREDIT	ACCOUNTS RECEIVABLE CREDIT	SALES TAX PAYABLE CREDIT	SALES CREDIT GRILLS	SALES CREDIT FURNITURE	SALES DISCOUNT DEBIT GRILLS	SALES DISCOUNT DEBIT FURNITURE	CASH DEBIT	
					1	2	3	4	5	6	7	8	9	
4	5	*Taylor Apartments*	*R844*	*175*			2 2 9 3 24				4 5 86		2 2 4 7 38	4
5														5

Date
Journal Page Number
Credit
Customer Account Number

CUSTOMER *Taylor Apartments* CUSTOMER NO. *175*

DATE		ITEM	POST. REF.	DEBIT	CREDIT	DEBIT BALANCE
July	*27*	*Balance*	*S7*	2 6 0 5 94		2 6 0 5 94
Aug.	*2*		*G8*		3 1 2 70	2 2 9 3 24
	4		*S8*	1 6 2 7 62		3 9 2 0 86
	5		*CR8*		2 2 9 3 24	1 6 2 7 62

Account Balance

Sales discounts are calculated on the amount owed at the time the invoice is paid. When a customer takes a discount after being granted a return or an allowance, the amount of the return or allowance must be deducted from the amount of the original sale before the discount can be calculated. To calculate the amount of cash received, (1) find the sales discount amount and (2) determine the amount of cash to be received.

This transaction is journalized the same way as a receipt of cash when there is no sales return or allowance. The only difference is the way in which the amounts are calculated. The steps for posting a cash receipt to an accounts receivable account are similar to the posting of sales on account. The letters CR and the journal page number are entered in the Post. Ref. column. Individual amounts in the Accounts Receivable Credit column are posted when the transaction is recorded in the cash receipts journal. This procedure keeps the customers' accounts up to date.

The accounts receivable account for Taylor Apartments shows the history of the original sales invoice, the credit memorandum, and the cash receipt. The calculation for each of these items is shown on the next page.

August 5. Received cash on account from Taylor Apartments, $2,247.38, covering Sales Invoice No. 816 for $2,605.94 ($2,458.43 plus sales tax of 6.00%, $147.51), less Credit Memorandum No. 30 for $312.70 ($295.00 plus sales tax, $17.70), less 2% discount, $45.86. Receipt No. 844.

GENERAL LEDGER

Cash

Debit	Credit
2,247.38	

Sales Discount—Grills

Debit	Credit
45.86	

Accounts Receivable

	Debit		Credit
S816	2,605.94	CM30	312.70
			2,293.24

ACCOUNTS RECEIVABLE LEDGER

Taylor Apartments

	Debit		Credit
S816	2,605.94	CM30	312.70
S864	1,627.62		2,293.24
(New Bal.	*1,627.62)*		

INPUT

- Use the math illustration on page 52 to explain how to calculate the amount owed with a discount after a return has been made.
- Explain that the cash received on account with a sales discount is journalized the same way whether or not there is a sales return or allowance.
- Explain that sales discounts are calculated on the amount owed at the time the invoice is paid. Therefore, a sales return or allowance reduces the amount owed.
- Point out that the steps for posting a cash receipt to an accounts receivable account are similar to the posting of sales on account.
- Explain that individual amounts often are posted to keep customer accounts up to date.
- Using the illustration, point out the arrows for steps in posting.

MODEL

Calculating sales discount

- Direct students to the math illustration on page 52 as you demonstrate calculating a sales discount when there is a sales return.
- Demonstrate on the board the process for adjusting the original invoice amounts for the amount of the sales return.
- Demonstrate the steps for calculating sales discounts and the cash received based on the invoice amounts adjusted for a sales return.

Posting from the cash receipts journal to the accounts receivable ledger

- Use a transparency of an account in the accounts receivable ledger to demonstrate posting the transaction dated August 5 to Taylor Apartments.
- Emphasize recording the posting references in the ledger account and the cash receipts journal.
- Remind students that posting individual accounts receivable is done as soon as the transaction is journalized to keep the accounts current.

INPUT

- Explain that the departmental cash receipts journal is proved and ruled in a manner similar to that used with other journals at the end of each month.
- Explain that special amount columns are totaled and the totals are posted to the general ledger at the end of the month.

MODEL

Proving and ruling the cash receipts journal

- Use a transparency of a departmental cash receipts journal.
- Explain that all amount columns are totaled at the end of the month.
- Explain how the equality of debits and credits is proved for the cash receipts journal.
- Explain the ruling of the cash receipts journal.

Posting to the general ledger

- Use a transparency of an account in the general ledger to demonstrate posting the total of the Accounts Receivable Credit column.
- Emphasize recording the posting references in the ledger account and the cash receipts journal.

	Sales Amount	+	Sales Tax	=	Invoice Amount
Original Sales Invoice Amount (S816)	$2,458.43	+	$147.51	=	$2,605.94
less Sales Return (CM30)	295.00	+	17.70	=	312.70
equals Sales Invoice Amount after Return	$2,163.43	+	$129.81	=	$2,293.24

Sales Invoice Amount after Return	×	Sales Discount Rate	=	Sales Discount
$2,293.24	×	2%	=	$45.86

Sales Invoice Amount after Return	−	Sales Discount	=	Net Sale (Cash Collected)
$2,293.24	−	$45.86	=	$2,247.38

Posting from a Cash Receipts Journal

CASH RECEIPTS JOURNAL — PAGE 8

	Date	Account Title	Doc. No.	Post. Ref.	1 General Debit	2 General Credit	3 Accounts Receivable Credit	4 Sales Tax Payable Credit	5 Sales Credit Grills	6 Sales Credit Furniture	7 Sales Discount Debit Grills	8 Sales Discount Debit Furniture	9 Cash Debit	
24	29	✓	T32	✓				331 95	2,618 14	3,319 84			6,269 93	24
25	30	Denison Landscapes	R860	125			1,359 00					27 18	1,331 82	25
26	31	Totals			—	—	28,948 16	859 18	7,415 95	9,148 25		348 19	46,023 35	26
27					(✓)	(✓)	(1205)	(2110)	(4105)	(4205)	(4110)	(4210)	(1105)	27
28														28

ACCOUNT *Accounts Receivable* — ACCOUNT NO. *1205*

Date		Item	Post. Ref.	Debit	Credit	Balance Debit	Balance Credit
20-- Aug.	1	Balance	✓			52,639 86	
	2		G8		312 70	52,327 16	
	31		S8	27,164 69		79,491 85	
	31		CR8		28,948 16	50,543 69	

Date · Journal Page Number · Column Total · Account Number · Account Balance

When the journal page is full or at the end of the month, the cash receipts journal is proved and ruled. Proving cash before the journal's column totals are posted helps to identify any errors in recording transactions. The cash columns of the cash receipts and cash payments journals are used to calculate an updated cash balance. This balance should match the outstanding cash balance on the next unused check stub.

Totals of the special amount columns in the cash receipts journal are posted to their respective accounts in the general ledger. The general ledger account number is written in parentheses immediately below the total. A check mark is placed in parentheses below the totals of the General Debit and Credit columns to show that the totals are not posted.

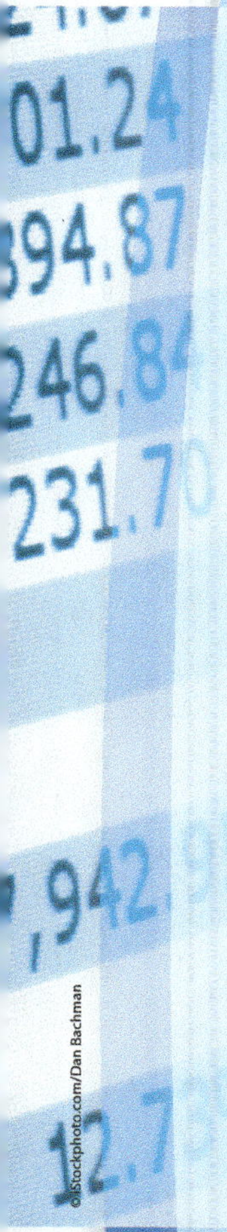

©iStockphoto.com/Dan Bachman

Evaluating Departmental Sales

Hua Wang was about to enter her first meeting with the board of directors of Breland Fashions. She had been hired just three days ago as Breland's first chief financial officer. Thus, she had to review quickly the following departmental sales report, which Bonita Alvarez, an accounting intern, had prepared for her:

Department	Budget	Actual		Budget Variance
Children's Apparel	$ 65,000	$ 63,084	↑	$ (1,916)
Gifts	32,000	30,180	↑	(1,820)
Housewares	48,000	51,982	↑	3,982
Jewelry	69,000	54,382	↓	(14,618)
Men's Apparel	124,000	118,917	→	(5,083)
Men's Shoes	28,000	29,079	↑	1,079
Women's Apparel	223,000	214,932	→	(8,068)
Women's Shoes	87,000	79,847	→	(7,153)

Hua recognized that the arrows in the Budget Variance column had been created by Excel's conditional formatting tool. "A good use of technology," she said. "But its application may confuse the board. What does this green arrow mean to you?" she said, pointing to the negative Budget Variance amount for the gifts department. She paused to allow Bonita to consider the question. "I think most people think green is good," she continued, "so I wonder if they'll understand green arrows next to negative amounts."

OPEN THE SPREADSHEET TLA_CH02

Follow the steps on the Instructions tab. Modify the report to provide better information on actual departmental sales relative to the budget. Use the spreadsheet to answer the following questions:

1. Determine the range of values that would result in a red, yellow, and green arrow in the Over (Under) Budget column.
2. Which department(s) sold 105% or more of its budget?
3. Which department(s) sold 95% or less of its budget?
4. Compare the arrows in the original and revised reports. State how the original application of conditional formatting of the amount of the budget variance was misleading.

THINK LIKE AN ACCOUNTANT

This activity requires students to modify and apply conditional formatting rules. Conditional formatting is a powerful tool; however, users must be careful when applying the tool to accounting information. The use of a three-arrow set to compare budget variance amounts for the departments yields confusing and misleading information. Students add a Budget Variance Percent column and correctly apply conditional formatting.

Answers

1. The range of values is $18,600 [$3,982 – ($14,618)]. The following calculations are required to determine the range for each arrow.

   ($14,618) + $18,600 × 67% = ($2,156)

   ($14,618) + $18,600 × 33% = ($8,480)

   Thus, the range of values to display for each arrow is as follows:

   Green arrow: >= ($2,156)

   Yellow arrow: >= ($8,480) and < ($2,156)

   Red arrow: < ($8,480)
2. Housewares, as shown by the green arrow.
3. Gifts, Jewelry, and Women's Shoes, as shown by the red arrows.
4. Answers may vary. A sample solution follows:

   The amount of change for the Gifts Department appeared with a green arrow, indicating a good result relative to other departments. However, as a percent of its budget, the Gifts Department was one of the worst performing departments. The red arrow of the Budget Variance Percent column more clearly indicates the performance of this department.

FORMATIVE ASSESSMENT

- This is an ongoing process. Circulate around the classroom or lab, observing which students have problems with the assignments.
- Troubleshooting: Diagnose the problems students have with this lesson. Students may have trouble (1) calculating the sales discount and related reduction in sales tax payable or (2) journalizing complex transactions having several parts, such as those involving returns.
- Assess student understanding by checking solutions to Independent Practice assignments and noting their answers to the Terms Review and Audit for Understanding questions.

CHECK FOR UNDERSTANDING

Terms Review

- Call on students to define each term in the Terms Review. Definitions are given in the Glossary.

Audit Your Understanding

- Call on students to answer the Audit Your Understanding questions. Answers are given in Appendix D of the textbook.

GUIDED PRACTICE

Work Together

- Have students write the solution to the Work Together problem as you guide the class through the examples.
- Direct students to record each transaction in the cash receipts journal as you elicit class participation in analyzing and recording each transaction.
- Call on students to describe each step in the process of posting separate amounts from the cash receipts journal to the accounts receivable ledger.
- Call on students to describe each step in the process of proving and ruling a departmental cash receipts journal.
- Ask a student to describe the steps for posting special column totals to the general ledger.

INDEPENDENT PRACTICE

On Your Own

- Assign the On Your Own problem to be worked independently.
- Use the Formative Assessment techniques to diagnose student understanding.

Application Problem

- Assign Application Problem 2-2.

Online Working Papers

- Students can access the Lesson 2-2 problems using this software.

RETEACH

- Give students several invoice amounts and discount rates to practice calculating sales discounts.
- Ask a student to make up an original cash receipt with a sales discount transaction statement that you write on the board.
- Ask another student to use T accounts to analyze the transaction.
- Using the departmental cash receipts journal, ask a student to record the transaction.

End of Lesson Review

LO4 Explain the impact of sales discounts on the collection of accounts receivable.

LO5 Journalize and post departmental cash receipts using a cash receipts journal.

Terms Review

sales discount

point-of-sale (POS) terminal

terminal summary

Audit your understanding

1. Why does a business offer cash discounts?
2. What does 2/10, n/30 mean?
3. What impact does a sales discount have on sales?
4. Why are credit card sales and cash sales recorded together in the sales journal?
5. How and when are entries in the Accounts Receivable Credit column posted?

Work together 2-2

Journalizing and posting departmental cash receipts

Columbus Hardware has two departments: Hardware and Lumber. The company offers credit terms of 2/10, n/30. Page 5 of a cash receipts journal and partial accounts receivable and general ledgers are provided in the *Working Papers*.

1. Journalize the following transactions completed during March of the current year. Post the items that are to be posted individually. The sales tax rate is 7.5%. Assume sales tax was paid on all cash and credit card sales. Source documents are abbreviated as follows: credit memorandum, CM; receipt, R; sales invoice, S; terminal summary, TS.

Transactions:

Mar. 3. Received cash on account from Andrews Homes for lumber purchased on S426 for $12,458.95, less discount. R445.
4. Recorded cash and credit card sales for the week: hardware, $3,194.18; lumber, $8,418.69; plus sales tax. TS12.
7. Received a check from Estate Housing for lumber on S428 for $9,248.17, less CM44 for $833.02, less discount. R446.
18. Received a check from Lisle Construction for hardware on S435 for $2,473.61, less CM45 for $325.51, less discount. R447.
22. Recorded cash and credit card sales for the week: hardware, $4,184.94; lumber, $6,148.71; plus sales tax. TS13.

2. Prove and rule the cash receipts journal. Post the totals to the general ledger.

On your own 2-2

Journalizing and posting departmental cash receipts

Forde Growers has two departments: Flowers and Plants. The company offers credit terms of 1/10, n/30. Page 5 of a cash receipts journal and partial accounts receivable and general ledgers are provided in the *Working Papers*. Work this problem independently.

1. Journalize the following transactions completed during April of the current year. The sales tax rate is 6.5%; assume sales tax was paid on all cash and credit card sales. Source documents are abbreviated as follows: credit memorandum, CM; receipt, R; sales invoice, S; terminal summary, TS.

Transactions:

Apr. 2. Received cash on account from Hillside Manor for flowers purchased on S297 for $615.17, less discount. R321.
5. Recorded cash and credit card sales for the week: flowers, $624.89; plants, $1,048.69; plus sales tax. TS16.
6. Received a check from Bakersville Gardens for plants purchased on S299 for $1,065.71, less discount. R322.
15. Recorded cash and credit card sales for the week: flowers, $1,097.43; plants, $1,190.45; plus sales tax. TS17.
21. Received a check from Grendon Clinic for plants purchased on March 22 on S278 for $229.61, less CM21 for $35.20, no discount. R323.
26. Received a check from Platte Hotels for flowers purchased on S428 for $841.95, less CM22 for $294.33, less discount. R324.

2. Prove and rule the cash receipts journal. Post the totals to the general ledger.

CLOSURE

- Ask students to summarize briefly the procedure for journalizing and posting cash receipts from cash sales and sales on account with a sales discount.

Essential Questions

- What return policies would I put in place for a business to guarantee honest returns? (*Deadline for return, condition of return, reason for return, and process for making the return.*)
- Is it necessary to give all customers a sales discount for early payment? Why or why not? (*A common answer might be to offer sales discounts to those customers who have a history of late payments as a management strategy to encourage timely payments.*)

EXTENDED LEARNING

- Assign Why Accounting on page 47.
- Review Careers in Accounting on page 50.
- Assign Think Like an Accountant on page 53.

A Look at Accounting Software

Receiving a Payment on Account

Managing accounts receivable is an important accounting function. In large companies, accounts receivable (AR) is usually a department, with its own employees, within the larger accounting department. The accounts receivable staff would include a credit manager who decides which customers can be extended credit and how much credit they are allowed. When customers fall behind in their payments, it is the AR staff that sends reminders and makes phone calls in an effort to collect. Dealing with customer accounts is an important part of maintaining good customer relations. Errors in handling customer billings and receipts can damage customer relations.

There are several errors that AR could make in receiving a customer payment. (1) The payment could be applied to the wrong customer account. (2) The amount of the payment could be entered incorrectly. (3) The payment might not be applied against the invoices and credit memos intended by the customer. (4) An earned discount might not be given or might be calculated incorrectly. (5) The debit could be posted to the wrong general ledger account. While computerized accounting systems improve accuracy and efficiency over manual systems, only errors 4 and 5 might be avoided with an automated system. Ultimately, it is the accounting staff that must take responsibility for correctly processing customer payments, whether their system is manual or automated.

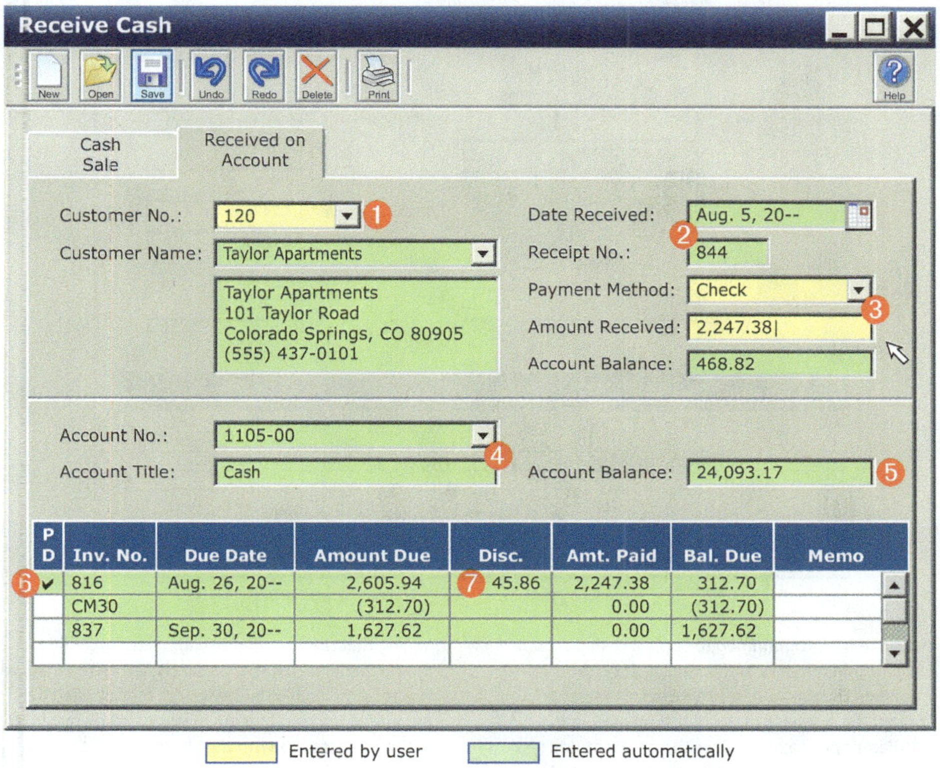

A Look at Accounting Software

This feature illustrates how a computerized accounting system would handle the transactions on page 51. It introduces a concept not taught in the chapter—how a cash discount is recalculated when an invoice is underpaid within the discount period. In a computerized accounting system, that calculation is done automatically. In a manual system, the accountant would need to know how to make the adjustment. Walking students through the calculations with some additional examples would be helpful.

Students might wonder what would happen if the check amount did not match a specific invoice and was higher than the amount of the oldest invoice. The first thing the accountant should do is verify that the correct customer account has been accessed. Sometimes customer names can be similar and the wrong account could have been brought up in the window. In that event, it makes sense that the payment would not match any of the invoices.

This feature presents how the system would apply a payment that did not match any specific invoice and was higher than the amount of the oldest invoice. The system would pay the oldest invoice in full; then it would apply the balance of the payment to the next oldest invoice. The process would continue until the payment was fully applied. Of course, the system might apply the payment in a manner not intended by the customer; so the accountant would examine the customer's check stub to see how the customer applied the payment. Then the payments that were applied automatically could be changed to match the customer's intent.

1. On the **Received on Account** tab, the user selects (by number or name) the customer whose check is being received. The system enters the address, contact information, and a list of open items—invoices and credit memorandums.
2. The current date is entered by the system, but it can be changed if the receipt occurred at an earlier date. The system automatically assigns the next sequential receipt number.
3. The user selects the type of payment—cash, check, credit card, or EFT (electronic fund transfer)—and keys the amount of the receipt. The system deducts the payment from the customer account balance and displays the new balance. Double-clicking the account balance would display a pop-up window with the customer's account. Clicking **New** on the menu bar would clear the window and allow the user to start over or enter another receipt.
4. The system enters the default Cash account. If another account is to be debited, the user can change this account number. The system displays the account title.
5. The system displays the new balance of account number 1105-00.
6. The system is programmed to apply the payment to the customer's account in a logical sequence. First, it would look for an invoice matching the amount of the payment. In this case, no invoice matches the amount of the payment, so the system would apply the payment to the oldest invoice.

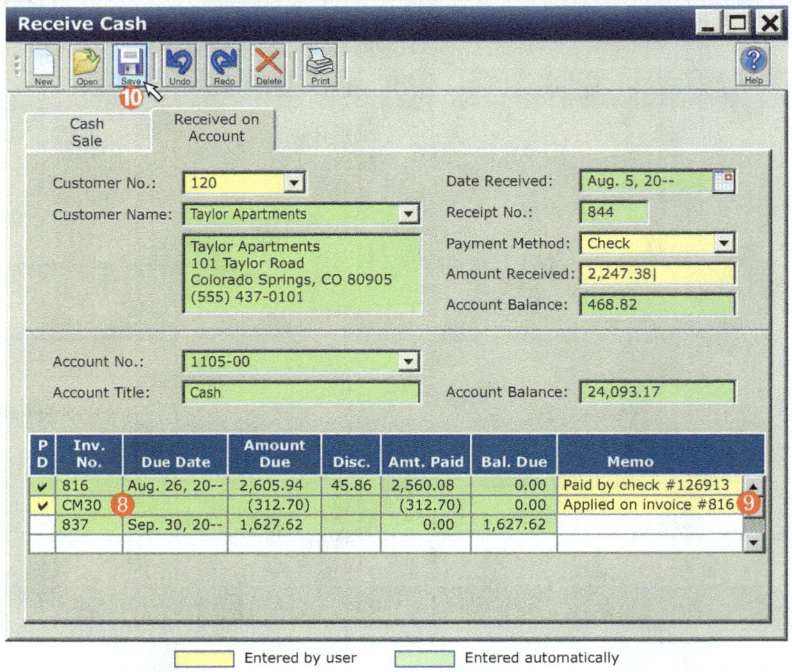

7. The system is programmed to apply a cash discount of 2% within ten days of the invoice date (see page 51). When the payment was entered, the system applied the payment to the oldest invoice and calculated the discount. Since the payment was less than the invoice amount, the system calculated the discount based on the amount paid ($2,247.38 ÷ 0.98 = $2,293.24; $2,293.24 × 0.02 = $45.86). The balance due would then be $312.70 ($2,605.94 – $45.86 – $2,247.38).
8. Seeing that the customer had applied the credit memo to the payment, the user clicked on the **PD** box for credit memo CM30. The system then applied the amount of the credit memo to invoice #816, resulting in the balances shown in the illustration.
9. The user has entered notes about how the payment was applied. The notes will be helpful if a question is ever raised about the payment.
10. The user clicks on **Save** to record the transaction and clear the window for the next receipt.

Chapter Summary

Managers use departmental data to make decisions relating to business operations. Sales on account are recorded in the sales journal. Cash collected from sales on account are recorded in the cash receipts journal. Departmental sales are recorded in the Sales Credit columns of each journal.

Individual amounts in the Accounts Receivable Debit column of each journal are posted when the transaction is recorded. This procedure keeps customer accounts up to date.

Each special journal contains a Sales Tax Payable Credit column. Most states require vendors to collect sales tax on sales of merchandise and services. Government agencies and not-for-profit organizations are typically exempt from paying sales taxes.

A business receives cash from collections of its sales on account and cash sales. To encourage early payment of sales on account, a business may grant a sales discount on the invoice amount. Many businesses offer terms of 2/10, n/30. A 2% discount off the amount owed is allowed when the invoice is paid within ten days. Sales discounts are recorded in a contra revenue account. A Sales Discount Debit account for each department is in the cash receipts journal.

Cash sales include sales to customers who paid with a credit or debit card. Department sales are recorded in Sales Credit columns from information contained in a terminal summary.

A credit memorandum is prepared to document the return of merchandise from a customer. The credit memorandum is the source document for an entry in a general journal. Sales returns and allowances are recorded in a contra revenue account. Sales returns and allowances are posted to the accounts receivable and general ledgers when the transactions are journalized.

The totals of the special columns of each special journal are posted to the general ledger.

Transfer Pricing

EXPLORE ACCOUNTING

Departmental accounting allows managers to evaluate the performance of individual departments. Some companies use departmental income from operations as a basis for rewarding effective managers. A management incentive plan could base a manager's salary on the amount of departmental income from operations, the percentage of income to net sales, or some other measure of profitability.

This type of incentive program becomes difficult to administer when a manager is responsible for a department in which the product is transferred to another department. Consider the following example. Cement Art has two departments: Design and Casting. The design department creates molds used by the casting department to make a variety of cement statues, bird baths, and planters. The casting department purchases its molds from the design department, pours cement in the molds, and sells the finished product to retail stores. The manager of each department receives a bonus equal to 0.05% of the department's profit.

The incentive plan would seem to be a good idea. However, if the casting department is required to purchase molds from the design department at any price, the design department manager has no incentive to control production costs. Thus, management must establish policies to determine the prices of molds transferred between the departments. Setting prices for the transfer of products between the departments is known as *transfer pricing*. Several transfer pricing methods are available:

1. **Set the price consistent with the prices charged by other suppliers of the same or similar products.**
2. **Set the price based on the price for which the product could be sold to other companies.**
3. **If the product is unique, use a percentage markup. This method must include a provision for containing increases in production costs.**

INSTRUCTIONS

With another student, assume the roles of the design and casting department managers. Assume that the current cost of producing a mold is $20.00, and the mold is sold to the casting department for $25.00. The casting department adds $10.00 of other materials and labor to the product and sells the finished product to customers for $60.00. Negotiate a transfer pricing policy that provides an incentive salary for each manager. The policy should include a provision for the design manager to increase the price of a mold for an increase in production costs.

© iStockphoto.com/Makhnach_M

CLOSURE

- Review the Chapter Summary.
- Review the new concepts introduced in this lesson.

Essential Questions

- What would the consequences be if the accounts receivable ledger were not current? (*The cash flow of the company could be negatively affected because customer payment information would not be up to date.*)
- Some businesses only allow customers to use major credit cards for purchases. Why would it be beneficial to your business to extend credit to customers? (*Answers will vary, but might include generating more sales by enhancing customer service and providing customers with another option for payment.*)

EXTENDED LEARNING

- Review A Look at Accounting Software on pages 55 and 56.
- Assign Explore Accounting on page 57.

EXPLORE ACCOUNTING

Assign students to work in two-person groups. One student should assume the role of the design department manager; the other student should be the casting department manager. Specific group solutions will vary, but all should include one of the three pricing schemes described in the feature.

CHECK FIGURES

For complete solutions to Chapter 2 problems, see the Teacher's Edition of the Working Papers.

Application Problem 2-1

Sales Journal column totals: $7,961.29; $234.29; $5,934.00; $1,793.00.

General Journal: Two return entries dated May 8 and 17.

May 31 balance in Accounts Receivable: $23,570.80.

Application Problem 2-2

Cash Receipts Journal column totals: $4,733.53; $1,517.00; $8,742.35; $14,596.03; $29.35; $58.84; $29,500.72.

Apply Your Understanding

INSTRUCTIONS: Download problem instructions for Excel, QuickBooks, and Sage 50 from the textbook companion website at www.C21accounting.com.

2-1 Application Problem: Journalizing and posting departmental sales on account and sales returns and allowances LO2, 3

The sales journal, general journal, and partial accounts receivable and general ledgers for Welch Furniture are provided in the *Working Papers*. Welch Furniture has two departments: Chairs and Tables. The general ledger and accounts receivable ledger are provided in the *Working Papers*.

Instructions:

1. Journalize the transactions completed during May of the current year. Use page 5 of a sales journal and page 8 of a general journal. Post the following transactions when journalized: (1) transactions affecting the accounts receivable subsidiary ledger and (2) transactions recorded in the general journal. The sales tax rate is 7%. Source documents are abbreviated as follows: sales invoice, S; credit memorandum, CM.

Transactions:

May 4. Sold six chairs for $259.00 each on account to Elrod Clinic, plus sales tax. S256.
8. Elrod Clinic received credit for returning one of the chairs sold on S256, plus sales tax. CM27.
12. Sold a table on account to Anna Patrick for $534.00, plus sales tax. S257.
16. Sold 20 chairs for $219.00 each on account to Lincoln City Schools. No sales tax. S258.
17. Granted credit to Anna Patrick for the return of the table sold on S257, plus sales tax. CM28.
23. Sold a table on account to Keller Stendal for $1,259.00, plus sales tax. S259.

2. Prove and rule the sales journal. Post the totals to the general ledger.

2-2 Application Problem: Journalizing and posting departmental cash receipts LO4, 5

Sage 50 Accounting

1. Journalize and post customer transactions on account to the cash receipts journal.
2. From the menu bar, select Reports & Forms; Accounts Receivable.
3. Print the sales journal and cash receipts journal.

QuickBooks

1. Journalize and post customer transactions on account in the Receive Payments window.
2. From the menu bar, select Reports; Banking, Deposit Detail.
3. From the menu bar, select Reports; Customers & Receivables, Customer Balance Detail.

Excel

1. Journalize and post customer transactions on account to the cash receipts journal and accounts payable ledger.
2. Print the worksheets.

AAONLINE

1. Go to www.cengage.com/login
2. Click on AA Online to access.
3. Go to the online assignment and follow the instructions.

The cash receipts journal, partial accounts receivable ledger, and partial general ledger for Nelson Auto Parts are provided in the *Working Papers*. Nelson Auto Parts has two departments: Parts and Tires. The company offers credit terms of 2/10, n/30.

Instructions:

1. Journalize the following transactions completed during June of the current year. Use page 7 of a cash receipts journal. The sales tax rate is 6.5%; assume sales tax was paid on all cash and credit card sales. Post transactions affecting the accounts receivable subsidiary ledger when journalized. Source documents are abbreviated as follows: credit memorandum, CM; receipt, R; sales invoice, S; terminal summary, TS.

Transactions:

June 3. Received cash on account from Sam's Service Station for parts purchased on S624 for $624.95, less discount. R668.
4. Received a check from Foreign Car Center for parts purchased on S599 for $498.18, less CM57 for $173.99, no discount. R669.
6. Recorded cash and credit card sales for the week: parts, $3,594.16; tires, $6,451.95; plus sales tax. TS21.
8. Received a check from Bob's Auto Repair for parts purchased on S625 for $842.62, less discount. R670.
20. Recorded cash and credit card sales for the week: parts, $5,148.19; tires, $8,144.08; plus sales tax. TS22.
22. Received a check from Delta Transportation for tires purchased on S634 for $3,221.94, less CM58 for $280.17, less discount. R671.

2. Prove and rule the cash receipts journal. Post the totals to the general ledger.

2-M Mastery Problem: Journalizing departmental sales, sales returns and allowances, and cash receipts LO2, 3, 4, 5

Sage 50 Accounting

1. Journalize and post customer transactions on account to the sales journal and cash receipts journal.
2. From the menu bar, select Reports & Forms; Accounts Receivable.
3. Print the sales journal and cash receipts journal.

QB

1. Journalize and post customer transactions on account in the Create Invoices window.
2. Journalize and post customer transactions on account in the Receive Payments window.
3. From the menu bar, select Reports; Sales, Sales by Customer Detail.

Excel

1. Journalize and post customer transactions on account to the sales journal and cash receipts journal.
2. Journalize and post sales returns to the general journal.
3. Print the worksheets.

AA ONLINE

1. Go to www.cengage.com/login
2. Click on AA Online to access.
3. Go to the online assignment and follow the instructions.

The sales journal, cash receipts journal, general journal, and partial accounts receivable and partial general ledgers for Maynard Office Supply are provided in the *Working Papers*. Maynard has two departments: Equipment and Supplies. The company offers credit terms of 2/10, n/30.

Instructions:

1. Journalize the transactions completed during May of the current year. Use page 5 of a sales journal, page 6 of a general journal, and page 8 of a cash receipts journal. The sales tax rate is 5%. Assume sales tax was paid on all cash and credit card sales. Post transactions affecting the accounts receivable subsidiary ledger and transactions in the general journal when journalized. Source documents are abbreviated as follows: credit memorandum, CM; receipt, R; sales invoice, S; terminal summary, TS.

Transactions:

May 3. Received cash on account from Lakeland Church for supplies purchased on April 26 covering S575 for $315.74, less discount. R603.
4. Sold equipment on account to Eastern Realty, $1,842.25, plus sales tax. S578.
5. Recorded cash and credit card sales: equipment, $6,148.27; supplies, $2,481.19; plus sales tax. TS21.
7. Granted credit to Eastern Realty for equipment returned, $295.00, plus sales tax, from S578. CM38.
12. Sold supplies on account to BLC Storage, $425.00, plus sales tax. S579.
13. Received cash on account from Eastern Realty for equipment purchased on May 4 on S578, less CM38, less discount. R604.
20. Received cash on account from BLC Storage for supplies purchased on May 12 on S579, less discount. R605.
23. Received $1,500.00 cash on account from Natural Products for equipment purchased on April 22, no discount. R606.
24. Sold supplies on account to Lakeland Church, $614.00. Lakeland Church is exempt from sales taxes. S580.
25. Recorded cash and credit card sales: equipment, $2,894.96; supplies, $3,148.09; plus sales tax. TS22.
26. Granted credit to Lakeland Church for supplies returned, $62.50, from S580. CM39.

2. Prove and rule the sales journal. Post the totals to the general ledger.
3. Prove and rule the cash receipts journal. Post the totals to the general ledger.

2-S Source Documents Problem: Journalizing departmental sales, sales returns and allowances, and cash receipts LO2, 4, 5

Ozark AV Shack sells audio and video equipment. Journals and source documents related to the sales and cash receipts are provided in the *Working Papers*. Post the following transactions when journalized: (1) transactions affecting the accounts receivable subsidiary ledger, (2) transactions recorded in the general journal, and (3) cash receipts entered in a general amount column of the cash payments journal. Ozark AV Shack uses a chart of accounts similar to the one Whiley Outdoor Living, Inc., uses.

Instructions:

1. Journalize the transactions shown in the source documents, by date, using page 11 of a sales journal, page 13 of a general journal, and page 14 of a cash receipts journal. All outstanding accounts receivable on November 1 relate to the sales of audio equipment. Post the items that are to be posted individually.
2. Prove and rule the sales journal. Post the totals.
3. Prove and rule the cash receipts journal. Post the totals.

Mastery Problem 2-M

Sales Journal column totals: $2,994.61; $113.36; $1,842.25; $1,039.00.

General Journal: Two return entries dated May 7 and 26.

Cash Receipts Journal column totals: General Debit and Credit columns, both $0; $3,886.60; $733.62; $9,043.23; $5,629.28; $32.49; $15.24; $19,245.00.

May 31 balance in Accounts Receivable: $26,885.37.

Source Documents Problem 2-S

Sales Journal column totals: $6,445.44; $449.69; $4,097.75; $1,898.00.

General Journal: Two return entries dated Nov. 3 and 18.

Cash Receipts Journal column totals: General Debit and Credit columns, both $0; $5,765.34; $2,345.24; $13,376.16; $17,893.78; $27.39; $63.06; $39,290.07.

Nov. 30 balance in Accounts Receivable: $29,001.34.

FORMATIVE ASSESSMENT

- Review solutions to the assigned problems in class, diagnosing trouble spots.

RETEACH

- Call on students to describe how they avoid the trouble spots diagnosed.
- Use reteaching suggestions from lesson plans as required.
- Assign Recycling Problem 2-R if needed.

INDEPENDENT PRACTICE

- Assign Mastery Problem 2-M for students as a culminating problem that combines all activities from the chapter.
- Assign Source Documents Problem 2-S, utilizing source documents related to sales and cash receipts.
- Assign Challenge Problem 2-C to accelerated students who work at a faster pace.
- Assign Study Guide 2.
- Students can access Online Working Papers to work end-of-chapter problems on the computer.
- Direct students to the C21 Accounting companion website for additional practice and review opportunities.

Challenge Problem 2-C

The problem involves the collection of sales to multiple departments on a single invoice. Three sales and a sales return are already presented in the sales and general journals. Students must devise a method of assigning the sales discount to each department to journalize three cash receipts. A sample of supporting calculations is provided in the solution. The solution calculates the sales, sales tax, and sales discount for each department individually. Some students may develop alternative methods of solving this problem. Small rounding differences may occur, depending on the method used, and should not be considered when grading this problem.

Discounts: June 12, $4.31 and $1.22; June 16, $8.09 and $5.39; June 20, $5.02 and $2.37.

EXTENDED LEARNING

- Assign 21st Century Skills on page 61.
- Assign Analyzing Home Depot's Financial Statements on page 61.

SUMMATIVE EVALUATION

- Chapter 2 Test
- Cognero for Chapter 2

2-C Challenge Problem: Journalizing departmental sales, sales returns and allowances, and cash receipts LO2, 3, 4, 5

Ellis Paint sells paint and paint supplies. Many customers purchase merchandise from both departments on a single sales invoice. Ellis Paint offers its customers terms of 2/10, n/30. Thus, any sales discount needs to be divided between the paint and supplies departments. Sales and sales return transactions are journalized in the sales and general journals shown below. A cash receipts journal is provided in the *Working Papers*.

SALES JOURNAL PAGE 6

	DATE		ACCOUNT DEBITED	SALE NO.	POST. REF.	1 ACCOUNTS RECEIVABLE DEBIT	2 SALES TAX PAYABLE CREDIT	3 SALES CREDIT PAINT	4 SALES CREDIT SUPPLIES	
1	20-- June	6	Daniel Painters	664	125	276 48	20 48	199 68	56 32	1
2		9	Hammond Construction	665	145	674 35	49 95	374 64	249 76	2
3		12	Rowell Designs	666	180	397 49	29 44	232 50	135 55	3

GENERAL JOURNAL PAGE 12

	DATE		ACCOUNT TITLE	DOC. NO.	POST. REF.	DEBIT	CREDIT	
1	20-- June	15	Sales Returns and Allowances—Supplies	CM55	4215	25 95		1
2			Sales Tax Payable		2110	2 08		2
3			Accounts Receivable/Rowell Designs		1205/180		28 03	3
4								4
5								5

Instructions:

Journalize the transactions completed during June of the current year. Use page 9 of a cash receipts journal. The sales tax rate is 8%. Source documents are abbreviated as follows: credit memorandum, CM; receipt, R; sales invoice, S.

Transactions:

June 12. Received cash on account from Daniel Painters covering S664, less discount. R701.
16. Received cash on account from Hammond Construction covering S665, less discount. R702.
20. Received cash on account from Rowell Designs covering S666, less CM55, less discount. R703.

COMMON CORE AND INTERDISCIPLINARY STUDIES

Extended learning features and activities present numerous opportunities to implement Common Core Standards through interdisciplinary studies. Practice is provided in the common core areas of English Language Arts & Literacy and Mathematical Practice. Many of these activities require short, critical-thinking and decision-making responses that apply reading, writing, speaking, listening, language, media and technology, and mathematical skills.

21st Century Skills

Bug Appétit!

Theme: Financial, Economic, Business, and Entrepreneurial Literacy

Skills: Creativity and Innovation, Critical Thinking and Problem Solving, Communication and Collaboration, ICT Literacy

PARTNERSHIP FOR 21ST CENTURY SKILLS

While restaurants are winning customers with dishes like caramelized mealworms and fried arachnid, entrepreneurs are creating new business opportunities. Organic insects by World Entomophagy, scorpion suckers by Hotlix, or arthropod-based nutritional supplements by BugMuscle are several of the new ventures.

Eating insects is actually an old tradition. Crickets, beetles, cicadas, and locusts are recorded in historical writings and have been consumed by humans for over ten thousand years. For example, fried winged termites are consumed in Ghana, grubs in New Guinea, and cicadas in Latin America. Experts say that insects are a food source for almost 80% of the world's population; yet Americans still prefer livestock.

Food preferences are usually determined by culture. Entomophagy, or eating insects, is gaining in popularity due to the nutritional value and environmental advantages. It could be the food of the future and an opportunity to increase sales. Perhaps the next time you eat BLTs, you will be eating beetles, locusts, and tarantulas!

APPLICATION

1. You are in the livestock business. It is estimated that the world population is expected to reach 9 billion people by 2050, and insects could be a viable option for food. With a partner, brainstorm three business opportunities involving insects that could help you maintain sales. Share your findings with the class.
2. Using the Internet, research advantages of eating insects. Then, create a commercial convincing others to get over the "yuck" factor and consume insects.

Source: www.time.com/time/magazine/article/0,9171,1810336,00.html; www.businessweek.com/magazine/on-the-menu-stinkbugs-and-mealworms-11172011.html.

Analyzing Home Depot's financial statements

Published financial statements include notes that provide a better understanding of some of the amounts, terms, and accounting policies used in preparing them. Home Depot's Consolidated Balance Sheets contain the heading "Cash and Cash Equivalents." The reader of the financial statements must refer to Home Depot's notes to learn what it reports in this amount on its balance sheets.

INSTRUCTIONS

1. Using the Consolidated Balance Sheets in Appendix B on page B-5, identify the actual amount of Home Depot's cash and cash equivalents as of February 3, 2013.
2. Referring to the Notes to Consolidated Financial Statements in Appendix B, identify the types of financial instruments included in cash and cash equivalents.

21ST CENTURY SKILLS

Answers

1. Answers will vary.
2. Public service announcements or infomercials should be (a) informative, (b) creative, and (c) persuasive.

ANALYZING HOME DEPOT'S FINANCIAL STATEMENTS

Answers

1. $2,494,000,000.
2. Home Depot "considers all highly liquid investments purchased with original maturities of three months or less to be cash equivalents . . . [and the company's investments in this category] consist primarily of money market funds."

Chapter 3

Calculating and Recording Departmental Payroll Data

Scope & Sequence

	New	Review/Enrich
Introduction		
Introduce the Chapter		
Lesson 3-1: Completing Payroll Records for Employee Earnings and Deductions		
Paying Employees		✓
Payroll Deductions		✓
Calculating Employee Earnings		✓
Commissions Record	✓	
Preparing a Payroll Register (Left Page)		✓
Preparing a Payroll Register (Right Page)		✓
Using the Federal Income Tax Withholding Tables		✓
Preparing an Employee Earnings Record		✓
Lesson 3-2: Recording a Payroll and Payroll Taxes		
Payroll Bank Account		✓
Automatic Check Deposit		✓
Journalizing Payment of a Payroll	✓	
Employer Payroll Taxes		✓
Calculating Employer Payroll Taxes	✓	
Journalizing Employer Payroll Taxes	✓	
Journalizing Payment of Federal Income Tax, Social Security Tax, and Medicare Tax Liabilities		✓
Journalizing Payment of Federal Unemployment Tax Liability		✓
Journalizing Payment of State Unemployment Tax Liability		✓
Closure		

Enhancing Instruction

Features	Common Core Standards
• Accounting in the Real World: Automatic Data Processing, Inc.	• ELAL—reading, media and technology
• Ethics in Action: The Danger of Social Media • Global Awareness: International Clubs • Forensic Accounting: Crazy Eddie	• ELAL—reading, media and technology • ELAL—reading, media and technology • Mathematics
• Think Like an Accountant: Labor Costs • Why Accounting?: Executive Compensation	• Mathematics • ELAL—reading, writing
• A Look at Accounting Software • Explore Accounting • 21st Century Skills • Source Documents Problem • Auditing for Errors • Analyzing Home Depot's Financial Statements	• ELAL—reading • ELAL—reading • ELAL—speaking, listening, writing • Mathematics • Mathematics

ELAL = English Language Arts & Literacy

Calculator: © iStockphoto.com/picstodisc; Paper: © iStockphoto.com/Qingwa

Practice and Assessment

Technology & Media	Teaching Strategies	Guided Practice	Independent Practice	Reteach/Enrich
• Instructor's Resource CD/Website: PowerPoint Slides Accounting Concepts • Online Working Papers • Transparency Masters: Commissions Record, Payroll Register, Tax Withholding Tables for Married and Single Persons, Employee Earnings Record	• Logical/Mathematical Learners • Tactile/Kinesthetic Learners • Visual/Spatial Students	• Terms Review • Audit Your Understanding • Work Together 3-1	• On Your Own 3-1 • Application Problem 3-1 • Formative Assessment, p. 74 • Online Working Papers	• Reteach, p. 75
• Instructor's Resource CD/Website: PowerPoint Slides Accounting Concepts • Online Working Papers • Transparency Masters: Payroll Register, Cash Payments Journal, General Journal	• Auditory/Linguistic Learners • Intrapersonal Learners	• Terms Review • Audit Your Understanding • Work Together 3-2	• On Your Own 3-2 • Application Problem 3-2 • Formative Assessment, p. 82 • Online Working Papers	• Reteach, p. 83
	• Common Core and Interdisciplinary Studies		• Mastery Problem 3-M • Study Guide 3 • Chapter 3 Test • Cognero Chapter 3	• Challenge Problem 3-C • Reteach, p. 88 • Recycling Problem 3-R

Introduce the Chapter

SET THE STAGE

GUIDING QUESTIONS

- Ask students how many have jobs, where they work, and what duties they perform.
- Ask students who have jobs to identify the different types of compensation that are paid by their employer. Explain the rationale for different methods of compensating employees.
- Ask students if they were ever surprised when they received their paycheck. Did they expect more? Why or why not?
- Ask students if they understand the difference between gross pay and net pay. Ask if they have thought about what happens to the money that is deducted. Explain that these deductions become liabilities to the employer.
- Ask students if they can choose to contribute to social security. Why or why not?
- Ask students to consider the role of the employer. Ask them to predict the taxes they think an employer must pay based on payroll.
- Ask students to predict the journals that will be used to record the payroll liability and payments to employees.
- Ask students if they have ever considered what government programs are available should they be laid off from a job. Ask students to consider who pays for these programs.

PREVIEW CHAPTER OBJECTIVES

- Introduce the topic of payroll by asking students how many have part-time jobs and how often they are paid.

TEACHING IDEA **Make a transparency of a payroll check stub (blocking out personal information). Ask students to identify all deductions listed on the stub. Have students determine which deductions are taxes and identify the type of tax.**

PREVIEW ACCOUNTING TERMS

- Read each term aloud to verify its pronunciation for students.
- Point out terms or parts of terms that should already be familiar to most students, such as *salary, pay period, payroll,* and *payroll taxes.*

Chapter 3 Calculating and Recording Departmental Payroll Data

LEARNING OBJECTIVES

After studying Chapter 3, in addition to defining key terms, you will be able to:

LO1 Explain how employees are paid.

LO2 Calculate employee earnings.

LO3 Prepare payroll reports.

LO4 Journalize the payment of a payroll.

LO5 Journalize the payment of payroll taxes.

Calculator: © iStockphoto.com/picstodisc; Paper: © iStockphoto.com/Qingwa

© iStockphoto.com/Michael DeLeon

- Lead an interactive discussion with students to review and explain the terms. Stress that special attention should be directed to all boldfaced and highlighted words presented in the text.

Accounting In The Real World
Automatic Data Processing, Inc.

Paying employees for their labors is a simple process. Multiply the hours worked by the hourly wage rate. Write a check for that amount. Oh, if it was only that easy!

In reality, payroll accounting can be complicated and confusing. Why? Companies must collect, pay, and report payroll taxes to several government agencies. Congress periodically changes federal tax laws and tax rates. State governments have their own unique payroll tax laws. Some cities require employees to pay an income tax. Each government agency specifies how and when to pay payroll taxes.

Automatic Data Processing, Inc. (ADP®) to the rescue! ADP® specializes in payroll services, allowing its clients to focus on their businesses. ADP® serves approximately 600,000 organizations worldwide. A business can "outsource" any or all tasks of its payroll function to ADP®. These tasks include the collection of employee hours, preparation of payroll checks, and filing of tax forms. A few of the other services ADP® can provide include candidate pre-screening, leave management, commuter and tuition benefit administration, and succession planning.

Each month, the government and financial community eagerly await the release of the ADP National Employment Report®. This report contains an estimate of the number of jobs gained or lost during the previous month.

Outsourcing payroll processing does not relieve a business of its responsibilities. The accountants must understand payroll tax laws and procedures to ensure the business complies with all federal, state, and city tax laws. The accountants must also work with ADP® professionals to ensure the business obtains the best payroll services available while minimizing its payroll processing costs.

CRITICAL THINKING

1. Search the Internet to identify the estimate of the jobs gained or lost on the latest ADP National Employment Report®.
2. Suppose the reports indicate job gains of 60,000 and 35,000 jobs in June and July, respectively. What does this information indicate about economic growth? What impact might this information have on the stock markets?

Source: www.adp.com.

Background: © iStockphoto.com/Steve cole images; Real World: Bob Goldberg/Feature Photo Service/Newscom

Key Terms

- wage
- salary
- pay period
- payroll
- payroll taxes
- withholding allowance
- tax base
- payroll register
- employee earnings record
- automatic check deposit
- electronic funds transfer (EFT)

Accounting In The Real World

Answers

1. Answers will vary depending on the months selected.
2. The numbers indicate that the economy is growing, but at a slower pace than in the prior month. The stock markets will likely view this as an unfavorable trend.

LESSON

3-1

BRIDGE

- Explain that the accounting concepts and practices related to a payroll system were presented in the first-year accounting course.
- Explain that this chapter will review the basic payroll procedures and present the preparation of a payroll for a departmentalized business.
- Ask students to identify the types of benefits they or their parents have received from their jobs.

TEACHING RESOURCES

- **Instructor's Resource CD/Website:**
  PowerPoint Slides
  Accounting Concepts
- **Working Papers:**
  Teacher's Edition of the Working Papers for Lesson 3-1
  Online Working Papers
- **Transparency Masters:**
  Commissions Record
  Payroll Register
  Tax Withholding Tables for Married and Single Persons
  Employee Earnings Record

ENGAGE

- Get students involved in discussing some of the ways of setting wages earned. (*hourly, salary, commissions, etc.*) Write responses on the board.
- Discuss the importance of maintaining accurate payroll records. Ask the class who might be interested in all or part of the payroll information.

PREVIEW

- Call on students to read the accounting terms and definitions introduced in this lesson: *wage, salary, pay period, payroll, payroll taxes, withholding allowance, tax base, payroll register,* and *employee earnings record.*
- Point out the learning objectives for this lesson.
- Direct students to read the headings in this lesson and to examine the illustrations.

© Lucky Business/Shutterstock.com

LESSON

3-1 Completing Payroll Records for Employee Earnings and Deductions

LO1 Explain how employees are paid.
LO2 Calculate employee earnings.
LO3 Prepare payroll reports.

Paying Employees LO1

Employees are an essential element of the business world. Businesses depend on competent employees in order to operate successfully. Employees provide services to a business in exchange for money. The amount paid to an employee for every hour worked is called a **wage**. A fixed annual sum of money divided among equal pay periods is called a **salary**. Federal, state, and local laws require employers to keep accurate records of payments to employees and other payments related to employee services. Payroll records are maintained for the business and for each employee. The payroll system used differs among businesses. A business protects itself by keeping complete and accurate payroll records of all required information.

The number of days or weeks of work covered by an employee's paycheck is called a **pay period**. The total amount earned by all employees for a pay period is called a **payroll**. In addition to salaries, a business must pay taxes based on the payroll. Taxes based on the payroll of a business are called **payroll taxes**. The law also requires employers to withhold certain payroll taxes from employee salaries each pay period.

Periodically, employers must pay government agencies all payroll taxes withheld from employee salaries as well as the employer payroll taxes. A business must also provide a yearly report to each employee showing the total salary earned and the total taxes withheld. The yearly report is provided to each employee on Form W-2. Businesses must distribute this form to their employees by January 31, reporting earnings and amounts withheld for the previous calendar year. Therefore, a business must keep records of each employee's earnings, amounts withheld, and net amount paid. Payroll records also must show the total amount of payroll taxes that a business must pay.

ETHICS IN ACTION

The Danger of Social Media

Angela is recognized as the best salesclerk in the juniors clothing department at Chandler's Fashions. She has a special talent for selecting brands that best fit a customer's size and shape. Angela's regular customers often communicate with her via her personal social media account. A recent exchange follows:

Maggie: When are the Christiana summer styles arriving?

Angela: Probably early April.

Maggie: I hear the colors are really bright. Can't wait!

Angela: Don't get too excited.

Maggie: ???

Angela: Unless you're a supermodel, you're not going to be able to pull it off.

Maggie: ☹

INSTRUCTIONS

Access the *Business Conduct Guide* of Target Stores. Using this code and the ethical model, determine whether Angela's posts demonstrate ethical behavior.

© iStockphoto.com/LdF

ETHICS IN ACTION

This activity involves ethics related to social media postings. The case is not intended to represent a significant violation of ethics. Use this activity to promote a discussion on the appropriate use of social media sites.

See a suggested solution for this feature in the Instructional Strategies section at the front of this book.

Payroll Deductions

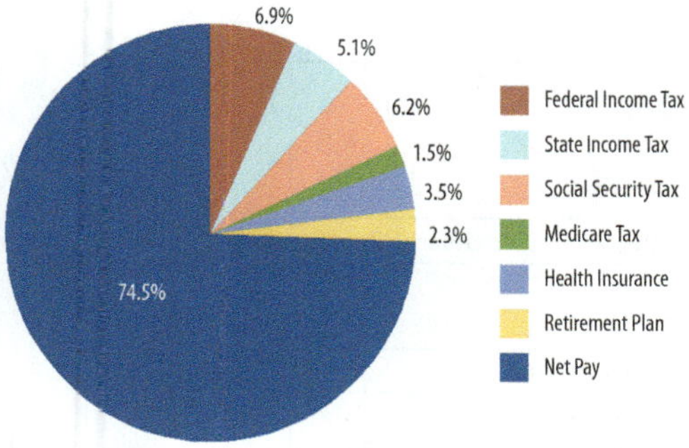

Whiley is required by law to withhold federal income tax and two FICA taxes (social security tax and Medicare tax) from each employee's pay. *FICA* is the abbreviation for the Federal Insurance Contributions Act.

The total earnings, marital status, and number of withholding allowances claimed by an employee determine the federal income tax amount to be withheld. For each person supported, including the employee, an employee is entitled to a reduction in the amount on which income tax is calculated. A deduction from total earnings for each person legally supported by a taxpayer, including the employee, is called a **withholding allowance**.

FICA provides for a federal system of old age, survivors, disability, and hospital insurance. The social security tax finances the old age, survivors, and disability insurance portion. The Medicare tax finances the hospital insurance portion. Each of these taxes is reported separately. Social security tax is calculated on employee earnings up to a maximum paid in a calendar year. The maximum amount of earnings on which a tax is calculated is called a **tax base**. Congress sets the tax base and the tax rates for social security tax. The social security tax rate and base used in this textbook are 6.2% of earnings up to a maximum of $113,700.00 in each calendar year. Medicare does not have a tax base. The Medicare tax rate used in this text is 1.45% of total employee earnings.

Some cities and states also require that employers deduct amounts for income and other taxes from employee earnings. Laws for handling state, city, and county taxes vary.

Some businesses also make deductions from employee earnings for health insurance, life insurance, retirement plans, and charitable contributions. Whiley makes deductions from its employee salaries for federal income tax, state income tax, social security tax, Medicare tax, health insurance, and retirement plans. The payroll components for Guiren L. Heng are shown in the graph above.

GLOBAL AWARENESS

International Clubs

Many students want to learn more about other cultures and peoples. Because of this, schools and colleges often sponsor international clubs or organizations. The focus of these clubs may vary, but most bring students together to promote understanding and appreciation of different cultures.

Club activities reflect the focus of the organization. Some clubs may sponsor and plan global awareness events featuring international art, food, dance, and speakers. Other clubs may enable students to practice speaking a foreign language—or help international students practice speaking English. Clubs can focus on support for international students, ranging from assistance on educational visas to helping them connect with other students from their homeland. Some clubs organize social events to foster new relationships. A popular activity is the celebration of holidays of different cultures, educating participants on the traditions and history of each holiday.

Many international clubs focus on travel by sponsoring study-abroad programs. Some study-abroad programs organize studies in a different foreign country each semester, with all participating students attending the same classes in that country. In other programs, each student is able to choose the foreign country in which he or she wishes to study.

© iStockphoto.com/Lusky

CRITICAL THINKING

1. Search the Internet to find an international club in your community. List at least one goal and one activity of the club.
2. Search the Internet to find out about a study-abroad program in your area—at either the high school or college level. List the name of the program and the sponsoring organization.

INPUT

- Explain that employees are required by law to withhold three federal taxes from each employee's pay—federal income tax, social security tax, and Medicare tax.
- Explain that in addition to the federal taxes, some states and/or cities have income taxes that employers must withhold from an employee's pay.
- Explain that in addition to taxes, employers may also make deductions from employee earnings for health insurance, life insurance, retirement savings, and savings deposits.
- Emphasize that the various payroll deductions can take a significant percentage of an employee's earnings.

MODEL

- Use the illustration to demonstrate how the payroll deductions represent a significant part of an employee's gross pay.

GLOBAL AWARENESS

Answers

1. Answers will vary.
2. Answers will vary.

DIFFERENTIATED INSTRUCTION

Logical/Mathematical learners enjoy reasoning and problem-solving activities. They enjoy learning through investigation. Provide students with several employer scenarios. Include a combination of employer benefits such as vacation, health care, and the matching of employee contributions. Ask students to select the employer they prefer based on the benefits offered and to explain their choice.

INPUT

- Ask students who have jobs how frequently they are paid. Write their responses on the board.
- Explain that companies may have weekly, semimonthly, or monthly pay periods.
- Explain that Whiley has a biweekly pay period and that the Hourly Employee Time Summary is designated for the two-week period.
- Point out that employees who are paid by the hour usually earn overtime pay after working 40 hours in a calendar week, regardless of the length of the pay period.
- Explain how regular hours are calculated.
- Explain how overtime hours are calculated.
- Explain how biweekly earnings are calculated.

MODEL

- Use the illustration in the book or demonstrate on the board how to calculate regular earnings, overtime earnings, and total earnings.

Calculating Employee Earnings LO2

Hourly Employee Time Summary

Pay Period: 6/29/20-- to 7/12/20--

Prepared on: 7/14/20--

Name	ID	Week Ended	Regular	Overtime	Totals
Denton, Juanita P.	14	7/5/20--	40	1	41
		7/12/20--	40	3	43
			80	4	84
Golden, Larry A.	35	7/5/20--	40		40
		7/12/20--	40		40
			80		80
Jewell, Mary B.	18	7/5/20--	37	2	39
		7/12/20--	35		35
			72	2	74

Whiley pays an hourly salary biweekly to most store and accounting department employees. Whiley's biweekly pay period is 80 hours, consisting of two regular 40-hour workweeks. The store is open six days a week. However, employees usually work only a five-day week of 40 hours. The pay rate for these employees is stated as an hourly rate.

Whiley uses an employee identification card scanner to log employee hours. All employees have badges with a magnetic strip coded to include their name and identification number. Employees slide the card through the card scanner when they begin and end each work period. At the end of a payroll period, a report listing employee hours worked provides the data for calculating employee earnings. The employee hours report for the biweekly period June 29 through July 12 is shown above. The software that supports the card scanner can produce a variety of reports. For example, to monitor employee attendance, a report of the actual times an employee arrives and leaves can also be generated.

All time worked in excess of 8 hours a day or 40 hours in any one week is considered overtime. Employees are paid 1½ times the regular rate for overtime hours. However, managers are paid a base salary and commissions, so their hours worked are not presented on this report.

Employee regular earnings are calculated by multiplying the hourly rate by the number of regular hours. Employee overtime earnings are calculated by multiplying the regular rate by 1.5 and multiplying the result by the number of overtime hours. The calculations are shown below for Juanita P. Denton.

Regular Hours	×	**Regular Rate**	=	**Regular Earnings**
80	×	$18.00	=	$1,440.00

Overtime Hours	×	**Regular Rate**	×	**1.5**	=	**Overtime Earnings**
4	×	$18.00	×	1.5	=	$108.00

Regular Earnings	+	**Overtime Earnings**	=	**Total Earnings**
$1,440.00	+	$108.00	=	$1,548.00

Commissions Record

COMMISSIONS RECORD

EMPLOYEE NO.	*9*	EMPLOYEE NAME	*Heng, Guiren L.*
PAY PERIOD ENDED	*July 12, 20--*	REGULAR BIWEEKLY SALARY	*$1,000.00*
DEPARTMENT	*Grills*	POSITION	*Department Manager*

	Grills	Furniture	
Sales on Account	*$ 8,143.36*	*$5,180.00*	
Cash and Credit Card Sales	*4,194.16*	*3,481.96*	
equal: Total Sales for the Month	*$12,337.52*	*$8,661.96*	
Less:			
Sales Discounts	*$ 109.68*	*$ 108.16*	
Sales Returns and Allowances	*612.19*	*325.99*	
equal: Total Reductions in Sales	*$ 721.87*	*$ 434.15*	
Equals:			
Net Sales	*$11,615.65*	*$8,227.81*	
times Commission Rate	*3.0%*	*5.0%*	
equal: Commission on Net Sales	*$ 348.47*	*$ 411.39*	*$759.86*

1 Heading Information

2 Calculate Net Sales by Department

3 Calculate Commissions

Other types of earnings may supplement an employee's basic salary. For example, an employee may receive commissions, cost-of-living adjustments, a share of profits, or a bonus.

At Whiley, department managers are paid a biweekly salary. This salary compensates the managers for their responsibility for the operations and appearance of their department. They are not paid for overtime hours.

To encourage increased sales, the managers are paid a commission on their net sales. While serving a customer, each manager often sells merchandise from both departments. Thus, they receive a commission based on their sales of merchandise from each department.

The departments have different commission rates. Whiley recognizes that customers need more assistance with furniture purchases than with grill purchases. Thus, furniture sales have a higher commission rate, 5%, than the 3% earned for grills sales.

The point-of-sale system provides a detailed report of each supervisor's sales from credit card and cash sales during the pay period. Amounts related to credit sales are accumulated by an analysis of sales invoices and credit memoranda. These amounts are used on a commissions record to calculate each supervisor's commission.

Preparing a Commissions Record

1. **Record the employee number, employee name, pay period, regular biweekly salary, department, and position at the top of the form.**
2. **Calculate department net sales for the month:**
   - **Write the amount of sales on account for each department.**
   - **Write the amount of cash and credit card sales for the month.**
   - **Add the two sales amounts and write the total sales for the pay period.**
   - **Write the amount of sales discounts.**
   - **Write the amount of sales returns and allowances.**
   - **Write the total of sales discounts and sales returns and allowances.**
3. **Calculate the commission on net sales for the month.**
   - **Calculate the difference between total sales for the month, less total sales discounts and returns and allowances. Write the amount of net sales.**
   - **Write the commission rate.**
   - **Multiply the commission rate times the net sales amount and write the commission on net sales.**
   - **The June commission for Guiren L. Heng is calculated as shown in the illustration.**

INPUT

- Explain that to provide employees with an incentive to achieve higher levels of effectiveness, employers sometimes pay employees a percentage of sales, called a commission. Whiley pays department managers in Grills a 3% commission, while department managers in Furniture earn a 5% commission.

MODEL

- Use the transparency or the illustration to illustrate the preparation of a commissions record.
- Demonstrate on the board how to calculate commissions as a percentage of net sales, using the process shown in the illustration.
- Record each item on the commissions record transparency, following the three steps shown.

INPUT

- Explain that a payroll register is used to record all essential payroll information for all employees for a specific payroll period.
- Explain that the employee's marital status and number of dependents is used later to determine the amount of federal income tax withheld from the employee's gross pay.
- Point out that the employees' and departmental managers' earnings are recorded in their respective departments. The store manager's and accounting and office employees' earnings are recorded under the Administrative classification.
- Explain that each business is unique and may design a payroll register to accumulate information that best serves the business as well as information required for federal and state reports.
- Explain that Whiley has three different types of earnings—regular, overtime, and commission. A separate column is provided in Whiley's payroll register for each type of earnings.

MODEL

- Prepare a transparency or refer to the illustrations on this page and the next page to illustrate entries in the payroll register form.
- From data for a selected employee, record each item on the payroll register form, following the nine steps shown for preparing a payroll register, emphasizing the importance of accuracy.

Preparing a Payroll Register (Left Page) LO3

1 Payroll Period Ending Date

4 Regular, Overtime, and Commission Earnings

3 Employee Name and Personal Information

9 Column Totals

PAYROLL REGISTER

SEMIMONTHLY PERIOD ENDED *July 12, 20--*

	EMPL. NO.	EMPLOYEE'S NAME	MARITAL STATUS	NO. OF ALLOWANCES	EARNINGS 1 REGULAR	EARNINGS 2 OVERTIME	EARNINGS 3 COMMISSION	EARNINGS 4 TOTAL
1	16	*Heng, Guiren L.*	M	2	1000 00		759 86	1759 86
2	22	*Denton, Juanita P.*	M	3	1440 00	108 00		1548 00
3	30	*Golden, Larry A.*	S	1	1600 00			1600 00
4	27	*Jewell, Jaylen B.*	M	3	1224 00	51 00		1275 00
5	18	*Lowe, Gerald K.*	M	4	1440 00			1440 00
6	29	*Odom, Keandre M.*	S	1	800 00		1055 40	1855 40
7	21	*Shelton, Emma T.*	S	3	1280 00	144 00		1424 00
8	33	*Watkins, James R.*	M	2	1292 00	76 50		1368 50
9		*Totals*			10076 00	379 50	1815 26	12270 76

An accounting form that summarizes the earnings, deductions, and net pay of all employees for one pay period is called a **payroll register**. Whiley prepares a separate payroll register for each biweekly (every two weeks) payroll.

To provide better cost control, Whiley separates employee earnings into three classifications: Grills Department, Furniture Department, and Administrative. The earnings of employees and departmental managers are recorded in their respective departmental classification. The earnings of the store manager and accounting and office employees are recorded in the Administrative classification.

Preparing a Payroll Register

For each pay period:

1. Enter the last day of the biweekly payroll period, July 12, 20--, at the top of the payroll register.
2. Record the date of payment, July 16, 20--, also at the top of the payroll register. The time between the end of a pay period and the date of payment is needed in order to prepare the payroll records and payroll checks.

For each employee:

3. Enter employee number, 16; name, Heng, Guiren L.; marital status, M; and number of allowances, 2. This information is taken from personnel records kept for each employee.
4. Write regular earnings, $1,000.00, and commissions, $759.86, in columns 1 and 3. An employee's overtime earnings would be entered in column 2. Write his total earnings, $1,759.86, in column 4.

   The regular earnings are calculated for hourly employees. Manager salaries are recorded in the Regular Earnings column, column 1. Add the regular earnings, overtime earnings, and commission earnings together to determine the total earnings for the biweekly pay period.
5. Extend total earnings to the appropriate department column or Administrative Salaries.

Preparing a Payroll Register (Right Page)

5 Earnings by Department — 6 Payroll Deductions — 7 Total Deductions — 2 Payment Date

PAYROLL REGISTER

DATE OF PAYMENT *July 16, 20--*

5	6	7	8	9	10	11	12	13	14	15		
DEPARTMENT			DEDUCTIONS									
GRILLS	FURNITURE	ADMINISTRATIVE	FEDERAL INCOME TAX	STATE INCOME TAX	SOCIAL SECURITY TAX	MEDICARE TAX	HEALTH INSURANCE	RETIREMENT PLAN	TOTAL	NET PAY	CHECK NO.	
1,348.47	411.39		135.00	70.39	109.11	25.52	60.00	40.00	440.02	1,319.84		1
	1,548.00		83.00	61.92	95.98	22.45	75.00	60.00	398.35	1,149.65		2
		1,600.00	189.00	64.00	99.20	23.20	45.00	20.00	440.40	1,159.60		3
1,275.00			50.00	51.00	79.05	18.49	75.00	50.00	323.54	951.46		4
		1,440.00	53.00	57.60	89.28	20.88	90.00	60.00	370.76	1,069.24		5
229.37	1,626.03		247.00	74.22	115.03	26.90	45.00	25.00	533.15	1,322.25		6
		1,424.00	117.00	56.96	88.29	20.65	75.00	50.00	407.90	1,016.10		7
	1,368.50		78.00	54.74	84.85	19.84	60.00	30.00	327.43	1,041.07		8
2,852.84	4,953.92	4,464.00	952.00	490.83	760.79	177.93	525.00	335.00	3,241.55	9,029.21		9

8 Net Pay

Preparing a Payroll Register

6 Enter the payroll deductions: federal income tax, $135.00; state income tax, $70.39; social security tax, $109.11; Medicare tax, $25.52; health insurance, $60.00; and retirement plan, $40.00. Federal income tax withholding is calculated using withholding tables, such as the ones shown on pages 70–71. The state in which Whiley operates calculates state income tax at 4% of total earnings. Guiren Heng's social security tax deduction for the biweekly pay period ended July 12 is calculated as shown here.

Total Earnings	×	Social Security Tax	=	Social Security Tax Deduction
$1,759.86	×	6.2%	=	$109.11

Guiren Heng's Medicare tax deduction for the biweekly pay period ended July 12 is calculated as shown here.

Total Earnings	×	Medicare Tax	=	Medicare Tax Deduction
$1,759.86	×	1.45%	=	$25.52

The number of dependents covered determines the health insurance deduction. A business determines what portion of monthly health insurance premium it requires its employees to pay.

Each employee determines the amount to be withheld for his or her contribution to the retirement plan.

7 Add the amounts for deductions and enter the total, $440.02, in column 14.

8 Subtract the total deductions from total earnings to determine net pay, $1,319.84. The net pay for Guiren Heng is calculated as shown here.

Total Earnings	−	Total Deductions	=	Net Pay
$1,759.86	−	$440.02	=	$1,319.84

At the end of the payroll period:

9 When the net pay has been entered for all employees, total each payroll register amount column. Subtract the Total Deductions column, $3,241.55, from the Total Earnings column, $12,270.76. The result should equal the total of the Net Pay column. If the totals do not agree, find and correct the errors. Rule the payroll register.

INPUT

- Explain that all of Whiley's employees have regular earnings. In addition, some have overtime and commissions earnings.
- Explain that Whiley keeps cost records by department for better cost control. Therefore, total earnings for employees are recorded in the Department column.
- Explain that federal income tax withholding amounts are determined using tables provided by the Internal Revenue Service. Some state income tax withholdings are determined using tables, and others are calculated as a percentage of federal income taxes.
- Explain that social security and Medicare tax withholdings are calculated as a percentage of total earnings.
- Explain that to provide separate cost information by department, Whiley includes a separate column for total earnings by department—Grills, Furniture, and Administrative.
- Point out some of the "Other" deductions.
- Remind students that the Check No. column of the payroll register is filled in only after the check is written.

MODEL

- Continue using the transparency or the illustration on this page and the previous page to complete the payroll register entries.
- Emphasize the importance of accuracy.
- Show how to prove the register. The totals of columns 14 and 15 should equal the total of column 4.
- Use the math illustrations to review some of the calculations needed to complete the payroll register.

DIFFERENTIATED INSTRUCTION

Tactile/Kinesthetic learners learn best through physical activity and contact with real objects. Allow students to participate in the process of preparing the payroll register. Have each student use a transparency to complete one or more steps of the recording process.

INPUT

- Explain that each employee is required to complete an Employee's Withholding Allowance form, which provides the information an employer needs to calculate the employee's income tax deduction.
- Explain that to simplify the process for employers to calculate employees' income tax withholding, the federal government prepares a series of employee's income tax withholding tables.
- Explain that a table is made for single and married persons for the various payroll periods—weekly, biweekly, semimonthly, monthly, and daily or miscellaneous. Each table has columns for number of dependents and horizontal lines for the different wage brackets.
- Explain that employers determine each employee's federal income tax withholding for each pay period using these tables.

Using the Federal Income Tax Withholding Tables

SINGLE Persons—**BIWEEKLY** Payroll Period

(For Wages Paid through December 20--)

And the wages are–		And the number of withholding allowances claimed is—										
At least	But less than	0	1	2	3	4	5	6	7	8	9	10
		The amount of income tax to be withheld is—										
$1,200	$1,220	$152	$129	$107	$84	$62	$39	$23	$ 8	$ 0	$ 0	$ 0
1,220	1,240	155	132	110	87	65	42	25	10	0	0	0
1,240	1,260	158	135	113	90	68	45	27	12	0	0	0
1,260	1,280	161	138	116	93	71	48	29	14	0	0	0
1,280	1,300	164	141	119	96	74	51	31	16	1	0	0
1,300	1,320	167	144	122	99	77	54	33	18	3	0	0
1,320	1,340	170	147	125	102	80	57	35	20	5	0	0
1,340	1,360	173	150	128	105	83	60	38	22	7	0	0
1,360	1,380	176	153	131	108	86	63	41	24	9	0	0
1,380	1,400	179	156	134	111	89	66	44	26	11	0	0
1,400	1,420	182	159	137	114	92	69	47	28	13	0	0
1,420	1,440	185	162	140	117	95	72	50	30	15	0	0
1,440	1,460	188	165	143	120	98	75	53	32	17	2	0
1,460	1,480	191	168	146	123	101	78	56	34	19	4	0
1,480	1,500	195	171	149	126	104	81	59	36	21	6	0
1,500	1,520	200	174	152	129	107	84	62	39	23	8	0
1,520	1,540	205	177	155	132	110	87	65	42	25	10	0
1,540	1,560	210	180	158	135	113	90	68	45	27	12	0
1,560	1,580	215	183	161	138	116	93	71	48	29	14	0
1,580	1,600	220	186	164	141	119	96	74	51	31	16	1
1,600	1,620	225	189	167	144	122	99	77	54	33	18	3
1,620	1,640	230	192	170	147	125	102	80	57	35	20	5
1,640	1,660	235	197	173	150	128	105	83	60	38	22	7
1,660	1,680	240	202	176	153	131	108	86	63	41	24	9
1,680	1,700	245	207	179	156	134	111	89	66	44	26	11
1,700	1,720	250	212	182	159	137	114	92	69	47	28	13
1,720	1,740	255	217	185	162	140	117	95	72	50	30	15
1,740	1,760	260	222	188	165	143	120	98	75	53	32	17
1,760	1,780	265	227	191	168	146	123	101	78	56	34	19
1,780	1,800	270	232	195	171	149	126	104	81	59	36	21
1,800	1,820	275	237	200	174	152	129	107	84	62	39	23
1,820	1,840	280	242	205	177	155	132	110	87	65	42	25
1,840	1,860	285	247	210	180	158	135	113	90	68	45	27
1,860	1,880	290	252	215	183	161	138	116	93	71	48	29
1,880	1,900	295	257	220	186	164	141	119	96	74	51	31
1,900	1,920	300	262	225	189	167	144	122	99	77	54	33
1,920	1,940	305	267	230	192	170	147	125	102	80	57	35
1,940	1,960	310	272	235	197	173	150	128	105	83	60	38
1,960	1,980	315	277	240	202	176	153	131	108	86	63	41
1,980	2,000	320	282	245	207	179	156	134	111	89	66	44
2,000	2,020	325	287	250	212	182	159	137	114	92	69	47
2,020	2,040	330	292	255	217	185	162	140	117	95	72	50
2,040	2,060	335	297	260	222	188	165	143	120	98	75	53
2,060	2,080	340	302	265	227	191	168	146	123	101	78	56
2,080	2,100	345	307	270	232	195	171	149	126	104	81	59

fyi

The taxes withheld from the earnings of single individuals are greater than those withheld from married individuals. For example, a single individual earning $1,900 with 2 allowances has $225 withheld. The same individual, if married, will have only $159 withheld. Depending on the spouse's earnings, the married individual may pay a higher annual tax bill. This unusual result of tax law has been dubbed the "marriage penalty."

MARRIED Persons—BIWEEKLY Payroll Period

(For Wages Paid through December 20--)

And the wages are—		And the number of withholding allowances claimed is—										
At least	But less than	0	1	2	3	4	5	6	7	8	9	10
		The amount of income tax to be withheld is—										
$1,200	$1,220	$ 99	$ 77	$ 59	$ 44	$ 29	$ 14	$ 0	$ 0	$ 0	$ 0	$ 0
1,220	1,240	102	80	61	46	31	16	1	0	0	0	0
1,240	1,260	105	83	63	48	33	18	3	0	0	0	0
1,260	1,280	108	86	65	50	35	20	5	0	0	0	0
1,280	1,300	111	89	67	52	37	22	7	0	0	0	0
1,300	1,320	114	92	69	54	39	24	9	0	0	0	0
1,320	1,340	117	95	72	56	41	26	11	0	0	0	0
1,340	1,360	120	98	75	58	43	28	13	0	0	0	0
1,360	1,380	123	101	78	60	45	30	15	0	0	0	0
1,380	1,400	126	104	81	62	47	32	17	2	0	0	0
1,400	1,420	129	107	84	64	49	34	19	4	0	0	0
1,420	1,440	132	110	87	66	51	36	21	6	0	0	0
1,440	1,460	135	113	90	68	53	38	23	8	0	0	0
1,460	1,480	138	116	93	71	55	40	25	10	0	0	0
1,480	1,500	141	119	96	74	57	42	27	12	0	0	0
1,500	1,520	144	122	99	77	59	44	29	14	0	0	0
1,520	1,540	147	125	102	80	61	46	31	16	1	0	0
1,540	1,560	150	128	105	83	63	48	33	18	3	0	0
1,560	1,580	153	131	108	86	65	50	35	20	5	0	0
1,580	1,600	156	134	111	89	67	52	37	22	7	0	0
1,600	1,620	159	137	114	92	69	54	39	24	9	0	0
1,620	1,640	162	140	117	95	72	56	41	26	11	0	0
1,640	1,660	165	143	120	98	75	58	43	28	13	0	0
1,660	1,680	168	146	123	101	78	60	45	30	15	0	0
1,680	1,700	171	149	126	104	81	62	47	32	17	2	0
1,700	1,720	174	152	129	107	84	64	49	34	19	4	0
1,720	1,740	177	155	132	110	87	66	51	36	21	6	0
1,740	1,760	180	158	135	113	90	68	53	38	23	8	0
1,760	1,780	183	161	138	116	93	71	55	40	25	10	0
1,780	1,800	186	164	141	119	96	74	57	42	27	12	0
1,800	1,820	189	167	144	122	99	77	59	44	29	14	0
1,820	1,840	192	170	147	125	102	80	61	46	31	16	1
1,840	1,860	195	173	150	128	105	83	63	48	33	18	3
1,860	1,880	198	176	153	131	108	86	65	50	35	20	5
1,880	1,900	201	179	156	134	111	89	67	52	37	22	7
1,900	1,920	204	182	159	137	114	92	69	54	39	24	9
1,920	1,940	207	185	162	140	117	95	72	56	41	26	11
1,940	1,960	210	188	165	143	120	98	75	58	43	28	13
1,960	1,980	213	191	168	146	123	101	78	60	45	30	15
1,980	2,000	216	194	171	149	126	104	81	62	47	32	17
2,000	2,020	219	197	174	152	129	107	84	64	49	34	19
2,020	2,040	222	200	177	155	132	110	87	66	51	36	21
2,040	2,060	225	203	180	158	135	113	90	68	53	38	23
2,060	2,080	228	206	183	161	138	116	93	71	55	40	25
2,080	2,100	231	209	186	164	141	119	96	74	57	42	27

EXAMPLE: Guiren Heng is married and claims 2 withholding allowances. His total earnings for the pay period are $1,759.86.

1. **Use the left two columns of the Biweekly Married Persons tax table shown here to locate the range containing the total earnings—At least $1,740 but less than $1,760.**
2. **Find the column with the correct number of withholding allowances, 2.**
3. **Find the intersection of the row and column. The amount of income tax to be withheld is $135.00.**

MODEL

- Prepare a transparency of the tax withholding table for married persons or direct students to the illustration.
- Determine the amount of federal income tax withholding for Guiren Heng, following the three steps shown.
- Ask students to determine the amount of tax withholdings for two or three additional situations—given wages and number of dependents.

TEACHING IDEA

Remind students that tax tables change periodically. To demonstrate, direct students to the website www.irs.gov and search for Circular E. Provide students with scenarios in which to compare using the tax table in the book and a more current tax table. Ask students to describe how taxes have changed and what legislation may have caused the change.

FORENSIC ACCOUNTING

The Excel file contains over 1,500 lines of daily sales information. Students create a series of formulas and use the filter tool to identify days where the cash portion of the daily deposit appears unusual. The relative amount of credit card, check, and cash sales changes over the four years as consumers change their buying and payment habits. For example, cash sales range from a low of 5.2% to a high of 50.3% of daily sales. Thus, comparing each day's cash percent to the four-year average of 31.6% is meaningless. The solution is to compare each day's cash sales percent to a number of preceding days. A 14-day moving average was selected for this exercise.

These data were created to mimic data of Crazy Eddie. Encourage students to suggest other tests that could be performed to find additional evidence of a skimming fraud similar to that of Crazy Eddie's.

Suggested Solution

1. Thirty (30) days are presented in the list. In each case, the percent of cash sales is more than 10% less than the 14-day moving average.
2. There is evidence that skimming may have begun in late 2009 and continued through 2012. During this period, the amounts of cash sales appear small relative to credit card and check sales. Beginning in mid-2012, there is evidence that sales were inflated by the deposit of checks. A visual review of the 30 days of sales reveals that there is a significant increase in the amounts of the check deposits relative to credit card and cash sales. Further investigation is required to gather evidence that fraudulent activities occurred.

FORENSIC ACCOUNTING

Crazy Eddie

Crazy Eddie was a chain of retail electronics stores in the New York region. Formed in the early 1970s by members of the Antar family, including Eddie Antar, the company grew to 43 stores, with annual sales of over $350 million.

Eddie Antar was born into a family of retailers. Through the generations, the Antars had learned how to operate a successful business. But according to Eddie's cousin, Sam Antar, they also learned how to avoid paying income taxes. Sam Antar, a former CPA, was the chief financial officer of Crazy Eddie. He states that skimming cash was a regular business practice for the Antar family. Skimming is the theft of cash before the sales transaction is recorded in the accounting records. Lower sales means less income and, thus, less income taxes.

The cash that the Antars skimmed from Crazy Eddie was deposited in foreign bank accounts. The fraud went undetected until the Antars decided to take the company public. To make the stock attractive for potential investors, the company had to report strong growth in profits. The Antars decided to stop the skimming gradually. From 1980 to 1984, Crazy Eddie reduced its skimming from $3 million per year to nearly zero. Reported income began to soar. To fuel its income growth further, the company began bringing skimmed funds back into the country. The funds, received in the form of a check, were included in daily receipts and recorded as sales.

Sam Antar contends that an examination of the components of daily deposits from sales would have revealed the fraud. The amount of daily sales paid with credit cards, checks, and cash should have been relatively consistent. Both the skimming and the depositing of money back into the company would have resulted in significant fluctuations.

ACTIVITY

BRT Enterprises is considering the purchase of Artic Dollar Stores. The director of the review team knows the history of the Crazy Eddie fraud. As a result, an analysis of daily cash receipts is performed as one method of detecting a skimming scheme.

The worksheet contains four years of daily sales receipts. The amount of credit card, check, and cash sales is presented for each day. A quick review of the data reveals changes in customers' payment methods. For example, customers' use of credit cards has gradually changed over the four years.

1. Prepare a list of daily cash that varies more than 10% from expectations. Summarize and explain the findings of this analysis.
2. What trend do you detect in the list? Support your conclusion.

INSTRUCTIONS

Open the spreadsheet FA_CH03 and complete the steps on the Instructions tab.

Source: www.whitecollarfraud.com.

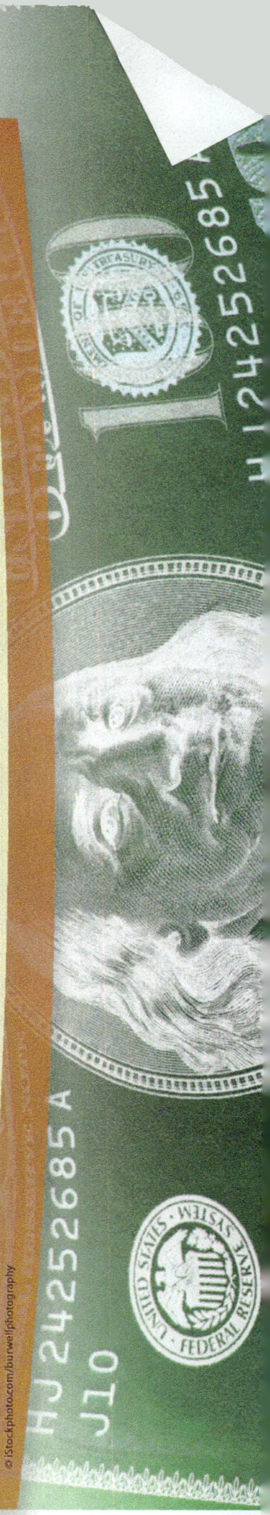

© iStockphoto.com/burwellphotography

Preparing an Employee Earnings Record

2 Personal Information

1 Last Day of Quarter

3 Previous Period Accumulated Earnings

EARNINGS RECORD FOR QUARTER ENDED *September 30, 20--*

EMPLOYEE NO. *16* NAME *Heng, Guiren L.* MARITAL STATUS *M* WITHHOLDING ALLOWANCES *2*

HOURLY WAGE ______ SALARY *$1,000.00* DEPARTMENT *Grills* POSITION *Department Manager*

		1	2	3	4	5	6	7	8	9	10
PAY PERIOD		TOTAL EARNINGS	DEDUCTIONS							NET PAY	ACCUMULATED EARNINGS
NO.	ENDED		FEDERAL INCOME TAX	STATE INCOME TAX	SOC. SEC. TAX	MEDICARE TAX	HEALTH INSURANCE	RETIREMENT PLAN	TOTAL		20 640 00
1	7/12	1 759 86	135 00	70 39	109 11	25 52	60 00	40 00	440 02	1 319 84	22 399 86
2											

4 Ending Date of Pay Period

5 Earnings and Deductions from Payroll Register

6 New Accumulated Earnings

Current Period Total Earnings	+	Previous Period Accumulated Earnings	=	New Accumulated Earnings
$1,759.86	+	$20,640.00	=	$22,399.86

A business must send a quarterly report to federal and state governments showing employee taxable earnings and taxes withheld from these earnings. A business form used to record details of an employee's earnings and deductions is called an **employee earnings record**. An employee's total earnings and deductions for each pay period are summarized on one line of the employee earnings record.

Whiley prepares a new earnings record for each employee each quarter. Guiren Heng's earnings record for the third quarter is shown here.

Accumulated earnings are often referred to as *year-to-date earnings*. Accumulated earnings are needed for each employee because some payroll taxes do not apply after an employee's earnings reach a certain tax base.

Preparing an Employee Earnings Record

1. Write the last day of the yearly quarter, **September 30, 20--**, at the top of the earnings record.
2. Enter the employee's number, name, marital status, withholding allowances, hourly rate or salary, department, and position in the appropriate space. This information is taken from the employee's personnel records.
3. Record the fiscal year's accumulated earnings, **$20,640.00**, for the beginning of the current quarter. This information is taken from the ending accumulated earnings for the previous quarter. The Accumulated Earnings column of the employee earnings record shows the accumulated earnings since the beginning of the fiscal year.
4. Write the ending date of the current pay period, **7/12**.
5. Enter the total earnings, deductions, and net pay in the assigned columns of the earnings record. This information is taken from the current pay period's payroll register.
6. Calculate and record the new accumulated earnings, **$22,399.86**, on the same line as the other payroll information for the pay period ended July 12.

INPUT

- Explain that a business must send a quarterly report to federal and state governments showing employee taxable earnings and taxes withheld from employee earnings. The employee earnings record is used to record the information needed for these reports.
- Emphasize that an earnings record is maintained for each employee.
- Explain that information for the earnings record is taken from the payroll register each pay period.

MODEL

- Prepare a transparency of the employee earnings record. Use the transparency or the illustration to show entries in the earnings record.
- Record each item in the earnings record, following the six steps shown.
- Direct students to the math illustration to demonstrate the calculation of new accumulated earnings.
- Emphasize that accumulated earnings are the employee's earnings for the year through the current pay period.
- Emphasize that total earnings, not net pay, are added to the accumulated earnings.

DIFFERENTIATED INSTRUCTION

Visual/Spatial students enjoy learning through drawing and physical imagery. Students can draw a picture, chart, or graph illustrating the relationship among the payroll register, commissions record, federal withholding tables, and employee earnings record.

CHECK FOR UNDERSTANDING

Terms Review

- Call on students to define each term in the Terms Review. Definitions are given in the Glossary.

Audit Your Understanding

- Call on students to answer the Audit Your Understanding questions. Answers are given in Appendix D of the textbook.

GUIDED PRACTICE

Work Together

- Have students write the solution to the Work Together problem as you guide the class through the examples.
- Direct students to record each entry in the commissions record, payroll register, and employee's earnings record as you elicit class participation in calculating and recording each entry.

End of Lesson Review

LO1 Explain how employees are paid.

LO2 Calculate employee earnings.

LO3 Prepare payroll reports.

Terms Review

wage
salary
pay period
payroll
payroll taxes
withholding allowance
tax base
payroll register
employee earnings record

Audit your understanding

1. What three federal taxes are withheld from an employee's pay?
2. How is the amount of federal income tax withholding determined?
3. What is the formula for calculating net pay on the payroll register?
4. What amount is added to the accumulated earnings to get the new accumulated earnings to date?

Work together 3-1

Completing payroll records

Coastline Flooring's partial payroll register for the pay period ended July 3, 20--, to be paid July 7, 20--, and a blank earnings record form are provided in the *Working Papers*. Use the appropriate withholding tax tables shown in this lesson to determine the federal income tax. Deductions for all employees are 5% of total earnings for state income tax, 6.2% for social security tax, and 1.45% for Medicare tax. Your instructor will guide you through the following examples. Save your work to complete Work Together 3-2.

1. Prepare a commissions record for Nigella K. Panuska, employee No. 12 and carpet department manager, for June of the current year. Nigella's biweekly salary of $1,200.00 is assigned to the carpet department. She also receives a monthly commission of 4% of carpet net sales and 2% of tile net sales. Commissions for the previous month are paid in the first pay period of the current month. Accounting records for the month ended June 30 of the current year are as follows:

	Carpet	Tile
Sales on account	$6,148.19	$1,706.22
Cash and credit card sales	2,491.96	2,882.03
Sales discounts	104.15	28.11
Sales returns and allowances	321.06	418.95

2. Prepare the payroll register entries for the following two employees:
   a. On line 5: Nigella K. Panuska, employee number 12, carpet department manager, married, and two allowances. Use the commission calculated in instruction 1. Her health insurance premium is $60.00 and retirement plan contribution is $100.00.
   b. On line 6: Andrew T. Webber, employee number 8, tile department clerk, single, one allowance, regular salary of $16.00 per hour with overtime paid at 1½ times the regular rate. He worked 80 hours regular time and 6 hours overtime. His medical insurance premium is $50.00 and retirement plan contribution is $60.00.
3. Complete the payroll register by totaling each amount column.
4. Prepare Andrew's earnings record for the first pay period of the quarter ended September 30, 20--. Accumulated earnings for the quarter ended June 30, 20--, are $18,240.00.

FORMATIVE ASSESSMENT

- This is an ongoing process. Circulate around the classroom or lab, observing which students have problems with the assignments.
- Troubleshooting: Students may have difficulty proving both the payroll register and the employee earnings record. They may need to be reminded that total earnings, not net pay, are added to the accumulated earnings.
- Assess student understanding by checking solutions to Independent Practice assignments and noting their answers to the Terms Review and Audit Your Understanding questions.

End of Lesson Review

On your own 3-1

Completing payroll records

Parker Electronics' partial payroll register for the pay period ended October 8, to be paid October 11, 20--, and a blank earnings record form are provided in the *Working Papers*. Use the appropriate withholding tax tables to determine the federal income tax. Deductions for all employees are 4% of total earnings for state income tax, 6.2% for social security tax, and 1.45% for Medicare tax. Work this problem independently. Save your work to complete On Your Own 3-2.

1. Prepare a commissions record for Destiny P. Tarton, employee No. 6 and video department manager, for September of the current year. Destiny's biweekly salary of $900.00 is assigned to the video department. She also receives a monthly commission of 8% on video net sales and 5% on audio net sales. Commissions for the previous month are paid in the first pay period of the current month. Accounting records for the month ended September 30 of the current year are as follows:

	Audio	Video
Sales on account	$1,483.96	$ 945.68
Cash and credit card sales	5,148.39	4,184.19
Sales discounts	22.04	14.15
Sales returns and allowances	415.16	319.41

2. Prepare the payroll register entries for the following two employees:
   a. On line 5: Destiny P. Tarton, employee number 6, video department manager, single, and three allowances. Use the commission calculated in instruction 1. Her health insurance premium is $100.00 and retirement plan contribution is $200.00.
   b. On line 6: Becky G. Wise, employee number 9, audio department clerk, married, two allowances, regular salary of $14.00 per hour with overtime paid at 1½ times the regular rate. She worked 80 hours regular time and 8 hours overtime. Her medical insurance premium is $80.00 and retirement plan contribution is $75.00.
3. Complete the payroll register by totaling each amount column.
4. Prepare Becky's earnings record for the first pay period of the quarter ended December 31, 20--. Accumulated earnings for the quarter ended September 30, 20--, are $24,652.00.

INDEPENDENT PRACTICE

On Your Own

- Assign the On Your Own problem to be worked independently.
- Use the Formative Assessment techniques to diagnose student understanding.

Application Problem

- Assign Application Problem 3-1.

Online Working Papers

- Students can access the Lesson 3-1 problems using this software.

Website

- Direct students to the C21 Accounting companion website for additional practice and review opportunities throughout the chapter.

RETEACH

- Provide the payroll and withholding information for several employees. Have students calculate the total deductions and net pay.
- Provide a partially completed employee earnings record for each employee. Have students calculate the accumulated earnings.

CLOSURE

- Ask students to summarize briefly the procedure for preparing a payroll register.
- Ask students to summarize the procedure for preparing an employee earnings record.

Essential Questions

- What kinds of premiums can you name that are paid at an overtime rate? (*weekends, holidays, a workday over 8 hours*)
- Would it ever be advantageous for the employee to be paid on commission? Explain. (*yes, if sales are good and regular commissions are predictable for budgeting payments*)

EXTENDED LEARNING

- Assign Accounting in the Real World on page 63.
- Assign Ethics in Action on page 64.
- Assign Global Awareness on page 65.
- Assign Forensic Accounting on page 72.

LESSON 3-2

BRIDGE

- Students learned how to calculate payroll in the previous lesson. However, to this point, nothing has been recorded in the accounting records.
- In this lesson, students will use the information from the payroll register to record the payroll in the proper journals and record and pay payroll taxes.

TEACHING RESOURCES

- **Instructor's Resource CD/Website:**
  PowerPoint Slides
  Accounting Concepts
- **Working Papers:**
  Teacher's Edition of the Working Papers for Lesson 3-2
  Online Working Papers
- **Transparency Masters:**
  Payroll Register
  Cash Payments Journal
  General Journal

ENGAGE

- Emphasize that until the payroll is recorded in the accounts, the accounting records are not affected. Therefore, it is extremely important that the payroll be journalized.
- Discuss the importance of paying withholding and payroll taxes accurately and on time.
- Discuss some of the consequences of not paying on time—additional interest and penalties will be assessed.

PREVIEW

- Call on students to read the accounting terms and definitions introduced in this lesson: *automatic check deposit* and *electronic funds transfer (EFT)*.
- Point out the learning objectives for this lesson.
- Direct students to read the headings in this lesson and to examine the illustrations.

INPUT

- Explain the importance for a business to have a separate bank account for payroll.
- Explain that Whiley writes a check from its general checking account each pay period for the exact amount of the total payroll checks to be prepared. This check is deposited in the payroll account.

LESSON 3-2 Recording a Payroll and Payroll Taxes

LO4 Journalize the payment of a payroll.
LO5 Journalize the payment of payroll taxes.

Payroll Bank Account LO4

Whiley pays its employees biweekly by check. A special payroll checking account and special payroll checks are used. After a biweekly payroll register has been completed, a check is written on Whiley's general checking account, payable to Payroll for the total net pay. This check is deposited in a special payroll checking account against which payroll checks are written for each employee's net pay. This account is reduced to zero as soon as all employees have cashed their payroll checks. Because the special payroll bank account has a balance only until all payroll checks are cashed, no special account is needed in the general ledger.

Automatic Check Deposit

Employees may authorize an employer to deposit payroll checks directly in their accounts at a specified bank. Depositing payroll checks directly to an employee's checking or savings account is called **automatic check deposit**.

Employers may also transfer payroll checks electronically from the employer's account directly to the employee's bank account. A computerized cash payments system that transfers funds without the use of checks, currency, or other paper documents is called **electronic funds transfer (EFT)**. Electronic funds transfer eliminates the need for preparing payroll checks. Under this system, each employee receives a statement of earnings and deductions similar to the detachable stub on a payroll check.

The use of automatic check deposit or electronic funds transfer for payroll does not change the accounting procedures for recording payroll. [CONCEPT: Consistent Reporting]

Journalizing Payment of a Payroll

1 Date
2 Salary Expense Accounts
3 Check Number
4 Salary Expense

CASH PAYMENTS JOURNAL — PAGE 13

	DATE	ACCOUNT TITLE	CK. NO.	POST. REF.	1 GENERAL DEBIT	2 GENERAL CREDIT	3 ACCOUNTS PAYABLE DEBIT	4 PURCH. DISCOUNT CR. GRILLS	5 PURCH. DISCOUNT CR. FURNITURE	6 CASH CREDIT	
13	16	Salary Expense—Grills	820		2 852 84					9 029 21	13
14		Salary Expense—Furniture			4 953 92						14
15		Salary Expense—Administrative			4 464 00						15
16		Employee Income Tax Payable—Federal				952 00					16
17		Employee Income Tax Payable—State				490 83					17
18		Social Security Tax Payable				760 79					18
19		Medicare Tax Payable				177 93					19
20		Medical Insurance Payable				525 00					20
21		Retirement Plan Payable				335 00					21
22											22

Liability Accounts 5
Liability Amounts 6
Net Pay 7

- Ask students what advantages automatic check deposit provides for the employee who chooses to have a payroll check deposited directly to a bank account.
- Ask students what advantages EFT (electronic funds transfer) provides for the employer who arranges to have payroll amounts electronically transferred to employee bank accounts.

Whiley's payroll register contains the information needed to journalize a payroll as shown in the cash payments journal. The source document for journalizing a payroll payment is the check written for the net payroll amount. [CONCEPT: Objective Evidence]

July 16. Paid cash for biweekly payroll, $9,029.21 (total payroll: grills, $2,852.84; furniture, $4,953.92; administrative, $4,464.00; less deductions: employee income tax—federal, $952.00; employee income tax—state, $490.83; social security tax, $760.79; Medicare tax, $177.93; medical insurance, $525.00; retirement plan, $335.00). Check No. 820.

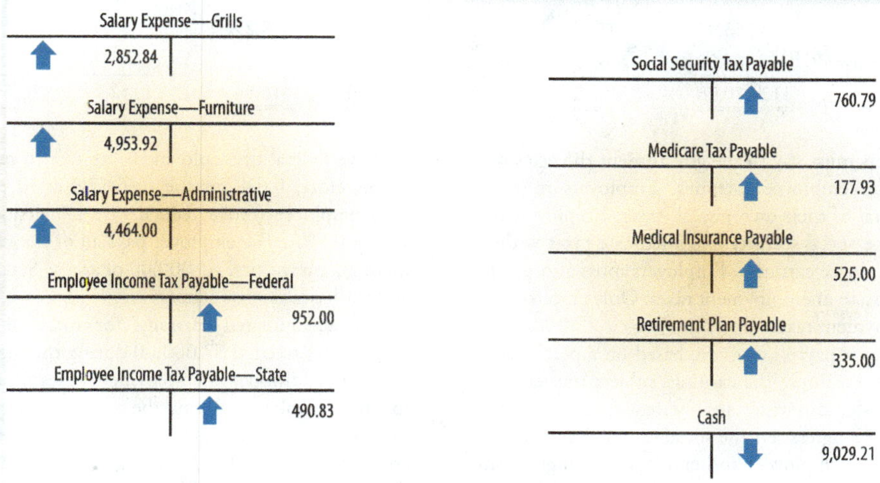

Journalizing Payment of a Payroll

1. Write the date, 16, in the Date column of the cash payments journal.
2. Record the salary expense accounts, Salary Expense—Grills, Salary Expense—Furniture, and Salary Expense—Administrative, in the Account Title column.
3. Enter the check number, 820, in the Ck. No. column.
4. Write the salary expense amounts, $2,852.84, $4,953.92, and $4,464.00 in the General Debit column.
5. Enter the liability accounts, Employee Income Tax Payable—Federal, Employee Income Tax Payable—State, Social Security Tax Payable, Medicare Tax Payable, Medical Insurance Payable, and Retirement Plan Payable, in the Account Title column.
6. Record the liability amounts, $952.00, $490.83, $760.79, $177.93, $525.00, and $335.00, in the General Credit column.
7. Write the net pay, $9,029.21, in the Cash Credit column.

Employer Payroll Taxes LO5

Most employers have four separate payroll taxes:

1. Employer social security tax
2. Employer Medicare tax
3. Federal unemployment tax
4. State unemployment tax

Unemployment taxes are used to pay cash benefits to qualified workers for limited periods of unemployment.

INPUT

- Explain that the payroll register column totals are the source of information needed to prepare a journal entry for the payroll.
- Explain that the departmental total earnings columns of the payroll register are the debit amounts for the departmental salary expense.
- Explain that the Net Pay column is the credit amount for Cash.
- Explain that all other columns provide the credit parts of the entry. These credits become liabilities; so if you add "Payable" to the end of each column heading, you have the liability account.
- Explain that because cash is paid out (net pay to employees), the payroll transaction is recorded in a cash payments journal.
- Because this journal entry uses a multiple-line entry, it is important to reinforce the concept that debits must always equal credits.
- Read the transaction statement.

MODEL

Analyze the transaction

- Use the transparency prepared for the previous lesson to review the information recorded in the various columns of a payroll register.
- Draw ten T accounts on the board.
- Read each column total from the payroll register.
- Ask students to analyze the treatment of each column total by determining the following: whether the total is part of the payroll entry, in which account the amount should be entered, and whether it is a debit or credit entry. Complete the T accounts as the information is provided.
- Emphasize that only the column totals for departmental total earnings are journalized.

Record the transaction

- Prepare a transparency of a cash payments journal to illustrate journalizing the payroll transactions.
- Record each item in the journal, following the seven steps shown.
- Add the debit entries and add the credit entries to show that the total debit entries equal the total credit entries.

INPUT

- Remind students that employers pay four separate payroll taxes: Two are the same amounts withheld from employees' pay—(1) social security tax and (2) Medicare tax. Two additional payroll taxes the employer must pay are (1) federal unemployment tax and (2) state unemployment tax.
- Explain that the total earnings subject to unemployment tax is referred to as unemployment taxable earnings.
- Explain that information for calculating the unemployment taxable earnings is found on the employee earnings record and the current payroll register.
- Explain that the effective tax rate in most states is 0.8% for federal unemployment tax and 5.4% for state unemployment tax. Both taxes are paid on the first $7,000.00 of each employee's earnings each year.
- Emphasize that payroll taxes are a direct result of the employees working in each department. For this reason, payroll taxes are reported by department.
- Emphasize that the total of all employer payroll taxes is an expense to the business.

MODEL

- Review the calculations shown in the illustration at the top of the page. Point out to students where the information was obtained for total taxable earnings, total social security tax, and total Medicare tax for the pay period.
- Review the calculations shown in the illustration at the bottom of the page.

TEACHING IDEA **Draw a Venn diagram on the board. Ask students to label the payroll taxes each employee paid, payroll taxes the employer paid, and taxes they both paid.**

Calculating Employer Payroll Taxes

Department	Social Security Earnings	Social Security 6.2%	Medicare 1.45%	FUTA Earnings	Federal Unemployment 0.6%	State Unemployment 5.4%	Total Payroll Taxes
Grills	$ 2,852.84	$176.88	$ 41.37	$1,275.00	$ 7.65	$ 68.85	$ 294.75
Furniture	4,953.92	307.14	71.83	1,548.00	9.29	83.59	471.85
Administrative	4,464.00	276.77	64.73	—	—	—	341.50
	$12,270.76	$760.79	$177.93	$2,823.00	$16.94	$152.44	$1,108.10

Employers must pay to the government the taxes withheld from employee earnings. Employers must also pay several of their own payroll taxes. Employers must match the social security and Medicare taxes withheld from employee earnings. Employers must also pay federal and state unemployment taxes. Only employers pay unemployment taxes.

Employer payroll taxes are based on a percentage of employee earnings. The earnings subject to social security and Medicare taxes are referred to as *social security earnings*. Congress sets the social security and Medicare tax rates for employees and employers. Congress often changes the tax rates and tax base. The social security tax rate used in this text is 6.2% of earnings up to the tax base—a maximum of $113,700.00 each calendar year. The Medicare tax rate used in this text is 1.45% of total employee earnings. The employer social security tax (6.2%) and Medicare tax (1.45%) rates are the same as the rates used for employees.

The calculation of social security and Medicare taxes for Whiley's latest payroll period is shown above. None of its employee's accumulated earnings has exceeded the $113,700.00 social security tax base. Therefore, the social security and Medicare taxes are calculated using total earnings for each department.

The federal unemployment tax used in this text is 6.0% of the first $7,000.00 earned by each employee. Earnings subject to unemployment taxes are referred to as *FUTA earnings*. An employer generally can deduct the amounts paid to state unemployment funds from federal unemployment payments. This deduction cannot be more than 5.4% of taxable earnings. The effective federal unemployment tax rate in most states is, therefore, 0.6% on the first $7,000.00 earned by each employee (6.0% federal – 5.4% deductible for state = 0.6%). The employer pays all of the unemployment tax on the first $7,000.00 of salary. State tax rates and tax bases vary by state.

The accumulated earnings for most of Whiley's employees exceeded $7,000.00 during the first quarter. Thus, no additional unemployment taxes must be paid for these employees during the second quarter. Whiley hired two employees during the second quarter. Neither employee's accumulated earnings exceeded $7,000.00 during the quarter. Whiley must pay unemployment on these earnings during the second quarter. The calculation of FUTA and SUTA taxes for Whiley's latest payroll period is shown above.

Whiley reports employee earnings by department to determine what expenses were incurred in earning each department's revenue. Payroll taxes are a direct result of the employees working in each department. Therefore, payroll tax expenses are also reported by department.

The salary column totals of the payroll register are used to calculate the employer's payroll taxes for each department. These calculations are summarized in the table at the top of the page. The calculations for the grills department are shown below as an example.

Rounding differences can occur when percentage calculations are performed on parts of a total amount and then compared with the percentage of the total. To correct the one-cent rounding error, add or subtract the rounding error to the larger of the department tax amounts.

	Total Taxable Earnings		Tax Rate		Grills Department Tax
Social Security	$2,852.84	×	6.20%	=	$176.88
Medicare	2,852.84	×	1.45%	=	41.37
Unemployment—Federal	1,275.00	×	0.60%	=	7.65
Unemployment—State	1,275.00	×	5.40%	=	68.85
Total Grills Department Payroll Tax Expense					$294.75

DIFFERENTIATED LEARNING

Auditory/Linguistic learners have highly developed auditory skills and often use language as a means to remember information. Invite someone who works for the IRS or the state tax office or a tax accountant to speak to the class. The speaker could explain unemployment payments and benefits in greater detail, as well as tax laws.

Journalizing Employer Payroll Taxes

1 Date
2 Department Expense Accounts
3 Memorandum Number
4 Departmental Payroll Tax Amounts
5 Liability Accounts
6 Liability Amounts

GENERAL JOURNAL — PAGE 10

	DATE		ACCOUNT TITLE	DOC. NO.	POST. REF.	DEBIT	CREDIT	
16		16	Payroll Taxes Expense—Grills	M69		294 75		16
17			Payroll Taxes Expense—Furniture			471 85		17
18			Payroll Taxes Expense—Administrative			341 50		18
19			Social Security Tax Payable				760 79	19
20			Medicare Tax Payable				177 93	20
21			Unemployment Tax Payable—Federal				16 94	21
22			Unemployment Tax Payable—State				152 44	22
23								23
24								24

July 16. Recorded employer payroll taxes for the biweekly pay period ended July 16. Taxes owed are social security tax, $760.79; Medicare tax, $177.93; federal unemployment tax, $16.94; state unemployment tax, $152.44; total payroll taxes by department are grills, $294.75; furniture, $471.85; and administrative, $341.50. Memorandum No. 69.

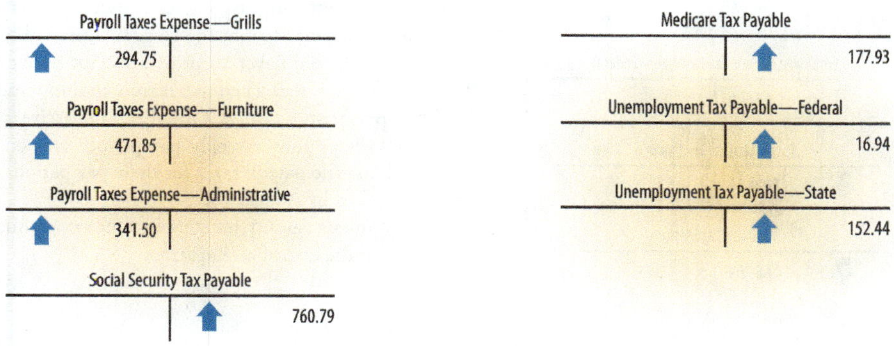

Journalizing Employer Payroll Taxes

1. Write the date, 16, in the Date column of the general journal.
2. Write the expense account titles, Payroll Taxes Expense—Grills, Payroll Taxes Expense—Furniture, and Payroll Taxes Expense—Administrative, in the Account Title column.
3. Enter the source document, M69, in the Doc. No. column.
4. Record each department's payroll taxes expense, $294.75, $471.85, and $341.50, in the Debit column.
5. Write the liability account titles, Social Security Tax Payable, Medicare Tax Payable, Unemployment Tax Payable—Federal, and Unemployment Tax Payable—State, in the Account Title column.
6. Enter the liability amounts, $760.79, $177.93, $16.94, and $152.44, in the Credit column.

INPUT

- Explain that because cash is not involved when the employer payroll taxes are recorded, the taxes must be recorded in the general journal.
- Emphasize the three departments that are debited for payroll taxes expense.

MODEL

Analyze the transaction

- Draw seven blank T accounts on the board.
- Read the transaction statement.
- Ask students to analyze the transaction. Determine whether each account is increased or decreased and whether the account is debited or credited. Complete the T accounts as the information is provided.

Record the transaction

- Prepare a transparency of a general journal to illustrate journalizing the employer payroll taxes.
- Record each item in the journal, following the six steps shown. Add the three debit entries. Add the four credit entries. Make sure that total debits equal total credits.

DIFFERENTIATED LEARNING

Intrapersonal learners often prefer to work alone. Ask students to research payroll processing companies. Students can report to the class the services provided by these companies and the costs involved.

INPUT

- Explain that the frequency and method of payment of withheld employees' federal income tax, social security tax, and Medicare tax plus employer's social security tax and Medicare tax is determined by the total amount of tax paid each year.
- Explain that businesses with large amounts of payroll taxes pay more frequently.
- Point out that most businesses are required to deposit federal payroll taxes using the Electronic Federal Tax Payment System and transferring the funds directly from their bank account to the government.
- Explain that employees' withheld income taxes, social security taxes, and Medicare taxes are paid in one payment.
- Point out that paying the liabilities for employee income tax, social security tax, and Medicare tax is a reduction in the liability accounts and a reduction in the Cash account; thus, the liability accounts are debited and Cash is credited.
- Ask students if any part of this transaction can be entered in a special column of the cash payments journal.
- Explain that the only account titles entered in the Account Title column are for those entries in the General Debit or General Credit columns.

MODEL

Analyze the transaction

- Draw a stack of four blank T accounts on the board.
- Read the transaction statement.
- Ask students to analyze the transaction, determining debit and credit parts. Complete the T accounts as the information is provided.

Record the transaction

- Use a cash payments journal transparency to illustrate recording the transaction.
- Record each item in the journal, following the five arrows shown in the illustration.

Journalizing Payment of Federal Income Tax, Social Security Tax, and Medicare Tax Liabilities

CASH PAYMENTS JOURNAL — PAGE 15

	DATE	ACCOUNT TITLE	CK. NO.	POST. REF.	1 GENERAL DEBIT	2 GENERAL CREDIT	3 ACCOUNTS PAYABLE DEBIT	4 PURCH. DISCOUNT CR. GRILLS	5 PURCH. DISCOUNT CR. FURNITURE	6 CASH CREDIT	
22	15	Employee Income Tax Payable—Federal	M76		2,047.00					5,655.90	22
23		Social Security Tax Payable			2,924.86						23
24		Medicare Tax Payable			684.04						24
25											25

Date — Liability Accounts — Memorandum Number — Liability Amounts — Payment Amount

Employers must pay to federal, state, and local governments all payroll taxes withheld from employee earnings as well as the employer payroll taxes. Federal and state laws govern the frequency of payments.

August 15. Made a deposit using the EFTPS for payroll tax liabilities: employee federal income tax, $2,047.00, employees' and employer's social security tax, $2,924.86, and Medicare tax, $684.04; total, $5,655.90. Memorandum No. 76.

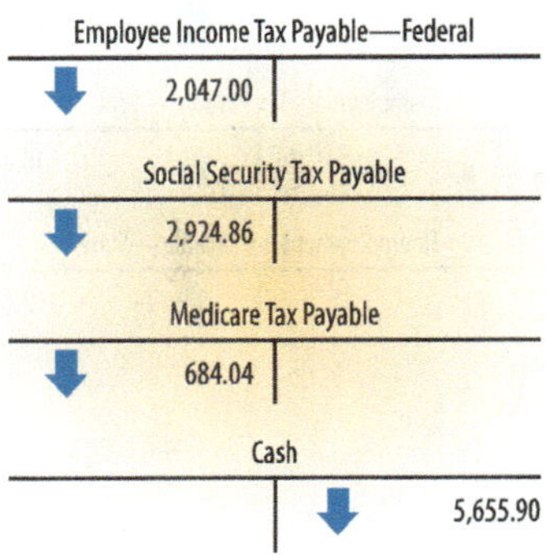

fyi Employers with large payroll tax liabilities must make more frequent deposits. A business that deposits more than $50,000 in a calendar year is classified as a semiweekly schedule depositor. If a payroll tax liability of $100,000 or more is accumulated on any day, the business must deposit the taxes on the next business day. Consult the most recent Internal Revenue Service publications for specific deposit rules.

The total amount of tax paid each year determines the frequency and method of payment of employee and employer payroll taxes. The greater the amount of taxes owed, the more frequently the liability must be paid. Whiley is classified as a monthly schedule depositor. A monthly schedule depositor must deposit the taxes by the 15th day of the next month.

Most employers are required to deposit federal payroll taxes using the Electronic Federal Tax Payment System (EFTPS). Either by computer or telephone, the business can have the deposit transferred directly from its bank account to the government. The EFTPS allows the employer to print a receipt of the deposit. This receipt is attached to a memorandum to document the payment of cash. [CONCEPT: Objective Evidence]

Whiley's July biweekly pay periods end on July 12 and 26. The payroll taxes for these pay periods must be deposited by August 15.

Whiley's liability for state income tax withholding is paid at the end of each quarter.

© vgstudio/Shutterstock.com

Journalizing Payment of Federal Unemployment Tax Liability

CASH PAYMENTS JOURNAL — PAGE 13

	DATE		ACCOUNT TITLE	CK. NO.	POST. REF.	1 GENERAL DEBIT	2 GENERAL CREDIT	3 ACCOUNTS PAYABLE DEBIT	4 PURCH. DISCOUNT CR. GRILLS	5 PURCH. DISCOUNT CR. FURNITURE	6 CASH CREDIT	
22		29	*Unemployment Tax Payable—Federal*	*M79*		501 75					501 75	22
23		29	*Unemployment Tax Payable—State*	*849*		735 75					735 75	23
24												24

Date — Liability Accounts — Document Number — Liability Amounts — Payment Amounts

If the federal unemployment tax liability for a business is $500.00 or more at the end of a quarter, it must pay the tax by the end of the following month. Any unpaid federal unemployment tax must be paid by January 31 of the following year.

Whiley's federal unemployment tax liability at the end of the first quarter did not exceed $500.00. Thus, no payment was made in April. The liability at the end of the second quarter is $501.75. Whiley must deposit this amount by the end of July, the following month.

Federal unemployment taxes are deposited using the EFTPS. A receipt of the deposit is attached to a memorandum to document the payment of cash. [CONCEPT: Objective Evidence]

July 29. Paid cash for federal unemployment tax liability for quarter ended June 30, $501.75. Memorandum No. 79.

Unemployment Tax Payable—Federal	
501.75	

Cash	
	501.75

THINK LIKE AN ACCOUNTANT

Labor Costs

The board of directors knows that the corporation will soon be required to renew its contract with its labor union. To ensure that management understands the money issues, the board asked the Accounting department to prepare an analysis of the labor costs. This analysis is to include all taxes and benefits paid.

Melinda Loggins, one of your colleagues, has prepared a first draft of the analysis. Her worksheet contains a schedule that calculates the employee and employer taxes for a worker having a $50,000 salary. The schedule also includes estimates of voluntary deductions, such as health insurance and retirement contributions. The corporation currently pays 60% of every employee's health insurance premiums. The corporation also matches the employee's retirement plan contributions.

"I used a pie chart, so that the board could see what portion of the total labor costs consists of employer taxes and contributions," Melinda stated proudly. "The supporting data, taken from the schedule, are to the right of the chart. So if you decide to make any changes, those are the data reflected in the chart."

OPEN THE SPREADSHEET TLA_CH03

The worksheet contains the pie chart and its supporting schedules. Follow the steps on the Instructions tab. Modify the chart to improve the information communicated to the board. Answer the following questions:

1. Which pie chart design provides the best information?
2. Prepare a brief statement that summarizes the information provided in the chart.
3. How does changing the chart type and format improve understanding?
4. What other changes would you propose?

INPUT

- Explain that federal unemployment insurance is paid by the end of the month following each quarter if the liability is more than $500.00. Explain that the payment is made through EFTPS.
- Explain that paying the liability for federal unemployment tax is a reduction in the liability account and a reduction in the Cash account; thus, the liability account, Unemployment Tax Payable—Federal, is debited and Cash is credited.
- Ask students if any part of this transaction can be entered in a special column of the cash payments journal.
- Explain that the only account titles entered in the Account Title column are for those entries in the General Debit or General Credit column.

MODEL

Analyze the transaction

- Draw two blank T accounts on the board.
- Read the transaction statement.
- Ask students to analyze the transaction, determining debit and credit parts. Complete the T accounts as the information is provided.

Record the transaction

- Use a cash payments journal transparency to illustrate recording the transaction.
- Record each item in the journal, following the five arrows shown.

THINK LIKE AN ACCOUNTANT

Answers

Although charts are a powerful tool for communicating data, charting tools and options must be applied correctly. This activity begins by enabling students to critique an existing pie-of-pie chart. Students are then directed to change the chart to a simple pie chart. By rotating the chart and reducing the number of data items, students are exposed to good charting techniques.

Answers will vary based on students' personal preferences.

See a suggested solution for this feature in the Instructional Strategies section at the front of this book.

INPUT

- Explain that requirements for paying state unemployment taxes vary from state to state. Explain that the payment is made through EFTPS.
- Explain that paying the liability for state unemployment tax is a reduction in the liability account and a reduction in the Cash account; thus, the liability account, Unemployment Tax Payable—State, is debited and Cash is credited.
- Ask students if any part of this transaction can be entered in a special column of the cash payments journal.
- Explain that the only account titles entered in the Account Title column are for those entries in the General Debit or General Credit column.

MODEL

Analyze the transaction

- Draw two blank T accounts on the board.
- Read the transaction statement.
- Ask students to analyze the transaction, determining debit and credit parts. Complete the T accounts as the information is provided.

Record the transaction

- Use a cash payments journal transparency to illustrate recording the transaction, as shown on page 81.
- Record each item in the journal, following the five arrows as shown for federal unemployment tax.

WHY ACCOUNTING?

Answers

1. Answers will vary, but should include some of the following points: Restricted stock is shares of stock that can be purchased once specific conditions have been met. The conditions can be financial goals, such as earnings per share or return on investment. The conditions could also require continued employment with the company for a specified number of years.
2. Answers will vary, but may include health insurance provided by the company, dental insurance, payments to an employee retirement plan, unemployment taxes (state and federal), sick days or days away from work, vacation pay, social security taxes, and Medicare taxes.

Journalizing Payment of State Unemployment Tax Liability

Requirements for paying state unemployment taxes vary from state to state. Usually, employers are required to pay the state unemployment tax during the month following each calendar quarter.

Whiley's state unemployment tax for the second quarter is $735.75.

July 29. Paid cash for state unemployment tax liability for quarter ended June 30, $735.75. Check No. 849.

Unemployment Tax Payable—State	
735.75	

Cash	
	735.75

WHY ACCOUNTING?

Executive Compensation

When determining how to configure a compensation plan for a company executive, the human resource manager has to consider many things. A compensation plan should motivate the executive to take actions that are in the best interests of the company. However, the compensation plan must also contain items important to the executive.

The human resource manager must also understand that not all forms of compensation affect the company's financial statements in the same way. One example of this is how stock options have been treated over time.

Prior to 2006, many companies offered stock options to their executives. A stock option is the right to purchase a share of stock in the future at a set price. An executive would exercise his or her option if the value of the stock increased above the option price. The benefit to the company was that the value of the option was not counted as an expense in the company's records. Therefore, executives could receive this benefit with no negative impact on the company's net income.

In 2006, GAAP began to require that stock options be expensed, thereby decreasing the company's net income. A human resource manager who was not aware of this accounting change might continue including stock options in compensation packages and greatly reduce the net income reported on the company's income statement.

CRITICAL THINKING

1. At the time of publication, restricted stock was not required to be expensed. Write a one-paragraph description of restricted stock.
2. Besides actual salary, what other items should be included when calculating the cost of hiring one employee?

© iStockphoto.com/Aleksko

FORMATIVE ASSESSMENT

- This is an ongoing process. Circulate around the classroom or lab, observing which students have problems with the assignments.
- Troubleshooting: Diagnose the problems students have with this lesson. Students sometimes have difficulty entering the affected accounts in the journals because each account title except Cash must be entered in the Account Title column. Also, students must ensure that total debits equal total credits for each transaction.
- Assess student understanding by checking solutions to Independent Practice assignments and noting their answers to the Terms Review and Audit Your Understanding questions.

End of Lesson Review

LO4 Journalize the payment of a payroll.

LO5 Journalize the payment of payroll taxes.

Terms Review

automatic check deposit

electronic funds transfer (EFT)

Audit your understanding

1. When a payroll is journalized, which account is credited for the total net amount paid to all employees?
2. What four separate payroll taxes do most employers have to pay?
3. How are most employers required to deposit federal payroll taxes?

Work together 3-2

Journalizing and paying payroll and payroll taxes

Use the solution from Work Together 3-1. A cash payments journal, page 15, and general journal, page 7, are provided in the *Working Papers*. Your instructor will guide you through the following examples.

1. Calculate departmental payroll taxes for the pay period ended July 3. No employees have earned more than the social security tax base. Unemployment taxes are due on the following earnings for this period: Carpet, $1,330.00; and Tile, $1,851.42.
2. Journalize the following transactions for July of the current year.

Transactions:

July 7. Paid the July 3 payroll. Check No. 568.

7. Recorded employer's payroll taxes for the pay period ended July 3. Memorandum No. 55.

15. Made a deposit using the EFTPS for employee and employer payroll taxes for the June pay periods: employee federal income tax withholding, $1,159.00; social security tax, $2,230.52; and Medicare tax, $521.67. Memorandum No. 56.

29. Made a deposit using the EFTPS for federal unemployment taxes for the first and second quarter, $523.69. Memorandum No. 57.

29. Paid state unemployment tax for the quarter ended June 30, $303.16. Check No. 579.

On your own 3-2

Journalizing and paying payroll and payroll taxes

Use the solution from On Your Own 3-1. A cash payments journal, page 18, and general journal, page 10, are provided in the *Working Papers*. Work independently to complete the following problem.

1. Calculate departmental payroll taxes for the pay period ended October 8. No employees have earned more than the social security tax base. Unemployment taxes are due on the following earnings for this period: Audio, $1,568.00; and Administrative, $1,628.00.
2. Journalize the following transactions for October of the current year.

Transactions:

Oct. 11. Paid the October 8 payroll. Check No. 772.

11. Recorded employer's payroll taxes for the pay period ended October 8. Memorandum No. 68.

15. Made a deposit using the EFTPS for employee and employer payroll taxes for the September pay periods: employee federal income tax withholding, $1,278.00; social security tax, $2,243.48; and Medicare tax, $524.73. Memorandum No. 69.

29. Made a deposit using the EFTPS for federal unemployment taxes for the first three quarters, $508.84. Memorandum No. 73.

29. Paid state unemployment tax for the quarter ended September 30, $331.99. Check No. 785.

CHECK FOR UNDERSTANDING

Terms Review

- Call on students to define each term in the Terms Review. Definitions are given in the Glossary.

Audit Your Understanding

- Call on students to answer the Audit Your Understanding questions. Answers are given in Appendix D of the textbook.

GUIDED PRACTICE

Work Together

- Have students write the solution to the Work Together problem as you guide the class through the examples.
- Direct students to record departmental payroll tax amounts as you elicit class participation in analyzing the transaction.
- Direct students to record each transaction in the cash payments journal or general journal as you elicit class participation in analyzing and recording the transaction.

INDEPENDENT PRACTICE

On Your Own

- Assign the On Your Own problem to be worked independently.
- Use the Formative Assessment techniques to diagnose student understanding.

Application Problem

- Assign Application Problem 3-2.

Online Working Papers

- Students can access the Lesson 3-2 problems using this software.

RETEACH

- Ask a student to make up an original payment of a payroll transaction statement. Write the statement on the board. Ask another student to explain how the transaction should be journalized, following the appropriate steps for journalizing payment of a payroll.
- Ask another student to make up an employer payroll taxes transaction for a company with two departments. Write the statement on the board. Ask another student to explain how the transaction should be journalized, following the appropriate steps.

CLOSURE

- Ask students to summarize briefly the procedure for journalizing and paying payroll and payroll taxes.

Essential Questions

- Do you think it is fair that an employer that has not reduced its workforce must pay the same amount of unemployment taxes as an employer who has had numerous layoffs? Explain. (*Answers will vary. Most students will think it is not fair.*)
- What are some ways companies can reduce the costs of payroll without changing the number of employees or changing salaries? (*Answers might include lobbying the government for reduced social security, changing insurance and/or benefit plans, locating in geographical areas with fewer or lower taxes, freezing wages and benefits, and minimizing or eliminating overtime.*)

EXTENDED LEARNING

- Assign Think Like an Accountant on page 81.
- Assign Why Accounting on page 82.

A Look at Accounting Software

Some students might think that the information that Whiley keeps on Juanita Denton, such as ethnicity and gender, encroaches on her privacy. All of the information is required by the IRS and other governmental agencies or is needed to manage her employment with the company. For example, the U.S. Department of Labor requires the data on ethnicity and gender to monitor compliance with equal opportunity employment.

Students could be asked to imagine how Ms. Denton's information would be used by the system. Examples: Her name and address would be printed on her deposit confirmation statement. (She is on direct deposit and does not receive a printed paycheck.) Her compensation information and number of allowances would be used to compute her wages, commission, benefits, taxes, and net pay. Her social security number would be used to report her tax withholding to the IRS. Her department number would enable the system to departmentalize her salary expense. Her employee number would enable the system to organize information related to her employment and to display or print that information as requested.

A Look at Accounting Software

Managing Employee Information

In a manual accounting system, information needed for managing and paying employees is maintained on several forms. Some payroll information is maintained in employee earnings records. Other information required by government regulatory and taxing agencies is kept in a file for each employee. In larger companies, a Human Resources (HR) Department maintains these files.

A computerized accounting system maintains all employee information in the Manage Employees module. Due to the confidentiality of the information, access to this module is strictly controlled by system security measures. Only authorized persons can view this information. Often, only a few individuals are authorized to enter and edit it.

The Set Up Accounts tab in the Enter/Edit Company Information window was illustrated in A Look at Accounting Software in Chapter 1. Many of the features on that tab operate in the same way on the Set Up Employees tab illustrated in this chapter.

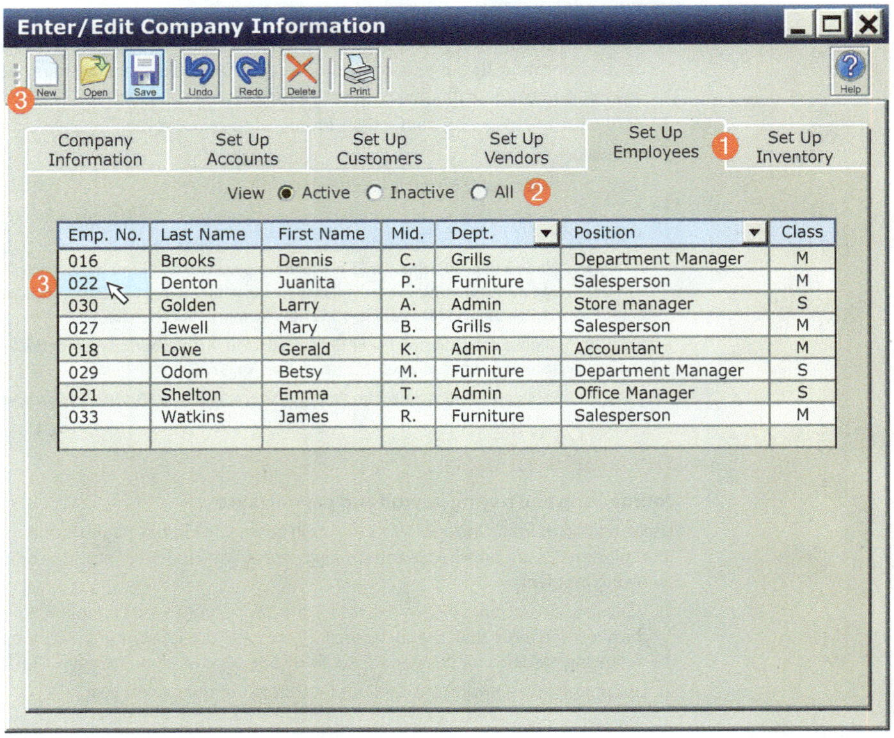

1. The user clicks on the **Set Up Employees** tab in the Enter/Edit Company Information window.
2. The **View Active** button is the system default setting. The user can narrow the list of employees displayed by selecting **Inactive** or **All** and by using the drop-down lists in the Dept. and Position columns.
3. To set up a new employee, the user clicks **New** on the menu bar. In this illustration, the user has double-clicked on employee number 022 to open the Manage Employees window for Juanita Denton.

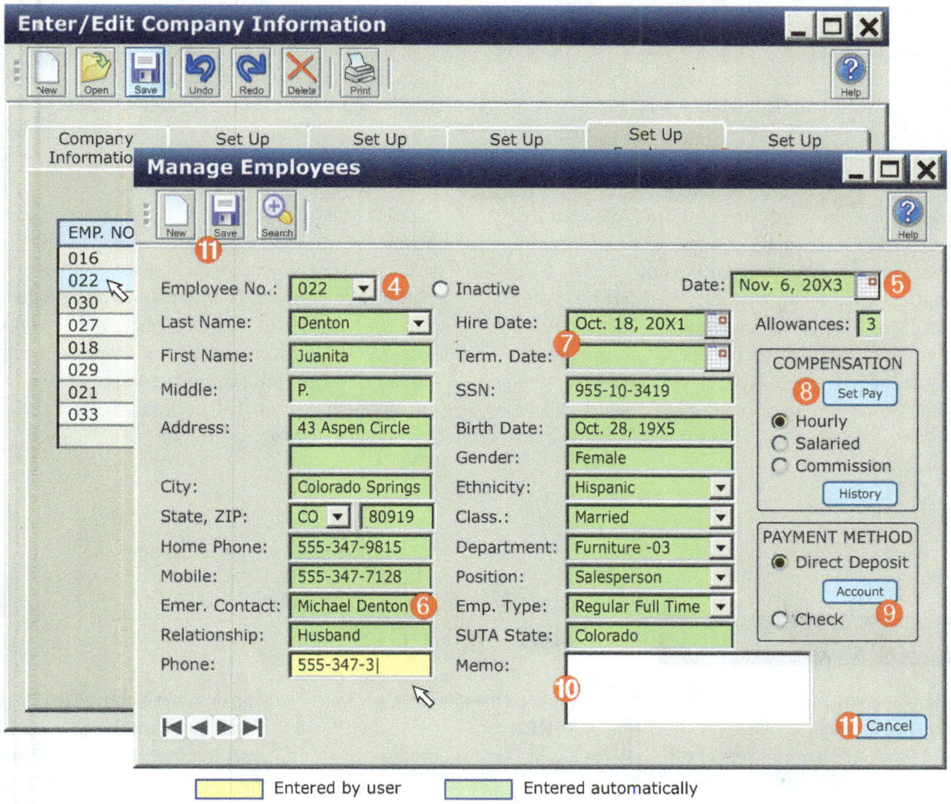

4 If the user were entering a new employee, this pop-up window would be mostly empty. The date would be displayed along with the next sequential employee number set by the system. Some fields would display default settings, such as Hourly and Direct Deposit, which were determined to be most likely when management programmed the system. Since Juanita Denton is already an employee, this screen is displayed with all her current data. The Manage Employees window collects all the information necessary to (1) prepare the payroll and (2) comply with federal, state, and local tax codes.

5 The system date is displayed. It cannot be changed.

6 Whiley maintains emergency contact information for each employee as part of its emergency preparedness plan. The user is keying a new phone number for Juanita Denton's emergency contact.

7 Other key information, required by the federal government, is the hire date and termination date of each employee.

8 Compensation data are required by the system to process payroll. Either **Hourly** or **Salaried** can be selected, but **Commission** can be selected in addition to either of those. Clicking the **Set Pay** button would open another pop-up window to enter the rate of pay, overtime, vacation, and benefits. The **History** button would let the user view all year-to-date payments to the employee or to select a range of payments.

9 When direct deposit is set up for an employee, the user would click the **Account** button and enter the routing number and account number for the linked bank account.

10 The memo field allows the user to enter notes pertaining to employee issues, problems, training, advancement potential, etc.

11 Clicking **Cancel** erases any changes and clears the screen. Clicking **Save** records the new information and prepares the window for the entry of a new employee.

CLOSURE

- Review the Chapter Summary.
- Demonstrate at least one activity or transaction from each lesson.

Essential Questions

- Paying taxes late carries serious implications. What procedures can be implemented to ensure that taxes are paid on time? (*Answers might include assigning two individuals who are responsible each month for the payment of taxes.*)
- Payroll fraud is costly to an employer. What policies might you put in place to prevent payroll fraud? (*Answers will vary, but could include fingerprinting employees instead of using time cards, verifying employees by checking photo identification, and having another employee, not the manager, complete payroll records.*)

EXTENDED LEARNING

- Review A Look at Accounting Software on pages 84 and 85.
- Assign Explore Accounting on page 86.

EXPLORE ACCOUNTING

Answers

1. The primary reason for Congress allowing employees to defer taxes is to encourage individuals to save for retirement and to pay for medical expenses.
2. Money cannot be withdrawn from retirement plans without penalty until employees are age 59½. Tax rates could be higher when individuals withdraw tax-deferred funds, resulting in higher taxes paid.
3. Amounts contributed to a tax-deferred health care plan can only be used for approved health care expenses. Amounts not spent during the plan period cannot be reimbursed to the individual.

Chapter Summary

Businesses must keep accurate records of employee earnings and the related payroll taxes. Employers are required to withhold federal income, social security, and Medicare taxes from the employees' total earnings. Some employers must also withhold state and city income taxes. Employees can elect to have medical insurance, retirement contributions, and other items deducted from their total earnings. These withholdings are liabilities of the business until paid.

Hourly employees are paid a set wage rate for all hours worked. Most employers are required to pay employees overtime pay for hours worked over 40 hours per week. The overtime pay rate is typically 1½ times the regular pay rate. Some employees earn a fixed salary each pay period. An employee's earnings can also include a commission on sales.

A payroll register summarizes the earnings, deductions, and net pay of all employees. A business can classify employee earnings by department. The payroll register is used to update an employee earnings record, a form useful in submitting quarterly and annual payroll tax reports to government agencies.

Employers must also pay payroll taxes. These taxes include social security, Medicare, federal unemployment, and state unemployment taxes. Employer payroll taxes can be classified by department. The federal government has rules that govern when and how taxes are to be deposited. Most employers must deposit employee and employer payroll taxes using the Electronic Federal Tax Payment System (EFTPS). Each state determines how its state taxes are deposited.

EXPLORE ACCOUNTING Pretax Benefits

© iStockphoto.com/Makhnach_M

Federal income tax is a major expense for most families. Current laws permit employers to set up retirement and health care plans that allow employees to set aside a portion of their earnings on a pretax basis. Employees pay no taxes in that tax year on the amounts withheld.

Retirement Plans

For amounts placed in many qualified retirement accounts, income tax is "deferred" on earnings. Individuals will pay income taxes on the amounts withdrawn from their retirement accounts when they retire. Because of the income tax deferral, the amount available at retirement will be much larger. The general requirements of most pretax retirement plans include the following:

1. The employer withholds the specified amount and deposits it in qualified investments, such as mutual funds.
2. The amount of earnings an employee can defer each year is limited.
3. Employees are assessed penalties if they withdraw amounts from their retirement account before the age of 59½.
4. Withdrawals from retirement plan accounts must begin by the time the person reaches age 70½.

Health Care and Childcare Plans

Employees may be permitted to have a portion of their pretax earnings deducted from their salaries. These amounts are then used to reimburse out-of-pocket medical or childcare expenses. The advantage is that payment is made with pretax dollars. However, the amount of earnings withheld is available only for the purpose designated. For example, if an employee authorizes $50.00 a month to be withheld for medical costs but uses only $500.00 during the year, the remaining $100.00 that was withheld is not paid back to the employee.

INSTRUCTIONS

1. Why would Congress allow employees to defer taxes on contributions to a retirement plan?
2. Are there any disadvantages to participating in a tax-deferred retirement plan?
3. Are there any disadvantages to participating in a tax-deferred health care plan?

Apply Your Understanding

INSTRUCTIONS: Download problem instructions for Excel, QuickBooks, and Sage 50 from the textbook companion website at www.C21accounting.com.

3-1 Application Problem: Completing payroll records LO1, 2, 3

Suburban Tractor's partial payroll register for the pay period ended July 8, 20--, payable on July 12, 20--, and a blank earnings record form are provided in the *Working Papers*. Use the appropriate withholding tax tables from this chapter to determine the federal income tax. Deductions for all employees are 5% of total earnings for state income tax, 6.2% for social security tax, and 1.45% for Medicare tax. Save your work to complete Application Problem 3-2.

Instructions:

1. Prepare a commissions record for Lien Y. Trang, employee No. 16 and equipment department manager, for June of the current year. Ms. Trang's biweekly salary of $1,000.00 is assigned to the equipment department. She also receives a monthly commission of 6% on equipment net sales and 1% on parts net sales. Commissions for the previous month are paid in the first pay period of the current month. Accounting records for the month ended June 30 of the current year are as follows:

	Equipment	Parts
Sales on account	$12,184.19	$3,149.62
Cash and credit card sales	3,148.22	4,107.15
Sales discounts	201.14	51.23
Sales returns and allowances	514.34	312.05

2. Prepare the payroll register entries for the following two employees:
   a. On line 4: Lien Y. Trang, employee number 16, equipment department manager, married, and three allowances. Use the commission calculated in instruction 1. Her health insurance premium is $100.00 and retirement plan contribution is $250.00.
   b. On line 5: Peter S. Valdez, employee number 20, parts department clerk, single, two allowances, regular salary of $18.00 per hour with overtime paid at 1½ times the regular rate. He worked 80 hours regular time and 1 hour of overtime. His medical insurance premium is $80.00 and retirement plan contribution is $100.00.
3. Complete the payroll register by totaling each amount column.
4. Prepare Peter Valdez's earnings record for the first pay period of the quarter ended September 30, 20--. Accumulated earnings for the quarter ended June 30, 20--, are $9,148.50.

3-2 Application Problem: Journalizing and paying payroll and payroll taxes LO4, 5

Use the solution from Problem 3-1. A cash payments journal, page 12, and general journal, page 9, are provided in the *Working Papers*.

Instructions:

1. Calculate departmental payroll taxes for the pay period ended July 8. No employees have earned more than the social security tax base. Unemployment taxes are due on the following earnings for this period: Equipment, $1,162.00; and Parts, $921.16.
2. Journalize the following transactions for July of the current year.

Transactions:

July	12.	Paid the July 8 payroll. Check No. 645.
	12.	Recorded employer's payroll taxes for the pay period ended July 8. Memorandum No. 50.
	15.	Made a deposit using the EFTPS for employee and employer payroll taxes for the June pay periods: employee federal income tax withholding, $1,267.00; social security tax, $2,102.43; and Medicare tax, $491.73. Memorandum No. 51.
	30.	Made a deposit using the EFTPS for federal unemployment taxes for the first three quarters, $529.16. Memorandum No. 54.
	30.	Paid state unemployment tax for the quarter ended June 30, $218.59. Check No. 653.

CHECK FIGURES

For complete solutions to Chapter 3 problems, see the Teacher's Edition of the Working Papers.

Application Problem 3-1

Lien Y. Trang commissions: Equipment, $877.02; Parts, $68.93.

Payroll Register column totals: Overtime, $141.00; Commission, $1,357.37; Equipment, $3,039.02; Parts, $2,855.93.

Application Problem 3-2

Departmental Total Payroll Taxes: Equipment, $302.20; Parts, $273.75; Administrative, $144.70.

July 12 Cash Payments Journal Cash Credit: $5,134.39.

Mastery Problem 3-M

DeShawn O. Ward commissions: Carpet, $703.63; Drapery, $232.81.

Payroll Register column totals: Overtime, $285.00; Commission, $1,548.59; Carpet, $4,243.48; Drapery, $3,502.11.

Departmental Total Payroll Taxes: Carpet, $383.02; Drapery, $267.91; Administrative, $181.28.

Oct. 7 Cash Payments Journal Cash Credit: $6,188.24.

INDEPENDENT PRACTICE

- Assign Mastery Problem 3-M for students as a culminating problem that combines all activities from the chapter.
- Assign Source Documents Problem 3-S, utilizing source documents related to payroll.
- Assign Challenge Problem 3-C to accelerated students who work at a faster pace.
- Assign Study Guide 3.
- Students can access Online Working Papers to work end-of-chapter problems on the computer.
- Direct students to the C21 Accounting companion website for additional practice and review opportunities.

FORMATIVE ASSESSMENT

- Review solutions to the assigned problems in class, diagnosing trouble spots.

RETEACH

- Call on students to describe how they avoid the trouble spots diagnosed.
- Use reteaching suggestions from lesson plans as required.
- Assign Recycling Problem 3-R if needed.

3-M Mastery Problem: Completing payroll records, journalizing payment of a payroll, and journalizing payroll taxes LO2, 3, 4, 5

Coastline Flooring's partial payroll register for the pay period ended October 4, 20--, a blank earnings record form, page 13 of a cash payments journal, and page 7 of a general journal are provided in the *Working Papers*. Use the appropriate withholding tax tables shown in this chapter to determine the federal income tax. Deductions for all employees are 3% of total earnings for state income tax, 6.2% for social security tax, and 1.45% for Medicare tax.

Instructions:

1. Prepare a commissions record for DeShawn O. Ward, employee No. 4 and carpet department manager, for September of the current year. DeShawn's biweekly salary of $1,000.00 is assigned to the carpet department. He also receives a monthly commission of 10% of carpet net sales and 15% of drapery net sales. Commissions for the previous month are paid in the first pay period of the current month. Accounting records for the month ended September 30 of the current year are as follows:

	Carpet	Drapery
Sales on account	$6,092.77	$1,019.14
Cash and credit card sales	1,049.25	594.10
Sales discounts	84.19	19.11
Sales returns and allowances	21.49	42.08

2. Prepare the payroll register entries for the following two employees:
   a. On line 5: Shekeia M. Shipp, employee number 8, drapery cutter, married, two allowances, regular salary of $18.00 per hour with overtime paid at 1½ times the regular rate. She worked 80 hours regular time and 8 hours overtime. Her medical insurance premium is $75.00 and retirement plan contribution is $200.00.
   b. On line 6: DeShawn O. Ward, employee number 4, carpet department manager, single, and one allowance. Use the commission calculated in instruction 1. His health insurance premium is $50.00 and retirement plan contribution is $100.00.
3. Complete the payroll register by totaling each amount column.
4. Prepare Shekeia Shipp's earnings record for the first pay period of the quarter ended September 30, 20--. Accumulated earnings for the quarter ended June 30, 20--, are $16,948.00.
5. Calculate departmental payroll taxes for the pay period ended October 4. No employees have earned more than the social security tax base. Unemployment taxes are due on the following earnings for this period: Carpet, $973.00; and Administrative, $1,328.00.
6. Journalize the following transactions for October of the current year.

Transactions:

Oct. 7. Paid the October 4 payroll. Check No. 841.
7. Recorded employer's payroll taxes for the pay period ended October 4. Memorandum No. 44.
15. Made a deposit using the EFTPS for employee and employer payroll taxes for the September pay periods: employee federal income tax withholding, $1,318.00; social security tax, $2,285.70; and Medicare tax, $534.61. Memorandum No. 45.
29. Made a deposit using the EFTPS for federal unemployment taxes for the first three quarters, $541.16. Memorandum No. 49.
29. Paid state unemployment tax for the quarter ended September 30, $346.57. Check No. 854.

Sage 50 Accounting

1. Journalize and post payroll transactions to the cash disbursements journal and general journal.
2. From the menu bar, select Reports & Forms; Accounts Payable, Cash Disbursements Journal.
3. From the menu bar, select Reports & Forms; General Ledger, General Journal.

QuickBooks

1. Journalize and post payroll transactions in the Write Checks window.
2. Journalize and post payroll transactions to the journal.
3. From the menu bar, select Reports; Banking, Check Detail.
4. From the menu bar, select Reports; Accountant & Taxes, Journal.

Excel

1. Complete the Payroll Register.
2. Journalize and post payroll transactions to the Cash Payments Journal and the General Journal.
3. Print the worksheets.

3-S Source Documents Problem: Completing payroll records, journalizing payment of a payroll, and journalizing payroll taxes LO1, 2, 3, 4, 5

Exterior Design sells doors and windows. Journals and source documents related to payroll are provided in the *Working Papers*. Use the appropriate withholding tax tables shown in this chapter to determine the federal income tax. Deductions for all employees are 4% of total earnings for state income tax, 6.2% for social security tax, and 1.45% for Medicare tax.

Instructions:

1. Prepare the commissions records for Daniel C. Pizzo and May E. Verdell. Each manager's regular salary is assigned to the department he or she manages. The information required to complete the commissions records is obtained from a Commission Sales Report and the Personnel Report. Overtime is paid at 1½ times the regular rate for hours worked over 8 hours per day or 40 hours per week.
2. Prepare the payroll register using information presented on the Hourly Employee Time Summary, each Commission Sales Report, and the Personnel Report. Withholdings for health insurance are based on each employee's allowances: one allowance, $100.00; two allowances, $150.00, three allowances, $180.00; and four allowances, $200.00.
3. Complete the employee earnings records.
4. Calculate departmental payroll taxes for the pay period ended July 9. Three of the employees have earned more than the FUTA tax base.
5. Journalize the following transactions for July of the current year.

Transactions:

July 13. Paid the July 9 payroll. Check No. 905.
13. Recorded employer's payroll taxes for the pay period ended July 9. Memorandum No. 65.
15. Deposited payroll taxes for the June pay periods. Memorandum No. 66.
30. Deposited federal unemployment taxes. Memorandum No. 72.
30. Paid state unemployment taxes. Check No. 916.

Sage 50 Accounting

1. Journalize and post payroll transactions to the cash disbursements journal and general journal.
2. From the menu bar, select Reports & Forms; Accounts Payable, Cash Disbursements Journal.
3. From the menu bar, select Reports & Forms; General Ledger, General Journal.

QB

1. Journalize and post payroll transactions in the Write Checks window.
2. Journalize and post payroll transactions to the journal.
3. From the menu bar, select Reports; Banking, Check Detail.
4. From the menu bar, select Reports; Accountant & Taxes, Journal.

Excel

1. Complete the payroll register.
2. Journalize and post payroll transactions to the Cash Payments Journal and the General Journal.
3. Print the worksheets.

Source Documents Problem 3-S

Daniel C. Pizzo commissions: Doors, $384.51; Windows, $51.23.

Payroll Register column totals: Overtime, $237.00; Commission, $1,449.64; Doors, $3,137.16; Windows, $3,140.48.

Departmental Total Payroll Taxes: Doors, $239.99; Windows, $317.54; Administrative, $262.76.

July 13 Cash Payments Journal Cash Credit: $5,260.02.

Challenge Problem 3-C

For Cooper: Federal income tax withholdings: $750.00; Earnings subject to withholding: $3,291.00; Minimum tax: $384.00; Additional tax: $45.75; Total tax: $429.75.

EXTENDED LEARNING

- Assign 21st Century Skills on page 91.
- Assign Auditing for Errors on page 92.
- Assign Analyzing Home Depot's Financial Statements on page 93.

SUMMATIVE EVALUATION

- Chapter 3 Test
- Cognero for Chapter 3

3-C Challenge Problem: Calculating federal income tax withholdings using the percentage method LO3

The Internal Revenue Service only provides tax withholding tables for a range of earnings. The table for biweekly single persons stops at earnings of $2,100.00. The tax withholdings for a single taxpayer earning over $2,100.00 in a biweekly payroll period must be calculated using the percentage method. A portion of the tax rate table available when this text was written is shown below.

TABLE 2—BIWEEKLY Payroll Period

(a) SINGLE person (including head of household)—				**(b) MARRIED person—**			
If the amount of wages (after subtracting withholding allowances) is:		The amount of income tax to withhold is:		If the amount of wages (after subtracting withholding allowances) is:		The amount of income tax to withhold is:	
Not over $85		$0		Not over $319		$0	
Over—	**But not over—**		**of excess over—**	**Over—**	**But not over—**		**of excess over—**
$85	—$428 . .	$0.00 plus 10%	—$85	$319	—$1,006 . .	$0.00 plus 10%	—$319
$428	—$1,479 . .	$34.30 plus 15%	—$428	$1,006	—$3,108 . .	$68.70 plus 15%	—$1,006
$1,479	—$3,463 . .	$191.95 plus 25%	—$1,479	$3,108	—$5,950 . .	$384.00 plus 25%	—$3,108
$3,463	—$7,133 . .	$687.95 plus 28%	—$3,463	$5,950	—$8,898 . .	$1,094.50 plus 28%	—$5,950
$7,133	—$15,406 . .	$1,715.55 plus 33%	—$7,133	$8,898	—$15,640 . .	$1,919.94 plus 33%	—$8,898
$15,406	—$15,469 . .	$4,445.64 plus 35%	—$15,406	$15,640	—$17,627 . .	$4,144.80 plus 35%	—$15,640
$15,469		$4,467.69 plus 39.6%	—$15,469	$17,627		$4,840.25 plus 39.6%	—$17,627

Adrianne Atkinson earns $4,000.00 each biweekly pay period. She is married and claims three withholding allowances. She is allowed to exclude $150.00 for each withholding allowance. Using the table above, her tax withholding is calculated as follows:

Total earnings		$4,000.00
Withholding allowance per person	$150.00	
Number of allowances	× 3	450.00
Earnings subject to withholding		$3,550.00
Minimum tax		$ 384.00
Additional tax ($3,550.00 – $3,108.00) × 25%		110.50
Taxes to be withheld		$ 494.50

Instructions:

Use the tax rate table above to calculate tax withholdings for five employees. A form is provided in the *Working Papers*. The amounts for Adrianne Atkinson are provided as a guide.

COMMON CORE AND INTERDISCIPLINARY STUDIES

Extended learning features and activities present numerous opportunities to implement Common Core Standards through interdisciplinary studies. Practice is provided in the common core areas of English Language Arts & Literacy and Mathematical Practice. Many of these activities require short, critical-thinking and decision-making responses that apply reading, writing, speaking, listening, language, media and technology, and mathematical skills.

21st Century Skills

Pay ... Attention

Theme: Financial, Economic, Business, and Entrepreneurial Literacy

Skills: Creativity and Innovation, Critical Thinking and Problem Solving, Communication and Collaboration,

ICT Literacy

PARTNERSHIP FOR 21ST CENTURY SKILLS

When it comes to employee pay, most managers try to determine an affordable amount that will attract and retain a quality employee. Most employees are trying to find the company that offers the highest pay for the skills offered. However, managers and employees must consider the total compensation package.

Compensation is your total gross earnings plus your benefits, or perks, that have monetary value and are often paid for, either totally or in part, by the employer. One study showed that the benefits most valued by employees were (in order of priority): retirement/savings plans; insurance plans, such as health, life, and disability; health/wellness programs; and childcare subsidies. However, the most common benefits offered by employers were: (1) life insurance, (2) vacation pay, (3) holiday pay, (4) medical insurance, (5) retirement plans, and (6) educational assistance programs.

Premiums on the insurance plans alone can cost a company tens of thousands of dollars per year, adding significantly to the compensation package of an employee. Yet, employee benefits have become so necessary to the employee that offering an attractive benefits package can help recruit and retain the best talent for a company.

Source: www.money-zine.com/Career-Development/Finding-a-Job/Top-Employee-Benefits.

APPLICATION

1. Use the Internet, make phone calls, or interview an adult to research benefits offered by three different companies. Compare your findings for similarities and differences.
2. Assume that you are a new start-up company. With a partner, create five benefits, or perks, that you could offer to your employees that would be attractive, yet inexpensive. Explain.

21ST CENTURY SKILLS

Answers

1. Answers will vary.
2. Answers will vary. Examples might include flexible work hours, work-from-home days, family days, fitness classes such as yoga, community service days, pizza Fridays, movie days, free car washes, retail discounts, and bring-a-pet-to-work day.

AUDITING FOR ERRORS

Answers

The following errors exist in the commissions record:

1. The cash and credit card sales amount for computers is incorrectly entered. The numbers 4 and 2 are reversed. (This is known as a transposition error.)
2. The sales discount amount for printers is incorrectly entered. An extra digit, a 6, is added to the number. (This error is known as a slide.)
3. For the Computers Department, the total reduction in sales is added rather than subtracted from the total sales for the month.

The printer's commission on net sales in incorrectly calculated. The correct commission is $682.78.

Auditing for errors

Kelly Sanders has prepared her first set of monthly commission records. She obtained sales data from the Commission Sales Report. The portion of the Commission Sales Report for Jane C. Kellogg and the commissions record Kelly prepared follow.

COMMISSION SALES REPORT

MONTH *August*
PREPARED ON *9/08/20--*

Name	Account Title	Computers	Printers
Kellogg, Jane C.	Sales on Account	$2,154.26	$1,089.66
	Cash and Credit Card Sales	9,142.36	3,048.15
	Sales Discounts	33.94	16.66
	Sales Returns and Allowances	648.16	319.90
	Commission Rate	5%	4%

COMMISSIONS RECORD

EMPLOYEE NO. *532* EMPLOYEE NAME *Kellogg, Jane C.*
PAY PERIOD ENDED *August 5, 20--* REGULAR BIWEEKLY SALARY *$1,000.00*
DEPARTMENT *Computers*

	Computers	Printers	
Sales on Account	*$ 2,154.26*	*$1,089.66*	
Cash and Credit Card Sales	*9,124.36*	*3,048.15*	
equals Total Sales for the Month	*$11,278.62*	*$4,137.81*	
Less:			
Sales Discounts	*$ 33.94*	*$ 166.66*	
Sales Returns and Allowances	*648.16*	*319.90*	
equals Total Reductions in Sales	*$ 682.10*	*$ 486.56*	
Equals:			
Net Sales	*$11,960.72*	*$3,651.25*	
times Commission Rate	*5.0%*	*4.0%*	
equals Commission on Net Sales	*$ 598.04*	*$ 279.26*	*$877.30*

As the senior accounting clerk, you have responsibility for reviewing the work prepared by new hires. Examine the commissions record Kelly prepared. Identify any errors. Calculate the correct commission if errors are found.

Analyzing Home Depot's financial statements

Expenses incurred in one fiscal period but not paid until a later date are called **accrued expenses**. During the last fiscal period of each year, Home Depot incurs salary and benefit expenses that are not paid until the following fiscal year. This occurs when a fiscal year ends in the middle of a payroll period. The accounting concept *Matching Revenue with Expenses* requires that financial statements must show all business expenses for a fiscal period. Consequently, Home Depot must report the unpaid salary and benefit amount even though it has not yet paid out cash. The unpaid amount owed for incurred employee salaries and benefits represents a liability. Use the material shown in Appendix B of this text to answer the questions below.

INSTRUCTIONS

1. Referring to the Consolidated Balance Sheets in Appendix B on page B-5, (a) list the title of the account that represents an amount owed for salaries and benefits and (b) list the amounts owed for this account on February 3, 2013, and January 29, 2012.
2. Referring to the Five-Year Operating and Financial Highlights on page B-15, identify one fact that would help explain the increase in this liability. List at least two other reasons that might explain the increase.

ANALYZING HOME DEPOT'S FINANCIAL STATEMENTS

Answers

1. a. Accrued Salaries and Related Expenses.
   b. $1,414,000,000 on February 3, 2013, and $1,372,000,000 on January 29, 2012.
2. Sales increased 6.2%, from $70,395,000,000 in fiscal year 2011 to $74,754,000,000 in fiscal year 2012. More employees would likely be required to support the increase in sales. Thus, the amount of accrued salaries would be larger with the increase in the number of employees. Other reasons might include increases in hourly pay rates and the cost of employee benefits.

Chapter 4 Financial Reporting for a Departmentalized Business

Scope & Sequence

	New	Review/Enrich
Introduction		
Introduce the Chapter	✓	
Lesson 4-1: Preparing Financial Information for a Departmentalized Business		
Preparing for End-of-Period Financial Reporting		✓
Proving the Accuracy of Subsidiary Ledgers		✓
Preparing an Unadjusted Trial Balance	✓	
Adjustment Information	✓	
Preparing an Adjusted Trial Balance	✓	
Calculating the Federal Income Tax Adjustment	✓	
Completing the Adjusted Trial Balance	✓	
Using a Work Sheet to Prepare Financial Statements	✓	
Lesson 4-2: Responsibility Statements for a Merchandising Business		
Features of a Responsibility Accounting System	✓	
Departmental Margin Statement	✓	
Vertical Analysis of Departmental Margin Statements	✓	
Lesson 4-3: Financial Statements for a Departmental Merchandising Business		
Income Statement with Departmental Margin	✓	
Statement of Stockholders' Equity		✓
Balance Sheet		✓
Statement of Cash Flows		✓
Lesson 4-4: End-of-Period Work for a Departmentalized Business		
Journalizing Closing Entries for a Departmentalized Business	✓	
Post-Closing Trial Balance		✓
Summary of the Accounting Cycle		✓
APPENDIX: Preparing a Work Sheet	✓	
Closure		

Enhancing Instruction

Features	Common Core Standards
• Accounting in the Real World: Whole Planet Foundation	• ELAL—reading
• Ethics in Action: Insider Trading • Financial Literacy: How Secure Is Social Security? • Careers in Accounting: Junior Accountant/Senior Accountant	• ELAL—reading • ELAL—reading, speaking, listening • ELAL—reading
• Why Accounting?: Accounting for Engineers • Think Like an Accountant: Allocating Corporate Expenses	• ELAL—writing, media and technology • Mathematics
• A Look at Accounting Software • Explore Accounting • 21st Century Skills • Auditing for Errors • Analyzing Home Depot's Financial Statements	• ELAL—reading • ELAL—reading, writing • ELAL—speaking, writing • Mathematics • Mathematics

ELAL = English Language Arts & Literacy

Calculator: © iStockphoto.com/picstodisc; Paper: © iStockphoto.com/Qingwa

Practice and Assessment

Technology & Media	Teaching Strategies	Guided Practice	Independent Practice	Reteach/Enrich
• Instructor's Resource CD/Website: PowerPoint Slides Accounting Concepts • Online Working Papers • Transparency Master: General Journal	• Tactile/Kinesthetic Learners	• Terms Review • Audit Your Understanding • Work Together 4-1	• On Your Own 4-1 • Application Problem 4-1 • Formative Assessment, p. 106 • Online Working Papers	• Reteach, p. 107
• Instructor's Resource CD/Website: PowerPoint Slides Accounting Concepts • Online Working Papers • Transparency Master: Statement (4-column with % of net sales)	• Gifted Learners	• Terms Review • Audit Your Understanding • Work Together 4-2	• On Your Own 4-2 • Application Problem 4-2 • Formative Assessment, p. 110 • Online Working Papers	• Reteach, p. 111
• Instructor's Resource CD/Website: PowerPoint Slides Accounting Concepts • Online Working Papers • Transparency Masters: Statement (4-column with Departmental, Company, and % net sales), Statement (3-column)	• Mathematical/Logical Learners	• Terms Review • Audit Your Understanding • Work Together 4-3	• On Your Own 4-3 • Application Problem 4-3 • Formative Assessment, p. 115 • Online Working Papers	• Reteach, p. 116
• Instructor's Resource CD/Website: PowerPoint Slides Accounting Concepts • Online Working Papers • Transparency Masters: General Journal, Post-Closing Trial Balance		• Terms Review • Audit Your Understanding • Work Together 4-4	• On Your Own 4-4 • Application Problem 4-4 • Formative Assessment, p. 121 • Online Working Papers	• Reteach, p. 122
			• Appendix Problem 4-1 • Appendix Problem 4-2 • Appendix Problem 4-3	
• Online Working Papers	• Common Core and Interdisciplinary Studies		• Mastery Problem 4-M • Study Guide 4 • Chapter 4 Test • Cognero Chapter 4	• Challenge Problem 4-C • Reteach, p. 128 • Recycling Problem 4-R • Reinforcement Activity 1

Introduce the Chapter

SET THE STAGE

GUIDING QUESTIONS

- Ask students to brainstorm consumer products sold by a single company. For example, Procter & Gamble sells Crest, Duracell, Tide, Downy, and Pampers. Explain that each of these product lines is often managed by a separate department in a company.
- Ask students why a manager of an individual department would want financial data specific to that department only. Provide an example.
- Ask for examples of decisions that might be made after the departmental financial statements are analyzed.

PREVIEW CHAPTER OBJECTIVES

- Point out that this chapter focuses on responsibility accounting for a departmentalized merchandising business.
- Explain that a departmentalized merchandising business prepares the same financial statements as a nondepartmentalized business. In addition, a departmentalized business prepares reports about how well each department is doing.

PREVIEW ACCOUNTING TERMS

- Read each term aloud to verify its pronunciation for students.
- Point out terms or parts of terms that should already be familiar to most students.
- Lead an interactive discussion that reviews and explains the terms. Stress that special attention should be directed to all boldfaced words presented in the text.

Chapter 4 Financial Reporting for a Departmentalized Business

LEARNING OBJECTIVES

After studying Chapter 4, in addition to defining key terms, you will be able to:

LO1 Identify the steps necessary to prepare for end-of-period financial reporting.

LO2 Prepare an unadjusted trial balance.

LO3 Journalize adjusting entries.

LO4 Prepare an adjusted trial balance.

LO5 Distinguish between direct and indirect expenses of a departmentalized business.

LO6 Prepare a departmental margin statement.

LO7 Calculate and analyze vertical analysis ratios.

LO8 Prepare financial statements for a departmentalized merchandising business.

LO9 Complete end-of-period work for a departmentalized merchandising business.

Calculator: © iStockphoto.com/picstodisc; Paper: © iStockphoto.com/Qingwa

© wavebreakmedia/Shutterstock.com

Background: © iStockphoto.com/hadynyah; Real World: Photo Courtesy of Whole Planet Foundation's Daniel Zaltani

Accounting In The Real World
Whole Planet Foundation

Corporate America has long recognized its responsibility to be a good citizen. Being a good citizen is also good business. Many corporations have foundations that donate money to charitable organizations.

Whole Foods Market, a leading retailer of natural and organic foods, created Whole Planet Foundation in 2005 to give back to global communities. The foundation's mission is to reduce poverty by making small loans to entrepreneurs in countries that supply Whole Foods Market with products. The foundation collaborates with local pro-poor organizations to assist in distributing funds to local entrepreneurs. These organizations, called *microfinance institutions*, can be nonprofit organizations or financial institutions.

Unlike most business loans, these "microloans" are usually $200 or less and do not require the borrower to sign a contract or to offer collateral. The foundation grants the loans most often to poor women so that they can start or expand a home-based business. The foundation's goal is that these loans will empower the women to escape poverty and provide food and shelter for their families.

To date, the nonprofit has authorized more than $37 million and disbursed $2 million through microlending partners worldwide. The average loan was $172, and 89% of the loans were granted to women. The most impressive number is the repayment rate of 96%!

CRITICAL THINKING

1. What advantages exist for Whole Foods Market to establish a separate organization to administer the granting of microloans?
2. What accounts or categories would you expect to see on the foundation's income statement?

Source: www.wholeplanetfoundation.org.

Key Terms

- fiscal period
- fiscal year
- schedule of accounts receivable
- schedule of accounts payable
- trial balance
- adjusting entries
- unadjusted trial balance
- plant assets
- depreciation expense
- adjusted trial balance
- tax bracket
- marginal tax rate
- work sheet
- responsibility accounting
- direct expense
- indirect expense
- responsibility statements
- departmental margin
- departmental margin statement
- gross profit
- financial ratio
- vertical analysis
- income statement
- statement of stockholders' equity
- capital stock
- retained earnings
- dividends
- balance sheet
- cash flow
- statement of cash flows
- operating activities
- investing activities
- financing activities
- closing entries
- post-closing trial balance
- accounting cycle

Accounting In The Real World

Answers

Unlike for-profit businesses, earning income is not the primary objective of a not-for-profit organization. For this reason, the income statement of a not-for-profit organization is titled a *statement of activities*.

1. Answers will vary. The activities of the Whole Planet Foundation are dramatically different from those of Whole Foods. Reporting both organizations' activities on a single set of financial statements would make it difficult, if not impossible, for the reader to interpret and analyze the financial statements.
2. Answers will vary. Students can be expected to identify contributions as a major component of revenue. Within the Expenses category, students should identify that program expenses are segregated from the fund-raising and administrative expenses. The foundation's statement of activities includes Contributions, Calendar Sales, and Other Revenue or Loss in the Revenues category. The statement includes Program, Management and General, and Fund-raising and Communications in the Expenses category.

LESSON

4-1

BRIDGE

- Point out that in the first-year accounting course, students have already learned the concepts and procedures related to end-of-period work for a merchandising business organized as a corporation.
- Remind students that they have already prepared adjusting entries and trial balances for service businesses, merchandising businesses, and corporations. Explain that the end-of-period work for a departmentalized business is similar to that of a non-departmentalized business.

TEACHING RESOURCES

- **Instructor's Resource CD/Website:**
  PowerPoint Slides
  Accounting Concepts
- **Working Papers:**
  Teacher's Edition of the Working Papers for Lesson 4-1
  Online Working Papers
- **Transparency Master:**
  General Journal

ENGAGE

- Ask students why financial statements are prepared by a business.
- Ask students how often a business should prepare financial statements. Lead into a discussion of the fiscal period and the concept of the accounting cycle.
- Point out that for tax purposes, businesses must prepare financial statements at least once per year.
- Explain that most businesses prepare financial statements monthly to analyze results and take corrective action.
- Explain that a departmentalized business plans adjustments to bring certain accounts up to date in preparing financial statements.

PREVIEW

- Call on students to read the accounting terms and definitions introduced in this lesson: *fiscal period, fiscal year, schedule of accounts receivable, schedule of accounts payable, trial balance, adjusting entries, unadjusted trial balance, plant assets, depreciation expense, adjusted trial balance, tax bracket, marginal tax rate,* and *work sheet.*
- Point out the learning objectives for this lesson.
- Direct students to read the headings in this lesson and to examine the illustrations.

LESSON

4-1 Preparing Financial Information for a Departmentalized Business

© Mike Flippo/Shutterstock.com

LO1 Identify the steps necessary to prepare for end-of-period financial reporting.
LO2 Prepare an unadjusted trial balance.
LO3 Journalize adjusting entries.
LO4 Prepare an adjusted trial balance.

Preparing for End-of-Period Financial Reporting LO1

Financial statements summarize the financial information that a business records. These statements are then analyzed to evaluate the financial position and progress of the business. The managers of a business use the statements to make financial decisions for future operations. A business also uses the financial statements in preparing tax reports and other reports, such as those required by the Securities and Exchange Commission (SEC).

The period for which financial statements are prepared depends on the needs of the business. An accounting period may be one month, three months, six months, or one year. For tax purposes, every business prepares financial statements at the end of each year. Successful businesses generally prepare financial statements monthly to analyze results and take corrective action when needed.

The length of time for which a business summarizes its financial information and reports its financial performance is called a **fiscal period**. [CONCEPT: Accounting Period Cycle] A fiscal period consisting of 12 consecutive months is called a **fiscal year**. Each business determines when its fiscal year ends. Whiley uses a fiscal year ending on December 31.

Before financial statements can be prepared, the business should ensure that its account balances are accurate. A business should:

- Ensure that all transactions have been journalized.
- Ensure that all journals have been posted.
- Perform bank reconciliations.

ETHICS IN ACTION

Insider Trading

David Robbins, a loan officer for a regional bank, has just closed a loan agreement with Rhett Industries. He was very impressed with the company's management and business plan. With the additional resources the loan will provide, Rhett Industries should experience rapid growth during the next few years. The corporation's stock should also show a dramatic increase in market price.

Upon returning to the office, David places an order to purchase 500 shares of the company's stock. This purchase is a substantial investment for David.

INSTRUCTIONS

Access the *Code of Conduct* of Citigroup Inc. and the insider trading information of the Securities and Exchange Commission. Using this information and the ethical decision-making model introduced in Chapter 2, determine whether David's purchase of the stock of Rhett Industries was ethical.

© iStockphoto.com/LdF

ETHICS IN ACTION

Detecting and prosecuting illegal insider trading is a priority for the SEC. Insider trading undermines investor confidence in the securities markets. This activity requires students to analyze whether the action is illegal and violates company policies. By searching the Internet for "SEC insider trading," students will access a page that provides clear guidance on insider trading rules (www.sec.gov/answers/insider.htm). Because the action is considered illegal, students are not required to consult the company code of conduct. However, as an extension of this activity, have students read the insider trading section of Citigroup's *Code of Conduct.*

See a suggested solution for this feature in the Instructional Strategies section at the front of this book.

Proving the Accuracy of Subsidiary Ledgers

Whiley Outdoor Living, Inc.		
Schedule of Accounts Receivable		
December 31, 20--		
Barnes Construction	3834	80
Central Community College	4190	70
Franklin Landscaping	1146	96
Jenkins Properties	2636	54
Lynch Construction	2898	49
Marist & Nelson, LLC	3138	77
Pratte Real Estate	1578	85
Taylor Apartments	2605	95
Wilson Properties	1484	21
Total Accounts Receivable	23515	27

Another step in preparing financial statements is to determine the accuracy of customer and vendor accounts. The total of the accounts receivable and accounts payable subsidiary ledgers should equal the amount of the related controlling accounts in the general ledger. A **schedule of accounts receivable** is a listing of customer accounts, account balances, and total amount due from all customers. Whiley's schedule of accounts receivable is shown above. The total of the schedule must equal the balance of the general ledger controlling account, Accounts Receivable. Whiley should correct any differences before preparing financial statements.

Whiley also prepares a report showing the total of all accounts payable ledger accounts. A listing of vendor accounts, account balances, and the total amount due all vendors is called a **schedule of accounts payable**. Some businesses call this listing an *accounts payable trial balance*. The total of the schedule must equal the balance of the general ledger controlling account, Accounts Payable.

FINANCIAL LITERACY

How Secure Is Social Security?

The Social Security Administration warns that, within just a few years, social security benefit payments will begin to exceed social security tax income.

Currently, more than 45 million people receive social security benefits. Social security has changed over the years to meet people's needs, and it must change again to meet future challenges. One of the changes that has been discussed is the privatization of social security. Privatization could include the ability of the individual to direct his or her benefits into a personal account. Other recommendations have been to (1) reduce benefits, (2) raise the payroll tax rate, (3) raise the payroll tax cap for wage-earner contributions, (4) increase the taxes on social security benefits, and (5) raise the retirement age.

© iStockphoto.com/Norebbo

ACTIVITIES

1. Research the recommended changes. Prepare a spreadsheet with the following information: (a) a summary of each recommendation, (b) its impact on the future recipient, and (c) its impact on either the employer or the employee (wage earner). Highlight the change you prefer and explain why.
2. Interview someone you know who is collecting social security and ask for his or her opinion. Share your findings with the class. Did this interview change your preference in question 1?

INPUT

- Review the preparation of the schedules of accounts receivable and accounts payable. Refer students to the illustration for the schedule of accounts receivable. Emphasize that the total of each schedule must equal the balance of the corresponding controlling account in the general ledger.

MODEL

- Show the relationship between several individual customer accounts and the controlling account by drawing separate T accounts for each customer account. Enter a balance in each account.
- Draw another T account representing the controlling account. Ask students what amount should appear as the balance in the controlling T account.
- Emphasize that the total of the individual customer accounts equals the total in the controlling account.

FINANCIAL LITERACY

Answers

1. Answers will vary, but should include the pros and cons for both the employee and employer.
2. Answers will vary. Students may change their recommendations after interviewing someone who is currently dependent on social security.

INPUT

- Explain that the first step in preparing financial statements is to create a list of all general ledger accounts and their balances.
- A proof of the equality of debits and credits is called the unadjusted trial balance. Once adjusting entries are made to bring certain accounts up to date, the trial balance is called an adjusted trial balance.
- Emphasize that all accounts are listed, even those with zero balances.

Preparing an Unadjusted Trial Balance LO2

Whiley Outdoor Living, Inc.
Unadjusted Trial Balance
December 31, 20--

ACCOUNT TITLE	DEBIT	CREDIT
Cash	62849 26	
Petty Cash	500 00	
Accounts Receivable	23515 27	
Allowance for Uncollectible Accounts		95 69
Merchandise Inventory—Grills	86148 68	
Merchandise Inventory—Furniture	106731 89	
Supplies	7610 87	
Prepaid Insurance	14000 00	
Office Equipment	32481 15	
Accumulated Depreciation—Office Equipment		14150 00
Dividends Payable		5000 00
Capital Stock		100000 00
Retained Earnings		114352 88
Dividends	19250 00	
Income Summary—General		
Income Summary—Grills		
Income Summary—Furniture		
Sales—Grills		472019 64
Sales Discount—Grills	8246 75	
Sales Returns and Allowances—Grills	9467 42	
Sales—Furniture		492187 31
Sales Discount—Furniture	5219 23	
Sales Returns and Allowances—Furniture	13810 76	
Purchases—Grills	254851 26	
Purchases Discount—Grills		3105 48
Purchases Returns and Allowances—Grills		6108 67
Purchases—Furniture	197084 64	
Purchases Discount—Furniture		2671 69
Purchases Returns and Allowances—Furniture		8094 21
Advertising Expense—Grills	14920 00	
Payroll Taxes Expense—Grills	6453 36	
Salary Expense—Grills	73011 20	
Advertising Expense—Furniture	5650 00	
Payroll Taxes Expense—Furniture	10926 17	
Salary Expense—Furniture	125806 20	
Credit Card Fee Expense	6842 20	
Depreciation Expense—Office Equipment		
Depreciation Expense—Store Equipment		
Insurance Expense		
Miscellaneous Expense	3495 04	
Payroll Taxes Expense—Administrative	7602 20	
Rent Expense	18400 00	
Salary Expense—Administrative	88028 80	
Supplies Expense		
Uncollectible Accounts Expense		
Utilities Expense	16204 68	
Federal Income Tax Expense	14000 00	
Totals	1297291 10	1297291 10

The process of preparing financial statements begins with a list of all general ledger accounts. A proof of the equality of debits and credits in a general ledger is called a **trial balance**. The trial balance lists all accounts, even those with a zero balance. Thus, it provides a complete list of accounts that may need to be adjusted.

Journal entries recorded to update general ledger accounts at the end of a fiscal period are called **adjusting entries**. A trial balance prepared before adjusting entries are posted is called an **unadjusted trial balance**. Beginning with the first account, a business should review each account to determine if an adjusting entry is required.

DIFFERENTIATED INSTRUCTION

Tactile/Kinesthetic learners learn best through physical activity and real objects. Allow students to use a work sheet to prepare end-of-period work.

Adjustment Information LO3

The next step in the preparation of financial statements is to collect the information required to bring selected account balances up to date. Whiley collected the following information necessary to prepare the adjusting entries.

Adjustment Information, December 31	
Estimate of uncollectible accounts	$ 2,210.61
Ending merchandise inventory—grills	89,349.72
Ending merchandise inventory—furniture	102,915.36
Supplies on hand	2,430.00
Value of prepaid insurance	2,000.00
Depreciation expense—office equipment	7,320.00
Depreciation expense—store equipment	8,370.00

UNCOLLECTIBLE ACCOUNTS ADJUSTMENT

GENERAL JOURNAL PAGE 20

	DATE		ACCOUNT TITLE	DOC. NO.	POST. REF.	DEBIT	CREDIT	
1			*Adjusting Entries*					1
2	20– Dec.	31	*Uncollectible Accounts Expense*			2 1 1 4 92		2
3			*Allowance for Uncollectible Accounts*				2 1 1 4 92	3

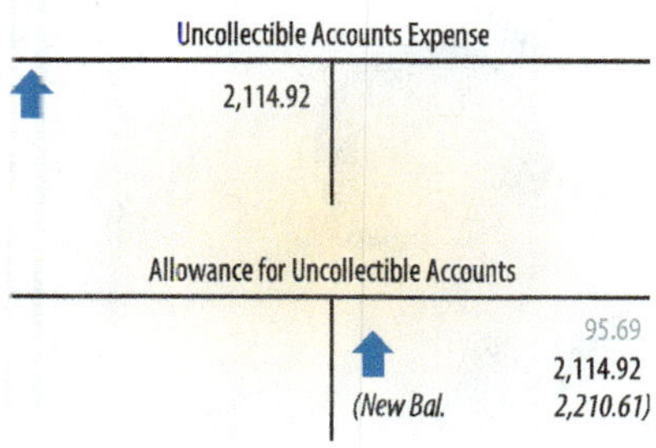

Merchandise is sometimes sold on account to customers who later are unable to pay the amounts owed. Amounts that cannot be collected from customers are business expenses. All expenses must be recorded in the fiscal period in which the expenses contribute to earning revenue. [CONCEPT: Matching Expenses with Revenue]

The Allowance for Uncollectible Accounts balance represents the total estimated amount of accounts receivable that Whiley believes will never be collected. Whiley estimates that $2,210.61 of its accounts receivable will eventually be uncollectible. The current balance in Allowance for Uncollectible Accounts is a $95.69 credit. An adjusting entry for $2,114.92 ($2,210.61 required balance less $95.69 current credit balance) is required to increase the account balance to $2,210.61. Uncollectible Accounts Expense increases by $2,114.92. Allowance for Uncollectible Accounts, a contra asset account, increases by $2,114.92. Write the words *Adjusting Entries* in the Account Title column before the first adjusting entry.

Adjusting entries are immediately journalized in a general journal. Adjusting entries are not typically posted to general ledger accounts until all adjusting entries have been journalized.

INPUT

- Emphasize that not all accounts in the general ledger are up to date. Point out that the trial balance on page 98 does not have a balance recorded for Uncollectible Accounts Expense. Lead into a discussion of uncollectible accounts and the accounting concept of Matching Expenses with Revenue.
- Point out that adjusting entries are used to bring specific accounts up to date.

MODEL

Analyze the transaction

- Write the calculations on the board for estimating the amount of uncollectible accounts expense.
- Use T accounts to show the adjustment for uncollectible accounts expense.
- Emphasize that, as with all transactions, there must be at least one debit part and one credit part and that both parts must be equal.
- Use the illustration to review the steps for journalizing adjusting entries.
- Point out that the heading Adjusting Entries is placed on the first line prior to the first adjusting entry.
- Point out that the adjusting entries presented in this lesson are similar to those presented in the first-year course for a merchandising business organized as a corporation.

INPUT

- Explain that there are three income summary accounts on the unadjusted trial balance: Income Summary—Grills, Income Summary—Furniture, and Income Summary—General.
- Explain that the departmental income summary accounts are used for adjusting the departmental merchandise inventory accounts.
- Explain that Income Summary—General is used for other closing entries in the future.

MODEL

Adjustment for departmental merchandise inventory

- Direct students to the Debit column of the unadjusted trial balance on page 98 as you demonstrate the beginning balance for Merchandise Inventory—Grills.
- Explain that a periodic inventory revealed that more grills are on hand at the end of the period than at the beginning. A debit adjustment to Merchandise Inventory—Grills brings the account up to date, showing the additional inventory.
- Explain that the inventory on hand for Furniture shows a decrease. A credit adjustment to Merchandise Inventory—Furniture brings the account up to date with the reduction in inventory.

MERCHANDISE INVENTORY ADJUSTMENTS

GENERAL JOURNAL PAGE 20

	DATE	ACCOUNT TITLE	DOC. NO.	POST. REF.	DEBIT	CREDIT	
4	31	*Merchandise Inventory—Grills*			3 201 04		4
5		*Income Summary—Grills*				3 201 04	5
6	31	*Income Summary—Furniture*			3 816 53		6
7		*Merchandise Inventory—Furniture*				3 816 53	7
8							8

The merchandise inventory account balances in the trial balance are the beginning inventory amounts for a fiscal period. The amount of the ending inventory is determined by taking a periodic inventory at the end of a fiscal period.

The beginning merchandise inventory of grills, $86,148.68, is shown in the Debit column of the unadjusted trial balance. The periodic inventory taken on December 31 shows that the cost of the grills inventory is $89,349.72. To bring the grills inventory up to date, the balance of Merchandise Inventory—Grills needs to be increased by $3,201.04 ($89,349.72 ending inventory less $86,148.68 beginning inventory).

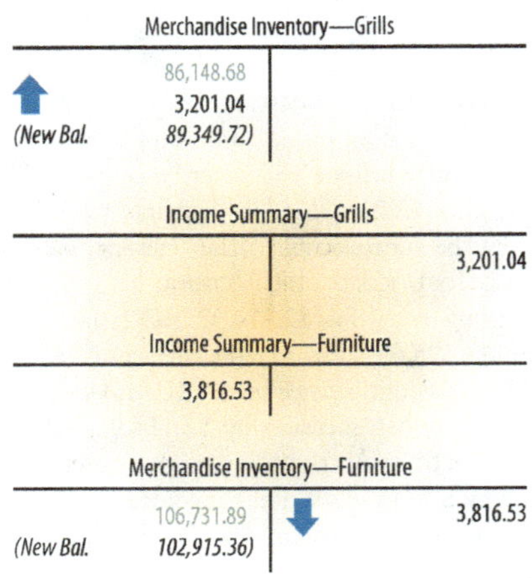

A similar adjusting entry is made for the furniture inventory. The $3,816.53 credit adjusting entry reduces the balance of Merchandise Inventory—Furniture.

Most accounts needing adjustment at the end of a fiscal period have a related expense account. Expense accounts are temporary accounts. For example, the adjustment to Allowance for Uncollectible Accounts included a debit to a related expense account, Uncollectible Accounts Expense. Merchandise Inventory, however, does not have a related expense account. Therefore, Income Summary, also a temporary account, is used to adjust Merchandise Inventory at the end of the fiscal year. Each department uses a separate income summary account.

© Leah-Anne Thompson/Shutterstock.com

SUPPLIES ADJUSTMENT

GENERAL JOURNAL — PAGE 20

	DATE		ACCOUNT TITLE	DOC. NO.	POST. REF.	DEBIT	CREDIT	
8		31	*Supplies Expense*			5 1 8 0 87		8
9			*Supplies*				5 1 8 0 87	9

Supplies Expense

Debit	Credit
5,180.87	

Supplies

Debit	Credit
7,610.87	5,180.87
(New Bal. 2,430.00)	

The Supplies account balance in the unadjusted trial balance includes two items: (1) the account balance on January 1 and (2) the cost of supplies bought during the year. The account balance does not reflect the cost of any supplies used during the year, which is an operating expense. The amount of the ending inventory is determined by taking a periodic inventory at the end of a fiscal period.

The Supplies balance is $7,610.87. The estimate of supplies on hand on December 31 is $2,430.00. To bring the account up to date, the balance must be decreased by $5,180.87 (December 31 balance, $7,610.87, less the estimate of supplies on hand, $2,430.00).

PREPAID INSURANCE ADJUSTMENT

GENERAL JOURNAL — PAGE 20

	DATE		ACCOUNT TITLE	DOC. NO.	POST. REF.	DEBIT	CREDIT	
10		31	*Insurance Expense*			12 0 0 0 00		10
11			*Prepaid Insurance*				12 0 0 0 00	11
12								12

Insurance Expense

Debit	Credit
12,000.00	

Prepaid Insurance

Debit	Credit
14,000.00	12,000.00
(New Bal. 2,000.00)	

The Prepaid Insurance account balance in the unadjusted trial balance includes two items: (1) the account balance on January 1 and (2) the amount of insurance premiums paid during the year. The account balance does not reflect the amount of any insurance used during the year, which is an operating expense. The amount of unexpired insurance is determined at the end of a fiscal period.

The Prepaid Insurance account balance is $14,000.00. The estimate of unexpired insurance on December 31 is $2,000.00. To bring the account up to date, the balance of Prepaid Insurance must be decreased by $12,000.00 (December 31 balance, $14,000.00, less unexpired insurance, $2,000.00).

INPUT

- Explain that the Supplies account listed in the unadjusted trial balance on page 98 reflects the balance of supplies at the beginning of the year as well as supplies purchased during the year. It does not reflect any supplies used during the year.
- Point out that a periodic inventory was taken to determine the value of supplies on hand at the end of the year.
- Review how to calculate the adjustment for supplies.
- Emphasize that students have already learned about adjusting for supplies for a non-departmentalized business in the first-year course.

MODEL

Adjustment for supplies

- Refer students to the unadjusted trial balance on page 98. Ask them to state the account balance for Supplies.
- Remind students that there was no previous account balance for supplies expense on the unadjusted trial balance.
- Demonstrate the calculations to determine the adjustment for supplies.
- Draw T accounts to illustrate the accounts used for the supplies adjustment.
- Remind students that expense amounts are entered as debits in the expense account and as a credit to the appropriate asset account.
- Refer students to the illustration in the book of the proper way to journalize the adjustment in the general journal.

INPUT

- Explain that the Prepaid Insurance account listed in the unadjusted trial balance on page 98 does not reflect the amount of insurance that has been used (or expired) during the year.
- Point out that the amount of unexpired insurance will need to be determined at the end of the year to calculate the adjustment for prepaid insurance.
- Review the adjustment for prepaid insurance.
- Emphasize that students have already learned about adjusting for prepaid insurance for a non-departmentalized business in the first-year course.

MODEL

Adjustment for prepaid insurance

- Refer students to the unadjusted trial balance on page 98. Ask them to state the amount of the account balance for Prepaid Insurance.
- Point out that the account balance represents the balance on January 1 plus the amount purchased during the year.
- Remind students that there was no previous account balance for insurance expense on the unadjusted trial balance.
- Draw T accounts for Insurance Expense and Prepaid Insurance to illustrate the accounts used for the insurance adjustment. Ask students for the amount of prepaid insurance recorded on the trial balance. Write the amount in the Prepaid Insurance T account.
- Remind students that expense amounts are entered as debits in the expense account and as a credit to the appropriate asset account.
- Refer students to the illustration in the book of the proper way to journalize the adjustment in the general journal.

INPUT

- Draw T accounts for Depreciation Expense—Office Equipment and Accumulated Depreciation—Office Equipment; label the normal balance sides. Show students how Whiley's estimate of $7,320.00 for yearly depreciation on office equipment is recorded. Emphasize that depreciation is an estimate.
- Review the concepts of plant assets and depreciation expense. Lead into a discussion of the accounting concept of Matching Expenses with Revenue.
- Stress that depreciation does not necessarily represent the actual decline in the value of an asset; instead, it is a method of allocating the cost of an asset over the years it will be used to generate revenue.
- Point out that a similar adjustment is made for Depreciation Expense—Store Equipment and Accumulated Depreciation—Store Equipment.

MODEL

Adjustment for depreciation expenses

- Continue to direct students to the illustration on page 98 as beginning balances are discussed.
- Draw T accounts to demonstrate the adjustments for depreciation.
- Refer students to the illustration for depreciation expense adjustments.
- Remind students that expense amounts are entered as debits.

DEPRECIATION EXPENSE ADJUSTMENTS

GENERAL JOURNAL — PAGE 20

	DATE	ACCOUNT TITLE	DOC. NO.	POST. REF.	DEBIT	CREDIT	
12	31	*Depreciation Expense—Office Equipment*			7 3 2 0 00		12
13		*Accumulated Depreciation—Office Equipment*				7 3 2 0 00	13
14	31	*Depreciation Expense—Store Equipment*			8 3 7 0 00		14
15		*Accumulated Depreciation—Store Equipment*				8 3 7 0 00	15
16							16

Depreciation Expense—Office Equipment	
7,320.00	

Accumulated Depreciation—Office Equipment	
	14,150.00
	7,320.00
	(New Bal. 21,470.00)

Depreciation Expense—Store Equipment	
8,370.00	

Accumulated Depreciation—Store Equipment	
	34,550.00
	8,370.00
	(New Bal. 42,920.00)

Physical assets that will be used for a number of years in the operation of a business are called **plant assets**. Plant assets are not bought for resale to customers in the normal course of business. Plant assets decrease in value because of use, the passage of time, and the availability of new models. The portion of a plant asset's cost that is transferred to an expense account in each fiscal period during that asset's useful life is called **depreciation expense**. The decrease in the value of equipment because of use and the passage of time is an operating expense. [CONCEPT: Matching Expenses with Revenue]

The amount of depreciation is an estimate. The actual decrease in equipment value is not known until equipment is disposed of or sold. For this reason, the estimated depreciation is recorded in a separate contra asset account for each type of equipment.

Whiley estimates that the annual depreciation on office equipment is $7,320.00. To adjust for the depreciation of office equipment, Depreciation Expense—Office Equipment increases by a $7,320.00 debit. The contra asset account, Accumulated Depreciation—Office Equipment, increases by a $7,320.00 credit.

A similar adjustment is made for Depreciation Expense—Store Equipment. Calculating the amount of depreciation is described more fully in Chapter 7.

© iStockphoto.com/Hocus Focus Studio

Preparing an Adjusted Trial Balance LO4

Whiley Outdoor Living, Inc.
Adjusted Trial Balance
December 31, 20--

ACCOUNT TITLE	DEBIT	CREDIT
Cash	62 849 26	
Petty Cash	500 00	
Accounts Receivable	23 515 27	
Dividends	19 250 00	
Income Summary—Grills	—	3 201 04
Income Summary—Furniture	3 816 53	—
Sales—Grills	—	472 019 64
Sales Discount—Grills	8 246 75	—
Sales Returns and Allowances—Grills	9 467 42	—
Sales—Furniture	—	492 187 31
Sales Discount—Furniture	5 219 23	—
Sales Returns and Allowances—Furniture	13 810 76	—
Purchases—Grills	254 851 26	—
Purchases Discount—Grills	—	3 105 48
Purchases Returns and Allowances—Grills	—	6 108 67
Purchases—Furniture	197 084 64	—
Purchases Discount—Furniture	—	2 671 69
Purchases Returns and Allowances—Furniture	—	8 094 21
Advertising Expense—Grills	14 920 00	
Payroll Taxes Expense—Grills	6 453 36	
Salary Expense—Grills	73 011 20	
Advertising Expense—Furniture	5 650 00	
Payroll Taxes Expense—Furniture	10 926 17	
Salary Expense—Furniture	125 806 20	
Credit Card Fee Expense	6 842 20	
Depreciation Expense—Office Equipment	7 320 00	
Depreciation Expense—Store Equipment	8 370 00	
Insurance Expense	12 000 00	
Miscellaneous Expense	3 495 04	
Payroll Taxes Expense—Administrative	7 602 20	
Rent Expense	18 400 00	
Salary Expense—Administrative	88 028 80	
Supplies Expense	5 180 87	
Uncollectible Accounts Expense	2 114 92	
Utilities Expense	16 204 68	
Federal Income Tax Expense		

1 Account Titles

2 Account Balances

3 Income Statement Credit Accounts

4 Income Statement Debit Accounts

Total of income statement credit accounts	$987,388.04
Less total of income statement debit accounts, excluding federal income tax expense	904,822.23
Income before income taxes	$ 82,565.81

5 Income before Income Taxes

An updated trial balance is prepared once all adjusting entries are posted to the general ledger. A trial balance prepared after adjusting entries are posted is called an **adjusted trial balance**. The adjusted trial balance is prepared in two steps. In the first step, all account balances, except for Federal Income Tax Expense, are entered on the trial balance. This procedure allows for the calculation of income before income taxes.

Calculating Income before Income Taxes

1. Enter the account titles of all general ledger accounts.
2. Enter the account balances of all accounts except **Federal Income Tax Expense**.
3. Calculate the total account balances of income statement credit accounts. Include the account balance of any **Income Summary** account having a credit balance.
4. Calculate the total account balances of income statement debit accounts, excluding the balance of **Federal Income Tax Expense**. Include the account balance of any **Income Summary** account having a debit balance.
5. Subtract the total of debits from the total of credits to calculate income before income taxes.

INPUT

- Explain that an updated list of accounts and balances is taken from the general ledger once accounts requiring adjustments have been updated.
- The trial balance that reflects the updated, adjusted accounts is called an adjusted trial balance.
- Point out that all accounts except Federal Income Tax Expense are recorded. This allows for the calculation of income before income taxes.

MODEL

Calculating income before income taxes

- Direct students through the five steps listed to calculate income before income taxes.
- Point out that when net income is finally known, federal income tax for the year can be calculated.

INPUT

- Point out that now that the net income is known, the federal income tax can be calculated.
- Remind students that the adjustment for federal income tax is for corporations only.
- Explain that the Internal Revenue Service provides the tax rate table used to calculate the federal income taxes owed based on net income.
- Explain that the line that expresses the tax rate and the taxable income amount is called the tax bracket.
- Point out that the tax rate associated with the tax bracket is called the marginal tax rate.
- Ask students what it means to use quarterly installments to pay for the estimated income tax. Point out that the amount of federal income tax in the unadjusted trial balance is the amount of tax that was paid in quarterly installments.
- Remind students that if the amount of the federal income tax calculated for the year exceeds the quarterly installment total, an adjustment is required to show the amount of additional tax that must be paid.

MODEL

Adjustment for federal income tax expense

- Direct students to the illustration or write on the board the first of three steps illustrated in the text—finding the tax bracket using the tax table.
- Direct students to the illustration or write on the board the second of three steps illustrated in the text—calculating the taxable income subject to the marginal rate.
- Direct students to the illustration or write on the board the third of three steps illustrated in the text—adding the bracket minimum income tax.
- Write on the board the amount of federal income tax, $16,322.38, as determined by Whiley at the end of the fiscal year.
- Demonstrate how to calculate the amount of the federal income tax expense adjustment when the total amount of tax is known. Point out that students must determine how much has been paid thus far by adding up the total federal income tax expense and subtracting this from the amount owed to determine how much additional is owed (or sometimes refunded if there is an overpayment).

Calculating the Federal Income Tax Adjustment

GENERAL JOURNAL — PAGE 20

	DATE		ACCOUNT TITLE	DOC. NO.	POST. REF.	DEBIT	CREDIT	
16		31	*Federal Income Tax Expense*			2 322 38		16
17			*Federal Income Tax Payable*				2 322 38	17
18								18

Now that the actual amount of income before income taxes is known, the actual amount of federal income tax is calculated. The amount of federal income tax a corporation must pay is calculated using a tax rate table issued by the Internal Revenue Service.

Different tax rates are applied to different levels of net income. Each tax rate and taxable income amount on one line of a tax table is called a **tax bracket**. The tax rate associated with a tax bracket is called a **marginal tax rate**.

The first step in calculating federal income tax is to find the correct tax bracket. Whiley's income before income taxes is $82,565.81. That amount of income, between $75,000.00 and $100,000.00, places Whiley in the third tax bracket (highlighted in the tax table). Whiley's income tax will be $13,750.00 plus 34% of the taxable income above the $75,000.00 minimum.

The second step is to calculate the amount of taxable income subject to the marginal tax rate. This amount, $7,565.81, is multiplied by the marginal tax rate, 34%, to calculate the marginal income tax, $2,572.38. The minimum amount of tax owed by a business in the $75,000 to $100,000 tax bracket is $13,750.00. This amount is provided in the third column of the tax table.

The third and final step is to add the bracket minimum income tax, $13,750.00, to the marginal income tax, $2,572.38. Whiley owes a total income tax of $16,322.38 for the fiscal year.

Tax Rate Schedule

If taxable income (line 30, Form 1120, or line 26, Form 1120-A) is:

Over—	But not over—	Tax is:	Of the amount over—
$0	50,000	15%	-0-
50,000	75,000	$7,500 + 25%	$50,000
75,000	100,000	13,750 + 34%	75,000
100,000	335,000	22,250 + 39%	100,000
335,000	10,000,000	113,900 + 34%	335,000
10,000,000	15,000,000	3,400,000 + 35%	10,000,000
15,000,000	18,333,333	5,150,000 + 38%	15,000,000
18,333,333	—	35%	-0-

Net Income before Federal Income Taxes	−	Tax Bracket Minimum Taxable Income	=	Net Income Subject to Marginal Tax Rate
$82,565.81	−	$75,000.00	=	$7,565.81

Net Income Subject to Marginal Tax Rate	×	Marginal Tax Rate	=	Marginal Income Tax
$7,565.81	×	34%	=	$2,572.38

Bracket Minimum Income Tax	+	Marginal Income Tax	=	Federal Income Tax
$13,750.00	+	$2,572.38	=	$16,322.38

Federal Income Tax Expense

Debit		Credit
4/15	3,500.00	
6/15	3,500.00	
9/15	3,500.00	
12/15	3,500.00	
12/31 Adj.	2,322.38	
(Adj. Bal.	16,322.38)	

Federal Income Tax Payable

Debit	Credit	
	12/31 Adj.	2,322.38

Corporations are required to make quarterly federal income tax payments. Estimating that it would owe $14,000.00 in federal income taxes for the year, Whiley made payments of $3,500.00 each quarter. The current balance of Federal Income Tax Expense, $14,000.00, needs to be brought up to date for the actual amount of federal income tax owed, $16,322.38. The adjusting entry increases Federal Income Tax Expense and increases the balance of Federal Income Tax Payable by $2,322.38. Whiley must pay an additional $2,322.38 when it files its tax return.

- Point out that the adjustment in this instance represents additional tax owed and is therefore debited to the expense account so that its balance reflects the amount of federal income tax. The same amount is credited to Federal Income Tax Payable.
- Draw T accounts for Federal Income Tax Expense and Federal Income Tax Payable to illustrate the accounts used for the federal income tax adjustment. Point out to students the illustration of the general journal and the proper way to journalize the adjustment for federal income taxes.

Careers In Accounting

Lian Vong

JUNIOR ACCOUNTANT/SENIOR ACCOUNTANT

© iStockphoto.com/VII-photo

Lian Vong graduated from college with a degree in accounting. Although she hoped someday to pass the CPA (certified public accountant) exam, she knew she needed some work experience before she could get her license. She decided to study for the exam while working full-time in an accounting position. She got a job as a junior accountant in one of the major accounting firms.

A junior accountant is an entry-level position in most accounting firms, and it usually requires a degree in accounting. As a junior accountant, Lian performed many tasks to support senior accountants. She double-checked calculations, performed tax calculations, posted journal entries, gathered data for monthly reports, and worked with receivables and payables.

The accounting firm paid for Lian to take a CPA exam review. She completed the course and passed the exam. After four years with the firm, Lian, now a CPA, was promoted to the position of senior accountant.

As a senior accountant, Lian had more responsibilities and performed higher-level work. She coordinated auditing procedures, performed financial analyses, and prepared tax returns and financial reports. She also communicated directly with clients on a regular basis. In addition, she supervised a team of junior accountants, including their training and scheduling.

Lian enjoys public accounting and hopes to stay with her firm for many years. She likes the variety and the opportunity for advancement.

Salary Range: A junior accountant typically earns 60 to 70% of a senior accountant's salary, with a salary range of $39,000 to $62,000. The range for a senior accountant is $49,000 to $79,000.

Qualifications: Both junior accountant and senior accountant positions require a degree in accounting. The position of senior accountant also usually requires three or more years of work experience and a CPA designation.

Occupational Outlook: Both junior and senior accounting positions are expected to experience above-average growth (over 20%) through 2018.

Sources: online.onetcenter.org; Ehow.com; Robert Half 2012 Salary Guide.

© iStockphoto.com/Mlenny

Careers In Accounting

Discuss careers as a junior and senior accountant.

INPUT

- Explain that the adjusted trial balance is completed after the account balances for Federal Income Tax Expense and Federal Income Tax Payable are updated.
- Point out that a work sheet is often used when accounting software is not available. Students learned how to use a work sheet in the first-year course. A sample work sheet is illustrated in the appendix at the end of this chapter, along with optional work sheet problems. Solutions for these problems can be found in the Teacher's Edition of the Working Papers.

TEACHING IDEA

Provide students with postcard-size paper. Ask students to write a postcard to you explaining one thing they learned well today and one area in which they need further clarification.

Completing the Adjusted Trial Balance

Whiley Outdoor Living, Inc.
Adjusted Trial Balance
December 31, 20--

ACCOUNT TITLE	DEBIT	CREDIT
Cash	62,849.26	
Petty Cash	500.00	
Accounts Receivable	23,515.27	
Allowance for Uncollectible Accounts		2,210.61
Merchandise Inventory—Grills	89,349.72	
Merchandise Inventory—Furniture	102,915.36	
Supplies	2,430.00	
Prepaid Insurance	2,000.00	
Office Equipment	32,481.15	
Accumulated Depreciation—Office Equipment		21,470.00
Store Equipment	64,184.07	
Accumulated Depreciation—Store Equipment		42,920.00
Accounts Payable		30,392.88
Sales Tax Payable		6,148.05
Employee Income Tax Payable—Federal		1,666.00
Employee Income Tax Payable—State		1,190.00
Social Security Tax Payable		2,950.80
Medicare Tax Payable		687.22
Medical Insurance Payable		1,050.00
Retirement Plan Payable		710.00
Unemployment Tax Payable—Federal		20.72
Unemployment Tax Payable—State		139.86
Federal Income Tax Payable		2,322.38
Depreciation Expense—Office Equipment	7,320.00	
Depreciation Expense—Store Equipment	8,370.00	
Insurance Expense	12,000.00	
Miscellaneous Expense	3,495.04	
Payroll Taxes Expense—Administrative	7,602.20	
Rent Expense	18,400.00	
Salary Expense—Administrative	88,028.80	
Supplies Expense	5,180.87	
Uncollectible Accounts Expense	2,114.92	
Utilities Expense	16,204.68	
Federal Income Tax Expense	16,322.38	
Totals	1,320,619.44	1,320,619.44

Federal Income Tax Amounts

Total, Prove, and Rule

After the income tax adjustment is posted, the balances for Federal Income Tax Payable and Federal Income Tax Expense are entered in the adjusted trial balance.

The trial balance is totaled, proved, and ruled. The trial balance provides the information necessary to prepare the financial statements.

Using a Work Sheet to Prepare Financial Statements

A **work sheet** is a columnar accounting form used to summarize the general ledger information needed to prepare financial statements. Prior to the use of computerized accounting systems, the work sheet was the most effective tool for collecting the information needed to prepare financial statements. Instructions for preparing a work sheet are located in the appendix at the end of this chapter.

FORMATIVE ASSESSMENT

- This is an ongoing process. Circulate around the classroom or lab, observing which students have problems with the assignments.
- Troubleshooting: Students may have difficulty remembering partner accounts for adjustment as well as calculating federal income tax payable.
- Assess student understanding by checking solutions to Independent Practice assignments and noting their answers to the Terms Review and the Audit Your Understanding questions.

End of Lesson Review

LO1 Identify the steps necessary to prepare for end-of-period financial reporting.

LO2 Prepare an unadjusted trial balance.

LO3 Journalize adjusting entries.

LO4 Prepare an adjusted trial balance.

Terms Review

fiscal period
fiscal year
schedule of accounts receivable
schedule of accounts payable
trial balance
adjusting entries
unadjusted trial balance
plant assets
depreciation expense
adjusted trial balance
tax bracket
marginal tax rate
work sheet

Audit your understanding

1. What two reports are prepared to prove the accuracy of posting to subsidiary ledgers?
2. Why are adjustments made to certain accounts at the end of the fiscal period?
3. Explain how income before income taxes is calculated using an adjusted trial balance.

Work together 4-1

Preparing an adjusted trial balance

Adjustment information for Foley's Interiors on December 31 is presented below.

Estimate of uncollectible accounts	$ 2,101.23
Ending merchandise inventory—kitchen	147,084.62
Ending merchandise inventory—bath	97,671.31
Supplies on hand	1,950.00
Value of prepaid insurance	2,500.00
Depreciation expense—office equipment	7,250.00
Depreciation expense—store equipment	8,490.00

A partially completed adjusted trial balance, a general journal, and selected accounts are provided in the *Working Papers*. Your instructor will guide you through the following examples. Save your work to complete Work Together 4-2.

1. Record the adjusting entries on page 20 of a general journal.
2. Post the adjusting entries to the general ledger accounts.
3. Enter the adjusted account balances on the adjusted trial balance.
4. Calculate federal income tax expense using the tax table presented in the lesson. Prepare and post the adjusting entry for federal income tax expense.
5. Complete the adjusted trial balance.

On your own 4-1

Preparing an adjusted trial balance

Adjustment information for Mixon Auto Supplies on December 31 is presented below.

Estimate of uncollectible accounts	$ 3,123.53
Ending merchandise inventory—parts	254,285.38
Ending merchandise inventory—accessories	114,223.95
Supplies on hand	1,480.00
Value of prepaid insurance	3,000.00
Depreciation expense—office equipment	4,850.00
Depreciation expense—store equipment	6,490.00

A partially completed adjusted trial balance, a general journal, and selected accounts are provided in the *Working Papers*. Work this problem independently. Save your work to complete On Your Own 4-2.

1. Record the adjusting entries on page 22 of a general journal.
2. Post the adjusting entries to the general ledger accounts.
3. Enter the adjusted account balances on the adjusted trial balance.
4. Calculate federal income tax expense using the tax table presented in the lesson. Prepare and post the adjusting entry for federal income tax expense.
5. Complete the adjusted trial balance.

CHECK FOR UNDERSTANDING

Terms Review

- Call on students to define each term in the Terms Review. Definitions are given in the Glossary.

Audit Your Understanding

- Call on students to answer the Audit Your Understanding questions. Answers are given in Appendix D of the textbook.

GUIDED PRACTICE

Work Together

- Have students write the solution to the Work Together problem as you guide the class through the examples. Elicit class participation in determining the solution.
- Ask a student to provide the adjusting entries needed to bring accounts up to date and to prepare an adjusted trial balance.
- Remind students to save their work to complete Work Together 4-2.

INDEPENDENT PRACTICE

On Your Own

- Assign the On Your Own problem to be worked independently.
- Remind students to save their work to complete On Your Own 4-2.

Application Problem

- Assign Application Problem 4-1.
- Remind students to save their work to complete Application Problems 4-2, 4-3, and 4-4.

Online Working Papers

- Students can access the Lesson 4-1 problems using this software.

RETEACH

- Analyze adjustments using four questions: (1) What is the balance of the account? (2) What should the balance be for the account? (3) What must be done to correct the account balance? (4) What adjustment is made?

Essential Questions

- Why would it be beneficial for a business to have an accounts payable subsidiary ledger? (*Answers might include knowing the account history of each vendor—how much is owed and how much has been paid.*)
- Would it ever be advantageous for a business to overpay federal taxes and receive a refund at the end of the fiscal year rather than owe an amount? Explain.

EXTENDED LEARNING

- Assign Accounting in the Real World on page 95.
- Assign Ethics in Action on page 96.
- Assign Financial Literacy on page 97.
- Review Careers in Accounting on page 105.

CLOSURE

- Ask students to summarize briefly what adjusting entries must be made and how to calculate the amounts.
- Ask students to explain the difference between an unadjusted trial balance and an adjusted trial balance.
- Ask students to explain briefly how to calculate net income, federal income taxes owed, and the federal income tax adjustment.

LESSON

4-2

BRIDGE

- Explain that students are already familiar with calculating gross profit from previous lessons in accounting. This lesson will help students apply what was previously learned about a non-departmentalized business to a departmentalized business.

TEACHING RESOURCES

- **Instructor's Resource CD/Website:**
  PowerPoint Slides
  Accounting Concepts
- **Working Papers:**
  Teacher's Edition of the Working Papers for Lesson 4-2
  Online Working Papers
- **Transparency Master:**
  Statement (4-column with % of Net Sales)

ENGAGE

- Ask students to imagine a company with two sales departments and to list the expenses of the company that do not directly involve either department. List these on the board and ask who is responsible for controlling each expense.
- Ask students to discuss why an individual department of a business would want to compare results from one period to the next.
- Ask students why a business would want to compare results from each department.

PREVIEW

- Call on students to read the accounting terms and definitions introduced in this lesson: *responsibility accounting, direct expense, indirect expense, responsibility statements, departmental margin, departmental margin statement, gross profit, financial ratio,* and *vertical analysis.*
- Point out the learning objectives for this lesson.
- Direct students to read the headings in this lesson and to examine the illustrations.

TEACHING IDEA **Ask students to summarize in 30–50 words what they learned in the previous lesson. Call on students to share their summaries with the class. If time permits, ask them to summarize in 10–15 words as well.**

LESSON

4-2 Responsibility Statements for a Merchandising Business

LO5 Distinguish between direct and indirect expenses of a departmentalized business.
LO6 Prepare a departmental margin statement.
LO7 Calculate and analyze vertical analysis ratios.

Features of a Responsibility Accounting System LO5

The two important features of a successful responsibility accounting system are as follows:

1. Each manager is assigned responsibility for only those revenues, cost, and expenses for which he or she can make decisions and affect the outcome.
2. The revenues, costs, and expenses for which a manager is responsible must be readily identifiable with the manager's unit. For example, if a manager is responsible for advertising expense, that manager should make decisions about advertising. In addition, a separate record should be kept for the manager's advertising expense. Thus, responsibility accounting traces revenues, costs, and expenses to the individual managers who are responsible for making decisions about those revenues, costs, and expenses.

Controlling costs is essential to a business's success. However, who should control a business's costs? Good management practices require that each manager be responsible for controlling all costs incurred by the manager's business unit. Assigning control of revenues, costs, and expenses to a specific manager is called **responsibility accounting**. Merchandising businesses with effective cost controls generally use some kind of responsibility accounting.

A typical merchandising business income statement reports net income earned during a fiscal period. However, the statement usually does not report specific information that a department manager can use to control departmental costs. Therefore, merchandising businesses often prepare departmental statements to show each department's contribution to net income.

In responsibility accounting, operating expenses are classified as either direct or indirect expenses. An operating expense identifiable with and chargeable to the operation of a specific department is called a **direct expense**. The cost of supplies used by a specific department is an example of a direct expense. An operating expense chargeable to overall business operations and not identifiable with a specific department is called an **indirect expense**. Therefore, the cost of electricity used by a business's overall operations is an example of an indirect expense. A department manager has little or no control over the use of electricity in the department.

Whiley uses responsibility accounting to help control costs and expenses. Whiley has two merchandising departments: Grills and Furniture. Each department's revenue, cost of merchandise sold, and direct expenses are recorded in separate departmental general ledger accounts as shown in Whiley's chart of accounts.

Each business develops a chart of accounts to meet its needs. Whiley groups its departmental accounts by type, such as operating revenue, cost of merchandise, direct expenses, and indirect expenses. For example, accounts under Direct Expenses—Grills are 6100 numbers. Accounts under Direct Expenses—Furniture are 6200 numbers.

INPUT

- Explain that responsibility accounting is assigning control of revenues, costs, and expenses only to the department manager who controls them.
- Direct students to the first column to explain two important features of responsibility accounting.
- Point out that direct expenses are under the control of and benefit a single department.
- Emphasize that expenses not separated by department are indirect expenses.

MODEL

- Write the two merchandising department titles for Whiley, Grills and Furniture, on the board.
- Ask for examples of direct expenses for each department. Write answers under the appropriate department heading. Examples might include advertising, salaries, payroll taxes, supplies, and sales.
- Ask for examples of indirect expenses Whiley might have. Write answers under the heading *Indirect Expenses*. An example might include Rent Expense.

Departmental Margin Statement LO6

	Whiley Outdoor Living, Inc.					
Statement Heading	Departmental Margin Statement—Grills					
	For Year Ended December 31, 20--					
						% of Net Sales
Operating Revenue Section	Operating Revenue:					
	Sales			472,019.64		
	Less: Sales Discount		8,246.75			
	Sales Returns and Allowances		9,467.42	17,714.17		
	Net Sales				454,305.47	100.0
Cost of Merchandise Sold Section	Cost of Merchandise Sold:					
	Merchandise Inventory, Jan. 1, 20--			86,148.68		
	Purchases		254,851.26			
	Less: Purchases Discount	3,105.48				
	Purchases Returns and Allowances	6,108.67	9,214.15			
	Net Purchases			245,637.11		
	Total Cost of Mdse. Available for Sale			331,785.79		
	Less Merchandise Inventory, Dec. 31, 20--			89,349.72		
	Cost of Merchandise Sold				242,436.07	53.4
Gross Profit	Gross Profit				211,869.40	46.6
Direct Expenses Section	Direct Expenses:					
	Advertising Expense			14,920.00		
	Payroll Taxes Expense			6,453.36		
	Salary Expense			73,011.20		
	Total Direct Expenses				94,384.56	20.8
Departmental Margin	Departmental Margin				117,484.84	25.9
	*Rounded to the nearest 0.1%.					

Financial statements reporting revenue, costs, and direct expenses under a specific department's control are called **responsibility statements**. Whiley prepares the usual end-of-fiscal-period financial statements. In addition, Whiley prepares a responsibility statement for each department.

The revenue earned by a department less its cost of merchandise sold and less its direct expenses is called **departmental margin**. A statement that reports departmental margin for a specific department is called a **departmental margin statement**.

Whiley's departmental margin statement—grills for the year ended December 31 is shown above. Information for this statement is obtained from the adjusted trial balance accounts having grills in the account title. The format of the statement is similar to an income statement. However, only direct expenses for the grills department are included on the departmental margin statement.

The operating revenue remaining after cost of merchandise sold has been deducted is called **gross profit**. Gross profit, therefore, shows the direct relationship between sales and sales price and merchandise inventory and the cost of merchandise inventory. By analyzing a department's gross profit data, managers can determine the amount of revenue remaining after the cost of merchandise has been deducted from net sales.

The departmental margin statements help department managers determine how revenue, costs, and direct expenses affect department results. With this knowledge, managers can make informed decisions to improve those results.

INPUT

- Point out that responsibility statements report revenue, costs, and direct expenses related to a specific department.
- Explain *departmental margin*.
- Direct students to the departmental margin statement illustrated and point out that the name of the department is not included in the account titles because all the accounts are the departmental accounts for Grills. This saves time and repetition and makes the statement easier to read.
- Refer students to the different sections of the departmental margin statement.
- Explain the difference between gross profit and departmental margin.

DIFFERENTIATED INSTRUCTION

Gifted learners need additional challenges, such as research, to maintain a high level of motivation. Students should interview a department manager from a company that uses responsibility accounting, asking him or her to address its importance. They should ask the manager to address motivation and competition between departments that can be enhanced or encouraged through responsibility accounting. Students should share their findings with the class.

Vertical Analysis of Departmental Margin Statements LO7

Departmental Margin	÷	Net Sales	=	Vertical Analysis Ratio for Departmental Margin
$117,484.84	÷	$454,305.47	=	25.9%

To help a manager analyze financial information, relationships between items in a financial statement are calculated. A comparison between two components of financial information is called a **financial ratio**. Reporting an amount on a financial statement as a percentage of another item on the same financial statement is called **vertical analysis**. Vertical analysis ratios may be shown in a separate column on a financial statement.

Whiley analyzes its departmental margin statements by calculating vertical analysis ratios for cost of merchandise sold, gross profit, direct expenses, and departmental margin. The ratios are calculated by dividing the amount on selected lines by the amount of departmental net sales. The calculation of the vertical analysis ratio for the departmental margin of the grills department is shown above.

A business may set departmental margin goals to encourage and determine acceptable performance by each of its department. Whiley set a minimum departmental margin goal of 25.0% for the grills department. Departmental goals are determined by reviewing many factors, including the department's previous achievements, economic and market trends, and changes in department costs.

Vertical analysis ratios for the current fiscal period are also compared to ratios for previous fiscal periods. The grills department's departmental margin ratios for the current and prior fiscal years are shown below.

	Current Year	Prior Year
Cost of Merchandise Sold	53.4%	54.1%
Gross Profit	46.6%	45.9%
Direct Expenses	20.8%	20.4%
Departmental Margin	25.9%	25.5%

When changes in vertical analysis ratios occur for an item on the departmental margin statement, the department manager seeks the reasons for the changes. If the changes are positive, the policies resulting in favorable changes are continued. If the changes are negative, the manager seeks to change policies to prevent further declines.

The departmental margin ratio for the grills department increased from 25.5% to 25.9%, a favorable trend. Still, the grills department manager should examine other vertical analysis ratios to ensure that unfavorable trends do not exist.

The cost of merchandise sold ratios indicate that the grills department was successful in controlling its cost of merchandise, resulting in a decrease in the cost of merchandise sold ratio from 54.1% to 53.4%, a favorable trend. The cost of merchandise sold ratio will increase by (1) increasing sales prices and (2) purchasing merchandise at a discounted unit price.

However, the grills department's direct expenses increased from 20.4% to 20.8% of net sales. The department manager needs to investigate the reasons for this unfavorable trend. Many factors and events can cause expenses to be higher than expected. The department may have contracted excessive advertising, scheduled too many workers, or allowed employees to work overtime hours.

Without the information on the departmental margin statement, a department manager will not know which policies to continue and which to change. The statements also provide information to assist company officers to evaluate the performance of department managers.

fyi Vertical analysis ratios are also known as *component percentages*.

INPUT

- Explain that a comparison between two components of financial information is called a financial ratio.
- Point out that reporting an amount on a financial statement as a percentage of another item on the same financial statement is called vertical analysis.
- Explain that a business may set departmental margin goals for each department to encourage acceptable performance or to evaluate performance.
- Explain that departmental goals are determined by reviewing previous performance, changes in costs, and economic and market trends.
- Explain that ratios for the current period are compared with the same percentages for previous periods to determine trends.
- Significant changes in ratios are evaluated to identify the reason for the change or to decide whether a policy resulting in a favorable change should be continued or a policy resulting in an unfavorable change should be discontinued.

MODEL

- Use the board or refer students to the math illustration to demonstrate calculating the ratio for departmental margin.
- Point out that the ratio of departmental margin to sales is calculated by dividing departmental margin by department net sales.
- Direct students to the bottom of the first column to compare the departmental margin for the current year with that of the prior year. Explain that the percentage is increasing, a positive trend for departmental margin.
- Refer to the illustration at the bottom of the page. Emphasize that increasing percentages for gross profit and departmental margin is a favorable trend, while increasing percentages for cost and expense items is an unfavorable trend.

FORMATIVE ASSESSMENT

- This is an ongoing process. Circulate around the classroom or lab, observing which students have problems with the assignments.
- Troubleshooting: Diagnose the kinds of problems students have with this lesson. They sometimes have difficulty with the format of the statement.
- Assess student understanding by checking solutions to Independent Practice assignments and noting their answers to the Terms Review and Audit Your Understanding questions.

End of Lesson Review

LO5 Distinguish between direct and indirect expenses of a departmentalized business.

LO6 Prepare a departmental margin statement.

LO7 Calculate and analyze vertical analysis ratios.

Terms Review

responsibility accounting
direct expense
indirect expense
responsibility statements
departmental margin
departmental margin statement
gross profit
financial ratio
vertical analysis

Audit your understanding

1. What two features are required if responsibility accounting is to be successful?
2. For what type of accounts does Whiley have separate departmental accounts in the general ledger?
3. How are the vertical analysis ratios for departmental margin calculated?

Work together 4-2

Preparing a departmental margin statement

Foley's Interiors has two departments: Kitchen and Bath. Use the adjusted trial balance or work sheet from Work Together 4-1. Your instructor will guide you through the following examples. Save your work to complete Work Together 4-3.

1. Prepare a departmental margin statement for each department.
2. Calculate vertical analysis ratios for cost of merchandise sold, gross profit, total direct expenses, and departmental margin.

On your own 4-2

Preparing a departmental margin statement

Mixon Auto Supplies has two departments: Parts and Accessories. Use the adjusted trial balance or work sheet from On Your Own 4-1. Work this problem independently. Save your work to complete On Your Own 4-3.

1. Prepare a departmental margin statement for each department.
2. Calculate vertical analysis ratios for cost of merchandise sold, gross profit, total direct expenses, and departmental margin.

Essential Question

- What decisions might be made based on the results of departmental margin statements? (*e.g., whether to discontinue a department, commit more resources to a department, or add or change department personnel*)

CHECK FOR UNDERSTANDING

Terms Review

- Call on students to define each term in the Terms Review. Definitions are given in the Glossary.

Audit Your Understanding

- Call on students to answer the Audit Your Understanding questions. Answers are given in Appendix D of the textbook.

GUIDED PRACTICE

Work Together

- Have students write the solution to the Work Together problems as you guide the class through the examples.
- Remind students to use their work completed in Work Together 4-1.
- Discuss each step of preparing the departmental margin statement.
- Calculate the ratios together before students record the answer in the Working Papers.
- Instruct students to save their work to complete Work Together 4-3.

INDEPENDENT PRACTICE

On Your Own

- Assign the On Your Own problem to be worked independently.
- Remind students to use their work from On Your Own 4-1 and to save their work to complete On Your Own 4-3.
- Use the Formative Assessment techniques to diagnose student understanding.

Application Problem

- Assign Application Problem 4-2. Use the adjusted trial balance or work sheet from Problem 4-1 to complete this problem.
- Remind students to save their work to complete Problem 4-3.

Online Working Papers

- Students can access the Lesson 4-2 problems using this software.

RETEACH

- Call on students to describe each step in preparing the departmental margin statement presented in this lesson.

CLOSURE

- Use the illustrations on pages 109–110 to review briefly the procedures for creating a departmental margin statement and calculating vertical analysis ratios.

LESSON

4-3

BRIDGE

- Explain that the financial statements presented in this lesson are similar to the financial statements students learned in the first-year accounting course.
- Point out that students have already learned how to calculate ratios.

TEACHING RESOURCES

- **Instructor's Resource CD/Website:**
  PowerPoint Slides
  Accounting Concepts
- **Working Papers:**
  Teacher's Edition of the Working Papers for Lesson 4-3
  Online Working Papers
- **Transparency Masters:**
  Statement (4-column with Departmental, Company, and % of Net Sales)
  Statement (3-column)

ENGAGE

- Ask students to summarize how to calculate departmental margin.

PREVIEW

- Call on students to read the accounting terms and definitions introduced in this lesson: *income statement, statement of stockholders' equity, capital stock, retained earnings, dividends, balance sheet, cash flow, statement of cash flows, operating activities, investing activities,* and *financing activities.*
- Point out the learning objective for this lesson.
- Direct students to read the headings in this lesson and to examine the illustrations.

INPUT

- Ask students what type of information is presented on an income statement. Emphasize that the income statement shows revenue, gross profit, expenses, and net income or loss. Lead into a discussion as to why this information is important to managers, owners, stockholders, investors, lenders, and other individuals associated with or interested in the company.
- Explain that although the details of a departmental margin statement are not reported on the company's income statement, summary information is reported.

LESSON

4-3 Financial Statements for a Departmental Merchandising Business

LO8 Prepare financial statements for a departmentalized merchandising business.

Income Statement with Departmental Margin LO8

Statement Heading

Whiley Outdoor Living, Inc.
Income Statement
For Year Ended December 31, 20--

	Departmental: Grills	Departmental: Furniture	Company		% of Net Sales*
Net Sales	454,305.47	473,157.32		927,462.79	100.0
Cost of Merchandise Sold	242,436.07	190,135.27		432,571.34	46.6
Gross Profit	211,869.40	283,022.05		494,891.45	53.4
Direct Expenses	94,384.56	142,382.37		236,766.93	25.5
Departmental Margin	117,484.84	140,639.68		258,124.52	27.8
Indirect Expenses:					
Credit Card Fee Expense			6,842.20		
Depreciation Exp.—Office Equipment			7,320.00		
Depreciation Exp.—Store Equipment			8,370.00		
Insurance Expense			12,000.00		
Miscellaneous Expense			3,495.04		
Payroll Taxes Expense			7,602.20		
Rent Expense			18,400.00		
Salary Expense—Administrative			88,028.80		
Supplies Expense			5,180.87		
Uncollectible Accounts Expense			2,114.92		
Utilities Expense			16,204.68		
Total Indirect Expenses				175,558.71	18.9
Income before Income Tax				82,565.81	8.9
Less Federal Income Tax Expense				16,322.38	1.8
Net Income				66,243.43	7.1

*Rounded to the nearest 0.1%.

Information from Departmental Margin Statements

Indirect Expenses from Adjusted Trial Balance

Income Taxes and Net Income

Vertical Analysis Ratios

A financial statement showing the revenue and expenses for a fiscal period is called an **income statement**. Whiley's income statement for the year ended December 31 is shown above. The income statement is prepared with five columns: two for departmental amounts and three for company amounts and vertical analysis ratios.

The amounts for the first section are obtained from the departmental margin statements. The remaining accounts and balances are obtained from the adjusted trial balance. Vertical analysis ratios are calculated by dividing each amount by company net sales.

- Point out that the format used for the income statement shown uses the two columns to the left to report information about departmental margins for the two departments.
- Explain that the format uses the two columns to the right to report information for the company. Note that the departmental margin information is totaled to show departmental information combined for the whole company.
- Explain that component percentages are calculated for each item on the income statement. Point out that a company can show whichever ratios it believes are relevant to understanding the income statement.

Statement of Stockholders' Equity

Statement Heading ①
Capital Stock Section ②
Beginning Retained Earnings ③
Change in Retained Earnings ④

Whiley Outdoor Living, Inc. Statement of Stockholders' Equity For Year Ended December 31, 20--			
Capital Stock:			
$1.00 Par Value			
January 1, 20--, 95,000 Shares Issued		95,000.00	
Issued during Current Year, 5,000 Shares		5,000.00	
Balance, December 31, 20--, 100,000 Shares Issued			100,000.00
Retained Earnings:			
Balance, January 1, 20--		114,352.88	
Net Income for 20--	66,243.43		
Less Dividends Declared during 20--	19,250.00		
Net Increase during 20--		46,993.43	
Balance, December 31, 20--			161,346.31
Total Stockholders' Equity, December 31, 20--			261,346.31

Total Stockholders' Equity ⑤

A financial statement that shows changes in a corporation's ownership for a fiscal period is called a **statement of stockholders' equity**. Whiley's statement of stockholders' equity for the fiscal year ended December 31 is shown above. Information for this statement is obtained from (1) the prior year's statement of stockholders' equity, (2) the income statement, and (3) the adjusted trial balance.

A statement of stockholders' equity contains two major sections:

1. Capital stock. Total shares of ownership in a corporation are called **capital stock**.
2. Retained earnings. An amount earned by a corporation and not yet distributed to stockholders is called **retained earnings**.

Net income increases the retained earnings of a corporation. A corporation may retain some income for business expansion. Some income may be distributed to stockholders as a return on their investment. Earnings distributed to stockholders are called **dividends**.

Preparing a Statement of Stockholders' Equity

① **Write the heading. Center the name of the company, name of the report, and date of the report on three separate lines at the top of the statement.**

② **Prepare the capital stock section. The stock information as of January 1 is obtained from the prior year's statement. The number of shares issued in the current year is obtained by analyzing the general ledger account. The December 31 amount equals the amount in the adjusted trial balance.**

③ **Begin the retained earnings section by entering the January 1 balance of retained earnings from the prior year's statement.**

④ **Complete the retained earnings section. The net income is obtained from the income statement. The dividends amount is found on the adjusted trial balance. Subtract the dividends from net income to determine the net increase in retained earnings. Add the increase to the January 1 balance to determine the December 31 balance.**

⑤ **Add the amount of capital stock and ending retained earnings to determine the total stockholders' equity as of December 31.**

INPUT

- Remind students that they have already learned how to prepare a statement of stockholders' equity.
- Ask students the purpose of the statement of stockholders' equity. Emphasize that the statement shows changes in a corporation's ownership for a stated fiscal period.
- Discuss and explain the two main sections of the statement of stockholders' equity—capital stock and retained earnings.
- Ask students the impact of net income and net loss on retained earnings.
- Ask students to explain a dividend and to describe its impact on retained earnings.
- Point out that the statement of stockholders' equity is the same for both departmentalized and non-departmentalized corporations.

MODEL

Prepare a statement of stockholders' equity

- Distribute a copy of a statement of stockholders' equity similar to the one presented on this page. Be sure to provide a price per share and the number of shares issued. However, do not include any figures in the three amount columns.
- Write three amounts on the board—a beginning balance for retained earnings, net income after federal income tax, and dividends declared. Ask students to complete the statement of stockholders' equity using the information provided on the statement and on the board. Allow students to work collaboratively and to use their texts.
- After students are finished, use a transparency of the same statement and demonstrate the process for completing a statement of stockholders' equity. Explain the origin of or show the calculation for each amount appearing in the amount columns.

INPUT

- Remind students that they have already prepared 3-column balance sheets during their accounting instruction.
- Ask students what is reported on a balance sheet. Emphasize that the balance sheet is simply a snapshot of a business showing what a business owns, owes, and is worth on a given day.
- Review the accounting concept that assets must always equal liabilities plus stockholders' equity. Point out that the balance sheet represents the accounting equation (A = L + OE) on paper.
- Discuss the difference between current assets and plant assets. Emphasize that these categories are based on the length of time the assets will be in use. For example, cash and other assets expected to be exchanged for cash or consumed within a year are known as current assets. Assets that will be used for a number of years in the operation of the business are known as plant assets.
- Remind students that the information for the preparation of the asset and liability portion of the balance sheet is obtained from the adjusted trial balance. The data used in preparing the stockholders' equity section of the balance sheet are obtained from the statement of stockholders' equity.
- Point out that the balance sheet is similar for both departmentalized and non-departmentalized corporations.

Balance Sheet

Whiley Outdoor Living, Inc.
Balance Sheet
December 31, 20--

				% OF ASSETS*
ASSETS				
Current Assets:				
Cash		62,849.26		
Petty Cash		500.00		
Accounts Receivable	23,515.27			
Less Allowance for Uncollectible Accounts	2,210.61	21,304.66		
Merchandise Inventory—Grills		89,349.72		
Merchandise Inventory—Furniture		102,915.36		
Supplies		2,430.00		
Prepaid Insurance		2,000.00		
Total Current Assets			281,349.00	89.7
Plant Assets:				
Office Equipment	32,481.15			
Less Accumulated Depreciation—Office Equipment	21,470.00	11,011.15		
Store Equipment	64,184.07			
Less Accumulated Depreciation—Store Equipment	42,920.00	21,264.07		
Total Plant Assets			32,275.22	10.3
Total Assets			313,624.22	100.0
LIABILITIES				
Current Liabilities:				
Accounts Payable		30,392.88		
Sales Tax Payable		6,148.05		
Employee Income Tax Payable—Federal		1,666.00		
Employee Income Tax Payable—State		1,190.00		
Social Security Tax Payable		2,950.80		
Medicare Tax Payable		687.22		
Medical Insurance Payable		1,050.00		
Retirement Plan Payable		710.00		
Unemployment Tax Payable—Federal		20.72		
Unemployment Tax Payable—State		139.86		
Federal Income Tax Payable		2,322.38		
Dividends Payable		5,000.00		
Total Liabilities			52,277.91	16.7
STOCKHOLDERS' EQUITY				
Capital Stock		100,000.00		
Retained Earnings		161,346.31		
Total Stockholders' Equity			261,346.31	83.3
Total Liabilities and Stockholders' Equity			313,624.22	100.0
*Rounded to the nearest 0.1%.				

A financial statement that reports assets, liabilities, and owners' equity on a specific date is called a **balance sheet**. A balance sheet reports the financial condition of a business on a specific date. Whiley's balance sheet for December 31 is shown above.

The data used in preparing the asset and liability sections of a balance sheet come from the adjusted trial balance. Assets are divided into two categories: current assets and plant assets. Accounts receivable, office equipment, and store equipment each have a contra account. The balance of the contra account is subtracted from the asset account. Liabilities are typically divided into two categories: current liabilities and long-term liabilities. Whiley does not currently have any long-term liabilities.

The data used in preparing the stockholders' equity section of a balance sheet come from the statement of stockholders' equity. Only the total amounts of capital stock and retained earnings are presented on the balance sheet. Information that is more detailed is available on the statement of stockholders' equity.

Vertical analysis ratios are calculated by dividing selected amounts by total assets.

DIFFERENTIATED INSTRUCTION

Mathematical/Logical learners enjoy solving problems and working with numbers. Using the Internet, ask students to obtain the statement of cash flows from two companies. Ask students to perform a vertical analysis by calculating the percent of net cash from operating activities, investing activities, and financing activities. Students should compare their analysis for each company and summarize their findings.

Statement of Cash Flows

Whiley Outdoor Living, Inc.			
Statement of Cash Flows			
For Year Ended December 31, 20--			
Cash flows from operating activities:			
Cash receipts from customers		914,108.26	
Cash payments for:			
Inventory purchases	(429,105.18)		
Salaries and wages	(311,827.93)		
Rent	(18,400.00)		
Taxes	(16,204.18)		
Insurance	(14,000.00)		
Other operating expenses	(55,418.10)		
Total cash payments		(844,955.39)	
Net cash provided (used) by operating activities			69,152.87
Cash flows from investing activities:			
Sale of equipment		5,200.00	
Purchase of equipment		(18,520.00)	
Net cash provided (used) by investing activities			(13,320.00)
Cash flows from financing activities:			
Issuance of stock		5,000.00	
Payment of cash dividends		(21,200.00)	
Net cash provided (used) by financing activities			(16,200.00)
Net change in cash			39,632.87
Cash balance, January 1, 20--			23,216.39
Cash balance, December 31, 20--			62,849.26

The income statement, statement of stockholders' equity, and balance sheet are prepared using the accrual basis of accounting. Understanding how a business receives and spends its cash provides a different perspective into its operations. The cash receipts and cash payments of a company are called **cash flow**. A financial statement that summarizes cash receipts and cash payments resulting from business activities during a fiscal period is called a **statement of cash flows**.

The statement of cash flows is divided into three sections. The cash receipts and payments necessary to operate a business on a day-to-day basis are called **operating activities**. These activities include receiving cash from customers, purchasing merchandise, and paying expenses. Cash receipts and cash payments involving the sale or purchase of assets used to earn revenue over a period of time are called **investing activities**. These activities include the sale and purchase of plant assets. Cash receipts and payments involving debt or equity transactions are called **financing activities**. These activities usually involve borrowing money from creditors and repaying the principal or selling stock and paying dividends.

The preparation and use of the statement of cash flows is presented in greater depth in Chapter 14.

INPUT

- Remind students that they have prepared a statement of cash flows in the first-year accounting course.
- A statement of cash flows summarizes the cash receipts (cash in) and cash payments (cash out) of a company during a fiscal period.
- Point out that cash receipts and payments pertaining to the day-to-day operations of a business are called operating activities. Those involving the sale or purchase of assets used to earn revenue are called investing activities. Activities that involve borrowing money, repaying borrowed money, and selling stock and paying dividends are called financing activities.

TEACHING IDEA **Ask students to list three things that a fellow student might misunderstand about this lesson. Collect lists and use them to determine what you need to review before beginning the next lesson.**

FORMATIVE ASSESSMENT

- This is an ongoing process. Circulate around the classroom or lab, observing which students have problems with the assignments.
- Troubleshooting: Students have prepared financial statements previously. However, they may have difficulty remembering the format of the statements.
- Assess student understanding by checking solutions to Independent Practice assignments and noting their answers to the Terms Review and Audit Your Understanding questions.

CHECK FOR UNDERSTANDING

Terms Review

- Call on students to define each term in the Terms Review. Definitions are given in the Glossary.

Audit Your Understanding

- Call on students to answer the Audit Your Understanding questions. Answers are given in Appendix D of the textbook.

GUIDED PRACTICE

Work Together

- Have students write the solution to the Work Together problem as you guide the class through the examples.
- Instruct students to use the adjusted trial balance or work sheet from Work Together 4-1 and the departmental margin statement from Work Together 4-2 to complete this problem.
- Direct students to record each amount on the proper form as you elicit class participation in determining and calculating each amount.
- Call on students to describe the various steps used to complete each problem.
- Remind students to save their work to complete Work Together 4-4.

INDEPENDENT PRACTICE

On Your Own

- Instruct students to use the adjusted trial balance or work sheet from On Your Own 4-1 and the departmental margin statement from On Your Own 4-2 to complete this problem.
- Assign the On Your Own problem to be worked independently.
- Use the Formative Assessment techniques to diagnose student understanding.

Application Problem

- Assign Application Problem 4-3.

Online Working Papers

- Students can access the Lesson 4-3 problems using this software.

RETEACH

- Call on students to describe each step in preparing the various financial statements presented in this lesson.

End of Lesson Review

LO8 Prepare financial statements for a departmentalized merchandising business.

Terms Review

income statement
statement of stockholders' equity
capital stock
retained earnings
dividends
balance sheet
cash flow
statement of cash flows
operating activities
investing activities
financing activities

Audit your understanding

1. Where does Whiley obtain the information to prepare the indirect expenses section of the income statement?
2. From where is the information to prepare the direct expenses section of the income statement obtained?
3. Where does Whiley obtain the stockholders' equity amounts reported on the balance sheet?

Work together 4-3

Preparing financial statements

Use the adjusted trial balance or work sheet for Foley's Interiors from Work Together 4-1 and the departmental margin statement from Work Together 4-2. Partially completed financial statements are provided in the *Working Papers*. Round percentage calculations to the nearest 0.1%. Save your work to complete Work Together 4-4.

1. Complete the income statement. Calculate and record the vertical analysis ratios for each amount in the fourth column of the statement.
2. Complete the statement of stockholders' equity. There were 74,000 shares of $1.00 par value stock issued as of January 1. There were 1,000 shares issued during the current year.
3. Complete the balance sheet. Calculate and record the vertical analysis ratios for each item in the third column of the statement.
4. Use the following information to complete the statement of cash flows. Foley's began the fiscal year with a cash balance of $2,375.14.

Cash received from:		Insurance	$ 16,000.00
Issuance of stock	$ 1,000.00	Inventory purchases	309,481.36
Sale of equipment	3,180.00	Other operating expenses	37,104.74
Sales to customers	697,018.61	Purchase of equipment	24,830.00
Cash payments for:		Rent	18,000.00
Dividends	16,000.00	Salaries and wages	231,648.69
Income taxes	14,048.17		

On your own 4-3

Preparing financial statements

Use the adjusted trial balance or work sheet for Mixon Auto Supplies from On Your Own 4-1 and the departmental margin statement from On Your Own 4-2. Partially completed financial statements are provided in the *Working Papers*. Round percentage calculations to the nearest 0.1%. Work this problem independently. Save your work to complete On Your Own 4-4.

1. Complete the income statement. Calculate and record the vertical analysis ratios for each amount in the fourth column of the statement.
2. Complete the statement of stockholders' equity. There were 19,500 shares of $10.00 par value stock issued as of January 1. There were 500 shares issued during the current year.
3. Complete the balance sheet. Calculate and record the vertical analysis ratios for each item in the third column of the statement.
4. Use the following information to complete the statement of cash flows. Mixon began the fiscal year with a cash balance of $15,826.01.

Cash received from:		Insurance	$ 13,000.00
Issuance of stock	$ 5,000.00	Inventory purchases	331,548.36
Sale of equipment	2,150.00	Other operating expenses	32,148.10
Sales to customers	701,483.39	Purchase of equipment	19,485.00
Cash payments for:		Rent	16,500.00
Dividends	36,000.00	Salaries and wages	201,483.17
Income taxes	12,940.74		

CLOSURE

- Use the illustrations on pages 112–115 to review briefly the procedures for preparing financial statements.

Essential Questions

- Which of the business activities—operating, investing, or financing—would generate the most cash for a student's landscaping company? Explain. (*More than likely, the most cash would be generated from operating activities through sales and services rendered.*)
- Is a statement of cash flows necessary? Doesn't the balance sheet already present the balance of the Cash account? Explain. (*The statement of cash flows is more important than just the cash account on the balance sheet because it traces the sources of cash input and output.*)

LESSON

4-4 End-of-Period Work for a Departmentalized Business

LO9 Complete end-of-period work for a departmentalized merchandising business.

Journalizing Closing Entries for a Departmentalized Business LO9

GENERAL JOURNAL PAGE 21

	DATE		ACCOUNT TITLE	DOC. NO.	POST. REF.	DEBIT	CREDIT	
1			*Closing Entries*					1
2	Dec.	31	*Income Summary—Grills*			3 2 0 1 04		2
3			*Sales—Grills*			472 0 1 9 64		3
4			*Sales—Furniture*			492 1 8 7 31		4
5			*Purchases Discount—Grills*			3 1 0 5 48		5
6			*Purchases Returns and Allowances—Grills*			2 6 7 1 69		6
7			*Purchases Discount—Furniture*			6 1 0 8 67		7
8			*Purchases Returns and Allowances—Furniture*			8 0 9 4 21		8
9			*Income Summary—General*				987 3 8 8 04	9

Heading

Temporary Accounts With Credit Balances

Total of Credit Accounts

Journal entries used to prepare temporary accounts for a new fiscal period are called **closing entries**. Whiley's closing entries made on December 31 are shown above. The information to journalize closing entries is obtained from the adjusted trial balance and other closing entries.

At the end of each fiscal period, Whiley records the following four closing entries:

1. Closing entry for income statement accounts with credit balances (revenue and contra cost accounts).
2. Closing entry for income statement accounts with debit balances (cost, contra revenue, and expense accounts).
3. Closing entry to record net income or net loss in the retained earnings account and to close the income summary account.
4. Closing entry for the dividends account.

CLOSING ENTRY FOR INCOME STATEMENT ACCOUNTS WITH CREDIT BALANCES

The closing entry for Whiley's income statement credit balance accounts on December 31 is shown above. The departmental income summary accounts with a credit balance are Income Summary—Grills and the revenue and contra cost accounts for each department. These accounts are closed to the account Income Summary—General. This account is used to collect the balances of all temporary accounts.

fyi Only temporary accounts are closed. Permanent account balances are needed to continue conducting business in the next accounting cycle.

LESSON 4-4

BRIDGE

- Point out that students have already learned about the importance of adjusting entries to bring certain accounts up to date and to prepare for the next fiscal period.
- Remind students that they have learned about closing entries in the first-year accounting course.

TEACHING RESOURCES

- **Instructor's Resource CD/Website:** PowerPoint Slides, Accounting Concepts
- **Working Papers:** Teacher's Edition of the Working Papers for Lesson 4-4 Online Working Papers
- **Transparency Masters:** General Journal, Post-Closing Trial Balance

ENGAGE

- Ask students how a company's Rent Expense account would look if the account had never been closed at the end of the fiscal year. Discuss that the current balance in the rent account would reflect not only this year's rent expense but also the total of all previous annual rent expenses. Lead into a discussion that closing entries are needed to bring certain accounts up to date and to prepare others for the next fiscal period. Emphasize that without current, up-to-date information, managers would have a difficult time making sound managerial decisions.

PREVIEW

- Call on students to read the accounting terms and definitions introduced in this lesson: *closing entries, post-closing trial balance,* and *accounting cycle*.
- Point out the learning objective for this lesson.
- Direct students to read the headings in this lesson and to examine the illustrations.

MODEL

Analyze closing entries

- Write on the board the four closing entries for a departmentalized business.
  1. Close income statement accounts with credit balances to Income Summary—General.
  2. Close income statement accounts with debit balances to Income Summary—General.
  3. Close Income Summary—General to Retained Earnings for the amount of net income or net loss.
  4. Close Dividends to Retained Earnings.
- Use the steps in the illustration to illustrate how Whiley's first closing entry is journalized.
- Use several T account transactions to illustrate the closing entry.

INPUT

- Ask students about the need for journalizing closing entries. Emphasize that closing entries are used to prepare temporary accounts for the next fiscal period. For example, revenue, cost, and expense accounts require zero balances at the start of each new fiscal period so that they can accumulate data for the new period of time.

INPUT

- Explain the need for Whiley to use two pages for its closing entries.

MODEL

- Use the steps in the illustration to illustrate how Whiley's second set of closing entries is journalized.
- Use several T account transactions to illustrate each closing entry. It is not necessary to write each expense for illustrative purposes.

WHY ACCOUNTING?

Answers

1. Answers will vary, but should include the goals of the course and the name of the organization that offers the course.
2. Answers will vary, but should include the name of the state and the number of PDH required for license renewal.

CLOSING ENTRY FOR INCOME STATEMENT ACCOUNTS WITH DEBIT BALANCES

GENERAL JOURNAL PAGE 21

DATE	ACCOUNT TITLE	DOC. NO.	POST. REF.	DEBIT	CREDIT
31	Income Summary—General			921,144.61	
	Income Summary—Furniture				3,816.53
	Sales Discount—Grills				8,246.75
	Sales Returns and Allowances—Grills				9,467.42
	Sales Discount—Furniture				5,219.23
	Sales Returns and Allowances—Furniture				13,810.76
	Purchases—Grills				254,851.26
	Purchases—Furniture				197,084.64
	Advertising Expense—Grills				14,920.00
	Payroll Taxes Expense—Grills				6,453.36
	Salary Expense—Grills				73,011.20
	Advertising Expense—Furniture				5,650.00
	Payroll Taxes Expense—Furniture				10,926.17
	Salary Expense—Furniture				125,806.20
	Credit Card Fee Expense				6,842.20
	Depreciation Expense—Office Equipment				7,320.00
	Depreciation Expense—Store Equipment				8,370.00
	Insurance Expense				12,000.00
	Miscellaneous Expense				3,495.04
	Payroll Taxes Expense—Administrative				7,602.20
	Rent Expense				18,400.00
	Salary Expense—Administrative				88,028.80
	Supplies Expense				5,180.87
	Uncollectible Accounts Expense				2,114.92
	Utilities Expense				16,204.68
	Federal Income Tax Expense				16,322.38

The closing entry for Whiley's income statement debit balance accounts on December 31 is shown above. The departmental income summary accounts with a debit balance are Income Summary—Furniture, the contra revenue accounts of each department, and all expense accounts. Similar to the closing entry for the income statement credit accounts, the accounts are closed to the account Income Summary—General.

WHY ACCOUNTING?

Accounting for Engineers

The requirements to become a professional engineer vary from state to state, but generally include a four-year degree from an accredited program, completion of two written exams, and engineering work experience. Professional engineers must also follow state requirements for continuing education called *professional development hours (PDH)*.

Professional engineers may encounter accounting courses. These courses are designed for engineers to give them an understanding of financial statements and budgeting, so that they can interact with accountants, financial analysts, and upper management.

Science, Technology, Engineering & Mathematics

CRITICAL THINKING

1. Search the Internet for accounting courses for engineers. Write a one-paragraph summary of the goals of the course and what organization offers it.
2. Search the Internet for the PDH requirement for your state for license renewal. If your state or a neighboring state. Report the number of PDH required and the name of the state.

© iStockphoto.com/AleksKo

CLOSING ENTRY TO RECORD NET INCOME OR NET LOSS

GENERAL JOURNAL — PAGE 21

	DATE		ACCOUNT TITLE	DOC. NO.	POST. REF.	DEBIT	CREDIT	
36		31	*Income Summary—General*			66,243.43		36
37			*Retained Earnings*				66,243.43	37
38								38

The closing entry to record Whiley's net income in the retained earnings account and to close Income Summary—General on December 31 is shown above. The balance of this account is the result of (1) closing all income statement credit accounts and (2) closing all income statement debit accounts. The difference between the two amounts is the net income.

After this closing entry is posted, Income Summary—General has a zero balance. The net income, $66,243.43, has been recorded as a credit to Retained Earnings. A corporation's net income increases its retained earnings.

Total of income statement credit accounts	$987,388.04
Total of income statement debit accounts	921,144.61
Net income	$ 66,243.43

THINK LIKE AN ACCOUNTANT

© iStockphoto.com/Dan Bachman

Allocating Corporate Expenses

Timeshare is an alternative way for individuals to vacation. In exchange for a one-time cost and annual maintenance fees, individuals purchase the right to occupy a vacation resort for a week every year. Some timeshare owners receive points that can be used to reserve a unit. The number of points required to book a reservation is based on the location of the resort, the season, the size of the unit, and the number of days being reserved. For example, a two-bedroom unit at a Florida beach in January will require more points than a one-bedroom unit in July.

Sunset Resorts operates 20 timeshare resorts in four southeastern states. Sunset Resorts' corporate office is located in Tampa, Florida. This office handles all management and accounting tasks that can be effectively performed from a central location. For example, it is more efficient for the corporate office to pay all vendors than for each division, or each resort, to process its own cash payments.

Corporate expenses are allocated to the company's five divisions. Corporate expenses are included in each division's income statement. Each division's net income has a direct impact on annual bonuses awarded to employees. Thus, each division manager wants his or her corporate expense allocation to be as small as possible.

For several years, some division managers have criticized how corporate expenses are allocated. The expenses of each department have been allocated based on the number of points redeemed at each location. The managers felt that more relevant measures should be used to allocate different departmental expenses. For example, the northern Florida region has, by far, the fewest number of complaints that might lead to lawsuits. Yet, that division is charged with nearly 17% of the legal department's expense.

OPEN THE SPREADSHEET TLA_CH04

The worksheet contains a schedule of departmental expenses and selected operational measures, including the points redeemed in each division. Follow the steps on the Instructions tab to calculate a more equitable allocation of corporate expenses. Prepare a statement that supports the method selected for allocating the Reservations departmental expense.

INPUT

- Direct students to the journal entry for closing net income into the Retained Earnings account.
- Point out that the amount of the entry is the difference between the income statement credit accounts and the income statement debit accounts, which equals net income in this example.

THINK LIKE AN ACCOUNTANT

Students apply critical-thinking skills to develop alternative methods for allocating corporate departmental expenses to the corporation's divisions. Students use the ROUND function and absolute reference tool to create the formulas. Students prepare a written statement supporting one of their decisions. This activity has many acceptable solutions. Encourage students to compare and debate their decisions.

Rounding errors may occur that result in a department's total allocations being $1,000 different from the total in column B. In practice, this rounding error would likely be resolved by adding or subtracting the rounding error from the largest division allocation.

A sample solution follows:

"The number of owner reservations is directly related to the number of owners and, therefore, the number of units available for sale. Many of the corporate departmental expenses relate more to the number of resorts rather than to the quality or number of units at each resort. As a result, the revised allocation method assigns more expenses to the number of resorts in each division."

The allocation methods for a reasonable solution are presented in a table in the Instructional Strategies section at the front of this book.

INPUT

- Direct students to the journal entry for closing the Dividends account to Retained Earnings.
- Point out that after this entry is posted, all temporary accounts have zero balances and are prepared for a new fiscal period.

INPUT

- Emphasize that total debits must equal total credits in the general ledger.
- Ask students how someone can determine if the general ledger is still in balance after the adjusting and closing entries have been posted. Discuss that mathematical errors might have occurred during the posting process. Lead into a discussion regarding the purpose of the post-closing trial balance. Stress that the preparation of a post-closing trial balance ensures that the equality of debits and credits has been maintained in preparation for a new fiscal period.

MODEL

Analyze the post-closing trial balance

- Direct students' attention to the illustration. Ask them about the source of information for preparing a post-closing trial balance.
- Point out that the debit and credit totals in the illustration are equal. Thus, Whiley's general ledger is ready for the start of the new fiscal period.
- Remind students that only temporary accounts are closed.

CLOSING ENTRY FOR THE DIVIDENDS ACCOUNT

GENERAL JOURNAL — PAGE 21

	DATE		ACCOUNT TITLE	DOC. NO.	POST. REF.	DEBIT	CREDIT	
38		31	*Retained Earnings*			19,250.00		38
39			*Dividends*				19,250.00	39

The closing entry for Whiley's **Dividends** account on December 31 is shown above. The debit balance of a **Dividends** account is the total amount of dividends declared during a fiscal period. Since dividends decrease the earnings that a corporation retains, the **Dividends** account is closed to **Retained Earnings**. The information needed for closing the **Dividends** account is obtained from the adjusted trial balance.

After the closing entry for the **Dividends** account is posted, **Dividends** has a zero balance. The amount of the dividends, $19,250.00, has been recorded as a debit to **Retained Earnings**.

After closing entries are posted, all temporary accounts have zero balances and are prepared for a new fiscal period.

Post-Closing Trial Balance

Debits must always equal credits in general ledger accounts. The trial balance proves that debits equal credits before adjusting and closing entries are posted. After adjusting and closing entries are posted, the equality of general ledger debits and credits is proved again. This procedure ensures that the equality of debits and credits has been maintained in preparation for a new fiscal period.

A trial balance prepared after the closing entries are posted is called a **post-closing trial balance**. Whiley's post-closing trial balance prepared on December 31 is shown above. The total debit balances, $380,224.83, is the same as the total credit balances. The equality of general ledger debits and credits is proved. Whiley's general ledger is ready for the next fiscal period. [CONCEPT: Accounting Period Cycle]

Whiley Outdoor Living, Inc.
Post-Closing Trial Balance
December 31, 20--

ACCOUNT TITLE	DEBIT	CREDIT
Cash	62,849.26	
Petty Cash	500.00	
Accounts Receivable	23,515.27	
Allowance for Uncollectible Accounts		2,210.61
Merchandise Inventory—Grills	89,349.72	
Merchandise Inventory—Furniture	102,915.36	
Supplies	2,430.00	
Prepaid Insurance	2,000.00	
Office Equipment	32,481.15	
Accumulated Depreciation—Office Equipment		21,470.00
Store Equipment	64,184.07	
Accumulated Depreciation—Store Equipment		42,920.00
Accounts Payable		30,392.88
Sales Tax Payable		6,148.05
Employee Income Tax Payable—Federal		1,666.00
Employee Income Tax Payable—State		1,190.00
Social Security Tax Payable		2,950.80
Medicare Tax Payable		687.22
Medical Insurance Payable		1,050.00
Retirement Plan Payable		710.00
Unemployment Tax Payable—Federal		20.72
Unemployment Tax Payable—State		139.86
Federal Income Tax Payable		2,322.38
Dividends Payable		5,000.00
Capital Stock		100,000.00
Retained Earnings		161,346.31
Totals	380,224.83	380,224.83

Summary of the Accounting Cycle

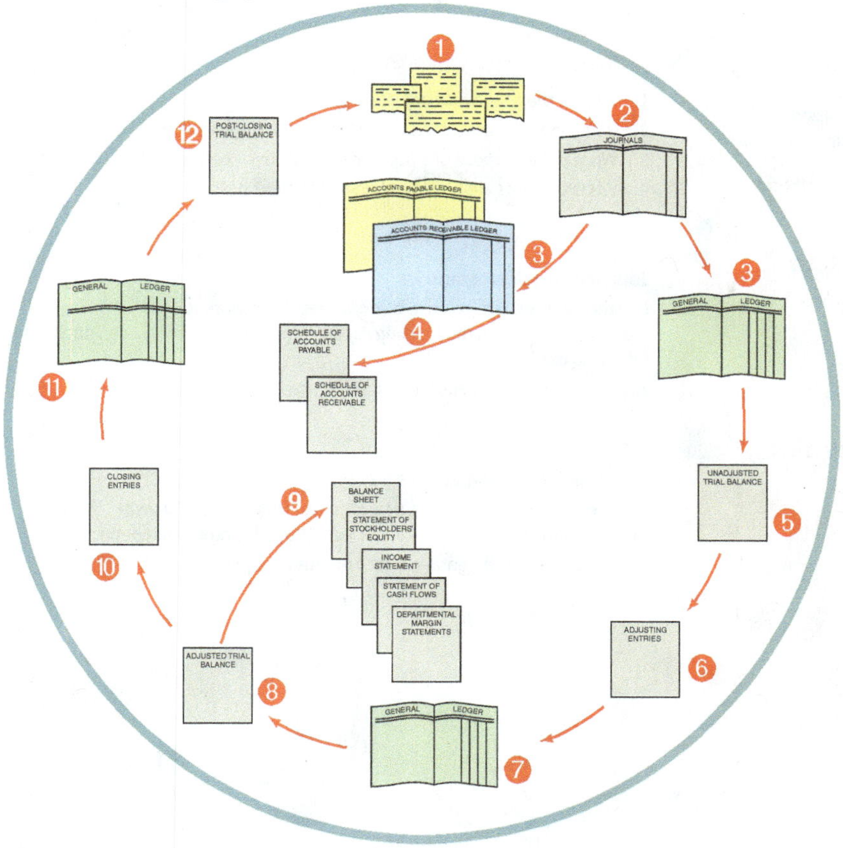

Accounting procedures used by Whiley, a departmentalized merchandising business, are described in Chapters 1 through 4. The same procedures are used from year to year. [CONCEPT: Consistent Reporting] The series of accounting activities included in recording financial information for a fiscal period is called an **accounting cycle**. Whiley's complete accounting cycle is shown above. Accounting cycle procedures provide information for preparing interim and end-of-fiscal-period financial statements. [CONCEPT: Accounting Period Cycle]

Accounting Activities in the Accounting Cycle for a Departmentalized Business

1. Source documents are checked for accuracy, and transactions are analyzed into debit and credit parts.
2. Transactions, from information on source documents, are recorded in journals.
3. Journal entries are posted to the accounts payable ledger, the accounts receivable ledger, and the general ledger.
4. Schedules of accounts payable and accounts receivable are prepared from the subsidiary ledgers.
5. An unadjusted trial balance is prepared from the general ledger.
6. Adjusting entries are journalized.
7. Adjusting entries are posted to the general ledger.
8. An adjusted trial balance is prepared from the general ledger.
9. Financial statements are prepared from the adjusted trial balance.
10. Closing entries are journalized.
11. Closing entries are posted to the general ledger.
12. A post-closing trial balance is prepared from the general ledger.

INPUT

- Review the accounting concept of Consistent Reporting by examining the steps of an accounting cycle for a departmentalized business.

MODEL

- Direct students' attention to the illustration. Review the steps of the accounting cycle. Ask students to explain and provide examples for each step.

FORMATIVE ASSESSMENT

- This is an ongoing process. Circulate around the classroom or lab, observing which students have problems with the assignments.
- Troubleshooting: Determine if students are having difficulty remembering the four closing entries. Some students may have trouble identifying the sources for adjusting and closing entries.
- Assess student understanding by checking solutions to Independent Practice assignments and noting their answers to the Terms Review and Audit Your Understanding questions.

CHECK FOR UNDERSTANDING

Terms Review

- Call on students to define each term in the Terms Review. Definitions are given in the Glossary.

Audit Your Understanding

- Call on students to answer the Audit Your Understanding questions. Answers are given in Appendix D of the textbook.

GUIDED PRACTICE

Work Together

- Have students write the solution to the Work Together problem as you guide the class through the examples.
- Instruct students to use the adjusted trial balance or work sheet from Work Together 4-1 to complete this problem.
- Direct students to record each amount on the proper form as you elicit class participation in determining and calculating each amount.
- Call on students to describe the various steps used to complete each problem.

INDEPENDENT PRACTICE

On Your Own

- Instruct students to use the adjusted trial balance or work sheet from On Your Own 4-1 to complete this problem.
- Assign the On Your Own problem to be worked independently.

Application Problem

- Assign Application Problem 4-4.

Online Working Papers

- Students can access the Lesson 4-4 problems using this software.

RETEACH

- Call on students to describe the accounting activities involved in the end-of-period work for a departmentalized business.

CLOSURE

- Review the illustration on page 121 showing the summary of the accounting cycle for a departmentalized business.

Essential Questions

- Why must the steps to the accounting cycle be done in order? (*Everything must be done in order. Otherwise, balances will be incorrect.*)
- If a work sheet is used, why do financial statements still need to be prepared? (*Work sheets are prepared for internal use to ensure that data are correct before preparing financial statements.*)
- Why aren't all accounts closed at the end of the year? (*Some accounts, such as assets, show amounts that have accumulated since they were set up.*)
- Why doesn't Income Summary appear on any of the financial statements? (*Income Summary is a temporary account, much like a recycle bin. It recycles the money and generates the outcome—either a net income or a net loss.*)

EXTENDED LEARNING

- Assign Why Accounting? on page 118.
- Assign Think Like an Accountant on page 119.

End of Lesson Review

LO9 Complete end-of-period work for a departmentalized merchandising business.

Terms Review

closing entries
post-closing trial balance
accounting cycle

Audit your understanding

1. What is the purpose of adjusting entries?
2. What accounts are closed by each of the closing entries?
3. What is the purpose of a post-closing trial balance?
4. What accounts are presented on a post-closing trial balance?

Work together 4-4

Journalizing closing entries

Use the adjusted trial balance or work sheet from Work Together 4-1. Page 21 of a general journal is provided in the *Working Papers*. Your instructor will guide you through the following example.

Journalize the closing entries for Foley's Interiors.

On your own 4-4

Journalizing closing entries

Use the adjusted trial balance or work sheet from On Your Own 4-1. Page 23 of a general journal is provided in the *Working Papers*. Work this problem independently.

Journalize the closing entries for Mixon Auto Supplies.

A Look at Accounting Software

Modifying a Report

Business managers and accountants need regular financial and operational reports in order to control their businesses. Ever since 1979, with the release of VisiCalc®, the first electronic spreadsheet, even users of manual accounting systems have been preparing reports with spreadsheet software. Spreadsheets today allow almost unlimited formatting capabilities—font styles, sizes, attributes, and colors; numbers with varying decimal places, rounding, and characteristics such as percentage and date forms; lines and symbols; and dozens of mathematical functions. However, with a manual accounting system, the data still must be keyed in, which can require a lot of time and is subject to error.

All computerized accounting systems provide some preprogrammed reports. Some provide report-writing modules with capabilities similar to spreadsheet software. The advantage to preparing a report in a computerized accounting system is that the data is already in the system, so a report can be displayed or printed in seconds. Changing the underlying data will immediately update the report.

No accounting system can ever provide all the reports that business managers or accountants may wish to see. That's why all accounting systems allow for some degree of report modification. All systems also allow report data to be exported to a spreadsheet where reports can be easily reformatted.

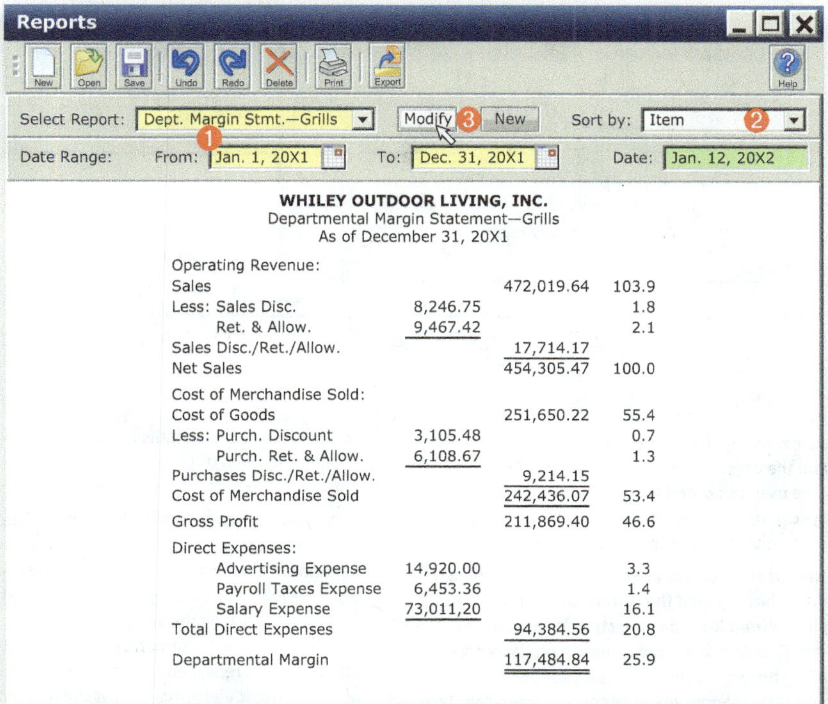

WHILEY OUTDOOR LIVING, INC.
Departmental Margin Statement—Grills
As of December 31, 20X1

Operating Revenue:			
Sales		472,019.64	103.9
Less: Sales Disc.	8,246.75		1.8
Ret. & Allow.	9,467.42		2.1
Sales Disc./Ret./Allow.		17,714.17	
Net Sales		454,305.47	100.0
Cost of Merchandise Sold:			
Cost of Goods		251,650.22	55.4
Less: Purch. Discount	3,105.48		0.7
Purch. Ret. & Allow.	6,108.67		1.3
Purchases Disc./Ret./Allow.		9,214.15	
Cost of Merchandise Sold		242,436.07	53.4
Gross Profit		211,869.40	46.6
Direct Expenses:			
Advertising Expense	14,920.00		3.3
Payroll Taxes Expense	6,453.36		1.4
Salary Expense	73,011.20		16.1
Total Direct Expenses		94,384.56	20.8
Departmental Margin		117,484.84	25.9

Entered by user   Entered automatically

1. The user has selected a report and set a date range for the fiscal year.
2. The **Sort by** selection block has been left in its default status (Item) to display the report in the order it was created. Options would include By account, By date, By amount/ascending, and By amount/descending. Sorting is most often used with custom reports.
3. Clicking on the **New** button would allow the user to create a new report form. Here, the user is clicking on the **Modify** button to make changes to the departmental margin statement in the window.

A Look at Accounting Software

There is so much to be said about creating, editing, and formatting reports in computerized systems that it is impossible to do more than scratch the surface with a feature of this length. Before students can begin to grasp the subject, they need to gain some understanding of database structures, which underlie all accounting systems. In databases, data are stored in individual fields of varying types—for example, numeric, alphanumeric, text, graphic, and audiovisual. Creating reports on top of that data requires the knowledge and skill needed to code report fields, such that those fields obtain and act upon specifically identified data from the database.

This feature takes some liberties with execution in the interest of brevity and expedience, but the objective described and the end result (a summary report) are everyday events in business.

Students who are interested might be encouraged to learn more about report writer software and give a presentation to the class as an extra credit activity.

One accounting detail that might be discussed is the use of Cost of Goods in the report in place of Purchases, as shown in the textbook. Because an automated system is being portrayed, it would use a perpetual inventory system. Therefore, as inventory is purchased, its cost is debited to an Inventory account. In real time then, as inventory is sold, its cost is credited to Inventory and debited to Cost of Goods (or Cost of Goods Sold). In the report illustrated, Cost of Merchandise Sold is used as a roll-up figure netting purchases discounts and purchases returns and allowances from Cost of Goods. In the real world, these account titles and report labels have many variations.

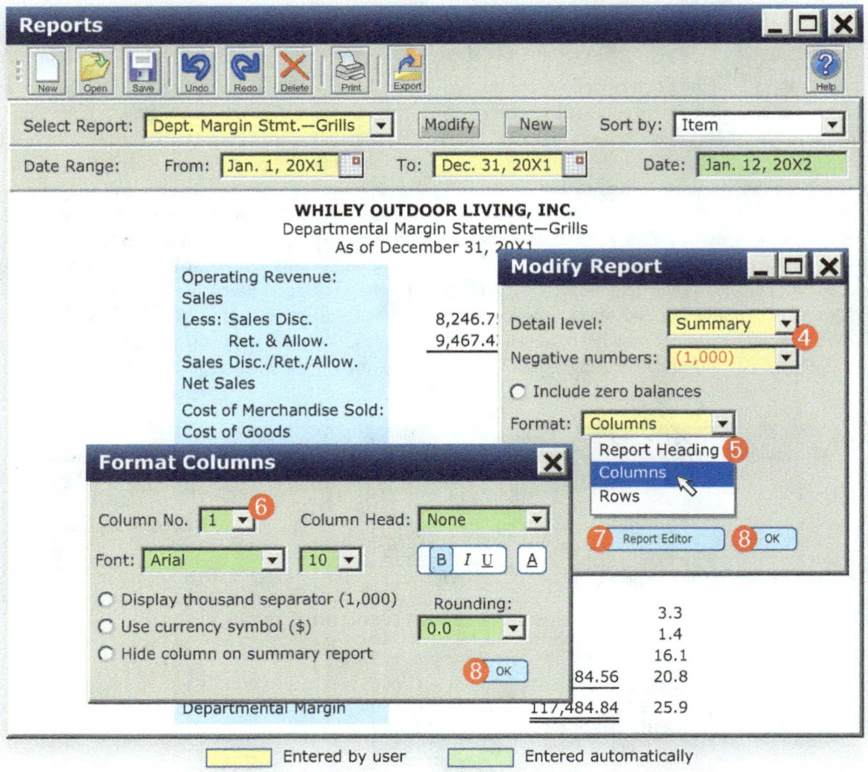

4 The system has opened the Modify Report dialog box, and the user has selected the Summary detail level. The user also opted to have negative numbers displayed in parentheses and in red, although there are no negative numbers in the current report.

5 The user has selected Columns from the **Format** field drop-list, which opened the Format Columns dialog box with **Column No. 1** pre-selected. At the same time, the system highlighted column 1 on the report. The dialog box shows the formatting currently set for column 1. Any changes made by the user would apply to all items in the column.

6 Selecting **Column No. 2** would move the highlighted area to the second column and show the format in that column. Options available to the user with these formatting dialog boxes allow quick modifications, but the choices are limited. For example, setting a column 1 format to an italic font would display all row headings in italic. It is not possible here to select just one row heading to display in italic.

7 If the user wanted to format the report at the field level—for example, the field for the heading **Operating Revenue** or the field for the amount of **Net Sales**—the report would have to be opened in the report editor. The report editor enables the coding of each individual cell for data content, format, calculation, and other attributes. The report editor would also be used for placing graphic elements, such as the underscores beneath the columns, in the report.

8 The user, having chosen not to change any column formats, would click the **OK** button or the **Close** box. Then, clicking **OK** on the Modify Report dialog box would accept the settings chosen by the user and display the modified report form.

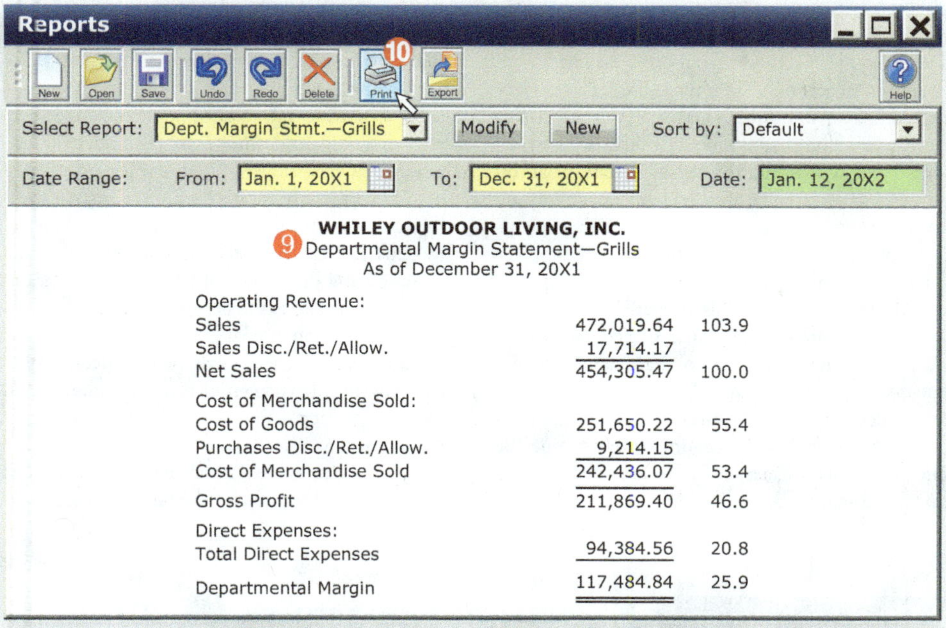

WHILEY OUTDOOR LIVING, INC.
Departmental Margin Statement—Grills
As of December 31, 20X1

Operating Revenue:		
Sales	472,019.64	103.9
Sales Disc./Ret./Allow.	17,714.17	
Net Sales	454,305.47	100.0
Cost of Merchandise Sold:		
Cost of Goods	251,650.22	55.4
Purchases Disc./Ret./Allow.	9,214.15	
Cost of Merchandise Sold	242,436.07	53.4
Gross Profit	211,869.40	46.6
Direct Expenses:		
Total Direct Expenses	94,384.56	20.8
Departmental Margin	117,484.84	25.9

Entered by user   Entered automatically

9 The user chose to display a summary report form, the same financial statement in a more condensed format. These options allow a report to be presented at different levels of detail appropriate for different levels of management. Attributes programmed in the report editor determine which rows get removed from the standard report to produce a summary report. The result is shown in the illustration above.

10 The user would click **Print** to print out the report.

CLOSURE

- Review the Chapter Summary.

Essential Questions

- What are some ways to enhance motivation and competition between departments of an organization through responsibility accounting?
- Would it ever be advantageous to complete the end-of-period report using a work sheet? Explain.
- Some companies refer to their departments as profit centers. Which departments might not directly make a profit for the company?

EXTENDED LEARNING

- Review A Look at Accounting Software on pages 123–125.
- Assign Explore Accounting on page 126.

EXPLORE ACCOUNTING

Answers

Reasons for paying a higher-than-budgeted price for fabric might include:

1. Purchasing a higher quality of fabric than is required.
2. Failing to obtain competitive bids.
3. Having to buy fabric for immediate delivery and incurring higher-than-normal shipping costs.

Reasons that a higher-than-budgeted quantity of fabric might be used, resulting in a large amount of scrap, might include:

1. Purchasing fabric of inferior quality.
2. Failing to train employees adequately.
3. Using old, obsolete, or poorly maintained equipment.
4. Failing to control employee theft.

Chapter Summary

The preparation of financial statements at the end of the fiscal year begins with the preparation of an unadjusted trial balance. All accounts, even those having a zero balance, are entered. The unadjusted trial balance acts as a checklist, enabling the business to determine which accounts need to be adjusted to up-to-date balances. Adjustments in the balance of merchandise inventory are recorded in an income summary account. Other adjustments involve a balance sheet account, such as Supplies, and a related expense account, such as Supplies Expense.

An adjusted trial balance is prepared after adjusting entries are posted. The balance of Federal Income Tax Expense is not included so that income before income taxes can be calculated. The total of the income statement debit accounts is subtracted from the total of income statement credit accounts to determine the income before income taxes. After federal income taxes are calculated, adjusted, and posted, the adjusted trial balance is completed. The adjusted trial balance is the source of information for financial statements.

A company having distinct product groups should use a departmental accounting system. Departmental revenues, costs, and direct expenses are accounted for to enable management to evaluate the performance of each department. Only those revenues, costs, and expenses that can be controlled by a manager should be recorded by department. The dollar amounts and vertical analysis ratios of a departmental income statement enable a business to evaluate the performance of a department.

A corporation prepares the traditional four financial statements. The format of the income statement contains the departmental revenue, gross profit, and margins for each department. The other financial statements are similar to those of other corporations.

Closing entries are journalized and posted to prepare the accounting records for the next fiscal year.

EXPLORE ACCOUNTING Exception Reports

© iStockphoto.com/Makhnach_M

The amount of financial information available to managers can become immense. Responsibility accounting is one way that managers focus accounting information on one aspect of the business. A departmental margin statement, for example, focuses on the revenue and expenses controlled by the manager of a single department. Even departmental margin statements can be overwhelming for a large company with hundreds of departments. How does an upper-level manager examine all of these statements to identify problems?

Rather than reviewing every line of every departmental statement, a manager can instruct the computer system to prepare a report of only those accounts for which the actual results differ significantly from expected results. These reports, often called *exception reports*, should identify both positive and negative situations. For example, an exception report could identify those accounts that differ by more than 10% from departmental budgets. This shorter report would allow the manager to focus quickly on areas that deserve attention.

Managers must gather information and be objective when investigating the reasons for excessive expenses. Does salary expense exceeding budget by 20% indicate that workers lack discipline? Although this explanation is possible, other reasons could cause even the best employees to be unproductive. For example, note these factors:

1. Workers have not received adequate training.
2. Equipment is obsolete and often broken.
3. Parts are frequently out of stock.

It is natural for managers to focus on negative situations. The manager can work with the department manager to correct the problem. Too often, managers neglect to investigate the reasons for positive performances. If a department has generated sales 20% more than its budget, the manager should investigate what strategies and methods can account for the successful results. This information can then be shared with other departments to improve sales throughout the company.

INSTRUCTIONS

A manager of Midwest Textiles receives an exception report showing that fabric costs of its toddler department are 14% above the budget. List possible explanations for the apparent problem in the purchase and use of fabric.

Apply Your Understanding

INSTRUCTIONS: Download problem instructions for Excel, QuickBooks, and Sage 50 from the textbook companion website at www.C21accounting.com.

4-1 Application Problem: Preparing an adjusted trial balance LO2, 3, 4

Sunset Sports, Inc., is a merchandising business that sells golf and tennis equipment. The company uses a calendar fiscal year. The following adjustment information for December 31 is available:

Estimate of uncollectible accounts	$ 1,740.79	Value of prepaid insurance	$1,000.00
Ending merchandise inventory—golf	64,933.31	Depreciation expense—office equipment	3,190.00
Ending merchandise inventory—tennis	47,687.92	Depreciation expense—store equipment	6,280.00
Supplies on hand	670.00		

Instructions:

A partially completed adjusted trial balance, a general journal, and selected general ledger accounts are provided in the *Working Papers*. Save your work to complete Problems 4-2, 4-3, and 4-4.

1. Record the adjusting entries on page 18 of a general journal.
2. Post the adjusting entries to the general ledger accounts.
3. Enter the adjusted general ledger account balances on the adjusted trial balance.
4. Calculate federal income tax expense using the tax table presented in the chapter. Prepare and post the adjusting entry for federal income tax expense.
5. Complete the adjusted trial balance.

AAONLINE

1. Go to www.cengage.com/login
2. Click on AA Online to access.
3. Go to the online assignment and follow the instructions.

4-2 Application Problem: Preparing a departmental margin statement LO6, 7

Use Sunset Sports' adjusted trial balance or work sheet from Problem 4-1. Save your work to complete Problem 4-3.

Instructions:

1. Prepare a departmental margin statement for each department.
2. Calculate vertical analysis ratios for cost of merchandise sold, gross profit, total direct expenses, and departmental margin.

AAONLINE

1. Go to www.cengage.com/login
2. Click on AA Online to access.
3. Go to the online assignment and follow the instructions.

4-3 Application Problem: Preparing financial statements LO8

Use Sunset Sports' adjusted trial balance or work sheet from Problem 4-1 and the departmental margin statement from Problem 4-2. Statement paper is provided in the *Working Papers*. Round percentage calculations to the nearest 0.1%.

Instructions:

1. Complete the income statement. Calculate and record the vertical analysis ratios for each amount in the fourth column of the statement.
2. Complete the statement of stockholders' equity. There were 58,000 shares of $1.00 par value stock issued as of January 1. There were 2,000 shares issued during the current year.
3. Complete the balance sheet. Calculate and record the vertical analysis ratios for each item in the third column of the statement.

CHECK FIGURES

For complete solutions to Chapter 4 problems, see the Teacher's Edition of the Working Papers.

Application Problem 4-1

Net Income before Federal Income Taxes, $62,244.57.

Federal Income Tax Payable, $561.14.

Adjusted Trial Balance column totals, $814,008.42.

Application Problem 4-2

Gross Profit, Golf: $204,351.00, 58.2%.

Departmental Margin, Golf: $148,011.27, 42.2%.

Gross Profit, Tennis: $106,206.02, 48.7%.

Departmental Margin, Tennis: $31,109.81, 14.3%.

Application Problem 4-3

Net Income: $51,683.43, 9.1%.

Total Stockholders' Equity, $155,051.78.

Total Assets, $191,473.95.

Net cash provided by operating activities, $63,578.14.

4. Use the following information to complete the statement of cash flows. Sunset Sports began the fiscal year with a cash balance of $26,534.33.

Cash received from:		Insurance	$ 12,000.00
Issuance of stock	$ 2,000.00	Inventory purchases	253,149.61
Sale of equipment	3,015.00	Other operating expenses	27,841.09
Sales to customers	567,148.14	Purchase of equipment	18,413.00
Cash payments for:		Rent	14,250.00
Dividends	23,400.00	Salaries and wages	186,414.68
Income taxes	9,914.62		

AA ONLINE

1. Go to www.cengage.com/login
2. Click on AA Online to access.
3. Go to the online assignment and follow the instructions.

Application Problem 4-4

Closing entry to close Income Summary to Retained Earnings, debit Income Summary—General, credit Retained Earnings, $51,683.43.

4-4 Application Problem: Journalizing closing entries LO9

Use Sunset Sports' adjusted trial balance or work sheet from Problem 4-1. Page 19 of a general journal is provided in the *Working Papers*.

Instructions:

Journalize the closing entries for Sunset Sports, Inc.

Sage 50 Accounting

1. Journalize and post adjusting and closing entries to the general journal.
2. From the menu bar, select Reports & Forms; General Ledger.
3. Print the general journal and trial balance.

QB

1. Journalize and post adjusting and closing entries to the journal.
2. From the menu bar, select Reports; Accountant & Taxes.
3. Print the journal and trial balance.

Excel

1. Journalize and post closing entries in the general journal.
2. Print the worksheet.

Mastery Problem 4-M

Net Income: $126,546.10, 9.5%.

Total Stockholders' Equity, $580,757.66.

Total Assets, $658,012.20.

Net cash provided by operating activities, $138,111.16.

Closing entry to close Income Summary to Retained Earnings, debit Income Summary—General, credit Retained Earnings, $126,546.10.

4-M Mastery Problem: Completing end-of-fiscal-period work for a departmentalized merchandising business LO2, 3, 4, 6, 7, 8, 9

Sage 50 Accounting

1. Journalize and post adjusting and closing entries to the general journal.
2. From the menu bar, select Reports & Forms; General Ledger.
3. Print the general journal and trial balance.

QB

1. Journalize and post adjusting and closing entries to the journal.
2. From the menu bar, select Reports; Accountant & Taxes.
3. Print the journal and trial balance.

Forde Furniture Gallery is a merchandising business that specializes in antiques and modern furniture. The company uses a calendar fiscal year. An adjusted trial balance as of December 31, general journals, selected general ledger accounts, and statement paper are provided in the *Working Papers*. Round percentage calculations to the nearest 0.1%. The adjustment information for December 31 follows.

Estimate of uncollectible accounts	$ 2,651.36
Ending merchandise inventory—antiques	249,183.92
Ending merchandise inventory—modern	228,540.53
Supplies on hand	1,295.00
Value of prepaid insurance	2,400.00
Depreciation expense—office equipment	3,240.00
Depreciation expense—store equipment	5,175.00

INDEPENDENT PRACTICE

- Assign Mastery Problem 4-M for students as a culminating problem that combines all activities from the chapter.
- Assign Challenge Problem 4-C to accelerated students who work at a faster pace.
- Assign Study Guide 4.
- Students can access Online Working Papers to work end-of-chapter problems on the computer.
- Direct students to the C21 Accounting companion website for additional practice and review opportunities.

FORMATIVE ASSESSMENT

- Review solutions to the assigned problems in class, diagnosing trouble spots.

RETEACH

- Call on students to describe how they avoid the trouble spots diagnosed.
- Use reteaching suggestions from lesson plans as required.
- Assign Recycling Problem 4-R if needed.

1. Journalize and post adjusting entries to the general journal.
2. Complete the departmental margin statements and other financial statements.
3. Journalize and post closing entries to the general journal.
4. Print the worksheets.

AA ONLINE

1. Go to www.cengage.com/login
2. Click on AA Online to access.
3. Go to the online assignment and follow the instructions.

Instructions:

1. Record the adjusting entries on page 24 of a general journal.
2. Post the adjusting entries to the general ledger accounts.
3. Enter the adjusted general account balances on the adjusted trial balance.
4. Calculate federal income tax expense using the tax table presented in the chapter. Prepare and post the adjusting entry for federal income tax expense.
5. Complete the adjusted trial balance.
6. Prepare a departmental margin statement for each department. Calculate vertical analysis ratios for cost of merchandise sold, gross profit, total direct expenses, and departmental margin.
7. Prepare the income statement, statement of stockholders' equity, and balance sheet. There were 11,800 shares of $25.00 par value stock issued as of January 1. There were 200 shares issued during the current year. Calculate and record the vertical analysis ratios for each amount in the fourth column of the income statement and third column of the balance sheet.
8. Use the following information to complete the statement of cash flows. Forde began the fiscal year with a cash balance of $24,569.20.

Cash received from:		Insurance	$ 13,600.00
Issuance of stock	$ 5,000.00	Inventory purchases	632,154.36
Sale of equipment	2,818.00	Other operating expenses	62,184.98
Sales to customers	1,318,614.61	Purchase of equipment	48,450.00
Cash payments for:		Rent	22,500.00
Dividends	60,000.00	Salaries and wages	400,915.61
Income taxes	49,148.50		

9. Journalize the closing entries. Use page 25 of a general journal.

4-C Challenge Problem: Analyzing a departmental margin statement LO2, 3

The departmental margin statement for the chemicals department of Crystal Pools for the years 20X6 and 20X7 is provided in the *Working Papers*. The company has set a goal for the chemicals department to contribute a minimum of 25.0% departmental margin. For the years 20X1 through 20X6, the departmental margin for the chemicals department has varied from 24.9% to 26.8% of net sales.

Instructions:

1. For 20X7, calculate and record the vertical analysis ratios to compare to the ratios given for 20X6. Round percentage calculations to the nearest 0.1%.
2. Calculate the changes in ratios from 20X6 to 20X7 for the following items: (a) cost of merchandise sold, (b) gross profit, (c) total direct expenses, and (d) departmental margin.
3. From an analysis of the departmental margin statement and the amounts obtained from instructions 1 and 2, answer the following questions:
   a. Is the departmental margin for the chemicals department at a satisfactory percentage of sales? Explain why it is or is not satisfactory.
   b. Is the trend of the cost of merchandise sold percentage favorable or unfavorable? Explain why it is or is not favorable. Suggest some possible reasons for the change in the cost of merchandise sold from 20X6 to 20X7.
   c. Is the trend of the total direct departmental expenses percentage favorable or unfavorable? Explain why the trend is or is not favorable.

EXTENDED LEARNING

- Assign 21st Century Skills on page 130.
- Assign Auditing for Errors on page 131.
- Assign Analyzing Home Depot's Financial Statements on page 131.

SUMMATIVE EVALUATION

- Chapter 4 Test
- Cognero for Chapter 4

Challenge Problem 4-C

Departmental Margin, 20X7: 24.2%.

Change in Gross Profit ratio, –1.8%.

21ST CENTURY SKILLS

Answers

1. Answers will vary, but might include the following: Shannon should be concerned that telephones are a falling market and that the advertising may not help increase sales of telephones, yet her department will incur the same advertising costs as the other departments. Also, her department produced the least amount of revenue. Applying advertising costs evenly across the departments, the Telephones Department will incur a higher percentage of costs for the advertising.
2. An advantage of adding a department for video games would be to increase the exposure of the success to management. With video as its own department, management should see the impact of the new products on the success of the company. By adding a new department, new costs are incurred.

21st Century Skills

Measuring Performance

Theme: Financial, Economic, Business, and Entrepreneurial Literacy

Skills: Creativity and Innovation, Critical Thinking and Problem Solving, Communication and Collaboration

PARTNERSHIP FOR 21ST CENTURY SKILLS

Home Electronics is a retailer of personal electronics products. Some of the products it sells are televisions, DVD players, cell phones, and computers for personal use. It has many outlets across the country, and annual sales range from $1.2 billion to $1.28 billion. Chart 1 shows the product sales for four years.

Chart 1
(in millions of dollars)

	Year 1	Year 2	Year 3	Year 4
Televisions	$ 425	$ 430	$ 420	$ 425
Music players and sound equipment	125	130	140	145
Telephones	50	45	40	35
Cell phones	200	210	230	240
Personal computers	400	430	440	435
	$1,200	$1,245	$1,270	$1,280

Some of the departmental accounting is based on the product line. There are other departments and cost centers that do not generate a profit. Each of the major product areas has a manager who is responsible for the success of his or her product line.

Management is concerned that sales are not growing fast enough and has decided to invest in advertising. Management is also considering taking on more product lines and possibly adding more departments.

APPLICATION

1. Shannon is the product manager of the Telephones Department. She has learned that one of management's proposals is to invest $500,000 in advertising. To track costs and to aid in evaluating the departmental areas, the costs of advertising will be spread evenly across the product departments. Discuss why Shannon would be for or against this method of tracking costs. What other proposals could Shannon suggest?
2. To increase sales, management is considering adding video games to the product selection. Compare and contrast the advantages and disadvantages of adding another department for the new product area, instead of adding the new products to an existing product department.

COMMON CORE AND INTERDISCIPLINARY STUDIES

Extended learning features and activities present numerous opportunities to implement Common Core Standards through interdisciplinary studies. Practice is provided in the common core areas of English Language Arts & Literacy and Mathematical Practice. Many of these activities require short, critical-thinking and decision-making responses that apply reading, writing, speaking, listening, language, media and technology, and mathematical skills.

Auditing for errors

A new accounting clerk for Lindsay Jewelry Company prepared the following post-closing trial balance:

Lindsay Jewelry Company *Post-Closing Trial Balance* *December 31, 20--*		
ACCOUNT TITLE	DEBIT	CREDIT
Cash	36,154.21	
Accounts Receivable	42,108.62	
Allowance for Uncollectible Accounts	4,093.68	
Merchandise Inventory—Gold	301,589.36	
Merchandise Inventory—Silver	104,847.31	
Supplies	3,250.00	
Prepaid Insurance	4,800.00	
Office Equipment	21,674.95	
Accumulated Depreciation—Office Equipment		10,845.00
Store Equipment	42,109.98	
Accumulated Depreciation—Store Equipment		19,265.41
Accounts Payable		31,087.91
Employee Income Tax Payable—Federal		2,194.56
Social Security Tax Payable		3,715.25
Medicare Tax Payable		881.15
Unemployment Tax Payable—Federal		51.36
Federal Income Tax Payable		4,194.00
Dividends Payable	20,000.00	
Capital Stock		250,000.00
Retained Earnings		195,343.76
Income Summary		14,862.35

1. Identify any errors in the trial balance.
2. Calculate the correct column totals.

Analyzing Home Depot's financial statements

The cost of merchandise is a significant cost for all merchandising businesses. In order to maximize profits, management attempts to keep this cost as low as possible. In this chapter, you have learned that the amount of revenue from sales less the cost of goods sold is called *gross profit*. The vertical analysis ratio for gross profit, most often referred to as *gross margin*, is an important measure of how effectively management is controlling its merchandise costs. Managers can compare the current ratio to prior years' ratios. Investors and other interested individuals can compare the ratios of companies operating in the same industry. Online investing sites, financial news publications, and company annual reports report gross margins.

INSTRUCTIONS

Refer to the Five-Year Summary of Financial and Operating Results in Appendix B on page B-15 to answer the following questions:

1. Identify the term used by Home Depot to refer to its gross margin.
2. List the gross margin for each fiscal year presented.
3. Identify the term used by Home Depot to refer to its net income vertical analysis ratio.
4. List the net income vertical analysis ratio for each fiscal year presented.
5. Would you classify Home Depot's trends identified in the previous questions as favorable or unfavorable?

AUDITING FOR ERRORS

Answers

1. a. The balance for Allowance for Uncollectible Accounts should be in the Credit column.
   b. The balance for Dividends Payable should be in the Credit column.
   c. The Income Summary account should be closed to Retained Earnings. The new balance of Retained Earnings would be $210,206.11 (the current balance of Retained Earnings, $195,343.76, plus the balance in Income Summary, $14,862.35).
2. The total of each column of the corrected adjusted trial balance is $556,534.43.

ANALYZING HOME DEPOT'S FINANCIAL STATEMENTS

Answers

1. Gross margin—% of sales.
2. The gross margin was 34.6%, 34.5%, 34.3%, 33.9%, and 33.7% for fiscal years 2012 to 2008, respectively.
3. Net earnings—% of sales.
4. The net earnings as a percent of sales were 6.1%, 5.5%, 4.9%, 4.0%, and 3.2% for fiscal years 2012 to 2008, respectively.
5. Favorable. Both ratios have increased consistently over the five-year period.

APPENDIX: Preparing a Work Sheet

DEPARTMENTAL WORK SHEET

A 12-column work sheet prepared using Whiley's account balances on December 31 is shown here. The additional columns provide the information for departmental margin statements. The adjustments planned on the work sheet are journalized and posted after the work sheet is completed.

1 List all accounts, even those with zero balances.

3 Extend adjusted balances to appropriate statement columns.

Whiley Outdoor Living, Inc.
Adjusted Trial Balance
December 31, 20--

	ACCOUNT TITLE	TRIAL BALANCE		ADJUSTMENTS		DEPARTMENTAL STATEMENTS				INCOME STATEMENT		BALANCE SHEET		
						GRILLS		FURNITURE						
		DEBIT	CREDIT	DEBIT	CREDIT	DEBIT	CREDIT	DEBIT	CREDIT	DEBIT	CREDIT	DEBIT	CREDIT	
1	*Cash*	62 849 26										62 849 26		1
2	*Petty Cash*	500 00										500 00		2
3	*Accounts Receivable*	23 515 27										23 515 27		3
4	*Allowance for Uncollectible Accounts*		95 69		(a) 2 114 92								2 210 61	4
5	*Merchandise Inventory—Grills*	86 148 68		(b) 3 201 04								89 349 72		5
6	*Merchandise Inventory—Furniture*	106 731 89			(c) 3 816 53							102 915 36		6
7	*Supplies*	7 610 87			(d) 5 180 87							2 430 00		7
8	*Prepaid Insurance*	14 000 00			(e) 12 000 00							2 000 00		8
9	*Office Equipment*	32 481 15										32 481 15		9
10	*Accumulated Depreciation—Office Equipment*		14 150 00		(f) 7 320 00								21 470 00	10
11	*Store Equipment*	64 184 07										64 184 07		11
12	*Accumulated Depreciation—Store Equipment*		34 550 00		(g) 8 370 00								42 920 00	12
13	*Accounts Payable*		30 392 88										30 392 88	13
14	*Sales Tax Payable*		6 148 05										6 148 05	14
15	*Employee Income Tax Payable—Federal*		1 666 00										1 666 00	15
16	*Employee Income Tax Payable—State*		1 190 00										1 190 00	16
17	*Social Security Tax Payable*		2 950 80										2 950 80	17
18	*Medicare Tax Payable*		687 22										687 22	18
19	*Medical Insurance Payable*		1 050 00										1 050 00	19
20	*Retirement Plan Payable*		710 00										710 00	20
21	*Unemployment Tax Payable—Federal*		20 72										20 72	21
22	*Unemployment Tax Payable—State*		139 86										139 86	22
23	*Federal Income Tax Payable*				(h) 2 322 38								2 322 38	23
24	*Dividends Payable*		5 000 00										5 000 00	24
25	*Capital Stock*		100 000 00										100 000 00	25

26	Retained Earnings		114,352.88										114,352.88	26
27	Dividends	19,250.00										19,250.00		27
28	Income Summary—General													28
29	Income Summary—Grills				(b) 3,201.04		3,201.04							29
30	Income Summary—Furniture			(c) 3,816.53				3,816.53						30
31	Sales—Grills		472,019.64				472,019.64							31
32	Sales Discount—Grills	8,246.75				8,246.75								32
33	Sales Returns and Allowances—Grills	9,467.42				9,467.42								33
34	Sales—Furniture		492,187.31						492,187.31					34
35	Sales Discount—Furniture	5,219.23						5,219.23						35
36	Sales Returns and Allowances—Furniture	13,810.76						13,810.76						36
37	Purchases—Grills	254,851.26				254,851.26								37
38	Purchases Discount—Grills		3,105.48				3,105.48							38
39	Purchases Returns and Allowances—Grills		6,108.67				6,108.67							39
40	Purchases—Furniture	197,084.64						197,084.64						40
41	Purchases Discount—Furniture		2,671.69						2,671.69					41
42	Purchases Returns and Allowances—Furniture		8,094.21						8,094.21					42
43	Advertising Expense—Grills	14,920.00				14,920.00								43
44	Payroll Taxes Expense—Grills	6,453.36				6,453.36								44
45	Salary Expense—Grills	73,011.20				73,011.20								45
46	Advertising Expense—Furniture	5,650.00						5,650.00						46
47	Payroll Taxes Expense—Furniture	10,926.17						10,926.17						47
48	Salary Expense—Furniture	125,806.20						125,806.20						48
49	Credit Card Fee Expense	6,842.20								6,842.20				49
50	Depreciation Expense—Office Equipment			(f) 7,320.00						7,320.00				50
51	Depreciation Expense—Store Equipment			(g) 8,370.00						8,370.00				51
52	Insurance Expense			(e) 12,000.00						12,000.00				52
53	Miscellaneous Expense	3,495.04								3,495.04				53
54	Payroll Taxes Expense—Administrative	7,602.20								7,602.20				54
55	Rent Expense	18,400.00								18,400.00				55
56	Salary Expense—Administrative	88,028.80								88,028.80				56
57	Supplies Expense			(d) 5,180.87						5,180.87				57
58	Uncollectible Accounts Expense			(a) 2,114.92						2,114.92				58
59	Utilities Expense	16,204.68								16,204.68				59
60						366,949.99	484,434.83	362,313.53	502,953.21					60
61	Department Margin—Grills					117,484.84					117,484.84			61
62	Department Margin—Furniture							140,639.68			140,639.68			62
63						484,434.83	484,434.83	502,953.21	502,953.21					63
64	Federal Income Tax Expense	14,000.00		(h) 2,322.38						16,322.38				64
65		1,297,291.10	1,297,291.10	44,325.74	44,325.74					191,881.09	258,124.52	399,474.83	333,231.40	65
66	Net Income									66,243.43			66,243.43	66
67										258,124.52	258,124.52	399,474.83	399,474.83	67

2 Plan adjustments and label using letters.

4 Excess of departmental revenue over expenses.

5 Adjust and extend Federal Income Tax Expense after calculating income before income tax.

6 Credit less debit column total equals net income.

Completing a Work Sheet

1. **Unadjusted trial balance.** Enter unadjusted account balances from the general ledger.
2. **Enter adjustments.** Adjustments are entered in the Adjustments columns. Letters are used to label each entry.
3. **Extend updated balances.** Adjusted account balances are extended to one of the four financial statement debit and credit columns. Asset, liability, and equity accounts are extended to the Balance Sheet Debit and Credit columns. Department revenue and expense accounts are extended to the appropriate department's debit and credit columns. All other revenue and expense accounts, except for Federal Income Tax Expense, are extended to the Income Statement Debit column.
4. **Calculate the difference of departmental revenue and expenses.** The department columns are totaled. The credit column total less the debit column total is the excess of departmental revenues over expenses. Enter the amount under the debit column total and in the Income Statement Credit column. Enter Department Margin and the department name in the Account Title column.
5. **Record the adjustment for income taxes.** The total of the Income Statement Credit column less the Income Statement Debit column (excluding federal income tax expense) equals income before income tax. Calculate federal income tax expense, enter an adjustment for any taxes due, and extend the income tax accounts to the appropriate columns.
6. **Calculate net income.** Enter the total of the Income Statement and Balance Sheet columns. The total of the Income Statement Credit column less the Income Statement Debit column is the net income for the fiscal period. The net income is written under the work sheet's Income Statement Debit column and the Balance Sheet Credit column. The net income amount makes each statement's debit and credit columns totals balance.

4-1 Appendix Problem: Preparing a work sheet

A partially completed work sheet for Foley's Interiors, based on Work Together 4-1, is provided in the *Working Papers*. The adjustment information for December 31 is presented below.

Estimate of uncollectible accounts	$ 2,101.23	Value of prepaid insurance	$2,500.00
Ending merchandise inventory—kitchen	147,084.62	Depreciation expense—office equipment	7,250.00
Ending merchandise inventory—bath	97,671.31	Depreciation expense—store equipment	8,490.00
Supplies on hand	1,950.00	Federal income tax expense	2,749.15

1. Enter the adjustments on the work sheet. Label each adjustment, using consecutive letters, (a), (b), etc.
2. Extend the adjusted account balances to the appropriate columns of the work sheet.
3. Complete the work sheet.

4-2 Appendix Problem: Preparing a work sheet

A partially completed work sheet for Mixon Auto Supplies, based on On Your Own 4-1, is provided in the *Working Papers*. The adjustment information for December 31 is presented below.

Estimate of uncollectible accounts	$ 3,123.53	Value of prepaid insurance	$3,000.00
Ending merchandise inventory—parts	254,285.38	Depreciation expense—office equipment	4,850.00
Ending merchandise inventory—accessories	114,223.95	Depreciation expense—store equipment	6,490.00
Supplies on hand	1,480.00	Federal income tax expense	3,392.43

1. Enter the adjustments on the work sheet. Label each adjustment, using consecutive letters, (a), (b), etc.
2. Extend the adjusted account balances to the appropriate columns of the work sheet.
3. Complete the work sheet.

4-3 Appendix Problem: Preparing a work sheet

A partially completed work sheet for Sunset Sports, Inc., based on Problem 4-1, is provided in the *Working Papers*. The adjustment information for December 31 is presented below.

Estimate of uncollectible accounts	$ 1,740.79	Value of prepaid insurance	$1,000.00
Ending merchandise inventory—golf	64,933.31	Depreciation expense—office equipment	3,190.00
Ending merchandise inventory—tennis	47,687.92	Depreciation expense—store equipment	6,280.00
Supplies on hand	670.00	Federal income tax expense	561.14

1. Enter the adjustments on the work sheet. Label each adjustment using consecutive letters, (a), (b), etc.
2. Extend the adjusted account balances to the appropriate columns of the work sheet.
3. Complete the work sheet.

Reinforcement Activity 1

Processing and Reporting Departmentalized Accounting Data

Sage 50 Accounting AAONLINE

This activity reinforces selected learning from Part 1, Chapters 1 through 4. The complete accounting cycle is for a departmentalized merchandising business organized as a corporation.

Jewel's Kitchen, Inc.

Jewel's Kitchen, Inc., sells kitchen merchandise in two departments: Equipment and Accessories. Jewel's Kitchen is open for business Monday through Saturday. It pays a monthly rent on the building. The business owns office equipment and store equipment. Most customers pay with cash or a credit card. A small number of customers have arranged to purchase merchandise on account.

Jewel's Kitchen's fiscal year is January 1 through December 31. The company uses the chart of accounts shown at the end of this activity. The journals and ledgers are similar to those illustrated in Part 1. The journals and ledger forms are provided in the *Working Papers*. Beginning balances have been recorded in the ledgers.

Recording Transactions

INSTRUCTIONS

1. Use the appropriate journal to record the following transactions completed during December of the current year. Calculate and record sales tax on all sales and sales returns and allowances as described in Chapter 2. The sales tax rate is 5.0%. Post the following transactions when journalized: (1) transactions affecting the accounts receivable or accounts payable subsidiary ledgers, (2) transactions recorded in the general journal, and (3) cash payments entered in the general columns of the cash payments journal. Source documents are abbreviated as follows: check, C; credit memorandum, CM; debit memorandum, DM; memorandum, M; purchase invoice, P; receipt, R; sales invoice, S; terminal summary, TS.

Dec. 1. Paid cash to SBG Properties for rent, $2,300.00. C796.
2. Purchased equipment on account from Burkes Industries, $3,484.15. P261.
2. Received cash on account from Denton Seafood, $4,108.62, covering S605 for accessories. R592.
4. Paid cash on account to Kitchen Concepts, $5,045.60, covering P258 for accessories for $5,148.57, less discount. C797.
4. Recorded cash and credit card sales: equipment, $6,148.26; accessories, $1,104.68; plus sales tax. TS48.
5. Sold accessories on account to Carlisle Steakhouse, $5,418.69, plus sales tax. S621.
6. Purchased accessories on account from Triangle Manufacturing, $6,148.17. P262.
6. Paid cash on account to Burkes Industries, $3,414.47, covering P260 for equipment for $3,484.15, less discount. C798.
8. Sold equipment on account to Virgie Berger, $614.25, plus sales tax. S622.
9. Paid cash for a miscellaneous expense, $275.00. C799.
9. Purchased accessories on account from Central Kitchen Supply, $5,174.68. P263.
10. Paid cash to Central Electric for a utility bill, $512.12. C800.
10. Sold accessories on account to Denton Seafood, $8,415.25, plus sales tax. S623.
11. Paid cash on account to Fulgham Pottery, $1,846.37, covering P257 for accessories. C801.
11. Granted credit to Virgie Berger for equipment returned, $120.00, plus sales tax, from S622. CM44.
13. Received cash on account from Carlisle Steakhouse, $5,575.83, covering S621 for accessories for $5,689.62, less discount. R593.
13. Returned accessories to Central Kitchen Supply, $614.62, from P263. DM55.
14. Purchased equipment on account from Specialty Supply, $4,914.74. P264.
14. Paid cash to Ganther Broadcasting for advertising a sale on accessories, $400.00. C802.
15. Received cash on account from Virgie Berger, $508.58, covering S622 for equipment for $644.96, less CM44 for $126.00, less discount. R594.

Reinforcement Activity

BRIDGE

- Reinforcement Activity 1 begins after Chapter 4 and reinforces the accounting cycle for a departmentalized merchandising business organized as a corporation.

TEACHING RESOURCES

- **Manual Accounting:**
  Working Papers for Reinforcement Activity 1
  Teacher's Edition of the Working Papers for Reinforcement Activity 1
  Online Working Papers
  Website for Audit Tests, Solutions, and Transparency Masters
- **Accounting Software:**
  QuickBooks, Excel, Sage 50 Accounting, and Automated Accounting Online may be used to automate this Reinforcement Activity.

INPUT FOR AUTOMATING

- Direct students to read the Help screens for specific requirements for automating Reinforcement Activity 1.

Reinforcement Activity 1 (Cont.)

Processing and Reporting Departmentalized Accounting Data

Dec. 15. Paid cash for liability for federal employee income tax, $524.00; social security tax, $961.85; Medicare tax, $224.95; total, $1,710.80. C803.
16. Sold accessories on account to LaFlore Café, $6,142.61, plus sales tax. S624.
16. Received cash on account from Hamilton Group, $2,000.00, in partial payment of its account. R595.
16. Paid cash on account to Hunley Equipment Co., $2,325.05, in partial payment of P255 for equipment. C804.
18. Paid cash on account to Central Kitchen Supply, $4,468.86, covering P263 for accessories for $5,174.68, less D55 for $614.62, less discount. C805.
18. Recorded cash and credit card sales: equipment, $7,813.25; accessories, $2,047.64; plus sales tax. TS49.
18. Declared a dividend of $0.50 per share on 15,000 shares outstanding. The dividend will be payable on January 18. M61.
21. Purchased accessories on account from Kitchen Concepts, $8,104.94. P265.
21. Sold accessories on account to Hamilton Group, $1,425.21, plus sales tax. S625.
22. Received cash on account from LaFlore Café, $6,320.75, covering S624 for accessories for $6,449.74, less discount. R596.
23. Received cash on account from Polk County Schools, $2,481.14, covering S618 for equipment. R597.
23. Sold equipment on account to Mary McCrory, $825.21, plus sales tax. S626.
27. Purchased accessories on account from Fulgham Pottery, $9,414.78. P266.
27. Sold accessories on account to Polk County Schools, $3,148.25; no sales tax. S627.
28. Paid cash to Davis Office Supply for supplies, $168.00. C806.
29. Paid cash on account to Triangle Manufacturing, $2,000.00, partially covering P262 for accessories. C807.
30. Sold accessories on account to LaFlore Café, $1,847.95, plus sales tax. S628.

Dec. 30. Paid credit card fee expense for December, $223.14. M62.
30. Recorded cash and credit card sales: equipment, $3,418.66; accessories, $845.60; plus sales tax. TS50.
30. Paid cash for monthly payroll, $5,017.56 (total payroll: equipment, $3,394.78; accessories, $2,801.69; administrative, $1,062.40; less deductions: employee income tax—federal, $498.00; employee income tax—state, $218.00; social security tax, $450.05; Medicare tax, $105.26; health insurance, $450.00; retirement contributions, $520.00). C808.
30. Recorded employer payroll taxes for the December pay period. Taxes owed are: social security tax, $450.05; Medicare tax, $105.26; federal unemployment tax, $2.80; state unemployment tax, $18.90. Payroll taxes are distributed among the departments as: equipment, $259.70; accessories, $236.04; and administrative, $81.27. M63.

2. Prove and total page 15 of the cash payments journal. Post the totals of the special columns to the general ledger.
3. Journalize the following transactions, applying the same posting procedures used above.

   Dec. 31. Paid cash to H&L Computers for office equipment, $961.25. C809.
   31. Paid cash to reimburse the petty cash fund, $203.83; advertising expense—accessories, $75.00; miscellaneous expense, $56.68; supplies, $72.15. C810.

4. Prove and rule the sales journal. Post the totals of the special columns.
5. Prove and rule the purchases journal. Post the totals of the special columns.
6. Prove the cash receipts journal and page 16 of the cash payments journal.
7. Prove cash. The balance on the next unused check stub is $50,712.48.
8. Rule the cash receipts journal. Post the totals of the special columns.
9. Rule page 16 of the cash payments journal. Post the totals of the special columns.

WINNING EDGE

Give students the *Winning Edge* by making competitive event prep part of their classroom materials throughout the year. Go to cengage.com/winningedge for a list of materials that prepare students for specific competitive events.

End-of-Fiscal-Period Work

INSTRUCTIONS

10. Prepare a schedule of accounts receivable and a schedule of accounts payable. Compare each schedule total with the balance of the controlling account in the general ledger. The total and the balance should be the same.
11. Record the adjusting entries on page 17 of a general journal.

Adjustment Information, December 31

Estimate of uncollectible accounts	$ 2,930.00
Ending merchandise inventory—equipment	89,626.86
Ending merchandise inventory—accessories	160,029.03
Supplies on hand	2,160.00
Value of prepaid insurance	1,400.00
Depreciation expense—office equipment	5,260.00
Depreciation expense—store equipment	6,120.00

12. Post the adjusting entries to the general ledger accounts.
13. Enter the general ledger account balances on the adjusted trial balance.
14. Calculate federal income tax expense using the tax table presented in Chapter 4. Prepare and post the adjusting entry for federal income tax expense.
15. Complete the adjusted trial balance.
16. Prepare departmental margin statements for Jewel's Kitchen's equipment and accessories departments. Calculate and record component percentages for each amount in the fourth column of the statements. Round percentage calculations to the nearest 0.1%.
17. Prepare an income statement. Calculate and record the vertical analysis ratios for each amount in the fourth column of the statement. Round percentage calculations to the nearest 0.1%.
18. Prepare a statement of stockholders' equity. There were 14,000 shares of $10.00 par value stock issued as of January 1. There were 1,000 shares issued during the current year.
19. Prepare a balance sheet. Calculate and record the vertical analysis ratios for each item in the third column of the statement.
20. Use the following information to complete the statement of cash flows. Jewel's Kitchen began the fiscal year with a cash balance of $21,311.88.

Cash received from:

Issuance of stock	$ 10,000.00
Sale of equipment	3,150.00
Sales to customers	621,548.61

Cash payments for:

Dividends	28,500.00
Income taxes	10,942.00
Insurance	14,800.00
Inventory purchases	339,141.45
Other operating expenses	51,449.76
Purchase of equipment	24,168.00
Rent	27,600.00
Salaries and wages	108,696.80

21. Use page 18 of a general journal. Journalize and post the closing entries.
22. Prepare a post-closing trial balance.

CHECK FIGURES

For the complete solution to Reinforcement Activity 1, see the Teacher's Edition of the Working Papers.

- Purchases Journal totals: $37,241.46; $8,398.89; $28,842.57.
- Cash Payments Journal page 15 totals: $12,847.93; $2,241.31; $19,364.20; $69.68; $194.17; $29,706.97.
- Sales Journal totals: $29,071.87; $1,234.45; $1,439.46; $26,397.96.
- Cash Receipts Journal totals: General Debit and Credit Column totals are both $0; $21,248.08; $1,068.90; $17,380.17; $3,997.92; $10.38; $242.78; $43,441.91.
- Federal Income Tax Payable, $3,824.40.
- Adjusted Trial Balance column totals, $1,047,076.90.
- Gross Profit, Equipment: $121,639.05, 55.5%.
- Departmental Margin, Equipment: $61,710.92, 28.2%.
- Gross Profit, Accessories: $185,905.15, 44.7%.
- Departmental Margin, Accessories: $132,746.06, 31.9%.
- Net Income before Income Tax: $67,297.58, 10.6%.
- Federal Income Tax Expense: $11,824.40, 1.9%.
- Total Current Assets: $321,552.90, 91.9%.
- Total Assets: $350,032.27.
- Total Liabilities: $58,755.18, 16.8%.
- Retained Earnings: $141,277.09.
- Net cash provided by operating activities, $68,918.60.
- Net cash used by investing activities, $21,018.00.
- Net cash used by financing activities, $18,500.00.
- Closing entry to close debit accounts: Income Summary—General, credit, $680,797.81.
- Closing entry to close credit accounts: Income Summary—General, debit, $625,324.63.
- Closing entry to close Retained Earnings: Income Summary—General, debit, $55,473.18.
- Post-Closing Trial Balance column totals, $392,752.27.

Reinforcement Activity 1 (Cont.)

Processing and Reporting Departmentalized Accounting Data

Chart of Accounts

General Ledger

Balance Sheet Accounts

(1000) ASSETS

1100–1400 CURRENT ASSETS
1105 Cash
1110 Petty Cash
1205 Accounts Receivable
1210 Allowance for Uncollectible Accounts
1305 Merchandise Inventory—Equipment
1310 Merchandise Inventory—Accessories
1405 Supplies
1410 Prepaid Insurance
1500 PLANT ASSETS
1505 Office Equipment
1510 Accumulated Depreciation—Office Equipment
1515 Store Equipment
1520 Accumulated Depreciation—Store Equipment

(2000) LIABILITIES

2105 Accounts Payable
2110 Sales Tax Payable
2115 Employee Income Tax Payable—Federal
2120 Employee Income Tax Payable—State
2125 Social Security Tax Payable
2130 Medicare Tax Payable
2135 Medical Insurance Payable
2140 Retirement Plan Payable
2145 Unemployment Tax Payable—Federal
2150 Unemployment Tax Payable—State
2155 Federal Income Tax Payable
2160 Dividends Payable

(3000) STOCKHOLDERS' EQUITY

3105 Capital Stock
3110 Retained Earnings
3115 Dividends
3205 Income Summary—General
3210 Income Summary—Equipment
3215 Income Summary—Accessories

Income Statement Accounts

(4000) OPERATING REVENUE

4105 Sales—Equipment
4110 Sales Discount—Equipment
4115 Sales Returns and Allowances—Equipment
4205 Sales—Accessories
4210 Sales Discount—Accessories
4215 Sales Returns and Allowances—Accessories

(5000) COST OF MERCHANDISE

5105 Purchases—Equipment
5110 Purchases Discount—Equipment
5115 Purchases Returns and Allowances—Equipment
5205 Purchases—Accessories
5210 Purchases Discount—Accessories
5215 Purchases Returns and Allowances—Accessories

(6000) DIRECT EXPENSES

6100 DIRECT EXPENSES—EQUIPMENT
6105 Advertising Expense—Equipment
6110 Payroll Taxes Expense—Equipment
6115 Salary Expense—Equipment
6200 DIRECT EXPENSES—ACCESSORIES
6205 Advertising Expense—Accessories
6210 Payroll Taxes Expense—Accessories
6215 Salary Expense—Accessories

(7000) INDIRECT EXPENSES

7105 Credit Card Fee Expense
7110 Depreciation Expense—Office Equipment
7115 Depreciation Expense—Store Equipment
7120 Insurance Expense
7125 Miscellaneous Expense
7130 Payroll Taxes Expense—Administrative
7135 Rent Expense
7140 Salary Expense—Administrative
7145 Supplies Expense
7150 Uncollectible Accounts Expense
7155 Utilities Expense

(8000) INCOME TAX

8105 Federal Income Tax Expense

Subsidiary Ledgers

Accounts Receivable Ledger

110 Virgie Berger
120 Carlisle Steakhouse
130 Denton Seafood
140 Hamilton Group
150 LaFlore Café
160 Mary McCrory
170 Polk County Schools
180 Waukawy Country Club

Accounts Payable Ledger

210 Burkes Industries
220 Central Kitchen Supply
230 Fulgham Pottery
240 Hunley Equipment Co.
250 Kitchen Concepts
260 Specialty Supply
270 Triangle Manufacturing

Organic Aisles is a departmentalized organic grocery store organized as a corporation. The company sells produce and grocery items. Separate accounting records are kept for two departments, Produce and Grocery. The activities included in the accounting cycle for Organic Aisles are listed here.

This simulation is available from the publisher in either manual or automated versions.

The following activities are included in this simulation:

1. Recording transactions in special journals and a general journal.
2. Calculating and recording departmental payroll data.
3. Posting items to be posted individually to a general ledger and subsidiary ledgers.
4. Proving and ruling journals.
5. Posting column totals to a general ledger.
6. Preparing schedules of accounts receivable and accounts payable.
7. Preparing a trial balance on a work sheet.
8. Planning adjustments and completing a work sheet.
9. Preparing financial statements.
10. Journalizing and posting adjusting entries.
11. Journalizing and posting closing entries.
12. Preparing a post-closing trial balance.
13. Completing Think Like an Accountant Financial Analysis.

139

Part 2
Accounting Adjustments and Valuation

OVERVIEW

Vaughn Distributors, Inc., is the business used in Part 2 to illustrate accounting adjustments and valuations. Vaughn operates from a large warehouse, part of which it rents to other businesses.

Chapter organization and content provide students with an expanded view of concepts that were presented in the first year of accounting study.

- **Chapter 5** describes inventory planning and valuation.
- **Chapter 6** describes accounting for uncollectible accounts.
- **Chapter 7** describes accounting for plant assets.
- **Chapter 8** describes accounting for notes Payable, prepaid expenses, and accrued expenses.
- **Chapter 9** describes accounting for unearned revenue, accrued revenue, and installment notes receivable.

ACCOUNTING SOFTWARE

For those instructors who want to integrate the accounting program fully, the problems at the end of each chapter are flagged to show when files are provided for completing a problem using QuickBooks, Excel, or Sage 50 Accounting. In addition, A Look at Accounting Software is provided at the end of each chapter in Part 2. This feature is designed to show how the accounting procedures described in these chapters are handled in commercial accounting software.

Part
2

Accounting Adjustments and Valuation

© iStockphoto.com/Alex Slobodkin

Reinforcement Activity

Reinforcement Activity 2, Processing Accounting Data for a Corporation, may be completed after Chapter 9.

THE BUSINESS—

VAUGHN DISTRIBUTORS, INC.

Vaughn Distributors, Inc., the business described in Part 2, purchases hand tools from foreign manufacturers and distributes the merchandise to independent hardware stores. Vaughn operates from a large warehouse, part of which it rents to other businesses.

© Flas100/Shutterstock.com

Chart of Accounts
VAUGHN DISTRIBUTORS, INC.

GENERAL LEDGER

Balance Sheet Accounts

(1000) ASSETS

1100 Current Assets
- 1110 Cash
- 1115 Petty Cash
- 1120 Accounts Receivable
- 1125 Allowance for Uncollectible Accounts
- 1130 Merchandise Inventory
- 1140 Supplies
- 1150 Prepaid Insurance
- 1155 Prepaid Advertising
- 1160 Notes Receivable
- 1165 Interest Receivable

1200 Plant Assets
- 1210 Land
- 1220 Building
- 1225 Accumulated Depreciation—Building
- 1230 Office Equipment
- 1235 Accumulated Depreciation—Office Equipment
- 1240 Warehouse Equipment
- 1245 Accumulated Depreciation—Warehouse Equipment

(2000) LIABILITIES

2100 Current Liabilities
- 2105 Accounts Payable
- 2110 Salaries Payable
- 2115 Employee Income Tax Payable
- 2120 Social Security Tax Payable
- 2125 Medicare Tax Payable
- 2130 Unemployment Tax Payable—Federal
- 2135 Unemployment Tax Payable—State
- 2140 Unearned Rent
- 2150 Federal Income Tax Payable
- 2160 Notes Payable
- 2165 Interest Payable

2200 Long-Term Liabilities
- 2205 Mortgage Payable

(3000) STOCKHOLDERS' EQUITY
- 3105 Capital Stock
- 3110 Retained Earnings
- 3115 Dividends
- 3120 Income Summary

Income Statement Accounts

(4000) OPERATING REVENUE
- 4105 Sales
- 4110 Sales Discount
- 4115 Sales Returns and Allowances

(5000) COST OF MERCHANDISE
- 5105 Purchases
- 5110 Purchases Discount
- 5115 Purchases Returns and Allowances

(6000) OPERATING EXPENSE
- 6105 Advertising Expense
- 6110 Depreciation Expense—Building
- 6115 Depreciation Expense—Office Equipment
- 6120 Depreciation Expense—Warehouse Equipment
- 6125 Insurance Expense
- 6130 Miscellaneous Expense
- 6135 Payroll Taxes Expense
- 6140 Property Tax Expense
- 6145 Salary Expense
- 6150 Supplies Expense
- 6155 Uncollectible Accounts Expense

(7000) OTHER REVENUE
- 7105 Gain on Plant Assets
- 7110 Interest Income
- 7115 Rent Income

(8000) OTHER EXPENSES
- 8105 Interest Expense
- 8110 Loss on Plant Assets

(9000) INCOME TAX
- 9105 Federal Income Tax Expense

The chart of accounts for Vaughn Distributors, Inc., is illustrated above for ready reference as you study Part 2 of this textbook.

Chart of Accounts

Vaughn Distributors, Inc., the business described in Part 2, purchases hand tools from foreign manufacturers and distributes the merchandise to independent hardware stores.

- Emphasize that students should refer to this chart of accounts throughout the chapters in Part 2.
- Stress that charts of accounts are extremely important to companies because they drive the accounting system used.
- Point out that the chart of accounts for Part 2 includes new account titles used in this part of the book, such as Notes Receivable, Land, Building, Notes Payable, and Other Revenue, and it includes only one revenue account (Sales).
- Emphasize that charts of accounts are used for determining the classification of accounts and show which accounts are temporary and permanent accounts.
- Stress that the chart of accounts is useful for completing automated accounting activities because account numbers are required for both data entry and file maintenance activities.

Chapter 5

Inventory Planning and Valuation

Scope & Sequence

	New	Review/Enrich
Introduction		
Introduce the Chapter		
Lesson 5-1 Determining Merchandise Inventory Quantities		
The Nature of Merchandise Inventory	✓	
Effects of Errors in Costing Merchandise Inventory	✓	
Costing and Counting the Inventory	✓	
Stock Record for a Perpetual Inventory System	✓	
Inventory Record Used for the Physical Inventory	✓	
Lesson 5-2 Inventory Costing Methods		
First-In, First-Out Inventory Costing Method		✓
Last-In, First-Out Inventory Costing Method		✓
Weighted-Average Inventory Costing Method		✓
Costing Inventory During Periods of Increasing Prices	✓	
Tax Limitations on Using LIFO	✓	
Costing Inventory During Periods of Decreasing Prices	✓	
Criticism of the LIFO Method	✓	
Lower of Cost or Market Inventory Costing Method		✓
Lesson 5-3 Estimating the Inventory		
Gross Profit Method of Estimating Inventory		✓
Retail Method of Estimating Inventory	✓	
Financial Analysis of Merchandise Inventory	✓	
Closure		

Enhancing Instruction

Features	Common Core Standards
• Accounting in the Real World: Johnson & Johnson	• ELAL—reading, writing
• Ethics in Action: Is Someone Reading Your E-mail? • Why Accounting?: Retraining after Workplace Injuries • Forensic Accounting: Restatement at Rite Aid Corporation	• ELAL—reading • ELAL—media and technology, reading • Mathematics
• Think Like an Accountant: Helping a Client Avoid Penalties	• Mathematics
• Global Awareness: Work/Holiday Visa	• ELAL—media and technology, writing
• A Look at Accounting Software • Explore Accounting • Auditing for Errors • 21st Century Skills • Analyzing Home Depot's Financial Statements	• ELAL—reading • ELAL—speaking, listening • Mathematics • ELAL—writing • Mathematics

ELAL = English Language Arts & Literacy

Calculator: © iStockphoto.com/picstodisc; Paper: © iStockphoto.com/Qingwa

Practice and Assessment

Technology & Media	Teaching Strategies	Guided Practice	Independent Practice	Reteach/Enrich
• Instructor's Resource CD/Website: PowerPoint Slides Accounting Concepts • Online Working Papers • Transparency Masters: Stock Record, Inventory Record	• Tactile/Kinesthetic Learners	• Terms Review • Audit Your Understanding • Work Together 5-1	• On Your Own 5-1 • Application Problem 5-1 • Formative Assessment, p. 149 • Online Working Papers	• Reteach, p. 150
• Instructor's Resource CD/Website: PowerPoint Slides Accounting Concepts • Online Working Papers	• Visual/Spatial Learners	• Terms Review • Audit Your Understanding • Work Together 5-2	• On Your Own 5-2 • Application Problem 5-2 • Formative Assessment, p. 157 • Online Working Papers	• Reteach, p. 158
• Instructor's Resource CD/Website: PowerPoint Slides Accounting Concepts • Online Working Papers • Transparency Master: Estimated Merchandise Inventory Sheet	• Auditory/Linguistic Learners	• Terms Review • Audit Your Understanding • Work Together 5-3	• On Your Own 5-3 • Application Problem 5-3 • Formative Assessment, p. 161 • Online Working Papers	• Reteach, p. 162
• Online Working Papers	• Common Core and Interdisciplinary Studies		• Mastery Problem 5-M • Study Guide 5 • Chapter 5 Test • Cognero Chapter 5	• Challenge Problem 5-C • Reteach, p. 168 • Recycling Problem 5-R

Introduce the Chapter

SET THE STAGE

GUIDING QUESTIONS

- Ask students if they have ever participated in taking inventory. If so, have them explain the process.
- Ask students if they think counting inventory can reflect stolen merchandise.
- Ask for examples of how a large merchandising retail store might take inventory.
- Ask students why it is important to take inventory.
- Ask students if they have ever gone to a store that did not change its inventory very often. How did this affect their purchases?

PREVIEW CHAPTER OBJECTIVES

- This chapter is unlike most chapters in that it contains no journal entries.
- This chapter focuses on accounting principles used to determine the amount and value of inventory.

PREVIEW ACCOUNTING TERMS

- Read each term aloud to verify its pronunciation for students.
- Point out terms or parts of terms that should already be familiar to most students, such as *inventory record*, *generally accepted accounting principles*, *inflation*, *turnover*, and *deflation*.
- Lead an interactive discussion that reviews and explains the terms. Stress that special attention should be directed to all boldfaced words presented in the text.

Chapter 5 Inventory Planning and Valuation

LEARNING OBJECTIVES

After studying Chapter 5, in addition to defining key terms, you will be able to:

LO1 Describe the nature of merchandise inventory.

LO2 Account for the quantity of merchandise inventory.

LO3 Determine the cost of merchandise inventory.

LO4 Determine the reported cost of merchandise inventory.

LO5 Estimate the cost of merchandise inventory.

LO6 Calculate the inventory turnover ratio and days' sales in inventory.

Calculator: © iStockphoto.com/picstodisc; Paper: © iStockphoto.com/Qingwa

© iStockphoto.com/GlobalStock

Accounting In The Real World
Johnson & Johnson

Merchandise inventory is the largest expenditure for most retail merchandising businesses. Management must ensure that purchasing decisions are made in accordance with the company's standards and policies. Employees must be free of any relationships that improperly influence their purchasing decisions. A relationship that causes an employee to make a decision at odds with the goals of a business is called a *conflict of interest*.

It is common for vendors to give small gifts to purchasing employees with whom they interact. Whether these gifts influence purchasing employees' decisions is difficult to determine. Gifts are more likely to be viewed as a conflict of interest.

A section in Johnson & Johnson's *Policy on Business Conduct* provides its employees with assistance on avoiding conflicts of interest. The document states that accepting gifts from a vendor is a conflict of interest. However, the company recognizes that entertainment, such as lunches and dinners, and modest gifts are customary in the normal course of business. Employees must use their professional judgment in deciding what is normal and modest. The document states, "If a disinterested third party would be likely to infer that it affected your judgment, then it is too much."

Johnson & Johnson encourages employees to seek the advice of their supervisor when faced with a potential conflict of interest. "Disclosure is the key." Disclosing the situation results in an open discussion that often eliminates any appearance of a conflict of interest.

CRITICAL THINKING

Many corporate codes of business conduct include sample situations of potential conflicts of interest. A sample situation might include a one-paragraph statement of the facts, and then state how the company would expect the employee to resolve the situation. Prepare a sample situation that could be added to the conflicts of interest section of Johnson & Johnson's *Policy on Business Conduct*.

Source: www.investor.jnj.com/governance/conduct.cfm.

Background: © iStockphoto.com/Gabor Izso; Real World: Emile Wamsteker/Bloomberg/Getty Images

Key Terms

- consignment
- consignee
- consignor
- stock record
- stock ledger
- inventory record
- generally accepted accounting principles
- first-in, first-out inventory costing method
- last-in, first-out inventory costing method
- weighted-average inventory costing method
- inflation
- deflation
- international financial reporting standards
- lower of cost or market inventory costing method
- gross profit method of estimating inventory
- retail method of estimating inventory
- inventory turnover ratio
- days' sales in inventory

Accounting In The Real World

Answers will vary. The following sample solution can be used to provide students with an example of the content and length of a case:

Situation: John is a purchasing agent who specializes in plastics for medical devices. Mary, a sales representative for a plastics company, has invited John to discuss delivery schedules over dinner at a very exclusive restaurant. John and Mary have worked together for years. Mary is well respected by other purchasing agents. Although John has attended many lunches and dinners with Mary, they have never gone to such an elegant restaurant. John expects that Mary will easily spend over $250.

Analysis: Having a working lunch or dinner paid for by a vendor representative is customary in the normal course of business. However, the dollar amount could be viewed as excessive by a disinterested third party. There appears to be no legitimate business reason to have dinner at such an exclusive restaurant. John should ask Mary to modify the dinner plans to include a more modest restaurant.

LESSON

5-1

BRIDGE

- Ask students why it is important to be able to determine the items of inventory that are and are not selling well.
- Ask any students who have experience with computerized inventory systems to explain what they know about such systems.
- Ask students to brainstorm advantages of computerized inventory systems: Records are more accurate, and inventory information is available more frequently.

TEACHING RESOURCES

- **Instructor's Resource CD/Website:**
  PowerPoint Slides
  Accounting Concepts
- **Working Papers:**
  Teacher's Edition of the Working Papers for Lesson 5-1
  Online Working Papers
- **Transparency Masters:**
  Stock Record
  Inventory Record

ENGAGE

- Ask students to list the kinds of information about a specific item of inventory that is needed to maintain an inventory system. (*e.g., item no., description, cost, selling price, quantity on hand, and quantity ordered*)

PREVIEW

- Call on students to read the accounting terms and definitions introduced in this lesson: *consignment, consignee, consignor, stock record, stock ledger,* and *inventory record.*
- Point out the learning objectives for this lesson.
- Direct students to read the headings in this lesson and to examine the illustrations.

TEACHING IDEA **Metacognition allows students to process what they did and why they did it. Ask students to use a piece of paper to write answers to the following questions as the lesson is being presented. What did we do today? Why did we do it? How can I apply it? What did I learn today?**

LESSON

5-1 Determining Merchandise Inventory Quantities

LO1 Describe the nature of merchandise inventory.
LO2 Account for the quantity of merchandise inventory.

The Nature of Merchandise Inventory LO1

For most merchandising businesses, the cost of inventory sold is the largest cost of doing business. Merchandising businesses implement good control measures in managing their inventory. A successful business must maintain an adequate amount of merchandise inventory that customers are willing to buy. A business may fail if it keeps too much or too little merchandise inventory on hand.

Business managers frequently analyze sales and inventory transactions to assist them in planning future inventory purchases. From this analysis, managers can determine the items of inventory that are selling well and the items that are not selling well. Managers also examine sales and inventory transactions to identify any seasonal trends in sales. This information allows managers to order the right kinds of merchandise at the right time.

Many businesses now maintain their inventory records on computer. Computerized inventory systems can keep more accurate records of the amount of inventory on hand. Computerized systems also provide more frequent inventory information to managers. Managers use this information to make effective business decisions.

ETHICS IN ACTION

Is Someone Reading Your E-mail?

Janice Tillman had just been escorted from the plant by security guards. Twenty minutes earlier, she lost her job because she sent e-mail messages containing threats directed toward Sylvia Hernandez, her supervisor. When confronted with the messages, Janice tried to dismiss them casually as a joke. Then she accused Sylvia of invading her privacy, claiming that she selected the "private message" option when sending the e-mails to a friend.

The company's code of conduct states, "E-mail communication on the company computer systems is subject to electronic monitoring."

INSTRUCTIONS

Use the ethical model to evaluate Sylvia's decision to fire Janice.

© iStockphoto.com/LdF

ETHICS IN ACTION

Students should be allowed to form their own conclusions unless the action is clearly illegal or a violation of a company or professional code of conduct. In this case, it would seem that Sylvia's action was ethical. However, students should be allowed the freedom to support alternative conclusions.

For more information about employee privacy issues, instruct students to visit the Privacy Rights Clearinghouse. This organization states that selecting an e-mail "private" option is not an issue unless the company has specifically promised its employees to keep these messages confidential. Even so, at least one civil case has demonstrated that the privacy of "private" messages can be mitigated.

Source: www.privacyrights.org.

See a suggested solution for this feature in the Instructional Strategies section at the front of this book.

Effects of Errors in Costing Merchandise Inventory

	Correct Ending Inventory = $700		Incorrect Ending Inventory = $500	
Net Sales		$6,000		$6,000
Cost of Merchandise Sold:				
Beginning Inventory	$ 600		$ 600	
Plus Net Purchases	3,200		3,200	
Cost of Merchandise Available for Sale	$3,800		$3,800	
Less Ending Inventory	700		500	
Cost of Merchandise Sold		3,100		3,300
Gross Profit		$2,900		$2,700
Operating Expenses		2,000		2,000
Net Income		$ 900		$ 700

An accurate ending merchandise inventory cost must be determined to report adequately the financial progress and condition of a merchandising business. [CONCEPT: Full Disclosure] The cost is reported in the Assets section of the balance sheet. The cost is also used on the income statement to determine the cost of merchandise sold. Any error made in costing the ending inventory has a significant effect on the income statement. An abbreviated income statement for Erin Company is shown above. On the left side, the income statement reflects the correct cost of Erin's ending inventory, $700. The right side shows the effect of using an incorrect cost of $500 for the ending inventory. The $200 understatement causes the cost of merchandise sold to be overstated. This error also affects the gross profit and the net income, which are understated.

An error in the ending inventory also affects other financial statements. The table below summarizes the effect of the $200 understatement of Erin's ending inventory on selected amounts of three financial statements. The statement of cash flows is the only financial statement not affected by the error.

Reports and Items Affected	Correct Amount	Effect of Understating Ending Inventory	Misstated Amount
Income Statement			
Cost of Merchandise Sold	$3,100	$+200	$3,300
Gross Profit	2,900	−200	2,700
Net Income	900	−200	700
Statement of Stockholders' Equity			
Net Income	900	−200	700
Retained Earnings	1,200	−200	1,000
Stockholders' Equity	1,700	−200	1,500
Balance Sheet			
Merchandise Inventory	700	−200	500
Total Assets	2,200	−200	2,000
Stockholders' Equity	1,700	−200	1,500

If the ending inventory is understated, the cost of merchandise sold will be overstated. The cost of merchandise sold overstatement results in an understatement of net income. Consequently, the understatement of net income results in an understatement of retained earnings and stockholders' equity. If the ending inventory is overstated, the reverse will be true, and additional income tax must be paid on the overstated income. In neither situation will the financial statements report accurate information. [CONCEPT: Full Disclosure]

INPUT

- Explain that an accurate inventory cost is important to report adequately the financial progress and condition of a business.
- Explain that if ending inventory is misstated, the income statement, balance sheet, and statement of stockholders' equity will be significantly affected.
- Point out the effects of errors on the income statement in the illustration at the top of the page.
- Direct students to the illustration at the bottom of the page to point out the magnitude of the effects of misstated amounts on the income statement, statement of stockholders' equity, and balance sheet.

DIFFERENTIATED INSTRUCTION

Tactile/Kinesthetic learners excel through physical activity and real objects. Ask students to take a physical inventory of ten items in their home. Students could prepare a stock record for each item. After several days, instruct students to perform another physical inventory and compare the actual quantity with the quantity on the stock record.

INPUT

- Explain that the cost of goods includes the price paid for them plus the cost involved in getting them delivered and ready for sale, including transportation charges paid by the buyer.
- Describe the two methods of determining the number of goods in inventory: taking a physical count and keeping a continuous record.
- Explain the importance of knowing who holds the title to goods in determining whether the goods are counted in inventory.
- Explain the difference between FOB shipping point (*goods in transit are part of the buyer's inventory*) and FOB destination (*goods in transit are not part of the buyer's inventory*).
- Explain that the person or business that receives goods on consignment does not include those goods as part of inventory.

Costing and Counting the Inventory LO2

Items in merchandise inventory are frequently referred to as *goods*. Typically, a business counts as part of its inventory all goods that it legally owns. The cost of these goods includes:

1. The price paid to vendors for the merchandise. This price is the purchase invoice amount less discounts, returns, and allowances granted by the vendors.
2. The cost of getting the goods to the place of business and ready for sale. This cost includes transportation charges paid by the buyer.

Merchandising businesses must know both the cost of the goods and the number of goods in inventory.

Businesses use two methods to determine the number of goods in inventory:

1. Taking a physical count of the items in inventory. All goods in inventory as of a given date are included in a physical inventory count.
2. Keeping a continuous record for each merchandise item showing the number purchased and the number sold. Using this method, a business can determine the number of goods in inventory at any point in time.

GOODS IN TRANSIT

Merchandising businesses purchase goods and services from vendors. A vendor that sells merchandise to a merchandising business is often referred to as a *supplier*. The supplier ships the goods to the business. For goods in transit at the time of a physical count of inventory, the business must determine who holds title to the goods. When title to goods in transit passes from the supplier to the buyer, the goods become part of the buyer's inventory regardless of where they are physically located.

A supplier's terms of sale may include the provision *FOB shipping point*. FOB is an abbreviation for the phrase *Free on Board*. FOB shipping point means that the buyer pays the transportation charges. Under FOB shipping point terms, the title to the goods passes to the buyer as soon as the vendor delivers the goods to a shipping company. These goods in transit, not yet received by the buyer, are part of the *buyer's* inventory.

If the terms of sale are *FOB destination*, the vendor pays the transportation charges. Title to the goods passes to the buyer when the buyer receives the goods. These goods in transit, not yet received by the buyer, are part of the *supplier's* inventory. The buyer does not include these goods in the cost of inventory.

GOODS ON CONSIGNMENT

Goods that are given to a business to sell but for which title remains with the vendor are called a **consignment**. The person or business that receives goods on consignment is called the **consignee**. The person or business that gives goods on consignment is called the **consignor**.

The consignee agrees to receive, care for, and attempt to sell the consigned goods. If the goods are sold, the consignee deducts a commission from the sale amount and sends the remainder to the consignor. In a consignment, title to the goods does not pass to the consignee. The goods on consignment are part of the consignor's inventory. The consignee does not include consigned goods in the cost of its inventory.

A consignee agrees to care for the goods on consignment and to make adequate attempts to sell them. Therefore, a consignee has implied liabilities if anything should happen to the goods before they are sold. A consignee often reports the cost of consigned goods as a footnote to its balance sheet.

Stock Record for a Perpetual Inventory System

STOCK RECORD

Description *6-inch drill extension* Stock No. *D-1643*

Reorder *60* Minimum *20* Location *Bin 253*

1	2	3	4	5	6	7
INCREASES			DECREASES			BALANCE
DATE	PURCHASE INVOICE NO.	QUANTITY	DATE	SALES INVOICE NO.	QUANTITY	QUANTITY
Oct. 1						*38*
			Oct. 22	*2065*	*20*	*18*
			Oct. 31	*2156*	*10*	*8*
Nov. 5	*816*	*60*				*68*
			Nov. 14	*2215*	*30*	*38*
			Dec. 9	*2295*	*25*	*13*
Dec. 23	*881*	*60*				*73*

(1) Item Description
(2) Beginning Quantity
(3) Sales Transactions
(4) Purchase Transactions

A continuous record of merchandise inventory increases and decreases and the balance on hand is known as a *perpetual inventory*. Vaughn Distributors maintains a perpetual inventory.

A perpetual inventory provides day-to-day records about the quantity of merchandise on hand. Based on the records, management knows when an item of inventory is low and needs to be reordered. For each inventory item, the record shows the number on hand, the number purchased, and the number sold. A form used to show the type of merchandise, quantity received, quantity sold, and balance on hand is called a **stock record**. A file of stock records for all merchandise on hand is called a **stock ledger**.

Vaughn's stock record for a 6-inch drill extension is shown above. It includes a notation of the minimum balance at which a reorder is to be placed. For example, Vaughn determines that two weeks are required to order and to receive a shipment from a vendor. In a two-week period, Vaughn will sell an average of 20 units. Therefore, Vaughn reorders the item when the inventory reaches 20 units. Each reorder is for 60 units. On October 22, the inventory balance falls below the reorder point. An order is immediately placed for 60 units. The order is received on November 5. A second order, placed on December 9, is received on December 23.

During the year, sales are recorded on the stock record when the sale is made. Purchases are recorded on the stock record when the goods are received. Unit prices are not recorded on the stock record. They are obtained from copies of the purchase invoices.

Maintaining a Stock Record

1. Record the description of the inventory item, 6-inch drill extension, the stock number, D-1643, the reorder quantity, 60, the minimum number, 20, and the warehouse location, Bin 253.
2. Write the beginning quantity. On Oct. 1, 20--, the quantity on hand was 38.
3. Record all sales transactions in the Decreases columns of the stock record. For the October 22 sale, enter the date, Oct. 22, sales invoice number, 2065, and quantity sold, 20. Subtract the amount sold from the previous balance and enter the new balance, 18.
4. Enter all purchase transactions in the Increases columns of the stock record when the goods are received. Enter the date, purchase invoice number, quantity, and balance.

INPUT

- Emphasize that stock records are used to maintain the continuous count of a perpetual inventory.
- Explain that all stock records comprise the stock ledger.
- Ask a student to identify information, other than the quantity on hand, that is recorded on a stock record.
- Explain how the Reorder and Minimum quantities are used in an inventory system.

MODEL

- Use the stock record transparency or direct students to the illustration to demonstrate how to maintain a stock record.
- Explain the use of the information at the top of the stock record.
- Demonstrate how to do the calculation for the Balance Quantity column for an entry in the Increases columns.
- Demonstrate how to do the calculation for the Balance Quantity column for an entry in the Decreases columns.
- Ask students to determine on which date the 6-inch drill extensions should have been reordered. (*Dec. 9, when the balance quantity, 13, fell below the minimum, 20*)

INPUT

- Explain what is involved in "taking an inventory."
- Emphasize that a business that uses a perpetual inventory also conducts a physical inventory once a year, usually at year-end.
- Explain that the inventory record is used in taking a physical inventory to record the quantity of units on hand for each item. After the count is taken, the unit price is recorded and the total cost is calculated.
- Explain that any differences between the inventory record and the perpetual inventory record are adjusted on the inventory records.
- Mention that if large or frequent differences are found, the recording and control procedures should be reviewed.

WHY ACCOUNTING?

Answers

1. The BLS is part of the U.S. Department of Labor.
2. Answers will vary.
3. Answer will vary from year to year.

Inventory Record Used for the Physical Inventory

INVENTORY RECORD

DATE *December 31, 20--* ITEM *Drill Accessories*

1 STOCK NUMBER	2 DESCRIPTIONS	3 NO. OF UNITS ON HAND	4 UNIT PRICE	5 TOTAL COST
D-0643-3	*3/16-in masonry bit*	*102*	*1.25*	*127.50*
D-1643	*6-in drill extension*	*47*	*40 @ 3.25*	*152.40*
			7 @ 3.20	
C-6432	*Grout mixer*	*48*	*4.98*	*239.04*
	Total			*6,018.47*

An inventory determined periodically by counting, weighing, or measuring items of merchandise on hand is known as a *physical inventory*. Counting, weighing, or measuring merchandise on hand for a physical inventory is commonly referred to as "taking an inventory." For businesses with a large quantity of merchandise on hand, taking an inventory is expensive. Therefore, businesses usually take an inventory only once each fiscal period.

Vaughn uses the perpetual inventory method to ensure that it maintains an adequate level of merchandise for sale. Errors can occur, however, even when the perpetual inventory method is used. Therefore, Vaughn takes a physical inventory once each year to check the accuracy of the perpetual inventory.

A form used during a physical inventory to record information about each item of merchandise on hand is called an **inventory record**. One inventory record is used for each item or category of items in inventory. When taking an inventory, Vaughn uses an inventory record for categories of merchandise as shown above.

The inventory count is compared to the perpetual inventory. Any differences are adjusted on the inventory records. If large differences are found, the business should review its recording and control procedures to ensure that the inventory and the inventory records are being properly maintained.

WHY ACCOUNTING?

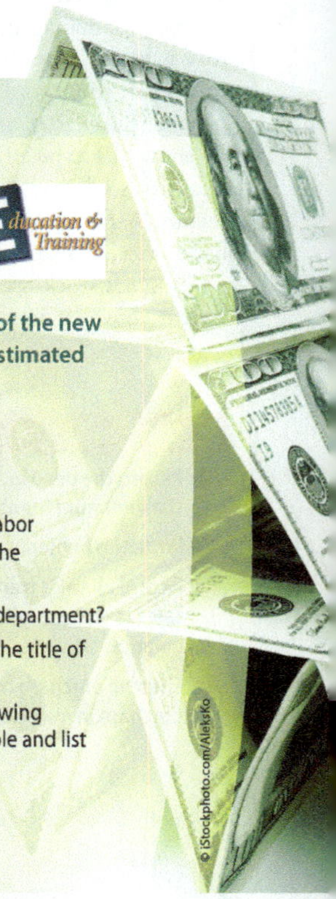

Retraining after Workplace Injuries

The Bureau of Labor Statistics (BLS) is a government agency whose mission is "to collect, analyze, and disseminate essential economic information. . . ." One item that the BLS tracks is the number of recordable injuries that occur in private industry each year. In 2010, there were over three million such injuries on the job.

An injured employee may have the right to collect payments through a workmen's compensation insurance program. These payments will continue until the employee recovers and is able to return to work. In many cases, the employee will never be able to return to the same position, and may be retrained for another position.

Retraining is feasible when the cost of the retraining is less than the cost of the continued workmen's compensation payments. This retraining may take place within the company, at an outside training facility, or at a college or university. The retraining plan must be based on the limitations of the injured employee and the requirements of the new position. The plan needs to include the estimated cost of the retraining.

Education & Training

CRITICAL THINKING

Go to the Internet website for the Bureau of Labor Statistics (www.bls.gov). Find the answers to the following questions:

1. The BLS is part of which federal government department?
2. Find one report published by the BLS. List the title of the report.
3. The BLS publishes a table of the fastest growing occupations. Search the website for the table and list the top occupation.

Source: Bureau of Labor Statistics (www.bls.gov/iif/).

© iStockphoto.com/AleksKo

© iStockphoto.com/burwellphotography

FORENSIC ACCOUNTING

Restatement at Rite Aid Corporation

If not for the country's fascination with Enron and WorldCom, the accounting fraud at the Rite Aid Corporation might have received more attention. About the same time that the Enron and WorldCom frauds were being revealed, the Securities and Exchange Commission (SEC) announced charges against several former senior Rite Aid executives. The SEC complaint alleged that Rite Aid overstated its net income by $1.6 billion between May 1997 and May 1999. When Rite Aid published corrected financial statements, it was the largest restatement ever recorded.

In a press release, the SEC outlined 13 different charges, ranging from improper accounting entries to false statements, abuse of vendor relationships, and improper related-party transactions. The extent of these frauds caused the regional director of the SEC's Northeast Regional Office to state:

> The charges announced today reveal a disturbing picture of dishonesty and misconduct at the highest level of a major corporation. Rite Aid's former senior management employed an extensive bag of tricks to manipulate the company's reported earnings and defraud its investors.

One of its "tricks" related to its transactions with vendors. Rite Aid was allowed to reduce amounts owed to vendors for the value of damaged and outdated products. Rite Aid overstated these amounts from vendors who did not require the unusable products to be returned to them. According to the SEC, Rite Aid overstated the value of damaged and outdated products by $36 million over a two-year period.

ACTIVITY

The internal auditors at Foster Stores are performing their regular examination of the purchasing function at each of the company's locations. A standard audit test is to search for any evidence that irregular transactions, such as those described above, are occurring.

The workbook contains two worksheets. One worksheet contains a list of all pharmaceutical items obtained from the computerized accounting system. The list includes the number of unit returns and purchases during the fiscal year for its Macon location. The list also contains an *Expire* column that provides instructions for how credit is obtained for outdated items. *None* indicates that the vendor does not accept credits for outdated items. *Return* indicates that the outdated items must be returned to the vendor for credit. *Discard* indicates that the vendor does not require the items to be returned in order to receive credit.

Use your analysis to answer the following questions.

1. Does any evidence exist that suggests that the location is inflating its credits for outdated items?
2. Is there a significant difference in the return rate between vendors that require the items to be returned, as compared to those that do not allow any credit for outdated items?

INSTRUCTIONS

Open the spreadsheet FA_CH05 and complete the steps on the Instructions tab.

Source: www.sec.gov/news/press/2002-92.htm.

FORENSIC ACCOUNTING

Students create a formula and use a PivotTable to analyze the rate of returns by vendor and method of obtaining credit for outdated items. The results attempt to simulate data that might have been available to auditors of Rite Aid. The drug names in the inventory list are fictional.

Answers

1. The return rates are higher for each vendor in the "discard" group. The average return rate for Davios Pharmaceuticals, 16.7%, is over seven times higher than the "return" group. Although less dramatic, the return rate for Quomai Drugs, 6.6%, is nearly triple the "return" vendor rate.
2. The return rate for vendors in the "none" group, 3.2%, is notably higher than the rate for vendors in the "return" group, 2.3%. However, neither vendor in the "none" group has a return rate that is higher than vendors in the "return" category.

EXTENDED LEARNING

- Assign Accounting in the Real World on page 143.
- Assign Ethics in Action on page 144.
- Assign Why Accounting on page 148.
- Assign Forensic Accounting on page 149.

FORMATIVE ASSESSMENT

- This is an ongoing process. Circulate around the classroom or lab, observing which students have problems with the assignments.
- Troubleshooting: Students may have difficulty understanding the relationship of the inventory record, stock record, and stock ledger.
- Assess student understanding by checking solutions to Independent Practice assignments and noting their answers to the Terms Review and Audit Your Understanding questions.

CHECK FOR UNDERSTANDING

Terms Review

- Call on students to define each term in the Terms Review. Definitions are given in the Glossary.

Audit Your Understanding

- Call on students to answer the Audit Your Understanding questions. Answers are given in Appendix D of the textbook.

GUIDED PRACTICE

Work Together

- Have students write the solution to the Work Together problem as you guide the class through the examples.
- Direct students to record each transaction in the stock record as you elicit class participation.
- Call on students to describe how to calculate the quantity balance.
- Remind students to save their work to complete the On Your Own problem.

INDEPENDENT PRACTICE

On Your Own

- Assign the On Your Own problem to be worked independently.
- Remind students that they will be using the work they saved in Work Together 5-1 to complete this problem.

Application Problem

- Assign Application Problem 5-1.

Online Working Papers

- Students can access the Lesson 5-1 problems using this software.

RETEACH

- Call on students to identify the two methods of determining the quantity of merchandise inventory.
- Call on students to explain the purpose of an inventory record.
- Call on students to identify the purpose of a stock record and its relationship to the stock ledger.

CLOSURE

- Ask students to summarize briefly the records used to determine the quantity of merchandise inventory.

End of Lesson Review

LO1 Describe the nature of merchandise inventory.

LO2 Account for the quantity of merchandise inventory.

Terms Review

consignment
consignee
consignor
stock record
stock ledger
inventory record

Audit your understanding

1. What two elements are included in the cost of merchandise available for sale?
2. If the ending merchandise inventory is understated, will the net income be overstated or understated?
3. Name two ways to determine the number of inventory items on hand.

Work together 5-1

Completing a stock record for a perpetual inventory system

A stock record form and an inventory record form for Harris Security are provided in the *Working Papers*. Your instructor will guide you through the following examples.

1. Fill in the top portion of the stock record form with the following information: Description, wireless monitoring camera; Stock No., C-4264; Reorder, 100; Minimum, 20; and Location, Bin 662.
2. Harris Security has 68 units of the item in stock on August 1. Record the following information. Save your work to complete On Your Own 5-1.

Date	Purchase Invoice No.	Sales Invoice No.	Quantity
Aug. 22		675	50
Aug. 31		712	12
Sept. 5	316		100
Sept. 14		785	18

On your own 5-1

Completing a stock record for a perpetual inventory system

Use the *Working Papers* from Work Together 5-1 above. Work independently to complete the following problem.

1. Record the remaining information for product number C-4264 on the stock record.

Date	Purchase Invoice No.	Sales Invoice No.	Quantity
Sept. 20		798	45
Sept. 22		802	30
Oct. 5	322		100
Oct. 26		834	25

2. Compare the ending balance in units from the stock record to the number of units on hand for item C-4264 in the inventory record. Make sure the quantities on the two records are equal.

Essential Questions

- In a merchandising business, how could a periodic inventory method be utilized and a computer still be used to monitor the inventory? (*A business could use the computer to record items sold and to generate needed reports. The perpetual inventory report could be compared to the periodic inventory for discrepancies.*)
- Could a business have gross profit but end up with a net loss for the year? Explain. (*Yes; it could have significant expenses that exceed gross profit.*)
- Why is it important to be accurate when taking a physical inventory count? (*Inaccurate inventory counts do not identify shrinkage and can be the difference between profit and loss as well as future reporting errors.*)

LESSON

5-2 Inventory Costing Methods

LO3 Determine the cost of merchandise inventory.
LO4 Determine the reported cost of merchandise inventory.

First-In, First-Out Inventory Costing Method LO3

FIFO Inventory Costing Method

Purchase Dates	Units Purchased	Unit Price	Total Cost	FIFO Units on Hand	FIFO Cost
January 1, beginning inventory	20	$ 9.40	$ 188.00		
March 12, purchases	12	9.80	117.60		
June 22, purchases	28	10.20	285.60		
August 7, purchases	24	10.70	256.80	20	$214.00
December 2, purchases	16	10.75	172.00	16	172.00
Totals	100		$1,020.00	36	$386.00

(1) Units from Most Recent Purchase
(2) Units Needed to Equal the Total Units on Hand
(3) Unit Price Times Units on Hand
(4) Total Units on Hand and Total Cost

The standards and rules that accountants follow while recording and reporting financial activities are called **generally accepted accounting principles**. These standards and rules are often referred to as *GAAP*. GAAP has been developed over time by the accounting profession in the United States. GAAP permit a business to use one of several methods to cost its merchandise inventory. A business selects the method that best matches the revenue and costs for that business. [CONCEPT: Matching Expenses with Revenue]

Once Vaughn takes a physical inventory, it must determine a dollar cost for each item. [CONCEPT: Unit of Measurement] Using the price of merchandise purchased first to calculate the cost of merchandise sold first is called the **first-in, first-out inventory costing method**. *FIFO* is an abbreviation for first in, first out. The FIFO method of determining the cost of merchandise on hand assumes that the merchandise purchased first (first in) is the merchandise sold first (first out). Thus, the FIFO method uses the most recent purchase prices to determine the cost of merchandise inventory remaining. For example, Vaughn has an inventory of 36 drill sets on December 31. If Vaughn used the FIFO method, the drill sets would be costed as shown above.

Using the FIFO method, the remaining four units from the August purchase and the units from the prior purchases and the beginning inventory are designated as the units that were sold. These drill sets are *first in*. Therefore, the business assumes that they are also the *first out*, or first sold.

Calculating Inventory Costs Using the FIFO Method

1. **Assign ending inventory units from the most recent purchase. The number of units in the ending inventory is 36. All 16 units from the December purchase are assigned to ending inventory.**
2. **If all units of the ending inventory have not been assigned, assign units from the next most recent purchase, August. This purchase included 24 units. Assign the lesser of the unassigned units, 20, or the number of units of the purchase, 24. Enter 20 units from the August purchase. All 36 units in ending inventory have now been assigned.**
3. **Multiply the units in the FIFO Units on Hand column by the unit prices. Enter the results, $214.00 and $172.00, in the FIFO Cost column.**
4. **Total the columns. The total number of units, 36, is the number of units on hand. The total cost assigned to these units using the FIFO method is $386.00.**

LESSON 5-2

BRIDGE

- Explain that in the first-year course, students learned about the cost of merchandise sold. In this course, they will learn how to use different methods to calculate the cost of merchandise sold.
- Point out that in the first-year course, students learned about International Financial Reporting Standards (IFRS). In this lesson, they will see some of the differences in reporting under IFRS instead of GAAP.

TEACHING RESOURCES

- **Instructor's Resource CD/Website:**
  PowerPoint Slides
  Accounting Concepts
- **Working Papers:**
  Teacher's Edition of the Working Papers for Lesson 5-2
  Online Working Papers

ENGAGE

- If the unit cost of items purchased remained constant, determining the cost of merchandise inventory would be a simple process. However, unit costs typically change during a fiscal year. Which unit costs should be used to cost the ending inventory? The methods presented in this lesson provide the answer to that question.

PREVIEW

- Call on students to read the accounting terms and definitions introduced in this lesson: *generally accepted accounting principles; first-in, first-out inventory costing method; last-in, first-out inventory costing method; weighted-average inventory costing method; inflation; deflation; international financial reporting standards;* and *lower of cost or market inventory costing method.*
- Point out the objectives for this lesson.
- Direct students to read the headings in this lesson and to examine the illustrations.

INPUT

- Explain the relationship between GAAP and inventory methods.
- Emphasize that FIFO uses the first costs to determine the cost of merchandise sold.
- Ask students to identify which costs are used to determine the cost of merchandise inventory remaining when the FIFO method is used. (*the unit costs of the most recent purchases*)

MODEL

- Direct students to draw five columns on a sheet of paper and copy the information in the first three columns of the illustration.
- Direct students to follow the four steps shown for costing merchandise inventory using the FIFO method.

INPUT

- Emphasize that LIFO uses the most recent purchases to determine the cost of merchandise sold.
- Point out that LIFO uses the earliest purchases to determine the cost of merchandise inventory remaining.

MODEL

- Direct students to draw five columns on a sheet of paper and copy the information in the first three columns of the illustration at the top of the page.
- Direct students to follow the arrows shown for costing merchandise inventory using the LIFO method.

THINK LIKE AN ACCOUNTANT

This activity introduces students to a time function. Students complete a schedule to determine the projected completion date of a construction project. The WORKDAY function is used to determine a future date that does not include Saturday, Sunday, or a holiday listed in a range of cells. A list of holidays covering 2013–2020 is presented on the worksheet. Students complete the schedule using the date 6/23/2013 and then use the schedule to determine the projected completion dates for two projects.

Excel dates are stored as serial numbers, with 1/1/1900 being the number 1. The number can be displayed in a variety of date formats. The following activity will help students understand serial numbers. Using a blank worksheet, enter the function =TODAY() in cell A1. This function calculates the current date. Enter the current date in cell A2. Enter an important date (e.g., your birthday). In cell A3, enter the formula +(A1-A2)/365. The cell, when formatted in a number format, will show the number of years since the important date. Change the format of all the numbers from date to numbers to show how the numbers are stored.

Last-In, First-Out Inventory Costing Method

LIFO Inventory Costing Method

Purchase Dates	Units Purchased	Unit Price	Total Cost	LIFO Units on Hand	LIFO Cost
January 1, beginning inventory	20	$ 9.40	$ 188.00	20	$188.00
March 12, purchases	12	9.80	117.60	12	117.60
June 22, purchases	28	10.20	285.60	4	40.80
August 7, purchases	24	10.70	256.80		
December 2, purchases	16	10.75	172.00		
Totals	100		$1,020.00	36	$346.40

Beginning Inventory Units

Unit Price Times Units on Hand

Units Needed to Equal the Total Units on Hand

Total Units on Hand and Total Cost

Using the price of merchandise purchased last to calculate the cost of merchandise sold first is called the **last-in, first-out inventory costing method**. *LIFO* is an abbreviation for last in, first out. The LIFO method uses the earliest purchase prices to determine the cost of merchandise inventory. If Vaughn used the LIFO method, the 36 drill sets would be costed as shown above.

Of the 36 units on hand, 20 units are assumed to be the units in the beginning inventory at $9.40 per unit. Another 12 units are assumed to have been purchased on the next earliest date, March 12, at $9.80 each. The remaining four units are assumed to have been purchased on the next earliest date, June 22, at $10.20 each. The total cost is $346.40.

The remaining 24 units from the June purchase and the units from the August and December purchases are designated as the units that were sold. These drill sets are last in. Therefore, the business assumes that they are also the first out, or first sold.

THINK LIKE AN ACCOUNTANT

Helping a Client Avoid Penalties

Jermaine Johnson's construction business has done very well building starter homes for lower-income families. His advertisements guarantee the quality and timely completion of the house.

While preparing Jermaine's tax return, you notice an unusual expense item—Penalty Expense. Giving him a quick call, you learn that this account reflects the costs of missing contract completion dates. Jermaine's contracts include a $50.00-per-day penalty for every day the house is not completed on time. Digging deeper, you learn that few houses are completed on time.

When Jermaine comes to your office to sign his return, you take the opportunity to ask him about how he determines target completion dates. He states that he estimates it requires 135 workdays to build a house. Accounting for weekends, he estimates it takes 180 days, or six months, to complete a house.

It is clear to you that Jermaine's method does not adequately account for the weekends, nor does it consider holidays. Therefore, you invite Jermaine to help you create a spreadsheet to assist him in setting completion dates.

OPEN THE SPREADSHEET TLA_CH05

The worksheet contains an incomplete schedule for estimating the start and end time for each significant stage of home construction. Follow the steps on the Instructions tab to complete the schedule. Answer these questions:

1. What is the projected completion date for a house with a start date of February 16 of the current year?
2. What is the projected completion date for a house with a start date of September 8 of the current year?
3. What additional changes to the schedule would you suggest that would help Jermaine estimate the completion dates of new contracts?

Answers

1. Answers will vary depending on the current year. A start date of 2/16/2014 results in a completion date of 8/26/2014. Start and completion dates for subsequent years are 2/16/2015 to 8/25/2015, 2/16/2016 to 8/25/2016, 2/16/2017 to 8/28/2017, 2/16/2018 to 8/28/2018, 2/16/2019 to 8/27/2019, and 2/16/2020 to 8/24/2020.
2. Answers will vary depending on the current year. A start date of 9/8/2014 results in a completion date of 3/24/2015. Start and completion dates for subsequent years are 9/8/2015 to 3/23/2016, 9/8/2016 to 3/20/2017, 9/8/2017 to 3/22/2018, 9/8/2018 to 3/25/2019, 9/8/2019 to 3/25/2020, and 9/8/2020 to 3/22/2021.
3. Answers will vary. Suggestions for change might include the following:
   a. Add columns for Jermaine to record the actual start date, end date, and actual duration for each stage. The information would enable him to determine the accuracy of his time estimates.
   b. Prepare a chart that compares the projected and actual duration for each stage.

Weighted-Average Inventory Costing Method

Weighted-Average Inventory Costing Method			
Purchase Dates	Units Purchased	Unit Price	Total Cost
January 1, beginning inventory	20	$ 9.40	$ 188.00
March 12, purchases	12	9.80	117.60
June 22, purchases	28	10.20	285.60
August 7, purchases	24	10.70	256.80
December 2, purchases	16	10.75	172.00
Totals	100		$1,020.00

Total Units and Cost of All Purchases

Total of Beginning Inventory and Purchases	÷	Total Units	=	Weighted-Average Price per Unit
$1,020.00	÷	100	=	$10.20

Average Price per Unit

Units in Ending Inventory	×	Weighted-Average Price per Unit	=	Cost of Ending Inventory
36	×	$10.20	=	$367.20

Cost of Ending Inventory

Using the average cost of the beginning inventory plus merchandise purchased during a fiscal period to calculate the cost of merchandise sold is called the **weighted-average inventory costing method**. This method is based on the assumption that the cost is an average of the price paid for similar items purchased during the fiscal period. If Vaughn used the weighted-average method, the 36 drill sets would be costed as shown above.

The total cost, $1,020.00, is divided by the total units purchased, 100, to calculate the weighted-average cost per unit, $10.20. The 36 units currently on hand are assumed to have been purchased at an average cost of $10.20 each. Therefore, the total cost of the ending merchandise inventory using the weighted-average method is $367.20. Vaughn would use the same weighted-average cost per unit, $10.20, to determine the cost of merchandise sold.

fyi

Inventory management consists of determining the quantity of goods on hand and developing procedures for ordering, receiving, and maintaining the inventory.

INPUT

- Explain that the weighted-average costing method is frequently used because it is the simplest to calculate.
- Ask students to identify which costs are used to determine the cost of merchandise inventory using the weighted-average method. (*All costs—beginning inventory and all purchases—are used to determine the unit cost.*)
- Explain that the three methods of costing ending inventory result in three different values.
- Point out the FYI at the bottom of the page, emphasizing that inventory management is determining the quantity of goods on hand and developing procedures for ordering, receiving, and maintaining the inventory.

MODEL

- Direct students to the illustration as you demonstrate the calculation of the weighted-average cost.
- Demonstrate calculating the total cost for each purchase by multiplying units by unit price.
- Show how the total cost amounts are added to get the total cost of all purchases.
- Demonstrate dividing the total cost by the number of units to get a weighted-average cost.
- Demonstrate multiplying weighted-average cost times units in ending inventory to get the cost of the ending inventory.

INPUT

- Explain that the rate at which the price for goods and services increases over time is called inflation and that inflation impacts the cost of the ending inventory using each of the inventory methods.
- Remind students that the value assigned to the ending inventory affects items on the income statement, statement of stockholders' equity, and balance sheet.
- Explain that prices usually increase under normal economic conditions and that the costing method that uses the latest prices to value ending inventory will give the highest value, FIFO.

MODEL

- Direct students to the illustration as you explain the effect of the three methods of costing the ending inventory.
- Have students point to each item in the table as you explain the effects of the ending inventory cost.
- Demonstrate that the FIFO method gives the highest ending inventory, the lowest cost of merchandise sold, and the highest net income. Create an income statement on the board, assign amounts to the items, and calculate the net income.
- Emphasize that the cost of goods available for sale (beginning inventory plus purchases) is the same for FIFO, LIFO, and weighted-average calculations.
- Summarize by pointing out that in a period of rising prices, the FIFO method usually results in the highest net income; the LIFO method, the lowest net income; and the weighted-average method, somewhere between the two.

INPUT

- Instruct a student to read the bottom of page 154 discussing tax limitations on using LIFO.
- Explain that the government permits a business to use LIFO or FIFO, whichever is advantageous to the business. However, the business must use the same method for financial and tax reporting.

Costing Inventory During Periods of Increasing Prices

Purchases		FIFO Method		LIFO Method		Weighted-Average Method
Date	Unit Price	Units	Cost	Units	Cost	
Beginning Inventory	$ 9.40			20	$188.00	
March	9.80			12	117.60	
June	10.20			4	40.80	$ 10.20
August	10.70	20	$214.00			
December	10.75	16	172.00			
Totals		36	$386.00	36	$346.40	$367.20
If prices are rising:						
Ending Inventory		Highest		Lowest		Intermediate
Cost of Merchandise Sold		Lowest		Highest		Intermediate
Reported Net Income		Highest		Lowest		Intermediate

The rate at which the price for goods and services increases over time is called **inflation**. Inflation impacts the cost of the ending inventory calculated using each of the inventory costing methods. The cost of the ending inventory affects the cost of merchandise sold amount on the income statement. The higher the ending inventory, the lower the cost of merchandise sold amount, and vice versa.

The prices for the drill sets illustrated in this lesson increased from $9.40 to $10.75 per unit. Three ways of costing the inventory of 36 drill sets during a period of increasing prices are summarized above. During an inflationary period, the FIFO method usually results in the highest cost of inventory. The most recent purchases are used to cost the inventory.

During an inflationary period, the LIFO method usually results in the lowest cost of inventory. The beginning inventory and the early purchases are used to cost the inventory. Therefore, the LIFO method results in the highest cost of merchandise sold and the lowest reported net income.

Tax Limitations on Using LIFO

The rate of inflation is influenced by many economic factors and varies by country each year. The United States has experienced inflation in 85% of the years since records have been maintained. Two periods of unusually high inflation occurred from 1917 to 1920 (16.6%) and 1979 to 1981 (11.7%).

In an inflationary period, a business would choose to use the FIFO method to prepare its financial statements. The FIFO method allows the business to report the highest level of net income. At the same time, a business would also choose to use the LIFO method to calculate its taxable income. The LIFO method would result in lower taxable income and a lower income tax liability.

Although lowering income taxes benefits a business, it also reduces tax revenues to the government. For this reason, early tax rules did not allow a business to use the LIFO method for calculating taxable income. During the late 1930s, Congress changed the tax laws to allow a business to use the LIFO method for calculating income taxes. However, it added an important requirement: the business must use the same method for financial and tax reporting.

remember FIFO uses the prices of the most recent purchases to determine the cost of merchandise inventory.

DIFFERENTIATED INSTRUCTION

Visual/Spatial learners enjoy learning through drawing and physical imagery. Allow students to work with partners. Supply students with several sheets of the same color of paper. Ask students to label the sheets of paper with costs of products and demonstrate to one another the three methods of costing inventory. Ask students to calculate the amount of the ending inventory and the cost of goods sold, using each of the three methods.

Costing Inventory During Periods of Decreasing Prices

Purchases		FIFO Method		LIFO Method		Weighted-Average Method
Date	Unit Price	Units	Cost	Units	Cost	
Beginning Inventory	$10.75			20	$215.00	
March	10.70			12	128.40	
June	10.20			4	40.80	$ 10.15
August	9.80	20	$196.00			
December	9.40	16	150.40			
Totals		36	$346.40	36	$384.20	$365.40
If prices are decreasing: Ending Inventory		Lowest		Highest		Intermediate
Cost of Merchandise Sold		Highest		Lowest		Intermediate
Reported Net Income		Lowest		Highest		Intermediate

The rate at which the price for goods and services decreases over time is called **deflation**. If Vaughn determined the cost of inventory during a period of decreasing prices, the three inventory costing methods would be summarized as shown above.

During a deflationary period, the FIFO method usually results in the lowest merchandise inventory cost. This lower inventory cost results in a higher cost of merchandise sold and a lower net income. In contrast, the LIFO method usually results in the highest ending inventory cost. This higher inventory cost results in a lower cost of merchandise sold and a higher net income.

The weighted-average method usually results in a total cost between the FIFO and LIFO total costs in both periods of increasing and decreasing prices. For businesses that purchase items with frequent fluctuations in price, the weighted-average method results in more consistent reporting of merchandise inventory costs.

Each business selects the method of costing merchandise inventory that best fits its policies and goals. Once selected, generally accepted accounting principles require that the business continue to use that method. In this way, the information on a series of financial statements can be compared easily. [CONCEPT: Consistent Reporting]

© shipfactory/Shutterstock.com

fyi Computer prices have declined over time despite dramatic advancements in technology. Electronic equipment has traditionally experienced declining prices.

INPUT

- Explain that deflation is the rate at which the price for goods and services decreases over time.
- Explain that in some circumstances, price levels can be decreasing, such as when more efficient production methods lead to less expensive manufacturing costs or when economic conditions result in lower prices in all merchandise.
- Direct students to the illustration as you explain that when prices are decreasing, the effects of the inventory costing methods are opposite of when prices are increasing.
- Explain that when prices are decreasing, the LIFO method results in the highest ending inventory cost and the lowest cost of merchandise sold and highest net income.
- Explain that with decreasing prices, the FIFO method has the opposite effect of the LIFO method and that the weighted-average method is between the two.

INPUT

- Ask a student to read page 156 explaining the criticism of the LIFO method.
- Explain the example provided. Although LIFO more accurately presents the cost of merchandise sold during an inflationary period, the cost of inventory is understated and can negatively affect the amount of federal income taxes owed.
- Point out that the International Financial Reporting Standards, which have been adopted around the world, do not allow the LIFO method.
- Companies that are not publicly traded may still use GAAP instead of IFRS and may use the LIFO method for the calculation of federal income taxes.

Criticism of the LIFO Method

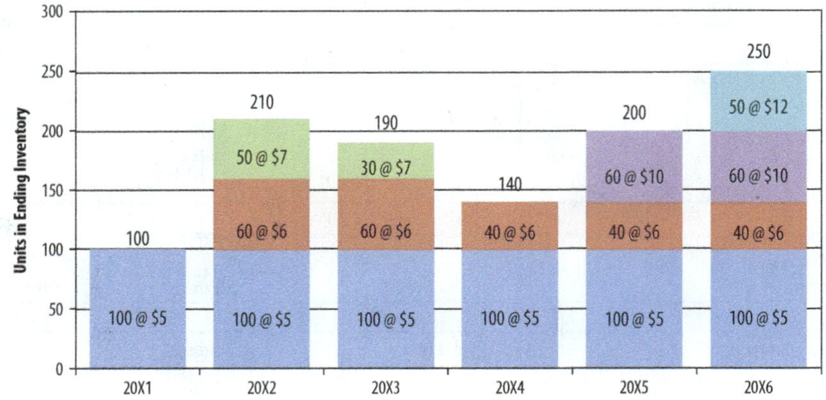

Inflation causes a conflict between the fair reporting of the cost of inventory and the cost of merchandise sold. In an inflationary period, the LIFO method more accurately presents the cost of merchandise sold but understates the cost of inventory.

In the example above, a company's first purchase of an item in 20X1 is 150 units @ $5.00 each. At the end of 20X1, the business has 100 units in inventory. The LIFO cost would be 100 units @ $5.00. In 20X2, the first two purchases are 60 units @ $6.00 and 180 units @ $7.00. At the end of 20X2, the business has 210 units in inventory. The LIFO cost would be 100 units @ $5.00, 60 units @ $6.00, and 50 units @ $7.00. In the years that follow the units in ending inventory vary between 140 and 250, but always stay above 100 units. Thus, the $5.00 unit cost continues to be used to cost 100 units, despite the fact that the latest market price has risen to $12.00.

Using the LIFO method, the cost of the 250 units in the 20X6 inventory is $1,940.00. If the FIFO method was used and the most recent purchase was for $12.00 per unit, the FIFO cost of these same units would be $3,000.00. The understatement of the cost of inventory grows over time. For a business selling the same product for decades, such as an oil business, the understatement can become large enough to distort the amount reported on the balance sheet.

INTERNATIONAL ACCOUNTING STANDARDS

The LIFO method has been criticized because of its understatement of inventory. As discussed earlier, the LIFO method was not initially accepted for the calculation of federal income taxes. In addition, the LIFO method has not been universally adopted in other countries.

The international financial community has also developed accounting standards. A set of accounting standards being adopted across the world is called **international financial reporting standards**, or *IFRS* (pronounced eye-fers). IFRS do not allow the LIFO method.

The Securities and Exchange Commission is committed to requiring publicly held corporations to submit financial statements prepared using IFRS rather than GAAP. However, businesses that are not publicly traded may still issue financial statements using GAAP. At the time this textbook was written, the LIFO method was still accepted for the calculation of federal income taxes.

remember

IFRS do not allow the LIFO method.

Lower of Cost or Market Inventory Costing Method LO4

Lower of Cost or Market Inventory Costing Method

Costing Method	Cost	Market Value (36 units × $10.15) current market price)	Lower of Cost or Market
FIFO	$386.00	$365.40	$365.40
LIFO	346.40	365.40	346.40
Weighted-average	367.20	365.40	365.40
	Determine Cost	Determine Market Price	Lower of Cost or Market Price

Regardless of the method used to cost inventory, the amount reported on the financial statements should not exceed the market value of the inventory. Using the lower of cost or market price to calculate the cost of the ending merchandise inventory is called the **lower of cost or market inventory costing method**. In this context, market refers to the current replacement cost of the merchandise item. For example, Vaughn may currently have to pay a vendor $10.15 to purchase a drill set. The market price, therefore, is $10.15. When merchandise is purchased, the unit price is used to record inventory costs. [CONCEPT: Historical Cost] The historical cost concept states that the actual amount paid for merchandise or other items bought is recorded.

If the unit price is higher than the market price at the end of a fiscal period, the inventory cost is reduced to the current market price. However, if the unit price is lower than the market price, the inventory cost is maintained at the unit price.

Two amounts are needed to apply the lower of cost or market method:

1. The cost of the inventory using the FIFO, LIFO, or weighted-average method.
2. The current market price of the inventory.

fyi The goal of the Japanese concept, the just-in-time (JIT) system, is to minimize inventory. Materials should be received only when they are needed for production; they should not be kept in inventory. The JIT system works well when vendors and buyers work together as business partners to plan inventory levels.

These two amounts are then compared, and the lower of the two is used to cost the inventory. For example, Vaughn uses the weighted-average method of costing inventory. The weighted-average cost and the current market price for 36 drill sets are shown above. The weighted-average cost is $367.20, and the current market price is $365.40. Using the lower of cost or market method, the market price of the drill sets is lower than the weighted-average cost. Therefore, the market price of $365.40 is used as the cost of the drill sets.

If Vaughn used the FIFO method, the FIFO cost would be $386.00. The $365.40 market price is lower than the FIFO cost, so the market price would be used instead of the FIFO cost. If Vaughn used the LIFO method, the LIFO cost would be $346.40. The LIFO cost is lower than the market price, so the LIFO cost would be used to cost the inventory.

© absolutimages/Shutterstock.com

INPUT

- Point out that regardless of the method used to cost inventory, the amount reported should not exceed the market value of the inventory.
- Point out that the lower of cost or market inventory costing method uses the current replacement cost of merchandise.
- Explain that two values are needed to determine the lower of cost or market cost: the cost using FIFO, LIFO, or weighted-average and the current market price.
- Point out that these two amounts are compared and that the lower of the two is used to cost the inventory.
- Direct students to the FYI. Explain the just-in-time system and its relationship to inventory.

TEACHING IDEA **Thumbs up, middle, or down. Ask students to provide a quick visual of lesson understanding. Ask them to give a thumbs up if they understand and can apply the new knowledge and skills. If they aren't sure or think they need further review, tell them to show thumbs in the middle. If they don't understand the material, ask them to give a thumbs down.**

FORMATIVE ASSESSMENT

- This is an ongoing process. Circulate around the classroom or lab, observing which students have problems with the assignments.
- Troubleshooting: Diagnose the kinds of problems students have with this lesson. Students may have difficulty (1) understanding which costs to use when calculating the cost of merchandise inventory using the FIFO and LIFO methods or (2) doing the calculations.
- Assess student understanding by checking solutions to Independent Practice assignments and noting their answers to the Terms Review and Audit Your Understanding questions.

CHECK FOR UNDERSTANDING

Terms Review

- Call on students to define each term in the Terms Review. Definitions are given in the Glossary.

Audit Your Understanding

- Call on students to answer the Audit Your Understanding questions. Answers are given in Appendix D of the textbook.

GUIDED PRACTICE

Work Together

- Have students write the solution to the Work Together problem as you guide the class through the examples.
- Direct students to determine the cost of the ending inventory using FIFO, LIFO, and weighted-average.

INDEPENDENT PRACTICE

On Your Own

- Assign the On Your Own problem to be worked independently.
- Use the Formative Assessment techniques to diagnose student understanding.

Application Problem

- Assign Application Problem 5-2.

Online Working Papers

- Students can access the Lesson 5-2 problems using this software.

RETEACH

- Put a set of inventory cost data on the board and direct students to walk through calculating the FIFO, LIFO, and weighted-average costs.
- Ask students how to calculate the cost of merchandise sold.
- Ask students to describe the effect of rising prices on the cost of merchandise sold using the FIFO, LIFO, and weighted-average methods.

CLOSURE

- Ask students to summarize briefly the procedures for calculating the cost of inventory using the FIFO, LIFO, and weighted-average inventory costing methods.

End of Lesson Review

LO3 Determine the cost of merchandise inventory.

LO4 Determine the reported cost of merchandise inventory.

Terms Review

generally accepted accounting principles

first-in, first-out inventory costing method

last-in, first-out inventory costing method

weighted-average inventory costing method

inflation

deflation

international financial reporting standards

lower of cost or market inventory costing method

Audit your understanding

1. Which inventory costing method uses the earliest purchase prices to determine the cost of merchandise inventory?
2. During an inflationary period, what inventory costing method will result in the highest reported net income?
3. What must a business do to qualify for using the LIFO method for tax reporting?
4. Which inventory costing method is not allowed by international financial reporting standards?
5. What two amounts are needed to apply the lower of cost or market inventory costing method?

Work together 5-2

Costing ending inventory using FIFO, LIFO, and weighted-average

Forms for calculating inventory costs for Jensen Auto are provided in the *Working Papers*. Your instructor will guide you through the following examples.

Jensen Auto had the following beginning inventory and purchases for an air filter. At the end of the year, 34 units remained in the inventory. Determine the cost of the ending inventory using the FIFO, LIFO, and weighted-average inventory costing methods.

	Units	Unit Price
Beginning inventory	8	$ 9.96
February purchase	20	10.24
May purchase	20	10.36
August purchase	20	10.46
November purchase	20	10.54

On your own 5-2

Costing ending inventory using FIFO, LIFO, and weighted-average

Forms for calculating inventory costs for Jensen Auto are provided in the *Working Papers*. Work independently to complete the following problem.

Jensen Auto had the following beginning inventory and purchases for an engine belt. At the end of the year, 226 units remained in the inventory. Determine the cost of the ending inventory using the FIFO, LIFO, and weighted-average inventory costing methods.

	Units	Unit Price
Beginning inventory	180	$4.00
February purchase	156	4.20
May purchase	160	4.50
August purchase	168	4.60
November purchase	176	4.80

Essential Questions

- Which inventory method would you select to yield the most net income for your business? (*In times of inflation, higher net income would be reflected using FIFO in most cases.*)
- Who can be harmed if a company changes its inventory costing methods each year? Why? (*The company could be negatively impacted by owing more in taxes and by the time and work necessary to apply a new method. Investors could be negatively affected if they do not base decisions on comparable costing methods.*)

EXTENDED LEARNING

- Assign Think Like an Accountant on page 152.

LESSON

5-3 Estimating the Inventory

LO5 Estimate the cost of merchandise inventory.
LO6 Calculate the inventory turnover ratio and days' sales in inventory.

Gross Profit Method of Estimating Inventory LO5

ESTIMATED MERCHANDISE INVENTORY SHEET

Gross Profit Method

DEPARTMENT *Discount Grocery* DATE *7/31/20--*

1	Beginning inventory, January 1		$ 32,150.00
2	Net purchases to date		202,950.00
3	Merchandise available for sale		235,100.00
4	Net sales to date	$401,900.00	
5	Less estimated gross profit (Net sales × Estimated gross profit percentage *48.0*%)	192,912.00	
6	Estimated cost of merchandise sold		208,988.00
7	Estimated ending inventory		$ 26,112.00

Callouts: Beginning Inventory; Net Purchases; Merchandise Available for Sale; Net Sales; Estimated Gross Profit; Estimated Cost of Merchandise Sold; Estimated Ending Inventory

A business needs to determine the cost of merchandise inventory to prepare monthly financial statements. Most merchandisers maintain a perpetual inventory using stock records or a computerized accounting system. The cost of the ending merchandise inventory can be obtained from accounting records.

For some small merchandisers, the cost of maintaining a perpetual inventory may exceed its benefit. Taking a monthly physical inventory is too expensive. A cost-effective alternative used by some small businesses is to estimate monthly ending inventories.

Estimating inventory by using the previous year's percentage of gross profit on operations is known as the **gross profit method of estimating inventory**. This method assumes that a continuing relationship exists between gross profit and net sales. Based on experience in previous fiscal periods, a gross profit to net sales percentage is calculated.

Discount Grocery does not maintain a perpetual inventory system. Instead, it estimates its monthly cost of merchandise inventory by using last year's actual gross margin of 48.0%. An ending merchandise inventory calculated using the gross profit method is an estimate and is not accurate. However, for monthly financial statements, the estimated amount is sufficiently accurate without taking a physical inventory.

In the illustration above, the net purchases on line 2 is the purchases amount from the general ledger, reduced by purchases discounts and purchases returns and allowances. The net sales on line 4 is the sales amount reduced by sales discounts and sales returns and allowances.

MODEL

- Direct students to the illustration as you demonstrate estimating the ending inventory using the gross profit method.
- Have students point to each amount as you explain the steps for estimating the ending inventory.

LESSON
5-3

BRIDGE

Point out that students have previously learned how to calculate the cost of goods sold. In this lesson, they will apply this information in analyzing merchandise inventory.

TEACHING RESOURCES

- **Instructor's Resource CD/Website:** PowerPoint Slides; Accounting Concepts
- **Working Papers:** Teacher's Edition of the Working Papers for Lesson 5-3; Online Working Papers
- **Transparency Master:** Estimated Merchandise Inventory Sheet

ENGAGE

- Taking a physical inventory is an expensive activity. Yet a company that does not keep a perpetual inventory needs to determine the cost of merchandise inventory to prepare monthly financial statements. Rather than incur the expense of a monthly physical inventory, a business can estimate its inventory.

PREVIEW

- Preview the accounting terms and definitions introduced in this lesson: *gross profit method of estimating inventory*, *retail method of estimating inventory*, *inventory turnover ratio*, and *days' sales in inventory*.
- Point out the learning objectives for this lesson.
- Direct students to read the headings in this lesson and to examine the illustrations.

TEACHING IDEA **Have students use the Internet to research ideas for effective inventory management. Have them agree on one idea and share it with the class.**

INPUT

- Emphasize that the gross profit method yields an estimate of the ending inventory.
- Emphasize that the gross profit percentage should be based on the prior periods' actual gross profit percentage.
- Remind students that they have already learned how to prepare an income statement with a cost of merchandise sold.

INPUT

- Point out that the ending inventory can also be estimated using the retail method.
- Explain that the retail method is based on the percentage ratio between the cost and retail prices of the cost of merchandise available for sale.
- Point out that to use the retail method of estimating inventory, a business must maintain separate records of both cost and retail prices for net purchases, net sales, and the beginning merchandise inventory.
- Mention that many businesses that need to estimate inventory use the gross profit method because it does not require keeping separate cost and retail price records.
- State that a business that keeps a perpetual inventory or has a computerized inventory system may have the figures needed for the retail method readily available.

MODEL

- Direct students to the illustration as you demonstrate the retail method of estimating inventory.
- Have students point to each item on the figure as you describe the steps for estimating the ending inventory.

GLOBAL AWARENESS

Answers

1. Answers will vary.
2. Answers will vary.

Retail Method of Estimating Inventory

ESTIMATED MERCHANDISE INVENTORY SHEET

Retail Method

COMPANY *F&G Stores* DATE *7/31/20--*

		Cost	Retail
1	Beginning inventory, January 1	$190,300.00	$325,300.00
2	Net purchases to date	116,700.00	198,700.00
3	Merchandise available for sale	$307,000.00	$524,000.00
4	Net sales to date		208,600.00
5	Estimated ending inventory at retail		$315,400.00
6	Estimated ending inventory	$184,824.40	
	(Inventory at retail × Percentage 58.6%)		

Beginning Merchandise Inventory at Cost and Retail

Merchandise Purchased at Cost and Retail

Merchandise Available at Cost and Retail

Sales to Date

Estimated Ending Inventory at Retail

Cost Divided by Retail

Estimated Ending Inventory Cost

Estimating inventory by using a percentage based on both cost and retail prices is called the **retail method of estimating inventory**. The retail method may be used instead of the gross profit method. To use the retail method, a business must keep separate records of both cost and retail prices for net purchases, net sales, and the beginning merchandise inventory.

An estimated ending merchandise inventory for F&G Stores, using the retail method, is shown above. In this illustration, the percentage used to estimate the ending inventory, 58.6%, is calculated by dividing the merchandise available for sale at cost, $307,000.00, by the merchandise available for sale at retail, $524,000.00.

Many businesses that need to estimate the ending merchandise inventory use the gross profit method rather than the retail method. The gross profit method does not require separate records for cost and retail prices.

GLOBAL AWARENESS

Work/Holiday Visa

If you are interested in working for a short time in a foreign country, you will most likely have to obtain a work visa, also called a *work/holiday visa*. This visa allows you to hold a temporary job in that country. The purpose of a work/holiday visa is to encourage an understanding of other countries.

Many countries put age restrictions and time limits on work/holiday visas. For example, Australia limits them to people aged 18 to 30, with a time limit of 12 months. Many countries allow work/holiday visas based on reciprocal agreements between countries. Because the United States does not usually grant work/holiday visas for citizens of other countries, U.S. citizens are limited in their options.

If you would like to live and work in a foreign country on a more permanent basis, further restrictions apply. Many countries require you to have a job before you can apply for a work permit. This is further complicated because, in many countries, you cannot enter the country to look for work. This means that you must be able to find a job and be hired without entering the country.

Some countries only allow work visas for positions that cannot be filled by a citizen of the country. In these cases, the employer must apply for the work visa for the new foreign employee. The employer must show evidence of unsuccessful attempts to fill the position with citizens of the country.

CRITICAL THINKING

1. Pick a country in which you would like to work while traveling. Use the Internet to determine the following:
   a. Can a U.S. citizen apply for a work/holiday visa for that country?
   b. What is the maximum length of time a work visa is valid?
   c. What are the age restrictions for a work/holiday visa?
2. Summarize your findings in a short written report.

© iStockphoto.com/Lusky

DIFFERENTIATED INSTRUCTION

Auditory/Linguistic learners have highly developed auditory skills and often have success using spoken language as a means to remember information. Ask students to compose a letter to their "employees" explaining why it is important to be accurate when taking inventory. Students should pair up and read their letters aloud to each other.

Financial Analysis of Merchandise Inventory LO6

The more rapidly a business sells merchandise, the more chance it has to make a satisfactory net income. For example, more revenue results from selling 100 drill sets per day than from selling 60 drill sets per day. Two measures of the speed with which merchandise inventory is sold are:

1. Inventory turnover ratio.
2. Days' sales in inventory.

INVENTORY TURNOVER RATIO

(January 1 Merchandise Inventory	+	December 31 Merchandise Inventory)	÷	2	=	Average Merchandise Inventory
($154,813.36	+	$162,048.14)	÷	2	=	$158,430.75

Cost of Merchandise Sold	÷	Average Merchandise Inventory	=	Inventory Turnover Ratio
$924,871.46	÷	$158,430.75	=	5.84

The number of times the average amount of merchandise inventory is sold during a specific period of time is called the **inventory turnover ratio**. An inventory turnover ratio expresses a relationship between an average inventory and the cost of merchandise sold. Merchandise inventory represents a large investment for most merchandising businesses. Therefore, a low inventory turnover ratio usually indicates a low return on investment.

A 5.84 inventory turnover ratio means that the business sold the average merchandise inventory 5.84 times during the current year. National trade associations and financial organizations publish average ratios for businesses in specific industries. Vaughn can compare its ratio with the ratio for similar businesses, which have an average inventory turnover ratio of 6.25 times. Vaughn's turnover ratio of 5.84 is below the industry standard of 6.25. To correct this situation, Vaughn's managers should consider taking action to better control the quantity of merchandise inventory on hand.

DAYS' SALES IN INVENTORY

The time needed to sell an average amount of merchandise inventory is called the **days' sales in inventory**. The days' sales in inventory, based on a 5.84 inventory turnover ratio, is calculated as shown below.

Days in Year	÷	Inventory Turnover Ratio	=	Days' Sales in Inventory
365	÷	5.84	=	63 Days

The number of days' sales in inventory is rounded to the nearest day. This level of accuracy provides managers with adequate information to make sound business decisions.

An average of 63 days means that, on average, each item in inventory is sold 63 days after it is purchased. Published averages show that businesses similar to Vaughn have an average number of days' sales in inventory of 58. Vaughn's management should seek ways to increase its turnover of inventory.

The higher the number of days in inventory, the longer merchandise tends to remain unsold. A business can increase the inventory turnover ratio and reduce the number of days' sales in inventory by reducing the size of the inventory kept on hand. However, a lower inventory level may not allow a business to meet customers' demands. A business also can improve its turnover ratio and the number of days' sales in inventory by increasing the amount of merchandise sold during a month or a year.

INPUT

- Explain that the more rapidly a business sells merchandise, the more chance it has to make a satisfactory net income.
- Explain that there are two measures of the speed at which merchandise is sold: the merchandise inventory turnover ratio and the average number of days' sales in merchandise inventory.
- Explain that a merchandise inventory turnover ratio expresses a relationship between an average inventory and the cost of merchandise sold.
- Explain that a low merchandise inventory turnover ratio means that inventory is not selling rapidly (turning over) and therefore return on investment is low.
- Explain that an inventory turnover ratio of 5.84 means that the average amount of merchandise inventory was sold 5.84 times during the fiscal period.
- Emphasize that inventory turnover ratios can be compared with those of similar businesses through national trade associations.
- Point out that if an inventory turnover ratio is low, managers need to control more effectively the quantity of merchandise inventory on hand.
- Explain that the inventory turnover ratio is divided into the number of days in a year to calculate the days' sales in inventory.

MODEL

- Use the board or direct students to the illustration to demonstrate the two steps in calculating the inventory turnover ratio.

INPUT

- Explain that the number of days' sales in inventory shows how many days it takes to sell an item in inventory. For example, if the number of days is 63, then it takes 63 days to sell each item in inventory after it is purchased.
- Explain that if management increases the turnover ratio, the number of days an item remains unsold will decrease.
- Explain that a business can improve the turnover and the number of days' sales figures by reducing the amount of inventory kept on hand. However, a lower inventory level may not satisfy customer demands.
- Point out that increasing sales is another way to improve the turnover ratio and the number of days' sales.

MODEL

- Use the board or direct students to the illustration to demonstrate calculating the number of days' sales in inventory.

FORMATIVE ASSESSMENT

- This is an ongoing process. Circulate around the classroom or lab, observing which students have problems with the assignments.
- Troubleshooting: Diagnose the problems students have with this lesson. Students may have difficulty (1) doing the calculations for the estimated inventory costing methods, (2) calculating the turnover ratio or the number of days' sales in inventory, or (3) understanding the meaning of the financial analysis results.
- Assess student understanding by checking solutions to Independent Practice assignments.

CHECK FOR UNDERSTANDING

Terms Review

- Call on students to define each term in the Terms Review. Definitions are given in the Glossary.

Audit Your Understanding

- Call on students to answer the Audit Your Understanding questions. Answers are given in Appendix D of the textbook.

GUIDED PRACTICE

Work Together

- Have students write the solution to the Work Together problem as you guide the class through the examples.
- Direct students to estimating inventory using the gross profit and retail methods and doing a financial analysis of merchandise inventory.

INDEPENDENT PRACTICE

On Your Own

- Assign the On Your Own problem to be worked independently.
- Use the Formative Assessment techniques to diagnose student understanding.

Application Problem

- Assign Application Problem 5-3.

Online Working Papers

- Students can access the Lesson 5-3 problems using this software.

RETEACH

- Give students additional sets of data for practicing the estimating methods. If necessary, require that they use blank ruled paper so that writing the descriptions helps reinforce the meaning of the calculations.
- Give students additional sets of data for calculating the two ratios.
- Ask students to define the two ratios and then ask them whether higher or lower numbers are more desirable.

CLOSURE

- Ask students to summarize the purpose of estimating inventory.
- Ask students to explain the meaning of the inventory turnover ratio and the number of days' sales in inventory.

End of Lesson Review

LO5 Estimate the cost of merchandise inventory.

LO6 Calculate the inventory turnover ratio and days' sales in inventory.

Terms Review

gross profit method of estimating inventory

retail method of estimating inventory

inventory turnover ratio

days' sales in inventory

Audit your understanding

1. On what assumptions is the gross profit method of estimating inventory based?
2. To use the retail method of estimating inventory, what records must be kept?
3. Explain an inventory turnover ratio of 5.0.
4. Explain a days' sales in inventory of 60.

Work together 5-3

Estimating inventory using the gross profit and retail methods; financial analysis of merchandise inventory

The following information is available for Debbie's Fabrics for the month of October. Estimated merchandise inventory sheets are provided in the *Working Papers*. Your instructor will guide you through the following examples.

	Cost	Retail
Beginning inventory, October 1	$96,850.00	$205,190.00
Net purchases for October	19,480.00	40,750.00
Net sales for October		40,510.00
Gross profit percentage	52.6%	

1. Estimate the ending inventory using the gross profit method.
2. Estimate the ending inventory using the retail method. Round the percentage to the nearest 0.1%.
3. The inventory for Debbie's Fabrics was $92,890.00 on January 1 and $101,700.00 on December 31. The cost of merchandise sold for the year was $496,710.00. Calculate the inventory turnover ratio and the days' sales in inventory. Round the inventory turnover ratio to two decimal places and the days' sales in inventory to the nearest day.

On your own 5-3

Estimating inventory using the gross profit and retail methods; financial analysis of merchandise inventory

The following information is available for Kelly Music for the month of July. Estimated merchandise inventory sheets are provided in the *Working Papers*. Work independently to complete the following problem.

	Cost	Retail
Beginning inventory, July 1	$65,180.00	$159,750.00
Net purchases for July	24,740.00	58,900.00
Net sales for July		62,730.00
Gross profit percentage	58.4%	

1. Estimate the ending inventory using the gross profit method.
2. Estimate the ending inventory using the retail method. Round the percentage to the nearest 0.1%.
3. Kelly Music's inventory was $63,250.00 on January 1 and $70,960.00 on December 31. The cost of merchandise sold for the year was $289,210.00. Calculate the inventory turnover ratio and the days' sales in inventory. Round the inventory turnover ratio to two decimal places and the days' sales in inventory to the nearest day.

Essential Questions

- Which industries might have higher days' sales in inventory compared with other industries? (*Typically, industries selling luxury goods will have higher days' sales in inventory.*)
- Which industries might have lower days' sales in inventory? Explain. (*Industries selling low-ticket items or consumables generally have lower days' sales in inventory.*)

EXTENDED LEARNING

- Assign Global Awareness on page 160.

A Look at Accounting Software

Setting Prices

In a manual accounting system, price lists would generally be maintained in a spreadsheet file and then printed out for use by sales staff, customers, and the accounting department. When a sales invoice was being prepared, the price sheet would be consulted to determine the prices to be charged. If variations to a listed price were needed for a particular type of customer or for a particular situation, all that would be required would be a written approval from an authorized manager.

Pricing is much more complicated in a computerized accounting system, but the business benefits by achieving much faster and more accurate recording of sales. The sales function of the accounting system is linked to the inventory function, and invoicing is done automatically. Therefore, it is necessary to set detailed rules for the way prices are to be charged when a sale is entered. Special situations need to be anticipated and rules set for alternate pricing in those situations.

The pricing function of a computerized accounting system is normally accessed from the primary navigation window. In this system, that is called the System Manager. Access to the price controls is strictly limited to only a few trusted individuals. While most users would be given the privilege of viewing prices, they would be unable to change them.

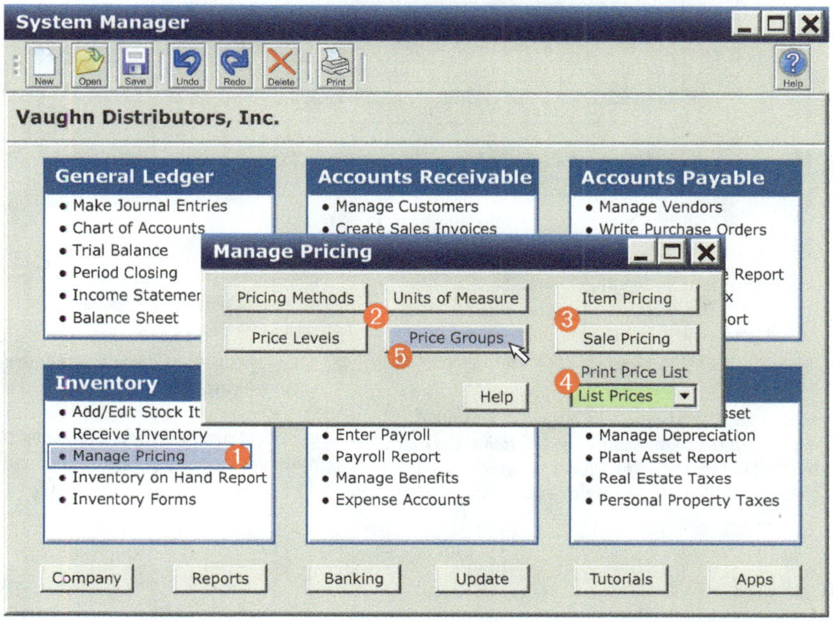

Entered by user   Entered automatically

1. The authorized user clicked on the **Manage Pricing** option from the System Manager, and the system opened a navigation pane providing access to the various parts of the pricing utility.
2. To calculate default selling prices on individual inventory items (9), the system uses four variables: Pricing Methods, Units of Measure, Price Levels, and Price Groups.
3. To set the price for an inventory item, the user would click on the **Item Pricing** button. Clicking the **Sale Pricing** button would enable the user to set temporary sale prices on selected groups of products without affecting normal selling prices.
4. Price lists for List Prices, Group Selling Prices, or special Sale Prices can be printed by selecting Print Price List. Sales price tags could also be printed for use on the sales floor.
5. The user has opened the Price Groups dialog box to set up a new Electric Tools price group.

A Look at Accounting Software

There is no simple explanation for the process of setting prices in a computerized accounting system. Perhaps the best way to help students understand the process is by replicating the system calculations. Using the variables shown in the third window, change just one variable each time. Ask students to imagine what will happen with each change.

1. Change Price Level to % of List Price and enter 90%: The Selling Price changes to $215.60 ($154.00 × 140%).
2. Change Unit of Measure to Dozen: Selling Price changes to $1,603.06 ($95.42 × 140% × 12). That might be high for a quantity sale, so the business might also change the Percent, perhaps to 98%, to bring the selling price down to $1,545.80 ($95.42 × 135% × 12).
3. Change Pricing Method to WHOLESALE, causing defaults to change. Price Level changes to % of List Price, Percent changes to 70%, and Unit of Measure changes to Case (assume 6). The selling price recalculates to ($154.00 × 70% × 6 = $646.80).

Have students imagine the variety of products carried in a home improvement store or a large retail store. Would the business want to use the same variables to price a light bulb as it would a lawn mower? A T-shirt the same as a mattress? That is the benefit of setting up price groups.

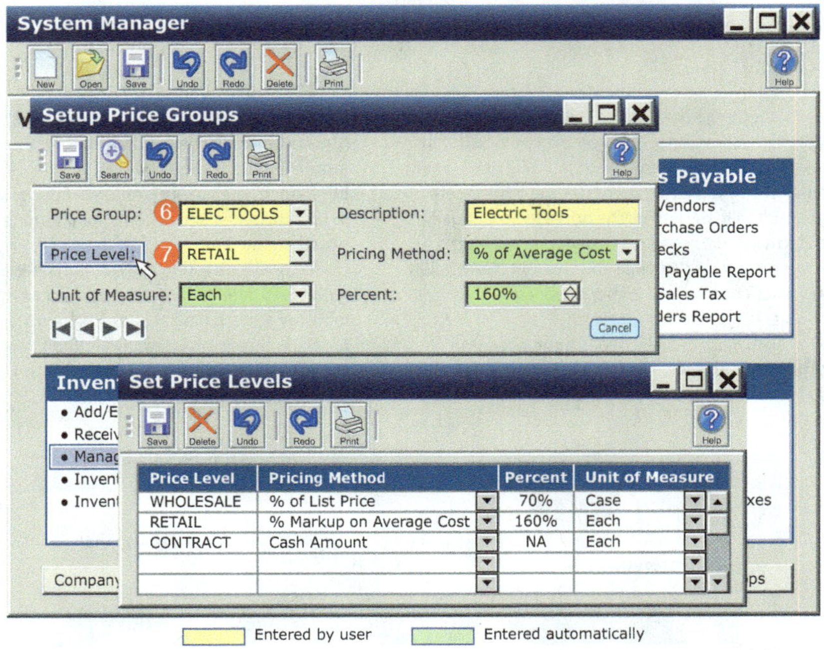

6 The system limits the length of some labels and sets their format. The Price Group label is formatted as all capital letters and is limited to ten characters, so the user has created the label ELEC TOOLS and entered its description.

7 Setting price levels allows the business to maintain different prices on the same inventory items. The user selected RETAIL. Values for Unit of Measure, Pricing Method, and Percent are entered automatically. The user wanted to see how the other price levels were set up and clicked on the **Price Level** label to open the Set Price Levels dialog box.

8 A merchandising business that sells to both wholesale and retail customers would have different price levels for each type of customer. Businesses might also sell to individual customers on a contract basis, where item prices are set by agreement with the customer.

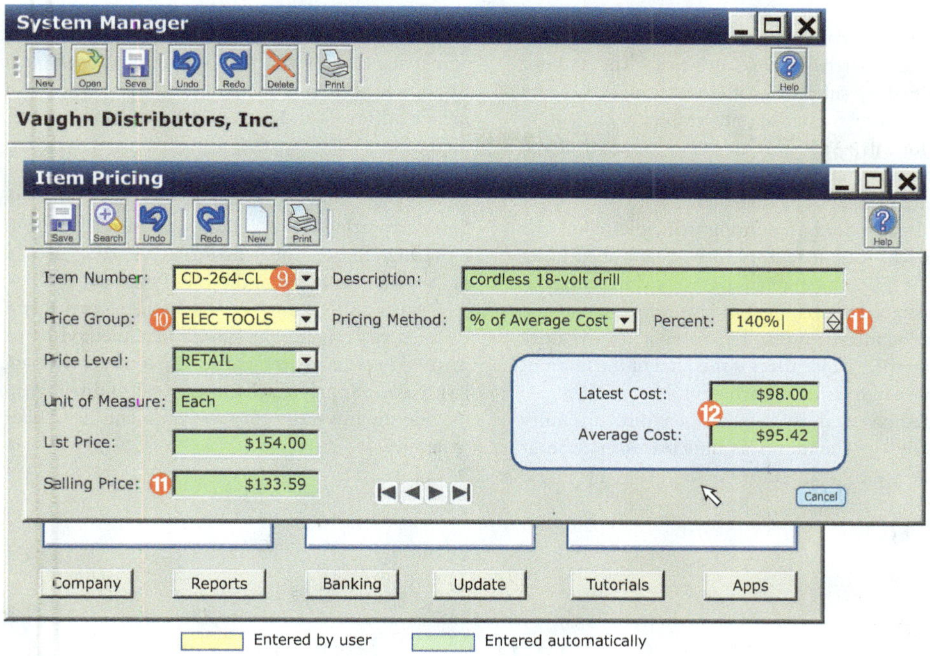

9 Having set up the ELEC TOOLS price group, the user returned to the Manage Pricing navigation pane and opened the Item Pricing dialog box. The user now is beginning the process of assigning individual inventory items to the new price group and has selected the cordless 18-volt drill.

10 When ELEC TOOLS is selected, the system populates all the other fields with their default values. These defaults can be changed by an authorized user. Price groups speed up the process of setting prices, and they maintain more uniformity in pricing.

11 The default Percent would have been entered as 160% (as seen in the Set Up Price Groups dialog box). If a sale were entered for this drill, the system would automatically use a selling price of $152.67 ($95.42 × 160%). Perhaps this drill has not sold well or a competitor is selling it for less. To reduce the regular selling price, the user changed Percent from 160% to 140%, and the selling price went down to $133.59 ($95.42 × 140%).

12 Computerized accounting systems maintain detailed records of the costs of each item purchased. Vaughn Distributors uses the FIFO method of inventory costing, and the accounting system maintains a perpetual inventory. Therefore, as each sale is made, the older items are deducted from inventory first. Also with each sale, the average cost of each item in inventory may change. This system displays both the average cost and the latest cost to assist the user in setting the item's price.

Chapter Summary

The cost of merchandise sold is the largest expense of most retail merchandising businesses. The amount is determined by subtracting the cost assigned to the ending inventory from the total cost of merchandise available for sale. Any error in the calculation of the ending inventory also causes the cost of merchandise sold and net income to be misstated.

Generally accepted accounting principles allow the cost of merchandise inventory to be determined using the LIFO, FIFO, or weighted-average costing method. The cost assigned to each item in inventory is compared to its current market price. The amount of inventory reported on the balance sheet is the total of the lower of the cost or market value of each item.

The method used to cost merchandise inventory results in different amounts as unit prices increase or decrease. The LIFO method results in the lowest cost of merchandise inventory during an inflationary period. As a result, the LIFO method yields the highest cost of merchandise sold and the lowest net income of the three methods.

The LIFO method has not been universally accepted. U.S. tax law only allows the use of the LIFO method for tax reporting if the method is also used for financial reporting. International financial reporting standards do not permit the use of the LIFO method.

A business that does not maintain perpetual inventory records can use the gross profit method or retail method to estimate its merchandise inventory. Financial ratios used to analyze activity in merchandise inventory include the inventory turnover ratio and days' sales in inventory.

EXPLORE ACCOUNTING

Computerized Purchasing Systems

© iStockphoto.com/Makhnach_M

The traditional method for purchasing inventory requires many documents and manual steps to complete. The process involves many employees, requires several days to place an order, and is subject to many clerical errors.

A modern, computerized purchasing system might work as follows: The company's computer continually monitors stock levels against minimum quantities established by management. When the quantity of any inventory item falls below its reorder point, the computer automatically sends a message to a vendor's computer with the order information. (Management frequently enters into long-term contracts with selected vendors that govern prices and delivery schedules.) The vendor's computer immediately informs its warehouse to ship the items. When the items are received, the company's computer sends a message to its bank's computer instructing the bank to transfer funds to the vendor's account.

The direct transfer of information between computers of two or more companies is called *electronic data interchange (EDI)*. EDI reduces the cost of placing an order by reducing paperwork and labor costs. The most important advantage, however, results from improved delivery times. The traditional manual ordering system required several days or weeks to process an order. An EDI system can have the order in transit on the same day the order is placed. Improved delivery time allows companies to reduce inventory levels, which results in substantial cost savings.

INSTRUCTIONS

Contact a local business and inquire if its computer system automatically contacts a vendor's computer with an order.

CLOSURE

- Review the Chapter Summary.
- Ask students to prepare a list of the new concepts introduced in this chapter.
- Remind students that the methods presented in this chapter are used to determine the actual historical cost or an estimate of merchandise inventory.

Essential Questions

- Which inventory costing method should be used if you own an automobile dealership? (*Since automobiles have unique identification numbers, they most likely will use Specific Identification Costing Method.*)
- Which inventory costing method should be used if you want to minimize income tax when inflation is occurring? (*With inflation, LIFO will incur lower profits.*)
- Who or which department would you want to conduct a physical count of inventory for your company? Why? (*The purpose of counting the inventory is to confirm its existence. The department in charge of the inventory should not be responsible for counting their own inventory because they may not note discrepancies if they are held accountable for the accuracy.*)
- What actions might you take if the inventory ratio is steadily declining? (*Promotions to increase sales, better controls of inventory management, or more efficient purchasing, as inventory could be out of date.*)
- How do you think theft and fraud impact merchandise inventory? Who is affected as a result of theft and fraud? (*Theft and fraud result in inventory shrinkage, which negatively affects the net income. In addition to the effects on the company, the consumer may have to pay higher prices to compensate for the losses incurred by theft or fraud.*)

EXTENDED LEARNING

- Review A Look at Accounting Software on pages 163–165.
- Assign Explore Accounting on page 166.

EXPLORE ACCOUNTING

Answers

This activity can be completed by groups of three or four students. Each group can be assigned a local business. Answers will vary depending on the willingness of the business to supply the information and the sophistication of its computer system. Because some groups may get a negative or limited response, evaluate the groups on their efforts to obtain the information rather than their actual findings. As an alternative approach, ask a local business professional who is familiar with EDI to speak to the class.

Apply Your Understanding

INSTRUCTIONS: Download problem instructions for Excel, QuickBooks, and Sage 50 from the textbook companion website at www.C21accounting.com.

5-1 Application Problem: Keeping perpetual inventory records LO2

Lambert Tools sells construction equipment to homebuilders. The company maintains a perpetual inventory system.

Instructions:

1. Complete the heading of a stock record for the following inventory item: description, scaffolding; stock number A-32; reorder quantity, 60; minimum quantity, 15; and location, aisle 6. Lambert has 32 units on hand on May 1.
2. Record on the stock record the merchandise items received and sold during May of the current year.

Transactions:

May 2. Sold 9 units of scaffolding to Schmidt Construction.
3. Sold 10 units of scaffolding to Davidson Homebuilders.
11. Central State University bought 7 units of scaffolding.
12. Received 60 units of scaffolding from Betts Manufacturing.
15. Twenty more units of scaffolding were sold to Schmidt Construction.
19. Sold 25 units of scaffolding to Kisner Contracting.
25. Received 60 units of scaffolding from Betts Manufacturing.

AA ONLINE

1. Go to www.cengage.com/login
2. Click on AA Online to access.
3. Go to the online assignment and follow the instructions.

5-2 Application Problem: Determining inventory cost using FIFO, LIFO, weighted-average, and lower of cost or market LO3, 4

Sage 50 Accounting

1. Journalize and post purchases of inventory in the Purchases/Receive Inventory window.
2. Print the purchase journal, sales journal and item costing report.

QB

1. Journalize and post purchases of inventory in the Enter Bills window.
2. From the menu bar, select Reports; Inventory
3. Print the inventory valuation summary and inventory valuation detail reports.

X

1. Key the inventory-related transactions on the stock record.
2. Use the inventory costing methods to calculate year-end inventory.
3. Print the worksheets.

AA ONLINE

1. Go to www.cengage.com/login
2. Click on AA Online to access.
3. Go to the online assignment and follow the instructions.

Forms containing the purchases and market prices of three inventory items of Bridges, Inc., are presented in the *Working Papers*. Units in the December 31 inventory and the market prices are shown below.

Stock Item	Quantity of Units on Hand	Market Price
B26	24	$ 6.90
C45	80	8.80
D55	18	11.75

Instructions:

1. For each item, calculate the inventory cost using the FIFO, LIFO, and weighted-average inventory costing methods. Identify whether the unit prices are increasing or decreasing. Identify whether each method results in the highest, lowest, or intermediate cost for ending inventory, cost of merchandise sold, and reported net income.
2. Assume that Bridges uses the FIFO method at the lower of cost or market. Complete the form in the *Working Papers* to determine the reported cost of the merchandise inventory.

CHECK FIGURES

For complete solutions to Chapter 5 problems, see the Teacher's Edition of the Working Papers.

Application Problem 5-1

Ending balance, 81 units.

Application Problem 5-2

1. Stock item B26, cost of ending inventory: FIFO, $163.20; LIFO, $157.80; weighted-average, $160.56.

5-3 Application Problem: Estimating cost of merchandise inventory; financial analysis of merchandise inventory LO5, 6

The following information is available for Cagle Company for the month of August. Estimated merchandise inventory sheets are provided in the *Working Papers*.

Item	Cost	Retail
Beginning inventory, August 1	$82,680.00	$173,690.00
Net purchases in August	26,150.00	54,930.00
Net sales in August		64,340.00
Gross profit percentage	52.4%	

Instructions:

1. Calculate the corporation's estimated ending inventory using the gross profit method of estimating inventory.
2. Calculate the corporation's estimated ending inventory using the retail method of estimating inventory. Round the percentage to the nearest 0.1%.
3. Cagle Company's inventory was $83,930.00 on January 1 and $82,750.00 on December 31. Cost of merchandise sold for the year was $369,940.00. Calculate the inventory turnover ratio and the days' sales in inventory. Round the inventory turnover ratio to two decimal places and the days' sales in inventory to the nearest day.

5-M Mastery Problem: Costing and financial analysis of merchandise inventory LO3, 4, 5, 6

On December 31 of the current year, Covert, Inc., took a physical inventory. Units in the December 31 inventory and the market prices are shown below.

Stock Item	Quantity of Units on Hand	Market Price
1548-C	23	$10.05
5324-B	60	6.85
0234-H	21	8.45

Instructions:

1. Calculate the inventory costs using the FIFO, LIFO, and weighted-average inventory costing methods. Use the form in the *Working Papers*.
2. Covert uses the LIFO inventory costing method to determine the cost of inventory. Use the market price given in the form at the beginning of the problem to determine the cost of inventory using the lower of cost or market. Total the Lower of Cost or Market column. Use the form in the *Working Papers*.
3. Calculate the corporation's estimated ending inventory using the gross profit method of estimating inventory. The corporation's records show the following on December 31 of the current year.

Item	Cost	Retail
Beginning inventory, January 1	$ 64,120.00	$132,950.00
Net purchases for year	164,260.00	336,180.00
Net sales for year		392,480.00
Gross profit percentage	51.6%	

Application Problem 5-3

1. Estimated ending inventory: gross profit method, $78,204.16.
2. Estimated ending inventory: retail method, $78,197.28.
3. Inventory turnover ratio, 4.44.

Mastery Problem 5-M

1. Stock item 1548-C, cost of ending inventory: FIFO, $228.15; LIFO, $220.82; weighted-average, $224.94.
3. Estimated ending inventory: gross profit method, $38,419.68.
4. Estimated ending inventory: retail method, $37,328.55.
5. Inventory turnover ratio, 3.71.

INDEPENDENT PRACTICE

- Assign Mastery Problem 5-M for students as a culminating problem that combines all new learning from the chapter.
- Assign Challenge Problem 5-C to accelerated students who work at a faster pace.
- Assign Study Guide 5.
- Students can access Online Working Papers to work end-of-chapter problems on the computer.
- Direct students to the C21 Accounting companion website for additional practice and review opportunities.

FORMATIVE ASSESSMENT

- Review solutions to the assigned problems in class, diagnosing trouble spots.

RETEACH

- Call on students to describe how they avoid the trouble spots diagnosed.
- Use reteaching suggestions from lesson plans as required.
- Assign Recycling Problem 5-R if needed.

4. Calculate the corporation's estimated ending inventory using the retail method of estimating inventory. Round the percentage to the nearest 0.1%.
5. Use the information and the estimated inventory calculated using the gross profit method. Calculate the corporation's inventory turnover ratio. Round the ratio to two decimal places.
6. Calculate the corporation's days' sales in inventory. Round the amount to the nearest day.

QB

1. Journalize and post purchases of inventory in the Enter Bills window.
2. From the menu bar, select Reports; Inventory.
3. Print the inventory valuation summary and inventory valuation detail reports.

X

1. Key the inventory-related transactions on the stock record.
2. Use the inventory costing methods to calculate year-end inventory.
3. Print the worksheets.

5-C Challenge Problem: Financial analysis of merchandise inventory LO6

Selected information for three corporations follows.

	Corporation		
Item	**A**	**B**	**C**
Beginning merchandise inventory	$ 6,500.00	$121,510.00	$ 65,180.00
Ending merchandise inventory	6,200.00	116,480.00	68,350.00
Cost of merchandise sold	294,910.00	351,490.00	998,450.00

Instructions:

1. For each corporation, calculate the inventory turnover ratio. Round the ratio to two decimal places.
2. For each corporation, calculate the days' sales in inventory. Round the amount to the nearest day.
3. Using your knowledge of retail stores gained from being a consumer, identify which corporation is most likely a grocery store, a gas station, and an auto parts store.

Challenge Problem 5-C

1. Corporation A, inventory turnover ratio: 46.44.

EXTENDED LEARNING

- Assign Auditing for Errors on page 170.
- Assign 21st Century Skills on page 171.
- Assign Analyzing Home Depot's Financial Statements on page 171.

SUMMATIVE EVALUATION

- Chapter 5 Test
- Cognero for Chapter 5

COMMON CORE AND INTERDISCIPLINARY STUDIES

Extended learning features and activities present numerous opportunities to implement Common Core Standards through interdisciplinary studies. Practice is provided in the common core areas of English Language Arts & Literacy and Mathematical Practice. Many of these activities require short, critical-thinking and decision-making responses that apply reading, writing, speaking, listening, language, media and technology, and mathematical skills.

AUDITING FOR ERRORS

Answers

1. Two digits in the net purchases to date are transposed; the amount should be $264,890.00.
2. The gross profit was calculated using 54.8%; the amount should be $302,990.84.
3. The amount of inventory lost in the fire is understated by $11,368.20; the amount should be $37,825.84 rather than $26,457.64.

Auditing for errors

On the evening of September 23, Douglass Music Store was heavily damaged by fire. Inventory with an estimated cost of $12,625.00 was salvaged. The remainder of the inventory was either burned or incurred heavy smoke damage. Many of the accounting records were also lost in the fire.

Based on the prior year's financial statements, Douglass began the fiscal year with inventory of $45,750.00. Using bank records, the company determined that its sales and inventory purchases through the date of the fire were $563,180.00 and $264,890.00, respectively. During the prior fiscal year, the company had a gross profit percentage of 53.8%.

Using this information, the bookkeeper prepared the following analysis to be submitted to the insurance company. Verify the numbers on the report, including the bookkeeper's additional items at the bottom of the report. List any errors and the correct amounts.

ESTIMATED MERCHANDISE INVENTORY SHEET

Gross Profit Method

DEPARTMENT *Douglass Music Store* DATE *9/23/20--*

1	Beginning inventory		$ 45,750.00
2	Net purchases to date		246,890.00
3	Merchandise available for sale		$292,640.00
4	Net sales to date	$563,180.00	
5	Less estimated gross profit (Net sales × Estimated gross profit percentage 53.8%)	308,622.64	
6	Estimated cost of merchandise sold		254,557.36
7	Estimated ending inventory		$ 38,082.64
	Salvaged inventory		12,625.00
	Inventory lost in fire		26,457.64

21st Century Skills

A Shrinking Dilemma

Theme: Financial, Economic, Business, and Entrepreneurial Literacy

Skills: Creativity and Innovation, Critical Thinking and Problem Solving, Communication and Collaboration, ICT Literacy

PARTNERSHIP FOR 21ST CENTURY SKILLS

Inventory shrinkage, when the physical count of inventory is less than the accounting records, costs U.S. retailers over $37 billion a year. This shrinkage is approximately 2% of sales revenue. Lost profits have forced some retailers out of business.

There are four primary sources for inventory shrinkage in retail:

1. Nearly 50% of inventory shrinkage comes from employee theft. Employees will often fake refunds, process fraudulent credit card sales, and manipulate inventory records.
2. The second major source of inventory shrinkage is shoplifting. There are an estimated 600,000 shoplifting incidents every day in the United States. Shoplifting consists of altering price tags as well as removing the merchandise from the store by concealment.
3. The third source for inventory shrinkage is administrative errors. Administrative errors include pricing mistakes and inaccuracies in paperwork.
4. The fourth source for inventory shrinkage is vendor fraud. Vendor fraud consists of receiving smaller shipments than invoiced.

APPLICATION

1. Using the Internet, find at least five loss prevention strategies that you would implement for your retail establishment to reduce inventory shrinkage.
2. Write a letter to your manager, describing new strategies that you would suggest for reducing inventory shrinkage.
3. Shrinkage affects the profitability of a business, but it also affects others. Describe at least two other stakeholders that could be affected by inventory shrinkage. Explain.

Source: 2010 National Retail Security Survey, conducted by the University of Florida.

Analyzing Home Depot's financial statements

Most companies include information about inventory in the first note to the financial statements, *Summary of Significant Accounting Policies*. This note usually tells the reader which method the company uses to value the cost of its ending inventory.

INSTRUCTIONS

1. Using Note 1, beginning on page B-10 of Appendix B in this textbook, locate the paragraph titled *Merchandise Inventories*. List the method Home Depot uses to value the majority of its merchandise inventory.
2. Identify the inventory turnover for each year reported in the Five-Year Summary of Financial and Operating Results on page B-15. Use the inventory turnover ratios to calculate the days' sales in inventory for each year.
3. Go to Home Depot's website (www.homedepot.com) and locate the financial statements for the most current year available. (Look for "Investor Relations" or a similar link.) Calculate Home Depot's inventory turnover ratio and days' sales in inventory for the most recent fiscal year.
4. Did these measures improve or worsen since fiscal year 2008?

21ST CENTURY SKILLS

Answers

1. Answers will vary, but might include fencing, locks, security tags, product placement, employee training, employee incentives, computer passwords, and all incoming merchandise being counted.
2. Letters should introduce the topic and explain the recommendations and rationale for each strategy.
3. Answers will vary, but might include employees not receiving bonuses and consumers paying more for merchandise.

ANALYZING HOME DEPOT'S FINANCIAL STATEMENTS

Answers

1. According to Note 1, "The majority of the Company's Merchandise Inventories are stated at the lower of cost (first-in, first-out) or market, as determined by the retail inventory method. Certain subsidiaries, including retail operations in Canada and Mexico, and distribution centers, record Merchandise Inventories at the lower of cost or market, as determined by a cost method."
2. The inventory ratio was 4.5, 4.3, 4.1, 4.1, and 4.0 for fiscal years 2012–2008, respectively. Using these values, the days' sales in inventory are 81, 85, 89, 89, and 91 days, respectively.
3. Answers will differ based on the fiscal year.
4. The ratios indicate a gradual improvement from 2008–2012. Answers for subsequent years will differ based on results of operations since 2012.

Chapter 6

Accounting for Uncollectible Accounts

Scope & Sequence

	New	Review/Enrich
Introduction		
Introduce the Chapter		
Lesson 6-1: Direct Write-Off Method of Recording Uncollectible Accounts		
Direct Write-Off of Losses from Uncollectible Accounts	✓	
Recording Uncollectible Accounts Expense	✓	
Collecting a Written-Off Account—Direct Write-Off Method	✓	
Lesson 6-2: Allowance Method of Recording Uncollectible Accounts Expense		
Selecting a Method for Accounting for Uncollectible Accounts	✓	
Estimating Uncollectible Accounts Expense		✓
Adjustment Using the Percentage of Sales Method	✓	
Adjustment Using Aging of Accounts Receivable		✓
Adjustment Using Percentage of Accounts Receivable	✓	
Writing Off an Uncollectible Account—Allowance Method		✓
Collecting a Written-Off Account—Allowance Method		✓
Lesson 6-3: Financial Analysis of Accounts Receivable		
Accounts Receivable Turnover Ratio	✓	
Analyzing Accounts Receivable Ratios	✓	
Closure		

Enhancing Instruction

Features	Common Core Standards
• Accounting in the Real World: Target Corporation	• ELAL—reading
• Ethics in Action: Integrity in Management Accounting	• ELAL—reading
• Financial Literacy: Avoid Debt Distress	• Mathematics
• Think Like an Accountant: Charting Sales and Accounts Receivable Trends	• Mathematics
• Careers in Accounting: Accounting Advisory Specialist	• ELAL—reading
• Why Accounting?: Cost of Preventing Workplace Injuries	• ELAL—speaking, reading
• A Look at Accounting Software	• ELAL—reading
• Explore Accounting	• ELAL—reading
• 21st Century Skills	• Mathematics
• Analyzing Home Depot's Financial Statements	• Mathematics

ELAL = English Language Arts & Literacy

Calculator: © iStockphoto.com/picstodisc; Paper: © iStockphoto.com/Qingwa

Practice and Assessment

Technology & Media	Teaching Strategies	Guided Practice	Independent Practice	Reteach/Enrich
• Instructor's Resource CD/Website: PowerPoint Slides Accounting Concepts • Online Working Papers • Transparency Masters: General Journal, Cash Receipts Journal (7-column)	• Intrapersonal Learners • Visual/Spatial Learners	• Terms Review • Audit Your Understanding • Work Together 6-1	• On Your Own 6-1 • Application Problem 6-1 • Formative Assessment, p. 176 • Online Working Papers	• Reteach, p. 177
• Instructor's Resource CD/Website: PowerPoint Slides Accounting Concepts • Online Working Papers • Transparency Masters: General Journal, Cash Receipts Journal (7-column)	• Auditory/Linguistic Learners	• Terms Review • Audit Your Understanding • Work Together 6-2	• On Your Own 6-2 • Application Problem 6-2 • Formative Assessment, p. 184 • Online Working Papers	• Reteach, p. 185
• Instructor's Resource CD/Website: PowerPoint Slides Accounting Concepts • Online Working Papers	• Gifted Learners	• Terms Review • Audit Your Understanding • Work Together 6-3	• On Your Own 6-3 • Application Problem 6-3 • Formative Assessment, p. 187 • Online Working Papers	• Reteach, p. 188
• Online Working Papers	• Common Core and Interdisciplinary Studies		• Mastery Problem 6-M • Study Guide 6 • Chapter 6 Test • Cognero Chapter 6	• Challenge Problem 6-C • Reteach, p. 193 • Recycling Problem 6-R

Introduce the Chapter

SET THE STAGE

GUIDING QUESTIONS

- Ask students why it would be advantageous for a business to offer credit to its customers.
- Ask students for examples of when it would not be advantageous to offer credit to customers.
- Ask students to brainstorm questions that could be asked of a customer wanting to buy merchandise on account to help ensure that the customer is a good credit risk.
- Ask students to predict what is meant by *bad debt*.
- Ask students for examples of why a customer may not pay when payment is due.
- Ask students to predict what happens to the Accounts Receivable account when a customer does not make a payment and when a customer makes a payment long after it is due.
- Ask students why a customer would pay past due amounts after all collection attempts had already been exhausted by the creditor.

PREVIEW CHAPTER OBJECTIVES

- Point out that students were introduced to uncollectible accounts in the first-year course.
- Emphasize that this chapter will review the concepts presented in the first-year course and introduce new concepts.
- Note that this chapter presents two methods for accounting for uncollectible accounts.

TEACHING IDEA **A credit rating is an evaluation of the willingness and ability of an individual or a business to pay debts on a timely basis. Invite a guest speaker from a local credit bureau to discuss the impact on an individual or a business when payment is not made on time or at all.**

PREVIEW ACCOUNTING TERMS

- Read each term aloud to verify its pronunciation for students.
- Point out terms or parts of terms that should already be familiar to most students, such as *uncollectible accounts*, *accounts receivable*, and *book value*.
- Lead an interactive discussion with students to review and explain the terms. Stress that special attention should be directed to all boldfaced and highlighted words presented in the text.

Chapter 6 Accounting for Uncollectible Accounts

LEARNING OBJECTIVES

After studying Chapter 6, in addition to defining key terms, you will be able to:

LO1 Calculate and record uncollectible accounts expense using the direct write-off method.

LO2 Calculate and record estimated uncollectible accounts expense using the allowance method.

LO3 Write off an uncollectible account receivable.

LO4 Account for the collection of an account receivable that was written off.

LO5 Calculate and analyze accounts receivable turnover ratios.

Calculator: © iStockphoto.com/picstodisc; Paper: © iStockphoto.com/Qingwa

Jose Luis Pelaez, Inc./Blend Images/Jupiter Images

Background: © iStockphoto.com/jdillontoole; Real World: AP Images/Sitthixay Ditthavong

Accounting In The Real World

Target Corporation

Would you like to receive 5% off your merchandise purchases? Would you be more likely to shop at a retailer that offers you a 5% discount? Would you spend more money with that retailer?

Of course, your answer to these questions is likely a resounding "yes." Thus was the motivation for Target's new *REDcard Rewards* program. Introduced in 2010, the *REDcard Rewards* program offers customers an immediate 5% discount on most merchandise. The *REDcard Rewards* program replaced an existing Target Visa that earned cardholders points toward a 10% coupon.

The *REDcard Rewards* program was an instant success. The number of card applications instantly rose. Total sales increased. Sales to *REDcard* cardholders became a larger percentage of total sales. *REDcard* cardholders are using their cards more often and spending more on each visit. In short, Target is benefiting from a heightened level of customer loyalty.

Unlike other credit cards, *REDcard* sales were initially accounted for as traditional credit sales, resulting in an increase in accounts receivable. In the notes to its financial statements, Target reported these sales in one of two segments: U.S. Retail and Canadian. But the transactions involved in collecting these accounts receivable were recorded in a third segment, U.S. Credit Card. This segment earned revenue by collecting finance charges from cardholders who carried outstanding balances. The possibility existed that some cardholders would not be able to pay their accounts. Thus, the segment's expenses included the cost of uncollectible accounts. During 2013, Target sold its U.S. Credit Card segment to a TD Bank Group, a business with expertise in processing credit card transactions. Customers can still use their *REDcard* and earn a 5% discount. Target continues to market the *REDcard* program, but cardholders now submit their payments to TD Bank Group.

CRITICAL THINKING

1. Target accounts for *REDcard Rewards* program discounts as a reduction of sales. What impact will the program have on Target's historical 30% gross margin?
2. What other advantages and disadvantages could the *REDcard Rewards* program have for Target over the Target VISA?

Source: www.target.com.

Key Terms

- uncollectible accounts
- writing off an account
- direct write-off method
- allowance method
- book value
- aging accounts receivable
- accounts receivable turnover ratio
- days' sales in accounts receivable

Accounting In The Real World

Answers

1. The discount reduces sales, whereas the cost of sales stays unchanged. Sales to customers using the *REDcard* reduce Target's gross margin.
2. Advantages: (a) Target continues to benefit from the customer loyalty generated by the *REDcard*. (b) Target can focus its efforts on selling merchandise. (c) Target does not need to manage the uncollectible accounts.

   Disadvantage: The finance charges are not income for Target.

LESSON
6-1

BRIDGE

- Point out that businesses often offer attractive credit terms. Ask students to explain why a business would offer these terms.

TEACHING RESOURCES

- **Instructor's Resource CD/Website:**
  PowerPoint Slides
  Accounting Concepts
- **Working Papers:**
  Teacher's Edition of the Working Papers for Lesson 6-1
  Online Working Papers
- **Transparency Masters:**
  General Journal
  Cash Receipts Journal (7-column)

ENGAGE

- Ask students to identify businesses in their community that are likely to make sales on account. Point out that sales on account differ from major credit card sales such as Visa and MasterCard.
- This lesson presents an alternative method of accounting for uncollectible accounts. The direct write-off method is useful for small businesses that have few accounts receivable.

PREVIEW

- Call on students to read the accounting terms and definitions introduced in this lesson: *uncollectible accounts*, *writing off an account*, and *direct write-off method*.
- Point out the learning objective for this lesson.
- Direct students to read the headings in this lesson and to examine the illustrations given.

INPUT

- Explain that sometimes a customer is unable or unwilling to pay when payment is due. These accounts receivable that cannot be collected are uncollectible accounts.
- Point out that when a customer is not expected to pay, the customer's accounts receivable is removed from the company's books. This is called writing off an account.
- Stress that sometimes in the future, a customer will make payment. The account balance is restored, and the receipt of cash is recorded.

LESSON 6-1 Direct Write-Off Method of Recording Uncollectible Accounts

LO1 Calculate and record uncollectible accounts expense using the direct write-off method.

Direct Write-Off of Losses from Uncollectible Accounts LO1

Many business transactions are completed on account rather than for cash. Businesses offer credit terms to attract new customers, increase sales to current customers, and encourage customer loyalty. Before a business sells merchandise on account, it should investigate the customer's credit rating to ensure that the customer will pay promptly.

Regardless of the care taken in granting credit, some customers will not pay when payment is due. Accounts receivable that cannot be collected are called **uncollectible accounts**. Uncollectible accounts are sometimes referred to as *bad debts*.

When a business makes a sale on account to a customer, it records the amount in a general ledger account titled Accounts Receivable. The amount remains recorded in this asset account until it is paid or until it is specifically known to be uncollectible.

When a customer account is believed to be uncollectible, it should be removed from the company's books. An uncollectible account should be canceled and removed from the assets of the business. Canceling the balance of a customer account because the customer does not pay is called **writing off an account.**

Occasionally, an account that has been written off is collected. The account balance is restored and the receipt of cash is recorded. A complete history of the transactions for each customer is maintained.

ETHICS IN ACTION

Integrity in Management Accounting

The Institute of Management Accountants (IMA) is an organization dedicated to providing its members with professional development opportunities in management accounting, financial management, and information management. The institute supports lifelong learning by its members through self-study courses, seminars, conferences, and webcasts. Members are encouraged to demonstrate their knowledge by becoming a Certified Management Accountant (CMA).

An important element of the IMA's mission is to encourage its members and their organizations to adopt ethical business practices. The IMA's *Statement of Ethical Professional Practice* states that IMA members must act ethically. Specific guidance is provided in the areas of competence, confidentiality, integrity, and credibility.

INSTRUCTIONS

Access the IMA's *Statement of Ethical Professional Practice*. What does the IMA state related to integrity?

Source: http://www.imanet.org.

© iStockphoto.com/LdF

ETHICS IN ACTION

The IMA's *Statement of Ethical Professional Practice* contains the following guidance regarding integrity:

"Each member has a responsibility to:

1. Mitigate actual conflicts of interest, and regularly communicate with business associates to avoid apparent conflicts of interest. Advise all parties of any potential conflicts.
2. Refrain from engaging in any conduct that would prejudice carrying out duties ethically.
3. Abstain from engaging in or supporting any activity that might discredit the profession."

Recording Uncollectible Accounts Expense

GENERAL JOURNAL — PAGE 11

	DATE		ACCOUNT TITLE	DOC. NO.	POST. REF.	DEBIT	CREDIT	
4		4	*Uncollectible Accounts Expense*	*M62*		182 00		4
5			*Accounts Receivable/Plaza Electronics*		✓		182 00	5
6								6

An amount owed by a specific customer is part of the Accounts Receivable account balance until it is paid or is written off as uncollectible. An uncollectible account is closed by transferring the balance to a general ledger account titled Uncollectible Accounts Expense.

Riverside Café operates a restaurant and catering business. Most of Riverside's sales are made for cash or are paid with a credit card. Riverside periodically makes a sale on account to cater an event for a business customer. Riverside has a small number of accounts receivable and very few of these accounts become uncollectible. Therefore, Riverside records uncollectible accounts expense only when a specific account is actually known to be uncollectible. Recording uncollectible accounts expense only when an amount is actually known to be uncollectible is called the **direct write-off method** of recording losses from uncollectible accounts.

On November 4, Riverside Café learned that Plaza Electronics is unable to pay its account. Riverside decides that Plaza Electronics' account is uncollectible. The entry to record the write-off is made in the general journal as shown above.

November 4. Wrote off Plaza Electronics' account as uncollectible, $182.00. Memorandum No. 62.

GENERAL LEDGER

Uncollectible Accounts Expense

Debit		Credit	
↑ 11/4	182.00		

Accounts Receivable

Debit		Credit	
Bal.	1,648.95	↓ 11/4	182.00
(New Bal.	*1,466.95)*		

ACCOUNTS RECEIVABLE LEDGER

Plaza Electronics

Debit		Credit	
Bal.	182.00	↓ 11/4	182.00
(New Bal.	*zero)*		

After this entry is journalized and posted, the balance of Accounts Receivable no longer includes the $182.00 as part of the business's assets. Also, Plaza Electronics' account has a zero balance and is written off.

© Austin Adams/Shutterstock.com

fyi A *credit rating* is an evaluation of the willingness and ability of an individual or a business to pay debts on a timely basis. Credit ratings are maintained by a several credit bureaus.

INPUT

- Use a general journal transparency to illustrate the general journal or direct students to the illustration.
- Point out that the direct write-off method writes off an account only when the account is known to be uncollectible.
- Explain to students that uncollectible accounts are referred to as bad debts; therefore, Uncollectible Accounts Expense could also be called Bad Debts Expense.
- Point out that a credit rating is an evaluation to determine if a customer is willing and able to pay debts on a timely basis.

MODEL

Analyze the transaction

- Draw three T accounts on the board.
- Read the transaction statement.
- Ask students to analyze the transaction by asking these questions: Which accounts are affected? Are they increased or decreased? Are they debited or credited? Complete the T accounts as the information is provided.
- Review the effect on the account for Plaza Electronics in the accounts receivable ledger.

Record the transaction

- Use a general journal transparency to illustrate recording the transaction in the general journal or direct students to the illustration.

DIFFERENTIATED INSTRUCTION

Intrapersonal learners often prefer to work alone (with their own strengths and weaknesses). Ask students to interview three businesses in their area that accept credit customers. Students should seek at least one reason each business chose to extend credit terms other than traditional bank cards (Visa, MasterCard, Discover, and American Express) so that their customers will buy on account.

Visual/Spatial learners enjoy learning through drawing and physical imagery. This activity requires two different credit card applications per student or group of students. Students should draw a Venn diagram to compare and contrast the questions asked on two different credit card applications to evaluate whether a business should sell to a customer on account.

INPUT

- Recording the collection of a written-off account requires two journal entries. One entry is documented by a memorandum. The second entry is documented by a receipt.
- Explain to students that the two entries enable the customer's Accounts Receivable account to reflect fully all activity of the account. Managers use this information when making future credit decisions for the customer.
- Ask students to explain why the credit is recorded to Uncollectible Accounts Expense.

MODEL

Reopen the account

- Draw four T accounts on the board and enter the balance amounts.
- Read the transaction statement.
- Enter in the T accounts the transaction to reopen the customer's account. Ask students to analyze the transaction by answering these questions: Which accounts are affected? Are they increased or decreased? Are they debited or credited?
- Use a general journal transparency to illustrate recording the transaction in the general journal or direct students to the illustration.

Record the cash received

- Read the transaction statement again.
- Enter in the T accounts the transaction to record the cash received. Ask students to analyze the transaction by answering these questions: Which accounts are affected? Are they increased or decreased? Are they debited or credited? Use a cash receipts journal transparency to illustrate recording the transaction in the cash receipts journal or direct students to the illustration.
- Ask students to identify the current balance of Plaza Electronics' account.

Collecting a Written-Off Account—Direct Write-Off Method

Reopen the Account ❶

GENERAL JOURNAL — PAGE 12

	DATE		ACCOUNT TITLE	DOC. NO.	POST. REF.	DEBIT	CREDIT	
10		6	Accounts Receivable/Plaza Electronics	M73	/	182 00		10
11			Uncollectible Accounts Expense				182 00	11
12								12

Record the Cash Receipt ❷

CASH RECEIPTS JOURNAL — PAGE 16

	DATE		ACCOUNT TITLE	DOC. NO.	POST. REF.	1 GENERAL DEBIT	2 GENERAL CREDIT	3 ACCOUNTS RECEIVABLE CREDIT	4 SALES CREDIT	5 SALES TAX PAYABLE CREDIT	6 SALES DISCOUNT DEBIT	7 CASH DEBIT	
7		6	Plaza Electronics	R321				182 00				182 00	7
8													8

A business should continue its efforts to collect an account even after it has been written off. If the account is later collected, a credit is recorded to Uncollectible Accounts Expense. The credit offsets the debit recorded when the account was written off. The write-off and collection also result in no impact on the balance of Uncollectible Accounts Expense.

December 6. Received cash in full payment of Plaza Electronics' account, previously written off as uncollectible, $182.00. Memorandum No. 73 and Receipt No. 321.

Riverside Café needs a complete history of each customer's credit activities. Therefore, two journal entries are recorded for the collection of a written-off account receivable as shown above.

1. A general journal entry to reopen the customer account.
2. A cash receipts journal entry to record the cash received on account.

GENERAL LEDGER

Cash

↑ 12/6	182.00			

Accounts Receivable

Bal.	1,648.95		11/4	182.00
↑ 12/6	182.00	↓	12/6	182.00
(New Bal.	1,466.95)			

Uncollectible Accounts Expense

11/4	182.00	↓	12/6	182.00
(New Bal.	zero)			

ACCOUNTS RECEIVABLE LEDGER

Plaza Electronics

Bal.	182.00		11/4	182.00
↑ 12/6	182.00	↓	12/6	182.00
(New Bal.	zero)			

Collecting a Written-Off Account Using the Direct Write-Off Method

❶ Record an entry in the general journal to debit **Accounts Receivable/Plaza Electronics** and credit **Uncollectible Accounts Expense** for the amount of the receipt, **$182.00**.

❷ Record an entry in the cash receipts journal to debit **Cash** and credit **Accounts Receivable** for the amount of the receipt, **$182.00**.

remember

Uncollectible accounts are also referred to as *bad debts*. Thus, the account used could be titled Bad Debt Expense.

FORMATIVE ASSESSMENT

- This is an ongoing process. Circulate around the classroom or lab, observing which students have problems with the assignments.
- Troubleshooting: Students may have trouble understanding why an account is reopened when cash is received on a written-off account. Students may also have difficulty understanding why the receipt of cash results in a credit to Uncollectible Accounts Expense.
- Assess student understanding by checking solutions to Independent Practice assignments and observing their answers to the Terms Review and Audit Your Understanding questions.

End of Lesson Review

LO1 Calculate and record uncollectible accounts expense using the direct write-off method.

Terms Review

uncollectible accounts

writing off an account

direct write-off method

Audit your understanding

1. Why should the amount of an uncollectible account be removed from the assets of a business?
2. In the direct write-off method, how is an uncollectible account closed?
3. Why is the customer account reopened when cash is received for an account previously written off as uncollectible?

Work together 6-1

Journalizing entries to write off uncollectible accounts—direct write-off method

Winters, Inc., uses the direct write-off method of recording uncollectible accounts expense. A general journal and a cash receipts journal are provided in the *Working Papers*. Use page 2 of a general journal and page 4 of a cash receipts journal. Source documents are abbreviated as follows: memorandum, M; receipt, R. Your instructor will guide you through the following examples.

Transactions:

Feb. 3. Wrote off Loper Company's past due account as uncollectible, $115.81. M33.

Apr. 24. Wrote off Polk Supply's past due account as uncollectible, $95.00. M42.

May 14. Received cash in full payment of Loper Company's account, previously written off as uncollectible, $115.81. M51 and R221.

June 8. Received cash in full payment of Polk Supply's account, previously written off as uncollectible, $95.00. M64 and R259.

On your own 6-1

Journalizing entries to write off uncollectible accounts—direct write-off method

NorthStar, Inc., uses the direct write-off method of recording uncollectible accounts expense. A general journal and a cash receipts journal are provided in the *Working Papers*. Use page 1 of a general journal and page 3 of a cash receipts journal. Source documents are abbreviated as follows: memorandum, M; receipt, R. Work this problem independently.

Transactions:

Jan. 14. Wrote off Sylvia Mendoza's past due account as uncollectible, $92.45. M25.

Feb. 12. Wrote off Conisha Martin's past due account as uncollectible, $62.48. M31.

June 20. Received cash in full payment of Sylvia Mendoza's account, previously written off as uncollectible, $92.45. M54 and R148.

Aug. 25. Received cash in full payment of Conisha Martin's account, previously written off as uncollectible, $62.48. M89 and R195.

CHECK FOR UNDERSTANDING

Terms Review

- Call on students to define each term in the Terms Review. Definitions are given in the Glossary.

Audit Your Understanding

- Call on students to answer the Audit Your Understanding questions. Answers are given in Appendix D of the textbook.

GUIDED PRACTICE

Work Together

- Have students write the solution to the Work Together problem as you guide the class through the examples.
- Call on students to use the direct write-off method to journalize entries to write off uncollectible accounts.

INDEPENDENT PRACTICE

On Your Own

- Assign the On Your Own problem to be worked independently.
- Use the Formative Assessment techniques to diagnose student understanding.

Application Problem

- Assign Application Problem 6-1.

Online Working Papers

- Students can access the Lesson 6-1 problems using this software.

RETEACH

- Call on students to list the transactions necessary to write off an uncollectible account and subsequently record the collection of the account.
- Write the five accounts affected by the transactions in this lesson. Ask students to make up original transaction statements and write them on the board.
- Ask another student to use T accounts to analyze the transaction statements.

CLOSURE

- Ask students to summarize briefly the procedures for journalizing transactions using the direct write-off method of accounting for uncollectible accounts.

Essential Questions

- Assume you own a business and want to allow customers to buy merchandise on account. What questions would you include on your credit application to evaluate the credit risk of customers wanting to buy merchandise on account? (*Questions might include employment, salary, length of time on job, others owed, rent or own home, and length of time at residence.*)
- How long would you wait for a customer to pay before deciding that the account is uncollectible? Explain. (*Some companies will attempt to collect for up to a year. Companies must decide at what point they will no longer spend resources attempting to collect versus focusing on other business.*)

EXTENDED LEARNING

- Assign Accounting in the Real World on page 173.
- Assign Ethics in Action on page 174.

LESSON
6-2

INPUT

- Compare and contrast the different methods of accounting for uncollectible accounts.
- Point out when the direct write-off method can be used appropriately.
- Stress what is meant by *immaterial* and the relevance of materiality and the direct write-off method.

BRIDGE

- Explain that this lesson reviews the journalizing of transactions for the allowance method that students learned in the first-year course.
- Point out that students have already learned to journalize transactions pertaining to accounts receivable accounts.

TEACHING RESOURCES

- **Instructor's Resource CD/Website:**
  PowerPoint Slides
  Accounting Concepts
- **Working Papers:**
  Teacher's Edition of the Working Papers for Lesson 6-2
  Online Working Papers
- **Transparency Masters:**
  General Journal
  Cash Receipts Journal (7-column)

ENGAGE

- The Matching Expenses with Revenue concept suggests that the expense of an uncollectible account should be recognized in the same fiscal period the sale on account is recorded. How can that be accomplished for a sale on the last day of the fiscal year? The allowance method is the solution.
- Explain that this lesson presents two methods for estimating uncollectible accounts expense.

PREVIEW

- Call on students to read the accounting terms and definitions introduced in this lesson: *allowance method, book value,* and *aging accounts receivable*.
- Point out the learning objectives for this lesson.
- Direct students to read the headings in this lesson and to examine the illustrations given.

LESSON
6-2 Allowance Method of Recording Uncollectible Accounts Expense

LO2 Calculate and record estimated uncollectible accounts expense using the allowance method.
LO3 Write off an uncollectible account receivable.
LO4 Account for the collection of an account receivable that was written off.

Selecting a Method for Accounting for Uncollectible Accounts

The direct write-off method of recording losses from uncollectible accounts is easy to apply. A business that uses this method only records the expense when a specific customer account is determined to be uncollectible. Thus, the expense may be recorded in a fiscal period different from the period of the sale. For this reason, the direct write-off method usually is not allowed under generally accepted accounting principles.

Uncollectible accounts expense should be recorded in the same fiscal period in which the sales revenue is received. [CONCEPT: Matching Expenses with Revenue] However, at the time sales on account are made, a business has no way to know for sure which customer will not pay an amount due. Therefore, the business makes an estimate based on its past history of uncollectible accounts. Crediting the estimated value of uncollectible accounts to a contra account is called the **allowance method** of recording losses from uncollectible accounts.

Business activities creating dollar amounts large enough to affect business decisions should be recorded in the accounting records using generally accepted accounting principles. [Business Concept: Materiality] An item that is not large enough to affect business decisions is referred to as being *immaterial*.

Accounts receivable must be reported on the balance sheet at their net realizable value. Only the allowance method achieves this reporting objective. However, a business can use the direct write-off method if the difference between using the two methods is immaterial.

Businesses having a small number and dollar amount of accounts receivable may be able to use the direct write-off method. Riverside Café, the business in Lesson 6-1, uses the direct write-off method. Most of its customers pay with cash or a credit card. Riverside only accepts credit sales for catering events with business customers. Thus, Riverside has a small number of accounts receivable and very few of these accounts become uncollectible.

Estimating Uncollectible Accounts Expense LO2

Two methods are commonly used to estimate uncollectible accounts expense:

1. Percentage of sales method.
2. Percentage of accounts receivable method.

The percentage of sales method assumes that a percentage of each sales dollar will become an uncollectible account. The percentage of accounts receivable method assumes that a percentage of accounts receivable at the fiscal year-end will become uncollectible. Regardless of the method used, the estimated amount is charged to Uncollectible Accounts Expense.

The difference between an asset's account balance and its related contra account balance is called **book value**. The book value of accounts receivable, reported on the balance sheet, represents an estimate of the total amount of accounts receivable the business expects to collect. When the accounts receivable are collected, the actual amount collected is said to have been realized. For this reason, the book value is often referred to as the *net realizable value*.

INPUT

- Ask students to identify the two methods for estimating uncollectible accounts.
- Ask students to describe the assumption that supports each of the two methods for estimating uncollectible accounts.
- Ask students to identify the name of the contra account used to record the uncollectible accounts expense.
- Point out the meaning of *book value* and explain that book value represents an estimate of the total amount of accounts receivable the business expects to collect in the future.
- Compare and contrast with students the difference between book value and net realizable value.

Adjustment Using the Percentage of Sales Method

Net Sales	×	Percentage	=	Estimated Uncollectible Accounts Expense
$618,194.37	×	0.4%	=	$2,472.78

1 Estimate of Uncollectible Accounts

GENERAL JOURNAL PAGE 16

	DATE		ACCOUNT TITLE	DOC. NO.	POST. REF.	DEBIT	CREDIT	
1			*Adjusting Entries*					1
2	*20-- Dec.*	*31*	*Uncollectible Accounts Expense*	*M62*		*2 4 7 2 78*		2
3			*Allowance for Uncollectible Accounts*				*2 4 7 2 78*	3
4								4

2 Adjusting Entry

Past experience of Noland Company indicates that approximately 0.4% of its net sales will prove to be uncollectible. On December 31, Noland estimated that 0.4% of its $618,194.37 net sales, $2,472.78, eventually will prove to be uncollectible.

At the end of a fiscal period, an adjustment for uncollectible accounts expense is journalized on the general journal. Before the adjustment is made, Noland's general ledger shows Allowance for Uncollectible Accounts with a $225.60 credit balance. This balance is what remains of estimates made in previous fiscal periods but not yet specifically identified by customer. The new balance, $2,698.38, is an estimate of the accounts receivable that will become uncollectible.

The balance of Allowance for Uncollectible Accounts may increase from year to year. A large increase may indicate that an incorrect percentage is being used to calculate the uncollectible amount. When this occurs, a new percentage should be calculated based on actual experience for the past two or three years. Other factors, such as an economic downturn, may cause a business to change the percentage.

Regardless of the percentage used, the estimate of the Allowance for Uncollectible Accounts must result in a reasonable and unbiased estimate of the money a business expects to collect in the future. A business must not change any estimate to achieve some other goal, such as reducing net income to avoid income taxes. It must make accounting estimates that are free from bias. [CONCEPT: Neutrality]

Uncollectible Accounts Expense

Debit		Credit
Adj.	2,472.78	

Allowance for Uncollectible Accounts

Debit	Credit	
	Bal.	225.60
	Adj.	2,472.78
	(New Bal.	*2,698.38)*

Estimating Uncollectible Accounts Expense by Using the Percentage of Sales Method

1. **Compute the estimated uncollectible accounts expense by multiplying net sales, $618,194.37, by the percentage estimate, 0.4%, which totals $2,472.78.**
2. **Record a debit to Uncollectible Accounts Expense and a credit to Allowance for Uncollectible Accounts for the amount of $2,472.78.**

fyi

A company can elect to base its estimate of uncollectible accounts expense on a percentage of total sales on account. The calculation of the allowance amount is the same as when total net sales is used.

INPUT

- Point out that estimated uncollectible accounts expense is a percentage of net sales.
- Point out that the current balance of Allowance for Uncollectible Accounts is not considered in calculating the estimate.
- Ask students to identify factors that might influence a business to increase or decrease the percentage from the amount indicated from past experience. (*changing economic conditions and changes in credit approval policies*)
- Ask students to identify two explanations for the prior balance of Allowance for Uncollectible Accounts. (*the amount of prior years' sales that may still become uncollectible or the inherent result of using estimates*)
- Remind students that adjustments for uncollectible accounts must be journalized in the general journal.
- Point out that a company can elect to base its estimate of uncollectible accounts expense on a percentage of total sales on account. The calculation of the allowance amount is the same as when net sales is used.

MODEL

Analyze the adjustment

- As you read Step 1, ask students to use a calculator to compute the allowance estimate.
- Draw two blank T accounts on the board.
- Ask students to analyze the adjustment by answering these questions: Which accounts are affected? Are they increased or decreased? Are they debited or credited? Complete the T accounts as the information is provided.

Record the adjustment

- As you read Step 2, use the general journal to demonstrate journalizing the adjustment or direct students to the illustration.

TEACHING IDEA

Pair up students and ask half of the pairs to draft a letter they would send to a customer who is 30 days past due on payment. Ask the other half to compose a letter they would send to a customer who is 180 days (6 months) past due on payment. Bring students together and ask for volunteers to read their letters. Ask the class to compare and contrast the two letters and determine if the tone or request sounds different.

INPUT

- Explain that the percentage of accounts receivable is an alternative method to the percentage of sales method.
- Point out that although a business can use either method to estimate uncollectible accounts expense, the business should use the same method from year to year.
- Point out that the aging of accounts receivable in one-month intervals is common practice but not a requirement of GAAP.

FINANCIAL LITERACY

Answers

1. Answers will vary.
2. Answers will vary.

Adjustment Using Aging of Accounts Receivable

Customer	Account Balance	Current	Days Account Balance Past Due			
			1–30	31–60	61–90	Over 90
Anderson Stores	$ 3,670.92	$ 2,184.61	$1,486.31			
Campbell Hardware	2,769.05		2,084.36	$ 684.69		
Vance Corporation	495.31					$ 495.31
Wallis Supply	1,068.68				$1,068.68	
York Tools	5,227.38	4,162.68	1,064.70			
	$31,098.44	$12,914.68	$8,436.81	$3,481.69	$2,084.31	$4,180.95
Percentages		2.0%	5.0%	10.0%	40.0%	80.0%

The percentage of accounts receivable method assumes that a percentage of the Accounts Receivable account balance is uncollectible. Therefore, emphasis is placed on estimating a percentage of accounts receivable that will not be collected. An amount that will bring the balance of Allowance for Uncollectible Accounts up to the estimated amount is recorded in that account.

Analyzing accounts receivable according to when they are due is called **aging accounts receivable**. Vaughn Distributors, Inc., ages accounts receivable at the end of each fiscal period, as shown above, to provide information for the uncollectible accounts expense adjustment. Vaughn sells on terms of 2/10, n/30. Vaughn offers customers a 2% discount for paying within 10 days. Vaughn expects customers to pay in full within 30 days.

FINANCIAL LITERACY

Avoid Debt Distress

Debt enslaves people and denies them financial freedom. It causes stress, prevents them from making purchases like a car or a home, damages their credit for many years, and can interfere with employment choices.

One of the leading reasons for debt problems in the United States is credit cards. The average American owns three credit cards and carries a balance of over $15,000. Credit cards are not bad when used appropriately. However, some of the following tactics used by credit card companies are often the culprits for excessive debt.

- Minimum monthly payment—Paying a minimum monthly payment allows the balance to grow steadily with interest charges.
- Low introductory rate—This gimmick will hook you and then switch your lower rate to a much higher rate, resulting in more interest charges.
- Fees—Many credit card companies tack on late payment fees, even if you are only a day late.
- Universal default—Sometimes your credit card company will increase your interest rate, based on one late payment with another company.

ACTIVITIES

1. Search through local newspapers or on the Internet for three advertisements that use any of the above tactics. Share with the class.
2. Obtain three different credit card applications. Read the fine print on the application. Then, draw a Venn diagram to compare/contrast the similarities and differences in interest rate, introductory interest rate, fees, universal default rules, and amount of minimum payment.

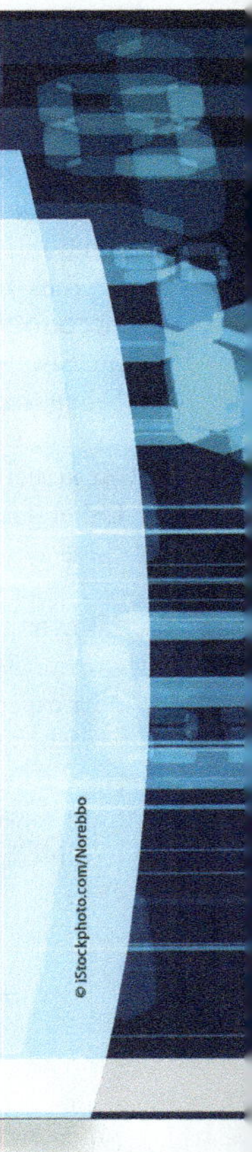

© iStockphoto.com/Norebbo

Adjustment Using Percentage of Accounts Receivable

Age Group	Amount	Percentage	Uncollectible
Current	$12,914.68	2.0%	$ 258.29
1–30	8,436.81	5.0%	421.84
31–60	3,481.69	10.0%	348.17
61–90	2,084.31	40.0%	833.72
Over 90	4,180.95	80.0%	3,344.76
	$31,098.44		$5,206.78
Current Balance of Allowance for Uncollectible Accounts			308.64
Estimated Addition to Allowance for Uncollectible Accounts			$4,898.14

1 Estimate for Each Age Group

2 Total Estimate

3 Addition to Allowance Account

Vaughn Distributors expects customers to pay in full within 30 days. If Vaughn has not received cash within 30 days, it mails reminders to the customers. If the business has not collected an amount from a customer after 90 days, it may stop selling on account to that customer until collection has been made.

Based on past records, Vaughn determines that a percentage of each accounts receivable age group will become uncollectible in the future. For example, 10.0% of the accounts receivable overdue 31–60 days will probably become uncollectible.

Using these percentages, Vaughn calculates the total amount of estimated uncollectible accounts receivable, as shown above. Of the total accounts receivable on December 31, $31,098.44, the business estimates that $5,206.78 will prove to be uncollectible in the future.

Vaughn's general ledger shows that Allowance for Uncollectible Accounts has a $308.64 credit balance. This balance is what remains of estimates made in previous fiscal periods but not yet specifically identified by customer. The allowance account is increased by a $4,898.14 credit. The new balance of the allowance account, $5,206.78 (previous balance, $308.64, plus adjustment, $4,898.14), equals the estimate of uncollectible accounts.

Estimating the Balance of Uncollectible Accounts Expense Using the Percentage of Accounts Receivable Method

1. **Compute the estimate for each age group. Multiply the amount of each age group by the percentage estimate.**
2. **Compute the total, $5,206.78, of the uncollectible estimates.**
3. **Subtract the current balance, $308.64, from the total estimate to determine the addition to the allowance account, $4,898.14. (If the allowance account has a debit balance, add the current balance to the total estimate.)**

THINK LIKE AN ACCOUNTANT

Charting Sales and Accounts Receivable Trends

Sales at Petaland Company had been increasing only modestly in past years. New management in 20X4 believed it could accelerate sales growth best by loosening its credit requirements for customers. Now five years later, the board of directors has requested an analysis of how the new credit policy has impacted sales and the collection of receivables.

OPEN THE SPREADSHEET TLA_CH06

The worksheet contains selected financial statement information for the past eight years. Follow the steps on the Instructions tab to prepare a chart. Answer these questions:

1. What is the annual trend in sales?
2. What is the relationship between sales and the accounts receivable turnover ratio?
3. What other data could be added to the chart to provide better information regarding the success of management's credit policies?

INPUT

- Point out that the amounts for each age group are obtained from the aging of accounts receivable.
- Remind students that the percentages are derived from past collection history. The longer a receivable is past due, the more likely it will become uncollectible.
- Point out to students that the balance in Allowance for Uncollectible Accounts is used in this estimation method as shown in the illustration.

MODEL

- As you read each step, ask students to use a calculator to compute the amounts.
- Draw two blank T accounts on the board.
- Ask students to analyze the adjustment by answering these questions: Which accounts are affected? Are they increased or decreased? Are they debited or credited? Complete the T accounts as the information is provided.

THINK LIKE AN ACCOUNTANT

This activity requires students to create a chart to show the relationship between sales and the accounts receivable turnover ratio. Charting two sets of amounts having dramatically different scales (one in millions, one less than 15) requires a chart with two axis scales.

Remind students to average accounts receivable to compute each year's ratio. For this reason, no ratio is calculated for 20X1. The formula for the 20X2 ratio is =+C5/((B12+C12)/2). Alternatively, this formula could use a function to determine the average accounts receivable balance: =C5/AVERAGE(B12,C12).

Question 3 requires students to consider the impact of bad debts expense on the analysis. Encourage students to create a chart that includes the operating expenses (because no detail of operating expenses is provided). This chart will reveal that the company's increase in sales has not translated to a similar increase in operating income.

A sample solution and chart can be found in the Instructional Strategies section at the front of this book.

INPUT

- Point out that both the direct and allowance methods are used to write off an account when the account is known to be uncollectible.
- Ask students to compare how writing off an account affects Uncollectible Accounts Expense using the direct and allowance methods. (*A direct method write-off increases the expense, whereas an allowance method write-off has no effect on the expense.*)
- Ask students to read the FYI feature to learn more about internal controls.

MODEL

Analyze the adjustment

- Draw three T accounts on the board.
- Read the transaction statement.
- Ask students to analyze the transaction by answering these questions: Which accounts are affected? Are they increased or decreased? Are they debited or credited? Complete the T accounts as the information is provided.
- Review the effect on the account for Vance Corporation in the accounts receivable ledger.

Record the transaction

- Use a general journal transparency to illustrate recording the transaction in the general journal or direct students to the illustration.
- Remind students that the abbreviation for the memorandum, M, and the memorandum number are recorded in the Doc. No. column.

Writing Off an Uncollectible Account—Allowance Method LO3

GENERAL JOURNAL PAGE *1*

	DATE		ACCOUNT TITLE	DOC. NO.	POST. REF.	DEBIT	CREDIT	
4		*23*	*Allowance for Uncollectible Accounts*	*M121*		*495 31*		4
5			*Accounts Receivable/Vance Corporation*				*495 31*	5
6								6

The procedures for writing off an account are the same regardless of the method used to calculate the estimated uncollectible accounts expense. When a specific customer account is thought to be uncollectible, the account balance is written off as shown above. Vaughn Distributors, Inc., determined that Vance Corporation will probably not pay the amount it owes, $495.31. The balance is no longer estimated to be uncollectible; it is actually determined to be uncollectible.

January 23. Wrote off Vance Corporation's past due account as uncollectible, $495.31. Memorandum No. 121.

After this entry is journalized and posted, Vance Corporation's account has a zero balance. Uncollectible Accounts Expense is not affected by this entry.

Vaughn did not notify Vance Corporation that it wrote off its account. Although Vaughn believes the account is probably uncollectible, it may continue its attempts to collect the account. In some cases, customers do subsequently pay accounts that have been written off.

In a previous fiscal period, an adjusting entry was recorded for estimated uncollectible accounts expense resulting in an Allowance for Uncollectible Accounts balance of $5,206.78. This balance is the estimated amount of uncollectible accounts. The $495.31 debit entry in this account removes an actual amount that is no longer estimated. As shown in the next column, the book value of accounts receivable is not affected by writing off an account.

GENERAL LEDGER

Allowance for Uncollectible Accounts

Debit		Credit	
1/23 Write off	495.31	Bal.	5,206.78
		(New Bal.	*4,711.47)*

Accounts Receivable

Debit		Credit	
Bal.	31,098.44	1/23 Write off	495.31
(New Bal.	*30,603.13)*		

ACCOUNTS RECEIVABLE LEDGER

Vance Corporation

Debit		Credit	
Bal.	495.31	1/23 Write off	495.31
(New Bal.	*zero)*		

	Before Account Written Off	After Account Written Off
Accounts Receivable	$31,098.44	$30,603.13
Allowance for Uncollectible Accounts	5,206.78	4,711.47
Book Value	$25,891.66	$25,891.66

fyi

Proper internal control requires that the custody, recording, and authority for a transaction be segregated. The employee responsible for writing off an account should not also have access to the cash received from customers paying their accounts.

Collecting a Written-Off Account—Allowance Method LO4

Reopen the Account ①

GENERAL JOURNAL PAGE 2

	DATE		ACCOUNT TITLE	DOC. NO.	POST. REF.	DEBIT	CREDIT	
1	20-- Feb.	3	*Accounts Receivable/Vance Corporation*	*M129*	/	495 31		1
2			*Allowance for Uncollectible Accounts*				495 31	2
3								3

Record the Cash Receipt ②

CASH RECEIPTS JOURNAL PAGE 3

	DATE	ACCOUNT TITLE	DOC. NO.	POST. REF.	1 GENERAL DEBIT	2 GENERAL CREDIT	3 ACCOUNTS RECEIVABLE CREDIT	4 SALES CREDIT	5 SALES TAX PAYABLE CREDIT	6 SALES DISCOUNT DEBIT	7 CASH DEBIT	
2	3	*Vance Corporation*	*R420*				495 31				495 31	2
3												3

February 3. Received cash in full payment of Vance Corporation's account, previously written off as uncollectible, $495.31. Memorandum No. 129 and Receipt No. 420.

GENERAL LEDGER

Cash

↑ 2/3 Received	495.31		

Accounts Receivable

Bal.	31,098.44	1/23 Write off	495.31
↑ 2/3 Reopen	495.31	↓ 2/3 Received	495.31
(New Bal.	30,603.13)		

Allowance for Uncollectible Accounts

1/23 Write off	495.31	Bal.	5,206.78
		↑ 2/3 Reopen	495.31
		(New Bal.	5,206.78)

ACCOUNTS RECEIVABLE LEDGER

Vance Corporation

Bal.	495.31	1/23 Write off	495.31
↑ 2/3 Reopen	495.31	↓ 2/3 Received	495.31
(New Bal.	zero)		

Later in the year, Vaughn Distributors received a check in full payment of the amount owed by Vance Corporation.

Vaughn Distributors' records must show a complete history of Vance Corporation's credit dealings. The collection of a written-off account receivable involves two journal entries as shown above.

A general journal entry is recorded to reopen the customer account. The $495.31 debit increases Accounts Receivable and Vance Corporation's account in the accounts receivable ledger. The account balances now appear as they were before Vance Corporation's account was written off as uncollectible.

The cash received from Vance Corporation is then recorded in the cash receipts journal. The $495.31 credit decreases Accounts Receivable and Vance Corporation's account in the accounts receivable ledger.

remember Entries for the collection of a written-off account present evidence of the customer's credit history. Managers can use this information to make informed decisions about extending credit to the customer in the future.

Journalizing the Collection of a Written-Off Account—Allowance Method

① Reopen the account by debiting Accounts Receivable and crediting Allowance for Uncollectible Accounts for the amount of the receipt, $495.31.

② Record an entry in the cash receipts journal to debit Cash and credit Accounts Receivable for the amount of the receipt, $495.31.

INPUT

- Recording the collection of a written-off account requires two journal entries. One entry is documented by a memorandum. The second entry is documented by a receipt.
- Explain to students that the two entries enable the customer's Accounts Receivable account to reflect all of the account activity. Managers use this information when making future credit decisions for the customer.
- Ask students to explain why the credit is recorded to Allowance for Uncollectible Accounts. (*Unlike the direct method, the write-off did not result in an expense. Thus, no entry to an expense or a revenue account should be made when a written-off account is collected.*)
- Ask students to read the Remember feature to learn more about how managers make customer credit decisions.

MODEL

Reopen the account

- Draw four T accounts on the board and enter the balance amounts.
- Read the transaction statement.
- Enter in the T accounts the transaction to reopen the customer's account. Ask students to analyze the transaction.
- Use a general journal transparency to illustrate recording the transaction in the general journal or direct students to the illustration.

Record the cash received

- Read the transaction statement again.
- Enter in the T accounts the transaction to record the cash received. Ask students to analyze the transaction.
- Use a cash receipts journal transparency to illustrate recording the transaction in the cash receipts journal or direct students to the illustration.
- Ask students to identify the current balance of Vance Corporation.

DIFFERENTIATED INSTRUCTION

Auditory/Linguistic learners have highly developed auditory skills and often have success using spoken language as a means to remember information. Invite a guest speaker from a local business to discuss which method of estimating uncollectibles is used in his or her place of business. Ask the speaker to discuss the correlation between the percentage used to estimate aging accounts and the economic factors considered when aging accounts.

Careers In Accounting

Review the accounting advisory specialist career.

Careers In Accounting

Abu Sarr

ACCOUNTING ADVISORY SPECIALIST

© Franco's Photos/Shutterstock.com

Abu Sarr works for a major international accounting firm, but he does not perform audits. He is an accounting advisory specialist who is part of a large staff of consultants that provide advisory services to businesses. His company offers advisory services in many areas, including accounting, risk management, performance improvement, tax, global expansion, and corporate leadership and development.

Abu graduated from a public college with a degree in accounting. He went to work in a regional public accounting firm, where he served as a junior accountant for three years. During that time, he became a CPA. He was hired by his current company in an entry-level accounting consulting position. After four years with the company, he was promoted to a senior consultant.

Abu has worked in many areas, including lease financing and the implementation of International Financial Reporting Standards (IFRS). Most recently, he has concentrated on mergers and acquisitions (M&A). In M&A, he helps companies make decisions about what companies to acquire and how to organize the merged companies. Because most M&As are quite complex, he works on a team with investment bankers, lawyers, financial analysts, tax specialists, and other consultants.

Abu took public speaking while in college and feels that this skill is very beneficial in his current position. He often must present complex issues to his clients and do so at a level that the client will understand.

Salary Range: Salaries for senior managers in the management services area average $87,700 to $173,500.

Qualifications: Extensive accounting knowledge, usually including the CPA designation, is required. In addition, the consultant must have excellent communication and presentation skills and must be able to work effectively in a team environment.

Occupational Outlook: As a career area, accounting is expected to experience much faster than average growth (over 20%) through 2018.

Sources: www.onetonline.org; Robert Half 2012 Salary Guide.

© iStockphoto.com/Mlenny

FORMATIVE ASSESSMENT

- This is an ongoing process. Circulate around the classroom or lab, observing which students have problems with the assignments.
- Troubleshooting: Diagnose the kinds of problems students have with this lesson. Students may have difficulty understanding the differences in the transactions using the direct and allowance methods.
- Assess student understanding by checking solutions to Independent Practice assignments and noting their answers to the Terms Review and Audit Your Understanding questions.

End of Lesson Review

LO2 Calculate and record estimated uncollectible accounts expense using the allowance method.

LO3 Write off an uncollectible account receivable.

LO4 Account for the collection of an account receivable that was written off.

Terms Review

allowance method

book value

aging accounts receivable

Audit your understanding

1. What are the two methods commonly used to estimate uncollectible accounts expense?
2. What is the formula for estimating uncollectible accounts expense based on net sales?
3. How is the addition to allowance for uncollectible accounts calculated using the percentage of accounts receivable method?
4. When can the direct write-off method be used?

Work together 6-2

Estimating amount of uncollectible accounts expense; journalizing the adjusting entry

General journals and a cash receipts journal are provided in the *Working Papers*. Your instructor will guide you through the following independent examples.

1. Lycum, Inc., had net sales of $642,453.29 during the current year ended December 31. It estimates that the amount of uncollectible accounts expense is equal to 0.8% of net sales. Record the adjusting entry for uncollectible accounts expense on December 31.
2. The aging of accounts receivable for Rollins, Inc., as of December 31 of the current year and estimated percentages of uncollectible accounts by age group are presented in the *Working Papers*. Calculate the estimated balance of Allowance for Uncollectible Accounts. Record the adjusting entry for uncollectible accounts expense. The balance of Allowance for Uncollectible Accounts on December 31 before adjusting entries are recorded is a $148.68 debit.
3. Journalize the following transactions completed during the current year.

Transactions:

Jan. 6. Wrote off Marcia Ayers' past due account as uncollectible, $621.23. Memorandum No. 225.

Apr. 14. Received cash in full payment of Marcia Ayers' account, previously written off as uncollectible, $621.23. Memorandum No. 259 and Receipt No. 630.

On your own 6-2

Estimating amount of uncollectible accounts expense; journalizing the adjusting entry

General journals and a cash receipts journal are provided in the *Working Papers*. Work this problem independently.

1. Goodrum, Inc., had net sales of $868,540.95 during the current year ended December 31. It estimates that the amount of uncollectible accounts expense is equal to 0.6% of net sales. Record the adjusting entry for uncollectible accounts expense.
2. The aging of accounts receivable for Nichols Supply is presented in the *Working Papers*. Record the adjusting entry for uncollectible accounts expense. The balance of Allowance for Uncollectible Accounts on December 31 before adjusting entries are recorded is a $248.68 credit.
3. Journalize the following transactions completed during the current year.

Transactions:

Jan. 4. Wrote off Patricia Webb's past due account as uncollectible, $492.16. Memorandum No. 123.

Mar. 29. Received a partial payment on Patricia Webb's account, previously written off as uncollectible, $200.00. Memorandum No. 162 and Receipt No. 456.

CHECK FOR UNDERSTANDING

Terms Review

- Call on students to define each term in the Terms Review. Definitions are given in the Glossary.

Audit Your Understanding

- Call on students to answer the Audit Your Understanding questions. Answers are given in Appendix D of the textbook.

GUIDED PRACTICE

Work Together

- Have students write the solution to the Work Together problem as you guide the class through the examples.
- Direct students to estimate and journalize the amount of uncollectible accounts expense.

INDEPENDENT PRACTICE

On Your Own

- Assign the On Your Own problem to be worked independently.
- Use the Formative Assessment techniques to diagnose student understanding.

Application Problem

- Assign Application Problem 6-2.

Online Working Papers

- Students can access the Lesson 6-2 problems using this software.

RETEACH

- Ask students to identify all the methods that are available to calculate the uncollectible accounts expense using the allowance method.
- Ask a student to make up original transactions to write off and subsequently collect an uncollectible account.
- Ask another student to analyze the transactions using T accounts.
- Ask a student to record the transactions in the journals.

Essential Question

- What methods might be employed to obtain past due payments from customers so that the account is not written off? (*Customers may be given extended time with interest or the option of making smaller payments over a longer period of time.*)

EXTENDED LEARNING

- Assign Financial Literacy on page 180.
- Assign Think Like an Accountant on page 181.
- Review Careers in Accounting on page 184.

CLOSURE

- Ask students to summarize briefly the procedures for accounting for uncollectible accounts.

LESSON

6-3

BRIDGE

- Explain to students that ratios or percentages are often used instead of dollar amounts to make decisions. Ask students to brainstorm examples of when ratios might provide a better understanding of a situation.

TEACHING RESOURCES

- **Instructor's Resource CD/Website:**
  PowerPoint Slides
  Accounting Concepts
- **Working Papers:**
  Teacher's Edition of the Working Papers for Lesson 6-3
  Online Working Papers

ENGAGE

- The accounting methods described in this chapter provide managers with the information they need to make decisions about extending credit to customers and collecting accounts receivable. The ratio presented in this section can help managers understand this information better.

PREVIEW

- Call on students to read the accounting terms and definitions introduced in this lesson: *accounts receivable turnover ratio* and *days' sales in accounts receivable.*
- Point out the learning objective for this lesson.
- Direct students to read the headings in this lesson and to examine the illustrations.

INPUT

- Explain that a ratio is a relationship of two amounts that enables a comparison with the same ratios from prior years, other companies, or industry averages.
- Point out that using the beginning and ending book values of accounts receivable is a cost-effective method for estimating an average book value of accounts receivable during the year, as shown in the illustration.
- Ask students to explain the purpose of each step shown in the illustration.

MODEL

- As you read each step, ask students to use a calculator to complete each step shown in the illustration.

LESSON

6-3 Financial Analysis of Accounts Receivable

LO5 Calculate and analyze accounts receivable turnover ratios.

Accounts Receivable Turnover Ratio LO5

	Total Accounts Receivable	−	Allowance for Uncollectible Accounts	=	Book Value of Accounts Receivable
Beginning	$29,481.67	−	$2,491.63	=	$26,990.04
Ending	$31,098.44	−	$2,698.38	=	$28,400.06

(Beginning Book Value of Accounts Receivable	+	Ending Book Value of Accounts Receivable)	÷	2	=	Average Book Value of Accounts Receivable
($26,990.04	+	$28,400.06)	÷	2	=	$27,695.05

Net Sales on Account	÷	Average Book Value of Accounts Receivable	=	Accounts Receivable Turnover Ratio
$229,715.64	÷	$27,695.05	=	8.3

A business needs cash to purchase additional merchandise and pay for operating expenses. If it does not collect amounts due from customers promptly, too large a share of the assets of the business will be in accounts receivable and not immediately usable. A business selling on account needs prompt collection from credit customers.

The number of times the average amount of accounts receivable is collected during a specified period is called the **accounts receivable turnover ratio**. The accounts receivable turnover ratio is calculated by dividing net sales on account by the average book value of accounts receivable. Vaughn Distributors' accounts receivable turnover ratio is calculated as shown above.

An accounts receivable turnover ratio of 8.3 times means that Vaughn Distributors turns over (or collects) its average accounts receivable 8.3 times a year.

DAYS' SALES IN ACCOUNTS RECEIVABLE

The average period of time to collect an account receivable is called the **days' sales in accounts receivable**. The ratio is also referred to as *days' sales outstanding.* The days' sales in accounts receivable based on an 8.3 accounts receivable turnover ratio is calculated as shown below

Days in Year	÷	Accounts Receivable Turnover Ratio	=	Days' Sales in Accounts Receivable
365	÷	8.3	=	44

The number of days' sales in accounts receivable is rounded to the nearest day. This level of accuracy provides managers with adequate information to make sound business decisions.

The terms of sale a business offers its credit customers influence its days' sales in accounts receivable. Vaughn offers 2/10, n/30 terms to its credit customers. Thus, Vaughn expects most of its customers to take advantage of the 2% discount and pay within 10 days. Some customers pay the net amount in 30 days and others have past due accounts. The longer time required to collect these accounts explains why Vaughn's average collection period is 44 days.

DIFFERENTIATED INSTRUCTION

Gifted learners need additional challenges to maintain a high level of motivation. Ask these learners to contact a local collection agency and discuss the fees and methods associated with the various ages of collection accounts. Students can ask about success rate in collecting past due accounts. They should organize the information and report it to the class.

Analyzing Accounts Receivable Ratios

Year	20X1	20X2	20X3	20X4	20X5	20X6	20X7
Accounts receivable turnover ratio	7.4	7.5	7.7	7.5	7.9	8.2	8.3
Days' sales in accounts receivable	49	49	47	49	46	45	44

The accounts receivable turnover ratio and days' sales in accounts receivable enable a business to analyze how frequently customers make payments on account. If customers are not paying promptly, the business can adopt new procedures to encourage more prompt collections.

From 20X1 through 20X7, Vaughn Distributors' accounts receivable turnover ratio increased from 7.4 to 8.3 times, as shown above. In 20X1, customers took an average of 49 days to pay their accounts in full. In 20X7, customers took an average of 44 days to pay their accounts in full, 5 days less than in 20X1.

With the exception of 20X4, the turnover ratio has been steadily increasing. On the average, customers have been paying their accounts in five fewer days over the seven-year period. Vaughn wants this favorable trend to continue.

However, Vaughn's days' sales in accounts receivable is still higher than would be expected. With 2/10, n/30 credit terms, a minimum goal should be to have a turnover ratio of 12.0 times (365 days/12.0 accounts receivable turnover ratio equals an average of 30 days for payment). The business might take several steps to create a more favorable accounts receivable turnover ratio.

1. Send account statements to customers more often, including a request for prompt payment.
2. Not sell on account to any customer who has an account for which payment is overdue more than 30 days.
3. Conduct a more rigorous credit check on new customers before extending credit to them.

Sometimes the demand for quicker payment can result in a loss of business. Some customers might start buying from competitors. A business must weigh a change in credit policies against the effect the change will have on total sales.

WHY ACCOUNTING?

Cost of Preventing Workplace Injuries

Health Science

Public health professionals in Minnesota worked with Minnesota teachers to develop a curriculum targeted to the health and safety of adolescents (under age 18) in the workplace. The curriculum, called *Work Safe Work Smart*, describes ways to protect the employee, such as adequate training, protective gear, and using shields and guards with dangerous machinery.

Steps taken to prevent workplace injuries usually come with a price tag. How much the employer is willing to pay to prevent injuries is dependent on a number of factors, including the likelihood of injury, the seriousness of the possible injury, the cost of preventive measures, and the losses that the company would incur if an injury occurs. Company personnel from many areas, such as accounting, human resources, risk management, operations, and upper management, need to work together to calculate these costs and determine what preventive measures to take.

CRITICAL THINKING

Select a workplace (yours or a friend's or relative's) and identify its required work safety procedures/equipment. Explain why you think these procedures/equipment are or are not useful.

Sources: Bureau of Labor Statistics (www.bls.gov/iff/); Health.state.mn.us.

© iStockphoto.com/Alekso

- Ask students to prepare a list of all the amounts needed to compute the accounts receivable turnover ratio.

INPUT

- Explain that computing the number of days' sales in accounts receivable, also known as days' sales outstanding, provides managers with information to make business decisions.
- Point out that the longer time required to collect from credit customers prohibits the business from making payments or purchasing additional merchandise.

INPUT

- Ask students to identify whether an increase in the accounts receivable turnover ratio indicates a positive or negative trend. (*positive*)
- Ask students to identify whether an increase in the days for payment indicates a positive or negative trend. (*negative*)
- Ask students to identify steps to improve the collection of accounts receivable.

TEACHING IDEA **Ask students to obtain the financial statements of a company with which they are familiar. Ask students to calculate and evaluate the accounts receivable turnover ratio for each year that financial information is available.**

WHY ACCOUNTING?

Answers

Answers will vary.

FORMATIVE ASSESSMENT

- This is an ongoing process. Circulate around the classroom or lab, observing which students have problems with the assignments.
- Troubleshooting: Diagnose the kinds of problems students have with this lesson. Students may have trouble understanding how to compute the average book value of accounts receivable.
- Assess student understanding by checking solutions to Independent Practice assignments and noting their answers to the Terms Review and Audit Your Understanding questions.

CHECK FOR UNDERSTANDING

Terms Review

- Call on students to define each term in the Terms Review. Definitions are given in the Glossary.

Audit Your Understanding

- Call on students to answer the Audit Your Understanding questions. Answers are given in Appendix D of the textbook.

GUIDED PRACTICE

Work Together

- Have students write the solution to the Work Together problem as you guide the class through the examples.
- Demonstrate how to calculate the accounts receivable turnover ratio for the current year.
- Demonstrate how to calculate the days' sales in accounts receivable.
- Ask students if this business is effective in collecting its accounts receivable.

INDEPENDENT PRACTICE

On Your Own

- Assign the On Your Own problem to be worked independently.

Application Problem

- Assign Application Problem 6-3.

Online Working Papers

- Students can access the Lesson 6-3 problems using this software.

RETEACH

- List the information required to compute the accounts receivable turnover ratio.
- Ask students to explain how to interpret the accounts receivable turnover ratio and the days' sales in accounts receivable.

CLOSURE

- Ask students to summarize briefly the procedure for calculating the accounts receivable ratio and the days' sales in accounts receivable.

End of Lesson Review

LO5 Calculate and analyze accounts receivable turnover ratios.

Terms Review

accounts receivable turnover ratio

days' sales in accounts receivable

Audit your understanding

1. What is the formula for calculating the accounts receivable turnover ratio?
2. How would you interpret the situation of a business that desires an accounts receivable turnover ratio of 12.0 times but actually has a turnover ratio of 6.0 times?
3. How can extremely restrictive credit terms have a negative impact on a business?

Work together 6-3

Financial analysis of accounts receivable

LMK Industries offers its customers n/30 credit terms. The turnover ratio for the prior year was 6.4. The following account balances were obtained from LMK Industries' records for the current year. Your instructor will guide you through the following examples.

	January 1	December 31
Accounts Receivable	$126,468.15	$135,643.58
Allowance for Uncollectible Accounts	4,123.27	5,754.77
Net Sales on Account		847,386.56

1. Calculate the accounts receivable turnover ratio for the current year.
2. Calculate the days' sales in accounts receivable.
3. Is LMK Industries effective in collecting its accounts receivable?

On your own 6-3

Financial analysis of accounts receivable

Yang Supply offers its customers 2/10, n/30 credit terms. The turnover ratio for the prior year was 15.9. The following account balances were obtained from the records of Yang Supply for the current year. Work this problem independently.

	January 1	December 31
Accounts Receivable	$65,856.05	$ 67,643.48
Allowance for Uncollectible Accounts	3,535.12	3,635.36
Net Sales on Account		982,435.94

1. Calculate the accounts receivable turnover ratio for the current year.
2. Calculate the days' sales in accounts receivable.
3. Is Yang Supply effective in collecting its accounts receivable?

Essential Questions

- How can someone go about determining if uncollectibles are within a reasonable range? (*Comparisons can be made on historical data.*)
- Why do we recognize revenue (sales) when the accounts receivable is uncollectible? We didn't receive the money, so why report the revenue? (*Revenue must be recognized when earned. Uncollectible expenses can be matched with revenue for that period.*)

EXTENDED LEARNING

- Assign Why Accounting on page 187.

A Look at Accounting Software

Setting Credit Limits

To minimize the number of write-offs of receivables, businesses take steps to reduce the risk of uncollectible accounts. One of the more important steps is determining the creditworthiness of each customer and limiting the amount of credit extended. In a manual accounting system, the credit limit would probably be written on a customer's ledger card. Before each credit sale, an accounting department employee would review the customer's account to be certain that the sale was within the customer's limit.

In a computerized accounting system, a business enters credit terms into each customer's record. The customer's credit limit is checked automatically prior to each sale. This process speeds credit sales and minimizes the chances of customers exceeding their credit limit.

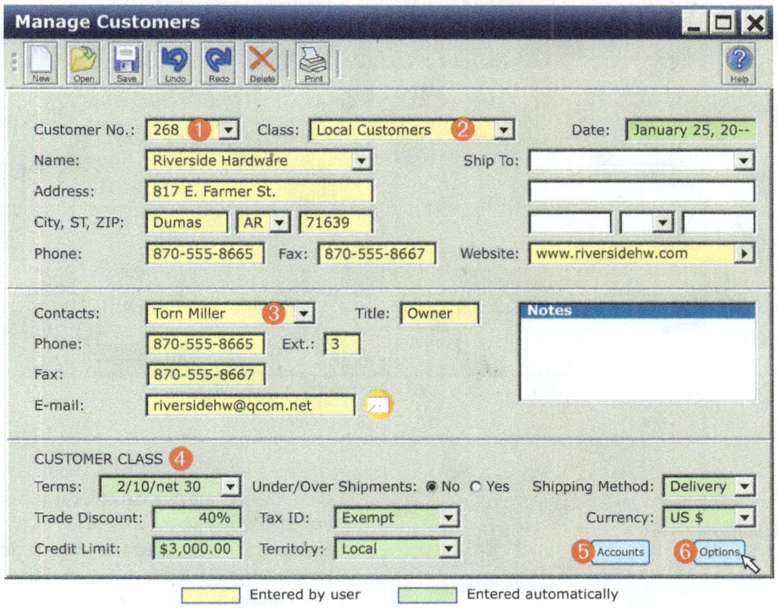

1. The accountant for Vaughn Distributors is setting up a new customer account for Riverside Hardware. On the Manage Customers window, the accountant accepted the next sequential customer number offered by the system.
2. The accountant selected Local Customers as the classification for Riverside Hardware. Having classifications allows the system to assign default settings for different types of customers.
3. After entering the customer's name, address, phone, fax, and website, the accountant entered the contact information for the customer's employee responsible for purchasing.
4. The Customer Class section of the window displays the default settings for the classification set in Step 2. The accountant can accept or change the settings. In addition to payment terms and trade discount, these settings indicate whether the customer will accept under- or over-shipments, the normal method of delivery, the amount of sales tax to collect (if any), the type of currency (for export sales), and the territory (for managing sales by salesperson or sales manager).
5. The **Accounts** button would be clicked to open a window where general ledger accounts could be assigned for handling transactions with this customer. Those accounts are assigned by default and would only be accessed to change them.
6. The accountant accepted all the defaults and clicked on the **Options** button to open the Credit Options dialog box.

A Look at Accounting Software

This feature focuses on how a business manages credit risk. The Chapter 14 Using Accounting Software feature in the first-year C21 Accounting text relates to aging of accounts receivable and collections. That feature could be reviewed to reinforce many of the concepts presented in this chapter. The Chapter 24 feature from the first-year text also presents the Manage Customers window. It, too, could be reviewed for more detail on managing customer information.

Students might be asked why Riverside Hardware would be exempt from sales tax. The answer is that Riverside purchases merchandise for resale and that sales taxes are collected when the items are sold at retail by the hardware store.

Balance forward billing is not commonly used in business-to-business commerce. It is most often used by professional businesses such as doctors, dentists, and attorneys. It is also the standard for credit card companies.

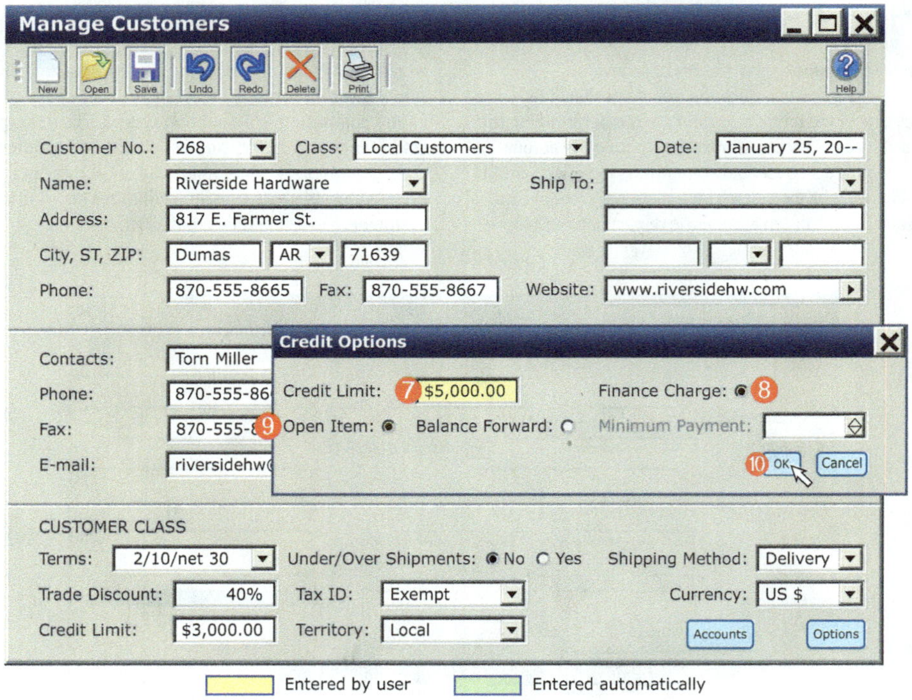

7 The accountant has changed the $3,000.00 default credit limit for local customers to $5,000.00 for Riverside Hardware.

8 Many businesses have a policy of assessing finance charges on customer balances when payments are late. The default setting is "on," but it can be turned off for select customers.

9 There are two methods of maintaining customer accounts—open item and balance forward. Open Item is the default. Under that method, the customer is expected to pay each invoice in full within the terms of payment. Some customers may be offered a Balance Forward account. Those customers can purchase merchandise up to their credit limit and are expected to pay a prescribed minimum amount of their account balance each period.

10 The accountant clicks **OK** to accept the settings and return to the main window.

Chapter Summary

A business may offer credit terms to attract new customers, increase sales to current customers, and encourage customer loyalty. The business will likely have some customers that will be unable to pay their accounts. An uncollectible account is no longer an asset and should be written off.

The two methods used to account for uncollectible accounts are the (1) direct write-off and (2) allowance methods. The direct write-off method recognizes an uncollectible account expense at the time the account is considered uncollectible. Although the method is easy to apply, it fails to always match the expense of the uncollectible account in the same accounting period as the related sale. For this reason, the method is not a generally accepted accounting principle. However, a business having an immaterial amount of uncollectible accounts may be able to use the direct write-off method.

A business using the allowance method records an estimate of uncollectible accounts expense in the same period as the related sales. Two methods of calculating an estimate are commonly used. The percentage of sales method assumes that a percentage of each sales dollar will become uncollectible. The percentage of accounts receivable method assumes that a percentage of accounts receivable at the fiscal year-end will become uncollectible. This method applies a series of percentages to age groups on an aging of accounts receivable. The accounts of the adjusting journal entry are the same regardless of the method used to estimate uncollectible accounts.

The accounts receivable turnover ratio and the days' sales in accounts receivable enable a business to analyze its effectiveness in collecting accounts receivable. The accounts receivable turnover ratio is calculated by dividing net sales on account by the average book value of accounts receivable. The days' sales in accounts receivable is calculated by dividing 365 by the accounts receivable turnover ratio. The ratio, stated in days, indicates the average length of time to collect an account.

Credit Scoring Systems

EXPLORE ACCOUNTING

To help reduce the amount of uncollectible accounts, a business should evaluate the creditworthiness of potential customers before granting credit. The most widely used credit score for individuals used in the United States is the FICO score. FICO stands for Fair Isaac Corporation, the company that developed the scoring model used to calculate credit scores.

The FICO score ranges between 300 and 850. The higher the score, the more creditworthy the customer. U.S. law enables individuals to obtain their credit score, free of charge, from three national credit bureaus. Each bureau collects financial information on individuals, such as payment history, types of credit, and use of credit. These data are entered into the FICO scoring model to calculate the FICO score. Since each bureau's financial information may vary, the FICO scores are often different.

Although individuals can obtain their credit scores free of charge, a business must pay a fee to the credit bureaus to obtain the same information. Similar sources of information are available for a business to evaluate the creditworthiness of business customers. A business must weigh the cost of evaluating a customer's creditworthiness against the benefit of reducing uncollectible accounts expense. The benefit of reducing uncollectible accounts expense should exceed the costs of performing credit evaluations. A business should not, for example, spend $60,000 in salaries and bureau fees to evaluate credit if the business can only reduce its annual uncollectible accounts expense by $40,000. Regardless of how credit is evaluated, a company must ensure that its decisions are consistent. Federal laws exist to ensure that individuals and businesses have equal access to credit.

INSTRUCTIONS

Research the FICO score. Identify the weight of each type of financial information used in the FICO score.

Source: myFICO.com.

© iStockphoto.com/Makhnach_M

CLOSURE

- Review the Chapter Summary.
- Discuss with students uncollectible accounts. Ask students to compare and contrast the various methods for calculating and adjusting uncollectible accounts.
- Have students explain what happens with an account that is collected after it had been written off.

Essential Questions

- Why wouldn't you show just the net balance of accounts receivable? Why bother showing the deduction of the allowance account on the balance sheet? (*The allowance account is only an estimate; therefore, the net balance may not truly reflect what is collected in accounts receivable. By showing the deduction, the balance sheet more accurately reflects the amount you think you will collect in the future.*)
- How accurate are companies with their estimates? Because these are guesses, could the estimates affect the net income reported? Explain. (*Companies should try to be as accurate as possible by using historical data to estimate uncollectibles. Net income is negatively affected because uncollectibles increase expenses.*)

EXTENDED LEARNING

- Review A Look at Accounting Software on pages 189 and 190.
- Assign Explore Accounting on page 191.

EXPLORE ACCOUNTING

Answers

Payment history (35%), credit utilization or amounts owed (30%), length of credit history (15%), types of credit used (10%), and recent searches for new credit (10%).

CHECK FIGURES

For complete solutions to Chapter 6 problems, see the Teacher's Edition of the Working Papers.

Application Problem 6-1

Accounts credited on general journal: Accounts Receivable, Jan. 23 and May 9; Uncollectible Accounts Expense, Mar. 6 and July 30.

Application Problem 6-2

1. Uncollectible Accounts Expense, $4,633.34.

Apply Your Understanding

INSTRUCTIONS: Download problem instructions for Excel, QuickBooks, and Sage 50 from the textbook companion website at www.C21accounting.com.

6-1 Application Problem: Journalizing entries to write off uncollectible accounts—direct write-off method LO1

Stallworth Company uses the direct write-off method of recording uncollectible accounts expense. A general journal and cash receipts journal are provided in the *Working Papers*.

Instructions:

Journalize the following transactions completed during the current year. Use page 4 of a general journal and page 6 of a cash receipts journal. Source documents are abbreviated as follows: memorandum, M; receipt, R.

Transactions:

Jan.	23.	Rochelle Company's legal counsel notified Stallworth of its plans to declare bankruptcy. Write off the $325.15 account balance as uncollectible. M42.
Mar.	6.	Received a $168.25 check from Norris Industries in full payment of its account. Norris Industries was never notified that Stallworth previously wrote off the account as uncollectible. M62 and R432.
May	9.	Based on conversations with managers at Guice Corporation, the account is expected to become uncollectible, $421.05. M73.
July	30.	Received a check from Zimmer Supply as a partial payment on its account that was previously written off as uncollectible, $250.00. M85 and R503.

AAONLINE

1. Go to www.cengage.com/login
2. Click on AA Online to access.
3. Go to the online assignment and follow the instructions.

6-2 Application Problem: Estimating amount of uncollectible accounts expense; journalizing the adjusting entry LO2, 3, 4

Sage 50 Accounting

1. Journalize and post transactions related to allowance for uncollectible accounts to the cash receipts journal.
2. Journalize and post accounts receivable transactions previously written off as uncollectible to the sales journal and cash receipts journal.
3. Print the sales journal and cash receipts journal.

QB

1. Journalize and post transactions related to allowance for uncollectible accounts to the journal.
2. Journalize and post accounts receivable transactions previously written off in the Create Invoices window and the Receive Payments window.
3. Print the journal and customer balance detail report.

General journals and a cash receipts journal are provided in the *Working Papers*.

Instructions:

1. eSystems, Inc. estimates that its uncollectible accounts expense will be approximately 0.9% of net sales. The current year's net sales is $514,815.35. Use page 20 of a general journal to record the adjusting entry for uncollectible accounts expense on December 31 of the current year.
2. Wimberly Corporation's aging of accounts receivable as of December 31 of the current year is presented in the *Working Papers*. Use the estimated percentages by age group to estimate the required balance of Allowance for Uncollectible Accounts. The balance of Allowance for Uncollectible Accounts on December 31 before adjusting entries are recorded is a $342.05 credit. Use page 13 of a general journal to record the adjusting entry for uncollectible accounts expense.
3. Journalize the following transactions for Wimberly Corporation completed during the current year. Use page 1 of a general journal and page 3 of a cash receipts journal. Source documents are abbreviated as follows: memorandum, M; receipt, R.

1. Journalize and post transactions related to allowance for uncollectible accounts.
2. Use the estimated percentages by age group to estimate the required balance of Allowance for Uncollectible Accounts to journalize the adjusting entry for December 31.
3. Print the worksheets.

AAONLINE

1. Go to www.cengage.com/login
2. Click on AA Online to access.
3. Go to the online assignment and follow the instructions.

Transactions:

Jan. 9. Concluded that Queen Industries is unable to pay its $450.00 outstanding account receivable. M148.

Mar. 3. Received a partial payment on Davis Manufacturing's account, previously written off as uncollectible, $800.00. M162 and R710.

May 14. Windle Supply has closed its doors. Write off its $900.00 account as uncollectible. M179.

June 22. Received a $580.00 check from Mattie Company in full payment of its account. The account was previously written off as uncollectible. M190 and R832.

6-3 Application Problem: Financial analysis of accounts receivable LO5

LampLight Industries offers its customers n/30 credit terms. The turnover ratio for the prior year was 11.0. The following account balances were obtained from LampLight Industries' records for the current year:

	January 1	December 31
Accounts Receivable	$45,364.23	$ 47,153.55
Allowance for Uncollectible Accounts	3,015.85	3,384.08
Net Sales on Account		484,047.53

Instructions:

1. Calculate the accounts receivable turnover ratio for the current year.
2. Calculate the days' sales in accounts receivable.
3. Is LampLight Industries effective in collecting its accounts receivable?

6-M Mastery Problem: Journalizing entries for uncollectible accounts—allowance method; calculating and journalizing the adjusting entry for uncollectible accounts expense LO2, 3, 4, 5

West River, Inc., uses the allowance method of recording uncollectible accounts expense. The following information was obtained from West River's records for the current year:

	January 1	December 31
Accounts Receivable	$65,184.26	$ 72,184.95
Allowance for Doubtful Accounts	3,481.62	4,048.78
Net Sales on Account		847,386.56

A general journal and cash receipts journal are provided in the *Working Papers*.

Transactions:

Feb. 2. A phone call to Alex Yarber, president of Yarber Supply, confirmed that the company is intending to file bankruptcy. Alex stated that no money would likely be available to pay Yarber Supply's creditors. The Yarber account of $6,215.48 is over 180 days past due. M166.

Mar. 24. Last year, you wrote off the $2,084.65 balance of Innovation Central. The account was over 180 days past due and collection seemed doubtful. Today, you received a $2,084.65 check from Innovation Central along with a letter stating that the company wished to reestablish a credit account with your company. M178 and R555.

Application Problem 6-3

1. Accounts receivable turnover ratio, 11.2.
2. Days' sales in accounts receivable, 33.

Mastery Problem 6-M

1. Accounts credited on general journal: Accounts Receivable, Feb. 2, June 12, and Oct. 17. Allowance for Uncollectible Accounts, Mar. 24, Nov. 3, and Dec. 31.
2. Dec. 31 Adjusting entry debited Uncollectible Accounts Expense, $9,150.85.
3. Accounts receivable turnover ratio, 13.1.

INDEPENDENT PRACTICE

- Assign Mastery Problem 6-M for students as a culminating problem that combines all new learning from the chapter.
- Assign Challenge Problem 6-C to accelerated students who work at a faster pace.
- Assign Study Guide 6.
- Students can access Online Working Papers to work end-of-chapter problems on the computer.
- Direct students to the C21 Accounting companion website for additional practice and review opportunities.

FORMATIVE ASSESSMENT

- Review solutions to the assigned problems in class, diagnosing trouble spots.

RETEACH

- Call on students to describe how they avoid the trouble spots diagnosed.
- Use reteaching suggestions from lesson plans as required.
- Assign Recycling Problem 6-R if needed.

EXTENDED LEARNING

- Assign 21st Century Skills on page 195.
- Assign Analyzing Home Depot's Financial Statements on page 195.

SUMMATIVE EVALUATION

- Chapter 6 Test
- Cognero for Chapter 6

Challenge Problem 6-C

1. Days account balance past due, 1–30: $3,982.40.
2. Uncollectible Accounts Expense, $3,597.81.

June 12. Received a reply to a collection request letter sent to Dennis Raborne. Dennis refuses to pay the remaining $62.00 of his bill, stating that the original bill was larger than the agreed-upon price. Although your records clearly indicate the $62.00 was an appropriate charge, your manager believes that further efforts to collect this account are pointless. M192.

Oct. 17. The U.S. Postal Service was unable to deliver a collection letter to Nancy Givens. Nancy owed $123.54 from an invoice dated January 16. M210.

Nov. 3. Today you received a $1,243.10 check from Yarber Supply. In the enclosed letter, Alex stated that the bankruptcy court ordered the company to pay 20 cents for every dollar owed to its creditors. Thus, the $1,243.10 is the only amount that Yarber Supply would ever be able to pay of its original account balance of $6,215.48. M222 and R621.

Instructions:

1. Journalize the selected transactions above that were completed during the current year. Use page 1 of a general journal and page 1 of a cash receipts journal. Source documents are abbreviated as follows: memorandum, M; receipt, R.
2. Journalize the adjusting entry for uncollectible accounts expense on December 31 of the current year. West River estimates that the amount of uncollectible accounts expense is equal to 1% of its net sales of $915,084.62.
3. Compute the accounts receivable turnover and days' sales in accounts receivable.

Sage 50 Accounting

1. Journalize and post transactions related to allowance for uncollectible accounts to the cash receipts journal.
2. Journalize and post accounts receivable transactions previously written off as uncollectible to the sales journal and cash receipts journal.
3. Print the sales journal and cash receipts journal.

QuickBooks

1. Journalize and post transactions related to allowance for uncollectible accounts to the journal.
2. Journalize and post accounts receivable transactions previously written off in the Create Invoices window and the Receive Payments window.
3. Print the journal and customer balance detail report.

AA ONLINE

1. Go to www.cengage.com/login
2. Click on AA Online to access.
3. Go to the online assignment and follow the instructions.

6-C Challenge Problem: Estimating amount of uncollectible accounts expense; journalizing the adjusting entry LO2

A form and general journal are provided in the *Working Papers*. A complete list of the accounts receivable, as of December 31, of Destin Warehouse follows:

Account	Amount	Invoice Date
Ballard Corporation	$2,383.70	August 11
Colister Company	3,874.80	October 12
Eads & Godfrey	1,260.30	November 19
Garrett, Inc.	2,031.00	September 16
Jeffries Distributors	1,406.50	August 14
McEwen Industries	2,722.10	November 5
Perryman Company	2,047.20	December 3
Ruffin Associates	3,615.20	October 23
Turnage Supply	5,664.80	December 14

Instructions:

1. Age the accounts receivable by determining the age group for each invoice and totaling the invoice amounts in each age group category. Destin Warehouse's credit terms are n/30.
2. Calculate the estimated balance of Allowance for Uncollectible Accounts, using the following percentages: not yet due, 0.5%; 1–30 days past due, 2.0%; 31–60 days, 5.0%; 61–90 days, 30%; and over 90 days, 60%.
3. Journalize the adjusting entry for uncollectible accounts expense on December 31 of the current year. Use page 12 of a general journal. The Allowance for Uncollectible Accounts has a debit balance of $221.68 on December 31 of the current year before adjusting entries are recorded.

COMMON CORE AND INTERDISCIPLINARY STUDIES

Extended learning features and activities present numerous opportunities to implement Common Core Standards through interdisciplinary studies. Practice is provided in the common core areas of English Language Arts & Literacy and Mathematical Practice. Many of these activities require short, critical-thinking and decision-making responses that apply reading, writing, speaking, listening, language, media and technology, and mathematical skills.

21st Century Skills

College Choices beyond Ramen Noodles

Theme: Financial, Economic, Business, and Entrepreneurial Literacy

Skills: Creativity and Innovation, Critical Thinking and Problem Solving, Communication and Collaboration, ICT Literacy

PARTNERSHIP FOR 21ST CENTURY SKILLS

Student loans now exceed credit card debt and total more than $1 trillion. Due to increases in the cost of college, students are relying more heavily on these loans to pay for their education, with the average student debt exceeding $25,000.

Any debt removes the financial freedom that a young person can have when starting a career. The debt can delay the purchase of a car or a home or impact lifestyle decisions, such as marriage or having children. The Department of Education estimates that almost 9% of student loans become uncollectible, damaging an individual's credit report for many years.

Students should consider the return on their investment. For instance, if they attend an expensive school but choose a career that does not have high earning potential, it may take years for them to pay off their debt.

Source: www.nytimes.com/2011/09/13/education/13loans.html.

APPLICATION

1. In addition to tuition and fees, students must budget other costs for attending college.
   a. Using the Internet, research five colleges of your choice to determine the breakdown in costs. Be sure to include at least three other areas of costs in addition to tuition and fees. Prepare a spreadsheet of your findings.
   b. Research the starting salary for a career of your choice. Determine which of the schools you researched would be the best choice. Explain why.
2. List three alternative ways you could pay for college besides student loans.
3. Interview a college graduate who has a student loan. Ask this person how the loan has impacted his or her lifestyle upon graduation and any advice he or she would provide to future students. Prepare a presentation using video, audio, or print, informing other students of the dangers and risks of student loan debt.

Analyzing Home Depot's financial statements

As shown in the financial statements in Appendix B of this textbook, Home Depot's Consolidated Balance Sheets list "Receivables, net" under the heading "Current Assets." This amount represents Home Depot's receivables after the allowance for uncollectible accounts estimate has been deducted. Additional information about these amounts is presented in Note No. 1, "Summary of Significant Accounting Policies."

INSTRUCTIONS

1. Refer to the Consolidated Balance Sheets on page B-5 to identify the net amount of accounts receivable on February 3, 2013, and January 29, 2012.
2. Using Note 1, beginning on page B-10, locate the paragraph titled "Accounts Receivable." Summarize the two types of accounts receivable described in the note.
3. How does the note describe the amount of the allowance for uncollectible accounts as of the end of fiscal 2012 or 2011?

21ST CENTURY SKILLS

Answers

1. Answers will vary for both (a) and (b) based on individual choices.
2. Alternative ways to pay for college might include part-time jobs, scholarships, endowments, grants, co-ops or internships, and employer-reimbursed tuition programs.
3. Presentations should include the negative long-term impact on financial freedom as well as lifestyle choices.

ANALYZING HOME DEPOT'S FINANCIAL STATEMENTS

Answers

1. 2013: $1,395,000,000; 2012: $1,245,000,000.
2. Accounts receivable result from (1) sales to customers using the company's private-label credit card and (2) amounts owed from selected customers resulting from transactions with company subsidiaries.
3. The allowance for uncollectible accounts is not material to the consolidated financial statements.

Chapter 7

Accounting for Plant Assets

Scope & Sequence

	New	Review/Enrich
Introduction		
Introduce the Chapter		
Lesson 7-1: Buying Plant Assets		
Plant Asset Costs	✓	
Buying a Plant Asset for Cash	✓	
Buying a Plant Asset on Account		✓
Allocating the Cost of Plant Assets		✓
International Accounting Standards	✓	
Plant Asset Record		✓
Property Taxes		✓
Lesson 7-2: Calculating and Journalizing Depreciation Expense		
Factors Used to Calculate Depreciation	✓	
Straight-Line Depreciation		✓
Recording Depreciation on Plant Asset Records	✓	
Journalizing Depreciation Expense	✓	
Journalizing Repair and Maintenance Payments	✓	
Lesson 7-3: Disposing of Plant Assets		
Discarding a Plant Asset with No Book Value	✓	
Discarding a Plant Asset with a Book Value	✓	
Selling a Plant Asset	✓	
Trading a Plant Asset	✓	
Selling Land and Buildings	✓	
Lesson 7-4: Other Methods of Depreciation		
Declining-Balance Method of Depreciation		✓
Units-of-Production Method of Depreciation	✓	
Calculating Depreciation Expense for Income Tax Reporting	✓	
Comparison of Depreciation Methods	✓	
Calculating Depletion on Natural Resources	✓	
Closure		

Enhancing Instruction

Features	Common Core Standards
• Accounting in the Real World: Union Pacific	• ELAL—reading, writing
• Ethics in Action: The Land of Opportunity? • Why Accounting?: Accounting for Environmental Costs in Agriculture • Global Awareness: Applying for a Passport	• ELAL—reading, writing • ELAL—reading, writing • ELAL—reading, writing
• Think Like an Accountant: Calculating Depreciation Expense	• Mathematics
• Forensic Accounting: A Pyramid Scheme at Equity Funding	• ELAL—writing, reading
• A Look at Accounting Software • Explore Accounting • 21st Century Skills • Auditing for Errors • Analyzing Home Depot's Financial Statements	• ELAL—reading • ELAL—reading, writing • ELAL—media and technology, listening, writing • Mathematics • Mathematics

ELAL = English Language Arts & Literacy

Calculator: © iStockphoto.com/picstodisc; Paper: © iStockphoto.com/Qingwa

Practice and Assessment

Technology & Media	Teaching Strategies	Guided Practice	Independent Practice	Reteach/Enrich
• Instructor's Resource CD/Website: PowerPoint Slides Accounting Concepts • Online Working Papers • Transparency Masters: Cash Payments Journal (5-column), General Journal	• Tactile/Kinesthetic Learners	• Terms Review • Audit Your Understanding • Work Together 7-1	• On Your Own 7-1 • Application Problem 7-1 • Formative Assessment, p. 203 • Online Working Papers	• Reteach, p. 204
• Instructor's Resource CD/Website: PowerPoint Slides Accounting Concepts • Online Working Papers • Transparency Master: General Journal	• Visual/Spatial Learners	• Terms Review • Audit Your Understanding • Work Together 7-2	• On Your Own 7-2 • Application Problem 7-2 • Formative Assessment, p. 210 • Online Working Papers	• Reteach, p. 210
• Instructor's Resource CD/Website: PowerPoint Slides Accounting Concepts • Online Working Papers • Transparency Masters: General Journal, Cash Receipts Journal (7-column), Cash Payments Journal (5-column)		• Audit Your Understanding • Work Together 7-3	• On Your Own 7-3 • Application Problem 7-3 • Formative Assessment, p. 216 • Online Working Papers	• Reteach, p. 217
• Instructor's Resource CD/Website: PowerPoint Slides Accounting Concepts • Online Working Papers	• Interpersonal Learners	• Terms Review • Audit Your Understanding • Work Together 7-4	• On Your Own 7-4 • Application Problem 7-4 • Formative Assessment, p. 222 • Online Working Papers	• Reteach, p. 223
• Online Working Papers	• Common Core and Interdisciplinary Studies		• Mastery Problem 7-M • Study Guide 7 • Chapter 7 Test • Cognero Chapter 7	• Challenge Problem 7-C • Reteach, p. 230 • Recycling Problem 7-R

Introduce the Chapter

SET THE STAGE

GUIDING QUESTIONS

- Ask students to provide examples of plant assets, around the school or at home, that may lose value over time. Explain these assets.
- Ask students if they have ever heard the term *book value*. Explain its meaning.
- Ask students why some assets depreciate and others don't.
- Ask students to predict why assets might need to be discarded.
- Ask students to brainstorm how property taxes are calculated on plant assets.

PREVIEW CHAPTER OBJECTIVES

- Point out that students were introduced to plant assets and depreciation in the first-year course.
- Point out that this chapter will review the concepts presented in the first-year course and introduce many new concepts related to plant assets.
- Note that this chapter presents several depreciation methods.

PREVIEW ACCOUNTING TERMS

- Read each term aloud to verify its pronunciation for students.
- Point out terms or parts of terms that should already be familiar to most students, such as *plant asset*, *book value*, and *depreciation*.
- Lead an interactive discussion with students to review and explain the terms. Stress that special attention should be directed to all boldfaced and highlighted words presented in the text.

TEACHING IDEA **Provide students with an index card that has a red object on one side and a green object on the other side. Ask students to place their card in front of them as you explain the chapter. When they miss information, need clarification, or don't understand something, they should turn the card to the red shape. This effective visual will help you determine student understanding.**

Chapter 7 Accounting for Plant Assets

LEARNING OBJECTIVES

After studying Chapter 7, in addition to defining key terms, you will be able to:

LO1 Journalize the purchase of plant assets.

LO2 Calculate and record depreciation expense using straight-line depreciation.

LO3 Journalize the disposal of plant assets.

LO4 Calculate depreciation expense using the declining-balance depreciation method.

LO5 Calculate depreciation expense using the units-of-production method.

LO6 Calculate and record depletion of a natural resource.

Calculator: © iStockphoto.com/picstodisc; Paper: © iStockphoto.com/Qingwa

© Tom Grill/Shutterstock.com

196 Chapter 7 Accounting for Plant Assets

Background: © iStockphoto.com/sqrt; Real World: © StonePhotos/Shutterstock.com

Accounting In The Real World

Union Pacific

From Chicago, St. Louis, Memphis, and New Orleans to the Pacific Ocean, the trademark yellow engines of Union Pacific are busy moving the goods that fuel the nation's economy. Union Pacific transports goods in 23 states. The company also connects with railways in Canada and Mexico. The company boasts over 10,000 customers.

Operating a railroad requires a huge investment in rails, engines, and cars. In a recent annual report, Union Pacific reported owning or leasing over 72,000 freight cars and 8,300 locomotives. The company owns or leases over 50,000 miles of track. Its capital investment represents over 89% of Union Pacific's $47 billion in assets. Despite this huge investment, Union Pacific spends billions each year to replace equipment and construct new facilities.

A business must establish accounting policies for assigning the useful life to different types of assets. These useful lives are used to determine annual depreciation expense. Computer equipment, for example, might have a three-year useful life, even though computers often last more than three years. Most companies assign useful lives based on tables provided by the Internal Revenue Service or other reliable sources. In contrast, capital intensive businesses such as Union Pacific expend more effort to reflect the actual useful lives of their assets.

Union Pacific's equipment is built to stand the test of time. The average age of a Union Pacific refrigerated car is over 25 years. The average age of a boxcar is 28 years. Its switching locomotives average 33 years old. For this reason, Union Pacific does not assign arbitrary useful lives to its equipment. Instead, the company regularly conducts studies to determine the actual service lives of its equipment. Management analyzes the results of these studies to adjust the useful lives used to calculate depreciation expense in subsequent years.

CRITICAL THINKING

1. What factors could cause the useful life of a locomotive to increase? decrease?
2. Identify another capital intensive business. Suggest how the business would assign a useful life and what factors could cause the useful life to increase or decrease.

Source: www.up.com/investors/secfiling/index.shtml.

Key Terms

- current assets
- plant asset record
- real property
- personal property
- assessed value
- millage rate
- salvage value
- straight-line method of depreciation
- book value of a plant asset
- half-year convention
- modified half-year convention
- declining-balance method of depreciation
- units-of-production method of depreciation
- Modified Accelerated Cost Recovery System (MACRS)
- depletion

Accounting In The Real World

Answers

1. Increase: lower usage rate, improved maintenance, and improved manufacturing methods.

   Decrease: technological obsolescence, improvements in fuel economy (the company would dispose of old equipment more quickly), and the reverse of all increase factors.

2. Industries include but are not limited to airlines, transportation companies (e.g., FedEx and UPS), cruise lines, oil refineries, and electric power companies. In addition to those items listed in question 1:

   Decrease: style obsolescence (e.g., customers' current expectation of cruise ship amenities), frequency of use over time (e.g., landings per day, which increase wear on an aircraft), and technological obsolescence (e.g., changes in how movies are delivered).

   Increase: the reverse of all increase factors.

LESSON
7-1

BRIDGE

- Ask students to predict what goes into the cost of a plant asset.

TEACHING RESOURCES

- **Instructor's Resource CD/Website:** PowerPoint Slides; Accounting Concepts
- **Working Papers:** Teacher's Edition of the Working Papers for Lesson 7-1; Online Working Papers
- **Transparency Masters:** Cash Payments Journal (5-column); General Journal

ENGAGE

- Every organization, including a school, must monitor and control the purchase, use, and disposition of its plant assets. Ask students to identify the types of plant assets required to operate their school, including the athletic, band, administrative, and maintenance departments. (*Students will quickly find this task overwhelming, demonstrating the need to have adequate records for plant assets.*)

PREVIEW

- Call on students to read the accounting terms and definitions introduced in this lesson: *current assets, plant asset record, real property, personal property, assessed value,* and *millage rate.*
- Point out the learning objective for this lesson.
- Direct students to read the headings in this lesson and to examine the illustrations.

LESSON 7-1 Buying Plant Assets

LO1 Journalize the purchase of plant assets.

Plant Asset Costs LO1

A business owns a variety of assets, all of which are used to help it earn a profit. Cash and other assets expected to be exchanged for cash or consumed within a year are called **current assets**.

Other assets, such as land, buildings, and equipment, are expected to help the business earn a profit for more than one year. Assets that will be used for a number of years in the operation of a business are known as *plant assets*. Plant assets are sometimes referred to as *fixed assets* or *long-term assets*.

Financial statements are prepared with the expectation that a business will remain in operation indefinitely. [CONCEPT: Going Concern] The going concern concept enables a business to record the cost of plant assets on the balance sheet. The cost of plant assets is recognized over many years through the recording of depreciation expense. Without the going concern concept, plant assets would have to be reported at the value for which they could be sold within the fiscal year.

All costs necessary to get the plant asset ready for its intended use are included in the cost of a plant asset. For example, the cost of equipment would include freight and installation. The cost of land would include surveying and realtor fees. Renovation costs to ensure compliance with fire codes and accessibility laws would be included in the cost of a building.

ETHICS IN ACTION

The Land of Opportunity?

As the director of corporate development, Kelly Maben is completing a proposal to locate a resort in Gulf Shores, Alabama. Confident the proposal will be approved, Kelly is considering the purchase of a family-owned restaurant across the street from the proposed building site.

INSTRUCTIONS

Obtain the *Code of Business Conduct and Ethics* of Hyatt Hotels Corporation. Using this information and the ethical model, provide Kelly with guidance on her proposed restaurant purchase. Is Kelly violating her company's code of conduct or simply seizing an opportunity?

© iStockphoto.com/Ldf

ETHICS IN ACTION

The section titled "Corporate Opportunities" contains guidance relevant to this decision. The section states that employees owe a duty to the company to advance its business interests. Business opportunities that employees discover in the function of their position are prohibited. Employees are prohibited from competing with the company. Kelly must inform the company that a competing business near the proposed resort site is available for purchase.

If the company elects not to purchase the restaurant and does not consider it to be a significant competitor, Kelly may be able to purchase it. However, Kelly should first consult with the company's Legal Department.

This activity focuses on business opportunities. However, some students may cite the "Conflicts of Interest" section that states that employees should avoid any private activities that influence their abilities to act in the interests of the company. That is a valid, but secondary, issue related to this activity.

Source: http://investors.hyatt.com.

Buying a Plant Asset for Cash

CASH PAYMENTS JOURNAL — PAGE 5

	DATE		ACCOUNT TITLE	CK. NO.	POST. REF.	1 GENERAL DEBIT	2 GENERAL CREDIT	3 ACCOUNTS PAYABLE DEBIT	4 PURCHASES DISCOUNT CREDIT	5 CASH CREDIT	
14		14	Warehouse Equipment	416		16 850 00				16 850 00	14
15		16	Warehouse Equipment	417		2 800 00				2 800 00	15
16											16

Vaughn Distributors, Inc., purchased an industrial storage system. The system will be used in the warehouse to store a new line of chemicals.

March 14. Paid cash to Metal Fabricators for a storage system, $16,850.00. Check No. 416.

Warehouse Equipment

Debit		Credit	
Mar. 14	16,850.00		
Mar. 16	2,800.00		

Cash

Debit		Credit	
		Mar. 14	16,850.00
		Mar. 16	2,800.00

The storage system requires assembly, including the services of a welder and an electrician. The assembly is required to get the system ready for its intended use. Thus, the cost of the assembly is part of the cost of the storage system.

March 16. Paid cash to Preston Construction to assemble the storage system, $2,800.00. Check No. 417.

Both transactions increase the cost of warehouse equipment, as shown in the T accounts.

© iStockphoto.com/AlekSko

WHY ACCOUNTING?

Accounting for Environmental Costs in Agriculture

Agriculture, Food & Natural Resources

As with any business, a farmer must estimate all costs and revenues when deciding what products to sell. A grain farmer will have different costs than a dairy farmer. If some costs are omitted from the estimate, the farmer's net income will be less than the estimated amount.

The market price for any farm product is the result of a combination of factors, one of which is the cost to produce the product. The ideal market price will cover all costs plus an adequate net income for the farmer.

Current costing methods for farmers do not include any environmental cost. For example, assume that a farmer applies a pesticide to a field, and the runoff from the pesticide flows into a nearby river. If the farmer does nothing to return the river to an undamaged state, the cost of repairing the river is not reflected in the cost of the farmer's products. Instead, the cost is passed on to someone down river, such as a fishery, where the fish die as a result of the chemicals in the river.

Many groups around the world are encouraging all businesses to include environmental costs when calculating the cost of products.

CRITICAL THINKING

List one industry that could impact the environment during the production of its product. List the possible environmental costs due to production.

Source: International Institute for Sustainable Development (www.iisd.org).

INPUT

- Explain the difference between current and plant assets.
- Ask students to predict which financial statement plant assets would be reported.
- Explain the accounting concept Going Concern.
- Describe the relationship between the Going Concern concept and plant assets.
- Remind students that the freight and other costs necessary to get the plant asset ready for use are included as part of the cost.

INPUT

- Explain that students have learned to record the purchase of a plant asset in the first-year course.
- Explain that the asset category is recorded in the Account Title column of the cash payments journal.

MODEL

- Draw two T accounts on the board and label them with the appropriate accounts.
- Read the transaction statements.
- Ask students to analyze the transactions by answering these questions: Which accounts are affected? Are they increased or decreased? Are they debited or credited? Complete the T accounts as the information is provided.
- Use a cash payments journal transparency to illustrate recording the transaction in the cash payments journal or direct students to the illustration at the top of the page.

WHY ACCOUNTING?

Answers

Answers will vary, but should include both the industry and the impact and cost on the environment. One example is drilling for oil in the Gulf of Mexico. The cost on the environment is the cost of an oil spill and its effect on marine life and the industries dependent on it, such as fishing and tourism.

DIFFERENTIATED INSTRUCTION

Tactile/Kinesthetic learners enjoy learning through physical activity and interaction with real objects. Ask students to take a walk around the school or a local business and list at least ten plant assets they observe.

INPUT

- Ask students to identify why the purchase of this office equipment is recorded in a general journal rather than a cash payments journal. (*The asset is purchased on account; therefore, no cash was paid.*)
- Remind students that office equipment that is purchased for resale to customers is recorded as merchandise rather than a plant asset.

MODEL

- Draw three T accounts on the board.
- Read the transaction statement.
- Ask students to analyze the transaction by answering these questions: Which accounts are affected? Are they increased or decreased? Are they debited or credited? Complete the T accounts as the information is provided.
- Use a general journal transparency to illustrate recording the transaction in the general journal or direct students to the illustration at the top of the page.

GLOBAL AWARENESS

Answers

Answers will vary.

Buying a Plant Asset on Account

GENERAL JOURNAL PAGE 3

	DATE		ACCOUNT TITLE	DOC. NO.	POST. REF.	DEBIT	CREDIT	
4		6	*Office Equipment*	*M23*		690 00		4
5			*Accounts Payable/Tech Systems*				690 00	5
6								6

Not all plant assets are bought for cash. Vaughn Distributors sometimes buys a plant asset on one date and pays for it on a later date.

March 6. Bought on account new monitors for three office computers from Tech Systems, $690.00. Memorandum No. 23.

This transaction does not involve the purchase of merchandise. Therefore, the entry is not recorded in a purchases journal. It is recorded in the general journal as shown above. The entry is posted to both the general ledger and the accounts payable ledger.

GENERAL LEDGER

Office Equipment

↑ 690.00	

Accounts Payable

	↑ 690.00

ACCOUNTS PAYABLE LEDGER

Tech Systems

	↑ 690.00

GLOBAL AWARENESS

Applying for a Passport

International travel usually requires a passport. A passport is a formal document that allows exit from and reentry into a country. It proves citizenship and provides identity for the traveler.

In the United States, first-time passport applicants over the age of 16 must present the following items:

1. Completed application form, which can be obtained online.
2. Proof of U.S. citizenship such as a certified birth certificate or a naturalization certificate.
3. Proof of identity, such as a driver's license or government ID.
4. A photocopy of the identification document.
5. A passport photo that meets specific criteria. Many local photo studios and photo centers offer passport photo services.
6. Fee ($110 plus an execution fee of $25, when this textbook was written).

Those items must be presented in person at an Acceptance Facility or Passport Agency. The locations of these offices and further information may be found at the U.S. Department of State, Bureau of Consular Affairs website: http://travel.state.gov/passport.

CRITICAL THINKING

Complete the following information that will be transferable to a passport application:

NAME: first, middle, and last name
DATE OF BIRTH: month, day, year
PLACE OF BIRTH: city, state, country
MAILING ADDRESS: street, city, state, country
CONTACT INFORMATION: e-mail, phone number
FAMILY: father's name, birth date, birthplace, U.S. citizen (yes or no), mother's name, birth date, birthplace, U.S. citizen (yes or no)
PERSONAL INFORMATION: height, color of hair, color of eyes

© iStockphoto.com/Lusky

Allocating the Cost of Plant Assets

GENERAL JOURNAL — PAGE 3

	DATE		ACCOUNT TITLE	DOC. NO.	POST. REF.	DEBIT	CREDIT	
16		12	*Land*	*M26*		*56 000 00*		16
17			*Building*			*224 000 00*		17
18			*Notes Payable*				*280 000 00*	18
19								19

Plants assets can be purchased as a group. Vaughn agreed to purchase a distribution center from NexTra Industries for $280,000.00. The purchase includes the land and building. NexTra is financing the purchase, allowing Vaughn to pay for the distribution center over 10 years.

March 12. Purchased a distribution center from NexTra Industries, signing a 10-year note. Memorandum No. 26.

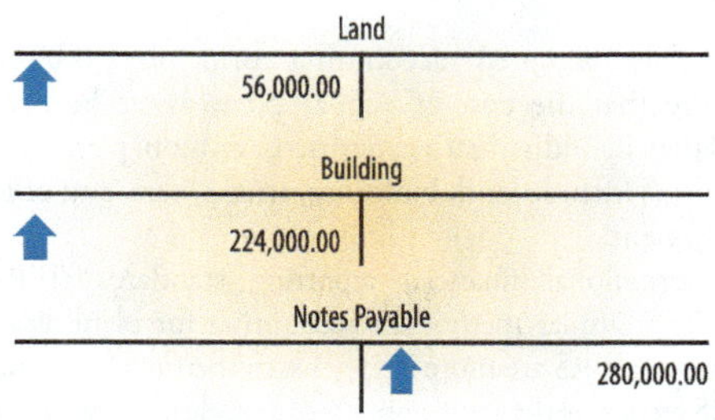

To help assign a cost to each plant asset, Vaughn hired an appraiser to assign market values to each item. The appraiser assigned a value of $60,000.00 to the land and $240,000.00 to the building. Thus, the total appraised value of the distribution center is $300,000.00. The appraised values are used to allocate the $280,000.00 cost to the land and building, as shown below.

	Appraised Value	Percentage of Total Appraised Value	Assigned Cost
Land	$ 60,000.00	20%	$ 56,000.00
Building	240,000.00	80%	224,000.00
Total	$300,000.00		$280,000.00

The land's appraised value is 20% of the total appraised value of $300,000.00. Thus, land is assigned 20% of the actual purchase price of the distribution center, as shown below.

Appraised Value	÷	Total Appraised Value	=	Percentage of Total Appraised Value
$60,000.00	÷	$300,000.00	=	20%

Percentage of Total Appraised Value	×	Total Purchase Price	=	Cost Allocated to Land
20%	×	$280,000.00	=	$56,000.00

INPUT

- Explain that a building and the land on which it is located are typically purchased for a single price. Separate values must be assigned to each asset. If a sales contract does not specify separate amounts for the land and building, a professional appraiser may be needed to determine the separate amounts.
- Point out that the appraiser assigned market values to each item.
- Explain the calculations at the bottom of the page.

MODEL

- Draw three T accounts on the board.
- Read the transaction statement.
- Ask students to analyze the transaction by answering these questions: Which accounts are affected? Are they increased or decreased? Are they debited or credited? Complete the T accounts as the information is provided.
- Use a general journal transparency to illustrate recording the transaction in the general journal or direct students to the illustration at the top of the page.

INPUT

- Explain that GAAP principles require that the cost of similar plant assets be accumulated in individual accounts.
- International financial reporting standards (IFRS) recognize that components of an individual plant asset may be used by the business for different periods of time. Therefore, each significant part of a plant asset is assigned a cost and is recorded in different plant asset accounts.
- Point out the individual components for the truck as shown in the illustration (frame, transmission, and tires). Explain that the business recognizes that the transmission and tires will need to be replaced in the period of time designated.
- Direct students to the calculations toward the bottom of the page to determine the costs assigned to each asset.

MODEL

- Use a cash payments journal transparency to illustrate recording the transaction in the cash payments journal or direct students to the illustration at the top of the page.

International Accounting Standards

CASH PAYMENTS JOURNAL PAGE 6

	DATE		ACCOUNT TITLE	CK. NO.	POST. REF.	GENERAL DEBIT (1)	GENERAL CREDIT (2)	ACCOUNTS PAYABLE DEBIT (3)	PURCHASES DISCOUNT CREDIT (4)	CASH CREDIT (5)	
17		7	*Truck—Frame*	523		23 100 00				30 000 00	17
18			*Truck—Transmission*			4 500 00					18
19			*Truck—Tires*			2 400 00					19
20											20
21											21

Generally accepted accounting principles (GAAP) require that the cost of similar plant assets be accumulated in individual accounts. Common plant asset accounts include land, buildings, trucks, cars, and office equipment.

International financial reporting standards (IFRS) require a similar method of accounting for plant assets. However, IFRS are more aggressive in their requirements. IFRS recognize that components of a single plant asset may be used by the business for different periods of time. Thus, each significant component of a plant asset is assigned a cost and recorded in different plant asset accounts.

Bethune Company purchased a delivery truck for $30,000.00. Using generally accepted accounting principles, Bethune would record the entire $30,000.00 purchase price in its Trucks plant asset account. However, Bethune prepares its financial statements using IFRS. The business recognizes that the transmission will have to be replaced after four years. In addition, the tires will only last for two years. Thus, Bethune records the truck in three plant asset accounts.

June 7. Bethune Company pays cash for a $30,000.00 delivery truck. Check No. 523.

The cost of the delivery truck is assigned in the same manner as Vaughn Distributors assigned the costs of its distribution center. An estimate of each component of the truck is used to allocate the total cost, as shown below.

	Appraised Value	Percentage of Total Appraised Value	Assigned Cost
Frame	$24,640.00	77%	$23,100.00
Transmission	4,800.00	15%	4,500.00
Tires	2,560.00	8%	2,400.00
Total	$32,000.00		$30,000.00

A set of replacement tires currently costs $2,560.00. This cost represents 8% of the total estimated value of the truck ($2,560.00 ÷ $32,000.00 = 8%). The tires are assigned 8% of the actual cost of the truck, $2,400.00 (8% × $30,000.00).

fyi It is not uncommon for the purchase price of a group of assets to be less than would be required to purchase the items individually.

© Iakov Filimonov/Shutterstock.com

Plant Asset Record

PLANT ASSET RECORD No. *215* General Ledger Account No. *1230*

Description *Copy machine* General Ledger Account *Office Equipment*

Date Bought *August 2, 20--* Serial Number *642-34632-63C* Original Cost *$1,400.00*

Estimated Useful Life *5 years* Estimated Salvage Value *$200.00* Depreciation Method *Straight-line*

Completed When Asset Is Purchased

Disposed of: Discarded ______ Sold ______ Traded ______

Date ______ Disposal Amount ______

Completed When Asset Is Disposed of

Year	Annual Depreciation Expense	Accumulated Depreciation	Ending Book Value

Completed Each Year to Record Depreciation

A business keeps a separate record of each plant asset it owns. An accounting form on which a business records information about each plant asset is called a **plant asset record**. Vaughn Distributors uses a printed card as its plant asset record as shown above.

Vaughn Distributors' plant asset record has three sections. Section 1 is prepared when the company buys a plant asset. Information in this section shows a description of the item, the general ledger account title and number, date bought, serial number, and information needed to calculate annual depreciation expense for the plant asset. Section 2 provides space for recording the disposition of the plant asset. Section 3 provides space for recording annual depreciation expense.

Calculating depreciation and disposing of plant assets are described later in this chapter.

Property Taxes

In most states, businesses have to pay taxes on plant assets. For tax purposes, state and federal governments define two kinds of property. Land and anything attached to it is called **real property**. Real property is sometimes referred to as *real estate*. All property not classified as real property is called **personal property**.

The value of an asset determined by tax authorities for the purpose of calculating taxes is called the **assessed value**. Assessed value is usually based on the judgment of persons referred to as assessors. Assessors are elected by citizens or are specially trained employees of a governmental unit.

The assessed value is assigned to an asset for tax purposes only. Often, the assessed value is only a part of the true value of the asset. Most governmental units with taxing power have a tax based on the value of real property. The tax rate used to calculate property taxes is called a **millage rate**. Some governmental units also tax personal property such as cars, boats, trailers, and airplanes. The millage rate is multiplied by an asset's assessed value to determine the property tax.

Payment of property taxes is necessary if a firm is to continue in business. Therefore, Vaughn Distributors classifies property tax as an operating expense. The transaction is journalized using the same steps as other operating expenses.

INPUT

- Point out that a plant asset record contains information in three distinct sections, as shown in the illustration.
- Ask students to describe the purpose of the three sections of a plant asset record.

INPUT

- Explain that property tax laws vary significantly from state to state. Local governments typically assess property taxes on real or personal property or on both.
- Ask students to identify the information needed to calculate property taxes.
- Point out that the assessed value is used to determine property taxes and may not be an appropriate value for making other business decisions.
- Explain how property taxes are calculated using the millage rate and the assessed value.

FORMATIVE ASSESSMENT

- This is an ongoing process. Circulate around the classroom or lab, observing which students have problems with the assignments.
- Troubleshooting: Students may have difficulty understanding why the assessed value, rather than the cost of plant assets, is used to compute property taxes.
- Assess student understanding by checking solutions to Independent Practice assignments and noting their answers to the Terms Review and Audit Your Understanding questions.

CHECK FOR UNDERSTANDING

Terms Review

- Call on students to define each term in the Terms Review. Definitions are given in the Glossary.

Audit Your Understanding

- Call on students to answer the Audit Your Understanding questions. Answers are given in Appendix D of the textbook.

GUIDED PRACTICE

Work Together

- Have students write the solution to the Work Together problem as you guide the class through the examples.
- Direct students to record each transaction on the plant asset record as you elicit class participation in analyzing and recording each transaction.
- Call on students to describe how to record the purchase of each plant asset on a plant asset record.
- Remind students to save their work to complete Work Together 7-2.

INDEPENDENT PRACTICE

On Your Own

- Assign the On Your Own problem to be worked independently.
- Remind students to save their work to complete On Your Own 7-2.

Application Problem

- Assign Application Problem 7-1.
- Instruct students to save their work to complete Application Problem 7-2.

Online Working Papers

- Students can access the Lesson 7-1 problems using this software.

RETEACH

- Call on students to identify the transactions for purchasing plant assets for cash and on account.
- Call on students to list the three sections of a plant asset record.
- Ask students to describe how property taxes are calculated and journalized.

CLOSURE

- Ask students to summarize briefly the procedures for journalizing transactions to record the buying of plant assets.

End of Lesson Review

LO1 Journalize the purchase of plant assets.

Terms Review

current assets

plant asset record

real property

personal property

assessed value

millage rate

Audit your understanding

1. What costs are included in the cost of a plant asset?
2. How is the cost assigned to plant assets purchased as a group?
3. How is the purchase of plant assets accounted for using IFRS?
4. What are the three sections of a plant asset record?
5. How is the amount of property tax determined?

Work together 7-1

Journalizing asset purchase transactions

Kellgren Corporation depreciates all plant assets using the straight-line method. Plant asset records, a general journal, and a cash payments journal are provided in the *Working Papers*. Source documents are abbreviated as: check, C; memorandum, M. Your instructor will guide you through the following examples.

Transactions:

Jan. 3. Paid cash for printer (plant asset no. 321), $840.00: no estimated salvage value; estimated useful life, three years; serial no. BO634BRE. C610.

Apr. 5. Bought a conveyor table (plant asset no. 326) on account from Packing Systems, $1,800.00: estimated salvage value, $200.00; estimated useful life, five years; serial no. HE26-3464. M67.

Oct. 8. Purchased a warehouse for $300,000.00. The building was appraised for $240,000.00 and the land for $80,000.00. The building has a useful life of 25 years and an estimated salvage value of $25,000.00; plant assets no. 341 and 342. C920.

1. Journalize the transactions completed during 20X1. General ledger accounts are: Land, 1210; Building, 1220; Office Equipment, 1230; and Warehouse Equipment, 1240.
2. Complete section 1 of a plant asset record for new asset purchases. Save your work to complete Work Together 7-2.

On your own 7-1

Journalizing asset purchase transactions

Hairston Stores depreciates all plant assets using the straight-line method. Depreciate all plant assets using the straight-line method. Plant asset records, a general journal, and a cash payments journal are provided in the *Working Papers*. Source documents are abbreviated as: check, C; memorandum, M. Work independently to complete the following problem.

Transactions:

Jan. 7. Bought a tablet computer (plant asset no. 403) on account from Computer Source, $650.00: no salvage value; estimated useful life, five years; serial no. 26-BT-327. M43.

July 12. Paid cash for a point-of-sale system (plant asset no. 410), $2,500.00: estimated salvage value, $500.00; estimated useful life, five years; serial no. 62-838C. C743.

Sept. 28. Purchased a store building for $200,000.00. The building was appraised for $132,000.00 and the land for $88,000.00. The building has a useful life of 25 years and an estimated salvage value of $20,000.00; plant assets no. 448 and 449. C993.

1. Journalize the transactions completed during 20X1. General ledger accounts are: Land, 1210; Building, 1220; Office Equipment, 1230; and Store Equipment, 1240.
2. Complete section 1 of a plant asset record for new asset purchases. Save your work to complete On Your Own 7-2.

Essential Questions

- Would it ever be advantageous to pay property tax on the cost rather than assessed value? Explain. (*Seldom would it be advantageous, as the assessed value is almost always less than the cost. Therefore, the taxes would be less when calculated on assessed value rather than cost.*)
- Think of a small business you would like to start if given the opportunity. List three plant assets you would need in your business. (*Answers might include buildings, land, furniture, equipment, and machinery pertaining to the type of business.*)

EXTENDED LEARNING

- Assign Accounting in the Real World on page 197.
- Assign Ethics in Action on page 198.
- Assign Why Accounting on page 199.
- Assign Global Awareness on page 200.

LESSON

7-2 Calculating and Journalizing Depreciation Expense

LO2 Calculate and record depreciation expense using straight-line depreciation.

Factors Used to Calculate Depreciation LO2

Plant assets may wear out, may no longer be needed in the operation of a business, or may become outdated by new models. To match revenue with the expenses incurred to earn it, the cost of a plant asset should be allocated to an expense account over the useful life of the plant asset. [CONCEPT: Matching Expenses with Revenue] As explained in Chapter 4, the portion of a plant asset's cost that is transferred to an expense account in each fiscal period during a plant asset's useful life is called *depreciation expense.*

Because of its permanent nature, land is not subject to depreciation. Increases or decreases in land value are usually recorded only when land is sold or otherwise disposed of.

Three factors are used to calculate a plant asset's annual depreciation expense:

1. Original cost.
2. Estimated salvage value.
3. Estimated useful life.

ORIGINAL COST

The original cost of a plant asset includes all costs paid to make the asset usable to a business. These costs include the purchase price, delivery costs, and any necessary installation costs. [CONCEPT: Historical Cost]

ESTIMATED SALVAGE VALUE

When a plant asset is disposed of, some part of its original value may remain. When a plant asset is bought, its final value can only be estimated. The estimated **salvage value** is the amount that will be received for an asset at the time of its disposal. Salvage value is also referred to as *residual value, scrap value,* or *trade-in value.*

Until a plant asset is disposed of, most businesses have difficulty determining its exact salvage value. Thus, until actually disposed of, a plant asset's salvage value can only be estimated. Because salvage value is used to calculate a plant asset's annual depreciation, the most accurate estimate possible is made when a plant asset is bought.

ESTIMATED USEFUL LIFE

The estimated useful life of a plant asset is the number of years it is expected to be useful to a business. A plant asset's useful life differs from one situation to another. Most businesses use past experience as the basis for estimating a plant asset's useful life. If a calculator usually lasts five years for a specific business, then the business uses five years as the estimated useful life of a new calculator. Sometimes, however, a business has difficulty estimating a plant asset's useful life. In these cases, it may use the Internal Revenue Service's guidelines that give the estimated useful life for many plant assets. [CONCEPT: Neutrality]

DEPRECIATION METHODS

Various depreciation methods are illustrated in this chapter. A business should select the depreciation method that provides the best financial information. A business typically uses the same depreciation method for all assets within a plant asset category.

© mast3r/Shutterstock.com

LESSON

7-2

BRIDGE

- Remind students that they have previously learned two depreciation methods in the first-year course (straight-line and double declining-balance).

TEACHING RESOURCES

- **Instructor's Resource CD/Website:**
  PowerPoint Slides
  Accounting Concepts
- **Working Papers:**
  Teacher's Edition of the Working Papers for Lesson 7-2
  Online Working Papers
- **Transparency Master:**
  General Journal

ENGAGE

- Plant assets represent a significant investment for most businesses. Therefore, the methods and estimates used to expense this investment over time have a significant impact on the financial statements.

PREVIEW

- Call on students to read the accounting terms and definitions introduced in this lesson: *salvage value, straight-line method of depreciation, book value of a plant asset, half-year convention,* and *modified half-year convention.*
- Point out the learning objective for this lesson.
- Direct students to read the headings in this lesson and to examine the illustrations.

INPUT

- Remind students that depreciation is an estimate that attempts to match the cost of plant assets with the revenue earned using those plant assets.
- Ask students to identify and define the three factors used to calculate depreciation.
- Remind students that three of the factors are estimates.

INPUT

- Ask students to identify how the estimated total depreciation expense is calculated.
- Point out that the straight-line method results in an equal amount of depreciation each year.
- Point out that the book value of a plant asset is the cost of the asset less accumulated depreciation.

MODEL

Calculate annual depreciation

- Ask students to use a calculator to compute the annual depreciation expense in the illustration.
- Ask students to prepare a table, assuming that the estimated salvage value is $500, and describe the impact of this change.

Calculate the book value

- Ask students to use a calculator to compute the ending book value for any of the five years.
- Ask students to identify the amounts that would appear on the balance sheet (original cost, accumulated depreciation, and book value).

Straight-Line Depreciation

Original Cost: $4,000.00
Estimated Salvage Value: $1,000.00
Estimated Useful Life: 5 years

Year	Beginning Book Value	Annual Depreciation	Ending Book Value
1	$4,000.00	$ 600.00	$3,400.00
2	3,400.00	600.00	2,800.00
3	2,800.00	600.00	2,200.00
4	2,200.00	600.00	1,600.00
5	1,600.00	600.00	1,000.00
Total Depreciation		$3,000.00	

Recording an equal amount of depreciation expense for a plant asset in each year of its useful life is called the **straight-line method of depreciation**.

On January 2, 20X1, Vaughn Distributors bought a computer for $4,000.00 with an estimated salvage value of $1,000.00 and an estimated useful life of five years. The details of the purchase and the depreciation amounts for each year of the asset's estimated useful life are shown above.

The estimated total depreciation expense is divided by the estimated useful life to compute the annual depreciation expense. The annual depreciation expense is the same for each year if the asset is used for the entire year.

Original cost		$4,000.00
Estimated salvage value	−	1,000.00
Estimated total depreciation expense	=	$3,000.00
Years of estimated useful life	÷	5
Annual depreciation expense	=	$ 600.00

The original cost of a plant asset minus accumulated depreciation is called the **book value of a plant asset**. An alternate method for calculating the book value is to subtract the annual depreciation expense from the beginning book value. The beginning book value for a year is the ending book value of the prior year.

Beginning Book Value	−	Annual Depreciation	=	Ending Book Value
$2,800.00	−	$600.00	=	$2,200.00

Annual depreciation expense can also be calculated using an annual percentage rate. In the preceding example, the plant asset has an estimated useful life of five years. Therefore, the annual depreciation rate is 20% (100% divided by 5 equals 0.20, or 20%). Estimated total depreciation expense, $3,000.00, times the depreciation rate, 20%, equals the annual depreciation expense, $600.00.

remember

Two of the three values used to compute depreciation are estimates.

CALCULATING DEPRECIATION EXPENSE FOR PART OF A YEAR

Annual depreciation expense		$240.00
Months in a year	÷	12
Monthly depreciation expense	=	$ 20.00
Number of months asset is used	×	5
Partial year's depreciation expense	=	$100.00

A calendar month is the smallest unit of time typically used to calculate depreciation. A plant asset may be placed in service at a date other than the first day of a fiscal period. In such cases, depreciation expense can be calculated to the nearest first of a month. To calculate depreciation expense for part of a year, the annual depreciation expense is divided by 12 to determine depreciation expense for a month. The monthly depreciation is then multiplied by the number of months the plant asset was used that year.

Vaughn Distributors bought a copy machine on August 2, 20X1. The annual straight-line depreciation expense is $240.00. The depreciation expense for the part of the year that Vaughn Distributors used the copy machine (August through December equals 5 months) is $100.00.

ALTERNATE METHODS FOR PARTIAL-YEAR DEPRECIATION

Other methods of recording a partial year's depreciation are accepted. A method that recognizes one half of a year's depreciation in the year of acquisition is called the **half-year convention**. Regardless of when the plant asset is purchased, one half of the annual depreciation is recorded in the first year. Using the half-year convention, Vaughn would record $120.00 ($240.00 annual depreciation expense ÷ 2) for the copy machine in 20X1.

A method that recognizes a full year's depreciation if the asset is acquired in the first half of the year is called the **modified half-year convention**. If the asset is acquired in the second half of the year, no depreciation is recorded in the first year. Using the modified half-year convention, Vaughn would not record any depreciation for the copy machine in 20X1.

Whatever method a business selects, it should be used consistently from year to year. [CONCEPT: Consistent Reporting] Changing methods could result in material changes in depreciation expense that would not allow the financial statements to be comparable.

THINK LIKE AN ACCOUNTANT

Calculating Depreciation Expense

Auditors must perform their audits in accordance with standards set by the profession and by government agencies. The auditor's report states:

> Those standards require that we plan and perform the audit to obtain reasonable assurance about whether the financial statements are free of material misstatement. An audit includes examining, on a test basis, evidence supporting the amounts and disclosures in the financial statements.

Recalculation is one method of examining evidence. In the area of plant assets, an auditor should recalculate the client's depreciation expense.

Assume that you are preparing to join an audit team, and you will be responsible for testing plant assets. Create a straight-line depreciation schedule, assuming that the client has two classes of plant assets. For one class, first-year depreciation is calculated to the nearest month. For the other class, the half-year convention is used.

OPEN THE SPREADSHEET TLA_CH07

The worksheet contains an incomplete depreciation schedule. Follow the steps on the Instructions tab and answer the questions:

1. Complete the depreciation schedule for a $36,400.00 car purchased on April 14 of the current year. The car is assigned a five-year useful life and is estimated to have a $4,000.00 salvage value. Calculate depreciation to the nearest month. What is the amount of depreciation in the first year?
2. Modify the depreciation of the car in question 1 to use the half-year convention. What is the amount of depreciation in the first year?
3. Prepare an e-mail to be sent to your colleagues, promoting the use of assigning names to certain cells in a worksheet.

© iStockphoto.com/Dan Bachman

INPUT

- Point out that sometimes a plant asset is put into service on a date other than the first day of the fiscal period; therefore, depreciation expense must be calculated for a part of the year.
- Point out that calculating depreciation expense for a partial year is also used when a plant asset is discarded or sold during a fiscal year.
- Explain that the half-year convention and the modified half-year convention are alternatives to recording depreciation for a partial year.

MODEL

- Ask students to identify how many months of depreciation would be calculated for a plant asset purchased on March 4 *(10)*, June 26 *(6)*, and December 22 *(0)*.

THINK LIKE AN ACCOUNTANT

This activity requires students to complete a depreciation schedule that shows the use of two of the conventions presented in the chapter. By clicking a box, students will see that the schedule modifies the annual depreciation amounts based on the selected convention.

The formulas required to complete this schedule are relatively complex. IF functions and logical formulas are required to make many decisions that affect annual depreciation amounts. To help reduce the complexity, students learn how to assign a meaningful name to a cell. That name can be used in a formula instead of the typical cell reference. Thus, the function in cell L13 appears as =Annual_ Depreciation/2.

Students are instructed to calculate the annual depreciation for Years 2–8. A MIN (minimum) function calculates the lesser of the annual depreciation or the remaining amount to be depreciated.

Selected formulas for the completed worksheet follow:

K7: =Day<=15

I13: =IF(First_Half_Month,(12-Month+1)/12*Annual_Depreciation,(12-Month)/12*Annual_Depreciation)

I14: =MIN(Annual_Depreciation,Total_ Depreciation-J13)

L13: =Annual_Depreciation/2

L14: =MIN(Annual_Depreciation,Total_ Depreciation-M13)

E13: =IF(Half_Year_Convention,L13,I13)

E14: =IF(Half_Year_Convention,L14,I14)

Answers

1. $4,830.00.
2. $3,220.00.
3. Answers will vary. A sample solution follows.

"I've just discovered an Excel tool that was extremely helpful in creating some complex formulas. The Define Name tool lets you assign a meaningful name to a cell. While creating a depreciation schedule, I assigned the name Annual_Depreciation to cell D9 containing that amount. Then, instead of using cell D9 in a formula, I used Annual_ Depreciation. This tool allows you to read a formula in English rather than tracing the cell references to understand what's used in the formula."

INPUT

- Ask students to identify the two places where annual depreciation expense is recorded.
- Explain that the depreciation amounts recorded on the plant asset record are useful if the asset is sold or disposed of before the end of its useful life.
- Ask students how to determine the accuracy of the annual depreciation expense and book value calculations. (*The book value at the end of the useful life will equal the estimated salvage value.*)

MODEL

- Ask students to use a calculator to compute the accumulated depreciation for any year as illustrated.

Recording Depreciation on Plant Asset Records

PLANT ASSET RECORD No. *215*		General Ledger Account No. *1230*
Description *Copy machine*		General Ledger Account *Office Equipment*
Date Bought *August 2, 20--*	Serial Number *642-34632-63C*	Original Cost *$1,400.00*
Estimated Useful Life *5 years*	Estimated Salvage Value *$200.00*	Depreciation Method *Straight-line*
Disposed of:	Discarded ______ Sold ______	Traded ______
Date ______		Disposal Amount ______

Year	Annual Depreciation Expense	Accumulated Depreciation	Ending Book Value
20X1	*$100.00*	*$ 100.00*	*$1,300.00*
20X2	*240.00*	*340.00*	*1,060.00*
20X3	*240.00*	*580.00*	*820.00*
20X4	*240.00*	*820.00*	*580.00*
20X5	*240.00*	*1,060.00*	*340.00*
20X6	*140.00*	*1,200.00*	*200.00*

Depreciation Expense — Accumulated Depreciation — Book Value

Vaughn Distributors records annual depreciation expense in two places for each plant asset:

1. On the plant asset record.
2. As part of the adjusting entries that are posted to general ledger accounts.

On December 31, Vaughn Distributors recorded the annual depreciation expense on each plant asset record. The plant asset record for a copy machine used as office equipment is shown above.

In section 3 of the plant asset record, the year is recorded in the Year column. The depreciation expense for the plant asset is recorded in the Annual Depreciation Expense column. The amount recorded in the Annual Depreciation Expense column is $100.00, the depreciation expense for the months that the copy machine was used in 20X1. For a full year, the annual depreciation expense is $240.00. The amount of accumulated depreciation is recorded in the Accumulated Depreciation column. The accumulated depreciation is the sum of the previous year's accumulated depreciation and the annual depreciation expense for the current year. A new book value is calculated and recorded in the Ending Book Value column.

20X3 Depreciation Expense	+	20X2 Accumulated Depreciation	=	20X3 Accumulated Depreciation
$240.00	+	$340.00	=	$580.00

20X3 Beginning Book Value	–	20X3 Annual Depreciation	=	20X3 Ending Book Value
$1,060.00	–	$240.00	=	$820.00

At the end of the estimated useful life, the copy machine should be depreciated down to its estimated salvage value. At the end of the sixth year, the ending book value is equal to the estimated salvage value, $200.00.

The calculation for depreciation uses an estimated useful life. The copy machine's actual useful life may exceed the estimate made when the asset was put into use. If a plant asset is used longer than the estimated useful life, depreciation is not recorded once the book value equals the estimated salvage value.

DIFFERENTIATED INSTRUCTION

Visual/Spatial learners enjoy learning through drawing and physical imagery. Allow students to create a poster-size illustration of a plant asset record with depreciation recorded.

Journalizing Depreciation Expense

GENERAL JOURNAL — PAGE 16

	DATE		ACCOUNT TITLE	DOC. NO.	POST. REF.	DEBIT	CREDIT	
1			*Adjusting Entries*					1
22		31	*Depreciation Expense—Office Equipment*			12 080 00		22
23			*Accumulated Depreciation—Office Equipment*				12 080 00	23
24								24

After depreciation expense is recorded on the plant asset records, depreciation amounts for the year are totaled.

An adjusting entry is made to record the total depreciation expense for the fiscal year for each category of plant assets. Vaughn Distributors records separate adjusting entries for office equipment, store equipment, warehouse equipment, and building. The adjusting entry for office equipment is shown above.

Depreciation Expense—Office Equipment	
12,080.00	

Accumulated Depreciation—Office Equipment	
	36,140.00
	12,080.00
	(New Bal. 48,220.00)

Journalizing Repair and Maintenance Payments

When a long-term asset is purchased, it is recorded at its historical cost, the actual amount paid for the asset. There are some circumstances when that historical cost could change over the life of the asset.

After an asset is put into service, expenditures might be required to maintain, repair, or replace a part of the asset. The accountant will have to decide if the payment qualifies as a repair or an improvement. The decision determines the accounts affected by the transaction.

If the expenditure merely maintains the asset in its normal operation, it should be treated as an expense in the period the payment is made. This category would include painting the inside or outside of a building, minor repairs on a delivery truck, regular maintenance on a piece of factory equipment, repairing gutters, and engine tune-ups. These costs typically bring the asset back to its original condition. Therefore, the entry to record the payment of $500.00 for an engine tune-up would include a debit to Repair Expense.

If the expenditure adds to the value or extends the useful life of the asset, it must be added to the cost of the asset instead of treated as an immediate expense. This category would include adding a wing to a building, replacing the engine in a vehicle, and redoing the ventilation system of a building to include a state-of-the art air purification system. Therefore, the entry to record the payment of $10,000.00 to add an air purification system would include a debit to Building. By increasing the cost of the asset, the amount of depreciation to be recorded during the remaining useful life of the asset will also change.

remember The accounts used to record depreciation expense are the same regardless of the depreciation method used.

INPUT

- Point out that depreciation is journalized in the general journal. An optional work sheet may be used to record depreciation prior to journalizing, if preferred.
- Remind students that accumulated depreciation is a contra account for the related plant asset account.

MODEL

Analyze the transaction

- Draw two T accounts on the board.
- Read the transaction statement.
- Ask students to analyze the transaction. Complete the T accounts as the information is provided.

Record the transaction

- Use a general journal transparency to record the transaction in the general journal or direct students to the illustration.

FORMATIVE ASSESSMENT

- This is an ongoing process. Circulate around the classroom or lab, observing which students have problems with the assignments.
- Troubleshooting: Diagnose the kinds of problems students have with this lesson. The concepts and procedures in this section are relatively simple and are a review of the first-year course. Thus, students' mistakes will most likely result from simple mathematical errors. Encourage students to check their work.
- Assess student understanding by checking solutions to Independent Practice assignments and observing their answers to the Terms Review and Audit Your Understanding questions.

CHECK FOR UNDERSTANDING

Terms Review

- Call on students to define each term in the Terms Review.

Audit Your Understanding

- Call on students to answer the Audit Your Understanding questions. Answers are given in Appendix D of the textbook.

GUIDED PRACTICE

Work Together

- Have students write the solution to the Work Together problem as you guide the class through the examples.
- Instruct students to use the plant asset records from Work Together 7-1.
- Call on students to describe the calculation of the annual depreciation expense.
- Call on students to describe the calculation of the depreciation expense, accumulated depreciation, and book value for each year.
- Direct students to record each transaction in the general journal as you elicit class participation in analyzing and recording the transactions.
- Remind students to save their work to complete Work Together 7-3.

INDEPENDENT PRACTICE

On Your Own

- Remind students to use the plant asset records from On Your Own 7-1.
- Assign the On Your Own problem to be worked independently.
- Instruct students to save their work to complete On Your Own 7-3.

Application Problem

- Remind students to use the plant asset records from Problem 7-1.
- Assign Application Problem 7-2.
- Instruct students to save their work to complete Problem 7-3.

Online Working Papers

- Students can access the Lesson 7-2 problems using this software.

RETEACH

- Ask students to summarize the calculations of depreciation expense using the straight-line method.
- Ask students to summarize how to calculate depreciation expense for a partial year.

End of Lesson Review

LO2 Calculate and record depreciation expense using straight-line depreciation.

Terms Review

salvage value

straight-line method of depreciation

book value of a plant asset

half-year convention

modified half-year convention

Audit your understanding

1. Which accounting concept is being applied when depreciation expense is recorded for plant assets?
2. Why is annual depreciation for land not recorded?
3. What three factors are used to calculate a plant asset's annual depreciation expense?
4. Should the installation of an elevator in a retail store be accounted for as a repair or an addition to the historical cost of the building?
5. What is the smallest unit of time used to calculate depreciation?

Work together 7-2

Calculating and journalizing depreciation

Use the plant asset records from Work Together 7-1. Depreciation tables and a general journal are provided in the *Working Papers*. Your instructor will guide you through the following examples.

1. Complete the depreciation table for each asset using the straight-line depreciation method. If the asset was not purchased at the beginning of 20X1, compute the depreciation expense for the part of 20X1 that the company owned the asset.
2. Complete each plant asset record for 20X1 through 20X4.
3. Journalize the adjusting entries to record depreciation expense for 20X1. Save your work to complete Work Together 7-3.

On your own 7-2

Calculating and journalizing depreciation

Use the plant asset records from On Your Own 7-1. Depreciation tables and a general journal are provided in the *Working Papers*. Work this problem independently.

1. Complete the depreciation table for each asset using the straight-line depreciation method. If the asset was not purchased at the beginning of 20X1, compute the depreciation expense for the part of 20X1 that the company owned the asset.
2. Complete each plant asset record for 20X1 through 20X4.
3. Journalize the adjusting entries to record depreciation expense for 20X1. Save your work to complete On Your Own 7-3.

CLOSURE

- Ask students to summarize briefly the procedures for calculating and recording depreciation expense using the straight-line method.

EXTENDED LEARNING

- Assign Think Like an Accountant on page 207.

Essential Questions

- What repairs might be made to a building to bring the asset back to its original condition? (*Answers might include new plumbing, a new roof, or insulation.*)
- What would be the risk in not recording depreciation on plant asset records? (*Costs cannot be allocated over time, and the plant asset would still be shown in the books as being worth more than it actually is worth after a period of time.*)

LESSON

7-3 Disposing of Plant Assets

LO3 Journalize the disposal of plant assets.

Discarding a Plant Asset with No Book Value LO3

GENERAL JOURNAL PAGE 1

	DATE		ACCOUNT TITLE	DOC. NO.	POST. REF.	DEBIT	CREDIT	
7		4	*Accumulated Depreciation—Office Equipment*	*M4*		1,245.00		7
8			*Office Equipment*				1,245.00	8

Journalize Disposal

PLANT ASSET RECORD No. *9* General Ledger Account No. *1230*
Description *Notebook computer* General Ledger Account *Office Equipment*

Date Bought *January 9, 20X1* Serial Number *6432-DGC-738* Original Cost *$1,245.00*
Estimated Useful Life *5 years* Estimated Salvage Value *zero* Depreciation Method *Straight-line*

Disposed of: Discarded ✓ Sold ______ Traded ______
Date *January 4, 20X6* Disposal Amount *zero*

Date, Amount, and Type of Disposal

Year	Annual Depreciation Expense	Accumulated Depreciation	Ending Book Value
20X1	$249.00	$ 249.00	$996.00
20X2	249.00	498.00	747.00
20X3	249.00	747.00	498.00
20X4	249.00	996.00	249.00
20X5	249.00	1,245.00	0.00

Vaughn Distributors usually disposes of plant assets in one of three ways:

1. The plant asset is discarded because the asset is no longer usable.
2. The plant asset is sold because it is no longer needed, even though it might still be usable.
3. The plant asset is traded for another plant asset of the same kind.

If a plant asset has a salvage value of zero and its total accumulated depreciation is equal to the original cost, the plant asset has no book value. When a plant asset with no book value is discarded, a journal entry removes the original cost of the plant asset and its related accumulated depreciation.

January 4, 20X6. Discarded a notebook computer: original cost, $1,245.00; total accumulated depreciation through December 31, 20X5, $1,245.00. Memorandum No. 4.

Accumulated Depreciation—Office Equipment

Debit		Credit	
Disposal	1,245.00	Bal.	1,245.00

Office Equipment

Debit		Credit	
Bal.	1,245.00	Disposal	1,245.00
		(New Bal.	*zero)*

LESSON 7-3

BRIDGE

- Point out that students have already learned some of the concepts in the first-year course, such as selling a plant asset and calculating the gain on the sale of plant assets.

TEACHING RESOURCES

- **Instructor's Resource CD/Website:**
  PowerPoint Slides
  Accounting Concepts
- **Working Papers:**
  Teacher's Edition of the Working Papers for Lesson 7-3
  Online Working Papers
- **Transparency Masters:**
  General Journal
  Cash Receipts Journal (7-column)
  Cash Payments Journal (5-column)

ENGAGE

- A business should evaluate periodically the effectiveness of its plant assets. Some plant assets, such as computers, become obsolete over time. Other plant assets, such as trucks, simply wear out. A growing business often outgrows its buildings. In each case, the business must dispose of these plant assets.

PREVIEW

- Point out the learning objective for this lesson.
- Direct students to read the headings in this lesson and to examine the illustrations.

INPUT

- Point out that some plant assets are assumed to have no salvage value. When fully depreciated, these assets have no book value.
- Point out that a discarded plant asset is simply thrown away.
- Ask students to identify where the amounts in the journal entry are obtained.

MODEL

Analyze the transaction

- Draw two T accounts on the board.
- Read the transaction statement.
- Ask students to analyze the transaction. Complete the T accounts as the information is provided.

Record the transaction

- Use a general journal transparency to record the transaction in the general journal or direct students to the illustration.

INPUT

- Point out that most plant assets have a book value when discarded or sold.
- Ask students to describe the depreciation expense of a discarded plant asset. (*Calculate a partial year's depreciation for the period the plant asset was used.*)
- Ask students to explain why two journal entries are recorded to discard a plant asset. (*One entry updates depreciation; the second entry records the disposition.*)
- Ask students to describe how to determine the loss on the disposal of a plant asset. (*It equals the book value after the depreciation entry.*)
- Ask students to explain why Loss on Plant Assets is not classified as an operating expense. (*The disposal of plant assets is not considered to be directly related to the production of revenue.*)

MODEL

Analyze the transaction

- Draw four T accounts on the board.
- Read the transaction statement.
- Ask students to analyze the transaction. Complete the T accounts as the information is provided.
- As you read Steps 1–3, have students record the journal entry and update the plant asset record.

Record the transaction

- Use a general journal transparency to record the transaction in the general journal or direct students to the illustration.
- As you read Step 4, ask students to analyze the adjustment by answering these questions: Which accounts are affected? Are they increased or decreased? Are they debited or credited? Complete the T accounts as the information is provided.

Discarding a Plant Asset with a Book Value

GENERAL JOURNAL — PAGE 4

	DATE		ACCOUNT TITLE	DOC. NO.	POST. REF.	DEBIT	CREDIT	
10		28	*Depreciation Expense—Office Equipment*	*M92*		40 00		10
11			*Accumulated Depreciation—Office Equipment*				40 00	11
12		28	*Accumulated Depreciation—Office Equipment*	*M92*		400 00		12
13			*Loss on Plant Assets*			300 00		13
14			*Office Equipment*				700 00	14
15								15

❶ Journalize Partial Year's Depreciation

❹ Journalize Disposal

Disposed of: Discarded ✓ Sold ______ Traded ______

Date *April 28, 20X4* Disposal Amount *zero*

❸ Date, Amount, and Type of Disposal

Year	Annual Depreciation Expense	Accumulated Depreciation	Ending Book Value
20X1	*$120.00*	*$120.00*	*$580.00*
20X2	*120.00*	*240.00*	*460.00*
20X3	*120.00*	*360.00*	*340.00*
20X4	*40.00*	*400.00*	*300.00*

❷ Partial Year's Depreciation

A plant asset may be sold or disposed of at any time during its useful life. When a plant asset is disposed of, its depreciation from the beginning of the current year to the date of disposal is recorded as shown above.

When an asset with a book value is discarded, a journal entry is recorded to (1) remove the original cost of the plant asset and its related accumulated depreciation and (2) recognize the loss on disposal of the asset.

April 28, 20X4. Discarded office table: original cost, $700.00; total accumulated depreciation through December 31, 20X3, $360.00; additional depreciation to be recorded through April 28, 20X4, $40.00. Memorandum No. 92.

Depreciation Expense—Office Equipment

Debit		Credit	
↑ Add. Depr.	40.00		

Accumulated Depreciation—Office Equipment

Debit		Credit	
↓ Disposal	400.00	Bal.	360.00
		↑ Add. Depr.	40.00
		(New Bal.	zero)

Loss on Plant Assets

Debit		Credit	
↑ Disposal	300.00		

Office Equipment

Debit		Credit	
Bal.	700.00	↓ Disposal	700.00
		(New Bal.	zero)

The loss from discarding a plant asset with a book value is equal to the asset's book value. The loss is not an operating expense. Therefore, Loss on Plant Assets is classified as an Other Expense.

Discarding a Plant Asset

1. Record a partial year's depreciation expense, $40.00, by debiting Depreciation Expense—Office Equipment and crediting Accumulated Depreciation—Office Equipment.
2. Record the partial year's depreciation expense, $40.00, in section 3 of the plant asset record.
3. Check the type of disposal, Discarded, and write the date, April 28, 20X4, and the disposal amount, zero, on the plant asset record.
4. Record an entry to remove the original cost, $700.00, from Office Equipment and $400.00 from Accumulated Depreciation—Office Equipment. Record the loss on disposal, $300.00, as a debit to Loss on Plant Assets.

Selling a Plant Asset

Proceeds from sale		$13,400.00
Book value of asset sold:		
Original cost	$26,000.00	
Accumulated depreciation	(12,000.00)	14,000.00
Gain (loss) on sale or disposal		$ (600.00)

❶ Calculate Gain or Loss on Sale of Plant Asset

❸ Journalize Sale of Plant Asset

CASH RECEIPTS JOURNAL — PAGE 1

	DATE	ACCOUNT TITLE	DOC. NO.	POST. REF.	1 GENERAL DEBIT	2 GENERAL CREDIT	3 ACCOUNTS RECEIVABLE CREDIT	4 SALES CREDIT	5 SALES TAX PAYABLE CREDIT	6 SALES DISCOUNT DEBIT	7 CASH DEBIT	
2	3	Accum. Depr.—Warehouse Equip.	R2		12 000 00						13 400 00	2
3		Loss on Plant Assets			600 00							3
4		Warehouse Equipment				26 000 00						4

Disposed of: Discarded ______ Sold ✓ Traded ______
Date *January 3, 20X4* Disposal Amount *$13,400.00*

❷ Date, Amount, and Type of Disposal

Year	Annual Depreciation Expense	Accumulated Depreciation	Ending Book Value
20X1	*$4,000.00*	*$ 4,000.00*	*$22,000.00*
20X2	*4,000.00*	*8,000.00*	*18,000.00*
20X3	*4,000.00*	*12,000.00*	*14,000.00*

When a plant asset is sold, a journal entry is recorded to:

1. Remove the original cost of the plant asset and its related accumulated depreciation.
2. Recognize the cash received.
3. Recognize the gain or loss on disposal of the asset.

January 3, 20X4. Received cash from sale of a packing machine, $13,400.00: original cost, $26,000.00; total accumulated depreciation through December 31, 20X3, $12,000.00. Receipt No. 2.

The amount of gain or loss is calculated by subtracting the book value from the cash received. The $600.00 loss on disposal is recorded as a debit to Loss on Plant Assets as shown above.

Cash

↑	
Sale 13,400.00	

Accumulated Depreciation—Warehouse Equipment

↓ Sale 12,000.00	Bal. 12,000.00
	(New Bal. zero)

Loss on Plant Assets

↑	
Sale 600.00	

Warehouse Equipment

Bal. 26,000.00	↓ Sale 26,000.00
	(New Bal. zero)

The sale of plant assets is not a normal operating activity of Vaughn Distributors. A loss from the sale of plant assets is classified as Other Expense.

Selling a Plant Asset

❶ Compute the gain or loss, **$600.00** loss, by subtracting the book value of the asset, **$14,000.00**, from the cash received, **$13,400.00**.

❷ Check the type of disposal, **Sold**, and write the date, **January 3, 20X4**, and the disposal amount, **$13,400.00**, on the plant asset record.

❸ Record an entry in the cash receipts journal to remove the original cost, **$26,000.00**, from **Warehouse Equipment** and **$12,000.00** from **Accumulated Depreciation—Warehouse Equipment**. Record the loss the on sale, **$600.00**, as a debit to **Loss on Plant Assets**.

INPUT

- Point out that plant assets can be sold as a productive asset or sold for scrap.
- Ask students to describe the calculation of the gain or loss on the sale of the plant asset.
- Ask students to explain why, unlike the entries on the previous two pages, this transaction is recorded in a cash receipts journal (*because the plant asset was sold for cash*).
- Ask students to explain why a partial year's depreciation was not recorded. *(Because the plant asset was sold on January 3, it was not considered to have been used during 20X4.)*

MODEL

Analyze the transaction

- Read the transaction statement.
- As you read Steps 1 and 2, have students compute the gain or loss and update the plant asset record.
- Draw four T accounts on the board.
- Ask students to analyze the transaction by answering these questions: Which accounts are affected? Are they increased or decreased? Are they debited or credited? Complete the T accounts as the information is provided.

Record the transaction

- Use a cash receipts journal transparency to record the transaction in the cash receipts journal or direct students to the illustration.
- As you read Step 3, have students record the entry.
- Remind students that the abbreviation for the receipt, R, and the receipt number are recorded in the Doc. No. column.

INPUT

- Point out that no gain or loss is recognized when a plant asset is traded for a similar plant asset.
- Ask students to describe the calculation of the cost of the new plant asset.
- Ask students to explain why the transaction is recorded in a cash payments journal (*because a portion of the purchase price was paid in cash*).

MODEL

Analyze the transaction

- Read the transaction statement.
- As you read Steps 1–3, have students compute the gain or loss and update the plant asset record.
- Draw three T accounts on the board.
- Ask students to analyze the transaction by answering these questions: Which accounts are affected? Are they increased or decreased? Are they debited or credited? Complete the T accounts as the information is provided.

Record the transaction

- Use a cash payments journal to illustrate recording the transaction in the cash payments journal or direct students to the illustration.
- As you read Step 4, have students record the entry.
- Remind students that the source document is a check and that the check number is recorded in the Ck. No. column.

Trading a Plant Asset

Cash paid		$ 8,995.00
Book value of traded asset:		
Original cost	$12,950.00	
Accumulated depreciation	(6,000.00)	6,950.00
Assigned cost of new plant asset		$15,945.00

❶ Assign Cost to New Asset

❹ Journalize Sale of Plant Asset

CASH PAYMENTS JOURNAL — PAGE 24

	DATE		ACCOUNT TITLE	CK. NO.	POST. REF.	1 GENERAL DEBIT	2 GENERAL CREDIT	3 ACCOUNTS PAYABLE DEBIT	4 PURCHASES DISCOUNT CREDIT	5 CASH CREDIT	
13		20	*Warehouse Equipment*	*848*		15 945 00				8 995 00	13
14			*Accum. Depr.—Warehouse Equip.*			6 000 00					14
15			*Warehouse Equipment*				12 950 00				15

Disposed of:	Discarded ______	Sold ______	Traded ✓
Date *December 20, 20X5*		Disposal Amount *$6,950.00*	

❷ Date, Amount, and Type of Disposal

PLANT ASSET RECORD No. *258*		General Ledger Account No. *1240*
Description *Forklift*		General Ledger Account *Warehouse Equipment*
Date Bought *December 20, 20X5*	Serial Number *2432-672-7-32*	Original Cost *$15,945.00*
Estimated Useful Life *7 years*	Estimated Salvage Value *$5,000.00*	Depreciation Method *Straight-line*

❸ New Asset Information

Vaughn Distributors needed a new forklift. The vendor agreed to take cash and an old forklift in trade. The new plant asset's original cost equals the cash actually paid plus the book value of the asset traded. [CONCEPT: Historical Cost]

When an old plant asset is traded for a new plant asset, the journal entry:

1. Removes the original cost of the old plant asset and its related accumulated depreciation.
2. Recognizes the cash paid.
3. Records the new plant asset at its original cost.

Warehouse Equipment

Debit ↑		Credit ↓	
Bal.	12,950.00	Trade-in	12,950.00
New Equip.	15,945.00		
(New Bal.	*15,945.00)*		

Accumulated Depreciation—Warehouse Equipment

Debit ↓		Credit	
Trade-in	6,000.00	Bal.	6,000.00
		(New Bal.	*zero)*

Cash

Debit		Credit ↓	
			8,995.00

December 20, 20X5. Paid cash, $8,995.00, plus old forklift for new forklift: original cost of old forklift, $12,950.00; total accumulated depreciation through December 20, 20X5, $6,000.00. Check No. 848.

Trading a Plant Asset

1. Compute the original cost of the new asset, **$15,945.00**, by adding the book value of the asset traded, **$6,950.00**, and the cash paid, **$8,995.00**.
2. Check the type of disposal, **Traded**, and write the date, **December 20, 20X5**, and the disposal amount, **$6,950.00**, on the plant asset record of the traded asset.
3. Complete section 1 of the plant asset record for the new asset.
4. Record the journal entry to reflect the trade in of the original plant asset, original cost, **$12,950.00**, from **Warehouse Equipment** and **$6,000.00** from **Accumulated Depreciation—Warehouse Equipment**. Record the value assigned to the new asset, **$15,945.00**, as a debit to **Warehouse Equipment**.

Selling Land and Buildings

Proceeds from sale		$97,000.00	
Book value of asset sold:			
Original cost	$165,000.00		
Improvements	10,000.00		
Accumulated depreciation	(85,000.00)	90,000.00	
Gain (loss) on sale or disposal		$ 7,000.00	

❶ Calculate Gain or Loss on Sale of Plant Asset

❸ Journalize Sale of Plant Assets

CASH RECEIPTS JOURNAL — PAGE 1

	DATE	ACCOUNT TITLE	DOC. NO.	POST. REF.	1 GENERAL DEBIT	2 GENERAL CREDIT	3 ACCOUNTS RECEIVABLE CREDIT	4 SALES CREDIT	5 SALES TAX PAYABLE CREDIT	6 SALES DISCOUNT DEBIT	7 CASH DEBIT	
4	5	Accum. Depr.—Building	R4		85 000 00						97 000 00	4
5		Gain on Plant Assets				7 000 00						5
6		Building				150 000 00						6
7		Land				25 000 00						7

Disposed of: Discarded ______ Sold ✓ Traded ______

Date *January 5, 20X6* Disposal Amount *$97,000 with No. 188*

❷ Date, Amount, and Type of Disposal

January 5, 20X6. Fidelity Company sold land with a building for $97,000.00 cash; original cost of land, $25,000.00; original cost of building, $140,000.00; improvements to prepare the building for sale, $10,000.00; total accumulated depreciation on building through December 31, 20X5, $85,000.00. Receipt No. 4.

The journal entry:

1. Removes the original cost of the land and building and the building's related accumulated depreciation.
2. Recognizes the cash received.
3. Recognizes the gain on disposal of the plant assets.

Cash

Debit		Credit	
↑ Sale	97,000.00		

Accumulated Depreciation—Building

Debit		Credit	
↓ Sale	85,000.00	Bal.	85,000.00
		(New Bal.	zero)

Gain on Plant Assets

Debit		Credit	
		↑ Sale	7,000.00

Building

Debit		Credit	
Original Cost	140,000.00	↓ Sale	150,000.00
Improvements	10,000.00	(New Bal.	zero)

Land

Debit		Credit	
Bal.	25,000.00	↓ Sale	25,000.00
		(New Bal.	zero)

Land is considered to be a permanent plant asset. Therefore, its useful life is not estimated, and annual depreciation is not recorded for it. The book value of land is its original cost. [CONCEPT: Historical Cost]

Land is seldom discarded (abandoned). Usually, land is sold at the same time that the buildings on it are sold. A separate plant record is maintained for the land and the building. Each record is updated when a sale is made.

Some improvements may be required to prepare a plant asset for sale. Similar to repair expenses, if the expenditure merely maintains the asset in its normal operation, it should be treated as an expense in the period the payment is made. However, if the expenditure improves the asset, the cost should be included in the cost of the asset.

Selling Land and Building

❶ Compute the gain on the sale of plant assets, $7,000.00, by subtracting the book value of the land and buildings, $90,000.00, from the cash received, $97,000.00.

❷ Check the type of disposal, Sold, and write the date, January 5, 20X6, and the disposal amount, $97,000.00, on the plant asset record. Include a reference to the other plant asset included in the sale.

❸ Record an entry on the cash receipts journal to remove the cost of existing plant assets: Land, $25,000.00, and Building, $150,000.00, and to remove $85,000.00 from Accumulated Depreciation—Building. Record the gain on sale, $7,000.00, as a credit to Gain on Plant Assets.

INPUT

- Ask students to explain why land is not depreciated.
- Point out that buildings and land typically are sold for a single purchase price.
- Ask students to review the method to calculate the gain or loss on the sale of plant assets.

MODEL

Analyze the transaction

- Draw five T accounts on the board.
- Read the transaction statement.
- Ask students to compute the gain or loss on the sale.
- Ask students to analyze the transaction by answering these questions: Which accounts are affected? Are they increased or decreased? Are they debited or credited? Complete the T accounts as the information is provided.

Record the transaction

- Use a cash receipts journal transparency to illustrate recording the transaction in the cash receipts journal or direct students to the illustration.
- Record the entry in the journal and update the plant asset records using the three steps listed.

FORENSIC ACCOUNTING

Students use a LEFT function to extract the division number from the policy number. A PivotChart is created to show the trend of the number of policies sold at each division.

It is important for students to realize that the analysis of data does not necessarily indicate that a fraud exists. Lead a classroom discussion on other reasons that could explain unusual trends.

Suggested Solution

1. After the first year, each division generally sells between 80 and 110 policies each year.
2. Yes, the sales for 5 of the 6 divisions declined during 2008 and for 4 of 6 of the divisions in 2012.
3. The sales in Division 04 show a different trend from other divisions. The division experienced a sharp decline in 2005, when sales at most other divisions held steady or increased slightly. Then in 2008, when sales in all other divisions were markedly lower, Division 04's sales surged to over 140 policies. Since 2006, Division 04's sales have outpaced the other divisions significantly.
4. Not necessarily. Division 04 may be doing a much better job than the other divisions in selling insurance policies. However, in light of our knowledge of the Equity Funding fraud, an audit of the operations of Division 04 is warranted.

FORENSIC ACCOUNTING

A Pyramid Scheme at Equity Funding

Equity Funding Corporation of America collapsed 13 years after its founding, a victim of an aggressive management team resolved to achieve growth at all costs.

Equity Funding's principal line of business was selling life insurance. As was typical in the insurance industry, Equity Funding would sell its policies to other insurance carriers. In exchange, Equity Funding received a one-time payment as its fee for selling the policy. For example, John Stanton purchases a $100,000 life insurance policy from Equity Funding. The policy requires that John pay an annual premium of $600. Equity Funding sells the policy to Excel Life Insurance (ELI) for $1,000. John continues to pay his $600 annual premium to Equity Funding, who remits the premium to ELI. Should John die while the policy is in force, ELI would be responsible for paying his estate $100,000.

Equity Funding first sold its stock to the public in 1964. At that time, the company earned a modest $0.6 million on assets of $9 million. The 1969 appointment of Fred Levin as the top executive of life insurance operations was a turning point for the company. Mr. Levin had a reputation for being a ruthless manager who could achieve results. His reputation was well founded, as the company's 1972 income soared to $26 million on assets of $500 million. Equity Funding had quickly become one of the nation's top life insurance companies.

These dramatic results were achieved with the help of an elaborate pyramid scheme. Equity Funding began selling fake insurance policies to other insurance companies. Equity Funding would instantly earn revenue from the one-time payment by the insurance carrier. But Mr. Levin faced two problems in maintaining the fraud. First, the insurance carriers would expect to receive the annual premiums from the fake policyholders. Thus, Equity Funding had to sell more fake policies to obtain the cash to pay the annual premiums. Using the example above, Equity Funding would have to sell two policies to pay John Stanton's $600 premium and have enough cash left over to report the continued growth in sales that Mr. Levin demanded. Second, ELI would be alerted that something was unusual if none of the Equity Funding policies were ever collected. Thus, Equity Funding had to create fake documents supporting the death of some of the policyholders. The number of policies that had to be sold grew larger every year, a trend that resembles an inverted pyramid.

The scheme unraveled in 1973, when a disgruntled former employee blew the whistle on the scheme. When insurance investigators took control of the company and its records, they soon learned that Equity Funding used a special code to distinguish fake from real policies. The fake policies began with the digits 99.

ACTIVITY

Blaylock Insurance assigns a nine-digit code for its policy numbers. The code uses the format AABBCCCCC where AA is the number of the division that sold the policy, BB is the year the policy was sold, and CCCCC is a sequential number.

The workbook contains a list of insurance policies sold by each of Blaylock Insurance's six divisions. Perform an analysis of the policies to determine if any unusual trends exist in the sale of policies at any of the company's divisions.

Use your analysis to answer the following questions:

1. Describe the general trend in the number of insurance policies sold each year.
2. Is there any year when the number of insurance policies sold declined for most of the divisions?
3. Do the sales for any division vary from the general trend? Support your answer.
4. Does your analysis indicate that a fraud exists?

INSTRUCTIONS

Open the spreadsheet FA_CH07 and complete the steps on the Instructions tab.

Source: Contemporary Auditing, 6e, Michael C. Knapp, Cengage Learning, 2007.

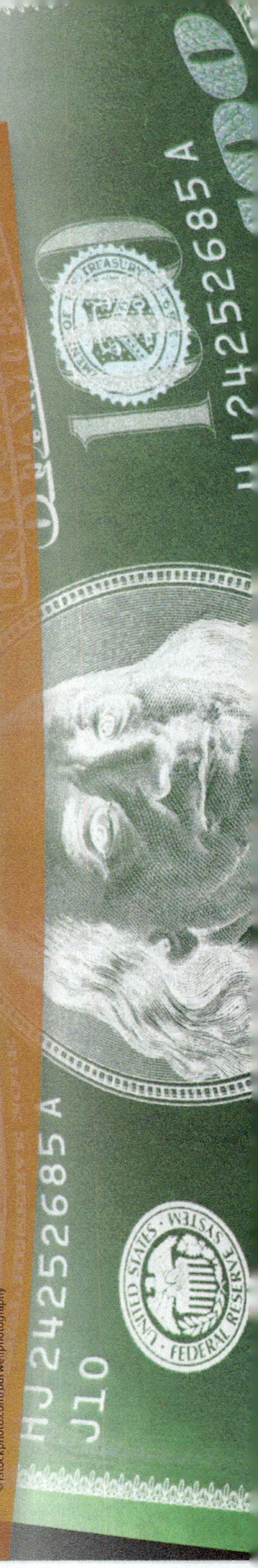

© iStockphoto.com/burwellphotography

FORMATIVE ASSESSMENT

- This is an ongoing process. Circulate around the classroom or lab, observing which students have problems with the assignments.
- Troubleshooting: Diagnose the kinds of problems students have with this lesson. Students may have difficulty (1) calculating the gain or loss on the sale of a plant asset, (2) identifying the accounts involved in a sale or disposition of a plant asset, or (3) identifying the appropriate journal to use when recording a plant asset disposition.
- Assess student understanding by checking solutions to Independent Practice assignments and noting their answers to the Audit Your Understanding questions.

End of Lesson Review

LO3 Journalize the disposal of plant assets.

Audit your understanding

1. What is recorded on a plant asset record for a plant asset that has been discarded?
2. When an asset is disposed of after the beginning of the fiscal year, what entry may need to be recorded before an entry is made for a discarded plant asset?
3. What is the formula to compute the gain or loss on the sale of a plant asset?
4. When cash is paid and old store equipment is traded for new store equipment, what is the formula for calculating the new equipment's original cost?

Work together 7-3

Recording the disposal of plant assets

Use the plant asset records from Work Together 7-2. A general journal, cash receipts journal, cash payments journal, and additional plant asset records are provided in the *Working Papers*. The following transactions occurred in 20X5. Source documents are abbreviated as follows: check, C; memorandum, M; receipt, R. Your instructor will guide you through the following examples.

Transactions:

Jan. 6. Discarded printer, no. 321. M165.
Mar. 29. Received cash for sale of conveyor table, no. 326, $500.00. M182 and R321.
June 25. Received cash for sale of a desk, no. 289, $600.00. M195 and R467.
Dec. 27. Paid cash, $23,000.00, plus old truck, no. 332, for new truck, no. 392. M256 and C887.
29. Sold a warehouse, nos. 341 and 342, for $273,400.00. M258 and R687.

1. Journalize additional depreciation, if needed. Journalize the disposal of each plant asset.
2. Make appropriate notations in the plant asset records.

On your own 7-3

Recording the disposal of plant assets

Use the plant asset records from On Your Own 7-2. A general journal, cash receipts journal, cash payments journal, and additional plant asset records are provided in the *Working Papers*. The following transactions occurred in 20X5. Source documents are abbreviated as follows: check, C; memorandum, M; receipt, R. Work this problem independently.

Transactions:

Mar. 23. Paid cash, $3,000.00, plus old point-of-sale system, no. 410, for a new system, no. 501. M89 and C753.
27. Received cash, $300.00, for an office chair, no. 460. M91 and R699.
June 17. Received cash for sale of a display case, no. 233, $3,300.00. M103 and R789.
Aug. 8. Discarded a tablet computer, no. 403. M117.
Oct. 3. Sold land, no. 449, and a building, no. 448, for $175,000.00. M143 and R884.

1. Journalize additional depreciation, if needed. Journalize the disposal of each plant asset.
2. Make appropriate notations in the plant asset records.

CHECK FOR UNDERSTANDING

Audit Your Understanding

- Call on students to answer the Audit Your Understanding questions. Answers are given in Appendix D of the textbook.

GUIDED PRACTICE

Work Together

- Have students write the solution to the Work Together problem as you guide the class through the examples.
- Remind students to use the plant asset records from Work Together 7-2.
- Ask students to calculate the gain or loss, if any, on the disposition of the plant asset.
- Ask a student to identify the appropriate journal in which to record the entry.
- Direct students to record the transactions in the journal.
- Direct students to record the appropriate information on the plant asset record.

INDEPENDENT PRACTICE

On Your Own

- Assign the On Your Own problem to be worked independently.
- Remind students to use the plant asset records from On Your Own 7-2.
- Use the Formative Assessment techniques to diagnose student understanding.

Application Problem

- Assign Application Problem 7-3.
- Remind students to use the plant asset records from Problem 7-1.

Online Working Papers

- Students can access the Lesson 7-3 problems using this software.

RETEACH

- Ask students to prepare a list of all the transactions presented in this section.
- Remind students that a partial year's depreciation expense should be recorded before the gain or loss on any plant asset is calculated. Stated another way, students should make sure that the book value of the plant asset is up to date.
- Ask students to make up original entries that result in both gains and losses on the sale of plant assets.
- Direct students to journalize the entries.

CLOSURE

- Ask students to list the information required to record the sale or disposition of a plant asset.
- Ask students to explain how to calculate the gain or loss on the sale or disposition of a plant asset.

Essential Questions

- Look around your school and determine three plant assets that will most likely be discarded in the near future. Explain your response.
- Is the book value important to the buyer? Explain. (*Yes, because it provides insight into recent asking prices for similar vehicles.*)

EXTENDED LEARNING

- Assign Forensic Accounting on page 216.

LESSON

7-4

BRIDGE

- Point out that students have previously learned the units-of-production method of depreciation and depletion in the first-year course.

TEACHING RESOURCES

- **Instructor's Resource CD/Website:** PowerPoint Slides Accounting Concepts
- **Working Papers:** Teacher's Edition of the Working Papers for Lesson 7-4 Online Working Papers

ENGAGE

- Generally accepted accounting principles (GAAP) require plant assets to be depreciated. However, GAAP do not specifically state how to depreciate plant assets. Over time, several methods have become accepted by accountants. A business should choose the method it believes results in the most accurate financial statements and use that method consistently.

PREVIEW

- Call on students to read the accounting terms and definitions introduced in this lesson: *declining-balance method of depreciation, units-of-production method of depreciation, Modified Accelerated Cost Recovery System (MACRS),* and *depletion.*
- Point out the learning objectives for this lesson.
- Direct students to read the headings in this lesson and to examine the illustrations.

INPUT

- Point out that students learned the double declining-balance method in the first-year course.
- Ask students how the declining-balance rate is calculated.
- Remind students that the salvage value is only used to limit the annual depreciation in the last year of the asset's useful life.
- Explain how to calculate depreciation expense if the book value of the plant asset is calculated to be less than its estimated salvage value.

LESSON

7-4 Other Methods of Depreciation

LO4 Calculate depreciation expense using the declining-balance depreciation method.
LO5 Calculate depreciation expense using the units-of-production method.
LO6 Calculate and record depletion of a natural resource.

Declining-Balance Method of Depreciation LO4

Plant Asset: Automobile
Depreciation Method: Double Declining-Balance

Original Cost: $35,000.00
Estimated Salvage Value: $3,000.00
Estimated Useful Life: 5 years

Year	Beginning Book Value	Declining-Balance Rate	Annual Depreciation	Ending Book Value
1	$35,000.00	40%	$14,000.00	$21,000.00
2	21,000.00	40%	8,400.00	12,600.00
3	12,600.00	40%	5,040.00	7,560.00
4	7,560.00	40%	3,024.00	4,536.00
5	4,536.00	—	1,536.00	3,000.00
Total Depreciation			$32,000.00	

Double Declining-Balance Rate
Annual Depreciation Expense
Final Year's Depreciation Expense

Many plant assets depreciate more in the early years of useful life than in the later years. Charging more depreciation expense in the early years of a plant asset may be more accurate than charging the same amount each year.

A type of accelerated depreciation that multiplies the book value of an asset by a constant depreciation rate to determine annual depreciation is called the **declining-balance method of depreciation**. Although the depreciation rate is the same each year, the annual depreciation expense declines from year to year.

The declining-balance depreciation rate is based on the straight-line rate. A declining-balance rate that is twice the straight-line rate is commonly used. This method of depreciation is referred to as the *double declining-balance method*. For example, a plant asset with an estimated useful life of five years would have a depreciation rate of 40%. The rate is used each year of the asset's useful life.

	Total depreciation expense		100%
÷	Estimated useful life	÷	5 years
=	Straight-line rate	=	20%
×	Double the rate	×	2
=	Double declining-balance rate	=	40%

The annual depreciation expense is calculated using the beginning book value for each year. In the asset's first year of service, the beginning book value equals its original cost. In later years, the beginning book value is the same as the ending book value from the previous year.

	Beginning Book Value	×	Depreciation Rate	=	Annual Depreciation Expense
Year 3	$12,600.00	×	40%	=	$5,040.00

MODEL

- Draw five columns on the board and label the columns as shown in the illustration.
- Ask a student to calculate the declining-balance rate.
- Ask a student to calculate and record the amounts for Year 1.
- Ask students to take turns completing the table.
- Discuss how the depreciation expense for Year 5 is determined.

Using this formula, the annual depreciation in year 5 would be $1,814.40 ($4,536.00 book value multiplied by the 40% depreciation rate). This amount would cause the book value of the plant asset to be less than its estimated salvage value. Therefore, in the last year, only enough depreciation expense is recorded to reduce the book value of the plant asset to its salvage value.

	Beginning Book Value	−	Salvage Value	=	Annual Depreciation Expense
Year 5	$4,536.00	−	$3,000.00	=	$1,536.00

Units-of-Production Method of Depreciation LO5

Plant Asset: Van
Depreciation Method: Units-of-Production
Original Cost: $24,200.00
Estimated Salvage Value: $5,000.00

Estimated Total Depreciation: $19,200.00
Estimated Useful Life: 120,000 miles
Depreciation Rate: $0.16 per mile driven

Year	Beginning Book Value	Miles Driven	Annual Depreciation	Ending Book Value
1	$24,200.00	22,600	$3,616.00	$20,584.00
2	20,584.00	24,300	3,888.00	16,696.00
3	16,696.00	28,100	4,496.00	12,200.00
4	12,200.00	20,400	3,264.00	8,936.00
5	8,936.00	16,200	2,592.00	6,344.00

Annual Depreciation Expense

Unit Depreciation Rate

Sometimes the useful life of a plant asset depends on how much the asset is used. For example, an automobile will wear out faster if it is driven 80,000 miles a year rather than 60,000 miles. Calculating the estimated annual depreciation expense based on the amount of production expected from a plant asset is called the **units-of-production method of depreciation**.

Mariah Delivery Service owns a delivery van. The van originally cost $24,200.00 and had an estimated salvage value of $5,000.00 and an estimated useful life of 120,000 miles. The depreciation rate for the truck is calculated by dividing the estimated total depreciation expense by the estimated useful life.

Depreciation expense for each year of the truck's estimated useful life is calculated at 16 cents per mile driven.

	Original cost		$24,200.00
−	Estimated salvage value	−	5,000.00
=	Total depreciation expense	=	$19,200.00
÷	Estimated useful life	÷	120,000 miles
=	Unit depreciation rate	=	$ 0.16

The annual depreciation expense for the truck is calculated by multiplying the total number of miles driven by the depreciation rate. After five years, $17,856.00 of depreciation has been expensed, as shown above. Additional depreciation expense will be recorded in future years as the truck approaches its 120,000 miles of useful life.

	Total Miles Driven	×	Unit Depreciation Rate	=	Annual Depreciation Expense
Year 3	28,100	×	$0.16	=	$4,496.00

fyi A company can select any generally accepted depreciation method. Once it has selected a method, however, the company cannot change the method unless it can show that the new method would better report the company's financial activities.

INPUT

- Point out that the three depreciation methods presented earlier in this chapter are based on the passage of time.
- Ask students to identify the basis for depreciation using the units-of-production method. (*units produced or used; e.g., truck miles driven*)
- Explain how the salvage value is used in the units-of-production method.
- Point out that the company must collect the production units for each asset to calculate depreciation. This can be a difficult task for a large company.

MODEL

- Draw five columns on the board and label the columns as shown in the illustration.
- Ask a student to calculate the depreciation rate.
- Ask a student to calculate and record the amounts for Year 1.
- Ask students to take turns completing the table.
- Point out that the useful life of the truck is stated in miles rather than years.

INPUT

- Point out that some businesses use the previous GAAP methods to calculate depreciation for financial reporting and use MACRS for income tax reporting.
- Discuss that MACRS classifies all assets into property classes.
- Ask students to explain why the rates for five-year property extend over six years. (*MACRS assumes that all assets are placed into service during the middle of Year 1; thus, five years of depreciation ends in the middle of Year 6.*)

MODEL

- Draw three columns on the board and label the columns as shown in the illustration.
- Ask a student to calculate and record the amounts for Year 1.
- Ask students to take turns completing the table.
- Point out that MACRS totally depreciates the asset, leaving no salvage value.

Calculating Depreciation Expense for Income Tax Reporting

Plant Asset: Computer **Original Cost:** $1,800.00
Depreciation Method: MACRS **Property Class:** 5-year

Year	Depreciation Rate	Annual Depreciation
1	20.00%	$ 360.00
2	32.00%	576.00
3	19.20%	345.60
4	11.52%	207.36
5	11.52%	207.36
6	5.76%	103.68
Total Depreciation	100.00%	$1,800.00

Most businesses use one of the generally accepted accounting methods to calculate depreciation for financial reporting purposes. A depreciation method required by the Internal Revenue Service to be used for income tax calculation purposes for most plant assets is called the **Modified Accelerated Cost Recovery System (MACRS)**.

MACRS is a depreciation method with prescribed periods for nine classes of plant assets. A property is assigned to a specified class based on its characteristics and general life expectancy. The two most common classes, other than real estate, are the five- and seven-year property classes. The five-year property class includes cars, general-purpose trucks, computers, manufacturing equipment, and office machinery. The seven-year property class includes office furniture and fixtures.

To calculate depreciation using MACRS, the Internal Revenue Service has prescribed methods that use annual

3-, 5-, 7-, 10-, 15-, and 20-Year Property Half-Year Convention

Year	Depreciation rate for recovery period					
	3-year	5-year	7-year	10-year	15-year	20-year
1	33.33%	20.00%	14.29%	10.00%	5.00%	3.750%
2	44.45	32.00	24.49	18.00	9.50	7.219
3	14.81	19.20	17.49	14.40	8.55	6.677
4	7.41	11.52	12.49	11.52	7.70	6.177
5		11.52	8.93	9.22	6.93	5.713
6		5.76	8.92	7.37	6.23	5.285
7			8.93	6.55	5.90	4.888
8			4.46	6.55	5.90	4.522
9				6.56	5.91	4.462
10				6.55	5.90	4.461
11				3.28	5.91	4.462
12					5.90	4.461
13					5.91	4.462
14					5.90	4.461
15					5.91	4.462
16					2.95	4.461
17						4.462
18						4.461
19						4.462
20						4.461
21						2.231

percentage rates to determine depreciation for each class of plant asset. These rates are applied to the total cost of the plant asset without considering a salvage value.

The depreciation rate for six asset classes is shown below. The rates assume the use of the half-year convention. As a result, an asset is depreciated over one year more than its asset class. For example, the five-year property class depreciation is spread over six years.

The rates shown in the table are based on two depreciation methods. The double declining-balance method is used for most of an asset's useful life. The depreciation method switches to the straight-line method as the asset approaches the end of its useful life. The switch can be seen in the 11.52% rates for years 4 and 5 of the five-year class. The next year's depreciation rate, 5.76%, is half of the 11.52% straight-line rate. In the sixth year, assets in this class are only depreciated for half of the year.

Annual depreciation is calculated by multiplying the plant asset's original cost times the depreciation rate for its specific class. A computer is classified as five-year property.

	Original Cost	×	Depreciation Rate	=	Annual Depreciation Expense
Year 3	$1,800.00	×	19.20%	=	$345.60

The remaining three MACRS asset classes apply to different types of real property. MACRS requires these plant assets to be depreciated using the straight-line method over useful lives ranging from 25 to 39 years.

Comparison of Depreciation Methods

Original Cost: $4,000.00
Estimated Salvage Value: $350.00
Estimated Useful Life: 5 years

Year	Straight-Line Method	Double Declining-Balance Method	MACRS
1	$ 730.00	$1,600.00	$ 800.00
2	730.00	960.00	1,280.00
3	730.00	576.00	768.00
4	730.00	345.60	460.80
5	730.00	168.40	460.80
6	—	—	230.40
Total Depreciation	$3,650.00	$3,650.00	$4,000.00

A business can elect to use one depreciation method for financial reporting and MACRS depreciation for its federal tax return. Each year, the depreciation expense and accumulated depreciation will differ between the two methods. Thus, the business must maintain depreciation records for each depreciation method.

A comparison of three depreciation methods for an asset having a five-year useful life is shown above. The comparison assumes that the asset was purchased at the beginning of the fiscal year. The total depreciation differs because only the MACRS method ignores the asset's salvage value.

Each of these depreciation methods conforms to generally accepted accounting principles. The straight-line method results in the same amount of depreciation expense recorded for each of the five years of estimated life. The double declining-balance method records a larger depreciation expense in the early years than the straight-line method.

MACRS uses percentages provided by the Internal Revenue Service. MACRS is based on a combination of the double declining-balance and straight-line methods. Because MACRS uses the half-year convention, a five-year asset is depreciated over six years.

INPUT

- Remind students that a business can use one depreciation method for financial reporting and MACRS depreciation for its income tax reporting.
- Explain the table comparing the three depreciation methods.
- Remind students that the straight-line and double declining-balance methods result in the same depreciation over the useful life of the asset.

DIFFERENTIATED INSTRUCTION

Interpersonal learners are people-oriented and learn best when they are with cooperative learning groups or a partner. Assign students to a partner. Using the Internet, each group should research three public corporations' financial statements and share with the class the plant assets that show depreciation or depletion of natural resources.

INPUT

- Explain that depletion is the depreciation of a natural resource.
- Discuss that the salvage value of the land is used to estimate the value of the resource being extracted.
- Ask students to explain how the depletion rate per unit is calculated.
- Point out that the method used to compute depletion is the same as the units-of-production method of depreciation.
- Ask students to provide examples of natural resources that would be depleted. (*oil, gas, coal, gravel, minerals, and timber*)

MODEL

- Draw five columns on the board and label the columns as shown in the illustration.
- Ask a student to calculate the depletion rate.
- Ask a student to calculate and record the amounts for Year 1.
- Ask students to take turns completing the table.

Calculating Depletion on Natural Resources LO6

Plant Asset: Coal Mine
Depletion Method: Units-of-Production
Original Cost: $2,500,000.00
Estimated Salvage Value: $400,000.00

Estimated Total Depletion: $2,100,000.00
Estimated Tons of Recoverable Coal: 800,000 tons
Depletion Rate: $2.625

Year	Beginning Book Value	Tons Recovered	Annual Depletion	Ending Book Value
1	$2,500,000.00	69,000	$181,125.00	$2,318,875.00
2	2,318,875.00	125,000	328,125.00	1,990,750.00
3	1,990,750.00	162,000	425,250.00	1,565,500.00
4	1,565,500.00	185,000	485,625.00	1,079,875.00

Annual Depletion Expense   Depletion Rate

Some plant assets decrease in value because part of these plant assets is physically removed in the operation of a business. For example, a lumber business owns land on which many trees grow. The business removes the trees to use for lumber. The land with the trees still growing on it is more valuable than the land from which the trees have been removed. The decrease in the value of a plant asset because of the removal of a natural resource is called **depletion**.

Powerland Company owns land on which a coal mine is located. The land with the coal has an original cost of $2,500,000.00. The company's experts estimate that the land contains 800,000 tons of recoverable coal. The estimated value of the remaining land after the coal is removed is $400,000.00. Therefore, each ton of coal taken from the land decreases the land's value by $2.625.

	Original cost		$2,500,000.00
−	Estimated salvage value	−	400,000.00
=	Estimated value of coal	=	$2,100,000.00
÷	Estimated tons of coal	÷	800,000
=	Depletion rate	=	$ 2.625

In the third year of operations, the business removed 162,000 tons of coal. The depletion expense for the third year is $425,250.00 as shown. Powerland uses the general ledger accounts Mine, Accumulated Depletion—Mine, and Depletion Expense—Mine to record depletion.

	Tons Recovered	×	Depletion Rate	=	Annual Depletion Expense
Year 3	162,000	×	$2.625	=	$425,250.00

fyi: Depletion is used to charge the cost of a variety of natural resources, including oil, gas, coal, gravel, minerals, and timber.

Knut Wiarda/Fotolia LLC

FORMATIVE ASSESSMENT

- This is an ongoing process. Circulate around the classroom or lab, observing which students have problems with the assignments.
- Troubleshooting: Diagnose the kinds of problems students have with this lesson. This section presents four depreciation methods that vary in their use of book value, salvage value, useful life, and depreciation rate. Students may have trouble remembering how to apply each method.
- Assess student understanding by checking solutions to Independent Practice assignments and noting their answers to the Terms Review and Audit Your Understanding questions.

End of Lesson Review

LO4 Calculate depreciation expense using the declining-balance depreciation method.

LO5 Calculate depreciation expense using the units-of-production method.

LO6 Calculate and record depletion of a natural resource.

Terms Review

declining-balance method of depreciation

units-of-production method of depreciation

Modified Accelerated Cost Recovery System (MACRS)

depletion

Audit your understanding

1. Which depreciation method ignores the estimated salvage value?
2. What is the basis for the units-of-production method of calculating depreciation?
3. Describe the types of assets in the MACRS five- and seven-year property classes.
4. How does a mining company calculate the amount of depletion for a year?

Work together 7-4

Computing depreciation using various depreciation methods and calculating depletion

1. The following information relates to a machine purchased on January 8, 20X1. Depreciation tables are provided in the *Working Papers*. Your instructor will guide you through the following examples.

		Production Hours	
Original cost	$24,000.00	20X1	2,880
Estimated salvage value	$3,000.00	20X2	3,220
Estimated useful life	5 years or 16,000 hours	20X3	3,150
MACRS property class	5-year	20X4	2,800

Complete depreciation tables showing depreciation expense calculated using the double declining-balance, units-of-production, and MACRS methods of depreciation. Round the double declining-balance depreciation rate to two decimal places. Round the units-of-production depreciation rate to the nearest cent.

2. The following data relate to a gas well owned by Southern Energy, Inc. The amount of gas taken from the well is measured in million cubic feet (MCF). A depletion table is provided in the *Working Papers*.

		MCF Recovered	
Original cost	$840,000.00	20X1	42,000
Estimated salvage value	$60,000.00	20X2	52,000
Estimated MCF of recoverable gas	800,000 MCF	20X3	48,500
		20X4	56,400

Complete a table showing depletion expense calculated using the units-of-production method. Round the depletion rate to the nearest cent.

CHECK FOR UNDERSTANDING

Terms Review

- Call on students to define each term in the Terms Review. Definitions are given in the Glossary.

Audit Your Understanding

- Call on students to answer the Audit Your Understanding questions. Answers are given in Appendix D of the textbook.

GUIDED PRACTICE

Work Together

- Have students write the solution to the Work Together problem as you guide the class through the examples.
- Direct students to complete a depreciation table for one depreciation method as you elicit class participation in calculating each amount.
- Call on students to explain the calculations so that you can assess their understanding before they begin the next depreciation table.
- Instruct students to complete the depletion table as you elicit class participation in calculating each amount.

INDEPENDENT PRACTICE

On Your Own

- Assign the On Your Own problem to be worked independently.
- Use the Formative Assessment techniques to diagnose student understanding.

Application Problem

- Assign Application Problem 7-4.

Online Working Papers

- Students can access the Lesson 7-4 problems using this software.

RETEACH

- List the information required to depreciate a plant asset using each of the depreciation methods.
- Ask students to explain each depreciation method.

CLOSURE

- Ask students to summarize briefly the various depreciation and depletion methods.
- Ask students to compare the impact of the depreciation methods on the amount of depreciation expense recorded at the beginning and end of a plant asset's useful life.

Essential Question

- Must you use the units-of-production method to depreciate a truck? Explain. *(Generally, the units-of-production method is reserved for equipment that is depreciated based on the amount of use. A truck depreciates not only on its use but the age of the vehicle as well.)*

End of Lesson Review

On your own 7-4

Computing depreciation using various depreciation methods and calculating depletion

1. The following information relates to a truck purchased on January 12, 20X1. Depreciation tables are provided in the *Working Papers*. Work independently to complete the following problem.

		Miles Driven	
Original cost	$38,000.00	20X1	79,500
Estimated salvage value	$3,000.00	20X2	62,800
Estimated useful life	3 years or 300,000 miles	20X3	52,800
MACRS property class	5-year	20X4	66,900

Complete tables showing depreciation expense calculated using the double declining-balance, units-of-production, and MACRS methods of depreciation. Round the double declining-balance depreciation rate to two decimal places. Round the units-of-production depreciation rate to the nearest cent.

2. The following data relate to a mineral mine owned by Bachmann Enterprises.

		Tons Mined	
Original cost	$420,000.00	20X1	33,500
Estimated salvage value	$80,000.00	20X2	42,500
Estimated tons of recoverable minerals	120,000 tons	20X3	25,600
		20X4	10,600

Complete a depletion table for this mine; show depletion expense calculated using the units-of-production method. Round the depletion rate to the nearest cent.

A Look at Accounting Software

Applying Depreciation

Vaughn Distributors, Inc., the company described in this chapter, uses a manual system for calculating and recording depreciation. The company has elected to use straight-line depreciation for all plant assets, for both corporate analysis and tax reporting. Imagine that Vaughn Distributors uses a computerized accounting system. The speed and efficiency of an automated system enables a company to more simply keep two sets of financial records—one for its corporate use, retaining the straight-line method, and the other to meet the requirements of the IRS for accelerated depreciation. In this example, the software labels the corporate records "Book" and the federal records "Tax."

As described in the chapter, Vaughn records depreciation and produces financial statements just once at the end of the year. Most companies prefer to see financial statements at least quarterly, or even monthly, to better manage their business activity. Since the IRS requires quarterly estimated payments of a company's annual tax liability, it is assumed here that Vaughn calculates and records depreciation at the end of every quarter so it can prepare financial reports for the period.

Calculating and recording depreciation in an automated system is very easy. Once the settings are made, plant assets can be depreciated by category or in total simply by clicking on Depreciate.

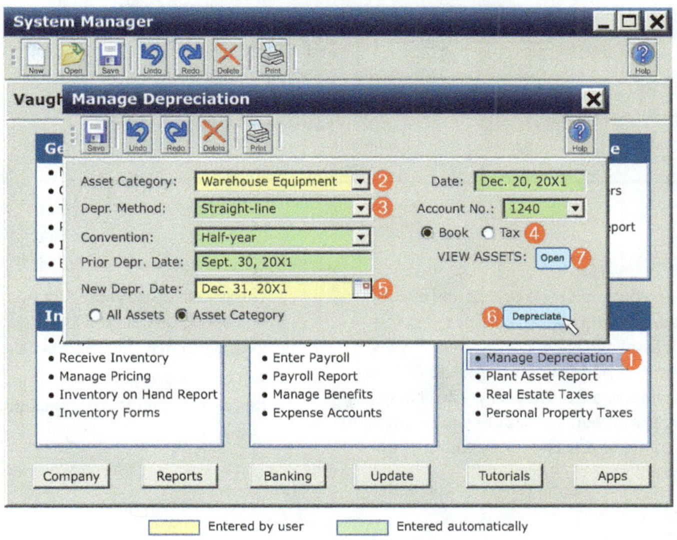

1. The accountant clicked on the **Manage Depreciation** option from the System Manager, and the system opened a dialog box that is used to set the depreciation variables for each plant asset category. Once those variables are set, the accountant can elect to depreciate all plant assets or to select a category of assets.
2. The accountant has selected the Warehouse Equipment category for depreciation.
3. Prior settings for depreciation method and convention are displayed along with the account number and prior depreciation date.
4. The default setting for the choice of financial records is Book. Clicking on **Tax** would display different settings such as double-declining balance or MACRS.
5. On December 20, the accountant has set December 31 as the next posting date for depreciation amounts.
6. The choice was made to depreciate just the Warehouse Equipment category of assets at this time, and the **Depreciate** button was clicked. The system will store the command until December 31, the new depreciation date. On that date, it will calculate and post the depreciation for each item of warehouse equipment, and it will post a journal entry for the total depreciation of all warehouse equipment.
7. To see the status of a specific asset, the accountant would click the **Open** button.

A Look at Accounting Software

Setting up depreciation in a real computerized accounting system is more complicated than represented in this feature. More variables are employed, usually in several different windows and dialog boxes. The windows in this feature have been designed to comport with the content of the chapter. The fundamental operation of the depreciation utility, however, is realistic.

The Manage Depreciation dialog box only accepts depreciation settings and commands. The Assets dialog box only allows for viewing the depreciation status of a plant asset. A review of the Chapter 19 feature in the first-year 10th Edition *Century 21 Accounting* text will show where in the system plant asset information is entered and edited.

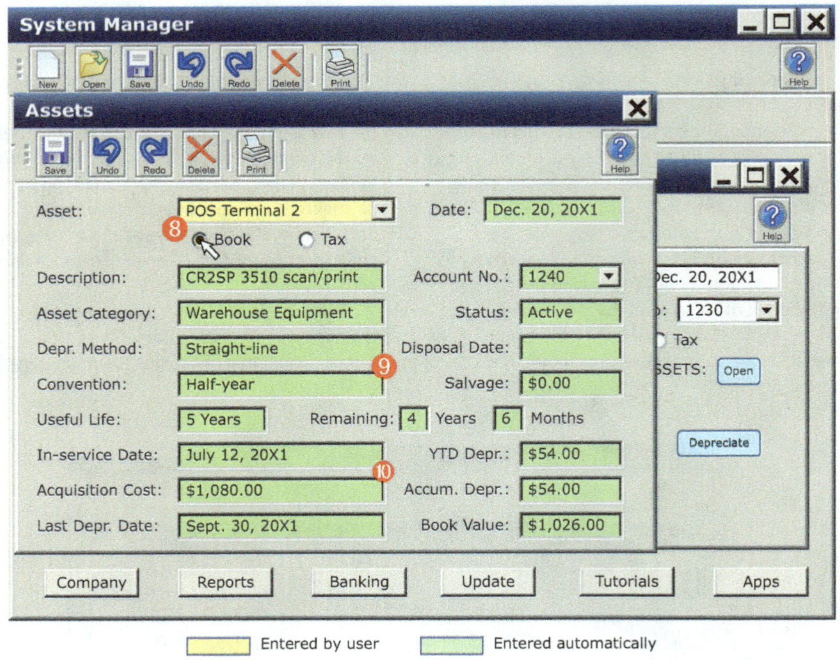

8 When the **Open** button is clicked, a second dialog box is opened, allowing the accountant to select a specific plant asset and to choose whether to view depreciation for corporate or tax purposes. All other fields in this window are display only—no changes can be made. The accountant has opened this item to verify the accuracy of the data for an audit.

9 The system displays the depreciation settings, as in the first dialog box, as well as the status of the item. If the item is inactive, the disposal date would be displayed.

10 The system displays the current depreciation status of that asset including the remaining useful life.

226

Chapter Summary

Plant assets, such as land, buildings, and equipment, are expected to help the business earn a profit for more than one year. The historical cost of each plant asset and related information is recorded on a plant asset record.

Except for land, a plant asset is depreciated over its estimated useful life. The original cost, estimated salvage value, and estimated useful life are used to calculate a plant asset's annual depreciation expense. Several depreciation methods conform to generally accepted accounting principles. The straight-line method of depreciation charges an equal amount of depreciation expense each year of a plant asset's useful life. The straight-line method is the easiest of the depreciation methods to calculate.

Accelerated depreciation methods depreciate more in the early years of a plant asset's useful life than in the later years. The double declining-balance method depreciates a plant asset at twice the straight-line rate. The useful life of some plant assets depends on how much the assets are used. The units-of-production method of depreciation can be used for plant assets, such as trucks and machines. This method is also used to account for the depletion of natural resources, such as gas and mineral reserves.

The Modified Accelerated Cost Recovery System (MACRS) is used for income tax purposes. For equipment in the five- and seven-year property classes, MACRS is based on the half-year convention using an accelerated depreciation method with a switch to the straight-line method later in the asset's useful life.

When a plant asset is sold, the accumulated depreciation of the asset is brought up to date. Any gain or loss on the sale is determined by subtracting the updated book value of the asset from the sale price. If the asset is traded for a similar asset, the purchase price of the new asset is the book value of the old asset plus any additional money paid to the seller.

Tax Laws Encourage Plant Asset Purchases

EXPLORE ACCOUNTING

The primary purpose of federal income tax laws is to guide the government's collection of tax revenue. However, Congress also uses income tax law to influence business activities. To promote economic development, Congress provides businesses with financial incentives to purchase plant assets. A business that purchases plant assets will likely hire more employees, purchase additional raw materials, and earn a higher net income—all resulting in increasing economic activity and income tax revenues.

Tax law allows businesses to expense certain plant assets in the year the assets are purchased. Assets that qualify for this election are known as *Section 179 property*, named for the applicable section of the Internal Revenue Code. In general, a business can expense up to $500,000.00 of Section 179 property purchases during a tax year. Many exceptions to this tax law can increase or limit the amount a particular business can deduct. Thus, tax accountants with a thorough knowledge of the current tax law must be consulted.

Section 179 property includes tangible personal property (e.g., computers, office desks, store displays) and manufacturing equipment. Thus, most buildings and storage structures do not qualify as Section 179 property.

INSTRUCTIONS

Obtain a copy of IRS Form 4562, *Depreciation and Amortization*. Identify the parts of the form. Prepare a list of amounts and other required information to report Section 179 property and MACRS depreciation.

© iStockphoto.com/Makhnach_M

CLOSURE

- Review the Chapter Summary.
- Ask students to prepare a list of the new concepts introduced in this chapter.
- Remind students that the journalizing of depreciation expense and the gain or loss on the disposition of assets is the same, regardless of the depreciation method used.

Essential Questions

- Why do we have various methods of depreciation? (*Having several methods allows a business to select the method that will benefit it the most when allocating costs.*)
- Why is it important to use the gain and loss accounts when recording disposals of assets? Couldn't we just credit revenue and debit expense on the sales of assets? (*Since the loss is like an expense and the gain is like revenue, having gain and loss accounts allows the business to keep track of the specific expense and revenue from the disposal of an asset.*)
- Would it be acceptable not to update depreciation before the asset is removed? Explain. (*No, it would not be acceptable because the appropriate gain or loss would not be allocated, leaving the financial records inaccurate.*)

EXTENDED LEARNING

- Review A Look at Accounting Software on pages 225 and 226.
- Assign Explore Accounting on page 227.

EXPLORE ACCOUNTING

Answers

Form 4562 is divided into six sections:

I. Election to Expense Certain Property Under Section 179

II. Special Depreciation Allowance and Other Depreciation

III. MACRS Depreciation

IV. Summary

V. Listed Property

VI. Amortization

Part I (Section 179 property) requires the total cost of property purchased and the amount of any limitations specified in the form instructions. Section A of Part III (MACRS) requires the total amount of depreciation for all assets placed into service in prior years. For each property class in Section B, the form requires the cost, recovery period, convention, method, and depreciation amount for assets purchased in the current year.

CHECK FIGURES

For complete solutions to Chapter 7 problems, see the Teacher's Edition of the Working Papers.

Application Problem 7-1

1. Sept. 27 debits: Building, $180,000.00; Land, $45,000.00.

Application Problem 7-2

1. Depreciation, shelving unit: 20X1, $253.33; 20X2, $760.00.

Apply Your Understanding

INSTRUCTIONS: Download problem instructions for Excel, QuickBooks, and Sage 50 from the textbook companion website at www.C21accounting.com.

7-1 Application Problem: Journalizing asset purchase transactions LO1

McKenzie Corporation depreciates all plant assets using the straight-line method. Plant asset records, a general journal, and a cash payments journal are provided in the *Working Papers*. Source documents are abbreviated as: check, C; memorandum, M.

Transactions:

Jan. 12. Wrote a $2,400.00 check to purchase a copy machine (plant asset no. 116, serial no. 46-36364). McKenzie believes the machine will have a five-year useful life and a $200.00 salvage value. C525.

Aug. 22. Bought a store shelving unit (plant asset no. 121, serial number GE-25BK) on account from Harris Supply for $4,800.00. Payment terms of the sale are n/30. The unit is expected to last for five years and has been assigned a salvage value of $1,000.00. M77.

Sept. 27. Purchased a storage building for $225,000.00 from Platte Industries. A licensed appraiser set the value of the building at $200,000.00 and the land at $50,000.00. McKenzie depreciates buildings over a 25-year useful life. The estimated salvage value of the building is set at $60,000.00. Assign the assets numbers 133 and 134. C722.

Instructions:

1. Journalize the transactions completed during 20X1. General ledger accounts are: Land, 1210; Building, 1220; Office Equipment, 1230; Store Equipment, 1240; and Transportation Equipment, 1250.
2. Complete section 1 of a plant asset record for new asset purchases. Save your work to complete Problem 7-2.
3. Assume that McKenzie Corporation uses IFRS to depreciate plant assets. McKenzie purchased a truck for $69,000.00. The truck had a sticker price of $79,000.00. The major items on the sticker include: engine, $31,600.00; transmission, $19,750.00; tires, $3,950.00; and frame (and remaining sticker items), $23,700.00. Determine the assigned cost to each item.

AA ONLINE

1. Go to www.cengage.com/login
2. Click on AA Online to access.
3. Go to the online assignment and follow the instructions.

7-2 Application Problem: Calculating and journalizing depreciation LO2

Use the plant asset records from Problem 7-1. Depreciation tables and a general journal are provided in the *Working Papers*.

Instructions:

1. Complete the depreciation table for each asset using the straight-line depreciation method. If the asset was not purchased at the beginning of 20X1, compute the depreciation expense for the part of 20X1 that the company owned the asset.
2. Complete each plant asset record for 20X1 through 20X4.
3. Journalize the adjusting entries to record depreciation expense for 20X1. Save your work to complete Problem 7-3.

AA ONLINE

1. Go to www.cengage.com/login
2. Click on AA Online to access.
3. Go to the online assignment and follow the instructions.

7-3 Application Problem: Recording the disposal of plant assets LO3

Sage 50 Accounting

1. Journalize and post transactions related to recording the disposal of plant assets to the cash receipts journal.
2. Journalize and post depreciation entries related to the disposal of plant assets to the general journal.
3. From the menu bar, select Reports & Forms; Accounts Receivable.
4. Print the cash receipts journal.

QB

1. Journalize and post transactions related to recording the disposal of plant assets to the journal.
2. Journalize and post depreciation entries related to the disposal of plant assets to the journal.
3. From the menu bar, select Reports; Accountant & Taxes.
4. Print the Journal.

X

1. Journalize and post transactions related to recording the disposal of plant assets to the cash receipts journal.
2. Journalize and post depreciation entries related to the disposal of plant assets in the general journal.
3. Print the worksheets.

AAONLINE

1. Go to www.cengage.com/login
2. Click on AA Online to access.
3. Go to the online assignment and follow the instructions.

Use the plant asset records from Problem 7-1. A general journal, cash receipts journal, cash payments journal, and additional plant asset records are provided in the *Working Papers*. The following transactions occurred in 20X5. Source documents are abbreviated as follows: check, C; memorandum, M; receipt, R.

Transactions:

Feb. 7. Sold a storage building, including the related land, to Esterine Corporation for $194,500.00, receiving a check for the total amount. Plant assets no. 133 and 134. M201 and R445.

June 25. Sold a desk, no. 289, to Second Act for $600.00. M222 and R687.

July 12. Received a $2,000.00 check for the sale of a shelving unit, no. 121, to Gaston Nursery. M244 and R884.

Oct. 6. A copy machine, no. 116, was beyond repair and has been discarded. M277.

Dec. 27. Traded in a truck, no. 332, and paid $23,000.00 to Nelson's Auto Mart on a new truck, no. 392. M280 and C887.

Instructions:

1. Journalize additional depreciation, if needed. Journalize the disposal of each plant asset.
2. Make appropriate notations in the plant asset records.

7-4 Application Problem: Computing depreciation using various depreciation methods and calculating depletion LO4, 5, 6, 7

Instructions:

1. The following information relates to a car purchased on January 8, 20X1. Depreciation tables are provided in the *Working Papers*.

		Miles Driven	
Original cost	$30,000.00	20X1	28,600
Estimated salvage value	$3,000.00	20X2	22,600
Estimated useful life	5 years or 100,000 miles	20X3	23,800
MACRS property class	5-year	20X4	25,900

Complete depreciation tables showing depreciation expense calculated using the double declining-balance, units-of-production, and MACRS methods of depreciation. Round the double declining-balance depreciation rate to two decimal places. Round the units-of-production depreciation rate to the nearest cent.

(continued on the next page)

Application Problem 7-3

1. Gains and losses on disposal of plant assets: Feb. 7, $14,500.00 loss; June 25, $200.00 gain; July 12, $113.33 gain.

Application Problem 7-4

1. Car, Year 2 annual depreciation: double declining-balance, $7,200.00; units-of-production, $6,102.00; MACRS, $9,600.00.
2. Coal mine, Year 2 annual depletion: $85,100.00.

Mastery Problem 7-M

1. Sept. 6 loss on plant assets, $176.67.
2. Computer, plant asset no. 233, 20X1 depreciation: $100.00.
3. Office desk, Year 2 annual depreciation: double declining-balance, $530.60; MACRS, $636.74.
4. Assigned costs: land, $108,000.00; structure, $84,000.00.

INDEPENDENT PRACTICE

- Assign Mastery Problem 7-M for students as a culminating problem that combines all new learning from the chapter.
- Assign Challenge Problem 7-C to accelerated students who work at a faster pace.
- Assign Study Guide 7.
- Students can access Online Working Papers to work end-of-chapter problems on the computer.
- Direct students to the C21 Accounting companion website for additional practice and review opportunities.

FORMATIVE ASSESSMENT

- Review solutions to the assigned problems in class, diagnosing trouble spots.

RETEACH

- Call on students to describe how they avoid the trouble spots diagnosed.
- Use reteaching suggestions from lesson plans as required.
- Assign Recycling Problem 7-R if needed.

EXTENDED LEARNING

- Assign 21st Century Skills on page 231.
- Assign Auditing for Errors on page 232.
- Assign Analyzing Home Depot's Financial Statements on page 233.

SUMMATIVE EVALUATION

- Chapter 7 Test
- Cognero for Chapter 7

2. The following data relate to a mineral mine owned by Chester Mining Company. A depletion table is provided in the *Working Papers.*

		Tons Mined	
Original cost	$925,000.00	20X1	86,600
Estimated salvage value	$100,000.00	20X2	92,500
Estimated tons of recoverable minerals	900,000 tons	20X3	105,900

Complete a table showing depletion expense calculated using the units-of-production method. Round the depletion rate to the nearest cent.

7-M Mastery Problem: Recording entries for plant assets LO1, 2, 3, 4, 7

Sage 50 Accounting

1. Journalize and post transactions related to recording the disposal of plant assets to the cash receipts journal.
2. Journalize and post depreciation entries related to the disposal of plant assets to the general journal.
3. From the menu bar, select Reports & Forms; Accounts Receivable.
4. Print the cash receipts journal.

QB

1. Journalize and post transactions related to recording the disposal of plant assets to the journal.
2. Journalize and post depreciation entries related to the disposal of plant assets to the journal.
3. From the menu bar, select Reports; Accountant & Taxes.
4. Print the Journal.

X

1. Journalize and post transactions related to recording the disposal of plant assets to the cash receipts journal.
2. Journalize and post depreciation entries related to the disposal of plant assets in the general journal.
3. Print the worksheets.

AAONLINE

1. Go to www.cengage.com/login
2. Click on AA Online to access.
3. Go to the online assignment and follow the instructions.

Eastern, Inc., uses the straight-line method of calculating depreciation expense. The plant asset records, depreciation schedules, and journals for Eastern are given in the *Working Papers.*

Transactions:

Mar. 2, 20X1	Paid cash, $660.00, and traded in an old computer, plant asset no. 233, for a new computer; serial no. C23656M, plant asset no. 315. The new computer has been assigned a three-year useful life and has an estimated salvage value of $300.00. M270 and C722.
Sept. 6, 20X3	Sold a computer, plant asset no. 315, to an employee for $400.00. M399 and R935.
Sept. 9, 20X3	Purchased an apartment complex from Williams Communities. The $900,000.00 purchase price includes six apartment buildings and an office. The complex was appraised for $1,000,000.00, with $820,000.00 assigned to the buildings. Eastern, Inc., paid $50,000.00 down and financed the remainder, signing a note with First American Bank. C839.

Instructions:

1. Journalize the transactions. Journalize an entry for additional depreciation expense if needed. Use page 3 of a general journal, page 9 of a cash receipts journal, and page 3 of a cash payments journal. Source documents are abbreviated as follows: check, C; memorandum, M; receipt, R.
2. Make needed notations on plant asset records 233 and 315.
3. Prepare double declining-balance and MACRS depreciation schedules for a $2,600.00 office desk purchased on January 10 of the current year. The desk has an estimated salvage value of $400.00 and a useful life of seven years. Round the double declining-balance depreciation rate to two decimal places.
4. Eastern has elected to begin using IFRS to depreciate plant assets. On September 22, 20X5, Eastern purchased a warehouse for $240,000.00, paying $50,000.00 down and signing a note with the seller for the remainder. The warehouse has an appraised value of $250,000.00, of which 45% is attributed to the land. The warehouse is structurally sound but requires significant repairs to the roof. Thus, the costs attributed to the building are estimated as follows: structure, 35%; electrical systems, 12%; roof, 5%; and landscaping, 3%. Determine the cost assigned to each item.

7-C Challenge Problem: Calculating depletion with a change in estimates LO7

The following data relate to a coal mine owned by Platson Resources. A depletion table is provided in the *Working Papers*.

		Tons Mined	
Original cost	$650,000.00	20X1	54,200
Estimated salvage value	$50,000.00	20X2	69,500
Estimated tons of recoverable minerals	326,000 tons	20X3	62,800

Instructions:

1. Complete a table showing depletion expense calculated using the units-of-production method. Round the depletion rate to the nearest cent.
2. In January 20X4, Platson Resources discovered a significant coal seam below the depths analyzed to determine its initial estimate of 326,000 tons. The company now estimates the mine still has 210,000 tons remaining to be recovered. Adjust the depletion rate and record depletion of 72,300 tons in 20X4 and 74,300 tons in 20X5.

21st Century Skills

A Salvage Title—Junk or Gem?

PARTNERSHIP FOR 21ST CENTURY SKILLS

Theme: Financial, Economic, Business, and Entrepreneurial Literacy

Skills: Creativity and Innovation, Critical Thinking and Problem Solving, Communication and Collaboration, ICT Literacy

You find the car of your dreams, and better yet, the price is too good to be true! Chances are it may have a salvage title, a branded title given by the state motor vehicle agency. It might be a good deal for someone thrifty. However, caution should be taken when purchasing a car with a salvage title.

Vehicles that have been in an accident, flood, or hailstorm; vandalized; or (in some states) previously stolen are issued a salvage title when the cost of repair exceeds the value of the car. Usually, the insurance company sells these cars to a salvage yard that dismantles and sells the parts. Other times, the car may be sold to someone who wants to make the needed repairs and resell the car. The salvage title protects future owners, so that they are aware of the damaged vehicle's past.

Purchasing a car with a salvage title can have potential problems. Repairs may not have been completed in their entirety by a reputable mechanic or body shop. Insurance companies may not insure the vehicle for the amount needed, and auto dealerships may be reluctant to take vehicles with salvage titles as trade-ins.

Sometimes, people take a car with a salvage title to another state, where it may be given a "clean" title. To avoid getting stuck with a car that has had its title "washed," the Edmunds automotive website recommends ordering a vehicle history report, which spans states and looks into the vehicle's entire history

If you don't mind having an imperfect car, one with a salvage title can save you a lot of money!

APPLICATION

1. Search the Internet and create a visual comparing and contrasting the following types of vehicle titles: salvage, clean, and clear.
2. a. Go to www.vehiclehistory.gov. Research and explain the five key indicators of a National Motor Vehicle Title Information System (NMVTIS) Vehicle History Report.
   b. With a partner, create a poster informing others about the importance of obtaining a Vehicle History Report.

Challenge Problem 7-C

1. Depletion rates: Years 1–3, $1.84; Years 4–5, $1.22.

21ST CENTURY SKILLS

Answers

1. Salvage—previous major damage to the vehicle; Clean—no major recorded damage; Clear—no liens (outstanding loans) on the vehicle.
2. a. The five key indicators are (i) State and Date of Title, (ii) Brand History, (iii) Odometer Reading, (iv) Total Loss History, and (v) Salvage History. Brief explanations should be provided for each.
   b. Information should be obtained from the five indicators to inform others of the importance of running a Vehicle History Report.

COMMON CORE AND INTERDISCIPLINARY STUDIES

Extended learning features and activities present numerous opportunities to implement Common Core Standards through interdisciplinary studies. Practice is provided in the common core areas of English Language Arts & Literacy and Mathematical Practice. Many of these activities require short, critical-thinking and decision-making responses that apply reading, writing, speaking, listening, language, media and technology, and mathematical skills.

AUDITING FOR ERRORS

Answers

1. The 20X1 annual depreciation expense amount is not calculated correctly.
2. Answers will vary but should identify that the accounting staff incorrectly used the salvage value in calculating the depreciation expense for 20X1. The salvage value is not used in the annual calculation of depreciation expense when the declining-balance depreciation method is used. The correct calculation is $9,600.00 × 28.57% = $2,742.72. The corrected ending book value is $6,857.28.

Auditing for errors

On May 5, 20X1, Tolstore, Inc., purchased a new drill press for use in its factory. The machine cost $9,600.00, has an estimated salvage value of $1,000.00, and an estimated useful life of seven years. Tolstore used the double declining-balance method of depreciation and the modified half-year convention. The bookkeeper prepared the following plant asset record.

PLANT ASSET RECORD No. *516* General Ledger Account No. *1240*

Description *Drill press* General Ledger Account *Production Equipment*

Date Bought *January 14, 20X1* Serial Number *26-32674-75* Original Cost *$9,600.00*

Estimated Useful Life *7 years* Estimated Salvage Value *$1,000.00* Depreciation Method *Double declining-balance*

Disposed of: Discarded ______ Sold ______ Traded ______

Date ______ Disposal Amount ______

Year	Annual Depreciation Expense	Accumulated Depreciation	Ending Book Value
20X1	*$2,457.02*	*$2,457.02*	*$7,142.98*

1. Find the error in the plant asset record.
2. Write a written explanation of the error to the bookkeeper. In your explanation, give the correct calculation.

Analyzing Home Depot's financial statements

An income statement is a financial statement prepared on an accrual basis. A statement of cash flows is a financial statement prepared on a cash basis. It shows how and where the company received cash and spent cash. On a statement of cash flows, outflows of cash are usually shown in parentheses. Inflows of cash are shown as positive amounts. These inflows and outflows of cash are organized into three categories—operating activities, investing activities, and financing activities. Buying and selling plant assets are classified as investing activities.

INSTRUCTIONS

1. Go to the Consolidated Statements of Cash Flows for Home Depot in Appendix B on page B-9. Find the heading "Cash flows from investing activities." How much cash has been used to purchase property and equipment over the last three years?
2. How much cash has been received from the sale of property and equipment over the last three years?
3. Using Note 1, beginning on page B-10, identify the method Home Depot uses to depreciate its buildings, furniture, fixtures, and equipment.

ANALYZING HOME DEPOT'S FINANCIAL STATEMENTS

Answers

1. 2012, $1,312,000,000; 2011, $1,221,000,000; 2010, $1,096,000,000.
2. 2012, $50,000,000; 2011, $56,000,000; 2010, $84,000,000.
3. Straight-line method.

Chapter 8

Accounting for Notes Payable, Prepaid Expenses, and Accrued Expenses

Scope & Sequence

	New	Review/Enrich
Introduction		
Introduce the Chapter		
Lesson 8-1: Notes Payable		
Borrowing Money with a Note Payable		✓
Calculating the Maturity Date		✓
Calculating Interest		✓
Paying a Note Payable	✓	
Drawing from a Line of Credit		✓
Paying a Line of Credit		✓
Lesson 8-2: Prepaid Expenses		
Description of Prepaid Expenses		✓
Adjusting Entry for Supplies Initially Recorded as an Expense		✓
Closing Entry for Supplies Expense		✓
Reversing Entry for Supplies Initially Recorded as an Expense	✓	
Advertising Initially Recorded as an Asset	✓	
Closing Entry for Prepaid Advertising	✓	
Comparison of Prepaid Expense Accounting Procedures	✓	
Lesson 8-3: Accrued Expenses		
Journalizing Accrued Interest Expense		✓
Procedure for Recording Accrued Expenses	✓	
Reversing Entry for Accrued Interest		✓
Payment of a Note At Maturity		✓
Journalizing Warranty Expense	✓	
Journalizing Warranty Payments	✓	
Accounting for Warranty Expense and Uncollectible Accounts Expense	✓	
Closure		

Enhancing Instruction

Features	Common Core Standards
• Accounting in the Real World: Tanger Outlets	• ELAL—reading
• Ethics in Action: The Boss Made Me Do It	• ELAL—reading
• Why Accounting?: Cost of ADA Implementation	• ELAL—reading
• Think Like an Accountant: Calculating Accrued Interest • Financial Literacy: Fun with FAFSA • Careers in Accounting: Tax Preparer/Tax Advisor	• Mathematics • ELAL—reading, writing • ELAL—reading
• A Look at Accounting Software • Explore Accounting • Auditing for Errors • 21st Century Skills • Analyzing Home Depot's Financial Statements	• ELAL—reading • Mathematics • Mathematics • ELAL—speaking, reading • ELAL—reading

ELAL = English Language Arts & Literacy

Calculator: © iStockphoto.com/picstodisc; Paper: © iStockphoto.com/Qingwa

Practice and Assessment

Technology & Media	Teaching Strategies	Guided Practice	Independent Practice	Reteach/Enrich
• Instructor's Resource CD/Website: PowerPoint Slides Accounting Concepts • Online Working Papers • Transparency Masters: Cash Receipts Journal (7-column), Cash Payments Journal (5-column)	• Musical Learners	• Terms Review • Audit Your Understanding • Work Together 8-1	• On Your Own 8-1 • Application Problem 8-1 • Formative Assessment, p. 240 • Online Working Papers	• Reteach, p. 241
• Instructor's Resource CD/Website: PowerPoint Slides Accounting Concepts • Online Working Papers • Transparency Master: General Journal	• ESL Students	• Terms Review • Audit Your Understanding • Work Together 8-2	• On Your Own 8-2 • Application Problem 8-2 • Formative Assessment, p. 246 • Online Working Papers	• Reteach, p. 247
• Instructor's Resource CD/Website: PowerPoint Slides Accounting Concepts • Online Working Papers • Transparency Masters: General Journal, Cash Payments Journal (5-column)	• Intrapersonal Learners	• Term Review • Audit Your Understanding • Work Together 8-3	• On Your Own 8-3 • Application Problem 8-3 • Formative Assessment, p. 253 • Online Working Papers	• Reteach, p. 254
• Online Working Papers	• Common Core and Interdisciplinary Studies		• Mastery Problem 8-M • Study Guide 8 • Chapter 8 Test • Cognero Chapter 8	• Challenge Problem 8-C • Reteach, p. 259 • Recycling Problem 8-R

Introduce the Chapter

SET THE STAGE

GUIDING QUESTIONS

- Ask students if they have ever borrowed money for a car or a similar item. Ask them to explain the process and the paperwork involved.
- Ask students what terms they would require if they were to loan money to someone in the class.
- Ask students to provide examples of payments that are made in advance.
- Ask how many students pay for car insurance. Explain how this works.
- Ask students to explain the purpose of warranties and if anyone has ever had to return or repair an item under warranty.
- Ask students to predict how warranties would be recorded in the accounting records.

PREVIEW CHAPTER OBJECTIVES

- Point out that students were introduced to notes, interest, prepaid expenses, and accrued expenses in the first-year course.
- Point out that this chapter will review the concepts presented in the first-year course and introduce many new concepts related to notes, prepaid expenses, and accrued expenses.

PREVIEW ACCOUNTING TERMS

- Read each term aloud to verify its pronunciation for students.
- Point out terms or parts of terms that should already be familiar to most students, such as *notes payable*, *interest*, *principal*, and *prepaid expense*.
- Lead an interactive discussion with students to review and explain the terms. Stress that special attention should be directed to all boldfaced and highlighted words presented in the text.

Chapter 8

Accounting for Notes Payable, Prepaid Expenses, and Accrued Expenses

LEARNING OBJECTIVES

After studying Chapter 8, in addition to defining key terms, you will be able to:

LO1 Journalize transactions for notes payable.

LO2 Journalize adjusting and reversing entries for prepaid expenses.

LO3 Compare and contrast prepaid expense accounting procedures.

LO4 Journalize adjusting and reversing entries for accrued expenses.

LO5 Account for warranty expenses.

LO6 Compare the accounting principles supporting the recognition of warranty expense and uncollectible accounts expense.

Calculator: © iStockphoto.com/picstodisc; Paper: © iStockphoto.com/Qingwa

© iStockphoto.com/ampyang

Accounting In The Real World

Tanger Outlets

What do Park City, Branson, Myrtle Beach, and Williamsburg have in common? Each city offers travelers an exciting vacation experience. Each city is also the home of a Tanger Outlet. With ownership in over 40 outlet centers in 26 states and Canada, frequent travelers are drawn to Tanger's upscale outlet shopping centers.

Tanger earns its revenue by renting space in its outlet shopping centers to retailers. Tanger boasts an impressive list of retailer tenants, including Ann Taylor, Banana Republic, Coach, Eddie Bauer, Guess, Kate Spade, Nike, Reebok, Timberland, and Tommy Hilfiger, just to name a few. Tanger's outlets contain over 12 million square feet of shopping space. That's the size of more than 220 football fields!

A review of Tanger's balance sheet reveals that over 80% of its assets are comprised of rental property. A large portion of this $1.4 billion investment is funded through proceeds from short- and long-term liabilities. Investors seeking to understand Tanger's financial condition need more information about each type of liability and its impact on Tanger's future operations.

The notes to the financial statements provide this detailed information. Any significant change in its liabilities, such as a new loan, is explained in detail. The notes include a schedule of the long-term debt that must be paid in each of the next five years.

CRITICAL THINKING

Assume your business is considering renting a location in a Tanger Outlet.

1. Why would your business be interested in how Tanger has financed its rental property?
2. What ratio could provide a measure of Tanger's effectiveness in operating its outlet shopping centers?

Source: www.tangeroutlet.com, Tanger Outlet's 2012 Annual Report.

Background: © iStockphoto.com/dlewis33; Real World: Mark Gail/The Washington Post/Getty Images

Key Terms

- debt financing
- promissory note
- notes payable
- date of a note
- principal
- maturity date
- interest
- interest rate
- current liabilities
- interest expense
- maturity value
- interest-bearing note
- noninterest-bearing note
- line of credit
- prime interest rate
- prepaid expense
- reversing entry
- accrued expenses

Accounting In The Real World

Answers

1. Answers will vary. Opening a retail location is a significant investment for a retailer. Before making this investment, the retailer needs to have confidence that the outlet operator is financially stable and can continue to operate the outlet for many years.
2. Answers will vary. In its annual report, Tanger includes its occupancy rate on a page titled *Financial Highlights*. In fiscal year 2010, the company maintained an impressive 98.4% occupancy. A retailer wants to be located in an outlet mall that is in high demand.

LESSON
8-1

BRIDGE

- Explain to students that when they obtain an automobile loan, they will most likely sign a promissory note for repayment.
- Ask students what information should be included on the promissory note.

TEACHING RESOURCES

- **Instructor's Resource CD/Website:**
  PowerPoint Slides
  Accounting Concepts
- **Working Papers:**
  Teacher's Edition of the Working Papers for Lesson 8-1
  Online Working Papers
- **Transparency Masters:**
  Cash Receipts Journal (7- column)
  Cash Payments Journal (5-column)

ENGAGE

- A growing business typically will have a need for additional cash. Short-term cash needs can be satisfied by using notes payable to borrow money from a bank or another lending source.

PREVIEW

- Call on students to read the accounting terms and definitions introduced in this lesson: *debt financing, promissory note, notes payable, date of a note, principal, maturity date, interest, interest rate, current liabilities, interest expense, maturity value, interest-bearing note, noninterest-bearing note, line of credit, and prime interest rate.*
- Point out the learning objective for this lesson.
- Direct students to read the headings in this lesson and to examine the illustrations.

TEACHING IDEA

Call on students to recite any poems or songs they learned to remember how many days are in each month. This will be helpful in calculating the maturity date. Demonstrate the "knuckle approach" as an aid in recalling the number of days in each month. Ask students to form a fist with both hands. Tell them to hold both fists in front of their body and to begin counting the first knuckle of the left hand, pinky finger as January. The space between the knuckles is February. Tell them to continue with knuckles and spaces, remembering not to leave a space between the two fists. Each knuckle represents a month (January, March, May, July, August, October, and December) that has 31 days. The non-knuckle months have 30 days, except February.

LESSON
8-1 Notes Payable

LO1 Journalize transactions for notes payable.

Borrowing Money with a Note Payable LO1

A business needs an adequate supply of cash to pay its operating expenses, buy inventory, and purchase plant assets. It is not unusual for a profitable business to be short of cash. When this occurs, the business must obtain additional capital to fund its operations. Obtaining capital by borrowing money for a period of time is called **debt financing**. A common way of obtaining debt financing is to get a loan from a financial institution.

A written and signed promise to pay a sum of money at a specified time is called a **promissory note**. Promissory notes signed by a business and given to a creditor are called **notes payable**. An example of a promissory note is shown below. Although the format of a promissory note may vary, each note will contain certain important information. The day a note is issued is called the **date of a note**. The original amount of a note is called the **principal**. The date on which the principal of a note is due to be repaid is called the **maturity date**. An amount paid for the use of money for a period of time is called **interest**. The percentage of the principal that is due for the use of the funds secured by a note is called the **interest rate**.

PROMISSORY NOTE

NOTE NO.: *6142* DATE: *March 8*, 20--

NAME: *Vaughn Distributors, Inc.*
ADDRESS: *1523 Fuller Drive*
Trenton, NJ 08604

For the value received, the signer promises to pay to the order of **First American Banking** of Trenton, New Jersey, *180* days from date, the principle sum of *$25,000.00* . *Twenty five thousand and xx/100* Dollars with interest from the date at an annual rate of *8%* per year, due on *September 4, 20--* . This promissory note may be paid with interest, in total or in part, without penalty.

SIGNEE: *M. David Vaughn*
President
Vaughn Distributors, Inc.

WITNESS: *Mary T. Gattis, Trenton, NJ*
Rayford P. Vicks, Trenton, NJ

INPUT

- Point out that it is not unusual for a business to borrow money when cash falls short.
- Point out that a note is a promise to pay between two individuals or businesses.
- Call on students to define each term.
- Direct students to the illustration on the page and explain the different parts of the promissory note.

CASH RECEIPTS JOURNAL — PAGE 3

	DATE	ACCOUNT TITLE	DOC. NO.	POST. REF.	GENERAL DEBIT (1)	GENERAL CREDIT (2)	ACCOUNTS RECEIVABLE CREDIT (3)	SALES CREDIT (4)	SALES TAX PAYABLE CREDIT (5)	SALES DISCOUNT DEBIT (6)	CASH DEBIT (7)	
7	8	Notes Payable	R98			25 000 00					25 000 00	7
8												8
9												9

March 8. Signed a 180-day, 8% note, $25,000.00. R98.

Cash	
↑ 25,000.00	

Notes Payable	
	↑ 25,000.00

Liabilities due within a short time, usually within a year, are called **current liabilities**. A note payable that will be repaid during the next fiscal year should be recorded in an account classified as a current liability. A note payable scheduled to mature in later fiscal periods should be classified as a long-term liability.

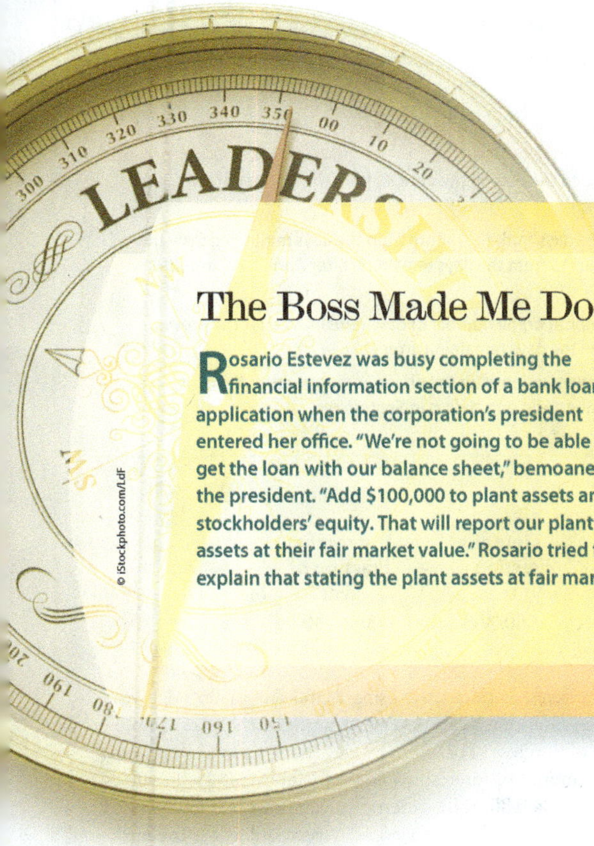

© iStockphoto.com/LdF

ETHICS IN ACTION

The Boss Made Me Do It

Rosario Estevez was busy completing the financial information section of a bank loan application when the corporation's president entered her office. "We're not going to be able to get the loan with our balance sheet," bemoaned the president. "Add $100,000 to plant assets and stockholders' equity. That will report our plant assets at their fair market value." Rosario tried to explain that stating the plant assets at fair market value violated GAAP, but the president wouldn't listen. "Just do it, Rosario. I'll take responsibility should anyone question it. I expect that document in the mail today. The future of this corporation and its 300 jobs depends on this loan."

INSTRUCTIONS

Using the ethical model, provide Rosario with guidance on whether she should mail the bank loan application with the altered financial statement information. Assume the corporation has yet to adopt a code of conduct.

INPUT

- Explain that a note payable that will be repaid during the year is recorded in an account classified as a current liability.
- A note payable that is scheduled to mature in later periods is a long-term liability.

MODEL

- Draw two T accounts on the board and label them with the appropriate accounts.
- Read the transaction statements.
- Ask students to analyze the transactions by answering these questions: Which accounts are affected? Are they increased or decreased? Are they debited or credited? Complete the T accounts as the information is provided.
- Use a cash receipts journal transparency to illustrate recording the transaction in the cash receipts journal or direct students to the illustration.

ETHICS IN ACTION

Knowingly mailing a document containing false representation is illegal. The action is considered to be mail fraud. In addition, submitting false documents with the intent of defrauding a bank is bank fraud. The penalty for these crimes can result in a fine not to exceed $1,000,000 or 30 years in prison. Thus, you should advise Rosario that she should not, under any circumstances, mail the loan application. The fact that the president stated that he will accept responsibility will not protect Rosario from prosecution.

Source: Title 18 of the U.S. Code, Part I, Chapter 63, §1341.

DIFFERENTIATED INSTRUCTION

Musical learners find their strengths in remembering melodies. Allow students to work by themselves or in groups to create a song to teach something they learned in this chapter. This can be the calculation of maturity date, facts about notes payable, or ways to remember the meaning of terms.

INPUT

- Explain that students learned how to calculate maturity dates in the first-year course.
- Point out that the number of days in the term of the note must be determined so that this figure can be used to calculate interest.
- Remind students that the date of the note is not included as one of the days on which interest is incurred.

MODEL

- Write the first month on the board and explain how to calculate the number of days.
- Write the next month on the board and ask students to calculate the total number of days.
- Continue the process of writing one month and updating the total number of days, as shown in the illustration at the top of the page.
- Explain how to determine the maturity date.
- Ask students to make up original note principals, interest rates, and terms for several notes.
- Direct students to calculate the maturity date for each note.

INPUT

- Ask students to explain why time as a fraction of a year is included in the interest calculation.
- Multiply the principal by the interest rate and ask students to identify the meaning of the amount (*the interest owed on $25,000 if borrowed for an entire year*).
- Explain that most financial institutions calculate interest using a 360-day year rather than a 365-day year.
- Point out that a 360-day year results in a slightly higher amount of interest.

MODEL

- Ask students to use a calculator to determine the interest shown in the illustration at the bottom of the page.
- Ask students to make up original note principals, interest rates, and terms for several notes (or use previous notes).
- Direct students to calculate the interest for each note.

Calculating the Maturity Date

1 Days in First Month

	Days from the Month	Days Remaining
Term of the Note		180
March 8–March 31	*23*	*157*
April	*30*	*127*
May	*31*	*96*
June	*30*	*66*
July	*31*	*35*
August	*31*	*4*
September 1–September 4	*4*	*0*

2 Days Remaining from Prior Month

3 Lesser of Days Remaining and Days of the Month

4 Days Remaining in Last Month

The number of days in each month during the term of a note impacts the maturity date. The maturity date for Vaughn Distributors' 180-day, March 8 note payable is September 4. The maturity date is determined as shown above.

Calculating the Maturity Date

1. **Compute the number of days in the first month, 23, by subtracting the date of the note, 8, from the number of days in the month the note was signed, 31.**
2. **For each month, calculate the days remaining by subtracting the days from the month from the days remaining from the previous month. For example, the days from May, 31, are subtracted from the days remaining after April, 127, to calculate the days remaining after May, 96.**
3. **For each month, enter the lesser of the number of days in the month or the number of days remaining after the previous month. For example, the number of days in June, 30, is less than the days remaining after May, 96.**
4. **When the number of days in the month is greater than the days remaining after the previous month, enter the days remaining. Because *4* is less than the number of days in September, add only 4 days in September.**

Calculating Interest

Principal	×	Interest Rate	×	Time as a Fraction of Year	=	Interest for Fraction of Year
$25,000.00	×	8%	×	180/365	=	$986.30

The interest rate of the note is stated as an annual rate. The interest paid on the note is calculated by applying the annual rate for the portion of the year that the note is outstanding as shown above. Vaughn's bank uses a 365-day year to calculate interest.

A financial institution may calculate its interest using a 360-day year. The loan agreement will specify whether interest is calculated using a 360-day or 365-day year. A 360-day year results in a slightly higher amount of interest. For the 180-day note shown above, the amount of interest would be $1,000.00 ($25,000.00 × 8% × 180/360). Interest calculations in this textbook are assumed to use a 365-day year, unless the use of the 360-day year is noted.

Paying a Note Payable

CASH PAYMENTS JOURNAL — PAGE 18

	DATE	ACCOUNT TITLE	CK. NO.	POST. REF.	1 GENERAL DEBIT	2 GENERAL CREDIT	3 ACCOUNTS PAYABLE DEBIT	4 PURCHASES DISCOUNT CREDIT	5 CASH CREDIT	
14	4	*Notes Payable*	*667*		*25 000 00*				*25 986 30*	14
15		*Interest Expense*			*986 30*					15

Interest accrued on borrowed funds is called **interest expense**. On the maturity date, the borrower pays both the principal of the note payable and the interest expense. The interest on short-term notes payable is typically paid at the maturity date. The payment of the note is recorded in the cash payments journal as shown above. The amount that is due on the maturity date of a note is called the **maturity value**. Vaughn Distributors pays the maturity value of its note on the maturity date.

September 4. Paid cash for the maturity value of the March 3 note: principal, $25,000.00, plus interest, $986.30; total, $25,986.30. Check No. 667.

Operating expenses, such as salaries and advertising, are incurred to support the normal operations of the business, which is sales. In contrast, the amount of interest expense is influenced by how the business elects to obtain its working capital. For this reason, Interest Expense is listed as an Other Expense on Vaughn Distributors' chart of accounts. Only expenses that are incurred to conduct normal business activities are classified as operating expenses. This method of reporting interest expense enables the comparison of operating income between companies in the same industry.

NONINTEREST-BEARING NOTES

A note having a stated interest rate is called an **interest-bearing note**. On the maturity date, the borrower pays the face value of the note plus interest at the stated interest rate. An alternative type of note does not require a stated interest rate. The proceeds of the note are less than the maturity value of the note. The maturity value less the note proceeds equals the amount of interest. A note that deducts interest from the face value of the note is called a **noninterest-bearing note**.

Vaughn Distributors purchased $36,096.51 of merchandise from Jenkins Industries, signing a 60-day noninterest-bearing note for $36,500.00. The amount of interest Vaughn Distributors pays is the difference, $403.49. Although the note does not have a stated interest rate, an implied rate of interest can be calculated as follows:

Interest	÷	Note Proceeds	÷	Time as a Fraction of Year	=	Implied Interest Rate
$403.49	÷	$36,096.51	÷	60/365	=	6.8%

fyi

The term of a note can be stated in months or years. Thus, a six-month note dated March 2 matures on September 2. The number of days between March 2 and September 2 must be determined in interest calculations.

INPUT

- Explain that both the principal and any unpaid interest are paid on the maturity date.
- Ask students to identify how Interest Expense is classified on the income statement.
- Explain why Interest Expense is classified as an Other Expense. (*An Other Expense does not impact income from operations, a measure of the company's effectiveness in buying and selling its product. Interest Expense is a reflection of the company's ability to fund its operations.*)
- Ask students to read the FYI.
- Explain the difference between an interest-bearing note and a noninterest-bearing note.

MODEL

Analyze the transaction

- Draw three T accounts on the board and enter the balance amounts.
- Read the transaction statement.
- Ask students to analyze the transaction.
- Record the amounts on the proper T accounts.

Record the cash payment

- Use a cash payments journal transparency to illustrate recording the transaction in the cash payments journal or direct students to the illustration.

Drawing from a Line of Credit

CASH RECEIPTS JOURNAL — PAGE 5

	DATE		ACCOUNT TITLE	DOC. NO.	POST. REF.	1 GENERAL DEBIT	2 GENERAL CREDIT	3 ACCOUNTS RECEIVABLE CREDIT	4 SALES CREDIT	5 SALES TAX PAYABLE CREDIT	6 SALES DISCOUNT DEBIT	7 CASH DEBIT	
10		20	*Line of Credit*	*R129*			*8 400 00*					*8 400 00*	10
11													11
12													12

The process of submitting and having a loan application approved can take days, even weeks. A business may need more immediate access to cash. A bank loan agreement that provides immediate short-term access to cash is called a **line of credit**, or *credit line*. The loan agreement sets the maximum amount that can be borrowed, the interest rate, and the repayment terms. The business can draw any amount it needs within the terms of the loan agreement.

May 20. Drew $8,400.00 on a line of credit. Receipt No. 129.

The interest rate for a note payable is fixed for the term of the loan. In contrast, the interest rate on a line of credit can change based on market interest rates. The interest rate charged to a bank's most creditworthy customers is called the **prime interest rate**. Line-of-credit interest rates are often based on the prime interest rate. For example, a line of credit may have an interest rate of 1.5% over the prime interest rate. This rate would be stated as *prime plus 1.5%*.

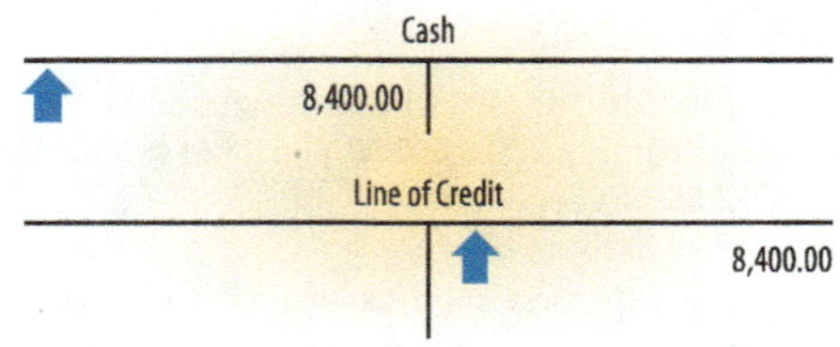

Paying a Line of Credit

CASH PAYMENTS JOURNAL — PAGE 10

	DATE		ACCOUNT TITLE	CK. NO.	POST. REF.	1 GENERAL DEBIT	2 GENERAL CREDIT	3 ACCOUNTS PAYABLE DEBIT	4 PURCHASES DISCOUNT CREDIT	5 CASH CREDIT	
23		31	*Line of Credit*	*722*		*1 000 00*				*1 092 60*	23
24			*Interest Expense*			*92 60*					24
25											25

A business can repay a portion of the outstanding principal of a line of credit at any time. Vaughn's line of credit requires monthly payments of interest and a partial principal payment.

May 31. Paid cash for the principal and interest on the line of credit: principal, $1,000.00, plus interest, $92.60; total, $1,092.60. Check No. 722.

Interest on a line of credit is typically calculated daily because the principal amount and interest rate can change during a month. The amount of interest due at the end of the month is obtained from the bank.

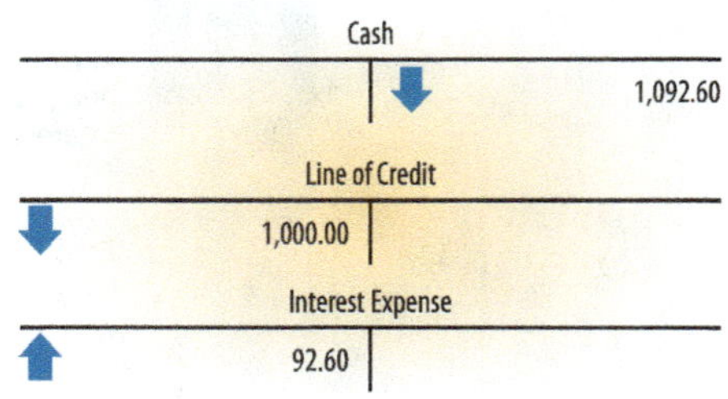

INPUT

- Explain that sometimes cash is needed before the loan application can be approved.
- A bank can provide immediate short-term access to cash by extending a line of credit.
- Point out that the interest rate on a line of credit, unlike a note payable, can change based on the market interest rates.
- Explain that the bank's most creditworthy customers are offered a lower interest rate, called the prime interest rate.

INPUT

- Point out that although a business can repay a portion of the outstanding principal of a line of credit at any time, the example shown requires monthly payments of interest and principal amounts.

MODEL

Analyze the transaction

- Draw three T accounts on the board and enter the balance amounts.
- Read the transaction statement.
- Ask students to analyze the transaction.
- Record the amounts on the proper T accounts.

Record the cash payment

- Use a cash payments journal transparency to illustrate recording the transaction in the cash payments journal or direct students to the illustration.

EXTENDED LEARNING

- Assign Accounting in the Real World on page 235.
- Assign Ethics in Action on page 237.

FORMATIVE ASSESSMENT

- This is an ongoing process. Circulate around the classroom or lab, observing which students have problems with the assignments.
- Troubleshooting: Students may have difficulty understanding (1) the fact that interest rates are stated as annual interest rates and (2) the calculation of interest expense for a fraction of a year.
- Assess student understanding by checking solutions to Independent Practice assignments and noting their answers to the Terms Review and Audit Your Understanding questions.

End of Lesson Review

LO1 Journalize transactions for notes payable.

Terms Review

debt financing
promissory note
notes payable
date of a note
principal
maturity date
interest
interest rate
current liabilities
interest expense
maturity value
interest-bearing note
noninterest-bearing note
line of credit
prime interest rate

Audit your understanding

1. What method of reporting interest expense enables the comparison of operating income between companies in the same industry?
2. Why is interest on a line of credit calculated daily?
3. A business purchased $9,629.05 of merchandise, signing a 90-day, $9,800.00 noninterest-bearing note. What is the implied rate of interest on the note?

Work together 8-1

Journalizing notes payable transactions

A cash receipts journal and a cash payments journal are provided in the *Working Papers*. Source documents are abbreviated as: check, C; receipt, R. Your instructor will guide you through the following examples.

1. Using the current year, journalize the following transactions.

   Transactions:

   June 4. Signed a 90-day, 10% note with Second National Bank, $5,000.00. R223.
   July 15. Signed a 120-day, 8% note with Commerce Bank, $8,000.00. R240.
   Dec. 6. Drew $5,600.00 from a line of credit. R368.

2. Calculate the maturity date of each note payable and the total amount of interest due at the maturity date.
3. Journalize the following transactions. Use the maturity dates and interest amounts calculated in the previous instruction.

   Transactions:

   Paid cash for the maturity value of the $5,000.00 note. C345.
   Paid cash for the maturity value of the $8,000.00 note. C652.
   Dec. 31. Paid cash on the line of credit: principal, $500.00; December interest, $46.00. C887.

On your own 8-1

Journalizing notes payable transactions

A cash receipts journal and a cash payments journal are provided in the *Working Papers*. Source documents are abbreviated as: check, C; receipt, R. Work this problem independently.

1. Using the current year, journalize the following transactions.

   Transactions:

   May 16. Signed a 180-day, 10% note with First National Bank, $16,000.00. R335.
   Aug. 8. Signed a 120-day, 9% note with American Bank, $20,000.00. R456.
   Dec. 3. Drew $16,900.00 from a line of credit. R615.

2. Calculate the maturity date of each note payable and the total amount of interest due at the maturity date.
3. Journalize the following transactions. Use the maturity dates and interest amounts calculated in the previous instruction.

   Transactions:

   Paid cash for the maturity value of the $16,000.00 note. C668.
   Paid cash for the maturity value of the $20,000.00 note. C702.
   Dec. 31. Paid cash on the line of credit: principal, $1,500.00; December interest, $138.00. 722.

CHECK FOR UNDERSTANDING

Terms Review

- Call on students to define each term in the Terms Review. Definitions are given in the Glossary.

Audit Your Understanding

- Call on students to answer the Audit Your Understanding questions. Answers are given in Appendix D of the textbook.

GUIDED PRACTICE

Work Together

- Have students write the solution to the Work Together problem as you guide the class through the examples.
- Direct students to record each transaction in the journals as you elicit class participation in analyzing and recording each transaction.
- Call on students to describe how to calculate the maturity date for the notes.
- Ask students to write their interest calculations on the board.

INDEPENDENT PRACTICE

On Your Own

- Assign the On Your Own problem to be worked independently.

Application Problem

- Assign Application Problem 8-1.

Online Working Papers

- Students can access the Lesson 8-1 problems using this software.

RETEACH

- Call on students to identify the information needed to journalize the signing of a note payable.
- Call on students to describe how to calculate the maturity date of a note.
- Ask students how to calculate interest expense for a fraction of a year.
- Call on a student to identify the transaction to record the payment of a note on the maturity date.

CLOSURE

- Ask students to summarize the procedures for journalizing transactions to record borrowing money with a note payable and later paying the maturity value of the note.

Essential Questions

- Describe situations when it would be advantageous to *receive* a line of credit rather than issue a note payable. (*A line of credit would be advantageous if the business may have ongoing borrowing needs. Once established, a line of credit does not require the business to reapply each time it needs to borrow.*)
- If a business were to extend a note to a customer, what terms would it place on the note? Would the terms differ among customers? Why or why not? (*The terms would include amount borrowed, interest rate, and due date. Yes, terms may differ among customers based on previous payment history, customer loyalty, and volume or amount of order.*)

LESSON

8-2

BRIDGE

- Remind students that they have previously studied adjusting and closing entries in the first-year course.
- Ask students to predict the types of accounts that would require adjustments.

TEACHING RESOURCES

- **Instructor's Resource CD/Website:**
  PowerPoint Slides
  Accounting Concepts
- **Working Papers:**
  Teacher's Edition of the Working Papers for Lesson 8-2
  Online Working Papers
- **Transparency Master:**
  General Journal

ENGAGE

- Many students will have begun to drive, and their experiences with insurance are useful. Ask students to identify the period of time that a single insurance payment covers. Have students discuss whether the insurance payment is an expense on the payment date or over the entire coverage period.

PREVIEW

- Call on students to read the accounting terms and definitions introduced in this lesson: *prepaid expense* and *reversing entry*.
- Point out the learning objectives for this lesson.
- Direct students to read the headings in this lesson and to examine the illustrations.

INPUT

- Ask students to identify several expenses that may be prepaid.
- Review how Whiley recorded these expenses to prepaid expense accounts and adjusted these accounts at year-end.
- Ask students to identify whether copy paper is merchandise inventory or supplies for an office supplies business. (*Office supplies sold by the business are merchandise inventory, whereas office supplies used by the business are an expense.*)

LESSON

8-2 Prepaid Expenses

LO2 Journalize adjusting and reversing entries for prepaid expenses.
LO3 Compare and contrast prepaid expense accounting procedures.

Description of Prepaid Expenses LO2

Most expenses occur in the same period in which a cash payment is made for the expense. Some expenses, such as insurance and advertising, require a payment before the benefit is received. Thus, a cash payment for these expenses may occur in the fiscal period before the related expense should be recognized.

Cash paid for an expense in one fiscal period that is not used until a later period is called a **prepaid expense**. Prepaid expenses include items such as supplies, insurance, and advertising. Only that portion of cash payment for expenses that have been used in the current fiscal period should be reported as an expense in that fiscal period. [CONCEPT: Matching Expenses with Revenue]

WHY ACCOUNTING?

Cost of ADA Implementation

The Americans with Disabilities Act (ADA) of 1990 and the ADA Amendments Act (ADAAA) of 2008 prohibit discrimination based on disability. Under these acts, the definition of disability is an "impairment that substantially limits one or more major life activities..., a record of such an impairment, or being regarded as having such an impairment."

ADA has broad implications in the workplace. It requires an employer to "provide reasonable accommodation" to an employee with a disability. Examples of typical accommodations are modifying equipment, adjusting the work schedule, reassigning the person to another position, and restructuring the job.

These accommodations may have a cost attached to them. In companies that are departmentalized, the cost may be assigned to the overall company, allocated in total to the department, or split between the company and the department. If any of this cost is allocated to the department, it will affect the net income of that department. The manager of the department should understand the cost of the accommodation and the portion of that cost that will be allocated to the department.

Business Management & Administration

CRITICAL THINKING

Assume you are the manager of a department. Ken, an employee, has a job which requires him to stand near a machine. Ken has developed a back problem and must be able to sit while working.

1. What accommodations might you investigate in order to allow Ken to remain employed?
2. How would you estimate the cost of these accommodations?

Source: U.S. Department of Justice, Americans with Disabilities Act (www.ada.gov).

© iStockphoto.com/Aleksko

WHY ACCOUNTING?

Answers

1. Perhaps the workstation can be redesigned so that Ken sits while performing his tasks, or Ken could be reassigned to another position.
2. If the workstation is redesigned, it would be easy to estimate its cost. In addition, the new workstation may need to be evaluated to ensure that it is as efficient as the prior one. If not, the cost of the loss of efficiency should also be included in the estimate. If Ken is reassigned to another position, the cost of training Ken and the cost of training a new employee to do Ken's former job would be included in the cost.

Prepaid expenses may be recorded initially as assets or as expenses. Both procedures require that the account balances be adjusted before financial statements are prepared. In Part 1, Whiley Outdoor Living, Inc., initially recorded its prepaid expenses as assets.

Prepaid expenses are assets until they are actually used. For example, Vaughn Distributors has a quantity of supplies on hand on any given day during the year. The company will use these supplies in the current and future fiscal periods. Vaughn initially records its prepaid expenses in expense accounts. Thus, the amount recorded in the account Supplies Expense prior to the fiscal year-end adjustments represents a mixture of an expense (supplies already used) and an asset (supplies not yet used).

Vaughn records an adjusting entry to recognize as an expense only those supplies used. This adjusting entry is made when financial statements need to be prepared. [CONCEPT: Full Disclosure] Vaughn records adjustments on December 31, the end of its fiscal year.

Adjusting Entry for Supplies Initially Recorded as an Expense

Debit the Asset Account

GENERAL JOURNAL — PAGE 16

	DATE		ACCOUNT TITLE	DOC. NO.	POST. REF.	DEBIT	CREDIT	
1			*Adjusting Entries*					1
4		31	*Supplies*			760 00		4
5			*Supplies Expense*				760 00	5
6								6

Credit the Expense Account

When Vaughn Distributors buys supplies, Supplies Expense is debited and Cash is credited. The $4,850.00 debit balance of Supplies Expense represents the amount of the beginning supplies inventory plus the total amount of all supplies bought during the fiscal period. Nothing has been recorded in Vaughn's Supplies account during the fiscal year.

On December 31, Vaughn takes a physical count of the supplies on hand. It determines that the supplies ending inventory is $760.00 and records the necessary adjusting entry as shown above.

Supplies

	Debit		Credit
Adj.	760.00		

Supplies Expense

	Debit		Credit
12/31 Bal.	4,850.00	Adj.	760.00
(New Bal.	*4,090.00)*		

The new balance of Supplies, $760.00, represents the ending supplies inventory on December 31. The new balance of Supplies Expense, $4,090.00, recognizes the amount of supplies used during the current year.

Closing Entry for Supplies Expense

To prepare a general ledger for the next fiscal period, closing entries are journalized and posted. After the closing entry is recorded, the Supplies Expense account balance is zero. The debit balance of $760.00 in Supplies represents the amount of supplies on hand on December 31.

Supplies

	Debit		Credit
Adj.	760.00		

Supplies Expense

	Debit		Credit
12/31 Bal.	4,850.00	Adj.	760.00
(New Bal.	*zero)*	Clos.	4,090.00

Income Summary

	Debit		Credit
Clos.	4,090.00		

INPUT

- Ask students to describe how the amount of an adjusting entry is determined.
- Ask why a closing entry must be prepared.
- Point out that the procedure for recording a closing entry is the same, regardless of the method used for initially recording supplies and other prepaid expenses.

MODEL

Record the adjusting entry

- Draw three T accounts on the board.
- Describe the adjusting entry.
- Ask students to analyze the adjusting entry by answering these questions: Which accounts are affected? Are they increased or decreased? Are they debited or credited? Complete the T accounts as the information is provided.
- Use a general journal transparency to illustrate recording the adjusting entry in the general journal or direct students to the illustration.

Record the closing entry

- Use the same three T accounts on the board.
- Describe the closing entry.
- Ask students to analyze the closing entry. Enter the closing entry in the T accounts and calculate the new balances.
- Use a general journal transparency to illustrate recording the closing entry in the general journal.

INPUT

- Point out that reversing entries are required only when prepaid expenses are initially recorded as expenses.
- Ask students to describe each of the prior year's entries shown in the T accounts.
- Ask students to repeat the rule for determining whether an adjusting entry should be reversed.

MODEL

- Draw two T accounts on the board and enter the pre-adjustment balances.
- Ask students to describe the adjusting and closing entries as they are recorded in the T accounts.
- Describe the reversing entry.
- Ask students to analyze the reversing entry by answering these questions: Which accounts are affected? Are they increased or decreased? Are they debited or credited? Complete the T accounts as the information is provided.
- Use a general journal transparency to illustrate recording the transaction in the general journal or direct students to the illustration.

Reversing Entry for Supplies Initially Recorded as an Expense

Debit the Expense Account

GENERAL JOURNAL — PAGE 1

	DATE		ACCOUNT TITLE	DOC. NO.	POST. REF.	DEBIT	CREDIT	
1			*Reversing Entries*					1
2	20— Jan.	1	*Supplies Expense*			760 00		2
3			*Supplies*				760 00	3
4								4

Credit the Asset Account

Vaughn initially records the amount of all supplies bought in an expense account. On December 31, the amount of Vaughn's supplies inventory, $760.00, is the debit balance of Supplies. To prepare the general ledger accounts for the next year, the $760.00 should be returned as a debit in Supplies Expense. The $760.00 debit can then be added to the amount of supplies bought during the next year.

Businesses that initially record prepaid items as expenses reverse the adjusting entries for prepaid expenses at the beginning of each fiscal period. An entry made at the beginning of one fiscal period to reverse an adjusting entry made in the previous fiscal period is called a **reversing entry**. Thus, a reversing entry is the exact opposite of the related adjusting entry.

Vaughn initially records supplies as expenses and, therefore, needs to record reversing entries. Accountants use the following rule of thumb to determine whether a reversing entry is needed: *If an adjusting entry creates a balance in an asset or a liability account, the adjusting entry is reversed.* This rule applies to expenses that will be used early during the next fiscal year.

Because Vaughn's adjusting entry for supplies created a balance in Supplies, a reversing entry is needed. The reversing entry is shown above.

After the reversing entry is posted, the cost of the supplies inventory, $760.00, is recorded in Supplies Expense. Vaughn expects these supplies will be used during the next fiscal year. Thus, the supplies will be expensed in the same fiscal year they are used to earn revenue. [CONCEPT: Matching Expenses with Revenue] The balance of Supplies is zero, as it was before the adjusting entry.

Supplies Expense

Debit		Credit	
12/31 Bal.	4,850.00	Adj.	760.00
Rev.	760.00	Clos.	4,090.00
(New Bal.	*760.00)*		

Supplies

Debit		Credit	
Adj.	760.00	Rev.	760.00
(New Bal.	*zero)*		

remember

Most adjustments that create an asset or a liability should be reversed.

© StockLite/Shutterstock.com

Advertising Initially Recorded as an Asset

Debit the Expense Account

GENERAL JOURNAL PAGE 16

	DATE		ACCOUNT TITLE	DOC. NO.	POST. REF.	DEBIT	CREDIT	
1			*Adjusting Entries*					1
8		31	*Advertising Expense*			25 000 00		8
9			*Prepaid Advertising*				25 000 00	9
10								10

Credit the Asset Account

During May of a prior fiscal year, Vaughn Distributors entered into an endorsement contract with a celebrity. Vaughn paid the celebrity $100,000.00 for the right to use the celebrity's image in its advertising and on its website. During the four-year contract, the celebrity must also make an appearance at an annual trade show.

Vaughn uses a different procedure for accounting for this prepaid expense. The procedure is the same as that used by Whiley Outdoor Living in Part 1. Expenditures are initially recorded in a prepaid asset account. At the end of the fiscal year, Vaughn records an adjusting entry to expense the portion of the prepaid expense used during the current fiscal year. Vaughn uses this procedure since, unlike supplies, the prepaid expense will be expensed over several fiscal years.

Vaughn initially recorded the $100,000.00 payment in Prepaid Advertising. During prior fiscal years, $40,000.00 of the payment was adjusted to Advertising Expense. The $60,000.00 balance in

Advertising Expense

	Debit		Credit
↑ Adj.	25,000.00		

Prepaid Advertising

	Debit		Credit
12/31 Bal.	60,000.00	↓ Adj.	25,000.00
(New Bal.	*35,000.00)*		

Prepaid Advertising represents the value of advertising to be expensed in future fiscal years.

Vaughn expenses the $100,000.00 payment evenly over the four years of the endorsement contract. An adjusting entry of $25,000.00 ($100,000.00 ÷ 4 years) is necessary to account for the advertising expense incurred during the current fiscal year.

After recording the adjustment, the new balance of Prepaid Advertising, $35,000.00, is the value of the endorsement contract to be received in future fiscal years.

Closing Entry for Prepaid Advertising

To prepare a general ledger for the next fiscal period, closing entries are journalized and posted.

The adjusting entry did not create a balance in an asset account. Therefore, no reversing entry is required.

Vaughn can use either procedure for recording prepaid expenses. Regardless of the procedure used, the financial statements must reflect the same value of prepaid expenses.

Income Summary

	Debit		Credit
Clos.	25,000.00		

Advertising Expense

	Debit		Credit
Adj.	25,000.00	↓ Clos.	25,000.00
(New Bal.	*zero)*		

INPUT

- Point out that this procedure is the same as what students learned in Part 1.
- Explain that this transaction is initially recorded in a prepaid expense account; therefore, an adjusting entry to expense the portion of advertising used during the current period is necessary.
- Remind students that the example provided is for advertising over a four-year contract. The amount of advertising used for the current year must be expensed.

MODEL

- Draw two T accounts on the board and enter the pre-adjustment balances.
- Describe the adjusting entry.
- Ask students to analyze the adjusting entry. Complete the T accounts as the information is provided.
- Use a general journal transparency to illustrate recording the adjusting entry in the general journal or direct students to the illustration at the top of the page.

INPUT

- Ask students to explain why a closing entry, rather than a reversing entry, is prepared for Prepaid Advertising.
- Point out that the effect of the closing entry is shown in the T accounts.

MODEL

- Continue to use the T accounts from the prior demonstration.
- Describe the closing entry and record the entry in the T accounts.
- Use a general journal transparency to illustrate recording the adjusting entry in the general journal or direct students to the illustration at the top of the page.

DIFFERENTIATED INSTRUCTION

ESL students are encouraged to and usually enjoy sharing their cultures with other students. Many businesses blunder when doing business internationally by not understanding other cultures. Ask students to select a country and prepare a brochure that lists, in the language of the country, ten common phrases used by travelers in that country, as well as ten tips when working with others in that culture.

INPUT

- Explain that a business can initially record a prepaid expense as an asset or an expense. Either procedure requires an adjustment before financial statements are prepared.
- Compare and contrast the two procedures illustrated.
- Remind students that each procedure requires that the expense account be closed at the end of the accounting period.

Comparison of Prepaid Expense Accounting Procedures LO3

A business can elect to initially record a prepaid expense as an asset or as an expense. Both procedures require that the account balances be adjusted before financial statements are prepared. Each procedure requires that the expense account be closed at the end of the accounting period.

The adjusting, closing, and reversing entries Vaughn recorded for supplies are shown in the left column of the following illustration. The adjusting entry recognized that $760.00 of supplies were on hand at the end of the fiscal period. The remaining balance in Supplies Expense, $4,090.00, represents the value of supplies used during the fiscal year. After accounts were closed, the balance in Supplies was reversed, resulting in a $760.00 debit in Supplies Expense.

The right side of the illustration shows the adjusting and closing entries for Vaughn if it initially records prepaid expenses as expenses. The adjusting entry recognized that $4,090.00 of supplies were used during the fiscal period. The remaining balance in Supplies, $760.00, represents the value of supplies on hand at the end of the fiscal year. Because the adjusting entry did not create a balance in an asset or a liability account, no reversing entry is required.

Note that the adjusted balances of Supplies and Supplies Expense are identical, regardless of the procedure used. As a result, the entry to close Supplies Expense is also identical. Only the procedure that initially records prepaid expenses to an expense account requires that a reversing entry be recorded.

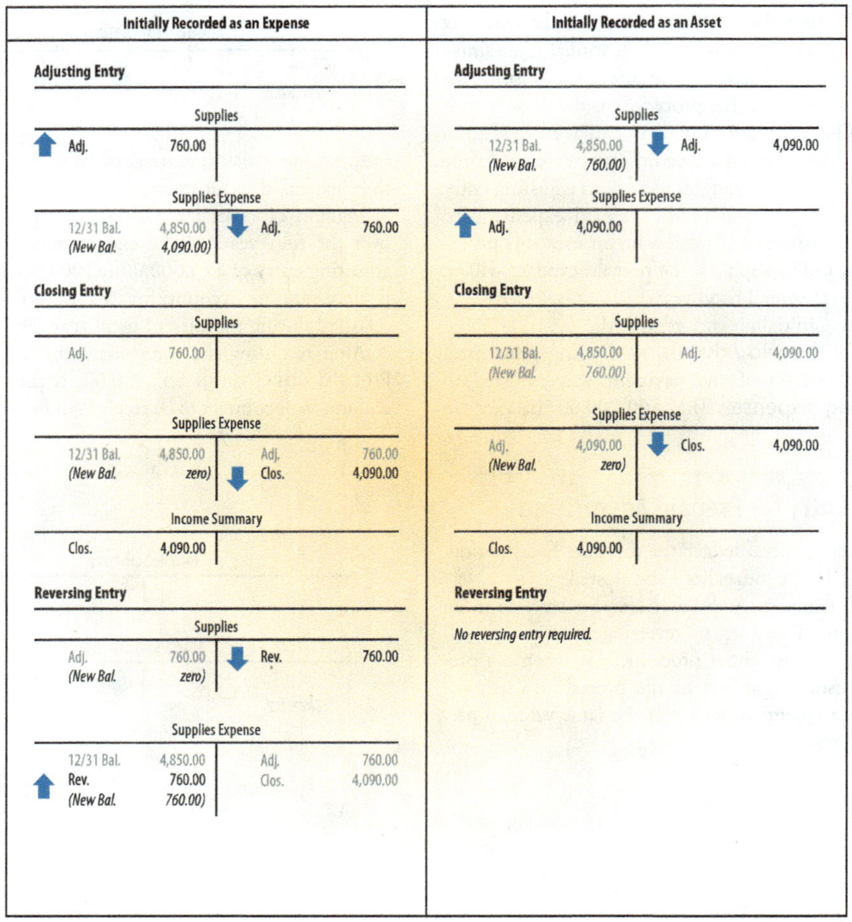

FORMATIVE ASSESSMENT

- This is an ongoing process. Circulate around the classroom or lab, observing which students have problems with the assignments.
- Troubleshooting: Diagnose the kinds of problems students have with this lesson. The concepts and procedures in this section are relatively simple because they review concepts presented in the first-year course. Students may have difficulty understanding when to record a reversing entry.
- Assess student understanding by checking solutions to Independent Practice assignments and observing their answers to the Terms Review and Audit Your Understanding questions.

End of Lesson Review

LO2 Journalize adjusting and reversing entries for prepaid expenses.

LO3 Compare and contrast prepaid expense accounting procedures.

Terms Review

prepaid expense

reversing entry

Audit your understanding

1. Which accounting concept is being applied when an adjusting entry is recorded for prepaid expenses?
2. Why is an adjusting entry made for supplies at the end of a fiscal period?
3. What rule of thumb can accountants follow to determine whether a reversing entry is needed?
4. How does the procedure used to account for prepaid expenses affect the balance reported in the financial statements?
5. Identify the similarities and differences between the adjusting, closing, and reversing entries of the two methods used to account for prepaid expenses.

Work together 8-2

Journalizing adjusting and reversing entries for prepaid expenses

Praxson, Inc., has the following general ledger account balances on December 31 of the current year before it records adjusting entries. A general journal is provided in the *Working Papers*. Your instructor will guide you through the following examples.

Supplies Expense	$ 3,200.00
Insurance Expense	8,000.00
Prepaid Advertising	80,000.00

1. Using the following adjustment information, journalize the adjusting entries on December 31 of the current year.

Supplies inventory	$ 400.00
Value of prepaid insurance	600.00
Advertising used	30,000.00

2. Journalize the reversing entries on January 1 of the next year.

On your own 8-2

Journalizing adjusting and reversing entries for prepaid expenses

WRP Industries has the following general ledger account balances on December 31 of the current year before it records adjusting entries. A general journal is provided in the *Working Papers*. Work this problem independently.

Insurance Expense	$ 8,600.00
Rent Expense	13,000.00
Prepaid Advertising	20,000.00

1. Using the following adjustment information, journalize the adjusting entries on December 31 of the current year.

Value of prepaid insurance	$ 900.00
Value of prepaid rent	1,000.00
Advertising used	6,000.00

2. Journalize the reversing entries on January 1 of the next year.

CHECK FOR UNDERSTANDING

Terms Review

- Call on students to define each term in the Terms Review. Definitions are given in the Glossary.

Audit Your Understanding

- Call on students to answer the Audit Your Understanding questions. Answers are given in Appendix D of the textbook.

GUIDED PRACTICE

Work Together

- Have students write the solution to the Work Together problem as you guide the class through the examples.
- Direct students to record the three adjusting entries in the general journal as you elicit class participation in analyzing and recording the transactions.
- Ask students to explain why reversing entries should be recorded.
- Direct students to record the three reversing entries in the general journal as you elicit class participation in analyzing and recording the transactions.

INDEPENDENT PRACTICE

On Your Own

- Assign the On Your Own problem to be worked independently.
- Use the Formative Assessment techniques to diagnose student understanding.

Application Problem

- Assign Application Problem 8-2.

Online Working Papers

- Students can access the Lesson 8-2 problems using this software.

RETEACH

- Ask students to describe the two methods used for accounting for prepaid expenses.
- Ask students to explain how to determine the amount for the adjusting entry.
- Ask students to identify when a reversing entry should be recorded.

CLOSURE

- Ask students to summarize briefly the recording of adjusting, closing, and reversing entries for prepaid expenses initially recorded as expenses.

Essential Question

- What would be the danger in just crediting the asset, rather than recording an adjusting entry at the end of each period? Explain the effect either way. (*Adjusting entries bring the account balances up to date and show why the change was made.*)

EXTENDED LEARNING

- Assign Why Accounting on page 242.

LESSON
8-3

BRIDGE

- Ask what is included in the payment for a note.
- Ask students to predict how warranties might be similar to uncollectible accounts.

TEACHING RESOURCES

- **Instructor's Resource CD/Website:**
  PowerPoint Slides
  Accounting Concepts
- **Working Papers:**
  Teacher's Edition of the Working Papers for Lesson 8-3
  Online Working Papers
- **Transparency Masters:**
  General Journal
  Cash Payments Journal (5-column)

ENGAGE

- Ask the class if any students have a part-time job for which their employer owes them for time worked. If that employer prepared financial statements today, should the amount owed to the students be shown as a liability? Amounts owed to one individual or business are also amounts owed by another individual or business.

PREVIEW

- Call on a student to read the accounting term and definition introduced in this lesson: *accrued expenses.*
- Point out the learning objectives for this lesson.
- Direct students to read the headings in this lesson and to examine the illustrations.

INPUT

- Point out that accruing interest expense was presented in the first-year course.
- Ask students to explain why interest is accrued on a note payable that matures in the next fiscal period.
- Point out that several accrued expenses may need to be recorded. Examples include payroll, payroll taxes, and income taxes.

LESSON

8-3 Accrued Expenses

LO4 Journalize adjusting and reversing entries for accrued expenses.
LO5 Account for warranty expenses.
LO6 Compare the accounting principles supporting the recognition of warranty expense and uncollectible accounts expense.

Journalizing Accrued Interest Expense LO4

Principal	×	Interest Rate	×	Time as a Fraction of Year	=	Interest for Fraction of Year
$9,000.00	×	8%	×	25/365	=	$49.32

Debit the Expense Account

Calculate the Accrual Amount

GENERAL JOURNAL PAGE 1

	DATE		ACCOUNT TITLE	DOC. NO.	POST. REF.	DEBIT	CREDIT	
1			*Adjusting Entries*					1
22		31	*Interest Expense*			49 32		22
23			*Interest Payable*				49 32	23
24								24

Credit the Liability Account

Expenses incurred in one fiscal period but not paid until a later fiscal period are called **accrued expenses**. On December 31, Vaughn Distributors has a 60-day, 8% note payable for $9,000.00, dated December 6. Vaughn owes the bank for interest on the note from December 6 to the end of the month. On December 31, Vaughn owes 25 days' worth of accrued interest on the note, $49.32. However, Vaughn will not pay any interest on this note until its maturity date.

The accrued interest expense for this note should be reported in the current fiscal period. [CONCEPT: Matching Expenses with Revenue] The adjusting entry shown above records the accrued interest adjustment. Vaughn uses the account titled Interest Payable to account for accrued interest. Another account title commonly used is Accrued Interest.

Interest Expense	
Adj. 49.32	

Interest Payable	
	Adj. 49.32

Procedure for Recording Accrued Expenses

A business may need to record several accrued expenses, such as payroll, payroll taxes, and income taxes. The same procedure is used to record any accrued expense.

With one exception, the transaction to record an accrued expense is the same as the transaction to record the payment of the expense. Rather than recording a credit to Cash, the credit is recorded to a liability account.

MODEL

Calculate accrued interest

- Ask students to calculate the number of days the note payable should be accrued, using the formula shown in the illustration.
- Ask students to use a calculator to compute the amount of accrued interest.

Analyze and record the transaction

- Draw two T accounts on the board.
- Describe the adjusting entry.
- Ask students to analyze the adjusting entry. Complete the T accounts as the information is provided. (*Students should refer to the math box and record the interest payment in the T accounts.*)
- Use a general journal transparency to illustrate recording the adjusting entry in the general journal or direct students to the illustration.

Reversing Entry for Accrued Interest

Debit the Liability Account

GENERAL JOURNAL — PAGE 1

	DATE		ACCOUNT TITLE	DOC. NO.	POST. REF.	DEBIT	CREDIT	
1			*Reversing Entries*					1
20		1	*Interest Payable*			49 32		20
21			*Interest Expense*				49 32	21
22								22

Credit the Expense Account

After preparing its financial statements, Vaughn Distributors journalizes and posts closing entries. To prepare the accounts for the next year, Vaughn records a reversing entry for accrued interest expense, as shown above. Vaughn's adjusting entry for accrued interest expense creates a balance in a liability account. Accountants generally reverse an adjusting entry that creates a balance in a liability account.

When Vaughn pays the note on February 4 of the following year, the total interest expense payment is $118.36. The total interest expense should be divided between the two fiscal periods. Interest for the prior year, $49.32, is charged for the 25 days the note was outstanding in that year. Interest for the current period, $69.04, relates to the 35 days from the start of the fiscal year to the maturity date.

THINK LIKE AN ACCOUNTANT

© iStockphoto.com/Dan Bachman

Calculating Accrued Interest

For years, BLT Corporation maintained a $1 million line of credit with a large financial institution. The money drawn from the line of credit was used to finance inventory and accounts receivable for the corporation's primary selling season.

BLT Corporation has 30 locations across the nation. BLT generally locates its manufacturing plants in small towns and, therefore, is often the largest employer in each town. A new chief financial officer has directed that the corporation begin borrowing from banks in the towns in which the corporation has plants. BLT believes that doing business with local banks is part of being a good community citizen and helps each local economy.

The corporation regularly has 20 to 30 notes outstanding at any time. Because the corporation prepares monthly financial statements, monthly calculations of accrued interest expense are required. You have been assigned the task of creating a schedule to calculate the interest for each note and the total amount to be used in the monthly interest expense accrual.

OPEN THE SPREADSHEET TLA_CH08

The worksheet contains a list of outstanding notes payable. Follow the steps on the Instructions tab to complete the schedule. Answer these questions:

1. What is the amount of the interest accrual for November 30, 2013?
2. Delete from the list all notes that matured during December 2013. On December 2, 2013, the corporation signed an 80-day, $50,000.00, 7.8% note with Mitchell National Bank of Mitchell, Iowa. What is the total amount of the interest accrual for December 31, 2013?
3. What other features could be added to the spreadsheet to provide more information to management regarding its notes payable?

INPUT

- Review the rule for recording reversing entries.
- Ask students to identify how reversing a prepaid expense differs from reversing an accrued liability. (*The procedures are the same; the adjusting entry for prepaid expenses initially recorded as an expense created an asset, whereas the adjusting entry for accrued interest created a liability.*)
- Ask students to explain why the reversing entry results in a credit balance in Interest Expense.

MODEL

Analyze the transaction

- Draw two T accounts on the board and record the balance before the adjusting entry.
- Review the adjusting and closing entries while recording these transactions in the T accounts.
- Describe the reversing entry.
- Ask students to analyze the reversing entry. Complete the T accounts as the information is provided.

Record the transaction

- Use a general journal transparency to illustrate recording the reversing entry in the general journal or direct students to the illustration at the top of the page.

THINK LIKE AN ACCOUNTANT

This activity requires students to create formulas using dates. Before assigning this activity, tell students to open a blank worksheet and enter the current date in MM/DD/YYYY format. Instruct students to format the cell using the Comma style. The number displayed in the cell is the number of days since January 1, 1900. For example, the date 12/27/2014 is the 42,000th day since January 1, 1900. Excel uses these numbers, known as serial numbers, to calculate and display dates. Students will use serial numbers to calculate the maturity date and the number of days to accrue each note.

Answers

1. $8,703.43.
2. $10,940.40.
3. Answers will vary. Added features might include the following:
   a. A column that compares the term of a note to the accrual days to assist in identifying notes that have matured.
   b. A calculation of the total loan principal.
   c. A calculation of the average interest rate.

INPUT

- Explain that when a note is issued in one period and matures in another, the interest expense is divided between the two periods. Use the illustration at the top of the page to identify the portion of interest expense recorded in the current period.

MODEL

Analyze the transaction

- Draw three T accounts on the board and record the balance before the payment of a note.
- Ask students to analyze the transaction. Complete the T accounts as the information is provided.

Record the transaction

- Use a cash payments journal transparency to illustrate recording the payment of a note at maturity in the cash payments journal or direct students to the illustration at the top of the page.

TEACHING IDEA This chapter presents many opportunities to display visuals around the room correlating to new learning. You may obtain sample product warranties and display them. Also, a large illustration of a promissory note, with each part labeled, makes a good reference while students are studying the chapter.

FINANCIAL LITERACY

Answers

1. Grants, work-study programs, and federal loans.
2. Answers will vary, but may include being a U.S. citizen, having a social security number, registering with selective service if applicable, maintaining satisfactory academic progress, and earning a high school diploma or GED.
3. a. Answers will vary. Grants are free money based on need. Loans are borrowed money paid back with interest. Scholarships are free money based on predetermined selection criteria. Work-study programs place students in paid jobs to work part time while attending school.

   b. Loans require promissory notes.

   c. **Optional:** Spreadsheets should be organized so that they are easy to read and compare program features.

Payment of a Note At Maturity

Principal	×	Interest Rate	×	Time as a Fraction of Year	=	Total Interest Due
$9,000.00	×	8%	×	60/365	=	$118.36

CASH PAYMENTS JOURNAL PAGE 1

	DATE	ACCOUNT TITLE	CK. NO.	POST. REF.	1 GENERAL DEBIT	2 GENERAL CREDIT	3 ACCOUNTS PAYABLE DEBIT	4 PURCHASES DISCOUNT CREDIT	5 CASH CREDIT	
5	4	Notes Payable	855		9 0 0 0 00				9 1 1 8 36	5
6		Interest Expense			1 1 8 36					6
7										7
8										8

On the maturity date, Vaughn Distributors writes a check for the maturity value of $9,118.36.

This transaction to pay the maturity of a note is the same as illustrated in Lesson 9-1. Notes Payable will be decreased by a debit for $9,000.00, the principal of the note. The debit entry to Interest Expense is for $118.36, the interest for the entire term of the note.

The $118.36 debit entry to Interest Expense, less the $49.32 credit balance created by the reversing entry, equals the $69.04 interest expense for the current period.

Notes Payable

Debit		Credit	
2/4 Pay.	9,000.00	Bal.	9,000.00
(New Bal.	*zero)*		

Interest Expense

Debit		Credit	
2/4 Pay.	118.36	Rev.	49.32
(New Bal.	*69.04)*		

Cash

Debit		Credit	
		2/4 Pay.	9,118.36

February 4. Paid cash for the maturity value of the December 6 note: principal, $9,000.00, plus interest, $118.36; total, $9,118.36. Check No. 855.

FINANCIAL LITERACY

Fun with FAFSA

Each year, the U.S. Congress budgets billions of dollars to help students with financing for college. One of the most important steps for students is completing the U.S. Department of Education's *Free Application for Federal Student Aid* (*FAFSA*). This application is required for federal and state financial aid programs and should be completed annually regardless of admission status.

The FAFSA application is evaluated using the Department of Education's special formula to determine a family's financial situation. The result is the Expected Family Contribution, or EFC. The EFC measures the eligibility for federal student aid, since many of these programs are based on financial need. Schools use the EFC to determine the financial package offered, including eligibility for institutional scholarships and grants.

Other options, such as private loans, are also available. However, private loans generally come with higher interest rates.

ACTIVITIES

Go to the website www.studentaid.ed.gov and answer the following questions:

1. What are the three types of Federal Student Aid programs?
2. List at least five basic eligibility requirements to receive student aid.
3. a. Compare and contrast the features of the following: grant, loan—subsidized and unsubsidized, scholarship, and work-study.

   b. Indicate which programs require a promissory note.

   c. **Optional:** Prepare a spreadsheet comparing your findings.

© iStockphoto.com/Norebbo

Careers In Accounting

Judy Romano

TAX PREPARER/TAX ADVISOR

© iStockphoto.com/espiegle

Judy Romano started her career as a tax preparer. She worked for a major tax preparation company. In the beginning, she prepared tax returns for individuals and small businesses. Although many of the tax returns only required basic tax knowledge, some tax returns were more challenging. In these instances, Ms. Romano would need to research tax bulletins, published by the Internal Revenue Service, to ensure that the tax return was completed correctly.

Ms. Romano took additional classes offered by her company and began preparing tax returns for small corporations. She enjoyed working with these clients. However, she soon realized that many of her clients were paying more federal income tax than necessary because they were not aware of ways to lessen their tax liability. In her position, she did not have the opportunity to educate her clients on tax law and how to use it to their advantage.

At that point, Ms. Romano decided to open her own tax advice and preparation service. A major portion of her work was to study her client's prior tax returns and give them ideas on how to legally reduce their tax liability. When her clients follow her advice, it is rewarding for her to see results in the form of lower taxes for those clients.

When Ms. Romano started as a tax preparer, there were very few laws or restrictions covering paid tax return preparers. Now, the federal government and several state governments have established rules for paid tax preparers, including having a practitioner tax identification number (PTIN).

Salary Range: The median salary for a tax preparer is $31,000 per year.

Qualifications: Paid tax preparers (other than certified public accountants, attorneys, and enrolled agents) have to pass a competency test to become a registered tax return preparer. Finally, all registered tax return preparers must complete continuing education requirements each year.

Occupational Outlook: The career area of tax preparers is expected to experience slower than average growth (from 3% to 6%) through 2018.

Source: www.onetonline.org.

© iStockphoto.com/Mlenny

Careers In Accounting

Review a career as a tax preparer/tax advisor.

INPUT

- Explain that businesses that offer warranties must estimate the cost of the repair per item sold.
- Point out the Matching Expenses with Revenue concept when applied to warranties.
- Direct students to the math illustration to compute the estimated warranty expense.

MODEL

Analyze the transaction

- Draw two T accounts on the board.
- Refer to the math illustration to determine the amount used for the transaction.
- Ask students to analyze the transaction by answering these questions: Which accounts are affected? Are they increased or decreased? Are they debited or credited? Complete the T accounts as the information is provided.

Record the transaction

- Use a general journal to illustrate recording the transaction in the general journal or direct students to the illustration.

Journalizing Warranty Expense LO5

Debit the Expense Account

GENERAL JOURNAL — PAGE 1

	DATE	ACCOUNT TITLE	DOC. NO.	POST. REF.	DEBIT	CREDIT	
1		*Adjusting Entries*					1
24	31	*Warranty Expense*			51 000 00		24
25		*Accrued Warranty Liability*				51 000 00	25
26							26

Credit the Liability Account

Any business that offers customers a warranty on its merchandise must account for the cost of repairs and replacements. Jackson Sports offers its customers a two-year warranty on its golf carts. Jackson Sports makes all repairs resulting from defective parts free of charge to the customer.

When Jackson Sports sells a golf cart, it does not know the extent of repairs that will be required during the warranty period. Some carts have no problems; other carts may require extensive repairs. Jackson Sports estimates that it spends an average of $60.00 on warranty repairs for each cart.

The expenses associated with earning revenue should be recorded in the same accounting period. Thus, repair costs during the warranty period should be expensed in the same period as the cart sale. [CONCEPT: Matching Expenses with Revenue] Jackson Sports sold 850 carts during the fiscal year. The business estimates that $51,000.00 of repairs will be required for these carts during the warranty period.

Number of Units Sold	×	Estimated Warranty per Unit	=	Estimated Warranty Expense
850	×	$60.00	=	$51,000.00

Warranty Expense

Adj. 51,000.00	

Accrued Warranty Liability

Bal. 620.00	Adj. 51,000.00 *(New Bal. 50,380.00)*

Jackson Sports began the current year with a $49,000.00 credit balance in Accrued Warranty Liability. During the year $49,620.00 of warranty claims was paid, resulting in a $620.00 debit balance in the accrual account. Accountants must periodically review the estimates used to calculate accruals to determine if changes are necessary.

© iStockphoto.com/STILLFX

remember

Although Whiley Outdoor Living and Vaughn Distributors use different procedures, both correctly separate and record the asset and expense portions of the cost of supplies. Both procedures meet the requirements of the *Matching Expenses with Revenue* concept.

DIFFERENTIATED INSTRUCTION

Intrapersonal learners prefer to work alone. These students enjoy the success that comes from their own self-discovery. Ask students to use the Internet to research a popular process used in many industries to control costs, called Six Sigma. Students should prepare a newspaper article to inform others of the purpose of Six Sigma and its correlation to warranties.

Journalizing Warranty Payments

CASH PAYMENTS JOURNAL — PAGE 1

	DATE	ACCOUNT TITLE	CK. NO.	POST. REF.	1 GENERAL DEBIT	2 GENERAL CREDIT	3 ACCOUNTS PAYABLE DEBIT	4 PURCHASES DISCOUNT CREDIT	5 CASH CREDIT	
17	16	Accrued Warranty Liability	225		125 00				125 00	17
18										18
19										19

Jackson Sports accrues its warranty costs when it sells a golf cart. When cash is paid to make repairs, the payment reduces the estimated future warranty liability.

January 16. Paid cash to replace a defective battery, $125.00. Check No. 225.

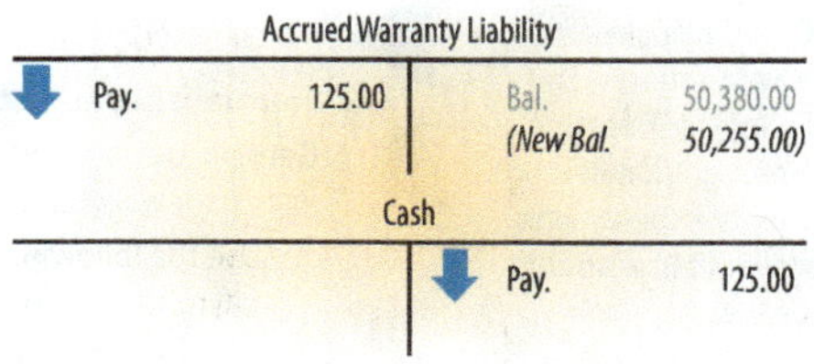

Accountants must periodically analyze the Accrued Warranty Liability account. If the actual costs incurred are significantly more or less than the $60.00 per cart, a new warranty expense estimate is computed.

With each sale on account, there is a chance that Jackson Sports will incur warranty costs. An estimate of these expenses is recorded in the same fiscal period as the sale. No expense is recorded when Jackson Sports incurs a warranty expenditure.

Accounting for Warranty Expense and Uncollectible Accounts Expense LO6

The accounting concept that supports the accounting for uncollectible accounts also applies to the accounting for warranty expenses. The *Matching Expenses with Revenue* principle requires that expenses associated with earning revenue be recorded in the same accounting period.

With each sale on account, there is a chance that the customer will not pay its account. There is also a chance that the business will be required to incur repairs or replace items in a future fiscal period. These expenses should be recorded in the same fiscal period as the revenue. The exact amount of each expense is not known at the time the sale is recorded. Thus, accountants must estimate these expenses and regularly evaluate the adequacy of their estimates.

Accrued Warranty Liability and Allowance for Uncollectible Accounts each have natural credit balances. These credit balances recognize that future, but unknown, expenses exist. The reporting for these accounts differs slightly. Allowance for Uncollectible Accounts has a related asset account and, therefore, is reported on the balance sheet as a contra asset account. In contrast, Warranty Payable does not have a related asset. As a result, Accrued Warranty Liability is reported as a liability on the balance sheet.

Accountants generally reverse an adjusting entry that creates a balance in a liability account. The accounting for uncollectible accounts and warranty expenses is an exception to this rule. Neither of the adjustments to estimate uncollectible accounts or warranty expenses is reversed.

© T.W. van Urk/Shutterstock.com

INPUT

- Explain that an entry must be made in the cash payments journal when a warranty payment is made for making a repair.
- Point out that each repair made will reduce the estimated future warranty liability.

MODEL

- Draw two T accounts on the board.
- Read the transaction statement.
- Ask students to analyze the transaction by answering these questions: Which accounts are affected? Are they increased or decreased? Are they debited or credited? Complete the T accounts as the information is provided.
- Use a cash payments journal transparency to illustrate recording the transaction in the cash payments journal or direct students to the illustration.

INPUT

- Point out that the accounting concept Matching Expenses with Revenue that applies to uncollectible accounts also applies to warranty expenses.
- Explain that with each sale on account, there is a chance the customer will not pay. With each warranty, there is also a chance that a repair will not have to be made.
- Warranty Payable is a liability account on the balance sheet that does not have a related asset account.

FORMATIVE ASSESSMENT

- This is an ongoing process. Circulate around the classroom or lab, observing which students have problems with the assignments.
- Troubleshooting: Diagnose the kinds of problems students have with this lesson. Students may have difficulty understanding why a reversing entry creates a credit balance in an expense account.
- Assess student understanding by checking solutions to Independent Practice assignments and noting their answers to the Terms Review and Audit Your Understanding questions.

CHECK FOR UNDERSTANDING

Term Review

- Call on students to define the term in the Term Review. A definition is given in the Glossary.

Audit Your Understanding

- Call on students to answer the Audit Your Understanding questions. Answers are given in Appendix D of the textbook.

GUIDED PRACTICE

Work Together

- Have students write the solution to the Work Together problem as you guide the class through the examples.
- Ask students to prepare T accounts for each account affected by the adjusting entries.
- Direct students to record the adjusting and reversing entries and warranty transactions.

INDEPENDENT PRACTICE

On Your Own

- Assign the On Your Own problem to be worked independently.
- Use the Formative Assessment techniques to diagnose student understanding.

Application Problem

- Assign Application Problem 8-3.

Online Working Papers

- Students can access the Lesson 8-3 problems using this software.

RETEACH

- Ask students to prepare a list of all transactions presented in this section.
- Ask students to explain the rule for determining if an adjusting entry should be reversed.
- Ask students to explain how the accounts and amounts of a reversing entry are determined.

CLOSURE

- Ask students to list the accrued expenses adjusted and reversed in this section.
- Ask students to explain how to determine if an accrued expense should be reversed.

End of Lesson Review

LO4 Journalize adjusting and reversing entries for accrued expenses.

LO5 Account for warranty expenses.

LO6 Compare the accounting principles supporting the recognition of warranty expense and uncollectible accounts expense.

Term Review

accrued expenses

Audit your understanding

1. What are the three steps to accrue an expense?
2. How do accountants determine if an adjusting entry for an accrued expense should be reversed?
3. When should the cost of repairing an item under warranty be expensed?
4. Identify the similarities and differences between the accounting for warranty costs and uncollectible accounts.

Work together 8-3

Journalizing adjusting and reversing entries for accrued expenses

General journals and a cash payments journal are provided in the *Working Papers*. Your instructor will guide you through the following examples.

1. Use the following information to journalize the adjusting entries for interest, payroll, payroll taxes, and warranties on December 31 of the current year.
   a. One note is outstanding on December 31: 90-day, 10% note with First Commercial Bank, $30,000.00, dated November 16.
   b. Payroll information for December 28 to December 31 is as follows:

Payroll and Employee Payroll Taxes		Employer Payroll Taxes	
Salaries	$3,200.00	Social security tax	$198.40
Federal income tax withheld	280.00	Medicare tax	46.40
Social security tax	198.40	Federal unemployment tax	4.80
Medicare tax	46.40	State unemployment tax	32.40

   c. Estimated warranty costs per item sold, $8.00. Units sold, 18,900.
2. Journalize the appropriate reversing entries on January 1 of the next year.
3. Journalize the following transactions.

Transactions:

Feb. 2. Paid cash to Electronic Service & Repair for warranty work performed for the company during January, $325.00. Check No. 667.
Paid cash for the maturity value of the November 16 note. Check No. 675.

On your own 8-3

Journalizing adjusting and reversing entries for accrued expenses

General journals and a cash payments journal are provided in the *Working Papers*. Work independently to complete the following problem.

1. Use the following information to journalize the adjusting entries for accrued interest, federal income tax, and warranties on December 31 of the current year.
   a. One note is outstanding on December 31: 120-day, 8% note with First American Bank, $16,000.00, dated September 20.
   b. The company owes additional federal income tax, $4,569.00.
   c. Estimated warranty costs per item sold, $2.25. Units sold, 32,600.
2. Journalize the appropriate reversing entries on January 1 of the next year.
3. Journalize the following transactions.

Transactions:

Jan. 12. Paid cash to D&D Service for warranty work performed for the company, $168.00. Check No. 552.
Paid cash for the maturity value of the September 20 note. Check No. 560.

Essential Questions

- A warranty provided by a company sets aside a certain amount to cover the cost of repairing deficiencies found in products after shipping. What can a company do before shipping to help reduce warranty costs? (*Protective packaging, employee training on proper handling, selection of reputable shipping companies, etc.*)
- What would be the terms of a warranty provided by your business? Explain. (*Answers might include period of time and a stipulation for normal wear and tear.*)

EXTENDED LEARNING

- Assign Think Like an Accountant on page 249.
- Assign Financial Literacy on page 250.
- Review Careers in Accounting on page 251.

A Look at Accounting Software

Drawing on a Line of Credit

Vaughn Distributors, Inc., has negotiated a line of credit with its bank. Within the terms of this agreement, Vaughn can draw cash against its line of credit as needed. The way a draw on the line of credit is handled is similar in a manual accounting system and an automated accounting system. In either case, the transaction likely takes place on the bank's web site and is recorded with a journal entry in the financial records.

One difference between a manual system and an automated system might be the method of accessing the bank's web site. In Vaughn's computerized accounting system, the banking module links directly to the bank's web site. Another difference is that the transaction is entered into the automated accounting system instead of recording a journal entry manually on paper.

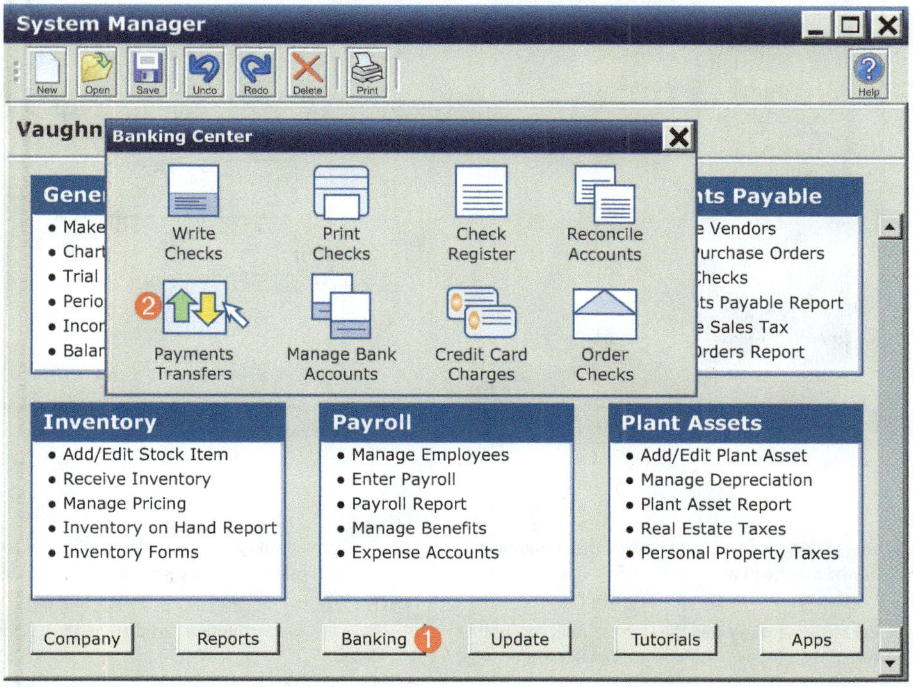

1. The accountant clicked on the **Banking** button on the System Manager window, which opened the Banking Center dialog box. The accounting system's security measures ensure that only authorized individuals can access specific functions within the banking module.
2. The accountant clicked on **Payments/Transfers.** That opened the browser, which automatically linked to the company's bank accounts, including its line of credit. A security window (not shown) opened with Vaughn's user name and password already entered along with a **Log In** button.

A Look at Accounting Software

Online banking offers individuals and businesses efficient ways to do business with a bank. This feature focuses on one simple function—transferring money between accounts. As anyone who uses online banking knows, these services are generally easy to use and very convenient. Students might be asked, based on their own or their parents' experience, to make a list of the banking services used online. These usually include viewing account activity and balances and transferring money. Paying bills online, accessing customer service, and ordering checks are common activities as well.

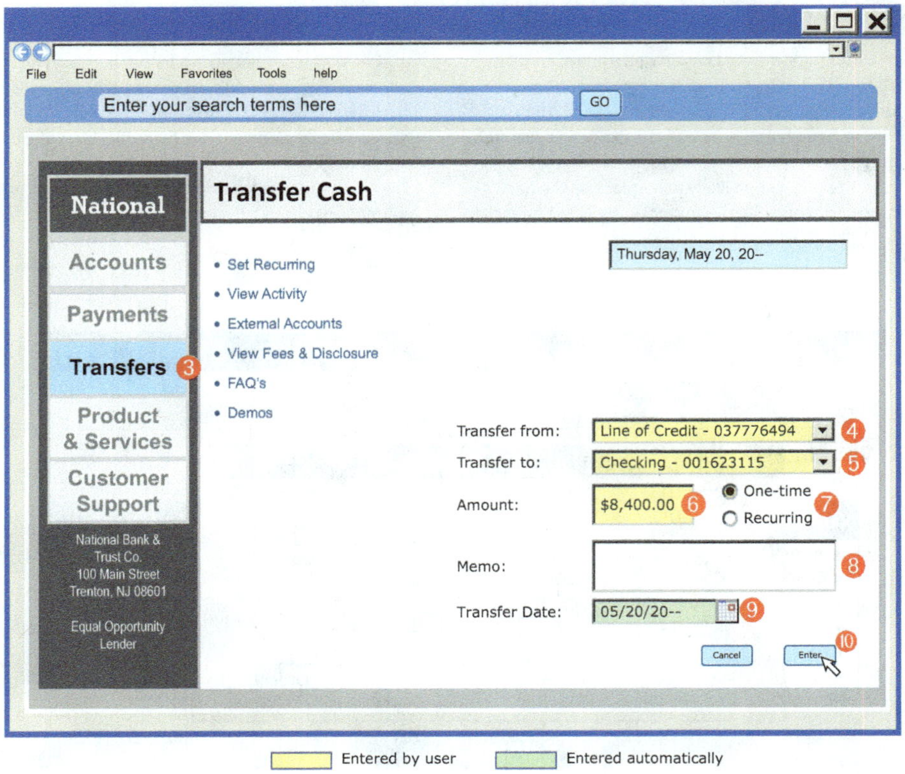

3. After clicking on the **Log In** button, the accountant viewed a menu of options. **Transfers** was selected, opening the Transfer Cash web page.
4. The accountant selected the Line of Credit account from the drop-down list labeled **Transfer from.**
5. In **Transfer to,** the checking account was selected.
6. The accountant entered the amount of the draw.
7. The default choice is for a one-time transaction, but the web site offers the company the option of setting up recurring transactions. For example, a bi-weekly draw might be set up to help the company meet its payroll obligations. If a recurring transaction had been set up, the bank would send a confirmation to the company via text message or email each time it executed the transfer.
8. The accountant could have entered a brief description of the transaction in the **Memo** field.
9. The transfer date defaults to the current date; however, the accountant can change it to a future date.
10. The accountant could click **Cancel** to clear all fields. Here the accountant has clicked on **Enter** to make the transfer. A new page would open, giving the accountant the opportunity to print or download a confirmation statement. The confirmation would be used as the source document for a journal entry to record the draw. From that page, the accountant could select another option from the main menu or log out.

Chapter Summary

A business needing capital to fund its operations may elect to obtain debt financing. One of the most common methods of debt financing is to sign a note payable with a financial institution. The interest on a note payable is calculated using the principal, annual interest rate, and the term of the note. Interest Expense is classified as Other Expense on the income statement.

A line of credit is a bank loan agreement that provides immediate short-term access to cash. The interest rate can change based on changes in market interest rates. Although a business can repay a line of credit at any time, monthly payments of principal and interest are typically required.

A prepaid expense is an expense paid in one fiscal period but not reported as an expense until a later fiscal period. Prepaid expenses may be recorded initially as assets or as expenses. In either case, an adjusting entry is required to recognize the expenses used during the current fiscal period. The adjusting entry creates a balance in an asset account. If an adjusting entry creates a balance in an asset or a liability account, the adjusting entry is reversed. This procedure is used when the prepaid expense will be used early in the next fiscal period.

The payment of an expense that will be used over several fiscal periods is initially recorded as an asset. An adjusting entry is required to recognize the portion of the expense used during the current fiscal period. However, no reversing entry is required.

An accrued expense is incurred in one fiscal period but not paid until a later fiscal period. An adjusting entry records the expense and creates a liability. Similar to prepaid expenses, accrued liabilities that will be paid early in the next fiscal period are reversed. A liability that extends over several periods is initially recorded as a liability. The procedure is similar to the accounting for uncollectible accounts receivable.

Impact of Changes in Foreign Exchange Rates on a Note Payable

U.S. companies often purchase products from foreign suppliers. Any changes in foreign exchange rates can have an impact on a firm's accounts payable and notes payable.

Suppose AmCorp, a U.S. company, gives ChiCorp, a Chinese corporation, a 12-month, 5% note payable for 1,000,000 yuan. Including the interest of 50,000 yuan (1,000,000 yuan × 5%), AmCorp will pay ChiCorp 1,050,000 yuan when the note matures. If the exchange rate at the beginning and at the end of the note remains the same (one yuan = $0.14), 1,050,000 yuan will cost $147,000 (1,050,000 yuan × $0.14).

Suppose, however, that during the 12-month period, the exchange rate between the yuan and the dollar declines from $0.14 to $0.13. Since a yuan costs less, AmCorp can now purchase 1,050,000 yuan for $136,500 (1,050,000 yuan × $0.13). Due to the one-cent decline in the exchange rate, AmCorp realizes a gain of $10,500 ($147,000 – $136,500) through the currency exchange process. AmCorp accounts for the gain on accounts payable using the entry below.

Notes Payable	140,000	
Interest Expense	7,000	
Cash		136,500
Gain or Loss on Foreign Currency Exchange		10,500

EXPLORE ACCOUNTING

INSTRUCTIONS

An American company, Fashion Clothiers, purchases men's clothing on account from a Canadian firm, Delmar, Inc., for 50,000 Canadian dollars. At the time of the sale, the exchange rate is one Canadian dollar equals 0.98 U.S. dollar. Thirty days later, when Fashion Clothiers pays the 50,000 Canadian dollars, the exchange rate has risen. One Canadian dollar can now be exchanged for 1.02 dollars. How much will it cost Fashion Clothiers to purchase Canadian dollars at the new rate? Use T accounts to show the impact on Fashion Clothiers.

© iStockphoto.com/Makhnach_M

CLOSURE

- Review the Chapter Summary.
- Ask students to prepare a list of the new concepts introduced in this chapter.

Essential Questions

- Should terms and conditions be assigned to each warranty provided? Explain. (*Each product warranty should have its own terms and conditions, as each product has its own lifetime and different variables in determining if it should be replaced or repaired.*)
- Why do most companies have to borrow cash? (*Answers might include to obtain assets or to manage cash shortages.*)

EXTENDED LEARNING

- Review A Look at Accounting Software on pages 255 and 256.
- Assign Explore Accounting on page 257.

EXPLORE ACCOUNTING

Answers

The inventory would be purchased for $49,000 (50,000 Canadian dollars × $0.98). At the time of payment, it would cost $51,000 (50,000 Canadian dollars × $1.02) to pay the account. The result is a $2,000 loss on the foreign currency exchange.

Inventory

Debit		Credit	
Purchase	49,000.00		

Accounts Payable

Debit		Credit	
Payment	49,000.00	Purchase	49,000.00

Cash

Debit		Credit	
		Payment	51,000.00

Gain or Loss on Foreign Currency Exchange

Debit		Credit	
Payment	2,000.00		

CHECK FIGURES

For complete solutions to Chapter 8 problems, see the Teacher's Edition of the Working Papers.

Application Problem 8-1

Interest Expense debits: Sept. 21, $99.86; Nov. 12, $493.15; Dec. 31, $67.25.

Application Problem 8-2

Adjusting entries credits: Supplies Expense, $940.00; Insurance Expense, $1,200.00; Prepaid Advertising, $40,000.00.

Apply Your Understanding

INSTRUCTIONS: Download problem instructions for Excel, QuickBooks, and Sage 50 from the textbook companion website at www.C21accounting.com.

8-1 Application Problem: Journalizing notes payable transactions LO1

A cash receipts journal and a cash payments journal are provided in the *Working Papers*. Source documents are abbreviated as: check, C; memorandum, M; receipt, R.

Instructions:

1. Using the current year, journalize the following transactions in the cash receipts journal.

Transactions:

May 16.	Obtained a note from Farmers Bank. The $10,000.00 is due in 180 days and has a 10% interest rate. R445.
June 23.	Negotiated a 90-day, 9% note with American Bank. The $4,500.00 proceeds were deposited in the corporation's checking account. R490.
Dec. 12.	Used an Internet banking site to transfer $6,000.00 from its line of credit to its checking account. R580.

2. Calculate the maturity date of each note payable and the total amount of interest due at the maturity date.
3. Journalize the following transactions in the cash payments journal. Use the maturity dates and interest amounts calculated in the previous instruction to journalize the payments of the notes payable.

Transactions:

	Wrote Check No. 446 to pay the maturity value of the $4,500.00 note.
	Paid cash for the maturity value of the $10,000.00 note. C588.
Dec. 31.	Used the Internet banking site to pay the December interest, $67.25 plus $500.00 of principal on its line of credit. M71 (enter the memorandum number in the Check No. column).

AAONLINE

1. Go to www.cengage.com/login
2. Click on AA Online to access.
3. Go to the online assignment and follow the instructions.

8-2 Application Problem: Journalizing adjusting and reversing entries for prepaid expenses LO2

West River, Inc., has the following general ledger account balances on December 31 of the current year before it records adjusting entries. A general journal is provided in the *Working Papers*.

Supplies Expense	$ 5,900.00
Insurance Expense	16,000.00
Prepaid Advertising	90,000.00

Instructions:

1. Using the following adjustment information, journalize the adjusting entries on December 31 of the current year.

Supplies inventory	$ 940.00
Value of prepaid insurance	1,200.00
Advertising used	40,000.00

2. Journalize the reversing entries on January 1 of the next year.

8-3 Application Problem: Journalizing adjusting and reversing entries for accrued expenses LO4, 5

General journals and a cash payments journal are provided in the *Working Papers*.

Instructions:

1. Use the following information to journalize the adjusting entries for accrued interest, accrued payroll, accrued employer payroll taxes, warranties, and federal income tax on December 31 of the current year.
   a. One note is outstanding on December 31: 180-day, 9% note with Windstar Bank, $50,000.00, dated October 10.
   b. Payroll information for December 29 to December 31:

Payroll and Employee Payroll Taxes		Employer Payroll Taxes	
Salaries	$2,850.00	Social security tax	$176.70
Federal income tax withheld	240.00	Medicare tax	41.33
Social security tax	176.70	Federal unemployment tax	3.60
Medicare tax	41.33	State unemployment tax	24.30

   c. Estimated warranty costs per item sold, $30.00. Units sold during fiscal year, 6,900.
   d. The company owes additional federal income tax, $3,248.00.
2. Journalize the appropriate reversing entries on January 1 of the next year.
3. Journalize the following transaction.

Transactions:

Mar. 12. Paid cash to John Patterson for parts he purchased to repair an item under warranty, $89.95. Check No. 334.
Paid cash for the maturity value of the October 10 note: principal, $50,000.00, plus interest. Check No. 401.

Sage 50 Accounting

1. Journalize and post adjusting and reversing entries to the general journal.
2. From the menu bar, select Reports & Forms; General Ledger.
3. Print the general journal and general ledger trial balance.

QB Quick Books

1. Journalize and post adjusting and reversing entries to the journal.
2. From the menu bar, select Reports; Accountant & Taxes.
3. Print the journal and trial balance.

Excel

1. Journalize and post adjusting and reversing entries to the general journal.
2. Print the worksheets.

8-M Mastery Problem: Journalizing notes payable transactions and adjusting and reversing entries LO1, 2, 4, 5

Sage 50 Accounting

1. Journalize and post notes payable transactions to the cash receipts journal.
2. Journalize and post adjusting and reversing entries to the general journal.
3. From the menu bar, select Reports & Forms; General Ledger.
4. Print the general journal and general ledger trial balance.

QB Quick Books

1. Journalize and post notes payable transactions to the cash receipts journal.
2. Journalize and post adjusting and reversing entries to the journal.
3. From the menu bar, select Reports & Forms; General Ledger.
4. Print the journal and general ledger trial balance.

Roberts, Inc., completed the following transactions during the current year. Roberts initially records supplies and insurance as expenses and maintains a liability account for estimated warranty expenses. Source documents are abbreviated as follows: check, C; memorandum, M; receipt, R.

Instructions:

1. Journalize the following transactions in a cash receipts journal.

Transactions:

Aug. 10. Agreed to a 180-day, 8% note with National Bank for $20,000.00. R123.
Oct. 20. Received $25,000.00 from First American Bank, signing a 90-day, 10% note. R149.
Nov. 5. Signed a $13,000.00, 90-day, 9% note with First Commerce Bank. R152.
Dec. 9. Drew $6,200.00 from its First American Bank line of credit. The bank deposited the funds directly to its checking account. R165.

2. Use the following information to journalize adjusting entries for prepaid expenses and accrued expenses on December 31 of the current year. Include the adjusting entry for the accrued interest on the outstanding notes payable.

Supplies inventory	$ 480.00
Value of prepaid insurance	2,400.00
Advertising used	20,000.00
Additional federal income tax owed	875.00

Application Problem 8-3

Selected adjusting entries credits: Interest Payable, $1,010.96; Accrued Warranty Liability, $207,000.00; Federal Income Tax Payable, $3,248.00.

Mastery Problem 8-M

Interest Expense debits: Jan. 18, $616.44; Jan. 31, $75.69; Feb. 3, $288.49; Feb. 6, $789.04.

Adjusting entries credits: Supplies Expense, $480.00; Insurance Expense, $2,400.00; Prepaid Advertising, $20,000.00; Interest Payable, $1,299.51; Federal Income Tax Payable, $875.00.

INDEPENDENT PRACTICE

- Assign Mastery Problem 8-M for students as a culminating problem that combines all new learning from the chapter.
- Assign Challenge Problem 8-C to accelerated students who work at a faster pace.
- Assign Study Guide 8.
- Students can access Online Working Papers to work end-of-chapter problems on the computer.
- Direct students to the C21 Accounting companion website for additional practice and review opportunities.

RETEACH

- Call on students to describe how they avoid the trouble spots diagnosed.
- Use reteaching suggestions from lesson plans as required.
- Assign Recycling Problem 8-R if needed.

FORMATIVE ASSESSMENT

- Review solutions to the assigned problems in class, diagnosing trouble spots.

EXTENDED LEARNING

- Assign 21st Century Skills on page 261.
- Assign Analyzing Home Depot's Financial Statements on page 261.

SUMMATIVE EVALUATION

- Chapter 8 Test
- Cognero for Chapter 8

Challenge Problem 8-C

Answers may vary. Product Claims Expense, $4,920.00 (based on 0.45% estimated claim ratio).

1. Journalize and post notes payable transactions to the cash receipts journal.
2. Journalize and post adjusting and reversing entries to the general journal.
3. Print the worksheets.

AA ONLINE

1. Go to www.cengage.com/login
2. Click on AA Online to access.
3. Go to the online assignment and follow the instructions.

3. Journalize the appropriate reversing entries on January 1 of the next year.
4. Calculate the maturity date for each note payable and the total amount of interest due at the maturity date.
5. Journalize the following transactions on a cash payments journal. For the payment of each note payable, use the maturity dates calculated in the prior step.

Transactions:

Jan. 12. Wrote a check to John Patterson for parts he purchased to repair an item under warranty, $89.95. C394.
Issued Check No. 405 for the maturity value of the First American Bank note, plus interest.

31. Used the bank's Internet site to pay $1,000.00 plus $75.69 interest on its line of credit. M84 (enter the memorandum number in the Check No. column).
Paid the maturity value of the First Commerce Bank note, plus interest. C423.
Wrote Check No. 428 to pay off the National Bank note, plus interest. C428.

8-C Challenge Problem: Accruing for self-insurance losses LO4

Presto Pizza operates a pizza delivery business. An unfortunate cost of operating the business is that customers may sue the company if they get sick after eating its pizza. Presto Pizza believes that most of these claims are unfounded. There is rarely ever any evidence that the pizza, rather than other factors, caused the customers to get sick.

For years, Pesto Pizza carried insurance coverage to protect it against these claims. However, the insurance premiums had risen dramatically in recent years, despite Presto Pizza filing fewer and fewer claims. To save money, Presto Pizza has decided to drop its insurance coverage effective January 1, 20X6. Instead, Presto Pizza will self-insure against these claims. Any future claims will be paid directly by Presto Pizza.

The following table presents information related to sales, product claims, and insurance premiums for the past five fiscal years.

	20X1	20X2	20X3	20X4	20X5
Sales	$823,632	$856,528	$896,800	$928,540	$970,463
Product claims	4,637	4,454	4,314	4,243	4,173
Insurance premiums	6,000	7,000	9,000	9,000	12,000

Instructions:

1. Identify accounts to be used to accrue the expense of product claims beginning in 20X6. Create a T account for each account. Use the forms in the *Working Papers*.
2. Use the T accounts to record the following transactions:

Transactions:

Feb. 6. Paid Family Medical Clinic $450 for the treatment of a customer who claimed the pizza made her sick.
June 9. Agreed to settle Mary Stephenson's lawsuit for $3,600.
Oct. 15. Wrote a check to Davidson County Hospital for the treatment of a customer who claimed there were foreign objects in her pizza, $89.

3. Record an adjusting entry for the expense of product claims. Use the form in the *Working Papers* to calculate the past ratios of claims to sales. Use this information to calculate an accrual for product claims. Sales for 20X6 were $1,093,267.

21st Century Skills

The Cost of Staying Connected

Theme: Financial, Economic, Business, and Entrepreneurial Literacy

Skills: Critical Thinking and Problem Solving, Communication and Collaboration, ICT Literacy

PARTNERSHIP FOR 21ST CENTURY SKILLS

Insurance is a common prepaid expense. Protecting a business with insurance minimizes the risk associated with unexpected losses and liabilities. Business owners, as well as consumers, must evaluate the different types of insurance available and buy the coverage needed. Almost every gadget can be insured. These costs can add up, so one must evaluate if the small risks *should* be insured.

Popular property insurance applicable to most everyone today, including teens, is cell phone insurance. Most new cell phones come with a manufacturer's warranty, but this usually only covers defects. Sales brochures promote "replacement is just a call away" if a phone is lost, broken, or stolen. However, a closer look at the insurance policy will provide the details and limitations. For example, what is considered normal wear and tear that may not be covered? What is a replacement phone? When is a phone repaired instead of replaced?

Although the transaction to purchase insurance takes place with the cell phone company, the coverage is usually provided by a third party. While insurance may be worthwhile if one owns an expensive cell phone or is prone to loss or damage, be sure to read the policy and know that the local cell phone provider may not be able to assist with your misfortune.

APPLICATION

1. Use the Internet or visit stores to obtain the cell phone insurance policies for three different cell phone carriers. Compare and contrast: (a) what is considered normal wear and tear, (b) what is a replacement phone, (c) when is a phone repaired instead of replaced, (d) what is the cost of the insurance, (e) what is the deductible, if any. Report your findings.
2. Explain whether cell phone insurance is worth the cost.
3. If you lost your phone and did not have cell phone insurance, what are your options to maintain service?

Analyzing Home Depot's financial statements

An investor interested in learning how much Home Depot spends on advertising must read beyond its Consolidated Statement of Earnings. Home Depot's advertising expense is not listed separately on the statement but is included in selling, general, and administrative expenses. Information regarding advertising can be obtained in the Notes to Consolidated Financial Statements. Note 1, Summary of Significant Accounting Policies, beginning on page B-10 in Appendix B, contains two sections that reveal how Home Depot accounts for advertising expenses.

INSTRUCTIONS

1. In the section Prepaid Advertising, when are the costs of producing television advertising recognized as an expense?
2. Refer to the Vendor Allowances section to identify the gross advertising expense for each fiscal year presented.
3. What are vendor allowances, and how does Home Depot account for these allowances?

COMMON CORE AND INTERDISCIPLINARY STUDIES

Extended learning features and activities present numerous opportunities to implement Common Core Standards through interdisciplinary studies. Practice is provided in the common core areas of English Language Arts & Literacy and Mathematical Practice. Many of these activities require short, critical-thinking and decision-making responses that apply reading, writing, speaking, listening, language, media and technology, and mathematical skills.

21ST CENTURY SKILLS

Answers

1. Answers will vary. Normal wear and tear may include shattered screens and malfunctions. A replacement phone could include a refurbished phone with limited capabilities. A policyholder may not have the option to obtain a new, similar phone for replacement. Costs will vary but usually include a monthly fee ranging from \$4–\$12 per month with an average of \$100 deductible.
2. Answers will vary. Considerations should include the cost to replace the phone with a new, similar model; the amount of time the phone will be owned; the cost of the insurance; and the deductible.
3. Answers will vary. Options might include paying for a new replacement phone, purchasing a refurbished phone from a cell phone carrier, or purchasing a used phone from a private individual.

ANALYZING HOME DEPOT'S FINANCIAL STATEMENTS

Answers

1. Television and radio advertising production costs, along with media placement costs, are expensed when the advertisement first appears.
2. Gross advertising expense was \$831 million, \$846 million, and \$864 million in fiscal years 2012, 2011, and 2010, respectively.
3. Vendor allowances are rebates paid to Home Depot by its vendors. Home Depot earns vendor allowances by reaching established volume targets and by advertising the vendors' products. Volume rebates and some advertising rebates are initially recorded as a reduction to merchandise inventories. Certain advertising rebates are recorded as an offset to advertising expense.

Chapter 9

Accounting for Unearned Revenue, Accrued Revenue, and Installment Notes Receivable

Scope & Sequence

	New	Review/Enrich
Introduction		
Introduce the Chapter		
Lesson 9-1: Unearned and Accrued Revenue		
Adjusting Entry for Unearned Revenue	✓	
Reversing Entry for Unearned Revenue	✓	
Adjusting Entry for Accrued Interest Income		✓
Reversing Entry for Accrued Interest Income		✓
Lesson 9-2: Accounting for Gift Cards		
Recording the Sale of a Gift Card	✓	
Recording a Sale with a Gift Card	✓	
Accounting for Unredeemed Gift Cards	✓	
Reporting of Gift Card Breakage	✓	
Lesson 9-3: Accounting for Installment Notes Receivable		
Issuing an Installment Note Receivable	✓	
Receiving a Monthly Payment on an Installment Note Receivable	✓	
Reclassification Entry for Installment Notes Receivable	✓	
Reversing Entry for a Reclassification Entry	✓	
Closure		

Enhancing Instruction

Features	Common Core Standards
• Accounting in the Real World: Southwest Airlines Co.	• ELAL—reading
• Ethics in Action: Sharing Nonpublic Information	• ELAL—reading
• Global Awareness: Legal Rights in Foreign Countries	• ELAL—reading, technology and media, writing
• Why Accounting?: Getting What They Want to Sell	• ELAL—reading, writing
• Think Like an Accountant: Creating an Amortization Schedule	• Mathematics
• Forensic Accounting: A Royal Disaster	• Mathematics
• A Look at Accounting Software	• ELAL—reading
• Explore Accounting	• ELAL—reading, writing
• 21st Century Skills	• ELAL—speaking, media and technology
• Analyzing Home Depot's Financial Statements	• Mathematics

ELAL = English Language Arts & Literacy

Calculator: © iStockphoto.com/picstodisc Paper: © iStockphoto.com/Qingwa

Practice and Assessment

Technology & Media	Teaching Strategies	Guided Practice	Independent Practice	Reteach/Enrich
• Instructor's Resource CD/Website: PowerPoint Slides Accounting Concepts • Online Working Papers • Transparency Master: General Journal		• Terms Review • Audit Your Understanding • Work Together 9-1	• On Your Own 9-1 • Application Problem 9-1 • Formative Assessment, p. 268 • Online Working Papers	• Reteach, p. 269
• Instructor's Resource CD/Website: PowerPoint Slides Accounting Concepts • Online Working Papers • Transparency Masters: General Journal, Cash Receipts Journal (7-column)	• Gifted Learners	• Term Review • Audit Your Understanding • Work Together 9-2	• On Your Own 9-2 • Application Problem 9-2 • Formative Assessment, p. 272 • Online Working Papers	• Reteach, p. 273
• Instructor's Resource CD/Website: PowerPoint Slides Accounting Concepts • Online Working Papers • Transparency Masters: Cash Receipts Journal (7-column), General Journal	• Mathematical/Logical Learners	• Terms Review • Audit Your Understanding • Work Together 9-3	• On Your Own 9-3 • Application Problem 9-3 • Formative Assessment, p. 278 • Online Working Papers	• Reteach, p. 279
• Online Working Papers	• Common Core and Interdisciplinary Studies		• Mastery Problem 9-M • Study Guide 9 • Chapter 9 Test • Cognero Chapter 9	• Challenge Problem 9-C • Reteach, p. 284 • Recycling Problem 9-R • Reinforcement Activity 2

Introduce the Chapter

SET THE STAGE

GUIDING QUESTIONS

- Ask students if they have ever received money before earning it. Have them explain their answers.
- Ask students to predict how they will calculate interest for a fraction of a year.
- Ask why interest is sometimes calculated based on a 360-day year instead of a 365-day year.
- Ask students if they have an unused gift card. Ask how long they have owned the card. Ask students to predict how a business might account for unused gift cards.
- Ask students to brainstorm situations when they would request an installment loan.
- Ask students to explain the relationship between a loan, the monthly payments, and the ending balance over a period of time.

PREVIEW CHAPTER OBJECTIVES

- Point out that students were introduced to installment notes, unearned revenue, and accrued revenue in the first-year course.
- Point out that this chapter will review the concepts presented in the first-year course and introduce many new concepts related to installment notes, unearned revenue, and accrued revenue.

PREVIEW ACCOUNTING TERMS

- Read each term aloud to verify its pronunciation for students.
- Point out terms or parts of terms that should already be familiar to most students, such as *unearned revenue*, *accrued revenue*, and *installment note*.
- Lead an interactive discussion with students to review and explain the terms. Stress that special attention should be directed to all boldfaced and highlighted words presented in the text.

Chapter 9

Accounting for Unearned Revenue, Accrued Revenue, and Installment Notes Receivable

LEARNING OBJECTIVES

After studying Chapter 9, in addition to defining key terms, you will be able to:

LO1 Describe and illustrate the adjusting and reversing entries for unearned revenue.

LO2 Describe and illustrate the adjusting and reversing entries for accrued revenue.

LO3 Journalize transactions for gift cards.

LO4 Record an adjusting entry for gift card breakage.

LO5 Describe how gift card breakage is reported in the financial statements.

LO6 Journalize transactions for installment notes receivable.

LO7 Describe and illustrate the reclassification and reversing entries for installment notes receivable.

Calculator: © iStockphoto.com/picstodisc; Paper: © iStockphoto.com/Qingwa

Accounting In The Real World

Southwest Airlines Co.

From the moment you begin boarding a Southwest Airlines flight, you know that this is not your typical airline. You can pick your seat when you board the aircraft. Don't be surprised if a flight attendant shares a joke while announcing the beverage service. From its ticket agents to baggage handlers, Southwest employees strive to make flying fun. However, what can you expect from a company whose stock symbol is LUV? In addition, unlike some of its competitors, Southwest consistently earns a profit.

In many industries, the company provides the goods or services to a customer and is paid either immediately or at a later date. However, the airline industry does not operate that way. In the airline industry, the company gets paid when the customer purchases a ticket, but it usually does not provide the service until sometime in the future. Another way in which the airline industry is unique is the frequent flyer program that many companies offer. This provides free transportation after the customer accumulates a certain number of miles or flights.

Both of these situations affect the financial statements of an airline. Southwest Airlines records these events as liabilities, called *air traffic liability*. This liability can make up a substantial portion of a company's current liabilities.

CRITICAL THINKING

1. Assume an airline company records a liability when a customer purchases a ticket for a future flight. When will the company decrease the liability?
2. When the company reduces the liability, what other account will be affected?

Source: www.southwest.com.

Background: © iStockphoto.com/Marchcattle; Real World: Jeff Haynes/Reuters/Landov

Key Terms

- unearned revenue
- accrued revenue
- breakage
- installment note
- amortization schedule
- reclassification entry

Accounting In The Real World

Answers

1. The company will decrease the liability when the ticket is used for the flight for which it was purchased.
2. A revenue account will be increased when the liability is decreased because the airline will have then earned the revenue.

LESSON

9-1

BRIDGE

- Students learned about unearned revenue in the first-year course. Ask students to provide some examples of unearned revenue.
- Ask students to predict when they think unearned revenue will appear in the accounting records as revenue actually earned.

TEACHING RESOURCES

- **Instructor's Resource CD/Website:** PowerPoint Slides Accounting Concepts
- **Working Papers:** Teacher's Edition of the Working Papers for Lesson 9-1 Online Working Papers
- **Transparency Master:** General Journal

ENGAGE

- Ask students to prepare a list of prepaid expenses. Describe how an expense for one business is usually revenue for another business. Apply this concept to the list of prepaid expenses.

PREVIEW

- Call on students to read the accounting terms and definitions introduced in this lesson: *unearned revenue* and *accrued revenue*.
- Point out the learning objectives for this lesson.
- Direct students to read the headings in this lesson and to examine the illustrations.

INPUT

- Ask students to determine why Rent Income is classified as Other Revenue. (*Vaughn Distributors is not in the business of renting buildings; thus, this revenue should not be mixed with its primary revenue source—selling appliances.*)
- Instruct students to read the FYI on page 265 to learn how a business can initially record unearned revenue as a liability.

LESSON

9-1 Unearned and Accrued Revenue

LO1 Describe and illustrate the adjusting and reversing entries for unearned revenue.
LO2 Describe and illustrate the adjusting and reversing entries for accrued revenue.

Adjusting Entry for Unearned Revenue LO1

Debit Rent Income

GENERAL JOURNAL — PAGE 13

	DATE		ACCOUNT TITLE	DOC. NO.	POST. REF.	DEBIT	CREDIT	
1			*Adjusting Entries*					1
12		31	*Rent Income*			5 000 00		12
13			*Unearned Rent*				5 000 00	13

Credit Unearned Rent

Cash received for goods or services which have not been provided is called **unearned revenue**. Unearned revenue is also known as *deferred revenue.*

Unearned revenue may be recorded initially as a liability or as revenue. Vaughn Distributors, Inc., rents part of its building to Keller Construction. During the year, Vaughn receives four checks from Keller, each for the next three months' rent. Most of these rental payments will be earned during the current fiscal year. For this reason, Vaughn has elected to record rent receipts initially as revenue.

On December 1, Vaughn Distributors received $7,500.00 from Keller Construction ($2,500.00 per month for December, January, and February rent). The receipt was recorded initially as rent income and is included in the $35,000.00 balance of Rent Income.

ETHICS IN ACTION

Sharing Nonpublic Information

Juanita Suarez, CPA, is a financial analyst for Natural Stores. The company manufactures a line of organic and gluten-free snack foods. As a result, Natural Stores purchases large quantities of corn and rice. Juanita's job is to track production costs and provide management with projections of future grain prices.

While attending a tailgate party before a football game, Juanita's friends were involved in a spirited conversation about the rising cost of going to the supermarket. "Have you seen what's happened to cereal prices lately?" bemoaned one friend. "Just another example of big business padding their wallets at our expense!" added another friend.

Juanita could not stay quiet any longer. "Oh, quit complaining. So much of the grain supply is being diverted for the production of alternative fuels. Our grain costs have skyrocketed. We're only passing part of the cost on to the consumer. People are going to be surprised when we report earnings."

INSTRUCTIONS

Access *A Champion's Code of Conduct* of General Mills. Use this code as a guide and the ethical model to help determine whether Juanita's comments demonstrate ethical behavior. Does this statement represent the disclosure of nonpublic information?

© iStockphoto.com/LdF

ETHICS IN ACTION

Encourage students to evaluate each of Juanita's statements. Juanita can discuss the change in grain prices, assuming that this information is available publicly. However, she should not discuss the impact of these costs on the financial results of the company.

This activity illustrates how easily an employee can reveal nonpublic information while participating in casual conversations with friends and family. As an extension of this activity, ask students with part-time jobs to suggest statements they could make regarding the financial performance of their employer that would constitute the sharing of nonpublic information.

See a suggested solution for this feature in the Instructional Strategies section at the front of this book.

Rent Income			
Adj.	5,000.00	12/31 Bal.	35,000.00
		(New Bal.	30,000.00)

Unearned Rent			
		Adj.	5,000.00

Only that part of the rent actually earned should be recorded as revenue in a fiscal period. An adjusting entry is recorded to separate the earned and unearned portions of the rent recorded in Rent Income, as shown above. The January and February rent is unearned and should be reported in Unearned Rent.

The $5,000.00 balance of Unearned Rent, a liability account, represents the value of two months of rental use owed to Keller Construction. The new balance of Rent Income, $30,000.00, correctly reflects 12 months of rent at $2,500.00 per month.

Unearned Rent is classified as a current liability, since the rent will be earned during the next fiscal period. Because Vaughn Distributors is not in the business of renting buildings, Rent Income is classified as Other Revenue.

fyi

A company can elect to record rent payments as Unearned Rent during the year. At December 31, it records an adjusting entry to recognize the revenue earned during the year. Recording unearned revenue initially either as a liability or as revenue is acceptable accounting practice. Vaughn Distributors prefers recording unearned revenue as revenue because the unearned revenue eventually will become revenue as the building space is used.

Cozyta/Fotolia LLC

INPUT

- Ask students to explain the meaning of a $5,000.00 balance in Unearned Rent as illustrated in the T account on page 265. (*If Keller Construction was able to cancel its rental agreement on December 31, Vaughn Distributors would owe Keller a $5,000.00 refund.*)

MODEL

Analyze the transaction

- Draw two T accounts on the board and enter the balance amount.
- Describe the adjusting entry.
- Ask students to analyze the adjusting entry.

Record the transaction

- Use a general journal transparency to illustrate recording the adjusting entry in the general journal or direct students to the illustration on page 264.

INPUT

- Point out that the rule for determining if an adjusting entry should be reversed applies to both revenue and expense adjusting entries.
- Ask students to describe each of the prior years' entries shown in the T accounts.
- Ask students to identify what the $5,000.00 credit balance in Rent Income represents.

MODEL

- Draw two T accounts on the board and enter the pre-adjustment balances.
- Ask students to describe the adjusting and closing entries as you record them in the T accounts.
- Describe the reversing entry.
- Ask students to analyze the reversing entry by answering these questions: Which accounts are affected? Are they increased or decreased? Are they debited or credited? Complete the T accounts as the information is provided.
- Use a general journal transparency to illustrate recording the transaction in the general journal or direct students to the illustration.

GLOBAL AWARENESS

Answers

Answers will vary.

Reversing Entry for Unearned Revenue

Debit Unearned Rent

GENERAL JOURNAL — PAGE 1

	DATE		ACCOUNT TITLE	DOC. NO.	POST. REF.	DEBIT	CREDIT	
1			*Reversing Entries*					1
10		1	*Unearned Rent*			5 000 00		10
11			*Rent Income*				5 000 00	11

Credit Rent Income

Unearned Rent

Rev.	**5,000.00**	Adj.	5,000.00

Rent Income

Adj.	5,000.00	12/31 Bal.	35,000.00
Clos.	30,000.00	**Rev.**	**5,000.00**
		(New Bal.	***5,000.00)***

On December 31, Rent Income is closed as part of Vaughn Distributors' closing entries. After closing entries are posted, the balance in Rent Income is zero and ready to record transactions in the next fiscal period.

Reversing entries for prepaid and accrued expenses are described in Chapter 8. If an adjusting entry creates a balance in an asset or liability account, the adjusting entry is normally reversed. Reversing entries for unearned revenue are made for the same reason as for prepaid expenses. The amount of unearned revenue must be returned to the account in which it was recorded initially.

Vaughn Distributors' adjusting entry created a balance in the liability account, Unearned Rent. Therefore, Vaughn Distributors needs to make a reversing entry for unearned rent on January 1, as shown above.

On January 1, after the reversing entry is posted, the new balance of Unearned Rent is zero, as it was before the adjusting entry. Rent Income has a $5,000.00 credit balance. The rent received in advance for January and February, $5,000.00, is part of the rent revenue earned in the new fiscal period.

GLOBAL AWARENESS

Legal Rights in Foreign Countries

While traveling, working, or living in a foreign country, U.S. citizens are expected to obey the laws of that country. Some of these laws may be very different from those in the United States. The punishment for a specific crime in a foreign country may be much harsher than that for the same crime in the United States.

A U.S. citizen arrested for a crime in a foreign country must follow that country's legal process for being charged with a crime, convicted, or sentenced, and for appealing a conviction. Usually, however, the U.S. citizen does not have to go through this process without help.

The United States has embassies in many countries. These embassies as well as the U.S. Department of State (the State Department) provide help to U.S. citizens who have been jailed in a foreign country. The website for the Department of State notes that "The State Department is committed to ensuring fair and humane treatment for American citizens imprisoned overseas ... within the limits of our authority in accordance with international law."

The State Department website gives specific information for many countries. This information includes a description of the country and its political climate, entry/exit requirements for U.S. citizens, and other information.

CRITICAL THINKING

Go to the website for the U.S. Department of State (www.state.gov). Pick a country you would like to visit. Search the site for specific information about that country. Summarize your findings in the following categories:

a. Country description.
b. Address of one embassy in this country.
c. Criminal penalties.

© iStockphoto.com/Lusky

Adjusting Entry for Accrued Interest Income LO2

Note	Principal	×	Interest Rate	×	Fraction of Year	=	Accrued Interest Income
18	$8,250.00	×	8%	×	31/365	=	$56.05
19	7,400.00	×	10%	×	16/365	=	32.44
							$88.49

Debit Interest Receivable

GENERAL JOURNAL — PAGE 13

	DATE		ACCOUNT TITLE	DOC. NO.	POST. REF.	DEBIT	CREDIT	
1			Adjusting Entries					1
17		31	Interest Receivable			88.49		17
18			Interest Income				88.49	18

Credit Interest Income

Revenue earned in one fiscal period but not received until a later fiscal period is called **accrued revenue**. For example, a business accepts a 30-day note on December 15. During December, the business earned interest for 16 days. However, the business will not receive any of the interest until the note's maturity in January. Interest for the first 16 days must be recorded in the current fiscal period. [CONCEPT: Matching Expenses with Revenue]

Vaughn Distributors periodically accepts a note from a customer who is unable to pay its account. On December 31, Vaughn Distributors has two notes receivable outstanding.

- Note Receivable No. 18, a 60-day, 8% note dated November 30, $8,250.00.
- Note Receivable No. 19, a 90-day, 10% note dated December 15, $7,400.00.

Accrued interest for each note is calculated from the date of the note through the end of the fiscal period, as shown above.

The accrued interest for all notes is totaled to compute the adjusting entry amount. The adjusting entry increases the balance of Interest Income to include interest that has been earned but not received in cash. Interest Income is reported in the Other Revenue section of the income statement.

The amount of interest owed to the company is reported as Interest Receivable. Interest Receivable is reported in the Current Assets section of the balance sheet.

Interest Receivable

Debit		Credit
Adj.	88.49	

Interest Income

Debit	Credit	
	12/31 Bal.	615.12
	Adj.	88.49
	(New Bal.	*703.61)*

© DenisNata/Shutterstock.com

INPUT

- Point out that students have already learned how to calculate interest for a fraction of a year.
- Remind students that they have already learned to accrue interest expense.
- Ask students to discuss the difference between accruing interest expense and accruing interest income. [*The calculation is the same; interest is an expense of the business that is required to pay the interest and income (or revenue) of the business entitled to receive the interest.*]
- Discuss that a company may have several notes receivable outstanding and that accrued interest for all notes can be adjusted with one adjusting entry.
- Ask students to explain why the adjusting entry debits an asset account.

MODEL

- Draw two T accounts on the board and enter the pre-adjustment balance.
- Describe the adjusting entry.
- Ask students to analyze the adjusting entry by answering these questions: Which accounts are affected? Are they increased or decreased? Are they debited or credited? Complete the T accounts as the information is provided.
- Use a general journal transparency to illustrate recording the adjusting entry in the general journal or direct students to the illustration.

INPUT

- Ask students to explain why accrued revenue is reversed.

MODEL

- Draw two T accounts on the board and enter the pre-adjustment balance.
- Describe the adjusting and closing entries while recording these entries in the T accounts.
- Describe the reversing entry.
- Ask students to analyze the reversing entry. Complete the T accounts as the information is provided.
- Use a general journal transparency to illustrate recording the reversing entry in the general journal or direct students to the illustration.

Reversing Entry for Accrued Interest Income

Debit Interest Income

GENERAL JOURNAL PAGE 1

	DATE		ACCOUNT TITLE	DOC. NO.	POST. REF.	DEBIT	CREDIT	
1			*Reversing Entries*					1
2	20-- Jan.	1	*Interest Income*			88 49		2
3			*Interest Receivable*				88 49	3
4								4

Credit Interest Receivable

Interest Income

Clos.	703.61	12/31 Bal.	615.12
Rev.	**88.49**	Adj.	88.49
(New Bal.	*88.49)*		

Interest Receivable

Adj.	88.49	**Rev.**	**88.49**
(New Bal.	*zero)*		

Interest Income is closed as part of Vaughn Distributors' closing entries. After closing entries are posted, Interest Income has a zero balance. The $88.49 balance in Interest Receivable represents interest that Vaughn Distributors has earned but has not yet received in cash.

The adjusting entry for accrued interest income created a balance in the asset account Interest Receivable. Therefore, on January 1, Vaughn Distributors needs to reverse the adjusting entry that created the balance in Interest Receivable, as shown above.

The new balance of Interest Receivable is zero, as it was before the adjusting entry. The new debit balance, $88.49, in Interest Income is not the normal balance in that account. When cash is received on the maturity date of each note, a credit to Interest Income will offset the debit balance.

Stockbyte/Getty Images

FORMATIVE ASSESSMENT

- This is an ongoing process. Circulate around the classroom or lab, observing which students have problems with the assignments.
- Troubleshooting: Diagnose the kinds of problems students have with this section. The concepts and procedures in this section are relatively simple, and some concepts are a review of the first-year course. Students may have difficulty understanding how to identify the revenue transactions that should be adjusted.
- Assess student understanding by checking solutions to Independent Practice assignments and noting their answers to the Terms Review and Audit Your Understanding questions.

End of Lesson Review

LO1 Describe and illustrate the adjusting and reversing entries for unearned revenue.

LO2 Describe and illustrate the adjusting and reversing entries for accrued revenue.

Terms Review

unearned revenue

accrued revenue

Audit your understanding

1. What is another term used to describe unearned revenue?
2. How is the account Unearned Rent classified on the financial statements?
3. What is the rule for determining whether an adjusting entry should be reversed?
4. In which section of the income statement is the account Interest Income reported?

Work together 9-1

Journalizing adjusting and reversing entries for unearned and accrued revenue

Winston, Inc., is preparing its December 31 financial statements for the current year. On December 1, the company received a $4,200.00 rent payment from Youngston Company. The payment is the $1,400.00 per month rent for December of the current year through February of the next year. Winston records rent receipts initially as revenue. General journal pages are provided in the *Working Papers*. Your instructor will guide you through the following examples.

Winston, Inc., has two notes receivable outstanding on December 31 of the current year.

Note No.	Interest Rate	Term	Principal	Date
22	8%	60 days	$6,000.00	November 22
23	9%	90 days	$5,000.00	December 8

1. Journalize the adjusting entries for unearned rent and accrued interest income. Use page 13 of a general journal.
2. Journalize the reversing entries for unearned rent and accrued interest income. Use page 14 of a general journal.

On your own 9-1

Journalizing adjusting and reversing entries for unearned and accrued revenue

K-109 Radio is preparing its December 31 financial statements for the current year. On October 30, City Recycling paid $3,500.00 to K-109 Radio for advertising. The advertising contract requires K-109 to provide City Recycling with $700.00 of advertising time per month for November of the current year through March of the next year. K-109 records advertising receipts initially as revenue. General journal pages are provided in the *Working Papers*. Work this problem independently.

K-109 Radio has two notes receivable outstanding on December 31 of the current year.

Note No.	Interest Rate	Term	Principal	Date
16	10%	120 days	$2,300.00	November 6
17	8%	60 days	$1,800.00	December 2

1. Journalize the adjusting entries for unearned advertising revenue and accrued interest income. Use page 19 of a general journal.
2. Journalize the reversing entries for unearned advertising revenue and accrued interest income. Use page 20 of a general journal.

CHECK FOR UNDERSTANDING

Terms Review

- Call on students to define each term in the Terms Review. Definitions are given in the Glossary.

Audit Your Understanding

- Call on students to answer the Audit Your Understanding questions. Answers are given in Appendix D of the textbook.

GUIDED PRACTICE

Work Together

- Have students write the solution to the Work Together problem as you guide the class through the examples.
- Ask students to explain their calculation of total interest income.
- Direct students to record the adjusting entry in the general journal as you elicit participation in analyzing and recording the transaction.
- Ask why a reversing entry should be recorded.
- Direct students to record the reversing entry in the general journal as you elicit class participation in analyzing and recording the transaction.

INDEPENDENT PRACTICE

On Your Own

- Assign the On Your Own problem to be worked independently.
- Use the Formative Assessment techniques to diagnose student understanding.

Application Problem

- Assign Application Problem 9-1.

Online Working Papers

- Students can access the Lesson 9-1 problems using this software.

Website

- Direct students to the C21 Accounting companion website for additional practice and review opportunities throughout the chapter.

CLOSURE

- Ask students to summarize briefly the recording of adjusting, closing, and reversing entries for unearned and accrued revenue.

Essential Question

- When would it be advantageous to calculate interest on a 360-day year instead of a 365-day year? (*Using the 360-day year yields more interest when you are the lender.*)

EXTENDED LEARNING

- Assign Accounting in the Real World on page 263.
- Assign Ethics in Action on page 264.
- Assign Global Awareness on page 266.

RETEACH

- Ask students to explain how to record the adjusting and reversing entries for unearned revenue.
- Ask students to discuss how to calculate an adjustment for interest on notes receivable.
- Ask students to identify how to record the adjusting and reversing entries for accrued revenue.

LESSON

9-2

BRIDGE

- Ask students to name the different forms of payment for a sale.
- Point out that students have already learned that credit card sales made with a bank credit card are recorded like cash.
- Explain that the use of gift cards, another method of payment, has increased in recent years. Students will learn how to account for gift cards sold and redeemed.

TEACHING RESOURCES

- **Instructor's Resource CD/Website:**
  PowerPoint Slides
  Accounting Concepts
- **Working Papers:**
  Teacher's Edition of the Working Papers for Lesson 9-2
  Online Working Papers
- **Transparency Masters:**
  General Journal
  Cash Receipts Journal (7-column)

ENGAGE

- Ask students to raise their hands if they ever received a gift card as a gift.
- Ask students how many have unused gift cards at home or in their possession.
- Ask students if they are aware that some of the gift cards they own may not be redeemable for the full amount or may have been cancelled.

PREVIEW

- Call on students to read the accounting term and definition introduced in this lesson: *breakage.*
- Point out the learning objectives for this lesson.
- Direct students to read the headings in this lesson and to examine the illustrations.

INPUT

- Point out that gift cards require different accounting procedures than those used for credit and debit cards.
- Explain that the sale of a gift card does not result in revenue. It results in a promise to allow someone to purchase merchandise in the future.
- Explain that until the card is redeemed, the outstanding balance is unearned revenue.
- Point out that the sale of gift cards is recorded in Gift Cards Outstanding, which is a current liability account.
- Explain the provisions of the Credit CARD Act of 2009.

LESSON

9-2 Accounting for Gift Cards

LO3 Journalize transactions for gift cards.
LO4 Record an adjusting entry for gift card breakage.
LO5 Describe how gift card breakage is reported in the financial statements.

Recording the Sale of a Gift Card LO3

CASH RECEIPTS JOURNAL PAGE 7

	DATE		ACCOUNT TITLE	DOC. NO.	POST. REF.	1 GENERAL DEBIT	2 GENERAL CREDIT	3 ACCOUNTS RECEIVABLE CREDIT	4 SALES CREDIT	5 SALES TAX PAYABLE CREDIT	6 SALES DISCOUNT DEBIT	7 CASH DEBIT	
1	20-- Apr.	1	Gift Cards Outstanding	R522			625 00					625 00	1
2													2

Credit Gift Cards Outstanding — Debit Cash

Retailers have traditionally accepted three forms of payment for a sale—cash, check, and credit card. The use of debit cards has increased in recent years as this technology has enabled customers to access their checking accounts without having to carry checks. Sales paid for with a debit card are processed and accounted for like a credit card. Thus, no new accounting procedures were required to account for debit card sales.

Most recently, the use of gift cards has increased dramatically. At first, customers purchased gift cards directly from the retailer. As the popularity of gift cards grew, displays of gift cards from many retailers began to appear in stores. Retailers often issue a gift card to a customer returning merchandise. These cards resemble a credit card—a plastic card with a magnetic strip where the amount of the card balance is stored. Websites and smartphones enable gift cards to be purchased and redeemed electronically. These virtual gift cards, unlike plastic gift cards, enable the retailer to collect the name and contact information of the cardholder and track the unused card balance.

Although they may look like credit and debit cards, gift cards require very different accounting treatment. The sale of a gift card does not result in revenue. The retailer receives cash and promises to allow the cardholder to purchase merchandise at some time in the future. Until the card is redeemed, the outstanding balance of the card is unearned revenue.

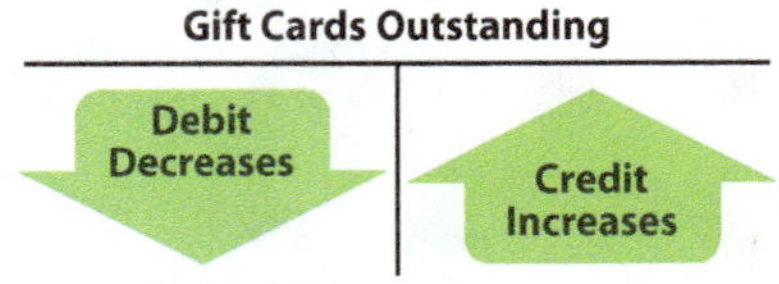

Riverside Lighting sells gift cards at its store and through its website. The company records the sale of gift cards in Gift Cards Outstanding, a current liability account.

April 1. Received cash for the sale of gift cards, $625.00. Receipt No. 522.

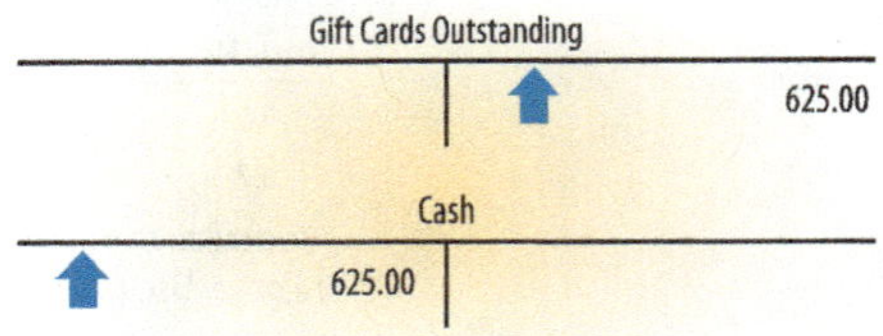

Gift cardholders expect they can redeem the full amount of the card at any future date. The Credit Card Accountability Responsibility and Disclosure Act of 2009 (Credit CARD Act) includes provisions designed to protect the value of gift cards. Retailers are not allowed to charge fees on unredeemed cards for 12 months. Unredeemed cards cannot be canceled until five years after the date of issuance.

MODEL

- Draw two T accounts on the board.
- Read the transaction.
- Ask students to analyze the transaction by answering these questions: Which accounts are affected? Are they increased or decreased? Are they debited or credited? Complete the T accounts as the information is provided.
- Use a cash receipts journal transparency to illustrate recording the transaction in the cash receipts journal or direct students to the illustration.

TEACHING IDEA

This activity emphasizes the importance of redeeming gift cards. Ask students to bring in unused gift cards that they own. Have them place a sticky note on each gift card with their name and the balance of the card. Place all cards in the front of the room. Ask a student to calculate the total value of unused cards in students' homes or wallets.

Recording a Sale with a Gift Card

Debit Gift Cards Outstanding

GENERAL JOURNAL — PAGE 8

	DATE		ACCOUNT TITLE	DOC. NO.	POST. REF.	DEBIT	CREDIT	
1	20-- Aug.	2	*Gift Cards Outstanding*	*M325*		*339 20*		1
2			*Sales*				*320 00*	2
3			*Sales Tax Payable*				*19 20*	3

Credit Sales

Credit Sales Tax Payable

A sale is recorded when a customer pays for merchandise using a gift card. Riverside Lighting's point-of-sale system records the daily amount of sales paid for with a gift card.

August 2. Customers redeemed gift cards for the sale of merchandise, $320.00, plus sales tax, $19.20. Memorandum No. 325.

The redemption of a gift card reduces the amount of gift cards outstanding. The debit to Gift Cards Outstanding reduces the balance of this liability account.

Gift Cards Outstanding

Debit	Credit
339.20	

Sales

Debit	Credit
	320.00

Sales Tax Payable

Debit	Credit
	19.20

The unused balance of a gift card is electronically recorded to the plastic card's magnetic strip. The balance of a virtual gift card is updated in the retailer's computer system.

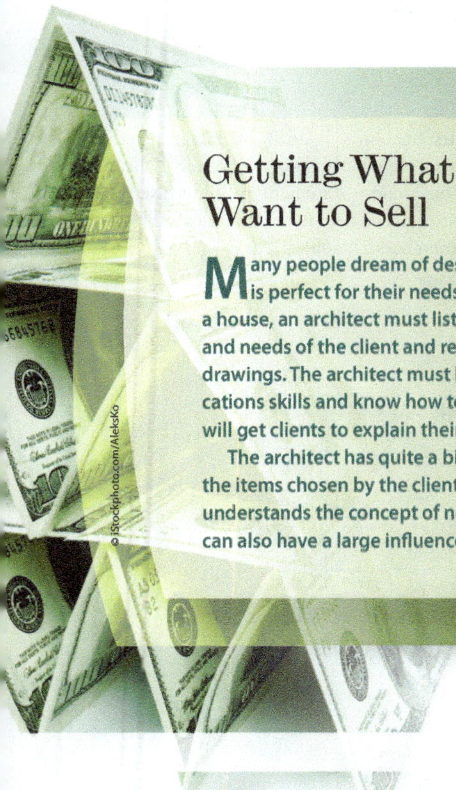

© iStockphoto.com/AleksKo

WHY ACCOUNTING?

Getting What They Want to Sell

Many people dream of designing a home that is perfect for their needs. When designing a house, an architect must listen to the wants and needs of the client and reflect these in the drawings. The architect must have good communications skills and know how to ask questions that will get clients to explain their expectations clearly.

The architect has quite a bit of influence over the items chosen by the clients. If the architect understands the concept of net income, he or she can also have a large influence on the bottom line of the construction company. The architect can choose items with a high profit margin, such as handmade bookshelves, and include those items in the drawings for a client. This will only be successful if the cost of the bookshelves has been calculated accurately and if the architect understands accounting.

Architecture & Construction

CRITICAL THINKING

Make a list of items with a high profit margin that could be included in the plans for a house.

INPUT

- Explain that the redemption of a gift card reduces the amount of gift cards outstanding and is now considered revenue; thus, it is recorded in sales.

MODEL

- Draw two T accounts on the board.
- Read the transaction.
- Ask students to analyze the transaction by answering these questions: Which accounts are affected? Are they increased or decreased? Are they debited or credited? Complete the T accounts as the information is provided.
- Use a general journal transparency to illustrate recording the transaction in the general journal or direct students to the illustration.

WHY ACCOUNTING?

Answers

Answers may vary, but could include such items as custom molding, specialized cabinets, upgraded light fixtures, and upgraded floor coverings.

DIFFERENTIATED INSTRUCTION

Gifted learners need additional challenges, such as research, to maintain a high level of motivation. Students should be asked to select three popular businesses that sell gift cards. They should interview a manager or use the Internet to research the provisions for use and redemption of the gift card.

INPUT

- Explain *breakage*.
- Point out that many gift cards are unredeemed in their entirety for many reasons.
- Explain that breakage is an estimate similar to uncollectible receivables and the depreciation of plant assets.
- Point out that a business should allow several years to pass before recognizing gift card breakage as revenue.

MODEL

- Draw two T accounts on the board.
- Describe the transaction.
- Record the breakage amount in the T accounts. Explain that this is an estimation.
- Use a general journal transparency to illustrate recording the breakage revenue in the general journal or direct students to the illustration.
- Use a general journal transparency to illustrate recording the adjusting entry in the general journal.

INPUT

- Point out that Breakage Revenue is located in the Operating Revenue section of the income statement. However, it is recorded separately so that users can compare the amount of revenue from sales with the related cost of merchandise sold.

Accounting for Unredeemed Gift Cards LO4

Debit Gift Cards Outstanding

GENERAL JOURNAL — PAGE 13

	DATE		ACCOUNT TITLE	DOC. NO.	POST. REF.	DEBIT	CREDIT	
1			*Adjusting Entries*					1
22		31	*Gift Cards Outstanding*			8 2 9 0 00		22
23			*Breakage Revenue*				8 2 9 0 00	23

Credit Breakage Revenue

Some gift cards are never redeemed. A cardholder may lose the card or discard a card having a very small remaining value. The cardholder of an electronic gift card may forget about the card or be unable to remember login, password, and security questions necessary to redeem the card's value.

The value of unredeemed gift cards is called **breakage**. When a business concludes that a gift card will never be redeemed, the value of the card is no longer a liability. Depending on state laws, the card value may be recognized as revenue. An adjusting entry records the gift card breakage. The adjusting entry reduces Gift Cards Outstanding to reflect the amount the business expects cardholders to redeem in the future. Vaughn operates in a state that allows it to recognize revenue from gift card breakage. The adjusting entry increases Breakage Revenue for the amount of the gift cards the business estimates will never be redeemed.

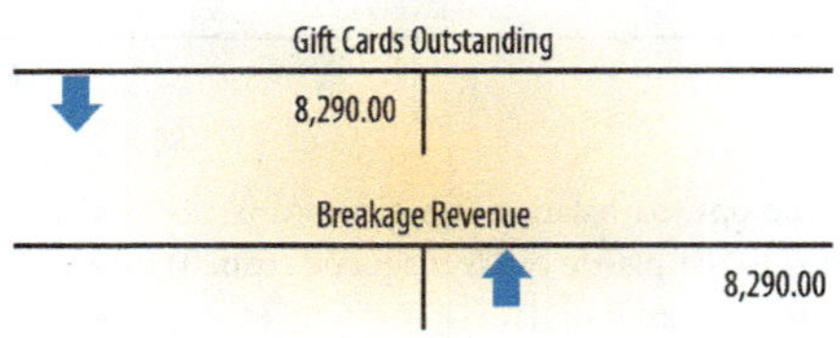

Breakage revenue is an estimate. Similar to the accounting for uncollectible accounts and the depreciation of plant assets, the business must use a generally accepted method consistently for making an unbiased estimate. [CONCEPT: Neutrality] At a minimum, a business should allow several years to pass before recognizing gift card breakage as revenue.

Reporting of Gift Card Breakage LO5

Riverside Lighting uses the account Breakage Revenue to record unredeemed cards. The account is included in the Net Sales section of the income statement, as shown below.

Breakage revenue is a normal part of business operations. Most businesses elect to include breakage revenue with other sales accounts instead of including the amount as other revenue. Breakage Revenue is listed separately on the income statement to allow users to compare the amount of revenue from sales with the related cost of merchandise sold.

Riverside Lighting
Income Statement
For Year Ended December 31, 20--

Operating Revenue:		
Sales		2101 8 6 4 17
Less: Sales Discounts	21 8 4 2 16	
Sales Returns and Allowances	16 4 9 7 14	38 3 3 9 30
Revenue from Sales		2063 5 2 4 87
Breakage Revenue		32 0 8 4 00
Net Sales		2095 6 0 8 87

FORMATIVE ASSESSMENT

- This is an ongoing process. Circulate around the classroom or lab, observing which students have problems with the assignments.
- Troubleshooting: Diagnose the kinds of problems students have with this lesson. Students may have difficulty understanding at what point the gift card is considered revenue.
- Assess student understanding by checking solutions to Independent Practice assignments and noting their answers to the Term Review and Audit Your Understanding questions.

End of Lesson Review

LO3 Journalize transactions for gift cards.

LO4 Record an adjusting entry for gift card breakage.

LO5 Describe how gift card breakage is reported in the financial statements.

Term Review

breakage

Audit your understanding

1. How do plastic and virtual gift cards differ in the information they provide to the retailer?
2. How does the Credit Card Accountability Responsibility and Disclosure Act of 2009 protect gift cardholders?
3. When is a sale recorded from the issuance of a gift card?
4. In what section of the income statement is the account Breakage Revenue reported?
5. Identify information related to gift cards that is disclosed in the notes to the financial statements.

Work together 9-2

Journalizing gift card transactions

Salter Stores uses gift cards to help increase its sales. A cash receipts journal and general journals are provided in the *Working Papers*. Your instructor will guide you through the following examples.

1. Record the following transactions on page 24 of a cash receipts journal and page 18 of a general journal. Salter Stores uses the accounts Gift Cards Outstanding and Breakage Revenue to account for gift card transactions. Source documents are abbreviated as follows: memorandum, M; receipt, R.

   Transactions:

   Dec. 29. Received cash for the sale of gift cards, $450.00. R456.

   29. Customers redeemed gift cards for the sale of merchandise, $148.15, plus $8.89 sales tax. M334.

   30. Received cash for the sale of gift cards, $550.00. R457.

   30. Customers redeemed gift cards for the sale of merchandise, $92.68, plus $5.56 sales tax. M335.

2. Salter Stores estimates that $4,525.00 of gift cards will never be redeemed. Record the adjusting entry on page 19 of a general journal.

On your own 9-2

Journalizing gift card transactions

Main Street Gifts sells gift cards at its store and via a website. A cash receipts journal and general journals are provided in the *Working Papers*. Work this problem independently.

1. Record the following transactions on page 18 of a cash receipts journal and page 14 of a general journal. Main Street Gifts uses the accounts Gift Cards Outstanding and Breakage Revenue to account for gift card transactions. Source documents are abbreviated as follows: memorandum, M; receipt, R.

   Transactions:

   Dec. 28. Received cash for the sale of gift cards, $920.00. R888.

   28. Customers redeemed gift cards for the sale of merchandise, $895.44, plus $62.68 sales tax. M167.

   31. Customers redeemed gift cards for the sale of merchandise, $1,648.07, plus $115.36 sales tax. M170.

   31. Received cash for the sale of gift cards, $625.00. R914.

2. Main Street Gifts estimates that $3,150.00 of gift cards will never be redeemed. Record the adjusting entry on page 15 of a general journal.

CHECK FOR UNDERSTANDING

Term Review

- Call on a student to define the term in the Term Review. A definition is given in the Glossary.

Audit Your Understanding

- Call on students to answer the Audit Your Understanding questions. Answers are given in Appendix D of the textbook.

GUIDED PRACTICE

Work Together

- Have students write the solution to the Work Together problem as you guide the class through the examples.
- Direct students to record the gift card transactions in the general journal as you elicit class participation in analyzing and recording the transactions.

INDEPENDENT PRACTICE

On Your Own

- Assign the On Your Own problem to be worked independently.
- Use the Formative Assessment techniques to diagnose student understanding.

Application Problem

- Assign Application Problem 9-2.

Online Working Papers

- Students can access the Lesson 9-2 problems using this software.

RETEACH

- Ask students to describe how to journalize the sale of gift cards.
- Ask students to explain *breakage*.
- Ask students to describe when to report gift cards as revenue.

EXTENDED LEARNING

- Assign Why Accounting on page 271.

CLOSURE

- Ask students to summarize briefly the journalizing of gift cards.

Essential Questions

- How are prepaid bank cards similar to gift cards? (*The revenue is already collected; however, the company has now incurred a liability to the cardholder.*)
- Why would a place of business establish expiration dates on gift cards? Why not? (*Many states have laws about expiration dates; however, they may be established so that the liability does not remain indefinitely. Businesses may not impose expiration dates, but may impose fees for unused balances.*)

LESSON

9-3

BRIDGE

- Ask students if they have car payments.
- Ask what information was provided so that they knew how much they would pay, how long they would pay, and when they would make each payment.

TEACHING RESOURCES

- **Instructor's Resource CD/Website:**
  PowerPoint Slides
  Accounting Concepts
- **Working Papers:**
  Teacher's Edition of the Working Papers for Lesson 9-3
  Online Working Papers
- **Transparency Masters:**
  Cash Receipts Journal (7-column)
  General Journal

ENGAGE

- To promote sales, some businesses offer customers the opportunity to expand their payment over time by making a monthly payment that includes principal and interest.

PREVIEW

- Call on students to read the accounting terms and definitions introduced in this lesson: *installment note*, *amortization schedule*, and *reclassification entry*.
- Point out the learning objectives for this lesson.
- Direct students to read the headings in this lesson and to examine the illustrations.

INPUT

- Explain that a note requiring a monthly payment of principal and interest over a period of time is called an installment note.
- Point out that the amount to be received, the cash down payment, and the total amount of the sale are recorded in the cash receipts journal.
- Ask students to read the FYI at the bottom of the page.

MODEL

- Draw three T accounts on the board.
- Read the transaction.
- Ask students to analyze the transaction by answering these questions: Which accounts are affected? Are they increased or decreased? Are they debited or credited? Complete the T accounts as the information is provided.
- Use a cash receipts journal transparency to illustrate recording the transaction in the cash receipts journal or direct students to the illustration.

LESSON

9-3 Accounting for Installment Notes Receivable

LO6 Journalize transactions for installment notes receivable.
LO7 Describe and illustrate the reclassification and reversing entries for installment notes receivable.

Issuing an Installment Note Receivable LO6

CASH RECEIPTS JOURNAL — PAGE 9

	DATE		ACCOUNT TITLE	DOC. NO.	POST. REF.	1 GENERAL DEBIT	2 GENERAL CREDIT	3 ACCOUNTS RECEIVABLE CREDIT	4 SALES CREDIT	5 SALES TAX PAYABLE CREDIT	6 SALES DISCOUNT DEBIT	7 CASH DEBIT	
4		3	Notes Receivable	NR325		15,000 00			17,144 66	514 34		2,659 00	4
5													5

Debit Notes Receivable for Note Principal — Credit Sales for Sales Amount — Credit Sales Tax Payable — Debit Cash for Down Payment

May 3. Sold a car to Mark Carver for $17,144.66 plus sales tax of $514.34, receiving a $2,659.00 down payment and accepting a 60-month, 10% installment note receivable for the balance, $15,000.00. Note Receivable No. 325.

To promote sales, some businesses must offer customers the opportunity to sign a note extending their payment over time. Retailers who sell expensive items, such as cars, boats, and recreational vehicles, typically finance their customers' purchases. Customers are generally required to make monthly payments over the term of the loan.

A note resulting from a sale that requires monthly payments of principal and interest is called an **installment note**. The procedures used to account for installment notes receivable must ensure that interest earned on the note is recorded in the correct accounting period. The business must also ensure that the total principal of outstanding notes is properly reported on the balance sheet.

Candor Auto Mart sells previously owned cars obtained from car rental companies. Candor offers creditworthy customers the opportunity to finance up to 90% of the purchase price of any car. Past experience has taught Candor that customers who can make a significant down payment are more likely to make their monthly payments.

Cash	
↑ 2,659.00	

Notes Receivable	
↑ 15,000.00	

Sales	
	↑ 17,144.66

Sales Tax Payable	
	↑ 514.34

Similar to sales on account, the sale is recorded as revenue at the time of sale, regardless of when the payment is made. [CONCEPT: Realization of Revenue]

fyi

A company that accepts a large number of notes might benefit from using a ledger system that enables management to identify the amount of notes outstanding with any customer. Thus, management could make informed decisions about extending additional credit to a particular customer.

Receiving a Monthly Payment on an Installment Note Receivable

CASH RECEIPTS JOURNAL — PAGE 15

	DATE		ACCOUNT TITLE	DOC. NO.	POST. REF.	1 GENERAL DEBIT	2 GENERAL CREDIT	3 ACCOUNTS RECEIVABLE CREDIT	4 SALES CREDIT	5 SALES TAX PAYABLE CREDIT	6 SALES DISCOUNT DEBIT	7 CASH DEBIT	
1	20-- Aug.	2	Notes Receivable	R503			196 95					318 71	1
2			Interest Income				121 76						2
3													3

Credit Notes Receivable for Principal Amount — Credit Interest Income for Interest Amount — Debit Cash for Total Payment

Candor Auto Mart provides its customers with a note agreement that includes a payment schedule. A schedule of the periodic payments on a note is called an **amortization schedule**. Mark Carver purchased the car on May 3. Thus, the note agreement requires that he make a payment by the third day of every month.

August 2. Received cash for Mark Carver's August payment, $196.95, and interest, $121.76; total, $318.71. Receipt No. 503.

Mark Carver is required to pay $318.71 each month. A portion of the payment is interest on the outstanding balance of the loan. The remaining amount reduces the outstanding loan principal. The monthly payment will enable Mark Carver to repay the loan fully by the end of the 5 years (60 months). Candor Auto Mart uses a 360-day year to prepare its amortization schedules.

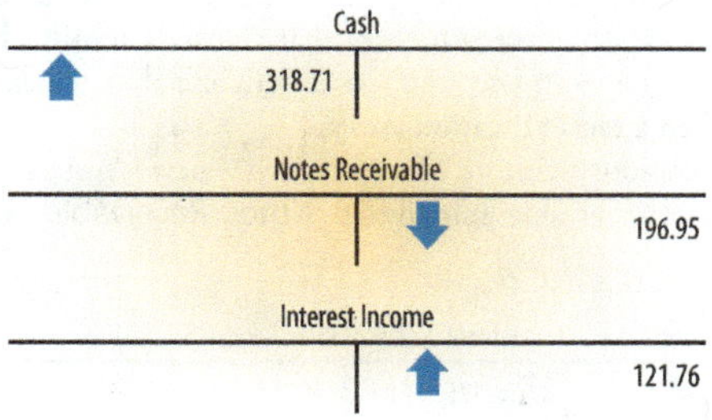

Amount Borrowed			$15,000.00		
Term of Note (Months)			60		
Annual Interest Rate			10%		
Monthly Payment			$318.71		
Monthly Due Date			3rd		
Payment Number	**Month**	**Beginning Balance**	**Interest**	**Principal**	**Ending Balance**
1	June	$15,000.00	$125.00	$193.71	$14,806.29
2	July	$14,806.29	$123.39	$195.32	$14,610.97
3	August	$14,610.97	$121.76	$196.95	$14,414.02
4	September	$14,414.02	$120.12	$198.59	$14,215.43
5	October	$14,215.43	$118.46	$200.25	$14,015.18
6	November	$14,015.18	$116.79	$201.92	$13,813.26
7	December	$13,813.26	$115.11	$203.60	$13,609.66
8	January	$13,609.66	$113.41	$205.30	$13,404.36

INPUT

- Explain the amortization schedule.
- Point out that Candor uses a 360-day year to calculate its interest.
- Explain how to record the payment received for the installment note.

MODEL

Analyze the transaction

- Draw three T accounts on the board.
- Read the transaction.
- Ask students to analyze the transaction.

Record the transaction

- Use a cash receipts journal transparency to illustrate recording the transaction in the cash receipts journal or direct students to the illustration at the top of the page.

DIFFERENTIATED INSTRUCTION

Mathematical/Logical learners enjoy solving problems and working with numbers. Ask students to create an example of an installment loan as well as an amortization table based on the example.

INPUT

- Explain why it is necessary to transfer account balances between accounts on one financial statement.
- Remind students of the meaning of *current assets*.
- Explain that reclassification does not affect total assets.

MODEL

Analyze the transaction

- Draw two T accounts on the board and record the balance before the reclassification entry.
- Ask students to analyze the transaction.
- Complete the T accounts as the information is provided.
- Point out the effect of the reclassification on the balance sheet.

Record the transaction

- Use a general journal transparency to illustrate recording the reclassification entry in the general journal or direct students to the illustration at the top of the page.

Reclassification Entry for Installment Notes Receivable LO7

Debit Current Portion of Notes Receivable

GENERAL JOURNAL — PAGE 14

	DATE		ACCOUNT TITLE	DOC. NO.	POST. REF.	DEBIT	CREDIT	
1			*Reclassification Entries*					1
2	20-- Dec.	31	*Current Portion of Notes Receivable*			175,212.00		2
3			*Notes Receivable*				175,212.00	3
4								4

Credit Notes Receivable

At the end of a fiscal period, a company records adjusting entries to bring account balances up to date. Adjusting entries change the balances of revenue and expense accounts. An entry that transfers account balances between accounts on one financial statement is called a **reclassification entry**.

Candor Auto Mart reports new installment notes receivable initially in Notes Receivable, as a noncurrent asset. When a balance sheet is prepared, Candor determines the total principal payments it expects to collect during the next fiscal period. A reclassification entry is recorded to transfer the amount from Notes Receivable to Current Portion of Notes Receivable, a current asset.

On December 31, Candor has $584,040.00 of notes receivable. Of that amount, $175,212.00 is expected to be collected during the next fiscal period. The total is reclassified from a noncurrent asset account to a current asset account. The entry has no effect on total assets or net income.

The impact of the reclassification entry is shown in the following section from Candor's balance sheet. Current Portion of Notes Receivable appears in the Current Assets section. Notes Receivable, the noncurrent portion of future principal payments, is presented after plant assets.

Current Portion of Notes Receivable

Debit	Credit
↑ Recl. 175,212.00	

Notes Receivable

Debit	Credit
12/31 Bal. 584,040.00	↓ Recl. 175,212.00
(New Bal. 408,828.00)	

Candor Auto Mart
Balance Sheet
December 31, 20--

Inventory	648,153.00	
Current Portion of Notes Receivable	175,212.00	
Other Current Assets	21,495.00	
Total Current Assets		914,613.00
Property and Equipment, net		159,148.00
Notes Receivable		408,828.00
Other Assets		32,084.00
Total Assets		1514,673.00

Reversing Entry for a Reclassification Entry

Debit Notes Receivable

GENERAL JOURNAL PAGE 1

	DATE		ACCOUNT TITLE	DOC. NO.	POST. REF.	DEBIT	CREDIT	
1			*Reversing Entries*					1
4	20-- Jan.	1	*Notes Receivable*			175 212 00		4
5			*Current Portion of Notes Receivable*				175 212 00	5
6								6

Credit Current Portion of Notes Receivable

The recording of customer note payments is simplified by using a single account to credit principal payments. Candor Auto Mart reverses the reclassification entry after the financial statements are prepared. After the reversing entry is posted, the balance of Notes Receivable represents the total outstanding principal of installment notes receivable.

Current Portion of Notes Receivable

Debit		Credit	
Recl.	175,212.00	Rev.	175,212.00
(New Bal.	*zero)*		

Notes Receivable

Debit		Credit	
12/31 Bal.	584,040.00	Recl.	175,212.00
Rev.	175,212.00		
(New Bal.	*584,040.00)*		

© iStockphoto.com/Dan Bachman

THINK LIKE AN ACCOUNTANT

Creating an Amortization Schedule

Hwy 66 RVs sells recreational vehicles. The business has been purchasing a license for software to prepare loan agreements. The owner, who prepares the loan documents, believes that the cost of the software outweighs its benefits. The owner also believes that using Microsoft Office products to prepare the documents would reduce administrative expenses. The owner has created a loan agreement in word processing but does not know how to create an amortization schedule.

OPEN THE SPREADSHEET TLA_CH09

The workbook contains an incomplete amortization schedule for a 60-month installment loan. Follow the steps on the Instructions tab. Prepare an amortization schedule for a $20,000.00, 10%, 60-month loan to Caleb Barfield. The note was signed on November 19, 2012. Answer the following questions.

1. What are the interest and principal amounts for the December 2013 payment?
2. Mandy Everson is buying a $35,000.00 recreational vehicle. Prepare an amortization schedule for an 8%, 60-month loan, using today's date. What are the date, monthly payment, and the interest and principal amounts for the 48th payment?
3. Hwy 66 RVs is considering having a special financing sale. Customers would be offered 10% off the sale price, but the interest rate would be increased by 1%. Modify Mandy Everson's loan as a method of analyzing the impact on the company. Would you recommend Hwy 66 RVs adopt this plan?

Answers

1. Interest, $139.62; principal, $285.32.
2. Date of 48th payment, answers will vary; monthly payment, $709.67; interest, $59.26; principal, $650.41.
3. No. The total interest earned on the 9% loan, $7,774.03, is only $107.20 greater than what would be earned on the 8% loan. The additional interest income does not offset the loss of $3,500 ($35,000 × 10%) in revenue.

INPUT

- Explain that a reversing entry updates Notes Receivable to represent the total outstanding principal of installment notes receivable.

MODEL

- Draw two T accounts.
- Point out the amount that has been added to Notes Receivable for the current period.
- Calculate the new balance of Notes Receivable as a result of the reversing entry.
- Use a general journal to illustrate recording the transaction in the general journal or direct students to the illustration.

THINK LIKE AN ACCOUNTANT

This activity requires students to complete an amortization schedule. Selected formulas used to calculate the month and year of payment have been entered in the spreadsheet. The first-year formulas have also been entered. By deleting the first-year formulas from the spreadsheet provided to students, you can increase the challenge level of the activity. A further challenge would be to require the amortization schedule to adapt automatically to any reasonable number of payments (e.g., 24 to 72 months).

The activity requires students to create several formulas and use the PMT (payment) and ROUND (rounding) functions. Some cell references must be changed to be absolute references. If necessary, review when and how to create an absolute reference. If a cell reference in a formula is to remain the same when the formula is copied, the cell reference should be an absolute reference. While students enter or edit the formula, ensure that they select the cell reference and press the F4 function key. Dollar signs will appear before the column and row reference of the cell. Alternatively, students can enter the dollar signs into the formula.

The formulas created in this activity are as follows:

C7: =ROUND(-PMT(C5/12,60,C4),2)

D11: =+G10

E11: =ROUND(+D11*$C$5/12,2)

F11: =+$C$7-E11

G11: =+D11-F11

F69: =+D69

FORENSIC ACCOUNTING

The Excel file contains a list of 65 outstanding installment notes receivable held by Helman Auto Mart. The list includes an analysis of the loan information for calculating the monthly principal payments for each note. A total of these amounts yields the amount that Helman used in its reclassification entry to recognize the current portion of installment notes receivable.

With one exception, students can view the formulas used to create the analysis. The outstanding balance, however, is suspiciously an entered value. This value is the basis for the formulas that calculate the current portion of the installment notes. Students use the ROUND and PV functions to calculate this value and discover that Helman's amounts are incorrect. The difference results in a significant decrease in the amount of current installment notes receivable.

Answers

1. The audited value, $856,113.58, is $36,226.57 less than the reported value of $892,340.15.
2. The audited value, $255,318.64, is $15,464.70 less than the reported value of $270,783.34.
3. Although the outstanding balance could have been calculated, the amounts were entered, making it impossible to understand how the amounts were calculated. Differences existed only for older loans having ten or more payments. It would have been more difficult to increase significantly the outstanding balances of more recent loans. An outstanding balance greater than the original loan amount would be an obvious red flag of a fraud.

FORENSIC ACCOUNTING

A Royal Disaster

Restatement may be one of the most feared words in the financial community. A restatement occurs when a corporation must publish revised financial statements due to a misstatement in previously published financial statements. A restatement often results in the corporation reporting a reduction in sales and net income. More importantly, a restatement brings into question the competency and integrity of management.

The restatement of Royal Ahold's financial statements in 2003 was a financial disaster for its home country, the Netherlands. The roots of Ahold can be traced back to a grocery store opened by Albert Heijn in 1887. Within 10 years, the business had expanded to 23 stores and had created its own brand of products. Thus, a corporate culture of expansion was established early in Ahold's history. Over the next 100 years, Ahold expanded into new markets, often acquiring entire grocery chains in other countries. By the late 20th century, Ahold had become a global leader in the grocery industry.

A pivotal event in Ahold's history was its 2000 acquisition of U.S. Foodservice. To inflate its earnings, U.S. Foodservice was fraudulently misstating payments from food manufacturers, an industry practice known as *promotional allowances*. Ahold was also incorrectly including in its financial statements the sales of other corporations in which it was part owner.

In 2003, Ahold announced the restatement of its financial statements for fiscal years 1999 to 2001. The restatement resulted in a $25.8 billion reduction in sales and a $1.1 billion reduction in operating income. Four corporate executives were forced to resign amid accusations they were involved in the frauds and concealed information from external auditors.

Fortunately, Ahold survived the scandal and remains a vibrant business today. However, the corporation was required to sell several of its acquisitions.

ACTIVITY

Helman Auto Mart has been struggling over the past several years. The auto market has declined, hurting Helman's sales and having a negative impact on its balance sheet. Helman's primary bank loan requires the company to maintain at least a 1.5 ratio of current assets to current liabilities. If the actual ratio drops below 1.5, the bank can immediately demand repayment of the loan.

The bank received a tip that Helman might be misstating its financial statements. Taking advantage of a provision of its loan agreement, the bank sent an audit team to review the statements.

As a member of that audit team, you have been instructed to examine the support for Helman's reclassification entry for the current portion of its installment notes receivable. The worksheet contains a list of Helman's installment notes receivable and the calculations supporting the reclassification entry.

1. What is the difference, if any, between the reported and audited totals of outstanding notes receivable?
2. Helman's worksheet calculated the current portion of installment notes receivable to be $270,783.34. How did the change in the outstanding balances affect this amount?
3. What evidence suggests that Helman's management may have intentionally misstated the outstanding balances?

INSTRUCTIONS

Open the spreadsheet FA_CH09 and complete the steps on the Instructions tab.

Sources: www.sec.gov/news/press/2004-144.htm; www.ahold.com.

© iStockphoto.com/burwellphotography

FORMATIVE ASSESSMENT

- This is an ongoing process. Circulate around the classroom or lab, observing which students have problems with the assignments.
- Troubleshooting: Diagnose the kinds of problems students have with this lesson. Students may have difficulty understanding the difference between reclassification entries and reversing entries for notes receivable.
- Assess student understanding by checking solutions to Independent Practice assignments and noting their answers to the Terms Review and Audit Your Understanding questions.

End of Lesson Review

LO6 Journalize transactions for installment notes receivable.

LO7 Describe and illustrate the reclassification and reversing entries for installment notes receivable.

Terms Review

installment note

amortization schedule

reclassification entry

Audit your understanding

1. When would the sale of a boat financed with an installment note be recorded as revenue?
2. What dollar amounts are presented on an amortization schedule?
3. Over the term of an installment note, what changes occur to the monthly payment, interest, and principal?
4. What amount of installment notes receivable should be classified as a current asset?

Work together 9-3

Journalizing installment notes receivable transactions

The journals and a loan payment schedule for Danny's Used Cars are given in the *Working Papers*. Your instructor will guide you through the following examples.

1. Using May of the current year, journalize these transactions. Refer to the amortization schedule when journalizing the May 9 transaction. Source documents are abbreviated as follows: note receivable, NR; receipt, R.

   Transactions:

   May 7. Sold a car to Jill Shelton for $14,860.00 plus $445.80 sales tax, receiving a $2,305.80 down payment and accepting a 60-month, 8% installment note receivable for the balance, $13,000.00. NR369.

   9. Received cash for Daniel Toney's May payment, $243.32. R787.

2. On December 31, $93,467.00 of the installment notes receivable of Danny's Used Cars is expected to be collected during the next fiscal period. Record the reclassification entry using page 15 of a general journal.
3. Use page 16 of a general journal to journalize the reversing entry of the December 31 reclassification entry for installment notes receivable.

On your own 9-3

Journalizing installment notes receivable transactions

The journals and a loan payment schedule for Riverside Marine are given in the *Working Papers*. Work these problems independently.

1. Using June of the current year, journalize these transactions. Refer to the amortization schedule when journalizing the June 10 and 16 transactions. Source documents are abbreviated as follows: note receivable, NR; receipt, R.

   Transactions:

   June 7. Sold a boat to Tyesha Anderson for $3,550.00 plus $177.50 sales tax, receiving a $527.50 down payment and accepting a 36-month, 9% installment note receivable for the balance, $3,200.00. NR283.

   10. Received cash for Wayne Wood's June payment, $120.84. R490.

   16. Received cash for Patrick Morgan's June payment, $127.20. R498.

   24. Sold a boat to Marie Mims for $4,000.00 plus $200.00 sales tax, receiving a $600.00 down payment and accepting a 36-month, 9% installment note receivable for the balance, $3,600.00. NR285.

2. On December 31, $48,475.00 of the installment notes receivable of Riverside Marine is expected to be collected during the next fiscal period. Record the reclassification entry using page 18 of a general journal.
3. Use page 19 of a general journal to journalize the reversing entry of the December 31 reclassification entry for installment notes receivable.

CHECK FOR UNDERSTANDING

Terms Review

- Call on students to define each term in the Terms Review. Definitions are given in the Glossary.

Audit Your Understanding

- Call on students to answer the Audit Your Understanding questions. Answers are given in Appendix D of the textbook.

GUIDED PRACTICE

Work Together

- Have students write the solution to the Work Together problem as you guide the class through the examples.
- Direct students to record each transaction as you elicit class participation in analyzing and recording each transaction.

INDEPENDENT PRACTICE

On Your Own

- Assign the On Your Own problem to be worked independently.
- Use the Formative Assessment techniques to diagnose student understanding.

Application Problem

- Assign Application Problem 9-3.

Online Working Papers

- Students can access the Lesson 9-3 problems using this software.

RETEACH

- Ask students to prepare a list of all transactions presented in this section.
- Ask what information is needed to journalize the reclassification entry.
- Call on students to describe how to journalize the reversing entry for a reclassification entry.

EXTENDED LEARNING

- Assign Think Like an Accountant on page 277.
- Assign Forensic Accounting on page 278.

CLOSURE

- Ask students to summarize briefly the procedures for journalizing transactions for notes receivable.

Essential Questions

- When would an amortization schedule be valuable to a consumer? (*It allows the consumer to visualize and calculate what happens to the loan as time progresses.*)
- What benefit would an amortization schedule be to a lender? (*It provides the lender with a breakdown of the schedule of payments along with payoff values.*)
- What is the effect of paying an extra amount each month on an installment loan? (*Adding extra amounts to the mortgage payment will reduce the total amount paid and shorten the term of the loan.*)

A Look at Accounting Software

Financing sales of high-priced merchandise is done every day in retail businesses such as furniture, automobile, and recreational vehicle dealers. Families of most students will have had the experience of signing notes for such purchases.

Accounting for these transactions is routine. You might ask students to list the steps required for the transactions in the Create Sales Invoice window if done in a manual accounting system: An accounts receivable ledger card would need to be created for Mark Carver, a journal entry would need to be made in the cash receipts journal, two inventory stock records would need to be updated and a new stock record prepared for the trade-in vehicle, calculations would need to be done for interest and payment amounts or looked up in interest tables, and a promissory note form would need to be filled out. In this example, the accounting system performs all of these tasks.

It is also a common practice for retailers who write notes to sell, or factor, the notes to a finance company to acquire cash more quickly. Many families of students will likely have had the experience of receiving notice that payments originally made to a retailer should subsequently be made to the finance company. Students might be asked to research factoring and to describe the accounting transactions that result from the sale of a note receivable.

A Look at Accounting Software

Setting Up a Note Receivable

Merchandising companies, especially those that deal in high-priced goods, will generally provide customers options for financing their purchases. Most often, the financing is done by another company that specializes in making loans. The merchandiser simply takes an application, seeks approval from the finance company, and then completes the transaction. The customer makes payments directly to the financing company. When a sale is financed by another company, the transaction is accounted for as a cash sale, with a corresponding account receivable from the finance company entered.

Merchandisers will sometimes extend credit themselves. The merchandiser may choose to hold a note to maturity or sell it to a finance company to raise cash. In this example, Candor Auto Mart has completed the sale of an automobile to Mark Carver and is financing the sale itself.

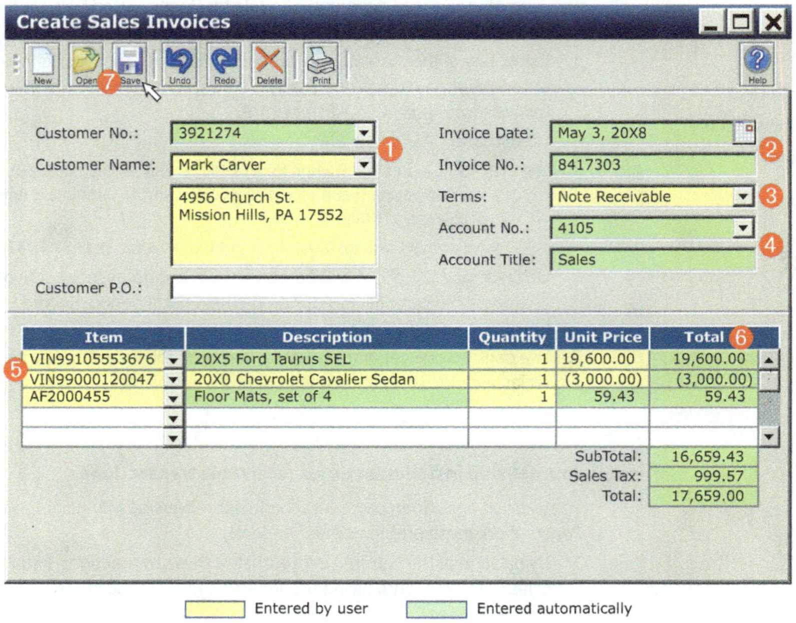
Create Sales Invoices

New Open Save Undo Redo Delete Print Help

Customer No.: 3921274 (1)
Customer Name: Mark Carver
4956 Church St.
Mission Hills, PA 17552
Customer P.O.:

Invoice Date: May 3, 20X8 (2)
Invoice No.: 8417303
Terms: Note Receivable (3)
Account No.: 4105
Account Title: Sales (4)

Item	Description	Quantity	Unit Price	Total (6)
VIN99105553676	20X5 Ford Taurus SEL	1	19,600.00	19,600.00
VIN99000120047	20X0 Chevrolet Cavalier Sedan	1	(3,000.00)	(3,000.00)
AF2000455	Floor Mats, set of 4	1	59.43	59.43
			SubTotal:	16,659.43
			Sales Tax:	999.57
			Total:	17,659.00

Entered by user Entered automatically

1. The finance manager at Candor Auto Mart has entered an auto sale to Mark Carver. The customer number was entered in sequence automatically by the system. If Mark were an existing customer, his account could have been selected from the customer list by name or number.
2. The invoice date and number were entered automatically by the system.
3. Since Candor is financing this sale, Notes Receivable was selected from the **Terms** drop-down list.
4. The default general ledger account is Sales. It could be changed if needed.
5. Mark is purchasing a Ford Taurus, trading in a Chevy Cavalier, and buying new floor mats for the Taurus. The Taurus and floor mats are inventory items; so when their stock numbers were selected, their descriptions and prices were automatically entered by the system. Here, the price of the Taurus was changed, probably due to negotiation. The Chevy is not an inventory item, so its description and trade-in value had to be entered.
6. The system calculated and entered all totals.
7. The system is programmed to request loan origination information whenever Note Receivable is selected in **Terms.** When the finance manager clicked **Save,** the system opened the Notes Receivable window.

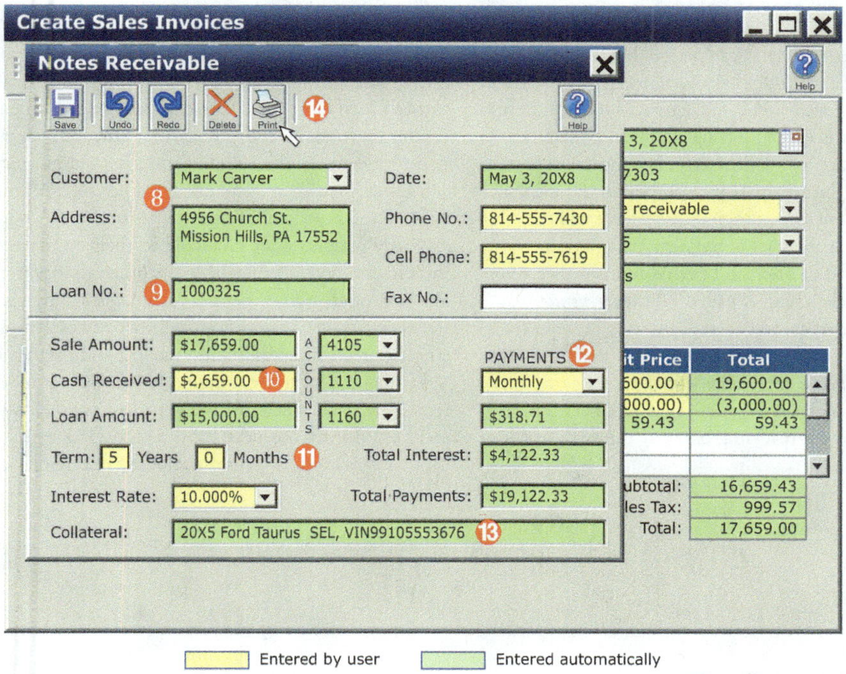

8 The customer name and address were entered automatically by the system. Phone numbers were entered by the finance manager.

9 The loan number was entered in sequence by the system.

10 The sale amount was brought forward automatically. The finance manager entered the amount of the down payment and the system calculated and entered the loan amount. Account numbers were entered by default, but could be changed.

11 The finance manager has entered the term of the note and selected the interest rate.

12 After the frequency of payments (Monthly) was selected, the system calculated and entered the monthly payment, the total interest, and the total payments.

13 Candor assumes that each note receivable will be collateralized with the vehicle sold. That means that if Mr. Carver fails to make payments as agreed, Candor can repossess the vehicle. The system automatically enters the vehicle's description.

14 The finance manager has saved the information and will print out the note so it can be signed. An amortization schedule can also be printed for the customer.

CLOSURE

- Review the Chapter Summary.
- Ask students to prepare a list of the new concepts introduced in this chapter.

Essential Questions

- What would be more advantageous for a future business—offering gift cards or offering coupons to customers? Explain. (*Opinions will vary. Some students will prefer gift cards because they provide immediate revenue. Others may prefer coupons because the business does not incur a liability.*)
- What would be the advantage of offering installment loans rather than extending credit through an Accounts Receivable account? (*Interest can be charged on installment loans. Accounts Receivable is an agreement to pay within a short period of time, usually 30 days.*)

EXTENDED LEARNING

- Review A Look at Accounting Software on pages 280 and 281.
- Assign Explore Accounting on page 282.

EXPLORE ACCOUNTING

Answers

1. Answers will vary. Danover should begin by sending e-mails to the cardholder. This process is relatively inexpensive as it requires minimal employee time. The next step would be to attempt to contact the cardholder by phone, a more expensive process that requires additional employee effort. As a last resort, a Danover employee could use an Internet people search site to locate the individual.

   Dr. Gift Cards Outstanding

   Cr. Cash
2. Answers will vary depending on state laws.

Chapter Summary

Revenue received in one fiscal period but not earned until the next fiscal period is called *unearned revenue.* An adjusting entry is recorded to recognize as income only that amount that is earned during the fiscal period. The adjustment creates a liability equal to the amount of revenue to be earned during the next fiscal period. A business that records the cash receipt initially as revenue will record a reversing entry at the start of the next fiscal period.

Revenue earned in one fiscal period but not received until a later fiscal period is called *accrued revenue.* An adjusting entry is recorded to recognize as income the amount that is earned during the fiscal period. The adjustment creates a receivable equal to the amount owed to the business. A business that records accrued revenue will record a reversing entry at the start of the next fiscal period.

The proceeds from the sale of gift cards are recorded initially in an unearned revenue account, such as Gift Cards Outstanding. Revenue is recognized when the customer redeems the gift card. Some gift cards are never redeemed. The value of unredeemed gift cards is called *breakage.* At the end of a fiscal period, the amount of breakage is generally recorded as revenue.

Many retailers offer financing to their customers. An installment note enables the customer to pay for the amount owed over a period of time. An amortization schedule is used to determine the portion of each monthly payment recognized as interest income and principal.

At the end of a fiscal period, a reclassification entry records as a current asset the principal payments to be collected during the next fiscal period. The reclassification entry is reversed at the start of the next fiscal period.

EXPLORE ACCOUNTING Legal Issues Surrounding Breakage

© iStockphoto.com/Makhnach_M

Accountants of a retail business that issues gift cards need to understand state laws related to unclaimed property. All states have rules that govern the ownership of all unclaimed property. Unclaimed property ranges from land to cars to checking accounts. Once all efforts to identify the owner have been exhausted, the unclaimed property becomes the property of the state.

Unredeemed gift cards represent a new form of unclaimed property. Some states have enacted legislation that exempts gift cards from unclaimed property rules. In these states, the issuing retailer can claim the unclaimed property, recording the breakage as revenue.

In all other states, the retailer must turn over the value of unclaimed property to the state. The state that receives the property is determined by the last known address of the cardholder. If the owner's address is unknown, the state where the retailer is located has the right to the unclaimed property.

The form of the gift card has a significant impact on the application of unclaimed property rules. No personal information of the cardholder is obtained when a plastic card is purchased at a retail store. Thus, there is no way to identify the last known address of the cardholder. Information about the cardholder is obtained at the time a virtual card is purchased. However, unless a cardholder notifies the retailer of any address change, the information stored by the retailer may be out of date.

INSTRUCTIONS

1. Danover Stores sold a $50.00 virtual gift card five years ago. The card has never been used. Danover has the name, address, phone number, and e-mail address of the cardholder. What efforts would be considered reasonable to contact the cardholder? Assuming those efforts are unsuccessful, identify the journal entry that would be required to account for unredeemed gift cards in a state that claims unclaimed property.
2. Research breakage laws in your state. How do your findings change the answers to question 1?

Apply Your Understanding

INSTRUCTIONS: Download problem instructions for Excel, QuickBooks, and Sage 50 from the textbook companion website at www.C21accounting.com.

9-1 Application Problem: Journalizing adjusting and reversing entries for unearned and accrued revenue LO1, 2

JMB Properties is preparing its December 31 financial statements for the current year. On September 30, Mixon & Sheppard, LLP, paid $12,000.00 to JMB Properties for the rental of office space. The payment is the monthly rent for October of the current year through March of the next year. JMB Properties records rent receipts initially as revenue. General journal pages are provided in the *Working Papers*.

Instructions:

1. Journalize the adjusting entry for unearned rent revenue. Use page 16 of a general journal.
2. Journalize the reversing entry for unearned rent revenue. Use page 17 of a general journal.

JMB Properties has two notes receivable outstanding on December 31 of the current year.

Note No.	Interest Rate	Term	Principal	Date
16	10%	120 days	$2,300.00	October 22
17	8%	60 days	$1,800.00	November 26

3. Journalize the adjusting entry for accrued interest income. Use page 16 of a general journal.
4. Journalize the reversing entry for accrued interest income. Use page 17 of a general journal.

9-2 Application Problem: Journalizing gift card transactions LO3, 4

Discount Hardware sells $25.00 and $50.00 gift cards. A cash receipts journal and general journals are provided in the *Working Papers*.

Instructions:

1. Record the following transactions on page 16 of a cash receipts journal and page 12 of a general journal. Discount Hardware uses the accounts Unearned Gift Card Revenue and Breakage Revenue to account for gift card transactions. Source documents are abbreviated as follows: memorandum, M; receipt, R.

Transactions:

Dec. 28. Customers redeemed gift cards for the sale of merchandise, $315.08, plus $18.90 sales tax. M223.
29. Received cash for the sale of gift cards, $250.00. R789.
30. Customers redeemed gift cards for the sale of merchandise, $221.67, plus $13.30 sales tax. M226.
30. Received cash for the sale of gift cards, $150.00. R792.

2. Discount Hardware estimates that $1,721.00 of gift cards will never be redeemed. Record the adjusting entry on page 13 of a general journal.

CHECK FIGURES

For complete solutions to Chapter 9 problems, see the Teacher's Edition of the Working Papers.

Application Problem 9-1

Adjusting entries credits: Unearned Rent, $6,000.00; Interest Income, $57.92.

Reversing entries credits: Rent Income, $6,000.00; Interest Receivable, $57.92.

Application Problem 9-2

Dec. 28 debit: Gift Cards Outstanding, $333.98

Dec. 29 credit: Gift Cards Outstanding, $250.00.

Adjusting entry credit: Breakage Revenue, $1,721.00.

Application Problem 9-3

July 3 credit: Interest Income, $392.81.

July 6 debit: Notes Receivable, $48,350.00.

July 12 credit: Interest Income, $301.78.

July 16 debit: Notes Receivable, $52,950.00.

Mastery Problem 9-M

Dec. 20 credit: Gift Cards Outstanding, $650.00.

Dec. 23 debit: Gift Cards Outstanding, $180.78.

Dec. 29 credit: Interest Income, $28.12.

Adjusting entries credits: Unearned Advertising, $1,800.00; Interest Income, $53.75; Breakage Revenue, $5,820.00.

Reclassification entry debit: Current Portion of Notes Receivable, $22,365.00.

Reversing entries credits: Advertising Revenue, $1,800.00; Interest Receivable, $53.75; Current Portion of Notes Receivable, $22,365.00.

INDEPENDENT PRACTICE

- Assign Mastery Problem 9-M for students as a culminating problem combining all new learning from the chapter.
- Assign Challenge Problem 9-C to accelerated students who work at a faster pace.
- Assign Study Guide 9.
- Students can access Online Working Papers to work end-of-chapter problems on the computer.
- Direct students to the C21 Accounting companion website for additional practice and review opportunities.

9-3 Application Problem: Journalizing installment notes receivable transactions LO6, 7

Sage 50 Accounting

1. Journalize and post notes receivable transactions to the cash receipts journal.
2. Journalize and post the reclassification entry to the general journal.
3. Journalize and post the reversing entry to the general journal.

QB

1. Journalize and post notes receivable transactions to the Journal.
2. Journalize and post the reclassification entry and reversing entry to the journal.

X

1. Journalize notes receivable transactions to the cash receipts journal.
2. Journalize the reclassification entry and reversing entry to the general journal.

AAONLINE

1. Go to www.cengage.com/login
2. Click on AA Online to access.
3. Go to the online assignment and follow the instructions.

The journals and a loan payment schedule for Maben RV Center are given in the *Working Papers*.

Instructions:

1. Using July of the current year, journalize these transactions on page 7 of a cash receipts journal. Refer to the amortization schedule when journalizing the July 3 and 12 transactions. Source documents are abbreviated as follows: note receivable, NR; receipt, R.

Transactions:

July 3. Received cash for Berk Hyde's July payment, $1,264.23. R369.

6. Sold a recreational vehicle to Blair Jordan for $53,350.00 plus $2,667.50 sales tax, receiving a $7,667.50 down payment and accepting a 60-month, 7% installment note receivable for the balance, $48,350.00. NR172.

12. Received cash for Altoria Johnwick's July payment, $985.84. R378.

16. Sold a recreational vehicle to Matt Payne for $61,450.00 plus $3,072.50 sales tax, receiving an $11,572.50 down payment and accepting a 48-month, 7% installment note receivable for the balance, $52,950.00. NR173.

2. On December 31, Maben RV Center has $675,474.90 of installment notes receivable outstanding. Of that amount, $134,643.00 is expected to be collected during the next fiscal period. Record the reclassification entry using page 20 of a general journal.
3. Journalize the reversing entry of the December 31 reclassification entry for installment notes receivable. Record the reversing entry using page 21 of a general journal.

9-M Mastery Problem: Journalizing unearned revenue, accrued revenue, and gift card and installment note receivable transactions LO1, 2, 3, 4, 6, 7

Sage 50 Accounting

1. Journalize and post transactions to the cash receipts journal.
2. Journalize and post the reclassification entry to the general journal.
3. Journalize and post adjusting and reversing entries to the general journal.

QB

1. Journalize and post transactions to the journal.
2. Journalize and post the reclassification entry to the general journal.
3. Journalize and post adjusting and reversing entries to the journal.

Marist Entertainment completed the following transactions during December of the current year. Marist records unearned items initially as revenue. The company uses the accounts Gift Cards Outstanding and Breakage Revenue to account for gift card transactions. The sales tax rate is 7.0%. A cash receipts journal and general journals are provided in the *Working Papers*.

Instructions:

1. Journalize the following transactions. Refer to the amortization schedule when journalizing cash receipts on installment notes receivable.

Transactions:

Dec. 19. Sold an entertainment system to Donna Tuttle for $3,000.00 plus $210.00 sales tax, receiving a $510.00 down payment and accepting a 36-month, 12% installment note receivable for the balance, $2,700.00. NR226.

20. Received cash for the sale of gift cards, $650.00. R820.

22. Received cash for Lisa Renfroe's December payment, $88.02. R825.

23. Customers redeemed gift cards for the sale of merchandise, $168.95. M301.

27. Received cash for the sale of gift cards, $150.00. R834.

29. Received cash for Rose Cribbs' December payment, $108.94. R841.

30. Customers redeemed gift cards for the sale of merchandise, $2,180.68. M312.

31. Sold a home theatre system to Rocky Holman for $4,762.50 plus $333.38 sales tax, receiving an $833.38 down payment and accepting a 36-month, 12% installment note receivable for the balance, $4,262.50. NR227.

FORMATIVE ASSESSMENT

- Review solutions to the assigned problems in class, diagnosing trouble spots.

RETEACH

- Call on students to describe how they avoid the trouble spots diagnosed.
- Use reteaching suggestions from lesson plans as required.
- Assign Recycling Problem 9-R if needed.

1. Journalize transactions in the cash receipts journal.
2. Journalize the reclassification entry to the general journal.
3. Journalize the adjusting and reversing entries to the general journal.

AAONLINE

1. Go to www.cengage.com/login
2. Click on AA Online to access.
3. Go to the online assignment and follow the instructions.

2. Use the following information to record adjusting entries on December 31 of the current year. Use page 21 of a general journal.
   a. On November 1, Marist Entertainment received $5,400.00 from Logistic Games for advertising of its electronic games. The payment is to pay for $1,800.00 of monthly advertising for November, December, and January. Marist Entertainment records advertising receipts initially as revenue.
   b. Marist Entertainment periodically loans money to employees. The company has two notes outstanding to employees on December 31.

Note No.	Interest Rate	Term	Principal	Date
E31	6%	120 days	$3,500.00	October 23
E32	5%	180 days	$1,800.00	November 4

   c. Marist Entertainment estimates that $5,820.00 of gift cards will never be redeemed.
3. On December 31, Marist Entertainment has $42,675.50 of installment notes receivable outstanding. Of that amount, $22,365.00 is expected to be collected during the next fiscal period. Record the reclassification entry using page 22 of a general journal.
4. Journalize any adjusting or reclassification entries that should be reversed. Use page 23 of a general journal.

9-C Challenge Problem: Journalizing sales and gift card transactions from a point-of-sale system LO3

The point-of-sale system for Teton Designs prepares a terminal summary that summarizes all cash and sales transactions, including transactions involving gift cards. Teton Designs records the amounts from the terminal summary in a single entry in the cash receipts journal. To provide a history of gift card transactions in the Gift Cards Outstanding account, the amounts of sales and redemptions of gift cards are listed individually in the journal entry.

Instructions:

Record the following transactions that occurred during August of the current year. Use page 5 of a cash receipts journal.

Transactions:

Aug. 4. Recorded the output of the terminal summary: cash and credit card sales, $2,532.55; sales tax, $145.34; sales of gift cards, $625.00; redemptions of gift cards, $208.34. Terminal Summary No. 28.

11. Recorded the output of the terminal summary: cash and credit card sales, $2,842.04; sales tax, $184.15; sales of gift cards, $200.00; redemptions of gift cards, $489.12. Terminal Summary No. 29.

EXTENDED LEARNING

- Assign 21st Century Skills on page 286.
- Assign Analyzing Home Depot's Financial Statements on page 286.

SUMMATIVE EVALUATION

- Chapter 9 Test
- Cognero for Chapter 9

Challenge Problem 9-C

Aug. 4 Gift Cards Outstanding: debit, $208.34; credit, $625.00.

21st Century Skills

Mobile Money

Theme: Financial, Economic, Business, and Entrepreneurial Literacy

Skills: Critical Thinking and Problem Solving, Communication and Collaboration, ICT Literacy

PARTNERSHIP FOR 21ST CENTURY SKILLS

Consumers are turning to prepaid cards as a convenient way to manage money. According to MyBankTracker, over $409 billion was uploaded on prepaid debit cards in a recent year. Prepaid cards—like iTunes, prepaid game cards, and other gift cards—are not credit cards, which means that only the money paid in advance can be spent.

Plastic long ago surpassed cash as the choice of payment for most consumers. While plastic is convenient, many people have found themselves in excessive debt due to overspending. According to Dave Ramsey, author and personal money-management advisor, when cash is used instead of plastic, one will spend less because spending cash hurts. *Carnegie Mellon Magazine* reports that researchers studying the neurological impact of big purchases found that spending cash registered as pain on a medical test.

Prepaid cards are appealing because they enable the user to avoid debt. They are offered by banks, with recognizable names like Visa and MasterCard, or by individual stores as reloadable gift cards. They can be used with the benefits of a bank account or given as gifts.

It should not come as a surprise that prepaid cards are now leading the trend for mobile apps. Mobile payment processing increases the convenience and decreases the debt risk, since a limit has already been set. Starbucks reports that 26 million mobile transactions were conducted in 2011, and customers loaded more than $100 million in funds onto the prepaid app.

In Haiti, where two-thirds of the population has mobile phones but only 10% have bank accounts, money is being transferred to prepaid accounts via mobile phones to help survivors with post-earthquake reconstruction. Mobile apps are not only safer and more convenient than cash, but they also help prevent the spread of diseases that could occur from handling currency. Clearly, new uses for prepaid cards are driving the way we spend our money.

APPLICATION

1. Using the Internet, research three prepaid debit cards. Compare and contrast the following for each card: activation fee, monthly fee, ATM withdrawal fee, maximum deposit balance, ATM balance inquiry fee, inactivity fee, closed account fee, card replacement fee, and one other interesting fact learned.
2. Select a presentation method and share your findings as a comparison.

Sources: http://www.mybanktracker.com/bank-news/2012/02/17/mobile-helps-prepaid-market-growth/; *Foundations in Personal Finance* by Dave Ramsey; www.un.org.

21ST CENTURY SKILLS

Answers

1. Answers will vary. Other interesting facts might include a per-usage fee or a statement fee.
2. Presentation methods will vary. Flow charts, diagrams, or spreadsheets may be used.

Analyzing Home Depot's financial statements

Like most national retailers, Home Depot offers its customer the opportunity to purchase gift cards. The cash received from the sale of gift cards is recorded in Deferred Revenue on Home Depot's Consolidated Balance Sheet.

INSTRUCTIONS

Refer to the Notes to Consolidated Financial Statements in Appendix B beginning on page B-10 to answer the following questions:

1. In which account does Home Depot record the redemption of gift cards?
2. How does Home Depot estimate the amount of gift card breakage?
3. Identify the amount of gift card breakage recognized in the three years presented on the Consolidated Statements of Earnings on page B-6.
4. How does Home Depot report breakage income?

ANALYZING HOME DEPOT'S FINANCIAL STATEMENTS

Answers

1. In Net Sales.
2. Based on historical redemption patterns.
3. 2012, $33 million; 2011, $42 million; 2010, $46 million.
4. As a reduction in selling, general, and administrative expenses.

COMMON CORE AND INTERDISCIPLINARY STUDIES

Extended learning features and activities present numerous opportunities to implement Common Core Standards through interdisciplinary studies. Practice is provided in the common core areas of English Language Arts & Literacy and Mathematical Practice. Many of these activities require short, critical-thinking and decision-making responses that apply reading, writing, speaking, listening, language, media and technology, and mathematical skills.

Reinforcement Activity 2

Processing Accounting Data for a Corporation

Sage 50 Accounting QB AAONLINE

This activity reinforces selected learning from Part 2, Chapters 5 through 9.

Franklin Auto Parts, Inc.

Franklin Auto Parts, Inc. (Franklin), a merchandising business, is organized as a corporation. The business sells a complete line of automotive parts to businesses and individuals. The business owns the land and building where its store is located.

Franklin's fiscal year ends on December 31. Franklin uses the chart of accounts shown on page 289. The journals used by Franklin are similar to those used in Part 2.

Franklin uses the following accounting policies:

- The allowance method of accounting for uncollectible accounts is used.
- The last-in, first-out and lower of cost or market costing methods are used.
- The straight-line method is used to calculate depreciation expense.
- Supplies, insurance, and advertising are initially recorded as expenses.
- A liability account is maintained for estimated warranty expenses.
- Receipts received in advance of sales are initially recorded as revenue.
- A liability account is maintained for outstanding gift cards.
- Gift card breakage is recorded as revenue.
- Interest on bank notes is calculated using a 365-day year. Amortization schedules for installment notes receivable are based on a 360-day year.

Recording Transactions

INSTRUCTIONS

1. Use the appropriate journal to record the following transactions completed during December of the current year. The sales tax rate is 6.0%. Journals and selected note amortization schedules are given in the *Working Papers*. Source documents are abbreviated as follows: check, C; memorandum, M; receipt, R; note receivable, NR.

   Transactions:

   Dec. 2. Drew $19,200.00 from its First Commerce Bank line of credit. The bank deposited the funds directly to Franklin's checking account. R892.

   3. Received cash for the sale of gift cards, $860.00. R893.

   4. Received an e-mail from James Daniels, the legal counsel for Mattre Enterprises, stating that Mattre has filed for bankruptcy. Mr. Daniels stated that it will likely take several years for the bankruptcy proceedings to be completed. Even then, there is little chance that Franklin will receive any payment from Mattre. The Mattre account of $2,486.31 is over 180 days past due. M135.

   5. Discarded an office desk: original cost, $1,650.00; estimated salvage value, $250.00; estimated useful life, 7 years; total accumulated depreciation through December 31 of last year, $900.00. M136.

   7. Customers redeemed gift cards for merchandise, $548.68, plus $27.43 sales tax. M137.

   9. Purchased at auction the store of a bankrupt merchandising business. The $380,000.00 purchase price included land appraised for $180,000.00 and a building appraised for $270,000.00. Franklin paid $80,000.00 down and financed the remainder by signing a note with First Commerce Bank. C769.

   12. May Stenson, owner of May's Mints, stated that she does not intend to pay the remaining $45.50 of her bill. May maintains that she did not receive all the items listed on the sales invoice. Although your records clearly indicate the correct number of items was delivered, your manager believes that further efforts to collect this account could damage your relationship with a valued customer. M138.

   13. GPR Landscape dishonored its $500.00, 60-day, 10% note due today. M139.

   14. Paid the maturity value of a $25,000.00, 180-day, 7.5% note with First Commerce Bank, plus interest. C770.

   16. Wrote a check to City Handyman for parts and labor to repair equipment under warranty, $155.95. C771.

   18. Earlier in the year, Franklin wrote off the $1,662.95 balance of Dan's Garage. The account was over 210 days past due and collection seemed doubtful. Today, Franklin received a $1,000.00 check from Dan's Garage. M140 and R894.

Reinforcement Activity

BRIDGE

- Reinforcement Activity 2 begins after Chapter 9 and reinforces processing accounting data for a corporation.

TEACHING RESOURCES

- **Manual Accounting:**
  Working Papers for Reinforcement Activity 2
  Teacher's Edition of the Working Papers for Reinforcement Activity 2
  Online Working Papers
  Website for Audit Tests, Solutions, and Transparency Masters
- **Accounting Software:**
  QuickBooks, Excel, Sage 50, and Automated Accounting Online may be used to automate this Reinforcement Activity.

INPUT FOR AUTOMATING

- Direct students to read the Help screens for specific requirements for automating Reinforcement Activity 2.

WINNING EDGE

Give students the *Winning Edge* by making competitive event prep part of their classroom materials throughout the year. Go to cengage.com/winningedge for a list of materials that prepare students for specific competitive events.

CHECK FIGURES

General Journal debits:

- Uncollectible Accounts Expense, $2,486.31.
- Depreciation Expense—Office Equipment, $183.33.
- Accumulated Depreciation—Office Equipment, $1,083.33.
- Loss on Plant Assets, $566.67.
- Gift Cards Outstanding, $576.11.
- Uncollectible Accounts Expense, $45.50.
- Accounts Receivable/GPR Landscape, $508.22.
- Accounts Receivable/Dan's Garage, $1,000.00.
- Depreciation Expense—Office Equipment, $420.00.
- Depreciation Expense—Office Equipment, $400.00.
- Gift Cards Outstanding, $2,305.24.

Adjusting Entries debits:

- Uncollectible Accounts Expense, $5,803.09.
- Income Summary, $915.45.
- Supplies, $689.00.
- Prepaid Insurance, $2,800.00.
- Prepaid Advertising, $3,500.00.
- Warranty Expense, $20,185.13.
- Gift Cards Outstanding, $1,920.00.
- Interest Receivable, $690.00.
- Interest Expense, $63.12.
- Federal Income Tax Expense, $5,092.00.

Cash Receipts Journal, select General Credit column entries:

- Dec. 3, Gift Cards Outstanding, $860.00.
- Dec. 21, Interest Income, $15.01.
- Dec. 27, Gain on Plant Asset, $60.00.
- Dec. 28, Notes Receivable, $201.47.

Cash Payments Journal, select General Debit column entries:

- Dec. 9, Land, $152,000.00.
- Dec. 14, Interest Expense, $924.66.
- Dec. 16, Accrued Warranty Liability, $155.95.
- Dec. 23, Office Equipment, $2,560.00.
- Dec. 30, Notes Payable, $244.52.

Reinforcement Activity 2 (Cont.)

Processing Accounting Data for a Corporation

Dec. 19. Sold merchandise to David Anderson for $2,000.00 plus $100.00 sales tax, receiving a $350.00 down payment and accepting a 12-month, 12% installment note receivable for the balance, $1,750.00. NR226.

20. Received cash for the sale of gift cards, $1,590.00. R895.

21. Received the December note payment from Danielle Petrus on her $4,200.00, 12-month, 10.0% note. R896.

22. Received $32,000.00 from First American Bank, signing a 180-day, 8% note. R897.

23. Paid cash, $1,460.00, and traded in an old copy machine for a new copy machine. The old copy machine had an original cost of $2,500.00, an estimated salvage value of $400.00, and a useful life of 5 years. Total accumulated depreciation recorded on the copy machine through December 31 of last year was $980.00. M141 and C772.

27. Received cash from the sale of a notebook computer, $360.00: original cost, $1,400.00; estimated salvage value, $200.00; useful life, 3 years; total accumulated depreciation through December 31 of last year, $700.00. M142 and R898.

28. Received the December note payment from David Lander on his $2,480.00, 12-month, 12.0% note. R899.

29. Customers redeemed gift cards for merchandise, $2,195.47, plus $109.77 sales tax. M143.

30. Paid the December payment on a $40,000.00 installment note with Platt Equipment. C773.

31. Used the bank's Internet site to pay $2,000.00 plus $134.95 interest on its line of credit. M144.

2. Journalize the adjusting entry for uncollectible accounts expense on December 31 of the current year. Franklin estimates that the amount of uncollectible accounts expense is equal to 0.9% of its net sales on account. The following information was obtained from Franklin's accounting records for the current year:

	January 1	December 31
Accounts Receivable	$ 58,161.32	$67,218.49
Allowance for Doubtful Accounts	4,671.34	265.22
Net Sales (on account)	644,787.46	

3. Franklin uses the perpetual inventory system. On December 31, the unadjusted balance of Merchandise Inventory was $22,330.01. On December 31, Franklin took a physical inventory to determine the actual quantity of each item in inventory. Using the forms in the *Working Papers*, determine the FIFO value of these items and the lower-of-cost-or-market value of total inventory. Units in the December 31 inventory and the market prices are shown below.

Stock Item	Quantity of Units on Hand	Market Price per Item
C-362	26	$ 35.50
A-342	42	84.50
B-164	16	1,062.25

Prepare an adjusting entry for inventory.

4. Use the following information to journalize adjusting entries on December 31 of the current year.

a. Current values of selected expense items are shown below.

Supplies inventory	$ 689.00
Value of unexpired insurance	2,800.00
Unused advertising	3,500.00

b. Warranty expense is estimated to be 1.5% of total sales. Total sales for the current fiscal year are $1,345,675.34.

c. Gift cards that will never be redeemed are estimated to be $1,920.00.

d. Interest revenue earned but not yet recorded on notes receivable is estimated to be $690.00.

e. No payment has been made on the $32,000.00 note payable with First American Bank, signed on December 22.

f. After recording all adjusting entries, Franklin determines that it owes additional federal income tax of $5,092.00.

Franklin Auto Parts, Inc., Chart of Accounts

General Ledger

Balance Sheet Accounts

(1000) ASSETS

1100 Current Assets
1110 Cash
1115 Petty Cash
1120 Accounts Receivable
1125 Allowance for Uncollectible Accounts
1135 Interest Receivable
1140 Merchandise Inventory
1150 Supplies
1160 Prepaid Insurance
1165 Prepaid Advertising
1200 Plant Assets
1210 Land
1220 Building
1225 Accumulated Depreciation—Building
1230 Office Equipment
1235 Accumulated Depreciation—Office Equipment
1240 Store Equipment
1245 Accumulated Depreciation—Store Equipment

(2000) LIABILITIES

2100 Current Liabilities
2105 Accounts Payable
2110 Salaries Payable
2115 Accrued Warranty Liability
2120 Unearned Rent
2125 Gift Cards Outstanding
2130 Employee Income Tax Payable
2135 Social Security Tax Payable
2140 Medicare Tax Payable
2145 Unemployment Tax Payable—Federal
2150 Unemployment Tax Payable—State
2160 Federal Income Tax Payable
2170 Line of Credit
2180 Notes Payable
2190 Interest Payable
2200 Long-Term Liability
2205 Mortgage Payable

(3000) STOCKHOLDERS' EQUITY

3105 Capital Stock
3110 Retained Earnings
3115 Dividends
3120 Income Summary

Income Statement Accounts

(4000) OPERATING REVENUE

4105 Sales
4110 Sales Discount
4115 Sales Returns and Allowances
4120 Breakage Revenue

(5000) COST OF MERCHANDISE

5105 Purchases
5110 Purchases Discount
5115 Purchases Returns and Allowances

(6000) OPERATING EXPENSE

6105 Advertising Expense
6110 Depreciation Expense—Building
6115 Depreciation Expense—Office Equipment
6120 Depreciation Expense—Warehouse Equipment
6125 Insurance Expense
6130 Miscellaneous Expense
6135 Payroll Taxes Expense
6140 Property Tax Expense
6145 Salary Expense
6150 Supplies Expense
6155 Uncollectible Accounts Expense
6160 Warranty Expense

(7000) OTHER REVENUE

7105 Gain on Plant Assets
7110 Interest Income
7115 Rent Income

(8000) OTHER EXPENSES

8105 Interest Expense
8110 Loss on Plant Assets

(9000) INCOME TAX

9105 Federal Income Tax Expense

Part 3
Corporation Accounting

OVERVIEW

Forest Equipment, Inc., is the business used in Part 3 to illustrate corporation accounting. Forest sells to other businesses as well as to retail customers.

Chapter organization and content provide students with an expanded view of concepts and topics that were presented in the first year of accounting study.

- **Chapter 10** describes how to organize a corporation and issue stock.
- **Chapter 11** describes corporate dividends and treasury stock.
- **Chapter 12** describes accounting for bonds.
- **Chapter 13** describes financial reporting and analysis for a corporation.
- **Chapter 14** describes the statement of cash flows.

ACCOUNTING SOFTWARE

For those instructors who want to integrate the accounting program fully, problems at the end of each chapter are flagged to show when files are provided for completing a problem using QuickBooks, Excel, or Sage 50. In addition, A Look at Accounting Software is provided at the end of Chapter 10. This feature is designed to show how the accounting procedures described in these chapters are handled in commercial accounting software.

Part 3 Corporation Accounting

© iStockphoto.com/AlexSlobodkin

Reinforcement Activity

Reinforcement Activity 3, Processing and Analyzing Accounting Data for a Corporation, may be completed after Chapter 14.

THE BUSINESS—

FOREST EQUIPMENT, INC.

Forest Equipment, Inc., is a corporation that sells farming and logging equipment. It purchases equipment from manufacturers to sell to a variety of agricultural businesses. Forest also has a store that sells to retail customers.

© Artur_eM/Shutterstock.com

Chart of Accounts

FOREST EQUIPMENT, INC.

GENERAL LEDGER

Balance Sheet Accounts

(1000) ASSETS

1100 Current Assets
1105 Cash
1110 Petty Cash
1115 Marketable Securities
1120 Accounts Receivable
1125 Allowance for Uncollectible Accounts
1130 Merchandise Inventory
1140 Supplies—Store
1145 Supplies—Administrative
1150 Prepaid Insurance
1155 Prepaid Interest
1160 Notes Receivable
1165 Interest Receivable
1200 Long-Term Investments
1205 Investment Securities
1300 Plant Assets
1310 Land
1320 Building
1325 Accumulated Depreciation—Building
1330 Office Equipment
1335 Accumulated Depreciation—Office Equipment
1340 Store Equipment
1345 Accumulated Depreciation—Store Equipment
1400 Intangible Assets
1405 Trademarks

(2000) LIABILITIES

2100 Current Liabilities
2105 Accounts Payable
2110 Sales Tax Payable
2115 Salaries Payable
2120 Employee Income Tax Payable
2125 Social Security Tax Payable
2130 Medicare Tax Payable
2135 Unemployment Tax Payable—Federal
2140 Unemployment Tax Payable—State
2145 Medical Insurance Payable
2150 Retirement Plan Payable
2155 Federal Income Tax Payable
2160 Dividends Payable
2165 Interest Payable
2170 Notes Payable
2175 Current Portion of Long-Term Debt
2200 Long-Term Liabilities
2205 Bonds Payable
2210 Discount on Bonds Payable
2215 Premium on Bonds Payable

(3000) STOCKHOLDERS' EQUITY

3105 Capital Stock—Common
3110 Paid-In Capital in Excess of Par Value—Common
3115 Capital Stock—Preferred
3120 Paid-In Capital in Excess of Par Value—Preferred
3125 Treasury Stock
3130 Paid-In Capital from Sale of Treasury Stock
3135 Retained Earnings
3140 Dividends—Common
3145 Dividends—Preferred
3150 Income Summary

Income Statement Accounts

(4000) OPERATING REVENUE

4105 Sales
4110 Sales Discount
4115 Sales Returns and Allowances

(5000) COST OF MERCHANDISE

5105 Purchases
5110 Purchases Discount
5115 Purchases Returns and Allowances

(6000) OPERATING EXPENSES

6100 Selling Expenses
6105 Advertising Expense
6110 Credit Card Fee Expense
6115 Depreciation Expense—Store Equipment
6120 Miscellaneous Expense—Sales
6125 Salary Expense—Sales
6130 Supplies Expense—Sales
6200 Administrative Expenses
6205 Depreciation Expense—Building
6210 Depreciation Expense—Office Equipment
6215 Insurance Expense
6220 Miscellaneous Expense—Administrative
6225 Payroll Taxes Expense
6230 Property Tax Expense
6235 Salary Expense—Administrative
6240 Supplies Expense—Administrative
6245 Uncollectible Accounts Expense
6250 Utilities Expense

(7000) OTHER REVENUE

7105 Gain on Plant Assets
7110 Interest Income

(8000) OTHER EXPENSES

8105 Interest Expense
8110 Loss on Plant Assets

(9000) INCOME TAX

9105 Federal Income Tax Expense

The chart of accounts for Forest Equipment, Inc., is illustrated above for ready reference as you study Part 3 of this textbook.

Chart of Accounts

- Emphasize that students should refer to this chart of accounts throughout the chapters in Part 3.
- Point out that this chart of accounts includes new stockholders' equity accounts that include common and preferred stock sales.

Chapter 10 Organizing a Corporation

Scope & Sequence

	New	Review/Enrich
Introduction		
Introduce the Chapter		
Lesson 10-1: Starting a Corporation		
Corporate Form of Business Ownership	✓	
Capital Stock	✓	
Advantages and Disadvantages of Corporations	✓	
Issuing Capital Stock	✓	
Issuing Stock with No Par Value	✓	
Issuing Common Stock with a Stated Value	✓	
Lesson 10-2: Accounting for Preferred Stock		
Issuing Preferred Stock	✓	
Issuing Preferred Stock at Par Value	✓	
Issuing Preferred Stock for more than Par Value	✓	
Issuing Stock for Assets Other than Cash	✓	
Convertible Preferred Stock	✓	
Closure		

Enhancing Instruction

Features	Common Core Standards
• Accounting in the Real World: E. I. du Pont de Nemours and Company	• ELAL—reading, writing
• Ethics in Action: Good Investing or Insider Trading?	• ELAL—reading
• Financial Literacy: Making Cents of Dollar-Cost Averaging	• Mathematics
• Think Like an Accountant: Charting the Capital Structure	• Mathematics
• Why Accounting?: Getting Paid to Communicate	• ELAL—reading, writing
• Careers In Accounting: Financial Planner	• ELAL—reading
• A Look at Accounting Software	• ELAL—reading
• Explore Accounting	• ELAL—reading, media and technology
• 21st Century Skills	• ELAL—media and technology, writing
• Analyzing Home Depot's Financial Statements	• Mathematics

ELAL = English Language Arts & Literacy

Calculator: © iStockphoto.com/picstodisc; Paper: © iStockphoto.com/Qingwa

Practice and Assessment

Technology & Media	Teaching Strategies	Guided Practice	Independent Practice	Reteach/Enrich
• Instructor's Resource CD/Website: PowerPoint Slides Accounting Concepts • Online Working Papers • Transparency Master: Cash Receipts Journal (7-column)	• Interpersonal Learners	• Terms Review • Audit Your Understanding • Work Together 10-1	• On Your Own 10-1 • Application Problem 10-1 • Formative Assessment, p. 301 • Online Working Papers	• Reteach, p. 302
• Instructor's Resource CD/Website: PowerPoint Slides Accounting Concepts • Online Working Papers • Transparency Masters: Cash Receipts Journal (7-column), General Journal	• Gifted Learners • Visual/Spatial Learners	• Terms Review • Audit Your Understanding • Work Together 10-2	• On Your Own 10-2 • Application Problem 10-2 • Formative Assessment, p. 308 • Online Working Papers	• Reteach, p. 309
• Online Working Papers	• Common Core and Interdisciplinary Studies		• Mastery Problem 10-M • Study Guide 10 • Chapter 10 Test • Cognero Chapter 10	• Challenge Problem 10-C • Reteach, p. 314 • Recycling Problem 10-R

Introduce the Chapter

SET THE STAGE

GUIDING QUESTIONS

- Ask if any students or their parents have stock certificates. If so, ask for the names of the companies for which they have stock certificates and the number of shares involved.
- Ask students why they would select certain companies in which to invest.
- Ask students if they have ever traded for something valuable using something besides cash. If so, ask them to explain.

PREVIEW CHAPTER OBJECTIVES

- Point out that this chapter describes many of the transactions that are unique to corporations, including initial stock issues.
- Note that two kinds of capital stock—common and preferred—are described and that the characteristics of each are detailed.
- Ask students to describe those characteristics that make the corporate form of business unique.
- Instruct a student to read each chapter objective aloud.

PREVIEW ACCOUNTING TERMS

- Read each term aloud to verify its pronunciation for students.
- Point out terms or parts of terms that should already be familiar to most students, such as *corporation*, *share of stock*, and *partnership*.
- Point out that five terms are types of stock and that it will be important to distinguish between them.

Chapter 10 Organizing a Corporation

LEARNING OBJECTIVES

After studying Chapter 10, in addition to defining key terms, you will be able to:

LO1 Describe the process for forming a corporation.

LO2 Describe the two basic kinds of stock.

LO3 Identify advantages and disadvantages of the corporate form of business.

LO4 Record the issuances of par-value, no-par-value, and stated-value common stock.

LO5 Record the issuance of preferred stock.

LO6 Explain how to account for convertible preferred stock.

Calculator: © iStockphoto.com/picstodisc; Paper: © iStockphoto.com/Qingwa

Klaus Tiedge/Blend Images/Getty Images

Background: © iStockphoto.com/Elenathewise; Real World: AP Images/ Keystone, Laurent Gillieron

Accounting In The Real World

E. I. du Pont de Nemours and Company

Few corporations can brag about being more than 200 years old. Throughout its history, DuPont has consistently looked for opportunities to grow its business by entering new markets. DuPont brands are now used in a diverse group of industries, including agriculture, construction, electronics, energy, food and beverage, health care, packaging, and transportation, just to name a few.

Another constant at DuPont has been its commitment to provide value to its stockholders. One way a company can achieve this goal is to pay a dividend. DuPont has paid a dividend every year since 1904. In 2000, DuPont paid a $1.40 per share dividend. By 2012, that amount had increased to $1.70, an annual increase of over 1.6%.

A financial ratio that communicates a company's commitment to paying dividends is the dividend payout ratio. This ratio is calculated by dividing dividends by net income.

In its 2012 report, DuPont's average payout ratio for the most recent three years was 45%. Thus, DuPont returns nearly half of its earnings to stockholders as a dividend. The ideal payout ratio is unique to each company and each investor. Management must weigh the financial requirements of the company with meeting its obligation to its stockholders. For over 100 years, DuPont has been successful in achieving both of these objectives.

CRITICAL THINKING

1. What two factors does DuPont consider when determining whether to declare a dividend?
2. DuPont must have an adequate supply of cash to pay a dividend. Suggest other factors that management should consider when determining the portion of earnings to pay as a dividend.
3. Work in a group to identify three corporations that have a large amount of cash. Based on your knowledge of the dividend payout ratio, why do you think the corporations are not using this cash to pay dividends? Do you think any of the corporations should begin paying or increasing their dividends?

Source: www.dupont.com.

Key Terms

- corporation
- share of stock
- stockholder
- board of directors
- articles of incorporation
- charter
- common stock
- preferred stock
- stock certificate
- par value
- par-value stock
- no-par-value stock
- stated-value stock
- proprietorship
- partnership
- double taxation
- limited liability corporation
- privately held corporation
- initial public offering
- publicly held corporation
- registration statement
- conversion option
- conversion ratio
- convertible preferred stock
- conversion price

Accounting In The Real World

Answers

1. a. DuPont has a long-standing commitment to its stockholders to return a significant portion of its earnings as a dividend.
   b. DuPont must ensure that ample resources are available to meet the financial requirements of the company.
2. Answers will vary and might include the following:
   - Opportunities for expansion
   - Level of debt
   - Needs for reserve funding for emergencies
   - Tax implications
3. In recent years, some corporations have been accumulating large amounts of cash, especially in their foreign subsidiaries. Financial news sources have frequently discussed the need for these corporations to either return this cash to stockholders or invest it to create jobs. Tax law has provided corporations with an incentive to retain cash in foreign subsidiaries.

   At the time this textbook was written, Apple Inc., Google Inc., and General Electric Company are three examples of corporations that possess significant amounts of cash.

LESSON
10-1

BRIDGE

- Explain that students are already familiar with certain aspects of a corporation. In this lesson, they will receive additional information on organizing a corporation.

TEACHING IDEA **Display a large sheet of paper in the room. At the top of the paper, write the heading "Characteristics of a Corporation." Instruct students to go to the paper and add characteristics as they learn them.**

TEACHING RESOURCES

- **Instructor's Resource CD/Website:**
  PowerPoint Slides
  Accounting Concepts
- **Working Papers:**
  Teacher's Edition of the Working Papers for Lesson 10-1
  Online Working Papers
- **Transparency Master:**
  Cash Receipts Journal (7-column)

ENGAGE

- Ask students to review the financial or business section of the newspaper or Internet sites for announcements of new stock issues and to bring copies to class. Discuss the number of shares offered, the type of stock, the price per share, and the name of the company offering the stock issue. Review some of the vocabulary used in the announcements, such as *securities, prospectus*, and *solicitation*.

PREVIEW

- Call on students to read the accounting terms and definitions introduced in this lesson: *corporation, share of stock, stockholder, board of directors, articles of incorporation, charter, common stock, preferred stock, stock certificate, par value, par-value stock, no-par-value stock, stated-value stock, proprietorship, partnership, double taxation*, and *limited liability corporation*.
- Point out the learning objectives for this lesson.
- Direct students to read the headings in this lesson and to examine the illustrations.

INPUT

- Ask students to read about selecting a corporate form of business ownership.

LESSON
10-1 Starting a Corporation

LO1 Describe the process for forming a corporation.
LO2 Describe the two basic kinds of stock.
LO3 Identify advantages and disadvantages of the corporate form of business.
LO4 Record the issuances of par-value, no-par-value, and stated-value common stock.

Corporate Form of Business Ownership LO1

Selecting the form of business ownership is an important decision of new business owners. An organization with the legal rights of a person which many persons or other corporations may own is called a **corporation**. [CONCEPT: Business Entity] A corporation is organized by law to exist separately and apart from its owners. Corporations differ from other forms of businesses principally in the nature of ownership and management.

A corporation's ownership is divided into units. A unit of ownership in a corporation is called a **share of stock**. The total shares of ownership in a corporation is known as *capital stock*. The owner of one or more shares of stock is called a **stockholder**. A stockholder is also referred to as a *shareholder*.

Stockholders share in a corporation's earnings. Many corporations distribute a portion of their earnings to stockholders by paying a dividend. Corporations may retain some or all of their earnings to finance future business expansion and improvement.

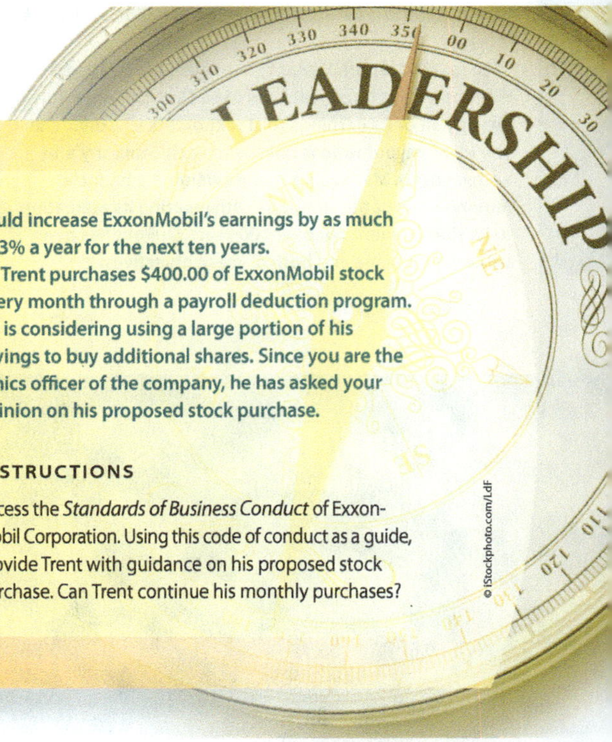

ETHICS IN ACTION

Good Investing or Insider Trading?

The discovery of alternative fuels has led most oil companies to become involved in the search for natural gas in shale located throughout the United States. As a geological engineer for ExxonMobil Corporation, Trent Hendrix has been working to develop estimates of the amount of natural gas reserves in a recent discovery in the Marcellus Shale.

Trent's findings are nothing short of spectacular. His data indicate the reserves are four times any previously published estimates. This discovery could increase ExxonMobil's earnings by as much as 3% a year for the next ten years.

Trent purchases $400.00 of ExxonMobil stock every month through a payroll deduction program. He is considering using a large portion of his savings to buy additional shares. Since you are the ethics officer of the company, he has asked your opinion on his proposed stock purchase.

INSTRUCTIONS

Access the *Standards of Business Conduct* of ExxonMobil Corporation. Using this code of conduct as a guide, provide Trent with guidance on his proposed stock purchase. Can Trent continue his monthly purchases?

© iStockphoto.com/LdF

ETHICS IN ACTION

Answers will vary and should incorporate ExxonMobil's *Code of Conduct*.

Suggested Solution

Trent should not make a special purchase of stock. In its Conflict of Interest Policy section, ExxonMobil's code states the following: "Directors, officers, and employees are expected to avoid securities transactions based on material, nonpublic information learned through their positions with the Corporation." The purchase Trent is considering is based on nonpublic information that he learned through his position as a geological engineer. Trent can continue to make his monthly purchases. He decided to make these purchases before he knew about the natural gas discovery.

ARTICLES OF INCORPORATION OF FOREST EQUIPMENT, INC.

ARTICLE I – NAME

The name of this corporation is Forest Equipment, Inc.

ARTICLE II – NATURE OF BUSINESS

This corporation may engage in or transact any and all lawful activities or business permitted under the laws of the United States and of the State of Alabama.

ARTICLE III – CAPITAL STOCK

The maximum authorized capital stock is:
Common stock: 10,000,000 shares, $1.00 par value
Preferred stock: 500,000 shares, 6%, $100.00 par value

ARTICLE IV – ADDRESS

The present street address of the principle office of this corporation is 15320 Shellhorn Road, Troy, Alabama, 36079.

ARTICLE V – TERM OF EXISTENCE

The duration of the corporation is perpetual unless otherwise stated.

ARTICLE VI – DIRECTORS

M. Dale Pearson	725 Garden Lane	Troy, AL 36079
Matthew H. Tillman	4362 University Ave.	Troy, AL 36079
Stephen P. Pearson	326 Woodside Circle	Montgomery, AL 36117
Mary E. McMullan	1634 Three Notch St.	Troy, AL 36079
Jeannie P. Donovan	9304 Briarwood Dr.	Troy, AL 36079

ARTICLE VII – INCORPORATORS

M. Dale Pearson	725 Garden Lane	Troy, AL 36079
Betty H. Pearson	725 Garden Lane	Troy, AL 36079
Stephen P. Pearson	326 Woodside Circle	Montgomery, AL 36117

IN WITNESS THEREOF, the undersigned incorporator executed these Articles of Incorporation on this the 31st day of March, 20--.

M. Dale Pearson

M. Dale Pearson

A corporation may have many owners. In many small corporations, the owners often participate in the management of the business. Members of a single family often own these businesses. In contrast, the owners of large national and international corporations do not participate in the management of the business. A group of persons elected by the stockholders to govern a corporation is called a **board of directors**. A board of directors represents the stockholders' interests and monitors the management of the corporation.

LEGAL REQUIREMENTS FOR FORMING A CORPORATION

Persons seeking to form a corporation must submit an application to the state in which the company is to be incorporated. A legal document that identifies basic characteristics of a corporation, which is a part of the application submitted to a state to become a corporation, is called the **articles of incorporation**. Some articles of incorporation are submitted to the federal government, but most are submitted to a state government. A state approves the formation of a corporation by issuing a **charter**, the legal right for a business to conduct operations as a corporation. The articles of incorporation submitted for Forest Equipment, Inc., are shown above.

Forest Equipment, Inc., is a corporation that sells farming and logging equipment. However, Article II of its articles of incorporation describes the nature of the business in broad, general terms. This broad purpose enables Forest to expand into other kinds of business activities, if it desires, without applying for a new charter.

INPUT

- Explain that the purpose of the board of directors is to represent the interests of owners not participating in the day-to-day management of the company.
- Point out that although each company's articles of incorporation are unique, the articles address similar items.
- Explain that individuals seeking to form a corporation must submit an application to the state, requesting permission to form a corporation. Point out that even businesses organized as corporate not-for-profit entities must comply.

DIFFERENTIATED INSTRUCTION

Interpersonal learners are people-oriented and learn best in cooperative learning groups or with a partner. Assign students to groups of three. Have each group plan the organization of a corporation. Each corporation is to be authorized 250,000 shares of $2.00 stated-value common stock and 50,000 shares of 10%, $100.00 par-value preferred stock. Have each group draft articles of incorporation following the illustration shown in this lesson. Each group should decide on its own corporation name and address.

INPUT

- Point out that the type of stock, such as common or preferred, has an effect on certain stockholder rights. For example, preferred stock gives stockholders a preference in earnings.
- Discuss the three basic rights of most stockholders.
- Refer students to the illustration as stock certificates are discussed.
- Ask students to describe the distinction between par-value stock and stated-value stock. (*Par-value stock has an authorized value printed on the stock certificate; stated-value stock does not.*) Emphasize that from an accounting standpoint, par-value and stated-value stock are recorded in the same manner.

Capital Stock LO2

No. 00001 *Shares* 20,000

FOREST EQUIPMENT, INC.

This Certifies that M. Dale Pearson *is the registered holder of* 20,000 *shares of the Common Stock transferable only on the books of the Corporation by the holder hereof in person of by Attorney upon surrender of this Certificate properly endorsed.*

In Witness Whereof, the said Corporation has caused this Certificate to be signed by its duly authorized officers this 2nd day of April, A.D. 20--.

M. Dale Pearson	Matthew H. Tillman
M. Dale Pearson	*Matthew H. Tillman*
Chairman of the Board	Secretary

Corporations may issue two basic kinds of stock. Stock that does not give stockholders any special preferences is called **common stock**. A class of stock that gives preferred shareholders preference over common shareholders in dividends along with other rights is called **preferred stock**. Forest is authorized to issue both common and preferred stock as described in Article III of the illustration on the previous page.

Most common stockholders have three basic rights.

1. To vote at stockholders' meetings, unless an exception is made for holders of a particular kind of stock.
2. To share in a corporation's earnings.
3. To share in the distribution of the assets of the corporation if it ceases operations and sells all its assets.

Written evidence of the number of shares that each stockholder owns in a corporation is called a **stock certificate**. A corporation issues a stock certificate when it receives full payment for the stock. A stock certificate, such as the one shown above, usually states the issue date, certificate number, number of shares, and name of the stockholder.

A stock certificate was once the only way of documenting ownership of a stock. Electronic recording of stock ownership has gradually eliminated the need for a corporation to issue stock certificates. Most large corporations now only issue a stock certificate on the request of the stockholder. Small corporations may still elect to issue stock certificates to their stockholders.

A corporation keeps a record of stock issued to each stockholder. A stockholder may later decide to sell some or all shares of stock owned. Changing ownership of stock is referred to as a *stock transfer*. Some corporations handle the issuing and transferring of stock certificates as well as the recording of stock ownership. Most corporations, however, engage a transfer agent, such as a bank, to maintain stock ownership records.

VALUE OF STOCK

Shares of stock are frequently assigned a value. A value assigned to a share of stock and printed on the stock certificate is called the **par value**. The par value has no relationship to the market value of the stock. The par value is set based on other factors, including state laws. A share of stock that has par value is called **par-value stock**.

A share of stock that has no authorized value printed on the stock certificate is called **no-par-value stock**. Some states require that no-par-value stock be assigned a stated or specific value. No-par-value stock that is assigned a value by a corporation is called **stated-value stock**. Stated-value stock is similar to par-value stock except that the value is not printed on the stock certificates.

COMMON STOCK

If a corporation issues only one type of stock, that stock is common stock. If a corporation issues only common stock, the common stockholders are entitled to all of the dividends. In most corporations, only owners of common stock have a right to vote on matters brought before the stockholders. The most common matters voted on by common stockholders are the members of the board of directors and the appointment of the independent auditor. Forest is authorized to issue $1.00 par-value common stock.

PREFERRED STOCK

To attract more investors, a corporation may offer preferred stock with preferences beyond the basic stockholders' rights. Preferred stockholders usually do not have voting rights and cannot influence when and how much is paid in dividends. Therefore, a typical preference given to preferred stockholders is to receive dividends before common stockholders. Other preferences granted preferred stockholders might include the following:

1. Unpaid dividends may accumulate and be paid in a later quarter. Accumulated preferred dividends must be paid before any common stock dividends are paid.
2. Dividends may be shared with common stockholders above a stated percentage or amount. Once the dividend to common stockholders equals the stated percentage of the preferred stock, additional dividends may be shared between preferred and common stockholders.

Every preference granted to preferred stockholders comes at the expense of common stockholders. For example, if preferred stockholders share in dividends above a stated percentage, common stockholders give up a right to some dividends. However, regardless of the type of stock issued, no stockholder is entitled to dividends until a corporation's board of directors votes to pay dividends.

Preferred stock dividends may be stated as an annual percentage of par value or as an amount per share. For example, Forest has authorized the issuance of 6%, $100.00 par-value preferred stock. Preferred stockholders will expect Forest to pay them a $6.00 (6% × $100.00) dividend per share.

CAPITAL ACCOUNTS OF A CORPORATION

Because of the number of owners, a corporation does not keep a separate capital account for each stockholder. Instead, it maintains a single summary general ledger capital account for each kind of stock issued. When a corporation issues only common stock, the value of all stock issued is recorded in a single capital stock account. When a corporation issues both common and preferred stock, separate capital stock accounts are used for common and preferred stock.

A corporation's net income is recorded in the capital account Retained Earnings. Using this account keeps the net income separate from the recorded values of issued capital stock. A net income is credited and a net loss is debited to Retained Earnings.

fyi

Most stock issued today is common stock.

© StockLite/Shutterstock.com

INPUT

- Explain that if a company chooses to issue only one type of stock, that stock is common stock. Stress that each share of common stock gives the owner the right to share in earnings distributions, vote on matters brought before the stockholders, and share in the assets if the corporation liquidates.
- Point out that some corporations issue two types of stock—common stock and preferred stock. Emphasize that preferred stock grants the holder certain preferences superior to those of common stock.
- Point out that one typical preference includes receiving dividends before common stockholders do. Mention that sometimes unpaid dividends accumulate and that dividends over a stated percentage may be shared with common stockholders.
- Explain that preferred stockholders usually do not have voting rights and cannot influence the amount of dividend paid.
- Point out the difficulty of maintaining a separate general ledger capital account for each owner if there were 200,000 different stockholders. Emphasize that companies maintain a single summary account for each kind of stock issued, such as Capital Stock—Common or Capital Stock—Preferred.
- Emphasize that the Retained Earnings account is used to record a corporation's earnings to keep income separate from issued stock.

INPUT

- Explain the advantages and disadvantages of the different forms of ownership.
- Point out the advantages a corporation has over a proprietorship and a partnership.
- Point out some of the disadvantages of a corporation.
- Explain the concept of double taxation.
- Stress that many states allow a limited liability corporation, or LLC, which has the advantages of each form of ownership.
- Point out that limited liability partnerships, or LLPs, are often organized in states that do not permit LLCs.

Advantages and Disadvantages of Corporations LO3

A corporation is only one of several forms of business. Several factors influence the form of business that is best at any particular time. Many businesses start as a **proprietorship**, a business owned by one person. As the business grows, the owner may need the expertise and financial resources of others. The form of ownership must change to account for multiple owners. A **partnership** is a business in which two or more persons combine their assets and skills. Most successful businesses will ultimately elect to adopt a corporate form of business.

Each form of business has advantages and disadvantages. The most significant difference is the extent to which the owner is responsible for the debts, taxes, and losses of the business. The personal assets of the owners of a proprietorship and partnership can be taken to satisfy the debts of the business.

The corporate form of business organization has several advantages over a proprietorship and a partnership:

- **Ease of formation.** Organizing a corporation is as simple as filing an application with the appropriate state agency. The approved application establishes the corporation as a legal entity, giving the corporation many of the same legal rights and risks as individuals have, including owning assets, borrowing money, paying taxes, and being sued.
- **Limited liability.** The liability of stockholders is limited to their investment in the corporation.
- **Supply of capital.** Individuals are more willing to invest in a corporation because their personal assets are protected by limited liability. Reporting requirements by government agencies reduce the perceived risk to investors.
- **Term of existence.** A corporation has a life independent of its owners. Most corporations have a perpetual term of existence.
- **Transfer of ownership.** Shares of stock can be bought and sold directly between individuals. The stock of some corporations can be traded on stock markets. The value of these shares is more readily available to help individuals make investment decisions. Individual investors can trade stock using Internet trading sites.

There are also some disadvantages to a corporation:

- **Regulation.** Corporations that issue stock to the public must follow the reporting requirements of the Securities and Exchange Commission (SEC) and the Public Company Accounting Oversight Board (PCAOB).
- **Loss of decision making.** Stockholders delegate the governance and decision making to the board of directors and executive officers. Some business decisions require approval of the stockholders. Although stockholders have the right to vote, most small investors have little chance of influencing the outcome of the vote.
- **Shared profits.** The earnings of the corporation are divided among the stockholders. The board of directors decides what portion of earnings is returned to the stockholders as a dividend.
- **Taxation.** The earnings of a corporation may be subject to federal and state income taxes. When the earnings of the corporation are distributed to the stockholders, individual stockholders may also have to pay income taxes on the dividends. The taxation of earnings to the corporation and to the stockholders when they receive dividends is called **double taxation**.

To help promote business development, many states now allow a form of business that combines certain characteristics of partnerships and corporations. A **limited liability corporation**, or LLC, offers its owners (known as members) the limited liability afforded to corporate stockholders. However, an LLC does not pay taxes on its earnings. Like a proprietorship or partnership, the earnings are divided among its members. The earnings are only taxed on the members' personal tax returns, thus eliminating the disadvantage of double taxation.

Many accounting firms operate as limited liability partnerships (LLPs). LLPs have the same advantages of limited liability and taxation as LLCs. LLPs are used when the business operates in states that do not recognize LLCs.

fyi

A business operating as a limited liability corporation must include the letters LLC in its formal business name.

Issuing Capital Stock LO4

	Number of Shares	×	Amount per Share	=	Amount
Total received	20,000	×	$5.00	=	$100,000.00
Par value	20,000	×	$1.00	=	20,000.00
Amount received in excess of par value					$ 80,000.00

Calculate Amounts

Credit the Capital Stock Account for the Par Value

CASH RECEIPTS JOURNAL PAGE 1

	DATE		ACCOUNT TITLE	DOC. NO.	POST. REF.	1 GENERAL DEBIT	2 GENERAL CREDIT	3 ACCOUNTS RECEIVABLE CREDIT	4 SALES CREDIT	5 SALES TAX PAYABLE CREDIT	6 SALES DISCOUNT DEBIT	7 CASH DEBIT	
1	20-- Apr.	2	Capital Stock—Common	R1			20 000 00					100 000 00	1
2			Paid-In Capital in Excess of										2
3			Par Value—Common				80 000 00						3

Credit the Paid-In Capital Account for the Excess Over Par Value

Debit Cash

Forest's charter is its legal authorization to begin business in the name of the corporation. The first step for Forest to begin operations is to raise the capital needed to purchase inventory, rent a building, and hire employees. It obtains capital by issuing stock to the incorporators.

When the corporation is formed, each of Forest's incorporators agreed to buy a minimum of 10,000 shares of common stock at $5.00 per share.

Paid-In Capital in Excess of Par Value—Common

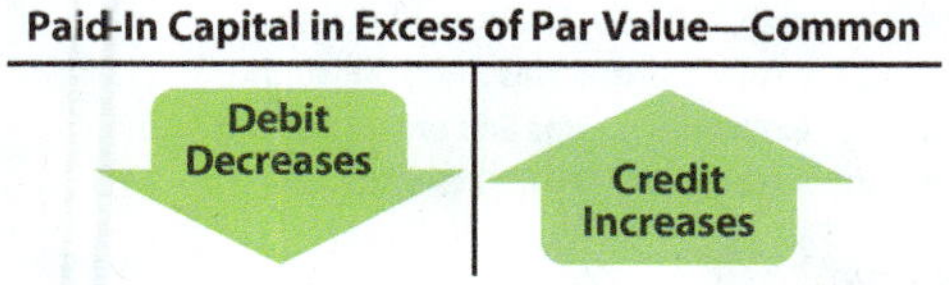

Common stock par values are arbitrary amounts that rarely have any relationship to the market value of the stock. Most issues of common stock are for an amount in excess of the par value.

The excess of proceeds from the issue of stock over the par value is recorded in the account Paid-In Capital in Excess of Par Value—Common. This account is an equity account and has a normal credit balance.

April 2. Received cash from M. Dale Pearson for 20,000 shares of $1.00 par-value common stock, valued at $5.00 per share, $100,000.00. Receipt No. 1.

Cash is debited for $100,000.00. Capital Stock—Common is credited for $20,000.00, the number of shares issued multiplied by the par value. The excess of the amount received over the par value of the stock issued, $80,000.00, is credited to Paid-In Capital in Excess of Par Value—Common.

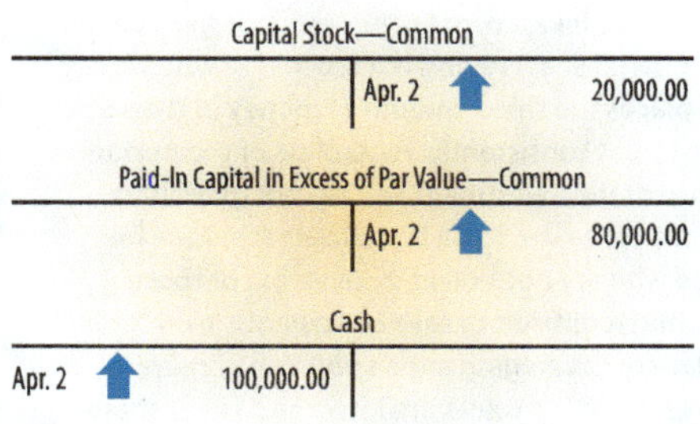

fyi

International Financial Reporting Standards (IFRS) use the title *Share Premium for Paid-In Capital in Excess of Par Value.*

INPUT

- Explain that the first step to begin operations is to raise the capital needed.
- Point out that par values are arbitrary and rarely have a relationship to the market value of stock.
- Explain that the excess of proceeds from the issue of stock over the par value is recorded in the account Paid-In Capital in Excess of Par Value—Common. This is an equity account with a normal credit balance.
- Explain the math illustration to demonstrate how the amounts journalized are calculated.

MODEL

- Draw three T accounts on the board.
- Read the transaction statement.
- Ask students to analyze the transaction. Complete the T accounts as the information is provided.
- Use the transparency of a cash receipts journal to illustrate the process for recording the entry in the journal or refer students to the illustration.
- Record each item in the journal.

INPUT

- Explain that when stock has no par value, the entire amount received from its issuance is recorded in the Capital Stock account.

MODEL

- Read the transaction statement.
- Ask students to analyze the transaction.
- Use the transparency of a cash receipts journal to illustrate the process for recording the entry in the journal or refer students to the illustration.
- Record each item in the journal.

Issuing Stock with No Par Value

CASH RECEIPTS JOURNAL — PAGE 12

	DATE	ACCOUNT TITLE	DOC. NO.	POST. REF.	1 GENERAL DEBIT	2 GENERAL CREDIT	3 ACCOUNTS RECEIVABLE CREDIT	4 SALES CREDIT	5 SALES TAX PAYABLE CREDIT	6 SALES DISCOUNT DEBIT	7 CASH DEBIT	
22	29	Capital Stock—Common	R199			5 000 00					5 000 00	22
23												23

Credit the Capital Stock Account for the Amount Received

Debit Cash

Common stock sometimes has no par value assigned to it. With no-par-value stock, the entire amount paid by an investor is recorded in the capital stock account. Wheeler, Inc., issues no-par-value common stock. The journal entry to record the transaction is shown above.

December 29. Received cash from Elizabeth Griffin for 1,000 shares of no-par-value common stock at $5.00 per share, $5,000.00. Receipt No. 199.

Cash is debited for $5,000.00. Capital Stock—Common is credited for $5,000.00, the total amount received for the 1,000 shares of stock.

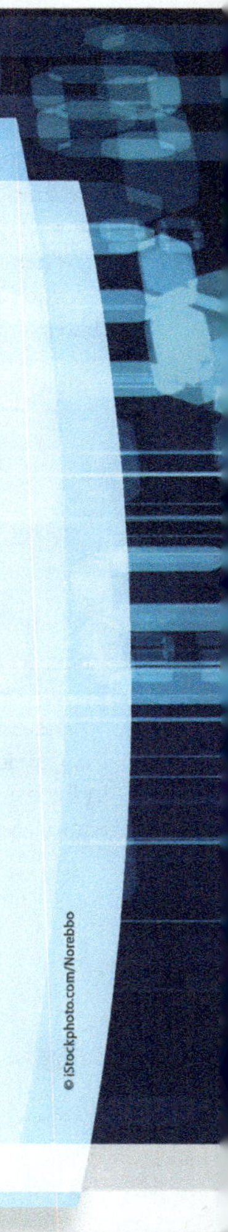

FINANCIAL LITERACY

Making Cents of Dollar-Cost Averaging

Investing in the stock market can be tricky. Some people are uncomfortable determining the best time to invest, and then they become concerned because the investment fluctuates over a short period.

Dollar-cost averaging is a technique whereby one places the same amount of money in the same investment consistently, regardless of the performance of the investment. It does not guarantee a profit. However, it is a beneficial technique for those who are not skilled in investing or those who find it difficult to save consistently over time. Dollar-cost averaging allows you to buy more shares when the prices are lower and fewer shares when the prices are higher.

Below is an example of dollar-cost averaging, assuming you plan to invest $100.00 per month.

June 28: Widgets cost $1 each. You buy 100 widgets.
July 27: Widgets now cost 75 cents each. You buy 133 widgets.
August 28: Widgets drop to 65 cents each. You buy 153 widgets.
September 27: Widgets cost $1.25 each. You buy 80 widgets.

At the end of September, you own 466 widgets. The cost of the units is now $1.25, so your total investment is worth $582.50. The cost of the 466 widgets over the four months was $400.00, so the average cost of each widget was 86 cents. Your investment increased from $400.00 to $582.50.

ACTIVITY

Using the following information, calculate the number of shares bought and the average cost per share. The monthly investment is $150.00. Round to two decimal places.

Date of Investment	Investment Amount	Cost per Share	Shares Bought*
January	$150.00	$12	
February	150.00	10	
March	150.00	8	
April	150.00	13	
TOTAL			

*Calculated by dividing investment by number of shares bought.

FINANCIAL LITERACY

Date of Investment	Investment Amount	Cost per Share	Shares Bought
January	$150.00	$12.00	12.5 ($150/$12)
February	150.00	10.00	15 ($150/$10)
March	150.00	8.00	18.75 ($150/$8)
April	150.00	13.00	11.54 ($150/$13)
TOTAL	600.00	10.38*	57.79

*Calculated by dividing investment of $600 by number of shares bought.

Issuing Common Stock with a Stated Value

Credit the Capital Stock Account for the Stated Value

CASH RECEIPTS JOURNAL PAGE 3

	DATE	ACCOUNT TITLE	DOC. NO.	POST. REF.	1 GENERAL DEBIT	2 GENERAL CREDIT	3 ACCOUNTS RECEIVABLE CREDIT	4 SALES CREDIT	5 SALES TAX PAYABLE CREDIT	6 SALES DISCOUNT DEBIT	7 CASH DEBIT	
4	2	*Capital Stock—Common*	*R233*			500 00					10 000 00	4
5		*Paid-In Capital in Excess of*										5
6		*Stated Value—Common*				9 500 00						6

Credit the Paid-In Capital Account for the Excess Over Stated Value

Debit Cash

Corporations may assign a value to common stock. The value is known as the *stated value*. A stated value serves the same function as par value. Therefore, no-par-value common stock with a stated value is recorded using the same procedures as par-value stock.

Lampkin Corporation's common stock has a stated value of $10.00 per share. Lampkin issued 500 shares of common stock to Alice Blake for $200.00 a share. The excess of the amount per share is recorded in Paid-In Capital in Excess of Stated Value—Common. This account is similar to the account used by Forest Equipment, except the description includes "Stated Value" rather than "Par Value."

March 2. Received cash from Alice Blake for 50 shares of $10.00 stated-value common stock at $200.00 per share, $10,000.00. Receipt No. 233.

Cash is debited for $10,000.00, the total amount received. Capital Stock—Common is credited for $500.00, the total stated value of the 50 shares. Paid-In Capital in Excess of Stated Value—Common is credited for $9,500.00, the amount received in excess of the stated value.

THINK LIKE AN ACCOUNTANT

© iStockphoto.com/Dan Bachman

Charting the Capital Structure

The board of directors of P&J Industries begins each meeting with an overview of the corporation's financial condition. The board consists of a diverse group of individuals, including a banker, a lawyer, a rancher, an educator, and a philanthropist. Each member brings unique talents and perspectives that have enabled the board to direct the corporation effectively. However, that diversity comes with a price. Some of the board members have little experience with reading financial statements.

To communicate the corporation's financial condition effectively to all board members, the Accounting Department prepares a report containing a series of charts. The controller recently learned of a new chart type and wants it incorporated into this quarter's report. The chart is known as a *pie of pie chart*. Unlike a single pie chart, a secondary chart shows the components of a single slice of the primary pie chart.

OPEN THE SPREADSHEET TLA_CH10

The worksheet contains a table containing the liability and stockholders' equity accounts of the balance sheet. Follow the steps on the Instructions tab to prepare two charts, and answer the following questions:

1. What percent is the stockholders' equity of the total liabilities and stockholders' equity?
2. What percent are the current liabilities of the total liabilities and stockholders' equity?
3. Each chart could be improved by reducing the number of items in the chart. Suggest changes in the items included in the charts.
4. Describe the charts that could communicate effectively the information provided on an income statement.

INPUT

- Explain that the same procedures for recording par-value stock are used for stated-value stock.

MODEL

- Read the transaction statement.
- Calculate the amount of excess over stated value.
- Demonstrate how the amounts are derived.
- Use the transparency of a cash receipts journal to illustrate the process for recording the entry in the journal or refer students to the illustration.

THINK LIKE AN ACCOUNTANT

This activity requires students to create two pie charts that focus on (1) stockholders' equity and (2) current liabilities. Students are required to make decisions on how to consolidate selected accounts to provide the appropriate number of slices in each chart. Students use their acquired knowledge to describe how the pie of pie chart can be used to communicate information on an income statement.

Answers

1. 43%
2. 18%
3. Because common stock is a very small amount relative to the other accounts, common stock and paid-in capital should be combined into a single amount and titled Capital Stock.
4. Answers will vary. The secondary pie could display the components of operating or departmental expenses.

FORMATIVE ASSESSMENT

- This is an ongoing process. Circulate around the classroom or lab, observing which students have problems with the assignments.
- Troubleshooting: Diagnose the kinds of problems students have with this section. Students may have difficulty understanding par value and stated value.
- Assess student understanding by checking solutions to Independent Practice assignments and noting their answers to the Terms Review and Audit Your Understanding questions.

CHECK FOR UNDERSTANDING

Terms Review

- Call on students to define each term in the Terms Review. Definitions are given in the Glossary.

Audit Your Understanding

- Call on students to answer the Audit Your Understanding questions. Answers are given in Appendix D of the textbook.

GUIDED PRACTICE

Work Together

- Have students write the solution to the Work Together problem as you guide the class through the examples.
- Direct students to record the transactions in the cash receipts journal as you elicit participation in analyzing and recording the transactions.

INDEPENDENT PRACTICE

On Your Own

- Assign the On Your Own problem to be worked independently.
- Use the Formative Assessment techniques to diagnose student understanding.

Application Problem

- Assign Application Problem 10-1.

Online Working Papers

- Students can access the Lesson 10-1 problems using this software.

Website

- Direct students to the C21 Accounting companion website for additional practice and review opportunities throughout the chapter.

RETEACH

- Ask students to compare and contrast the advantages of different types of ownership.
- Ask students to explain the rights of stockholders.
- Ask students to describe the types of stock.
- Ask students to explain how to account for par and stated value.

CLOSURE

- Ask students to write a brief paragraph on the significance of selecting the corporate form of business ownership. Students should define the term *corporation* and explain how corporations differ from other forms of businesses.

End of Lesson Review

LO1 Describe the process for forming a corporation.

LO2 Describe the two basic kinds of stock.

LO3 Identify advantages and disadvantages of the corporate form of business.

LO4 Record the issuances of par-value, no-par-value, and stated-value common stock.

Terms Review

corporation
share of stock
stockholder
board of directors
articles of incorporation
charter
common stock
preferred stock
stock certificate
par value
par-value stock
no-par-value stock
stated-value stock
proprietorship
partnership
double taxation
limited liability corporation

Audit your understanding

1. What are the responsibilities of a corporation's board of directors?
2. What two basic kinds of stock may a corporation issue?
3. What three basic rights do stockholders usually have?
4. In place of a general ledger capital account for each owner, how does a corporation show stock ownership?
5. How are the earnings of a corporation subject to double taxation?
6. How does a limited liability corporation differ from a traditional corporation?

Work together 10-1

Issuing common stock

Page 6 of a cash receipts journal is provided in the *Working Papers*. The source document is abbreviated as follows: receipt, R. Your instructor will guide you through the following examples.

Transaction:

June 5. Harold Davis purchased 6,000 shares of GlassTown, Inc., common stock for $8.00 per share. R242.

Journalize the transaction using each of the following assumptions regarding the common stock:

a. $1.00 par-value common stock.
b. No-par-value common stock.
c. $1.00 stated-value common stock.

On your own 10-1

Issuing common stock

Page 15 of a cash receipts journal is provided in the *Working Papers*. The source document is abbreviated as follows: receipt, R. Work this problem independently.

Transaction:

Aug. 9. Mandy Reston purchased 500 shares of First National Bank common stock for $14.00 per share. R334.

Journalize the transaction using each of the following assumptions regarding the common stock:

a. $5.00 par-value common stock.
b. No-par-value common stock.
c. $5.00 stated-value common stock.

Essential Question

- When would it be advantageous to form an LLC instead of a corporation? (*When the business is looking for a lower tax rate, needs more flexibility in organization, and is not interested in going public.*)

EXTENDED LEARNING

- Assign Accounting in the Real World on page 293.
- Assign Ethics in Action on page 294.
- Assign Financial Literacy on page 300.
- Assign Think Like an Accountant on page 301.

LESSON
10-2 Accounting for Preferred Stock

LO5 Record the issuance of preferred stock.
LO6 Explain how to account for convertible preferred stock.

Issuing Preferred Stock LO5

As a corporation grows, it may require additional capital to finance its expansion. The portion of a corporation's net income not paid to stockholders as dividends is a primary source of additional capital. However, retained earnings may not provide an adequate source of capital for a corporation. Both new and existing corporations may require a large increase in capital to finance rapid expansion. Thus, a corporation can acquire additional capital by issuing stock to investors, borrowing money, or both.

Usually, the articles of incorporation permit a corporation to issue more shares of stock than it sells to initial investors. As the need arises for more capital, a corporation can issue some of the remaining authorized stock.

Three members of the Pearson family incorporated Forest Equipment, Inc. A corporation owned by a small number of individuals is called a **privately held corporation**. Many of today's largest corporations began as small, privately held corporations. As these businesses grew, the need to raise additional capital required them to issue stock to the public. The initial issue of a security on a public exchange is called an **initial public offering**. An initial public offering is commonly referred to as an *IPO*. A corporation having its stock traded on public exchanges is called a **publicly held corporation**. The process of issuing an IPO is commonly referred to as *taking a company public*. Although the initial investors may retain a large portion of the outstanding stock, a corporation with stock traded on a public exchange is a publicly held corporation.

A publicly held corporation is required to file its financial statements with the Securities and Exchange Commission. The document submitted to the SEC for permission to sell a security on a public exchange is called a **registration statement**.

Once a corporation becomes publicly held, it must submit many documents to the SEC. The two statements most commonly used by investors are the 10-Q (quarterly) and 10-K (annual) reports. Each statement contains financial statements and other financial information. These statements are available free to the public on the SEC's and the corporation's Internet sites.

© Monkey Business Images/Shutterstock.com

LESSON
10-2

BRIDGE

- Point out that students have already learned how to journalize common stock sold in excess of par value or in excess of stated value. In this lesson, they will learn to account for preferred stock sold in excess of par value or in excess of stated value.

TEACHING RESOURCES

- **Instructor's Resource CD/Website:**
  PowerPoint Slides
  Accounting Concepts
- **Working Papers:**
  Teacher's Edition of the Working Papers for Lesson 10-2
  Online Working Papers
- **Transparency Masters:**
  Cash Receipts Journal (7- column)
  General Journal

ENGAGE

- Ask students if they have ever owned preferred stock. If so, ask them to explain why they purchased preferred stock instead of common stock.
- Ask students if they are familiar with any companies that sell stock to a limited number of individuals.
- Ask students to predict how they might account for purchasing stock for an asset other than cash.

PREVIEW

- Call on students to read the accounting terms and definitions introduced in this lesson: *privately held corporation, initial public offering, publicly held corporation, registration statement, conversion option, conversion ratio, convertible preferred stock*, and *conversion price*.
- Point out the learning objectives for this lesson.
- Direct students to read the headings in this lesson and to examine the illustrations.

INPUT

- Explain that many large corporations started as privately held corporations.
- Point out the difference between a privately held corporation and a publicly held corporation.
- Explain that publicly held corporations are required to submit quarterly and annual reports to the SEC.

DIFFERENTIATED INSTRUCTION

Gifted learners need additional challenges, such as research, to maintain a high level of motivation. Using the Internet, students should obtain the names of privately held and publicly held corporations in their community, city, or nearest large municipality. Students should share the list with the class.

Visual/Spatial learners like to see the topic being discussed. Display a large map in the room. Ask these students to label the map with the names of privately held and publicly held corporations in their community.

INPUT

- Explain that privately held corporations can issue preferred stock to a small number of investors; however, those with preferred stock do not have voting rights.

MODEL

- Draw two T accounts on the board.
- Read the transaction.
- Ask students to analyze the transaction by answering these questions: Which accounts are affected? Are they increased or decreased? Are they debited or credited? Complete the T accounts as the information is provided.
- Use a cash receipts journal transparency to illustrate recording the transaction in the journal or direct students to the illustration.

WHY ACCOUNTING?

Answers will vary.

Issuing Preferred Stock at Par Value

Credit the Capital Stock Account for the Par Value

CASH RECEIPTS JOURNAL — PAGE 14

	DATE	ACCOUNT TITLE	DOC. NO.	POST. REF.	1 GENERAL DEBIT	2 GENERAL CREDIT	3 ACCOUNTS RECEIVABLE CREDIT	4 SALES CREDIT	5 SALES TAX PAYABLE CREDIT	6 SALES DISCOUNT DEBIT	7 CASH DEBIT	
1	20-- *Nov.* 2	*Capital Stock—Preferred*	*R235*			*30 000 00*					*30 000 00*	1
2												2

Debit Cash

Forest Equipment is authorized by its charter to issue a total of 10,000,000 shares of common stock and 500,000 shares of preferred stock. However, Forest initially issued only 65,000 shares of common stock to its three stockholders. Thus, Forest may issue some of the remaining shares of common or some shares of preferred stock to raise additional capital.

Forest's three initial stockholders, all members of the Pearson family, want to retain full management control. Selling common stock to another investor, or taking the company public, would cause the Pearson family to lose some of its control over the business. In addition, Forest does not want to incur the cost and effort required to file its financial statements with the SEC.

After weighing its options, Forest elects to issue preferred stock to a small number of local investors. Issuing this stock will not cause Forest to become a publicly held corporation. Forest's preferred stock does not offer any voting rights. Thus, the current stockholders can retain management control of the business.

Forest negotiated an issue of 300 preferred shares of preferred stock at par value to Zach Ruston.

Capital Stock—Preferred

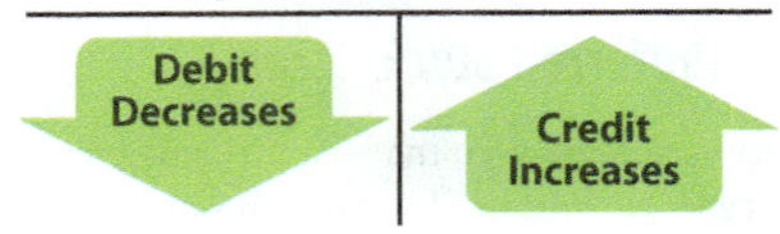

November 2. Received cash from Zach Ruston for 300 shares of 6%, $100.00 par-value preferred stock at par value, $30,000.00. Receipt No. 235.

Capital Stock—Preferred

		Nov. 2	30,000.00

Cash

Nov. 2	30,000.00		

Cash is debited for $30,000.00, the total amount received. Capital Stock—Preferred is credited for $30,000.00, the total par value of the preferred stock issued.

WHY ACCOUNTING?

Getting Paid to Communicate

Peter Drucker, a well-known management specialist, once said, "The most important thing in communication is to hear what isn't being said." Other similar statements point out that communicating can be a challenging art. A major in communications can lead to a variety of career fields such as broadcasting, journalism, government, public relations, arbitration, grant writing, and education.

Many public relations (PR) positions require more than good communication skills. For example, a PR director for a company that makes pacemakers may be the one to announce a research breakthrough or to explain why the company's income statement is being restated. He or she should have some knowledge of medicine and an understanding of how revenues and expenses are measured.

A/V Technology & Communications

CRITICAL THINKING

Using the Internet or the "Help Wanted" section of a local newspaper, find a job opening in the communications/public relations area. List the education and work experience requirements for the position.

© iStockphoto.com/AlekcKo

Issuing Preferred Stock for More than Par Value

	Number of Shares	×	Amount per Share	=	Amount
Total received	200	×	$103.00	=	$20,600.00
Par value	200	×	$100.00	=	20,000.00
Amount received in excess of par value					$ 600.00

Calculate Amounts

Credit the Capital Stock Account for the Par Value

CASH RECEIPTS JOURNAL PAGE 14

	DATE		ACCOUNT TITLE	DOC. NO.	POST. REF.	1 GENERAL DEBIT	2 GENERAL CREDIT	3 ACCOUNTS RECEIVABLE CREDIT	4 SALES CREDIT	5 SALES TAX PAYABLE CREDIT	6 SALES DISCOUNT DEBIT	7 CASH DEBIT	
1	20-- Nov.	23	Capital Stock—Preferred	R489			20 000 00					20 600 00	1
2			Paid-In Capital in Excess of										2
3			Par Value—Preferred				600 00						3

Credit the Paid-In Capital Account for the Excess Over Par Value

Debit Cash

Investors purchase preferred stock to earn the dividend. A preferred stock's dividend rate can be compared to the rate of interest earned on alternative investments. As a result, the value of a preferred stock is dependent on market interest rates and the investor's confidence that the dividend will be paid without interruption. These factors may cause the preferred stock to be issued at a price other than its par value.

Market interest rates fluctuate based on many economic factors. When market interest rates fall below the preferred stock's dividend rate, investors will pay more than the par value. When market interest rates rise above the preferred stock's dividend rate, investors will pay less than the par value.

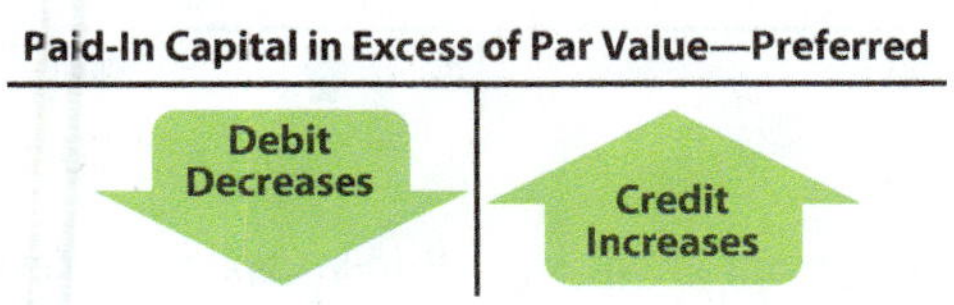

The payment of preferred dividends is not guaranteed. A company in financial distress may not generate enough cash to pay the dividend. Thus, investors must attempt to predict the future economic health of the company. Investors should evaluate the financial statements, research the expertise and experience of management, and consider the future market for the company's products and services.

The excess of proceeds from the issue of preferred stock over the par value is recorded in the account Paid-In Capital in Excess of Par Value—Preferred. This account is an equity account and has a normal credit balance.

Forest negotiated an issue of 200 preferred shares to Sophia Sanchez. Market interest rates had declined since the preferred stock was first issued. Thus, Sophia is willing to pay $103.00 per share.

November 23. Received cash from Sophia Sanchez for 200 shares of 6%, $100.00 par-value preferred stock at $103.00 per share, $20,600.00. Receipt No. 489.

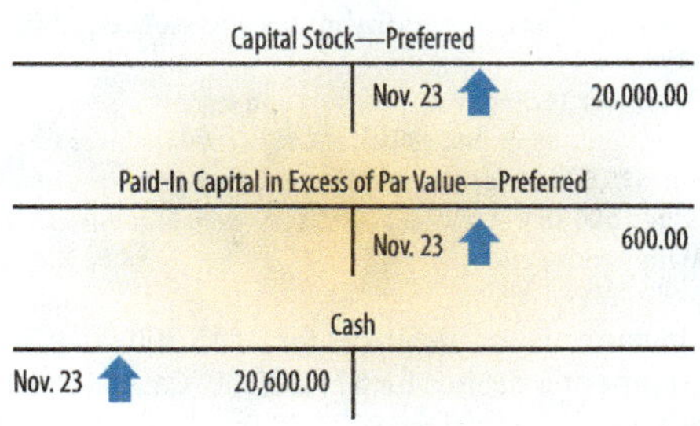

Cash is debited for $20,600.00, the total amount received. Capital Stock—Preferred is credited for $20,000.00, the total par value of the preferred stock issued. Paid-In Capital in Excess of Par Value—Preferred is credited for $600.00, the amount received in excess of the par value. Regardless of the amount received, the credit to the capital stock account always equals the total par or stated value of the stock issued.

INPUT

- Point out that dividends for preferred stock are not guaranteed and depend on the financial condition of the company.
- Explain that preferred stock may be issued at a higher or lower price than its par value, based on economic factors.
- Point out that Paid-In Capital in Excess of Par Value—Preferred is similar to the account used for common stock when an excess over par value is recorded.

MODEL

- Draw three T accounts on the board.
- Read the transaction.
- Ask students to analyze the transaction by answering these questions: Which accounts are affected? Are they increased or decreased? Are they debited or credited? Complete the T accounts as the information is provided.
- Use a cash receipts journal transparency to illustrate recording the transaction in the journal or direct students to the illustration.

INPUT

- Explain that sometimes corporations issue capital stock in exchange for assets other than cash.
- Explain the math illustration at the top of the page.
- Point out that the business and the investor have agreed on the value of the assets and the capital stock.

MODEL

- Draw three T accounts on the board.
- Read the transaction.
- Ask students to analyze the transaction by answering these questions: Which accounts are affected? Are they increased or decreased? Are they debited or credited? Complete the T accounts as the information is provided.
- Use a general journal transparency to illustrate recording the transaction in the journal or direct students to the illustration.

Issuing Stock for Assets Other than Cash

	Number of Shares	×	Amount per Share	=	Amount
Total received	600	×	$101.50	=	$60,900.00
Par value	600	×	$100.00	=	60,000.00
Amount received in excess of par value					$ 900.00

Calculate Amounts

Debit the Asset Accounts for the Assets Received

GENERAL JOURNAL — PAGE 13

	DATE		ACCOUNT TITLE	DOC. NO.	POST. REF.	DEBIT	CREDIT	
11		16	*Inventory*	*M53*		45 300 00		11
12			*Store Equipment*			15 600 00		12
13			*Capital Stock—Preferred*				60 000 00	13
14			*Paid-In Capital in Excess of*					14
15			*Par Value—Preferred*				900 00	15

Credit the Capital Stock Account

Credit the Paid-In Capital Account for the Excess Over Par Value

Occasionally, corporations issue capital stock in exchange for assets other than cash. When other assets are used to pay for capital stock, the investor and corporation must agree on the value of the assets and the capital stock.

BSF Supply is going out of business and has agreed to sell selected assets to Forest Equipment for $60,900.00. BSF Supply agreed to accept 600 shares of preferred stock in exchange for its inventory and store equipment.

December 16. Received inventory and store equipment from BSF Supply at agreed values of $45,300.00 for inventory and $15,600.00 for store equipment. Forest Equipment issued 600 shares of 6%, $100.00 par-value preferred stock. Memorandum No. 53.

Inventory

Dec. 16 ↑ 45,300.00	

Store Equipment

Dec. 16 ↑ 15,600.00	

Capital Stock—Preferred

	Dec. 16 ↑ 60,000.00

Paid-In Capital in Excess of Par Value—Preferred

	Dec. 16 ↑ 900.00

Inventory is debited for $45,300.00. Store Equipment is debited for $15,600.00. Capital Stock—Preferred is credited for $60,000.00, the total par value of the preferred stock issued. Paid-In Capital in Excess of Par Value—Preferred is credited for $900.00, the amount received in excess of the par value.

fyi

International Financial Reporting Standards (IFRS) use the title *Ordinary Shares* for Common Stock *and Preferred Shares* for Preferred Stock.

Convertible Preferred Stock LO6

A preferred stock is a contractual agreement between the corporation and the stockholder. The stockholder agrees to permanently invest an amount of money with the corporation. In exchange, the corporation gives preferred stockholders the right to receive any declared dividends before common stockholders receive dividends.

When preparing to issue preferred stock, a corporation has to balance two naturally conflicting objectives:

1. Maximize the price that investors are willing to pay for the preferred stock.
2. Minimize the amount of dividends that might be declared in the future.

A provision that helps a corporation achieve both objectives is a one that lets the stockholder trade preferred stock for common stock. The ability of a security to be traded for a specified number of shares of another security is called a **conversion option**. The number of shares of common stock received when a security is converted is called the **conversion ratio**. Preferred stock that can be exchanged for a specified number of common shares is called **convertible preferred stock**.

Convertible preferred stock gives the stockholder the ability to share in the income of the corporation through an increase in the market price of the common stock. Thus, this option adds value to the preferred stock and enables the corporation to issue the stock with a lower dividend rate.

Five years ago, Chandler Corporation issued 1,000 shares of $100.00 par-value, 4.5% preferred stock. The preferred stock has a conversion option, allowing the stockholder to convert each preferred share into five shares of common stock. The par or stated value of the preferred stock divided by the conversion ratio is called the **conversion price**. The conversion price of Chandler's preferred stock is $20.00, as shown below.

Par Value of Preferred Stock	÷	Conversion Ratio	=	Conversion Price
$100.00	÷	5	=	$20.00

Agnes Moreland purchased 50 of Chandler's preferred shares when its common stock had a market value of $8.00 per share. Since the market price of the common stock is less than $20.00, Agnes should hold her preferred shares and receive any dividends. However, when the common stock increases to $20.00 or more per share, Agnes has a decision to make. She can hold her preferred shares and continue to receive the 4.5% dividend, or she can elect to convert her 50 shares to common stock. Upon conversion, Agnes would receive 250 shares of common stock, as shown below.

Number of Preferred Shares	×	Conversion Ratio	=	Number of Common Shares
50	×	5	=	250

Agnes will only benefit from converting her preferred shares if the market value of the common stock increases by at least 4.5% each year, less the effect of any dividends paid on common stock.

The conversion affects the corporation in two ways. After the conversion, dividends can be declared to common stockholders without having to first pay preferred stockholders. However, the earnings of the corporation and any declared dividends must now be shared among a larger number of shares.

Neither the corporation nor potential investors can predict the future market price of the common stock. Thus, the ultimate value of the conversion option is difficult to determine. If the market price never reaches $20.00, the conversion option is worthless to the stockholders. However, if Chandler sets the conversion price too high, such as $60.00, investors may not perceive the conversion option to be of any value.

© wavebreakmedia/Shutterstock.com

INPUT

- Explain why a corporation would allow a provision for converting stock.
- Explain conversion option, conversion ratio, convertible preferred stock, and conversion price.
- Point out the math illustrations that demonstrate the conversion price and the number of common shares received if converted.

Careers In Accounting

Review a career as a financial planner.

Careers In Accounting

Edward O'Brien

FINANCIAL PLANNER

© iStockphoto.com/Squaredpixels

Edward O'Brien is a financial planner. He works with individuals and families to help them develop financial objectives, form a plan for reaching those objectives, and implement the plan. His clients hire him for a variety of tasks over a wide range of areas.

Many clients only want help in relation to tax strategies or estate planning. However, Mr. O'Brien offers a broad range of services, including cash flow management, investments, insurance and risk management, budgeting, saving for educational costs, and planning for retirement.

Before Mr. O'Brien can help a client make financial decisions, he must understand the client's goals and the client's comfort with the risk related to various investments. He must also have a good understanding of the client's current financial position and other nonfinancial factors that may affect the achievement of the client's goals.

Mr. O'Brien feels that excellent communications skills are extremely important in his work. He needs to make his clients feel comfortable sharing personal information with him. He also needs to ask the right questions in the right way to ensure that he and his client establish appropriate goals and objectives.

Most states and countries do not highly regulate the financial planning career field. In many states, people can call themselves financial planners with little or no education or experience in the field.

In order for his clients to have more trust in him, Mr. O'Brien completed the requirements to be called a Certified Financial Planner (CFP). These requirements include earning a bachelor's degree, completing educational requirements in the financial planning area, passing an examination, and acquiring work experience.

Salary Range: Salary varies greatly, depending on how many clients a financial planner has and how successful the financial planner is. In 2010, the median wage for a financial planner was $64,750.

Qualifications: As stated above, the qualifications to be a financial planner vary from state to state. In order to sell services as a CFP, one must have completed the requirements of that certification. However, it is possible to sell services as a financial planner with only a high school education.

Occupational Outlook: The growth for financial planner positions is projected to be much faster than average (29% or higher) through 2020.

Sources: www.onetonline.org; www.cfp.net.

© iStockphoto.com/Mlenny

FORMATIVE ASSESSMENT

- This is an ongoing process. Circulate around the classroom or lab, observing which students have problems with the assignments.
- Troubleshooting: Diagnose the kinds of problems students have with this lesson. Students may have difficulty understanding the conversion of preferred stock.
- Assess student understanding by checking solutions to Independent Practice assignments and noting their answers to the Terms Review and Audit Your Understanding questions.

End of Lesson Review

LO5 Record the issuance of preferred stock.

LO6 Explain how to account for convertible preferred stock.

Terms Review

privately held corporation
initial public offering
publicly held corporation
registration statement
conversion option
conversion ratio
convertible preferred stock
conversion price

Audit your understanding

1. To finance rapid expansion, how can a corporation acquire additional capital?
2. Must all corporations file their financial statements with the SEC?
3. How can a business issue stock without causing the voting rights of current common stockholders to be diminished?
4. What is the relationship between an investor's desired dividend rate and the price at which a preferred stock is issued?
5. Why does a conversion option add value to preferred stock?
6. A 6%, $100.00 par-value preferred stock has a conversion ratio of 10. The corporation's common stock is currently valued at $12.00. Should preferred stockholders convert their stock?

Work together 10-2

Journalizing preferred stock transactions

Journalize each transaction completed during the current year. A general journal and a cash receipts journal are provided in the *Working Papers*. Your instructor will guide you through the following examples.

Transactions:

Mar. 17. Received cash from Lataya Davis for 200 shares of 6%, $50.00 par-value preferred stock at par value, $10,000.00. Receipt No. 443.

May 2. Received cash from Richard Estes for 100 shares of 6%, $50.00 par-value preferred stock at $53.00 per share, $5,300.00. Receipt No. 589.

July 12. Received office equipment from Isabella Hubbard at an agreed-upon value of $7,300.00 for 130 shares of 6%, $50.00 par-value preferred stock. Memorandum No. 133.

On your own 10-2

Journalizing preferred stock transactions

Journalize each transaction completed during the current year. A general journal and a cash receipts journal are provided in the *Working Papers*. Work independently to complete the following problem.

Transactions:

Feb. 6. Received inventory from Ella McMurtry at an agreed-upon value of $6,210.00 for 60 shares of 8%, $100.00 par-value preferred stock. Memorandum No. 87.

Apr. 12. Received cash from HGL Investments for 70 shares of 8%, $100.00 par-value preferred stock at par value, $70,000.00. Receipt No. 233.

May 22. Received cash from Lashundra Green for 150 shares of 8%, $100.00 par-value preferred stock at $102.50 per share, $15,375.00. Receipt No. 279.

CHECK FOR UNDERSTANDING

Terms Review

- Call on students to define each term in the Terms Review. Definitions are given in the Glossary.

Audit Your Understanding

- Call on students to answer the Audit Your Understanding questions. Answers are given in Appendix D of the textbook.

GUIDED PRACTICE

Work Together

- Have students write the solution to the Work Together problem as you guide the class through the examples.
- Direct students to record the preferred stock transactions in the cash receipts journal as you elicit participation in analyzing and recording the transactions.

INDEPENDENT PRACTICE

On Your Own

- Assign the On Your Own problem to be worked independently.
- Use the Formative Assessment techniques to diagnose student understanding.

Application Problem

- Assign Application Problem 10-2.

Online Working Papers

- Students can access the Lesson 10-2 problems using this software.

RETEACH

- Ask students to describe the features of preferred stock and the process of issuing preferred stock for more than par value.
- Ask students to explain how to issue stock for assets other than cash.
- Ask students to explain converting preferred stock.

CLOSURE

- Ask students to summarize briefly the issuing of preferred stock.

Essential Questions

- Would it be worthwhile for a corporation to offer convertible preferred stock? Explain. (*Yes, when it needs to raise revenue very quickly.*)
- What assets might be worthwhile to accept as a trade for stock in lieu of cash for a personal athletic training business? (*Ellipticals, treadmills, or other fitness equipment.*)

EXTENDED LEARNING

- Assign Why Accounting on page 304.
- Review Careers in Accounting on page 308.

A Look at Accounting Software

Many aspects of stock trading could be explored beyond what is covered in the chapter and in this feature. Students might be challenged to survey members of their extended family to see how many of them own stock. Shares could be held directly or in a brokerage account, a mutual fund, or a retirement account. Shares could also be held in the company in which a relative works as part of an ESOP (employee stock ownership plan). A relative might own shares in a privately held company, where trading is regulated by a shareholder agreement.

Regarding communications with shareholders, relatives might be asked about the types of notices and documents they have received. Students could collect and share examples with the class. A discussion could be held on the purpose of those documents.

Some stockholders are active traders with online trading accounts, whereas others may have accounts with financial advisors who buy and sell securities (both stocks and bonds) for their investors. Students might be asked to investigate the advantages and disadvantages of trading on one's own vs. working with a financial advisor.

Investors accept a certain amount of risk when they buy stock. Stock prices can fall, or the shares can even become worthless. A stockbroker or financial advisor might be invited to speak to the class about managing risk.

Finally, students might be asked to research the costs of owning and trading stock. What fees might be charged? What taxes are owed on capital gains? What are the tax implications of losses on stock transactions?

A Look at Accounting Software

Maintaining Shareholder Records

This chapter covered the accounting transactions recorded by a corporation when stock is issued. The initial sale of issued shares is just a small step in the process of accounting for capital stock. The corporation must notify shareholders of stockholder meetings, elections of directors, declaration and payment of dividends, and regulatory filings. Thus, a corporation must have records of all its shareholders—how to contact them, how many shares each holds, and the dates of their stock purchases and sales.

Small corporations, often closely held, are usually able to maintain these records in a spreadsheet. Large corporations may have thousands or even millions of shareholders. The largest corporations, especially those that are publicly traded, contract with agents to manage record keeping for, and communications with, their shareholders. Many corporations, though, are able to maintain these records with the help of specially designed accounting programs, generally referred to as *shareholder accounting software*.

Since shareholder accounting software is not often included with accounting software packages, it is usually necessary to purchase it separately. Add-on programs like these are called *modules* or *applications*, and they may function separately from the company's main accounting system or be integrated with it.

In this feature, it is assumed that the shareholder software is a fully integrated module that is launched from the System Manager. The Main Menu illustrates the functions performed by this module.

1. The user clicked the **Apps** button, which brought up a dialog box showing the icons of all add-on modules.
2. The user then clicked on the **Shareholder Accounting** icon to open that module's main menu.
3. To record a sale of stock from one shareholder to another, the user clicked on **Stock Transfers**, and the system opened the Stock Transfers window.

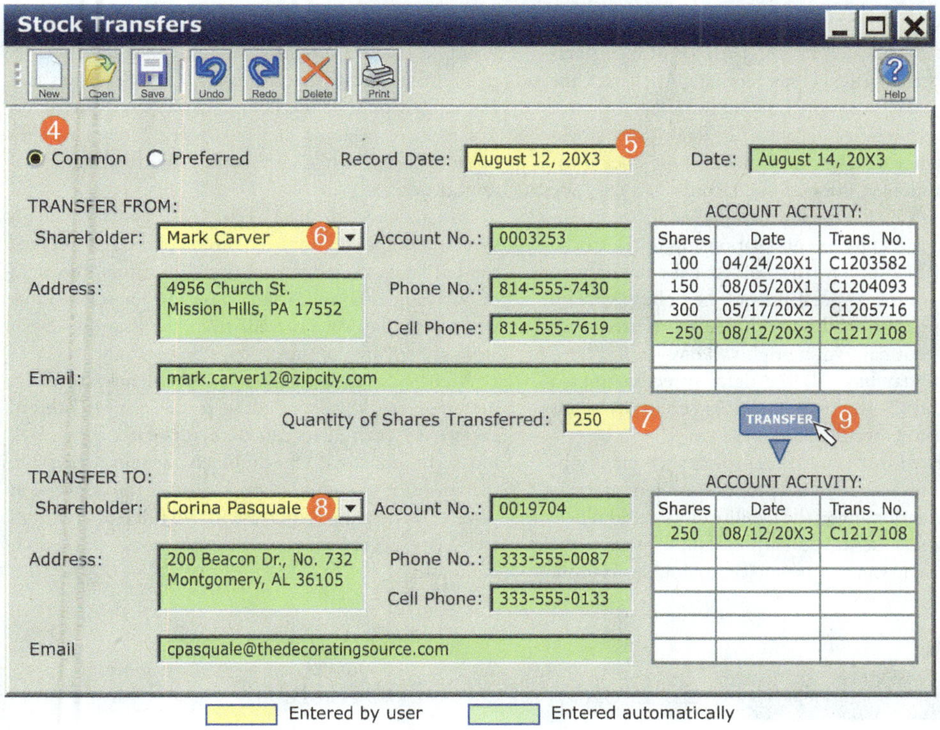

4 Forest Equipment has issued both common and preferred shares, so the type of shares to be transferred must be selected. Since there is more activity in the company's common shares, **Common** is the default setting.

5 The record date is the date on which the sale of the stock actually took place. The date on which the transaction is entered may be later, as it is here.

6 The user selected the account of Mark Carver, the shareholder who sold some of his shares. His account number, address, phone numbers, e-mail address, and account activity were entered automatically by the system.

7 The user entered **250** in the Quantity of Shares Transferred field.

8 Corina Pasquale was selected as the purchaser of Mark Carver's shares. If she were a new shareholder, the user would first have had to use the Account Maintenance feature on the main menu to set up an account for her. The amount paid for the shares is of no consequence to the corporation. Forest Equipment is only interested in knowing how to contact Corina and where to send her dividends. If she elected to have dividends automatically deposited, that information would also appear in her account.

9 The user clicked the **Transfer** button, and the system automatically assigned a transaction number and recorded the entries in the shareholder accounts.

CLOSURE

- Review the Chapter Summary.
- Ask students to prepare a list of the new concepts introduced in this chapter.

Essential Questions

- Which form of business ownership would be best for a landscaping business owned by a high school student? Explain. (*A sole proprietorship would probably be best, since it is the easiest to form. A landscaping business provides a service, so a small amount of cash will be needed for start-up.*)
- Which form of business ownership would be best for a landscaping business that wants to establish a location in every state within the next six months? Explain. (*An LLC would probably be best because it would provide protection from personal assets as growth occurs, yet be taxable like a partnership.*)
- Why might someone choose to become a privately held corporation rather than a publicly held corporation? (*They might want the protection of personal assets but might not want to share ownership.*)

EXTENDED LEARNING

- Review A Look at Accounting Software on pages 310 and 311.
- Assign Explore Accounting on page 312.

EXPLORE ACCOUNTING

Answers

1. The home page of the Division of Corporations contains a heading entitled "Why Choose Delaware as Your Corporate Home?" that includes a link to the booklet "Why Corporations Choose Delaware."
2. The registered agent is an individual or a business assigned to receive official documents issued by the state on behalf of the corporation.
3. Some individuals have incorporated businesses whose only purpose is to launder cash generated through illegal activities. Some corporations have been created to make political contributions while protecting the identity of the individual(s) providing the funds.

Chapter Summary

A corporation is created by filing articles of incorporation with a state agency. Upon receiving its charter, the corporation can issue up to its authorized number of common and preferred shares. Although some stockholders may receive a stock certificate, most stock ownership is maintained in electronic records.

A stock can be a par-value, no-par-value, or stated-value stock. The value has no relationship to the stock's market value. Common stockholders have the right to the earnings of the corporation and the right to vote on matters brought before the stockholders. Preferred stock usually does not have voting rights. However, preferred stockholders may have (1) the right to receive unpaid dividends and (2) the right to participate in dividends equal to the common stockholders.

A corporate form of business provides several advantages and disadvantages over a proprietorship or partnership. A corporation limits the liability of its stockholders to their investment in the corporation. However, the earnings of a corporation are subject to double taxation. A publicly held corporation also incurs significant costs to file its financial statements with the Securities and Exchange Commission. A limited liability corporation is a form of business that retains the limited liability of stockholders while eliminating the disadvantage of double taxation.

The stock issued above its par value results in a credit to a capital stock account. The excess of the amount over the par value is credited to a paid-in capital in excess of par value account. The accounting for stated-value stock is similar. All proceeds from the issue of no-par stock are credited to the capital stock account.

A corporation can lower the dividend rate of its preferred stock by including a conversion option. Preferred stockholders can elect to convert their stock for common stock. Stockholders benefit when the market price of common stock exceeds the conversion price and the annual increase in the price of common stock is expected to exceed the preferred stock dividend rate.

EXPLORE ACCOUNTING A Delaware Corporation

© iStockphoto.com/Makhnach_M

In 1960, Sam Walton opened his first store in Rogers, then a small town of 5,700 in northwest Arkansas. Initially, members of the Walton family owned the new company. When the company's stock was listed on the New York Stock Exchange in 1972, Wal-Mart Stores, Inc., had grown to 51 stores in five states: Arkansas, Missouri, Oklahoma, Kansas, and Louisiana. The corporation is headquartered in Bentonville, Arkansas.

Readers of Wal-Mart's annual 10-K report filed with the Securities and Exchange Commission are likely to notice something unusual on the cover page. Wal-Mart is incorporated in the state of Delaware.

Since the early 1900s, Delaware has been a popular state in which to incorporate. Nearly half of all public corporations in the United States are incorporated in Delaware. These corporations do not have to be headquartered in Delaware. They do not even have to do business or have a bank account in the state. Delaware is only their legal home. The only requirement is that the corporation maintain a registered agent in the state.

By drafting corporation-friendly laws, Delaware has attracted corporations in the United States and across the world. Delaware corporations pay an annual tax known as a *franchise tax*. There are two methods to calculate this tax. For most corporations, the tax is calculated based on the amount of total assets, the number of authorized and issued shares of stock, and the par value of the stock. There is also a limit on what a corporation must pay.

These taxes provide a significant amount of funds to operate the state government. The amount of legal activity in the state also employs many Delaware residents. Thus, like any business that provides a service, the state of Delaware is eager to encourage corporations around the world to call Delaware home.

INSTRUCTIONS

Conduct research on the Internet to answer the following questions.

1. How does the Division of Corporations for the state of Delaware advertise Delaware's interest in attracting incorporation in the state?
2. What are the requirements of a registered agent?
3. Identify any negative events that have occurred that might suggest that Delaware's laws of incorporation may be too liberal.

Sources: http://corp.delaware.gov/; *Why Corporations Choose Delaware*, Lewis J. Black, Jr., Delaware Department of State, Division of Corporations, 2007.

INDEPENDENT PRACTICE

- Assign Mastery Problem 10-M for students as a culminating problem combining all new learning from the chapter.
- Assign Challenge Problem 10-C to accelerated students who work at a faster pace.
- Assign Study Guide 10.
- Students can access Online Working Papers to work end-of-chapter problems on the computer.
- Direct students to the C21 Accounting companion website for additional practice and review opportunities.

Apply Your Understanding

INSTRUCTIONS: Download problem instructions for Excel, QuickBooks, and Sage 50 from the textbook companion website at www.C21accounting.com.

10-1 Application Problem: Issuing common stock LO4

A cash receipts journal is provided in the *Working Papers*. The source document is abbreviated as follows: receipt, R.

Transaction:

July 2. John Abrams purchased 4,000 shares of GDT Tractors common stock for $6.00 per share. R553.

Instructions:

Journalize the transaction using each of the following assumptions regarding the common stock:

A. $0.10 par-value common stock.
B. No-par-value common stock.
C. $0.10 stated-value common stock.

10-2 Application Problem: Journalizing preferred stock transactions LO5

Instructions:

Journalize each transaction completed during the current year. A cash receipts journal and a general journal are provided in the *Working Papers*. Source documents are abbreviated as follows: memorandum, M; receipt, R.

Transactions:

Jan. 7. Received cash from Kelly Everland for 400 shares of $25.00 par-value preferred stock at par value, $10,000.00. R199.

Mar. 12. Received cash from Brienna Terrell for 300 shares of $25.00 par-value preferred stock at $27.00 per share, $8,100.00. R274.

Apr. 6. Received store equipment from Weldon Bester at an agreed-upon value of $5,800.00 for 220 shares of $25.00 par-value preferred stock. M93.

June 3. Received cash from Cliff Jemison for 400 shares of $25.00 par-value preferred stock at $26.50 per share, $10,000.00. R433.

Sage 50 Accounting

1. Journalize and post preferred stock transactions to the cash receipts journal.
2. Journalize and post issuance of preferred stock for store equipment to the general journal.
3. Print the cash receipts journal, general journal and general ledger trial balance.

QuickBooks

1. Journalize and post preferred stock transactions to the journal.
2. Print the journal and trial balance.

Excel

1. Journalize preferred stock transactions to the cash receipts journal and general journal.
2. Print the spreadsheets.

CHECK FIGURES

For complete solutions to Chapter 10 problems, see the Teacher's Edition of the Working Papers.

Application Problem 10-1

Assumption A: credit Paid-In Capital in Excess of Par Value—Common, $23,600.00.

Assumption B: credit Capital Stock—Common, $24,000.00.

Assumption C: credit Paid-In Capital in Excess of Stated Value—Common, $23,600.00.

Application Problem 10-2

Credits to Paid-In Capital in Excess of Par Value—Preferred: Mar. 12, $600.00; Apr. 6, $300.00; June 3, $600.00.

Mastery Problem 10-M

Credits to Paid-In Capital in Excess of Stated Value—Common: Apr. 1, $40,000.00; Apr. 3, $100,000.00.

Credits to Paid-In Capital in Excess of Par Value—Preferred: Apr. 4, $2,600.00; Apr. 28, $1,500.00.

FORMATIVE ASSESSMENT

- Review solutions to the assigned problems in class, diagnosing trouble spots.

RETEACH

- Call on students to describe how they avoid the trouble spots diagnosed.
- Use reteaching suggestions from lesson plans as required.
- Assign Recycling Problem 10-R if needed.

Challenge Problem 10-C

Credits to Paid-In Capital in Excess of Par Value—Common: Feb. 11, $146,060.00; July 4, $28,500.00; Sept. 22, $190,000.00.

Credits to Paid-In Capital in Excess of Par Value—Preferred: Mar. 7, $4,000.00; Aug. 13, $6,400.00.

EXTENDED LEARNING

- Assign 21st Century Skills on page 315.
- Assign Analyzing Home Depot's Financial Statements on page 315.

SUMMATIVE EVALUATION

- Chapter 10 Test
- Cognero for Chapter 10

10-M Mastery Problem: Journalizing stock transactions LO4, 5

After operating as a partnership for several years, Temika Clark and Terry Friesen decided to incorporate their business, Modern Landscapes. The new corporation received its charter on March 31 of the current year. The corporation is authorized to issue 150,000 shares of $1.00 stated-value common stock and 50,000 shares of 8%, $100.00 par-value preferred stock.

Instructions:

Journalize the following transactions. A general journal and a cash receipts journal are provided in the *Working Papers*. Source documents are abbreviated as follows: memorandum, M; receipt, R.

Transactions:

Apr. 1. Received cash from Temika Clark for 10,000 shares of common stock at $5.00 per share, $50,000.00. Receipt No. 1.
2. Received cash from Harris Financial Advisors for 800 shares of preferred stock at par value. Receipt No. 2.
3. Received cash from Terry Friesen for 25,000 shares of common stock at $5.00 per share, $125,000.00. Receipt No. 3.
4. Received equipment from Marshall Glenn at an agreed-upon value of $27,600.00 in exchange for 250 shares of preferred stock. M3.
28. Received cash from State Retirement Fund for 500 shares of preferred stock at $103.00 per share, $51,500.00. Receipt No. 16.

Sage 50 Accounting

1. Journalize and post preferred stock transactions to the cash receipts journal.
2. Journalize and post issuance of preferred stock for store equipment to the general journal.
3. Print the cash receipts journal, general journal and general ledger trial balance.

QB

1. Journalize and post preferred stock transactions to the journal.
2. Print the journal and trial balance.

X

1. Journalize preferred stock transactions to the cash receipts journal and general journal.
2. Print the spreadsheets.

10-C Challenge Problem: Journalizing stock transactions LO4, 5, 6

Tullos Technologies is authorized to issue 100,000 shares of $1.00 par-value common stock and 80,000 shares of 5%, $100.00 par-value preferred stock. The preferred stock has a conversion option that allows one share to be exchanged for five shares of common stock.

Instructions:

Journalize the following transactions. A general journal and a cash receipts journal are provided in the *Working Papers*. Source documents are abbreviated as follows: memorandum, M; receipt, R.

Transactions:

Feb. 11. Received land from Development Partners at an agreed-upon value of $155,600.00 in exchange for 9,540 shares of common stock. M33.
Mar. 7. Received cash from Salmar Equity Partners for 2,000 shares of preferred stock at $102.00 per share. R56.
July 4. Lisle Motors exchanged 300 shares of preferred stock for common stock. M47.
Aug. 13. Received $68,900.00 from Melton Pension Fund for 625 shares of preferred stock. R196.
Sept. 22. Salmar Equity Partners exchanged its 2,000 shares of preferred stock for common stock. M156.

COMMON CORE AND INTERDISCIPLINARY STUDIES

Extended learning features and activities present numerous opportunities to implement Common Core Standards through interdisciplinary studies. Practice is provided in the common core areas of English Language Arts & Literacy and Mathematical Practice. Many of these activities require short, critical-thinking and decision-making responses that apply reading, writing, speaking, listening, language, media and technology, and mathematical skills.

21st Century Skills

The Dow ... and How

Theme: Financial, Economic, Business, Entrepreneurial Literacy, and History

Skills: Critical Thinking and Problem Solving, Communication and Collaboration, ICT Literacy, Life and Career Skills

PARTNERSHIP FOR 21ST CENTURY SKILLS

If you read or listen to investment news, you might hear that the Dow is up or the Dow is down. Upward trends are referred to as *bull markets*, and downward trends are referred to as *bear markets*. These terms give us the pulse of the stock market. The Dow Jones Industrial Average, called *Dow* for short, is the oldest index and probably the most widely followed stock market index in the world.

With an index, the number is not important. What is important is the percentage of change over time from an original value. The movement of the index, up or down, tells you how companies traded on the stock market are doing, in general.

Charles Dow and Edward Jones created the Dow Jones Industrial Average (DJIA) in 1896. It represented the average stock price of companies in 12 industries, including cotton, sugar, tobacco, gas, electric, coal, iron, leather, and rubber. The average was calculated as a simple average.

The companies of the DJIA have changed 48 times in its history. Today, the Dow's 30 stocks reflect a portion of the actual industries in the market, including technology and fast-food companies. These stocks are averaged using a special formula. To be included in the index, a stock must be a leader in its industry. General Electric is the only original company that is still included in the Dow.

APPLICATION

1. Use the Internet with a partner and research the performance of the Dow over the last 100 years. Create a timeline depicting historical events that influenced gains or losses in the market.
2. Use the Internet and obtain a list of the 30 companies currently listed in the DJIA. Select one company to research. Write a one-page paper describing how the company was started, when and why it went public, when it became a part of the DJIA, a history of its stock performance, and events that affected its performance. Present your findings to the class. **Optional:** Create a sample page on social media, outlining the above for a company of your choice.
3. Look over the list of 30 companies currently listed in the DJIA. If one company could be replaced, explain what public company you would add, describe its industry, and justify your reason.

Analyzing Home Depot's financial statements

Home Depot is authorized to issue one class of common stock. The corporation has only issued a fraction of the number of shares authorized. Information about the par value of the stock and the number of shares authorized, issued, and outstanding can be found in the Equity section of Home Depot's balance sheet.

INSTRUCTIONS

Use Home Depot's Consolidated Balance Sheets and Consolidated Statements of Stockholders' Equity in Appendix B on pages B-5 and B-8 to answer the following questions:

1. What is the par value of Home Depot's common stock?
2. How many shares of common stock are authorized, issued, and outstanding as of February 3, 2013?
3. Use the Consolidated Statements of Stockholders' Equity to determine the dollar amount of common stock issued under employee stock plans.

21ST CENTURY SKILLS

Answers

1. Answers will vary based on the historical events.
2. Answers will vary.
3. Answers will vary. Students should select a company that is a leader in its industry.

ANALYZING HOME DEPOT'S FINANCIAL STATEMENTS

Answers

1. $0.05 par value.
2. Authorized, 10 billion shares; issued: 1.754 billion shares; outstanding: 1.484 billion shares.
3. $679 million ($1 million to Common Stock, $678 million to Paid-In Capital).

Chapter 11

Corporate Dividends and Treasury Stock

Scope & Sequence

	New	Review/Enrich
Introduction		
Introduce the Chapter		
Lesson 11-1: Calculating and Journalizing Dividends for a Corporation		
Cash Dividends	✓	
Calculating a Dividend	✓	
Journalizing the Declaration of a Dividend	✓	
Journalizing the Payment of a Dividend	✓	
Declaring a Stock Dividend	✓	
Paying a Stock Dividend	✓	
Impact of a Stock Dividend	✓	
Lesson 11-2: Treasury Stock Transactions		
Treasury Stock	✓	
Buying Treasury Stock	✓	
Selling Treasury Stock for More Than Original Cost	✓	
Selling Treasury Stock for Less Than Original Cost	✓	
Lesson 11-3: Purchasing and Selling Capital Stock of Other Corporations		
Purchasing Capital Stock	✓	
Receiving a Dividend on a Marketable Security	✓	
Selling a Marketable Security	✓	
Closure		

Enhancing Instruction

Features	Common Core Standards
• Accounting in the Real World: Pandora Media, Inc.	• ELAL—reading
• Ethics in Action: Exercising Stock Options • Global Awareness: Importing and Exporting Goods • Why Accounting?: How the Bottom Line Can Affect Jail Sentences	• ELAL—reading • ELAL—reading, technology and media, writing • ELAL—reading, technology and media, writing
• Forensic Accounting: Insider Trading	• Mathematics
• Think Like an Accountant: Evaluating a Stock Buyback Program	• Mathematics
• Explore Accounting • 21st Century Skills • Analyzing Home Depot's Financial Statements	• Mathematics • ELAL—reading, writing • Mathematics

ELAL = English Language Arts & Literacy

Calculator: © iStockphoto.com/picstodisc; Paper: © iStockphoto.com/Qingwa

Practice and Assessment

Technology & Media	Teaching Strategies	Guided Practice	Independent Practice	Reteach/Enrich
• Instructor's Resource CD/Website: PowerPoint Slides Accounting Concepts • Online Working Papers • Transparency Masters: General Journal, Cash Payments Journal (5-column)	• Intrapersonal Learners	• Terms Review • Audit Your Understanding • Work Together 11-1	• On Your Own 11-1 • Application Problem 11-1 • Formative Assessment, p. 323 • Online Working Papers	• Reteach, p. 324
• Instructor's Resource CD/Website: PowerPoint Slides Accounting Concepts • Online Working Papers • Transparency Masters: Cash Payments Journal (5-column), Cash Receipts Journal (7-column), General Journal	• Visual/Spatial Learners	• Terms Review • Audit Your Understanding • Work Together 11-2	• On Your Own 11-2 • Application Problem 11-2 • Formative Assessment, p. 328 • Online Working Papers	• Reteach, p. 329
• Instructor's Resource CD/Website: PowerPoint Slides Accounting Concepts • Online Working Papers • Transparency Masters: Cash Payments Journal (5-column), Cash Receipts Journal (7-column)	• Musical Learners	• Audit Your Understanding • Work Together 11-3	• On Your Own 11-3 • Application Problem 11-3 • Formative Assessment, p. 332 • Online Working Papers	• Reteach, p. 333
	• Common Core and Interdisciplinary Studies		• Mastery Problem 11-M • Study Guide 11 • Chapter 11 Test • Cognero Chapter 11	• Challenge Problem 11-C • Reteach, p. 336 • Recycling Problem 11-R

Introduce the Chapter

SET THE STAGE

GUIDING QUESTIONS

- Ask students if, given the option to purchase stock that paid dividends or stock that did not pay dividends, which they would select and why.
- Ask students if they have ever considered corporations purchasing stock from other corporations.
- Ask students to predict how dividends would be reported by the corporation receiving them from another corporation.

PREVIEW CHAPTER OBJECTIVES

- Point out that this chapter describes transactions related to declaring and paying dividends, both cash and stock.
- Note that sometimes a corporation will purchase its own stock or the stock of other corporations.
- Instruct a student to read each chapter objective aloud.

PREVIEW ACCOUNTING TERMS

- Read each term aloud to verify its pronunciation for students.
- Point out terms or parts of terms that should already be familiar to most students, such as *dividend* and *stock*.

Chapter 11

Corporate Dividends and Treasury Stock

LEARNING OBJECTIVES

After studying Chapter 11, in addition to defining key terms, you will be able to:

LO1 Account for the declaration and payment of a cash dividend.

LO2 Account for the declaration and payment of a stock dividend.

LO3 Explain why a corporation would purchase its own stock.

LO4 Journalize entries for buying and selling treasury stock.

LO5 Journalize transactions for the purchase and sale of the capital stock of other corporations.

Calculator: © iStockphoto.com/picstodisc; Paper: © iStockphoto.com/Qingwa

Stockbyte/Getty Images

Accounting In The Real World

Pandora Media, Inc.

Pandora Media, Inc., offers a revolutionary way to listen to music. By streaming songs over the Internet, Pandora offers access to a vast array of songs from every genre. Customers can create "radio stations" that identify their listening preferences. As music is streamed, customers can click "thumbs-up" and "thumbs-down" buttons to refine future song selections. Pandora offers both an audio and a visual experience. While listening to a song, a customer can view the lyrics, read a profile of the artist, and view a list of similar artists.

Pandora's common stock, listed on the New York Stock Exchange, was first offered to the public in 2011. The history of the corporation, however, dates back more than a decade. Documents filed with Pandora's initial public offering (IPO) provide insight into how the corporation was financed during this time.

A startup corporation can rarely issue its stock to the public. Instead, the corporation has to seek financing from private investors. When the amounts required exceed the limits of individual investors, a startup corporation often seeks financing from venture capital firms. These firms combine the investments of many individuals and organizations, such as pension funds. They also provide management expertise to assist the corporation in managing its growth and improving its chance of success.

Pandora received most of its funding by issuing preferred stock to several venture capital firms. Just prior to the IPO, this investment was more than $128 million. The IPO enabled the venture capital firms to earn a return on their investments. More than half of the proceeds of Pandora's IPO allowed the firms to receive unpaid dividends and sell their stock. The remaining proceeds provided the corporation with additional operating capital.

Many startup corporations are not successful. In these cases, a venture capital firm may lose most or all of its investment. However, when a corporation is successful, venture capital firms can earn a substantial profit by selling their investment. More importantly, venture capital firms provide the seed money necessary to enable corporations to create jobs and grow the economy.

CRITICAL THINKING

1. Identify three factors that would be unique to a venture capital firm, as compared to a bank, when deciding to invest in a startup corporation.
2. Research a corporation that recently had an IPO. Was the amount paid to the venture capital firms consistent with their risk? Can the amount paid in comparison to the venture capital firm's investment be the only measure for answering this question?

Source: www.sec.gov/edgar.shtml.

Background: © iStockphoto.com/Jamie Farrant/eeljoyvnz; Real World: Spencer Platt/Getty Images News/Getty Images

Key Terms

- declaring a dividend
- date of declaration
- date of record
- date of payment
- stock dividend
- treasury stock
- buyback

Accounting In The Real World

Answers

1. Answers will vary. Factors might include the following:
   a. Estimated time to the IPO.
   b. Total investment required.
   c. Number of others participating.
   d. Extent of management assistance required.
   e. Management's prior experience with start-up corporations.
2. Answers will vary. Depending on the research results, many students may be shocked to learn about the profit the venture capital firms earned upon their "exit" from the corporation. Remind students that the profit earned in these cases must offset the losses incurred on unsuccessful ventures.

LESSON
11-1

BRIDGE

- Point out that principles for forming a corporation and issuing capital stock to investors were presented earlier in this book. In this lesson, the transactions to distribute earnings of a corporation to stockholders (dividends) will be journalized. Explain that dividends are one reason stockholders invest in a corporation.

TEACHING RESOURCES

- **Instructor's Resource CD/Website:**
  PowerPoint Slides
  Accounting Concepts
- **Working Papers:**
  Teacher's Edition of the Working Papers for Lesson 11-1
  Online Working Papers
- **Transparency Masters:**
  General Journal
  Cash Payments Journal (5-column)

ENGAGE

- Share the names of five companies that have declared a dividend recently. Point out names of larger, well-known companies that do not pay dividends.

PREVIEW

- Call on students to read the accounting terms and definitions introduced in this lesson: *declaring a dividend, date of declaration, date of record, date of payment,* and *stock dividend.*
- Point out the learning objectives for this lesson.
- Direct students to read the headings in this lesson and to examine the illustrations.

INPUT

- Point out that businesses usually retain a portion of earnings for expansion and improvement. However, another portion may be distributed in the form of dividends to stockholders.
- Point out that no stockholder is guaranteed a dividend.

LESSON
11-1 Calculating and Journalizing Dividends for a Corporation

LO1 Account for the declaration and payment of a cash dividend.
LO2 Account for the declaration and payment of a stock dividend.

Cash Dividends LO1

A primary goal of a corporation's board of directors is to increase stockholder wealth. A corporation can achieve this goal in two ways. It can reinvest its earnings to finance growth, causing the stock price to increase. It can distribute a portion of its earnings to its stockholders. Corporate earnings distributed to stockholders are known as *dividends*. The board of directors must weigh the financing needs of the business against the desire of its stockholders to receive a dividend.

Action by a board of directors to distribute corporate earnings to stockholders is called **declaring a dividend**. The board determines when and what amount of the retained earnings will be distributed. A corporation has no obligation to distribute retained earnings to stockholders until the board of directors has declared a dividend.

Three important dates are involved in distributing a dividend:

1. Date of declaration. The date on which a board of directors votes to distribute a dividend is called the **date of declaration**.
2. Date of record. The date that determines which stockholders are to receive dividends is called the **date of record**. Stockholders may buy and sell stock at any time. However, only persons listed as stockholders on the date of record will receive dividends.
3. Date of payment. The date on which dividends are actually to be paid to stockholders is called the **date of payment**. Ordinarily, the date of payment occurs several weeks after the date of record. Thus, a corporation has time to determine who is entitled to receive dividends and to distribute the dividends on the date of payment.

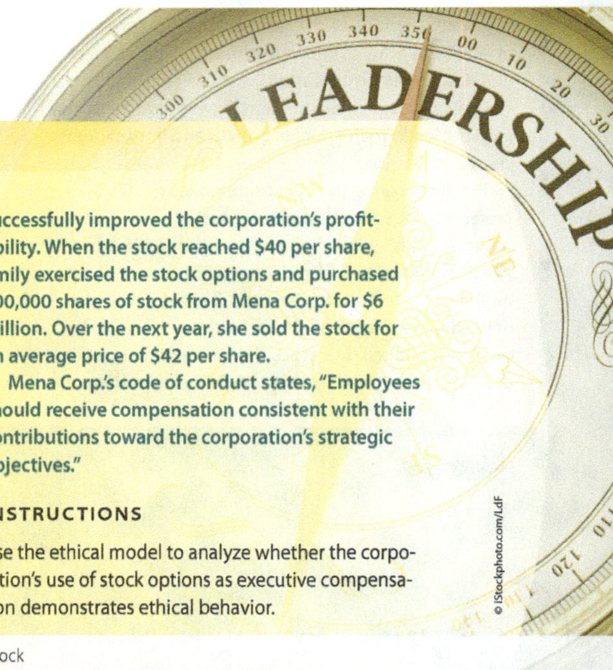

ETHICS IN ACTION

Exercising Stock Options

Corporations often compensate executives with more than a salary. The compensation package often includes **stock options**—the right to purchase company stock at a specified price. The option price is set higher than the current market price. If the stock price increases above the option price, the option enables the executive to purchase the stock at less than the market price. If the stock's market price never exceeds the option price, the option is worthless.

Four years ago, Mena Corp. offered its new chief executive officer, Emily Tillman, an annual salary of $500,000 plus 200,000 stock options at $30. The stock was selling for $18 at the time. Emily successfully improved the corporation's profitability. When the stock reached $40 per share, Emily exercised the stock options and purchased 200,000 shares of stock from Mena Corp. for $6 million. Over the next year, she sold the stock for an average price of $42 per share.

Mena Corp.'s code of conduct states, "Employees should receive compensation consistent with their contributions toward the corporation's strategic objectives."

INSTRUCTIONS

Use the ethical model to analyze whether the corporation's use of stock options as executive compensation demonstrates ethical behavior.

© iStockphoto.com/LdF

ETHICS IN ACTION

Most students will conclude that issuing stock options as part of the CEO's compensation package appears to be ethical. However, excessive management compensation continues to be a controversial issue. Although the management compensation packages of public corporations may seem excessive, the compensation is warranted if the executive can increase the profitability of the company and the wealth of its stockholders. In too many instances, however, executives have received excessive compensation, even when their corporations were declining.

As an extension of this activity, ask students to search current business magazines and newspapers for articles relating to excessive management compensation.

See a suggested solution for this feature in the Instructional Strategies section at the front of this book.

Calculating a Dividend

When a board of directors declares a dividend, the corporation is obligated to pay it. At the date of declaration, the corporation incurs a liability that must be recorded.

The board of directors of Hariton, Inc., has decided to declare a quarterly dividend of $10,000.00. On December 31, the date of record, the corporation has issued 2,000 shares of 8%, $100.00 par-value preferred stock and 64,000 shares of $10.00 par-value common stock. The par value of preferred stock is used to calculate the dividend on preferred stock. The amount of the $10,000.00 distributed to the preferred stock is calculated as follows:

Number of Preferred Shares	×	Par Value	=	Par Value of Preferred Stock
2,000	×	$100.00	=	$200,000.00

Par Value of Preferred Stock	×	Quarterly Dividend Rate	=	Preferred Dividend Amount
$200,000.00	×	8%/4	=	$4,000.00

The dividend rate on preferred stock is stated as an annual rate. The annual rate is divided by 4 to calculate a quarterly dividend. Any dividends above the amount paid to preferred stock are available for common stock.

Total Amount Available for Dividends	−	Preferred Dividend Amount	=	Amount Available for Common Dividends
$10,000.00	−	$4,000.00	=	$6,000.00

In subsequent years, Hariton may elect to increase its quarterly dividend. Hariton's preferred stock dividend will never exceed an annual rate of 8% of its par value. Therefore, additional dividends will be distributed to common stock.

© iStockphoto.com/Lusky

GLOBAL AWARENESS

Importing and Exporting Goods

Many businesses, large and small, operate in the global market. Some companies import goods to sell or to use in manufacturing, and other companies export goods to foreign markets. These companies must adhere to government regulations in both the importing and the exporting country.

When shipping goods overseas, appropriate documentation must accompany the package to verify its contents. Customs officials will read the documentation and may open the packages. If the documentation is incomplete or inaccurate, the shipment may be delayed or returned to the sender.

All major trading nations use the Harmonized Commodity Description and Coding System (HS). HS allows all products to be classified and more easily identified. HS establishes a single ten-digit code for each type of commodity, and this code is included on all paperwork connected with a shipment. This helps customs officials in both countries determine if the product is subject to import/export restrictions or special duties.

The World Customs Organization (WCO) maintains HS. The WCO is an international intergovernmental organization. Its goal is to "improve the effectiveness and efficiency" of international customs to support global trade while maintaining security. By encouraging international standards for imports and exports, the WCO also supports developing nations with their global trade. WCO membership consists of customs administrators from 176 countries.

CRITICAL THINKING

Go to the website for the World Customs Organization (www.wcoomd.org). Search for information about the WCO to answer the following questions:

1. List five countries (other than the United States) that belong to the WCO. Look for members of the Customs Co-Operation Council (CCC) of the WCO.
2. List the name of the secretary general of the WCO and one item of information from the secretary general's biography.

INPUT

- Emphasize that a corporation does not have to pay dividends. However, once declared, dividends must be paid.
- Point out that the dividends on common stock do not necessarily equal the dividends on preferred stock.

MODEL

- Use the math illustrations to explain the process for calculating the amount of dividends on preferred stock and common stock.
- Show on the board how the amount for preferred dividends is calculated. Emphasize that this amount must be paid first and that the remainder is distributed to the common stockholders.
- Point out that the preferred dividend rate is divided by 4 to calculate the quarterly dividend.
- Continue to show how each calculation is performed.

GLOBAL AWARENESS

Answers

1. Lists will vary.
2. Answers will vary. At the time of publication, Mr. Kunio Mikuriya of Japan was the secretary general of the WCO.

DIFFERENTIATED INSTRUCTION

Intrapersonal learners often prefer to work alone using their own strengths and weaknesses. Direct students to MSN Money Central, CBS Market Watch, or the New York Stock Exchange to research five companies that pay dividends. Tell students to record the rate of the dividend for each company and to be prepared to share their results with others in the class.

INPUT

- Remind students that once dividends are declared, they must be paid. Point out that because cash is not paid out the same day dividends are declared, the Cash account cannot be credited.
- Emphasize that because cash is owed as a result of the declaration of dividends, Dividends Payable is credited.
- Ask students how they would classify Dividends—Common (*contra capital*).

MODEL

Analyze the transaction

- Draw three blank T accounts on the board.
- Read the transaction statement.
- Ask students to analyze the transaction. Complete the T accounts as the information is provided. Remind students that calculations were completed on the previous page.

Record the transaction

- Use the general journal transparency to illustrate the process for recording the entry or direct students to the illustration in the book.

INPUT

- Explain that when the dividends are paid, Dividends Payable is debited to show the decrease in the amount owed.
- Ask students which journal should be used to record the cash payment of dividends.

MODEL

Analyze the transaction

- Draw two blank T accounts on the board.
- Read the transaction statement.
- Ask students to analyze the transaction. Complete the T accounts as the information is provided.

Record the transaction

- Use the cash payments journal transparency to illustrate the process for recording the entry or direct students to the illustration in the book.

Journalizing the Declaration of a Dividend

Debit Each Dividend Account

GENERAL JOURNAL — PAGE 24

	DATE		ACCOUNT TITLE	DOC. NO.	POST. REF.	DEBIT	CREDIT	
16	Dec.	15	Dividends—Common	M456		6 000 00		16
17			Dividends—Preferred			4 000 00		17
18			Dividends Payable				10 000 00	18

Credit Dividends Payable

A journal entry is recorded on the date the dividend is declared.

December 15. Hariton's board of directors declared an annual dividend of $10,000.00. Memorandum No. 456.

Dividends—Common

Debit	Credit
↑ 12/15 6,000.00	

Dividends—Preferred

Debit	Credit
↑ 12/15 4,000.00	

Dividends Payable

Debit	Credit
	↑ 12/15 10,000.00

The journal entry creates a current liability for the total amount of the dividends declared. The action of the board of directors creates an obligation to pay the dividend on January 15, the payment date.

No journal entry is recorded on December 31, the date of record. Stockholders owning the stock on the date of record receive the declared dividend. On the next day, a buyer would purchase the shares *ex-dividend* (without the dividend).

Journalizing the Payment of a Dividend

CASH PAYMENTS JOURNAL — PAGE 1

	DATE		ACCOUNT TITLE	CK. NO.	POST. REF.	1 GENERAL DEBIT	2 GENERAL CREDIT	3 ACCOUNTS PAYABLE DEBIT	4 PURCHASES DISCOUNT CREDIT	5 CASH CREDIT	
14	Jan.	15	Dividends Payable	745		10 000 00				10 000 00	14
15											15
16											16

Debit Dividends Payable

Credit Cash

On January 15, Hariton issued a single check for $10,000.00, the total amount of the dividends to be paid.

January 15. Paid cash for annual dividend declared on December 15, $10,000.00. Check No. 745.

Dividends Payable

Debit	Credit
↓ 1/15 10,000.00	↓ 12/15 Decl. 10,000.00 (New Bal. zero)

Cash

Debit	Credit
	↓ 1/15 10,000.00

The dividend check is issued to an agent who handles the details of preparing and mailing stockholders' checks. The agent writes a separate check to each eligible stockholder. This procedure avoids a large number of entries in Hariton's cash payments journal.

TEACHING IDEA Provide a large sheet of paper or a section of the board for students to record the name of a company and the rate of the dividend. Students can use the data collected in the Differentiated Instruction activity for comparison purposes.

Declaring a Stock Dividend LO2

Number of Common Shares	×	Dividend Percent	=	Number of Shares to Be Issued
100,000	×	2%	=	2,000

Number of Shares to Be Issued	×	Market Price per Share	=	Stock Dividend Amount
2,000	×	$5.30	=	$10,600.00

Calculate the Stock Dividend Amount

Credit Stock Dividends Distributable

GENERAL JOURNAL PAGE 6

	DATE		ACCOUNT TITLE	DOC. NO.	POST. REF.	DEBIT	CREDIT	
1	20-- June	1	*Stock Dividends*	*M235*		*10 600 00*		1
2			*Stock Dividends Distributable*				*200 00*	2
3			*Paid-In Capital in Excess of Par Value—Common*				*10 400 00*	3
4								4

Debit Stock Dividends

Credit Paid-In Capital in Excess of Par Value—Common

The payment of a dividend with the stock of the corporation is called a **stock dividend**. Similar to cash dividends, transactions are recorded on the declaration date and the payment date.

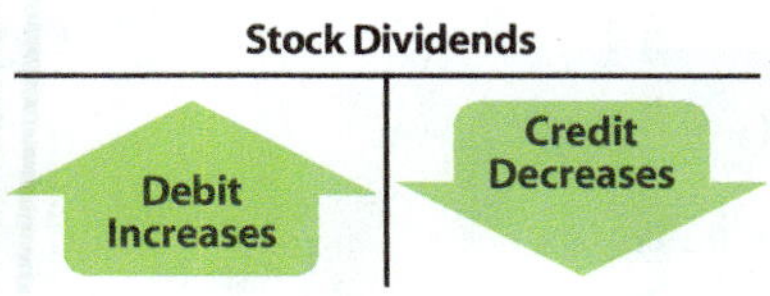

The debit portion of the journal entry to record the declaration of a stock dividend is similar to that used for a cash dividend. To distinguish between cash and stock dividends, the amount of the stock dividend is debited to Stock Dividends rather than Dividends. Stock Dividends is a temporary equity account and has a normal debit balance.

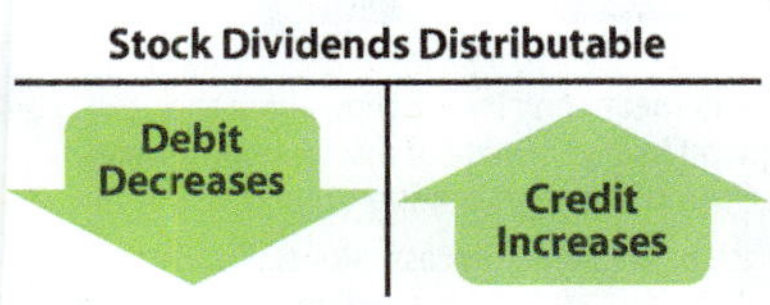

The credit part of the journal entry resembles the issuance of common stock. Because the stock will not be issued until the payment date, the par value of the stock to be issued is credited to Stock Dividends Distributable rather than Common Stock. Stock Dividends Distributable is an equity account and has a normal credit balance.

June 1. Abraham Corporation's board of directors declared a 2% stock dividend, payable on June 30. The corporation has 100,000 shares of $0.10 par-value common stock outstanding. The current market price of the stock is $5.30. Memorandum No. 235.

Stock Dividends	
6/1 Decl. 10,600.00	

Stock Dividends Distributable	
	6/1 Decl. 200.00

Paid-In Capital in Excess of Par Value—Common	
	6/1 Decl. 10,400.00

The amount of the stock dividend is based on the market price of the stock. The credit to Stock Dividends Distributable is the number of shares issued, 2,000, multiplied by the par value of the stock, $0.10. The difference between the value of the stock dividend, $10,600.00, and the par value of the stock to be issued, $200.00, is credited to Paid-In Capital in Excess of Par Value—Common.

INPUT

- Explain that sometimes the payment of a dividend is paid in stock rather than in cash.
- Point out that Stock Dividends is debited rather than Dividends.
- Explain that Stock Dividends Distributable is an equity account with a normal credit balance.
- Point out that the difference between the value of the stock dividend and the par value of the stock to be issued is the amount credited to Paid-In Capital in Excess of Par Value—Common.

INPUT

- Explain that paying the stock dividend moves the balance from Stock Dividends Distributable to Capital Stock—Common.
- Point out the calculation for the entry.

MODEL

- Draw two T accounts on the board.
- Read the transaction statement.
- Ask students to analyze the transaction. Complete the T accounts as the information is provided.
- Use the transparency of a general journal to illustrate the process for recording the entry in the journal or refer students to the illustration.

WHY ACCOUNTING?

Answers

1. Answers will vary.
2. Answers will vary but could include how much of a threat the released inmates will be to society; if potential criminals know they will not go to jail for committing a lesser crime; if more crimes will be committed; if businesses and families move out of cities that release inmates; and if tax revenues will decrease.

Paying a Stock Dividend

Debit Stock Dividends Distributable

GENERAL JOURNAL PAGE 6

	DATE		ACCOUNT TITLE	DOC. NO.	POST. REF.	DEBIT	CREDIT	
22	June	30	*Stock Dividends Distributable*	M246		2 0 0 00		22
23			*Capital Stock—Common*				2 0 0 00	23
24								24

Credit Capital Stock—Common

Abraham Corporation declared a 2% stock dividend on June 1. The company had 100,000 of its $0.10 par-value stock outstanding. The stock dividend will result in the issuance of 2,000 shares (100,000 shares × 2%). On the declaration date, the par value of the 2,000 shares, $200.00, was debited to Stock Dividends Distributable.

June 30. Abraham Corporation issued 2,000 shares of common stock in payment of its June 1 stock dividend, $200.00. Memorandum No. 246.

Stock Dividends Distributable

Debit		Credit	
6/30 Issue	200.00	6/1 Decl.	200.00
		(New Bal.	*zero)*

Capital Stock—Common

Debit		Credit	
		6/30 Issue	200.00

The journal entry removes the balance from Stock Dividends Distributable to Capital Stock—Common.

WHY ACCOUNTING?

How the Bottom Line Can Affect Jail Sentences

Many prison and jail systems throughout the United States are dealing with the issue of overcrowding. In California, a gymnasium is being used to house 213 prisoners. Bunk beds are aligned in rows and columns. The tight living arrangements are being blamed for numerous riots and fights that occur at the facility.

One way to solve overcrowding is to build more facilities. Because of the high cost to build more jails, many jurisdictions are taking a different approach. Instead of raising taxes to build jails, they are releasing prisoners who have lesser offenses. In many cases, these prisoners will be in monitored probation programs, increasing the costs to administer these programs.

Law, Public Safety, Corrections & Security

Administrators of jails and prisons need to adhere to budgets that usually are set by governmental organizations. When trying to keep expenses within the budget, they have to analyze the costs of different options. Knowledge of how to identify and measure costs is essential.

CRITICAL THINKING

1. Search the Internet to find information about the prison population in your state or a neighboring state. Summarize the information in a short report.
2. Not all decisions are based on costs alone. What other items should be considered when making a decision to release inmates rather than build new jails?

© iStockphoto.com/AleksKo

Impact of a Stock Dividend

GENERAL JOURNAL — PAGE 15

	DATE		ACCOUNT TITLE	DOC. NO.	POST. REF.	DEBIT	CREDIT	
1			*Closing Entries*					1
23	*Dec.*	*31*	*Retained Earnings*			*10 600 00*		23
24			*Stock Dividends*				*10 600 00*	24

Stock Dividends

6/1 Decl. 10,600.00 *(New Bal. zero)*	12/31 Clos. 10,600.00

Stock Dividends Distributable

6/30 Issue 200.00	6/1 Decl. 200.00 *(New Bal. zero)*

Paid-In Capital in Excess of Par—Common

	6/1 Decl. 10,400.00

Capital Stock—Common

	6/30 Issue 200.00

Retained Earnings

12/31 Clos. 10,600.00	

All dividends, whether for cash or stock, are closed to Retained Earnings at the end of the fiscal period. The impact of declaring and paying a stock dividend on the accounts of Abraham Corporation is shown in the T accounts.

The stock dividend has no impact on the assets or liabilities of the corporation. The journal entries simply transfer amounts among equity accounts. Retained Earnings is reduced by the amount of the dividend. Common Stock and Paid-In Capital in Excess of Par—Common, together, increase by the amount of the dividend.

Because the corporation gives nothing of value, the stockholders do not receive anything of value. The transaction increases the number of shares outstanding. Each stockholder retains his or her share of the corporation. For example, Gail Winston owned 4,000, or 4%, of Abraham's 100,000 shares prior to the stock dividend. She receives 80 shares with the 2% stock dividend. After the stock dividend, she owns 4,080 of the 102,000 shares outstanding, still exactly 4%.

If stockholders receive nothing of value, why would a corporation pay a stock dividend? Two common reasons are:

- A corporation's stockholders may expect a dividend, but the corporation lacks the necessary funds to pay a cash dividend. A stock dividend allows the corporation to pay a dividend without using any financial resources.
- A stock dividend will cause an immediate decline in the market price per share. The total market value of the corporation remains constant, while the number of shares increases. As shown below, Abraham's 2% stock dividend should cause the market price to drop from $5.30 to $5.20 per share.

Number of Shares Before Stock Dividend	×	Market Price Before Stock Dividend	=	Total Market Value
100,000	×	$5.30	=	$530,000.00

Total Market Value	÷	Number of Shares After Stock Dividend	=	Market Price After Stock Dividend
$530,000.00	÷	102,000	=	$5.20

A stock dividend helps to maintain investor demand for a stock. As a corporation continues to grow, its stock market price will also grow. An investor who perceives the stock price to be too expensive might not consider buying the stock. The stock dividend is an effective tool for the corporation to keep its stock price within a desired price range.

INPUT

- Explain that all dividends, cash or stock, are closed to Retained Earnings at the end of the fiscal period.
- Point out that a stock dividend helps to maintain investor demand for stock.
- Explain that corporations may pay stock dividends (1) if the company lacks the funds to pay a cash dividend and (2) if the stock dividend will cause a decline in the market price per share, resulting in an increase in the number of shares.
- Point out the math illustration at the bottom of the page to show the impact of a stock dividend.

MODEL

- Draw five T accounts on the board.
- Ask students to analyze the transaction. Complete the T accounts as the information is provided.
- Demonstrate with a general journal transparency or direct students to the illustration on the page to show how to close Stock Dividends to Retained Earnings.

FORMATIVE ASSESSMENT

- This is an ongoing process. Circulate around the classroom or lab, observing which students have trouble with the assignments.
- Troubleshooting: Diagnose the kinds of problems students have with this section. Students may have difficulty understanding (1) the difference between declaring and paying dividends and (2) the difference in journalizing the payment for cash dividends and stock dividends.
- Assess student understanding by checking solutions to Independent Practice assignments and noting their answers to the Terms Review and Audit Your Understanding questions.

CHECK FOR UNDERSTANDING

Terms Review

- Call on students to define each term in the Terms Review. Definitions are given in the Glossary.

Audit Your Understanding

- Call on students to answer the Audit Your Understanding questions. Answers are given in Appendix D of the textbook.

GUIDED PRACTICE

Work Together

- Have students write the solution to the Work Together problem as you guide the class through the examples.
- Direct students to record the transactions in the cash payments journal as you elicit participation in analyzing and recording the transactions.

INDEPENDENT PRACTICE

On Your Own

- Assign the On Your Own problem to be worked independently.
- Use the Formative Assessment techniques to diagnose student understanding.

Application Problem

- Assign Application Problem 11-1.

Online Working Papers

- Students can access the Lesson 11-1 problems using this software.

RETEACH

- Use four T accounts to demonstrate the declaration and payment of cash dividends: Dividends—Preferred, Dividends—Common, Dividends Payable, and Cash.
- Use three T accounts to demonstrate the declaration and payment of stock dividends: Stock Dividends, Stock Dividends Distributable, and Paid-In Capital in Excess of Par Value—Common.

CLOSURE

- Ask students to prepare a list of new accounts introduced in this lesson and to explain each.
- Ask students to draw T accounts for each new account under the appropriate headings Asset, Liabilities, and Stockholders' Equity.
- Ask students to place a + or – on the appropriate increase or decrease side of each account.

End of Lesson Review

LO1 Account for the declaration and payment of a cash dividend.

LO2 Account for the declaration and payment of a stock dividend.

Terms Review

declaring a dividend
date of declaration
date of record
date of payment
stock dividend

Audit your understanding

1. Who determines when and what amount of retained earnings a corporation will distribute as dividends?
2. Why does a corporation record a liability when a dividend is declared?
3. What transaction is recorded on the date of record?
4. What term is used to describe a stock purchased after the date of record?
5. What is the normal balance of the account Stock Dividends Distributable?
6. Describe the effect of a stock dividend on (a) the stockholders and (b) the corporation.

Work together 11-1

Journalizing dividend transactions

On April 1 of the current year, Western Tours, Inc., had 8,000 shares of 6%, $100.00 par-value preferred stock and 50,000 shares of $1.00 par-value common stock outstanding.

Journalize each transaction completed during the current year. Page 5 of a general journal and page 7 of a cash payments journal are provided in the *Working Papers*. Source documents are abbreviated as follows: check, C; memorandum, M. Your instructor will guide you through the following examples.

Transactions:

Apr. 1. The board of directors declared a quarterly cash dividend of $25,000.00, payable on April 30. M32.
30. Paid the April 1 dividend. C533.
July 1. An economic downturn made it impossible for Western Tours to declare its regular quarterly cash dividend. In lieu of a cash dividend, the board of directors declared a 5% stock dividend on common stock. The market price of the common stock on July 1 was $6.90. M57.
31. Issued the July 1 stock dividend. M68.

On your own 11-1

Journalizing dividend transactions

On July 1 of the current year, TPE Industries had 10,000 shares of 8%, $50.00 par-value preferred stock and 60,000 shares of $0.10 par-value common stock outstanding.

Journalize each transaction completed during the current year. Page 7 of a general journal and page 12 of a cash payments journal are provided in the *Working Papers*. Source documents are abbreviated as follows: check, C; memorandum, M. Work this problem independently.

Transactions:

July 1. The board of directors declared a quarterly cash dividend of $30,000.00, payable on August 1. M66.
Aug. 1. Paid the July 1 dividend. C765.
15. In an effort to reduce its stock price, the board of directors declared a 10% stock dividend on common stock. The market price of the common stock was $78.60. M87.
Sept. 15. Issued the August 15 stock dividend. M99.

Essential Question

- How would I determine the amount of dividends to pay if I wanted to reinvest in my company as well? (*The amount of the dividend is based on the cash available as well as the corporation's desire to reinvest in the company.*)

EXTENDED LEARNING

- Assign Accounting in the Real World on page 317.
- Assign Ethics in Action on page 318.
- Assign Global Awareness on page 319.
- Assign Why Accounting on page 322.

LESSON

11-2 Treasury Stock Transactions

LO3 Explain why a corporation would purchase its own stock.
LO4 Journalize entries for buying and selling treasury stock.

Treasury Stock LO3

A corporation with a significant amount of excess cash has several options. For most corporations, the first option is to use excess cash to purchase more equipment, open new locations, or purchase other businesses. The corporation can also consider issuing or increasing the dividend paid to stockholders. In addition, the corporation can elect to pay outstanding debt.

Another option is to purchase its own stock. A corporation's own stock that has been issued and reacquired is called **treasury stock**. When a corporation buys treasury stock, it reduces the number of shares outstanding.

A corporation usually intends to use the treasury stock for a specific purpose. For example, a corporation may acquire treasury stock to be given to employees as bonus payments.

Publicly held corporations frequently purchase their own stock. A program approved by a board of directors authorizing the corporation to repurchase its stock is called a **buyback**. A buyback often occurs when a corporation believes that its stock is undervalued by the stock market. Remaining stockholders benefit because the net income of the corporation is divided among a fewer number of shares.

Buying Treasury Stock LO4

CASH PAYMENTS JOURNAL PAGE 3

	DATE		ACCOUNT TITLE	CK. NO.	POST. REF.	1 GENERAL DEBIT	2 GENERAL CREDIT	3 ACCOUNTS PAYABLE DEBIT	4 PURCHASES DISCOUNT CREDIT	5 CASH CREDIT	
5	Feb.	3	Treasury Stock	887		18 000 00				18 000 00	5
6											6

Debit Treasury Stock — Credit Cash

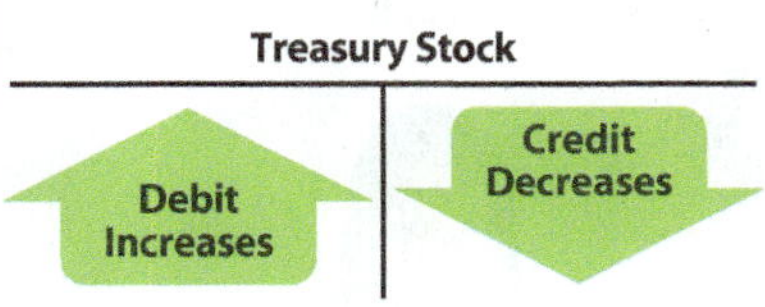

February 3. Paid cash to Kate Mason for 2,000 shares of $5.00 par-value common stock at $9.00 per share, $18,000.00. Check No. 887.

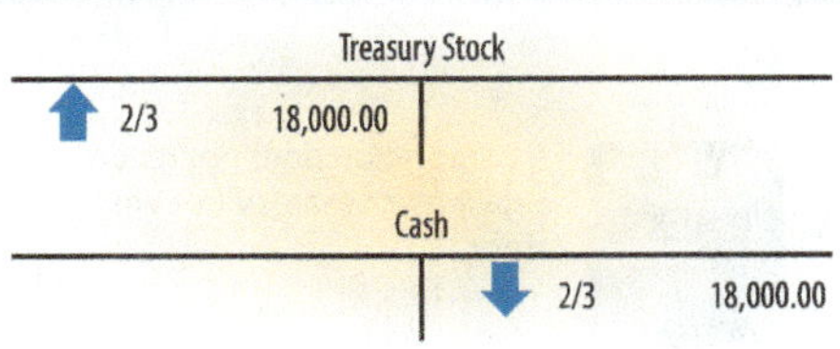

Capital stock accounts have normal credit balances. Treasury Stock is a contra capital stock account and therefore has a normal debit balance.

Forest Equipment has an excess amount of cash and does not have any need for new equipment or other plant assets. The board of directors authorizes the corporation to repurchase up to 10,000 shares of its common stock.

A corporation records treasury stock at the price paid, regardless of the stock's par or stated value. [CONCEPT: Historical Cost] Treasury Stock is debited and Cash is credited for $18,000.00, the total amount paid for the stock.

MODEL

Analyze the transaction

- Draw two T accounts on the board.
- Read the transaction statement.
- Ask students to analyze the transaction. Complete the T accounts as the information is provided.

Record the transaction

- Use the transparency of a cash payments journal to illustrate the process for recording the entry in the journal.

LESSON 11-2

BRIDGE

- Point out that students have already learned how to journalize stock sold. In this lesson, they will learn how to journalize purchasing and reselling a corporation's own stock.

TEACHING RESOURCES

- **Instructor's Resource CD/Website:**
  PowerPoint Slides
  Accounting Concepts
- **Working Papers:**
  Teacher's Edition of the Working Papers for Lesson 11-2
  Online Working Papers
- **Transparency Masters:**
  Cash Payments Journal (5-column)
  Cash Receipts Journal (7-column)

ENGAGE

- Divide the class into groups of four or five students. Have students brainstorm why a corporation would need (or want) to buy back shares of stock it had previously issued. One member of each group should be appointed the recorder and write the group's list on the board. This cooperative learning activity should not take more than 10 to 15 minutes of class time.

PREVIEW

- Call on students to read the accounting terms and definitions introduced in this lesson: *treasury stock* and *buyback*.
- Point out the learning objectives for this lesson.
- Direct students to read the headings in this lesson and to examine the illustrations.

INPUT

- Stress the difference between treasury stock and stock that has never been issued. Emphasize that treasury stock is not an asset of the corporation, does not have voting rights, and does not receive dividends as long as it is held by the corporation.
- Emphasize that the Capital Stock account is not affected when treasury stock is bought or sold. The balance of the Capital Stock account is equal to the number of shares issued times the par value of the stock.
- Explain the purpose of a buyback.

INPUT

- Remind students that a corporation records treasury stock at the price paid, regardless of the stock's par or stated value. It follows, then, that when treasury stock is sold, it is removed from the Treasury Stock account at the same value for which it was originally purchased.
- Point out that sometimes, however, treasury stock is sold for more than its original cost. In this instance, the amount received in excess of the treasury stock's original cost is credited to Paid-In Capital from Sale of Treasury Stock. Refer to the illustration.
- Emphasize that Paid-In Capital from Sale of Treasury Stock is a stockholders' equity account. It is increased with a credit and decreased with a debit.

MODEL

Calculate excess amount

- Read the transaction statement.
- Use the math illustration on the page to explain the process for calculating the amount received in excess of original cost.
- Use the board to show how the excess amount is calculated manually.
- Ask students to verify amounts with a calculator.

Analyze the transaction

- Draw three blank T accounts on the board.
- Ask a student to read the transaction statement.
- Ask students to analyze the transaction by answering these questions: Which accounts are affected? What is the classification of each account? Are the accounts increased or decreased? Are they debited or credited? Complete the T accounts as the information is provided.

Record the transaction

- Use the cash receipts journal transparency to illustrate the process for recording the entry in the journal.

Selling Treasury Stock for More Than Original Cost

	No. of Shares	×	Value per Share	=	Value
Total received	300	×	$16.00	=	$4,800.00
Original cost	300	×	$ 9.00	=	2,700.00
Amount received in excess of original cost					$2,100.00

Calculate the Amounts to Be Recorded

Credit Treasury Stock for Its Cost

CASH RECEIPTS JOURNAL — PAGE 16

	DATE		ACCOUNT TITLE	DOC. NO.	POST. REF.	1 GENERAL DEBIT	2 GENERAL CREDIT	3 ACCOUNTS RECEIVABLE CREDIT	4 SALES CREDIT	5 SALES TAX PAYABLE CREDIT	6 SALES DISCOUNT DEBIT	7 CASH DEBIT	
13	Aug.	6	Treasury Stock	R657			2 700 00					4 800 00	13
14			Paid-In Capital from										14
15			Sale of Treasury Stock				2 100 00						15

Credit the Paid-In Capital Account for the Excess over Cost of Treasury Stock

Debit Cash

August 6. Received cash from DeMarcus Long for 300 shares of treasury stock at $16.00 per share, $4,800.00. Treasury stock was bought on February 3 for $9.00 per share. Receipt No. 657.

Cash

Debit		Credit	
↑ 8/6 Sale	4,800.00		

Treasury Stock

Debit		Credit	
Bal.	18,000.00	↓ 8/6 Sale	2,700.00
(New Bal.	15,300.00)		

Paid-In Capital from Sale of Treasury Stock

Debit		Credit	
		↑ 8/6 Sale	2,100.00

A corporation needing to raise additional capital may elect to sell its treasury stock rather than issue additional shares.

Cash is debited for $4,800.00, the total amount received from the sale of the treasury stock. Treasury Stock is credited for $2,700.00, the original cost of the 300 shares of treasury stock. Paid-In Capital from Sale of Treasury Stock is credited for $2,100.00, the amount received in excess of the treasury stock's original cost.

Treasury stock is not an asset of a corporation. Since treasury stock is not owned by a stockholder, the stock does not involve voting rights. Dividends are not paid on treasury stock. Once treasury stock is given or sold to a stockholder, it ceases to be treasury stock and is again capital stock outstanding.

remember A corporation does not record a gain on the sale of its own stock.

© wavebreakmedia/Shutterstock.com

Selling Treasury Stock for Less Than Original Cost

	No. of Shares	×	Value per Share	=	Value
Original cost	200	×	$9.00	=	$1,800.00
Total received	200	×	$7.50	=	1,500.00
Amount received less than original cost					$ 300.00

Calculate the Amounts to Be Recorded

Credit Treasury Stock for Its Cost

CASH RECEIPTS JOURNAL — PAGE 22

	Date		Account Title	Doc. No.	Post. Ref.	1 General Debit	2 General Credit	3 Accounts Receivable Credit	4 Sales Credit	5 Sales Tax Payable Credit	6 Sales Discount Debit	7 Cash Debit	
7	Dec.	13	Treasury Stock	R922			1 800 00					1 500 00	7
8			Paid-In Capital from										8
9			Sale of Treasury Stock			300 00							9

Debit Paid-In Capital for the Excess of the Cost of Treasury Stock over the Cash Received

Debit Cash

A corporation with excess cash may purchase its stock when it believes the stock is undervalued by the market. Like many investors, the corporation cannot always predict future stock prices. The market price of the stock may continue to decline. If the corporation needs to sell treasury stock to raise capital, the sales price may be less than the cost of the treasury stock.

December 13. Received cash from Granger Hollins for 200 shares of treasury stock at $7.50 per share, $1,500.00. Treasury stock was bought originally on February 3 at $9.00 per share. Receipt No. 922.

Cash

Debit		Credit	
12/13 Sale	1,500.00		

Treasury Stock

Debit		Credit	
Bal.	15,300.00	12/13 Sale	1,800.00
(New Bal.	*13,500.00)*		

Paid-In Capital from Sale of Treasury Stock

Debit		Credit	
12/13 Sale	300.00	Bal.	2,100.00
		(New Bal.	*1,800.00)*

Cash is debited for $1,500.00, the total amount of cash received. Treasury Stock is credited for $1,800.00, the original cost. Paid-In Capital from Sale of Treasury Stock is debited for $300.00, the amount received that is less than the treasury stock's original cost.

Treasury stock is still considered to be issued stock. When treasury stock transactions occur, no entry is made in Capital Stock—Common. The difference between the balance of the capital stock account and the treasury stock account is the value of outstanding stock. After recording the entry on December 13 for the sale of treasury stock, the number of outstanding shares of common stock is calculated as follows:

No. of Shares Issued	−	No. of Shares of Treasury Stock	=	No. of Shares Outstanding
80,000	−	1,500	=	78,500

fyi The par or stated value of a stock has no impact on the amounts of treasury stock transactions.

INPUT

- Point out that sometimes treasury stock is sold for less than its original purchase cost. In this instance, the amount received less than the treasury stock's original cost is debited to Paid-In Capital from Sale of Treasury Stock.
- Stress that the Capital Stock account is not affected when treasury stock is bought or sold.
- Point out that capital stock less treasury stock equals outstanding stock. Outstanding stock represents the value of the number of shares of stock in the hands of stockholders.

MODEL

Analyze the transaction

- Draw three blank T accounts on the board.
- Ask students to read the transaction statement.
- Ask students to analyze the transaction. Use the math illustration to help students calculate the amount received less than the original cost. Complete the T accounts as the information is provided.

Record the transaction

- Use the cash receipts journal transparency to illustrate the process for recording the entry in the journal.

Compute shares outstanding

- Review the treasury stock transactions presented in this lesson. Point out that 2,000 shares were originally purchased by the corporation and 500 were then sold, leaving a balance of 1,500 shares.
- Use the math illustration and the board to show the process for calculating the number of shares outstanding.

DIFFERENTIATED INSTRUCTION

Visual/Spatial learners like to see the topic being discussed. Ask these students to print a financial statement from a company of their choice and to highlight the treasury stock on the statement. Display these financial statements around the room so that other students can see how treasury stock is reported.

FORENSIC ACCOUNTING

The workbook contains a list of (1) employees and (1) stock transactions. Students combine selected text fields to create a unique identification code for each employee and the buyer in each stock transaction. The VLOOKUP function is used to match the codes between the two lists.

The VLOOKUP function is limited to looking up a single value in a table. Because members of employees' families can execute stock transactions, comparing names is not a solution. Instead, students are directed to combine and compare street addresses and zip codes. Thus, stock transactions of any person living at an employee's address can be matched to the employee.

Answers

Answers will vary. A suggested solution follows.

A comparison was made between employee addresses and the buyer addresses of Blanchard Corporation stock. Seven transactions that require further analysis were detected. The following information was obtained:

1. Four "buy" transactions were executed for two employees (or related individuals). These transactions violate the corporation's code of conduct. The stock prices are consistent with other transactions during that period of time.
2. Three transactions were executed by two employees. None of these transactions were authorized, which was a violation of the code of conduct. The stock prices are consistent with other transactions made during that period of time.
3. The "sell" transactions by Maggie Watt and Jennifer Watt were executed within four days before a significant drop in the stock price on October 1. These sales were executed at $41.74 (September 27) and $42.39 (September 30) per share. In contrast, the first transaction on October 1 was priced at $34.50. These individuals live at the same address as Blanchard employee Gordon Watt. None of these transactions were authorized, which was a violation of the code of conduct. Although the timing of these sales may be a coincidence, a reasonable person would question whether insider information motivated these transactions.

FORENSIC ACCOUNTING

Insider Trading

Martha Stewart has built a media empire by selling a distinct lifestyle. Martha Stewart Living Omnimedia offers a wide range of products, from recipe books to cookware, furniture to paint, and towels to bedding. Stewart shares cooking, decorating, gardening, and craft ideas through magazines, books, radio and television shows, and social media.

During one period, Martha Stewart's name was in the media for the wrong reason. In 2003, the Securities and Exchange Commission (SEC) filed securities fraud charges against Stewart and her former stockbroker, Peter Bacanovic. The complaint alleged that the receipt of insider information motivated Stewart to sell her shares of a biopharmaceutical company, ImClone Systems, Inc. Subsequently, during the SEC investigation, she attempted to conceal facts.

In 2001, investors were awaiting the government's decision to approve ImClone's new cancer drug Erbitux. ImClone chief executive officer, Sam Waksal, knew that the government was about to reject Erbitux. Waksal instructed his stockbroker, Peter Bacanovic, to sell all his ImClone stock that was held by Bacanovic's firm, Merrill Lynch. Waksal used his insider information to his benefit, which resulted in his being convicted of violating insider trading laws.

Bacanovic was also Stewart's stockbroker. On December 27, 2001, Bacanovic executed a sale of all of Stewart's shares in ImClone. The next day, ImClone publicly announced that the government did not approve Erbitux. ImClone's stock price dropped instantly. By selling her shares before the official announcement, Stewart avoided losses of $45,673.

Stewart was not convicted of using this insider information. However, she was accused of lying to investigators, stating that she did not recall anyone telling her that Waksal was selling his stock. Stewart was convicted of obstruction of justice and served five months in prison.

ACTIVITY

Blanchard Corporation's common stock is traded publicly. To avoid any appearance of insider trading, Blanchard has a code of conduct that restricts how its employees can buy and sell its stock. Employees may only purchase Blanchard stock by scheduling monthly purchases, thus avoiding any appearance of using insider information to make purchase decisions. Employees must provide a 30-day written notice of their intent to sell any of their shares. These rules apply to the employees and members of their immediate family.

Blanchard's internal auditors have obtained from its stock agent a listing of all stock transactions during the past fiscal year. The list does not include scheduled employee purchases. No employees submitted written requests for the sale of stock. Write an e-mail to the chief financial officer, describing any information that seems to indicate an employee used insider information to execute stock trades.

INSTRUCTIONS

Open the spreadsheet FA_CH11 and complete the steps on the Instructions tab.

Source: www.sec.gov/news/press/2003-69.htm.

© iStockphoto.com/burwellphotography

FORMATIVE ASSESSMENT

- This is an ongoing process. Circulate around the classroom or lab, observing which students have trouble with the assignments.
- Troubleshooting: Diagnose the kinds of problems students have with this lesson. Students may have difficulty remembering the rules for increasing and decreasing Treasury Stock and Paid-In Capital from Sale of Treasury Stock.
- Assess student understanding by checking solutions to Independent Practice assignments and noting their answers to the Terms Review and Audit Your Understanding questions.

End of Lesson Review

LO3 Explain why a corporation would purchase its own stock.

LO4 Journalize entries for buying and selling treasury stock.

Terms Review

treasury stock

buyback

Audit your understanding

1. What is the normal balance of the Treasury Stock account?
2. What often causes a corporation to authorize a buyback?
3. How do remaining stockholders benefit from a buyback?
4. How does treasury stock affect the amount of dividends paid by the corporation?

Work together 11-2

Journalizing treasury stock transactions

Journalize each transaction completed during the current year. Page 12 of a cash receipts journal and page 2 of a cash payments journal are provided in the *Working Papers*. Source documents are abbreviated as follows: check, C; receipt, R. Your instructor will guide you through the following examples.

Transactions:

Jan. 25. Paid cash to Mike Straton for 400 shares of $1.00 par-value common stock at $16.00 per share, $6,400.00. C688.

May 7. Received cash from Patti Edwards for 200 shares of treasury stock at $16.50 per share, $3,300.00. R456.

19. Received cash from Kathryn Welch for 50 shares of treasury stock at $15.00 per share, $750.00. R468.

On your own 11-2

Journalizing treasury stock transactions

Journalize each transaction completed during the current year. Page 16 of a cash receipts journal and page 4 of a cash payments journal are provided in the *Working Papers*. Source documents are abbreviated as follows: check, C; receipt, R. Work independently to complete the following problem.

Transactions:

Feb. 14. Paid cash to Jill Goforth for 3,000 shares of $10.00 stated-value common stock at $24.00 per share, $72,000.00. C554.

Aug. 2. Received cash from Chandra Gunter for 600 shares of treasury stock at $24.50 per share, $14,700.00. R732.

13. Received cash from Dewey Jaynes for 300 shares of treasury stock at $23.25 per share, $6,975.00. R748.

CHECK FOR UNDERSTANDING

Terms Review

- Call on students to define each term in the Terms Review. Definitions are given in the Glossary.

Audit Your Understanding

- Call on students to answer the Audit Your Understanding questions. Answers are given in Appendix D of the textbook.

GUIDED PRACTICE

Work Together

- Have students write the solution to the Work Together problem as you guide the class through the examples.
- Direct students to record the treasury stock transactions in journals as you elicit participation in analyzing and recording the transactions.

INDEPENDENT PRACTICE

On Your Own

- Assign the On Your Own problem to be worked independently.
- Use the Formative Assessment techniques to diagnose student understanding.

Application Problem

- Assign Application Problem 11-2.

Online Working Papers

- Students can access the Lesson 11-2 problems using this software.

RETEACH

- Draw three T accounts arranged in a vertical column on the board.
- Label the top account Cash, the middle account Treasury Stock, and the bottom account Paid-In Capital from Sale of Treasury Stock.
- Ask a student to record a corporation's $20,000 cash purchase of 1,000 shares of its own stock at $20 a share.
- Ask a student to record a transaction showing the sale of 200 shares of treasury stock at $22 a share.
- Ask a student to record a transaction showing the sale of 100 shares of treasury stock at $16 a share.

EXTENDED LEARNING

- Assign Forensic Accounting on page 328.

CLOSURE

- Ask students to prepare a list of all new accounts learned in this lesson and the definition or purpose of each account.
- Ask students to draw T accounts for each new account under the appropriate heading: Assets, Liabilities, or Stockholders' Equity.
- Ask students to place a + or – in the appropriate increase or decrease side of each account.

Essential Questions

- Why would a gain or loss not be recorded on the sale of treasury stock? (*A gain or loss cannot be recorded because the corporation is reacquiring its own stock and has all the "insider" information.*)
- Why wouldn't you pay dividends on treasury stock? (*Since the stock has been reacquired by its own company, it does not have shareholder rights, such as voting or dividends.*)

LESSON

11-3

BRIDGE

- Point out that students have already learned how to journalize the selling of a corporation's own stock and the payment of dividends. In this lesson, they will learn how to account for purchasing the stock of other publicly held corporations and receiving dividends from other corporations as an additional form of revenue.

TEACHING RESOURCES

- **Instructor's Resource CD/Website:** PowerPoint Slides Accounting Concepts
- **Working Papers:** Teacher's Edition of the Working Papers for Lesson 11-3 Online Working Papers
- **Transparency Masters:** Cash Payments Journal (5-column) Cash Receipts Journal (7-column)

ENGAGE

- Ask students for examples of how they earn a return on their cash.
- Ask students if they are familiar with any companies that own the stock of other corporations.

PREVIEW

- Point out the learning objective for this lesson.
- Direct students to read the headings in this lesson and to examine the illustrations.

INPUT

- Explain that many corporations purchase the capital stock of other publicly held corporations to earn a return on their cash assets.
- Explain that Marketable Securities is an asset account with a normal debit balance and is the name of the account that shows the purchase of the capital stock of another corporation.

MODEL

Analyze and record the transaction

- Draw two blank T accounts on the board.
- Ask students to read the transaction statement.
- Ask students to analyze the transaction.
- Use the cash payments journal transparency to illustrate the process for recording the entry in the journal.

LESSON

11-3 Purchasing and Selling Capital Stock of Other Corporations

LO5 Journalize transactions for the purchase and sale of the capital stock of other corporations.

Purchasing Capital Stock LO5

CASH PAYMENTS JOURNAL PAGE 2

	DATE		ACCOUNT TITLE	CK. NO.	POST. REF.	1 GENERAL DEBIT	2 GENERAL CREDIT	3 ACCOUNTS PAYABLE DEBIT	4 PURCHASES DISCOUNT CREDIT	5 CASH CREDIT	
4	Jan.	23	Marketable Securities	268		52 000 00				52 000 00	4
5											5
6											6

Debit Marketable Securities — Credit Cash

A corporation that earns a net income usually generates a positive cash flow. The corporation must decide what to do with the cash. Alternative uses of the cash include reinvesting in the business, paying a dividend, or reducing liabilities.

A period often exists between the time a corporation generates the cash and when the cash will be used. During this time, the corporation should attempt to earn a return on its cash assets. Depositing the cash in a bank is an easy and safe method to earn interest. A corporation can also make a temporary investment by purchasing the capital stock of another corporation.

The purchase of the capital stock of another corporation is recorded in the account Marketable Securities. This account is a current asset that has a normal debit balance. Forest uses Marketable Securities to account for short-term investments and Investment Securities to account for long-term investments.

Marketable Securities

Debit Increases	Credit Decreases

Forest Equipment, Inc., has excess cash it intends to use to purchase new store equipment. However, the equipment will not be purchased for several months. Thus, Forest decides to make a temporary investment in the stock market. After an evaluation of alternative investments, the board of directors approved the purchase of the common stock of Ellisville Steel. On the date of purchase, the market price of the stock is $26.00 per share.

January 23. Purchased 2,000 shares of Ellisville Steel at the current market price of $26.00 per share, $52,000.00. Check No. 268.

Marketable Securities

↑ 1/23 52,000.00	

Cash

	↓ 1/23 52,000.00

The debit to Marketable Securities is the number of shares purchased, 2,000, multiplied by the market price of the stock, $26.00. Cash is credited for the total amount of the purchase, $52,000.00.

Purchasing the capital stock of publicly held corporations is a common method of investing excess cash. The corporation can sell its investment quickly and easily on a national stock exchange.

Receiving a Dividend on a Marketable Security

CASH RECEIPTS JOURNAL — PAGE 5

	DATE		ACCOUNT TITLE	DOC. NO.	POST. REF.	1 GENERAL DEBIT	2 GENERAL CREDIT	3 ACCOUNTS RECEIVABLE CREDIT	4 SALES CREDIT	5 SALES TAX PAYABLE CREDIT	6 SALES DISCOUNT DEBIT	7 CASH DEBIT	
1	20-- Mar.	1	Dividend Revenue	R456			280 00					280 00	1
2													2
3													3

Credit Dividend Revenue — Debit Cash

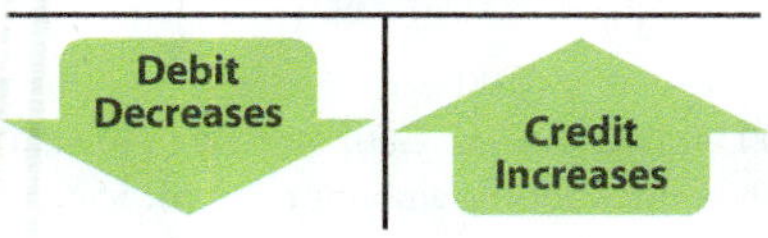

Like individual stockholders, a corporation may receive a dividend on capital stock owned as a temporary investment. Dividends earned on marketable securities are recorded in Dividend Revenue. This account is classified as an other revenue account and has a normal credit balance.

The credit to Dividend Revenue is the number of shares owned, 2,000, multiplied by the dividend per share, $0.14. Cash is debited for the amount received, $280.00.

March 1. Forest Equipment received a $0.14 per share dividend on its 2,000 shares of Ellisville Steel, $280.00. Receipt No. 456.

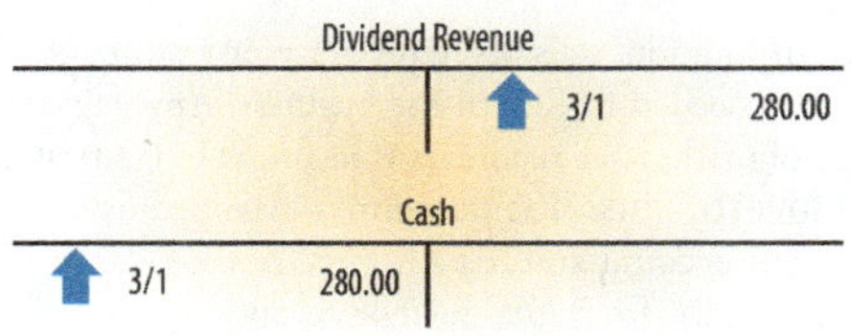

© iStockphoto.com/Dan Bachman

THINK LIKE AN ACCOUNTANT

Evaluating a Stock Buyback Program

A corporation must make important decisions, such as how to spend the cash generated from earning net income. Many corporations invest the cash in additional plant assets to expand the business. Others use the cash to pay down long-term liabilities. Cash is also used to pay dividends.

Hillman Corporation recently sold its international operations, resulting in a one-time increase in cash. After fully funding its expansion plans, reducing the level of debt, and paying annual dividends, Hillman Corporation still has $40 million more than its normal cash balance. The board of directors is meeting to debate what, if anything, should be done with this unusual amount of available cash. One idea that has been suggested is for the corporation to implement its first stock buyback program.

The board of directors has requested an analysis of the impact of a $20 million buyback or using $20 million to increase the annual dividend.

OPEN THE SPREADSHEET TLA_CH11

The worksheet contains the structure required to prepare the analysis. Follow the steps on the Instructions tab to create the formulas required to calculate the requested information. Answer these questions:

1. How many shares of stock could be repurchased?
2. What effect would the buyback have on the current amount of the total annual dividends?
3. The board has expressed concern over increasing the dividend above a level it could not sustain for at least eight years. Recommend a new amount for the annual dividend.

DIFFERENTIATED INSTRUCTION

Musical learners can be taught by turning lessons into lyrics. Have students share new accounts and concepts related to dividends, treasury stock, and marketable securities by preparing a rap or a music video demonstrating their knowledge.

INPUT

- Explain that any dividends received on a marketable security are recorded in Dividend Revenue. This is an additional revenue account with a normal credit balance.

MODEL

Analyze and record the transaction

- Draw two blank T accounts on the board.
- Ask students to read the transaction statement.
- Ask students to analyze the transaction.
- Use the cash receipts journal transparency to illustrate the process for recording the entry in the journal.

THINK LIKE AN ACCOUNTANT

Students are provided with an incomplete analysis. Formulas are created to calculate most of the values in the analysis. Students are expected to be able to use the integer (INT) function to calculate the number of shares that could be repurchased.

Encourage students to perform an Internet search to identify a corporation that has a buyback program. These programs typically generate a substantial number of news releases and articles. Have students assess whether the financial community believes the buyback program will have a favorable impact on stockholders who retain their shares.

Answers

1. 357,142.
2. Total annual dividends would decrease by $857,141, assuming the dividend per share remains at $2.40.
3. Assuming there is no stock buyback, distributing the $20 million over eight years would support a $0.25 increase in the annual dividend per share.

INPUT

- Explain that a marketable security, considered a temporary investment, is sold when the business needs cash.
- Point out that any gains are recorded in Gain on Sale of Investments and losses are recorded in Loss on Sale of Investments.

MODEL

Analyze and record the transaction

- Draw three blank T accounts on the board.
- Ask students to read the transaction statement.
- Ask students to analyze the transaction, determining if there is a gain or loss on the sale.
- Use the cash receipts journal transparency to illustrate the process for recording the entry in the journal.

Selling a Marketable Security

Credit Marketable Securities

CASH RECEIPTS JOURNAL — PAGE 9

	DATE		ACCOUNT TITLE	DOC. NO.	POST. REF.	1 GENERAL DEBIT	2 GENERAL CREDIT	3 ACCOUNTS RECEIVABLE CREDIT	4 SALES CREDIT	5 SALES TAX PAYABLE CREDIT	6 SALES DISCOUNT DEBIT	7 CASH DEBIT	
10	May	4	Marketable Securities	R677			52,000.00					54,400.00	10
11			Gain on Sale of Investments				2,400.00						11
12													12

Credit Gain on Sale of Investments

Debit Cash

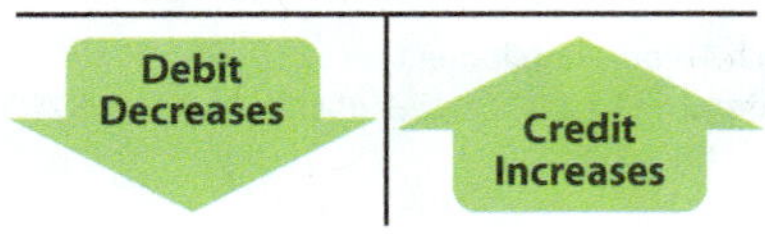

A corporation sells its temporary investments when cash is needed for use in the business. Any gain on the sale of marketable securities is recorded in Gain on Sale of Investments. The account is classified as an other revenue account and has a normal credit balance.

Any loss from the sale of temporary investments would be recorded in Loss on Sale of Investments.

Forest Equipment is beginning its purchase of new store equipment. Since the common stock of Ellisville Steel has reached its highest market price of the year, Forest decides to sell its shares in the corporation.

The credit to Marketable Securities is the original purchase price of the stock, $52,000.00. The stock was sold for $27.20 per share, a $1.20 gain over the original cost of $26.00 per share. The resulting gain of $2,400.00 is credited to Gain on Sale of Investments. Cash is debited for the amount received, $54,400.00.

May 4. Forest Equipment sold its investment in Ellisville Steel, 2,000 shares at $27.20 per share, $54,400.00. Receipt 677.

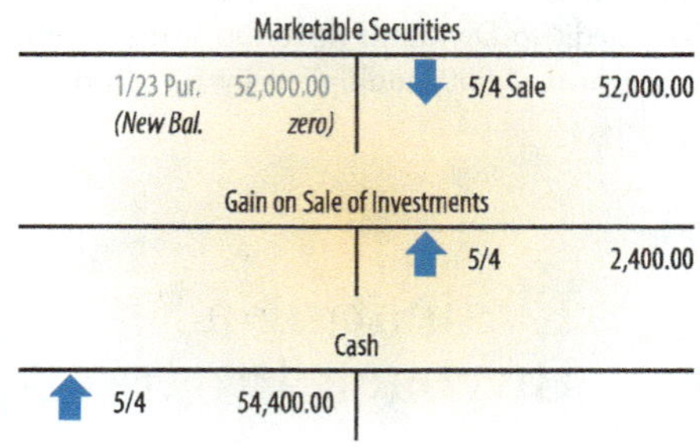

© Mike Flippo/Shutterstock.com

FORMATIVE ASSESSMENT

- This is an ongoing process. Circulate around the classroom or lab, observing which students have trouble with the assignments.
- Troubleshooting: Diagnose the kinds of problems students have with this lesson. Students may have difficulty understanding the meaning and purpose of marketable securities.
- Assess student understanding by checking solutions to Independent Practice assignments and noting their answers to the Audit Your Understanding questions.

End of Lesson Review

LO5 Journalize transactions for the purchase and sale of the capital stock of other corporations.

Audit your understanding

1. Why would a corporation purchase the capital stock of another corporation?
2. How is the account Marketable Securities classified?
3. How is the account Dividend Revenue classified?
4. How is the account Gain on Sale of Investments classified?

Work together 11-3

Journalizing the purchase and sale of the capital stock of other corporations

MPL Industries has decided to purchase stock of Rowen Corporation as a temporary investment of excess cash.

Journalize each transaction completed during the current year. Page 3 of a cash payments journal and page 8 of a cash receipts journal are provided in the *Working Papers*. Source documents are abbreviated as follows: check, C; receipt, R. Your instructor will guide you through the following examples.

Transactions:

Feb. 8. MPL purchased 3,000 shares of Rowen Corporation at $16.80 per share, $50,400.00. C258.

Apr. 2. Received a $0.12 per share cash dividend from Rowen Corporation, $360.00. R322.

June 13. MPL sold its 3,000 shares of Rowen Corporation for $19.40 per share, $58,200.00. R367.

On your own 11-3

Journalizing the purchase and sale of the capital stock of other corporations

Keller Mining's board of directors approved the use of excess cash to purchase stock in HPC Equipment.

Journalize each transaction completed during the current year. Page 1 of a cash payments journal and page 6 of a cash receipts journal are provided in the *Working Papers*. Source documents are abbreviated as follows: check, C; receipt, R. Work this problem independently.

Transactions:

Jan. 23. Keller Mining purchased 700 shares of HPC Equipment with a current market price of $56.25 per share, $39,375.00. C456.

Mar. 15. Received a $0.25 per share cash dividend from HPC Equipment, $175.00. R443.

May 22. Keller Mining sold all of its shares of HPC Equipment for $62.90 per share, $44,030.00. R532.

CHECK FOR UNDERSTANDING

Audit Your Understanding

- Call on students to answer the Audit Your Understanding questions. Answers are given in Appendix D of the textbook.

GUIDED PRACTICE

Work Together

- Have students write the solution to the Work Together problem as you guide the class through the examples.
- Direct students to record the transactions in journals as you elicit participation in analyzing and recording the transactions.

INDEPENDENT PRACTICE

On Your Own

- Assign the On Your Own problem to be worked independently.
- Use the Formative Assessment techniques to diagnose student understanding.

Application Problem

- Assign Application Problem 11-3.

Online Working Papers

- Students can access the Lesson 11-3 problems using this software.

RETEACH

- Ask students to describe the purpose of marketable securities.
- Ask students to explain how to record the sale of a marketable security.
- Ask students to describe how to account for dividends received for marketable securities.

CLOSURE

- Ask students to summarize briefly marketable securities.

Essential Question

- What are other options for earning a return on cash? Compare the advantages of these options to those of marketable securities. (*Examples might include savings or checking accounts. These are very liquid as well, but marketable securities usually offer a better return on a short-term investment.*)

EXTENDED LEARNING

- Assign Think Like an Accountant on page 331.
- Assign Explore Accounting on page 334.

EXPLORE ACCOUNTING Stock Splits

© iStockphoto.com/Makhnach_M

The method for trading stock has changed dramatically since 1990. The Internet led to the founding of numerous online trading sites allowing individual investors to trade any number of shares for a fixed fee. Despite these changes, many corporations continue to manage their stock prices. At the end of 2012, the average stock price of the 30 stocks comprising the Dow Jones Industrial Average was $56.

To reduce the market price, a corporation can increase the number of shares outstanding by dividing each outstanding share into two or more shares. Dividing a share of stock into a larger number of shares is called a **stock split.** In a 2-for-1 stock split, the company doubles the number of shares and reduces each share's par value by half. Thus, an investor holding 100 shares of $10 par-value stock then owns 200 shares of $5 par-value stock. More importantly, the market price of the stock, once at $60 per share, immediately drops to $30 per share.

Similar to a stock dividend, a stock split does not increase stockholders' ownership in the company and the value of their investment. Before the stock split, the investor owned 100 shares of $60 stock valued at $6,000. After the stock split, the investor owns 200 shares of $30 stock, also valued at $6,000. Because all stockholders now own twice the number of shares, each investor's percentage ownership in the corporation remains the same.

Stock split information is available from a variety of sources. The following stock split information for The Coca-Cola Company was obtained from the Investor Relations section of its website.

HISTORY OF STOCK SPLITS FOR THE COCA-COLA COMPANY

Record Date	Activity	Cumulative Shares
07/27/2012	2-for-1 Stock Split	9,216
05/01/1996	2-for-1 Stock Split	4,608
05/01/1992	2-for-1 Stock Split	2,304
05/01/1990	2-for-1 Stock Split	1,152
06/16/1986	3-for-1 Stock Split	576
05/09/1977	2-for-1 Stock Split	192
05/13/1968	2-for-1 Stock Split	96
01/22/1965	2-for-1 Stock Split	48
01/22/1960	3-for-1 Stock Split	24
11/15/1935	4-for-1 Stock Split	8
04/25/1927	1-for-1 Stock Dividend	2
09/05/1919		1

Source: http://www.coca-colacompany.com/investors/stock-history/investors-info-splits.

Suppose an investor purchased 100 shares of The Cola-Cola Company on March 1, 1990, for $73.60 per share.

Record Date	Split (X-for-1)	Number of Shares	Cost Basis	Total Cost
07/27/2012	2	1,600	$ 4.60	$7,360.00
05/01/1996	2	800	$ 9.20	$7,360.00
05/01/1992	2	400	$18.40	$7,360.00
05/01/1990	2	200	$36.80	$7,360.00
Initial investment		100	$73.60	$7,360.00

Assuming a current market price of $42.00 per share, the 100 shares initially purchased for $7,360.00 are now worth $67,200.00 ($42.00 × 1,600).

Without any stock splits, the 100 shares would likely have a market price $672.00 per share ($67,200.00/100 shares). Instead, the investor has 1,600 shares with a cost basis of $4.60 per share.

INSTRUCTIONS

Assume an investor purchased 100 shares of The Coca-Cola Company on July 1, 1985, for $72.00 per share. Determine the current value of the shares, assuming a $42.00 market price. How many shares would the investor own?

EXPLORE ACCOUNTING

Answers

The investor would now own 4,800 shares having a total market value of $201,600.00 ($42.00 per share × 4,800 shares). The following schedule supports the calculation of the number of shares.

Record Date	Split (X-for-1)	Number of Shares	Cost Basis	Total Cost
07/27/2012	2	4,800	$ 1.50	$7,200.00
05/01/1996	2	2,400	$ 3.00	$7,200.00
05/01/1992	2	1,200	$ 6.00	$7,200.00
05/01/1990	2	600	$12.00	$7,200.00
06/16/1986	3	300	$24.00	$7,200.00
Initial investment		100	$72.00	$7,200.00

Chapter Summary

A cash dividend distributes a corporation's earnings to its stockholders. A corporation incurs a liability when the board of directors declares a dividend. Stockholders who own the stock on the date of record receive the dividend. A stock dividend results in the issuance of additional shares of stock, but does not provide stockholders with anything of value. A corporation may issue a stock dividend to reduce the stock's market price.

Treasury stock is a corporation's own stock that has been issued and reacquired. A corporation may approve a program to buy treasury stock if it believes that its stock is undervalued by the stock market. Treasury stock may later be sold. Any gain or loss from the sale of treasury stock is recorded in stockholders' equity.

A corporation may make a temporary investment in the capital stock of another corporation. Dividends earned and any gain from the sale of the investment are classified as other revenue on the income statement.

Apply Your Understanding

INSTRUCTIONS: Download problem instructions for Excel, QuickBooks, and Sage 50 from the textbook companion website at www.C21accounting.com.

11-1 Application Problem: Journalizing dividend transactions LO1, 2

On January 1 of the current year, Southeast Supply had 5,000 shares of 6%, $100.00 par-value preferred stock and 200,000 shares of $10.00 par-value common stock outstanding.

Instructions:

Journalize each transaction completed during the current year. Page 1 of a general journal and page 2 of a cash payments journal are provided in the *Working Papers*. Source documents are abbreviated as follows: check, C; memorandum, M.

Transactions:

Jan.	1.	The board of directors declared a quarterly cash dividend of $40,000.00, payable on January 31. M3.
	31.	Paid the January 1 dividend. C223.
Apr.	1.	The board of directors raised its quarterly cash dividend to $42,000.00, payable on April 30. M23.
	30.	Paid the April 1 dividend. C345.
May	15.	The board of directors declared a 2% stock dividend on common stock. The market price of the common stock on May 15 was $84.00. M78.
June	15.	Issued the May 15 stock dividend. M93.

11-2 Application Problem: Journalizing treasury stock transactions LO3, 4

HPT Corporation has 50,000 shares of $1.00 par stock outstanding.

Instructions:

Journalize each transaction completed during the current year. Page 12 of a cash receipts journal and page 2 of a cash payments journal are provided in the *Working Papers*. Source documents are abbreviated as follows: check, C; receipt, R.

Transactions:

Jan.	6.	Paid cash to Debra Joiner for 600 shares of common stock at $24.00 per share, $14,400.00. C325.
June	2.	Received cash from Imani Locke for 200 shares of treasury stock at $24.60 per share, $4,920.00. R628.
	12.	Received cash from Bernard Laws for 100 shares of treasury stock at $23.80 per share, $2,380.00. R634.
	29.	Received cash from Lynda Lann for 150 shares of treasury stock at $24.90 per share, $3,735.00. R651.

CLOSURE

- Review the Chapter Summary.
- Ask students to prepare a list of the new concepts introduced in this chapter.

Essential Questions

- Why isn't treasury stock an asset? (*It is considered a reduction in net worth, not an asset, because the company cannot own stock in itself.*)
- Why does treasury stock have a normal debit balance? (*It is a reduction in the company's net worth.*)
- Would a corporation specifically purchase stock in other publicly held corporations that offered dividends? Why or why not? (*Yes, they might if they were looking for a liquid, short-term investment on which to obtain a greater return than on other short-term investments.*)

CHECK FIGURES

For complete solutions to Chapter 11 problems, see the Teacher's Edition of the Working Papers.

Application Problem 11-1

General journal debits: Apr. 1, Dividends—Common, $34,500.00; May 15, Stock Dividends, $336,000.00; June 15, Stock Dividends Distributable, $40,000.00.

General journal credits: Jan. 1, Dividends Payable, $40,000.00; Apr. 1, Dividends Payable, $42,000.00.

Application Problem 11-2

Paid-In Capital from Sale of Treasury Stock: June 2, credit $120.00; June 12, debit $20.00; June 29, credit $135.00.

Application Problem 11-3

Oct. 15: credit Dividend Revenue, $660.00.

Nov. 3: credit Marketable Securities, $38,940.00; credit Gain on Sale of Investments, $1,210.00.

Mastery Problem 11-M

General journal debits: July 1, Dividends—Common, $2,500.00; Aug. 6, Stock Dividends, $5,775.00.

General journal credits: July 1, Dividends Payable, $3,000.00; Aug. 6, Stock Dividends Distributable, $350.00.

Cash receipts journal credits: Sept. 30, Dividend Revenue, $114.00; Gain on Sale of Investments, $690.00; Oct. 25, Paid-In Capital from Sale of Treasury Stock, $300.00.

INDEPENDENT PRACTICE

- Assign Mastery Problem 11-M for students as a culminating problem combining all new learning from the chapter.
- Assign Challenge Problem 11-C to accelerated students who work at a faster pace.
- Assign Study Guide 11.
- Students can access Online Working Papers to work end-of-chapter problems on the computer.
- Direct students to the C21 Accounting companion website for additional practice and review opportunities.

FORMATIVE ASSESSMENT

- Review solutions to the assigned problems in class, diagnosing trouble spots.

RETEACH

- Call on students to describe how they avoid the trouble spots diagnosed.
- Use reteaching suggestions from lesson plans as required.
- Assign Recycling Problem 11-R if needed.

11-3 Application Problem: Journalizing the purchase and sale of the capital stock of other corporations LO5

SkyFore Corporation invests excess cash in the stock market.

Instructions:

Journalize each transaction completed during the current year. Page 15 of a cash payments journal and page 10 of a cash receipts journal are provided in the *Working Papers*. Source documents are abbreviated as follows: check, C; receipt, R.

Transactions:

Aug.	30.	SkyFore purchased 1,100 shares of Plancing Corporation for $35.40 per share, $38,940.00. C664.
Oct.	15.	Received a $0.60 per share cash dividend from Plancing Corporation, $660.00. R621.
Nov.	3.	SkyFore sold all of its shares of Plancing Corporation at the current market price of $36.50 per share, $40,150.00. R764.

11-M Mastery Problem: Journalizing dividend, treasury stock, and investment transactions LO1, 2, 3, 4, 5

TA Post Corporation has 35,000 shares of $1.00 stated-value common stock and 250 shares of 8%, $100.00 par-value preferred stock outstanding.

Instructions:

Journalize each transaction completed during the current year. Page 4 of a general journal, page 6 of a cash receipts journal, and page 7 of a cash payments journal are provided in the *Working Papers*. Source documents are abbreviated as follows: check, C; memorandum, M; receipt, R.

Transactions:

July	1.	The board of directors declared a quarterly cash dividend of $3,000.00, payable on July 31. M22.
	31.	Paid the July 1 dividend. C55.
Aug.	6.	The board of directors declared a 1% stock dividend on common stock. An independent appraisal service has estimated that the common stock has a market value of $16.50 on August 6. M31.
	9.	Purchased 300 shares of MXZ Corporation for $52.00 per share, $15,600.00. C68.
	23.	Paid cash to Darius Henderson for 250 shares of the corporation's common stock at $17.00 per share, $4,250.00. C79.
Sept.	6.	Issued the August 6 stock dividend. M42.
	30.	Received a $0.38 per share cash dividend from MXZ Corporation, $114.00. R69.
Oct.	12.	Sold all of its shares of MXZ Corporation for $54.30 per share, $16,290.00. R81.
	25.	Received cash from Tatyanna Jamley for 150 shares of treasury stock at $19.00 per share, $2,850.00. R92.

Sage 50 Accounting

1. Journalize and post corporate dividend and treasury stock transactions to the cash disbursements journal.
2. Journalize and post stock dividend transactions to the general journal.
3. Print the cash disbursements journal, cash receipts journal, and general journal.

QuickBooks

1. Journalize and post corporate dividend and treasury stock transactions in the Write Checks window.
2. Journalize and post stock dividend transactions to the journal.
3. Print the check detail and journal.

Excel

1. Journalize corporate stock dividend and treasury stock transactions to the cash payments journal and cash receipts journal.
2. Print the spreadsheets.

COMMON CORE AND INTERDISCIPLINARY STUDIES

Extended learning features and activities present numerous opportunities to implement Common Core Standards through interdisciplinary studies. Practice is provided in the common core areas of English Language Arts & Literacy and Mathematical Practice. Many of these activities require short, critical-thinking and decision-making responses that apply reading, writing, speaking, listening, language, media and technology, and mathematical skills.

11-C Challenge Problem: Journalizing stock and dividend transactions LO1, 2, 3, 4

KCL Stores began the current year with the following capital stock outstanding: 82,000 shares of $1.00 par-value common stock and 12,000 shares of 7.5%, $50.00 par-value preferred stock. KCL's preferred stock has the right to receive unpaid dividends from previous quarters before common stockholders can share in any future cash dividends.

Instructions:

Journalize the following transactions. Page 1 of a general journal, page 4 of a cash receipts journal, and page 3 of a cash payments journal are provided in the *Working Papers*. Source documents are abbreviated as follows: check, C; memorandum, M; receipt, R.

Transactions:

Jan. 5. The board of directors, concerned over the company's cash flows, decided to limit the quarterly dividend to $10,000.00, payable on January 31. M4.
5. The board of directors declared a 5% stock dividend on common stock. An independent appraisal service estimated that the common stock has a market value of $62.50 on January 5. M31.
31. Paid the January 5 cash dividend. C298.
Feb. 2. Issued the January 5 stock dividend. M42.
Apr. 1. With cash flow problems continuing, the board of directors decided to suspend any dividends during the current quarter.
2. Received cash for the sale of 3,000 shares of preferred stock for $52.00 per share, $156,000.00. R234.
July 1. The board of directors decided to resume a quarterly cash dividend, declaring a $25,000.00 dividend payable on July 31. M62.
31. Paid the July 1 cash dividend. C334.
Oct. 1. The board of directors declared a quarterly cash dividend of $25,000.00, payable on October 31. M83.
31. Paid the October 1 cash dividend. C456.

Sage 50 Accounting

1. Journalize and post corporate dividend and treasury stock transactions to the cash disbursements journal.
2. Journalize and post stock dividend transactions to the general journal.
3. Print the cash disbursements journal, cash receipts journal, and general journal.

QB

1. Journalize and post corporate dividend and treasury stock transactions in the Write Checks window.
2. Journalize and post stock dividend transactions to the journal.
3. Print the check detail and journal.

X

1. Journalize corporate stock dividend and treasury stock transactions to the cash payments journal and cash receipts journal.
2. Print the spreadsheets.

Challenge Problem 11-C

General journal debits: Jan. 5, Dividends—Preferred, $10,000.00; Jan. 5, Stock Dividends, $256,250.00; July 1, Dividends—Preferred, $25,000.00; Oct. 1, Dividends—Common, $9,375.00.

General journal credits: Jan. 5, Paid-In Capital in Excess of Par Value—Common, $252,150.00; Feb. 2, Capital Stock—Common, $4,100.00.

Cash receipts journal credits: Apr. 2, Capital Stock—Preferred, $150,000.00; Paid-In Capital in Excess of Par Value—Preferred, $6,000.00.

EXTENDED LEARNING

- Assign 21st Century Skills on page 338.
- Assign Analyzing Home Depot's Financial Statements on page 339.

SUMMATIVE EVALUATION

- Chapter 11 Test
- Cognero for Chapter 11

21ST CENTURY SKILLS

Answers

1. Answers will vary, but possible companies include Hasbro, Johnson & Johnson, The Coca-Cola Company, Target, Home Depot, and Walmart.
2. A minor must have a parent or legal guardian serve as custodian of the account.
3. Announcements should be informative, grammatically correct, and easy for a potential investor to understand.

21st Century Skills

Build Wealth DRIP by DRIP

PARTNERSHIP FOR 21ST CENTURY SKILLS

Theme: Financial, Economic, Business, and Entrepreneurial Literacy

Skills: Critical Thinking and Problem Solving, Information Literacy, Creativity and Innovation, and Communication and Collaboration

Many corporations sell stock only through brokers, with a hefty minimum investment. However, many quality corporations offer direct stock plans (DSP). An individual share of stock can be purchased directly from the company with minimal or no fees and commissions. This makes investing more affordable for those with small amounts of money to invest.

Instead of receiving cash dividends, over one thousand companies offer direct reinvestment programs (DRIPS). DRIPS allow the investor to reinvest cash dividends by purchasing additional company stock. The investor can watch his or her shares and investment grow.

DSP and DRIPS are ideal for young people just starting to invest. With very little money, one can learn the value of investing through these programs.

APPLICATION

1. Using the Internet, find three companies that offer direct stock plans. List the names of the companies, the minimum initial purchase, the minimum purchase, the maximum purchase, and the fees, if any, to purchase the stock.
2. Using the Internet, research DSP and DRIPS. What are the conditions for a minor (someone under age 18) to purchase a share of stock?
3. Create a public service announcement using print or video to educate young investors about DSP and DRIPS. Be sure to include the names of at least three companies that offer these plans and that would also be familiar to students.

Analyzing Home Depot's financial statements

A corporation's board of directors decides the dividend policy for the corporation. Home Depot has paid a quarterly dividend since 1987. During fiscal years 2011–2012, Home Depot raised its quarterly dividend from $0.29 to $0.39 per share.

A ratio of interest to stockholders is the dividend yield. It is calculated as the dividend per share divided by the market price per share.

INSTRUCTIONS

1. Look at Home Depot's Consolidated Balance Sheets in Appendix B on page B-5 to determine the number of shares of common stock issued and outstanding as of February 3, 2013.
2. In fiscal year 2012, Home Depot's board of directors declared and paid dividends of $1.16 per share of common stock. Using the number of shares of common stock that were issued and outstanding at the end of fiscal year 2012, estimate the total dividends Home Depot would have paid that year.
3. Look at Home Depot's Consolidated Statements of Stockholders' Equity, on page B-8, and locate the dollar amount of cash dividends actually paid during fiscal year 2012. How does your amount of total dividends calculated in part (2) compare with the actual cash dividends paid? Why do you think the two amounts are different?
4. During fiscal year 2012, Home Depot's stock reached a high of $67.82 per share. Use this market price to determine the dividend yield for fiscal year 2012.

ANALYZING HOME DEPOT'S FINANCIAL STATEMENTS

Answers

1. Issued, 1.754 billion shares; outstanding, 1.484 billion shares.
2. Outstanding shares of 1.484 billion shares × $1.16 per share = $1.721 billion.
3. Total dividends paid were $1.743 billion during fiscal year 2012, more than the amount estimated. Dividends are paid on shares outstanding, which decreased from 1.537 billion to 1.484 billion shares. Based on this information, the average number of shares outstanding during fiscal year 2012 is estimated to be $1.503 billion ($1.743 billion dividends ÷ $1.16 dividends per share).
4. Dividends per share, $1.16, divided by the stock price, $67.82, results in a dividend yield of 1.71%.

Chapter 12 Accounting for Bonds

Scope & Sequence

	New	Review/Enrich
Introduction		
Introduce the Chapter		
Lesson 12-1: Bonds Payable Transactions		
Corporate Bonds Payable	✓	
Issuing Bonds at a Discount	✓	
Issuing Bonds at a Premium	✓	
Lesson 12-2: Paying Interest on Bonds		
Calculating Bond Interest	✓	
Paying Interest on Bonds Issued at a Discount	✓	
Paying Interest on Bonds Issued at a Premium	✓	
Lesson 12-3: Effect of Redeeming and Converting Bonds		
Retiring a Bond Issue	✓	
Calling a Bond Issue at a Loss	✓	
Accounting for Convertible Bonds	✓	
Lesson 12-4: Bond Investments		
Purchasing Bonds	✓	
Receiving Interest on Bonds Purchased at a Discount	✓	
Receiving Interest on Bonds Purchased at a Premium	✓	
Closure		

Enhancing Instruction

Features	Common Core Standards
• Accounting in the Real World: The U.S. Treasury	• ELAL—reading, media and technology
• Ethics in Action: Reporting Ethics Violations	• ELAL—reading, writing
• Think Like an Accountant: Financing a Takeover • Careers In Accounting: Tax Examiner/Collector	• Mathematics • ELAL—reading
• Financial Literacy: Superman and Savings Bonds • Why Accounting?: How Marketing Can Use Accounting Ratios	• ELAL—reading, writing, media and technology • Mathematics
• Explore Accounting • 21st Century Skills • Analyzing Home Depot's Financial Statements	• ELAL—reading • ELAL—reading, writing, media and technology • Mathematics

ELAL = English Language Arts & Literacy

Calculator: © iStockphoto.com/picstodisc; Paper: © iStockphoto.com/Qingwa

Practice and Assessment

Technology & Media	Teaching Strategies	Guided Practice	Independent Practice	Reteach/Enrich
• Instructor's Resource CD/Website: PowerPoint Slides Accounting Concepts • Online Working Papers • Transparency Master: Cash Receipts Journal (7-column)	• Visual/Spatial Learners • Interpersonal learners	• Terms Review • Audit Your Understanding • Work Together 12-1	• On Your Own 12-1 • Application Problem 12-1 • Formative Assessment, p. 344 • Online Working Papers	• Reteach, p. 345
• Instructor's Resource CD/Website: PowerPoint Slides Accounting Concepts • Online Working Papers • Transparency Master: Cash Payments Journal (5-column)	• Logical/Mathematical Learners	• Terms Review • Audit Your Understanding • Work Together 12-2	• On Your Own 12-2 • Application Problem 12-2 • Formative Assessment, p. 348 • Online Working Papers	• Reteach, p. 349
• Instructor's Resource CD/Website: PowerPoint Slides Accounting Concepts • Online Working Papers • Transparency Master: Cash Payments Journal (5-column)		• Terms Review • Audit Your Understanding • Work Together 12-3	• On Your Own 12-3 • Application Problem 12-3 • Formative Assessment, p. 353 • Online Working Papers	• Reteach, p. 354
• Instructor's Resource CD/Website: PowerPoint Slides Accounting Concepts • Online Working Papers • Transparency Masters: Cash Payments Journal (5-column), Cash Receipts Journal (7-column)	• Visual/Spatial Learners	• Term Review • Audit Your Understanding • Work Together 12-4	• On Your Own 12-4 • Application Problem 12-4 • Formative Assessment, p. 359 • Online Working Papers	• Reteach, p. 360
	• Common Core and Interdisciplinary Studies		• Mastery Problem 12-M • Study Guide 12 • Chapter 12 Test • Cognero Chapter 12	• Challenge Problem 12-C • Reteach, p. 363 • Recycling Problem 12-R

Introduce the Chapter

SET THE STAGE

GUIDING QUESTIONS

- Ask students what they would prefer, if given the option to purchase stock or bonds, and why.
- Ask students if they would prefer to receive interest payments every few months or receive a large lump sum in 10 years. Explain.
- Ask students if they have heard of mutual funds. Explain.
- Ask students if they have considered how companies save money needed to pay retirees. Explain.

PREVIEW CHAPTER OBJECTIVES

- Note that transactions for bond issues are covered, including the issue of bonds at a discount and at a premium.
- Instruct a student to read each chapter objective aloud.

PREVIEW ACCOUNTING TERMS

- Read each term aloud to verify its pronunciation for students.
- Point out terms or parts of terms that should already be familiar to most students, such as *bonds* and *interest rate*.

Chapter 12 Accounting for Bonds

LEARNING OBJECTIVES

After studying Chapter 12, in addition to defining key terms, you will be able to:

LO1 Explain why and how a corporation issues bonds.

LO2 Journalize the issue of bonds at a discount and at a premium.

LO3 Account for the payment of bond interest.

LO4 Journalize the retiring of a bond issue.

LO5 Account for the early redemption of a bond issue.

LO6 Explain how to account for convertible bonds.

LO7 Journalize the purchase and sale of an investment in bonds.

Calculator: © iStockphoto.com/picstodisc; Paper: © iStockphoto.com/Qingwa

© bikeriderlondon/Shutterstock.com

Accounting In The Real World

The U.S. Treasury

Background: © iStockphoto.com/chictype; Real World: © Richard Cavalleri/Shutterstock.com

Organizations of all kinds often need to raise large amounts of cash. The cash might be used for any number of reasons, from funding an expansion plan, to replacing aging equipment, or simply paying daily expenses during an economic downturn.

An organization that regularly needs to raise cash is the federal government of the United States of America. In recent history, the taxes and fees collected by the federal government have rarely exceeded its cash expenditures. The U.S. Department of the Treasury (the Treasury Department) is charged with the task of ensuring an adequate amount of cash is available to fund the federal government's daily operations. The Treasury Department borrows the cash from individual investors, investment funds, and pension funds all over the world. In return, the Treasury Department pays the investors interest for use of their cash.

The Treasury Department offers investors other ways of loaning money to the federal government. These financial instruments include savings bonds, Treasury bills, Treasury notes, Treasury inflation-protected securities (TIPS), and Treasury bonds. Each financial instrument offers a variety of interest payments, interest rates, and terms.

Accountants at the Treasury Department maintain detailed records of the Treasury's transactions and generate a variety of reports. Over 15 daily, monthly, and annual reports provide information on financial instrument activity, outstanding borrowings, and the public debt. The Treasury Department even reports a monthly statement of gifts received to reduce the public debt.

CRITICAL THINKING

Access the Internet site for the Treasury Department and find answers to the following questions:

1. How often is interest paid on a Treasury bill? Why would the Treasury Department issue a financial instrument with these terms?
2. How is interest paid on Treasury inflation-protected securities (TIPS)? How does the interest rate on the date the securities are issued compare with the rate on Treasury notes or bonds?

Source: http://www.treasurydirect.gov.

Key Terms

- bond
- bond issue
- face value
- stated interest rate
- effective interest rate
- bond amortization
- carrying value
- retiring a bond issue
- term bonds
- serial bonds
- call option
- callable bond
- institutional investors

Accounting In The Real World

Answers

1. No periodic interest payments are made. Instead, interest is paid when the Treasury bill is redeemed. For example, a Treasury bill that sold for $960 may be redeemed for $1,000. Thus, the investor earns $40 of interest when the Treasury bill is redeemed. Treasury bills are short-term investments of no more than one year. Paying the interest at the maturity date is more convenient and less costly than making periodic interest payments.
2. Interest is paid twice a year. The interest rate on TIPS on the date of issue is lower than the interest rate on Treasury notes or bonds. Investors are willing to accept a lower initial interest rate, knowing that the principal of the TIPS will be adjusted for future inflation.

LESSON

12-1

BRIDGE

- Point out that students have learned about selling capital stock to acquire additional capital. In this lesson, they will learn about going into debt to gain additional capital.

TEACHING RESOURCES

- **Instructor's Resource CD/Website:**
  PowerPoint Slides
  Accounting Concepts
- **Working Papers:**
  Teacher's Edition of the Working Papers for Lesson 12-1
  Online Working Papers
- **Transparency Master:**
  Cash Receipts Journal (7-column)

ENGAGE

- Display the financial pages of a newspaper to make students aware of the terms of corporate bonds.

PREVIEW

- Call on students to read the accounting terms and definitions introduced in this lesson: *bond, bond issue, face value,* and *stated interest rate*.
- Point out the learning objectives for this lesson.
- Direct students to read the headings in this lesson and to examine the illustrations.

INPUT

- Discuss the advantages and disadvantages of acquiring additional capital from the three sources: using retained earnings, issuing additional capital stock, and borrowing the funds.
- Direct students' attention to the table at the bottom of the page comparing capital stock and bonds as a source of capital.

LESSON

12-1 Bonds Payable Transactions

LO1 Explain why and how a corporation issues bonds.
LO2 Journalize the issue of bonds at a discount and at a premium.

Corporate Bonds Payable LO1

For a growing business, the capital needed to expand may come from three sources:

1. Using retained earnings.
2. Issuing additional capital stock.
3. Borrowing the funds.

A business's management team may find that capital needed for expansion could be accumulated from retained net income during the next five to ten years. However, the business may need the additional capital within the next year. A corporation's board of directors must decide whether to raise the needed capital by issuing additional stock or by borrowing the money.

An advantage of issuing stock is that the additional capital becomes part of a corporation's permanent capital. Permanent capital does not have to be returned to stockholders as long as the business continues to operate. Another advantage is that dividends do not have to be paid to stockholders unless the earnings are sufficient to warrant such payments. A disadvantage of issuing more stock to raise additional capital is that the ownership is spread over more shares and more owners.

An advantage of borrowing the additional capital is that stockholders' equity is not spread over additional shares of stock. A disadvantage is that interest must be paid on the loan, which decreases the net income. This decrease in net income decreases the amount available for dividends. Another disadvantage of borrowing additional capital is that the amount borrowed must be repaid in the future.

Large loans are sometimes difficult to obtain for short periods. Corporations frequently borrow needed capital with the provision that the loan be repaid several years in the future. Therefore, the loan can be paid out of future earnings accumulated over several years.

Large loans may also be difficult to obtain from one bank or one individual. A long-term promise to pay a specified amount on a specified date and to pay interest at stated intervals is called a **bond**. Bonds are similar to notes payable because both are written promises to pay. However, most notes payable are for one year or less, but bonds generally run for a long period of time, such as 5, 10, or 20 years. Also, bonds payable tend to be issued for larger amounts than notes payable.

All bonds representing the total amount of a loan are called a **bond issue**. A corporation usually sells an entire bond issue to a securities dealer, who sells individual bonds to the public.

COMPARISON OF CAPITAL STOCK AND BONDS AS A SOURCE OF CORPORATE CAPITAL

Decisions of how to obtain capital can impact a corporation's future significantly. A board of directors must consider the short- and long-term impact of the following qualities of capital stock and bonds:

	Capital Stock	Bonds
Status of security holder	Corporate owners	Creditors
Account classification	Stockholders' equity	Liability
Claim on corporate assets	Secondary claim	Primary claim
Nature of periodic payments	Dividends	Interest expense
Requirement to make periodic payments	Optional, subject to adequate net income and board approval	Required; payment of interest does not depend on net income
Length of access to capital	Permanent	Must be repaid to the bondholders on the bonds' maturity date

SETTING A BOND ISSUE PRICE

It can take several months for a company to issue bonds. The registration process begins when the company determines what type of security it will issue. Public accountants are hired to audit the information that will be included in the registration statement filed with the Securities and Exchange Commission. The amount to be paid to a bondholder at the bond maturity date is called the **face value**. The face value is also known as *par value*, *principal*, or *maturity value*. The rate of interest used to calculate periodic interest payments on a bond is called the **stated interest rate**.

As the registration process nears conclusion, the corporation will decide on the number, face value, interest rate, and term of the bonds. The company must then arrange for a securities dealer, known as an *underwriter*, to sell the bonds. This final process may require several weeks.

A corporation will attempt to assign a stated interest rate that approximates the current market rate of interest. That rate, however, rarely equals the market interest rate on the day the bonds are issued. Two factors cause this difference. Unlike market interest rates, the stated interest rate is often a rounded percentage, such as 6.0%, 6.5%, or 7.0%. During the final weeks of the registration process, market interest rates can be expected to change.

Investors will adjust the price they are willing to pay for the bond, based on the current market interest rate. If the market interest rate is above the stated interest rate, investors are not willing to pay full price for a bond that yields a below-market rate. Thus, the bond will be issued at a discount. However, if the market interest rate is below the stated interest rate, investors are willing to pay extra to earn an above-market rate. This bond will be issued at a premium.

Issuing Bonds at a Discount LO2

Credit Bonds Payable for the Face Value

CASH RECEIPTS JOURNAL — PAGE 13

				1	2	3	4	5	6	7
DATE	ACCOUNT TITLE	DOC. NO.	POST. REF.	GENERAL DEBIT	GENERAL CREDIT	ACCOUNTS RECEIVABLE CREDIT	SALES CREDIT	SALES TAX PAYABLE CREDIT	SALES DISCOUNT DEBIT	CASH DEBIT
20X1 July 1	Bonds Payable	R559			100 000 00					99 151 32
	Discount on Bonds Payable			848 68						

Debit the Difference to Discount on Bonds Payable

Debit Cash for the Bond Proceeds

A securities dealer purchases the bonds at a price that yields the market interest rate. As a result, the bonds are almost always issued for an amount above or below the bonds' face value. Regardless of the amount received, the face value of the bonds is credited to Bonds Payable. Bonds issued for an amount below the face value are accounted for using a contra account, Discount on Bonds Payable. Because it is a contra account to a liability account, Discount on Bonds Payable has a normal debit balance.

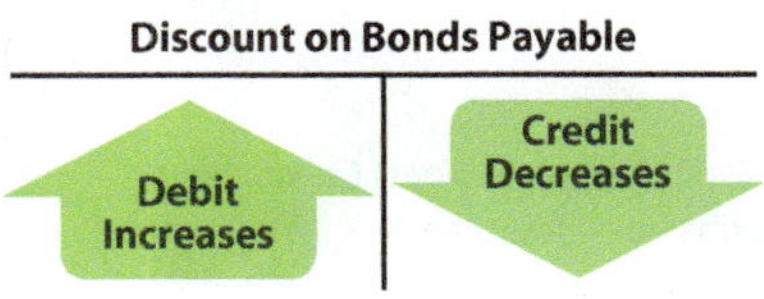

Forest Equipment issued bonds to finance the expansion of its store. The market interest rate on the bond issue date was above the bonds' stated interest rate.

July 1, 20X1. Received cash for 100 five-year, 6.0%, $1,000.00 face-value bonds, issued to yield 6.2%, $99,151.32. Receipt No. 559.

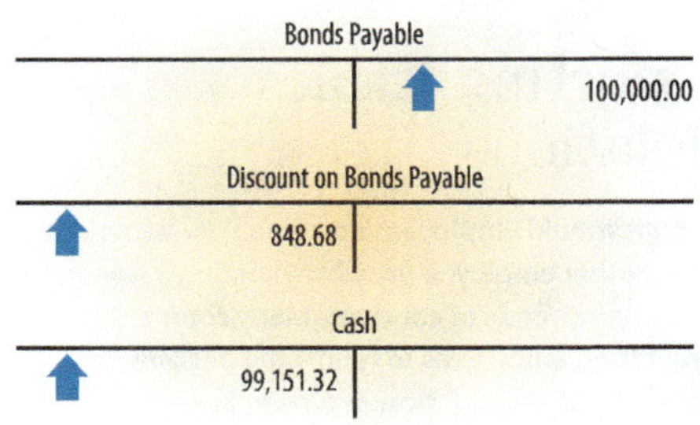

Bonds Payable is credited for $100,000.00, the face value of the bonds. Cash is debited for $99,151.32, the proceeds from the issuance of the bonds. The difference, $848.68, is debited to Discount on Bonds Payable.

INPUT

- Explain the process for setting a bond issue price.
- Point out that in spite of accurate processes to assign a stated interest rate approximating the current market rate of interest, seldom are bonds issued at the market rate due to fluctuations in the market and the amount of time it takes to complete the bond registration process.

TEACHING IDEA **Collect copies of financial statements from a newspaper to show students different municipalities, including schools, that are offering bonds for sale. Pass these around and discuss the terms of the bonds.**

INPUT

- Point out that Bonds Payable is credited for the face value amount, regardless of how much is received.
- Point out that bonds issued for an amount less than face value are accounted for in a contra account called Discount on Bonds Payable.

MODEL

Analyze the transaction

- Draw three blank T accounts on the board.
- Read the transaction statement.
- Ask students to analyze the transaction. Complete the T accounts as the information is provided.

Record the transaction

- Use the cash receipts journal transparency to illustrate the process for recording the entry or direct students to the illustration in the book.

DIFFERENTIATED INSTRUCTION

Visual/Spatial learners learn best by creating visual images using three-dimensional space. Ask students to write the following headings on poster board: Using Retained Earnings, Selling Capital Stock, and Issuing Bonds. Under each heading, write *Advantages* and *Disadvantages*. Ask students to list the *advantages* and *disadvantages* for each category of acquiring additional funds. For example, advantages for using retained earnings might include money not spent until saved; pay-as-you-go basis; and no interest or dividends to pay. Disadvantages might include too long of a wait to accumulate needed funds and funds needed immediately or in the near future.

Interpersonal learners will enjoy completing this activity with a partner.

INPUT

- Explain that when bonds are issued for an amount above the face value, they are sold at a premium.
- Emphasize again that Bonds Payable is credited for the face value amount, regardless of how much is received.

MODEL

Analyze the transaction

- Draw three blank T accounts on the board.
- Read the transaction statement.
- Ask students to analyze the transaction. Complete the T accounts as the information is provided.

Record the transaction

- Use the cash receipts journal transparency to illustrate the process for recording the entry or direct students to the illustration in the book.

ETHICS IN ACTION

Answers

1. The FedEx Alert Line is available 24/7 and is toll-free. It is available anywhere in the world where permitted by local laws. Trained operators who are not FedEx employees answer the Alert Line. The operators forward the information to the appropriate level of FedEx management, which may include the Legal, Security, Human Resources, and Internal Audit departments.
2. While answers may vary, the following is a possible example of a script that may be used for a hotline. "My name is [operator name]. Before you tell me anything, let me assure you that what you share with me today will remain confidential. Our system can't even track your phone number, so I have no idea where you are calling from. And I would suggest that you don't even say your name, where you work, or your position. Can I call you [any name] for today? [Name], do you have any questions before we talk about why you called?"

Issuing Bonds at a Premium

Credit Bonds Payable for the Face Value

CASH RECEIPTS JOURNAL — PAGE 7

	DATE		ACCOUNT TITLE	DOC. NO.	POST. REF.	GENERAL DEBIT (1)	GENERAL CREDIT (2)	ACCOUNTS RECEIVABLE CREDIT (3)	SALES CREDIT (4)	SALES TAX PAYABLE CREDIT (5)	SALES DISCOUNT DEBIT (6)	CASH DEBIT (7)	
1	20-- Apr.	1	Bonds Payable	R123			500 000 00					510 800 10	1
2			Premium on Bonds Payable				10 800 10						2
3													3

Credit the Difference to Premium on Bonds Payable

Debit Cash for the Bond Proceeds

A bond may be issued to yield an interest rate below the market rate. The proceeds from the issue will be greater than the face value of the bonds. Bonds issued for an amount above the face value are accounted for using the account Premium on Bonds Payable. This account has a normal credit balance.

TYP Corporation issued bonds to finance the purchase of a competing corporation. The market interest rate on the bond issue date was below the bonds' stated interest rate.

April 1. Received cash for 500 five-year, 6.0%, $1,000.00 face-value bonds, issued to yield 5.5%, $510,800.10. Receipt No. 123.

Bonds Payable is credited for $500,000.00, the face value of the bonds. Cash is debited for $510,800.10, the proceeds from the issuance of the bonds. The difference, $10,800.10, is credited to Premium on Bonds Payable.

Premium on Bonds Payable

Debit Decreases	Credit Increases

Bonds Payable

	500,000.00

Premium on Bonds Payable

	10,800.10

Cash

510,800.10	

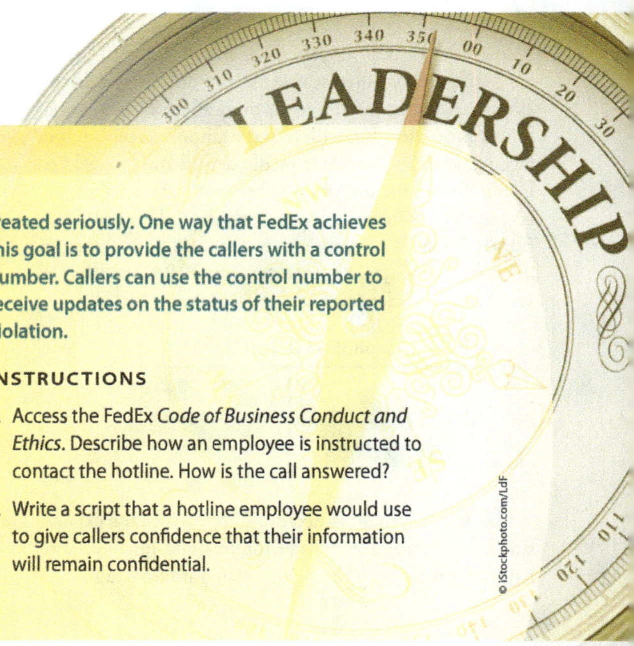

ETHICS IN ACTION

Reporting Ethics Violations

What should employees do when they witness another employee possibly violating a law or the company's code of conduct? Many companies instruct their employees to report the possible violation to an ethics officer or a compliance department. The company may have a phone number or "hotline" that allows an individual to provide confidential information regarding possible ethics violations.

For a hotline to be effective, employees must have confidence that their information is being treated seriously. One way that FedEx achieves this goal is to provide the callers with a control number. Callers can use the control number to receive updates on the status of their reported violation.

INSTRUCTIONS

1. Access the FedEx *Code of Business Conduct and Ethics*. Describe how an employee is instructed to contact the hotline. How is the call answered?
2. Write a script that a hotline employee would use to give callers confidence that their information will remain confidential.

© iStockphoto.com/LdF

FORMATIVE ASSESSMENT

- This is an ongoing process. Circulate around the classroom or lab, observing which students have problems with the assignments.
- Troubleshooting: Diagnose the kinds of problems students have with this section. Students may have difficulty understanding how to record premiums and discounts on bonds.
- Assess student understanding by checking solutions to Independent Practice assignments and noting their answers to the Terms Review and Audit Your Understanding questions.

End of Lesson Review

LO1 Explain why and how a corporation issues bonds.

LO2 Journalize the issue of bonds at a discount and at a premium.

Terms Review

bond

bond issue

face value

stated interest rate

Audit your understanding

1. What are two advantages of raising needed capital by issuing stock?
2. What is an advantage of raising additional capital by borrowing?
3. What is a disadvantage of borrowing additional capital?
4. What are three names for the face value of a bond?
5. What are two reasons why the stated interest rate of a bond will vary from the market interest rate?

Work together 12-1

Journalizing bond transactions

Journalize the following transactions. Page 7 of a cash receipts journal is provided in the *Working Papers*. Your instructor will guide you through the following examples.

Transactions:

July 1, 20X1. Received cash for 50 five-year, 7.0%, $5,000.00 face-value bonds, issued to yield 6.7%, $253,142.42. Receipt 291.

July 1, 20X6. Received cash for 600 five-year, 6.5%, $1,000.00 face-value bonds, issued to yield 6.6%, $595,658.06. Receipt 888.

On your own 12-1

Journalizing bond transactions

Journalize the following transactions. Page 8 of a cash receipts journal is provided in the *Working Papers*. Work independently to complete the following problem.

Transactions:

July 1, 20X1. Received cash for 40 five-year, 8.0%, $5,000.00 face-value bonds, issued to yield 8.25%, $197,984.83. Receipt 334.

July 1, 20X6. Received cash for 300 five-year, 7.5%, $1,000.00 face-value bonds, issued to yield 7.0%, $310,659.31. Receipt 986.

EXTENDED LEARNING

- Assign Accounting in the Real World on page 341.
- Assign Ethics in Action on page 344.

CHECK FOR UNDERSTANDING

Terms Review

- Call on students to define each term in the Terms Review. Definitions are given in the Glossary.

Audit Your Understanding

- Call on students to answer the Audit Your Understanding questions. Answers are given in Appendix D of the textbook.

GUIDED PRACTICE

Work Together

- Have students write the solution to the Work Together problem as you guide the class through the examples.
- Direct students to record the transactions in the cash receipts journal as you elicit participation in analyzing and recording the transactions.

INDEPENDENT PRACTICE

On Your Own

- Assign the On Your Own problem to be worked independently.
- Use the Formative Assessment techniques to diagnose student understanding.

Application Problem

- Assign Application Problem 12-1.

Online Working Papers

- Students can access the Lesson 12-1 problems using this software.

Website

- Direct students to the C21 Accounting companion website for additional practice and review opportunities.

RETEACH

- Ask a student to use T accounts to demonstrate issuing bonds at a discount.
- Ask another student to use T accounts to demonstrate issuing bonds at a premium.

CLOSURE

- Ask students to explain briefly the relationship between issuing a bond, face value, and the stated interest rate.

Essential Question

- Why would a company issue bonds when it could just sell more stock? (*Sample answers: Bonds do not add owners to the company; the obligation to the bondholder ends on the maturity date.*)

LESSON

12-2

BRIDGE

- Point out that students have already learned how to journalize issuing bonds at a premium and at a discount. In this lesson, they will learn how to pay interest on bonds.

TEACHING RESOURCES

- **Instructor's Resource CD/Website:** PowerPoint Slides Accounting Concepts
- **Working Papers:** Teacher's Edition of the Working Papers for Lesson 12-2 Online Working Papers
- **Transparency Master:** Cash Payments Journal (5-column)

ENGAGE

- Ask what incentives a company might provide to keep investors.
- Ask students if they receive any incentives from their bank to keep their account open.
- Ask students how frequently they receive an incentive from their bank.

PREVIEW

- Call on students to read the accounting terms and definitions introduced in this lesson: *effective interest rate, bond amortization*, and *carrying value*.
- Point out the learning objective for this lesson.
- Direct students to read the headings in this lesson and to examine the illustrations.

INPUT

- Direct students' attention to the math illustration at the bottom of the page to calculate the interest payment.
- Emphasize that a trustee is usually appointed to handle the details of paying each bondholder.
- Explain the difference between face value and carrying value.
- Explain bond amortization and review the amortization schedule, pointing out the effective interest rate and the meaning of the bond discount when the bonds mature.
- Direct students' attention to the math illustration toward the top of page 347 to calculate the interest expense.

LESSON

12-2 Paying Interest on Bonds

LO3 Account for the payment of bond interest.

Calculating Bond Interest LO3

Amortization Schedule

Face Value:	$100,000.00	Bond Proceeds:	$99,151.32
Stated Interest Rate:	6.0%	Effective Interest Rate:	6.2%
Term of Bonds:	5 years	Bond Discount:	$848.68
Interest Payments:	semiannual		

Period	Beginning Carrying Value	Interest Expense	Interest Payment	Amortization of Bond Discount	Ending Carrying Value
1	$99,151.32	$3,073.69	$3,000.00	$73.69	$ 99,225.01
2	99,225.01	3,075.98	3,000.00	75.98	99,300.99
3	99,300.99	3,078.33	3,000.00	78.33	99,379.32
4	99,379.32	3,080.76	3,000.00	80.76	99,460.08
5	99,460.08	3,083.26	3,000.00	83.26	99,543.34
6	99,543.34	3,085.84	3,000.00	85.84	99,629.18
7	99,629.18	3,088.50	3,000.00	88.50	99,717.68
8	99,717.68	3,091.25	3,000.00	91.25	99,808.93
9	99,808.93	3,094.08	3,000.00	94.08	99,903.01
10	99,903.01	3,096.99	3,000.00	96.99	100,000.00

Forest Equipment issued $100,000.00 of bonds with a stated interest rate of 6.0%. As with most bonds, Forest is required to pay semiannual interest payments. Forest pays the interest amount to a trustee, who handles the payments to each individual bondholder. The total payment is calculated using the face value of the bonds and the stated interest rate, as shown below.

Forest issued its bonds at an $848.68 discount. The stated interest rate of 6.0% was below the market interest rate on the date the bonds were issued. As a result, investors were not willing to pay the face value for the bonds. The discounted bonds were issued at a price that will earn investors a 6.2% return, the market interest rate on the issue date. The market interest rate at the time bonds are issued is called the **effective interest rate**. When the bonds are retired, the bondholders will receive $848.68 more than they paid for the bonds. This payment, equal to the discount, is the extra interest that enables the bondholders to earn an effective interest rate above the stated interest rate.

Face Value of Bonds	×	Stated Interest Rate	×	Time as Fraction of a Year	=	Interest Payment
$100,000.00	×	6.0%	×	1/2	=	$3,000.00

Generally accepted accounting principles require that a portion of the bond discount or premium be expensed over the term of the bonds. Reducing the amount of a bond discount or premium over time is called **bond amortization**. The face value of a bond adjusted for any unamortized discount or premium is called the **carrying value**.

Interest expense is calculated based on the carrying value of the bonds multiplied by the effective interest rate. The amount of the first semiannual interest expense is calculated below.

The amortization schedule on the previous page shows the changes in the amount of interest expense recognized each period. The amortization of the discount reduces the balance in Discount on Bonds Payable, thus increasing the carrying value of the bonds. The amount of interest expense on bonds issued at a discount will increase each year. At the maturity date of the bonds, the carrying value is equal to the face value of the bonds.

Carrying Value of Bonds	×	Effective Interest Rate	×	Time as Fraction of a Year	=	Interest Expense
$99,151.32	×	6.2%	×	1/2	=	$3,073.69

Paying Interest on Bonds Issued at a Discount

CASH PAYMENTS JOURNAL — PAGE 24

	DATE	ACCOUNT TITLE	CK. NO.	POST. REF.	1 GENERAL DEBIT	2 GENERAL CREDIT	3 ACCOUNTS PAYABLE DEBIT	4 PURCHASES DISCOUNT CREDIT	5 CASH CREDIT	
25	31	*Interest Expense*	521		3 073 69				3 000 00	25
26		*Discount on Bonds Payable*				73 69				26
27										27

Debit Interest Expense — Credit Discount on Bonds Payable for the Difference — Credit Cash

Forest Equipment issued its $100,000.00 bonds for $99,151.32. The discount of $848.68 will be amortized over the ten semiannual interest payments. The amortization schedule on the previous page provides the amounts to be recorded for each payment.

December 31, 20X1. Paid cash to trustee for first semiannual interest payment on bond issue, $3,000.00. Check No. 521.

Interest Expense

Pay. 3,073.69	

Discount on Bonds Payable

Bal. 848.68	Pay. 73.69
(New Bal. 774.99)	

Cash

	3,000.00

Interest Expense is debited for $3,073.69. Discount on Bonds Payable is credited for $73.69. Cash is credited for $3,000.00.

After the interest payment is posted, the new balance of Discount on Bonds Payable is $774.99. The new carrying value of the bonds, $99,225.01, is calculated as shown at the right. The new carrying value matches the ending carrying value for period 1, as shown in the amortization schedule.

Bonds Payable	–	Discount on Bonds Payable	=	Carrying Value of Bonds
$100,000.00	–	$774.99	=	$99,225.01

remember: The amount of interest paid on a bond is the same whether the bond is issued at a discount or a premium.

INPUT

- Explain that when interest is paid, the journal entry must show the amount paid as well as the discount amortized for each interest payment.
- Direct students' attention to the math illustration at the bottom of the page to calculate the carrying value of bonds after the discount.

MODEL

Analyze the transaction

- Draw three T accounts on the board.
- Read the transaction statement.
- Ask students to analyze the transaction. Complete the T accounts as the information is provided.

Record the transaction

- Use the transparency of a cash payments journal to illustrate the process for recording the entry in the journal.

DIFFERENTIATED INSTRUCTION

Logical/Mathematical learners enjoy reasoning and problem-solving activities. They enjoy learning through investigations. Provide students with note cards. Ask students to create different scenarios of transactions involving paying interest on bonds. Tell them to write the scenario on one side of the note card and the answer on the other side. Ask them to exchange note cards and solve the problems by journalizing the interest transactions correctly.

INPUT

- Explain that over time, the carrying value is reduced each period; as a result, the amount of interest expense declines each period.
- Point out that the difference between the interest payment and the interest expense is debited to the Premium on Bonds Payable account.

MODEL

Calculate excess amount

- Read the transaction statement.
- Use the math illustration on the page to explain the process for calculating the carrying amount, the interest expense, and the interest payment.
- Use the board to show how the Premium on Bonds Payable is calculated.
- Ask students to verify amounts with a calculator.

Analyze the transaction

- Draw three blank T accounts on the board.
- Ask a student to read the transaction statement.
- Ask students to analyze the transaction by answering these questions: Which accounts are affected? What is the classification of each account? Are they increased or decreased? Are they debited or credited? Complete the T accounts as the information is provided.

Record the transaction

- Use the cash payments journal transparency to illustrate the process for recording the entry in the journal.

Paying Interest on Bonds Issued at a Premium

Face Value of Bonds	+	Premium on Bonds Payable	=	Carrying Value of Bonds	
$500,000.00	+	$10,800.10	=	$510,800.10	← Calculate the Carrying Value

Carrying Value of Bonds	×	Effective Interest Rate	×	Time as Fraction of a Year	=	Interest Expense	
$510,800.10	×	5.5%	×	1/2	=	$14,047.00	← Calculate the Interest Expense

Face Value of Bonds	×	Stated Interest Rate	×	Time as Fraction of a Year	=	Interest Payment	
$500,000.00	×	6.0%	×	1/2	=	$15,000.00	← Calculate the Interest Payment

CASH PAYMENTS JOURNAL — PAGE 21

	DATE		ACCOUNT TITLE	CK. NO.	POST. REF.	1 GENERAL DEBIT	2 GENERAL CREDIT	3 ACCOUNTS PAYABLE DEBIT	4 PURCHASES DISCOUNT CREDIT	5 CASH CREDIT	
1	20-- Oct.	1	*Interest Expense*	867		14 047 00				15 000 00	1
2			*Premium on Bonds Payable*			9 53 00					2

Debit Interest Expense — Debit Premium on Bonds Payable for the Difference — Credit Cash

TYP Corporation issued $500,000.00 of bonds for $510,800.10, a premium of $10,800.10. The 6.0% stated-value bonds were issued to yield 5.5%. The interest expense is calculated using the current carrying value of the bonds, multiplied by the effective interest rate, as shown above.

October 1. Paid cash to trustee for first semiannual interest payment on bond issue, $15,000.00. Check No. 867.

Interest Expense

Debit	Credit
↑ Pay. 14,047.00	

Premium on Bonds Payable

Debit	Credit
↓ Pay. 953.00	Bal. 10,800.10
	(New Bal. 9,847.10)

Cash

Debit	Credit
	↓ Pay. 15,000.00

When the bonds are issued, their carrying value is the face value plus the premium, or $510,800.10. As shown in the partial amortization schedule below, the carrying value is reduced each period. As a result, the amount of interest expense declines each period.

Amortization Schedule

Face Value:	$500,000.00	Bond Proceeds:	$510,800.10
Stated Interest Rate:	6.0%	Effective Interest Rate:	5.5%
Term of Bonds:	5 years	Bond Premium:	$10,800.10
Interest Payments:	semiannual		

Period	Beginning Carrying Value	Interest Expense	Interest Payment	Amortization of Bond Premium	Ending Carrying Value
1	$510,800.10	$14,047.00	$15,000.00	$ (953.00)	$509,847.10
2	509,847.10	14,020.80	15,000.00	(979.20)	508,867.90
10	501,216.55	13,783.45	15,000.00	(1,216.55)	500,000.00

FORMATIVE ASSESSMENT

- This is an ongoing process. Circulate around the classroom or lab, observing which students have problems with the assignments.
- Troubleshooting: Diagnose the kinds of problems students have with this lesson. Students may have difficulty remembering the differences between accounting for bonds issued at a premium and bonds issued at a discount.
- Assess student understanding by checking solutions to Independent Practice assignments and noting their answers to the Terms Review and Audit Your Understanding questions.

End of Lesson Review

LO3 Account for the payment of bond interest.

Terms Review

effective interest rate

bond amortization

carrying value

Audit your understanding

1. What is the formula for calculating periodic interest expense on a bond?
2. How does the effective interest rate impact the amount of interest paid on bonds with semiannual interest payments?
3. How does the amount of interest expense change over the term of a bond issued at a discount?
4. How does the amount of the carrying value change over the term of a bond issued at a premium?

Work together 12-2

Journalizing bond interest payments

Journalize each transaction completed during the current year. Round calculated amounts to two decimal places. Page 20 of a cash payments journal is provided in the *Working Papers*. Your instructor will guide you through the following examples.

Transactions:

June 30. Paid cash to trustee for the semiannual interest payment on a $300,000.00, 6.0% bond issue having a carrying value of $296,190.63 and a 6.3% effective interest rate. Check No. 654.

Dec. 31. Paid cash to trustee for the semiannual interest payment on a $500,000.00, 6.5% bond issue having a carrying value of $506,365.13 and a 6.2% effective interest rate. Check No. 776.

On your own 12-2

Journalizing bond interest payments

Journalize each transaction completed during the current year. Round calculated amounts to two decimal places. Page 12 of a cash payments journal is provided in the *Working Papers*. Work independently to complete the following problem.

Transactions:

June 30. Paid cash to trustee for the semiannual interest payment on a $400,000.00, 7.0% bond issue having a carrying value of $396,690.07 and a 7.2% effective interest rate. Check No. 543.

Dec. 31. Paid cash to trustee for the semiannual interest payment on a $300,000.00, 6.0% bond issue having a carrying value of $303,868.15 and a 5.7% effective interest rate. Check No. 622.

CHECK FOR UNDERSTANDING

Terms Review

- Call on students to define each term in the Terms Review. Definitions are given in the Glossary.

Audit Your Understanding

- Call on students to answer the Audit Your Understanding questions. Answers are given in Appendix D of the textbook.

GUIDED PRACTICE

Work Together

- Have students write the solution to the Work Together problem as you guide the class through the examples.
- Direct students to journalize bond interest payments in the cash payments journal as you elicit participation in analyzing and recording the transactions.

INDEPENDENT PRACTICE

On Your Own

- Assign the On Your Own problem to be worked independently.
- Use the Formative Assessment techniques to diagnose student understanding.

Application Problem

- Assign Application Problem 12-2.

Online Working Papers

- Students can access the Lesson 12-2 problems using this software.

RETEACH

- Ask a student to explain an amortization table and the relationship between the beginning carrying amount and the ending carrying amount.
- Ask a student to draw three T accounts on the board and to explain how to pay interest on bonds issued at a discount. Ask the class to provide a sample transaction.
- Ask a student to draw three T accounts on the board and to explain how to pay interest on bonds issued at a premium. Ask the class to provide a sample transaction.

CLOSURE

- Ask students to prepare a list of all new accounts presented in this lesson and the definition or purpose of each account.
- Ask students to draw T accounts for each new account under the appropriate heading: Assets, Liabilities, or Stockholders' Equity.
- Ask students to place a + or − in the appropriate increase or decrease side on each account.

Essential Question

- Why is the market rate of interest different from the stated rate of interest? (*The market rate of interest fluctuates based on internal and external factors, such as global events and perceptions. The stated rate of interest is the rate promised for the life of the bond and promised to the bondholder when the bond was purchased.*)

LESSON

12-3 Effect of Redeeming and Converting Bonds

LO4 Journalize the retiring of a bond issue.
LO5 Account for the early redemption of a bond issue.
LO6 Explain how to account for convertible bonds.

Retiring a Bond Issue LO4

CASH PAYMENTS JOURNAL PAGE 13

	DATE		ACCOUNT TITLE	CK. NO.	POST. REF.	1 GENERAL DEBIT	2 GENERAL CREDIT	3 ACCOUNTS PAYABLE DEBIT	4 PURCHASES DISCOUNT CREDIT	5 CASH CREDIT	
1	20X6 July	1	Bonds Payable	954		100 000 00				100 000 00	1
2											2
3											3

Debit Bonds Payable — Credit Cash

When Forest's bonds are due, the corporation issues a single check to a trustee for the total maturity value of the bonds. The trustee writes checks to individual bondholders. Paying the amounts owed to bondholders for a bond issue is called **retiring a bond issue**.

July 1, 20X6. Retired a bond issue at its face value, $100,000.00. Check No. 954.

Bonds Payable	
7/1/06 Retire 100,000.00	7/1/01 Issue 100,000.00
(New Bal. zero)	

Cash	
	7/1/06 Retire 100,000.00

Bonds Payable is debited for $100,000.00, the total amount of the bond issue. Cash is credited for $100,000.00. After this entry is posted, Bonds Payable has a zero balance.

All of Forest's bond issue matures on the same date. Bonds that all mature on the same date are called **term bonds**. Sometimes portions of a bond issue mature on different dates. Portions of a bond issue that mature on different dates are called **serial bonds**. For example, a 10-year bond issue with one-tenth of the bonds maturing every year is a serial bond issue. An advantage of serial bonds is that interest does not have to be paid on the total bond issue for the total 10 years.

Calling a Bond Issue at a Loss LO5

A corporation can benefit from having the legal right to repurchase outstanding bonds. The right of a corporation to repurchase its security for a specified price is called a **call option**. A bond that can be called before its maturity date is called a **callable bond**.

A corporation sets the stated interest rate of a bond issue to approximate the current market interest rates. Without a call option, the corporation is obligated to pay the stated interest rate for the term of the bond. If market interest rates increase, the corporation benefits

LESSON 12-3

BRIDGE

- Point out that students have learned how to issue and pay interest on bonds. In this lesson, they will learn how to redeem bonds and convert bonds to common stock.

TEACHING RESOURCES

- **Instructor's Resource CD/Website:** PowerPoint Slides; Accounting Concepts
- **Working Papers:** Teacher's Edition of the Working Papers for Lesson 12-3; Online Working Papers
- **Transparency Master:** Cash Payments Journal (5-column)

ENGAGE

- Ask students if they ever owned savings bonds. Ask if all savings bonds mature at the same time.

PREVIEW

- Call on students to read the accounting terms and definitions introduced in this lesson: *retiring a bond issue, term bonds, serial bonds, call option,* and *callable bond.*
- Point out the learning objectives for this lesson.
- Direct students to read the headings in this lesson and to examine the illustrations.

INPUT

- Point out that a trustee oversees the payment to the individual bondholders when the bonds are due.
- Stress that bonds maturing on a single date are called term bonds.
- Ask a student to contrast term bonds with serial bonds. (*A corporation pays off a portion of a serial bond every year, whereas with a term bond, a corporation waits until the maturity date to pay off the entire bond issue.*)

MODEL

Analyze the transaction

- Draw two blank T accounts on the board. Record the previous balances in the T accounts.
- Ask a student to read the transaction statement.
- Ask students to analyze the transaction by answering these questions: Which accounts are affected? What is the classification of each account? Are they increased or decreased? Are they debited or credited? Complete the T accounts as the information is provided.
- Record these amounts in the T accounts.
- Use the cash payments journal transparency to illustrate the process for recording the entry in the journal or refer students to the illustration at the top of the page.

Debit Bonds Payable

CASH PAYMENTS JOURNAL — PAGE 9

	DATE		ACCOUNT TITLE	CK. NO.	POST. REF.	1 GENERAL DEBIT	2 GENERAL CREDIT	3 ACCOUNTS PAYABLE DEBIT	4 PURCHASES DISCOUNT CREDIT	5 CASH CREDIT	
1	20-- July	1	Bonds Payable	622		500 000 00				525 000 00	1
2			Discount on Bonds Payable				20 000 00				2
3			Loss on Redemption of Bonds			45 000 00					3

Debit Loss on Redemption of Bonds — Credit Discount on Bonds Payable — Credit Cash

from having issued bonds at lower rates. If current market interest rates fall, the corporation is burdened by having to pay higher-than-market interest rates.

A call option protects a corporation from declines in market interest rates. Chandler Corporation issued $500,000.00 of 10.5%, 20-year callable bonds. Five years later, the market interest rate dropped to 7.0%. Thus, Chandler is paying $17,500.00 more in interest each year than it would if it could pay current interest rates, as shown below.

Chandler has decided to call its bond issue. The bond issue requires bondholders be paid 105% of the bonds' face value. Thus, Chandler will have to pay $525,000.00 to call the bonds.

The redemption amount is almost always above the carrying value, resulting in a loss. The loss is recorded in Loss on Redemption of Bonds. This account is classified as an Other Expense on the income statement.

Loss on Redemption of Bonds

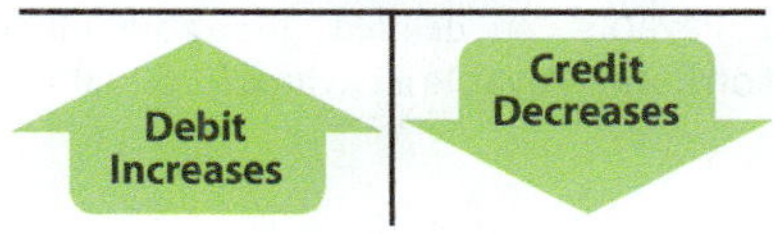

	Face Value of Bond Issue	×	Interest Rate	=	Interest Payment
Market rate at issue date	$500,000.00	×	10.5%	=	$52,500.00
Current market rate	500,000.00	×	7.0%	=	35,000.00
					$17,500.00

THINK LIKE AN ACCOUNTANT

Financing a Takeover

Kelsay Corporation is the fourth largest security service provider in its region. Over the past few years, the market has been consolidating, meaning that smaller corporations are purchased by larger competitors. Kelsay's management believes that market forces and competition will only allow three businesses to survive. As a result, it is considering the bold move of acquiring one of its larger competitors.

Kelsay's board has a proposal to generate the $7.5 million necessary to buy one of its competitors. The proposal calls for a 10%, 5-year, $2,000,000 bank note, issuing 60,000 shares of 6%, $50.00 preferred stock, and issuing100,000 shares of common stock at the current market price of $25.00. The proposal does not include the issuance of any bonds.

Three board members subsequently submitted different proposals:

Proposal A: Obtain a 12%, 6-year, $2,000,000 bank note and issue 220,000 shares of common stock.

Proposal B: Obtain a 9%, 3-year, $500,000 bank note and issue 5,000 of 7%, 20-year, $1,000 bonds, 10,000 shares of preferred stock, and 60,000 shares of common stock.

Proposal C: Issue 5,000 bonds and 50,000 shares of preferred stock.

OPEN THE SPREADSHEET TLA_CH12

The workbook contains a detailed 10-year projection of Kelsay's cash flows from purchasing its competitor. Follow the steps on the Instructions tab to prepare a chart. Answer these questions:

1. Which of the four proposals results in the highest total projected income available to common stockholders?
2. Prepare a statement for the board of directors, explaining the results of the analysis.

INPUT

- Explain that corporations can have the legal right to repurchase outstanding bonds.
- Point out that having a call option protects the corporation from declines in market interest rates.
- Stress that the redemption value is usually above the carrying value.

THINK LIKE AN ACCOUNTANT

Students are provided with a completed analysis for determining the projected 10-year income from the purchase of the competitor. Using Excel's Scenario Manager tool, students prepare an analysis of the projected results of the four alternatives. The Define Name tool is used to assign meaningful names to the values included in the scenario summary.

Answers

1. Proposal A yields the highest projected income of $2,464,499 in total and $3.24 for each common share.
2. Answers will vary. Each of the proposals generates the required $7.5 million of capital necessary to purchase the competitor. Proposal A generates the largest proportion of capital through the issuance of common stock. This alternative requires the smallest amount of interest and preferred dividend payments. The result is that a large projected amount of income is available to the common stockholders.

MODEL

Calculate a loss on redemption

- Read the transaction statement.
- Use the math illustration on page 352 to explain the process for calculating the redemption amount and the loss on redemption.
- Ask students to verify amounts with a calculator.

Analyze and record the transaction

- Draw four blank T accounts on the board. Write the previous balance for Bonds Payable and Discount on Bonds Payable from the issuance of the bond.
- Ask a student to read the transaction statement.
- Ask students to analyze the transaction by answering these questions: Which accounts are affected? What is the classification of each account? Are they increased or decreased? Are they debited or credited? Complete the T accounts as the information is provided.
- Record these amounts on the T accounts.
- Use the cash payments journal transparency to illustrate the process for recording the entry in the journal or refer students to the illustration at the top of page 351.

INPUT

- Explain that investors may pay more for a bond issue that has a conversion option.
- Point out that a conversion option allows bondholders to elect to convert bonds to common stock.
- Direct students to the math illustration that demonstrates calculating the conversion price.
- Stress that GAAP requires that the bonds be recorded at face value.
- Point out that IFRS recognize the conversion option as a contribution to stockholders' equity when the transaction is recorded.

July 1. Chandler Corporation redeemed its $500,000.00 bond issue with a call option of 105%, $525,000.00. The bonds have a carrying value of $480,000.00. Check 622.

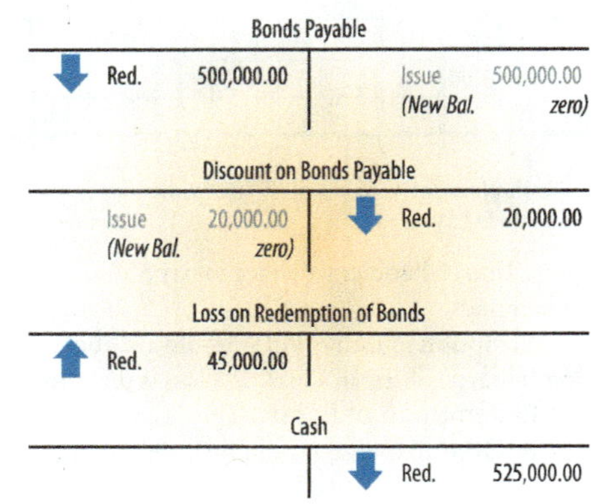

Bonds Payable is debited for $500,000.00. Discount on Bonds Payable is credited for $20,000.00. Cash is credited for $525,000.00. The difference, $45,000.00, is debited to Loss on Redemption of Bonds.

Chandler is willing to incur a loss of $45,000.00 in the current year to eliminate the annual $17,500.00 overpayment of interest for the remaining 15 years of the bond term.

The redemption of a bond issue with a premium would be journalized using similar steps. The entry would include a debit to Premium on Bonds Payable.

Face Value of Bond Issue	×	Call Option	=	Redemption Amount
$500,000.00	×	105%	=	$525,000.00

Redemption Amount	–	Carrying Value of Bond Issue	=	Loss on Redemption
$525,000.00	–	$480,000.00	=	$45,000.00

Accounting for Convertible Bonds LO6

Similar to preferred stock, bonds can be issued with a conversion option. If the market price of the corporation's common stock rises above the conversion price, bondholders may elect to convert their bonds to common stock. Investors are willing to pay more for a bond issue that has a conversion option. As a result, the conversion option reduces the corporation's interest expense.

Bennett Corporation needed to raise $800,000.00 of capital to finance a major expansion. The corporation was relatively young and had only become profitable in the past year. As a result, management knew that it would have to offer investors additional incentives to purchase its bonds.

Bennett elected to issue 800, $1,000.00, 7.5%, 10-year convertible bonds at a premium, $820,000.00. The bonds have a conversion rate of 20 shares of common stock for each bond. Thus, the conversion price is $50.00.

Par Value of Bonds	÷	Conversion Ratio	=	Conversion Price
$1,000.00	÷	20	=	$50.00

Prior to issuing the bonds, Bennett's underwriter projected that the bonds would be sold at $750,000.00, which is a $50,000.00 discount without the conversion option. Thus, investors were willing to pay $70,000.00 more for the bonds with the conversion option.

GENERALLY ACCEPTED ACCOUNTING PRINCIPLES

As illustrated earlier in the chapter, generally accepted accounting principles require the bonds to be recorded at face value, $800,000.00, with the premium being recorded in Premium on Bonds Payable. The following journal entry illustrates the issuance of a convertible bond at a premium:

Account	Debit	Credit
Cash	820,000.00	
Bonds Payable		800,000.00
Premium on Bonds Payable		20,000.00

INTERNATIONAL FINANCIAL REPORTING STANDARDS

IFRS account for bond issuance transactions differently. IFRS recognize the estimated value of the conversion option. The estimated value of the bonds without the conversion option is recorded in Bonds Payable. The estimated value of the conversion option is recorded in a stockholders' equity account, Conversion Option. IFRS consider the value of the conversion option to be a contribution to stockholders' equity.

Account	Debit	Credit
Cash	820,000.00	
Bonds Payable		750,000.00
Conversion Option (Stockholders' Equity)		70,000.00

Careers In Accounting

Review a career as a tax examiner/collector.

Careers In Accounting

Olguita Mendez

TAX EXAMINER/COLLECTOR

© Andre_Popov/Shutterstock.com

Olguita Mendez works for the Internal Revenue Service (IRS) as a tax examiner. She has held this position since she graduated from college three years ago with a degree in accounting. Her main activity in this position is to verify the accuracy of tax returns. When she first started, she focused on the tax returns of individuals. In the last year, she has been working on business tax returns.

In her position, Ms. Mendez must have a good understanding of the federal tax code. She had extensive training when she was first hired by the IRS, and she is required to attend classes every year in order to stay current.

When verifying a tax return, Ms. Mendez may find that the return is not complete. A document, a supplemental schedule, or a signature may be missing. In that case, she corresponds with the taxpayer or business, seeking to obtain the missing information or document. If an error is found, she will correct the error and recalculate the taxes due, again contacting the taxpayer to request the amount due.

Most of Ms. Mendez's time is spent in a local office of the IRS. Occasionally, she finds a return that contains questionable data. She then may inform the taxpayer that she will be performing an audit. Audits are usually performed in the home of an individual taxpayer or in the office of a representative of a business.

Although Ms. Mendez enjoys the challenges of her job, she is training to be a tax collector. A tax collector contacts individuals and businesses who owe back taxes and negotiates a plan for the payment of these taxes. A tax collector almost exclusively works out in the field, in contact with taxpayers and businesses.

Salary: The median wage for tax examiners is $50,440.

Qualifications: Most positions require training in a vocational school or an associate's degree. A four-year degree in accounting is helpful.

Occupational Outlook: The growth for tax examiner positions is projected to be slower than average (3% to 9%) for the period from 2010 to 2020.

Source: www.onetonline.org.

© iStockphoto.com/Mlenny

FORMATIVE ASSESSMENT

- This is an ongoing process. Circulate around the classroom or lab, observing which students have problems with the assignments.
- Troubleshooting: Diagnose the kinds of problems students have with this lesson. Students may have difficulty understanding the difference between redeeming and converting bonds.
- Assess student understanding by checking solutions to Independent Practice assignments and noting their answers to the Terms Review and Audit Your Understanding questions.

CHECK FOR UNDERSTANDING

Terms Review

- Call on students to define each term in the Terms Review. Definitions are given in the Glossary.

Audit Your Understanding

- Call on students to answer the Audit Your Understanding questions. Answers are given in Appendix D of the textbook.

GUIDED PRACTICE

Work Together

- Have students write the solution to the Work Together problems as you guide the class through the examples.
- Direct students to journalize the redemption and call of a bond issue as you elicit participation in analyzing and recording the transactions.

INDEPENDENT PRACTICE

On Your Own

- Assign the On Your Own problem to be worked independently.
- Use the Formative Assessment techniques to diagnose student understanding.

Application Problem

- Assign Application Problem 12-3.

Online Working Papers

- Students can access the Lesson 12-3 problems using this software.

RETEACH

- Ask students to use T accounts to record the retirement of a bond issue.
- Ask students to create an original bond issue transaction statement that you write on the board.
- Ask another student to analyze the transaction using T accounts.
- Ask a student to use T accounts to show calling a bond at a loss.
- Ask a student to explain convertible bonds.

CLOSURE

- Ask students to summarize briefly the retirement of bonds, accounting for the early redemption of a bond, and accounting for convertible bonds.

End of Lesson Review

LO4 Journalize the retiring of a bond issue.

LO5 Account for the early redemption of a bond issue.

LO6 Explain how to account for convertible bonds.

Terms Review

retiring a bond issue
term bonds
serial bonds
call option
callable bond

Audit your understanding

1. What is the primary difference between a term bond and a serial bond?
2. What would encourage a corporation to call a bond issue?
3. What is the conversion price of a $5,000.00 bond having a conversion ratio of 25?
4. A corporation issues $600,000.00 of convertible bonds for $610,000.00. The underwriters projected that the bonds would be sold for $585,000.00, until the corporation added a conversion option. What amount should be recorded in Bonds Payable, using GAAP? IFRS?

Work together 12-3

Redeeming and calling a bond issue

Journalize each transaction completed during the current year. Page 6 of a cash payments journal is provided in the *Working Papers*. Your instructor will guide you through the following examples.

Transactions:

Apr.	1.	Retired a bond issue at its face value, $250,000.00. Check No. 558.
July	1.	Redeemed an $800,000.00 bond issue with a call option of 103%. The bonds have a carrying value of $765,000.00. Check No. 740.
Oct.	1.	Redeemed a $600,000.00 bond issue with a call option of 105%. The bonds have a carrying value of $610,000.00. Check No. 941.

On your own 12-3

Redeeming and calling a bond issue

Journalize each transaction completed during the current year. Page 10 of a cash payments journal is provided in the *Working Papers*. Work independently to complete the following problem.

Transactions:

July	1.	Retired a bond issue at its face value, $200,000.00. Check No. 621.
Oct.	1.	Redeemed a $700,000.00 bond issue with a call option of 105%. The bonds have a carrying value of $732,000.00. Check No. 842.
Nov.	1.	Redeemed a $600,000.00 bond issue with a call option of 106%. The bonds have a carrying value of $584,000.00. Check No. 969.

Essential Question

- Why would I want to call bonds and incur a loss? (*Calling a bond gives the issuer an opportunity to respond to lower interest rates by refinancing the debt at a lower rate of interest.*)

EXTENDED LEARNING

- Assign Think Like an Accountant on page 351.
- Review Careers in Accounting on page 353.

LESSON

12-4 Bond Investments

LO7 Journalize the purchase and sale of an investment in bonds.

Purchasing Bonds LO7

CASH PAYMENTS JOURNAL — PAGE 7

	DATE		ACCOUNT TITLE	CK. NO.	POST. REF.	1 GENERAL DEBIT	2 GENERAL CREDIT	3 ACCOUNTS PAYABLE DEBIT	4 PURCHASES DISCOUNT CREDIT	5 CASH CREDIT	
1	20-- July	1	Investment Securities	754		24 7 8 7 75				24 7 8 7 75	1
2											2
3											3

Debit Investment Securities — Credit Cash

A corporation uses an underwriter to sell its bonds to the public. The underwriter can sell the bonds to individual investors or to other corporations. However, most bonds are sold to organizations that manage the investments of individual investors. These organizations are called **institutional investors**. Mutual funds and pension plans are examples of institutional investors.

In an effort to maximize the return of its investments, an institutional investor will generally purchase a variety of investments. Short-term investments usually consist of capital stock. Long-term investments usually consist of capital stock and bonds. Bonds tend to provide the institutional investor with a stable and predictable return on its investment.

A bond issued at a discount or premium is also purchased at a discount or premium. Bonds purchased by an institutional investor are recorded in Investment Securities. Unlike the issuing corporation, the buyer does not record the discount or premium in a separate account.

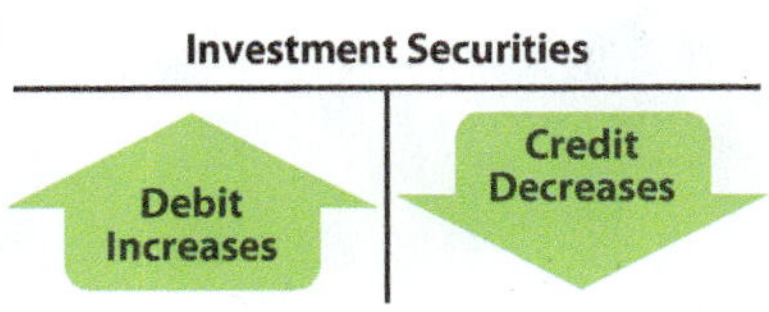

On July 1, Forest Equipment issued 100, five-year, 6.0%, $1,000.00 face-value bonds for $99,151.32. Thus, each bond was issued for $991.51 ($99,151.32 ÷ 100 bonds). The Albreck Investment Fund purchased 25 of Forest's bonds for $24,787.75 ($991.51 × 25 bonds). The fund intends to hold the bonds for several years.

July 1. The Albreck Investment Fund purchased 25 of Forest Equipment's $1,000 face-value bonds at $991.51 each. Check No. 754.

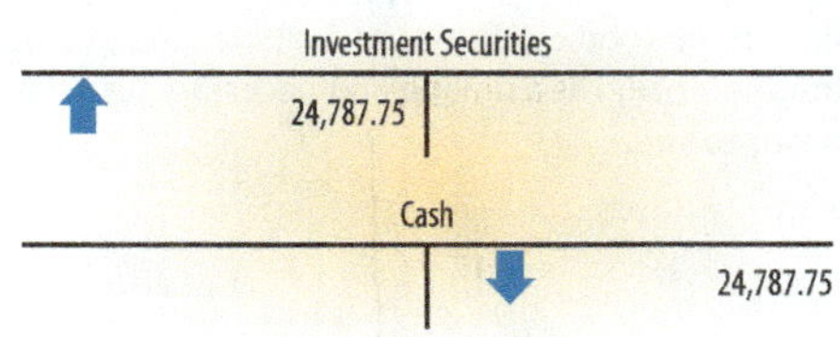

Investment Securities is debited for $24,787.75, the total amount paid for the bonds. Cash is credited for $24,787.75.

The market price of capital stock can change significantly over a short period of time. In contrast, a change in the market price of bonds tends to be more gradual. As a result, an institutional investor is unlikely to make a short-term investment in bonds.

LESSON 12-4

BRIDGE

- Point out that students have already learned about selling bonds. In this lesson, they will learn how to account for investing in bonds as the buyer of the bonds.

TEACHING RESOURCES

- **Instructor's Resource CD/Website:** PowerPoint Slides; Accounting Concepts
- **Working Papers:** Teacher's Edition of the Working Papers for Lesson 12-4; Online Working Papers
- **Transparency Masters:** Cash Payments Journal (5-column); Cash Receipts Journal (7-column)

ENGAGE

- Ask students if they realize that some companies buy bonds as investments to help fund retirement packages for their employees.

PREVIEW

- Call on a student to read the accounting term and definition introduced in this lesson: *institutional investors*.
- Point out the learning objective for this lesson.
- Direct students to read the headings in this lesson and to examine the illustrations.

INPUT

- Explain that institutional investors are organizations that purchase a variety of investments, such as capital stock and bonds.
- Point out that the buyer does not record the discount or premium.
- Explain that investors are unlikely to make a short-term investment in bonds because bond market price changes tend to be more gradual than those of capital stock.

MODEL

Analyze and record the transaction

- Draw two blank T accounts on the board.
- Ask students to read the transaction statement.
- Ask students to analyze the transaction.
- Use the cash payments journal transparency to illustrate the process for recording the entry in the journal.

FINANCIAL LITERACY

Answers

1. You can access the website www.treasurydirect.gov/forms/mar0023.pdf to see a comparison of the two bonds. Some answers might include the following: Series I bonds are different because they can be purchased with federal tax refunds. Series I can be purchased electronically or in paper form. Series EE earn a fixed rate of interest. Series I bonds ensure that you are earning interest above inflation.
2. Advertising methods may vary. However, all should be creative and persuasive and include at least three advantages of buying bonds, such as no state or local taxes on the interest earned when cashing in a savings bond at retirement or no age-related withdrawal penalties when cashing in a bond prior to retirement.
3. Answers will vary, but might include that the War Bond campaign allowed Americans to have a moral and financial stake in the war.

FINANCIAL LITERACY

Superman and Savings Bonds

Paying for the American Revolutionary War was the start of the country's debt. To help the government pay for World War I, Americans bought *Liberty Bonds.* In 1935, *U.S. Savings Bonds* were first sold. These bonds were designed so that the owners could *lend* money to the government and be paid interest for the use of their money. During World War II, U.S. Savings bonds became known as *War Bonds*. After September 11, 2001, U.S. Savings Bonds were sold as *Patriot Bonds* to help fight the war on global terrorism.

Savings bonds can be owned by anyone, including children, and are unique because they cannot be sold by brokers or dealers to other people in the secondary market. Initially, savings bonds could be purchased at financial institutions and through the mail. Smart investors would store their savings bonds in a safe place, such as a safe deposit box, until the bonds matured. In 2012, the Treasury Department discontinued the practice of selling paper savings bonds. They can be purchased through the U.S. Government Treasury Direct website, making it easier for individuals to loan money to the federal government.

Savings bonds are purchased at face value and can be bought for as little as $25. They are often referred to as an "All American Investment" because they are an easy way to save money safely and receive a low interest rate. In addition, they are considered very safe, since they are "backed by the full faith and credit of the U.S. Government."

ACTIVITIES

1. There are two different types of U.S. Savings Bonds. The most common is the Series EE. There is also another, called the Series I Bond. Using the library or the Internet, research the differences. Then, compose a letter to a classmate, comparing and contrasting Series EE and Series I Savings Bonds available for purchase.
2. Different media have been used over the years to persuade people to buy bonds. Go to http://www.treasurydirect.gov/kids/art/art.htm and view some of the posters, newspaper ads, and commercials used by the government. Choose and create an advertising medium to convince your classmates to buy savings bonds today. Research at least three advantages of buying bonds, and be sure to use these advantages as well as creativity and a persuasive tone in your advertisement.
3. Many Hollywood celebrities participated in bond drives during World War II. Many think of the War Bond campaign as a unique and necessary fusion of nationalism and consumerism. Explain what this means to you.

Source: www.treasurydirect.gov.

© iStockphoto.com/Norebbo

Receiving Interest on Bonds Purchased at a Discount

Carrying Value of Bonds	×	Effective Interest Rate	×	Time as Fraction of a Year	=	Interest Revenue
$24,787.75	×	6.2%	×	1/2	=	$768.42 ← Calculate the Interest Revenue

Face Value of Bonds	×	Stated Interest Rate	×	Time as Fraction of a Year	=	Interest Payment
$25,000.00	×	6.0%	×	1/2	=	$750.00 ← Calculate the Interest Payment

Credit Interest Revenue

CASH RECEIPTS JOURNAL — PAGE 1

	DATE	ACCOUNT TITLE	DOC. NO.	POST. REF.	1 GENERAL DEBIT	2 GENERAL CREDIT	3 ACCOUNTS RECEIVABLE CREDIT	4 SALES CREDIT	5 SALES TAX PAYABLE CREDIT	6 SALES DISCOUNT DEBIT	7 CASH DEBIT	
1	20-- Jan. 4	*Interest Revenue*	R678			768 42					750 00	1
2		*Investment Securities*			18 42							2
3												3

Debit the Difference to Investment Securities

Debit Cash for the Interest Payment

Forest Equipment issued its 6.0% bonds to yield 6.2%. The calculation of the first period's semiannual interest payment is shown above. The interest revenue is calculated using the current carrying value of the bonds multiplied by the effective interest rate.

January 4. The Albreck Investment Fund received the semiannual interest payment on 25 bonds of Forest Equipment, $750.00. Receipt No. 678.

© wavebreakmedia/Shutterstock.com

Interest Revenue

	↑ Rec. 768.42

Investment Securities

Buy 24,787.75	
↑ Rec. 18.42	
(New Bal. 24,806.17)	

Cash

↑ Rec. 750.00	

Interest Revenue is credited for $768.42. Cash is debited for $750.00. The difference, $18.42, is debited to Investment Securities.

The carrying value of the bonds increased by $18.42. If the fund keeps the bonds until maturity, the carrying value will gradually increase to equal the bonds' total face value of $25,000.00.

fyi The calculation method is the same for interest revenue and interest expense.

INPUT

- Remind students that interest revenue is calculated using the current carrying value of the bonds multiplied by the effective interest rate.

MODEL

Analyze and record the transaction

- Draw three blank T accounts on the board.
- Ask students to read the transaction statement.
- Ask students to analyze the transaction.
- Refer to the math illustration at the top of the page to calculate interest revenue and the interest payment.
- Use the cash receipts journal transparency to illustrate the process for recording the entry in the journal.

TEACHING IDEA **Invite a representative from an investment company to speak to the class about mutual funds and how decisions are made to purchase bonds.**

INPUT

- Point out that the interest payment is more than the interest revenue when interest on bonds purchased at a premium is received.

MODEL

Analyze and record the transaction

- Direct students to the math illustration at the top of the page to calculate interest revenue and the interest payment.
- Use the cash receipts journal transparency to illustrate the process for recording the entry in the journal.
- Draw three blank T accounts.
- Ask students to read the transaction statement.
- Ask students to analyze the transaction and record the amounts on the T accounts.

WHY ACCOUNTING?

Answers

1. Before the Promotion = $1,300.00/$130,000.00 = 1.0%.

   After the Promotion = $2,175.00/$145,000.00 = 1.5%.

2. Before the promotion, advertising expense was 1 cent for every $1.00 of sales. After the promotion, it was 1.5 cents for every $1.00 of sales. This indicates that the increase in advertising expenses as a percentage of sales may not be as advantageous to the company's bottom line as was initially anticipated.

Receiving Interest on Bonds Purchased at a Premium

Carrying Value of Bonds	×	Effective Interest Rate	×	Time as Fraction of a Year	=	Interest Revenue
$81,728.00	×	5.5%	×	1/2	=	$2,247.52 ← Calculate the Interest Revenue

Face Value of Bonds	×	Stated Interest Rate	×	Time as Fraction of a Year	=	Interest Payment
$80,000.00	×	6.0%	×	1/2	=	$2,400.00 ← Calculate the Interest Payment

Credit Interest Revenue

CASH RECEIPTS JOURNAL — PAGE 20

	DATE		ACCOUNT TITLE	DOC. NO.	POST. REF.	1 GENERAL DEBIT	2 GENERAL CREDIT	3 ACCOUNTS RECEIVABLE CREDIT	4 SALES CREDIT	5 SALES TAX PAYABLE CREDIT	6 SALES DISCOUNT DEBIT	7 CASH DEBIT	
1	20-- Oct.	3	*Interest Revenue*	*R544*			2 247 52					2 400 00	1
2			*Investment Securities*				152 48						2
3													3

Credit the Difference to Investment Securities

Debit Cash for the Interest Payment

TYP Corporation issued 500, five-year, 6.0%, $1,000.00 face-value bonds. The bonds were sold for $510,800.10, or $1,021.60 ($510,800.10 ÷ 500 bonds) per bond.

The bonds were sold at a premium, and therefore, the effective interest rate of 5.5% is less than the 6.0% stated interest rate.

WHY ACCOUNTING?

How Marketing Can Use Accounting Ratios

The American Marketing Association defines marketing as "... the activity, set of institutions, and processes for creating, communicating, delivering, and exchanging offerings that have value for customers, clients, partners, and society at large."

The Marketing Department may develop and implement a marketing campaign, but how does it determine if the campaign was effective? The Accounting Department may be able to provide the data needed to measure the effectiveness of the plan. One way to measure this would be to determine the ratio of advertising expense to net sales before and after the campaign. While the Accounting Department would produce the calculations, Marketing Department personnel must understand what is being measured and how to interpret the results. For example, if sales are recorded on the accrual basis, the receipt of cash from a sale in the previous period would not be included in the measurement. Without this knowledge, the Marketing Department may misinterpret the results.

CRITICAL THINKING

The Accounting Department provided the following data measuring the items before and after a sales promotion:

	Before the Promotion	After the Promotion
Sales	$130,000.00	$145,000.00
Advertising expense	1,300.00	2,175.00

1. Calculate the ratio of advertising expense to sales before the promotion and after the promotion. Put your answer in the form of a percentage, rounded to the nearest tenth (0.1).
2. What does the answer for question 1 indicate?

Source: www.marketingpower.com.

DIFFERENTIATED INSTRUCTION

Visual/Spatial learners use tools such as multimedia and texts with pictures to assist with learning. Students should research mutual funds and prepare a brochure or a multimedia presentation discussing how they work, the advantages and disadvantages of investing in mutual funds, and the names of three investment companies in the area that sell mutual funds.

The Albreck Investment Fund purchased 80 of these bonds, paying $81,728.00 ($1,021.60 × 80 bonds). The calculation of the first period's semiannual interest payment is shown on the previous page. The interest revenue is calculated using the current carrying value of the bonds multiplied by the effective interest rate.

Interest Revenue is credited for $2,247.52. Cash is debited for $2,400.00. The difference, $152.48, is credited to Investment Securities.

The carrying value of the bonds decreased by $152.48. If the fund keeps the bonds until maturity, the carrying value will gradually decrease to equal the bonds' total face value of $80,000.00.

October 3. The Albreck Investment Fund received the semiannual interest payment on 80 bonds of TYP Corporation, $2,400.00. Receipt No. 544.

Interest Revenue	
	↑ Rec. 2,247.52

Investment Securities	
Buy 81,728.00 (New Bal. 81,575.52)	↓ Rec. 152.48

Cash	
↑ Rec. 2,400.00	

SELLING A BOND INVESTMENT

Credit Investment Securities

CASH RECEIPTS JOURNAL — PAGE 14

	DATE		ACCOUNT TITLE	DOC. NO.	POST. REF.	1 GENERAL DEBIT	2 GENERAL CREDIT	3 ACCOUNTS RECEIVABLE CREDIT	4 SALES CREDIT	5 SALES TAX PAYABLE CREDIT	6 SALES DISCOUNT DEBIT	7 CASH DEBIT	
4		5	*Investment Securities*	*R432*			24 885 74					27 636 25	4
5			*Gain on Sale of Investments*				2 750 51						5
6													6

Credit the Difference to Gain on Sale of Investments

Debit Cash

The Albreck Investment Fund held its 25 bonds of Forest Equipment for several years. On the receipt of each semiannual interest payment, a debit was recorded that included an increase in the carrying value of the bonds. After three years, the carrying value of the bonds had increased to $24,885.74.

After receiving the latest interest payment, the Albreck Investment Fund decided to sell the bonds. Changes in market interest rates have caused the market value of the bonds to increase $1,105.45 per bond.

Investment Securities is credited for $24,885.74, the current carrying value of the bonds. Cash is debited for $27,636.25, the total amount received from the sale. The difference, $2,750.51, is credited to Gain on Sale of Investments.

July 1. The Albreck Investment Fund sold its 25 bonds of Forest Equipment for $1,105.45 per bond. Receipt No. 432.

Investment Securities	
Bal 24,885.74 (New Bal. zero)	↓ Sell 24,885.74

Gain on Sale of Investments	
	↑ Sell 2,750.51

Cash	
↑ Sell 27,636.25	

Proceeds from Sale of Investment Security	−	Carrying Value of Investment Security	=	Gain on Sale of Investments
$27,636.25	−	$24,885.74	=	$2,750.51

An institutional investor is in the business of purchasing and selling securities to earn a return for its investors. The gains and losses from the sale of investments are reported in a special section of its income statement.

In contrast, most corporations are not in the business of purchasing and selling securities. Any gain or loss from the sale of investments is reported by the corporation as Other Revenue or Other Expense.

INPUT

- Explain that when the investor decides to sell bonds, changes in market interest rates are reflected by a gain or loss on sale of investments.

MODEL

Analyze and record the transaction

- Draw three blank T accounts on the board.
- Ask students to read the transaction statement.
- Ask students to analyze the transaction, determining if there is a gain or loss on the sale.
- Use the cash receipts journal transparency to illustrate the process for recording the entry in the journal.

FORMATIVE ASSESSMENT

- This is an ongoing process. Circulate around the classroom or lab, observing which students have problems with the assignments.
- Troubleshooting: Diagnose the kinds of problems students have with this lesson. Students may have difficulty remembering how to journalize the purchase and sale of a bond investment by the buyer, rather than by the seller.
- Assess student understanding by checking solutions to Independent Practice assignments and noting their answers to the Term Review and Audit Your Understanding questions.

CHECK FOR UNDERSTANDING

Term Review

- Call on a student to define the term in the Term Review. The definition is given in the Glossary.

Audit Your Understanding

- Call on students to answer the Audit Your Understanding questions. Answers are given in Appendix D of the textbook.

GUIDED PRACTICE

Work Together

- Have students write the solution to the Work Together problem as you guide the class through the examples.
- Direct students to journalize bond investment transactions as you elicit participation in analyzing and recording the transactions.

INDEPENDENT PRACTICE

On Your Own

- Assign the On Your Own problem to be worked independently.
- Use the Formative Assessment techniques to diagnose student understanding.

Application Problem

- Assign Application Problem 12-4.

Online Working Papers

- Students can access the Lesson 12-4 problems using this software.

RETEACH

- Ask students to describe the purpose of investment securities.
- Ask students to explain the difference in receiving interest on bonds purchased at a discount and those purchased at a premium.
- Ask a student to generate a transaction for selling an investment for a gain and to draw three T accounts to demonstrate the sale.

CLOSURE

- Ask students to summarize briefly investment securities.

Essential Question

- Why would an investor sell bonds at a loss? (*Answers will vary, but might include that the owner needs the principal for other obligations or investments.*)

End of Lesson Review

LO7 Journalize the purchase and sale of an investment in bonds.

Term Review

institutional investors

Audit your understanding

1. What are two examples of an institutional investor?
2. How does the accounting for a bond discount differ between the issuing corporation and an institutional investor?
3. What amounts are used to calculate the amount of interest revenue earned on a bond investment?
4. At the maturity date of a bond investment, what will be the amount in the Investment Securities account?
5. How would most corporations report a gain or loss on the sale of a bond investment?

Work together 12-4

Journalizing bond investment transactions

FTR Investments specializes in investing retirement funds for teachers. On January 1, FTR Investments has the following bond investments:

- PlatMat Corporation, $75,000.00 of 5.0% bonds, purchased to yield 5.2%; $74,588.27 carrying value.
- OpeLin Industries, $120,000.00 of 6.0% bonds, purchased to yield 5.9%; $120,422.07 carrying value.

Journalize each transaction completed during the current year. Page 5 of a cash payments journal and page 3 of a cash receipts journal are provided in the *Working Papers*. Source documents are abbreviated as follows: check, C; receipt, R. Your instructor will guide you through the following examples.

Transactions:

June	30.	Purchased 40 of Mason Electronic Corporation's $5,000.00 face-value bonds at $5,158.16 each, totaling $206,326.40. C624.
July	1.	Received the semiannual interest payment on the PlatMat Corporation bonds. R642.
	1.	Received the semiannual interest payment on the OpeLin Industries bonds. R643.
	1.	Sold the OpeLin bonds, $122,754.00. R644.

On your own 12-4

Journalizing bond investment transactions

Davidson Securities has the following bond investments as of January 1:

- Greatlin Industries, $50,000.00 of 6.0% bonds, purchased to yield 5.8%; $50,271.76 carrying value.
- PESC Corporation, $90,000.00 of 6.5% bonds, purchased to yield 6.8%; $89,068.12 carrying value.

Journalize each transaction completed during the current year. Page 7 of a cash payments journal and page 4 of a cash receipts journal are provided in the *Working Papers*. Source documents are abbreviated as follows: check, C; receipt, R. Work independently to complete the following problem.

Transactions:

July	1.	Received the semiannual interest payment on the Greatlin Industries bonds. R599.
	1.	Received the semiannual interest payment on the PESC Corporation bonds. R600.
	1.	Sold the PESC Corporation bonds, $89,900.00. R601.
	14.	Purchased 50 of Larsson Corporation's $1,000.00 face-value bonds at $998.60 each, totaling $49,930.00. C591.

EXTENDED LEARNING

- Assign Financial Literacy on page 356.
- Assign Why Accounting on page 358.

Chapter Summary

A corporation may elect to acquire capital by issuing bonds. Bonds enable the corporation to obtain a large amount of debt for an extended period of time. A bond is typically identified by its stated interest rate, term, and face value, such as 6%, 20-year, $5,000.00 bonds. A bond with a callable option can be redeemed by the corporation prior to the maturity date. An early redemption typically results in a loss that is recorded as an Other Expense.

Changes in market interest rates may cause bonds to be issued at a discount or a premium. The effective interest rate is the rate that will be earned by the bondholder over the term of the bond. The discount or premium is amortized over the remaining term of the bond. The amount of interest expense recorded is based on the carrying value of the bonds and the effective interest rate. The amount of the interest payment is based on the face value and the stated interest rate of the bonds. The interest payment amount is the same, regardless of the price at which the bonds were issued.

Institutional investors, such as mutual funds and pension plans, are significant buyers of corporate bonds. Unlike the issuing corporation, institutional investors record investments in Investment Securities, net of any premium or discount. The interest revenue earned on a bond is calculated using the same method the corporation uses to determine interest expense—the carrying value of the bonds multiplied by the effective interest rate.

Bond Sinking Funds

EXPLORE ACCOUNTING

To assure bondholders that the bond issue will be paid at maturity, some bonds require the corporation to make periodic payments to a restricted fund. The fund is referred as a *bond sinking fund*. The payments are made to a trustee, which is a person or an institution given legal authorization to administer property for the benefit of the property owners.

Each time the corporation pays interest on the bonds, it also makes a payment into the bond sinking fund. The amount of the payment is typically the total face value of the bond issue divided by the number of payments. Thus, a corporation that issues $100,000.00 of 20-year bonds would be required to make $5,000.00 semiannual payments.

Although the trustee has control over the funds, the bond sinking fund is an asset of the corporation. The trustee is expected to invest the balance of the bond sinking fund on behalf of the corporation. Any interest earned reduces the amount the corporation must deposit. For example, Porterville Corporation is responsible for making a $5,000.00 payment into the bond sinking fund. The fund has earned $400.00 of interest since the last payment. The journal entry to record the deposit into the bond sinking fund would be as follows:

Account	Debit	Credit
Bond Sinking Fund	5,000.00	
Interest Income		400.00
Cash		4,600.00

As the bond sinking fund balance increases, the amount of interest earned in a year usually increases. Thus, the amount the corporation must deposit each year will generally decrease. At the maturity date of the bonds, the trustee uses the bond sinking fund to pay the maturity value to the bondholders.

INSTRUCTIONS

Assume your corporation is planning to issue bonds that will contain a sinking fund provision. The bond trustee will be required to invest sinking fund cash in short-term (one year or less) bank certificates of deposit. Research how the sinking fund will be disclosed on the financial statements. Do you agree with the findings of your research?

© iStockphoto.com/Makhnach_M

CLOSURE

- Review the Chapter Summary.
- Ask students to prepare a list of the new concepts introduced in this chapter.

Essential Question

- What advantage do bonds have over long-term notes? (*Usually the interest rate is lower for bonds than for a long-term note.*)

EXTENDED LEARNING

- Assign Explore Accounting on page 361.

EXPLORE ACCOUNTING

Answer

A sinking fund should be reported on the balance sheet as a long-term asset immediately after current assets. The fact that the sinking fund is invested in short-term investments is not a factor. The money in the sinking fund is not available to pay current operating expenses. The sinking fund is restricted to paying the maturity value of a long-term liability. Thus, reporting the sinking fund as a long-term asset is appropriate.

CHECK FIGURES

For complete solutions to Chapter 12 problems, see the Teacher's Edition of the Working Papers.

Application Problem 12-1

July 1, 20X1, debit Discount on Bonds Payable, $2,507.66.

July 1, 20X6, credit Premium on Bonds Payable, $4,494.34.

Application Problem 12-2

July 1, Premium on Bonds Payable, debit $186.93.

Aug. 1, Discount on Bonds Payable, credit $432.61.

Application Problem 12-3

Apr. 1, Discount on Bonds Payable, credit $11,000.00.

July 1 debits: Premium on Bonds Payable, $21,000.00; Loss on Redemption of Bonds, $27,000.00.

Apply Your Understanding

INSTRUCTIONS: Download problem instructions for Excel, QuickBooks, and Sage 50 from the textbook companion website at www.C21accounting.com.

12-1 Application Problem: Journalizing bond transactions LO2

Instructions:

Journalize the following transactions. Page 8 of a cash receipts journal is provided in the *Working Papers*.

Transactions:

July 1, 20X1. Received cash for 200 five-year, 6.5%, $1,000.00 face-value bonds, issued to yield 6.8%, $197,492.34. Receipt 450.

July 1, 20X6. Received cash for 400 five-year, 6.0%, $1,000.00 face-value bonds, issued to yield 5.85%, $404,494.34. Receipt 890.

12-2 Application Problem: Journalizing bond interest payments LO3

Instructions:

Journalize each transaction completed during the current year. Page 18 of a cash payments journal is provided in the *Working Papers*.

Transactions:

July 1. Paid cash to trustee for the semiannual interest payment on a 6.0%, $500,000.00 bond issue having a carrying value of $502,138.00 and a 5.9% effective interest rate. Check No. 446.

Aug. 1. Paid cash to trustee for the semiannual interest payment on a 6.5%, $800,000.00 bond issue having a carrying value of $794,965.73 and a 6.65% effective interest rate. Check No. 538.

12-3 Application Problem: Redeeming and calling a bond issue LO4, 5

After making its semiannual interest payments, Cutform Corporation elected to call three of its bond issues.

Instructions:

Journalize each transaction completed during the current year. Page 9 of a cash payments journal is provided in the *Working Papers*.

Transactions:

Apr. 1. Redeemed a $900,000.00 bond issue with a call option of 104%. The bonds have a carrying value of $889,000.00. Check No. 554.

June 1. Retired a bond issue at face value, $300,000.00. Check No. 721.

July 1. Redeemed an $800,000.00 bond issue with a call option of 106%. The bonds have a carrying value of $821,000.00. Check No. 763.

12-4 Application Problem: Journalizing bond investment transactions LO6

Betterson Mutual Funds has the following bond investments as of January 1:

- Ocean Import, $100,000.00 of 6.0% bonds, purchased to yield 5.9%; $100,271.32 carrying value.
- Washington Corporation, $60,000.00 of 5.5% bonds, purchased to yield 5.7%; $59,576.14 carrying value.

Betterson Mutual Funds accrued earned but unpaid interest income on its December 31 financial statements. These accruals were reversed at the start of the current fiscal year.

Instructions:

Journalize each transaction completed during the current year. Page 5 of a cash payments journal and page 3 of a cash receipts journal are provided in the *Working Papers*. Source documents are abbreviated as follows: check, C; receipt, R.

Transactions:

Mar. 1. Purchased 50 of PC Corporation's $1,000.00 face-value bonds at $998.60 each, totaling $49,930.00. C591.
1. Received the semiannual interest payment on the Ocean Import bonds. R289.
Apr. 1. Received the semiannual interest payment on the Washington Corporation bonds. R325.
1. Sold the Ocean Import bonds, $102,100.00. R326.

12-M Mastery Problem: Journalizing bond transactions LO2, 3, 4, 5, 6

TA Post Corporation has the following bonds outstanding as of January 1:

- 6%, 10-year, $1,000 face-value bonds, $500,000.00, issued at a 5.9% effective interest rate, callable at 105%.
- 6.5%, 20-year, $5,000 face-value bonds, $750,000.00, issued at a 6.7% effective interest rate.

The corporation accrued interest income and interest expense when preparing its December 31 financial statements. These accruals were reversed at the start of the current fiscal year.

Instructions:

Journalize each transaction completed during the current year. Page 6 of a cash receipts journal and page 3 of a cash payments journal are provided in the *Working Papers*. Source documents are abbreviated as follows: check, C; receipt, R.

Transactions:

Apr. 1. Purchased ten of DRB Corporation's 6.25% $1,000.00 face-value bonds at $1,008.52 each, resulting in a yield of 6.05%. C445.
27. Paid cash to trustee for the semiannual interest payment on the $750,000.00 bond issue, which has a carrying value of $749,274.31. C468.
May 1. Paid cash to trustee to retire the $750,000.00 bond issue at its face value. C492.
June 1. Received cash for 400 ten-year, 5.0%, $1,000.00 face-value bonds, issued to yield 5.2%, $396,517.20. R161.
July 1. Paid cash to trustee for the semiannual interest payment on the $500,000.00 bond issue, which has a carrying value of $501,560.51. C589.
1. Redeemed the $500,000.00 bond issue with a call option of 105%. C590.
Oct. 1. Received the semiannual interest payment on its DRB Corporation bonds. R268.
1. Sold its investment in DRB Corporation bonds for $1,025.00 per bond. R269.

Sage 50 Accounting

1. Journalize and post bond transactions to the cash receipts journal and cash disbursements journal.
2. Print the cash receipts journal and cash disbursements journal.

QB

1. Journalize and post bond transactions to the journal.
2. Journalize and post bond transactions in the Write Checks window.
3. Print the journal and check detail.

Excel

1. Journalize bond transactions to the cash receipts journal and cash payments journal.
2. Print the spreadsheets.

Application Problem 12-4

Cash receipts journal credits: Mar. 1, Interest Securities, $42.00; Apr. 1, Interest Revenue, $1,697.92; Gain on Sale of Investments, $1,870.68.

Mastery Problem 12-M

Cash receipts journal: June 1, Discount on Bonds Payable, debit $3,482.80.

Cash payments journal debits: Apr. 27, Interest Expense, $25,100.69; July 1, Premium on Bonds Payable, $203.96; Loss on Redemption of Bonds, $23,643.45.

INDEPENDENT PRACTICE

- Assign Mastery Problem 12-M for students as a culminating problem combining all new learning from the chapter.
- Assign Challenge Problem 12-C to accelerated students who work at a faster pace.
- Assign Study Guide 12.
- Students can access Online Working Papers to work end-of-chapter problems on the computer.
- Direct students to the C21 Accounting companion website for additional practice and review opportunities.

FORMATIVE ASSESSMENT

- Review solutions to the assigned problems in class, diagnosing trouble spots.

RETEACH

- Call on students to describe how they avoid the trouble spots diagnosed.
- Use reteaching suggestions from lesson plans as required.
- Assign Recycling Problem 12-R if needed.

Challenge Problem 12-C

Cash payments journal debits: Apr. 1, Premium on Bonds Payable, $603.30; June 23, Interest Expense, $7,902.05; June 23, Loss on Redemption of Bonds, $16,845.90.

EXTENDED LEARNING

- Assign 21st Century Skills on page 365.
- Assign Analyzing Home Depot's Financial Statements on page 365.

SUMMATIVE EVALUATION

- Chapter 12 Test
- Cognero for Chapter 12

12-C Challenge Problem: Journalizing bond transactions LO3, 5

PR&K Corporation has 480 of its 7.5%, ten-year, $1,000 face-value bonds outstanding. The bonds were issued to yield a 7.2% effective interest rate. The bonds pay interest on April 1 and October 1 each year and have a call option at 104%.

PR&K Corporation called the bonds on June 23 of the current year. Bond transactions that occur during a semiannual period require that accrued interest be recorded.

Instructions:

Journalize each transaction. Page 3 of a cash payments journal is provided in the *Working Papers*.

Transactions:

Apr.	1.	Paid cash to trustee for the semiannual interest payment on the $480,000.00 bond issue, which has a carrying value of $483,241.65. Check No. 654.
June	23.	Paid cash to trustee for the interest accrued on the $480,000.00 bond issue since the last semiannual interest payment. Check No. 728.
	23.	Redeemed the $480,000.00 bond issue. Check No. 729.

Sage 50 Accounting

1. Journalize and post bond transactions to the cash disbursements journal.
2. Print the cash disbursements journal.

QB

1. Journalize and post bond transactions in the Write Checks window.
2. Print the check detail.

X

1. Journalize bond transactions to the cash receipts journal and cash payments journal.
2. Print the spreadsheets.

COMMON CORE AND INTERDISCIPLINARY STUDIES

Extended learning features and activities present numerous opportunities to implement Common Core Standards through interdisciplinary studies. Practice is provided in the common core areas of English Language Arts & Literacy and Mathematical Practice. Many of these activities require short, critical-thinking and decision-making responses that apply reading, writing, speaking, listening, language, media and technology, and mathematical skills.

21st Century Skills

Bond Investment Options

Theme: Financial, Economic, Business, and Entrepreneurial Literacy

Skills: Critical Thinking and Problem Solving, Information Literacy, ICT Literacy

PARTNERSHIP FOR 21ST CENTURY SKILLS

Bonds are issued as a way to raise capital. An investor who purchases bonds lends money in return for a promise to be paid a fixed rate of interest plus the capital at a future date. Bonds can be purchased online or through a broker or a bank.

Most bonds are issued by one of three groups. First, the U.S. government issues Treasury bonds to finance the national debt and the ongoing business of the federal government. State and local governments also issue bonds to raise money for public projects, such as schools, bridges, and roads. These bonds, called *municipal bonds* or *munis*, offer special tax exemptions that attract investors.

Corporations issue bonds to help finance major purchases or ongoing activities. Corporate bonds are the most lucrative, but have greater risk.

Bonds are given credit ratings, much like grades, that range from AAA to DDD. These ratings help the investor determine the credit risk of the bond. Bonds with lower ratings usually pay a higher yield, or rate of return, due to their higher risk. Treasury bonds are considered the safest bond investment, since the government has less risk of defaulting than a corporation.

APPLICATION

1. Using the Internet, find the names of the three main rating agencies for bonds.
2. Using websites like www.bondsonline.com, compare and contrast the bond rating definitions of the three rating agencies. Create a spreadsheet or other visual to share your findings.
3. Some bonds are referred to as "junk" bonds. Using the Internet, explain the meaning of junk bonds. Explain why an investor would buy a bond called "junk."

Analyzing Home Depot's financial statements

Home Depot uses a variety of financial instruments to finance its operations and fund its expansion. As of February 3, 2013, Home Depot had six bond issues outstanding with due dates ranging from 2013 to 2041 and interest rates ranging from 3.95% to 5.95%.

INSTRUCTIONS

Use Home Depot's Consolidated Balance Sheets and Consolidated Statements of Cash Flows found in Appendix B on pages B-5 and B-9 to answer the following questions:

1. What were the proceeds from long-term borrowings for each of the three fiscal years?
2. Identify the amount of payments of long-term debt for each fiscal year.
3. For each year presented on the Consolidated Balance Sheets, determine the amount of long-term debt as a percent of total liabilities and stockholders' equity. Include the current installments of long-term debt.

21ST CENTURY SKILLS

Answers

1. Moody's, Standard & Poor's, and Fitch Ratings.
2. Visuals will vary. Agency ratings should match the appropriate agency.
3. A junk bond is a high-yield bond that pays a higher rate of interest but has more risk of default. As a result, junk bonds have lower ratings.

ANALYZING HOME DEPOT'S FINANCIAL STATEMENTS

Answers

1. Fiscal year 2012, zero; 2011, $1,994 million; 2010, $988 million.
2. Fiscal year 2012, $32 million; 2011, $1,028 million; 2010, $1,029 million.
3. As the following table shows, the amount of long-term debt has remained relatively unchanged as a percent of total liabilities and stockholders' equity over the periods presented.

	February 3, 2013	January 29, 2012
Current installments of long-term debt	$ 1,321	$ 30
Long-term debt	9,475	10,758
Total long-term debt	$10,796	$10,788
Total liabilities and stockholders' equity	41,084	40,518
Long-term debt as a percent of total liabilities and stockholders' equity	26.3%	26.6%

Chapter 13

Financial Reporting and Analysis for a Corporation

Scope & Sequence

	New	Review/Enrich
Introduction		
Introduce the Chapter		
Lesson 13-1: Measuring and Analyzing Financial Strength		
Financial Statement Analysis		✓
Financial Analysis Objectives	✓	
Short-Term Financial Strength	✓	
Long-Term Financial Strength	✓	
Lesson 13-2: Measuring and Analyzing Profitability		
Profitability Analysis	✓	
Lesson 13-3: Calculating and Analyzing Efficiency Measures and Market Ratio		
Analyzing Efficiency	✓	
Market Ratios	✓	
Lesson 13-4: Advanced Topics in Financial Reporting		
Net Income and Taxable Income	✓	
Comprehensive Income	✓	
Closure		

Enhancing Instruction

Features	Common Core Standards
• Accounting in the Real World: Chipotle Mexican Grill	• ELAL—reading
• Ethics in Action: Client Referrals • Why Accounting?: Uniform System of Accounts for Restaurants	• ELAL—reading • ELAL—reading, media and technology
• Forensic Accounting: Channel Stuffing • Global Awareness: World Trade Organization	• Mathematics • ELAL—reading, media and technology, writing
• Think Like an Accountant: Charting Earnings per Share	• ELAL—reading, writing
• Explore Accounting • 21st Century Skills • Analyzing Home Depot's Financial Statements	• ELAL—reading • ELAL—reading, writing, media and technology • Mathematics

ELAL = English Language Arts & Literacy

Calculator: © iStockphoto.com/picstodisc; Paper: © iStockphoto.com/Qingwa

Practice and Assessment

Technology & Media	Teaching Strategies	Guided Practice	Independent Practice	Reteach/Enrich
• Instructor's Resource CD/Website: PowerPoint Slides Accounting Concepts • Online Working Papers	• Logical/Mathematical Learners	• Terms Review • Audit Your Understanding • Work Together 13-1	• On Your Own 13-1 • Application Problem 13-1 • Formative Assessment, p. 376 • Online Working Papers	• Reteach, p. 377
• Instructor's Resource CD/Website: PowerPoint Slides Accounting Concepts • Online Working Papers	• Auditory/Linguistic Learners	• Terms Review • Audit Your Understanding • Work Together 13-2	• On Your Own 13-2 • Application Problem 13-2 • Formative Assessment, p. 383 • Online Working Papers	• Reteach, p. 384
• Instructor's Resource CD/Website: PowerPoint Slides Accounting Concepts • Online Working Papers		• Terms Review • Audit Your Understanding • Work Together 13-3	• On Your Own 13-3 • Application Problem 13-3 • Formative Assessment, p. 389 • Online Working Papers	• Reteach, p. 390
• Instructor's Resource CD/Website: PowerPoint Slides Accounting Concepts • Online Working Papers	• Visual/Spatial Learners	• Terms Review • Audit Your Understanding • Work Together 13-4	• On Your Own 13-4 • Application Problem 13-4 • Formative Assessment, p. 392 • Online Working Papers	• Reteach, p. 393
	• Common Core and Interdisciplinary Studies		• Mastery Problem 13-M • Study Guide 13 • Chapter 13 Test • Cognero Chapter 13	• Challenge Problem 13-C • Reteach, p. 397 • Recycling Problem 13-R

Introduce the Chapter

SET THE STAGE

GUIDING QUESTIONS

- Ask students if they could determine whether a company is financially healthy by reviewing the financial statements.
- Ask students what tax rate is used on corporations' federal taxes on taxable income.
- Ask students what they would use to determine if it were safe to invest in a company.

PREVIEW CHAPTER OBJECTIVES

- Note that many financial ratios will be learned in this chapter to analyze a company's financial strength.
- Instruct a student to read each chapter objective aloud.

PREVIEW ACCOUNTING TERMS

- Read each term aloud to verify its pronunciation for students.
- Point out terms or parts of terms that should already be familiar to most students, such as *equity*, *average*, *capital*, *market value*, and *ratio*.

Chapter 13 Financial Reporting and Analysis for a Corporation

LEARNING OBJECTIVES

After studying Chapter 13, in addition to defining key terms, you will be able to:

LO1 Analyze the financial strength of a business.

LO2 Analyze the profitability of a business.

LO3 Perform efficiency analysis of a business.

LO4 Calculate the market ratios of a business.

LO5 Calculate permanent and temporary differences in net income and taxable income.

LO6 Understand the concept of comprehensive income.

Calculator: © iStockphoto.com/picstodisc; Paper: © iStockphoto.com/Qingwa

© Goodluz/Shutterstock.com

Accounting In The Real World

Chipotle Mexican Grill

With over 1,200 stores in 41 states, chances are you have heard of Chipotle Mexican Grill. You may have even sampled one of its famous foil-wrapped burritos.

As a consumer, you may be mostly concerned with the quality of your burrito. Chipotle supports local family farmers and aims for using only naturally raised animals and organic ingredients. Chipotle's customers reflect the growing number of consumers who are not only interested in good food, but also concerned about sustainably raised food.

As an investor, you may be interested in more than the items listed on the menu. You may want to study the financial statements of Chipotle Mexican Grill to compare it with other investments. Many financial ratios can be calculated using the financial statements of the company. Other measures may require some research.

One measure used by company management and by investors is known as *same-store sales* or *comparable restaurant sales*. Same-store sales is used to evaluate sales trends at individual restaurant locations. This measure requires that the company separately measure sales of restaurants by the length of time the restaurant has been open. Same-store sales is calculated by dividing the change in sales by the prior period's sales. It can be calculated for a week, a month, or a year.

Restaurants strive to generate consistent increases in same-store sales. Popular methods of increasing sales include expanding menu options, offering value menus, and increasing prices. In 2011, Chipotle's same-store sales grew 11.2%, which is an increase over its 2010 same-store sales of 9.4%. Chipotle's 2011 annual report states "Comparable restaurant sales growth in 2011 was due primarily to increases in customer visits, as well as the impact of menu price increases implemented during the year."

It is risky for a business to implement menu price increases. The company might lose customers to another similar restaurant. Customers might make fewer trips to Chipotle. However, at Chipotle, customer visits increased even as menu prices increased.

CRITICAL THINKING

1. Why might a Chipotle customer continue choosing Chipotle despite increases in menu prices?
2. If a business does not report its same-store sales growth, would an investor be able to calculate it by using published financial statements?

Source: www.chipotle.com.

Background: © iStockphoto.com/AdShooter; Real World: © iStockPhoto.com/marcnorman

Key Terms

- comparative financial statements
- cash equivalents
- working capital
- current ratio
- quick assets
- quick ratio
- debt ratio
- equity ratio
- common equity per share
- EBIT
- interest coverage ratio
- gross margin
- operating margin
- rate earned on average total assets
- rate earned on average stockholders' equity
- free cash flow
- capital expenditures
- earnings per share (EPS)
- market value of a share of stock
- price-earnings ratio
- dividend yield
- permanent difference
- temporary difference
- comprehensive income

Accounting In The Real World

Answers

1. Answers will vary, but could include these: (1) Chipotle's customers may believe that their desire for sustainably raised food is worth the increase in price and that there are not many alternatives. (2) Customers may think that the value is still good even with higher prices. (3) There may not be similar restaurants in the area.
2. If the business reported the dollar amount of same-store sales from year to year, the investor could calculate the change from year to year. However, if the business only reports total sales and does not separate the dollar amount of new-store sales and existing-store sales, the investor will not be able to calculate the change over time.

LESSON
13-1

BRIDGE

- Point out that students have already learned to prepare financial statements. In this lesson, they will use financial data to compare financial information from other fiscal periods and calculate ratios.

TEACHING RESOURCES

- **Instructor's Resource CD/Website:**
  PowerPoint Slides
  Accounting Concepts
- **Working Papers:**
  Teacher's Edition of the Working Papers for Lesson 13-1
  Online Working Papers

ENGAGE

- Show students the financial section of a newspaper or a website. Point out some of the ratios that will be presented in this lesson.

PREVIEW

- Call on students to read the accounting terms and definitions introduced in this lesson: *comparative financial statements, cash equivalents, working capital, current ratio, quick assets, quick ratio, debt ratio, equity ratio, common equity per share, EBIT,* and *interest coverage ratio*.
- Point out the learning objective for this lesson.
- Direct students to read the headings in this lesson and to examine the illustrations.

INPUT

- Explain that financial statements help in understanding the financial condition of a business.
- Point out that the SEC determines the standards and rules so that statements are structured similarly from company to company.
- Stress that financial statements of public companies are submitted quarterly and annually.
- Ask who might use the financial information prepared on these statements.
- Point out that financial statements alone only provide snapshots of the whole picture (financial condition).
- Explain that analyzing financial statements involves calculating the relationships among the different items on the statements.

LESSON
13-1 Measuring and Analyzing Financial Strength

LO1 Analyze the financial strength of a business.

Financial Statement Analysis

Financial statements contain all information necessary to understand a business's financial condition. [CONCEPT: Full Disclosure] The structure of these statements is similar from company to company in order to meet the requirements of the Securities and Exchange Commission (SEC). Congress established the SEC in 1933. The SEC was given the authority to develop accounting principles and rules.

To ensure that information provided to external users is accurate and complete, the SEC requires public companies to submit quarterly and annual reports. These reports must include specific disclosures and discussions. The SEC makes these reports available to all current and potential investors through an online database called EDGAR (the Electronic Data Gathering, Analysis, and Retrieval system).

Financial statements are prepared for both internal and external users. Managers use financial information to identify areas for improving the profitability of their corporation. Banks and lending agencies use the information to decide whether to loan money to a business. Owners and potential owners use the information to decide whether to buy, sell, or keep their investment. Each group uses the financial information in a different way to assist with decision making.

Although financial statements provide useful information, they can be difficult to understand. For example, is a significant increase in the cost of merchandise sold an unfavorable trend? This question cannot be answered without considering information provided by other financial statement items, such as net sales. Financial statement analysis provides this information, since it calculates the relationships among financial statement items.

Financial Analysis Objectives LO1

Financial analysis objectives are determined by a business's characteristics and achievements that are important to the analyst. Information is analyzed to obtain more knowledge about the business's strengths and weaknesses. Common objectives for analyzing financial information are to determine (1) financial strength, (2) profitability (3) efficiency, and (4) market value.

Financial statements, with supporting schedules, are the primary information sources to be analyzed. A statement showing two or more years' information permits a reader to compare year-to-year differences. Financial statements that provide information for multiple fiscal periods are known as **comparative financial statements**. To be useful, financial statements must be prepared by using the same accounting principles in each period. [CONCEPT: Consistent Reporting]

© iStockphoto.com/Nano

INPUT

- Explain the four objectives for analyzing financial information.
- Point out that comparative financial statements provide information for multiple fiscal periods for comparison purposes.

TEACHING IDEA **Collect copies of financial statements from companies familiar to students and display them as you discuss the statements.**

Comparative financial statements for Forest Equipment, Inc., are shown below and on the next several pages. These financial statements will be used as the basis for the financial analysis discussed in this chapter.

INCOME STATEMENT

Forest Equipment, Inc. Income Statement For Years Ended December 31, 20X3, 20X2, and 20X1	20X3	20X2	20X1
Net Sales	646,017.54	645,212.32	642,578.45
Cost of Merchandise Sold:	391,035.52	398,600.20	395,452.15
Gross Profit	254,982.02	246,612.12	247,126.30
Operating Expenses:			
Selling, General and Administrative	109,435.14	105,265.14	104,698.20
Depreciation and Amortization	26,053.00	22,421.30	21,535.28
Total Operating Expenses	135,488.14	127,686.44	126,233.48
Income from Operations	119,493.88	118,925.68	120,892.82
Other Revenue and Expenses:			
Interest Income	1,087.50	1,095.54	989.54
Dividend Revenue	3,000.00	2,500.00	1,500.00
Gain on Sale of Investments	5,700.00	6,500.00	—
Interest Expense	(11,708.33)	(7,850.00)	(4,554.25)
Total Other Revenue and Expenses	(1,920.83)	2,245.54	(2,064.71)
Net Income before Federal Income Tax	117,573.05	121,171.22	118,828.11
Less: Federal Income Tax Expense	29,103.49	30,506.78	29,592.96
Net Income	88,469.56	90,664.44	89,235.15

The income statement is presented in an abbreviated format normally used in annual reports. The cost of merchandise sold section has been reduced to a single line, and the operating expenses are divided into two categories: selling, general and administrative expenses and depreciation and amortization expenses.

ETHICS IN ACTION

Client Referrals

Feng Entertainment Group asked its public accounting firm, Aquino, Mendoza & Ruett, to develop a comprehensive health and retirement program. Aquino, Mendoza & Ruett conducts Feng Entertainment's annual audit. Knowing that it lacked the expertise needed to perform these services, Halina Aquino, a CPA and the managing partner of the accounting firm, refers Feng Entertainment to another firm, Moreno and Cote. In appreciation for the referral, Moreno and Cote gives Halina Aquino an all-expense-paid trip to St. Thomas. Neither accounting firm informs Feng Entertainment of the trip.

INSTRUCTIONS

Determine whether the referral was made in accordance with the AICPA *Code of Professional Conduct*.

© iStockphoto.com/LdF

INPUT

- Emphasize that the income statement for a corporation is similar to that for any other form of business organization.
- Direct students to the illustration on this page.
- Point out that the primary difference in an income statement for a corporation is the federal income tax expense section at the end of the income statement.

ETHICS IN ACTION

Rule 503(C) states "Any member who accepts a referral fee for recommending or referring any service of a CPA to any person or entity or who pays a referral fee to obtain a client shall disclose such acceptance or payment to the client." The rule ensures that clients are billed only for the services received. If referral fees were allowed, Moreno and Cote may attempt to recover the cost of the referral.

Suggested Solution

No. Although a referral fee is not prohibited, Rule 503(C) prohibits a member of the AICPA from accepting a referral fee without informing the client.

Source: www.aicpa.org/Research/Standards/CodeofConduct/Pages/default.aspx.

INPUT

- Direct students to the illustration on this page.
- Point out the different sections of the statement of stockholders' equity.
- Explain how common stock, preferred stock, and retained earnings show the beginning balance, changes during the fiscal period, and the ending balance.
- Point out the listing of the additional paid-in capital in the paid-in capital section.
- Explain that treasury stock is deducted from the total of the paid-in capital and retained earnings because the stock is held by the corporation and is not outstanding.

STATEMENT OF STOCKHOLDERS' EQUITY

Forest Equipment, Inc.
Statement of Stockholders' Equity
For Years Ended December 31, 20X3, 20X2, and 20X1

	20X3	20X2	20X1
Paid-In Capital:			
Common Stock, $1.00 Par Value:			
Balance, January 1	65,000.00	65,000.00	65,000.00
Additional Common Stock Issued	0.00	0.00	0.00
Balance, December 31	65,000.00	65,000.00	65,000.00
Preferred Stock, 6%, $100.00 Par Value:			
Balance, January 1	127,500.00	50,000.00	50,000.00
Additional Preferred Stock Issued	0.00	77,500.00	0.00
Balance, December 31	127,500.00	127,500.00	50,000.00
Total Value of Capital Stock Issued	192,500.00	192,500.00	115,000.00
Additional Paid-In Capital:			
Paid-In Capital in Excess of Par Value—Common	100,000.00	100,000.00	100,000.00
Paid-In Capital in Excess of Par Value—Preferred	6,000.00	6,000.00	1,500.00
Paid-In Capital from Sale of Treasury Stock	2,718.00	1,000.00	0.00
Total Additional Paid-In Capital	108,718.00	106,100.00	101,500.00
Total Paid-In Capital	301,218.00	298,600.00	216,500.00
Retained Earnings:			
Balance, January 1, 20--	143,841.26	77,726.82	6,441.67
Net Income after Federal Income Tax	88,469.56	90,664.44	89,235.15
Less Preferred Dividends Declared	(7,650.00)	(7,650.00)	(3,000.00)
Less Common Dividends Declared	(14,950.00)	(16,900.00)	(14,950.00)
Balance, December 31	209,710.82	143,841.26	77,726.82
Treasury Stock			
Balance, December 31	(22,000.00)	(30,000.00)	(18,000.00)
Total Stockholders' Equity, December 31, 20--	488,928.82	412,441.26	276,226.82
Common Shares Outstanding	65,000.00	65,000.00	65,000.00
Preferred Shares Outstanding	1,275.00	1,275.00	500.00
Treasury Shares	2,500.00	3,500.00	2,000.00

Forest's statement of stockholders' equity is presented for three years. When beginning and ending balances are shown, the ending balance for one period is equal to the beginning balance for the following period. A comparative statement allows the user to identify changes over several accounting periods.

remember Businesses present abbreviated financial statements in the annual report. Major subtotals are given, but details of individual accounts are not.

Forest Equipment, Inc.
Balance Sheet
December 31, 20X3 and 20X2

	20X3	20X2
Assets		
Current Assets:		
Cash and Cash Equivalents	47,277.30	45,378.52
Accounts Receivable, net	66,706.43	55,647.10
Merchandise Inventory	144,066.40	95,214.25
Other Receivables	8,250.00	8,531.40
Other Current Assets	70,694.98	71,456.21
Total Current Assets	336,995.11	276,227.48
Total Plant Assets, net	397,650.00	366,480.00
Intangible Assets	1,440.00	1,440.00
Total Assets	736,085.11	644,147.48
Liabilities		
Current Liabilities:		
Accounts Payable	52,939.05	54,225.68
Accrued Salaries and Related Expenses	26,183.69	25,700.40
Sales Tax Payable	1,616.05	1,545.22
Federal Income Tax Payable	5,103.49	4,830.06
Other Current Liabilities	62,415.33	59,221.33
Total Current Liabilities	148,257.61	145,522.69
Long-Term Liabilities:		
Bonds Payable, net	98,898.68	86,183.53
Total Liabilities	247,156.29	231,706.22
Stockholders' Equity		
Paid-In Capital	301,218.00	298,600.00
Retained Earnings	209,710.82	143,841.26
Treasury Stock	(22,000.00)	(30,000.00)
Total Stockholders' Equity	488,928.82	412,441.26
Total Liabilities and Stockholders' Equity	736,085.11	644,147.48

Forest's balance sheet is also presented in an abbreviated format. Short-term, liquid investments that are readily convertible to cash and which mature in three months or less are called **cash equivalents**. Cash and cash equivalents are summarized on the first line of the balance sheet. Accounts receivable are shown at net realizable value. Plant assets are shown at net book value and are presented as a total on one line of the balance sheet. Bonds payable are shown net of any bond premium or bond discount.

remember

Comparative financial statements allow the reader to compare results and determine trends more easily.

INPUT

- Remind students that a corporate balance sheet reports assets, liabilities, and stockholders' (owners') equity on a certain date, just like any other form of business organization.
- Direct students to the illustration as you review the sections of the balance sheet.
- Point out that comparative financial statements allow the reader to compare results quickly.
- Explain cash equivalents.

INPUT

- Direct students to the illustration as you review the statement of cash flows.
- Remind students that comparative statements allow the reader to compare results quickly over two accounting periods.
- Point out the different sections and how each step is recorded on the statement.

STATEMENT OF CASH FLOWS

Forest Equipment, Inc.
Statement of Cash Flows
For Years Ended December 31, 20X3 and 20X2

	20X3	20X2
Cash flows from operating activities:		
Cash receipts from:		
Sales	646,720.30	610,444.85
Interest	422.10	650.42
Total cash receipts	647,142.40	611,095.27
Cash payments for:		
Inventory purchases	(355,654.12)	(342,336.89)
Salaries and wages	(68,937.82)	(69,312.25)
Insurance	(12,000.00)	(10,650.00)
Interest	(11,690.10)	(6,489.33)
Taxes	(29,452.47)	(30,015.45)
Other operating expenses	(105,022.11)	(95,405.22)
Total cash payments	(582,756.62)	(554,209.14)
Net cash provided/(used) by operating activities	64,385.78	56,886.13
Cash flows from investing activities:		
Sale of investment securities	41,000.00	13,000.00
Purchase of office equipment	(25,462.00)	(35,214.00)
Purchase of store equipment	(82,525.00	(87,639.00)
Net cash provided/(used) by investing activities	(66,987.00)	(109,853.00)
Cash flows from financing activities:		
Issuance of bonds	15,000.00	
Issuance of preferred stock		82,000.00
Sale of treasury stock	9,000.00	
Purchase of treasury stock		(13,500.00)
Payment of cash dividends	(19,500.00)	(22,050.00)
Net cash provided/(used) by financing activities	4,500.00	46,450.00
Net change in cash	1,898.78	(6,516.87)
Cash balance, January 1	45,378.52	51,895.39
Cash balance, December 31	47,277.30	45,378.52

Forest's statement of cash flows is presented in comparative format for two periods. The ending cash balance for 20X2 is equal to the beginning balance for 20X3. The comparative format allows the user to compare sources and uses of cash over two accounting periods.

remember

The statement of cash flows reports all cash flows in and out of the company.

Short-Term Financial Strength

A successful business needs adequate capital. A business gets capital from two sources: (1) owners' investments and retained earnings and (2) loans. Some capital, either owned or borrowed, will be used for long periods. Some capital is borrowed for short periods. A business can invest capital in assets (such as equipment and buildings) for long periods. A business also invests in assets (such as merchandise) that will be converted back to cash in a short period. Short-term assets are referred to as current assets because they are consumed in a business's daily activities or exchanged for cash. Long-term assets are referred to as *plant assets* and are used over a long period.

Forest uses three measures to analyze its short-term financial strength: (1) working capital, (2) current ratio, and (3) quick ratio.

WORKING CAPITAL

	Total Current Assets	−	Total Current Liabilities	=	Working Capital
20X3	$336,995.11	−	$148,257.61	=	$188,737.50
20X2	$276,227.48	−	$145,522.69	=	$130,704.79

The amount of total current assets less total current liabilities is known as **working capital**. Working capital, stated in dollars is the amount of current assets available to the business after current liabilities are paid. It is not the amount of cash available to the business. Comparing the amount of working capital from year to year reveals trends.

Forest's working capital for December 31, 20X3, and December 31, 20X2, is calculated as shown above, using information from the balance sheet (page 371). Forest's working capital increased from $130,704.79 to $188,737.50, a favorable trend. A review of other financial information suggests that part of the reason for the lower working capital in 20X2 was the company's fast expansion. Frequently, when a business expands rapidly, it borrows money to buy more inventory and pay more employees. The rate of increased costs for merchandise and payroll may be initially greater than the rate of increase in sales and net income. In 20X3, Forest increased its current assets more than its current liabilities by increasing long-term liabilities and paying out less dividends.

WHY ACCOUNTING?

Uniform System of Accounts for Restaurants

The National Restaurant Association (NRA) is, by membership, the largest foodservice trade association in the world. The NRA held its first meeting in 1919 and has worked to promote the restaurant industry and support restaurant owners ever since. On its website, the NRA lists its four main benefits of membership as advocacy and representation, education and networking, tools and solutions, and research and insights.

In 2012, the NRA released the 8th edition of its standardized chart of accounts, *The Uniform System of Accounts for Restaurants*. This guide for the restaurant industry contains nearly 300 possible accounts to be used by restaurant owners. It also includes a precise income statement format that "provides guidance for accurate and consistent accounting."

According to Joe Erickson, vice president of RestaurantOwner.com, the guide is helpful to independent restaurant owners, many of whom "seem to have problems properly recording sales or are challenged by cash controls."

Hospitality & Tourism

CRITICAL THINKING

1. In *The Uniform System of Accounts for Restaurants*, two categories were added under "Sales." One of these new categories is "Merchandise Sales." What items could be included in this category, and why do you think this category was added?
2. Go to www.restaurant.org and search the site for current issues facing the restaurant industry. Write a one-paragraph summary of one of these issues and how the NRA is addressing it.

Sources: www.restaurant.org; www.RestaurantOwner.com.

INPUT

- Point out that financial strength analysis examines a company's potential to generate the necessary funds to pay off its financial obligations. This type of analysis can be conducted for the short term and the long term.
- Explain the three measures used to analyze short-term financial strength.

MODEL

- Emphasize that a successful business needs adequate capital if it intends to expand, develop new products, or offer consumers more choices.
- Ask students to explain the difference between short- and long-term assets. Lead into a discussion that short-term assets are usually consumed or converted into cash within a year. Examples include cash, supplies, accounts receivable, and prepaid insurance. Long-term assets are used over a longer period of time. Examples include office furniture, equipment, land, or buildings.
- Emphasize that working capital is the amount of current assets available to the business after current liabilities are paid.
- Review the calculation presented in the illustration.

WHY ACCOUNTING?

Answers

1. Answers will vary, but could include hats, T-shirts, key chains, sauces, mixes, sweatshirts, jackets, and other items sold by restaurants. This category was added because more restaurants are selling merchandise to increase net profit.
2. Answers will vary. At the time of publication, current issues included the large-beverage ban in New York City, food safety, food labeling, sustainability, labor and workforce issues, and tax issues.

INPUT

- Emphasize that Forest uses ratios to help analyze its ability to pay its current liabilities.
- Point out that the current ratio shows the relationship of current assets to current liabilities. Note that companies rely on the cash on hand plus the cash soon to be received from other current assets to pay current liabilities. Generally, a business with a current ratio of less than 2.0 has difficulty raising cash to pay current liabilities on time.
- Review the calculation presented in the illustration.

INPUT

- Explain that quick assets are cash and other current assets that can be converted into cash. Quick assets include cash, accounts receivable, and marketable securities.
- A ratio that measures the relationship of quick assets to current liabilities is the quick ratio.
- Explain that another name for quick ratio is the acid-test ratio.
- Point out that the ratio indicates that for each $1.00 needed to pay current liabilities, this amount (ratio) is available in quick assets.
- Review the calculation presented in the illustration.

CURRENT RATIO

	Total Current Assets	÷	Total Current Liabilities	=	Current Ratio
20X3	$336,995.11	÷	$148,257.61	=	2.3
20X2	$276,227.48	÷	$145,522.69	=	1.9

A ratio that measures the relationship of current assets to current liabilities is called the **current ratio**. Normally, current liabilities are expected to be paid from cash on hand and cash soon to be received from other current assets.

The current ratio is calculated by dividing total current assets by total current liabilities. Forest's current ratios for 20X3 and 20X2 are calculated as shown above, using information from the balance sheet (page 371). The 20X3 current ratio of 2.3 means that Forest owns $2.30 in current assets for each $1.00 needed to pay current liabilities.

Businesses similar to Forest try to maintain a current ratio of 2.0. Industry experience has shown that a business with a current ratio of less than 2.0 has difficulty raising cash to pay current liabilities on time. At the same time, industry experience shows that a current ratio can be too high. If the current ratio is 3.0 or higher, the business has more capital invested in current assets than is needed to run the business.

In 20X2, Forest's current ratio of 1.9 was slightly below the desired ratio. However, the 20X3 ratio, 2.3, is at a satisfactory level. Forest's expansion may also have contributed to the lower current ratio in 20X2. In 20X3, Forest lowered its current liabilities by increasing long-term liabilities.

QUICK RATIO

	Total Quick Assets (Cash + Accounts Receivable)	÷	Total Current Liabilities	=	Quick Ratio
20X3	$113,983.73	÷	$148,257.61	=	0.8
20X2	$101,025.62	÷	$145,522.69	=	0.7

Cash and other current assets that can be converted quickly into cash are called **quick assets**. Quick assets include cash, accounts receivable, and marketable securities, but not merchandise inventory or prepaid expenses. On Forest's balance sheet, cash and cash equivalents and accounts receivable are quick assets. A ratio that measures the relationship of quick assets to current liabilities is called the **quick ratio**. The quick ratio is also called the *acid-test* ratio. This ratio shows the ability of a business to pay all its current liabilities almost immediately, if necessary.

Forest's quick ratios for 20X3 and 20X2 are calculated as shown above. The 20X3 ratio of 0.8 indicates that for each $1.00 needed to pay current liabilities, Forest has $0.80 available in quick assets. For companies similar to Forest, the desired industry standard for a quick ratio is between 0.9 and 1.3. Therefore, Forest's quick ratio for 20X3 is slightly lower than desired.

Forest's quick ratio has increased from 0.7 to 0.8. While this is a favorable trend, Forest must do more to increase its quick ratio. This could be accomplished by increasing cash from the sale of capital stock or by borrowing for a long term to pay off current liabilities.

© Rehan Qureshi/Shutterstock.com

Long-Term Financial Strength

Businesses that are successful and are able to continue operating through both strong and weak economic periods usually have long-term financial strength. Long-term financial strength requires a balance between stockholders' capital and borrowed capital. A profitable business can be even more profitable by using borrowed capital wisely. However, borrowed capital must be repaid with interest. Continuing operation of a business with a large percentage of borrowed capital may be jeopardized if net income declines and it cannot make loan payments. In addition, creditors are reluctant to loan additional money to companies with a high level of liabilities. A well-managed company monitors its long-term financial strength to ensure that it maintains a reasonable balance between stockholders' capital and borrowed capital.

Forest uses four measures to analyze long-term financial strength: (1) debt ratio, (2) equity ratio, (3) equity per share, and (4) interest coverage ratio.

DEBT RATIO

	Total Liabilities	÷	Total Assets	=	Debt Ratio
20X3	$247,156.29	÷	$736,085.11	=	33.6%
20X2	$231,706.22	÷	$644,147.48	=	36.0%

Total liabilities divided by total assets is called the **debt ratio**. This ratio shows the percentage of assets that are financed with borrowed capital (liabilities).

Forest's debt ratios for 20X3 and 20X2 are calculated as shown above, using information from the balance sheet (page 371). The 20X3 ratio of 33.6% indicates that for each $1.00 of assets owned by Forest, the company has borrowed 33.6 cents.

The average debt ratio for companies similar to Forest is 30.0%. Forest's ratios are above the industry average, an unfavorable condition. Rapid growth over the past two or three years, financed primarily through borrowed capital, has caused the unfavorable liabilities level. However, Forest's 20X3 debt ratio has decreased from 20X2, which is a favorable trend. The company should consider increasing assets without increasing liabilities by issuing more capital stock. This action would reduce the debt ratio.

EQUITY RATIO

	Total Stockholders' Equity	÷	Total Assets	=	Equity Ratio
20X3	$488,928.82	÷	$736,085.11	=	66.4%
20X2	$412,441.26	÷	$644,147.48	=	64.0%

The ratio found by dividing stockholders' equity by total assets is called the **equity ratio**. This ratio shows the percentage of assets that are provided by stockholders' equity.

Forest's equity ratios for 20X3 and 20X2 are calculated as shown above, using information from the statement of stockholders' equity (page 370) and the balance sheet (page 371). Forest's ratio for 20X3, 66.4%, indicates that for each $1.00 of assets owned by the company, 66.4 cents' worth was acquired with stockholders' capital. The average equity ratio for companies similar to Forest is 70.0%. Forest's ratios are below the industry average, an unfavorable condition.

The debt and equity ratios show the mix of capital provided by capital borrowed and capital provided by stockholders. The sum of the two ratios equals 100%, as shown here because total liabilities and stockholders' equity represent the source of all asset ownership.

	20X3	20X2
Debt Ratio	33.6%	36.0%
Equity Ratio	66.4%	64.0%
Totals	100.0%	100.0%

Due to rapid expansion, Forest's 20X2 equity ratio declined to an unfavorable level, and its debt ratio increased to an unfavorable level. In 20X3, both ratios have improved but remain unfavorable. Forest can continue efforts to increase its equity ratio by reducing liabilities and issuing additional stock.

fyi An unfavorable ratio in one year may be balanced by previous actual positive results and future expected positive results. The trend in a ratio may be more important than the ratio for a particular year.

INPUT

- Emphasize that long-term financial strength is demonstrated by companies that maintain the proper ratio between borrowed capital and stockholders' capital.
- Point out the four measures used to analyze long-term financial strength.
- Point out that companies with high percentages of borrowed capital sometimes find it difficult to make loan payments. Companies with high debt ratios do not have much of an operating cushion when earnings are low or there is a down cycle in the economy. During these declines, some businesses do not generate the cash flow needed to repay debts; consequently, they fail.
- Emphasize that the debt ratio shows the percentage of assets financed with borrowed capital, representing money owed or liabilities.
- Point out that the debt ratio shows the percentage of assets financed with borrowed capital (liabilities) and that the equity ratio shows the percentage of assets financed with owners' capital (stockholders' equity).
- Emphasize that the total of the debt ratio and the equity ratio must always equal 100%. In other words, all of Forest's assets were financed by either borrowed capital (liabilities) or stockholders' capital.

MODEL

- Direct students to the math illustration. Review the amounts and calculate the debt ratio.
- Ask a student to explain the meaning of Forest's debt ratio.
- Direct students to the math illustration. Review the amounts and calculate the equity ratio.
- Ask a student to explain the meaning of Forest's equity ratio.

DIFFERENTIATED INSTRUCTION

Logical/Mathematical learners enjoy reasoning and problem-solving activities. They enjoy learning through investigations and by working through problems in a systematic way. Ask students to go to http://money.msn.com or a comparable website and locate the financial statements for five companies. Instruct students to use the correct financial statements to compute the working capital, current ratio, quick ratio, debt ratio, equity ratio, and earnings per share for each of the five companies. Tell students to be prepared to explain their findings to the class.

INPUT

- Point out that the portion of stockholders' equity belonging to a single share of outstanding stock is called equity per share.
- Emphasize that the information for stock comes from the statement of stockholders' equity.

MODEL

- Direct students to the math illustration for calculating equity per share on common stock.
- Review the amounts and demonstrate on the board where the data were obtained and how to calculate equity per share.

INPUT

- Explain that the interest coverage ratio is the number of times a company can cover its interest expense with its earnings.
- Explain EBIT in calculating the interest coverage ratio.

MODEL

- Direct students to the math illustration for calculating the interest coverage ratio.

EQUITY PER SHARE ON COMMON STOCK

	Par Value of Preferred Stock	×	Shares of Preferred Stock Outstanding	=	Preferred Stockholders' Share of Stockholders' Equity
20X3	$100.00	×	1,275	=	$127,500.00
20X2	$100.00	×	1,275	=	$127,500.00

	Total Stockholders' Equity	–	Preferred Stockholders' Share of Stockholders' Equity	=	Common Stockholders' Share of Stockholders' Equity
20X3	$488,928.82	–	$127,500.00	=	$361,428.82
20X2	$412,441.26	–	$127,500.00	=	$284,941.26

	Common Stockholders' Share of Stockholders' Equity	÷	Shares of Common Stock Outstanding	=	Common Equity per Share
20X3	$361,428.82	÷	65,000	=	$5.56
20X2	$284,941.26	÷	65,000	=	$4.38

The amount of common stockholders' equity belonging to a single share of common stock is known as **common equity per share**. When a company has both common and preferred stock outstanding, the preferred stockholders' share of stockholders' equity must be subtracted from the total stockholders' equity. The preferred stockholders' share of stockholders' equity is equal to the par value of the preferred stock multiplied by the number of preferred shares outstanding.

Forest's common equity per share for 20X3 and 20X2 is calculated as shown above, using information from the statement of stockholders' equity (page 370). Forest's common equity per share in 20X3, $5.56, indicates that on December 31, 20X3, each share of common stock represents ownership in $5.56 of the assets.

Common equity per share tells stockholders how much ownership of the company each share represents. For example, Forest's common stockholders know that each share represents a $5.56 equity in the total company assets. This ownership has increased from $4.38 per share in 20X2, a significant increase and a favorable trend.

INTEREST COVERAGE RATIO AND EBIT

	EBIT	÷	Interest Expense	=	Interest Coverage Ratio
20X3	$129,281.38	÷	$11,708.33	=	11.0
20X2	$129,021.22	÷	$ 7,850.00	=	16.4
20X1	$123,382.36	÷	$ 4,554.25	=	27.1

Earnings before interest expense and taxes is called **EBIT** (pronounced ē - bĭt). EBIT is used in the calculation of several financial ratios. The easiest way to calculate EBIT is to start with net income and add interest expense and taxes. EBIT for 20X3 is $129,281.38 ($88,469.56 + $11,708.33 + $29,103.49).

The number of times a company can cover its interest expense with its earnings is called the **interest coverage ratio**. Forest's interest coverage ratios for the most recent three years are shown at the bottom of the first column, using information from the income statement (page 369). Forest's interest coverage ratio of 11.0 for 20X3 means that Forest's earnings can cover its interest expense 11.0 times.

Forest has been increasing its debt as it experiences rapid growth and increases in inventory. With increased debt comes increased interest expense. While Forest's net income has been relatively stable, its interest expense has grown each of the past two years. This growth has caused Forest's interest coverage ratio to decrease dramatically. However, it is still well above the acceptable ratio of 2.0.

If a company's interest coverage ratio falls below 2.0, it runs the risk of not being able to pay its annual interest expense. When this happens, banks may hesitate to loan additional funds to the company.

fyi *Dun & Bradstreet* publications list various ratios for numerous industries.

FORMATIVE ASSESSMENT

- This is an ongoing process. Circulate around the classroom or lab, observing which students have problems with the assignments.
- Troubleshooting: Diagnose the kinds of problems students have with this section. Students may have difficulty remembering the various formulas used for calculating financial strength.
- Assess student understanding by checking solutions to Independent Practice assignments and noting their answers to the Terms Review and Audit Your Understanding questions.

End of Lesson Review

LO1 Analyze the financial strength of a business.

Terms Review

comparative financial statements
cash equivalents
working capital
current ratio
quick assets
quick ratio
debt ratio
equity ratio
common equity per share
EBIT
interest coverage ratio

Audit your understanding

1. What three measures can be used to analyze short-term financial strength?
2. Why does a well-managed company monitor its long-term financial strength?
3. What is the formula for calculating debt ratio?

Work together 13-1

Analyzing short- and long-term financial strength

Information taken from S & T Company's comparative income statement and balance sheet is provided in the *Working Papers*. Your instructor will guide you through the following examples.

1. Calculate the following financial strength ratios for the current year and the prior year. Round ratios to the nearest tenth.
   a. Working capital
   b. Current ratio
   c. Quick ratio
   d. Debt ratio
   e. Equity ratio
   f. Common equity per share
   g. Interest coverage ratio
2. List two ways that S & T Company can increase its interest coverage ratio.

On your own 13-1

Analyzing short- and long-term financial strength

Information taken from OfficeWorld Supply Company's comparative income statement and balance sheet is provided in the *Working Papers*. Work independently to complete the following problem.

1. Calculate the following financial strength ratios for the current year and the prior year. Round ratios to the nearest tenth.
   a. Working capital
   b. Current ratio
   c. Quick ratio
   d. Debt ratio
   e. Equity ratio
   f. Common equity per share
   g. Interest coverage ratio
2. List one way that OfficeWorld Supply Company can decrease its debt ratio.

CHECK FOR UNDERSTANDING

Terms Review

- Call on students to define each term in the Terms Review. Definitions are given in the Glossary.

Audit Your Understanding

- Call on students to answer the Audit Your Understanding questions. Answers are given in Appendix D of the textbook.

GUIDED PRACTICE

Work Together

- Have students write the solution to the Work Together problem as you guide the class through the examples.
- Direct students to calculate and analyze the financial strength ratios.

INDEPENDENT PRACTICE

On Your Own

- Assign the On Your Own problem to be worked independently.
- Use the Formative Assessment techniques to diagnose student understanding.

Application Problem

- Assign Application Problem 13-1.

Online Working Papers

- Students can access the Lesson 13-1 problems using this software.

Website

- Direct students to the C21 Accounting companion website for additional practice and review opportunities throughout the chapter.

RETEACH

- Have students make a reference sheet listing the formulas they learned for financial strength ratios.

CLOSURE

- Write the formulas for financial strength analysis on the board.
- Organize students in small groups and have them prepare an example using each formula.

Essential Question

- Why would short-term financial strength be important? *(Short-term financial strength indicates a company's ability to pay off its debt as it comes due over the next year.)*

EXTENDED LEARNING

- Assign Accounting in the Real World on page 367.
- Assign Ethics in Action on page 369.
- Assign Why Accounting on page 373.

LESSON
13-2

BRIDGE

- Point out that students have already learned how to prepare financial statements. In this lesson, they will learn how to use the data on the financial statements to analyze a company's financial health.

TEACHING RESOURCES

- **Instructor's Resource CD/Website:**
  PowerPoint Slides
  Accounting Concepts
- **Working Papers:**
  Teacher's Edition of the Working Papers for Lesson 13-2
  Online Working Papers

ENGAGE

- Ask why ratios would be used for comparisons, rather than dollar amounts.

PREVIEW

- Call on students to read the accounting terms and definitions introduced in this lesson: *gross margin, operating margin, rate earned on average total assets, rate earned on average stockholders' equity, free cash flow,* and *capital expenditures.*
- Point out the learning objective for this lesson.
- Direct students to read the headings in this lesson and to examine the illustrations.

INPUT

- Explain that profitability is an important measure of a business's success.
- Point out the five profitability measures.
- Explain that gross margin is the gross profit as a percent of net sales.
- Direct students to the math illustration demonstrating the calculation of gross margin over three years.

LESSON 13-2 Measuring and Analyzing Profitability

LO2 Analyze the profitability of a business.

Profitability Analysis LO2

The amounts and consistency of earnings are important measures of a business's success. The earnings of a business must be satisfactory to continue operations. [CONCEPT: Going Concern] Consequently, managers, owners, and creditors are interested in an analysis of the profitability of the company. Forest calculates five profitability measures for the three most recent years: (1) gross margin, (2) operating margin, (3) rate earned on average total assets, (4) rate earned on average stockholders' equity, and (5) free cash flow.

GROSS MARGIN

	Gross Profit	÷	Net Sales	=	Gross Margin
20X3	$254,982.02	÷	$646,017.54	=	39.5%
20X2	$246,612.12	÷	$645,212.32	=	38.2%
20X1	$247,126.30	÷	$642,578.45	=	38.5%

The ratio of the money earned relative to the amount of the investment is known as the *return on investment.* There are several measures used to analyze return on investment. The measures differ as to the investment that is identified and the dollar amount used for the earnings.

Gross profit as a percent of net sales is called **gross margin**. Forest's gross margins for 20X3 and the two prior years are calculated as shown above, using information from the income statement (page 369). The 39.5% gross margin for 20X3 indicates that for each $1.00 of sales, Forest earns 39.5 cents in gross profit. The remaining amount from the sales dollar, 60.5 cents ($1.00 − $0.395), represents the cost of merchandise sold. Gross profit must be high enough to cover operating expenses, other expenses, taxes, and profit. Gross margin can be improved by increasing sales at a faster rate than the cost of merchandise sold.

Forest's gross margin decreased from 20X1 to 20X2, even though net sales increased significantly. This decrease was the result of the cost of merchandise sold increasing at a faster rate than net sales. Forest's gross margin increased from 20X2 to 20X3. Net sales increased only slightly during this period, but the cost of merchandise sold actually decreased. Forest was able to lower its cost of merchandise sold, possibly due to lower employee costs or finding a less expensive inventory source.

Forest feels that an acceptable gross margin is not less than 40.0%. Forest must try to increase its gross margin in the future.

© zhu difeng/Shutterstock.com

OPERATING MARGIN

	Income from Operations	÷	Net Sales	=	Operating Margin
20X3	$119,493.88	÷	$646,017.54	=	18.5%
20X2	$118,925.68	÷	$645,212.32	=	18.4%
20X1	$120,892.82	÷	$642,578.45	=	18.8%

Income from operations as a percent of net sales is called **operating margin**. This ratio is also referred to as the *rate of return on sales*. Forest's operating margins for 20X3 and the two prior years are calculated as shown above, using information from the income statement (page 369).

Forest's 18.5% operating margin for 20X3 indicates that for each $1.00 of sales, it earns 18.5 cents in operating income. This amount is available to cover other expenses, taxes, and profit.

Operating margin is used by investors to determine how effective a business is at earning a profit from its normal operations. Investors can compare Forest's operating margin with that for other companies in the same industry. This measure of a company's profitability is better than a ratio using net income because the managers of a company have more control over income from operations. Net income is affected by the income statement category "Other Revenues and Expenses" and by taxes. The items included in Other Revenues and Expenses do not reflect the normal operations of the business, and managers cannot easily control the amount of taxes paid to the government.

Forest has set an operating margin of at least 18.0% as its benchmark goal. Therefore, even though Forest's gross margin is lower than desired, the company has done a very good job of controlling operating expenses and has an operating margin that is acceptable.

© Blend Images/Shutterstock.com

INPUT

- Explain that income from operations as a percent of net sales is called operating margin.
- Point out that this measure only uses income from operations as a measurement, rather than net income that is used in the gross margin. This is because managers have more control over income from operations.
- Direct students to the math illustration demonstrating the calculation of operating margin over three years.

FORENSIC ACCOUNTING

The workbook contains the history of sales orders. Channel stuffing may be indicated when orders are shipped before the customer requests the merchandise. Students calculate the number of days between the order, requested delivery, and delivery dates. Filters are used to search for transactions where the dates occurred at unusual intervals.

Answers

Step 16: 30.8 days.

Step 22: Most of the 20 transactions (1) occurred in September, just before the end of the third quarter; (2) were packed by the employee having the initials PJL; and (3) were invoiced during September.

Step 28: Deliveries are made an average of 1.9 days before the customer's requested delivery date. All 20 transactions delivered the highest number of days before the merchandise was requested (1) occurred in September or October, (2) were packed by the employee having the initials PJL, and (3) were invoiced in September.

Step 29: There is strong, but not absolute, evidence that employee PJL shipped merchandise to customers early. More evidence would be required to determine whether the early deliveries were for legitimate reasons or for channel stuffing. Further tests might include:

1. Interviewing customers.
2. Comparing the frequency of differences between the order and invoice values.
3. Interviewing employee PJL and other employees in shipping.
4. Analyzing order, delivery, and invoicing activity after 9/30/14.

FORENSIC ACCOUNTING

Channel Stuffing

It seems to happen earlier every year. Retail store shelves have barely been cleared of their Halloween candy when gifts and supplies for the important Thanksgiving through New Year's Day selling season begin to appear.

Commonly, retailers take delivery of seasonal items well before the selling season. In fact, it is a business necessity. Items for sale in December might be ordered during the spring and be delivered in October. Retailers and suppliers both benefit from early ordering. The retailer is assured that the merchandise will be available for sale and will be delivered at the desired time. A supplier can plan its production schedules better, ensuring that it has an adequate supply of raw materials and labor.

Suppose that a supplier offers customers a 20% discount to order and pay for merchandise a full 12 months before the selling season. In exchange, the supplier will warehouse the merchandise until requested by each retailer.

When should the supplier record the sale? When the order is received, when the merchandise is produced, when the merchandise is delivered, or when cash is exchanged? Generally accepted accounting principles (GAAP) require that the sale be recorded when the merchandise is transferred between the parties. The transfer most often occurs when the goods are delivered.

Sunbeam, a maker of household appliances, began to offer its customers similar terms in 1997. Customers were offered discounts for ordering merchandise well before it was needed. Sunbeam would hold the items until the normal delivery date. However, contrary to GAAP, Sunbeam recorded the sales when the orders were received. This practice, known as *channel stuffing*, is illegal because it fraudulently inflates sales by recording future sales in the current period. When Sunbeam's fraudulent financial statements were revealed, the reported net income of $110 million was reduced to $38 million. As sales continued to decline, Sunbeam's stock price plummeted.

ACTIVITY

The quarterly income statement of Chopra Novelties reported a sharp increase in sales. This was the "break-out" quarter that the new chief executive officer had been promising. As a member of the board of directors, you are pleased with this higher level of sales. Yet, you wonder whether some imaginative accounting could have been used to achieve these results. Thus, you direct the internal auditor to perform some basic tests related to the timing of sales and to look specifically for signs of channel stuffing.

INSTRUCTIONS

Open the spreadsheet FA_CH13 and complete the steps on the Instructions tab.

Source: Called to Account: Fourteen Financial Frauds that Shaped the American Accounting Profession, Paul M. Clikeman, Routledge, New York, 2009.

© iStockphoto.com/burwellphotography

RATE EARNED ON AVERAGE TOTAL ASSETS

$$\left[\begin{array}{c}\text{January 1, 20X3}\\ \text{Total Assets}\end{array} + \begin{array}{c}\text{December 31, 20X3}\\ \text{Total Assets}\end{array}\right] \div 2 = \begin{array}{c}\text{Average}\\ \text{Total Assets}\end{array} \quad (1)$$

$$[\$644{,}147.48 + \$736{,}085.11] \div 2 = \$690{,}116.30$$

$$\begin{array}{c}\text{Net}\\ \text{Income}\end{array} \div \begin{array}{c}\text{Average}\\ \text{Total Assets}\end{array} = \begin{array}{c}\text{Rate Earned on}\\ \text{Average Total Assets}\end{array} \quad (2)$$

$$\$88{,}469.56 \div \$690{,}116.30 = 12.8\%$$

A business uses its assets to earn net income. If a business uses all assets as efficiently as possible, it should earn the best possible net income. The relationship between net income and average total assets is called the **rate earned on average total assets**. This rate is also referred to as *return on assets* (*ROA*), and it shows how well a business is using its assets to earn net income. Forest's rate earned on average total assets is calculated as shown above, using income statement and balance sheet information.

Calculating the Rate Earned on Average Total Assets

1. **Calculate average total assets. Average total assets is the average amount of assets held during a year.**
   a. **Add January 1 total assets and December 31 total assets. (Total assets for January 1 are the same as the total assets on the prior year's December 31 balance sheet.)**
   b. **Divide the total by 2.**
2. **Divide net income by average total assets to determine the rate earned on average total assets.**

A 12.8% rate earned on average total assets means that for each $1.00 of assets, the business earned 12.8 cents. A table comparing this result to the rate for 20X2 is shown below.

	20X3	20X2*
Net income	$ 88,469.56	$ 90,664.44
January 1 total assets	644,147.48	645,298.12
December 31 total assets	736,085.11	644,147.48
Average total assets	690,116.30	644,722.80
Rate earned on average total assets	12.8%	14.1%

*Some information for 20X2 is taken from financial statements that are not illustrated.

Forest compares this rate to rates of return on alternative investments. Forest's goal is to earn a rate of return that is at least as high as other types of investments. For example, if Forest can earn more by placing extra cash in government bonds, the company is not meeting its earnings goal.

Investment sources available to Forest are earning 12.0%. Although both years' rates of return are above this goal, the rate earned on average total assets for 20X3 has dropped significantly from 20X2. Forest must take measures to ensure that this trend does not continue. To increase this rate, Forest must either earn more net income with the same amount of assets or earn the same amount of income with less invested assets.

INPUT

- Explain that the relationship between net income and average total assets is called the rate earned on average total assets.
- Stress that this rate shows how well a business is using its assets to earn net income.
- Point out that this rate is also called ROA (return on asset).

MODEL

Calculate the rate earned on average total assets

- Direct students to the two steps for calculating the rate.
- Use the math illustration on the page to explain the process for calculating the rate earned on average total assets.
- Use the board to show how the rate is calculated.
- Discuss what this rate means to Forest.

INPUT

- Explain that investors use this rate to measure and compare the best investment.

MODEL

Calculate the rate earned on average stockholders' equity

- Direct students to the two steps for calculating the rate.
- Use the math illustration on the page to explain the process for calculating the rate earned on average stockholders' equity.
- Use the board to show how the rate is calculated.
- Discuss what this rate means to Forest.

RATE EARNED ON AVERAGE STOCKHOLDERS' EQUITY

$$\left[\begin{array}{c}\text{January 1, 20X3} \\ \text{Stockholders' Equity}\end{array} + \begin{array}{c}\text{December 31, 20X3} \\ \text{Stockholders' Equity}\end{array}\right] \div 2 = \begin{array}{c}\text{Average} \\ \text{Stockholders' Equity}\end{array} \quad (1)$$

$$[\$412{,}441.26 + \$488{,}928.82] \div 2 = \$450{,}685.04$$

$$\text{Net Income} \div \begin{array}{c}\text{Average} \\ \text{Stockholders' Equity}\end{array} = \begin{array}{c}\text{Rate Earned on} \\ \text{Average Stockholders' Equity}\end{array} \quad (2)$$

$$\$88{,}469.56 \div \$450{,}685.04 = 19.6\%$$

Investors use financial measures to compare businesses to determine the best investment. The relationship between net income and average stockholders' equity is called the **rate earned on average stockholders' equity**. Forest's rate earned on average stockholders' equity is calculated as shown above.

Calculating the Rate Earned on Average Stockholders' Equity

1. Calculate average stockholders' equity.
   a. Add January 1 stockholders' equity and December 31 stockholders' equity. (Stockholders' equity for January 1 is the same as the stockholders' equity on the prior year's December 31 balance sheet.)
   b. Divide the total by 2.
2. Divide net income by average stockholders' equity to determine the rate earned on average stockholders' equity.

A 19.6% rate earned on average stockholders' equity means that for each $1.00 of stockholders' equity, the business earned 19.6 cents. The following table compares the 20X3 rate to the 20X2 rate.

	20X3	20X2*
Net income	$ 88,469.56	$ 90,664.44
January 1 stockholders' equity	412,441.26	401,276.21
December 31 stockholders' equity	488,928.82	412,441.26
Average stockholders' equity	450,685.04	406,858.74
Rate earned on average stockholders' equity	19.6%	22.3%

*Some information for 20X2 is taken from financial statements that are not illustrated.

Forest's rate is well above the industry standard of 12.0%. However, its rate has decreased significantly from 22.3% to 19.6%. Even though a comparison with industry standards shows that Forest achieved a satisfactory rate earned on average stockholders' equity, the trend is one that should be investigated. Forest does not want this trend to continue. To keep the rate from decreasing, Forest must maintain the level of net income with the same amount of stockholders' equity.

DIFFERENTIATED INSTRUCTION

Auditory/Linguistic learners have highly developed auditory skills and often use language as a means to express themselves in writing and speaking. Tell students to select one business and analyze its finances using the financial ratios presented in this lesson. Ask students to write a letter to a company suggesting where it should focus its attention based on the results of their analysis.

FREE CASH FLOW

	Cash Flow from Operating Activities	–	Capital Expenditures	=	Free Cash Flow
20X3	$64,385.78	–	$107,987.00	=	($43,601.22)
20X2	$56,886.13	–	$122,853.00	=	($65,966.87)

Cash flow data are important information for company managers, creditors, and investors. If a company cannot pay its bills by their due date, it must arrange for short-term loans or cash advances. **Free cash flow** is a measure equal to cash flows from operations less cash used for capital expenditures. **Capital expenditures** are purchases of plant assets used in the operation of a business. Forest's free cash flow for 20X3 and 20X2 is calculated as shown above, using information from the statement of cash flows (page 372). For Forest, capital expenditures are the purchases of office equipment and store equipment.

Forest's free cash flow is negative for both years. This means that each year Forest used more cash for purchases of equipment than the cash flow from operating activities. The negative free cash flow for 20X3 ($43,601.22) is less than the negative cash flow for 20X2 ($65,966.87). This is a result of an increase in cash flow from operating activities and a decrease in capital expenditures.

While a negative free cash flow is not acceptable in the long run, Forest was aware of the need to invest in capital items. Over the last three years, company managers took steps to increase cash flows by issuing bonds and selling preferred stock.

GLOBAL AWARENESS

World Trade Organization

A company looking to expand its business can try to sell its goods and services in foreign markets. Goods or services shipped out of a seller's home country to another country are known as *exports*.

Companies can also buy products from foreign markets. A foreign company may sell materials, component parts, or finished goods at a lower price than a domestic company. Goods or services shipped into the buyer's home country from another country are known as *imports*.

Doing business in a foreign country can help a company grow, but it also brings potential challenges. Business practices can vary from country to country. In some countries, the government can block imports to or exports from specific countries. In other countries, the government can institute tariffs on imports or exports.

An organization that works "to ensure that trade flows as smoothly, predictably and freely as possible" between nations is the World Trade Organization (WTO). The WTO states on its website that it "is the only international organization dealing with the global rules of trade between nations." The WTO was established on January 1, 1995. As of March 2013, the WTO had 159 member countries.

The basis for smooth, predictable, and free trade flows is a WTO trading agreement. A country signs such an agreement and is then bound to follow it. The WTO supports the negotiation and enforcement of these agreements. If a country is not adhering to a trade agreement, the WTO will oversee a dispute settlement process.

The WTO also focuses efforts on helping developing countries, which are given some leeway in implementing trade agreements. Most trade agreements also contain measures to increase the trading opportunities of developing countries.

CRITICAL THINKING

Visit the WTO website at www.wto.org to answer these questions.

1. Find the current list of WTO member countries. List three countries that joined the WTO on January 1, 1995. List the newest member of the WTO and the date it became a member.
2. List the name of the director-general and when his or her term as director-general ends.
3. Why might the government of a country limit the importing of goods to that country?

© iStockphoto.com/Lusky

INPUT

- Explain that analyzing cash flow helps a company determine if it can pay its bills by their due date to avoid short-term loans.
- Point out that free cash flow is a measure equal to cash flows from operations less cash used for capital expenditures.
- Emphasize that capital expenditures are purchases of plant assets used in the operations of a business.

MODEL

- Direct students to the math illustration for calculating free cash flow.
- Use the board to show how the rate is calculated.
- Discuss what this rate means to Forest.

GLOBAL AWARENESS

Answers

1. Answers will vary. At time of publication, the current membership list included 76 countries that joined the WTO on January 1, 1995. At the time of publication, the newest member on this list was Tajikistan, which joined the WTO on March 2, 2013.
2. Answers will vary depending on the date. At the time of publication, Roberto Azevêdo was the director-general of the WTO. He was appointed for a four-year term on September 1, 2013.
3. The government might be trying to support the domestic market for a product. By prohibiting imports, its citizens must buy the product produced in their own country. A government may also limit the importing of goods from a specific country for political purposes. Such a sanction could harm the economy of the prohibited country, forcing it to make changes or lift its own limits on imports.

FORMATIVE ASSESSMENT

- This is an ongoing process. Circulate around the classroom or lab, observing which students have problems with the assignments.
- Troubleshooting: Diagnose the kinds of problems students have with this lesson. Students may have difficulty remembering the formulas for the various ratios for analyzing the profitability of a business.
- Assess student understanding by checking solutions to Independent Practice assignments and noting their answers to the Terms Review and Audit Your Understanding questions.

CHECK FOR UNDERSTANDING

Terms Review

- Call on students to define each term in the Terms Review. Definitions are given in the Glossary.

Audit Your Understanding

- Call on students to answer the Audit Your Understanding questions. Answers are given in Appendix D of the textbook.

GUIDED PRACTICE

Work Together

- Have students write the solution to the Work Together problem as you guide the class through the examples.
- Direct students to calculate profitability measures. Ask students to explain the meaning of the operating margin.

INDEPENDENT PRACTICE

On Your Own

- Assign the On Your Own problem to be worked independently.
- Use the Formative Assessment techniques to diagnose student understanding.

Application Problem

- Assign Application Problem 13-2.

Online Working Papers

- Students can access the Lesson 13-2 problems using this software.

RETEACH

- Have students make a reference sheet listing the formulas for analyzing profitability.

CLOSURE

- Write on the board the formulas used for profitability analysis.
- Organize students in small groups and ask them to prepare an example using each formula.

Essential Questions

- Why isn't the amount of net income a good evaluator of a company's profitability? (*The net income alone does not provide company history of net income/net loss nor industry averages for comparisons.*)
- Why would measuring free cash flow be an indicator of profitability? (*When free cash flow is positive, it indicates that there is cash to reinvest and grow the business.*)

End of Lesson Review

LO2 Analyze the profitability of a business.

Terms Review

gross margin
operating margin
rate earned on average total assets
rate earned on average stockholders' equity
free cash flow
capital expenditures

Audit your understanding

1. What is the formula for operating margin?
2. What does the rate earned on average total assets show?
3. What does the rate earned on average stockholders' equity show?

Work together 13-2

Calculating profitability measures

Information taken from KL Marketing Group's financial statements is provided in the *Working Papers*. Your instructor will guide you through the following examples.

1. Calculate the following profitability measures for the current year and the prior year. Round percentage calculations to the nearest 0.1% and dollar amounts to the nearest $0.01.
   a. Gross margin
   b. Operating margin
   c. Rate earned on average total assets
   d. Rate earned on average stockholders' equity
   e. Free cash flow
2. Explain what its operating margin from the current year tells KL Marketing Group.

On your own 13-2

Calculating profitability measures

Information taken from GreenWay Corporation's financial statements is provided in the *Working Papers*. Work independently to complete the following problem.

1. Calculate the following profitability measures for the current year and the prior year. Round percentage calculations to the nearest 0.1% and dollar amounts to the nearest $0.01. Your instructor will guide you through the examples.
   a. Gross margin
   b. Operating margin
   c. Rate earned on average total assets
   d. Rate earned on average stockholders' equity
   e. Free cash flow
2. Explain what the gross margin from the current year tells GreenWay Corporation.

LESSON

13-3 Calculating and Analyzing Efficiency Measures and Market Ratio

LO3 Perform efficiency analysis of a business.
LO4 Calculate the market ratios of a business.

Analyzing Efficiency LO3

The profitability and continued growth of a business are influenced by how efficiently the business utilizes its assets. The operating cycle of a merchandising business consists of three phases: (1) purchasing merchandise, (2) selling merchandise (frequently on account), and (3) collecting the accounts receivable. Much of a business's assets are in accounts receivable and merchandise inventory. The faster a business can convert these assets to cash and begin another operating cycle, the more efficient and profitable the business will be.

ACCOUNTS RECEIVABLE TURNOVER RATIO

Calculate average book value of accounts receivable

[Beginning Book Value of Accounts Receivable	+	Ending Book Value of Accounts Receivable]	÷	2	=	Average Book Value of Accounts Receivable
[$55,647.10	+	$66,706.43]	÷	2	=	$61,176.77

Calculate accounts receivable turnover ratio

Net Sales	÷	Average Book Value of Accounts Receivable	=	Accounts Receivable Turnover Ratio
$646,017.54	÷	$61,176.77	=	10.6

A business accepts accounts receivable to encourage sales. However, the earnings process is not complete until the business receives cash for sales on account. Thus, an efficient company closely monitors the length of time required to collect its receivables. The number of times the average amount of accounts receivable is collected during a specified period is known as the *accounts receivable turnover ratio*. This ratio monitors a business's accounts receivable collection efficiency.

Forest's accounts receivable turnover ratio for 20X3 is calculated as shown above, using the information from the balance sheet and income statement. Forest's turnover ratio indicates that accounts are being collected 10.6 times a year.

DAYS' SALES IN ACCOUNTS RECEIVABLE

The average period of time to collect an account receivable is known as *days' sales in accounts receivable*.

Calculate days' sales in accounts receivable

Days in Year	÷	Accounts Receivable Turnover Ratio	=	Days' Sales in Accounts Receivable
365	÷	10.6	=	34 days

The days' sales in accounts receivable is calculated above.

The accounts receivable turnover ratio for 20X2 was 11.4. The days' sales in accounts receivable was 32 days. Forest's credit terms are n/30. Thus, the company's goal is to collect accounts receivable in 30 days or less. Neither year's results meet that goal. In addition, the ratio has decreased from 11.4 to 10.6. This unfavorable trend may be a result of Forest's growth and should be monitored carefully so that it does not continue. The unfavorable trend could also result from a relaxation of credit restrictions.

LESSON 13-3

BRIDGE

- Point out that students have learned how to use ratios to measure profitability. In this lesson, they will learn ratios for analyzing efficiency and market ratios.

TEACHING RESOURCES

- **Instructor's Resource CD/Website:**
  PowerPoint Slides
  Accounting Concepts
- **Working Papers:**
  Teacher's Edition of the Working Papers for Lesson 13-3
  Online Working Papers

ENGAGE

- Ask students if new merchandise has ever attracted them to a retail store.
- Ask students to predict how the market price of a company's share of stock might be used to analyze the company's financial health.

PREVIEW

- Call on students to read the accounting terms and definitions introduced in this lesson: *earnings per share (EPS), market value of a share of stock, price-earnings ratio,* and *dividend yield.*
- Point out the learning objectives for this lesson.
- Direct students to read the headings in this lesson and to examine the illustrations.

INPUT

- Explain the importance of efficiency.
- Explain that the accounts receivable turnover ratio is the number of times the average amount of accounts receivable is collected annually.
- Point out that the turnover ratio is a measure of a company's efficiency in collecting its accounts receivable.
- Point out that the days' sales in accounts receivable calculation determines the average number of days it takes for payment to be received.

MODEL

- Use the board or direct students to the math illustration to demonstrate calculating the accounts receivable turnover ratio.
- Point out that the first step is to calculate the average book value of accounts receivable.
- Demonstrate dividing the net sales on account from the income statement by the average book value of accounts receivable to get the accounts receivable turnover ratio.
- Use the board or direct students to the math illustration to demonstrate calculating the days' sales in accounts receivable.
- Ask students to explain what the accounts receivable turnover ratio and the days' sales in accounts receivable mean to the company.

INPUT

- Point out that the faster a company sells its merchandise, the faster it earns income.
- Explain that there are two measures of the speed at which merchandise is sold: the merchandise inventory turnover ratio and the average number of days' sales in merchandise inventory.
- Explain that the merchandise inventory turnover ratio indicates how many times the inventory was turned over, or sold, during a specific period of time.
- Direct students to the math illustration and demonstrate how to calculate the inventory turnover ratio.
- Explain that the inventory turnover ratio is used to calculate the average number of days' sales in merchandise inventory by dividing it into the number of days in a year.
- Direct students to the math illustration and demonstrate how to calculate the days' sales in inventory.

INVENTORY TURNOVER RATIO

Calculate average merchandise inventory

[January 1 Merchandise Inventory	+	December 31 Merchandise Inventory]	÷	2	=	Average Merchandise Inventory
[$95,214.25	+	$144,066.40]	÷	2	=	$119,640.33

Calculate inventory turnover ratio

Cost of Merchandise Sold	÷	Average Merchandise Inventory	=	Inventory Turnover Ratio
$391,035.52	÷	$119,640.33	=	3.3

A company earns income when it sells merchandise. The faster it sells its inventory, the more efficient and generally the more profitable the business. The number of times the average amount of merchandise inventory is sold during a specific period is known as the *inventory turnover ratio*. This ratio can be used to monitor merchandise inventory efficiency.

Forest's inventory turnover ratio for 20X3 is calculated as shown above, using information from the income statement and balance sheet. The turnover ratio of 3.3 indicates that the inventory is being sold 3.3 times in a year.

DAYS' SALES IN INVENTORY

Calculate days' sales in inventory

Days in Year	÷	Inventory Turnover Ratio	=	Days' Sales in Inventory
365	÷	3.3	=	111 days

The time needed to sell an average amount of merchandise inventory is known as *days' sales in inventory*. The days' sales in inventory is calculated above.

The inventory turnover ratio for 20X2 was 3.2. The days' sales in inventory was 114 days. An optimum merchandise inventory turnover ratio is determined by two factors: (1) amount of sales and (2) number of days needed to replenish the inventory. Previous experience indicates that Forest needs to maintain an inventory turnover ratio between 3.3 and 3.6. Forest's inventory turnover ratio is slightly lower than desired. That means that Forest has slightly more inventory on hand than would be necessary. A turnover ratio considerably lower than the acceptable range would indicate too much inventory on hand. A turnover ratio considerably higher than the acceptable range would mean that Forest is at risk for lost sales because some items could be out of stock before new inventory is received. Overall, Forest's current inventory level is satisfactory.

INPUT

- Explain that market ratios relate an amount to the market price of the company's stock.
- Point out that earnings per share is calculated on shares of stock outstanding. The calculation does not use shares that are treasury stock because these shares are not outstanding.
- Emphasize the difference between a simple capital structure and a complex capital structure.
- Explain diluted earnings per share.
- Direct students to the math illustration at the bottom of the page. Review the calculations for determining earnings per share.

Market Ratios LO4

Most ratios classified as market ratios relate an amount from the financial statements of a company with the market price of the company's stock. Market ratios, therefore, are somewhat objective because the market price of a stock is determined by the marketplace.

EARNINGS PER SHARE

	[Net Income	−	Preferred Dividends]	÷	Shares of Common Stock Outstanding	=	Earnings per Share
20X3	[$88,469.56	−	$7,650.00]	÷	65,000	=	$1.24
20X2	[$90,664.44	−	$7,650.00]	÷	65,000	=	$1.28
20X1	[$89,235.15	−	$3,000.00]	÷	65,000	=	$1.33

Net income after federal income tax divided by the number of outstanding shares of stock is known as **earnings per share (EPS)**. Stockholders and management frequently use earnings per share as a measure of success. As earnings per share increase, more people become interested in buying stock. This demand for stock causes stock prices to go up. The company then finds it easier to issue stock or borrow money.

Forest's earnings per share for 20X3 and the two prior years are calculated as shown above, using information from the income statement and the statement of stockholders' equity. Although net income increased from 20X1 to 20X2, earnings per share decreased from $1.33 to $1.28. This was caused by an increase in preferred dividends due to more preferred shares outstanding. More dividends paid to preferred stockholders decreased the amount of net income available to common shareholders. Earnings per share decreased again in 20X3, due to a decrease in net income. Forest knows that a positive trend is important to the company and must try to increase its earnings per share in the future.

Forest Equipment, Inc., has what is called a *simple capital structure*. This means that it does not have any convertible preferred stock or convertible bonds payable or stock options outstanding. If a company has convertible preferred stock or bonds or stock options, it is considered to have a *complex capital structure*, and it must complete additional calculations for earnings per share. Earnings per share calculated as if all convertible securities and stock options are converted to shares of common stock is called *diluted earnings per share*.

For example, assume that during 20X3, Forest Equipment, Inc., issued bonds that could be converted to 5,000 shares of common stock. Even though the bonds were not converted during 20X3, the company would have to calculate and disclose diluted earnings per share in addition to regular (or basic) earnings per share. The only part of the calculation that would change would be the number of shares of common stock outstanding. For calculating diluted earnings per share, it is assumed that all 5,000 shares of common stock have been issued. Forest's diluted earnings per share would be $1.15 [($88,469.56 − $7,650.00) ÷ 70,000 = $1.15]. Notice that this calculation indicates that each share only earned $1.15 instead of $1.24. Diluted earnings per share gives the stockholder a "worst-case scenario of earnings. This lower earnings per share would only come true if everyone holding the convertible bonds converted his or her shares.

THINK LIKE AN ACCOUNTANT

© iStockphoto.com/Dan Bachman

Charting Earnings per Share

LMP Technology has been a privately held corporation since its inception. A major source of the corporation's capital has been the sale of preferred stock to venture capitalists. The corporation also manages a stock incentive program that awards its 20 employees with stock in lieu of competitive market salaries.

The corporation's strategies have worked well. The corporation has grown to become a major supplier of computer networking equipment. At the urging of its venture capitalist investors, LMP has decided it is time to take the corporation public.

LMP's Accounting Department has been charged with creating the documents required to file an initial public offering with the Securities and Exchange Commission. The Accounting Department was also given responsibility for creating a presentation that management would deliver to various brokerage firms and institutional investors to raise awareness of, and demand for, LMP's common stock. Charts showing the growth in earnings per share would be critical to communicating the success of the corporation.

OPEN THE SPREADSHEET TLA_CH13

The workbook contains ten years of earnings and stock information. Follow the steps on the Instructions tab to prepare two charts. Answer these questions:

1. Describe the growth in earnings per share over the past ten years.
2. Compare and contrast the two charts. Identify what charting options should be selected to create the chart for the presentation.

THINK LIKE AN ACCOUNTANT

Students are given net income and stock information for a ten-year period. Students begin by calculating earnings per share. These data are then used to create two versions of a chart showing the growth in the corporation's earnings per share. The questions require students to prepare written statements describing the trend in earnings per share and supporting their selection of options of the two charts.

Solutions will vary.

Suggested Solution

1. Earnings per share has remained relatively steady during the ten-year period, ranging from a low of $3.57 to a high of $3.77. The issuance of additional preferred stock resulted in a drop in earnings per share in 20X4. However, earnings have shown steady growth since that time.
2. Although Version A focuses on annual changes in earnings per share, the chart tends to distort the magnitude of these changes. Version B, having a $0.00 minimum vertical scale, more clearly shows that the corporation has experienced relatively stable earnings over the ten-year period. The expansion of individual bars is more visually appealing and better communicates a trend, similar to a continuous line.

INPUT

- Point out that the P/E ratio should only be used in conjunction with other financial measures as a predictor of the future success of a company.
- Ask students to define the price-earnings ratio. Lead a discussion showing the P/E ratio as the relationship between the market value per share and the earnings per share of a stock. Point out that the P/E ratio is based on a company's growth potential and future profitability. When investors think a company's future growth and earnings show excellent potential, they are usually willing to pay more for the stock.
- Stress that a high P/E ratio means that investors expect high growth and earnings in the future.
- Point out that the price-earnings ratio is often reported in the stock market section of the newspaper.
- Ask what Forest's P/E ratios mean for the three years illustrated.

MODEL

- Direct students to the math illustration.
- Review the information on how to calculate the price-earnings ratio.
- Write and explain the calculation on the board.

TEACHING IDEA **Provide students with extra practice by writing additional amounts for market price per share and earnings per share.**

PRICE-EARNINGS RATIO

	Market Price per Share	÷	Earnings per Share	=	Price-Earnings Ratio
20X3	$ 9.50	÷	$1.24	=	7.7
20X2	$10.00	÷	$1.28	=	7.8
20X1	$10.00	÷	$1.33	=	7.5

The price at which a share of stock may be sold on the stock market at any given time is called the **market value of a share of stock**. The market price of a share of stock is determined by the amount that investors are willing to pay for it. Thus, the market price of a company's stock is influenced strongly by what potential investors think the company's earnings will be in the future. Market value can change frequently and dramatically for heavily traded stocks.

The relationship between the market value per share and earnings per share of a stock is called the **price-earnings ratio** (P/E ratio). Investors usually want to buy stock in companies that are earning a reasonable amount of net income. The P/E ratio can be compared to those of similar companies.

Forest's P/E ratio of 7.7 means that the price of one share of stock is 7.7 times the earnings per share. In 20X3, the decrease in the market price caused the P/E ratio to decrease. The market is not willing to pay as much per share as in the past. This may be due to several unfavorable trends revealed by an analysis of Forest's financial statements. Forest may need to try to increase earnings per share to maintain investor confidence.

It is also important to realize that Forest's P/E ratio for 20X3 would have decreased even more if not for the decrease in earnings per share from 20X2 to 20X3. Had its earnings per share stayed at $1.28, its P/E ratio would have been only 7.4.

What is a typical P/E ratio? P/E ratios vary considerably from industry to industry. When analyzing a company, it is best to compare its P/E ratio with other companies in the same industry. In addition, while a higher P/E ratio usually is considered better than a lower P/E ratio, there are some exceptions. A low P/E ratio (a low market price compared to the earnings) indicates that the market is not confident about the future of the stock. However, it could also mean that the stock is undervalued, which would indicate a good time to buy its shares. On the other hand, a high P/E ratio (a high market price compared to the earnings) indicates that the market has confidence in the future earnings of the company. However, it may mean that the stock is overpriced and ready for a correction.

A smart investor will not make an investment decision based on P/E ratio alone. The P/E ratio should be used in conjunction with other financial measures and with nonfinancial data that would help one predict the future success of a company.

© shipfactory/Shutterstock.com

fyi *The Wall Street Journal* and many local newspapers report price-earnings ratios in their stock quotations.

DIVIDEND YIELD

	Common Dividends	÷	Common Shares Outstanding	=	Common Dividend per Share
20X3	$14,950.00	÷	65,000	=	$0.23
20X2	$16,900.00	÷	65,000	=	$0.26
20X1	$14,950.00	÷	65,000	=	$0.23

	Common Dividend per Share	÷	Market Price per Share	=	Common Dividend Yield
20X3	$0.23	÷	$ 9.50	=	2.4%
20X2	$0.26	÷	$10.00	=	2.6%
20X1	$0.23	÷	$10.00	=	2.3%

The relationship between dividends per share and market price per share is called the **dividend yield**. Dividend yield can be calculated for both common and preferred stock. Forest's common dividend yield for 20X3 and the two prior years is calculated above.

Forest's common dividend yield of 2.4% for 20X3 means that stockholders are earning 2.4% on their investment in Forest stock. An investor will compare the earnings on Forest's stock with other investment opportunities. However, even though the dividend yield is low, investors who are not looking for immediate cash inflow from dividends may hold on to their Forest stock because of an expectation that the market value of the stock will increase.

	Preferred Dividends	÷	Preferred Shares Outstanding	=	Preferred Dividend per Share
20X3	$7,650.00	÷	1,275	=	$6.00
20X2	$7,650.00	÷	1,275	=	$6.00
20X1	$3,000.00	÷	500	=	$6.00

	Preferred Dividend per Share	÷	Market Price per Share	=	Preferred Dividend Yield
20X3	$6.00	÷	$107.00	=	5.6%
20X2	$6.00	÷	$112.00	=	5.4%
20X1	$6.00	÷	$110.00	=	5.5%

Forest's preferred dividend yield for 20X3 and the two prior years is calculated above. Forest's preferred dividend yield of 5.6% for 20X3 means that stockholders are earning 5.6% on their investment in Forest stock. Note that the dividend yield decreased in 20X2 because the market price of the stock increased. The dividend yield increased in 20X3 because the market price of the stock decreased.

INPUT

- Ask students to define *dividend yield*.
- Point out that dividend yield can be calculated for both common and preferred stock.
- Direct students to the math illustration and review how to calculate the dividend yield.
- Write and explain the calculation on the board.

FORMATIVE ASSESSMENT

- This is an ongoing process. Circulate around the classroom or lab, observing which students have problems with the assignments.
- Troubleshooting: Diagnose the kinds of problems students have with this lesson. Students may have difficulty remembering the formulas to analyze efficiency measures and market ratios of a business.
- Assess student understanding by checking solutions to Independent Practice assignments and noting their answers to the Terms Review and Audit Your Understanding questions.

CHECK FOR UNDERSTANDING

Terms Review

- Call on students to define each term in the Terms Review. Definitions are given in the Glossary.

Audit Your Understanding

- Call on students to answer the Audit Your Understanding questions. Answers are given in Appendix D of the textbook.

GUIDED PRACTICE

Work Together

- Have students write the solution to the Work Together problems as you guide the class through the examples.
- Direct students to calculate and analyze efficiency measures and market ratios.

INDEPENDENT PRACTICE

On Your Own

- Assign the On Your Own problem to be worked independently.
- Use the Formative Assessment techniques to diagnose student understanding.

Application Problem

- Assign Application Problem 13-3.

Online Working Papers

- Students can access the Lesson 13-3 problems using this software.

RETEACH

- Call on students to describe how to calculate each ratio in the lesson.
- Provide a set of different data and call on students to calculate each ratio.
- Provide a set of analysis results and ask whether the performance is acceptable or unacceptable.

CLOSURE

- Ask students to summarize briefly efficiency measures and market ratios.

Essential Questions

- Why would efficiency ratios be needed to assess a company's financial health if profitability ratios were used? (*The profitability of a company depends on how efficient the company is in collecting money and controlling its assets, such as inventory.*)
- Why do market indicators matter when evaluating a company's financial health? (*The stock's worth is important because you are acquiring a piece of the company. It's profitability is an important consideration.*)

End of Lesson Review

LO3 Perform efficiency analysis of a business.

LO4 Calculate the market ratios of a business.

Terms Review

earnings per share (EPS)

market value of a share of stock

price-earnings ratio

dividend yield

Audit your understanding

1. What does earnings per share show?
2. What is the formula for the price-earnings ratio?
3. If the dividend paid remains the same from Year 1 to Year 2, but the market value of the stock decreases, how will the dividend yield be affected?

Work together 13-3

Calculating and analyzing efficiency measures and market ratios

Information taken from Bonita Bay Supply's financial statements is provided in the *Working Papers*. Your instructor will guide you through the following examples.

1. Calculate the following efficiency measures and market ratios for the current year and the prior year. Round percentage calculations to the nearest 0.1%, dollar amounts to the nearest $0.01, and the price-earnings ratio to the nearest tenth.
   a. Accounts receivable turnover ratio
   b. Days' sales in accounts receivable
   c. Inventory turnover ratio
   d. Days' sales in inventory
   e. Earnings per share
   f. Price-earnings ratio
   g. Dividend yield
2. Bonita Bay Supply's credit terms are n/30. Analyze the company's days' sales in accounts receivable in terms of its credit policy and state any trend this measure reveals.

On your own 13-3

Calculating and analyzing efficiency measures and market ratios

Information taken from Morgan Enterprise's financial statements is provided in the *Working Papers*. Work independently to complete the following problem.

1. Calculate the following efficiency measures and market ratios for the current year and the prior year. Round percentage calculations to the nearest 0.1%, dollar amounts to the nearest $0.01, and the price-earnings ratio to the nearest tenth.
   a. Accounts receivable turnover ratio
   b. Days' sales in accounts receivable
   c. Inventory turnover ratio
   d. Days' sales in inventory
   e. Earnings per share
   f. Price-earnings ratio
   g. Dividend yield
2. Analyze the company's days' sales in inventory and state any trend this measure reveals.

EXTENDED LEARNING

- Assign Think Like an Accountant on page 387.

LESSON

13-4 Advanced Topics in Financial Reporting

LO5 Calculate permanent and temporary differences in net income and taxable income.

LO6 Understand the concept of comprehensive income.

Net Income and Taxable Income LO5

The net income reported by a company on its income statement is usually not the same amount reported on the company's tax return as "taxable income." The difference between net income and taxable income is caused by the rules that must be followed to calculate each amount.

Net income is calculated following accounting rules, called generally accepted accounting principles (GAAP). GAAP are developed by the accounting profession and are designed to provide important information that is accurate, reliable, comparable, and consistent.

Taxable income is calculated following U.S. tax laws. Tax laws are developed by Congress, enforced by the Internal Revenue Service, and designed to collect government revenue in an equitable manner. In addition, most tax laws are cash-based, where amounts are included in revenue when the cash is actually received and count as an expense when the cash is paid out.

Because two different sets of rules are followed, net income rarely equals taxable income. The differences between net income and taxable income fall into two categories: permanent differences and temporary differences.

PERMANENT DIFFERENCES

A difference between net income and taxable income only for that year and that is never balanced out in a future year is called a **permanent difference**. An example of a permanent difference in revenues is interest revenue on a tax-exempt bond. This interest revenue is never subject to income tax. The company receiving the interest will not have to include it in its taxable income, but will include it on its income statement. Thus, its net income will be higher than its taxable income.

Company ABC bought a tax-exempt bond on January 1, 20X1, and sold the bond on December 31, 20X1. The company earned and received $1,000 of interest revenue on the bond. Before considering the interest revenue from the bond, Company ABC's net income and taxable income both equal $50,000. What effect does the $1,000 of interest revenue have on both taxable income and net income? As shown, taxable income is not affected by the interest revenue on the tax-exempt bond. However, net income is increased by $1,000 because the interest revenue was earned in 20X1 and GAAP require that it be added to net income. The difference of $1,000 is a permanent difference because the interest revenue will never be included in taxable income.

Taxable Income	
Taxable income before interest revenue	$50,000.00
+ Taxable interest revenue	—
Taxable income	$50,000.00

Net Income	
Net income before interest revenue	$50,000.00
+ Interest revenue	1,000.00
Net Income	$51,000.00

Permanent differences include cash payments that are not deductible for tax purposes but are listed as expenses for net income calculations. Some examples are premiums paid on life insurance policies for key employees, lobbying and political expenses, fines, and one-half the cost of business meals.

TEMPORARY DIFFERENCES

A difference between net income and taxable income for more than one period that reverses out over the entire period is called a **temporary difference**. A temporary difference is also known as a *timing difference*. Once the difference has been reversed, the total net income will equal the total taxable income.

DIFFERENTIATED INSTRUCTION

Visual/Spatial learners enjoy learning through drawing and physical imagery. Students can draw a mind map to represent graphically the ratios they learned in this chapter. The mind map is a visual thinking tool that helps students structure the information around the term *financial analysis*. Students should include the financial ratios presented in this chapter and explain what each ratio tells them.

LESSON

13-4

BRIDGE

- Point out that students have already learned how to calculate net income. In this lesson, they will learn about net income and taxable income. They will also learn why the difference exists.

TEACHING RESOURCES

- **Instructor's Resource CD/Website:**
  PowerPoint Slides
  Accounting Concepts
- **Working Papers:**
  Teacher's Edition of the Working Papers for Lesson 13-4
  Online Working Papers

ENGAGE

- Ask students if all income is taxable.

PREVIEW

- Call on students to read the accounting terms and definitions introduced in this lesson: *permanent differences, temporary differences,* and *comprehensive income.*
- Point out the learning objectives for this lesson.
- Direct students to read the headings in this lesson and to examine the illustrations.

INPUT

- Compare and contrast net income and taxable income.
- Explain that net income is calculated following GAAP rules and that taxable income is calculated using laws enforced by the IRS.
- Explain that differences between taxable and financial income occur because tax regulations and GAAP are frequently different.
- Explain why a temporary difference is also known as a timing difference.
- Point out the temporary difference pertaining to depreciation.
- Direct students to the illustrations on the page that compare taxable income to net income.

INPUT

- Explain comprehensive income.
- Direct students to the illustration toward the bottom of the page to explain how comprehensive income can be different from net income.
- Explain that many of the reasons for comprehensive income are explained in other accounting courses.

Accrued items often lead to temporary differences between taxable income and net income. These differences arise because the expenses must be recognized in net income when they are incurred, while taxable deductions are taken in the period the cash is paid. Company XYZ paid $1,000 cash for insurance on December 15, 20X1, for the next year. Before considering the insurance expense, Company XYZ's net income and taxable income both equal $50,000. What effect does the $1,000 of insurance expense have on taxable income and net income? As shown above, net income will not include the $1,000 as an expense in 20X1, but it will show the expense on the 20X2 income statement because the insurance premium was for 20X2. For tax purposes, the $1,000 will be a deduction against taxable income for 20X1, not 20X2.

The total taxable income and the total net income over the two-year period is the same, $99,000.00. The difference is a timing difference.

Taxable Income—20X1	
Taxable income before insurance expense	$50,000.00
– Tax deductible insurance expense	1,000.00
Taxable income	$49,000.00

Net Income—20X1	
Net income before insurance expense	$50,000.00
– Insurance expense	—
Net Income	$50,000.00

Taxable Income—20X2	
Taxable income before insurance expense	$50,000.00
– Tax deductible insurance expense	—
Taxable income	$50,000.00

Net Income—20X2	
Net income before insurance expense	$50,000.00
– Insurance expense	1,000.00
Net Income	$49,000.00

The largest temporary difference is often associated with depreciation. Many companies use straight-line depreciation for the calculation of net income so that the amount of depreciation is level over the life of the asset. For the same asset, the company will usually use an accelerated method of depreciation for the calculation of taxable income. This allows the company to pay fewer taxes in the early years of the asset, because the deductible expense is higher. The company pays more taxes in the later years of the asset, because of a lower deductible expense. Again, over the life of the asset the total amount of depreciation will be the same.

Comprehensive Income LO6

Income Statement	
Revenues	$50,000.00
Expenses	15,000.00
Income from operations	$35,000.00
Other revenues and expenses	(2,000.00)
Income before fed. income tax	$33,000.00
Federal income tax	(4,950.00)
Net income	$28,050.00

Statement of Comprehensive Income	
Net income	$28,050.00
Other comprehensive income	
Foreign currency translation	4,200.00
Unrealized loss on securities	(3,000.00)
Comprehensive Income	$29,250.00

How revenue is measured and when it is recognized is determined by GAAP. Not everyone agrees with GAAP and there is controversy about some areas of revenue recognition. Most items that increase or decrease equity are stated on the income statement. There are some items, however, that are not on the income statement but are included as increases or decreases directly to equity.

All changes in equity for the period, except changes caused by owner investments and owner distributions, is called **comprehensive income**. Companies must disclose comprehensive income either as a separate statement or as part of the traditional income statement.

Most of these items shown above on the statement of comprehensive income are beyond the scope of this book. The illustration shows how these items can cause comprehensive income to be more or less than net income.

FORMATIVE ASSESSMENT

- This is an ongoing process. Circulate around the classroom or lab, observing which students have problems with the assignments.
- Troubleshooting: Diagnose the kinds of problems students have with this lesson. Students may have difficulty understanding what determines permanent and temporary differences and the concept of comprehensive income.
- Assess student understanding by checking solutions to Independent Practice assignments and noting their answers to the Terms Review and Audit Your Understanding questions.

End of Lesson Review

LO5 Calculate permanent and temporary differences in net income and taxable income.

LO6 Understand the concept of comprehensive income.

Terms Review

permanent difference

temporary difference

comprehensive income

Audit your understanding

1. What rules are followed to prepare the income statement?
2. What rules are followed when preparing a tax return?
3. Name the two types of differences between taxable income and net income.
4. What is included in comprehensive income?

Work together 13-4

Calculating permanent and temporary differences in net income and taxable income

Klitzke Corporation had net income and taxable income of $95,000.00 for 20X1 before depreciation and interest revenue. In addition, Klitzke Corporation identified the following two items that will cause differences between net income and taxable income:

a. On January 1, 20X1, Klitzke Corporation bought office furniture for $49,000. For net income purposes, Klitzke Corporation will depreciate it using straight-line depreciation. Estimated life is 7 years. Estimated salvage value is zero. For taxable income purposes, depreciation for 20X1 is $12,250.00.

b. On December 31, 20X1, Klitzke Corporation received a check for $2,500.00 for interest earned in 20X1 on a tax-exempt bond.

1. Identify each difference between net income and taxable income as permanent or temporary.
2. Calculate the straight-line depreciation for 20X1 for the office furniture.
3. Calculate net income for Klitzke Corporation.
4. Calculate taxable income for Klitzke Corporation.

On your own 13-4

Calculating permanent and temporary differences in net income and taxable income

Hill Company had net income and taxable income of $88,000.00 for 20X1 before rent revenue and interest revenue. In addition, Hill Company identified the following two items that will cause differences between net income and taxable income:

a. On December 20, 20X1, Hill Company received a $12,000 check for rent revenue for the first six months of 20X2.

b. On December 31, 20X1, Hill Company received a check for $1,200.00 for interest earned in 20X1 on a tax-exempt bond.

1. Identify each difference between net income and taxable income as permanent or temporary.
2. Calculate net income for Hill Company.
3. Calculate taxable income for Hill Company.

CHECK FOR UNDERSTANDING

Terms Review

- Call on students to define each term in the Terms Review. Definitions are given in the Glossary.

Audit Your Understanding

- Call on students to answer the Audit Your Understanding questions. Answers are given in Appendix D of the textbook.

GUIDED PRACTICE

Work Together

- Have students write the solution to the Work Together problem as you guide the class through the examples.
- Direct students to calculate permanent and temporary differences in net income and taxable income.

INDEPENDENT PRACTICE

On Your Own

- Assign the On Your Own problem to be worked independently.
- Use the Formative Assessment techniques to diagnose student understanding.

Application Problem

- Assign Application Problem 13-4.

Online Working Papers

- Students can access the Lesson 13-4 problems using this software.

RETEACH

- Ask students to explain the difference between net income and taxable income.
- Ask students to provide an example of permanent and temporary differences on taxable income and net income.
- Ask students to explain the concept of comprehensive income.

CLOSURE

- Ask students to summarize briefly the concepts presented in this lesson.

Essential Question

- How can a company take advantage of temporary and permanent differences as a more efficient way of paying taxes? (*Temporary differences in GAAP rules and accounting rules allow tax payments to be made in the future.*)

CLOSURE

- Review the Chapter Summary.
- Ask students to prepare a list of the new concepts introduced in this chapter.

Essential Question

- Do you think any of these ratios are related? Explain. What do these formulas really tell us about the company? *(Individually, the ratios allow us to strategically analyze the financial performance of the company and help distinguish among companies that may fail.)*

EXTENDED LEARNING

- Assign Explore Accounting on page 394.

EXPLORE ACCOUNTING

Answer

Answers will vary. However, in all cases, EBIT should be equal to or higher than net earnings and EBITDA should be equal to or higher than EBIT.

Chapter Summary

Financial statements are prepared periodically and used by company management and external users such as investors, creditors, and government agencies. The information contained in the financial statements is analyzed to help the user determine the company's financial strength, profitability, efficiency, and market value.

Short-term financial strength measures indicate the short-term liquidity of the business. These measures include working capital, the current ratio, and the quick ratio. Long-term financial strength focuses on how a company obtains long-term capital. Long-term measures are the debt ratio, the equity ratio, equity per share, and the interest coverage ratio.

Profitability analysis helps the user determine the consistency of the company's earnings. Profitability measures are gross margin, operating margin, rate of return on average total assets, rate of return on average stockholders' equity, and free cash flow. Viewing these measures over time will reveal favorable and/or unfavorable trends.

Efficiency measures indicate how the business utilizes its resources. They include measures for collection of accounts receivable and turnover of inventory. An efficient business will collect accounts receivable on a timely basis and only have enough inventory on hand to meet customer demand.

Market ratios tie together the financial statements and the stock market. The value of a share of stock not only indicates past performance, but also reflects how the market views the future of a company. Market measures include the earnings per share, the price-earnings ratio, and the dividend yield.

Net income and taxable income can be different because of permanent differences and temporary differences. Permanent differences will never balance out. Temporary differences will balance out over the term of the difference.

Comprehensive income is a more inclusive measure of income and includes all changes in equity except those resulting from owner investments or owner distributions.

EXPLORE ACCOUNTING EBIT and EBITDA

© iStockphoto.com/Makhnach_M

As described on page 376, EBIT is net earnings before interest expense and taxes. EBITDA (pronounced ē - bĭt - dah) is net earnings before interest expense, taxes, depreciation, and amortization. Both EBIT and EBITDA are often used in place of net income in calculations such as the rate of return on average total assets and the rate earned on average stockholders' equity. When more than one calculation is available for a financial measure, a company must decide which calculation is the best measure to use in making decisions. Once decided, the company should use the same calculation from period to period. If the same calculation is used over time, the company can compare results over the period to determine trends.

While EBIT is a generally accepted measure used by accountants and analysts, EBITDA is quite controversial. Since EBITDA begins with net earnings and then adds back not only interest expense and taxes, but also depreciation and amortization, some feel that this is an easy way to change negative earnings into a positive number. Those who support the calculation of EBITDA say that it is a true measure of cash flows because depreciation and amortization are expenses that do not require a cash outflow.

Perhaps the biggest argument against the use of EBITDA is that it does not adhere to GAAP. It allows a company to ignore several components of net income that are required by GAAP. To add to the discussion, some companies do not want to stop at EBITDA. In recent times, companies are calculating EBITDAR, which also adds back any rent expense paid by the company.

INSTRUCTIONS

Obtain the annual reports of three public corporations. List the net earnings of each company. For each company, calculate EBIT and EBITDA. Compare the differences between the three amounts for each company. Write a paragraph describing the relationship between net earnings, EBIT, and EBITDA. State which measure you feel is most accurate.

Apply Your Understanding

INSTRUCTIONS: Download problem instructions for Excel, QuickBooks, and Sage 50 from the textbook companion website at www.C21accounting.com.

13-1 Application Problem: Analyzing short- and long-term financial strength LO1

1. Create and key formulas to compute the financial strength ratios.
2. Print the worksheets.

Information taken from Rogness Corporation's comparative income statement and balance sheet is provided in the *Working Papers*.

Instructions:

1. Calculate the following financial strength ratios for the current year and the prior year. Round ratios to the nearest tenth. Use the results to determine whether the trend between the prior year and the current year appears to be favorable or unfavorable. Give reasons for your responses.
   a. Working capital
   b. Current ratio
   c. Quick ratio
   d. Debt ratio
   e. Equity ratio
   f. Common equity per share
   g. Interest coverage ratio
2. Explain any change in the quick ratio for Rogness Corporation.

13-2 Application Problem: Calculating profitability measures LO2

1. Create and key formulas to compute ratios related to profitability measures.
2. Print the worksheets.

Information taken from Emerald Resort Incorporated's financial statements is provided in the *Working Papers*.

Instructions:

1. Calculate the following profitability measures for the current year and the prior year. Round percentage calculations to the nearest 0.1% and dollar amounts to the nearest $0.01. Use the results to determine whether the trend between the prior year and the current year appears to be favorable or unfavorable. Give reasons for your responses.
   a. Gross margin
   b. Operating margin
   c. Rate earned on average total assets
   d. Rate earned on average stockholders' equity
   e. Free cash flow
2. Explain what free cash flow from the current year tells Emerald Resort Incorporated.

CHECK FIGURES

For complete solutions to Chapter 13 problems, see the Teacher's Edition of the Working Papers.

Application Problem 13-1

1. a. Working capital prior year, $180,540.00.
   b. Current ratio current year, 2.1.
   c. Quick ratio current year, 0.8.
   d. Debt ratio prior year, 47.8%.
   e. Equity ratio current year, 57.2%.
   f. Common equity per share prior year, $80,040.00.
   g. Interest coverage ratio prior year, $86,500.00.

Application Problem 13-2

1. a. Gross margin current year, 30.1%.
   b. Operating margin current year, 18.5%.
   c. Rate earned on average total assets prior year, 5.5%.
   d. Rate earned on average stockholders' equity prior year, 10.6%.
   e. Free cash flow current year, $17,316.00.

Application Problem 13-3

1. a. Accounts receivable turnover ratio prior year, 7.0.
   b. Days' sales in accounts receivable current year, 39.
   c. Inventory turnover ratio current year, 6.7.
   d. Days' sales in inventory prior year, 64.
   e. Earnings per share prior year, $3.09.
   f. Price-earnings ratio prior year, 8.3.
   g. Dividend yield current year, $1.00.

Application Problem 13-4

2. $8,000.00.
3. $72,500.00.
4. $52,000.00.

13-3 Application Problem: Calculating and analyzing efficiency measures and market ratios LO3, 4

1. Create and key formulas to analyze efficiency measures and market ratios.
2. Print the worksheets.

Information taken from Hartmann Company's financial statements is provided in the *Working Papers*.

Instructions:

1. Calculate the following efficiency measures and market ratios for the current year and the prior year. Round percentage calculations to the nearest 0.1%, dollar amounts to the nearest $0.01, and the price-earnings ratio to the nearest tenth. Use the results to determine whether the trend between the prior year and the current year appears to be favorable or unfavorable. Give reasons for your responses.
   a. Accounts receivable turnover ratio
   b. Days' sales in accounts receivable
   c. Inventory turnover ratio
   d. Days' sales in inventory
   e. Earnings per share
   f. Price-earnings ratio
   g. Dividend yield
2. Hartmann Company's credit terms are n/30. Analyze the company's days' sales in accounts receivable in terms of its credit policy and state any trend this measure reveals.

13-4 Application Problem: Calculating permanent and temporary differences in net income and taxable income LO5

CMS Corporation had net income and taxable income of $77,000.00 for 20X1 before depreciation, interest revenue, and rent expense. In addition, CMS Corporation identified the following three items that will cause differences between net income and taxable income:

a. On January 1, 20X1, CMS Corporation bought office furniture for $40,000. For net income purposes, CMS Corporation will depreciate it using straight-line depreciation. Estimated life is five years. Estimated salvage value is zero. For taxable income purposes, depreciation for 20X1 is $10,000.00.
b. On December 31, 20X1, CMS Corporation received a check for $3,500.00 for interest earned in 20X1 on a tax-exempt bond.
c. On December 20, 20X1, CMS Corporation paid $15,000 for rent expense for the first three months of 20X2.

Instructions:

1. Identify each difference between net income and taxable income as permanent or temporary.
2. Calculate the straight-line depreciation for 20X1 for the office furniture.
3. Calculate net income for CMS Corporation.
4. Calculate taxable income for CMS Corporation.

13-M Mastery Problem: Analyzing financial statements LO1, 2, 3, 4, 5

1. Create and key formulas related to Eiler Enterprise's financial statements to calculate financial ratios and measures.
2. Print the worksheets.

Information taken from Eiler Enterprise's financial statements is provided in the *Working Papers*.

Instructions:

Calculate the following ratios and measures for the current year and the prior year. Round percentage calculations to the nearest 0.01%, dollar amounts to the nearest $0.01, and ratios to the nearest tenth. Use the results to determine whether the trend between the prior year and the current year appears to be favorable or unfavorable. Give reasons for your responses.

1. Working capital
2. Current ratio
3. Quick ratio
4. Debt ratio
5. Equity ratio
6. Common equity per share
7. Interest coverage ratio
8. Gross margin
9. Operating margin
10. Rate earned on average total assets
11. Rate earned on average stockholders' equity
12. Free cash flow
13. Accounts receivable turnover ratio
14. Days' sales in accounts receivable
15. Inventory turnover ratio
16. Days' sales in inventory
17. Earnings per share
18. Price-earnings ratio
19. Dividend yield

13-C Challenge Problem: Calculating the effect of transactions on the current ratio LO1

1. Create and key formulas to compute current ratios.
2. Print the worksheets.

Clausen Company is nearing the end of its fiscal year, and the Accounting Department has estimated that the current ratio for the current year will be 1.5, with estimated current assets of $150,000 and estimated current liabilities of $100,000. The company wants to increase the current ratio to at least 2.0 by the end of the period. It has the following options:

a. Borrow $50,000 by signing a short-term note payable, due in six months.
b. Borrow $50,000 by signing a long-term note payable, due in 18 months.
c. Sell $50,000 of common stock.
d. Pay off $25,000 of accounts payable with cash.
e. Replace $25,000 of accounts payable with a long-term note payable, due in 24 months.

Instructions:

1. For each option above, calculate the new totals for the current assets and the current liabilities, and calculate the new current ratio.
2. Identify which options would achieve the company's goal of a current ratio of 2.0.

Mastery Problem 13-M

1. Working capital current year, $286,224.00.
3. Quick ratio prior year, 0.7.
5. Equity ratio prior year, 47.7%.
7. Interest coverage ratio current year, 2.1.
9. Operating margin current year, 5.0%.
11. Rate earned on average stockholders' equity prior year, 15.8%.
13. Accounts receivable turnover ratio prior year, 14.4.
15. Inventory turnover ratio current year, 2.8.
17. Earnings per share current year, $1.11.
19. Dividend yield prior year

    Common stock, 15.0%.

    Preferred stock, 7.4%.

Challenge Problem 13-C

1. a. Current assets, $200,000.00.

   b. Current liabilities, $100,000.00.

   c. Current ratio, 2.00.

   d. Current liabilities, $75,000.00.

   e. Current assets, $150,000.00.

INDEPENDENT PRACTICE

- Assign Mastery Problem 13-M for students as a culminating problem combining all new learning from the chapter.
- Assign Challenge Problem 13-C to accelerated students who work at a faster pace.
- Assign Study Guide 13.
- Students can access Online Working Papers to work end-of-chapter problems on the computer.
- Direct students to the C21 Accounting companion website for additional practice and review opportunities.

FORMATIVE ASSESSMENT

- Review solutions to the assigned problems in class, diagnosing trouble spots.

RETEACH

- Call on students to describe how they avoid the trouble spots diagnosed.
- Use reteaching suggestions from lesson plans as required.
- Assign Recycling Problem 13-R if needed.

EXTENDED LEARNING

- Assign 21st Century Skills on page 398.
- Assign Analyzing Home Depot's Financial Statements on page 399.

SUMMATIVE EVALUATION

- Chapter 13 Test
- Cognero for Chapter 13

21ST CENTURY SKILLS

Answers

1. Answers will vary but might include ensuring security, keeping items that belong together intact, reordering, collecting data for informational purposes, and tracking pets.
2. Answers will vary. Many who oppose may indicate privacy or religious concerns.
3. Smart Cards are becoming popular in many industries. Student research may indicate ethical and privacy concerns, particularly in health and/or financial areas.

21st Century Skills

Radio Frequency Identification Tags—Music for Inventory Turnover

PARTNERSHIP FOR 21ST CENTURY SKILLS

Theme: Financial, Economic, Business, and Entrepreneurial Literacy

Skills: Critical Thinking and Problem Solving and Information Literacy

Every company's goal should be to optimize inventory turnover. After all, a company has a limited amount of money to invest in inventory. To pay a bill and generate a profit, the inventory must be sold. The inventory turnover rate measures how quickly a business is moving its inventory.

Understanding the market and understanding the customer are two important factors that can improve inventory turnover rates. Technology allows companies to go one step further to improve inventory turnover.

Radio frequency identification, or RFID, tags are used to identify and track objects. Many different industries use RFID tags. For example, schools use them to track the whereabouts of students. Walmart has recently started using RFID tags to keep stock current. RFID tags are considered the next generation in managing inventory and improving inventory turnover.

Sources: http://dailynightly.nbcnews.com/_news/2012/10/14/14425733-rfid-chips-let-schools-track-students-and-retain-funding-but-some-parents-object?lite; http://www.arkansasbusiness.com/article/85508/wal-mart-used-technology-to-become-supply-chain-leader?page=all.

APPLICATION

1. Using the Internet, research and list three new applications for the use of RFID tags.
2. Many students are opposed to the use of RFID tags for attendance purposes. Write one paragraph explaining your point of view.
3. With a partner, research Smart Cards. Explain to another group the similarities of Smart Cards with RFID tags and the pros and cons of the use of Smart Cards in different industries.

COMMON CORE AND INTERDISCIPLINARY STUDIES

Extended learning features and activities present numerous opportunities to implement Common Core Standards through interdisciplinary studies. Practice is provided in the common core areas of English Language Arts & Literacy and Mathematical Practice. Many of these activities require short, critical-thinking and decision-making responses that apply reading, writing, speaking, listening, language, media and technology, and mathematical skills.

Analyzing Home Depot's financial statements

The annual reports of publicly traded companies describe some of the financial ratios presented in this chapter. Other ratios must be calculated using the information provided in the financial statements.

Income statement amounts are the result of operations over an entire year or fiscal period. However, balance sheet amounts are the balances on a particular date. Therefore, when financial ratios use both an income statement amount and a balance sheet amount, the balance sheet amount is expressed commonly as an average of the amount at the beginning of the fiscal period and the amount at the end of the fiscal period. For example, average total assets for a company that uses the calendar year as its fiscal year would be the sum of the total assets on January 1 and the total assets on December 31, divided by 2.

Because the balance sheet contains only two years of information, investors rely on information in multiple-year summaries to obtain the required information. Home Depot's Five-Year Summary of Financial and Operating Results found in Appendix B on page B-15 enables readers to calculate financial ratios for several fiscal periods.

INSTRUCTIONS

Identify or calculate the following financial ratios for the years 2012 and 2011, using the financial statements and the Five-Year Summary of Financial and Operating Results, as appropriate. Use amounts in millions of dollars, except for per-share data.

1. Rate earned on average total assets
2. Rate earned on average stockholders' equity
3. Diluted earnings per share
4. Working capital
5. Current ratio
6. Debt ratio
7. Free cash flow

ANALYZING HOME DEPOT'S FINANCIAL STATEMENTS

Answers

		2012	2011
1.	Rate earned on average total assets	11.1%	9.6%
2.	Rate earned on average stockholders' equity	25.4%	21.1%
3.	Diluted earnings per share (as reported in summary)	$3.00	$2.47
4.	Working capital (as reported in summary)	$3,910	$5,144
5.	Current ratio (as reported in summary)	1.34	1.55
6.	Debt ratio	56.7%	55.8%
7.	Free cash flow	$5,663	$5,430

Chapter 14

Statement of Cash Flows

Scope & Sequence

	New	Review/Enrich
Introduction		
Introduce the Chapter		
Lesson 14-1: Preparing the Operating Activities Section of a Statement of Cash Flows		
Cash Flows	✓	
Direct Method and Indirect Method	✓	
Determining Cash Flows from Operating Activities	✓	
Reporting Cash Flows from Operating Activities	✓	
Lesson 14-2: Completing the Statement of Cash Flows		
Preparing the Investing Activities Section		✓
Preparing the Financing Activities Section		✓
Completing the Statement of Cash Flows		✓
Cash Flow Analysis	✓	
Closure		

Enhancing Instruction

Features	Common Core Standards
• Accounting in the Real World: EMC Corporation	• Mathematics
• Ethics in Action: Bribing Government Officials	• ELAL—reading
• Why Accounting?: Bottom Line May Affect Theatrical Performance	• ELAL—writing
• Think Like an Accountant: Charting the Statement of Cash Flows	• Mathematics
• Financial Literacy: Money Chase	• ELAL—reading, writing, media and technology
• Careers In Accounting: Financial Analyst	• ELAL—reading
• Explore Accounting	• ELAL—reading, writing
• 21st Century Skills	• ELAL—reading, writing, speaking
• Auditing for Errors	• Mathematics
• Analyzing Home Depot's Financial Statements	• Mathematics

ELAL = English Language Arts & Literacy

Calculator: © iStockphoto.com/picstodisc; Paper: © iStockphoto.com/Qingwa

Technology & Media	Teaching Strategies	Guided Practice	Independent Practice	Reteach/Enrich
• Instructor's Resource CD/Website: PowerPoint Slides Accounting Concepts • Online Working Papers • Transparency Master: 3-column Financial Statement Form	• Gifted Learners • Auditory/Linguistic Learners • Intrapersonal Learners	• Terms Review • Audit Your Understanding • Work Together 14-1	• On Your Own 14-1 • Application Problem 14-1 • Formative Assessment, p. 409 • Online Working Papers	• Reteach, p. 410
• Instructor's Resource CD/Website: PowerPoint Slides Accounting Concepts • Online Working Papers • Transparency Master: 3-column Financial Statement Form	• Tactile/Kinesthetic Learners • Visual/Spatial Learners	• Audit Your Understanding • Work Together 14-2	• On Your Own 14-2 • Application Problem 14-2 • Formative Assessment, p. 416 • Online Working Papers	• Reteach, p. 417
• Online Working Papers			• Mastery Problem 14-M • Study Guide 14 • Chapter 14 Test • Cognero Chapter 14	• Challenge Problem 14-C • Reteach, p. 421 • Recycling Problem 14-R • Reinforcement Activity 3

Practice and Assessment

Introduce the Chapter

SET THE STAGE

GUIDING QUESTIONS

- Ask for examples of problems that a business may encounter if there is an insufficient supply of cash.
- Ask students why it is critical that financial analysis include a study of a company's ability to produce cash. Emphasize than an incoming flow of cash is necessary for the continued operation of a business. Without an inflow of cash, companies cannot pay for expenses, purchase additional merchandise, or invest in updated equipment.
- Ask students why businesses in financial trouble seem to lay off employees before cutting other expenses. Point out that wages and salaries are generally the largest expense of a company and that it is the fastest way to improve cash flow.
- Ask students to list ways that a company might invest in its own business.

PREVIEW CHAPTER OBJECTIVES

- Point out that three cash flow activities are presented in this chapter. Mention that a clear understanding of each activity is necessary to prepare the statement of cash flows.
- Instruct a student to read each chapter objective aloud.

PREVIEW ACCOUNTING TERMS

- Read each term aloud to verify its pronunciation for students.
- Point out the terms that should already be familiar to most students, such as *direct method* and *indirect method*

Chapter 14 Statement of Cash Flows

LEARNING OBJECTIVES

After studying Chapter 14, in addition to defining key terms, you will be able to:

LO1 Understand the difference between the direct and indirect methods of preparing the statement of cash flows.

LO2 Use the indirect method to complete the operating activities section of a statement of cash flows.

LO3 Complete the investing and financing activities sections of a statement of cash flows.

LO4 Calculate the operating cash flow ratio and the cash flow margin ratio.

Calculator: © iStockphoto.com/picstudio; Paper: © iStockphoto.com/Qingwa

© Monkey Business Images/Shutterstock.com

Accounting In The Real World

EMC Corporation

EMC Corporation is an American multinational company that assists companies worldwide with their data storage and security needs. EMC's customers range in size from startup companies to Fortune Global 500 companies. Employing over 60,000 people and operating in over 86 countries, EMC ranked 139 in the 2012 Fortune 500 list.

EMC values sustained research and development, investing $16.5 billion in this area since 2003. Using collaborative teams to work with customers enables innovation and the opportunity to develop custom solutions. The company offers extremely fast access to cloud storage for faster backups and recoveries.

According to its website, EMC is "committed to acting in a socially and environmentally responsible manner and to being an attentive and thoughtful neighbor in our local and global communities." In 2012, EMC was included in the Dow Jones Sustainability Index for North America, which "tracks the financial performance of leading sustainability-driven companies."

As a large corporation, EMC has not lost sight of its employees. It has won numerous awards, including the 2013 Top 50 Employers award from *CAREERS & the disABLED Magazine*, being ranked the 19th best multinational company in the Best Workplaces in Europe 2012, and a score of 100 on the Human Rights Campaign 2013 Corporate Equality Index.

Like other publicly held corporations, EMC publishes an annual report, which includes a statement of cash flows. EMC's statement of cash flows is prepared using one of two methods approved by GAAP. The two different methods will be discussed in this chapter.

CRITICAL THINKING

1. Using the Internet, find the most recent annual report for EMC. For the most recent year, find and list the following amounts from the statement of cash flows: net cash provided by (used for) operating activities, net cash provided by (used for) investing activities, net cash provided by (used for) financing activities, and net increase (decrease) in cash and cash equivalents.
2. How does the net increase (decrease) in cash for the most current year compare to the same figure for the two prior years?

Source: www.emc.com.

Background: © iStockphoto.com/Alex Slobodkin; Real World: Jin Lee/Bloomberg/Getty Images

Key Terms

- direct method
- indirect method

Accounting In The Real World

Answers

Answers will vary depending on the year chosen.

LESSON
14-1

BRIDGE

- Point out that students have already studied several topics related to cash flows, including budgeting, comparative financial statements, financial statement analysis, and financial strength analysis.
- In this lesson, students will expand on preparing the operating activities section of a statement of cash flows. This section will report and explain the sources and uses of the company's cash related to operating the business.

TEACHING RESOURCES

- **Instructor's Resource CD/Website:** PowerPoint Slides; Accounting Concepts
- **Working Papers:** Teacher's Edition of the Working Papers for Lesson 14-1; Online Working Papers
- **Transparency Master:** 3-column financial statement form

ENGAGE

- Ask students how a company earning a net income of $1 million could not have enough cash to pay its bills. Stress that even though a company reports the revenue when it is generated, it may not have received the cash for the sale. Therefore, it could lack the cash to pay bills.

PREVIEW

- Call on students to read the accounting terms and definitions introduced in this lesson: *direct method* and *indirect method*.
- Point out the learning objectives for this lesson.
- Direct students to read the headings in this lesson and to examine the illustrations.

INPUT

- Point out the four reasons for analyzing cash flow, listed in the middle of the page.
- Emphasize that studying cash flows provides additional information about a company's present and future financial condition.

TEACHING IDEA **Obtain copies of cash flow statements from companies of interest to students. Display statements of cash flows on the bulletin board, highlighting or comparing and contrasting the ways in which the corporations present their statements of cash flows.**

LESSON
14-1 Preparing the Operating Activities Section of a Statement of Cash Flows

LO1 Understand the difference between the direct and indirect methods of preparing the statement of cash flows.
LO2 Use the indirect method to complete the operating activities section of a statement of cash flows.

Cash Flows

Some investors and financial analysts rely heavily on an examination of income statements and balance sheets to judge a company's performance. However, impressive profits are not always a guarantee of success in the future. For example, despite reporting a substantial net income for the year, a business may experience a cash shortage and have difficulty paying its bills. Cash flow analysis helps owners, creditors, and other interested parties:

1. Determine a company's potential to produce cash in the future.
2. Judge a company's ability to pay bills and repay debts.
3. Explain changes in the Cash account balance.
4. Evaluate a company's investment and equity transactions.

The statement of cash flows is prepared on a cash basis. It reports cash flows in and out of the company, using three categories of cash flows: operating activities, investing activities, and financing activities.

ETHICS IN ACTION

Bribing Government Officials

Companies that operate throughout the world are exposed to different cultures, social norms, and acceptable business practices. In some countries, giving bribes to government officials to gain favorable business terms is both acceptable and expected. In our society, however, giving bribes to government officials is unethical and illegal.

In 1977, Congress passed the Foreign Corrupt Practices Act, which made it illegal for U.S. companies to bribe foreign government officials.

INSTRUCTIONS

Access *Everyday Values*, the code of conduct for Harley-Davidson. What guidance does Harley-Davidson provide its employees in the following situations involving foreign government officials?

a. An employee, at the end of a business meeting with a government official, is considering paying for everyone's lunch.
b. To thank a mayor's staff for their help with a bike rally, an employee wants to give the mayor's staff Harley-Davidson hats or T-shirts.
c. An employee learns that a marketing company hired by Harley-Davidson has given a free motorcycle to a government official in thanks for closing a road to film a commercial.
d. An employee submits an expense reimbursement request that includes a $1,000 payment to a customs official, a payment described as necessary to get a shipment of parts through customs.

© iStockphoto.com/LdF

ETHICS IN ACTION

Harley-Davidson's *Everyday Values* is a comprehensive code of conduct. You may want to guide students to the Government section of the document to limit their search.

See a suggested solution for this feature in the Instructional Strategies section at the front of this book.

Direct Method and Indirect Method LO1

Direct Method

Statement of Cash Flows			
Cash flows from operating activities:			
Cash receipts from:			
Sales	xxx		
Interest	xxx		
Total cash receipts		xxx	
Cash payments for:			
Inventory purchases	xxx		
Salaries and wages	xxx		
Interest	xxx		
Federal income tax	xxx		
Total cash payments		xxx	
Cash provided by (used for) operating activities			xxx

Indirect Method

Statement of Cash Flows		
Cash flows from operating activities:		
Net income		xxx
Adjustments to net income:		
Depreciation and amortization expense	xxx	
Changes in current assets and liabilities:		
Decrease in accounts receivable	xxx	
Increase in merchandise inventory	(xxx)	
Decrease in accounts payable	(xxx)	
Increase in federal income tax payable	xxx	
Total adjustments to net income		xxx
Cash provided by (used for) operating activities		xxx

The operating activities section of the statement of cash flows reports the cash inflows and cash outflows resulting from the operation of a business. This section can be prepared using either of two formats. Listing cash flows from operating activities as cash receipts and cash payments is called the **direct method**. Listing cash flows from operating activities by starting with net income and adjusting for noncash items is called the **indirect method**.

Two important facts are true when comparing the direct method and the indirect method:

1. Only the cash flows from operating activities differ. The cash flows from investing activities and the cash flows from financing activities are prepared in the same manner under the two methods.
2. Regardless of the method used, the total cash provided by (used for) operating activities equals the same amount. The only thing that is different is the way the cash flows are presented.

GAAP allow either method, but prefer the direct method. The direct method is easier to understand because:

1. The direct method lists the actual cash receipts and cash payments within categories that are understood easily.
2. The indirect method starts with net income that results from using accrual-based accounting. Thus, the relationship between net income and actual cash flows is not obvious.

When the direct method is used, GAAP require that a separate schedule be prepared. This schedule reconciles net income to total cash provided by (used for) operating activities. The supplemental schedule is very similar to the format used for the indirect method. Because the direct method requires this schedule, most companies use the indirect method to prepare the statement of cash flows.

Chapter 4 focused on the direct method of preparing the statement of cash flows. This chapter will focus on the indirect method of preparing the statement of cash flows.

© Hugo Felix/Shutterstock.com

INPUT

- Explain the difference between the direct and indirect methods of preparing the operating activities section of the statement of cash flows.
- Direct students to the illustration on the page to point out the differences between the methods.
- Point out that the net amount of cash provided by (used for) operating activities will be the same with both methods.
- Emphasize that GAAP allow either method. Because the direct method was presented in Chapter 4, the indirect method will be presented in this lesson.

DIFFERENTIATED INSTRUCTION

Gifted learners need additional challenges, such as research, to maintain a high level of motivation. Ask students to use the Internet to research the financial statements for a company of interest. Tell students to compare the balance sheet with the statement of cash flows and explain how the change occurred, presenting their findings to the class or a small group.

Auditory/Linguistic learners have highly developed auditory skills and often use language as a means to remember information.

Intrapersonal learners enjoy writing. Instruct these learners to write a one-page paper describing where the money came from and where it went.

Determining Cash Flows from Operating Activities LO2

The cash flows from operating activities can be determined indirectly by identifying the net income for the period and making several adjustments.

NET INCOME

Net income presented on an income statement summarizes revenues and expenses generated by the operating activities of a business during the fiscal period. For this reason, net income is a good starting point for calculating the cash flows from operating activities. A net income is viewed as a *source of cash*, because it brings additional money into a firm eventually. A net loss reduces the amount of money available for expenditures and is considered to be a *use of cash*.

Since the income statement is prepared using the accrual basis of accounting and the statement of cash flows is prepared using the cash basis of accounting, the recognition of revenues and expenses occurs at different times. Adjustments are made to net income to recognize the timing differences.

ADJUSTING NET INCOME FOR DEPRECIATION AND AMORTIZATION

Depreciation Expense

	Debit		Credit
Dec. 31	9,284.00		

Effect on cash: None; add amount to net income

Accumulated Depreciation

	Debit		Credit
		Dec. 31	9,284.00

Depreciation expense is recognized on the income statement. However, it does not involve an outflow of cash. Since depreciation expense does not use cash, the amount is added back to the net income amount.

At the end of the fiscal year, Cradle Mountain Corporation uses the straight-line method of depreciation to expense an appropriate amount of the original cost of equipment. Depreciation for the year is recorded by debiting Depreciation Expense and crediting Accumulated Depreciation as shown above.

Notice that the credit for this transaction is Accumulated Depreciation, not Cash. Depreciation expense does not affect the balance in the Cash account. However, depreciation expense is deducted from company revenues to determine net income. Since no cash is paid out, the amount of depreciation expense reported on the income statement must be added back to net income to determine the actual cash generated from operating activities.

The amount of total depreciation expense added back to net income is one of the adjustments to net income to determine the actual *source of cash* from operations. Amortization expense is also a noncash expense and is treated in a similar manner.

remember

Sources of cash represent cash inflows, which are added on the statement of cash flows. Uses of cash represent cash outflows, which are subtracted on the statement of cash flows.

INPUT

- Explain that cash received from operating activities can be determined indirectly by identifying the net income and then making some adjustments. Point out that this will seem like a backwards approach to calculating cash by starting with net income.
- Point out that net income is a source of cash that brings money into the business. Subsequently, a net loss is considered a use of cash.
- Point out that the indirect method first identifies net income/net loss. Net income is an appropriate starting point because it summarizes the cash receipts and cash payments generated by the operating activities of a business.

INPUT

- Because the income statement is prepared using the accrual basis of accounting and the statement of cash flows is prepared using a cash basis of accounting, revenues and expenses occur at different times. Therefore, adjustments must be made.
- Explain that depreciation was an expense on the income statement and would have been subtracted from revenues to calculate net income. However, depreciation does not involve cash. Therefore, the amount of depreciation expense is added back to the net income figure. Point out that amortization is treated in the same manner.

Prior Year

Cash

Cash received from sales	322,810.00		

Accounts Receivable

Jan. 1 Bal.	201,500.00	Cash received	322,810.00
Credit sales	240,760.00		
Dec. 31 Bal.	119,450.00		

Decrease in noncash current asset is an $82,050.00 *source of cash.*

Sales

		Sales on account	240,760.00

Current Year

Cash

Cash received from sales	313,321.00		

Accounts Receivable

Jan. 1 Bal.	119,450.00	Cash received	313,321.00
Credit sales	401,744.00		
Dec. 31 Bal.	207,873.00		

Increase in noncash current asset is an $88,423.00 *use of cash.*

Sales

		Sales on account	401,744.00

The second adjustment to net income involves changes in *noncash current assets* (current assets other than cash). Increases and decreases in noncash current assets affect cash flows and require an adjustment to net income. For example, an increase in the current asset Accounts Receivable indicates that not all of the sales on account reported for a period were collected. Consequently, an increase in Accounts Receivable means that cash received from sales is less than the sales amount reported on the income statement.

During the prior year, Cradle Mountain Corporation's Accounts Receivable decreased $82,050.00. Assuming that all sales were made on account, this decrease means that the actual cash inflow for sales on account was $322,810.00, which is more than the $240,760.00 reported as sales on the income statement. For this reason, net income is adjusted by adding $82,050.00 for the decrease in a current asset. A decrease in a noncash current asset is considered to be a *source of cash.*

How can a company collect $322.810.00 of receivables if sales on account for the year are only $240,760.00? In this instance, Cradle Mountain collected a portion of the $201,500.00 balance in Accounts Receivable due from the previous year. Noncash current assets may also increase during a fiscal period. During the current year, Cradle Mountain collected $88,423.00 less than it sold on account. An increase in a noncash current asset represents a *use of cash* and is subtracted from the net income amount. This use of cash supports the company's daily operations by allowing the business to offer customers the option to buy now and pay later. A use of cash means a specified sum of money is no longer available for other business activities.

Each noncash asset account is analyzed in a similar manner to Accounts Receivable to determine cash flows from operations.

fyi

Determine if the increase or decrease in an account represents a source of cash or a use of cash. If a change in an account represents a source of cash, it is always added on the statement of cash flows. If a change represents a use of cash, it is always subtracted.

remember

The cash inflows and outflows of a business are identified using the information presented on a company's financial statements.

INPUT

- Point out that a decrease in a noncash current asset is considered a source of cash. An increase in a noncash current asset represents a use of cash. Write these statements on the board.
- Emphasize that the noncurrent asset in this example is accounts receivable.
- Emphasize that a portion of the accounts receivable collected may have been from sales made in the previous year.

MODEL

- Draw six T accounts on the board. Provide two sets of the following accounts: Cash, Accounts Receivable, and Sales.
- Ask a student to read the second and third paragraphs on this page, explaining the current and prior years' accounts receivable.
- Emphasize that the $88,423.00 increase in accounts receivable, a current asset, represents a use of cash because this money is not available to the business for other purposes. Because $88,423.00 of the year's sales on account was not collected, this amount must be deducted from the net income figure so that the true cash flow from sales is reported accurately.
- Use the same approach described above for explaining that a decrease in a current asset represents a source of cash.

INPUT

- Point out that the third adjustment to net income involves changes in current liabilities.
- Use the transactions provided in the illustration to demonstrate that an increase in a current liability represents a source of cash and that a decrease in a current liability represents a use of cash. Write these two statements on the board.

MODEL

- Draw three T accounts on the board. Label them Accounts Payable, Purchases, and Cash.
- Ask a student to read the second and third paragraphs on page 407.
- Refer to the current-year illustration on page 406.
- Ask a student which accounts are debited and credited to record a $193,192.00 purchase of merchandise on account (*debit Purchases, credit Accounts Payable*). Record the correct response in the T accounts.
- Ask a student which accounts are debited and credited to record a $149,252.00 cash payment on account (*debit Accounts Payable, credit Cash*). Record the correct response in the T accounts.
- Ask students to review the T accounts. Ask them the amount of purchases for the year (*$193,192.00*). Ask them how much of the $193,192.00 was actually paid in cash (*$149,252.00*). Ask students to state the ending balance for accounts payable (*$76,310.00*).
- Emphasize that the $76,310.00 increase in accounts payable, a current liability, represents a source of cash because this amount was not paid out during the year for purchases and is therefore available to the business for other purposes. Because $76,310.00 of the year's purchases on account was not paid, this amount must be added to the net income figure so that the true cash flow for purchases is accurately reported.
- Emphasize that the actual cash outflow for purchases was $149,252.00 and not the full $193,192.00 reported on the income statement.
- Use the same approach described above to explain that a decrease in a current liability represents a use of cash.

ANALYZING CHANGES IN CURRENT LIABILITIES

Prior Year

Cash

Debit		Credit	
		Cash payments on account	111,886.00

Accounts Payable

Debit		Credit	
Cash payments	111,886.00	Jan. 1 Bal.	40,000.00
		Credit purchases	104,256.00
		Dec. 31 Bal.	32,370.00

Decrease in current liability is a $7,630.00 use of cash.

Purchases

Debit		Credit	
Purchases on account	104,256.00		

Current Year

Cash

Debit		Credit	
		Cash payments on account	149,252.00

Accounts Payable

Debit		Credit	
Cash payments	149,252.00	Jan. 1 Bal.	32,370.00
		Credit purchases	193,192.00
		Dec. 31 Bal.	76,310.00

Increase in current liability is a $43,940.00 source of cash.

Purchases

Debit		Credit	
Purchases on account	193,192.00		

WHY ACCOUNTING?

Bottom Line May Affect Theatrical Performance

The last time you went to see a play, you probably didn't wonder if the production would make a net income. You were probably more interested in the acting and the set design. However, someone does have to worry about the bottom line generated by the production. That task usually is the responsibility of the theater's general manager. He or she must make sure that all operations stay within the budget. The budget may determine how many performances are offered, the set design, and who fills each acting role. The budget is also affected by the anticipated size of the audience, the grants received, and the fund-raising efforts. If any of these revenue sources are less than budgeted, decisions must be made to cut expenses during the run of the play.

A/V Technology & Communications

CRITICAL THINKING

1. Assume that your school is putting on a play. Make a list of the costs that may be incurred.
2. List sources of revenue that could help offset these costs.

© iStockphoto.com/AleksKo

WHY ACCOUNTING?

Answers

1. Answers will vary. Possible costs include costumes; set design; props; royalties; duplication of programs; and pay for the director, the conductor, the musical director, and supervisors.
2. Answers will vary. Possible sources of revenue include advertisements in programs; ticket sales; concession sales; sales of programs; contributions from local businesses; grants; and merchandise sales related to the play, such as T-shirts, hats, and CDs.

The third adjustment to net income involves changes in current liabilities. During the operation of a business, increases and decreases in current liabilities occur as debts are added and paid off in the process of generating revenues.

During the prior year, Cradle Mountain Corporation was extremely aggressive in paying off its debts. In fact, assuming that all purchases were on account, the company paid off $111,886.00 of accounts payable, which is $7,630.00 more than the total purchases on account of $104,256.00. Why would a company pay more than it owes? In this instance, Cradle Mountain paid a portion of the $40,000.00 accounts payable balance owed for the previous year. A decrease in a current liability represents a *use of cash* and is subtracted from net income.

The $43,940.00 increase in accounts payable at the end of the current year means that the actual cash outflow for purchases on account was $149,252.00 and not the full $193,192.00 reported as purchases on the income statement. For this reason, net income is adjusted by adding back $43,940.00 for the increase in a current liability. Since the company has use of the $43,940.00, the increase in a current liability represents a *source of cash*.

Each current liability is analyzed in a similar manner to accounts payable.

© iStockphoto.com/Dan Bachman

THINK LIKE AN ACCOUNTANT

Charting the Statement of Cash Flows

A publicly held corporation must publish an annual report. The report includes its financial statements, a discussion of its operations, and other information that management considers useful to investors. Charts are often used to communicate changes in sales, income, and other key financial statement amounts.

While attending a seminar, the controller for Walthal Corporation learned about a *waterfall chart*. The seminar leader used the chart to show the source and use of an item of inventory. He demonstrated how to create the chart by using a stacked column chart design.

The controller realized that a waterfall chart is uniquely qualified to communicate the information on a statement of cash flows. The chart could show the beginning cash balance, the sources of cash, the uses of cash, and the ending cash balance. Thus, the chart quickly enables the user to see how cash was used.

OPEN THE SPREADSHEET TLA_CH14

The worksheet contains the sample waterfall chart provided by the seminar leader and Walthal's statement of cash flows. Follow the steps on the Instructions tab to prepare the chart. Answer the following questions:

1. What colors could be selected to reinforce the concepts of sources and uses of cash?
2. Prepare a statement to be included in an accounting procedures manual that provides guidance on when a waterfall chart should be selected to communicate information.

fyi The Financial Accounting Standards Board (FASB), in Statement No. 95, classifies the interest paid on borrowed money as an operating activity. The reason for this classification is that the payment of interest expense on a loan is considered to have a direct effect on a firm's net income.

THINK LIKE AN ACCOUNTANT

This activity requires students to use Excel's stacked column chart design to create a waterfall chart. The logic of the numbers displayed in the chart can be confusing. A sample of a waterfall and its supporting schedule are provided as an illustration. Students are directed to use the Trace Precedents tool to analyze the logic of the formulas. Students must then apply this knowledge to complete a schedule containing the chart data and to create the chart.

The questions allow students to apply higher-level thinking skills. The first question requires students to assign chart colors that support the message communicated by the chart. Encourage students to search the Internet for color theory to learn the message conveyed by individual colors and combinations of colors. For example, blue is generally perceived to communicate peace and loyalty.

The second question requires students to express a rule for when a waterfall chart is used. Begin by asking students to express a rule for a more common chart type, such as a pie chart. For example, "A pie chart is used to show the relative amounts of individual items that comprise a meaningful total amount. The total of all the pie chart slices should equal 100% of an amount." Students could also be instructed to identify the similarities between the model chart shown in the Excel file and the chart created for the statement of cash flows.

Sample Solution

1. Green is typically considered the color of money and could be used for sources of cash. Red typically represents a loss of money and could be used for uses of cash.
2. A waterfall chart is useful in showing activity where the item has a beginning and ending balance. The bars between these balances can show additions and deletions to the item. Thus, the chart could be used to show the activity in a general ledger account.

INPUT

- Refer students to the illustration.
- Ask students to name the three financial statements presented in the illustration (*income statement, statement of cash flows, and balance sheet*).
- Point out that the income statement is presented in abbreviated form for illustrative purposes.
- Ask students to state the amount of net income after federal income taxes for the current year (*$80,275.00*). Ask students if this is a source of cash or a use of cash. Emphasize that net income eventually brings money into the company; therefore, it is viewed as a source of cash.
- Ask students to state the amount of depreciation expense (*$9,284.00*). Ask students if this is a source of cash or a use of cash (*source of cash*). Emphasize that depreciation expense is recognized on the income statement, but it does not involve a cash payment during the identified fiscal period.
- Ask students to state the account titles of noncash current assets. Write the account titles on the board. Ask students to state the amount of increase or decrease from the prior year. Write the amounts beside the appropriate account titles. Ask students if the increase or decrease represents a source of cash or a use of cash. Write the correct responses [*Accts. Rec., ($88,423.00), use of cash; Supplies, $319.00, source of cash; Merchandise Inventory, ($93,312.00), use of cash*].
- Ask students to state the account titles of current liabilities. Write the account titles on the board. Ask students to state the amount of increase or decrease from the prior year. Write the amounts beside the appropriate account titles. Ask students if the increase or decrease represents a source of cash or a use of cash. Write the correct responses (*Notes Payable, $31,191.00, source of cash; Accts. Pay., $43,940.00, source of cash*).
- Emphasize that a source of cash is added to net income and that a use of cash is subtracted from net income.

MODEL

- Direct students to the illustration at the top of page 409 to review the five steps necessary to report cash flows from operating activities or use a transparency of a three-column financial statement form to demonstrate preparation of the operating activities section of the statement of cash flows.

Reporting Cash Flows from Operating Activities

Cradle Mountain Corporation
Comparative Income Statement
For Years Ended December 31, 20X2 and 20X1

	20X2	20X1	Increase (Decrease)
Net Sales	$401,744.00	$240,760.00	$160,984.00
Cost of Merchandise Sold	193,192.00	104,256.00	88,936.00
Gross Profit on Operations	$208,552.00	$136,504.00	$ 72,048.00
Operating Expenses:			
Depreciation Expense	$ 9,284.00	$ 8,204.00	$ 1,080.00
Other Operating Expenses	90,788.00	63,380.00	27,408.00
Total Operating Expenses	$100,072.00	$ 71,584.00	$ 28,488.00
Net Income before Federal Income Tax Expense	$108,480.00	$ 64,920.00	$ 43,560.00
Less Federal Income Tax Expense	28,205.00	16,879.00	11,326.00
Net Income after Federal Income Tax Expense	$ 80,275.00	$ 48,041.00	$ 32,234.00

Add depreciation expense. (2)

(1) Enter net income.

Cradle Mountain Corporation
Statement of Cash Flows
For Year Ended December 31, 20X2

Cash flows from operating activities:			
Net income		$ 80,275.00	
Adjustments to net income:			
Depreciation expense	$ 9,284.00		
Changes in current assets and liabilities:			
Increase in accounts receivable	(88,423.00)		
Decrease in supplies	319.00		
Increase in merchandise inventory	(93,312.00)		
Increase in notes payable	31,191.00		
Increase in accounts payable	43,940.00		
Total adjustments to net income		$(97,001.00)	
Cash used for operating activities			$(16,726.00)

Enter changes in current assets. (3)

Calculate cash flows from operating activities. (5)

Cradle Mountain Corporation
Comparative Balance Sheet
December 31, 20X2 and 20X1

	20X2	20X1	Increase (Decrease)
ASSETS			
Current Assets:			
Cash	$ 6,748.00	$ 10,056.00	$ (3,308.00)
Accounts Receivable (book value)	207,873.00	119,450.00	88,423.00
Supplies	1,001.00	1,320.00	(319.00)
Merchandise Inventory	248,256.00	154,944.00	93,312.00
Total Current Assets	$463,878.00	$285,770.00	$178,108.00
Plant Assets:			
Equipment	$ 66,400.00	$ 49,856.00	$ 16,544.00
Building	96,000.00	96,000.00	—
Land	48,000.00	72,000.00	(24,000.00)
Less Accum. Depr.—Equipment and Land	17,488.00	8,204.00	9,284.00
Total Plant Assets (book value)	$192,912.00	$209,652.00	$(16,740.00)
Total Assets	$656,790.00	$495,422.00	$161,368.00
LIABILITIES			
Current Liabilities:			
Notes Payable	$ 40,602.00	$ 9,411.00	$ 31,191.00
Accounts Payable	76,310.00	32,370.00	43,940.00
Total Current Liabilities	$116,912.00	$ 41,781.00	$ 75,131.00
Long-Term Liabilities:			
Mortgage Payable	$117,162.00	$117,600.00	$ (438.00)
Total Liabilities	$234,074.00	$159,381.00	$ 74,693.00
STOCKHOLDERS' EQUITY			
Total Stockholders' Equity	$422,716.00	$336,041.00	$ 86,675.00
Total Liabilities and Stockholders' Equity	$656,790.00	$495,422.00	$161,368.00

(4) Enter changes in current liabilities.

Reporting Cash Flows from Operating Activities

1. Enter net income, $80,275.00, as shown on Cradle Mountain's comparative income statement.
2. Add the amount of depreciation expense, $9,284.00, to net income.
3. Enter the changes in current assets as indicated in the table below.

Change in Account	20X2	20X1	Increase (Decrease)	Source or Use of Cash
Increase in Accts. Rec.	$207,873.00	$119,450.00	$88,423.00	use of cash
Decrease in Supplies	1,001.00	1,320.00	(319.00)	source of cash
Increase in Mdse. Inv.	248,256.00	154,944.00	93,312.00	use of cash

4. Enter the changes in current liabilities as indicated in the table below.

Change in Account	20X2	20X1	Increase (Decrease)	Source or Use of Cash
Increase in Notes Pay.	$40,602.00	$ 9,411.00	$31,191.00	source of cash
Increase in Accts. Pay.	76,310.00	32,370.00	43,940.00	source of cash

5. Determine the cash provided by operating activities (if cash increases) or the cash used for operating activities (if cash decreases). After reporting the individual adjustments to net income, the statement of cash flows shows that the actual cash requirement for Cradle Mountain's operating activities exceeded net income by $16,726.00. This shortfall places Cradle Mountain in a very serious position regarding the company's ability to meet its short-term demands for cash.

FINANCIAL LITERACY

Money Chase

A budget, or spending plan, is necessary for financial planning. Many individuals have a well-planned budget, yet find themselves running out of money at the end of the month. Why? While the budget is helpful for establishing financial goals, the user may not take into account the timing and fluctuations of the inflows and outflows of cash.

Each day, financial events take place. Paychecks or other monies are received. Payments and other expenditures are made. A personal income and expenditures statement, also known as a *cash flow statement*, is helpful for analyzing the timing of inflows and outflows of cash. Once the cash flow has been determined, smart money management strategies can be used. A surplus, or positive cash flow, allows monies to be set aside for an emergency fund or an investment or to pay off debt. Managing cash helps eliminate the need for borrowing or using credit in the future.

ACTIVITIES

1. Sometimes there is a negative cash flow, or a deficit in cash, at the end of the month. Together with a partner, list three money management strategies that could be implemented to avoid a deficit.
2. a. Using the Internet, research the difference between discretionary income and disposable income. Write a letter to a middle-school-aged student, explaining the difference.
   b. Explain what is meant by the following: "Teenagers with discretionary income determine new trends." What trends are being determined today by teenagers? What trends do you think teenagers may have impacted with discretionary income in the 1960s?
3. Many U.S. companies have expanded into China in recent years as its economy has expanded. Using the Internet, research some of the reasons why approximately one-third of Chinese income is discretionary, in spite of Chinese workers earning lower wages than U.S. workers.

Source: http://money.cnn.com/2012/06/26/news/economy/china-middle-class/index.htm.

© iStockphoto.com/Norebbo

FINANCIAL LITERACY

Answers

1. Answers will vary but might include increase inflows of cash by adding income with a second job or by selling personal items, prioritize spending by determining wants versus needs, use coupons to spend less, request that due dates be adjusted to fit better with inflows of money.
2. a. Discretionary income is the amount of income left after paying necessary expenses. Disposable income is the income left after paying taxes only. Letters should be easy to understand by the intended audience.
   b. Answers will vary. Those with extra money can buy more, thereby making items more popular or trendy. Examples of trends today might include iPods, camera phones, social networks, and fantasy leagues. Examples of trends in the 1960s might include transistor radios, lava lamps, mood rings, and records.
3. Answers will vary but might include few have credit obligations; many use public transportation and have no car payment; many live in small quarters, thereby eliminating expensive housing costs; their average cell phone bills are less expensive than in the United States.

FORMATIVE ASSESSMENT

- This is an ongoing process. Circulate around the classroom or lab, observing which students have difficulty with the assignments.
- Troubleshooting: Diagnose the kinds of problems students have with this lesson. Students may become confused that an increase in a current asset is subtracted from net income whereas an increase in a current liability is added to the net income to determine cash flows.
- Assess student understanding by checking solutions to Independent Practice assignments and noting their answers to the Terms Review and Audit Your Understanding questions.

CHECK FOR UNDERSTANDING

Terms Review

- Call on students to define each term in the Terms Review. Definitions are given in the Glossary.

Audit Your Understanding

- Call on students to answer the Audit Your Understanding questions. Answers are given in Appendix D of the textbook.

GUIDED PRACTICE

Work Together

- Have students write the solution to the Work Together problem as you guide the class through the examples. Direct students to record answers on the proper form as you elicit class participation in determining the solution.
- Call on students for solutions.
- Ask a student to prepare the operating activities section of a statement of cash flows.
- Remind students to save their work to complete Work Together 14-2.

INDEPENDENT PRACTICE

On Your Own

- Assign the On Your Own problem to be worked independently.
- Remind students to save their work to complete On Your Own 14-2.
- Use the Formative Assessment techniques to diagnose student understanding.

Application Problem

- Assign Application Problem 14-1.
- Remind students to save their work to complete Application Problem 14-2.

Online Working Papers

- Students can access the Lesson 14-1 problems using this software.

RETEACH

- Write the operating activities given below. Do not write the information shown in parentheses. Ask students to identify the following increases and decreases as sources of cash or uses of cash.
  - Net income (*source of cash*)
  - Net loss (*use of cash*)
  - Depreciation expense (*source of cash*)
  - Decrease in noncash current asset (*source of cash*)
  - Increase in current liability (*source of cash*)
  - Decrease in current liability (*use of cash*)

End of Lesson Review

LO1 Understand the difference between the direct and indirect methods of preparing the statement of cash flows.

LO2 Use the indirect method to complete the operating activities section of a statement of cash flows.

Terms Review

direct method

indirect method

Audit your understanding

1. Although depreciation expense is recognized on the income statement under the accrual basis of accounting, it does not involve an outflow of cash. Why?
2. What does a decrease in the balance of supplies indicate?
3. What does an increase in the balance of merchandise inventory indicate?
4. What is the starting point for calculating the cash flow from operating activities, using the indirect method?

Work together 14-1

Preparing the operating activities section of a statement of cash flows

A comparative balance sheet for Western Wear, Inc., is provided in the *Working Papers*. The income statement for 20X2 indicates that net income was $5,080.00 and depreciation expense was $13,650.00. Statement paper and a form for analyzing changes in accounts are also provided in the *Working Papers*. Your instructor will guide you through the following examples.

1. For each item listed on the form:
   a. Record the appropriate December 31 balances for 20X2 and 20X1.
   b. Classify it as a current asset or a current liability.
   c. Compute the amount of increase or decrease from 20X1.
   d. Indicate if the increase or decrease represents a source of cash or a use of cash.
2. Prepare the operating activities section of the statement of cash flows for the current year ended December 31, using the indirect method.

Save your work to complete Work Together 14-2.

On your own 14-1

Preparing the operating activities section of a statement of cash flows

A comparative balance sheet for Southern Gulf Corporation is provided in the *Working Papers*. The income statement for 20X2 indicates that net income was $41,800.00 and depreciation expense was $9,800.00. Statement paper and a form for analyzing changes in accounts are also provided in the *Working Papers*. Work independently to complete the following problem.

1. For each item listed on the form:
   a. Record the appropriate December 31 balances for 20X2 and 20X1.
   b. Classify it as a current asset or a current liability.
   c. Compute the amount of increase or decrease from 20X1.
   d. Indicate if the increase or decrease represents a source of cash or a use of cash.
2. Prepare the operating activities section of the statement of cash flows for the current year ended December 31, using the indirect method.

Save your work to complete On Your Own 14-2.

CLOSURE

- Label and write amounts on the board that represent net income, net loss, depreciation expense, and changes in current assets and current liabilities. Ask students to state if the amounts represent sources of cash or uses of cash. Ask them to explain their answers.

Essential Question

- If the cash flow statement is important, why don't we prepare all financial statements on a cash basis? (*Revenues and expenses are matched better when the accrual basis of accounting is used.*)

EXTENDED LEARNING

- Assign Accounting in the Real World on page 401.
- Assign Ethics in Action on page 402.
- Assign Why Accounting on page 406.
- Assign Think Like an Accountant on page 407.
- Assign Financial Literacy on page 409.

LESSON

14-2 Completing the Statement of Cash Flows

LO3 Complete the investing and financing activities sections of a statement of cash flows.
LO4 Calculate the operating cash flow ratio and the cash flow margin ratio.

Preparing the Investing Activities Section LO3

Cradle Mountain Corporation
Comparative Balance Sheet
December 31, 20X2 and 20X1

	20X2	20X1	Increase (Decrease)
ASSETS			
Plant Assets:			
Equipment	$ 66,400.00	$ 49,856.00	$ 16,544.00
Building	96,000.00	96,000.00	—
Land	48,000.00	72,000.00	(24,000.00)
Less Accum. Depr.—Equipment and Land	17,488.00	8,204.00	9,284.00
Total Plant Assets (book value)	$192,912.00	$209,652.00	$(16,740.00)

Enter changes in long-term assets. 1

Cradle Mountain Corporation
Statement of Cash Flows
For Year Ended December 31, 20--

Cash flows from investing activities:		
Addition to equipment	$(16,544.00)	
Proceeds from sale of property	24,000.00	
Cash provided by investing activities		$ 7,456.00

Determine the effect on cash from investing activities. 2

Responsible investing activities are critical to the long-term success of a company. Cash flows resulting from investing activities are identified by analyzing the changes in long-term assets (plant assets). Cradle Mountain's investing activities section for the statement of cash flows is shown above.

Reporting Cash Flows from Investing Activities

1 **Analyze changes in long-term assets. The $16,544.00 increase in equipment represents a cash outflow. The increase in a long-term asset is a use of cash. During the year, Cradle Mountain Corporation sold a parcel of land for $24,000, the same amount paid for the land one year earlier. The $24,000.00 decrease in the long-term asset, Land, represents a cash inflow and is a source of cash. The following table summarizes the changes.**

Change in Account	20X2	20X1	Increase (Decrease)	Source or Use of Cash
Increase in Equipment	$66,400.00	$49,856.00	$ 16,544.00	use of cash
Decrease in Land	48,000.00	72,000.00	(24,000.00)	source of cash

2 **Determine the cash provided by investing activities (if cash increases) or the cash used for investing activities (if cash decreases). Cradle Mountain's investing activities provided $7,456.00 in cash during the current year.**

LESSON
14-2

BRIDGE

- Point out that students are already familiar with investing and financing activities. In this lesson, students will learn the formal procedure for listing investing and financing activities on the statement of cash flows.

TEACHING RESOURCES

- **Instructor's Resource CD/Website:**
  PowerPoint Slides
  Accounting Concepts
- **Working Papers:**
  Teacher's Edition of the Working Papers for Lesson 14-2
  Online Working Papers
- **Transparency Master:**
  3-column financial statement form

ENGAGE

- Distribute statements of cash flows from various companies of interest to students. Discuss and highlight the way corporations present their statements of cash flows.

PREVIEW

- Point out the learning objectives for this lesson.
- Direct students to read the headings in this lesson and to examine the illustrations.

INPUT

- Ask students why investing activities are critical to the long-term success of the firm. Point out that investing activities are primarily involved with the sale and purchase of long-term assets needed to operate a business. For example, investing activities include the purchases of land, buildings, furniture, equipment, machinery, and other items that will help the company earn revenue.
- Refer students to the illustration. Ask them to state the account titles of long-term assets (*Plant Assets*). Write the account titles on the board. Ask students to state the amount of increase or decrease from the prior year. Write the amounts beside the appropriate titles. Ask students if the increase or decrease represents a source of cash or a use of cash. Write the correct responses (*Equipment, $16,544.00, use of cash; Building, $0.00, no impact; Land, $24,000.00, source of cash*).

- Ask students why the increase of $9,284.00 in accumulated depreciation for equipment and land can be ignored. Ask them if they remember seeing $9,284.00 somewhere else (*Depreciation Expense under Operating Activities*). Emphasize that the increase in accumulated depreciation equals the depreciation expense reported on the income statement and was already accounted for under operating activities.
- Review with students the two rules at the top of page 412 regarding the increases and decreases of long-term assets.

MODEL

- Prepare the investing activities section for the statement of cash flows.
- Continue to use the transparency started in Lesson 14-1 to demonstrate the preparation of the investing activities section for the statement of cash flows.
- Review Steps 1 and 2 for reporting cash flows from investing activities. Demonstrate how each step is recorded on the statement. Emphasize the origin of each amount by pointing out the financial statement used to determine the amounts.
- Remind students that a use of cash is subtracted and that a source of cash is added.
- Ask students to verify the cash provided by the investing activities figure, $7,456.00.
- Emphasize that a use of cash represents a negative cash flow and that a source of cash represents a positive cash flow.

MODEL

- Continue to use the transparency used earlier in this lesson to demonstrate preparation of the financing activities section for the statement of cash flows.
- Review Steps 1–3 on the following page for reporting cash flows from financing activities. Demonstrate how each step is recorded on the statement. Emphasize the origin of each amount by pointing out the financial statements used to determine the amounts. Refer students to the illustration on page 412 for a visual example.
- Remind students that a use of cash is subtracted and that a source of cash is added.

ANALYZING CASH FLOWS FROM INVESTING ACTIVITIES

The increase in accumulated depreciation for equipment and building ($9,284.00) can be ignored. This increase matches the depreciation expense that was recorded on the income statement. The effect on cash flows was already accounted for under operating activities.

When calculating the cash flows from investing activities, it is useful to remember that:

- Increases in long-term assets generally result in cash outflows (*uses of cash*) that are subtracted on the statement of cash flows.
- Decreases in long-term assets generally result in cash inflows (*sources of cash*) that are added on the statement of cash flows.

Preparing the Financing Activities Section

Cradle Mountain Corporation
Comparative Balance Sheet
December 31, 20X2 and 20X1

	20X2	20X1	Increase (Decrease)
Long-Term Liabilities:			
Mortgage Payable	$117,162.00	$117,600.00	$(438.00)

1 Analyze change in long-term liability.

Cradle Mountain Corporation
Statement of Cash Flows
For Year Ended December 31, 20X2

Cash flows from financing activities:		
Repayment of mortgage	$ (438.00)	
Proceeds from issuance of common stock	32,000.00	
Dividend payment	(25,600.00)	
Cash provided by financing activities		$5,962.00

3 Determine cash flows from financing activities.

2 Analyze changes in cash identified on the statement of stockholders' equity.

Cradle Mountain Corporation
Comparative Statement of Stockholders' Equity
For Years Ended December 31, 20X2 and 20X1

	20X2	20X1	Increase (Decrease)
Capital Stock:			
$10.00 Per Share			
Balance, January 1	$ 288,000.00	$ —	$ 288,000.00
Additional Capital Stock Issued	32,000.00	288,000.00	(256,000.00)
Balance, December 31	$ 320,000.00	$288,000.00	$ 32,000.00
Retained Earnings:			
Balance, January 1	$ 48,041.00	$ —	$ 48,041.00
Net Income after Federal Income Tax	80,275.00	48,041.00	32,234.00
Total	$ 128,316.00	$ 48,041.00	$ 80,275.00
Less Dividend Payment	25,600.00	—	25,600.00
Balance, December 31	$ 102,716.00	$ 48,041.00	$ 54,675.00
Total Stockholders' Equity, December 31	$ 422,716.00	$336,041.00	$ 86,675.00

- Ask students to verify the cash provided by the financing activities, $5,962.00.

TEACHING IDEA Prepare a bulletin board or other visual to match business transactions with the type of activity (operating, investing, financing) and whether the transaction represents a cash inflow or outflow.

Reporting Cash Flows from Financing Activities

1. **Analyze changes in long-term liabilities. The $438.00 decrease in Mortgage Payable represents a cash outflow.**
2. **Analyze changes in cash identified on the statement of stockholders' equity. Cradle Mountain issued $32,000.00 of additional capital stock during the year. This activity resulted in a receipt of $32,000.00 from the issuance of 3,200 shares of capital stock at $10.00 per share. The sale of stock provides a source of cash. A cash dividend of $25,600.00 was paid during the year. The dividend payment represents a use of cash.**
3. **Determine the cash provided by financing activities (if cash increases) or the cash used for investing activities (if cash decreases). Cradle Mountain's financing activities provided $5,962.00 in cash during the current year.**

ANALYZING CASH FLOWS FROM FINANCING ACTIVITIES

Financing activities are often used to maintain an adequate balance in the Cash account. These activities usually involve borrowing money from creditors and repaying the principal or acquiring capital from owners and providing a return on their investment. Cash flows originating from a company's financing activities are identified by examining the changes in long-term liabilities reported on the balance sheet and the changes in stockholders' equity reported on the statement of stockholders' equity. This analysis is shown on the previous page.

The statement of stockholders' equity also shows a change in Retained Earnings due to the net income of the business. Net income was the starting point for the analysis of changes in the operating activities of the business. Net income does not affect the financing activities of the business.

When calculating the cash flows from financing activities, remember that:

- Increases in long-term liabilities and the issuance of stock generally result in cash inflows (*sources of cash*) that are added on the statement of cash flows.
- Decreases in long-term liabilities and the payment of cash dividends generally result in cash outflows (*uses of cash*) that are subtracted on the statement of cash flows.

remember

Financing activities involve debt or equity transactions.

© Orange Line Media/Shutterstock.com

INPUT

- Ask students which business activity occurs first—operating, investing, or financing—when a corporation gets started (*financing activities*). Explain that a corporation acquires cash through financing activities. Stress that these funds are then used to purchase assets (*investing activities*) so that the business can produce revenue (*operating activities*).
- Point out that another use of financing activities is to maintain an adequate balance in the Cash account. Remind students that budget projections may indicate an upcoming shortage of cash, in which case money is borrowed from creditors or acquired from owners through the sale of additional stock.
- Emphasize that cash flows from a company's financing activities are identified by changes in long-term liabilities and stockholders' equity.
- Remind students that a change in retained earnings due to the net income or net loss of a business can be ignored when reporting cash flows from financing activities. This is because the net income or net loss results from the operating activities of the business and has already been reported under that section of the statement of cash flows.
- Review the two rules for increases and decreases in cash flows related to financing activities.

DIFFERENTIATED INSTRUCTION

Tactile/Kinesthetic students learn best through experiences and activities. Allow students to create a flash card game. Each flash card should be labeled with the name of an operating, investing, or financing activity. The opposite side of the flash card should be labeled with *source of cash* or *use of cash*.

Visual/Spatial learners usually recall what they have seen. They can benefit from the flash card game as well.

MODEL

- Review Steps 1–4 for completing the statement of cash flows.
- Continue to use the transparency, which now shows completed operating, investing, and financing activities sections. Refer students to the illustration on this page for an example.
- Complete the transparency and emphasize that the statement of cash flows cannot be double-ruled unless the Cash balance, end-of-period amount matches the current-year Cash account balance listed on the comparative balance sheet.

Completing the Statement of Cash Flows

Cradle Mountain Corporation
Statement of Cash Flows
For Year Ended December 31, 20X2

Cash flows from operating activities:			
Net income		$ 80,275.00	
Adjustments to net income:			
Depreciation expense	$ 9,284.00		
Changes in current assets and liabilities:			
Increase in accounts receivable	(88,423.00)		
Decrease in supplies	319.00		
Increase in merchandise inventory	(93,312.00)		
Increase in notes payable	31,191.00		
Increase in accounts payable	43,940.00		
Total adjustments to net income		$(97,001.00)	
Cash used for operating activities			$(16,726.00)
Cash flows from investing activities:			
Addition to equipment		$(16,544.00)	
Proceeds from sale of property		24,000.00	
Cash provided by investing activities			$ 7,456.00
Cash flows from financing activities:			
Repayment of mortgage		$ (438.00)	
Proceeds from issuance of common stock		32,000.00	
Dividend payment		(25,600.00)	
Cash provided by financing activities			$ 5,962.00
Net decrease in cash			$ (3,308.00)
Cash balance, beginning of period			10,056.00
Cash balance, end of period			$ 6,748.00

Compute ending cash balance.

$10,056.00
– 3,308.00
$ 6,748.00

③ Compute ending cash balance.
④ Verify calculation.
② Identify beginning cash balance.
① Compute net increase or decrease.

Cradle Mountain Corporation
Comparative Balance Sheet
December 31, 20X2 and 20X1

	20X2	20X1	Increase (Decrease)
ASSETS			
Current Assets:			
Cash	$6,748.00	$10,056.00	$(3,308.00)

The completed statement of cash flows is shown above. The cash balances at the beginning and end of the period, shown on the statement of cash flows, must match the amounts shown on the comparative balance sheet.

Completing the Statement of Cash Flows

1. Compute the net increase or decrease in Cash resulting from operating, investing, and financing activities.
2. Identify the beginning cash balance from the comparative balance sheet. The beginning cash balance for the current year is the ending cash balance from the prior year, $10,056.00.
3. Compute the ending cash balance, $6,748.00 ($10,056.00 – $3,308.00 decrease in cash).
4. Verify that the Cash balance, end of period, matches the ending cash balance shown on the comparative balance sheet.

Cash Flow Analysis LO4

The intent of the statement of cash flows is to report and explain the sources and uses of a company's cash and to clarify changes in other account balances. Cradle Mountain's statement of cash flows helps explain the difference between solid profits and a decrease in the Cash account. Among other things, the large increases in accounts receivable and merchandise inventory (uses of cash) hampered Cradle Mountain's ability to pay its bills. Studying cash flows along with analyzing the income statement, the statement of stockholders' equity, and the balance sheet provides a more accurate overview of a company's present and future financial condition.

In addition to free cash flow, which was explained in Chapter 13, additional ratios are sometimes used to analyze cash flows.

The **operating cash flow ratio** is calculated as:

$$\text{Operating Cash Flow Ratio} = \text{Cash Flows from Operating Activities} \div \text{Current Liabilities}$$

The operating cash flow ratio for Cradle Mountain for 20X2 is calculated as:

$$(14.3) = (\$16{,}726.00) \div \$116{,}912.00$$

Similar to the current ratio, the operating cash flow ratio indicates how likely the company is to be able to pay off current liabilities with its cash flows from operations. A ratio of 1.0 or greater is desirable. Cradle Mountain's ratio of (14.3) is not desirable. It can improve its ratio by selling inventory and decreasing the receivables.

The **cash flow margin ratio** is calculated as:

$$\text{Cash Flow Margin Ratio} = \text{Cash Flows from Operating Activities} \div \text{Net Sales}$$

The cash flow margin ratio for Cradle Mountain for 20X2 is calculated as:

$$(4.16) = (\$16{,}726.00) \div \$401{,}744.00$$

This ratio shows the cash flow from operations for every $1.00 of net sales. Net income is necessary for the long-term success of a business, but a company must also be able to pay its bills when due. The operations of a business must provide cash on a timely basis so that it can remain in business. Cradle Mountain's ratio of (4.16) is not desirable. As stated above, Cradle Mountain needs to achieve a positive cash flow from its operating activities to remain in business.

© Yuri Arcurs/Shutterstock.com

INPUT

- Explain the intent of the cash flow statement.
- Point out that a profitable business is desirable. However, a company must be able to pay its bills on time to stay in business.
- Point out how changes in certain accounts hindered the ability of Cradle Mountain to pay its bills on time.
- Explain the operating cash flow ratio and the cash flow margin ratio.

MODEL

- Write on the board the formula for calculating the operating cash flow ratio.
- Explain the steps of the calculation.
- Write on the board the formula for calculating the cash flow margin ratio.
- Explain the steps of the calculation.
- Point out the meanings of these ratios and how they are used to analyze a company's financial health.

Careers In Accounting

Review a career as a financial analyst.

Careers In Accounting

Rebecca Martin

FINANCIAL ANALYST

© StockLite/Shutterstock.com

Rebecca Martin enjoys her job as a senior financial analyst for an investment company in New York City. She has been with the company for six years. She was promoted to her current position after three years as a junior financial analyst.

An investment company receives money from its clients. The company invests the money in stocks and other investments and charges a fee for its services. The entire set of investments is called a **portfolio**. The portfolio managers continually sell stocks from the portfolio and add new stocks to it. The clients then share in the net profits and losses of the investments.

In her position, Rebecca Martin does extensive research on potential investments. She makes recommendations on which stocks should be included in the portfolio. She also tracks funds in the portfolio and recommends when stocks should be sold.

Rebecca uses basic financial ratios and measures to analyze an investment's performance, paying attention to historic data and trends. She also needs to gather other information that could affect the value of stock. She tracks economic forecasts and reads financial newspapers and journals. She searches the Internet for data and press releases about companies. She then puts all these data together and determines the value of an investment by forecasting its future earnings.

Soon after starting in her current position, at the suggestion of her manager, Rebecca began to focus on investments in technology. She has acquired a sound understanding of the field and now analyzes only technology investments. She finds it very challenging to stay up to date on the latest developments in the ever-changing world of technology. Many weeks she works 50 to 70 hours.

When asked what she likes best about her position, Rebecca stated that she likes the fact that she can evaluate her decisions by tracking the value of the investments she recommends. She is results-oriented, and she can easily determine the results of her work.

Because technology changes quickly, Rebecca attends several conferences and seminars each year. She is also working to earn the designation of Chartered Financial Analyst (CFA). To obtain this, she must complete a program of study and pass three exams. Once she becomes a CFA, she hopes to move up to the position of portfolio manager.

A financial analyst must have excellent written and oral communications skills. The analyst must also be able to synthesize information, pay attention to details, and use critical thinking and investigative skills. Expertise in using electronic spreadsheet and presentation software is essential.

Salary Range: In 2010, the median wage for a financial analyst was $75,650, with top salaries at $141,000.

Qualifications: The minimum requirement is a bachelor's degree in a related field, such as accounting, economics, or finance. A master's degree is often preferred.

Occupational Outlook: The growth for financial analyst positions is projected to be faster than average (20% to 28%) for the period from 2010 to 2020. However, competition is strong in this career area. A graduate degree and/or certification are very helpful.

Sources: www.onetonline.org; www.cfainstitute.org.

© iStockphoto.com/Mlenny

FORMATIVE ASSESSMENT

- This is an ongoing process. Circulate around the classroom or lab, observing which students have difficulty with the assignments.
- Troubleshooting: Diagnose the kinds of problems students have with this lesson. Students may become confused that a decrease in a long-term asset is added as an increase on the statement of cash flows whereas a decrease in a long-term liability is subtracted as a decrease on the statement of cash flows.
- Assess student understanding by checking solutions to Independent Practice assignments and noting their answers to the Audit Your Understanding questions..

End of Lesson Review

LO3 Complete the investing and financing activities sections of a statement of cash flows.

LO4 Calculate the operating cash flow ratio and the cash flow margin ratio.

Audit your understanding

1. How are the cash flows resulting from a company's investing activities identified?
2. Why is an increase in accumulated depreciation on the balance sheet ignored when analyzing the cash flows from investing activities?
3. How are the cash flows originating from a company's financing activities identified?
4. How does an individual know if all cash transactions have been properly accounted for on the statement of cash flows?

Work together 14-2

Completing the statement of cash flows

Use the *Working Papers* from Work Together 14-1. A comparative balance sheet and forms for analyzing changes in long-term assets, long-term liabilities, and stockholders' equity are provided in the *Working Papers*. Your instructor will guide you through the following examples.

1. Complete the changes in the long-term assets and long-term liabilities form.
2. Prepare the investing activities section of the statement of cash flows.
3. Complete the changes in stockholders' equity form.
4. Prepare the financing activities section of the statement of cash flows.
5. Complete the statement of cash flows.
6. Calculate the following ratios:
   a. Operating cash flow ratio
   b. Cash flow margin ratio (Net sales equal $24,645.00)

On your own 14-2

Completing the statement of cash flows

Use the Working Papers from On Your Own 14-1. A comparative balance sheet and forms for analyzing changes in long-term assets, long-term liabilities, and stockholders' equity are provided in the Working Papers. Work independently to complete the following problem.

1. Complete the changes in the long-term assets and long-term liabilities form.
2. Prepare the investing activities section of the statement of cash flows.
3. Complete the changes in stockholders' equity form.
4. Prepare the financing activities section of the statement of cash flows.
5. Complete the statement of cash flows.
6. Calculate the following ratios:
   a. Operating cash flow ratio
   b. Cash flow margin ratio (Net sales equal $70,110.00)

CHECK FOR UNDERSTANDING

Audit Your Understanding

- Call on students to answer the Audit Your Understanding questions. Answers are given in Appendix D of the textbook.

GUIDED PRACTICE

Work Together

- Have students write the solution to the Work Together problem as you guide the class through the examples.
- Remind students to use Work Together 14-1 to complete Work Together 14-2.
- Direct students to complete the statement of cash flows.

INDEPENDENT PRACTICE

On Your Own

- Assign the On Your Own problem to be worked independently.
- Remind students to use On Your Own 14-1 to complete On Your Own 14-2.
- Use the Formative Assessment techniques to diagnose student understanding.

Application Problem

- Assign Application Problem 14-2.
- Remind students to use Application Problem 14-1 to complete Application Problem 14-2.

Online Working Papers

- Students can access the Lesson 14-2 problems using this software.

RETEACH

- Write the following investing and financing activities on the board. Do not write the information in parentheses. Ask students to identify the following increases and decreases as sources of cash or uses of cash.

Investing Activities:
- Purchases of plant assets (*use of cash*)
- Decreases in long-term assets (*source of cash*)

Financing Activities:
- Capital stock issue (*source of cash*)
- Mortgage issue (*source of cash*)
- Payment of cash dividends (*use of cash*)
- Repayment of loan principal (*use of cash*)

CLOSURE

- Direct students to the statement of cash flows on page 414.
- Ask students to state the origin of each amount shown. Answers should identify the financial statement used or indicate that the amount is the result of a calculation.

Essential Question

- Can it be assumed that a company is financially healthy if it has a positive cash flow? Explain. (*The cash flow statement is just a piece of the puzzle. For example, it does not show profit earned or lost because profitability is composed of things that are not all cash-based.*)

EXTENDED LEARNING

- Review Careers in Accounting on page 416.

CLOSURE

- Review the Chapter Summary.
- Ask students to prepare a list of the new concepts introduced in this chapter.

Essential Questions

- In times of cash flow difficulties, what options are available to help a business overcome its cash flow dilemma? (*Options might include review pricing, renegotiate costs and/or terms, and improve bank relations to help with overdrafts or loans.*)
- Who are the users of the cash flow statement (because it only tells where the company's money came from and where it was spent)? (*A company can use a cash flow statement to predict future cash flows, which helps with budgeting. For investors, the cash flows reflect a company's financial health.*)

EXTENDED LEARNING

- Assign Explore Accounting on page 418.

EXPLORE ACCOUNTING

Answers

1. At the time of publication, the proposed revenue recognition rule had not yet been adopted. Once adopted, it is expected to have an effective date of January 1, 2017.
2. Answers will vary.

Chapter Summary

The statement of cash flows can be prepared by using the direct method or the indirect method. The method used affects only the cash flows from operating activities section. The direct method lists the cash receipts and cash payments from operating activities. The indirect method begins with net income and makes adjustments for the differences between net income and actual cash flows.

When using the indirect method, the first adjustment is for depreciation and amortization. These two noncash expenses are added to net income. The second adjustment analyzes all noncash current assets. Increases in current assets are subtracted from net income. Decreases in current assets are added to net income. The third adjustment analyzes all current liabilities. Increases in current liabilities are added to net income. Decreases in current liabilities are subtracted from net income. Cash provided by or used for operating activities is net income plus or minus all adjustments.

Cash flows from investing activities involve long-term (plant) assets. Increases in plant assets represent a use of cash. Decreases in plant assets represent a source of cash.

Cash flows from financing activities involve long-term liabilities and changes in stockholders' equity. Increases in these accounts represent a source of cash. Decreases in these accounts represent a use of cash.

The statement of cash flows is completed by netting out the cash flows from operating, investing, and financing activities to determine the change in cash during the fiscal period. The change is then verified by taking the beginning cash balance and adding a cash increase or subtracting a cash decrease to arrive at the ending cash balance as found on the balance sheet.

EXPLORE ACCOUNTING — Changing Rules for the Recognition of Revenue

© iStockphoto.com/Makhnach_M

At the time of publication, a new rule relating to when revenue is recognized was being proposed. The proposal is a joint project of the Financial Accounting Standards Board (FASB) and the International Accounting Standards Board (IASB). The FASB develops the generally accepted accounting principles (GAAP) that must be followed in the United States. The IASB develops International Financial Reporting Standards (IFRS). This joint proposal means that GAAP and IFRS will use the same standards to measure and record revenue.

Current GAAP for revenue recognition contain different rules for revenue recognition in different industries. Current IFRS can be difficult to use when the sales contract is complex. The new standard will eliminate some inconsistencies in the current revenue recognition standards and will provide a single model that can be used across a range of industries.

The new rule still provides that revenue be recognized when the transfer of goods or services is essentially complete and in the amount that the company expects to receive. The major differences relate to long-term contracts and contracts that have multiple elements.

Once the new standard is passed by both organizations, it is expected to take effect on January 1, 2017. Since companies use comparative financial statements, the revenue must be measured the same way for all years shown. [CONCEPT: Consistent Reporting] Therefore, companies will have to measure revenue using both methods until 2017. For financial statements before 2017, all years will be shown on financial statements using the old standard. In 2017, the current and prior years will all be shown using the new standard.

INSTRUCTIONS

Go to www.fasb.org and do the following:

1. Search for information about revenue recognition. Find out if the new revenue recognition standard was adopted. If so, list the date of adoption and the effective date of the new standard.
2. Continue searching the site to find at least one new proposed standard. List the name of the proposed standard and write a one-sentence summary of the topic of the proposal.

Sources: www.ifrs.org; www.fasb.org.

Apply Your Understanding

INSTRUCTIONS: Download problem instructions for Excel, QuickBooks, and Sage 50 from the textbook companion website at www.C21accounting.com.

14-1 Application Problem: Preparing the operating activities section of a statement of cash flows LO1, 2

The comparative income statement of NLC Corporation reveals the following net income and depreciation expense for the current year:

Net income	$182,920
Depreciation expense	25,000

The comparative balance sheet of NLC Corporation lists the following current assets and current liabilities and their ending balances for the current and prior years:

	Current Year	Prior Year
Accounts Receivable (book value)	$111,030	$ 96,000
Merchandise Inventory	236,632	242,000
Supplies	12,296	11,000
Accounts Payable	99,524	88,000

Instructions:

1. In the forms provided in the *Working Papers*, record the appropriate amount for net income. Indicate if this item represents a source of cash or a use of cash.
2. Record the appropriate amount for depreciation expense. Indicate if this item represents a source of cash or a use of cash.
3. For each current asset and current liability, write the balances for the current year and the prior year. Classify each account as a current asset or a current liability. Compute the amount of increase or decrease from the prior year. Indicate if the increase or decrease represents a source of cash or a use of cash.
4. Using the indirect method and the information collected, prepare the cash flows from operating activities section of the statement of cash flows for the current year ending December 31, 20X2. Save your work to complete Problem 14-2.

1. Compute the increase (decrease) of the corresponding accounts to operating activities of the statement of cash flows.
2. Print the worksheet.

14-2 Application Problem: Completing the statement of cash flows LO1, 2, 3

Use the statement of cash flows started in Problem 14-1. The comparative balance sheet of NLC Corporation lists the following long-term assets and long-term liabilities, with their ending balances for the current and prior years:

	Current Year	Prior Year
Office Equipment	$ 45,600	$ 25,000
Office Furniture	24,420	18,000
Land (decrease due to sale)	200,000	280,000
Mortgage Payable	160,200	184,000

The comparative statement of stockholders' equity of NLC Corporation reveals the following stock and dividend information for the current year:

Sale of additional common stock	$ 40,000
Payment of cash dividend	100,000

CHECK FIGURES

For complete solutions to Chapter 14 problems, see the Teacher's Edition of the Working Papers.

Application Problem 14-1

2. Depreciation expense: $25,000.00; source of cash.
3. Merchandise inventory: current asset; decrease ($5,368.00); source of cash.

   Supplies: current asset; increase $1,296.00; use of cash.
4. Cash provided by operating activities, $208,486.00.

Application Problem 14-2

1. Office equipment: long-term asset; increase $20,600.00; use of cash.

   Mortgage payable: long-term liability; decrease ($23,800.00); use of cash.
2. Sale of additional common stock: $40,000.00; source of cash.
3. Cash provided by investing activities, $52,980.00.
4. Cash used for financing activities, ($83,800.00).
5. Net increase in cash, $177,666.00.
10. Operating cash flow ratio, 2.09.

Instructions:

1. For each long-term asset and long-term liability, write the balances for the current year and the prior year. Compute the amount of increase or decrease from the prior year. Indicate if the increase or decrease represents a source of cash or a use of cash.
2. For each amount taken from the comparative statement of stockholders' equity, record the appropriate amount. Indicate if these activities represent a source of cash or a use of cash.
3. Using the statement of cash flows started in Problem 14-1, prepare the cash flows from investing activities section of the statement of cash flows.
4. Prepare the cash flows from financing activities section of the statement of cash flows.
5. Compute the net increase or decrease resulting from operating, investing, and financing activities.
6. Record the cash balance for the beginning of the period in the form provided. NLC Corporation started the year with a beginning cash balance of $135,860.00.
7. Compute the cash balance for the end of the fiscal period by adding the amount of increase or decrease in cash and the beginning cash amount.
8. Complete the statement of cash flows for NLC Corporation by entering the net increase or decrease in cash, the beginning cash balance, and the ending cash balance.
9. Verify the accuracy of the statement of cash flows by comparing the statement's ending cash balance with the cash balance of $313,526.00 listed for the current year on NLC's comparative balance sheet.
10. Calculate the following ratios:
    a. Operating cash flow ratio
    b. Cash flow margin ratio (Net sales equal $270,220.00)

1. Compute the increase (decrease) of the corresponding accounts to investing activities and to financing activities of the statement of cash flows.
2. Complete the statement of cash flows.
3. Print the worksheets.

14-M Mastery Problem: Preparing a statement of cash flows LO1, 2, 3

Use the abbreviated comparative financial statements for Alpine Corporation in the *Working Papers*.

Instructions:

1. Review the comparative income statement and identify the amounts of net income (or net loss) and depreciation expense for the period. Indicate if each item represents a source of cash or a use of cash.
2. Analyze the comparative balance sheet and complete the following steps:
    a. Prepare a list of current assets and current liabilities.
    b. Write the balances for 20X2 and 20X1.
    c. Classify each account as a current asset or a current liability.
    d. Compute the amount of increase or decrease from 20X1.
    e. Indicate if the increase or decrease represents a source of cash or a use of cash.
3. Analyze the comparative balance sheet and complete the following steps:
    a. Prepare a list of long-term assets.
    b. Write the balances for 20X2 and 20X1.
    c. Compute the amount of increase or decrease from 20X1.
    d. Indicate if the increase or decrease represents a source of cash or a use of cash.

Mastery Problem 14-M

1. Net income: $21,599.00; source of cash.
2. Accounts receivable (book value): current asset; decrease ($23,836.00); source of cash.

   Notes payable: current liability; decrease ($1,257.00); use of cash.
3. Equipment: long-term asset; increase $8,000.00; use of cash.
4. Mortgage payable: long-term liability; decrease ($1,873.00); use of cash.
5. Payment of cash dividend: $22,000.00; use of cash.
6. Cash provided by operating activities, $45,668.00.

   Net increase in cash, $25,795.00.

10. Cash flow margin ratio, 0.08.

INDEPENDENT PRACTICE

- Assign Mastery Problem 14-M for students as a culminating problem combining all new learning from the chapter.
- Assign Challenge Problem 14-C to accelerated students who work at a faster pace.
- Assign Study Guide 14.
- Students can access Online Working Papers to work end-of-chapter problems on the computer.
- Direct students to the C21 Accounting companion website for additional practice and review opportunities.

FORMATIVE ASSESSMENT

- Review solutions to the assigned problems in class, diagnosing trouble spots.

4. Reexamine the comparative balance sheet and complete the following steps:
   a. Prepare a list of long-term liabilities.
   b. Compute the amount of increase or decrease from 20X1.
   c. Indicate if the increase or decrease represents a source of cash or a use of cash.
5. Review the comparative statement of stockholders' equity and (1) identify the amounts of any additional stock issued or cash dividends paid and (2) indicate if each item represents a source of cash or a use of cash.
6. Prepare the operating, investing, and financing activities sections of a statement of cash flows, using the indirect method.
7. Enter the cash balance at the beginning of the year as shown on the comparative balance sheet.
8. Compute the cash balance for the end of the period to complete the statement of cash flows.
9. Verify the accuracy of the statement of cash flows by comparing the statement's ending cash balance with the cash balance listed for 20X2 on Alpine's comparative balance sheet.
10. Calculate the following ratios:
    a. Operating cash flow ratio
    b. Cash flow margin ratio
11. Assume that for 20X1, Alpine Corporation's operating cash flow ratio was 0.40, and its cash flow margin ratio was 0.06. Compare the two-year trend for each calculation and write a short summary of each trend.

1. Complete the comparative income statement, the comparative statement of stockholders' equity and the comparative balance sheet.
2. Compute the increase (decrease) of the corresponding accounts to operating activities, to investing activities and to financing activities of the statement of cash flows.
3. Complete the statement of cash flows.
4. Print the worksheets.

14-C Challenge Problem: Preparing a statement of cash flows with amortization expense LO1, 2, 3

Use the abbreviated comparative financial statements for Southwest Electronics, Inc., in the *Working Papers*. The comparative balance sheet for Southwest Electronics lists an intangible asset, Patents. The patents were granted in the first year of the business's existence. Southwest Electronics has estimated that the patents have a five-year useful life. Although the expense is recognized on the income statement under the accrual basis of accounting, it does not involve an outflow of cash. The cash was actually spent in an earlier period. Since the amortized patent expense shown on Southwest Electronics' comparative income statement does not use cash, it is handled the same way as depreciation expense. Both patents and depreciation expense are adjustments to net income (or net loss), which are presented before changes in current assets and liabilities.

Instructions:

Prepare a statement of cash flows for 20X2 for Southwest Electronics, Inc., using the indirect method.

1. Complete the comparative income statement, the comparative statement of stockholders' equity, and the comparative balance sheet.
2. Complete the statement of cash flows.
3. Print the worksheets.

RETEACH

- Call on students to describe how they avoid the trouble spots diagnosed.
- Use reteaching suggestions from lesson plans as required.
- Assign Recycling Problem 14-R if needed.

EXTENDED LEARNING

- Assign 21st Century Skills on page 422.
- Assign Auditing for Errors on page 423.
- Assign Analyzing Home Depot's Financial Statements on page 423.

SUMMATIVE EVALUATION

- Chapter 14 Test
- Cognero for Chapter 14

Challenge Problem 14-C

Cash used for operating activities, ($24,820.00).

Cash used for investing activities, ($14,255.00).

Cash provided by financing activities, $42,045.00.

COMMON CORE AND INTERDISCIPLINARY STUDIES

Extended learning features and activities present numerous opportunities to implement Common Core Standards through interdisciplinary studies. Practice is provided in the common core areas of English Language Arts & Literacy and Mathematical Practice. Many of these activities require short, critical-thinking and decision-making responses that apply reading, writing, speaking, listening, language, media and technology, and mathematical skills.

21ST CENTURY SKILLS

Answers

1. Answers will vary but might include reconsidering extending credit to all customers, as some customers may not have a good payment history and would be considered a credit risk; the amount of credit extended may be evaluated as well as the terms. Short-term solutions might include offering discounts or free shipping in exchange for early payment.
2. Venn diagrams will vary based on the businesses selected. You may need to remind students that accounts receivable are different from credit extended by national credit cards such as Visa, MasterCard, and Discover.

21st Century Skills

Dash for Cash

PARTNERSHIP FOR 21ST CENTURY SKILLS

Theme: Financial, Economic, Business, and Entrepreneurial Literacy

Skills: Critical Thinking and Problem Solving, Communication and Collaboration

If businesses were paid the instant they made a sale, they would never have a cash flow problem. Unfortunately, that does not happen. It seems simple enough to collect accounts receivable as fast as possible. However, most customers are using the same strategy of collecting receivables fast and slowing down their own accounts payable. Many companies find themselves owing payables prior to collecting receivables. Nonetheless, some top-performing companies have found strategies to help improve their cash flow by managing their accounts receivable.

To shorten the accounts receivable collection period, a good system needs to be in place. Evaluating the customer terms, the length of time it takes to be paid, and the process for contacting customers past due is a good place to begin. The whole idea is to improve the speed in which payment is received.

APPLICATION

1. Marilla Manufacturing produces screens for smartphones. It is currently experiencing a cash shortage and is having difficulty purchasing manufacturing supplies and meeting weekly payroll. It extends credit to all customers and allows them 90 days to pay on receivables. Its sales have grown dramatically this year, and it maintains outstanding relations with its customers. Marilla Manufacturing is having difficulty understanding why there is a shortage of cash. What suggestions would you offer the president of the company regarding its credit policy? What recommendations would you make in the short term to help overcome the shortage of cash? Explain your recommendations.
2. Interview two local small business owners who extend credit to customers. Create a Venn diagram on a poster to compare and contrast their credit policies and credit terms.

Auditing for errors

Henry Hunter, a newly hired accountant, has prepared the following statement of cash flows. Henry has asked you to examine his statement because the ending cash balance does not equal the balance of the cash account. Prepare a list of any errors you identify in the statement and calculate the correct ending cash balance.

Westside Corporation Statement of Cash Flows For Year Ended December 31, 20X2			
Cash flows from operating activities:			
Net income		91,460.00	
Adjustments to net income:			
Depreciation expense	13,000.00		
Changes in current assets and liabilities:			
Increase in accounts receivable	7,510.00		
Decrease in merchandise inventory	(2,733.00)		
Increase in accounts payable	1,045.00		
Decrease in notes payable	(6,500.00)		
Total adjustments to net income		12,322.00	
Cash provided by operating activities			103,782.00
Cash flows from investing activities:			
Addition to machinery		(15,000.00)	
Repayment of mortgage		12,650.00	
Addition to office furniture		(3,800.00)	
Cash provided by investing activities			(6,150.00)
Cash flows from financing activities:			
Proceeds from sale of land		15,000.00	
Proceeds from issuance of common stock		(25,000.00)	
Dividend payment		50,000.00	
Cash used for financing activities			40,000.00
Net increase in cash			137,632.00
Cash balance, beginning of period			135,860.00
Cash balance, end of period			1,772.00

Analyzing Home Depot's financial statements

Home Depot's Comparative Statement of Cash Flows is given on page B-9 of Appendix B.

INSTRUCTIONS

Using Home Depot's statement of cash flows, answer the following questions:

1. Which method does Home Depot use for its statement of cash flows?
2. In the operating activities section, looking only at changes in assets and liabilities, list by both title and amount the largest source of cash for 2013. Did this item increase or decrease during the current fiscal period?
3. For 2013, what was Home Depot's Net Cash Used in Investing Activities?
4. For 2013, what was Home Depot's largest use of cash from financing activities?

AUDITING FOR ERRORS

Answers

1. The statement should include "For Year Ended December 31, 20--."
2. Increases and decreases of current assets are reversed. An increase in a current asset is a use of cash; a decrease in a current asset is a source of cash.
3. The repayment of the mortgage should be in the financing activities section. In addition, the amount is a use of cash.
4. The proceeds from the sale of land should be in the investing activities section.
5. The proceeds from the issuance of common stock are a source of cash.
6. The dividend payment is a use of cash.
7. The end-of-period cash balance should be calculated by adding the beginning cash balance to the net increase in cash.
8. The revised ending cash balance should be $188,638.00.

ANALYZING HOME DEPOT'S FINANCIAL STATEMENTS

Answers

1. Indirect.
2. Accounts Payable and Accrued Expenses, $698 million. Because it is listed as a source of cash, Accounts Payable and Accrued Expenses must have increased during the fiscal period. Increases in current liabilities are added to net income.
3. $1,432 million.
4. Repurchases of Common Stock, $3,984 million.

Reinforcement Activity

BRIDGE

- Reinforcement Activity 3 begins after Chapter 14 and reinforces processing and analyzing accounting data for a corporation.

TEACHING RESOURCES

- **Manual Accounting:**
  Working Papers for Reinforcement Activity 3
  Teacher's Edition of the Working Papers for Reinforcement Activity 3
  Online Working Papers
  Website for Audit Tests, Solutions, and Transparency Masters
- **Accounting Software:**
  QuickBooks, Excel, Sage 50, or Automated Accounting Online may be used to automate this Reinforcement Activity.

INPUT FOR AUTOMATING

- Direct students to read the Help screens for specific requirements for automating Reinforcement Activity 3.

Reinforcement Activity 3

Processing and Analyzing Accounting Data for a Corporation

This activity reinforces selected learning from Part 3, Chapters 10 through 14.

Peterson Pet Supply, Inc.

Peterson Pet Supply, Inc., organized as a corporation, sells a complete line of pet supplies. Peterson owns the land and building where its store is located.

Peterson's fiscal year ends on December 31. It has recorded and posted all journal entries through December 14. It uses the chart of accounts shown on page 426.

INSTRUCTIONS

1. Use the appropriate journal to record the following selected transactions completed from December 15 through December 31, 20X3. Source documents are abbreviated as follows: check, C; memorandum, M; receipt, R.

   Transactions:

   Dec. 15. The board of directors declared a $2,800.00 semiannual cash dividend on preferred stock, payable on December 31. M432.
   18. Received cash for 10,000 shares of common stock, $10 par value, at $12.40 per share, $124,000.00. R512.
   19. Received cash for 100 shares of 8%, $100 par-value preferred stock at $120.00 per share, $12,000.00. R513.
   23. Received office equipment at an agreed-upon value of $20,000.00 in exchange for 1,600 shares of common stock. M433.
   31. Paid the December 15 dividend. C818.
   31. Paid cash to trustee for the semiannual interest payment on a $30,000.00, 8% bond, which was issued at face value. C819.
   31. Purchased 1,000 shares of Apex Corporation stock as an investment for $85.00 per share, $85,000.00. C820.
   31. Received cash for 30 five-year, 6.0%, $1,000.00 bonds, issued at face value, $30,000.00. R514.

2. A comparative income, a statement of stockholders' equity, and a balance sheet for Peterson Pet Supply, Inc., are given in the *Working Papers*. Use these statements and the following information to prepare a statement of cash flows (indirect method) for 20X3.
   a. The change in the Investment Securities account is due to the cash purchase of additional investments throughout 20X3.
   b. Land was sold for its cost, $25,000.00.
   c. Equipment was purchased for cash as follows: office equipment, $50,000.00; store equipment, $35,000.00.
   d. Bonds were issued at face value, $30,000.00.
   e. Common stock was issued for $310,000.00.
   f. Preferred stock was issued for $24,000.00.
   g. All common and preferred dividends declared were paid in cash.

3. Using the financial statements, calculate the following ratios and measures for the years indicated. Round percentage calculations to the nearest 0.1%, dollar amounts to the nearest $0.01, and ratios to the nearest 0.1. Use the results to determine whether the trend appears to be favorable or unfavorable. Give reasons for your responses.
   a. Profitability ratios:
      (1) Gross margin
      (2) Operating margin
      (3) Rate earned on average total assets (total assets, January 1, 20X2: $975,223.55)
      (4) Rate of return on average stockholders' equity (total stockholders' equity, January 1, 20X2: $967,852.88)
   b. Efficiency ratios:
      (1) Accounts receivable turnover (net accounts receivable, January 1, 20X2: $67,248.25)
      (2) Inventory turnover (total merchandise inventory, January 1, 20X2: $98,254.10)
   c. Short-term financial strength ratios:
      (1) Working capital
      (2) Current ratio
      (3) Quick ratio
   d. Long-term financial strength ratios:
      (1) Debt ratio
      (2) Equity ratio
      (3) Common equity per share
      (4) Interest coverage ratio
   e. Market ratios:
      (1) Earnings per share
      (2) Price-earnings ratio (market for fiscal year-end 20X3, 20X2, and 20X1, respectively: $12.10, $12.00, $11.50)
      (3) Dividend yield—common stock

f. Cash ratios:
   (1) Free cash flow (20X2: cash provided by operating activities, $75,521.11; capital expenditures, $10,000.00)
   (2) Operating cash flow ratio
   (3) Cash flow margin ratio

4. Using a new journal page, journalize the following selected transactions from 20X4:

Transactions:

Jan. 1. Paid cash to Courtney Hoff for 100 shares of Peterson Pet Supply, Inc., stock at $12.00 per share, $1,200.00. C821.

1. Received cash for 100 ten-year, 6.0%, $1,000.00 face-value bonds paying interest semiannually, issued to yield 7.0%, $92,894.20. R515.

June 30. Received a $0.75 per share cash dividend from Apex Corporation, $750.00. R586.

June 30. Paid cash to trustee for the semiannual interest payment on the bonds issued on January 1. C875.

July 1. Sold all 1,000 shares of Apex Corporation stock at $87.00 per share, $87,000.00. R587.

1. Paid cash to trustee to retire bonds at maturity. Bonds were issued at face value, $25,000.00. C876.

Aug. 15. Received cash from Teresa Fischer for 200 shares of treasury stock at $12.50 per share, $2,500.00. This treasury stock was purchased for $10.00 per share. R598.

Dec. 31. Paid cash to trustee for the semiannual interest payment on the bonds issued on January 1. C923.

31. Paid cash to trustee to redeem its $100,000.00 bond issue of January 1, with a call option of 101%, $101,000.00. The bonds have a carrying value of $93,405.59. C924.

CHECK FIGURES

1. General journal Dec. 23 entry: Debit Office Equipment, $20,000.00; Credit Capital Stock—Common, $16,000.00 and Paid-In Capital in Excess of Par Value—Common, $4,000.00.

   Cash receipts journal Dec. 19 entry: Debit Cash, $12,000.00; Credit Capital Stock—Preferred, $10,000.00 and Paid-In Capital in Excess of Par—Preferred, $2,000.00.

2. Cash provided by operating activities, $77,698.78.

   Net increase in cash, $1,898.78.

3. a. Gross margin 20X3, 36.6%.

      Operating margin 20X1, 9.0%.

      Rate earned on average stockholders' equity 20X2, 4.8%.

   b. Accounts receivable turnover 20X3, 10.2.

      Inventory turnover 20X2, 4.0.

   c. Current ratio 20X2, 2.4.

      Quick ratio 20X3, 1.3.

   d. Debt ratio, 20X2, 18.2%.

      Equity ratio, 20X3, 84.2%.

      Interest coverage ratio 20X1, 10.1.

   e. Earnings per share, 20X2 $0.58.

      Price-earnings ratio 20X3, $27.50.

   f. Free cash flow 20X3, $17,698.78.

      Operating cash flow ratio 20X2, 0.5.

4. Cash receipts journal, Jan. 1 entry: Debit Cash, $92,894.20 and Discount on Bonds Payable, $7,105.80; credit Bonds Payable, $100,000.00.

   Cash payments journal, July 1 entry: Debit Bonds Payable, $25,000.00; credit Cash, $25,000.00.

Reinforcement Activity 3 (Cont.)

Processing and Analyzing Accounting Data for a Corporation

Peterson Pet Supply, Inc., Chart of Accounts

General Ledger

Balance Sheet Accounts

(1000) ASSETS

1100 Current Assets
1105 Cash
1110 Petty Cash
1115 Marketable Securities
1120 Accounts Receivable
1125 Allowance for Uncollectible Accounts
1130 Merchandise Inventory
1135 Supplies—Store
1140 Supplies—Administrative
1145 Prepaid Insurance
1200 Long-Term Investments
1205 Investment Securities
1300 Plant Assets
1310 Land
1320 Building
1325 Accumulated Depreciation—Building
1330 Office Equipment
1335 Accumulated Depreciation—Office Equipment
1340 Store Equipment
1345 Accumulated Depreciation—Store Equipment

(2000) LIABILITIES

2100 Current Liabilities
2105 Accounts Payable
2110 Sales Tax Payable
2115 Salaries Payable
2120 Employee Income Tax Payable
2125 Social Security Tax Payable
2130 Medicare Tax Payable
2135 Unemployment Tax Payable—Federal
2140 Unemployment Tax Payable—State
2145 Federal Income Tax Payable
2150 Dividends Payable
2155 Interest Payable
2160 Notes Payable
2200 Long-Term Liabilities
2205 Bonds Payable
2210 Discount on Bonds Payable
2215 Premium on Bonds Payable

(3000) STOCKHOLDERS' EQUITY

3105 Capital Stock—Common
3110 Paid-In Capital in Excess of Par—Common
3115 Capital Stock—Preferred
3120 Paid-In Capital in Excess of Par—Preferred
3125 Treasury Stock
3130 Paid-In Capital from Sale of Treasury Stock
3135 Retained Earnings
3140 Dividends—Common
3145 Dividends—Preferred
3150 Income Summary

Income Statement Accounts

(4000) OPERATING REVENUE

4105 Sales
4110 Sales Discount
4115 Sales Returns and Allowances

(5000) COST OF MERCHANDISE

5105 Purchases
5110 Purchases Discount
5115 Purchases Returns and Allowances

(6000) OPERATING EXPENSE

6100 Selling Expenses
6105 Advertising Expense
6110 Cash Short and Over
6115 Depreciation Expense—Store Equipment
6120 Miscellaneous Expense—Sales
6125 Salary Expense—Sales
6130 Supplies Expense—Sales
6200 Administrative Expenses
6205 Depreciation Expense—Building
6210 Depreciation Expense—Office Equipment
6215 Insurance Expense
6220 Miscellaneous Expense—Administrative
6225 Payroll Taxes Expense
6230 Property Tax Expense
6235 Salary Expense—Administrative
6240 Supplies Expense—Administrative
6245 Uncollectible Accounts Expense
6250 Utilities Expense

(7000) OTHER REVENUE

7105 Dividend Revenue
7110 Gain on Plant Assets
7115 Gain on Sale of Investments
7120 Interest Income

(8000) OTHER EXPENSES

8105 Interest Expense
8110 Loss on Plant Assets
8115 Loss on Redemption of Bonds

(9000) INCOME TAX

9105 Federal Income Tax Expense

WINNING EDGE

Give students the *Winning Edge* by making competitive event prep part of their classroom materials throughout the year. Go to cengage.com/winningedge for a list of materials that prepare students for specific competitive events.

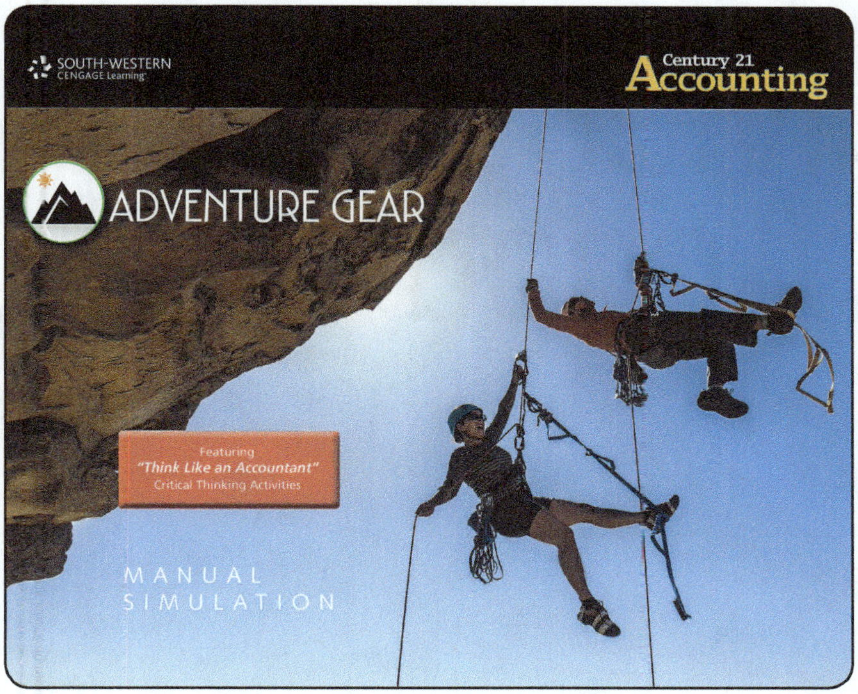

Adventure Gear is a dynamic merchandising business organized as a corporation. This business simulation covers the realistic transactions completed by Adventure Gear, which sells gear and accessories for adventure sports such as rock climbing, snowboarding, ziplining, kayaking, mountain biking, and more. The activities included in the accounting cycle for Adventure Gear are listed below.

This simulation is available from the publisher in either manual or automated versions.

The following activities are included in this simulation:

1. Recording transactions in special journals and a general journal.
2. Posting items to be posted individually to a general ledger and subsidiary ledgers.
3. Proving and ruling journals.
4. Posting column totals to a general ledger.
5. Preparing schedules of accounts receivable and accounts payable.
6. Preparing a trial balance on a work sheet.
7. Planning adjustments and completing a work sheet.
8. Preparing financial statements.
9. Journalizing and posting adjusting entries.
10. Journalizing and posting closing entries.
11. Preparing a post-closing trial balance.
12. Completing Think Like an Accountant Financial Analysis.

427

Part 4
Management Accounting

OVERVIEW

Tint My Windows, Inc., is the business described in Chapters 15 and 16 to illustrate management accounting. Tint My Windows purchases window tinting material and sells it to commercial businesses and individual consumers. Tint My Windows operates from a rented warehouse.

Chapter organization and content provide students with an expanded view of concepts related to management accounting.

- **Chapter 15** describes budgetary planning and control.
- **Chapter 16** describes management decision making using cost-volume-profit analysis.
- **Chapter 17** describes job order costing.
- **Chapter 18** describes management decision making using differential analysis.
- **Chapter 19** describes process costing, activity-based costing, and product pricing.

ACCOUNTING SOFTWARE

For those instructors who want to integrate the accounting program fully, problems at the end of each chapter are flagged to show when files are provided for completing a problem using QuickBooks, Excel, or Sage 50. In addition, A Look at Accounting Software is provided at the end of Chapter 15. This feature is designed to show how the accounting procedures described in these chapters are handled in commercial accounting software.

Part 4
Management Accounting

© iStockphoto.com/Aleksandr Bobodkin

Reinforcement Activity

Reinforcement Activity 4, Processing and Analyzing Cost Accounting Data for a Manufacturing Business, may be completed after Chapter 19.

THE BUSINESS—

TINT MY WINDOWS, INC.

Tint My Windows, Inc., the business described in Chapters 15 and 16, purchases window tinting material in large quantities and sells it to commercial businesses and individual consumers. Tint My Windows operates from a rented warehouse.

© Timo Kohlbacher/Shutterstock.com

Chart of Accounts

TINT MY WINDOWS, INC.

GENERAL LEDGER

Balance Sheet Accounts

(1000) ASSETS

1100 Current Assets
1105 Cash
1110 Petty Cash
1115 Accounts Receivable
1120 Allowance for Uncollectible Accounts
1125 Notes Receivable
1130 Interest Receivable
1135 Merchandise Inventory
1140 Supplies—Sales
1145 Supplies—Administrative
1150 Prepaid Insurance
1200 Plant Assets
1205 Equipment—Delivery
1210 Accumulated Depreciation—Delivery Equipment
1215 Equipment—Office
1220 Accumulated Depreciation—Office Equipment
1225 Equipment—Warehouse
1230 Accumulated Depreciation—Warehouse Equipment

(2000) LIABILITIES

2100 Current Liabilities
2105 Accounts Payable
2110 Sales Tax Payable
2115 Notes Payable
2120 Interest Payable
2125 Employee Income Tax Payable
2130 Social Security Tax Payable
2135 Medicare Tax Payable
2140 Unemployment Tax Payable—Federal
2145 Unemployment Tax Payable—State
2150 Federal Income Tax Payable
2155 Dividends Payable
2200 Long-Term Liabilities
2205 Bonds Payable

(3000) STOCKHOLDERS' EQUITY

3105 Capital Stock
3110 Retained Earnings
3115 Dividends
3120 Income Summary

Income Statement Accounts

(4000) OPERATING REVENUE

4105 Sales
4110 Sales Discount
4115 Sales Returns and Allowances

(5000) COST OF MERCHANDISE

5105 Purchases
5110 Purchases Discount
5115 Purchases Returns and Allowances

(6000) OPERATING EXPENSE

6100 Selling Expenses
6105 Advertising Expense
6110 Delivery Expense
6115 Depreciation Expense—Delivery Equipment
6120 Depreciation Expense—Warehouse Equipment
6125 Miscellaneous Expense
6130 Salary Expense—Commissions
6135 Salary Expense—Regular
6140 Supplies Expense—Sales
6200 Administrative Expenses
6205 Depreciation Expense—Office Equipment
6210 Insurance Expense
6215 Miscellaneous Expense—Administrative
6225 Payroll Taxes Expense
6230 Rent Expense
6235 Salary Expense—Administrative
6240 Supplies Expense—Administrative
6245 Uncollectible Accounts Expense
6250 Utilities Expense

(7000) OTHER REVENUE

7105 Interest Income
7110 Gain on Plant Asset

(8000) OTHER EXPENSES

8105 Interest Expense
8110 Loss on Plant Asset

(9000) INCOME TAX

9105 Federal Income Tax Expense

The chart of accounts for Tint My Windows, Inc., is illustrated above for reference as you study Chapters 15 and 16 of this textbook.

Chart of Accounts

- Emphasize that students should refer to this chart of accounts in Chapters 15 and 16.
- Stress that charts of accounts are extremely important to companies because they drive the accounting system used by that business.
- Emphasize that charts of accounts are used for determining the classification of accounts and show which accounts are temporary and which are permanent.

Chapter 15 Budgetary Planning and Control

Scope & Sequence

	New	Review/Enrich
Introduction		
Introduce the Chapter		
Lesson 15-1: Budget Planning and the Sales and Purchases Budgets		
Budget Planning	✓	
Budget Functions	✓	
Budget Period	✓	
Sources of Budget Information	✓	
Comparative Income Statement		✓
Annual Operational Plans and Goals	✓	
Sales Budget	✓	
Purchases Budget	✓	
Lesson 15-2: Expense Budgets and the Budgeted Income Statement		
Selling Expenses Budget	✓	
Administrative Expenses Budget	✓	
Other Revenue and Expenses Budget	✓	
Budgeted Income Statement	✓	
Lesson 15-3: Cash Budgets		
Cash Receipts Budget	✓	
Analysis of Cash Receipts	✓	
Cash Payments Budget	✓	
Cash Budget	✓	
Lesson 15-4: Performance Reports		
Performance Report	✓	
Preparing a Performance Report	✓	
Balanced Scorecard	✓	
Closure		

Enhancing Instruction

Features	Common Core Standards
• Accounting in the Real World: Walmart	• ELAL—reading, writing, media and technology
• Ethics in Action: Sharing Your Knowledge	• ELAL—reading
• Why Accounting?: State Parks and Sources of Revenue • Think Like an Accountant: Charting Financial Ratios	• ELAL—reading, writing • Mathematics
• Global Awareness: Foreign Corrupt Practices Act	• ELAL—reading, writing, media and technology
• Forensic Accounting: Shell Companies	• Mathematics
• A Look at Accounting Software • Explore Accounting • 21st Century Skills • Analyzing Home Depot's Financial Statements	• ELAL—reading • ELAL—reading, writing • ELAL—reading, writing, media and technology • Mathematics

ELAL = English Language Arts & Literacy

Calculator: © iStockphoto.com/picstodisc; Paper: © iStockphoto.com/Qingwa

Practice and Assessment

Technology & Media	Teaching Strategies	Guided Practice	Independent Practice	Reteach/Enrich
• Instructor's Resource CD/Website: PowerPoint Slides Accounting Concepts • Online Working Papers • Transparency Master: Blank Budget Form		• Terms Review • Audit Your Understanding • Work Together 15-1	• On Your Own 15-1 • Application Problem 15-1 • Formative Assessment, p. 437 • Online Working Papers	• Reteach, p. 438
• Instructor's Resource CD/Website • Online Working Papers • Transparency Master: Blank Budget Form	• Gifted Learners	• Terms Review • Audit Your Understanding • Work Together 15-2	• On Your Own 15-2 • Application Problem 15-2 • Formative Assessment, p. 444 • Online Working Papers	• Reteach, p. 445
• Instructor's Resource CD/Website • Online Working Papers • Transparency Master: Blank Budget Form	• ESL Learners	• Terms Review • Audit Your Understanding • Work Together 15-3	• On Your Own 15-3 • Application Problem 15-3 • Formative Assessment, p. 450 • Online Working Papers	• Reteach, p. 451
• Instructor's Resource CD/Website • Online Working Papers • Transparency Master: Blank Budget Form	• Visual/Spatial Learners	• Terms Review • Audit Your Understanding • Work Together 15-4	• On Your Own 15-4 • Application Problem 15-4 • Formative Assessment, p. 455 • Online Working Papers	• Reteach, p. 456
• Online Working Papers	• Common Core and Interdisciplinary Studies		• Mastery Problem 15-M • Study Guide 15 • Chapter 15 Test • Cognero Chapter 15	• Challenge Problem 15-C • Reteach, p. 463 • Recycling Problem 15-R

Introduce the Chapter

SET THE STAGE

GUIDING QUESTIONS

- Ask students if they have ever created a budget. If so, have them explain.
- Ask students to brainstorm who should create the budget for a company.
- Ask students why a company would spend time creating a budget.
- Ask for examples of other ways that a company's performance could be evaluated besides financially.

PREVIEW CHAPTER OBJECTIVES

- Note that students will learn how to prepare various budgets that help determine the operating budget. All budgets will be used to analyze the targeted projections against the actual performance of a company on the performance report.
- Instruct a student to read each chapter objective aloud.

PREVIEW ACCOUNTING TERMS

- Read each term aloud to verify its pronunciation for students.
- Point out terms or parts of terms that should already be familiar to most students, such as *budget*, *cash payments*, and *cash receipts*.

Chapter 15 Budgetary Planning and Control

LEARNING OBJECTIVES

After studying Chapter 15, in addition to defining key terms, you will be able to:

LO1 Prepare a sales budget.
LO2 Prepare a purchases budget.
LO3 Prepare a selling expenses budget.
LO4 Prepare an administrative expenses budget.
LO5 Prepare an other revenue and expenses budget.
LO6 Prepare a budgeted income statement.
LO7 Prepare a cash receipts budget.
LO8 Prepare a cash payments budget.
LO9 Prepare a cash budget.
LO10 Prepare a performance report.
LO11 Identify performance measures in a balanced scorecard system.

Calculator: © iStockphoto.com/picstudisc; Paper: © iStockphoto.com/Qingwa

© mast3r/Shutterstock.com

Accounting In The Real World

Walmart

With 2.2 million associates worldwide and serving over 245 million customers each week, Walmart is the largest retailer in the world. Although it is a publicly traded corporation, the Walton family, with 48 percent of the stock, still controls the company.

Sam Walton founded the company in 1962 and established the motto, "Lowest Prices Anytime, Anywhere." The emphasis on low prices has continued throughout Walmart's growth. In 1992, Sam Walton said, "If we work together, we'll lower the cost of living for everyone ... we'll give the world an opportunity to see what it's like to save and have a better life."

Walmart makes up for a lower profit margin by achieving a high volume of sales. The goal of low prices and high-volume sales has a significant impact on Walmart's financial budget. As this chapter illustrates, a company begins the budget process by setting revenue goals. Expenses are then estimated, so that the company can predict its profitability for the year.

With a commitment to low prices, Walmart must do all it can to keep its costs as low as possible. One way to accomplish this is by tightly controlling the amount and type of inventory on hand. Walmart has been a leader in inventory control. As customers buy goods at Walmart, the sales data for each store are electronically tracked. Computers automatically issue purchase orders, so that replacement goods are delivered with incredible efficiency. However, inventory costs are only part of the budgeting process. Walmart must also keep other operating costs, such as employee wages, utilities, and administrative costs, as low as possible.

CRITICAL THINKING

1. Go to www.stock.walmart.com and search for the most recent annual report for Walmart. Using the income statement, calculate the ratio of operating income to net sales for each of the three years given. Analyze your results and write a two- or three-sentence summary of your findings.
2. Assume that Walmart's managers are thinking of increasing its advertising budget. What should the managers consider before deciding how much, if any, to increase this budget item?

Source: www.stock.walmart.com.

Background: © 06photo/Shutterstock.com; Real World: © iStockphoto.com/Shaunl

Key Terms

- budgeting
- budget
- budget period
- sales budget
- purchases budget
- selling expenses budget
- administrative expenses budget
- other revenue and expenses budget
- budgeted income statement
- cash receipts budget
- cash payments budget
- cash budget
- performance report
- balanced scorecard

Accounting In The Real World

Answers

1. Answers will vary. Students should calculate operating income divided by net sales for each of the three years given. Their analysis should determine any trends that are evident and/or determine how the ratio changed over the three-year period.
2. Before deciding to increase its advertising budget, Walmart's managers should estimate how effective the additional ads will be. They need to determine that the increase in advertising expense will be less than the increase in net sales the ads cause.

LESSON

15-1

BRIDGE

- Point out that students have learned about income statements earlier in accounting. In this lesson, they will learn how to use comparative income statements for establishing a budget and goals for the next period of time.

TEACHING RESOURCES

- **Instructor's Resource CD/Website:**
  PowerPoint Slides
  Accounting Concepts
- **Working Papers:**
  Teacher's Edition of the Working Papers for Lesson 15-1
  Online Working Papers
- **Transparency Master:**
  Blank Budget Form

ENGAGE

- Ask students if it is important only for corporations to budget. Lead into a discussion of personal budgets. Ask students why it is important that families prepare a basic budget.
- Emphasize that for most families, money is not an unlimited resource; therefore, a plan is needed to select the best alternatives for spending the money that is available.
- Ask students if any of them or their families use a budget to plan for certain expenditures or to save for a vacation.

PREVIEW

- Call on students to read the accounting terms and definitions introduced in this lesson: *budgeting*, *budget*, *budget period*, *sales budget*, and *purchases budget*.
- Point out the learning objectives for this lesson.
- Direct students to read the headings in this lesson and to examine the illustrations.

INPUT

- Have students read the text on the page. Ask one student to read aloud.
- Emphasize that a budget is a financial plan or look into the company's future.
- Ask students to identify several company goals that may have an impact on budget preparation.
- Ask students the difference between a budgeted income statement and a regular income statement. Point out that the budgeted income statement consists of estimated figures and that a regular income statement contains actual figures.

LESSON

15-1 Budget Planning and the Sales and Purchases Budgets

LO1 Prepare a sales budget.
LO2 Prepare a purchases budget.

Budget Planning

Planning the financial operations of a business is called **budgeting**. A financial road map used by individuals and companies as a guide for spending and saving is called a **budget**. Many businesses prepare a variety of budgets, choosing those budgets that fit the needs of that company. Each budget provides managers with detailed information about a specific area of the business's operations.

A budget is a view into the future—a financial estimate of future business activities. Budget preparation begins with identifying company goals. Company goals might be to increase sales, reduce the cost of merchandise sold, or increase net income. All of these goals affect budget preparation because the budget is a business's financial plan.

Two budgets commonly prepared in businesses are the budgeted income statement and the cash budget. The budgeted income statement is a projection of a business's sales, costs, expenses, and net income for a fiscal period. It is similar to a regular income statement and is sometimes known as an *operating budget*. The cash budget is a projection of a business's cash receipts and payments for a fiscal period. It is used to manage cash and estimate cash shortages and overages.

ETHICS IN ACTION

Sharing Your Knowledge

John Oglesby is a certified public accountant who works as a computer consultant. He has just helped a local movie theater install a new ticketing system that tracks when and how often individuals come to the theater. The system will enable the theater to analyze its customers and select movies that target customers having specific movie preferences.

John has received a phone call from another theater in the same city. The theater owner explained that his business had been steadily declining over the past few years. He was particularly disturbed that his teenage daughter had received a text message containing a special movie premier offer from one of his competitors. After talking for over ten minutes, the owner finally got around to the purpose of his call—offering to hire John to evaluate his existing computer systems and to suggest any recommendations. After allowing the theater owner to present his request, John politely declined to accept the engagement.

INSTRUCTIONS

Use the AICPA *Code of Professional Conduct* to determine if John's actions violate the confidentiality rule. When researching the AICPA *Code of Professional Conduct*, begin by selecting the section title that most closely relates to the issue. Read the Rule and any related Interpretations. Then scan the titles of the Ethics Rulings for any case that may be similar to the issue.

Source: http://www.aicpa.org/Research/Standards/CodeofConduct/Pages/sec300.aspx.

© iStockphoto.com/LdF

ETHICS IN ACTION

Sample Solution

John followed the guidance in the *Code of Professional Conduct* in declining the engagement. Ethics Ruling 15, Section Rule 391.029–.030, prohibits a member from using information gained from one client to benefit another client if the prospective client would know the origin of the information. It is likely that the theater manager knew that John worked with the competing theater. Therefore, John can only accept the engagement with the permission of his existing theater client.

Budget Functions

A carefully prepared budget reflects the best financial projections possible by those persons who prepare it. A completed budget shows the projected course of action for a business. A budget serves three important business functions.

1. **Planning.** In preparing a budget, managers plan actions that will meet desired goals.
2. **Operational control.** A budget projects the accomplishments of a business. It specifies the type and the amount of projected activities. By comparing actual performance with projected performance, management can judge how well a business is achieving its goals.
3. **Department coordination.** Profitable business growth requires all managers to be aware of the company's plans. A budget reflects these plans. Each phase of a business operation must be coordinated with all related phases. For example, to achieve projected sales, the Purchasing Department must know when and how much merchandise to purchase. Therefore, all management personnel must help plan and use a budget as a guide to control and coordinate sales, costs, and expenses.

Budget Period

The length of time covered by a budget is called the **budget period**. Usually, this period is one year. Some companies also prepare a long-range budget of five years or more for special projects and plant and equipment purchases. However, the annual budget is the one used to compare current financial performance with budget plans.

An annual budget is normally prepared for a company's fiscal year. The annual budget is commonly divided into quarterly and monthly budgets. Such budget subdivisions provide frequent opportunities to evaluate how actual operations compare with budgeted operations.

A budget must be prepared in sufficient time to be communicated to the appropriate managers prior to the beginning of a budget period. Large and complex companies start gathering budget information long before the beginning of a new budget year.

Sources of Budget Information

A budget cannot be exact, since it shows only projected sales, costs, and expenses. However, a company should project future operations as accurately as possible. A company uses many information sources.

COMPANY RECORDS

The accounting and sales records of a business contain much of the information needed to prepare budgets. Accounting information about previous years' operations is used to determine trends in sales, purchases, and operating expenses. Expected price changes, sales promotion plans, and market research studies also are important in projecting activity for a budget period.

GENERAL ECONOMIC INFORMATION

A general slowdown or speedup in the national economy may affect budget decisions. Unusually high inflation rates affect budgeted amounts. A labor strike may affect some related industries and thus affect company operations. New product development, changes in consumer buying habits, merchandise availability, international trade, and general business conditions all must be considered when preparing budgets.

COMPANY STAFF AND MANAGERS

Sales personnel estimate the amount of projected sales. Considering projected sales for the new budget period, other department managers project budget items for their areas of responsibility in the business.

GOOD JUDGMENT

Good judgment by the individuals preparing the budgets is essential to realistic budgets. Even after evaluating all available information, answers to many budget questions are seldom obvious. Since some information will conflict with other information, final budget decisions are based on good judgment.

remember National magazines and newspapers are a good source of information regarding general economic conditions.

INPUT

- Point out that budgets are estimates of what will happen in the future.
- Emphasize the three functions of budgeting: planning, operational control, department coordination.
- Point out that planning helps managers create action plans to reach goals.
- Explain that operational control helps managers determine if their action plans were appropriate for reaching goals.
- Stress the importance of department coordination in reaching goals. All departments must contribute to the overall plan for it to be successful.
- Emphasize the effort necessary to prepare a budget. Budgets need to be prepared well in advance and require information gathering, analysis, estimating, and approval.

INPUT

- Emphasize that although budgets rely on estimated figures, these projections need to be as accurate as possible. Stress that unless budgets are based on realistic assumptions, their value in operational control is lessened.
- Ask students where companies gather most of their information for the budget process. Stress that a company's own records and market research are extremely useful in projecting trends and identifying activities that will affect prices, promotional expenses, and other related items.
- Ask students what information or activities outside the company may affect its plans. Discuss economic factors, global competition, union contracts, new product development, and technology.
- Ask students which department or group of individuals within a corporation would be best suited to develop an estimate of projected sales for the upcoming year. Discuss the importance of involving sales personnel in this component of the budget process.
- Emphasize that sales personnel interact with customers on a daily basis and often can provide valuable input regarding projected sales for the next year.

INPUT

- Ask students to review the comparative income statement presented in the illustration.
- Ask students what type of information is provided by the statement. Discuss net sales, cost of merchandise sold, expense amounts, federal income tax, and units of tint sold. Point out that there are amounts for two years as well as figures representing the dollar and percentage amounts of increase or decrease from the previous year.
- Ask students how Tint My Windows, Inc., might use the information presented on the comparative income statement during budget planning. Emphasize that one purpose for analyzing the comparative income statement is to identify trends in sales, costs, and expenses. Another is to develop reasonable expectations and amounts for the next fiscal period's sales, costs, and expenses.
- Point out that the comparative income statement is also helpful in identifying those items that are increasing or decreasing at a higher-than-normal rate.

Comparative Income Statement

Tint My Windows, Inc.
Comparative Income Statement
For Years Ended December 31, 20X2 and 20X1

			Increase (Decrease)	
	20X2	20X1	Amount	Percentage*
Operating Revenue:				
Net Sales	$2,350,250	$2,100,000	$ 250,250	11.9
Cost of Merchandise Sold	1,343,000	1,188,000	155,000	13.0
Gross Profit on Operations	$1,007,250	$ 912,000	$ 95,250	10.4
Operating Expenses:				
Selling Expenses:				
Advertising Expense	$ 56,400	$ 47,250	$ 9,150	19.4
Delivery Expense	188,010	175,800	12,210	6.9
Depr. Expense—Delivery Equipment	9,000	8,750	250	2.9
Depr. Expense—Warehouse Equipment	13,500	13,500	0	0.0
Miscellaneous Expense—Sales	14,360	14,950	(590)	(3.9)
Salary Expense—Commissions	94,000	85,000	9,000	10.6
Salary Expense—Regular	42,700	35,400	7,300	20.6
Supplies Expense	14,100	13,560	540	4.0
Total Selling Expenses	$ 432,070	$ 394,210	$ 37,860	9.6
Administrative Expenses:				
Depr. Expense—Office Equipment	$ 18,000	$ 15,000	$ 3,000	20.0
Insurance Expense	6,000	5,620	380	6.8
Miscellaneous Expense—Administrative	48,460	42,050	6,410	15.2
Payroll Taxes Expense	28,170	25,740	2,430	9.4
Rent Expense	37,500	37,500	0	0.0
Salary Expense—Administrative	97,280	94,050	3,230	3.4
Supplies Expense—Administrative	17,030	18,250	(1,220)	(6.7)
Uncollectible Accounts Expense	14,100	12,785	1,315	10.3
Utilities Expense	12,600	9,150	3,450	37.7
Total Administrative Expenses	$ 279,140	$ 260,145	$ 18,995	7.3
Total Operating Expenses	$ 711,210	$ 654,355	$ 56,855	8.7
Income from Operations	$ 296,040	$ 257,645	$ 38,395	14.9
Other Expenses:				
Interest Expense	3,600	8,120	$ (4,520)	(55.7)
Net Income before Federal Income Tax	$ 292,440	$ 249,525	$ 42,915	17.2
Federal Income Tax Expense	97,300	80,560	16,740	20.8
Net Income after Federal Income Tax	$ 195,140	$ 168,965	$ 26,175	15.5
Units (sq. ft.) of Tint Sold	671,500	600,000	71,500	11.9

*Percentages rounded to the nearest 0.1%

Preparing a budget involves analyzing available financial information. An analysis of previous years' sales, costs, and expenses is an important part of budget preparations. A comparative income statement provides the information for Tint My Windows' analysis of previous years' sales, costs, and expenses and also shows trends that may be occurring. The statement also highlights items that may be increasing or decreasing at a higher rate than other items on the statement. Tint My Windows' comparative income statement is shown above.

Annual Operational Plans and Goals

Goals for 20X3:

1. The economy is projected to remain strong throughout 20X3. Therefore, the sales goal is to increase unit sales to 700,000, about a 4.2% increase. The unit sales price will be increased in the second quarter from $3.50 to $3.70 per square foot to recover merchandise cost increases in 20X2 and projected increases in the budget year.
2. Sales distribution by quarters is projected to be consistent with prior quarters.
3. The unit cost of merchandise is projected to rise from $2.00 to $2.10 in the first quarter, a 5% increase.
4. An automated cutting machine has been ordered. It will cost $50,000 and is projected to save approximately $15,000 per year in salary expense.
5. All sales employees on salary will receive a 6.0% increase in wages. Administrative employees on salary will receive a 3.0% increase in wages.
6. An effort will be made to maintain rigid controls on all expenditures.

After previous years' records have been analyzed, a business sets goals, develops operational plans, and projects sales, costs, and expenses for the coming year. Annual company goals establish targets that the company will work toward in the coming year. Goals help a company coordinate the efforts of all areas toward a common direction. An operational plan provides general guidelines for achieving the company's goals. Operational plans and goals generally are determined by a planning group consisting of the company's executive officers and department managers.

At Tint My Windows, the planning group includes the president and all department managers. The planning group reviews the analysis of the previous year's comparative income statement and considers possible changes in economic conditions that may affect the company. From these discussions, the company's operational plan and goals for the coming year are determined. After reviewing company records and considering general economic conditions, Tint My Windows' planning group develops the planning guidelines shown above.

The operational plan is converted into a more precise plan expressed in dollars by preparing a budgeted income statement. Tint My Windows prepares separate budgets for the major parts of the budgeted income statement. Separate budgets are prepared for sales, purchases, selling expenses, administrative expenses, and other revenue and expenses. To permit more frequent comparisons between actual and budgeted amounts, budgets are separated into quarterly projections.

At Tint My Windows, the Accounting Department is responsible for coordinating budget preparation. The sales manager is responsible for preparing the sales, purchases, and selling expenses budgets. The administrative manager is responsible for preparing the administrative expenses budget and the other revenue and expenses budget. The Accounting Department then prepares the budgeted income statement. The completed budgeted income statement, with attached supporting budgets, is submitted to the budget committee for approval. The budget committee consists of the president and two members of Tint My Windows' board of directors.

fyi Most budgets are based on forecasts of increases or decreases over previous years' performances. In zero-based budgeting, however, the data are prepared each year as though operations were being started for the first time.

© Valua Vitaly/Shutterstock.com

INPUT

- Direct students to the goals listed at the top of the page. Ask one student to read them aloud.
- Discuss how a business sets goals.
- Point out that after a company's records for the preceding year(s) have been analyzed, goals and targets are set for the coming year.
- Ask students how these goals could provide a direction.
- Explain the difference between goals and an operational plan.
- Stress that goals help all departments come together toward a common direction.
- Explain that the actual budgeted income statement is a combination of several specific budget schedules contributed by various department managers.

INPUT

- Stress that the sales budget is the basis for all other budgets. Refer to the sales budget as other budgets are introduced.
- Direct students to the illustration. Ask them to state the amount of projected sales for the coming year, 20X3. Ask students how 700,000 units were projected. Direct students to the list of goals on page 435 and review Tint My Windows' first goal for 20X3.
- Discuss Tint My Windows' policy for rounding off projected amounts. Point out that the company rounds unit projections to the nearest hundred units and dollar projections to the nearest $10. Emphasize that rounding off simplifies the budgeting process.

MODEL

- Distribute copies of a blank budget. Guide students through the preparation of Tint My Windows' sales budget, using the illustration on this page.
- Read each step aloud or ask a student to read them. Explain how each amount for each step is calculated or determined.
- Point out to students where each step's amount appears on the sales budget.
- Provide extensive practice in rounding off based on Tint My Windows' policy. Have students practice rounding off with a variety of unit projections and dollar projections.

Sales Budget LO1

Determine sales percentages:

20X2 Actual Unit Sales First Quarter	÷	20X2 Actual Unit Sales	=	20X2 Sales Percentage First Quarter
149,800	÷	671,500	=	22.3%

1 Enter actual and projected units.

2

4 Enter unit sales price.

Tint My Windows, Inc.
Sales Budget
For Year Ended December 31, 20X3

Schedule 1

	Annual Budget	Quarter 1st	2nd	3rd	4th
Actual Unit Sales, 20X2	671,500	149,800	157,200	218,200	146,300
Sales Percentage by Quarter		22.3%	23.4%	32.5%	21.8%
Projected Unit Sales, 20X3	700,000	156,100	163,800	227,500	152,600
Times Unit Sales Price		$3.50	$3.70	$3.70	$3.70
Net Sales	$2,558,780	$546,350	$606,060	$841,750	$564,620

6 Calculate total net sales.

$ 546,350
606,060
841,750
564,620
$2,558,780

3 Calculate unit sales volume:

20X2 Sales Percentage First Quarter	×	20X3 Projected Unit Sales	=	20X3 Projected Unit Sales First Quarter
22.3%	×	700,000	=	156,100

5 Calculate projected net sales:

20X3 Projected Unit Sales First Quarter	×	Unit Sales Price	=	20X3 Projected Net Sales First Quarter
156,100	×	$3.50	=	$546,350

A statement that shows the projected net sales for a budget period is called a **sales budget**. The sales budget is prepared first because the other budgets are affected by the projected net sales. Projected net sales are used to estimate the amount of merchandise to purchase and the amount that may be spent for salaries, advertising, and other selling and administrative expenses.

Tint My Windows' sales manager, with knowledge of the budget guidelines and with the assistance of sales representatives, prepares the sales budget shown above. Based on the planning group's goal of a 4.2% increase in unit sales, the budget reflects projected sales of 700,000 units. The sales manager plans to increase the unit sales price from $3.50 to $3.70 in the second quarter. The timing of this increase was planned after reviewing competitors' selling prices and analyzing projected costs of merchandise.

Accurate projections are important for effective budgeting. However, since budgets are based on estimates, most businesses round the projected amounts to simplify the budgeting process. Tint My Window rounds unit projections to the nearest hundred units and dollar projections to the nearest $10.

Preparing a Sales Budget

1. Enter the number of actual units, 671,500, and projected units, 700,000, in the Annual Budget column.
2. Determine the sales percentages by quarter. Dividing the annual budget into quarterly segments provides more frequent opportunities to compare actual with budgeted operations.
3. Calculate the unit sales volume for each quarter. Tint My Windows' planning group believes that quarterly sales percentages will remain the same. Therefore, 22.3% of annual sales are expected to occur in the first quarter.
4. Enter the unit sales prices for each quarter.
5. Calculate projected net sales for each quarter.
6. Calculate total net sales for 20X3.

Purchases Budget LO2

Enter projected unit sales. ②

Determine purchases: ⑤
205,200 units
−46,800
158,400 units

Enter beginning inventory. ④

Enter unit cost. ⑥

Tint My Windows, Inc.
Purchases Budget
For Year Ended December 31, 20X3 — Schedule 2

	Quarter			
	1st	2nd	3rd	4th
Unit Sales for Quarter	156,100	163,800	227,500	152,600
Ending Inventory	49,100	68,300	45,800	48,500
Total Units Needed	205,200	232,100	273,300	201,100
Less Beginning Inventory	46,800	49,100	68,300	45,800
Purchases	158,400	183,000	205,000	155,300
Times Unit Cost	$2.10	$2.10	$2.10	$2.10
Cost of Purchases	$332,640	$384,300	$430,500	$326,130

① Calculate ending inventory for each quarter:

20X3 Unit Sales Second Quarter	×	Ending Inventory Unit Sales Percentage	=	20X3 Ending Inventory Second Quarter
163,800	×	30.0%	=	49,140 rounded to 49,100

⑦ Determine cost of purchases:

Purchases First Quarter	×	Unit Cost	=	Cost of Purchases First Quarter
158,400	×	$2.10	=	$332,640

③ Determine total units needed:
156,100
+49,100
205,200

After the planning group approves the sales budget, the remaining budgets are prepared. A statement prepared to show the projected amount of purchases that will be required during a budget period is called a **purchases budget**. The following factors are considered when projecting purchases:

1. Projected unit sales.
2. The quantity of merchandise on hand at the beginning of the budget period.
3. The quantity of merchandise needed to fill projected sales orders without having excessive inventory.
4. The price trends of merchandise to be purchased.

The sales manager prepares the purchases budget shown above. The sales manager determines that the number of units in the ending inventory should be about 30.0% of the number of units projected to be sold in the subsequent quarter.

Preparing a Purchases Budget

1. Calculate the ending inventory for each quarter. Round estimates to the nearest hundred. Use 48,500 units for the fourth quarter's ending inventory (161,700 units projected to be sold in the first quarter of 20X4 × 30%).
2. Enter projected unit sales for the quarter from the sales budget.
3. Add projected sales units and the ending inventory units to determine the total units needed per quarter.
4. Enter the beginning inventory, which is the same as the ending inventory for the preceding quarter. Tint My Windows' ending inventory of 46,800 units on December 31, 20X2, becomes its January 1 beginning inventory.
5. Subtract the beginning inventory from the total units needed to determine total unit purchases for the quarter.
6. Enter the unit cost for each quarter. Tint My Windows' planning group has projected that materials costs will rise from $2.00 to $2.10 per unit in the first quarter of 20X3.
7. Multiply the unit purchases each quarter by the unit cost to determine the cost of purchases.

INPUT

- Remind students that the sales budget is prepared first because the other schedules are affected by the projected net sales.
- Point out that projected sales determine the amount of purchases necessary during a particular budget period.
- Ask students what factors should be considered when determining the amount of purchases required for a budget period. Review the four factors presented in the text.
- Ask students what problems might be associated with owning an excessive inventory. Discuss the possibility of model changes, changes in consumer tastes, the inability to recover cost if not sold, and reduced prices due to technological advances, for example.
- Direct students to the list of goals on page 435. Review Goal 3.

MODEL

- Distribute copies of a blank budget. Guide students through the preparation of Tint My Windows' purchases budget, using the illustration on this page.
- Read each step aloud or ask a student to read them. Explain or ask how each amount for each step is calculated or determined.
- Point out to students where each step's amount appears on the purchases budget.

FORMATIVE ASSESSMENT

- This is an ongoing process. Circulate around the classroom or lab, observing which students have difficulty with the assignments.
- Troubleshooting: Diagnose the kinds of problems students have with this section. Students may have difficulty determining favorable and unfavorable trends when making comparisons, or they may have difficulty computing the appropriate answers for the different budgets.
- Assess student understanding by checking solutions to Independent Practice assignments and noting their answers to the Terms Review and Audit Your Understanding questions.

CHECK FOR UNDERSTANDING

Terms Review

- Call on students to define each term in the Terms Review. Definitions are given in the Glossary.

Audit Your Understanding

- Call on students to answer the Audit Your Understanding questions. Answers are given in Appendix D of the textbook.

GUIDED PRACTICE

Work Together

- Have students write the solution to the Work Together problem as you guide the class through the examples.
- Direct students to prepare a sales budget and a purchases budget.
- Remind students to save their work to complete Work Together 15-2.

INDEPENDENT PRACTICE

On Your Own

- Assign the On Your Own problem to be worked independently.
- Remind students to save their work to complete On Your Own 15-2.
- Use the Formative Assessment techniques to diagnose student understanding.

Application Problem

- Assign Application Problem 15-1.
- Remind students to save their work to complete Problem 15-2.

Online Working Papers

- Students can access the Lesson 15-1 problems using this software.

Website

- Direct students to the C21 Accounting companion website for additional practice and review opportunities.

End of Lesson Review

LO1 Prepare a sales budget.

LO2 Prepare a purchases budget.

Terms Review

budgeting
budget
budget period
sales budget
purchases budget

Audit your understanding

1. What is the first step in budget preparation?
2. What two budgets are commonly prepared by a business?
3. What is the length of time generally covered by a company's budget?
4. How do annual goals help a company?

Work together 15-1

Preparing a sales budget and a purchases budget

Maddox Corporation wishes to prepare a sales budget and a purchases budget for 20X3. Management has set a sales goal of 100,000 units. After reviewing price trends, the sales manager projects that Maddox Corporation will need to increase its unit sales price from $14.50 to $15.00 in the first quarter.

The sales manager, after checking with the company's merchandise suppliers, projects that the cost of merchandise will remain at $7.00 per unit throughout 20X3.

Quarterly unit sales for 20X2 are as follows:

1st quarter	17,000 units	3rd quarter	24,000 units
2nd quarter	19,000 units	4th quarter	30,000 units

After considering the time required to reorder merchandise, the sales manager requests that 20.0% of the next quarter's unit sales be available in the prior quarter's ending inventory. Ending inventory for 20X2 is 3,800 units. Management projects that 22,600 units will be sold in the first quarter of 20X4.

A partially completed sales budget and purchases budget are given in the *Working Papers*.

1. Complete the sales budget (Schedule 1) for the four quarters ended December 31, 20X3. Maddox Corporation rounds unit amounts to the nearest hundred units, dollar amounts to the nearest $10, and percentage amounts to the nearest 0.1%.
2. Complete the purchases budget (Schedule 2) for the four quarters ended December 31, 20X3.

Save your work for use in Work Together 15-2.

On your own 15-1

Preparing a sales budget and a purchases budget

Northstar, Inc., wishes to prepare a sales budget and a purchases budget for 20X3. Management has set a sales goal of 220,000 units. After reviewing price trends, the sales manager projects that Northstar, Inc., will need to increase its unit sales price from $8.00 to $8.25 in the first quarter.

The sales manager, after checking with the company's merchandise suppliers, projects that the cost of merchandise will increase from $3.25 to $3.50 in the first quarter of 20X3.

Quarterly unit sales for 20X2 are as follows:

1st quarter	40,000 units	3rd quarter	52,000 units
2nd quarter	48,000 units	4th quarter	60,000 units

After considering the time required to reorder merchandise, the sales manager requests that 25.0% of the next quarter's unit sales be available in the prior quarter's ending inventory. Ending inventory for 20X2 is 11,000 units. Management projects that 48,000 units will be sold in the first quarter of 20X4.

A partially completed sales budget and purchases budget are given in the *Working Papers*.

1. Complete the sales budget (Schedule 1) for the four quarters ended December 31, 20X3. Northstar rounds unit amounts to the nearest hundred units, dollar amounts to the nearest $10, and percentage amounts to the nearest 0.1%.
2. Complete the purchases budget (Schedule 2) for the four quarters ended December 31, 20X3.

Save your work for use in On Your Own15-2.

RETEACH

- Arrange the class in groups of three or four students. Distribute copies of a blank 4-column financial form.
- Ask each group to create two simplified comparative income statements. The first comparative income statement is to show a percentage increase in sales; the second, a percentage decrease in sales.
- Direct students to use only five expense accounts and to ignore federal income tax.
- Ask students to indicate if the percentage changes in expenses are favorable or unfavorable.
- Ask each group to write its examples on the board. Ask students in other groups if they spot any errors in calculations, percentage amounts, or trend analysis.
- Review the steps necessary to prepare a sales budget and a purchases budget.

CLOSURE

- Ask students to explain briefly the three functions of a budget.

Essential Question

- What three goals could I set for myself this year that would help in creating a personal budget? (*Answers might include the following: obtain a job, spend less on gas or clothing, save for college or an automobile.*)

EXTENDED LEARNING

- Assign Accounting in the Real World on page 431.
- Assign Ethics in Action on page 432.

LESSON

15-2 Expense Budgets and the Budgeted Income Statement

LO3 Prepare a selling expenses budget.
LO4 Prepare an administrative expenses budget.
LO5 Prepare an other revenue and expenses budget.
LO6 Prepare a budgeted income statement.

Selling Expenses Budget LO3

Tint My Windows, Inc.
Selling Expenses Budget
For Year Ended December 31, 20X3 — Schedule 3

	Annual Budget	Quarter 1st	2nd	3rd	4th
Advertising Expense	$ 61,410	$13,110	$ 14,550	$ 20,200	$13,550
Delivery Expense	189,010	42,150	44,230	61,430	41,200
Depr. Expense—Delivery Equipment	9,000	2,250	2,250	2,250	2,250
Depr. Expense—Warehouse Equipment	16,875	3,375	4,500	4,500	4,500
Miscellaneous Expense—Sales	12,790	2,730	3,030	4,210	2,820
Salary Expense—Commissions	102,340	21,850	24,240	33,670	22,580
Salary Expense—Regular	29,360	6,550	6,870	9,540	6,400
Supplies Expense—Sales	15,360	3,280	3,640	5,050	3,390
Total Selling Expenses	$436,145	$95,295	$103,310	$140,850	$96,690

A statement prepared to show projected expenditures related directly to the selling operations is called a **selling expenses budget**. The sales manager projects the information for the selling expenses budget. However, other sales personnel may provide specific information. For example, the advertising manager supplies much of the advertising expense information. After selling expenses information has been projected, a selling expenses budget is prepared.

Some selling expense items are relatively stable and require little planning. For example, depreciation expenses for delivery and warehouse equipment are reasonably stable from year to year unless new equipment is bought. On the other hand, several selling expenses increase and decrease in relation to sales increases and decreases. Tint My Windows has a seasonal business, with higher sales during the second and third quarters. The company hires more personnel and spends more for advertising and sales supplies during the heavy sales season. All of these factors are considered when a selling expenses budget is made. Tint My Windows' selling expenses budget is shown above.

The company's sales manager uses a number of approaches to project the various selling expenses. Most selling expenses are linked closely to the amount of quarterly net sales. Management uses the following projection guides to prepare its selling expenses budget.

1. **Advertising expense.** This expense is closely related to sales and sales promotions for the year. Advertising expense for 20X2 was 2.4% ($56,400 ÷ $2,350,250) of net sales. Sales promotion emphasis will be maintained at about the same level this year. Thus, 2.4% of each quarter's projected net sales will be allocated to advertising expense. The first-quarter projected advertising expense is $13,110 (2.4% × $546,350 = $13,112, rounded to $13,110).

LESSON

15-2

BRIDGE

- Point out that in the previous lesson, students learned to create sales and purchases budgets. In this lesson, they will learn how to create a selling expenses budget, an administrative expenses budget, an other revenue and expenses budget, and a budgeted income statement.

TEACHING RESOURCES

- **Instructor's Resource CD/Website:** PowerPoint Slides; Accounting Concepts
- **Working Papers:** Teacher's Edition of the Working Papers for Lesson 15-2; Online Working Papers
- **Transparency Master:** Blank Budget Form

ENGAGE

- Ask students to brainstorm items that might contribute to selling expenses.
- Ask students to predict the items that might be included in a budgeted income statement.
- Ask students how frequently they might compare budgeted data to actual data.

PREVIEW

- Call on students to read the accounting terms and definitions introduced in this lesson: *selling expenses budget, administrative expenses budget, other revenue and expenses budget,* and *budgeted income statement.*
- Point out the learning objectives for this lesson.
- Direct students to read the headings in this lesson and to examine the illustrations.

INPUT

- Ask students to state some of the factors a business must consider when projecting selling expenses for the coming year. Write the answers on the board and discuss. (*Answers might include increases in sales goals, implementation of new advertising strategies, purchase of new vehicles for sales personnel, raises in salaries or commissions, and purchases of cell phones for sales force.*)

MODEL

Use projection guides to determine expense amounts

- Distribute copies of a blank budget. Guide students through the preparation of Tint My Windows' selling expenses budget, using the illustration on page 439 as a guide.
- Direct students to the illustration on page 434. Ask students to state the amounts of advertising expense and net sales for 20X2. Write these amounts on the board (*$56,400; $2,350,250*). Review with students the procedure for determining component percentage of net sales (*$56,400/$2,350,250 = 2.4%*). Indicate to students that 2.4% of each quarter's projected net sales will be allocated to advertising.
- Direct students to the illustration on page 436. Ask them to state the amount of projected net sales for the first quarter (*$546,350*). Show students the mathematical process for calculating the advertising expense for the first quarter. Write the figures on the board (*$546,350 × 2.4% = $13,112.40*). Remind students that Tint My Windows rounds dollar amounts to the nearest $10 amount (*$13,110*). Ask students to calculate the amount of advertising expense for the remaining quarters.

- Point out that Tint My Windows' delivery expense is projected to be $0.27 per unit. Direct students to the illustration on page 436. Ask them to state the amount of projected unit sales for the first quarter of 20X3 (*156,100 units*). Show students the mathematical process for calculating the delivery expense for the first quarter. Write the figures on the board (*156,100 units × $0.27 = $42,147*).
- Direct students to the illustration on page 434. Point out that the depreciation expense for delivery equipment was $9,000 for 20X2. Indicate that Tint My Windows has determined that this amount will remain the same for the year, or $2,250 per quarter (*$9,000/4*).
- Direct students to the list of goals on page 435. Ask a student to read Goal 4 for 20X3.
- Direct students' attention to the illustration on page 434. Point out that the depreciation expense for warehouse equipment was $13,500 for 20X2. Explain to students that this amount equals $3,375 depreciation per quarter (*$13,500/4*). Point out that Tint My Windows has determined that this amount will increase to $4,500 per quarter due to the purchase of the automated cutter.
- Use the illustration on page 434 to explain the 0.6% (*$14,360/$2,350,250*) component percentage for miscellaneous expense for 20X2. Indicate that Tint My Windows is determined to reduce miscellaneous expense to 0.5% of net sales for 20X3. Show students the calculation for the first-quarter miscellaneous expense, $2,730 (*$546,350 × 0.5% = $2,732, rounded to $2,730*).
- Indicate that Tint My Windows will continue to pay a 4% commission on net sales. Show students the calculation for first-quarter salary expense—commissions, $21,850 (*$546,350 × 4% = $21,854, rounded to $21,850*).

2. **Delivery expense.** This expense is closely related to the number of units sold and delivered. The previous year's delivery expense increased significantly because an external freight company was used for some deliveries until Tint My Windows could acquire an additional truck. Rigid cost control measures will be applied to reduce future unit delivery expenses. Delivery expense is projected to be $0.27 per unit (sq. ft.) sold times each quarter's projected unit sales. The first-quarter projected delivery expense is $42,150 ($0.27 × 156,100 units = $42,147, rounded to $42,150).
3. **Depreciation expense—delivery equipment.** No new delivery equipment will be added. Thus, depreciation expense will remain the same as for the previous year ($2,250 per quarter).
4. **Depreciation expense—warehouse equipment.** A new automated cutter will be acquired at the beginning of the second quarter, increasing quarterly depreciation expense from $3,375 to $4,500 per quarter in the second, third, and fourth quarters.
5. **Miscellaneous expense—sales.** Miscellaneous expense was 0.6% ($14,360 ÷ $2,350,250) of net sales in 20X2. Management is committed to reducing miscellaneous expense to 0.5% of net sales in 20X3. The first-quarter miscellaneous expense is projected as $2,730 (0.5% × $546,350 = $2,732, rounded to $2,730).
6. **Salary expense—commissions.** Salespersons will continue to earn a 4.0% commission on net sales. The first-quarter commissions are projected as $21,850 (4.0% × $546,350 = $21,854, rounded to $21,850).
7. **Salary expense—regular.** Regular salary expense is determined by salary increases and changes in activity that affect the number of people employed. The new automated cutter will reduce regular salary expense by $15,000. A 6.0% raise will be added to remaining salaries. Thus, the projected annual amount is calculated as shown.

Salary Expense: 20X2 Comparative Income Statement	$42,700
Less Reduction from Automated Cutter	−15,000
Total	$27,700
Plus 6.0% Rate Increase	+ 1,660
Projected Salary Expense—Regular	$29,360

The projected amount is allocated among the four quarters in relation to the sales percentage from the sales budget. The first-quarter regular salaries are projected as $6,550 (22.3% × $29,360 = $6,547, rounded to $6,550).

8. **Supplies expense—sales.** Supplies expense was 0.6% ($14,100 ÷ $2,350,250) of net sales in 20X2. The same percentage relationship is expected in 20X3. The first-quarter supplies expense is projected as $3,280 (0.6% × $546,350 = $3,278, rounded to $3,280).

After the quarterly amounts have been calculated and entered, the annual budget amounts are determined by totaling the quarterly amounts.

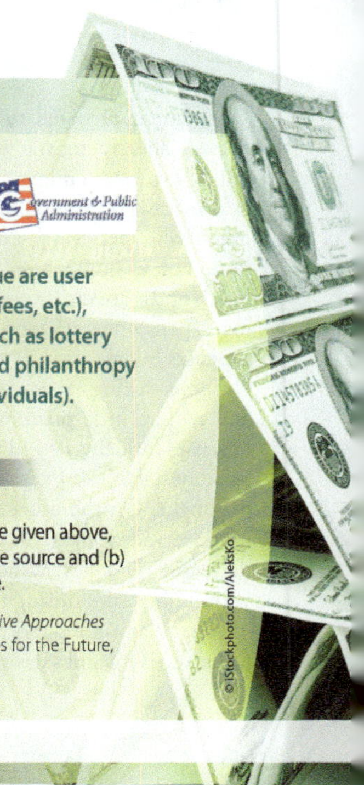

WHY ACCOUNTING?

State Parks and Sources of Revenue

A state government must establish budgets for its revenues and operating expenses and for the services it provides to its residents. One cost item for most states is a state park system. The state governing body must allocate a specific amount of money for the operation of these parks. To do this, the governing body will rely on the specialized skills of government accountants.

If state tax revenues decrease, the governing body must make corresponding decreases in monies allocated to specific programs and services. If this happens, the state park system has two choices: decrease the budgeted costs and expenses (usually by decreasing the services offered), or identify other sources of revenue (to maintain the same level of services).

Government & Public Administration

Some sources of additional revenue are user fees (such as entrance fees, camping fees, etc.), dedicated public revenue sources (such as lottery profits earmarked for state parks), and philanthropy (donations by businesses and/or individuals).

CRITICAL THINKING

For each of the sources of additional revenue given above, list (a) one comment supporting the revenue source and (b) one comment opposing the revenue source.

Source: *Paying for State Parks: Evaluating Alternative Approaches for the 21st Century*, by Margaret Wells, Resources for the Future, January 2013.

WHY ACCOUNTING?

Answers

Answers will vary. Suggested answers follow.

User fees:

(a) Those people who use the state park system pay more for the system than those who don't use it.

(b) At some point, the user fee may discourage people from visiting the park, thereby reducing revenue.

Dedicated public revenue sources:

(a) Those people who support the state parks can choose to support the funding source (i.e., participate in the lottery so that more dollars will be dedicated to the state park system).

(b) If the funding source's revenues decrease, the revenue given to the state park system will decrease—even if there is no correlation between the two, such as a portion of the state's sales tax going to the state park system.

Philanthropy:

(a) People who support the state park system can choose to contribute to it. Those who do not support it will not have to pay for it.

(b) Because people can use the state parks without contributing, they let others pay their way.

Administrative Expenses Budget LO4

Tint My Windows, Inc. Administrative Expenses Budget For Year Ended December 31, 20X3					Schedule 4
	Annual Budget	Quarter			
		1st	2nd	3rd	4th
Depr. Expense—Office Equipment	$ 18,000	$ 4,500	$ 4,500	$ 4,500	$ 4,500
Insurance Expense	7,000	1,750	1,750	1,750	1,750
Miscellaneous Expense—Administrative	45,080	11,270	11,270	11,270	11,270
Payroll Taxes Expense	28,980	6,680	7,020	8,530	6,750
Rent Expense	37,800	9,450	9,450	9,450	9,450
Salary Expense—Administrative	100,200	25,050	25,050	25,050	25,050
Supplies Expense—Administrative	17,900	3,820	4,240	5,890	3,950
Uncollectible Accounts Expense	15,360	3,280	3,640	5,050	3,390
Utilities Expense	13,630	3,040	3,190	4,430	2,970
Total Administrative Expenses	$283,950	$68,840	$70,110	$75,920	$69,080

A statement that shows the projected expenses for all operating expenses not directly related to selling operations is called an **administrative expenses budget**. The administrative manager prepares this budget, using information from these sources:

1. Past records.
2. Company plans.
3. Sales and selling expenses budgets.
4. Discussions with other managers.

After the administrative expenses have been projected, the administrative expenses budget is prepared. Tint My Windows' administrative expenses budget is shown above.

Most administrative expenses are known and remain the same each period. Some administrative expenses need to be budgeted as a percentage of another amount from another budget. The following information was used to prepare the administrative expenses budget.

1. **Depreciation expense—office equipment.** Recently purchased office equipment increased annual depreciation to $18,000. Annual depreciation is divided equally over the four quarters.
2. **Insurance expense.** Annual insurance is projected to increase to $7,000 primarily because of added coverage for the new automated cutting machine. An equal amount is paid each quarter.
3. **Miscellaneous expense—administrative.** This expense is based on Salary Expense—Administrative. Therefore, Salary Expense—Administrative must be calculated first. Closely related to administrative salaries, miscellaneous expense was 49.8% ($48,460 ÷ $97,280) of administrative salaries in 20X2. Management is committed to reducing miscellaneous expense to 45.0% of projected administrative salaries in 20X3. The first-quarter miscellaneous expense is projected as $11,270 (45.0% × $25,050 = 11,273, rounded to $11,270).
4. **Payroll taxes expense.** This expense is based on the total of three salary expense amounts. Therefore, all salary expense amounts must be calculated before calculating payroll tax expense. Based on current payroll tax rates, payroll taxes expense is 12.5% of all salaries each quarter. The first-quarter salaries are projected as $53,450 (Salary Expense—Commissions, $21,850 + Salary Expense—Regular, $6,550 + Salary Expense—Administrative, $25,050). Thus, payroll taxes expense is projected as $6,680 (12.5% × $53,450 = $6,681, rounded to $6,680). Tint My Windows chooses to put all payroll tax expenses into the administrative expenses budget, even though some of these taxes relate to the sales department. Other companies may choose to list payroll taxes in both budgets.
5. **Rent expense.** Tint My Windows leases the building for a known rental fee. Rent will increase to $3,150 per month. Thus, rent expense can be projected at $9,450 each quarter.
6. **Salary expense—administrative.** No new administrative personnel will be hired. Salary expense is projected as $100,200, equal to the 20X2 amount, $97,280, adjusted for a 3.0% salary increase. An equal amount is paid each quarter. Thus, each quarter's salary expense is projected as $25,050 ($100,200 ÷ 4).

- Ask a student to read Goals 4 and 5 in the list of goals on page 435. Use the math illustration to explain the changes in salary expense—regular for 20X3. Point out that total salary expense—regular (*$29,360*) is allocated among quarters, using the same sales percentage rates shown in the illustration on page 436. Show the calculation for determining regular salaries for the first quarter, $6,550 (*$29,360 × 22.3%*).
- Use the illustration on page 434 to explain the 0.6% (*$14,100/$2,350,250*) component percentage for supplies expense—sales for 20X2. Indicate that Tint My Windows will use the same rate for 20X3. Show students the calculation for the first-quarter supplies expense, $3,280 (*$546,350 × 0.6% = $3,278, rounded to $3,280*).

INPUT

- Ask students to state some of the factors a business might consider when projecting administrative expenses for the coming year. Write answers on the board and discuss. (*Answers might include increases in sales goals for next year, purchases of new office equipment, changes in insurance rates, increase in payroll tax percentages, changes in employee benefits, increases in rent, purchases of new office buildings, raises for employees, fluctuations in uncollectible accounts, and changes in utility rates.*)
- Review Tint My Windows' projection guides for determining administrative expenses for 20X3.

MODEL

Use projection guides to determine expense amounts

- Distribute copies of a blank budget. Guide students through the preparation of Tint My Windows' administrative expenses budget, using the illustration on this page.
- Using the board, demonstrate how each amount is calculated.
- Ask a student to read projection guide 1 for depreciation expense—office equipment. Ask students to explain how Tint My Windows determined that the first-quarter amount for depreciation expense is $4,500 (*$18,000/4*).
- Use this same strategy for demonstrating guides 2–9. Ask students to explain the sources for various numbers. Ask them to point out the figures from which amounts were derived. Ask students to demonstrate on the board the mathematical computations for calculating certain amounts or percentages.

INPUT

- Direct students to the comparative income statement shown on page 434. Ask students if Tint My Windows earned any revenue or incurred any expenses outside the normal operations of the business during 20X2. Point out that the comparative income statement shows that Tint My Windows earned no "other" revenue and incurred only one "other" expense, interest expense for $3,600.
- Emphasize that Tint My Windows prepares an other revenue and expenses budget to account for revenue and expense amounts earned or incurred outside normal operations. These amounts might reflect interest income, interest expense, and gains or losses on the sale of plant assets.

MODEL

- Distribute copies of a blank budget. Guide students through the preparation of Tint My Windows' other revenue and expenses budget, using the illustration on this page.
- Show students where each amount appears on the budget by completing the transparency on the overhead. Point out that Tint My Windows intends to pay off a $25,000 loan at the start of the fourth quarter. Consequently, interest expense of $940 is shown in each of the first three quarters and no interest expense is shown for the fourth quarter.

7. **Supplies expense—administrative.** Supplies expense was 0.7% ($17,030 ÷ $2,350,250) of net sales for 20X2. The same percentage will be used in 20X3. The first-quarter supplies expense is projected as $3,820 (0.7% × $546,350 = $3,824, rounded to $3,820).
8. **Uncollectible accounts expense.** Closely related to net sales, uncollectible accounts expense was 0.6% ($14,100 ÷ $2,350,250) of net sales in 20X2. The first-quarter uncollectible accounts expense is projected as $3,280 (0.6% × $546,350 = $3,278, rounded to $3,280).
9. **Utilities expense.** Utilities expense is based on the amount of power, heat, telephone, and other utilities used in 20X2. Costs are projected to increase by 8.2%, consisting of a 4.2% projected increase in activity and a 4.0% increase in rates. The utilities expense by quarter in 20X2 is multiplied by 108.2% (100.0% + 8.2%) and 20X3's projected utilities expense is calculated as follows:

	20X2 Actual Utilities Expense	×	108.2%	=	20X3 Projected Utilities Expense
1st Quarter	$ 2,810	×	108.2%	=	$ 3,040
2nd Quarter	2,950	×	108.2%	=	3,190
3rd Quarter	4,095	×	108.2%	=	4,430
4th Quarter	2,745	×	108.2%	=	2,970
Total	$12,600	×	108.2%	=	$13,630

Other Revenue and Expenses Budget LO5

Tint My Windows, Inc.
Other Revenue and Expenses Budget
For Year Ended December 31, 20X3 — Schedule 5

	Annual Budget	Quarter 1st	2nd	3rd	4th
Other Expenses:					
Interest Expense	$2,820	$940	$940	$940	

Budgeted revenue and expenses from activities other than normal operations are shown in a statement called the **other revenue and expenses budget**. Typical items in this budget are interest income, interest expense, and gains or losses on the sale of plant assets. Tint My Windows' other revenue and expenses budget is shown above. Tint My Windows has only one other expense item and no other revenue items.

Tint My Windows' administrative manager is responsible for projecting the information in the other revenue and expenses budget. The projected interest expense is based on the interest due on a $25,000 loan used to acquire the automated cutter. Since Tint My Windows plans to repay the $25,000 loan at the beginning of the fourth quarter, the budget shows interest expense for only three quarters.

remember Even though budgets are based on estimates, much care is taken to ensure that the estimates are as accurate as possible.

Budgeted Income Statement LO6

Tint My Windows, Inc. Budgeted Income Statement For Year Ended December 31, 20X3					Schedule 6
	Annual Budget	Quarter 1st	2nd	3rd	4th
Operating Revenue:					
Net Sales (Schedule 1)	$2,558,780	$546,350	$606,060	$841,750	$564,620
Cost of Merchandise Sold:					
Beginning Inventory	$ 93,600	$ 93,600	$103,110	$143,430	$ 96,180
Purchases (Schedule 2)	1,473,570	332,640	384,300	430,500	326,130
Total Merchandise Available	$1,567,170	$426,240	$487,410	$573,930	$422,310
Less Ending Inventory	101,850	103,110	143,430	96,180	101,850
Cost of Merchandise Sold	$1,465,320	$323,130	$343,980	$477,750	$320,460
Gross Profit on Sales	$1,093,460	$223,220	$262,080	$364,000	$244,160
Operating Expenses:					
Selling Expenses (Schedule 3)	$ 436,145	$ 95,295	$103,310	$140,850	$ 96,690
Administrative Expenses (Schedule 4)	283,950	68,840	70,110	75,920	69,080
Total Operating Expenses	$ 720,095	$164,135	$173,420	$216,770	$165,770
Income from Operations	$ 373,365	$ 59,085	$ 88,660	$147,230	$ 78,390
Other Expenses (Schedule 5)	2,820	940	940	940	—
Net Income before Federal Income Tax	$ 370,545	$ 58,145	$ 87,720	$146,290	$ 78,390
Federal Income Tax Expense	125,990	31,500	31,500	31,500	31,490
Net Income after Federal Income Tax	$ 244,555	$ 26,645	$ 56,220	$114,790	$ 46,900

1. Beginning inventory:
46,800 units × $2.00 = $93,600

2. Ending inventory:
49,100 units × $2.10 = $103,110

A statement that shows a company's projected sales, costs, expenses, and net income is called a **budgeted income statement**. Since the five budgets contain detailed items, Tint My Windows prepares a shortened budgeted income statement and attaches the supporting budgets. Tint My Windows' budgeted income statement is shown above.

The first-quarter beginning inventory is calculated using the 20X2 unit cost, $2.00. Other inventory amounts are calculated using the unit cost for 20X3, $2.10.

© Andresr/Shutterstock.com

INPUT

- Review the different budgets that students have learned thus far.
- Emphasize that due to the detailed nature of each of these budgets, Tint My Windows presents a summary on a single form referred to as a budgeted income statement.
- Review the procedure for calculating federal income tax for a corporation. Use the tax rate table presented in the math illustration on the next page.

MODEL

Prepare a budgeted income statement

- Distribute copies of a blank budget. Guide students through preparation of the Annual Budget and 1st-Quarter columns of Tint My Windows' budgeted income statement, using the illustration on this page.
- Ask students the origin of each amount presented in the Annual Budget and 1st-Quarter columns of Tint My Windows' budgeted income statement. Ask students to name the proper budget, identify the related illustration, or show the calculation related to a corresponding amount. Point out that the beginning inventory for the annual budget and the first quarter (*$93,600*) is determined using a unit cost amount of $2.00 (*46,800 units × $2.00 = $93,600*). All other beginning and ending inventory amounts are calculated using a unit cost of $2.10.
- Organize students into groups of three or four. Ask the groups to review the amounts for the second quarter and determine their origin.

DIFFERENTIATED INSTRUCTION

Gifted learners need additional challenges to maintain a high level of motivation. Ask students to use the Internet to study the current economic conditions affecting U.S. businesses today. Ask students to create a new comparative income statement and explain how economic factors affected the figures they generated.

THINK LIKE AN ACCOUNTANT

This activity requires students to apply absolute references and create a bar chart. Students must evaluate the effectiveness of charting a group of values having a wide range. Students are then directed to create a second set of ratios that are scaled so that 100% indicates that the target ratio has been achieved.

This activity can be extended by requiring students to:

1. Modify the schedule, using the formula suggested by the sample solution to question 3.
2. Identify the trend in each of the ratios as being positive or negative.
3. Modify the chart to include a heading.

Sample Solutions

1. Some of the bars are too small to detect the trend. The ratio amounts range from a low of 10.5% to a high of 9.8%. Because the chart is scaled between zero and the largest amount, the ratios represented by percentages are too small to be viewed effectively.
2. a. Has the target been achieved, as evidenced by a bar that extends beyond the 100% line?
   b. Is the trend improving, as evidenced by the bars increasing in length from 20X1 to 20X3?
3. The current ratio and inventory ratio have increased and exceeded the target ratio. The accounts receivable ratio is improving and, if the trend continues, can be expected to achieve the target before 20X5. In contrast, the gross margin and rate earned on average total assets are declining. The debt ratio is declining toward its target.
4. Except for the debt ratio, an increasing amount relative to the target ratio is a positive trend. The downward trend of the debt ratio is a positive sign. To be consistent with the other ratios, the relationship between the actual and target ratios needs to be shown, where a positive trend is represented by increasingly larger bars. This goal can be achieved by subtracting the difference between the actual and target ratios, dividing the amount by the target ratio, and subtracting the result from 100%. Thus, the formula in cell F8 would be =1 – (C8 – $B$8)/B8.

Amounts from the five supporting budgets allow Tint My Windows to project net income before federal income tax. Federal income taxes are estimated using a tax rate table furnished by the Internal Revenue Service. Tint My Windows uses the tax rate table shown at the right. Using these rates, Tint My Windows calculates its federal income tax.

Quarterly income tax payments are $31,500 ($125,990 ÷ 4 = $31,498, rounded to $31,500). Thus, Tint My Windows' payments equal $94,500 ($31,500 × 3 quarters) through the third quarter. The fourth-quarter amount equals the unpaid amount of federal income taxes, $31,490 ($125,990 − $94,500).

Tax Rate Schedule

If taxable income is:

Over—	But not over—	Tax is:	Of the amount over—
$0	50,000	15%	-0-
50,000	75,000	$7,500 + 25%	$50,000
75,000	100,000	13,750 + 34%	75,000
100,000	335,000	22,250 + 39%	100,000
335,000	10,000,000	113,900 + 34%	335,000
10,000,000	15,000,000	3,400,000 + 35%	10,000,000
15,000,000	18,333,333	5,150,000 + 38%	15,000,000
18,333,333	—	35%	-0-

Flat Dollar Amount	+	Percentage × Amount in Excess of $335,000	=	Federal Income Tax Expense
$113,900	+	34% × $35,545	=	
$113,900	+	$12,085.30	=	$125,985.30 rounded to $125,990

At this point, the net income has been estimated by quarter for the next fiscal year. Tint My Windows' management must analyze these results to determine if the estimated net income is adequate for current stockholders and to attract new investors. If not, management must adjust the supporting budgets by either increasing revenue or decreasing expenses.

THINK LIKE AN ACCOUNTANT

Charting Financial Ratios

Aretha Johnson, the owner of Johnson Stores, was ready to retire but faced a serious problem. None of her children had any interest in operating her farming supply stores. Wanting to retain an equity interest in the business to benefit her grandchildren, she elected to recruit a partner, Wayne Hillman. Mr. Hillman purchased a 40% stake in the business and set in motion a five-year plan to improve its financial performance.

Mr. Hillman set targets for six financial ratios that he considered critical measures of success. He has requested a chart that shows the three-year progress in meeting those targets. He intends to use the information to assist in preparing the budgets for the coming year.

OPEN THE SPREADSHEET TLA_CH15

The worksheet contains a schedule of six financial ratios. The schedule presents the actual ratios for the past three years and Mr. Hillman's target ratios. Follow the steps on the Instructions tab to prepare a chart. Answer these questions:

1. Explain why the chart does not effectively communicate the trend in all of the financial ratios.
2. Each set of bars communicates the change in the actual ratios relative to the target ratios. What two questions can be answered by evaluating each set of bars?
3. Is Johnson Stores making progress in achieving its five-year targets? Support your answer.
4. Is there a ratio where the message communicated by the chart is inconsistent with the other ratios? How would you correct this problem?

© iStockphoto.com/Dan Bachman

FORMATIVE ASSESSMENT

- This is an ongoing process. Circulate around the classroom or lab, observing which students have difficulty with the assignments.
- Troubleshooting: Diagnose the kinds of problems students have with this lesson. Students may have difficulty obtaining or computing the appropriate answers for the different budgets and the budgeted income statement.
- Assess student understanding by checking solutions to Independent Practice assignments and noting their answers to the Terms Review and Audit Your Understanding questions.

End of Lesson Review

LO3 Prepare a selling expenses budget.

LO4 Prepare an administrative expenses budget.

LO5 Prepare an other revenue and expenses budget.

LO6 Prepare a budgeted income statement.

Terms Review

selling expenses budget
administrative expenses budget
other revenue and expenses budget
budgeted income statement

Audit your understanding

1. What sources of information are used in preparing an administrative expenses budget?
2. What items are typically included in the other revenue and expenses budget?
3. If the budgeted income statement does not show adequate net income, what must be done?

Work together 15-2

Preparing budgets for selling expenses, administrative expenses, and other expenses and preparing a budgeted income statement

Use the information given and the budgets prepared in Work Together 15-1. Additional information is given below. Expenses for 20X3 are projected as follows: Except where noted, percentages are based on projected net sales. For these items, calculate each quarter's amount by multiplying the percentage times that quarter's net sales. Calculate the annual total by adding the four quarterly amounts. When a dollar amount is given, the total amount should be divided equally among the four quarters.

Selling Expenses		Administrative Expenses	
Advertising Expense	2.5%	Depr. Exp.—Office Equip.	$4,000.00
Delivery Expense	5.0%	Insurance Expense	$6,000.00
Depr. Exp.—Delivery Equip.	$8,000.00	Misc. Exp.—Admin.	$3,000.00
Depr. Exp.—Warehouse Equip.	$5,000.00	Payroll Taxes Expense	12.0% of total salaries
Misc. Exp.—Sales	4.0%	Rent Expense	$24,000.00
Salary Exp.—Sales	6.0%	Salary Exp.—Admin.	$20,000.00
Supplies Expense—Sales	2.0%	Supplies Exp.—Admin.	$8,000.00
		Uncoll. Accts. Expense	0.5%
		Utilities Expense	2.5%

Interest Expense is estimated to be $2,520.00. Federal income taxes are calculated using the tax rate table shown in this chapter. Equal quarterly income tax payments are based on the projected annual federal income tax expense.

Partially completed budget forms are given in the *Working Papers*.

1. Complete the selling expenses budget (Schedule 3) for the four quarters ended December 31, 20X3. Maddox Corporation rounds all amounts to the nearest $10.
2. Complete the administrative expenses budget (Schedule 4) for the four quarters ended December 31, 20X3.
3. Complete the other revenue and expenses budget (Schedule 5) for the four quarters ended December 31, 20X3.
4. Complete the budgeted income statement for the four quarters ended December 31, 20X3.
   Save your work for use in Work Together 15-3.

CHECK FOR UNDERSTANDING

Terms Review

- Call on students to define each term in the Terms Review.

Audit Your Understanding

- Call on students to answer the Audit Your Understanding questions. Answers are given in Appendix D of the textbook.

GUIDED PRACTICE

Work Together

- Have students write the solution to the Work Together problem as you guide the class through the examples.
- Remind students to use the information given and budgets prepared in Work Together 15-1.
- Direct students to save their work to complete Work Together 15-3.

INDEPENDENT PRACTICE

On Your Own

- Assign the On Your Own problem to be worked independently.
- Remind students to use the information given and budgets prepared in On Your Own 15-1.
- Direct students to save their work to complete On Your Own 15-3.

Application Problem

- Remind students to use the information given and budgets prepared in Application Problem 15-1.
- Assign Application Problem 15-2.
- Direct students to save their work to complete Application Problem 15-3.

Online Working Papers

- Students can access the Lesson 15-2 problems using this software.

RETEACH

- Review the budgets presented in this lesson, their purposes, and the interrelationship among the budgets presented thus far.

CLOSURE

- Ask students to name the budgets and the statement they learned to prepare.
- Ask students to explain the basic content and purpose of each budget or statement. Write responses under each heading.

Essential Questions

- Would it be advantageous to calculate federal income tax on gross profit? Explain. (*Seldom is it advantageous because expenses usually reduce the amount of net income that is taxable. However, if Other Revenue is greater than Operating Revenue, it could be advantageous.*)
- Why must department managers work as a team to obtain information for their budget(s) when it is prepared only for a specific department? (*Managers still must work as a team to align with overall company goals.*)

EXTENDED LEARNING

- Assign Why Accounting on page 440.
- Assign Think Like an Accountant on page 444.

End of Lesson Review

On your own 15-2

Preparing budgets for selling expenses, administrative expenses, and other expenses and preparing a budgeted income statement

Use the information given and the budgets prepared in On Your Own 15-1. Additional information is given below. Expenses for 20X3 are projected as follows: Except where noted, percentages are based on projected net sales. For these items, calculate each quarter's amount by multiplying the percentage times that quarter's net sales. Calculate the annual total by adding the four quarterly amounts. When a dollar amount is given, the total amount should be divided equally among the four quarters.

Selling Expenses	
Advertising Expense	4.0%
Delivery Expense	6.5%
Depr. Exp. —Delivery Equip.	$10,000.00
Depr. Exp.—Warehouse Equip.	$20,000.00
Misc. Exp.—Sales	5.0%
Salary Exp.—Sales	7.0%
Supplies Expense—Sales	2.0%

Administrative Expenses	
Depr. Exp. —Office Equip.	$15,000.00
Insurance Expense	$12,000.00
Misc. Exp. —Admin.	$8,000.00
Payroll Taxes Expense	12.0% of total salaries
Rent Expense	$24,000.00
Salary Exp. —Admin.	$35,000.00
Supplies Exp. —Admin.	$14,400.00
Uncoll. Accts. Expense	0.4%
Utilities Expense	6.0%

Interest Expense is estimated to be $4,000.00. Federal income taxes are calculated using the tax rate table shown in this chapter. Equal quarterly income tax payments are based on the projected annual federal income tax expense.

Partially completed budget forms are given in the *Working Papers*.

1. Complete the selling expenses budget (Schedule 3) for the four quarters ended December 31, 20X3. Northstar, Inc., rounds all amounts to the nearest $10.
2. Complete the administrative expenses budget (Schedule 4) for the four quarters ended December 31, 20X3.
3. Complete the other revenue and expenses budget (Schedule 5) for the four quarters ended December 31, 20X3.
4. Complete the budgeted income statement for the four quarters ended December 31, 20X3. Save your work for use in On Your Own15-3.

LESSON

15-3 Cash Budgets

LO7 Prepare a cash receipts budget.
LO8 Prepare a cash payments budget.
LO9 Prepare a cash budget.

Cash Receipts Budget LO7

Tint My Windows, Inc.
Cash Receipts Budget
For Year Ended December 31, 20X3 — Schedule A

	Quarter 1st	2nd	3rd	4th
Cash Receipts from Sales:				
Prior Year's 4th-Quarter Sales ($512,050) . . .	$150,540			
1st-Quarter Sales ($546,350).	382,450	$160,630		
2nd-Quarter Sales ($606,060).		424,240	$178,180	
3rd-Quarter Sales ($841,750)			589,230	$247,470
4th-Quarter Sales ($564,620)				395,230
Total Cash Receipts from Sales	$532,990	$584,870	$767,410	$642,700
Cash Receipts from Other Sources:				
Note Payable to Bank.	25,000			
Total Cash Receipts.	$557,990	$584,870	$767,410	$642,700

Collection Percentage	×	First-Quarter Sales	=	Second-Quarter Cash Receipts
29.4%	×	$546,350	=	$160,627, rounded to $160,630

Collection Percentage	×	Second-Quarter Sales	=	Second-Quarter Cash Receipts
70.0%	×	$606,060	=	$424,242, rounded to $424,240

Good cash management requires planning and controlling cash so that it will be available to meet obligations when they come due. Tint My Windows prepares a cash budget to help analyze cash inflows and cash outflows. The treasurer prepares Tint My Windows' cash budget in consultation with the budget committee. A treasurer is a corporate officer who is usually responsible for planning the corporation's requirement for and use of cash. The treasurer analyzes:

1. Projected receipts from cash sales, customers on account, and other sources.
2. Projected cash payments for ordinary expenses, such as rent, payroll, and payments to vendors on account.
3. Other cash payments for assets, such as plant assets or supplies.

Projected cash receipts for a budget period are reported on a statement called a **cash receipts budget**. Tint My Windows' cash receipts budget is shown above. To prepare a cash receipts budget, projections are composed of the following:

1. Quarterly cash sales.
2. Quarterly collections on account from customers. The amounts received from customers will not be the same as the amount of sales on account. Normally, cash is received for sales on account made during the previous one or two months. In addition, some sales returns and allowances and uncollectible accounts are likely.
3. Cash to be received quarterly from other sources.

LESSON

15-3

BRIDGE

- Point out that the procedures for planning and preparing a budgeted income statement were presented earlier in this chapter. Explain that a business also needs to plan and control the amount of cash on hand. In this lesson, a cash budget will be planned and prepared.

TEACHING RESOURCES

- **Instructor's Resource CD/Website:** PowerPoint Slides; Accounting Concepts
- **Working Papers:** Teacher's Edition of the Working Papers for Lesson 15-3; Online Working Papers
- **Transparency Master:** Blank Budget Form

ENGAGE

- Ask students how predicting cash receipts and cash payments can assist with budgeting.
- Ask students if they have ever prepared a budget that was not effective. Explain. Point out that sometimes cash is not received as expected or payments occur due to unforeseen circumstances. The cash affected could have resulted in a budget not being met.

PREVIEW

- Call on students to read the accounting terms and definitions introduced in this lesson: *cash receipts budget*, *cash payments budget*, and *cash budget*.
- Point out the learning objectives for this lesson.
- Direct students to read the headings in this lesson and to examine the illustrations.

INPUT

- Emphasize that good cash management requires analyzing cash inflows and cash outflows to determine if a company will have sufficient funds to purchase new equipment, pay expenses, buy additional merchandise, and provide owners with a return on their investment.
- Ask students to name the sources of a company's cash receipts. Discuss cash sales; amounts received for sales on account; and other cash sources, such as loans and sales of assets.

INPUT

- Discuss Tint My Windows' pattern of net sales per quarter. Emphasize that approximately 70% of net sales are collected during the same quarter.

MODEL

Prepare a cash receipts budget

- Distribute copies of a blank budget. Guide students through the preparation of Tint My Windows' cash receipts budget, using the illustration as a guide.
- Direct students to the illustration on page 447. Ask students how the first figure in the first quarter, $150,540, was calculated. Point out that 29.4% of prior-quarter sales are collected in the subsequent period (*$512,050 × 29.4% = $150,542.70, rounded to $150,540*).
- Ask students how the figure of first-quarter sales in the first column, $546,350, was calculated. Emphasize that 70% of all net sales are collected during the same period (*$546,350 × 70% = $382,445, rounded to $382,450*).
- Ask students the origin of Tint My Windows' first-quarter net sales of $546,350. (See the illustration of the sales budget on page 436.)
- Show students that the total receipts from sales, $532,990, was simply calculated by adding $150,540 and $382,450.
- Point out that after cash receipts and cash payments were projected for the first quarter, Tint My Windows' treasurer decided the company was very low on cash. To ensure there was adequate cash to pay company bills, the treasurer made arrangements to borrow $25,000 during the first quarter.
- Ask students to verify the amounts of Tint My Windows' projected cash receipts for the second, third, and fourth quarters. Circulate around the classroom and assist students having difficulties.

GLOBAL AWARENESS

Answers

1. Answers will vary. At the time of publication, both the DOJ and the SEC listed recent enforcement activities.
2. Answers will vary but may include the following: Bribery encourages market inefficiencies and instability. It threatens security by facilitating criminal activity. It is anticompetitive and may lead to distorted prices. It places honest businesses at a disadvantage. Contracts acquired through bribery may not be legally enforceable. The corrupt foreign official may increase demands in the future. Bribery encourages a climate of permissiveness. It may cause employees, investors, and customers to lose trust in a company.

Analysis of Cash Receipts

An analysis of Tint My Windows' sales for previous years shows the following pattern of net sales per quarter:

1. About 40.0% are cash sales.
2. About 30.0% are sales on account collected in the same quarter. Thus, 70.0% of a quarter's net sales are collected during the same quarter.
3. About 29.4% are collected in the following quarter.
4. About 0.6% prove to be uncollectible.

As shown in the cash receipts budget, the total cash receipts from sales in the first quarter ($532,990) include $105,540 from 20X2's fourth-quarter sales on account (29.4% × $512,050 = $150,543, rounded to $150,540) plus $382,450 from 20X3's first-quarter sales (70.0% × $546,350 = $382,445, rounded to $382,450). Cash sales and collections on account provide most of the cash receipts. If additional cash is needed, other sources of cash should be planned. For example, Tint My Windows' treasurer determines that cash on hand will be reduced in the first quarter to an unusually low level. This condition could prevent the company from making timely payments for its expenditures. Therefore, the treasurer arranges to borrow $25,000 during the first quarter.

GLOBAL AWARENESS

Foreign Corrupt Practices Act

In the United States, it is illegal for any person or business to bribe a government official in order to have that official act or fail to act in a manner that benefits the person or business. However, in some countries, bribery is a legal, accepted way to conduct business.

During investigations by the Securities and Exchange Commission (SEC) in the mid-1970s, more than 400 U.S. companies admitted to such bribery. As a result, the Foreign Corrupt Practices Act (FCPA) was enacted by Congress and signed into law in 1977. The purpose of the FCPA was to stop corrupt practices, "create a level playing field" for businesses so that honest competition could prevail, and restore the public's trust in the marketplace.

The FCPA focuses on two methods of preventing corruption. First, it prohibits individuals and firms from engaging in the bribery of foreign officials. Second, it requires specific control measures to prevent the falsifying of accounting records or the failure to use a system of internal control. A 1998 amendment to the FCPA extends the prohibition of bribery to foreign individuals and firms doing business in the United States.

A company found guilty of violating the FCPA could be required to pay back with interest any illegally acquired profits and be subject to penalties. In addition, it may have to be overseen by a consultant. The total financial loss could be substantial and could include the loss of exporting rights.

The Department of Justice (DOJ) and the SEC have developed guidelines for implementing the FCPA. These guidelines cover to whom the act applies, what actions are prohibited, and what sanctions may be enforced, and they include an outline of an effective compliance program. They are available at the following websites:
www.justice.gov/criminal/fraud/fcpa
www.sec.gov/spotlight/fcpa.shtml

CRITICAL THINKING

1. Go to the website for either the DOJ or the SEC. Search for the FCPA and find a recent case brought against a U.S. company. List the name of the company and how it violated the FCPA.
2. Using the case found in Part 1, list several ways in which bribery is bad for business.

© iStockphoto.com/Lusky

Cash Payments Budget LO8

Tint My Windows, Inc. Cash Payments Budget For Year Ended December 31, 20X3				Schedule B
	Quarter			
	1st	2nd	3rd	4th
From Purchases:				
Prior Year's 4th Quarter ($276,800)	$ 83,040			
1st-Quarter Purchases ($332,640)	232,850	$ 99,790		
2nd-Quarter Purchases ($384,300)		269,010	$115,290	
3rd-Quarter Purchases ($430,500)			301,350	$129,150
4th-Quarter Purchases ($326,130)				228,290
Total Payments from Purchases	$315,890	$368,800	$416,640	$357,440
For Operating Expenses:				
Cash Selling Expenses	$ 89,670	$ 96,560	$134,100	$ 89,940
Cash Administrative Expenses	61,060	61,970	66,370	61,190
Total Cash Operating Expenses	$150,730	$158,530	$200,470	$151,130
Other Cash Payments:				
Federal Income Tax Expense	$ 31,500	$ 31,500	$ 31,500	$ 31,490
Fixed Asset Purchases	50,000			
Cash Dividend		55,000		55,000
Investment				100,000
Note Payable and Interest				27,500
Total Other Cash Payments	$ 81,500	$ 86,500	$ 31,500	$213,990
Total Cash Payments	$548,120	$613,830	$648,610	$722,560

Projected cash payments for a budget period are reported on a statement called a **cash payments budget**. Tint My Windows' cash payments budget is shown above. To prepare the cash payments budget, the accountant and treasurer make the following projections:

1. Quarterly cash payments for accounts payable or notes payable to vendors.
2. Quarterly cash payments for each expense item. This projection requires an analysis of the selling expenses, administrative expenses, and other revenue and expenses budgets.
3. Quarterly cash payments for buying equipment and other assets.
4. Quarterly cash payments for dividends.
5. Quarterly cash payments for investments.

Tint My Windows' treasurer uses the following guides to prepare the cash payments budget.

1. **Cash payments for merchandise.** An analysis of past records for payments to vendors on account shows the following pattern of purchases in a quarter:
   a. About 20.0% are cash purchases.
   b. About 50.0% are on account and are paid for in the quarter. Thus, 70.0% (20.0% + 50.0%) of a quarter's purchases are paid for during the same quarter.
   c. The remaining 30.0% are purchases on account paid for in the following quarter.

Cash payments are calculated using the same procedure used for cash receipts. Purchase amounts are from the purchases budget. The first-quarter cash payments for the first-quarter purchases are $232,850 (70.0% × $332,640 = $232,848 rounded to $232,850).

DIFFERENTIATED INSTRUCTION

ESL learners learn best by building engagement with other learners. Ask students to explain why a company budget should or should not be distributed to all employees at all levels of the company. Use Think/Pair/Share as an activity that allows for engagement with other learners. Give students a few minutes to think of their response to the question. Then ask them to pair with another student and share their response.

INPUT

- Ask students to name the types of cash payments Tint My Windows might make during a quarter. Lead into a discussion of cash payments for accounts or notes payable, various selling and administrative expenses, equipment purchases, dividends, and investments.
- Ask students the names of the budgets that provide information related to cash payments (*purchases, selling expenses, administrative expenses, and other revenue and expenses budgets*).
- Discuss the projection guides used by Tint My Windows to determine cash payments for merchandise, operating expenses, and other cash payments.

MODEL

Prepare a cash payments budget

- Distribute copies of a blank budget. Guide students through the preparation of Tint My Windows' cash payments budget using the illustration.
- Direct students to the illustration on this page. Ask students how the first figure in the 1st-Quarter column, $83,040, was calculated. Point out that 30% of the prior-quarter purchases are paid for during the subsequent quarter (*$276,800 × 30% = $83,040*). Show all math calculations on the board.
- Ask students how the second figure in the 1st-Quarter column, $232,850, was calculated. Emphasize that 70% of all purchases are paid for during the quarter (*$332,640 × 70% = $232,848, rounded to $232,850*).
- Ask students the origin of Tint My Windows' first-quarter purchases of $332,640. (See the illustration of the purchases budget on page 437.)
- Use the math illustration in projection guide 2 to explain the process for determining the cash payments for operating expenses. Ask students the origin of the selling and administrative expenses. (See the illustrations on pages 439 and 441.) Emphasize that cash is not actually paid out for depreciation and uncollectible accounts expenses.
- Ask a student to read the projection guide for other cash payments. As the student reads, make notes on the board to identify other cash payments (*federal income tax, automated cutting machine, cash dividends, cash investment, and repayment of promissory note*). After the student has finished reading the paragraph, ask the class to state the amount of the cash payment for each category. Write the appropriate responses under each category.

- Identify the other cash payments related to the first quarter and calculate the totals for the first quarter.
- Ask students to verify the amounts of Tint My Windows' projected cash payments for the second, third, and fourth quarters. Circulate around the classroom and assist students having difficulties.

INPUT

- Explain that a cash budget summarizes cash receipts and cash payments and identifies the amount of cash available at the end of each quarter.

MODEL

Prepare a cash budget

- Distribute copies of a blank budget. Guide students through the preparation of Tint My Windows' cash budget, using the illustration on this page.
- Ask students to verify the amounts of Tint My Windows' cash budget for the second, third, and fourth quarters. Circulate around the classroom and assist students having difficulties.

2. **Cash payments for operating expenses.** Cash payments for most operating expenses are made in the quarter the expense is incurred. However, the selling expenses budget, shown on page 439, and the administrative expenses budget, page 441, include some projected items for which cash will not be paid. For example, cash is not paid for depreciation and uncollectible accounts expenses. Therefore, these amounts are not included in the cash payments budget. The first quarter's cash payments for selling expenses and for administrative expenses are calculated as follows:

Selling Expenses		$95,295
Less: Depr. Exp. —Del. Equip.	$2,250	
Depr. Exp. —Warehouse Equip.	3,375	5,625
Cash Payments for Selling Exp.		$89,670

Administrative Expenses		$68,840
Less: Depr. Exp. —Office Equip.	$4,500	
Uncollectible Accts. Exp.	3,280	7,780
Cash Payment for Admin. Exp.		$61,060

3. **Other cash payments.** Tint My Windows also plans for cash payments other than for merchandise, selling expenses, and administrative expenses. Federal income tax payments equal the quarterly federal income tax expense amounts on the budgeted income statement. Tint My Windows also plans to buy a new automated cutting machine for $50,000 at the end of the first quarter. The company expects to pay a $55,000 cash dividend to stockholders in the second and fourth quarters. Since a large cash balance is projected for the third quarter, Tint My Windows plans a $100,000 interest-earning investment in the fourth quarter. In addition, plans call for repaying the promissory note plus interest, $27,500, at the beginning of the fourth quarter.

The last line of the cash payments budget shows the total cash payments projected each quarter. This total indicates the minimum amount of cash that must be available each quarter.

Cash Budget LO9

Tint My Windows, Inc.
Cash Budget
For Year Ended December 31, 20X3

	Quarter			
	1st	2nd	3rd	4th
Cash Balance—Beginning	$ 26,225	$ 36,095	$ 7,135	$125,935
Cash Receipts Budget (Schedule A)	557,990	584,870	767,410	642,700
Cash Available	$584,215	$620,965	$774,545	$768,635
Less Cash Payments (Schedule B)	548,120	613,830	648,610	722,560
Cash Balance—Ending	$ 36,095	$ 7,135	$125,935	$ 46,075

A statement that shows for each month or quarter a projection of a company's beginning cash balance, cash receipts, cash payments, and ending cash balance is called a **cash budget**. Tint My Windows' cash budget, shown above, is prepared from the information in the cash receipts budget and the cash payments budget. The first-quarter beginning cash balance is taken from the balance sheet on December 31, 20X2.

At the end of each quarter of a budget period, Tint My Windows compares the actual cash balance with the projected cash balance shown on the cash budget. If the actual cash balance is less than the projected balance, the reasons for the decrease are determined and action is taken to correct the problem. One reason may be that some customers are not paying their accounts when they should. Another may be that expenses are exceeding budget projections. If the decrease continues, the company could have a quarter in which there is not enough cash to make all the required cash payments. If this shortage does occur, the business will have to borrow money until receipts and payments are brought into balance.

FORMATIVE ASSESSMENT

- This is an ongoing process. Circulate around the classroom or lab, observing which students have difficulty with the assignments.
- Troubleshooting: Diagnose the kinds of problems students have with this lesson. Students may have difficulty remembering or implementing projection guides when calculating various amounts.
- Assess student understanding by checking solutions to Independent Practice assignments and noting their answers to the Terms Review and Audit Your Understanding questions.

End of Lesson Review

LO7 Prepare a cash receipts budget.

LO8 Prepare a cash payments budget.

LO9 Prepare a cash budget.

Terms Review

cash receipts budget

cash payments budget

cash budget

Audit your understanding

1. What is the goal of good cash management?
2. What projections are needed to prepare a cash receipts budget?
3. What projections are needed to prepare a cash payments budget?
4. At the end of a period, if the actual cash balance is less than the projected cash balance, what should be done?

Work together 15-3

Preparing a cash receipts budget, a cash payments budget, and a cash budget

Use the information given and the budgets prepared in Work Together 15-1 and 15-2. Additional information is given below.

a. Actual amounts for the fourth quarter of 20X2: sales, $435,000.00; purchases, $168,000.00.
b. The balance of cash on hand on January 1, 20X3, is $9,500.00.
c. In each quarter, cash sales are 15.0% and collections of accounts receivable are 50.0% of the projected net sales for the current quarter. Collections from the preceding quarter's net sales are 34.5% of that quarter. Uncollectible accounts expense is 0.5% of net sales.
d. In each quarter, cash payments for cash purchases are 10.0% and for accounts payable 50.0% of the purchases for the current quarter. Cash payments for purchases of the preceding quarter are 40.0% of that quarter.
e. In the first quarter, Maddox will borrow $20,000.00 on a promissory note and will purchase equipment costing $55,000.00 for cash. In each quarter, dividends of $2,500.00 will be paid in cash. In the fourth quarter, the promissory note plus interest will be paid in cash, $22,500.00.
f. Quarterly income tax payments are 1/4 of the projected annual federal income tax.

Partially completed budget forms are given in the *Working Papers*. For the four quarters ended December 31, 20X3, complete the following budgets, rounding all amounts to the nearest $10: (1) Cash receipts budget (Schedule A), (2) Cash payments budget (Schedule B), (3) Cash budget.

On your own 15-3

Preparing a cash receipts budget, a cash payments budget, and a cash budget

Use the information given and the budgets prepared in On Your Own 15-1 and 15-2. Additional information is given below.

a. Actual amounts for the fourth quarter of 20X2: sales, $480,000.00; purchases, $146,250.00.
b. The balance of cash on hand on January 1, 20X3, is $7,250.00.
c. In each quarter, cash sales are 10.0% and collections of accounts receivable are 45.0% of the projected net sales for the current quarter. Collections from the preceding quarter's net sales are 44.6% of that quarter. Uncollectible accounts expense is 0.4% of net sales.
d. In each quarter, cash payments for cash purchases are 20.0% and for accounts payable 45.0% of the purchases for the current quarter. Cash payments for purchases of the preceding quarter are 35.0% of that quarter.
e. In the first quarter, Northstar will borrow $30,000.00 on a promissory note and will purchase equipment costing $100,000.00 for cash. In each quarter, dividends of $6,000.00 will be paid in cash. In the fourth quarter, the promissory note plus interest will be paid in cash, $34,000.00.
f. Quarterly income tax payments are 1/4 of the projected annual federal income tax.

Partially completed budget forms are given in the *Working Papers*. For the four quarters ended December 31, 20X3, complete the following budgets, rounding all amounts to the nearest $10: (1) Cash receipts budget (Schedule A), (2) Cash payments budget (Schedule B), (3) Cash budget.

CHECK FOR UNDERSTANDING

Terms Review

- Call on students to define each term in the Terms Review. Definitions are given in the Glossary.

Audit Your Understanding

- Call on students to answer the Audit Your Understanding questions. Answers are given in Appendix D of the textbook.

GUIDED PRACTICE

Work Together

- Have students write the solution to the Work Together problem as you guide the class through the examples.
- Direct students to prepare a cash receipts budget, a cash payments budget, and a cash budget.
- Remind students to use the information given and the budgets prepared in Work Together 15-1 and 15-2. Additional information is provided for this problem.

INDEPENDENT PRACTICE

On Your Own

- Assign the On Your Own problem to be worked independently.
- Remind students to use the information given and the budgets prepared in On Your Own 15-1 and 15-2. Additional information is provided for this problem.
- Use the Formative Assessment techniques to diagnose student understanding.

Application Problem

- Assign Application Problem 15-3.
- Remind students to use the information given and the budgets prepared in Application Problems 15-1 and 15-2. Additional information is provided for this problem.

Online Working Papers

- Students can access the Lesson 15-3 problems using this software.

RETEACH

- Review the cash receipts, cash payments, and cash budgets.
- Explain how to analyze the cash payments budget.

CLOSURE

- Ask students to describe similarities and differences between preparing a budgeted income statement and a cash budget.

Essential Question

- Isn't predicting cash receipts and cash payments just an estimate? How can preparing a cash budget help with the overall performance of a company? (*Yes, they are estimates. However, the estimates can help the company predict when to plan for loans or additional investments.*)

EXTENDED LEARNING

- Assign Global Awareness on page 448.

LESSON

15-4

BRIDGE

- Point out that students have learned how to prepare budgets in previous lessons as a means to reach targeted goals. In this lesson, they will compare their budget to what actually occurred, through a performance report.

TEACHING RESOURCES

- **Instructor's Resource CD/Website:**
  PowerPoint Slides
  Accounting Concepts
- **Working Papers:**
  Teacher's Edition of the Working Papers for Lesson 15-4
  Online Working Papers
- **Transparency Master:**
  Blank Budget Form

ENGAGE

- Ask students what else besides financial data can be measured to determine the performance of a company.
- Ask students how they would evaluate local businesses' performance if they were unaware of the financial data.

PREVIEW

- Call on students to read the accounting terms and definitions introduced in this lesson: *performance report* and *balanced scorecard.*
- Point out the learning objectives for this lesson.
- Direct students to read the headings in this lesson and to examine the illustrations.

LESSON

15-4 Performance Reports

LO10 Prepare a performance report.
LO11 Identify performance measures in a balanced scorecard system.

Performance Report LO10

Tint My Windows, Inc.
Performance Report
For Quarter Ended March 31, 20X3

	Budget	Actual	Over (Under) Amount	Over (Under) Percentage
Unit Sales	156,100	157,800	1,700	1.1
Operating Revenue:				
Net Sales	$546,350	$552,300	$ 5,950	1.1
Cost of Merchandise Sold	323,130	331,380	8,250	2.6
Gross Profit on Operations	$223,220	$220,920	$ (2,300)	(1.0)
Operating Expenses:				
Selling Expenses:				
Advertising Expense	$ 13,110	$ 13,000	$ (110)	(0.8)
Delivery Expense	42,150	42,606	456	1.1
Depr. Expense—Delivery Equipment	2,250	2,250	—	—
Depr. Expense—Warehouse Equipment	3,375	3,375	—	—
Miscellaneous Expense—Sales	2,730	2,750	20	0.7
Salary Expense—Commissions	21,850	22,092	242	1.1
Salary Expense—Regular	6,550	6,550	—	—
Supplies Expense—Sales	3,280	3,200	(80)	(2.4)
Total Selling Expenses	$ 95,295	$ 95,823	$ 528	0.6
Administrative Expenses:				
Depr. Expense—Office Equipment	$ 4,500	$ 4,500	$ —	—
Insurance Expense	1,750	1,750	—	—
Miscellaneous Expense—Administrative	11,270	11,250	(20)	(0.2)
Payroll Taxes Expense	6,680	6,712	32	0.5
Rent Expense	9,450	9,450	—	—
Salary Expense—Administrative	25,050	25,050	—	—
Supplies Expense—Administrative	3,820	3,780	(40)	(1.0)
Uncollectible Accounts Expense	3,280	3,200	(80)	(2.4)
Utilities Expense	3,040	3,200	160	5.3
Total Administrative Expenses	$ 68,840	$ 68,892	$ 52	0.1
Total Operating Expenses	$164,135	$164,715	$ 580	0.4
Income from Operations	$ 59,085	$ 56,205	$ (2,880)	(4.9)
Other Expenses	940	940	—	—
Net Income before Federal Income Tax	$ 58,145	$ 55,265	$ (2,880)	(5.0)
Federal Income Tax Expense	31,500	18,791	(12,709)	(40.3)
Net Income after Federal Income Tax	$ 26,645	$ 36,474	$ 9,829	36.9

At the end of each quarter, a business prepares an income statement that compares actual amounts with the budgeted income statement for the same period. This comparison shows variations between actual and projected items. A report showing a comparison of projected and actual amounts for a specific period is called a **performance report**.

Preparing a Performance Report

The quarterly performance report for Tint My Windows is shown on the previous page. This report is sent to the sales manager and the administrative manager. Knowing about significant differences between projected and actual income statement amounts helps the managers identify areas that need to be reviewed. By identifying large variations early, managers may be able to make changes that will correct negative effects on net income for the year. If conditions change significantly, the budget for the remainder of the year can be revised.

Preparation of a performance report is similar to preparation of a comparative income statement. However, a performance report compares actual amounts with projected amounts for the same period. A comparative income statement compares actual amounts of one period with actual amounts of a prior period.

The first amount column of the performance report shows the amounts projected for the first quarter. The second amount column shows the actual sales, costs, and expenses for the quarter. The third amount column shows how much the actual amount varies from the projected amount. For example, actual net sales, $552,300, *less* projected net sales, $546,350, *equals* the actual over projected amount, $5,950. The fourth column shows the percentage that the actual amount was over or under the projected amount. For example, the net sales increase, $5,950, *divided by* projected net sales, $546,350, *equals* the percentage by which actual exceeds projected, 1.1%. Percentages are rounded to the nearest 0.1%.

An analysis is made of all significant differences to determine why the differences occurred. Normally, Tint My Windows only considers changes of 5.0% or more to be significant. However, because the items influencing gross profit are large dollar amounts, small percentage changes affect net income significantly. Therefore, Tint My Windows' sales manager reviews changes in net sales and the cost of merchandise sold, regardless of the amount of change.

Tint My Windows' performance report indicates that three items should be reviewed:

1. Net sales.
2. Cost of merchandise sold.
3. Utilities expense.

Managers should determine what actions, if any, could correct the unfavorable situations, such as the 5.3% overage in utilities expense. If the utility service cost has increased, the manager cannot change that. However, if power is being wasted, procedures may need to be changed.

Managers should also determine what actions caused favorable results, such as the 1.1% overage in net sales, and encourage a continuation of those favorable actions.

Balanced Scorecard LO11

The performance report presented in this lesson focuses solely on financial data. While financial data are important, some managers feel that only using financial measures ignores other possible measures and feedback that may improve the efficiency and effectiveness of a business. This focus on financial data is said to be "out of balance." A more balanced approach is to include other nonfinancial data when measuring performance.

A **balanced scorecard** is a planning and measurement system developed by R. S. Kaplan and D. P. Norton[1] to use multiple performance measures to ensure that a company's vision and strategy are reflected in its goals and activities. The balanced scorecard develops performance measures in four areas: learning and growth, internal business, customer service, and financial.

LEARNING AND GROWTH

Learning and growth includes both research and development of company products or services as well as education of employees and customers. Learning and growth performance measures would answer the question, "To achieve our vision, how will we sustain our ability to change and improve?" Typical learning and growth performance measures could include the number of new products introduced, employee turnover, employee satisfaction ratings, the number of classes completed, and the number of employees trained for more than one task.

[1] R. S. Kaplan and D. P. Norton, *The Balanced Scorecard: Translating Strategy into Action,* published by Harvard Business School Press, 1996.

INPUT

- Direct students to the illustrations on pages 434 and 452. Ask students the difference between a comparative income statement and a performance report. Point out that the comparative income statement compares actual amounts of a prior period. A performance report compares actual amounts with projected amounts for the same period.
- Refer students to the illustration on page 452. Ask them to state the amount of increase or decrease for net sales (*$5,950 increase*). Quickly review with students how the amount was calculated (*$552,300 – $546,350 = $5,950*). Show and explain the calculations used to calculate the 1.1% increase in net sales (*$5,950/$546,350 = 1.1%*).
- Select several other lines on the performance report and show the calculations required to compute amounts and percentages. Be sure to include a negative amount and percentage.
- Ask students to identify favorable and unfavorable percentage changes. Remind students that not all positive percentage changes are favorable. Point out that a percentage increase in an expense is unfavorable.
- Emphasize that unfavorable trends require additional investigation. Factors causing favorable trends should be encouraged.
- Point out that a performance report can be used to evaluate a company's budgeting process.

TEACHING IDEA **Ask students to work together in groups of three or four. Tell them to brainstorm at least three suggestions they would offer a local retailer who did not meet targeted sales.**

INPUT

- Explain that sometimes a company can be measured in other areas besides financial data.
- Direct students to the performance measures. Ask a student to read the objective of each, how each is measured, and the target goal of each measure.

INTERNAL BUSINESS

Internal business includes the basic processes for providing a product or service that has value to customers and creates value for shareholders. Internal business performance measures would answer the question, "To satisfy our shareholders and customers, at what business processes must we excel?" Typical internal business performance measures could include the amount of materials wasted in a manufacturing process, the percentage of defective units produced, the time to produce a product, machinery down time due to lack of routine maintenance, and the number of sales returns.

CUSTOMER SERVICE

Customer service includes identifying customers and providing the products and/or services they desire. Customer service performance measures would answer the question, "To achieve our vision, how should we appear to our customers?" Typical customer service performance measures could include percentage of repeat customers, the percentage of customer referrals, and market share.

FINANCIAL

Financial, which businesses usually measure, includes traditional ratios and measures already discussed in this textbook. Financial performance measures would answer the question, "To succeed financially, how should we appear to our shareholders?" Typical financial performance measures could include earnings per share, the current ratio, the price/earnings ratio, the debt/equity ratio, return on investment, and profit margin.

OBJECTIVES, MEASURES, TARGETS, AND INITIATIVES

The balanced scorecard system is more than just setting performance objectives. Within each area, a company should identify its objectives, determine how outcomes will be measured, set target goals, and develop an initiative to help ensure its objectives are met. For example, in the customer service area, one objective could be to increase customer satisfaction. The measure used could be a follow-up survey that rates customer satisfaction on a scale of five to one. The target goal would be to receive a score of five from 75% of the surveys taken. An initiative to help ensure success would be to hold training classes on customer service.

The balanced scorecard system emphasizes that there is a cause-and-effect relationship between the four focus areas. Employees who are trained better will have a positive effect on internal business practices. Better and more efficient business practices will have a positive effect on customers. Satisfied customers will have a positive effect on the financial results of the company.

The balanced scorecard for Masonville College is shown below.

Performance Measure	Objective	How Measured	Target Goal
Learning/Growth	Increase the awareness and observance of confidentiality laws.	Number of employees who complete an online course on confidentiality laws.	25% of employees complete the online course each year.
	Improve employee use of computerized purchase order system.	Percent of purchase orders that are submitted electronically.	No less than 25% increase in percent of purchases orders submitted electronically each year.
Internal Business	Increase the number of applicants for faculty positions.	Average number of applications received for faculty positions.	No less than 10% increase in average number of applications received for faculty positions.
	Update faculty computers.	Number of new computers put into service.	No less than 20% of faculty computers replaced each year.
Customer Service	Decrease the number of days to process entrance applications that are complete.	Number of days from receipt of complete application to sending approval or non approval to applicant.	90% of applicants will have a response within 10 business days.
	Decrease the number of books returned to bookstore because the wrong book was purchased.	Number of returns processed because the wrong book was purchased.	No more than 6% of books purchased are returned because the incorrect book was purchased.
Financial	Increase the total credit hours enrolled by students	Total credit hours of tuition paid.	No less than a 2% increase in total credit hours per semester.
	Decrease utilities costs.	Total utilities costs incurred.	No less than a 5% decrease in utilities cost by the end of the fiscal period.

DIFFERENTIATED INSTRUCTION

Visual/Spatial learners learn best by creating visual images using three-dimensional space. Ask students to prepare and display a comparative income statement, sample budgets, and a performance report. Each should be labeled properly to show the interrelationship among the forms.

© iStockphoto.com/burwellphotography

FORENSIC ACCOUNTING

Shell Companies

Joseph Wells may be the most recognized name in forensic accounting. As the founder of the Association of Certified Fraud Examiners, Mr. Wells has led the charge to heighten accountants' and managers' awareness of the damage that fraud can have on business organizations. One method Mr. Wells uses to share his knowledge is to publish articles in the *Journal of Accountancy*, the monthly publication of the American Institute of Certified Public Accountants.

In a series of *Journal of Accountancy* articles, Mr. Wells identified several tests that auditors should perform to search for the signs, or "red flags," of expenditure fraud. With improper accounting controls, an employee may be able to create a false vendor and issue checks to the vendor. These false vendors are often referred to as "shell companies." A common red flag of a shell company includes an address consisting of a post office box. Because a shell company does not have a physical address, it must have a location for the check to be delivered. A fraudster can easily rent a post office box.

ACTIVITY

Malcolm Promotions has hired Webb & Associates, a public accounting firm, to perform the annual audit of its financial statements. Sari Mariza, a first-year staff auditor, has been assigned the task of performing tests on Malcolm's vendor data file. The file has been provided to Sari as a tab delimited text file. Thus, Sari must first import the data into Excel before searching for any red flags of a shell company. Each data item, such as company name and address, is separated by a tab. Excel uses the tabs to identify the data items and place them in the appropriate columns.

INSTRUCTIONS

Open the spreadsheet FA_CH15 and complete the steps on the Instructions tab.

FORENSIC ACCOUNTING

The series of articles can be obtained online at www.journalofaccountancy.com. Click the Open Advanced Search link; enter Wells as the author; and change the date range to July 2002 to September 2002.

When importing the tab delimited file, students are required to recognize that the vendor numbers should be entered as a text field. Examine the third record to ensure that both the vendor number and zip code begin with a zero.

When filtering the data, students are provided with an initial suggestion for the filter (P*O*). However, this filter results in some unintended results. Students must determine how to modify the filter to remove the unintended results. Most students will conclude that a filter of P*O*Box will solve the problem. However, one unintended address remains (5714 Potter's Sandbox). Adding a space before Box in the filter eliminates this final unintended result.

Students are instructed to describe the filter used by writing a statement such as "The results were obtained by filtering the Address column for items containing P*O* Box."

Answer

Nine vendors.

FORMATIVE ASSESSMENT

- This is an ongoing process. Circulate around the classroom or lab, observing which students have difficulty with the assignments.
- Troubleshooting: Diagnose the kinds of problems students have with this lesson. Students may have difficulty remembering or implementing projection guides when calculating various amounts.
- Assess student understanding by checking solutions to Independent Practice assignments and noting their answers to the Terms Review and Audit Your Understanding questions.

CHECK FOR UNDERSTANDING

Terms Review
- Call on students to define each term in the Terms Review. Definitions are given in the Glossary.

Audit Your Understanding
- Call on students to answer the Audit Your Understanding questions. Answers are given in Appendix D of the textbook.

GUIDED PRACTICE

Work Together
- Have students write the solution to the Work Together problem as you guide the class through the steps.
- Direct students to complete a performance report.

INDEPENDENT PRACTICE

On Your Own
- Assign the On Your Own problem to be worked independently.
- Use the Formative Assessment techniques to diagnose student understanding.

Application Problem
- Assign Application Problem 15-4.

Online Working Papers
- Students can access the Lesson 15-4 problems using this software.

RETEACH
- Ask students to describe the different parts of a performance report.
- Ask students to discuss the components of a balanced scorecard.

CLOSURE
- Ask students to describe similarities and differences between preparing a budgeted income statement and a performance report.
- Ask students to explain the purpose of a balanced scorecard.

Essential Question
- What should be measured on a balanced scorecard for a restaurant, a personal trainer, and a hair salon? *(Answers will vary, but might include the following: Restaurant—product sales, customer service, customer wait time; Personal Trainer—number of clients, client satisfaction, reduction in number of injuries; Hair Salon—number of haircuts, inventory of supplies needed, employee rewards for product sales.)*

End of Lesson Review

LO10 Prepare a performance report.

LO11 Identify performance measures in a balanced scorecard system.

Terms Review

performance report

balanced scorecard

Audit your understanding

1. Why is knowing about significant differences between projected and actual income statement amounts important?
2. How does a performance report differ from a comparative income statement?
3. A balanced scorecard system develops performance measures in what four areas?
4. In addition to identifying objectives in each of the four areas, what else is required by a balanced scorecard system?

Work together 15-4

Completing a performance report

A partially completed performance report for Maddox Corporation is in the *Working Papers*. Maddox Corporation has just completed its first quarter of the fiscal year ended December 31, 20X3. Management is interested in identifying significant favorable and unfavorable differences between projected and actual amounts. Maddox only considers changes of 5.0% or more to be significant. Management reviews changes in net sales and cost of merchandise regardless of the amount of change.

1. Complete the performance report by calculating the increase (decrease) from budget and percentage increase (decrease) from budget.
2. Place an asterisk (*) in the right margin by every item that is significant.

On your own 15-4

Completing a performance report

A partially completed performance report for Northstar, Inc., is in the *Working Papers*. Northstar has just completed its first quarter of the fiscal year ended December 31, 20X3. Management is interested in identifying significant favorable and unfavorable differences between projected and actual amounts. Northstar, Inc., only considers changes of 5.0% or more to be significant. Management reviews changes in net sales and cost of merchandise regardless of the amount of change.

1. Complete the performance report by calculating the increase (decrease) from budget and percentage increase (decrease) from budget.
2. Place an asterisk (*) in the right margin by every item that is significant.

EXTENDED LEARNING
- Assign Forensic Accounting on page 455.

A Look at Accounting Software

Preparing Budgets Using Open Database Connectivity (ODBC)

The *A Look at Accounting Software* feature illustrates generally the advantages of automated accounting systems compared to the manual systems presented in the content of a chapter. With analytical activity such as budgeting, however, spreadsheet software improves the efficiency of both manual and automated accounting systems. While it is possible to create detailed budgets in automated systems, the database structure of accounting software doesn't allow the kind of "what if" analysis that can be done in a spreadsheet. Still, it is important to have budget numbers in the automated accounting system so that reports can be created to compare actual performance with budgeted expectations.

One solution for creating spreadsheets for budgets is to use open database connectivity (ODBC) to export financial data from the accounting system. Using an ODBC transfer, data from the accounting system (e.g., end-of-period balances from the general ledger) are downloaded to a spreadsheet, where complex analysis can be performed as budgets are finalized. After the budgeting process is completed, the budget data are uploaded to the accounting system. If a budget needs to be modified, changes can be made directly in the accounting system or revised in the spreadsheet and uploaded again.

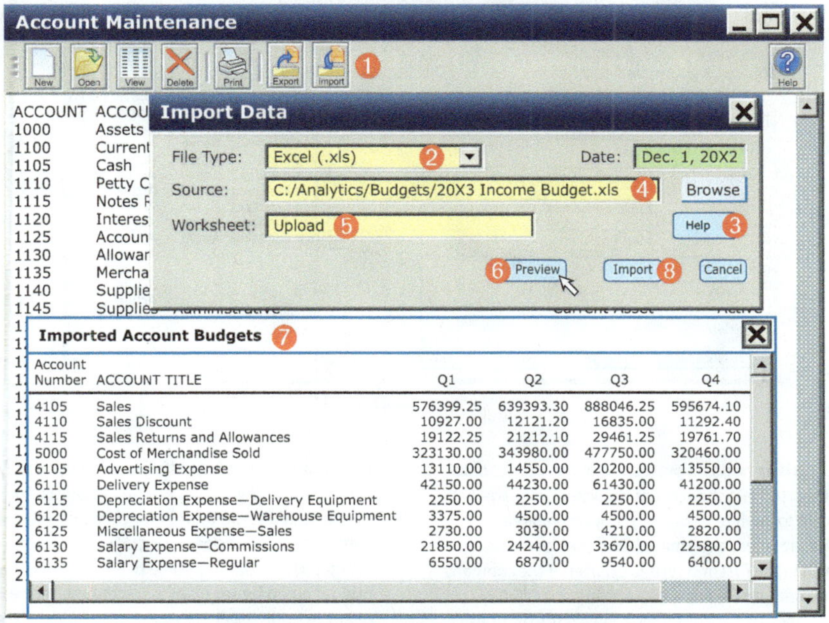

Account Number	ACCOUNT TITLE	Q1	Q2	Q3	Q4
4105	Sales	576399.25	639393.30	888046.25	595674.10
4110	Sales Discount	10927.00	12121.20	16835.00	11292.40
4115	Sales Returns and Allowances	19122.25	21212.10	29461.25	19761.70
5000	Cost of Merchandise Sold	323130.00	343980.00	477750.00	320460.00
6105	Advertising Expense	13110.00	14550.00	20200.00	13550.00
6110	Delivery Expense	42150.00	44230.00	61430.00	41200.00
6115	Depreciation Expense—Delivery Equipment	2250.00	2250.00	2250.00	2250.00
6120	Depreciation Expense—Warehouse Equipment	3375.00	4500.00	4500.00	4500.00
6125	Miscellaneous Expense—Sales	2730.00	3030.00	4210.00	2820.00
6130	Salary Expense—Commissions	21850.00	24240.00	33670.00	22580.00
6135	Salary Expense—Regular	6550.00	6870.00	9540.00	6400.00

Entered by user   Entered automatically

1. The controller for Tint My Windows, Inc., began working on budgets for the coming year (20X3) by exporting data from the accounting system to Excel. The controller and company management completed the budgets and are in the process of importing the budgets into the company's accounting system. On December 1, 20X2, the controller accessed the **Account Maintenance** window. The system displayed all accounts in the chart of accounts. Next, the controller clicked on the **Import** button. That action opened the Import Data dialog box.
2. The accounting system allows users to import data in several different formats. The controller selected Excel as the file type.

A Look at Accounting Software

Several different methods are usually applied in preparing budgets. Different methods may be applied to different types of accounts. For example, periodic insurance expenses may be equal for each period, whereas sales revenues might vary greatly from one period to the next. So dividing an annual insurance budget into equal amounts for each period makes sense, but to budget sales, it would be better to estimate changes for each period—perhaps for each product line—based on market projections. Alternatively, costs of merchandise might logically be estimated based on historical trends.

Budget Strategies

For each account,

- increase or decrease the prior year budgeted amount.
- increase or decrease the prior year actual amount.
- estimate a budget amount based on an analysis of market and economic conditions (zero-based budgeting).

Calculation Methods

For each account,

- apply an estimated percentage increase or decrease.
- apply an estimated dollar amount of increase or decrease.
- apply a historical percentage increase or decrease.

Range of Accounts

Choose a budget strategy and calculation method to apply to each single account.

Choose a budget strategy and calculation method to apply to a designated range of accounts.

Choose one budget strategy and calculation method and apply to all accounts.

Fiscal Periods

Apply the chosen budget strategy and calculation method to each account for each fiscal period.

Calculate an annual estimated budget for each account and divide into equal amounts for each fiscal period.

In a class discussion, you can challenge students to weigh the pros and cons of different budgeting methods for selected accounts.

3 Before data can be imported, it must be precisely formatted, so that the system knows how to enter the data to the proper accounts and budget periods. The Help button provides detailed guidance on how to format spreadsheet data.

4 The controller browsed to the Excel file containing the 20X3 income budget.

5 Since the budget spreadsheet is made up of several worksheets, it was necessary to tell the system which worksheet contained the budget data.

6 The controller clicked the **Preview** button to verify that the formats were correct and the data would be imported correctly.

7 The system opened a pop-up display showing each account affecting the income budget with the quarterly budget amounts set by management.

8 After verifying that the data would import correctly, the controller clicked the **Import** button to bring the data into the accounting system.

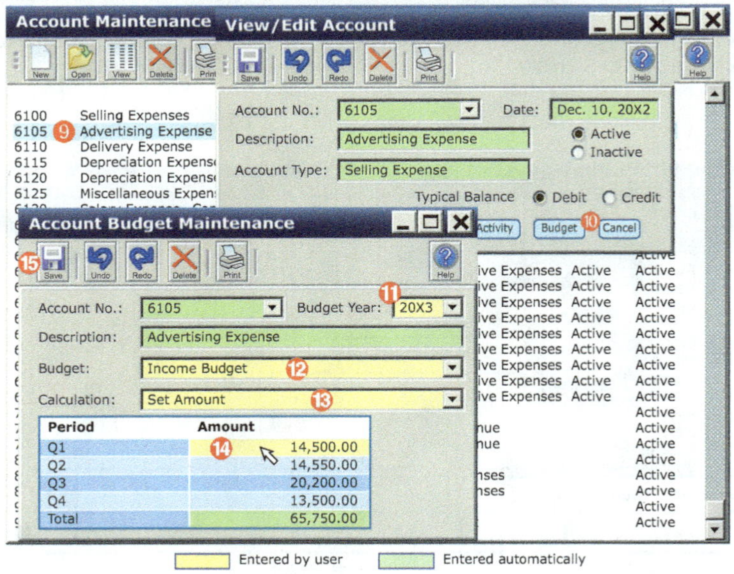

9 Budgeting is an ongoing process. After the budget data were imported into the accounting system, management continued to analyze its business opportunities and risks. Management determined that sales would be improved in the first and second quarters if the company took advantage of a unique advertising opportunity. On December 10, the controller accessed the **Account Maintenance** window again to modify a budget number. By scrolling down and clicking on account **6105**, the controller opened the **View/Edit Account** window displaying the advertising expense account.

10 The controller clicked the **Budget** button, which opened the Account Budget Maintenance window.

11 Budget year **20X3** was selected.

12 As you learned in this chapter, several budgets commonly are prepared. The controller selected the **Income Budget.**

13 The accounting system offers several options for calculating and entering budget amounts. For example, to set the budget for this account, the controller could choose to increase last year's budgeted amounts by some percentage. Or, the new budget could be set up as a percentage increase over the prior year's actual expense. In this case, the controller simply wanted to change one number and selected **Set Amount.** That option enabled the controller to enter or change each number.

14 The system displayed the quarterly budget amounts that were imported earlier, and the controller increased the Q1 advertising expense budget from $13,110.00 to $14,500.00.

15 After making the change, the controller must click **Save** to enter the new budget number.

Chapter Summary

A budget is an estimate of the financial future of a business. Preparing a budget requires a known set of company goals. Once a budget is developed, it should be communicated to all employees. Two major budgets are the budgeted income statement and the cash budget. Supporting budgets are used to develop the two major budgets.

Budgets are usually prepared for a one-year period and are prepared ahead of time, so that they can be communicated to the appropriate managers. Sources of budget information include company records, general economic information, and company staff and managers. Managers also need to use good judgment.

Once goals are determined, the budgets are developed in the following order: sales budget, purchases budget, selling expenses budget, administrative expenses budget, other revenue and expenses budget, budgeted income statement, cash receipts budget, cash payments budget, and the cash budget.

A performance report compares the budgeted and the actual revenues and expenses for a budget period. It calculates the differences between budgeted amounts and actual amounts, both on a dollar basis and a percentage basis. A performance report helps identify problem areas while there is still time to make adjustments.

The balanced scorecard is a method used to provide a more balanced approach to performance evaluation. A company using the balanced scorecard will determine performance objectives in four areas: learning and growth, internal business, customer service, and financial. In addition to setting objectives, the company will identify the measure to be used to determine if the objective is met, determine a target score to be achieved, and develop an initiative to help ensure success.

Contingent Liabilities

EXPLORE ACCOUNTING

Business transactions affect the accounts of a business and are reflected in journal entries, which are posted to accounts. However, other items that can affect the financial position of the company are not entered into the books automatically.

One such item is called a contingent liability. A contingent liability is a possible future obligation that arises from a current condition and is dependent upon a future event occurring. One example of a contingent liability is a pending lawsuit against a company. The possible future obligation is the chance that the company may lose the lawsuit and have to pay a penalty or fine. The current condition is the fact that the lawsuit has already been filed. The future event is the ruling of the court. Depending on the court ruling, the company may or may not have a financial obligation.

The accountant must analyze each contingent liability to determine if it must be included in the financial statements. The first step is to determine how likely it is that a loss will occur in the future. GAAP list three possibilities: probable, possible, and remote. If it is probable that the loss will occur and if the loss can be reasonably estimated, the company must add a liability to the balance sheet in the amount of the probable loss. At the same time, a loss must be shown on the income statement.

If it is probable that the loss will occur but the loss cannot be reasonably estimated, the company does not have to add a liability to its balance sheet. However, the company must disclose the possible loss in the notes that accompany the financial statements.

If the chance of loss is possible, the company must treat the possibility in the same way it would treat a probable loss. If the chance of loss is remote, the company does not have to do anything.

A company must budget for the actual payment of such a liability—if it is deemed to be a probable loss. Depending on the amount of the probable loss, a company may have to arrange to borrow money or sell other assets.

INSTRUCTIONS

For each of the following activities, state if a liability must be added to the balance sheet, if the company must disclose the activity in the notes, or if no reporting of the activity is required.

1. The company is involved in a lawsuit. The legal team thinks it is probable that the company will lose the case, but it has no idea of the amount of probable loss.
2. The company has published a $1-off coupon in the local paper. The company has estimated that 35% of the coupons will be redeemed.

© iStockphoto.com/Makhnach_M

CLOSURE

- Review the Chapter Summary.
- Ask students to prepare a list of the new concepts introduced in this chapter.

Essential Questions

- Why is it important for a business to obtain so many budgets from various departments? (*All department managers must work together to see their departments' impact on the overall budget and goals of the company.*)
- Who uses the performance report? How and why would they use it? (*All managers should use a performance report to compare their budgeted amounts with actual amounts. This information will allow management to determine future objectives.*)
- Couldn't a manager just prepare a budgeted income statement and a performance report? Explain. (*If a manager stops at this point, he or she is not creating an action plan for the future.*)

EXTENDED LEARNING

- Review A Look at Accounting Software on pages 457 and 458.
- Assign Explore Accounting on page 459.

EXPLORE ACCOUNTING

Answers

1. The loss is probable but cannot be estimated. Therefore, the company must disclose the lawsuit in the notes.
2. The chance of having to pay the coupon amount (for at least some of the coupons) is probable, and an estimate of the total cost can be made. The company must include a liability on the balance sheet for the estimated amount.

CHECK FIGURES

For complete solutions to Chapter 15 problems, see the Teacher's Edition of the Working Papers.

Application Problem 15-1

1. Net Sales, 1st Quarter, $1,750,000.
   Projected Unit Sales, 20X3, 2nd Quarter, $134,000.
   Net Sales, 4th Quarter, $1,316.000.
2. Cost of Purchases, 1st Quarter, $831,000.
   Purchases, 2nd Quarter, 137,900.
   Cost of Purchases, 4th Quarter, $786,000.

Application Problem 15-2

1. Total Selling Expenses, 1st Quarter, $442,250.
   Salary Expense—Sales, 2nd Quarter, $131,320.
   Total Selling Expenses, 3rd Quarter, $513,090.
2. Payroll Taxes Expenses, Annual Budget, $66,530.
   Total Administrative Expenses, 1st Quarter, $225,580.
   Uncollectible Accounts Expense, 2nd Quarter, $9,380.
   Total Administrative Expenses, 4th Quarter, $185,050.
3. Interest Expense, 3rd Quarter, $5,000.
4. Gross Profit on Sales, Annual Budget, $3,277,200.
   Income from Operations, 2nd Quarter, $162,420.
   Cost of Merchandise Sold, 3rd Quarter, $1,102,500.
   Federal Income Tax Expense, 4th Quarter, $49,800.

Apply Your Understanding

INSTRUCTIONS: Download problem instructions for Excel, QuickBooks, and Sage 50 from the textbook companion website at www.C21accounting.com.

15-1 Application Problem: Preparing a sales budget and a purchases budget LO1, 2

1. Complete the sales budget.
2. Complete the purchases budget.
3. Print the worksheets.

Craine Corporation wishes to prepare a sales budget and a purchases budget for 20X3. Management has set a sales goal of 500,000 units. After reviewing price trends, the sales manager projects that Craine Corporation will need to increase its unit sales price from $12.50 to $14.00 in the first quarter.

The sales manager, after checking with the company's merchandise suppliers, projects that the cost of merchandise will increase from $7.00 to $7.50 per unit in the first quarter of 20X3.

Quarterly unit sales for 20X2 are as follows:

1st quarter	117,000 units	3rd quarter	137,800 units
2nd quarter	125,400 units	4th quarter	87,800 units

After considering the time required to reorder merchandise, the sales manager requests that 30.0% of the next quarter's unit sales be available in the prior quarter's ending inventory. Ending inventory for 20X2 is 54,400 units. Management projects that 130,000 units will be sold in the first quarter of 20X4.

Instructions:

1. Prepare a sales budget (Schedule 1) for the four quarters ended December 31, 20X3. Craine Corporation rounds unit amounts to the nearest hundred units, dollar amounts to the nearest $10, and percentage amounts to the nearest 0.1%.
2. Prepare a purchases budget (Schedule 2) for the four quarters ended December 31, 20X3.
   Save your work for use in Problem 15-2.

15-2 Application Problem: Preparing budgets for selling expenses, administrative expenses, and other expenses and preparing a budgeted income statement LO3, 4, 5, 6

Use the information given and the budgets prepared in Problem 15-1. Additional information is given below.

Expenses for 20X3 are projected as follows: Except where noted, percentages are based on projected net sales. For these items, calculate each quarter's amount by multiplying the percentage times that quarter's net sales. Calculate the annual total by adding the four quarterly amounts. When a dollar amount is given, the total amount should be divided equally among the four quarters.

Selling Expenses		Administrative Expenses	
Advertising Expense	4.5%	Depr. Exp.—Office Equip.	$44,000.00
Delivery Expense	2.0%	Insurance Expense	$14,400.00
Depr. Exp.—Delivery Equipment	$75,000.00	Misc. Exp.—Admin.	$16,000.00
Depr. Exp.—Warehouse Equipment	$84,000.00	Payroll Taxes Expense	12.0% of total salaries
Misc. Exp.—Sales	5.5%	Rent Expense	$72,000.00
Salary Exp.—Sales	7.0%	Salary Exp.—Admin.	$64,400.00
Supplies Expense—Sales	4.0%	Supplies Exp.—Admin.	$30,000.00
		Uncoll. Accts. Exp.	0.5%
		Utilities Exp.	8.0%

Interest Expense is estimated to be $20,000.00. Federal income taxes are calculated using the tax rate table shown in this chapter. Equal quarterly income tax payments are based on the projected annual federal income tax expense.

Instructions:

1. Prepare a selling expenses budget (Schedule 3) for the four quarters ended December 31, 20X3. Craine Corporation rounds all amounts to the nearest $10.
2. Prepare an administrative expenses budget (Schedule 4) for the four quarters ended December 31, 20X3.
3. Prepare an other revenue and expenses budget (Schedule 5) for the four quarters ended December 31, 20X3.
4. Prepare a budgeted income statement for the four quarters ended December 31, 20X3.

   Save your work for use in Problem 15-3.

1. Complete the selling expenses budget.
2. Complete the administrative expense budget.
3. Complete the budgeted income statement.
4. Print the worksheets.

15-3 Application Problem: Preparing a cash receipts budget, a cash payments budget, and a cash budget LO7, 8, 9

1. Complete the cash receipts budget.
2. Complete the cash payments budget.
3. Complete the cash budget.
4. Print the worksheets.

Use the information given and the budgets prepared in Problems 15-1 and 15-2. Additional information is given below.

a. Actual amounts for the fourth quarter of 20X2: sales, $1,229,200.00; purchases, $369,600.00.

b. The balance of cash on hand on January 1, 20X3, is $122,500.00.

c. In each quarter, cash sales are 15.0% and collections of accounts receivable are 35.0% of the projected net sales for the current quarter. Collections from the preceding quarter's net sales are 49.5% of that quarter. Uncollectible accounts expense is 0.5% of net sales.

d. In each quarter, cash payments for cash purchases are 20.0% and for accounts payable 65.0% of the purchases for the current quarter. Cash payments for purchases of the preceding quarter are 15.0% of that quarter.

e. In the first quarter, Craine will borrow $200,000.00 on a promissory note and will purchase equipment costing $350,000.00 for cash. In each quarter, dividends of $15,000.00 will be paid in cash. In the fourth quarter, the promissory note plus interest will be paid in cash, $220,000.00.

f. Equal quarterly income tax payments are based on projected annual federal income tax expense.

Instructions:

1. Prepare a cash receipts budget (Schedule A) for the four quarters ended December 31, 20X3. Round all amounts to the nearest $10.
2. Prepare a cash payments budget (Schedule B) for the four quarters ended December 31, 20X3.
3. Prepare a cash budget for the four quarters ended December 31, 20X3.

Application Problem 15-3

1. Total Cash Receipts from Sales, 1st Quarter, $1,483,450.
   Total Cash Receipts, 2nd Quarter, $1,804,250.
   Total Cash Receipts, 4th Quarter, $1,676,710.
2. Total Payments from Purchases, 1st Quarter, $761,790.
   Total Cash Operating Expenses, 2nd Quarter, $648,450.
   Total Other Cash Payments, 3rd Quarter, $64,800.
   Fixed Asset Purchases, 4th Quarter, $0.
3. Cash Balance—Ending, 1st Quarter, $21,030.
   Cash Available, 2nd Quarter, $1,825,280.
   Cash Balance—Beginning, 4th Quarter, $303,790.

Application Problem 15-4

Advertising Expense, Amount over, $6,250; Percentage, 7.9.

Total Selling Expenses, Amount over, $13,650; Percentage 3.1.

Utilities Expense, Amount over, $1,500; Percentage, 1.1.

Mastery Problem 15-M

1. Net Sales, 3rd Quarter, $452,400.
2. Cost of Purchases, 2nd Quarter, $318,750.
3. Total Selling Expenses, 1st Quarter, $27,380.
4. Total Administrative Expenses, Annual Budget, $149,660.
6. Gross Profit on Sales, Annual Budget, $461,250.

   Net Income after Federal Income Tax, Annual Budget, $113,510.
7. Total Cash Receipts from Sales, 3rd Quarter, $447,310.
8. Total Cash Payments, 3rd Quarter, $407,730.
9. Cash Balance—Beginning, 3rd Quarter, $79,770.

INDEPENDENT PRACTICE

- Assign Mastery Problem 15-M for students as a culminating problem combining all new learning from the chapter.
- Assign Challenge Problem 15-C to accelerated students who work at a faster pace.
- Assign Study Guide 15.
- Students can access Online Working Papers to work end-of-chapter problems on the computer.
- Direct students to the C21 Accounting companion website for additional practice and review opportunities.

FORMATIVE ASSESSMENT

- Review solutions to the assigned problems in class, diagnosing trouble spots.

15-4 Application Problem: Completing a performance report LO10

1. Complete the Performance Report.
2. Print the worksheet.

AAONLINE

1. Go to www.cengage.com/login
2. Click on AA Online to access.
3. Go to the online assignment and follow the instructions.

A partially completed performance report for Craine Corporation is in the *Working Papers*.

Craine Corporation has just completed its first quarter of the fiscal year ended December 31, 20X3. Management is interested in identifying significant favorable and unfavorable differences between projected and actual amounts. Craine only considers changes of 5.0% or more to be significant. Management reviews changes in net sales and cost of merchandise regardless of the amount of change.

Instructions:

1. Complete the performance report by calculating the increase (decrease) from budget and percentage increase (decrease) from budget.
2. Place an asterisk (*) in the right margin by every item that is significant.

15-M Mastery Problem: Preparing a budgeted income statement and a cash budget with supporting budgets LO1, 2, 3, 4, 5, 6, 7, 8, 9

On December 31, 20X2, the accounting records of ZZZ Company show the following unit sales for 20X2:

1st quarter	44,000 units	3rd quarter	69,600 units
2nd quarter	68,800 units	4th quarter	57,600 units

The following are additional actual amounts for the 4th quarter of 20X2:

Sales (57,600 units @ $5.60)	$322,560
Purchases (52,800 units @ $4.00)	$211,200
Ending inventory	25,000 units

Management has established a unit sales goal of 260,000 units for 20X3 and 48,000 units for the first quarter of 20X4. The sales manager, after reviewing price trends and checking with the company's merchandise suppliers, projects that the unit cost of merchandise will increase from $4.00 to $4.25 in the first quarter of 20X3. Because of the increase in costs, the company will need to increase its unit sales price from $5.60 to $6.00 in the first quarter of 20X3.

After considering the time required to reorder merchandise, the sales manager requests that 40.0% of each quarter's unit sales be available in the prior quarter's ending inventory.

Expenses are projected as shown below. Except where noted, percentages are based on quarterly projected net sales. For these items, calculate each quarter's amount by multiplying the percentage times that quarter's net sales. Calculate the annual total by adding the four quarterly amounts. When a dollar amount is given, the total amount should be divided equally among the four quarters.

Interest expense for each quarter is projected to be $2,500.

Federal income taxes are calculated using the tax rate table shown in this chapter. Equal quarterly income tax payments are based on the projected annual federal income tax expense.

Additional information is as follows:

a. The balance of cash on hand on January 1, 20X3, is $83,200.

b. In each quarter, cash sales are 10.0% and collections of accounts receivable are 40.0% of the projected net sales for the current quarter. Collections from the preceding quarter's net sales are 49.4% of that quarter. Uncollectible accounts expense is 0.6% of net sales.

Selling Expenses		Administrative Expenses	
Advertising Expense	1.2%	Depreciation Expense—Office Equipment	$7,200
Delivery Expense	0.6%	Insurance Expense	$8,400
Depreciation Expense—Delivery Equipment	$ 4,800	Miscellaneous Expense— Administrative	$6,000
Depreciation Expense—Warehouse Equipment	$13,360	Payroll Taxes Expense	12.0% of salaries
Miscellaneous Expense—Sales	0.4%	Rent Expense	$19,200
Salary Expense—Sales	5.0%	Salary Expense—Administrative	$50,400
Supplies Expense—Sales	0.8%	Supplies Expense—Administrative	$5,600
		Uncollectible Accounts Expense	0.6%
		Utilities Expense	1.8%

c. In each quarter, cash payments for cash purchases are 10.0% and for accounts payable 55.0% of the purchases for the current quarter. Cash payments for purchases of the preceding quarter are 35.0% of that quarter.

d. In the first quarter, $80,000 will be borrowed on a promissory note, and equipment costing $60,000 will be purchased for cash. In each quarter, dividends of $20,000 will be paid in cash. In the fourth quarter, the promissory note plus interest will be paid in cash, $90,000.

Instructions:

Prepare the following budgets for the year ended December 31, 20X3. Round percentage amounts to the nearest 0.1%, unit amounts to the nearest 100 units, and dollar amounts to the nearest $10.

1. Prepare a sales budget (Schedule 1).
2. Prepare a purchases budget (Schedule 2).
3. Prepare a selling expenses budget (Schedule 3).
4. Prepare an administrative expenses budget (Schedule 4).
5. Prepare an other revenue and expenses budget (Schedule 5).
6. Prepare a budgeted income statement (Schedule 6).
7. Prepare a cash receipts budget (Schedule A).
8. Prepare a cash payments budget (Schedule B).
9. Prepare a cash budget.

1. Complete the sales budget and the purchases budget.
2. Complete the selling expenses budget and the administrative expenses budget.
3. Complete the budgeted income statement and the cash receipts budget.
4. Complete the cash payments budget and the cash budget.

RETEACH

- Call on students to describe how they avoid the trouble spots diagnosed.
- Use reteaching suggestions from lesson plans as required.
- Assign Recycling Problem 15-R if needed.
- Assign 21st Century Skills on page 464.
- Assign Analyzing Home Depot's Financial Statements on page 465.

SUMMATIVE EVALUATION

- Chapter 15 Test
- Cognero for Chapter 15

COMMON CORE AND INTERDISCIPLINARY STUDIES

Extended learning features and activities present numerous opportunities to implement Common Core Standards through interdisciplinary studies. Practice is provided in the common core areas of English Language Arts & Literacy and Mathematical Practice. Many of these activities require short, critical-thinking and decision-making responses that apply reading, writing, speaking, listening, language, media and technology, and mathematical skills.

Challenge Problem 15-C

Customer Service: One possible objective: Decrease the number of returned bicycles.

21ST CENTURY SKILLS

Answers

1. At the time of printing, 12 states prohibited payday loans or had regulations that made the payday loan business unprofitable in the state.
2. Answers will vary depending on the states selected.

15-C Challenge Problem: Balanced scorecard LO11

Superior Bicycles is implementing a balanced scorecard system. It has developed the following performance measures:

Increase the number of cross-trained employees

Increase the return on investment

Decrease the returns on parts purchased by Superior Bicycles

Decrease the number of times parts are out of stock

Improve employee turnover

Decrease the number of returned bicycles

Decrease operating costs

Decrease the time from sale to delivery of bicycle to customer

Use the form provided in the *Working Papers.* The first performance measure has been completed as an example.

Instructions:

1. Identify two performance measures for each of the four scorecard areas, and write them in the form next to the appropriate area (Learning/Growth, Internal Business, Customer Service, and Financial).
2. For each performance measure, list one way it could be measured and a possible target goal.

21st Century Skills

Avoid the Payday Trap

PARTNERSHIP FOR 21ST CENTURY SKILLS

Theme: Financial, Economic, Business, and Entrepreneurial Literacy

Skills: ICT Literacy, Communication and Collaboration, Critical Thinking and Problem Solving

Making wise financial decisions and sticking to a budget are the best ways to be prepared for unexpected financial emergencies. However, actual spending is not always the same as planned on a personal budget.

To help bridge the gap when temporary cash shortfalls result, some people turn to quick alternatives, such as short-term payday loans. These loans, also referred to as *cash advances*, provide quick cash without a credit check or collateral. These short-term loans are intended to carry one through to the next paycheck.

Payday loans are legal and regulated in many states, but they are illegal in some states, primarily due to the interest rates charged. At first, the interest rates may not appear to be excessive. However, when the rate is applied to the term of the loan, the borrower may be paying an interest rate of as much as 780% or more. Many people have difficulty paying back these loans in the required time, and they begin a cycle of loan traps.

APPLICATION

1. The Consumer Federation of America has created a website, www.paydayloaninfo.org, to help educate consumers about payday loans in each state.
   a. Using this website or others found through research, identify five states that prohibit payday loans and five states that permit payday loans.
   b. Prepare a spreadsheet with the following headings: Name of State, Legal Status, Maximum Amount per Loan, APR for 14-Day Loan on $100, Maximum Number of Outstanding Loans per Year.
2. Write a paragraph in which you compare and contrast the data obtained for the ten states.

Analyzing Home Depot's financial statements

From net sales to the average amount of each sales ticket, the Five-Year Summary of Financial and Operating Results on page B-15 of Appendix B in this textbook provides a historical perspective to Home Depot's growth. This Summary reports trends that are an important input in the budgeting process. The first step of the budgeting process is to establish operational goals.

INSTRUCTIONS

Use the information in the Summary to suggest operational goals for Home Depot for 2013. For each of the following items, examine the trend from 2009 to 2012 and decide what operational goal you believe Home Depot should attempt to achieve in 2013. Be prepared to defend your goals in class.

1. What percent increase in comparable store sales will Home Depot achieve during 2013?
2. Home Depot will control product costs and achieve what gross profit percentage in 2013? (*Hint:* Gross profit percentage and gross margin are similar terms.)
3. What average ticket price will Home Depot achieve in 2013? (*Hint:* Calculate the percent increase in the average ticket price each year.)

ANALYZING HOME DEPOT'S FINANCIAL STATEMENTS

Answers

Operational goals based on these trends will differ. An example of a solution follows:

1. Home Depot will achieve a 5.5% increase in comparable store sales during 2013.
2. Home Depot will control product costs and achieve a 35.0% gross profit percentage in 2013.
3. Home Depot will achieve an average ticket price of $56.81 in 2013, a 3.5% increase over 2012.

Chapter 16 Management Decision Making Using Cost-Volume-Profit Analysis

Scope & Sequence

	New	Review/Enrich
Introduction		
Introduce the Chapter		
Lesson 16-1: Cost Characteristics That Influence Decisions		
Management Decisions	✓	
Total Cost versus Unit Cost	✓	
Variable Cost Characteristics	✓	
Fixed Costs	✓	
Gross Profit and Contribution Margin Income Statements	✓	
Contribution Margin Per Unit	✓	
Contribution Margin Rate	✓	
Lesson 16-2: Determining Breakeven		
Calculating the Breakeven Point	✓	
Breakeven Income Statement	✓	
Calculating the Breakeven Point for New Products	✓	
Lesson 16-3: Decisions That Affect Net Income		
Calculating Sales to Earn a Planned Net Income	✓	
Effect of Volume Changes on Net Income	✓	
Effect of Cost Changes at Average Volume	✓	
Effect of Cost Changes at Above-Average Volume	✓	
Effect of Changes in Costs on the Contribution Margin Rate	✓	
Effect of a Change in the Sales Price	✓	
Using Breakeven to Plan a Sales Mix	✓	
Closure		

Enhancing Instruction

Features	Common Core Standards
• Accounting in the Real World: Nintendo	• ELAL—reading
• Ethics in Action: Fraud Awareness • Financial Literacy: House Poor	• ELAL—reading, writing • Mathematics
• Why Accounting?: Computerized Breakeven Analysis • Careers in Accounting: Loan Officer	• ELAL—reading, writing • ELAL—reading
• Think Like an Accountant: Analyzing Relationships to Predict Sales	• Mathematics
• Explore Accounting • 21st Century Skills • Analyzing Home Depot's Financial Statements	• Mathematics • ELAL—reading, writing • Mathematics

ELAL = English Language Arts & Literacy

Calculator: © iStockphoto.com/picstodisc; Paper: © iStockphoto.com/Qingwa

Practice and Assessment

Technology & Media	Teaching Strategies	Guided Practice	Independent Practice	Reteach/Enrich
• Instructor's Resource CD/Website: PowerPoint Slides Accounting Concepts • Online Working Papers • Transparency Master: Statement (2-column)	• Interpersonal Students	• Terms Review • Audit Your Understanding • Work Together 16-1	• On Your Own 16-1 • Application Problem 16-1 • Formative Assessment, p. 472 • Online Working Papers	• Reteach, p. 473
• Instructor's Resource CD/Website: PowerPoint Slides Accounting Concepts • Online Working Papers • Transparency Master: Statement (2-column)	• Logical/Mathematical Learners	• Terms Review • Audit Your Understanding • Work Together 16-2	• On Your Own 16-2 • Application Problem 16-2 • Formative Assessment, p. 477 • Online Working Papers	• Reteach, p. 478
• Instructor's Resource CD/Website: PowerPoint Slides Accounting Concepts • Online Working Papers	• Visual/Spatial Learners	• Terms Review • Audit Your Understanding • Work Together 16-3	• On Your Own 16-3 • Application Problem 16-3 • Formative Assessment, p. 485 • Online Working Papers	• Reteach, p. 486
• Online Working Papers	• Common Core and Interdisciplinary Studies		• Mastery Problem 16-M • Study Guide 16 • Chapter 16 Test • Cognero Chapter 16	• Challenge Problem 16-C • Reteach, p. 489 • Recycling Problem 16-R

Introduce the Chapter

SET THE STAGE

GUIDING QUESTIONS

- Ask students if increasing sales automatically translates to more net income. Ask them to explain their responses.
- Ask students what *breakeven* means.
- Ask students to predict how a breakeven point is determined.
- Ask students to brainstorm fixed costs associated with a high school.
- Ask students to brainstorm variable costs associated with a high school.
- Ask students how a business might determine how much net income is desirable.

PREVIEW CHAPTER OBJECTIVES

- Note that this chapter focuses on analyzing income statement information so that students understand how operations affect net income and how to plan strategies for increasing net income.
- Instruct a student to read each chapter objective aloud.

PREVIEW ACCOUNTING TERMS

- Read each term aloud to verify its pronunciation for students.
- Point out terms or parts of terms that should already be familiar to most students, such as *total costs*, *unit*, *contribution*, and *breakeven*.

Chapter 16 Management Decision Making Using Cost-Volume-Profit Analysis

LEARNING OBJECTIVES

After studying Chapter 16, in addition to defining key terms, you will be able to:

LO1 Differentiate fixed and variable costs.

LO2 Prepare an income statement reporting contribution margin.

LO3 Calculate the contribution margin per unit and the contribution margin rate.

LO4 Calculate the breakeven point.

LO5 Prepare a breakeven income statement.

LO6 Calculate the sales dollars and sales units required to earn a planned amount of net income.

LO7 Determine the effect of changes in sales volume, unit costs, and unit sales prices on net income.

LO8 Calculate a sales mix.

Calculator: © iStockphoto.com/picstodisc; Paper: © iStockphoto.com/Qingwa

© Goodluz/Shutterstock.com

Accounting In The Real World
Nintendo

For almost three decades, Nintendo has been a leader in the gaming industry around the globe. The basic strategy of the company is the "expansion of the gaming population, which is to encourage as many people in the world as possible, regardless of age, gender, or gaming experience, to embrace and enjoy playing video games."

Founded in 1889 as a card company, Nintendo introduced its Nintendo Entertainment System in North America in 1985. Nintendo has remained an industry leader by introducing new and exciting hardware and software. In fact, Nintendo has been listed on several "Most Innovative Companies" lists, including *Forbes* and *Businessweek*.

Nintendo users will recognize the company's main mascot, Mario, but are also familiar with Zelda, Metroid, Pokemon, and others. Many of these mascots have moved through the various hardware and software innovations introduced by Nintendo.

Introducing new hardware and software in the gaming industry is a risky business. Researchers must try to determine what new features users will want and how different a new product has to be in order to encourage the consumer to pay the price for it—and all the new software that it will require.

Before any company introduces a new product, its managers need to understand the relationship between the expected revenues and costs. How much of the new product must be sold to make the desired profit is an important question that must be answered.

CRITICAL THINKING

1. Not all new products are successful. Identify a company that was unsuccessful in introducing a new product and the unsuccessful product.
2. Why might Nintendo keep Mario (and others) as its mascot throughout a variety of games, rather than introducing new mascots with each new gaming system?

Sources: www.nintendo.co.jp; www.businessweek.com; www.forbes.com.

Background: © iStockphoto.com/adventtr, Real World: © Barone Firenze/Shutterstock.com

Key Terms

- total costs
- unit cost
- variable costs
- fixed costs
- contribution margin
- breakeven point
- sales mix

Accounting In The Real World

Answers

1. Answers will vary. An example of a Nintendo product that was relatively unsuccessful was the GameCube. Other possible products include Coke Classic, Pepsi A.M., and McDonald's Arch Deluxe.
2. Answers will vary. A possible reason is that Mario fans are very loyal and demand his games on each new gaming system.

LESSON
16-1

BRIDGE

- Point out that students have already learned about income statements. In this lesson, they will learn how to analyze income statements to influence managerial decisions.

TEACHING RESOURCES

- **Instructor's Resource CD/Website:**
  PowerPoint Slides
  Accounting Concepts
- **Working Papers:**
  Teacher's Edition of the Working Papers for Lesson 16-1
  Online Working Papers
- **Transparency Master:**
  Statement (2-column)

ENGAGE

- Ask students to explain how net income can be increased (*by increasing sales and/or decreasing costs and expenses*).
- Ask students to list the costs a company might incur in manufacturing a simple item such as a chair. Then ask students to identify which of these costs change as the number of chairs produced changes and which costs stay relatively the same no matter how many chairs are manufactured.

PREVIEW

- Call on students to read the accounting terms and definitions introduced in this lesson: *total costs, unit cost, variable costs, fixed costs,* and *contribution margin*.
- Point out the learning objectives for this lesson.
- Direct students to read the headings in this lesson and to examine the illustrations.

INPUT

- Discuss the enumerated items in the middle of the page.

LESSON
16-1 Cost Characteristics That Influence Decisions

LO1 Differentiate fixed and variable costs.
LO2 Prepare an income statement reporting contribution margin.
LO3 Calculate the contribution margin per unit and the contribution margin rate.

Management Decisions

Managers use financial statements, including the income statement, to make business decisions. An income statement includes information about operating revenue, the cost of merchandise sold, the gross profit on operations, operating expenses, and the net income or net loss. By analyzing the income statement, managers can gain an understanding of the relationship among sales, costs, and expenses.

Managers can increase net income by increasing sales and/or decreasing costs and expenses. Managers, with the advice and assistance of accountants, analyze the relationships among sales, costs, and expenses to:

1. Determine the level of sales necessary to achieve planned net income.
2. Evaluate the impact of changes in sales volume, unit sales prices, and unit costs on net income.
3. Identify the strengths and weaknesses of a company.

ETHICS IN ACTION

Fraud Awareness

The Association of Certified Fraud Examiners (ACFE) estimates that the typical organization loses 5% of its revenues to fraud. The ACFE periodically conducts an extensive survey of organizations to learn the impact of fraud, how fraud was detected, and what organizations are doing to combat fraud.

Every business owner can benefit by studying the findings of this survey. The information is particularly valuable to small business owners. The survey indicates that smaller organizations suffer greater losses than larger organizations. Most small organizations do not have the financial resources to segregate duties properly, a fundamental method for preventing fraud. Small organizations are also less likely to have formal anti-fraud controls.

An awareness of how fraud occurs, who is most likely to commit fraud, and how fraud can be detected enables business owners to implement controls that can help reduce the negative impact of fraud. Accountants need to take an active role in fraud prevention and detection.

INSTRUCTIONS

Access the *Report to the Nations on Occupational Fraud and Abuse* to answer the following questions:

1. What is the median dollar amount lost to fraud?
2. What is the most common type of occupational fraud?
3. What is the most common method used to detect frauds?
4. Identify another interesting fact from the survey.

Source: http://www.acfe.com.

© iStockphoto.com/LdF

ETHICS IN ACTION

The ACFE's report is a comprehensive document that presents the results and methodology of the survey. Encourage students to search for other interesting facts. Lead a classroom discussion on how this information can be used within an organization to reduce the negative impact of fraud.

The answer to question 1 will depend on the contents of the most recent survey. The answers to questions 2 and 3 have been consistent over past surveys and can be expected to continue in the future.

Answers

1. In its 2012 survey, the median loss was $140,000.
2. Asset misappropriation.
3. Tips.
4. Answers will vary.

Total Cost versus Unit Cost

Tint My Windows, Inc. Income Statement For Month Ended July 31, 20--		
Operating Revenue:		
Net Sales		$269,500.00
Cost of Merchandise Sold		161,700.00
Gross Profit on Operations		$107,800.00
Operating Expenses:		
Selling Expenses	$46,950.00	
Administrative Expenses	24,430.00	
Total Operating Expenses		71,380.00
Income from Operations		$ 36,420.00
Other Expenses		300.00
Net Income		$ 36,120.00

All costs for a specific period of time are called **total costs**. The abbreviated income statement above shows that the total cost of the merchandise sold by Tint My Windows, Inc., during July was $161,700.00. Total selling expenses were $46,950.00. These totals show how much money was spent for these activities during a specific period. [CONCEPT: Accounting Period Cycle]

An amount spent for one unit of a specific product or service is called a **unit cost**. Tint My Windows sold 77,000 square feet of tinting materials during July at a total cost of $161,700.00. The unit cost of each square foot of material is calculated as follows:

Total Cost of Merchandise Sold	÷	Units Sold	=	Unit Cost of Merchandise Sold
$161,700.00	÷	77,000	=	$2.10

Units may be expressed in many different terms. However, units should be expressed in terms that are meaningful to the people who are responsible for the costs. Some examples of other unit terms are gallons, liters, pounds, kilograms, inches, yards, meters, and hours. Knowing unit costs can be helpful to a manager in setting unit selling prices and in planning cost control.

© Andresr/Shutterstock.com

INPUT

- Explain the difference between total costs and unit cost. The concept of unit cost is a key component of the analysis in this chapter.
- Explain that the abbreviated income statement in the illustration shows total costs for many items on the statement, but it does not furnish enough information to determine what it costs to manufacture or sell one unit of product.
- Explain that units may be expressed in many terms, but they should be expressed in terms that are meaningful to the people who are responsible for the costs.

MODEL

- Use the board to demonstrate the calculation of unit cost as shown in the math illustration.
- Give a number of different amounts and direct students to calculate unit costs.

DIFFERENTIATED INSTRUCTION

Interpersonal students are people-oriented and learn best with cooperative learning groups or with a partner. Assign students to a partner. Each pair should think about their costs related to the classes in which they are currently enrolled. Ask them to list at least two costs that are fixed and two that are variable. If time permits, ask the pairs to brainstorm the fixed and variable costs associated with an amusement park.

INPUT

- Explain that total variable costs change with the number of units, whereas unit variable costs remain the same no matter how many units are produced. For example, if the wood for a chair costs $10, each chair will require $10 of wood. The total cost of wood depends on how many chairs are produced.
- Explain that fixed costs remain the same no matter how many units are produced. For example, the rent is the same each month no matter how many units are produced or sold.

MODEL

Variable costs

- Direct students to the illustration at the top of the page as you demonstrate the nature of variable costs.
- Demonstrate how the amounts in the Total Cost column of the table on the right are calculated by multiplying the number of units (square feet) purchased by the unit cost per square foot.
- Draw on the board a blank graph similar to the figure and ask students to suggest where the seven points should be placed for drawing the graph of unit costs.
- Point out that the total cost is different each month because the units sold amount is different each month (variable cost).

Fixed costs

- Direct students to the illustration at the bottom of the page as you demonstrate the nature of fixed costs.
- Draw on the board a blank graph similar to the figure and ask students to suggest where the seven points should be placed for drawing the graph of unit costs.
- Point out that the graph is a perfectly horizontal line because the rent is fixed at the same amount each month no matter how many units are sold (fixed cost).

Variable Cost Characteristics LO1

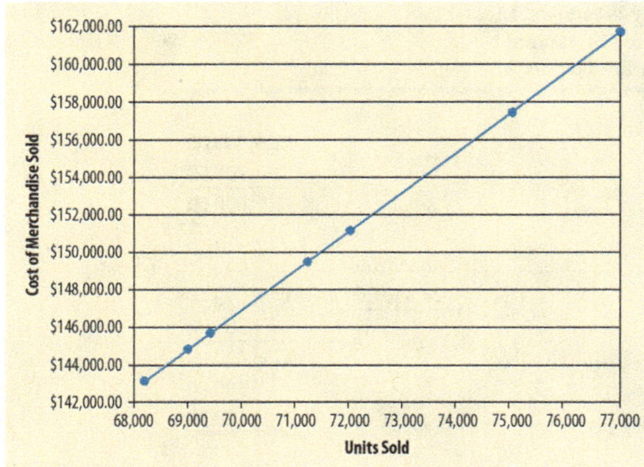

Tint My Windows, Inc.
Cost of Merchandise Sold
For Period January 1–July 31, 20--

Month	Units Sold	Unit Cost per Sq. Ft.	Total Cost
January	68,200	$2.10	$ 143,220.00
February	69,400	2.10	145,740.00
March	69,000	2.10	144,900.00
April	72,000	2.10	151,200.00
May	71,200	2.10	149,520.00
June	75,000	2.10	157,500.00
July	77,000	2.10	161,700.00
	501,800		$1,053,780.00

Costs may be separated into two parts: variable and fixed. Costs that change in direct proportion to a change in the number of units are called **variable costs**. The *total* variable cost *varies* with a change in the number of units. As the number of units increases, the cost increases. The *unit* variable cost *remains the same* regardless of the number of units.

For example, a business buys 1 hour of radio advertising for $300.00. Later, the business buys 10 more hours of advertising for $3,000.00 (10 × $300.00). Regardless of the number of hours purchased, the unit cost of an hour of advertising is $300.00 per hour. Thus, radio advertising is a variable cost.

Tint My Windows' materials purchases for the months of January through July are shown above. The volume of materials purchased ranges from a low of 68,200 square feet in January to a high of 77,000 square feet in July. However, the price paid per square foot (unit cost) remained at $2.10 throughout the seven-month period. Therefore, these costs have the characteristics of variable costs.

Tint My Windows' monthly costs for materials purchases are plotted on the graph above. The line between the plotted points indicates the relationship between the number of square feet of materials purchased and the total cost of materials. The straight, upward-sloping line shows that as the quantity of materials increases, the total cost also increases. The line is straight because Tint My Windows' unit cost per square foot remained the same, although the number of units purchased per month varied.

Fixed Costs

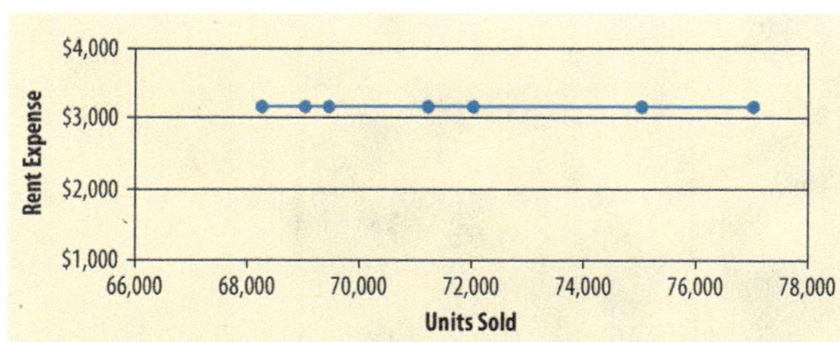

Costs that remain constant regardless of a change in business activity are called **fixed costs**. For example, Tint My Windows' rent is $3,150.00 per month. Rent is *fixed* because the amount has been set at $3,150.00 per month regardless of how many square feet of materials are purchased. If each monthly rental cost is plotted on a graph and the points are connected, the chart will appear as shown here. The fixed cost line is a straight line parallel to the base of the graph.

fyi

Businesses such as airlines, public utilities, and railroads have large fixed costs. These businesses may be considered riskier because much of their revenue is devoted to paying these fixed costs.

Gross Profit and Contribution Margin Income Statements LO2

Tint My Windows, Inc.
Income Statement
For Month Ended July 31, 20--

Operating Revenue:			
Net Sales (77,000 sq. ft. @ $3.50)			$269,500.00
Cost of Merchandise Sold (77,000 sq. ft. @ $2.10)			161,700.00
Gross Profit on Sales			$107,800.00
Operating Costs:			
Selling Costs:			
Sales Commissions (77,000 sq. ft. @ $0.14)	$10,780.00		
Delivery Expense (77,000 sq. ft. @ $0.27)	20,790.00		
Other Variable Selling Costs (77,000 sq. ft. @ $0.12)	9,240.00		
Other Fixed Selling Costs	6,140.00	$46,950.00	
Administrative Costs:			
Rent Expense	$ 3,150.00		
Insurance Expense	580.00		
Other Variable Administrative Costs (77,000 sq. ft. @ $0.03)	2,310.00		
Other Fixed Administrative Costs	18,390.00	24,430.00	
Total Operating Expenses			71,380.00
Income from Operations			$ 36,420.00
Other Expenses			300.00
Net Income			$ 36,120.00

Tint My Windows, Inc.
Income Statement
For Month Ended July 31, 20--

Operating Revenue:		
Net Sales (77,000 sq. ft. @ $3.50)		$269,500.00
Variable Costs:		
Cost of Merchandise Sold (77,000 sq. ft. @ $2.10)	$161,700.00	
Sales Commissions (77,000 sq. ft. @ $0.14)	10,780.00	
Delivery Expense (77,000 sq. ft. @ $0.27)	20,790.00	
Other Variable Selling Costs (77,000 sq. ft. @ $0.12)	9,240.00	
Other Variable Administrative Costs (77,000 sq. ft. @ $0.03)	2,310.00	
Total Variable Costs		204,820.00
Contribution Margin		$ 64,680.00
Fixed Costs:		
Rent Expense	$ 3,150.00	
Insurance Expense	580.00	
Other Fixed Selling Costs	6,140.00	
Other Fixed Administrative Costs	18,390.00	
Other Expenses	300.00	
Total Fixed Costs		28,560.00
Net Income		$ 36,120.00

An income statement reports operating revenue, the cost of merchandise sold, gross profit on operations, operating expenses, and the net income or net loss. Gross profit is determined by subtracting the cost of merchandise sold from net sales. On a typical income statement, as shown in the top portion of the illustration above costs are shown as the cost of merchandise sold, selling expenses, and administrative expenses.

Income determined by subtracting all variable costs from net sales is called the **contribution margin**. Tint My Windows' income statement, shown in the bottom portion of the illustration above, reports the contribution margin and the net income by grouping costs into two categories: variable costs and fixed costs.

INPUT

- Explain that the standard income statement reports gross profit on operations by subtracting the cost of merchandise sold from net sales and then deducting expenses to arrive at net income. Variable and fixed costs are mixed together.
- Explain that the contribution margin is the income left over after all variable costs are subtracted from net sales.
- Explain that an income statement reporting contribution margin separates fixed and variable costs and reports them in separate groups.

MODEL

- Use a 2-column transparency and direct students to the top income statement in the illustration. Explain each item on the statement and ask students to identify whether each selling and administrative expense is a fixed or variable cost.
- Use the transparency to build the income statement reporting contribution margin by referring to the gross profit income statement for each item.
- Point out that all of the variable costs appear above the contribution margin; the fixed costs, below it.

INPUT

- Explain the importance of the contribution margin per unit. Direct students to the second income statement on page 471. Ask students what appears below the contribution margin.
- Point out that the items below the contribution margin on the income statement are the items that must be covered by the contribution margin.
- Explain that the contribution margin per unit can be calculated.

MODEL

- Write the formula on the board as you demonstrate how to calculate the contribution margin per unit.
- Point out that the amounts are taken from the income statement in the illustration on page 471.

INPUT

- Explain the difference between the contribution margin per unit and the contribution margin rate.

MODEL

- Write the formula on the board as you demonstrate how to calculate the contribution margin rate.
- Point out that the amounts are taken from the income statement in the illustration on page 471.

FINANCIAL LITERACY

Answers

1. $1,456 ($5,200 × 0.28).
2. No. Fixed expenses are currently $3,240 – $925 for rent, or $2,315. Add the mortgage payment of $1,456, and fixed expenses become $3,771. Variable expenses are $2,260. The two expenses total $6,031. This means that they must adjust their variable expenses because their gross monthly pay is only $5,200.

Contribution Margin Per Unit LO3

The concept of contribution margin is important to managers because it allows them to determine the income available to cover fixed costs and provide a profit. Tint My Windows' managers can determine from this income statement that the contribution margin in July was $64,680.00. The contribution margin per unit is calculated as follows:

Contribution Margin	÷	Units Sold	=	Per Unit Contribution Margin
$64,680.00	÷	77,000	=	$0.84

Thus, Tint My Windows determined that it will earn an $0.84 contribution margin for each square foot of tinting materials sold. The managers also know that the company will have $28,560.00 of fixed costs each month, regardless of the number of square feet of tinting materials sold. In July, therefore, Tint My Windows earned net income of $36,120.00.

Contribution Margin Rate

Contribution Margin	÷	Net Sales	=	Contribution Margin Rate
$64,680.00	÷	$269,500.00	=	0.24 or 24%

The contribution margin rate measures the relationship between the contribution margin and net sales. The formula for the contribution margin rate is shown above, with the amounts taken from the financial statements. The rate for Tint My Windows means that for every $1.00 of new sales, $0.24 is contribution margin. The contribution margin rate is the portion of each dollar of revenue that is available to pay for fixed costs and provide a net income.

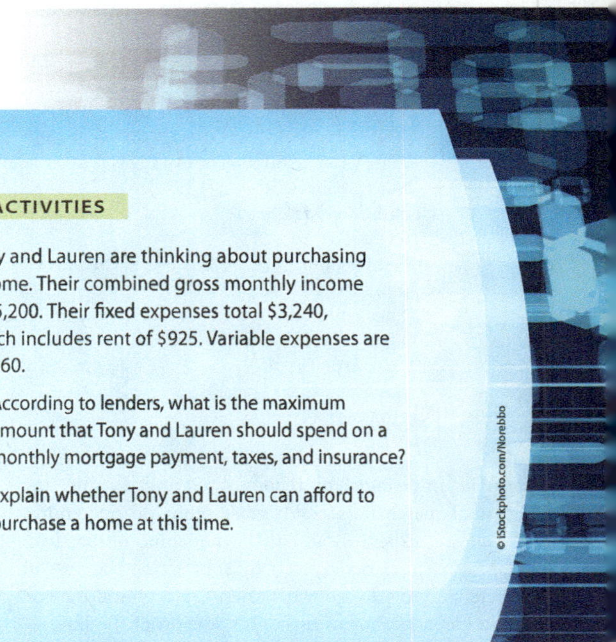

© iStockphoto.com/Norebbo

FINANCIAL LITERACY

House Poor

Fixed expenses for individuals include rent or house payments, insurance, and car payments. Variable expenses include electricity, water, and food.

Individuals who spend a large portion of their income on a house payment, leaving little for other variable expenses, may become "house poor." According to lenders, the monthly mortgage, taxes, and insurance should be less than 28% of the monthly gross income. In addition, monthly debt payments, such as car loan, mortgage, and credit card payments, should not exceed 36% of the monthly gross income.

ACTIVITIES

Tony and Lauren are thinking about purchasing a home. Their combined gross monthly income is $5,200. Their fixed expenses total $3,240, which includes rent of $925. Variable expenses are $2,260.

1. According to lenders, what is the maximum amount that Tony and Lauren should spend on a monthly mortgage payment, taxes, and insurance?
2. Explain whether Tony and Lauren can afford to purchase a home at this time.

FORMATIVE ASSESSMENT

- This is an ongoing process. Circulate around the classroom or lab, observing which students have difficulty with the assignments.
- Troubleshooting: Diagnose the kinds of problems students have with this section. Students may have difficulty (1) determining which costs are fixed and which are variable, (2) transferring information from a gross profit income statement to an income statement emphasizing contribution margin, or (3) using the correct format for an income statement with contribution margin.
- Assess student understanding by checking solutions to Independent Practice assignments and noting their answers to the Terms Review and Audit Your Understanding questions.

End of Lesson Review

LO1 Differentiate fixed and variable costs.

LO2 Prepare an income statement reporting contribution margin.

LO3 Calculate the contribution margin per unit and the contribution margin rate.

Terms Review

total costs
unit cost
variable costs
fixed costs
contribution margin

Audit your understanding

1. If total monthly variable costs for a company were plotted on a graph for ten months during a period of increasing sales, would the line drawn between the plotted points be parallel to the base or sloping? Explain why.
2. How does the contribution margin differ from the gross profit?

Work together 16-1

Preparing an income statement with contribution margin

A blank income statement form for Fullman Flooring is included in the *Working Papers*. Your instructor will guide you through the following examples.

1. Use the following information to prepare Fullman Flooring's January income statement reporting contribution margin. The February information will be used to complete On Your Own 16-1.

	January	February
Net sales	104,000 square feet	99,000 square feet
Unit sales price	$8.00 per square foot	$8.00 per square foot
Cost of merchandise sold	$4.50 per square foot	$4.55 per square foot
Selling expenses:		
Sales commission	$0.64 per square foot	$0.64 per square foot
Delivery cost	$1.00 per square foot	$1.00 per square foot
Other variable selling expenses	$0.70 per square foot	$0.70 per square foot
Other fixed selling expenses	$14,240.00	$14,240.00
Administrative expenses:		
Rent expense	$7,600.00	$7,600.00
Insurance expense	$900.00	$900.00
Other variable administrative expenses	$0.60 per square foot	$0.62 per square foot
Other fixed administrative expenses	$25,080.00	$25,080.00

2. Calculate the contribution margin per unit.
3. Calculate the contribution margin rate.

On your own 16-1

Preparing an income statement with contribution margin

Use the February information from Work Together 16-1. A blank income statement form for Fullman Flooring is included in the *Working Papers*. Work independently to complete this problem.

1. Prepare Fullman Flooring's February income statement reporting contribution margin.
2. Calculate the contribution margin per unit.
3. Calculate the contribution margin rate.

CHECK FOR UNDERSTANDING

Terms Review

- Call on students to define each term in the Terms Review. Definitions are given in the Glossary.

Audit Your Understanding

- Call on students to answer the Audit Your Understanding questions. Answers are given in Appendix D of the textbook.

GUIDED PRACTICE

Work Together

- Have students write the solution to the Work Together problem as you guide the class through the examples.
- Direct students to prepare an income statement with contribution margin.

INDEPENDENT PRACTICE

On Your Own

- Assign the On Your Own problem to be worked independently.
- Use the Formative Assessment techniques to diagnose student understanding.

Application Problem

- Assign Application Problem 16-1.

Online Working Papers

- Students can access the Lesson 16-1 problems using this software.

Website

- Direct students to the C21 Accounting companion website for additional practice and review opportunities throughout the chapter.

RETEACH

- Prepare a list of costs and call on students to identify which are fixed and which are variable.
- Direct students to the first income statement in the illustration on page 471. Call on students to describe where each item would appear on a contribution margin income statement.
- Call on students to suggest where, on a blank income statement form, items should appear for contribution margin.

CLOSURE

- Ask students to describe the difference between fixed and variable costs and to explain why contribution margin is important.

Essential Questions

- How should sales employees be paid? Consider wages and commissions, for example. (*Opinions will vary. Most will prefer a combination of wages and commissions. A good candidate may be attracted to the wages for dependable income. However, employees are more motivated to sell when earning commission.*)
- Are fixed costs always "fixed"? What changes could occur, and how would these affect the net income? (*Fixed costs could change over time due to factors such as increases in rent or insurance. Fixed costs generally rise rather than decrease; this would negatively affect net income.*)

EXTENDED LEARNING

- Assign Accounting in the Real World on page 467.
- Assign Ethics in Action on page 468.
- Assign Financial Literacy on page 472.

LESSON
16-2

BRIDGE

- Point out that students learned about contribution margin in the previous lesson. In this lesson, they will apply this learning to determining breakeven.

TEACHING RESOURCES

- **Instructor's Resource CD/Website**:
  PowerPoint Slides
  Accounting Concepts
- **Working Papers:**
  Teacher's Edition of the Working Papers for Lesson 16-2
  Online Working Papers
- **Transparency Master:**
  Statement (2-column)

ENGAGE

- Ask students what the word *breakeven* means to them. Ask students when they "broke even" in their personal lives. Point out that it is the same in accounting.

PREVIEW

- Call on a student to read the accounting term and definition introduced in this lesson: *breakeven point*.
- Point out the learning objectives for this lesson.
- Direct students to read the headings in this lesson and to examine the illustrations.

INPUT

- Point out that to make decisions affecting net income, a manager needs to know the amount of sales necessary to earn a favorable net income and the factors that contribute most to net income.
- Point out that at the breakeven point, there is neither a net income nor a net loss, but that all costs are paid for by net sales.
- Point out that at sales levels above the breakeven point, there is a net income. Conversely, at sales levels below the breakeven point, there is a net loss.
- Emphasize that the contribution margin rate must be calculated before breakeven sales can be calculated.
- Explain that the breakeven point can be calculated for either total sales dollars or total unit sales, but that the sales dollar breakeven point must be calculated first.

LESSON 16-2 Determining Breakeven

LO4 Calculate the breakeven point.
LO5 Prepare a breakeven income statement.

Calculating the Breakeven Point LO4

Contribution Margin	÷	Net Sales	=	Contribution Margin Rate	
$64,680.00	÷	$269,500.00	=	0.24 or 24%	1

Total Fixed Costs	÷	Contribution Margin Rate	=	Sales Dollar Breakeven Point	
$28,560.00	÷	0.24 or 24%	=	$119,000.00	2

Sales Dollar Breakeven Point	÷	Unit Sales Price	=	Unit Sales Breakeven Point	
$119,000.00	÷	$3.50	=	34,000	3

If a manager is to make decisions that yield a favorable net income for a company, the manager needs two important types of information:

1. The amount of merchandise or services the company must sell to earn a favorable net income.
2. The factors that contribute most to net income.

The amount of sales at which net sales is equal to total costs is called the **breakeven point**. At the breakeven point, neither a net income nor a net loss occurs. At sales levels above the breakeven point, a net income occurs. Conversely, at sales levels below the breakeven point, a net loss occurs. Knowing the breakeven point allows managers to determine the amount of sales needed to start earning a profit. The breakeven point can be stated in sales dollars or in unit sales, as shown above.

The amounts required to calculate a breakeven point are obtained from an income statement prepared to report contribution margin, such as the second income statement on page 471.

Calculating a Breakeven Point

1. Calculate the contribution margin rate. Variable costs change in direct proportion to changes in sales activity. Therefore, for every $1.00 of revenue, $0.76 is required for variable costs.
2. Calculate the sales dollar breakeven point by dividing the total fixed costs by the contribution margin rate. Tint My Windows uses total amounts rounded to the nearest $10 in breakeven point calculations. The sales dollar breakeven point is the amount of sales at which the entire contribution margin is used to pay for fixed costs. Tint My Windows must have total sales of $119,000.00 just to recover its variable and fixed costs. Sales must be more than $119,000.00 if the company is to earn a net income. At a sales level of exactly $119,000, total costs are $119,000 (fixed costs are $28,560 and variable costs are $90,440 [$119,000 × 0.76]), and Tint My Windows has no net income. Any sales level less than $119,000 results in a net loss.
3. Calculate the unit sales breakeven point by dividing the sales dollar breakeven point by the unit sales price. The unit sales breakeven point indicates the number of square feet of tinting materials that Tint My Windows must sell at $3.50 per square foot to achieve breakeven sales.

MODEL

- Refer students to the three steps listed at the bottom of page 474.
- Demonstrate the calculation of the contribution margin rate on the board.
- Demonstrate the calculation of the sales dollar breakeven point on the board.
- Demonstrate the calculation of the unit sales breakeven point on the board.

Breakeven Income Statement LO5

Tint My Windows, Inc. Breakeven Income Statement For Month Ended July 31, 20--		
Operating Revenue:		
Net Sales (34,000 sq. ft. @ $3.50)		$119,000.00
Variable Costs:		
Cost of Merchandise Sold (34,000 sq. ft. @ $2.10)	$71,400.00	
Sales Commissions (34,000 sq. ft. @ $0.14)	4,760.00	
Delivery Expense (34,000 sq. ft. @ $0.27)	9,180.00	
Other Variable Selling Costs (34,000 sq. ft. @ $0.12)	4,080.00	
Other Variable Administrative Costs (34,000 sq. ft. @ $0.03)	1,020.00	
Total Variable Costs		90,440.00
Contribution Margin		$ 28,560.00
Fixed Costs:		
Rent Expense	$ 3,150.00	
Insurance Expense	580.00	
Other Fixed Selling Costs	6,140.00	
Other Fixed Administrative Costs	18,390.00	
Other Expenses	300.00	
Total Fixed Costs		28,560.00
Net Income		$ 0.00

The breakeven income statement above shows the proof for Tint My Windows' breakeven point for materials sales. If the breakeven point is accurate, the net income is zero.

The breakeven income statement is a projection of sales and costs under specific assumptions. Tint My Windows reports projected amounts to the nearest $10. Total sales, *$119,000.00*, is equal to the sales dollar breakeven point. Each variable cost is calculated by multiplying the unit sales breakeven point, *34,000 units*, by the unit variable cost of each cost item. The amount of each fixed cost is taken from the July income statement. The contribution margin, *$28,560.00*, is 24% of net sales, *$119,000.00*. This verifies Tint My Windows' contribution margin rate of 24%.

WHY ACCOUNTING?

Computerized Breakeven Analysis

Members of the Information Technology (IT) Department of any business need to have a basic understanding of the operations they support. For example, in a manufacturing firm, the Accounting Department may have specific data it needs to gather to track production costs. In addition, the controller may want the data presented in a specific format. A member of the IT Department may need to rewrite the software program used by the Accounting Department so that reports will gather the data and print out a report in the desired format. To accomplish this, the IT person needs to have an understanding of what is included in the costs of production.

Arts, A/V Technology & Communications

CRITICAL THINKING

Assume that you work in the IT Department of a company that sells cellular phones. Explain how the understanding of variable costs and fixed costs can help you in your position.

© iStockphoto.com/AleksKG

INPUT

- Explain that an income statement can be prepared using the breakeven amounts to prove the calculations. If the calculations are correct, the net income on the breakeven income statement will be zero, the breakeven point.

MODEL

- Use a 2-column statement transparency or direct students to the illustration as you explain how to prepare a breakeven income statement.
- Demonstrate that the amount used for net sales is the sales dollar breakeven point.
- Demonstrate that variable costs are calculated by multiplying unit variable costs times the unit sales breakeven point.

WHY ACCOUNTING?

Answers

Answers will vary. Possible answers include that the knowledge of fixed and variable costs could be helpful in developing software to calculate the contribution margin and the breakeven point for each model of cellular phone.

Careers In Accounting

Review the career of a loan officer.

Careers In Accounting

Kumar Khan

LOAN OFFICER

© infocus/Shutterstock.com

Kumar Khan likes helping people achieve their goals. His position as a loan officer at a mid-size bank gives him the opportunity to do this every day.

Mr. Khan meets with bank customers who wish to apply for a loan. He explains the different types of loans, credit options, and payment schedules that are available. Kumar feels one of the most important tasks he performs is listening to the applicant's needs and matching those needs to the best loan option.

Once the applicant has determined the best option and has submitted an application, Mr. Khan will review the application for completeness and accuracy. A loan officer also verifies the financial status of the applicant to determine if the application is likely to be approved. The application may be sent to a credit analyst, who will report on the completeness of the application and/or ask for additional information. Mr. Khan's bank requires that all loan applications be presented to a loan committee for approval. Once approved, the loan officer completes the final paperwork and presents it to the applicant for signing.

In addition to processing loan applications, loan officers may also attempt to collect past-due loans. This might include setting up a revised payment plan with the borrowers. If the borrower fails to make payments, the loan officer may need to arrange to repossess the property used as collateral for the loan. This property is then sold to pay off the loan.

In large financial institutions, loan officers may specialize in specific types of loans, such as commercial or agricultural. Some loan officers, especially those who specialize in the mortgage market, may work evenings and weekends in order to meet customer schedules. Most loan officers spend some time outside the financial institution calling on businesses and meeting potential new customers.

Salary Range: In 2011, the median wage for a loan officer was $58,030.00. In some markets, compensation includes commissions on loans acquired.

Qualifications: Minimum requirement is a high school diploma. Most openings prefer an associate's degree or vocational school training. Some loan officers work their way up to the position, starting as tellers or in customer service.

Occupational Outlook: The growth for loan officer positions is projected to be average (10% to 19%) for the period from 2010 to 2020.

Source: www.onetonline.org

© iStockphoto.com/Mlenny

DIFFERENTIATED INSTRUCTION

Logical/Mathematical learners enjoy reasoning and problem-solving activities. They enjoy being taught through investigations. Provide students with additional data so that they can practice calculating the breakeven point.

Calculating the Breakeven Point for New Products

Unit Sales Price	−	Variable Cost per Unit	=	Contribution Margin per Unit	
$38.00	−	$18.00	=	$20.00	1

Total Fixed Costs	÷	Contribution Margin per Unit	=	Unit Sales Breakeven Point	
$25,000.00	÷	$20.00	=	1,250	2

Unit Sales Breakeven Point	×	Unit Sales Price	=	Sales Dollar Breakeven Point	
1,250	×	$38.00	=	$47,500.00	3

When a business plans to introduce a new product, management is interested in knowing how many units the company must sell to break even. Unfortunately, no financial statements exist from which sales and cost information can be obtained. Therefore, an alternative method of calculating the breakeven point is using the *contribution margin per unit* rather than the *contribution margin rate.*

Tint My Windows is considering selling seat covers at $38.00 per unit. Management expects variable costs of $18.00 per unit, with fixed costs of $25,000.00 per month. From the analysis, Tint My Windows determines that it must sell more than 1,250 seat covers per month before the company begins to make a net income. Thus, management will begin selling seat covers if it believes it can sell more than 1,250 per month.

This alternative method is also useful for calculating the breakeven point for existing products when complete financial statements are not available.

Calculating a Breakeven Point for a New Product

1. **Calculate the contribution margin per unit by subtracting the variable cost per unit from the unit sales price. The contribution margin per unit represents the amount available per unit to cover fixed costs and earn a profit.**
2. **Calculate the unit sales breakeven point by dividing the total fixed costs by the contribution margin per unit. The unit sales breakeven point indicates the number of units that must be sold at the projected unit sales price to cover all variable and fixed costs. If Tint My Windows sells exactly 1,250 units, it will earn no net income, nor will it incur a net loss.**
3. **Calculate the sales dollar breakeven point by multiplying the unit sales breakeven point by the unit sales price. This calculation gives the revenue earned by selling 1,250 units at the projected sales price, $38.00 per unit.**

INPUT

- Point out that when a business is going to introduce a new product, management wants to know how many units the company must sell to break even.
- Emphasize that for analyzing a new product introduction, no historical income statement information is available. Therefore, it is necessary to use the alternative contribution margin per unit rather than the historical contribution margin rate.

MODEL

- Demonstrate on the board the three steps for calculating the breakeven point, based on the contribution margin per unit.
- Calculate the contribution margin per unit by subtracting the variable cost per unit from the unit sales price. Point out that the contribution margin per unit represents the amount per unit that is available to cover fixed costs and net income.
- Calculate the unit sales breakeven point by dividing the total fixed costs by the contribution margin per unit. Explain that the unit sales breakeven point is the number of units that must be sold to cover all variable and fixed costs, before earning any net income.
- Calculate the sales dollar breakeven point by multiplying the unit sales breakeven point by the unit sales price.

FORMATIVE ASSESSMENT

- This is an ongoing process. Circulate around the classroom or lab, observing which students have difficulty with the assignments.
- Troubleshooting: Diagnose the kinds of problems students have with this lesson. Students may have difficulty (1) determining which breakeven calculation to use, (2) remembering the formulas for calculating the breakeven point, or (3) selecting the correct amounts to use in the breakeven calculations.
- Assess student understanding by checking solutions to Independent Practice assignments and noting their answers to the Term Review and Audit Your Understanding questions.

CHECK FOR UNDERSTANDING

Term Review

- Call on a student to define the term in the Term Review. A definition is given in the Glossary.

Audit Your Understanding

- Call on students to answer the Audit Your Understanding questions. Answers are given in Appendix D of the textbook.

GUIDED PRACTICE

Work Together

- Have students write the solution to the Work Together problem as you guide the class through the examples.
- Direct students to calculate breakeven in sales dollars and unit sales and prepare a breakeven income statement.

INDEPENDENT PRACTICE

On Your Own

- Assign the On Your Own problem to be worked independently.
- Use the Formative Assessment techniques to diagnose student understanding.

Application Problem

- Assign Application Problem 16-2.

Online Working Papers

- Students can access the Lesson 16-2 problems using this software.

RETEACH

- Prepare an alternative set of data for students to use in practicing the calculations. Use both an existing situation with a gross profit income statement and data for introducing a new product.
- Call on students to describe which method to use to calculate the breakeven point and to explain why.
- Call on students to give the steps for the calculations as another student writes them on the board.

CLOSURE

- Ask students to summarize briefly the procedures for calculating the breakeven point.

End of Lesson Review

LO4 Calculate the breakeven point.

LO5 Prepare a breakeven income statement.

Term Review

breakeven point

Audit your understanding

1. In what two ways can the breakeven point be stated?
2. What is the result of sales above the breakeven point?
3. What is the result of sales below the breakeven point?
4. If no historic information exists from which sales and cost information can be obtained, how can management calculate a breakeven point?
5. What is the simplest way to verify the accuracy of a breakeven calculation?

Work together 16-2

Calculating breakeven in sales dollars and unit sales and preparing a breakeven income statement

An income statement for July and blank forms for Cathy's Cakes are included in the *Working Papers*. Your instructor will guide you through the following examples.

1. Use the income statement to calculate the breakeven point in sales dollars and in unit sales for July.
2. Prepare a breakeven income statement for July of the current year. Save your work to complete Work Together 16-3.

On your own 16-2

Calculating breakeven in sales dollars and unit sales and preparing a breakeven income statement

An income statement for August and blank forms for Cathy's Cakes are included in the *Working Papers*. Work independently to complete this problem.

1. Use the income statement to calculate the breakeven point in sales dollars and in unit sales for August.
2. Prepare a breakeven income statement for August of the current year. Save your work to complete On Your Own 16-3.

Essential Question

- Wouldn't it be less time-consuming to produce a new product based on market research as an indicator of consumer demand than to calculate the breakeven point based on financial data alone? Explain. (*No. A company could be generating a lot of revenue based on consumer demand; but unless it knows the breakeven point, it may not be selling the product at the right price to make a profit.*)

EXTENDED LEARNING

- Assign Why Accounting on page 475.
- Review Careers in Accounting on page 476.

LESSON

16-3 Decisions That Affect Net Income

LO6 Calculate the sales dollars and sales units required to earn a planned amount of net income.
LO7 Determine the effect of changes in sales volume, unit costs, and unit sales prices on net income.
LO8 Calculate a sales mix.

Calculating Sales to Earn a Planned Net Income LO6

Total Fixed Costs	+	Planned Net Income	=	Required Contribution Margin ➊
$28,560.00	+	$10,500.00	=	$39,060.00

Required Contribution Margin	÷	Contribution Margin Rate	=	Sales Dollars ➋
$39,060.00	÷	0.24 or 24%	=	$162,750.00

Sales Dollars	÷	Selling Price per Unit	=	Sales Units ➌
$162,750.00	÷	$3.50	=	46,500

Determining the breakeven point provides management with important information about the relationship of sales, variable costs, and fixed costs. Businesses do not, however, operate merely to break even. Managers need information that will assist them in achieving a planned net income. Breakeven analysis can be used to calculate the dollar and unit sales needed to earn a specified amount of a planned net income.

Calculating Sales to Earn Planned Net Income

➊ Calculate the required contribution margin. The sum of the total fixed costs and the planned net income is the contribution margin necessary to cover fixed costs and to earn the planned amount of net income. Tint My Windows' managers want to know the amount of total sales required to earn $10,500.00 of net income.

➋ Calculate the amount of sales dollars by dividing the required contribution margin by the contribution margin rate. Thus, Tint My Windows must sell $162,750.00 of tinting materials in order to earn a net profit of $10,500.00.

➌ Calculate the unit breakeven point by dividing the unit sales dollars at the breakeven point by the selling price per unit. Thus, Tint My Windows must sell 46,500 square feet of tinting materials ($162,750.00 total sales *divided by* the unit sales price of $3.50) to earn $10,500.00 of net income.

There is another way to calculate the sales units required to make this profit. The required contribution margin, $39,060.00, divided by the contribution margin per unit, $0.84, is 46,500 units.

LESSON

16-3

BRIDGE

- Point out that in previous lessons, students learned about the contribution margin. In this lesson, they will learn how to make decisions that affect net income, using the contribution margin as part of the formula.

TEACHING RESOURCES

- **Instructor's Resource CD/Website:**
  PowerPoint Slides
  Accounting Concepts
- **Working Papers:**
  Teacher's Edition of the Working Papers for Lesson 16-3
  Online Working Papers

ENGAGE

- Explain that part of this lesson will involve determining required sales levels needed to obtain a specific net income. Students may not have considered that a business frequently determines the desired level of net income and then calculates the sales level needed to reach it.

PREVIEW

- Call on a student to read the accounting term and definition introduced in this lesson: *sales mix*.
- Point out the learning objectives for this lesson.
- Direct students to read the headings in this lesson and to examine the illustrations.

INPUT

- Point out that breakeven analysis can be used to calculate the sales needed to earn a specific amount of net income.

MODEL

- Using the board, demonstrate the calculation of the sales required to earn a planned net income, as shown in the math illustration.
- Remind students that the contribution margin is the amount left, after paying variable costs, to cover net income and fixed costs. Therefore, the first step is to calculate the contribution margin by adding fixed costs and the planned net income.
- Demonstrate calculating the required sales dollars by dividing the required contribution margin by the contribution margin rate.

INPUT

- Explain that now that students have an understanding of how sales, variable costs, and fixed costs affect contribution margin and net income, students also should be able to analyze how a change in one of these items would affect net income.
- Explain that some changes that affect net income are sales increases or decreases, changes in production methods, decreases in sales price, and increases in sales volume.
- Explain that the relationship among sales, costs, and net income can be expressed as net sales minus variable costs equals contribution margin and contribution margin minus fixed costs equals net income.

MODEL

- Direct students to the illustration or demonstrate on the board how to analyze the effect of volume changes on net income.
- Draw five columns on the board. In the first column, write an abbreviated income statement with contribution margin, showing Net sales, Variable costs, Contribution margin, Fixed costs, and Income from operations, as shown in the table.
- In the second column, write the per-unit costs shown in the table.
- Demonstrate calculating the items for each of the three levels of unit sales.
- Direct students to the graph as you demonstrate where each level of sales appears.
- Point out that when the Sales line is below the Total Costs line, there is a net loss; when the Sales line intersects the Total Costs line, there is breakeven (no net income or loss); and when the Sales line is above the Total Costs line, there is net income.

Effect of Volume Changes on Net Income LO7

	Per Unit	Number of Units		
		30,000	34,000	38,000
Net sales	$3.50	$105,000.00	$119,000.00	$133,000.00
Variable costs	2.66	79,800.00	90,440.00	101,080.00
Contribution margin	$0.84	$ 25,200.00	$ 28,560.00	$ 31,920.00
Fixed costs		28,560.00	28,560.00	28,560.00
Income from operations		$ (3,360.00)	$ —	$ 3,360.00

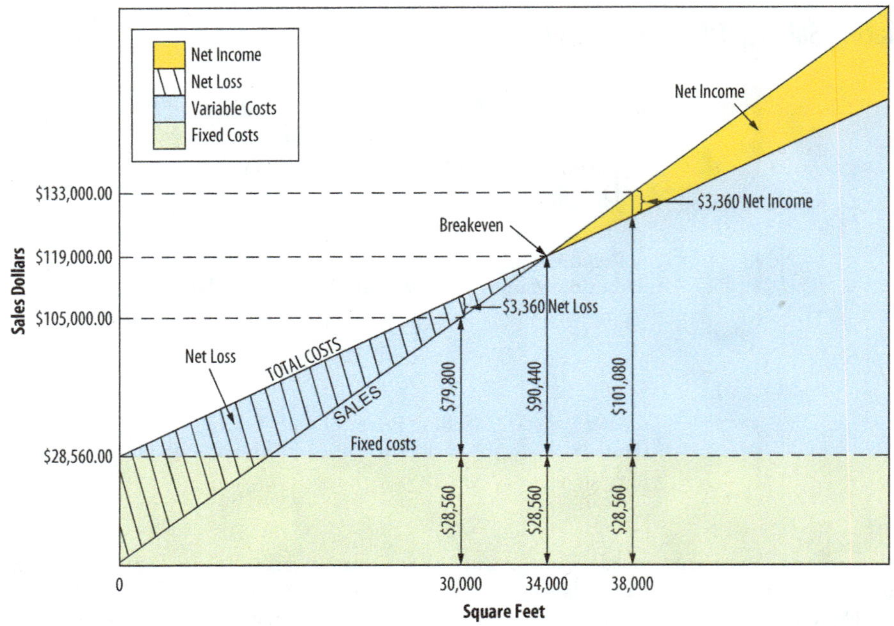

Businesses must be able to determine the change in net income that would result from changes in the relationship of sales, variable costs, and fixed costs. Tint My Windows' managers desire answers to questions such as these:

1. What would net income be if sales increase or decrease?
2. Would it be profitable to change production methods?
3. What would be the effect on net income of a decrease in unit sales price and an increase in sales volume?

Tint My Windows has calculated its unit breakeven point to be 34,000 square feet. The table above shows how net income changes for a decrease or an increase of 4,000 units. For each square foot of tinting materials that Tint My Windows sells, $0.84 of contribution margin is available for fixed costs and net income. At the 34,000-unit breakeven point, the $28,560.00 contribution margin pays for fixed costs, leaving no remaining amount for net income. For each square foot of tinting materials sold above 34,000 units, the $0.84 per square foot contribution margin increases net income. Therefore, when 38,000 square feet of tinting materials are sold, net income is expected to be $3,360.00 (4,000 square feet × $0.84 contribution margin per unit).

If only 30,000 square feet of tinting materials are sold during the month, the contribution margin of $25,200.00 would not cover the fixed costs of $28,560.00. At this sales volume, a net loss of $3,360.00 would result.

The graph on the previous page shows the relationship of sales, costs, and net income as the volume changes. The sales line, beginning at zero, represents the unit sales price times the number of units sold. The total cost line, starting at $28,560.00 (total fixed costs), represents the total fixed and variable costs for the number of units sold. No matter what the sales volume is, the fixed costs remain constant. The variable cost area represents 76% of sales ($2.66 ÷ $3.50), regardless of volume.

At the breakeven point, the sales and total cost lines intersect, indicating that neither a net income nor a net loss will occur. If 38,000 square feet of tinting materials are sold, the sales line is above the total cost line. At this sales volume, $133,000.00 of sales is higher than the sum of the fixed costs ($28,560.00) and the variable costs ($101,080.00), resulting in a net income of $3,360.00. If the sales volume is below 34,000 square feet, the total cost line is above the sales line, indicating a net loss.

Effect of Cost Changes at Average Volume

	Alternative 1 Manual Cutting			Alternative 2 Automated Cutting		
	Per Unit	Units Sold	Total	Per Unit	Units Sold	Total
Net sales	$3.50	38,000	$133,000.00	$3.50	38,000	$133,000.00
Variable costs	2.66	38,000	101,080.00	2.50	38,000	95,000.00
Contribution margin	$0.84	38,000	$ 31,920.00	$1.00	38,000	$ 38,000.00
Fixed costs			28,560.00			34,640.00
Income from operations			$ 3,360.00			$ 3,360.00

Two types of costs, variable and fixed, influence the decisions a company may make. Total variable costs increase or decrease as sales increase or decrease. Total fixed costs remain constant regardless of sales.

Tint My Windows' management is concerned that the relatively low contribution margin rate makes increasing the net income difficult. Tint My Windows is searching for ways to improve its percentage of net income per sales dollar. An alternate production method is being considered. The new method would automate the cutting of tinting materials. A cost comparison of the two methods, Alternative 1 and Alternative 2, is shown above and described below.

- *Alternative 1: Manual Cutting.* Variable costs per square foot of tinting materials are $2.66. Tint My Windows currently pays a crew to cut the tinting materials to dimensions ordered by its customers. Of the total variable costs, $0.16 per square foot represents the cost of this crew. Fixed costs are $28,560.00 per month.
- *Alternative 2: Automated Cutting.* The company buys an automated cutter and assigns the cutting crew to process orders of new product lines. The variable costs of the tinting materials decrease by $0.16 per square foot to $2.50 per square foot. However, the new method requires buying the automated cutter and employing an experienced cutter at a fixed salary. Thus, fixed costs increase by $6,080.00 per month, to a total of $34,640.00.

Sales have been averaging about 38,000 square feet of tinting materials per month. At a 38,000-unit sales level, net income is the same for both alternatives. With Alternative 2, the contribution margin is higher, but fixed costs also are higher. Thus, the higher fixed costs cancel the higher contribution margin.

INPUT

- Explain that breakeven analysis can also be used to analyze the effect of cost changes.
- Point out that the same abbreviated income statement format with contribution margin can be used for the analysis.

MODEL

- Direct students to the illustration or use the board to demonstrate how to analyze two different methods of production at the same sales level.
- Demonstrate the calculations in Alternative 1.
- Point out that with Alternative 2, the variable costs per unit decline because of an improved production method.
- Point out, however, that the production method in Alternative 2 requires new equipment and a new employee; so fixed costs increase.
- Explain that Alternative 2 has a higher contribution margin for covering fixed costs and net income, but that because fixed costs also have increased, there is no improvement in net income at this sales level.

MODEL

- Point out that this demonstration is continued for a higher sales volume, 42,000 units instead of 38,000 units.
- Direct students to the illustration at the top of the page as you demonstrate the calculations for the two alternatives at the higher sales level.
- Point out that at this higher sales level, Alternative 2 results in a larger contribution dollar amount and therefore greater net income than does Alternative 1.

INPUT

- Explain that when everything else is equal, the alternative with the highest contribution margin rate is the best alternative.
- Point out that everything else is rarely equal.
- Explain that the analysis just presented favors Alternative 2 only at higher levels of sales. Point out that when sales fall below $38,000, Alternative 1 is preferable.
- Point out that higher contribution margin rates are usually desirable, but that fixed costs must be in reasonable proportion to expected sales because the contribution margin must cover the fixed costs before there is any net income.

MODEL

- Direct students to the illustration in the middle of the page to demonstrate the calculation of the contribution margin rates of the two alternatives.

Effect of Cost Changes at Above-Average Volume

	Alternative 1 Manual Cutting			Alternative 2 Automated Cutting		
	Per Unit	Units Sold	Total	Per Unit	Units Sold	Total
Net sales	$3.50	42,000	$147,000.00	$3.50	42,000	$147,000.00
Variable costs	2.66	42,000	111,720.00	2.50	42,000	105,000.00
Contribution margin	$0.84	42,000	$ 35,280.00	$1.00	42,000	$ 42,000.00
Fixed costs			28,560.00			34,640.00
Income from operations			$ 6,720.00			$ 7,360.00

Tint My Windows is planning to increase unit sales. A cost comparison with a sales volume of 42,000 units is shown above. With the increased sales volume, Alternative 2 earns a higher net income. If Tint My Windows expects a permanent sales increase, Alternative 2 would be more profitable than Alternative 1.

Effect of Changes in Costs on the Contribution Margin Rate

	Alternative 1 Manual Cutting		Alternative 2 Automated Cutting	
	Dollars	Percent	Dollars	Percent
Net sales	$133,000	100.0%	$133,000	100.0%
Variable costs	101,080	76.0%	95,000	71.4%
Contribution margin	$ 31,920	24.0%	$ 38,000	28.6%

As long as sales increase as expected, Alternative 2 will be favored. However, if sales do not increase, the results will be much different. If the number of units actually sold falls below 38,000, the results will favor Alternative 1.

What is the reason for the change in favorable alternatives? The contribution margin rate favors Alternative 2. The illustration above shows that the contribution margin rate for Alternative 1 is 24.0% versus 28.6% for Alternative 2. This means that for every $1.00 of sales from Alternative 1, $0.24 is available for fixed costs and net income. However, for every $1.00 of sales from Alternative 2, $0.286 is available for fixed costs and net income.

A higher contribution margin rate is usually desirable. However, fixed costs must also be reasonable, since the contribution margin must cover the fixed costs before any net income is earned. The contribution margin rate, *28.6%*, for the automated cutting method is more favorable. However, fixed costs are $34,640.00—$6,080.00 more than the fixed costs for the manual cutting method. If the sales volume declines, the increased contribution margin is not enough to recover the increased fixed costs. Therefore, a reduction in the net income occurs.

A logical conclusion is "Everything else being equal, the activity with the higher contribution margin rate is more profitable." If "everything else" is equal, selecting the more profitable choice is very simple. However, alternatives are seldom that simple, because fixed costs probably differ for each alternative. Therefore, an effective manager looks for the best combination of fixed and variable costs.

Effect of a Change in the Sales Price

	Current Price			Price Reduction and Sales Volume Increase		
	Per Unit	Units Sold	Total	Per Unit	Units Sold	Total
Net sales	$3.50	38,000	$133,000.00	$3.25	45,600	$148,200.00
Variable costs	2.66	38,000	101,080.00	2.66	45,600	121,296.00
Contribution margin.	$0.84	38,000	$ 31,920.00	$0.59	45,600	$ 26,904.00
Fixed costs			28,560.00			28,560.00
Income from operations. . .			$ 3,360.00			$ (1,656.00)

Setting the sales price of a product is extremely important. If the price is set too high, potential customers will buy from another business. If the price is set too low, the company may not earn enough money to cover costs and may suffer a loss. The objective is to set sales prices that provide a reasonable amount of net income, while keeping prices competitive.

Tint My Windows earned a record net income in July, selling 38,000 units. Unfortunately, Tint My Windows' managers believe that a price reduction is necessary to sustain this sales volume. Management is considering a plan to reduce the unit sales price by $0.25 (from $3.50 to $3.25). Management projects that the price decrease will result in an increase in the average number of units sold (from 38,000 to 45,600 units). Should Tint My Windows implement this price reduction? The illustration above shows the effect of this price change on the sales volume and the net income.

Price cutting can be dangerous. In July, Tint My Windows had an $0.84 contribution margin per square foot of materials sold. The average sales of 38,000 units resulted in a $31,920.00 total contribution margin. A unit sales price reduction of $0.25 per unit to $3.25 per unit reduces the contribution margin to $0.59. The potential results of a price cut can be calculated. The unit sales required to maintain the net income using the new contribution margin is calculated as follows:

Contribution Margin	÷	New Contribution Margin per Unit	=	Unit Sales Required to Maintain Planned Net Income
$31,920.00	÷	$0.59	=	54,101.69 (Rounded to 54,100)

A decrease in unit sales price from $3.50 to $3.25 is projected to increase average sales from 38,000 to 45,600 units. However, at $3.25, the company would have to sell a total of 54,100 units to maintain the same net income as current sales at the $3.50 price. Reducing the unit sales price by $0.25 would not be a profitable decision if the company can sell only 45,600 units.

fyi Spreadsheet software is an ideal tool to use for calculating breakeven and for analyzing the effect of price, cost, and sales mix changes. An effective spreadsheet identifies the variables used in an analysis, for example, units sold, price per unit, variable costs, and fixed costs. The analysis is built by creating formulas that reference these variables. When the amounts of the variables are changed, the spreadsheet instantly recalculates the analysis and displays the results.

INPUT

- Explain the importance of setting prices at levels that will not discourage customers but will earn enough to cover costs and net income.
- Point out that reducing prices also reduces the contribution margin; so there must be an increase in sales volume to maintain the same net income.
- Explain that the abbreviated income statement format can be used to analyze the effect of a price cut.

MODEL

- Direct students to the illustration as you demonstrate the effects of a price cut and a sales volume increase.
- Explain that the contribution margin dropped 30% (*$0.25 decrease divided by $0.84*), whereas units sold increased only 20% (*7,600 increase divided by 38,000*). Point out that even with the sales volume increase, a net loss resulted from the price decrease.
- Use the board to demonstrate the calculation for the unit sales required to maintain net income with a price cut. Point out that in the example, 54,100 units were required to maintain net income, but sales were forecast to increase only to 45,600. Therefore, a price cut will not achieve the desired net income.

INPUT

- Explain that breakeven analysis can also be used with a sales mix (relative distribution of sales among various products).
- Point out that a sales mix must be calculated from information on the income statement before breakeven analysis can be calculated.
- Explain that after a sales mix percentage is calculated for each product, the usual breakeven analysis determines the total sales dollars required for the desired net income. Then the sales mix percentages are applied to the total sales dollars to determine the quantity of sales for each product.
- Explain that in the example given, the goal is to increase monthly net income to $15,000 from the $10,000 shown on the income statement.

MODEL

- Direct students to the income statement in the illustration as you demonstrate how the income statement shows information about net sales and variable costs for the two products, refrigerators and dishwashers.
- Use the board to demonstrate the calculations for sales mix, as shown in the math illustration.
- Demonstrate the first step in the calculation: calculating the sales mix.
- Demonstrate dividing the product sales, $320,000, by the total sales for refrigerators, $800,000. Explain that the percentage that results is the percentage of sales represented by refrigerators, 40%.
- Demonstrate dividing product sales, $480,000 by the total sales for dishwashers, $800,000. Explain that the percentage that results is the percentage of sales represented by dishwashers, 60%.

TEACHING IDEA **Invite a speaker from a local retail business to discuss important cost considerations that influence a manager's business decisions. Advise the speaker in advance that students have been studying fixed and variable costs and breakeven analysis applied to business decisions. Also ask the speaker to address decisions recently made pertaining to the sales mix of his or her business.**

Using Breakeven to Plan a Sales Mix LO8

Wicklund Appliances
Income Statement
For the Month Ended May 31, 20--

Operating Revenue:		
Net Sales		
Refrigerators (320 @ $1,000.00)	$320,000.00	
Dishwashers (800 @ $600.00)	480,000.00	$800,000.00
Variable Costs		
Refrigerators (320 @ $750.00)	$240,000.00	
Dishwashers (800 @ $500.00)	400,000.00	640,000.00
Contribution Margin		$160,000.00
Fixed Costs		150,000.00
Income from Operations		$ 10,000.00

1

	Product Sales	÷	Net Sales	=	Sales Mix
Refrigerators	$320,000.00	÷	$800,000.00	=	40.0%
Dishwashers	$480,000.00	÷	$800,000.00	=	60.0%

2

Contribution Margin	÷	Net Sales	=	Contribution Margin Rate
$160,000.00	÷	$800,000.00	=	20.0%

3

Total Fixed Costs	+	Planned Income from Operations	=	Required Contribution Margin
$150,000.00	+	$15,000.00	=	$165,000.00

4

Required Contribution Margin	÷	Contribution Margin Rate	=	Total Sales Dollars
$165,000.00	÷	20.0%	=	$825,000.00

5

	Sales Mix	×	Total Sales Dollars	=	Product Sales Dollars
Refrigerators	40.0%	×	$825,000.00	=	$330,000.00
Dishwashers	60.0%	×	$825,000.00	=	$495,000.00

6

	Product Sales Dollars	÷	Unit Sales Price	=	Product Unit Sales
Refrigerators	$330,000.00	÷	$1,000.00	=	330
Dishwashers	$495,000.00	÷	$ 600.00	=	825

DIFFERENTIATED INSTRUCTION

Visual/Spatial learners enjoy drawing, designing, and seeing relationships. Allow students to create a bulletin board or poster illustrating the various formulas they learned in this chapter. Students should include the formula, an example, and the purpose of the calculation.

The relative distribution of sales among various products is called the **sales mix**. The sales mix must be calculated to determine the breakeven point for a company that sells more than one product. Wicklund Appliances sells refrigerators and dishwashers. The income statement on the previous page reports Wicklund's sales and cost information for the month ended May 31.

Wicklund expects the relationship of refrigerator sales to dishwasher sales to remain relatively stable in future months. However, management has indicated its objective to improve monthly net income to $15,000.00. How many refrigerators and dishwashers should Wicklund plan to purchase and sell?

The procedures used to calculate the sales to earn a planned net income are similar to those previously described in this chapter.

Managers of the Refrigerators and Dishwashers departments can now plan to accomplish these sales objectives. For example, the Dishwashers Department manager knows that the department must sell 25 more dishwashers (825 – 800 = 25) each month. Thus, the manager can plan to increase purchases and devise new sales promotion and advertising campaigns to sell the increased number of dishwashers.

Sales Mix Needed to Earn a Planned Net Income

1. **Calculate the sales mix using information from the income statement. The sales amounts for each product are divided by net sales. The total product mix must equal 100%.**
2. **Calculate the contribution margin rate by dividing the contribution margin by net sales.**
3. **Add the total fixed costs and the planned net income to determine the required contribution margin.**
4. **Divide the required contribution margin by the contribution margin rate to determine the total sales dollars.**
5. **Multiply the sales mix percentage by the total sales dollars to determine the sales dollars needed for each product.**
6. **Divide the product sales dollars by the unit sales price to determine the product unit sales. The unit sales prices are found on the income statement. The product unit sales indicate the number of units of each product that must be sold to achieve the planned net income of $15,000.00.**

THINK LIKE AN ACCOUNTANT

© iStockphoto.com/Dan Bachman

Analyzing Relationships to Predict Sales

Denisa Cortez operates a coffee shop in a resort village in Colorado. Her instincts tell her that sales vary according to the weather. Since most of her sales occur before 10:00 A.M., Denisa believes the morning low temperature is a good predictor of sales.

Denisa wants to get more precise with her predictions in an effort to control inventory and employee hours better.

Your analysis will rely on a statistical method known as *regression*. The regression yields an equation containing constant and variable amounts. Assume that the relationship between sales and temperature is determined to be $400.00 + $2.00*X*. Given a temperature of 25, sales would be predicted to be $450.00 [$400.00 + ($2.00 × 25)].

The ability of the equation to make an accurate prediction is measured by the R^2 (R squared) statistic. R^2 is a value between zero and one. An R^2 near zero indicates that the equation has no predictive value. An R^2 near 1 indicates that the equation can generate very accurate predictions.

OPEN THE SPREADSHEET TLA_CH16

The worksheet contains sales data for each of 5 product lines—coffee, frozen drinks, cappuccinos, doughnuts, and muffins—for the past fiscal year, and daily low temperatures. Follow the steps on the Instructions tab to prepare a chart for each product line. Answer these questions:

1. Predict total sales for the following temperatures: 20, 40, 60.
2. Are you confident of the sales predictions for doughnuts? Explain.
3. Muffins must be baked prior to the shop's 6:00 A.M. opening. How can this prediction schedule help Denisa increase her net income?

THINK LIKE AN ACCOUNTANT

Students use the scatter chart to develop a sales prediction model. The scatter chart displays a regression line of the relationship between temperature and sales of a product line (e.g., coffee and doughnuts) at a coffee shop. Detailed instructions are provided for creating the first two charts. Students use this knowledge to determine the chart options that best show the relationship between temperature and the remaining three product lines.

Answers

1. 20, $2,357.91; 40, $2,382.29; 60, $2,537.72 (assumes a linear trend line for cappuccinos and doughnuts and an exponential trend line for muffins).
2. Answers will vary. The R^2 is very low, indicating the equation is not effective in predicting sales. Temperature appears to have little impact on doughnut sales.
3. Denisa can accurately predict the quantity of muffins that should be baked. Thus, she can plan for the number of employee hours required and limit the number of unsold muffins that must be discarded.

FORMATIVE ASSESSMENT

- This is an ongoing process. Circulate around the classroom or lab, observing which students have difficulty with the assignments.
- Troubleshooting: Diagnose the kinds of problems students have with this lesson. Students may have difficulty (1) determining which calculation methods to use or (2) understanding breakeven point and breakeven analysis.
- Assess student understanding by checking solutions to Independent Practice assignments and noting their answers to the Term Review and Audit Your Understanding questions.

CHECK FOR UNDERSTANDING

Term Review

- Call on a student to define the term in the Term Review. A definition is given in the Glossary.

Audit Your Understanding

- Call on students to answer the Audit Your Understanding questions. Answers are given in Appendix D of the textbook.

GUIDED PRACTICE

Work Together

- Have students write the solution to the Work Together problem as you guide the class through the examples.
- Direct students to calculate sales to earn a planned net income, the effect of volume and sales price changes, and sales mix.

INDEPENDENT PRACTICE

On Your Own

- Assign the On Your Own problem to be worked independently.
- Use the Formative Assessment techniques to diagnose student understanding.

Application Problem

- Assign Application Problem 16-3.

Online Working Papers

- Students can access the Lesson 16-3 problems using this software.

RETEACH

- For additional practice, give students different assumptions to use with the sample data in the lesson.
- Ask students to complete abbreviated income statements for the data to determine what is known and unknown about a scenario so that they can select the appropriate formulas.

CLOSURE

- Ask students to summarize the purpose of breakeven analysis.
- Ask students to explain what the contribution margin must be large enough to cover.

End of Lesson Review

LO6 Calculate the sales dollars and sales units required to earn a planned amount of net income.

LO7 Determine the effect of changes in sales volume, unit costs, and unit sales prices on net income.

LO8 Calculate a sales mix.

Term Review

sales mix

Audit your understanding

1. At the breakeven point on a graph, what is true about the sales line and the total costs line?
2. What is true about total variable costs as sales increase?
3. What is true about total fixed costs as sales increase?
4. To earn a planned net income, the required contribution margin must equal what two amounts?

Work together 16-3

Calculating sales to earn a planned net income, the effect of volume and sales price changes, and sales mix

Use your work and the data from Work Together 16-2. Forms are provided in the *Working Papers*. Your instructor will guide you through the examples.

1. Calculate the amount of sales dollars needed to achieve a net income of $6,000 for July.
2. Determine the net income or net loss if: (a) 4,000 units are sold; (b) 5,000 units are sold; (c) 6,000 units are sold.
3. Cathy's Cakes normally sells 7,500 cakes in July. If the selling price is reduced by $1.00, Cathy's Cakes expects to sell 9,000 cakes. Calculate this change's effect on net income.
4. In September, Cathy's Cakes expanded to sell pies at $20.00 each. Use the following results from September to calculate the product sales dollars and product unit sales necessary for Cathy's Cakes to earn a planned net income of $36,000.00.

	Cakes	Pies	Totals
Net sales	$120,000.00	$80,000.00	$200,000.00
Variable costs	105,000.00	45,000.00	150,000.00
Total contribution margin			$ 50,000.00
Fixed costs			19,000.00
Income from operations			$ 31,000.00

On your own 16-3

Calculating sales to earn a planned net income, the effect of volume and sales price changes, and sales mix

Use your work and the data from On Your Own 16-2. Forms are provided in the *Working Papers*. Work independently to complete this problem.

1. Calculate the amount of sales dollars needed to achieve a net income of $6,000 for August.
2. Determine the net income or net loss if: (a) 7,000 units are sold; (b) 8,000 units are sold; (c) 9,000 units are sold.
3. Cathy's Cakes normally sells 10,000 cakes in August. If the selling price is increased by $1.00, Cathy's Cakes expects to sell 9,500 cakes. Calculate this change's effect on net income.
4. In October, Cathy's Cakes' sales mix changed. Because of rising variable costs for cakes, Cathy's had to increase the price of cakes by $0.50 (to $16.50). By automating pie production, Cathy's was able to decrease the variable costs for pies, so it decreased the price of pies by $1.00 (to $19.00). Because of the price changes, Cathy's sold fewer cakes and more pies. The automation increased fixed expenses by $5,000 (to $24,000). Use the following results from October to calculate the product sales dollars and product unit sales necessary for Cathy's Cakes to continue earning a planned net income of $36,000.00. Round percentage calculations to one place after the decimal point.

	Cakes	Pies	Totals
Net sales	$82,500.00	$123,500.00	$206,000.00
Variable costs	72,700.00	71,500.00	144,200.00
Total contribution margin			$ 61,800.00
Fixed costs			24,000.00
Income from operations			$ 37,800.00

Essential Questions

- Is it possible to have a best-selling product that isn't the most profitable one? Explain. (*Yes, because the costs of making the product may exceed the revenue generated from selling the product.*)
- Why is sales mix important to managers? (*Managers need to analyze sales mix to determine if all products are profitable and to make decisions about any that aren't.*)

EXTENDED LEARNING

- Assign Think Like an Accountant on page 485.

Chapter Summary

Managers must evaluate the impact of changes in sales volume, unit sale prices, and unit costs on the net income of a company. Costs can be separated into two kinds: variable and fixed. Total variable costs increase as sales volume increases. Total fixed costs stay the same, regardless of sales volume.

The contribution margin can be used to assist in calculating the effect on net income of changes in costs and sales. The contribution margin is also useful in calculating the breakeven point in sales dollars or in sales units. Another useful calculation that uses the contribution margin is the sales required to earn a planned net income.

Companies that sell more than one product also must be concerned about the sales mix of the products sold. Since each product may have a different contribution margin, the sales mix of the units sold will produce differing results. If changes are to be made in sales volume, selling price, or costs, the relative sales mix must be considered in order to produce accurate predictions.

The High-Low Method

EXPLORE ACCOUNTING

A cost having both fixed and variable characteristics is called a *mixed cost*. For example, the electricity use in a factory is a mixed cost. As production increases, the cost of electricity for the production machinery increases. This is the variable portion of electricity expense. The cost of lights, which are on regardless of how many units of product are being manufactured, is the fixed portion of electricity expense. A graph of mixed costs is shown below.

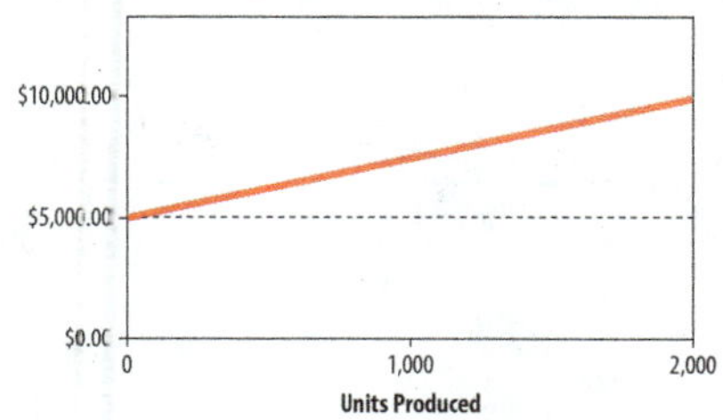

The fixed portion ($5,000.00) of the mixed cost is represented by the dotted horizontal line that is parallel to the base of the graph. The variable portion of the mixed cost is the space between the fixed cost line and the red line. The red line represents the total mixed cost.

When applying what-if scenarios to mixed costs, the fixed and variable components of these costs must be determined. Several measures can be used for this purpose, including the scattergraph, high-low, and least-squares regression methods. Regardless of the method used, a formula can be used to calculate the mixed cost. This formula, based on a fixed cost plus an amount per unit of output, is usually stated as:

Total Mixed Cost = Fixed Cost + (Variable Rate × Output)

The high-low method, while not the most accurate, is the easiest to use without the help of a computer. Using the electricity example, the high-low method requires tracking total electricity expense and units of production for past periods. Assume the following data:

	Expense	Units
January	$2,830.00	560
February	2,580.00	500
March	2,740.00	540
April	2,150.00	400
May	2,488.00	480

Identifying the highest and lowest levels, the variable rate is calculated using the formula:

$$\frac{\text{Highest Cost} - \text{Lowest Cost}}{\text{Highest Units} - \text{Lowest Units}} = \frac{\$2,830 - \$2,150}{560 - 400}$$

$$= \$4.25 \text{ per unit}$$

The variable cost of electricity is $4.25 per unit of production.

The fixed cost is determined by using either the high or low production point and solving for total fixed costs:

$$\$2,830 = X + (\$4.25 \times 560), \text{ or}$$
$$X = \$450$$

The cost of electricity can be estimated by solving the formula for any level of production:

Total Cost of Electricity = $450 + ($X$ × $4.25)

INSTRUCTIONS

Use the following data to develop the formula for total delivery expense:

Delivery Expense	Miles Driven
$10,000	70,000
9,498	65,000
8,705	57,000
9,802	68,000
8,500	55,000

© iStockphoto.com/Makhnach_M

CLOSURE

- Review the Chapter Summary.
- Ask students to prepare a list of the new concepts introduced in this chapter.

Essential Questions

- How can a change in sales mix have an impact on sales volume? (*If prices are changed for products within the mix, the sales volume could be impacted.*)
- How would knowing the breakeven point help an artist who only sells the product at craft shows on occasional weekends? (*The artist could predict how many products would need to be sold to determine if it is worth selling at the craft show, based on fixed costs and the variable costs per unit.*)
- How can knowing the breakeven point affect the business hours of operation? (*If the business provides services, calculating the breakeven point would tell it how many hours of service it would need to provide to break even.*)

EXTENDED LEARNING

- Assign Explore Accounting on page 487.

EXPLORE ACCOUNTING

Answers

$$\frac{\$10,000 - \$8,500}{70,000 - 55,000} = \$0.10 \text{ variable rate.}$$

To calculate fixed expense:

$10,000 = X + (70,000 × $0.10), or $3,000 fixed expense.

Formula for delivery expense: Total delivery expense = $3,000 + ($X$ × $0.10).

CHECK FIGURES

For complete solutions to Chapter 16 problems, see the Teacher's Edition of the Working Papers.

Application Problem 16-1

Contribution margin, $11,500,000.00.

Net income, $10,585,400.00.

Application Problem 16-2

1. Sales dollar breakeven point, $10,000.00.
2. Total variable costs, $4,000.00.

   Other fixed administrative costs, $2,500.00.

INDEPENDENT PRACTICE

- Assign Mastery Problem 16-M for students as a culminating problem combining all new learning from the chapter.
- Assign Challenge Problem 16-C to accelerated students who work at a faster pace.
- Assign Study Guide 16.
- Students can access Online Working Papers to work end-of-chapter problems on the computer.
- Direct students to the C21 Accounting companion website for additional practice and review opportunities.

Apply Your Understanding

INSTRUCTIONS: Download problem instructions for Excel, QuickBooks, and Sage 50 from the textbook companion website at www.C21accounting.com.

16-1 Application Problem: Preparing an income statement with contribution margin LO1, 2, 3

A blank income statement for Adams Paint Supply, Inc., is included in the *Working Papers*.

Instructions:

1. Use the following information to prepare Adams Paint Supply's March income statement reporting contribution margin.

	March
Net sales	2,875,000 gallons
Unit sales price	$10.00 per gallon
Cost of merchandise sold	$5.00 per gallon
Selling expenses:	
Sales commission	$0.15 per gallon
Delivery cost	$0.50 per gallon
Other variable selling expenses	$0.10 per gallon
Other fixed selling expenses	$650,000.00
Administrative expenses:	
Rent expense	$107,600.00
Insurance expense	$72,000.00
Other variable administrative expenses	$0.25 per gallon
Other fixed administrative expenses	$85,000.00

2. Calculate the contribution margin per unit.
3. Calculate the contribution margin rate.

1. Use Excel's Sum function to complete the income statement with contribution margin.
2. Print the worksheet.

16-2 Application Problem: Calculating breakeven in sales dollars and unit sales and preparing a breakeven income statement LO4, 5

An income statement for September and blank forms for Bountiful Boards, Inc., are included in the *Working Papers*.

Instructions:

1. Use the income statement to calculate the breakeven point in sales dollars and in unit sales for September.
2. Prepare a breakeven income statement for September of the current year. Save your work to complete Problem 16-3.

1. Use Excel's Sum function to complete the income statement.
2. Use Excel's Sum function to complete the breakeven income statement.
3. Print the worksheets.

16-3 Application Problem: Calculating sales, sales mix, and the effect of volume and price changes LO6, 7, 8

1. Calculate income from operations under three separate scenarios.
2. Complete the worksheet to calculate a planned net income of $302,000.00 with the added product of snowboards.
3. Print the worksheets.

Use the *Working Papers* and data from Problem 16-2. Forms for completing this problem are provided in the *Working Papers*.

Instructions:

1. Assume that Bountiful Boards wants a net income of $324,000.00 for September. Calculate the amount of sales dollars needed to achieve this net income.
2. Determine the net income or net loss if: (a) 4,500 units are sold; (b) 5,500 units are sold; (c) 6,500 units are sold.
3. Assume that Bountiful Boards normally sells 4,000 skateboards in September. If the selling price is reduced by $5.00, Bountiful Boards expects to sell 4,500 skateboards. Calculate this change's effect on net income.
4. In November, Bountiful Boards expanded to sell snowboards at $500.00 each. Use the following results from November to calculate the product sales dollars and product unit sales necessary for Bountiful Boards to earn a planned net income of $302,000.00.

	Skateboards	Snowboards	Totals
Net sales	$400,000.00	$100,000.00	$500,000.00
Variable costs	160,000.00	60,000.00	220,000.00
Total contribution margin			$280,000.00
Fixed costs			6,000.00
Income from operations			$274,000.00

16-M Mastery Problem: Calculating breakeven and the sales required for a desired income LO2, 3, 4, 5, 6

1. Complete the income statement.
2. Calculate the breakeven point in sales dollars and in unit sales for April.
3. Print the worksheets.

A blank income statement for Candle Scents, Inc., is included in the *Working Papers*.

Instructions:

1. Use the following information to prepare Candle Scents' income statement reporting contribution margin.

		April
Net sales		6,000 gallons
Unit sales price		$5.00 per gallon
Cost of merchandise sold		$2.00 per gallon
Selling expenses:		
Sales commission		$0.50 per gallon
Delivery cost		$0.10 per gallon
Other variable selling expenses		$0.15 per gallon
Other fixed selling expenses	$1,000.00	
Administrative expenses:		
Rent expense	$1,200.00	
Insurance expense	$200.00	
Other variable administrative expenses		$0.25 per gallon
Other fixed administrative expenses	$3,000.00	

2. Calculate the contribution margin per unit and the contribution margin rate.
3. Use the income statement to calculate the breakeven point in sales dollars and in unit sales for April.
4. Assume that Candle Scents wants a net income of $7,500.00 for April. Calculate the amount of sales dollars and unit sales needed to achieve this net income.

Application Problem 16-3

1. Sales dollars, $550,000.00.
2. Income from operations, 4,500 units, $264,000.00.

   Contribution margin, 6,500 units, $390,000.00.
3. Contribution margin, current price, $240,000.00.

   Income from operations, price reduction and sales volume increase, $241,500.00.
4. Required contribution margin, $308,000.00.

   Sales mix: skateboards, 80.0%; snowboards, 20.0%.

Mastery Problem 16-M

1. Contribution margin, $12,000.00.

   Net income, $6,600.00.
2. Contribution margin rate, $40.0%.
3. Unit sales breakeven point; 2,700.
4. Unit sales breakeven point, 6,450.

FORMATIVE ASSESSMENT

- Review solutions to the assigned problems in class, diagnosing trouble spots.

RETEACH

- Call on students to describe how they avoid the trouble spots diagnosed.
- Use reteaching suggestions from lesson plans as required.
- Assign Recycling Problem 16-R if needed.

EXTENDED LEARNING

- Assign 21st Century Skills on page 490.
- Assign Analyzing Home Depot's Financial Statements on page 491.

SUMMATIVE EVALUATION

- Chapter 16 Test
- Cognero for Chapter 16

COMMON CORE AND INTERDISCIPLINARY STUDIES

Extended learning features and activities present numerous opportunities to implement Common Core Standards through interdisciplinary studies. Practice is provided in the common core areas of English Language Arts & Literacy and Mathematical Practice. Many of these activities require short, critical-thinking and decision-making responses that apply reading, writing, speaking, listening, language, media and technology, and mathematical skills.

Challenge Problem 16-C

2. CM per minute, Model Y: $44.00.
3. Minutes available to produce Model Y: 45,000.

21ST CENTURY SKILLS

Answers

1. For members of households who have long and busy days, with little time or energy to accomplish other tasks, the need is someone to help with some of those tasks. Answers will vary, but tasks might include grocery shopping, housecleaning, pet sitting, and delivery services. Business opportunities might include grocery delivery service; housecleaning service; dog walking service; and various delivery services such as dry cleaning, children's taxi, and take-out food.
2. Answers will vary.
   a. Fixed costs might include automobile and automobile insurance. Variable costs might include gas, employee wages, boxes, bags, and cleaning supplies.
   b. Students should include the quantity needed to break even as well as the dollar amount to break even.
3. Service businesses typically do not have large facilities and equipment needed for operations, whereas manufacturers are highly capitalized.
4. Service businesses that might have high fixed costs are those that have high costs for equipment used in their service, such as excavators.

16-C Challenge Problem: Using contribution margin to analyze sales mix with constraint LO2

ABC Corporation makes two briefcases, Models X and Y. ABC Corporation is trying to determine the optimal sales mix for its products. The following per-unit data have been compiled by the Accounting Department:

	Model X	Model Y
Unit selling price	$200.00	$300.00
Unit variable expense	50.00	80.00
Unit contribution margin	$150.00	$220.00
Unit demand	25,000	15,000
Stitching time (minutes)	3	5

Since the unit contribution margin of Model Y is higher than that of Model X, it may appear that ABC Corporation should focus its efforts on Model Y. However, another issue must be considered.

A point in a system that limits the output of the entire system is called a *constraint* or *bottleneck*. ABC Corporation's constraint is its stitching machine, which is run 40 hours per week, 50 weeks of the year. The *theory of constraints* concept states that in order to optimize profits, a company should produce the product that gives the company the highest amount of contribution margin per unit of the constraint.

The formula for calculating the contribution margin per unit of constraint is:

$$\text{Contribution Margin per Unit of Constraint} = \frac{\text{Contribution Margin per Unit}}{\text{Amount of Constraint Required per Unit}}$$

The contribution margin per minute of stitching for Model X is calculated as follows:

$$\$50.00 = \frac{\$150.00}{3 \text{ minutes}}$$

Therefore, ABC Corporation earns $50.00 of contribution margin per minute while Model X is being stitched.

Instructions:

1. Calculate the contribution margin per minute for Model Y.
2. Which model earns the higher contribution margin per minute?
3. The theory of constraints states that the product with the higher contribution margin per unit of constraint should be produced up to its total demand. Any additional units of constraint should be used to produce the product with the lower contribution margin per unit of constraint. Using your results from parts (1) and (2) above, how many units of Models X and Y should ABC Corporation produce in a year? (*Hint:* ABC Corporation has only 120,000 minutes of stitching available per year.)

21st Century Skills

Pursue the Passion?

Theme: Financial, Economic, Business, and Entrepreneurial Literacy

Skills: Communication and Collaboration, Critical Thinking and Problem Solving, and Life and Career Skills

PARTNERSHIP FOR 21ST CENTURY SKILLS

Entrepreneurship plays a vital role in the U.S. economy. New ideas and opportunities create jobs, allow for global competition, create economic growth, and improve the quality of life. Entrepreneurs must investigate what consumers want in order to identify new ideas and opportunities. A good place to start is to look at trends, unmet needs, customer frustrations, or even their own experiences that could create business opportunities.

There is no guarantee that a new business venture will be profitable, or if it will break even. Entrepreneurs cannot assume that their great ideas will translate into profits. Therefore, all entrepreneurs should calculate the breakeven point before investing time and money in a new business.

APPLICATION

With a partner, answer the following:

1. **Many households are very busy with jobs and family.** Identify a need that households described by this statement would have. Then list three business opportunities that could be created due to this need.
2. Select one of the above business opportunities.
   a. List the fixed and variable costs that would be incurred by this business venture.
   b. Prepare a breakeven analysis.
3. Many service businesses have relatively low fixed costs and high variable costs, while manufacturers have relatively high fixed costs and low variable costs. Explain.
4. What types of service businesses might have high fixed costs?

Analyzing Home Depot's financial statements

Home Depot's Consolidated Statements of Earnings can be found in Appendix B on page B-6. Assume that Home Depot's fixed costs equal 75% of selling, general, and administrative expenses and 100% of depreciation and amortization and that Home Depot's variable costs consist only of 100% of the cost of sales plus 25% of the selling, general, and administrative expenses. Ignore all other costs.

INSTRUCTIONS

For 2012, calculate the following. Round dollar amounts to whole dollars. Round percents to one decimal place.

1. Total fixed expenses.
2. Total variable expenses.
3. Contribution margin
4. Contribution margin rate.
5. Breakeven sales dollars.

ANALYZING HOME DEPOT'S FINANCIAL STATEMENTS

Answers

1. ($16,508,000,000 × 0.75) + $1,568,000,000 = $13,949,000,000.
2. ($16,508,000,000 × 0.25) + $48,912,000,000 = $53,039,000,000.
3. $74,754,000,000 – $53,039,000,000 = $21,715,000,000.
4. $21,715,000,000 ÷ $74,754,000,000 = 29.0%.
5. $13,949,000,000 ÷ 29.0% = $48,100,000,000.

Chapter 17 Job Order Costing

Scope & Sequence

	New	Review/Enrich
Introduction		
Introduce the Chapter		
Lesson 17-1: Manufacturing Cost Flows, Direct Materials, and Direct Labor		
Manufacturing Businesses	✓	
Three Manufacturing Cost Elements	✓	
Inventories for a Manufacturing Business	✓	
Cost Records	✓	
Manufacturing Cost Flows	✓	
Records for Materials	✓	
Recording Direct Materials on a Cost Sheet	✓	
Recording Materials Purchases	✓	
Recording Materials Requisitions	✓	
Direct Labor on a Cost Sheet	✓	
Journal Entries to Record Factory Payroll for a Month	✓	
Lesson 17-2: Accounting for Factory Overhead		
Calculating and Recording Factory Overhead	✓	
Completing a Job Cost Sheet	✓	
Journalizing Actual Factory Overhead	✓	
Recording Applied Overhead	✓	
Disposing of Overapplied and Underapplied Factory Overhead Balances	✓	
Lesson 17-3: Accounting for Finished Goods and Cost of Goods Sold and Financial Reporting for a Manufacturing Business		
Recording Journal Entries for Manufacturing Accounts	✓	
Finished Goods Ledger Card	✓	
Recording Finished Goods Transactions	✓	
Recording Sales and Cost of Goods Sold	✓	
Statement of Cost of Goods Manufactured	✓	
Income Statement for a Manufacturing Business	✓	
Balance Sheet for a Manufacturing Business	✓	
Lesson 17-4: Standard Costs and Variance Analysis		
Standard Costs	✓	
Total Materials Variance	✓	
Materials Price Variance	✓	
Materials Quantity Variance	✓	
Total Labor Variance	✓	
Labor Price Variance	✓	
Labor Quantity Variance	✓	
Closure		

Enhancing Instruction

Features	Common Core Standards
• Accounting in the Real World: General Mills	• ELAL—reading
• Ethics in Action: Client Referrals • Why Accounting?: Limited Resources • Forensic Accounting: It Just Doesn't Add Up	• ELAL—reading • ELAL—reading, writing • Mathematics
• Global Awareness: Why Do Foreign Exchange Rates Change?	• ELAL—reading, writing
• Think Like an Accountant: Measuring Material Variances	• Mathematics
• Explore Accounting • Auditing for Errors • 21st Century Skills • Analyzing Home Depot's Financial Statements	• ELAL—reading • Mathematics • ELAL— reading, writing • Mathematics

ELAL = English Language Arts & Literacy

Calculator: © iStockphoto.com/picstodisc; Paper: © iStockphoto.com/Qingwa

Practice and Assessment

Technology & Media	Teaching Strategies	Guided Practice	Independent Practice	Reteach/Enrich
• Instructor's Resource CD/Website: PowerPoint Slides Accounting Concepts • Online Working Papers • Transparency Master: Cash Payments Journal		• Terms Review • Audit Your Understanding • Work Together 17-1	• On Your Own 17-1 • Application Problems 17-1.1, 17-1.2 • Formative Assessment, p. 505 • Online Working Papers	• Reteach, p. 506
• Instructor's Resource CD/Website: PowerPoint Slides Accounting Concepts • Online Working Papers • Transparency Master: Cost Sheet	• Logical/Mathematical Learners	• Terms Review • Audit Your Understanding • Work Together 17-2	• On Your Own 17-2 • Application Problem 17-2 • Formative Assessment, p. 510 • Online Working Papers	• Reteach, p. 511
• Instructor's Resource CD/Website: PowerPoint Slides Accounting Concepts • Online Working Papers • Transparency Masters: Finished Goods Ledger Card, 3-Column Income Statement with % of Net Sales Column, 3-Column Statement Paper	• Visual/Spatial Learners	• Term Review • Audit Your Understanding • Work Together 17-3	• On Your Own 17-3 • Application Problems 17-3.1, 17-3.2 • Formative Assessment, p. 517 • Online Working Papers	• Reteach, p. 518
• Instructor's Resource CD/Website: PowerPoint Slides Accounting Concepts • Online Working Papers	• Tactile/Kinesthetic Learners	• Terms Review • Audit Your Understanding • Work Together 17-4	• On Your Own 17-4 • Application Problem 17-4 • Formative Assessment, p. 523 • Online Working Papers	• Reteach, p. 524
• Online Working Papers	• Common Core and Interdisciplinary Studies		• Mastery Problem 17-M • Study Guide 17 • Chapter 17 Test • Cognero Chapter 17	• Challenge Problem 17-C • Reteach, p. 528 • Recycling Problem 17-R

Introduce the Chapter

SET THE STAGE

GUIDING QUESTIONS

- Ask students to identify companies that manufacture products in their town or city.
- Ask students if any of their family members work in manufacturing companies. If so, ask students to identify the products manufactured.
- Ask students how a business might keep track of the costs to manufacture products.
- Ask students to predict which employees' wages may be considered indirect labor when a product is manufactured.
- Ask students to think of accounting records that always provide the balance of an account. Ask them to think of different ways that materials could be recorded so that the balance and value are available readily and are up to date.
- Ask students to think of standards that exist in their school. Then ask what standards a manufacturing business might put into place.
- Ask students why standards are important.

PREVIEW CHAPTER OBJECTIVES

- Note that this chapter focuses on accounting for a manufacturing business.
- Instruct a student to read each chapter objective aloud.

PREVIEW ACCOUNTING TERMS

- Read each term aloud to verify its pronunciation for students.
- Point out terms or parts of terms that should be familiar to most students, such as *labor*, *overhead*, and *ledger*.

Chapter 17 Job Order Costing

LEARNING OBJECTIVES

After studying chapter 17, in addition to defining key terms, you will be able to:

LO1 Classify manufacturing costs as direct materials, direct labor, and factory overhead.

LO2 Prepare ledgers and cost sheets for a manufacturing business.

LO3 Maintain records and prepare journal entries for materials purchased and used in production.

LO4 Maintain records and prepare journal entries for labor costs used in production.

LO5 Maintain records and prepare journal entries for factory overhead.

LO6 Journalize the transfer of work in process to finished goods.

LO7 Journalize a sale and the related cost of goods sold.

LO8 Prepare a statement of cost of goods manufactured.

LO9 Understand the differences on the income statement and balance sheet for a manufacturing business.

LO10 Calculate and analyze variances related to direct materials.

LO11 Calculate and analyze variances related to direct labor.

Calculator: © iStockphoto.com/picstodisc; Paper: © iStockphoto.com/Qingwa

© Pressmaster/Shutterstock.com

Accounting In The Real World

General Mills

General Mills, a Fortune 500 company, can trace its roots back to the 1860s. From Betty Crocker coupons (from 1929 to 2006) to Boxtops for Education (from 1996 to present), many generations can recall their coupon and Boxtops ties to the company. Not everyone knows that General Mills at one time owned a radio station and the company that made Play-Doh. General Mills is one of the largest food companies in the world. It sells its products in more than 100 countries and has manufacturing operations or offices in 30 countries.

General Mills was founded on the Mississippi River in Minneapolis. The river played an important role in the success of General Mills. It served as a means of transportation to get the grains to the mills, and it also provided energy to run the mills that processed the grains.

At General Mills, giving back to the community is a way of life. In fact, the history of giving goes back to Cadwallader Washburn, a co-founder "... who left money in the 1880s for an orphanage to care for children of employees killed when the company's riverfront mill exploded."

General Mills ranked third on the Forbes 2012 list of companies that give the most back to their community in terms of percentage of net profits, giving 4.0% of company profits to nonprofit organizations. The General Mills Foundation awards grants for programs that focus on hunger and nutrition, wellness, education, and arts and culture. Since 1954, the foundation has awarded more than a half billion dollars to nonprofit organizations. The culture of giving extends to the employees at General Mills. More than 83% of the employees in the Twin Cities area volunteer in local organizations.

CRITICAL THINKING

1. What are the advantages of locating a manufacturing operation near a primary source of raw materials?
2. Do you believe General Mills' support of the community affected the success of this business?

Sources: "General Mills Finds Many Ways to Give," *StarTribune*, December 29, 2007; www.generalmills.com; www.forbes.com.

Key Terms

- direct materials
- direct labor
- factory overhead
- indirect materials
- indirect labor
- work in process
- finished goods
- job order costing
- process costing
- materials ledger
- cost ledger
- finished goods ledger
- applied overhead
- underapplied overhead
- overapplied overhead
- statement of cost of goods manufactured
- standard
- standard costing system
- materials quantity standard
- materials price standard
- labor quantity standard
- labor price standard
- total materials variance
- materials price variance
- materials quantity variance
- total labor variance
- labor price variance
- labor quantity variance

Accounting In The Real World

Answers

1. The raw materials will be fresh, and transportation costs will be minimized. In addition, the company may have some control over the quantity and quality of the production of raw materials.
2. Because General Mills gives to local organizations in the areas in which it is located, many consumers know of its charitable giving and may be more likely to have brand loyalty when making purchasing decisions.

Background: © iStockphoto.com/Lostinyonkers; Real World: Rob Kim Lancov

INPUT

- Explain that Custom Cyclery buys materials to manufacture bicycles and sells the bicycles to merchandisers who resell them to consumers.
- Direct students to the chart of accounts used by Custom Cyclery. Remind students that they will reference these accounts for the next thee chapters.

THE BUSINESS—

CUSTOM CYCLERY CORPORATION

Custom Cyclery Corporation, a custom bicycle manufacturing business, buys wheels, tires, frames, gears, and other materials.

Raphye Alexius/ Image Source/Getty Images

Chart of Accounts

CUSTOM CYCLERY CORPORATION

Balance Sheet Accounts

(1000) ASSETS

1100 Current Assets
1105 Cash
1110 Petty Cash
1115 Accounts Receivable
1120 Allowance for Uncollectible Accounts
1125 Materials
1130 Work in Process
1135 Finished Goods
1140 Supplies—Factory
1145 Supplies—Sales
1150 Supplies—Administrative
1155 Prepaid Insurance
1200 Plant Assets
1205 Factory Equipment
1210 Accumulated Depreciation—Factory Equipment
1215 Office Equipment
1220 Accumulated Depreciation—Office Equipment
1225 Store Equipment
1230 Accumulated Depreciation—Store Equipment
1235 Building
1240 Accumulated Depreciation—Building
1245 Land

(2000) LIABILITIES

2100 Current Liabilities
2105 Accounts Payable
2110 Employee Income Tax Payable
2115 Social Security Tax Payable
2120 Medicare Tax Payable
2125 Salaries Payable
2130 Unemployment Tax Payable—Federal
2135 Unemployment Tax Payable—State
2140 Federal Income Tax Payable
2145 Dividends Payable
2200 Long-Term Liabilities
2205 Mortgage Payable

(3000) STOCKHOLDERS' EQUITY

3105 Capital Stock
3110 Retained Earnings
3115 Dividends
3120 Income Summary

Income Statement Accounts

(4000) OPERATING REVENUE

4105 Sales

(5000) COST OF SALES

5105 Cost of Goods Sold

(5500) MANUFACTURING COSTS

5505 Factory Overhead
5510 Depreciation Expense—Factory Equipment
5515 Depreciation Expense—Building
5520 Heat, Light, and Power Expense
5525 Insurance Expense—Factory
5530 Miscellaneous Expense—Factory
5535 Payroll Taxes Expense—Factory
5540 Property Tax Expense—Factory
5545 Supplies Expense—Factory

(6000) OPERATING EXPENSE

6100 Selling Expenses
6105 Advertising Expense
6110 Delivery Expense
6115 Depreciation Expense—Store Equipment
6120 Miscellaneous Expense—Sales
6125 Salary Expense—Sales
6130 Supplies Expense—Sales
6200 Administrative Expenses
6205 Depreciation Expense—Office Equipment
6210 Insurance Expense—Administrative
6215 Miscellaneous Expense—Administrative
6220 Payroll Tax Expense—Administrative
6225 Property Tax Expense—Administrative
6230 Salary Expense—Administrative
6235 Supplies Expense—Administrative
6240 Uncollectible Accounts Expense
6245 Utilities Expense—Administrative

(7000) OTHER REVENUE

7105 Gain on Plant Assets
7110 Miscellaneous Revenue

(8000) OTHER EXPENSES

8105 Interest Expense
8110 Loss on Plant Assets

(9000) INCOME TAX

9105 Federal Income Tax Expense

The chart of accounts for Custom Cyclery Corporation is illustrated above for reference as you study Chapters 17 through 19 of this textbook.

LESSON
17-1 Manufacturing Cost Flows, Direct Materials, and Direct Labor

LO1 Classify manufacturing costs as direct materials, direct labor, and factory overhead.
LO2 Prepare ledgers and cost sheets for a manufacturing business.
LO3 Maintain records and prepare journal entries for materials purchased and used in production.
LO4 Maintain records and prepare journal entries for labor costs used in production.

Manufacturing Businesses

The three general types of businesses are service, merchandising, and manufacturing. Service businesses provide a needed service for their customers. Examples of service business are accounting firms, law firms, and medical practices.

Merchandising businesses sell products to customers. A merchandising business purchases products and, without changing the products' forms, sells those products to customers. Department stores and grocery stores are examples of merchandising businesses.

A manufacturing business buys materials and uses labor and machinery to change the materials into a finished product. A manufacturing business generally sells the finished product to a merchandising business, which then sells the product to customers.

Custom Cyclery Corporation, a custom bicycle manufacturing business, buys wheels, tires, frames, gears, and other materials. Using labor and machinery, Custom Cyclery combines the materials to make bicycles. Merchandising businesses buy the bicycles from Custom Cyclery for resale to customers.

A service business needs to know the cost of providing services to be able to calculate net income. A merchandising business needs to know the cost of merchandise sold to calculate net income. For the same reason, a manufacturing company needs to know the costs required to produce the finished products that it sells. To know how much finished products cost, Custom Cyclery keeps records of all costs involved in making the products.

ETHICS IN ACTION

Client Referrals

Karen Schwartz is a CPA whose practice focuses on computer applications in business. Karen helps her clients to select, install, and manage computerized accounting systems. Karen was recently engaged to help the internal audit staff of Golden Hotels to purchase and install AuditTech, a database designed specifically for auditors to search for the red flags of errors and fraud in accounting data. In addition, Karen will provide regular training to the audit staff.

AuditTech Software, Inc., provides monetary awards to consultants who refer new customers. The 20 software licenses purchased by Golden Hotels enabled Karen to reach the 100-license level of sales, earning her a $1,000 credit at a popular electronics store.

INSTRUCTIONS

Determine whether the referral was made in accordance with the AICPA *Code of Professional Conduct.*

© iStockphoto.com/LdF

LESSON
17-1

BRIDGE

- Point out that students have learned about accounting for a service business and a merchandising business. In this lesson, students will learn about accounting for a manufacturing business.

TEACHING RESOURCES

- **Instructor's Resource CD/Website:** PowerPoint Slides, Accounting Concepts
- **Working Papers:** Teacher's Edition of the Working Papers for Lesson 17-1, Online Working Papers
- **Transparency Master:** Cash Payments Journal

ENGAGE

- Ask students to describe how a manufacturing business, compared with a service or merchandising business, gets its product to consumers.
- Point out that the business described on this page, Custom Cyclery, will be used to illustrate the concepts in Chapters 17–19.

PREVIEW

- Call on students to read the accounting terms and definitions introduced in this lesson: *direct materials, direct labor, factory overhead, indirect materials, indirect labor, work in process, finished goods, job order costing, process costing, materials ledger, cost ledger*, and *finished goods ledger*.
- Point out the learning objectives for this lesson.
- Direct students to read the headings in this lesson and to examine the illustrations.

INPUT

- Ask students to list the three types of businesses and the kind of cost information each needs.

ETHICS IN ACTION

Rule 503(B) states "A member in public practice who is not prohibited by this rule from performing services for or receiving a commission and who is paid or expects to be paid a commission shall disclose that fact to any person or entity to whom the member recommends or refers a product or service to which the commission relates."

Source: www.aicpa.org/about/code/index.htm.

Suggested Solution

No. The $1,000 represents a commission subject to Rule 503. Rule 503(A) forbids a CPA from accepting a commission if the CPA performs audits or other services related to the client's financial statements. Because Karen does not perform these services for Golden Hotels, Rule 503(B) allows her to accept the commission. However, the rule also states that she must disclose the commission to the client. There is no evidence that Karen informed Golden Hotels of the commission.

INPUT

- List the three manufacturing cost elements: direct materials, direct labor, and factory overhead.
- Explain direct materials and ask for examples of direct materials used in manufacturing a local product.
- Explain direct labor. Discuss the kinds of labor that are not included in direct labor.
- Explain factory overhead. Discuss indirect materials and indirect labor. Discuss other elements of factory overhead.
- Explain the three kinds of inventory accounts for a manufacturing business. Discuss what is included in each.

Three Manufacturing Cost Elements LO1

The manufacturing cost of any finished product includes three elements: (1) direct materials, (2) direct labor, and (3) factory overhead.

DIRECT MATERIALS

Materials that are of significant value in the cost of a finished product and that become an identifiable part of the product are called **direct materials**. Direct materials include all items used in the manufacturing process that have sufficient value to justify charging the cost directly to the product. [CONCEPT: Materiality] The Materiality concept states that business activities creating dollar amounts large enough to affect business decisions should be recorded and reported as separate items. Dollar amounts that are small and not considered important in decision making may be combined with other amounts. For example, frames, wheels, gears, and seats used to manufacture bicycles are considered direct materials and accounted for separately. Screws, nuts, and glue used in the manufacture of bicycles are parts with a small enough dollar value that they are grouped together and only their total value is recorded in the accounting records.

DIRECT LABOR

Salaries of factory workers who make a product are called **direct labor**. Direct labor includes wages and salaries only of persons working directly on a product. Wages and salaries of supervisors, maintenance workers, and others whose efforts do not apply directly to the manufacture of a product are not considered to be direct labor.

FACTORY OVERHEAD

All expenses other than direct materials and direct labor that apply to making products are called **factory overhead**. Some materials used in manufacturing a product cost a very small amount for each unit produced. Materials used in the completion of a product that are of insignificant value to justify accounting for separately are called **indirect materials**. Indirect materials may include such items as screws, glue, solder, and nuts. Materials and supplies used by the factory, such as cleaning supplies and lubricants for the machinery, are also classified as indirect materials.

Some factory workers devote their time to supervisory, clerical, and maintenance tasks necessary to operate the factory. Such workers include time clerks, supervisors, maintenance people, receiving clerks, and inspectors. Salaries paid to factory workers who are not actually making products are called **indirect labor**.

Other costs incurred in the manufacturing process include: (1) depreciation of factory buildings and equipment; (2) repairs to factory buildings and equipment; (3) insurance on building, equipment, and stock; (4) taxes on property owned; and (5) heat, light, and power. All of these expenses, along with indirect materials and indirect labor, make up factory overhead.

Inventories for a Manufacturing Business

A merchandising business normally has one general ledger account for merchandise inventory. However, a manufacturing business has three inventory accounts related to the products manufactured: (1) Materials; (2) Work in Process; and (3) Finished Goods. These accounts are classified as Current Assets of Custom Cyclery Corporation.

A Materials inventory account shows the cost of materials on hand that have not yet been used in making a product. Products that are being manufactured but are not yet complete are called **work in process**. A Work in Process inventory account shows all costs that have been spent on products that are not yet complete. Manufactured products that are fully completed are called **finished goods**. A Finished Goods inventory account shows the cost of completed products still on hand and unsold.

fyi

Robots and advanced electronic systems are used to manufacture products in many factories. The use of automated equipment to perform routine, repetitive manufacturing tasks is often referred to as "computer integrated manufacturing" (CIM).

Cost Records LO2

Manufacturing businesses keep detailed cost records for three purposes: (1) to determine accurate costs for each product made, (2) to provide specific cost information to managers who must identify high cost areas so that corrective action can be taken, and (3) to provide cost summary information for journal entries.

Two general methods are used to measure manufacturing costs. Measuring the manufacturing costs of a specific order or batch as it goes through the production process is called **job order costing**. The end result is a total cost for that order or batch and a per-unit cost for each unit in the batch. Job order costing, illustrated in this chapter, is used when a company manufactures smaller batches of products that are significantly different from each other.

Measuring the manufacturing costs of similar goods as they flow continuously from one production process to another is called **process costing**. At the end of a period, costs are collected from each process to determine an average per-unit cost. Process costing is used when a company manufactures homogenous goods in a continuous process.

SUBSIDIARY COST LEDGERS

Three subsidiary ledgers provide the detailed cost information for the three manufacturing inventory accounts.

1. **Materials Ledger.** Custom Cyclery uses a perpetual inventory system for direct and indirect materials. A perpetual inventory record provides detailed cost information about each type of material. A ledger containing all records of materials is called a **materials ledger**.
2. **Cost Ledger.** Custom Cyclery keeps a record of all charges for direct materials, direct labor, and factory overhead for each job. The record is known as a *cost sheet.* A cost sheet is maintained for each manufacturing job. A ledger containing all cost sheets for products in the process of being manufactured is called a **cost ledger**.
3. **Finished Goods Ledger.** The company keeps a record of each kind of finished good to provide a perpetual inventory of each product produced and its cost. A ledger containing records of all finished goods on hand is called a **finished goods ledger**. This ledger is similar to a materials ledger.

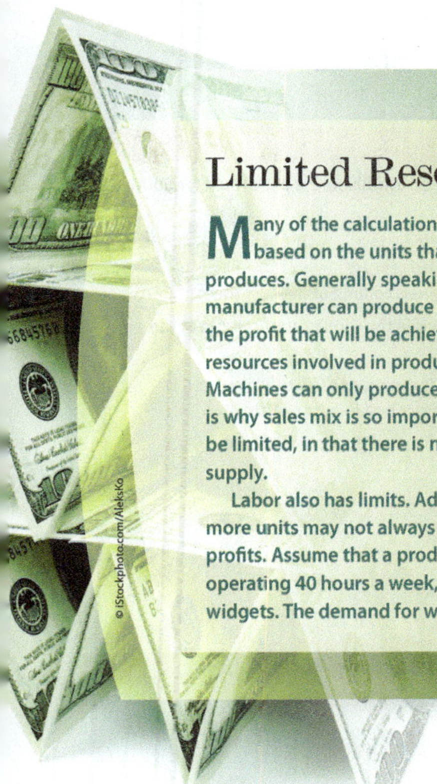

© iStockphoto.com/AleksKo

WHY ACCOUNTING?

Limited Resources

Many of the calculations in this chapter are based on the units that the manufacturer produces. Generally speaking, the more units a manufacturer can produce and sell, the greater the profit that will be achieved. However, most resources involved in production are limited. Machines can only produce so many units, which is why sales mix is so important. Materials may be limited, in that there is not always an endless supply.

Labor also has limits. Adding labor to produce more units may not always contribute to higher profits. Assume that a production process, operating 40 hours a week, can produce 10,000 widgets. The demand for widgets is 15,000. The company can obtain the raw materials necessary to produce 15,000 widgets.

The issue is direct labor. Should the company ask current employees to work overtime? Should the company put on a second shift? Could the company save money by operating two shifts of part-time workers?

Most of these questions can be answered by the Accounting Department and the Production Department working together and understanding the issues that affect the ultimate decision.

CRITICAL THINKING

List three issues that need to be considered when deciding to increase production to 15,000 widgets.

WHY ACCOUNTING?

Answers will vary. Possible responses include how overtime would affect the contribution margin per widget, how a second shift would affect fixed expenses, how two part-time shifts would affect the benefits provided to employees, and if quality employees could be found for full- or part-time employment.

INPUT

- Explain three purposes for keeping manufacturing cost records.
- Explain that three subsidiary ledgers are maintained for the three manufacturing inventory accounts.
- Point out that a number of forms are used for keeping detailed information in a cost system.
- Explain that a materials ledger uses a materials ledger card for each kind of direct and indirect material.
- Explain that entries are recorded on a materials ledger each time material is received and issued.
- Explain that a cost ledger uses a cost sheet for each manufacturing job.
- Point out that a materials requisition is completed for all direct materials issued for a particular job and that the information is recorded on the cost sheet for that job.
- Point out that employees complete a job-time record showing hours worked on each job and that those direct labor costs are recorded on the cost sheet for that job.
- Point out that when a job is completed, factory overhead is estimated and recorded on the cost sheet.
- Point out that a finished goods ledger card is kept for each type of product manufactured.
- Explain that entries are recorded on a finished goods ledger card each time a product is manufactured or received and each time a product is shipped or issued to a customer.
- Emphasize that the total of accounts in the subsidiary ledgers must equal the balance of the general ledger inventory accounts.
- The total of all materials ledger cards equals the balance of Materials in the general ledger.
- The total of all cost sheets for products in the process of being manufactured equals the balance of Work in Process in the general ledger.
- The total of all finished goods ledger cards equals the balance of Finished Goods in the general ledger.

MODEL

- Demonstrate the flow of costs from raw materials through work in process to finished goods by sketching the flow on the board or direct students to the illustration on page 498.
- Demonstrate that the number and cost of each kind of direct and indirect material purchased is recorded on the materials ledger cards (step 1).
- Demonstrate that a materials requisition is prepared (step 2a).
- Show students that direct materials used are subtracted (step 2b).
- Demonstrate that direct labor is completed on job-time records (step 3).
- Demonstrate that factory overhead is estimated and recorded on the cost sheet when a job is completed (step 4).
- Demonstrate that the total cost of a completed job is transferred to the finished goods ledger cards (step 5).

Manufacturing Cost Flows

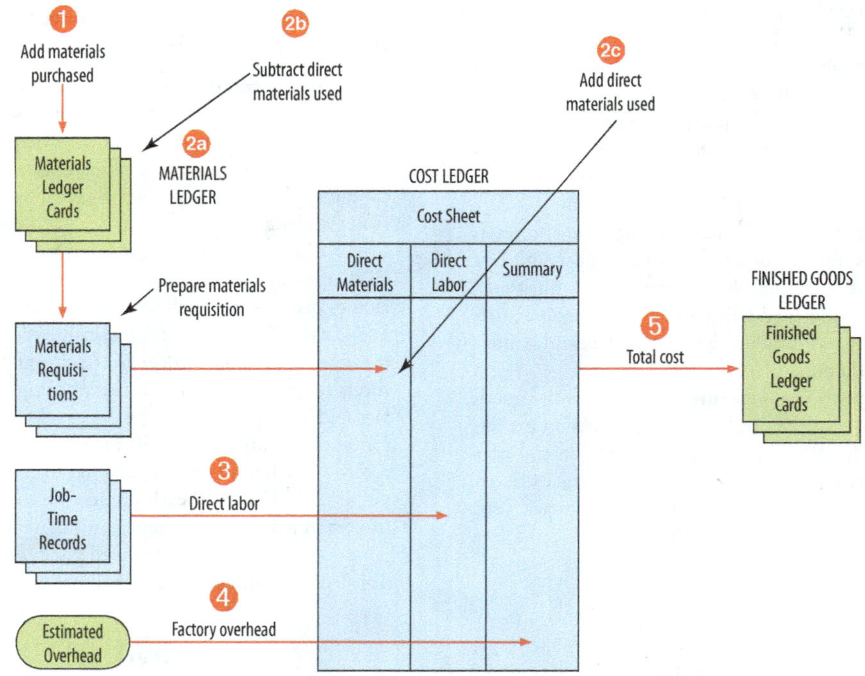

Recording Manufacturing Costs

1. Record the number and cost of each kind of material purchased on materials ledger cards. This step is performed for both direct and indirect materials.
2. a. Prepare a materials requisition to use when direct materials are issued for use in the factory.
   b. The amount of direct materials issued is recorded as a reduction on the materials ledger card.
   c. The amount of direct materials issued is recorded as an increase in the Direct Materials column of the cost sheet.
3. Prepare job-time records when direct labor is used. Time record amounts are recorded in the Direct Labor column of the cost sheet.
4. Estimate and record the amount of factory overhead when a product is completed. The amount of factory overhead is recorded in the Summary column of the cost sheet. Estimating factory overhead is described later in this chapter.
5. Total all costs on the cost sheet when a product is completed. Transfer the total to a finished goods ledger card.

remember Only the cost of direct materials and direct labor are recorded separately on the cost sheet for each job. Indirect materials and indirect labor are recorded as part of the estimated overhead recorded on the cost sheet.

Records for Materials LO3

1 Open a materials ledger card.

MATERIALS LEDGER CARD

Article *26" Men's Frame* Acct. No. *130*

Reorder *150* Minimum *110* Location *Aisle 15B*

ORDERED			RECEIVED					ISSUED					BALANCE			
DATE	PURCHASE ORDER NO.	QUANTITY	DATE	PURCHASE ORDER NO.	QUANTITY	UNIT PRICE	VALUE	DATE	REQUISITION NO.	QUANTITY	UNIT PRICE	VALUE	DATE	QUANTITY	UNIT PRICE	VALUE
													20-- Jan. 2	110	38.00	4,180.00
20-- Jan. 3	522	150						20-- Jan. 3	775	50	38.00	1,900.00	3	60	38.00	2,280.00
								10	780	45	38.00	1,710.00	10	15	38.00	570.00
			20-- Jan. 13	522	150	38.00	5,700.00						13	165	38.00	6,270.00

2 Record orders placed.

3 Record orders received.

4 Record the new balance.

A manufacturing business keeps a record of materials used in the manufacturing process. The business should have on hand sufficient materials so that the manufacturing process will not be interrupted. However, too large a stock of materials requires needless investment in inventory. To provide a perpetual inventory and detailed cost information about materials, Custom Cyclery keeps a materials ledger card for each type of material. A materials ledger card is shown above.

Notice that the materials ledger card also shows items that have been issued. The issuing of materials will be discussed later in the chapter. The total value for all the materials ledger cards equals the balance of the Materials general ledger account. The relationship of the general ledger accounts to the forms and ledgers will also be discussed later in the chapter.

Opening a Materials Ledger Card and Recording Materials Ordered

1. Open a materials ledger card for each type of material kept in the storeroom.
   a. Enter the name and account number of the item.
   b. Determine and record the reorder quantity and minimum quantities to be kept in stock. When the number on hand equals the minimum, the materials clerk notifies the purchasing agent to place a new order.
2. Record the date of an order, Jan. 3, the purchase order number, 522, and the quantity ordered, 150, in the Ordered columns. The data are recorded from a purchase order. The purchase order authorizes a seller to deliver goods with payment to be made later. The order was placed because the quantity on hand, 110 units, equaled the minimum level at which a new order is placed. Note that the quantity ordered equals the reorder quantity shown at the top of the ledger card.
3. When the items ordered are received, record the date, Jan. 13, the purchase order number, 522, the quantity, 150, the unit price, 38.00, and the total value of the order, 5,700.00, in the Received columns of the materials ledger card. The total value is the quantity, 150, multiplied by the unit price, $38.00.
4. Add the quantity and value to the previous balances and extend the amounts to the Balance columns.

INPUT

- Explain that a manufacturing business keeps a perpetual inventory of the materials used in the manufacturing process.
- Emphasize that the total of the materials ledger cards equals the balance of Materials in the general ledger.
- Point out that it is important to monitor the materials inventory and to reorder when quantities reach the minimum level because a shortage of one material might cause an expensive production process to be shut down.

MODEL

- Direct students to the illustration as you demonstrate maintaining a materials ledger card.
- Demonstrate how to open a materials ledger card by completing the top portion. Point out the reorder quantity and the minimum quantity.
- Demonstrate how to record amounts ordered, received, and issued, as well as to calculate the new balance after each entry. Point out that the unit price is also recorded.

INPUT

- Explain that a new cost sheet is started each time a new job begins.
- Point out that materials cannot be transferred to the factory without a materials requisition.
- Explain that each materials requisition form is prepared in triplicate. One copy is kept in the factory where the materials will be used, and the other two are sent to the materials storeroom. After the material is issued, one of the two copies is forwarded to the Cost Accounting Department for entry on the materials ledger card.
- Explain that a job is not necessarily started for a sale to a customer. The products may be needed to replenish stock for sale.

MODEL

Opening a cost sheet (step 1)

- Direct students to the first illustration to demonstrate how to open a cost sheet for a new job.
- Point out how to record the job number and item description in the top section of the cost sheet.
- Explain how to record the number of items to be manufactured and the reason for the order, "Stock."
- Explain how to record the date the cost sheet was started and the date the job should be finished (Date wanted).
- Explain that the Date completed is left blank until the job is completed.
- Direct students to examine the remaining columns in anticipation of their use in step 4.

Preparing a materials requisition (step 2)

- Direct students to the materials requisition form in the middle illustration as you demonstrate how to prepare a materials requisition.
- Demonstrate completing the top portion of the materials requisition. Point out that a company will either use prenumbered forms or write a sequential number on each form.
- Point out that the name and position of the person making the requisition and the date are also entered in the top portion.
- Emphasize the importance of checking whether the materials are direct or indirect. In this case, a Men's Frame is a significant part of a finished bicycle, so the Direct box is checked.

Recording Direct Materials on a Cost Sheet

COST SHEET

Job. No. *644* Date *January 17, 20--*
Item *Model SFM Bicycle* Date wanted *January 26, 20--*
No. of items *25* Date completed
Ordered for *Stock*

1 Open a cost sheet for each job.

DIRECT MATERIALS		DIRECT LABOR				SUMMARY	
REQ. NO.	AMOUNT	DATE	AMOUNT	DATE	AMOUNT	ITEM	AMOUNT
796	*$ 85.00*						
802	*950.00*						

4 Record the issuance of direct materials.

MATERIALS REQUISITION ☒ Direct ☐ Indirect

Requisition No. *802* Date *January 17, 20--*
Requisitioned by: *Cameron Wright* Position *Supervisor*

2 Prepare a materials requisition.

Job No.	Quantity	Description	Unit Price	Total Cost
644	*25*	*26″ Men's Frame*	*38.00*	*950.00*

Materials Issued *January 17, 20--* Recorded:
By *GFG* Materials Clerk

3 Update the materials ledger card.

MATERIALS LEDGER CARD

Article *26″ Men's Frame* Acct. No. *130*
Reorder *150* Minimum *110* Location *Aisle 15B*

ORDERED			RECEIVED					ISSUED					BALANCE			
DATE	PURCHASE ORDER NO.	QUANTITY	DATE	PURCHASE ORDER NO.	QUANTITY	UNIT PRICE	VALUE	DATE	REQUISITION NO.	QUANTITY	UNIT PRICE	VALUE	DATE	QUANTITY	UNIT PRICE	VALUE
			20-- Jan. 13	*522*	*150*	*38.00*	*5,700.00*						*13*	*165*	*38.00*	*6,270.00*
								20-- Jan. 17	*802*	*25*	*38.00*	*950.00*	*17*	*140*	*38.00*	*5,320.00*

During the manufacturing process, all costs of making a product must be recorded. All charges for direct materials, direct labor, and factory overhead for a particular job are recorded on a cost sheet, such as the one shown above.

When direct materials are needed for a job, they are requested from the storeroom using a materials requisition form. A materials requisition form is used to authorize transfer of items from the storeroom to the factory. When materials are issued to the factory from the storeroom, the materials ledger card is updated.

- Point out how to complete the remainder of the requisition. Note that the job number is required for each material listed on the form. Point out that whoever issues the materials initials the bottom of the form.

Updating a materials ledger card (step 3)

- Direct students to the materials ledger card in the third illustration.
- Point out how to enter the information from the materials requisition in the issued columns of the materials ledger card.
- Explain how to record the balance information.

Recording direct materials on a cost sheet (step 4)

- Direct students to the illustration as you explain how to record the direct materials on the cost sheet.
- Explain how to record the materials requisition number and the total cost of the issued materials in the Direct Materials columns on the cost sheet.

Recording Direct Materials on a Cost Sheet

1. Open a new cost sheet for each job started. When the Cost Accounting Department receives a request from the Factory Department supervisor for a job number, it assigns the number and prepares a new job cost sheet. To open a new job cost sheet:
   a. Enter the Job No., 644.
   b. Enter the stock number and the description of the product, Model SFM Bicycle.
   c. Enter the number of items to be manufactured, 25.
   d. Enter the customer that ordered the item. In this case, the product will replenish Custom Cyclery's stock of the bicycle. Therefore, Stock is entered on the Ordered for line.
   e. Enter the date the job number is assigned, January 17, 20--.
   f. Enter the date the item is wanted, January 26, 20--.
2. Prepare a materials requisition in triplicate. One copy of a materials requisition is kept in the factory. Two copies are sent to the materials storeroom.
   a. Enter the requisition number, 802. Requisitions are numbered in order. The next available number is assigned.
   b. Enter the name of the person who is making the requisition, Cameron Wright.
   c. Check the appropriate box to indicate whether the requisition is for direct or indirect materials. In this case, a bicycle frame is a major part of the finished product. Therefore, the Direct box is checked.
   d. Enter the date of the requisition, January 17, 20--.
   e. Enter the position of the person making the requisition, Supervisor. Usually, a supervisor or a manager has the authority to make the requisition.
   f. Enter the job number to which the materials are being issued, 644.
   g. Enter the quantity requisitioned, 25.
   h. Enter the description, 26" Men's Frame.
   i. Enter the unit price of the materials, 38.00.
   j. Enter the total cost of the materials being issued to the factory, 950.00. The total cost is determined by multiplying the quantity by the unit price (25 × $38.00 = $950.00).
   k. Record the date on which the materials are issued to the factory, January 17, 20--.
   l. The materials clerk initials the requisition to show that the materials have been issued. One copy of the completed materials requisition is kept in the storeroom. The original requisition is sent to the Cost Accounting Department.
3. Update the materials ledger card. When the materials requisition is received by the Cost Accounting Department, an entry is made in the materials ledger.
   a. Enter the date the materials are issued to the factory, Jan. 17, 20--, in the Date column of the Issued section of the materials ledger card.
   b. Enter the requisition number, 802.
   c. Enter the quantity issued, 25.
   d. Enter the unit price, 38.00.
   e. Enter the total value of the materials issued, 950.00.
   f. Enter the date in the Balance Date column.
   g. Enter the new quantity of the material, 140, in the Balance Quantity column. Subtract the quantity issued from the current quantity in inventory (165 – 25 = 140) to determine the new quantity.
   h. Enter the unit price, 38.00.
   i. Enter the total value of the materials, 5,320.00 (140 units × $38.00 = $5,320.00).
4. Record the issuance of direct materials on the cost sheet. When the Cost Accounting Department receives the materials requisition, an entry is made on the cost sheet.
   a. Enter the requisition number, 802, in the Req. No. column.
   b. Enter the total value of the materials issued, 950.00, in the Direct Materials Amount column.

501

FORENSIC ACCOUNTING

Students use the formula auditing tools to identify errors in the analysis. The errors involve (1) wrong cells being referenced, (2) an incomplete range in a sum function, and (3) amounts entered rather than being calculated with formulas. Remind students that the owners agreed with Rob's estimates of sales prices, quantities, variable costs, and fixed costs. In the case of payroll expenses and employee benefits, the owners would have agreed to the rates shown in A32:A33, not the calculated amounts of these estimates.

Answers

1. G8: Uses the subcontract unit price.
   H20: Payroll tax calculation does not include the manager's salary.
   J20: Amount is entered, rather than a formula being used.
   C26: Amount is entered, rather than a formula being used.
   H29: SUM function excludes the manager's salary.
   I29: Amount is entered, rather than a formula being used.
2. Yes, the owners would have made a different decision. The revised net income for the three alternatives is existing process, $15,529; automation, $28,610; and subcontract, $14,123.
3. Answers will vary. Rob may have inserted the errors to protect the jobs of the current workers. However, further evidence is necessary before any conclusion can be reached as to whether this was the result of unintentional errors or fraud.

FORENSIC ACCOUNTING

It Just Doesn't Add Up

For years, Crown Sports used the same employee-intensive process to produce its aluminum bats. When new owners purchased the company, they instructed Rob Jenkins, the manager of the Bat Department, to investigate alternative production methods. Rob submitted an analysis containing estimates of fixed and variable costs for the existing process, compared to installing new equipment to automate the process. (The automated process would result in the termination of many employees.) The analysis also included an option to subcontract the production of the bats from another vendor.

The units available for sale using each method differ. New automated equipment would be able to produce more bats. As more bats become available, Rob believes that the unit sales price must change to ensure that the higher quantity can be sold. The new owners met with Rob and concurred with the estimates in his analysis. Fortunately for Crown's employees, the analysis demonstrated that the current employee-intensive production process generates the highest net income.

ACTIVITY

A year has passed since the decision was made, and the owners are puzzled over the Bat Department's poor performance. The department had failed to achieve the net income projected in Rob's analysis. The owners have asked you to examine the analysis. Your first step is to check its accuracy.

INSTRUCTIONS

Open the spreadsheet FA_CH17 and complete the steps on the Instructions tab.
Answer the following questions:

1. Identify and correct the errors in the analysis.
2. Based on the corrected analysis, would the owners have made a different decision?
3. Do you believe that Rob committed a fraud by intentionally misstating the analysis? Explain your answer.

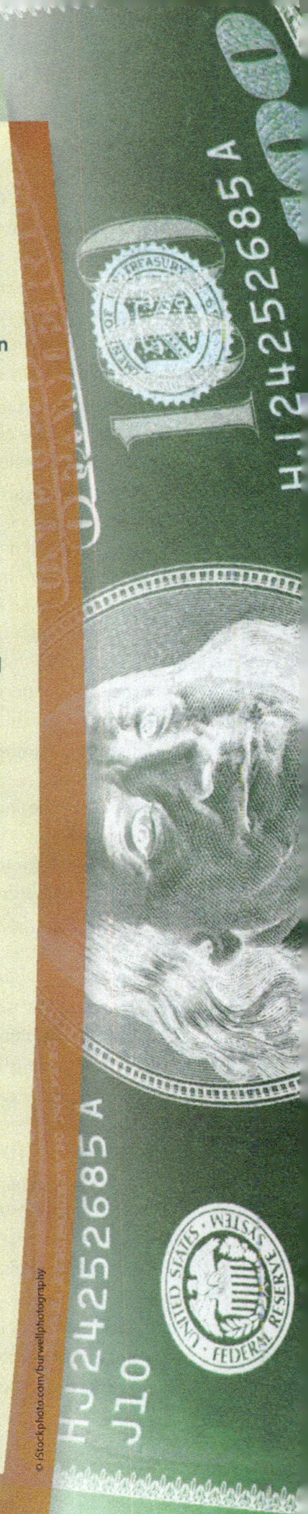

© iStockphoto.com/burwellphotography

Recording Materials Purchases

MATERIALS PURCHASES JOURNAL — PAGE 1

	DATE		ACCOUNT CREDITED	PURCH. NO.	POST. REF.	MATERIALS DR. ACCTS. PAY. CR.	
1	20-- Jan.	3	*Schwindley Gear Company*	501		3 278 85	1
23		31	*Total*			174 293 20	23

Custom Cyclery records the amount of direct and indirect materials purchased and issued in the general ledger account Materials. Custom Cyclery uses a perpetual inventory in the factory that permits the company to charge the cost of direct materials to a job as materials are issued. [CONCEPT: Matching Expenses with Revenue]

Custom Cyclery uses a special materials purchases journal to record all materials purchases. All purchases are made on account; therefore, the journal has a single amount column. An entry in the materials purchases journal is shown above.

At the end of a month, the total of the materials purchases journal is posted to Materials and Accounts Payable in the general ledger.

In the Materials account, the January 1 debit balance, $87,255.41, is the materials inventory at the beginning of the month. The January 31 debit, $174,293.20, is the total posted from the materials purchases journal. This represents the total cost of direct and indirect materials purchased during the month.

Materials

	Debit		Credit
Jan. 1 Bal.	87,255.41		
Jan. 31	174,293.20		

Accounts Payable

	Debit		Credit
		Jan. 31	174,293.20

Recording Materials Requisitions

GENERAL JOURNAL — PAGE 1

	DATE		ACCOUNT TITLE	DOC. NO.	POST. REF.	DEBIT	CREDIT	
1	20-- Jan.	31	*Work in Process*	M312		143 876 00		1
2			*Factory Overhead*			15 221 00		2
3			*Materials*				159 097 00	3
4								4

A materials requisition is prepared for direct materials issued for a specific job. After materials are issued, the requisition amount is recorded on a cost sheet and the requisition is filed. At the end of a month, the total value of all direct materials issued to specific jobs must be transferred from Materials to Work in Process.

A materials requisition is also prepared for indirect materials used in the factory. After the indirect materials are issued to the factory, the requisition is filed. At the end of the month, the total value of all indirect materials issued is transferred from Materials to Factory Overhead.

Custom Cyclery prepares a memorandum with monthly summary information of the direct materials requisitions and the indirect materials totals. The general journal entry to transfer these amounts is shown above.

Materials

	Debit		Credit
Jan. 1 Bal.	87,255.41		
Jan. 31	174,293.20		
		Jan. 31	159,097.00

Work in Process

	Debit		Credit
Jan. 1 Bal.	78,796.00		
Jan. 31 Dir. Mat.	143,876.00		

Factory Overhead

	Debit		Credit
Jan. 31 Ind. Mat.	15,221.00		

INPUT

- Explain that both direct and indirect materials are recorded in the Materials account.
- Explain that a special materials purchases journal is used to record all purchases of materials on account.

MODEL

- Draw a T account on the board for Materials. Explain that Materials is an asset account.
- Ask students to identify the increase, decrease, and normal balance sides of the Materials account. Label the accounts as the information is given.
- Direct students to the illustration of the materials purchases journal as you explain the transaction for buying materials on account. Point out that the materials purchases journal has a single column for debits to Materials and credits to Accounts Payable.
- Label two T accounts on the board with the account titles Materials and Accounts Payable and enter the balance shown for Materials.
- Explain posting the total of the materials purchases journal at the end of the month.

INPUT

- Remind students that as materials are issued from materials requisitions, the amounts are recorded on cost sheets.
- Explain that materials requisitions are prepared for issuing both direct and indirect materials.
- Explain that at the end of a month, the materials requisitions must be recorded in the general journal accounts, with direct materials debited to Work in Process and indirect materials debited to Factory Overhead.

INPUT

- Explain that the time a factory employee works on a job is a direct labor cost to that job.
- Point out that factory employees may work on different jobs in a single shift.
- Explain that factory employees must complete a job-time record for each job worked on during a shift.
- Emphasize that if employees did not complete a job-time record for each job worked on, there would be no accurate way to charge direct labor to specific jobs.
- Explain that the Cost Accounting Department collects all job-time records, calculates the direct labor cost for a job by multiplying the employee hours times the employee rate of pay for each employee for each job, and records the total cost for each job on its cost sheet.

MODEL

Completing a job-time record

- Direct students to the illustration as you explain the completion of the job-time record.
- Point out that a job-time record is completed by each factory employee for each job worked on.
- Point out that the hours an employee works on a job are multiplied by the employee's hourly rate of pay to calculate the direct labor for that employee.

Recording direct labor

- Direct students to the illustration as you explain recording direct labor costs on a cost sheet.
- Explain that the direct labor costs of all employees for a particular job are added and entered on the cost sheet in the Direct Labor column.

Direct Labor on a Cost Sheet LO4

JOB-TIME RECORD

Employee Number *521* Job Number *644*

Date *January 17, 20--*

Time Started *12:30 PM*

Time Finished *5:00 PM*

Total time spent on job *4.5 Hrs.*

❶ Each employee prepares a job-time record for each job worked on.

COST SHEET

Job. No. *644* Date *January 17, 20--*

Item *Model SFM Bicycle* Date wanted *January 26, 20--*

No. of items *25* Date completed

Ordered for *Stock*

DIRECT MATERIALS		DIRECT LABOR				SUMMARY	
REQ. NO.	AMOUNT	DATE	AMOUNT	DATE	AMOUNT	ITEM	AMOUNT
796	*$ 85.00*	*Jan. 17*	*$270.00*				
802	*950.00*						

❷ Record the total of all the job-time records for the job.

Factory employees may work on a number of different jobs each day. Therefore, a job-time record is kept to indicate the amount of time spent on each job. At the end of each day, all job-time records are summarized. The total direct labor cost for each job is recorded on each job's cost sheet.

A job-time record for one Custom Cyclery employee working 4.5 hours on Job No. 644 is shown above. All the direct labor costs for Job No. 644 are recorded in the Direct Labor columns of the cost sheet shown above.

Assigning Direct Labor to Jobs

Each factory employee:

❶ **Prepares a job-time record for each job worked on during the day. The record includes employee number, job number, date, time started, and time finished. The employee calculates and records the total time spent on the job.**

Accounting Department:

❷ **Totals the time on job-time records for each job and records the cost in the Direct Labor column of the cost sheet.**

Journal Entries to Record Factory Payroll for a Month

CASH PAYMENTS JOURNAL — PAGE 1

	DATE		ACCOUNT TITLE	CK. NO.	POST. REF.	GENERAL DEBIT (1)	GENERAL CREDIT (2)	ACCOUNTS PAYABLE DEBIT (3)	PURCHASES DISCOUNT CREDIT (4)	CASH CREDIT (5)	
1	20-- Jan.	15	Work in Process	1221		44 220 00				41 944 88	1
2			Factory Overhead			7 341 00					2
3			Employee Income Tax Payable				5 671 71				3
4			Social Security Tax Payable				3 196 78				4
5			Medicare Tax Payable				747 63				5
18		31	Work in Process	1260		42 875 00				39 993 29	18
19			Factory Overhead			6 287 00					19
20			Employee Income Tax Payable				5 407 82				20
21			Social Security Tax Payable				3 048 04				21
22			Medicare Tax Payable				712 85				22

Custom Cyclery pays all factory employees twice each month. A separate payroll register is prepared for factory employees. A cash payments journal entry is prepared for each factory payroll. The journal entries for the January 15 and January 31 factory payroll for Custom Cyclery are shown above.

Recording Factory Payroll

1. Debit Work in Process for direct labor and Factory Overhead for indirect labor.
2. Credit Employee Income Tax Payable, Social Security Tax Payable, and Medicare Tax Payable for the amounts withheld from employees.
3. Credit Cash for the net pay.

Work in Process

Debit		Credit	
Jan. 1 Bal.	78,796.00		
Jan. 15 Dir. Lab.	44,220.00		
Jan. 31 Dir. Lab.	42,875.00		
Jan. 31 Dir. Mat.	143,876.00		

Social Security Tax Payable

Debit		Credit	
		Jan. 15	3,196.78
		Jan. 31	3,048.04

Factory Overhead

Debit		Credit	
Jan. 15 Ind. Lab.	7,341.00		
Jan. 31 Ind. Lab.	6,287.00		
Jan. 31 Ind. Mat.	15,221.00		

Medicare Tax Payable

Debit		Credit	
		Jan. 15	747.63
		Jan. 31	712.85

Employee Income Tax Payable

Debit		Credit	
		Jan. 15	5,671.71
		Jan. 31	5,407.82

Cash

Debit		Credit	
		Jan. 15	41,944.88
		Jan. 31	39,993.29

The balance in Work in Process, $78,796.00, represents the costs associated with products that were in production at the end of the prior period. The other debits represent the total amounts of direct labor and direct materials used for all jobs during the month.

The debits to Factory Overhead represent the total amounts of indirect labor used and indirect materials issued during the month.

INPUT

- Explain that a separate payroll register is prepared for factory employees.
- Point out that rather than Salary Expense being debited, the factory payroll costs are debited to Work in Process and Factory Overhead.

MODEL

Analyzing factory cost accounts

- Draw T accounts on the board for Work in Process and Factory Overhead.
- Explain that Work in Process is an asset account and Factory Overhead is a cost account.
- Ask students to identify the increase, decrease, and normal balance sides of the accounts and label the accounts as the information is given.

Analyzing the factory payroll transaction

- Draw six T accounts on the board, with the account titles and balances shown.
- Explain that factory employee salaries are distributed as direct labor to Work in Process and as indirect labor to Factory Overhead. Record the debit amounts in the T accounts.
- Record the employee withholding amounts as credits to the usual payroll tax liability accounts.
- Record the net salary as a credit to Cash.

Recording the transaction

- Use a transparency of a cash payments journal or direct students to the illustration on this page as you demonstrate journalizing the transaction.
- Repeat the analysis and continue journalizing for the January 31 factory payroll.

FORMATIVE ASSESSMENT

- This is an ongoing process. Circulate around the classroom or lab, observing which students have difficulty with the assignments.
- Troubleshooting: Diagnose the kinds of problems students have with this section. Students may have difficulty remembering how to record the various manufacturing costs.
- Assess student understanding by checking solutions to Independent Practice assignments and noting their answers to the Terms Review and Audit Your Understanding questions.

CHECK FOR UNDERSTANDING

Terms Review

- Call on students to define each term in the Terms Review. Definitions are given in the Glossary.

Audit Your Understanding

- Call on students to answer the Audit Your Understanding questions. Answers are given in Appendix D of the textbook.

GUIDED PRACTICE

Work Together

- Have students write the solution to the Work Together problem as you guide the class through the examples.
- Direct students to classify manufacturing costs and to record and journalize materials and labor costs.

INDEPENDENT PRACTICE

On Your Own

- Assign the On Your Own problem to be worked independently.
- Use the Formative Assessment techniques to diagnose student understanding.

Application Problems

- Assign Application Problem 17-1.1.
- Assign Application Problem 17-1.2.

Online Working Papers

- Students can access the Lesson 17-1 problems using this software.

RETEACH

- Prepare a list of various costs and ask students to determine whether the costs should be classified as direct materials, direct labor, or factory overhead.
- Direct students to a job cost sheet and review how to record the items.
- Call on students to explain how to journalize materials and labor costs.

CLOSURE

- Ask students to describe the differences between direct materials, direct labor, and factory overhead.

End of Lesson Review

LO1 Classify manufacturing costs as direct materials, direct labor, and factory overhead.

LO2 Prepare ledgers and cost sheets for a manufacturing business.

LO3 Maintain records and prepare journal entries for materials purchased and used in production.

LO4 Maintain records and prepare journal entries for labor costs used in production.

Terms Review

direct materials
direct labor
factory overhead
indirect materials
indirect labor
work in process
finished goods
job order costing
process costing
materials ledger
cost ledger
finished goods ledger

Audit your understanding

1. What are the three manufacturing cost elements of a finished product?
2. What term is used to describe products that are being manufactured but are not yet complete?
3. What is the purpose of a cost sheet?
4. What is the purpose of a materials requisition?

Work together 17-1

Classifying manufacturing costs; recording and journalizing materials and labor costs

Wooddale Products Corporation manufactures furniture. A list of manufacturing costs, a cost sheet, and blank journals are included in the *Working Papers*. Your instructor will guide you through the following examples. Save your work for use in Work Together 17-2.

1. For each cost, determine whether the cost should be classified as direct materials, direct labor, or factory overhead.
2. Record the following items on the cost sheet for Job No. 218:
   a. Materials Requisition No. 335, for $200.00 of direct materials for Job No. 218.
   b. April 25 total of all Job-Time Records for Job No. 218 for the day, $250.00.
3. Journalize the following transactions for April of the current year:

Transactions:

Apr. 30. Requisitioned $2,350.00 of direct materials and $1,700.00 of indirect materials for the Production Department. M265.

30. Paid employees their semimonthly pay. Gross (pretax) direct labor costs were $13,200.00. Gross indirect labor costs were $8,950.00. Employee income tax was $2,436.50. Social security tax was 6.2% and Medicare tax was 1.45% of gross wages. C354.

On your own 17-1

Classifying manufacturing costs; recording and journalizing materials and labor costs

Morganstern Corporation manufactures gas grills. A list of manufacturing costs, a cost sheet, and blank journals are included in the *Working Papers*. Work independently to complete the following problems. Save your work for use in On Your Own 17-2.

1. For each cost, determine whether the cost should be classified as direct materials, direct labor, or factory overhead.
2. Record the following items on the cost sheet for Job No. 587:
   a. Materials Requisition No. 422, for $750.00 of direct materials for Job No. 587.
   b. May 28 total of all Job-Time Records for Job No. 587 for the day, $600.00.
3. Journalize the following transactions for May of the current year:

Transactions:

May 28. Requisitioned $8,425.00 of direct materials and $4,623.00 of indirect materials for the Production Department. M381.

31. Paid employees their semimonthly pay. Gross (pretax) direct labor costs were $14,500.00. Gross indirect labor costs were $6,000.00. Employee income tax was $2,255.00. Social security tax was 6.2% and Medicare tax was 1.45% of gross wages. C533.

Essential Question

- Ask students if they think all the records kept for manufacturing costs are worth the time and effort. (*All these records are worth keeping. Manufacturing involves so many different types of costs to produce a product that, without these records, a business would not know how to determine the selling price or if it were making a profit.*)

EXTENDED LEARNING

- Assign Accounting in the Real World on page 493.
- Assign Ethics in Action on page 495.
- Assign Why Accounting on page 497.
- Assign Forensic Accounting on page 502.

LESSON

17-2 Accounting for Factory Overhead

LO5 Maintain records and prepare journal entries for factory overhead.

Calculating and Recording Factory Overhead LO5

Estimated factory overhead for current year = $1,050,000.00 ← 1

Estimated total direct labor cost = $1,500,000.00 ← 2

Estimated Factory Overhead	÷	Estimated Total Direct Labor Cost	=	Factory Overhead Applied Rate
$1,050,000	÷	$1,500,000.00	=	0.70 or 70%

← 3

Total Direct Labor Costs (Job No. 644)	×	Factory Overhead Applied Rate	=	Applied Overhead (Job No. 644)
$750.00	×	70%	=	$525.00

← 4

Some factory overhead expenses occur regularly throughout a fiscal period, and others occur irregularly. Many factory overhead expenses are not known until the end of a fiscal period. Therefore, factory overhead expenses normally are charged to jobs by using an application rate based on a known cost such as direct labor. This method applies factory overhead expenses to all jobs and permits a company to record overhead on a cost sheet when a job is completed. Generally, three factors are considered in estimating factory overhead: (1) amount of factory overhead for the past several fiscal periods, (2) number of products the factory expects to produce in the next fiscal period, and (3) expected change in unit costs of factory overhead items. Base units are usually cost items that can be identified easily. Direct labor cost, direct labor hours, and direct materials costs are common bases. A base unit should be selected that most closely relates to the actual overhead costs. Custom Cyclery uses direct labor cost as a base unit because there is a close relationship between the amount of direct labor cost and factory overhead costs. The estimated amount of factory overhead recorded on cost sheets is called **applied overhead**. The applied overhead is calculated for Job No. 644 as shown above.

Applied overhead is recorded on cost sheets during the fiscal period and before all factory overhead for the current period is known. [CONCEPT: Matching Expenses with Revenue] Therefore, the factory overhead applied rate is calculated before the fiscal period begins.

Determining a Factory Overhead Applied Rate

1. **Estimate the amount of factory overhead costs for the next fiscal period. Custom Cyclery expects to produce 50,000 bicycles during the coming year. Considering this volume, the previous years' overhead, and anticipated cost increases, Custom Cyclery estimates factory overhead as $1,050,000.00.**
2. **Estimate the number of base units that will be used in the next fiscal period. Custom Cyclery estimates next year's direct labor cost as $1,500,000.00 (50,000 x 2 x $15.00).**
3. **Calculate the factory overhead applied rate. Divide estimated factory overhead costs by the estimated base unit. Custom Cyclery's factory overhead applied rate is 70% of direct labor cost.**
4. **Calculate and record the amount of applied overhead, *$525.00*, on the cost sheet for Job No. 644 (total direct labor for Job No. 644, $750.00, multiplied by the factory overhead rate, 70%).**

LESSON

17-2

BRIDGE

- Point out that students have learned about the three elements that go into the cost of manufacturing a product. In this lesson, they will learn how to account for factory overhead in greater detail.

TEACHING RESOURCES

- **Instructor's Resource CD/Website:** PowerPoint Slides Accounting Concepts
- **Working Papers:** Teacher's Edition of the Working Papers for Lesson 17-2 Online Working Papers
- **Transparency Master:** Cost Sheet

ENGAGE

- Ask students to define *factory overhead* and to explain why it is an important element when determining the cost of a product.

PREVIEW

- Call on students to read the accounting terms and definitions introduced in this lesson: *applied overhead*, *underapplied overhead*, and *overapplied overhead*.
- Point out the learning objective for this lesson.
- Direct students to read the headings in this lesson and to examine the illustrations.

INPUT

- Explain that materials requisitions and job-time records make identifying direct material and direct labor costs for a job relatively easy.
- Point out that other costs of a business may not be easy to identify when a job is completed and may not be known until the end of a fiscal period.
- Explain that because the exact value of many costs is not known, an estimated amount of factory overhead is applied to each job using an application rate based on a known cost.
- Explain that Custom Cyclery uses direct labor costs for calculating applied overhead.
- Explain that the factory overhead applied rate is calculated before a fiscal period begins.

MODEL

- Direct students to the math illustration as you demonstrate how to calculate the factory overhead applied rate.
- Demonstrate that the first step in determining the rate is to estimate the total factory overhead for the year. Estimates are based on the amount of overhead in previous periods, the number of products expected to be produced, and any expected changes in factory overhead items.
- Demonstrate how to calculate the estimated total direct labor cost (the basis of the overhead rate) by multiplying the number of units to be produced times the estimated direct labor hours per unit times the estimated hourly salary rate.
- Demonstrate how to calculate the rate by dividing the estimated factory overhead by the estimated direct labor cost.
- Demonstrate how to calculate the applied overhead amount by multiplying the total direct labor costs of a specific job times the factory overhead applied rate.

INPUT

- Explain that when a job is completed, the cost sheet columns are totaled and the totals are recorded in the Summary columns.
- Point out that the factory overhead is calculated using the applied rate and recorded in the Summary columns.
- Explain that the final step in completing a cost sheet is to calculate the cost per unit for the job.
- Explain that jobs that have not been completed at the end of a fiscal period need to be totaled to determine the ending inventory for Work in Process in the general ledger.

MODEL

- Use a transparency or direct students to the illustration as you explain how to complete a cost sheet.
- Explain how to total the Direct Materials and Direct Labor columns.
- Explain how to transfer the totals of the Direct Materials and Direct Labor columns to the Summary columns.
- Demonstrate how to calculate the applied overhead by multiplying the applied rate (70%) times the total Direct Labor ($750). Point out that the method of calculation is also recorded.
- Explain how to total the Summary column to obtain the total cost for the job.
- Write the number of units manufactured, pointing this out to students.
- Demonstrate how to calculate the cost per unit by dividing the total costs by the number of units. Point out that this amount is recorded as the last item in the Summary Amount column.

Completing a Job Cost Sheet

COST SHEET

Job. No. *644* Date *January 17, 20--*
Item *Model SFM Bicycle* Date wanted *January 26, 20--*
No. of items *25* Date completed *January 19, 20--*
Ordered for *Stock*

DIRECT MATERIALS		DIRECT LABOR				SUMMARY	
REQ. NO.	AMOUNT	DATE	AMOUNT	DATE	AMOUNT	ITEM	AMOUNT
796	$ 85.00	Jan. 17	$270.00			Direct Materials	$1,250.00
802	950.00	18	195.00			Direct Labor	750.00
810	215.00	19	285.00			Factory Overhead	
	$1,250.00		$750.00			(70% of direct	
						labor costs)	525.00
						Total Cost	$2,525.00
						No. of units finished	25
						Cost per unit	$ 101.00

1. Total direct materials.
2. Total direct labor.
3. Transfer amounts to Summary columns.
4. Calculate applied factory overhead.
5. Determine total job cost.
6. Determine cost per unit.

Total Costs (Job No. 644)	÷	No. of Units	=	Cost per Unit
$2,525.00	÷	25	=	$101.00

The completed cost sheet for Job No. 644 is shown above. When a job is completed, its total costs are calculated and recorded in the Summary columns of the cost sheet. Direct Materials and Direct Labor columns on the cost sheet are totaled and the totals are recorded in the Summary columns. Then factory overhead is applied to the job. A cost per unit is determined for each job.

Job No. 644 was completed on January 19. At the end of a fiscal period, cost sheets will also exist for jobs that have not been completed. The total value for all cost sheets for work still in process equals the balance of the Work in Process account in the general ledger. Thus, at the end of a fiscal period, cost sheets for work in process are totaled to determine the ending inventory for the general ledger account Work in Process.

fyi At the end of a fiscal period, factory overhead is applied to all jobs that are still in process. Therefore, the Work in Process account reflects direct materials, direct labor, and factory overhead costs for work still in process.

© iStockphoto.com/Jasantiso

Journalizing Actual Factory Overhead

GENERAL JOURNAL — PAGE 1

	DATE		ACCOUNT TITLE	DOC. NO.	POST. REF.	DEBIT	CREDIT	
4		31	Factory Overhead	M313		32 354 00		4
5			Depr. Expense—Factory Equipment				4 600 00	5
6			Depr. Expense—Building				4 000 00	6
7			Heat, Light, and Power Expense				4 600 25	7
8			Insurance Expense—Factory				750 00	8
9			Miscellaneous Expense—Factory				1 679 75	9
10			Payroll Taxes Expense—Factory				11 250 30	10
11			Property Tax Expense—Factory				3 543 70	11
12			Supplies Expense—Factory				1 930 00	12
13								13

Factory overhead includes various indirect factory expenses such as indirect labor, indirect materials, taxes, depreciation, and insurance. Actual factory overhead expenses are summarized in an account titled Factory Overhead.

Indirect labor and indirect materials are posted directly to Factory Overhead from the entries shown on pages 503 and 505. Other indirect expenses are recorded throughout the month in other manufacturing expense accounts. At the end of each month, these indirect expense account balances are transferred to Factory Overhead. The actual factory overhead can then be compared with the estimated amount of factory overhead recorded on the job cost sheets. Recall that factory overhead is estimated (applied) so that a company can record overhead on a cost sheet as soon as a job is completed.

Factory Overhead

Debit		Credit
Jan. 15 Ind. Lab.	7,341.00	
Jan. 31 Ind. Lab.	6,287.00	
Jan. 31 Ind. Mat.	15,221.00	
Jan. 31 OH Exp.	32,354.00	
(New Bal.	*61,203.00)*	

Adjusting entries are made at the end of a fiscal period. These adjusting entries include debits to Depreciation Expense, Insurance Expense, and Supplies Expense. The closing entry to transfer actual overhead expenses to Factory Overhead is shown above.

After postings are completed, all actual factory overhead expense accounts are summarized in the Factory Overhead account.

© ImageryMajestic/Shutterstock.com

INPUT

- Explain that in addition to direct and indirect labor and materials, a factory has many other kinds of overhead costs, such as depreciation, utilities, insurance, and taxes.
- Remind students that some expense accounts are adjusted at the end of a fiscal period, such as depreciation expense.
- Explain that all adjusting entries are journalized and posted, and then the balances of the manufacturing expense accounts are transferred to Factory Overhead.

MODEL

- Draw a T account for Factory Overhead on the board and record the entries for labor and materials already explained.
- Direct students to the illustration as you demonstrate journalizing the transaction. Point out that all the expense accounts are credited and that Factory Overhead is debited. Record the Factory Overhead amount in the T account. Emphasize that these are actual overhead amounts.

DIFFERENTIATED INSTRUCTION

Logical/Mathematical learners enjoy reasoning and problem-solving activities. They enjoy learning by conducting investigations. Ask students to form groups of three or four. Explain that service businesses often calculate the cost of materials and direct labor when performing different services. Tell students to brainstorm at least three types of service businesses and to create a list of costs that must be determined for each service.

INPUT

- Remind students that throughout the month as jobs are finished, an applied amount of factory overhead (an estimate) is recorded on each job cost sheet. At the end of the month, incomplete jobs also have an applied factory overhead amount recorded.
- Explain that this applied factory overhead amount must be journalized and posted.

MODEL

Recording applied overhead

- Draw T accounts for Work in Process and Factory Overhead and record the balances shown or direct students to the illustration at the top of this page as you demonstrate how to record applied overhead.
- Point out that the amount of applied overhead recorded on the job cost sheets is recorded as a debit to Work in Process and a credit to Factory Overhead, as shown in the general journal and the T accounts.
- Direct students to the Factory Overhead T account as you demonstrate that the Jan. 31 Act. OH amount, $61,203.00, is the amount of overhead transferred from the direct factory expense accounts, as shown on the page. Point out that the journal entry on this page is for the applied (estimated) overhead recorded on the job cost sheets, $60,966.50.

Recording underapplied and overapplied factory overhead

- Direct students to the T account for Factory Overhead shown at the top of the page. Point out that the actual overhead is greater than the applied overhead, so the overhead was underapplied and the debit balance must be closed.
- Explain that underapplied and overapplied overhead is closed by making entries to Income Summary and Factory Overhead.
- Direct students to the illustration as you demonstrate how to close Factory Overhead when there is underapplied overhead (debit balance). Explain that if the estimated (applied) overhead had been greater than the actual overhead, Factory Overhead would have had a credit balance and the closing entry would have been just the opposite.

Recording Applied Overhead

GENERAL JOURNAL — PAGE *1*

	DATE	ACCOUNT TITLE	DOC. NO.	POST. REF.	DEBIT	CREDIT	
13	31	*Work in Process*	*M314*		60 966 50		13
14		*Factory Overhead*				60 966 50	14
15							15

Work in Process

Debit		Credit	
Jan. 1 Bal.	78,796.00		
Jan. 15 Dir. Lab.	44,220.00		
Jan. 31 Dir. Lab.	42,875.00		
Jan. 31 Dir. Mat.	143,876.00		
Jan. 31 App. OH	60,966.50		

Factory Overhead

Debit		Credit	
Jan. 31 Act. OH	61,203.00	Jan. 31 App. OH	60,966.50
(New Bal.	*236.50)*		

Custom Cyclery applies factory overhead to each job at the rate of 70% of direct labor charges. At the end of each month, Custom Cyclery totals the applied factory overhead recorded on all job cost sheets. Its applied factory overhead for January is *$60,966.50*. The journal entry to record applied factory overhead is shown above.

The Factory Overhead debit, *$61,203.00*, is the actual factory overhead expense for the month. The credit, *$60,966.50*, is the applied factory overhead for the month. The account's $236.50 ending debit balance results from recording less applied factory overhead than the amount of actual factory overhead expenses for the month.

Disposing of Overapplied and Underapplied Factory Overhead Balances

GENERAL JOURNAL — PAGE *1*

	DATE	ACCOUNT TITLE	DOC. NO.	POST. REF.	DEBIT	CREDIT	
15	31	*Income Summary*	*M315*		2 3 6 50		15
16		*Factory Overhead*				2 3 6 50	16
17							17

The rate used to calculate applied factory overhead is only an estimate. Therefore, Factory Overhead may have an ending balance. The amount by which applied factory overhead is less than actual factory overhead is called **underapplied overhead**. The debit balance, *$236.50*, in Custom Cyclery's account indicates underapplied overhead for January. The journal entry to close Factory Overhead at the end of January is shown above.

A credit balance indicates that applied factory overhead is more than actual factory overhead. The amount by which applied factory overhead is more than actual factory overhead is called **overapplied overhead**. If Factory Overhead has a credit balance, Factory Overhead is debited and Income Summary is credited for the overapplied overhead amount.

Overhead may be overapplied or underapplied for two reasons: (1) actual expenses may be higher or lower than normal, an event that requires closer control over expenditures; (2) the factory overhead applied rate may be inaccurate. If the rate is found to be inaccurate, a revised rate is determined. The revised rate is used in the next fiscal period.

FORMATIVE ASSESSMENT

- This is an ongoing process. Circulate around the classroom or lab, observing which students have difficulty with the assignments.
- Troubleshooting: Diagnose the kinds of problems students have with this lesson. Students may have difficulty remembering the journal entries for factory overhead.
- Assess student understanding by checking solutions to Independent Practice assignments and noting their answers to the Terms Review and Audit Your Understanding questions.

End of Lesson Review

LO5 Maintain records and prepare journal entries for factory overhead.

Terms Review

applied overhead

underapplied overhead

overapplied overhead

Audit your understanding

1. After factory overhead has been applied to work in process, what does a credit balance in Factory Overhead indicate?
2. Explain the difference between actual factory overhead and applied factory overhead.

Work together 17-2

Completing a cost sheet and journalizing entries for overhead

Use the cost sheet and journals used in Work Together 17-1. Your instructor will guide you through the following examples. Save your work for use in Work Together 17-3.

1. Job No. 218 was completed on April 30. Complete the cost sheet for Job No. 218. Factory overhead is applied based on direct labor hours. Estimated factory overhead for the period was $35,000.00. The number of estimated direct labor hours was 1,750. A total of 29 direct labor hours was used on Job No. 218.
2. Journalize the following transactions for April of the current year:

Transactions:

Apr. 30. Obtained factory costs for the month: depreciation on building, $800.00; depreciation on equipment, $850.00; insurance, $640.00; property taxes, $710.00; utilities, $1,600.00. M266. Assume that these expenses have already been properly accounted for and now need to be closed.

30. Applied overhead at the rate of $20.00 per direct labor hour, with 1,740 direct labor hours worked this period. M267.

30. Closed the Factory Overhead account. Actual total overhead costs for the period were $35,700.00. M268.

On your own 17-2

Completing a cost sheet and journalizing entries for overhead

Use the cost sheet and journals used in On Your Own 17-1. Work independently to complete the following problems. Save your work for use in On Your Own 17-3.

1. Job No. 587 was completed on May 28. Complete the cost sheet for Job No. 587. Factory overhead is applied to each job as a percentage of direct labor charges. Estimated factory overhead for the year is $280,000.00. Estimated direct labor cost for the year is $350,000.00.
2. Journalize the following transactions for May of the current year:

Transactions:

May 31. Obtained factory costs for the month: depreciation on building, $750.00; depreciation on equipment, $200.00; insurance, $400.00; property taxes, $950.00; utilities, $2,600.00. M385. Assume that these expenses have already been properly accounted for and now need to be closed.

31. Applied overhead at the rate determined in part 1 above. Total direct labor cost for the month is $29,000.00. M386.

31. Closed the Factory Overhead account. Actual total overhead costs for the period were $23,000.00. M387.

CHECK FOR UNDERSTANDING

Terms Review

- Call on students to define each term in the Terms Review. Definitions are given in the Glossary.

Audit Your Understanding

- Call on students to answer the Audit Your Understanding questions. Answers are given in Appendix D of the textbook.

GUIDED PRACTICE

Work Together

- Have students write the solution to the Work Together problem as you guide the class through the examples.
- Direct students to complete a cost sheet and to journalize entries for overhead.

INDEPENDENT PRACTICE

On Your Own

- Assign the On Your Own problem to be worked independently.
- Use the Formative Assessment techniques to diagnose student understanding.

Application Problem

- Assign Application Problem 17-2.

Online Working Papers

- Students can access the Lesson 17-2 problems using this software.

RETEACH

- Call on students to complete a cost sheet and to explain the elements.
- Review the journal entries for factory overhead.

CLOSURE

- Ask students to summarize briefly the accounting for factory overhead.

Essential Question

- Wouldn't it be less time-consuming to ignore overapplied and underapplied factory overhead? Explain the impact. *(It would be less time-consuming. However, it is important because the true cost of the product—or the job—would not be known. Therefore, one could not price the product, or job, to make a profit.)*

LESSON
17-3

BRIDGE

- Point out that in previous lessons, students learned how to prepare financial statements for a corporation. Although the financial statements for a manufacturing business are somewhat similar, students will learn about those that differ.

TEACHING RESOURCES

- **Instructor's Resource CD/Website:**
  PowerPoint Slides
  Accounting Concepts
- **Working Papers:**
  Teacher's Edition of the Working Papers for Lesson 17-3
  Online Working Papers
- **Transparency Masters:**
  Finished Goods Ledger Card
  3-Column Income Statement with % of Net Sales Column
  3-Column Statement Paper

ENGAGE

- Ask students to explain when to use a perpetual inventory. Explain that a perpetual inventory is used to keep a record of inventory accounts of finished goods.

PREVIEW

- Call on a student to read the accounting term and definition introduced in this lesson: *statement of cost of goods manufactured*.
- Point out the learning objectives for this lesson.
- Direct students to read the headings in this lesson and to examine the illustrations.

INPUT

- Direct students to the illustration to review journalizing entries used to update the general ledger accounts for costs incurred in completing jobs.

LESSON

17-3 Accounting for Finished Goods and Cost of Goods Sold and Financial Reporting for a Manufacturing Business

LO6 Journalize the transfer of work in process to finished goods.
LO7 Journalize a sale and the related cost of goods sold.
LO8 Prepare a statement of cost of goods manufactured.
LO9 Understand the differences on the income statement and balance sheet for a manufacturing business.

Recording Journal Entries for Manufacturing Accounts

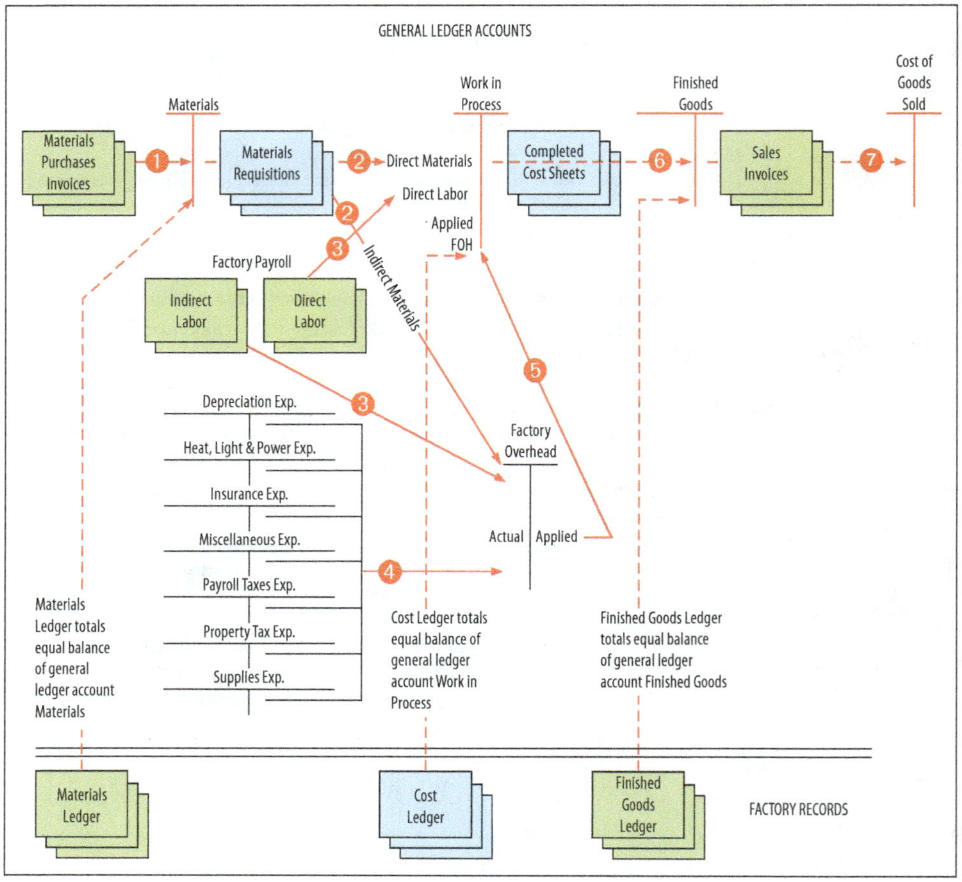

All manufacturing costs flow through the manufacturing accounts. These costs are recorded through each phase of the manufacturing process. Summary journal entries update general ledger accounts for costs incurred in completing jobs, as shown above. Thus, end-of-fiscal-period inventory adjustments are not required.

Recording Journal Entries for Manufacturing Accounts

1. Purchase materials.
2. Issue direct and indirect materials to the factory.
3. Record factory payroll.
4. Close individual manufacturing expense accounts.
5. Record applied overhead.
6. Record cost of products completed.
7. Record cost of products sold.

Finished Goods Ledger Card

1 Complete the Manufactured/Received columns.

2 Enter existing inventory balance.

FINISHED GOODS LEDGER CARD

Description *Bicycle* Stock No. *SFM*

Minimum *75* Location *Aisle 22L*

MANUFACTURED/RECEIVED					SHIPPED/ISSUED					BALANCE			
DATE	JOB NO.	QUANTITY	UNIT COST	TOTAL COST	DATE	SALES INVOICE NO.	QUANTITY	UNIT COST	TOTAL COST	DATE	QUANTITY	UNIT COST	TOTAL COST
										20-- *Jan. 1*	*106*	*98.00*	*10,388.00*
					17	*622*	*20*	*98.00*					
							30	*100.00*	*4,960.00*	*17*	*70*	*100.00*	*7,000.00*
19	*644*	*25*	*101.00*	*2,525.00*						*19*	*70*	*100.00*	
											25	*101.00*	*9,525.00*

3 Extend data for Job 644.

4 Calculate total cost.

When a job is completed, the finished goods are placed in the finished goods stock area. At this time, summary information from the cost sheet is recorded on the completed product's finished goods ledger card. The entry for the completed Job No. 644 is recorded on the finished goods ledger card shown above.

The total value for all finished goods ledger cards equals the Finished Goods inventory balance in the general ledger. After Custom Cyclery's Job No. 644 is completed and recorded, the company has 95 SFM bicycles on hand at a total cost of $9,525.00. This amount will be added to the total costs of all other finished goods still on hand to determine the balance of Finished Goods inventory in the general ledger.

Completing a Finished Goods Ledger Card

1. **Complete the Manufactured/Received columns of the finished goods ledger card.**
   (a) Record the date the finished goods are transferred to the finished goods inventory, 19; (b) enter the Job No., 644; (c) enter the quantity, 25; (d) enter the unit cost, 101.00; (e) enter the total cost, 2,525.00.
2. **Enter the existing inventory in the Balance columns.**
   (a) Enter the date, 19; (b) enter the previous quantity of fax machines in inventory, 70, and the unit cost, 100.00. Unit costs for each job may differ since the amount of direct materials and direct labor used may vary. Therefore, the unit costs for each job are kept separate.
3. **Extend the quantity, 25, and the unit cost, 101.00, for Job 644.**
4. **Calculate the total cost of all goods in inventory, 9,525.00 [(70 x $100.00) + (25 x $101.00)].** Although unit costs are kept separate, the total cost balance is combined for all units in the finished goods inventory. Custom Cyclery uses the first-in, first-out inventory method. Thus, the cost recorded first is the cost removed from inventory first when units are sold.

INPUT

- Explain that in the same way that completed jobs are moved from the factory floor to the finished goods area, the costs are transferred from Work in Process to Finished Goods by recording the quantity, unit cost, and total cost on the finished goods ledger card.
- Emphasize that the total value for all finished goods ledger cards equals the balance of Finished Goods in the general ledger.
- Explain that unit costs for each job may differ and therefore are kept separate on the finished goods ledger card.

MODEL

- Direct students to the illustration or use the transparency to explain transferring a job from Work in Process to Finished Goods.
- Explain recording information for Job No. 644 in the Manufactured/Received columns of the finished goods ledger card.
- Explain the completion of the Balance columns on January 19 after the job is completed.
- Point out that the first line on January 19 is for the 70 units still in inventory after the sale on the 17th.
- Explain that the increase from Job. No. 644 is recorded on the second line for the 19th. Point out that the 70 units in inventory have a different cost than the 25 units transferred from Work in Process.
- Demonstrate how to calculate the total cost for the quantities, using two different unit costs.

INPUT

- Remind students that when jobs are finished, the job cost sheets are completed. At the end of the month, the costs on these completed sheets are transferred to Finished Goods.
- Explain that the final two journal entries for the manufacturing accounts are (1) to transfer completed jobs out of Work in Process into Finished Goods and (2) to transfer goods that have been sold out of Finished Goods into Cost of Goods Sold.
- Students sometimes confuse the cost of products with the selling price of products. Point out that a company would have no net income if it sold products for the same price it cost to manufacture them.
- Explain that the cost of each unit sold is recorded on the company's copy of the sales invoice, and these costs are totaled and recorded in Cost of Goods Sold at the end of the month. Explain that this is a feature of a perpetual inventory system.

MODEL

Recording finished goods transactions

- Direct students to the illustration as you demonstrate the journal entry for transferring completed products from Work in Process to Finished Goods.
- Demonstrate that the total of the completed cost sheets, $288,543.25, is credited to Work in Process to remove those costs from that inventory account.
- Demonstrate that the total of the completed cost sheets is debited to Finished Goods to include those costs in that inventory account.

Recording sales and cost of goods sold

- Direct students to the illustration as you demonstrate how to record the cost of goods sold for products that have been sold during the month. Remind students that the amount is obtained by totaling the cost amounts recorded on each sales invoice during the month.
- Demonstrate that the costs are transferred out of Finished Goods with a credit, $268,115.00.
- Demonstrate that the costs are transferred into Cost of Goods sold with a debit for the same amount.

Recording Finished Goods Transactions LO6

GENERAL JOURNAL — PAGE 1

	DATE	ACCOUNT TITLE	DOC. NO.	POST. REF.	DEBIT	CREDIT	
17	31	*Finished Goods*	*M316*		*288 543 25*		17
18		*Work in Process*				*288 543 25*	18
19							19

Finished Goods

Debit		Credit	
Bal.	118,257.00		
Jan. 31 Completed Cost Sheets	288,543.25		

Work in Process

Debit		Credit	
Jan. 1 Bal.	78,796.00	Jan. 31 Completed Cost Sheets to Finished Goods	288,543.25
Jan. 15 Dir. Lab.	44,220.00		
Jan. 31 Dir. Lab.	42,875.00		
Jan. 31 Dir. Mat.	143,876.00		
Jan. 31 App. OH	60,966.50		
(New Bal. Jan. 31	*82,190.25)*		

Custom Cyclery totals the cost sheets for all jobs completed during the month. Its January total, *$288,543.25*, is the cost of work finished during the month. This amount is transferred from Work in Process to Finished Goods. The journal entry to record this transaction is shown above.

The balance in Finished Goods, *$118,257.00*, represents the beginning inventory. The January 31 debit to Finished Goods and credit to Work in Process, *$288,543.25*, represents the cost of finished goods transferred from the factory to the stockroom. The Work in Process balance, *$82,190.25*, is the total amount of direct labor, direct materials, and applied factory overhead charged to the jobs in the ending inventory of work in process.

Recording Sales and Cost of Goods Sold LO7

GENERAL JOURNAL — PAGE 1

	DATE	ACCOUNT TITLE	DOC. NO.	POST. REF.	DEBIT	CREDIT	
19	31	*Cost of Goods Sold*	*M317*		*268 115 00*		19
20		*Finished Goods*				*268 115 00*	20
21							21

Cost of Goods Sold

Debit		Credit	
Jan. 31 from Finished Goods	268,115.00		

Finished Goods

Debit		Credit	
Bal.	118,257.00	Jan. 31 Cost of Goods Sold	268,115.00
Jan. 31 Completed Cost Sheets	288,543.25		
(New Bal. Jan. 31	*138,685.25)*		

DIFFERENTIATED INSTRUCTION

Visual/Spatial learners enjoy drawing, designing, and seeing relationships. Allow students the opportunity to create a bulletin board with a map of manufacturing facilities in their community or a nearby city. Tell students to label the map with the name of the manufacturer and the items produced.

Custom Cyclery uses a perpetual inventory, one in which a continuous record is kept of increases and decreases to inventory accounts. Therefore, a different procedure is used to determine and record the cost of goods sold. A copy of each sales invoice is sent to the Accounting Department to record the sale. For each invoice, the unit cost of each product shipped and the total cost of all products shipped are calculated and recorded on the sales invoice copy.

At the end of the month, cost information on all sales invoices is totaled. The total costs recorded for Custom Cyclery's January sales, *$268,115.00*, is the cost of goods sold for the month. This number represents the total cost of products sold, not the revenue derived from sales (which is determined by the selling price). This total cost is transferred from the inventory account Finished Goods to the cost account Cost of Goods Sold, as shown on the previous page.

The debit to Cost of Goods Sold, *$268,115.00*, is the cost of goods sold during the month. The credit to Finished Goods, *$268,115.00*, is the cost of finished goods sold during the month and removed from inventory. The Finished Goods balance, *$138,685.25*, is the ending inventory of finished goods.

Statement of Cost of Goods Manufactured LO8

Custom Cyclery Corporation
Statement of Cost of Goods Manufactured
For Month Ended January 31, 20--

Direct Materials	$143,876.00
Direct Labor	87,095.00
Factory Overhead Applied	60,966.50
Total Cost of Work Placed in Process	$291,937.50
Work in Process Inventory, Jan. 1, 20--	78,796.00
Total Cost of Work in Process During January	$370,733.50
Less Work on Process Inventory, Jan. 31, 20--	82,190.25
Cost of Goods Manufactured	$288,543.25

Enter direct materials, direct labor, and factory overhead applied for the period.

Total the cost of work placed in process.

Add beginning work in process inventory.

Subtract ending work in process inventory.

A manufacturing business prepares an income statement, a statement of stockholders' equity, and a balance sheet. These statements are similar to those previously described for other kinds of businesses. A statement showing details about the cost of finished goods is called a **statement of cost of goods manufactured**. This statement shows the amounts of the cost elements—materials, direct labor, and factory overhead—spent on the goods completed in a fiscal period. A statement of cost of goods manufactured supplements the income statement. Custom Cyclery's statement of cost of goods manufactured is shown above.

The direct materials amount, *$143,876.00*, is the amount debited to Work in Process in the general journal on page 503. The direct labor amount, *$87,095.00*, is the total direct labor entered in the cash payments journal, page 505. The factory overhead amount, *$60,966.50*, is the total of the applied factory overhead recorded on the cost sheet and recorded in the general journal on page 510.

INPUT

- Explain that a cost of goods manufactured statement is unique to a manufacturing business.
- Point out that a cost of goods manufactured statement is a supplement to the income statement because it shows the details of one of the items on the income statement—the cost of goods manufactured.

MODEL

- Direct students to the illustration as you explain how to prepare a cost of goods manufactured statement.
- Explain that the total cost of work placed in process is calculated by adding direct materials from the total requisitions, direct labor gathered from the costs sheets, and applied factory overhead obtained from the job cost sheets.
- Demonstrate how to add the beginning balance of Work in Process from the general ledger to the total cost of work placed in process to get the total cost of Work in Process during the month.
- Demonstrate how to subtract the ending balance of Work in Process to get the cost of goods manufactured.

INPUT

- Explain the two ways that an income statement for a manufacturing business differs from that of a merchandising business.
- Point out that the partial income statement illustrated is the only part of the income statement that differs from those presented previously.

MODEL

- Use a transparency or direct students to the illustration as you demonstrate how to prepare an income statement for a manufacturing business.
- Demonstrate that the Cost of Goods Sold section is similar to that of a merchandising business. Demonstrate that the beginning inventory and the cost of goods manufactured are added to obtain the total cost of finished goods available for sale. Demonstrate that the ending finished goods inventory is then subtracted to obtain the cost of goods sold.
- Demonstrate that the cost of goods sold needs to be adjusted by the amount of overapplied or underapplied overhead. Demonstrate that underapplied overhead is added to the cost of goods sold to obtain the net cost of goods sold.
- Demonstrate how to calculate component percentages.

INPUT

- Explain that there is little difference between the balance sheet of a merchandising and a manufacturing business.
- Point out that the primary difference in a balance sheet for a manufacturing business is that there are three manufacturing inventory accounts—Materials, Work in Process, and Finished Goods—rather than a single merchandise inventory account.
- Explain that although a statement of stockholders' equity and a statement of cash flows are not illustrated, they would not differ from those of a merchandising business.

MODEL

- Use the transparency or direct students to the illustration as you explain the preparation of a balance sheet.
- Demonstrate the preparation of the Assets section. Point out that the three inventory accounts are listed separately in the Current Assets section.
- Explain that the remainder of the balance sheet is the same as what students learned previously.

Income Statement for a Manufacturing Business LO9

Custom Cyclery Corporation
Partial Income Statement
For Month Ended January 31, 20--

			% of Net Sales
Operating Revenue:			
Sales		$413,000.00	100.0%
Cost of Goods Sold:			
Finished Goods Inventory, Jan. 1, 20--	$118,257.00		
Cost of Goods Manufactured	288,543.25		
Total Cost of Finished Goods Available for Sale	$406,800.25		
Less Finished Goods Inventory, Jan. 31, 20--	138,685.25		
Cost of Goods Sold	$268,115.00		
Underapplied Overhead	236.50		
Net Cost of Goods Sold		268,351.50	65.0%
Gross Profit on Operations		$144,648.50	35.0%

The income statement for a manufacturing business differs in two ways from the income statements of merchandising businesses shown in previous chapters:

1. Cost of goods manufactured is used instead of purchases. This amount is taken from the statement of cost of goods manufactured.
2. The amount of underapplied overhead, *$236.50*, is added to the cost of goods sold. The amount is added because applied overhead is less than the actual overhead. The cost of goods manufactured, shown on the previous page, includes the applied overhead amount rather than the actual amount. The income statement must be adjusted to reflect actual factory overhead costs. Theoretically, the underapplied or overapplied overhead should be apportioned among the Work in Process inventory, Finished Goods inventory, and Cost of Goods Sold accounts. However, since the amount is small, it is charged entirely to Cost of Goods Sold. The partial income statement for Custom Cyclery Corporation, with these differences, is shown above. After Gross Profit on Operations, the remaining income statement is the same as those shown in previous chapters.

Balance Sheet for a Manufacturing Business

Custom Cyclery Corporation
Partial Balance Sheet
January 31, 20--

ASSETS			
Current Assets:			
Cash		$185,269.21	
Petty Cash		200.00	
Accounts Receivable	$234,112.75		
Less Allowance for Uncollectible Accounts	7,035.25	227,077.50	
Materials		102,451.61	
Work in Process		82,190.25	
Finished Goods		138,685.25	
Supplies—Factory		7,871.00	
Supplies—Sales		7,258.50	
Supplies—Administrative		1,945.00	
Prepaid Insurance		3,500.00	
Total Current Assets			$756,448.32

TEACHING IDEA **Explain that consumers often make decisions to spend more money to prevent further problems down the road. Ask students to identify problems that could occur if thought did not go into selecting the best supplier of materials. Then ask students to pair up with another student and make a list of 3–5 ways that consumers spend a little more money to prevent problems at a later date. Examples might include dental cleanings, yearly heating/cooling maintenance, physical exams, and driveway sealing.**

A partial balance sheet prepared by Custom Cyclery Corporation on January 31 of the current year is shown on the previous page.

Except for the list of inventories, the balance sheet of a manufacturing business is similar to the balance sheet of a merchandising business. In a manufacturing business, the Current Assets section of the balance sheet lists three types of inventories: (1) materials, (2) work in process, and (3) finished goods.

A statement of stockholders' equity and a statement of cash flows for a manufacturing business are similar to those of a merchandising business described in previous chapters.

© iStockphoto.com/Lusky

GLOBAL AWARENESS

Why Do Foreign Exchange Rates Change?

When a business transaction is completed between companies in different countries, one of the companies will be dealing with foreign currency. The price of the goods being sold will have to be stated in the currency of one of the countries. As discussed in Chapter 8 (p. 257), if the exchange rate changes between the time of the sale and the payment date, one company will report a foreign currency loss and the other company will report a foreign currency gain.

The exchange rate between two countries is based on the relative value of each country's currency in terms of supply and demand. For example, if the demand for Country A's currency is low compared to the currency for Country B, the value of Country A's currency will decrease. Thus, it will take more of Country A's currency to buy imported goods from Country B, so the demand for local goods in Country A will increase. In addition, it will take less of Country B's currency to buy goods from Country A, increasing the demand for exports to Country B.

What causes a country's currency to change value? While many factors influence the value of a currency, three major factors are commonly cited: balance of trade, inflation, and interest rates.

The difference between the value of a country's exports and the value of its imports is called its *balance of trade*. A *trade surplus* exists when exports exceed imports. A *trade deficit* exists when imports exceed exports. When a country has a trade surplus, the demand for its currency is high and, therefore, the value of its currency will increase. A trade deficit causes a decrease in the demand for the currency and a decrease in the currency's value.

Countries with a high inflation rate will produce products with a higher price, which will discourage exports. Products from countries with a lower inflation rate will have a lower cost, which will encourage imports. Therefore, inflation affects the balance of trade, which affects the value of a country's currency.

As the interest rates increase in a country, the interest rates on new bonds will also increase. This increases the demand for that country's bonds, which will increase the value of its currency. As interest rates decrease in a country, the value of its currency will also decrease.

CRITICAL THINKING

Prior to 2005, China had a fixed exchange rate. This can happen when a government buys or sells its own currency in order to have it maintain a fixed value. In 2005, China discontinued its fixed exchange rate. What impact would this have on the value of the Chinese currency?

GLOBAL AWARENESS

Answer

A fixed exchange rate eliminates the uncertainty involved in business transactions. With a fixed exchange rate, a company doing business with China does not have to worry about a foreign currency loss. Because China has discontinued its fixed exchange rate, companies doing business with China face the risk of foreign currency losses and gains. Also, China's currency will now fluctuate in value, which will affect its balance of trade with other countries.

FORMATIVE ASSESSMENT

- This is an ongoing process. Circulate around the classroom or lab, observing which students have difficulty with the assignments.
- Troubleshooting: Diagnose the kinds of problems students have with this lesson. Students may have difficulty (1) completing a finished goods ledger, (2) recording journal entries for manufacturing accounts, (3) completing a statement of cost of goods manufactured, and (4) remembering the differences between the financial statements for a corporation and those for a manufacturing business.
- Assess student understanding by checking solutions to Independent Practice assignments and noting their answers to the Term Review and Audit Your Understanding questions.

CHECK FOR UNDERSTANDING

Term Review

- Call on a student to define the term in the Term Review. A definition is given in the Glossary.

Audit Your Understanding

- Call on students to answer the Audit Your Understanding questions. Answers are given in Appendix D of the textbook.

GUIDED PRACTICE

Work Together

- Have students write the solution to the Work Together problem as you guide the class through the examples.
- Direct students to update a finished goods ledger card and to journalize entries for finished goods and cost of goods sold.

INDEPENDENT PRACTICE

On Your Own

- Assign the On Your Own problem to be worked independently.
- Use the Formative Assessment techniques to diagnose student understanding.

Application Problems

- Assign Application Problem 17-3.1.
- Assign Application Problem 17-3.2.

Online Working Papers

- Students can access the Lesson 17-3 problems using this software.

RETEACH

- Call on students to describe each line on the statement of cost of goods manufactured and to explain how it is calculated.
- Review financial statement preparation as needed.

CLOSURE

- Ask students to summarize briefly the procedures for completing end-of-period work for a manufacturing business.

Essential Question

- What would be the impact of not calculating cost of goods manufactured? (*A business would not know where its money is going at every stage of the manufacturing process.*)

End of Lesson Review

LO6 Journalize the transfer of work in process to finished goods.

LO7 Journalize a sale and the related cost of goods sold.

LO8 Prepare a statement of cost of goods manufactured.

LO9 Understand the differences on the income statement and balance sheet for a manufacturing business.

Term Review

statement of cost of goods manufactured

Audit your understanding

1. How is overapplied overhead accounted for on an income statement?
2. In which section of the balance sheet are the three inventory accounts of a manufacturing business listed?

Work together 17-3

Updating a finished goods ledger card; journalizing entries for finished goods and cost of goods sold

Use the forms and journals used in Work Together 17-2. Your instructor will guide you through the following examples.

1. Using the cost sheet for Job No. 218, update the finished goods ledger card for Desk G-78.
2. Journalize the following transactions for April of the current year:

Transactions:

Apr. 30. Transferred products costing $74,600.00 to finished goods during the month. M269.
30. Sold products costing $69,700.00 during the month. M270.

On your own 17-3

Updating a finished goods ledger card; journalizing entries for finished goods and cost of goods sold

Use the forms and journals used in On Your Own 17-2. Work independently to complete the following problems.

1. Using the cost sheet for Job No. 587, update the finished goods ledger card for grill Model SS412.
2. Journalize the following transactions for May of the current year:

Transactions:

May 31. Transferred products costing $92,500.00 to finished goods during the month. M388.
31. Sold products costing $89,700.00 during the month. M389.

EXTENDED LEARNING

Assign Global Awareness on page 517.

LESSON
17-4 Standard Costs and Variance Analysis

LO10 Calculate and analyze variances related to direct materials.
LO11 Calculate and analyze variances related to direct labor.

Standard Costs

To increase net income, management must control costs. Since direct materials and direct labor can comprise a large portion of total costs, these two items are often the focus of cost controls. Dixon Molding Corporation, a manufacturer of molded plastic items, makes plastic cell phone cases. Dixon management wants to determine if the cost of each cell phone case is as low as possible in terms of direct materials and direct labor.

One way of evaluating this is for Dixon to determine how much plastic should be used for each case, how much that plastic should cost, how much direct labor should be employed for each case, and how much that direct labor should cost. An estimated amount of direct materials or direct labor, usually in price or quantity, established for each unit produced is called a **standard**. A **standard costing system** is a system of setting standards for each cost of production. The estimated amount of direct materials to be used per unit of output is called the **materials quantity standard**. The estimated cost per unit of direct materials is called the **materials price standard**. The estimated amount of direct labor needed to produce one unit of output is called the **labor quantity standard**. The labor quantity standard is also referred to as the *labor efficiency standard.* The estimated cost per hour of direct labor is called the **labor price standard**. The labor price standard is also referred to as the *labor rate standard.*

Once standards are established, they can be compared to actual results to evaluate the efficiency of the manufacturing process. A standard costing system assists company management in planning and controlling company performance.

Dixon's management has established the following standards:

Material quantity standard	4 ounces per cell phone case
Material price standard	$0.03 per ounce
Labor quantity standard	0.1 hour per cell phone case
Labor price standard	$15.00 per hour

Using these standards, Dixon can calculate the total standard cost of one cell phone case as follows:

	Quantity Standard	×	Price Standard	=	Total
Direct materials	4 ounces	×	$0.03	=	$0.12
Direct labor	0.1 hour	×	$15.00	=	1.50
Total cost				=	$1.62

LESSON
17-4

BRIDGE

- Point out that in previous lessons students learned how to calculate the cost of manufacturing goods. In this lesson, they will learn how management analyzes and controls costs.

TEACHING RESOURCES

- **Instructor's Resource CD/Website:**
  PowerPoint Slides
  Accounting Concepts
- **Working Papers:**
  Teacher's Edition of the Working Papers for Lesson 17-4
  Online Working Papers

ENGAGE

- Explain that management must learn not only how to account for a manufacturing business but also how to analyze the data to make decisions to enhance products, reduce costs, or prevent costs.

PREVIEW

- Call on students to read the accounting terms and definitions introduced in this lesson: *standard, standard costing system, materials quantity standard, materials price standard, labor quantity standard, labor price standard, total materials variance, materials price variance, materials quantity variance, total labor variance, labor price variance,* and *labor quantity variance.*
- Point out the learning objectives for this lesson.
- Direct students to read the headings in this lesson and to examine the illustrations.

INPUT

- Explain that standards must be set to control costs.
- Direct students to the illustration for examples of quantity and pricing standards.
- Point out that standards can be used as comparisons to evaluate efficiency of the manufacturing process.

INPUT

- Explain that a comparison of standard costs and the actual costs allows management to analyze variances in total materials
- Point out the differences between favorable and unfavorable variances.

THINK LIKE AN ACCOUNTANT

Students complete a cost variance analysis schedule and use IF functions to identify variances as favorable or unfavorable.

Solution

1. Materials price variance, ($265) favorable; materials usage variance, $1,290 unfavorable.
2. Materials price variance, ($35) favorable; materials usage variance, $60 unfavorable.
3. Using too little material or purchasing cheaper material of lesser quality may result in favorable variances but negatively impact the quality of the finished product.

Total Materials Variance LO10

$$
\begin{array}{rcccc}
\text{Total Materials Variance} & = & \text{Actual Cost} & - & \text{Standard Cost} \\
 & = & (AP \times AQ) & - & (SP \times SQ) \\
 & = & (\$0.028 \times 890{,}000) & - & (\$0.03 \times 800{,}000) \\
 & = & \$24{,}920.00 & - & \$24{,}000.00 \\
 & = & \$920.00 & & \text{Unfavorable}
\end{array}
$$

Where:
AP = Actual Price
AQ = Actual Quantity
SP = Standard Price
SQ = Standard Quantity

The difference between the actual cost of materials and the expected standard cost of materials is called the **total materials variance**. Using the standard costs listed on page 519, Dixon Molding Corporation can calculate its total materials variance.

Assume that Dixon produced 200,000 cell phone cases in March. Dixon purchased and used 890,000 ounces of plastic at a cost of $24,920.00, or $0.028 per ounce ($24,920.00 ÷ 890,000 ounces). According to its materials quantity standard, Dixon should have used 800,000 ounces of plastic (200,000 units × 4 ounces per unit).

Filling in the above formula, the actual price per ounce of plastic purchased is $0.028. The actual quantity purchased and used in production is 890,000 ounces of plastic. The standard price per ounce of plastic is $0.03. The standard quantity is 800,000 ounces. Therefore, the actual cost is $24,920.00, and the standard cost for 200,000 units is $24,000.00. Since the actual cost is more than the standard cost, the $920.00 variance is said to be *unfavorable*. This unfavorable variance means that Dixon paid $920.00 more for materials than it should have according to the materials price and quantity standards.

THINK LIKE AN ACCOUNTANT

Measuring Material Variances

Management accountants are responsible for monitoring the costs of production. Accountants establish standards for the quantity and price of the material that should be used for each unit produced. For example, Dutch Bakery expects to use 3 cups of flour for each loaf of bread. Each cup of flour is expected to cost $0.30. These amounts are known as *standards*. Any variance from the standards should be investigated and appropriate actions taken.

Dutch Bakery used 48,600 pounds of flour last week to produce 16,200 loaves of bread. The company should have spent $14,580 for the flour. The job cost records indicate that the flour cost $15,606, or $0.295 per cup. Thus, the company spent $1,026 more on flour than it expected.

OPEN THE SPREADSHEET TLA_CH17

The workbook contains an incomplete materials variance analysis. Follow the steps on the Instructions tab to calculate what portion of the total variance can be attributed to the quantity and the price of material used.

1. Determine the materials price variance and materials usage variance for the flour used in last week's bread production.
2. During the same week, Dutch Bakery used 7,050 cups of the same flour to produce 2,900 pound cakes. The company expected to use 2.5 cups of flour for each cake. Calculate the materials price and material usage variances.
3. How can a favorable materials price or material usage variance require managers to take corrective actions?

© iStockphoto.com/Dan Bachman

Materials Price Variance

Materials Price Variance	=	AQ	×	(AP − SP)
	=	890,000	×	($0.028 − $0.03)
	=	890,000	×	$0.002
	=	$1,780.00		Favorable

Where:
AQ = Actual Quantity
AP = Actual Price
SP = Standard Price

The total materials variance of $920.00 can have one of two causes: (1) the quantity used is different from the standard quantity at that level of production or (2) the price paid for plastic is different from the standard price. To understand the cause of the variance in more detail, Dixon calculates two additional materials variances.

The difference between the actual price paid for materials and the materials price standard at the actual quantity purchased and used is called the **materials price variance**. Using the standards and the actual amounts previously given, Dixon calculates its materials price variance as shown above.

The actual quantity of plastic purchased and used in production is 890,000 ounces. The actual price paid for the plastic is $0.028 per ounce. The standard price for plastic is $0.03 per ounce. Because the actual price paid for plastic is less than the standard price for plastic, the $1,780.00 variance is said to be *favorable.*

Materials Quantity Variance

Materials Quantity Variance	=	SP	×	(AQ − SQ)
	=	$0.03	×	(890,000 − 800,000)
	=	$0.03	×	90,000
	=	$2,700.00		Unfavorable

Where:
SP = Standard Price
AQ = Actual Quantity
SQ = Standard Quantity

The difference between the actual quantity of materials purchased and used in production and the standard quantity of materials for that level of production at the standard price is called the **materials quantity variance**.

Dixon calculates its materials quantity variance as shown above. The standard price of plastic is $0.03 per ounce. The actual quantity of material used to produce 200,000 units is 890,000 ounces. The standard quantity is 800,000 ounces. Because the actual quantity used is more than the standard quantity, the $2,700.00 variance is said to be *unfavorable.*

The difference between the materials quantity variance ($2,700.00 Unfavorable) and the materials price variance ($1,780.00 Favorable) is equal to the total materials variance of $920.00 Unfavorable.

Dixon's management will want to investigate these variances to determine what actions need to be taken. Was the lower materials cost due to obtaining material of lesser quality? Were waste and spoilage higher than normal because of these materials? If so, since the total materials variance was unfavorable, it indicates that the less expensive plastic saved Dixon less money than the added cost caused by inferior materials. Are material costs decreasing? If so, Dixon may need to review the materials price standard to reflect new, lower costs.

INPUT

- Explain that the materials price variance can be calculated using the standards and the actual amounts.
- Point out the two reasons that there may be a materials price variance.
- Direct students to the math illustration while you explain the calculation for determining the materials quantity variance.
- Point out some of the reasons variances may be unfavorable and explain how this might relate to the materials price standard.

INPUT

- Explain how to calculate the total labor variance.
- Direct students to the math illustration while you explain the calculation for determining the total labor variance.
- Point out the two reasons there may be a labor variance—quantity and/or price variances on labor.

Total Labor Variance LO11

Total Labor Variance	=	Actual Cost	−	Standard Cost
	=	(AP × AQ)	−	(SP × SQ)
	=	($15.10 × 19,000)	−	($15.00 × 20,000)
	=	$286,900.00		$300,000.00
		$13,100.00		Favorable

Where:
AP = Actual Price
AQ = Actual Quantity
SP = Standard Price
SQ = Standard Quantity

The difference between the actual cost of labor and the expected standard cost of labor is called the **total labor variance**. Using the standard costs listed on page 519, Dixon Molding Corporation can calculate its total labor variance.

Assume, again, that Dixon produced 200,000 cell phone cases in March. Dixon used 19,000 hours of direct labor at a cost of $286,900.00, or $15.10 per hour ($286,900.00 ÷ 19,000). According to its labor quantity standard, Dixon should have used 20,000 hours of direct labor (200,000 × 0.1 hour per unit).

Filling in the above formula, the actual price per hour of direct labor is $15.10. The actual quantity of labor is 19,000 hours. The standard price of labor is $15.00 per hour. The standard quantity of labor is 20,000 hours. Therefore, the actual cost of labor is $286,900.00, and the standard cost of labor for 200,000 units is $300,000.00. Since the actual cost is less than the standard cost, the $13,100.00 variance is said to be *favorable*. This favorable variance means that Dixon paid $13,100.00 less for labor than it should have according to the labor price and quantity standards.

© Rob Marmion/Shutterstock.com

DIFFERENTIATED INSTRUCTION

Tactile/Kinesthetic learners enjoy learning by going outside the classroom, and **auditory/linguistic learners** enjoy conversing with others. Ask students to schedule a meeting with a local manufacturer. Instruct students to ask how hiring employees and selecting suppliers impacts the cost of goods manufactured. Tell students to be prepared to present their findings to the class.

Labor Price Variance

$$\begin{aligned} \text{Labor Price Variance} &= \text{AQ} \times (\text{AP} - \text{SP}) \\ &= 19{,}000 \times (\$15.10 - \$15.00) \\ &= 19{,}000 \times \$0.10 \\ &= \$1{,}900.00 \quad \text{Unfavorable} \end{aligned}$$

Where:
AQ = Actual Quantity
AP = Actual Price
SP = Standard Price

The total labor variance of $13,100.00 can be caused by two reasons: (1) the quantity used is different from the standard quantity at that level of production or (2) the price paid for labor is different from the standard price. To understand the cause of the variance in more detail, Dixon calculates two additional labor variances.

The difference between the actual price paid for labor and the labor price standard at the actual quantity used is called the **labor price variance**. Using the standards and the actual amounts previously given, Dixon calculates its labor price variance as shown above.

The actual quantity of labor used in production is 19,000 hours. The actual price paid for labor is $15.10 per hour. The standard price for labor is $15.00 per hour. Because the actual price paid for labor is more than the standard price for labor, the $1,900.00 variance is said to be *unfavorable*.

Labor Quantity Variance

$$\begin{aligned} \text{Labor Quantity Variance} &= \text{SP} \times (\text{AQ} - \text{SQ}) \\ &= \$15.00 \times (19{,}000 - 20{,}000) \\ &= \$15.00 \times 1{,}000 \\ &= \$15{,}000.00 \quad \text{Favorable} \end{aligned}$$

Where:
SP = Standard Price
AQ = Actual Quantity
SQ = Standard Quantity

The difference between the actual quantity of labor used in production and the standard quantity of labor for that level of production at the standard price is called the **labor quantity variance**.

Dixon calculates its labor quantity variance as shown above. The standard price of labor is $15.00 per hour. The actual quantity of labor used to produce 200,000 units is 19,000 hours. The standard quantity is 20,000 hours. Because the quantity used is less than the standard quantity, the $15,000.00 variance is said to be *favorable*.

The difference between the labor quantity variance ($15,000.00 Favorable) and the labor price variance ($1,900.00 Unfavorable) is equal to the total labor variance of $13,100.00 Favorable.

Even though the total labor variance is favorable, Dixon's management will want to investigate the labor variances to determine the cause of the variances. Are labor costs rising? If so, the labor price standard may have to be changed. Did Dixon employ more experienced workers than normal? If so, are these more experienced workers more efficient, causing the favorable variance for labor quantity? Should more experienced workers be used for this process in the future?

Labor variances may be related to materials variances. Any possible connection should be investigated. Did Dixon have to assign more experienced workers to the process because lesser quality materials were purchased? Would more materials have been used if less experienced workers were employed?

INPUT

- Explain how to determine labor price variances.
- Direct students to the math illustration while you explain the calculation for determining the total labor price variance.

INPUT

- Explain how to determine labor quantity variances.
- Direct students to the math illustration while you explain the calculation for determining the total labor quantity variance.
- Point out some of the questions that management should consider while analyzing the variance.

FORMATIVE ASSESSMENT

- This is an ongoing process. Circulate around the classroom or lab, observing which students have difficulty with the assignments.
- Troubleshooting: Diagnose the kinds of problems students have with this lesson. Students may have difficulty remembering the calculations for determining the variances and determining when the variances are favorable or unfavorable.
- Assess student understanding by checking solutions to Independent Practice assignments and noting their answers to the Terms Review and Audit Your Understanding questions.

CHECK FOR UNDERSTANDING

Terms Review

- Call on students to define each term in the Terms Review. Definitions are given in the Glossary.

Audit Your Understanding

- Call on students to answer the Audit Your Understanding questions. Answers are given in Appendix D of the textbook.

GUIDED PRACTICE

Work Together

- Have students write the solution to the Work Together problem as you guide the class through the examples.
- Direct students to calculate variances for materials and labor.

INDEPENDENT PRACTICE

On Your Own

- Assign the On Your Own problem to be worked independently.
- Use the Formative Assessment techniques to diagnose student understanding.

Application Problem

- Assign Application Problem 17-4.

Online Working Papers

- Students can access the Lesson 17-4 problems using this software.

RETEACH

- Give students different scenarios to use in calculating variances for materials and labor.
- Ask a student to explain how to complete a cost sheet.
- Ask students to review the differences in the financial statements for a manufacturing business and a corporation.

CLOSURE

- Ask students to summarize how to calculate variances related to direct materials and direct labor.
- Ask students to explain how to analyze variances related to direct materials and direct labor.

End of Lesson Review

LO10 Calculate and analyze variances related to direct materials.

LO11 Calculate and analyze variances related to direct labor.

Terms Review

standard
standard costing system
materials quantity standard
materials price standard
labor quantity standard
labor price standard
total materials variance
materials price variance
materials quantity variance
total labor variance
labor price variance
labor quantity variance

Audit your understanding

1. What is the formula for total materials variance?
2. If the actual materials cost is less than the standard cost, is the variance favorable or unfavorable?
3. How can the total materials variance be related to the total labor variance?

Work together 17-4

Calculating variances for materials and labor

Glommen Corporation makes jeans. Glommen's management has established the following standards:

Material quantity standard	3 yards per pair of jeans
Material price standard	$6.00 per yard
Labor quantity standard	1 hour per pair of jeans
Labor price standard	$12.00 per hour

Glommen actually produced 150,000 pairs of jeans this month. It purchased and used 445,000 yards of denim at a total cost of $2,714,500.00. A total of 151,200 hours of direct labor were used at a total cost of $1,829,520.00. Forms are provided in the *Working Papers*. Your instructor will guide you through the following examples.

1. Calculate the total materials variance, the materials price variance, and the materials quantity variance. Comment on your results.
2. Calculate the total labor variance, the labor price variance, and the labor quantity variance. Comment on your results.

On your own 17-4

Calculating variances for materials and labor

Northstar, Inc., produces wooden bird feeders. Northstar's management has established the following standards:

Material quantity standard	2 board feet per feeder
Material price standard	$1.50 per board foot
Labor quantity standard	0.5 hour per feeder
Labor price standard	$10.00 per hour

Northstar actually produced 1,000,000 bird feeders this year. It purchased and used 2,020,000 board feet of wood at a total cost of $2,949,200.00. A total of 480,000 hours of direct labor were used at a total cost of $4,790,400.00. Forms are provided in the *Working Papers*. Work independently to complete the following problems.

1. Calculate the total materials variance, the materials price variance, and the materials quantity variance. Comment on your results.
2. Calculate the total labor variance, the labor price variance, and the labor quantity variance. Comment on your results.

Essential Questions

- Why would favorable labor variances warrant further scrutiny by management? (*A favorable labor variance may indicate further investigation is needed to determine if all tasks are being completed on a job.*)
- How are standards determined? (*Standards are usually determined by industrial engineers through time and motion studies.*)

EXTENDED LEARNING

- Assign Think Like an Accountant on page 520.

Chapter Summary

The cost of a manufactured product consists of three cost elements: (1) direct materials, (2) direct labor, and (3) factory overhead. Direct materials are those materials that have significant value and become an identifiable part of the finished product. Direct labor is the cost of labor connected directly to the manufacture of the product. Factory overhead consists of all other manufacturing costs, such as indirect materials, indirect labor, cleaning supplies, factory depreciation, and insurance.

A manufacturing business uses three inventory accounts: (1) Materials, (2) Work in Process, and (3) Finished Goods. As these materials and labor costs flow through the manufacturing process, the related costs must flow through the accounts via journal entries. Overhead costs are recorded by using a predetermined overhead rate. At the end of the period, overapplied overhead or underapplied overhead must be transferred to Cost of Goods Sold.

The cost of each job order must also be recorded. A cost sheet is used to collect the direct materials, direct labor, and factory overhead costs for each job. When the job is complete, the total cost is known and a per-unit cost can be calculated.

The statement of cost of goods manufactured is used by a manufacturing company to calculate the cost of goods manufactured, which replaces the purchases line on the income statement. On the balance sheet, a manufacturing company must report all three inventory accounts.

Standard costs are established in a standard costing system. These standard costs can then be used to evaluate the performance of a company in terms of materials used, the price paid for materials, the labor hours employed, and the cost of labor through variance calculation and analysis.

ISO 9001 Certification

EXPLORE ACCOUNTING

A manufacturing company can make all of its component parts or purchase some of those parts from other companies. If the company purchases components from another company, it needs assurance about the quality of the parts. Rather than personally examining each supplier's manufacturing process, the purchasing company can require its suppliers to be ISO 9001 certified. ISO 9001 certification assures customers that the company has an effective quality management system that continually evaluates and improves the production process.

The ISO certification program was developed by the International Organization of Standardization (ISO), a worldwide federation of national standards organizations. ISO's role includes programs that certify the manufacturing process. To become ISO 9001 certified, a company must follow ISO's standards for various phases of the production process, including design, development, production, inspection, and servicing. The company must maintain an information system to record its compliance with ISO standards. Finally, the company must hire an independent organization to audit its initial and continuing compliance with ISO standards. ISO 9001 certification does not assure or guarantee the production of quality products. However, ISO 9001 certification does make a positive statement about a company's commitment to quality.

Other than helping to control costs, how does ISO 9001 certification impact accounting? Accountants assist in designing and operating the information system necessary to collect ISO 9001 compliance data. Accountants in public accounting firms are also involved in ISO 9001 certification. These firms can either assist a client to prepare for the ISO 9001 certification process or be the independent organization that audits the client and awards ISO 9001 certification.

INSTRUCTIONS

1. How is ISO certification similar to financial statement audits?
2. Several types of ISO certification are available. Explain the purpose of the ISO 14000 family of standards.
3. An acronym for the International Organization of Standardization would logically be "IOS." Explain why the ISO title is used for the organization and its certifications.

© iStockphoto.com/Makhnach_M

CLOSURE

- Review the Chapter Summary.
- Ask students to prepare a list of the new concepts introduced in this chapter.

Essential Questions

- Who would be responsible for variances? (*Answers will differ, but most will indicate the production manager.*)
- How can the poor selection of a vendor create an unfavorable materials variance? (*Vendors who supply poor-quality material or damaged products could create an unfavorable materials variance.*)
- How can poor employee hiring create an unfavorable labor variance? (*Hiring unskilled workers can result in labor costs that exceed the standard.*)

EXPLORE ACCOUNTING

Answers

1. An independent auditor tests documentation produced by the ISO information system to determine if the company is complying with the ISO standard. The auditor then issues a report certifying that the company is in conformance.
2. The ISO 14000 family of standards deals with environmental management systems. The standards require a company to be in compliance with environmental laws and to strive to improve the environmental impact of its manufacturing processes.
3. Because "International Organization of Standardization" would have different acronyms in different languages ("IOS" in English, "OIN" in French for "Organisation internationale de normalization," etc.), its founders decided to give it also a short, all-purpose name. They chose "ISO," derived from the Greek root "isos," meaning "equal." It was chosen to identify standards that use the same or equal specifications.

EXTENDED LEARNING

- Assign Explore Accounting on page 525.

CHECK FIGURES

For complete solutions to Chapter 17 problems, see the Teacher's Edition of the Working Papers.

Application Problem 17-1.1

1. Materials Ledger Card: Jan. 13 Balance, $7,800.00.

Application Problem 17-1.2

3. General Journal: Credit to Materials, $44,000.00.

   Cash Payments Journal: Credit to Cash, $50,437.00.

Apply Your Understanding

INSTRUCTIONS: Download problem instructions for Excel, QuickBooks, and Sage 50 from the textbook companion website at www.C21accounting.com.

17-1.1 Application Problem: Completing a materials ledger card and journalizing entries in a materials purchases journal LO2, 3

Wold Appliance makes all appliances, but specializes in washing machines and dryers. A partially completed materials ledger card and a materials purchases journal are given in the *Working Papers*.

Instructions:

1. Record the following transactions for FL7500 Washer Tubs on the materials ledger card. The price for this tub is $24.00 per unit. Update the balance when necessary.

Transactions:

Jan. 3. Recorded Purchase Order No. 613 for 200 units.
3. Recorded Requisition No. 775, moving 10 tubs into production.
10. Recorded Requisition No. 782, moving 45 tubs into production.
13. Received Purchase Order No. 613.

2. Record the following purchases in a materials purchases journal.

Transactions:

Jan. 3. Purchased materials on account from KB Manufacturing, $3,212.00. P610.
5. Purchased materials on account from Northend Motors, $21,567.00. P611.
12. Purchased materials on account from Gateway Gear, Inc., $6,765.00. P612.
13. Purchased materials on account from Washington Corporation, $4,800.00. P613.

17-1.2 Application Problem: Recording and journalizing materials and labor costs LO2, 3, 4

Lake Country Manufacturing produces plastic gears. A cost sheet and blank journals are included in the *Working Papers*.

Instructions:

1. Record the following items on the cost sheet for Job No. 335:
   a. Materials Requisition No. 230 for $1,900.00 of direct materials for Job No. 335.
   b. June 29 total of all Job-Time Records for Job No. 335 for the day, $2,725.00.
2. Journalize the following transactions:

Transactions:

June 30. Requisitioned $24,000.00 of direct materials and $20,000.00 of indirect materials for the Production Department. M421.
30. Paid employees their semimonthly pay. Gross (pretax) direct labor costs were $52,500.00. Gross indirect labor costs were $9,500.00. Employee income tax was $6,820.00. Social security tax was 6.2% and Medicare tax was 1.45% of gross wages. C574.

Save your work for use in Problem 17-2.

Sage 50 Accounting

1. Journalize and post transactions related to manufacturing materials and labor costs to the general journal.
2. Journalize and post transactions related to manufacturing materials and labor costs to the cash disbursements journal.
3. Print the general journal, cash disbursements journal, and trial balance.

QB

1. Journalize and post transactions related to manufacturing materials and labor costs to the journal.
2. Print the journal and the trial balance.

Excel

1. Complete the materials ledger card, cost sheet, and finished goods ledger card.
2. Journalize and post transactions to the general journal and cash payments journal.
3. Prepare a statement of cost of goods manufactured and partial income statement.
4. Print the worksheets.

17-2 Application Problem: Completing a cost sheet and journalizing entries for overhead LO5

Use the cost sheet and journals used in Problem 17-1.2.

Instructions:

1. Job No. 335 was completed on June 30. Complete the cost sheet for Job No. 335. Factory overhead is applied based on direct labor hours. Estimated factory overhead for the year was $600,000.00. The number of estimated direct labor hours for the year was 60,000. A total of 415 direct labor hours was used on Job No. 335.
2. Journalize the following transactions:

Transactions:

June 30. Obtained factory costs for the month: depreciation on building, $1,650.00; depreciation on equipment, $1,950.00; insurance, $1,750.00; property taxes, $2,250.00; utilities, $2,400.00. M422. Assume that these expenses have already been properly accounted for and now need to be closed.

30. Applied overhead at the rate of $10.00 per direct labor hour, with 5,000 direct labor hours worked this period. M423.

30. Closed the Factory Overhead account. Actual total overhead costs for the period were $49,500.00. M424.

Save your work for use in Problem 17-3.1.

17-3.1 Application Problem: Updating a finished goods ledger card; journalizing entries for finished goods and cost of goods sold LO6, 7

Use the forms and journals used in Problem 17-2.

Instructions:

1. Using the cost sheet for Job No. 335, update the finished goods ledger card for Magnetic Gear MEG3.
2. Journalize the following transactions:

Transactions:

June 30. Transferred products costing $135,000.00 to finished goods during the month. M425.

30. Sold products costing $118,550.00 during the month. M426.

17-3.2 Application Problem: Preparing a statement of cost of goods manufactured and completing financial statements for a manufacturing business LO8

The Accounting Department at Medford Manufacturing has compiled the following data for the month of April of the current year.

Cost of direct labor	$ 95,120.00
Direct materials issued into production	268,300.00
Factory overhead applied	122,600.00
Finished goods beginning inventory	63,540.00
Finished goods ending inventory	59,420.00
Materials ending inventory	32,690.00
Overapplied overhead	2,100.00
Work in process beginning inventory	63,250.00
Work in process ending inventory	61,720.00

Forms are provided in the *Working Papers*.

Instructions:

1. Prepare a statement of cost of goods manufactured for the month of April.
2. Complete the partial income statement through gross profit on operations for the month of April.
3. Complete the partial balance sheet through total current assets for April 30, 20--.

Application Problem 17-2

1. Cost Sheet: Total Cost, $20,000.00.
2. Entry to close expense accounts: Debit to Factory Overhead, $10,000.00.

Application Problem 17-3.1

1. Finished Goods Ledger Card: June 30 Balance, $109,550.00.
2. Entry to record cost of sales: Credit to Finished Goods, $118,550.00.

Application Problem 17-3.2

1. Statement of Cost of Goods Manufactured: Total Cost of Work Placed in Process, $486,020.00.
2. Income Statement: Cost of Goods Sold, $491,670.00.
3. Balance Sheet: Total Current Assets, $311,783.00.

Application Problem 17-4

1. Materials Price Variance, $710.00 Favorable.
2. Labor Quantity Variance, $750.00 Favorable.

Mastery Problem 17-M

1. Factory Overhead Applied Rate, 80%.
3. Cost Sheet: Cost per unit, $58.12.
5. Finished Goods Ledger Card: May 1 Balance, $8,526.00.
6. Finished Goods Ledger Card: May 18 Balance, $11,763.00.
7. Credit to Cash, $125,758.21.
8. a. Credit Materials, $140,358.00.
9. Credit Factory Overhead, $889.60.

INDEPENDENT PRACTICE

- Assign Mastery Problem 17-M for students as a culminating problem combining all activities from the chapter.
- Assign Challenge Problem 17-C to accelerated students who work at a faster pace.
- Assign Study Guide 17.
- Students can access Online Working Papers to work end-of-chapter problems on the computer.
- Direct students to the C21 Accounting companion website for additional practice and review opportunities.

FORMATIVE ASSESSMENT

- Review solutions to the assigned problems in class, diagnosing trouble spots.

17-4 Application Problem: Calculating variances for materials and labor LO10, 11

Arneson Corporation makes hand-dipped candles. Arneson's management has established the following standards for one of its candles:

Material quantity standard	10 ounces of wax
Material price standard	$0.20 per ounce
Labor quantity standard	0.25 hour per candle
Labor price standard	$15.00 per hour

Arneson actually produced 7,000 candles this month. It purchased and used 71,000 ounces of wax at a total cost of $13,490.00. A total of 1,700 hours of direct labor were used at a total cost of $25,840. Forms are provided in the *Working Papers*.

1. Calculate the total materials variance, the materials price variance, and the materials quantity variance. Comment on your results.
2. Calculate the total labor variance, the labor price variance, and the labor quantity variance. Comment on your results.

17-M Mastery Problem: Preparing cost records and journalizing entries that summarize cost records at the end of a fiscal period LO2, 3, 4, 5, 6, 7, 8

Mercury manufactures boots. The company records manufacturing costs by job number and uses a factory overhead applied rate to charge overhead costs to its products.

The company estimates Mercury will manufacture 50,000 boots next year. For this amount of production, total factory overhead is estimated to be $797,600.00. Estimated direct labor costs for next year are $997,000.00.

The following information is taken from the records of Mercury on May 31 of the current year.

a. The total factory payroll for the month according to the payroll register is $154,860.00, distributed as follows.

Work in Process	$116,320.00	Employee Income Tax Payable	$17,255.00
Factory Overhead	38,540.00	Social Security Tax Payable	9,601.32
Cash	125,758.21	Medicare Tax Payable	2,245.47

b. The total of all requisitions of direct materials issued during the month is $128,688.00. The total of all requisitions of indirect materials issued during the month is $11,670.00.

c. Manufacturing expense accounts and their balances for the month are as follows:

Depreciation Expense—Factory Equipment	$ 2,947.20	Miscellaneous Expense	$ 640.00
Depreciation Expense—Building	1,440.00	Payroll Taxes Expense—Factory	21,680.40
Heat, Light, and Power Expense	4,620.00	Property Tax Expense—Factory	3,624.00
Insurance Expense—Factory	768.00	Supplies Expense—Factory	8,016.00

d. The total of all cost sheets completed during the month is $332,850.00.

e. The total of costs recorded on all sales invoices for May is $517,410.00.

Instructions:

1. Calculate Mercury's factory overhead applied rate for next year as a percentage of direct labor cost.
2. On May 3, Mercury began work on Job No. 283. The order is for 150 pairs of No. 52L boots for stock; date wanted May 13. Open a cost sheet for Job No. 283 and record the following items.

Transactions:

May	3.	Direct materials, $1,725.00. Materials Requisition No. 392.
	3.	Direct labor, $258.00. Daily summary of job-time records.
	4.	Direct labor, $496.00. Daily summary of job-time records.
	5.	Direct materials, $945.00. Materials Requisition No. 399.
	5.	Direct labor, $350.00. Daily summary of job-time records.
	6.	Direct labor, $384.00. Daily summary of job-time records.
	7.	Direct labor, $590.00. Daily summary of job-time records.
	10.	Direct materials, $720.00. Materials Requisition No. 428.
	10.	Direct labor, $330.00. Daily summary of job-time records.
	11.	Direct labor, $304.00. Daily summary of job-time records.
	12.	Direct labor, $248.00. Daily summary of job-time records.

RETEACH

- Call on students to describe how they avoid the trouble spots diagnosed.
- Use reteaching suggestions from lesson plans as required.
- Assign Recycling Problem 17-R if needed.

3. Complete the cost sheet, recording factory overhead at the rate calculated in part (1).
4. Prepare a finished goods ledger card for Stock No. 52L boots. Minimum quantity is set at 100. Inventory location is Area C-50.
5. Record on the finished goods ledger card the beginning balance on May 1: 140 units at a unit cost of $60.90. Mercury uses the first-in, first-out method to record inventory costs.
6. Record the following transactions on the finished goods ledger card for 52L boots.

Transactions:

May	5.	Sold 60 pairs of 52L boots. Sales Invoice No. 633.
	12.	Received 150 pairs of 52L boots. Record cost from cost sheet for Job No. 283.
	18.	Sold 30 pairs of 52L boots. Sales Invoice No. 652.

7. Journalize the factory payroll entry on page 10 of a cash payments journal. C711.
8. Journalize the following entries on page 5 of a general journal.
   a. An entry to transfer the total of all direct materials requisitions to Work in Process and indirect materials to Factory Overhead. M211.
   b. An entry to close all individual manufacturing expense accounts to Factory Overhead. M212.
   c. An entry to record applied factory overhead to Work in Process. M213.
9. Continue using page 5 of the general journal. Journalize the entry to close the balance of the Factory Overhead account to Income Summary. M214.
10. Journalize the entry to transfer the total of all cost sheets completed from Work in Process to Finished Goods. M215.
11. Journalize the entry to transfer the cost of products sold from Finished Goods to Cost of Goods Sold. M216.

Sage 50 Accounting

1. Journalize and post transactions related to manufacturing materials and labor costs to the general journal.
2. Journalize and post transactions related to manufacturing materials and labor costs to the cash disbursements journal.
3. Print the general journal, cash disbursements journal, and trial balance.

QB Quick Books

1. Journalize and post transactions related to manufacturing materials and labor costs to the journal.
2. Print the journal and the trial balance.

Excel

1. Complete the cost sheet and finished good ledger card.
2. Journalize and post transactions to the general journal and cash payments journal.
3. Print the worksheets.

17-C Challenge Problem: Calculating overhead rate LO5

Owatonna, Inc., has made the following estimates for the current year: total factory overhead, $400,000.00; direct material costs, $1,000,000.00; direct labor costs, $1,600,000.00; direct labor hours, 50,000. It is trying to determine which method of applying an overhead rate is most accurate: (a) direct materials cost, (b) direct labor cost, or (c) direct labor hours.

Instructions:

1. Calculate Owatonna's factory overhead applied rate for each of the three bases.
2. Assume the following for Job No. 444: total direct materials, $150,000.00; total direct labor, $130,000.00; direct labor hours, 5,000; 4,000 units produced. Calculate the total cost and the per-unit cost for Job No. 444 using each of the three bases for factory overhead.
3. How should Owatonna decide which overhead basis to use to apply overhead?
4. What is the danger in using an inaccurate overhead basis to apply overhead?

EXTENDED LEARNING

- Assign Auditing for Errors on page 530.
- Assign 21st Century Skills on page 530.
- Assign Analyzing Home Depot's Financial Statements on page 531.

SUMMATIVE EVALUATION

- Chapter 17 Test
- Cognero for Chapter 17

Challenge Problem 17-C

1. c. Factory Overhead Applied Rate, $8.00.

2. b. Per-Unit Cost, $78.13.

2. c. Total Cost, $320,000.

COMMON CORE AND INTERDISCIPLINARY STUDIES

Extended learning features and activities present numerous opportunities to implement Common Core Standards through interdisciplinary studies. Practice is provided in the common core areas of English Language Arts & Literacy and Mathematical Practice. Many of these activities require short, critical-thinking and decision-making responses that apply reading, writing, speaking, listening, language, media and technology, and mathematical skills.

AUDITING FOR ERRORS

Answers

1. Advertising and promotion is a selling expense, not a manufacturing cost.
2. Delivery of finished goods to customers is a selling expense, not a manufacturing cost.
3. Packing materials is a direct material.
4. Sandpaper is an indirect material.

21ST CENTURY SKILLS

Answers

1. Answers will vary. Examples of direct labor should include all expenditures associated with the employee assisting the customer. These include wages and taxes.
2. Answers will vary. A discussion might be held regarding the amount of profit the student expects and the price a customer is willing to pay for the service.

Auditing for errors

East End Manufacturing is a new company that will produce a line of high-quality wood computer desks. The company's management is working on its accounting system and has prepared the following policy for classifying manufacturing costs. Determine whether any item in the policy violates generally accepted accounting principles.

Description	Direct Materials	Direct Labor	Indirect Material	Indirect Labor	Other
Advertising and promotion					X
Delivery of finished goods to customer		X			
Depreciation of machinery					X
Utilities					X
Inspector wages		X			
Insurance on factory					X
Maintenance wages				X	
Packing materials			X		
Production wages		X			
Sandpaper	X				
Screws			X		
Supervisor salaries				X	
Varnish	X				
Wood	X				

21st Century Skills

Making Green by Going Green

PARTNERSHIP FOR 21ST CENTURY SKILLS

Theme: Financial, Economic, Business, and Entrepreneurial and Environmental Literacy

Skills: Creative Thinking and Problem Solving

Many entrepreneurs are looking for business opportunities that help preserve environmental quality. Organic foods, alternative energy, energy efficiency, and green products and services are examples of business opportunities in an industry that is taking steps to protect our natural resources.

Green transportation is growing around the world in an effort to reduce carbon emissions. Many U.S. cities and college campuses are offering bike sharing as an alternative form of transportation to gasoline-powered cars. Traditional automobiles not only release greenhouse gases into the atmosphere, but also create smog, which can affect overall public health.

APPLICATION

Assume that you are going to start your own bike-share business, which will enhance your local school or community and will impact the environment positively. Your business will also provide bike repair services.

1. What would be the major costs of your business? Classify the costs as direct materials, direct labor, factory overhead, and selling and administrative expenses (if applicable).
2. Create a job cost sheet that includes estimates of the costs of serving one of your customers in bike rental or repair. What amount would you need to charge to cover all the costs for the service and make a profit for yourself?

Analyzing Home Depot's financial statements

This chapter discussed the accounting for a manufacturing business and how the financial statements for a manufacturer are different from those for a service business or a merchandising business.

INSTRUCTIONS

1. Is Home Depot a service business, a merchandising business, or a manufacturing business?
2. If Home Depot were a manufacturing business, it would list three inventory accounts on its balance sheet. Review Home Depot's balance sheet and list its inventory account(s).

ANALYZING HOME DEPOT'S FINANCIAL STATEMENTS

Answers

1. Merchandising business.
2. Merchandise Inventories.

Chapter 18

Management Decision Making Using Differential Analysis

Scope & Sequence

	New	Review/Enrich
Introduction		
Introduce the Chapter		
Lesson 18-1: Short-Term Management Decisions Using Differential Analysis		
Differential Analysis	✓	
Make or Buy Decision	✓	
Special Orders	✓	
Discontinue a Segment	✓	
Sell or Process Further	✓	
Lesson 18-2: Future and Present Value of Money		
Time Value of Money	✓	
Future Value of Money	✓	
Present Value of Money	✓	
Future Value of an Annuity	✓	
Present Value of an Annuity	✓	
Lesson 18-3: Long-Term Management Decisions Using Net Present Value		
Calculating the Net Present Value of an Investment	✓	
Calculating the Net Present Value with an Unequal Net Cash Flow	✓	
Lease or Buy Decision	✓	
Closure		

Enhancing Instruction

Features	Common Core Standards
• Accounting in the Real World: Verizon Communications	• ELAL—reading
• Ethics in Action: It's Just a Day or Two • Financial Literacy: Costs of Lost Productivity	• ELAL—reading, writing • Mathematics
• Why Accounting?: Selling Waste Products for a Profit? • Careers in Accounting: Enterprise Resource Planning Project Manager	• ELAL—reading, writing, media and technology • ELAL—reading
• Think Like an Accountant: Evaluating Projects with the Internal Rate of Return	• Mathematics
• Explore Accounting • 21st Century Skills • Auditing for Errors • Analyzing Home Depot's Financial Statements	• Mathematics • ELAL—reading, writing • Mathematics • Mathematics

ELAL = English Language Arts & Literacy

Calculator: © iStockphoto.com/picstodisc; Paper: © iStockphoto.com/Qingwa

Practice and Assessment

Technology & Media	Teaching Strategies	Guided Practice	Independent Practice	Reteach/Enrich
• Instructor's Resource CD/Website: PowerPoint Slides Accounting Concepts • Online Working Papers	• Interpersonal Learners • Gifted Learners	• Terms Review • Audit Your Understanding • Work Together 18-1	• On Your Own 18-1 • Application Problems 18-1.1, 18-1.2, 18-1.3, 18-1.4 • Formative Assessment, p. 538 • Online Working Papers	• Reteach, p. 539
• Instructor's Resource CD/Website: PowerPoint Slides Accounting Concepts • Online Working Papers	• Logical/Mathematical Learners	• Terms Review • Audit Your Understanding • Work Together 18-2	• On Your Own 18-2 • Application Problem 18-2 • Formative Assessment, p. 546 • Online Working Papers	• Reteach, p. 547
• Instructor's Resource CD/Website: PowerPoint Slides Accounting Concepts • Online Working Papers	• Auditory/Linguistic Learners	• Terms Review • Audit Your Understanding • Work Together 18-3	• On Your Own 18-3 • Application Problem 18-3 • Formative Assessment, p. 551 • Online Working Papers	• Reteach, p. 552
• Online Working Papers	• Common Core and Interdisciplinary Studies		• Mastery Problem 18-M • Study Guide 18 • Chapter 18 Test • Cognero Chapter 18	• Challenge Problem 18-C • Reteach, p. 556 • Recycling Problem 18-R

Introduce the Chapter

SET THE STAGE

GUIDING QUESTIONS

- Ask students if they realize that sometimes products with different labels are made by the same manufacturer.
- Ask students to predict how a manufacturer of plastic might process it further for consumer-ready products.
- Ask them how to determine how much money they will need each year if they are no longer working.
- Ask them to predict how much money to save for future needs, such as college.

PREVIEW CHAPTER OBJECTIVES

- Note that this chapter focuses on management decision making.
- Instruct a student to read each chapter objective aloud.

PREVIEW ACCOUNTING TERMS

- Read each term aloud to verify its pronunciation for students.
- Point out terms or parts of terms that should already be familiar to most students, such as *revenues* and *costs*.

Chapter 18 Management Decision Making Using Differential Analysis

LEARNING OBJECTIVES

After studying Chapter 18, in addition to defining key terms, you will be able to:

LO1 Use differential analysis for make or buy decisions.

LO2 Use differential analysis for special order decisions.

LO3 Use differential analysis for discontinuing a segment decisions.

LO4 Use differential analysis for sell or process further decisions.

LO5 Calculate the future value and present value of an amount.

LO6 Calculate the future value and present value of an annuity.

LO7 Use net present value of an annuity to evaluate business decisions.

LO8 Use net present value of unequal cash flows to evaluate business decisions.

LO9 Use net present value to evaluate a lease or buy decision.

Calculator: © iStockphoto.com/pictosdisc; Paper: © iStockphoto.com/Qingwa

Photos.com/Jupiter Images

Background: © iStockphoto.com/urbancow; Real World: © Northfoto/Shutterstock.com

Accounting In The Real World

Verizon Communications

Verizon Communications remains a leader in the cellular phone market year after year. In 2012, it was ranked No. 1 on *Fortune* magazine's list of the World's Most Admired Companies. One of the largest telecommunications companies, Verizon has a workforce of more than 181,000 and generates annual consolidated operating revenues of over $115 billion.

The Verizon name is derived from two words: *veritas*, the Latin word meaning certainty and reliability, and *horizon*, signifying forward-looking and visionary. To fulfill these objectives, Verizon must continually expand and upgrade its communications systems. Verizon's capital investments equal $16.2 billion. Verizon continues to invest in its communications systems each year on the expectation that it will generate additional revenues for years to come.

Verizon operates in an industry in which depreciation is a significant component of its operating expenses. As a result, the cash generated from fees occurs after the year that cash is paid to purchase communications equipment. When evaluating additional investments, Verizon managers must consider the timing of the investment and the related revenues.

CRITICAL THINKING

1. How are the costs of Verizon's communications equipment networks matched against the related revenues?
2. What does Verizon's continued investment in its communications networks indicate about today's technology?

Source: http://about.verizon.com.

Key Terms

- differential analysis
- relevant revenues
- relevant costs
- sunk cost
- joint products
- split-off point
- joint costs
- time value of money
- future value
- compounding
- present value
- annuity
- future value of an annuity
- present value of an annuity
- net cash flows
- net present value

Accounting In The Real World

Answers

1. Communications equipment is depreciated over its useful life. As a result, the cost of the communications system is matched against the revenue generated by the system.
2. Communications networks have a relatively short useful life. This equipment becomes technologically obsolete in a short time, forcing Verizon to upgrade its equipment with the latest technologies.

LESSON
18-1

BRIDGE

- Point out that students learned about overhead and direct labor and materials in previous lessons. In this lesson, they will apply these concepts when using differential analysis to make management decisions.

TEACHING RESOURCES

- **Instructor's Resource CD/Website:**
  PowerPoint Slides
  Accounting Concepts
- **Working Papers:**
  Teacher's Edition of the Working Papers for Lesson 18-1
  Online Working Papers

ENGAGE

- Ask students if they have ever spent money to make money. Explain whether this was a wise decision.
- Ask students if they think it would be a better financial choice for a fast-food restaurant to make its own ketchup or buy ketchup from another source. Explain.

PREVIEW

- Call on students to read the accounting terms and definitions introduced in this lesson: *differential analysis, relevant revenues, relevant costs, sunk cost, joint products, split-off point,* and *joint costs.*
- Point out the learning objectives for this lesson.
- Direct students to read the headings in this lesson and to examine the illustrations.

INPUT

- Explain that management often needs to make decisions, such as dropping a product, making or buying a new product, or accepting a special order. An analysis needs to be conducted to determine the financial impact of these decisions.
- Explain that sunk costs have already been incurred and cannot be changed by any decision made now or in the future; therefore, they are not considered relevant costs.

LESSON
18-1 Short-Term Management Decisions Using Differential Analysis

LO1 Use differential analysis for make or buy decisions.
LO2 Use differential analysis for special order decisions.
LO3 Use differential analysis for discontinuing a segment decisions.
LO4 Use differential analysis for sell or process further decisions.

Differential Analysis

Management makes many decisions in the course of operating a company. These decisions can affect the financial performance of the company for a few days or for many years. When comparing two options, management may look at the total revenues and expenses relating to each alternative. However, if some revenues and expenses are the same regardless of the alternative chosen, looking at total revenues and expenses may not be the best method. Analyzing only the differences between the revenues and expenses resulting from each of two options is called **differential analysis**. Differential analysis is useful for short-term management decisions.

Revenues that are different between two options are called **relevant revenues**. Costs that are different between two options are called **relevant costs**. Differential analysis considers only relevant revenues and relevant costs.

Relevant costs must be both future costs and costs that differ between alternatives. A cost that occurred in the past and cannot be recovered by a future decision is called a **sunk cost**. A sunk cost can never be a relevant cost. An example of a sunk cost is the depreciation incurred by an asset purchased three years ago. When considering whether to replace the asset, the depreciation associated with that asset is a sunk cost and, therefore, is not a relevant cost.

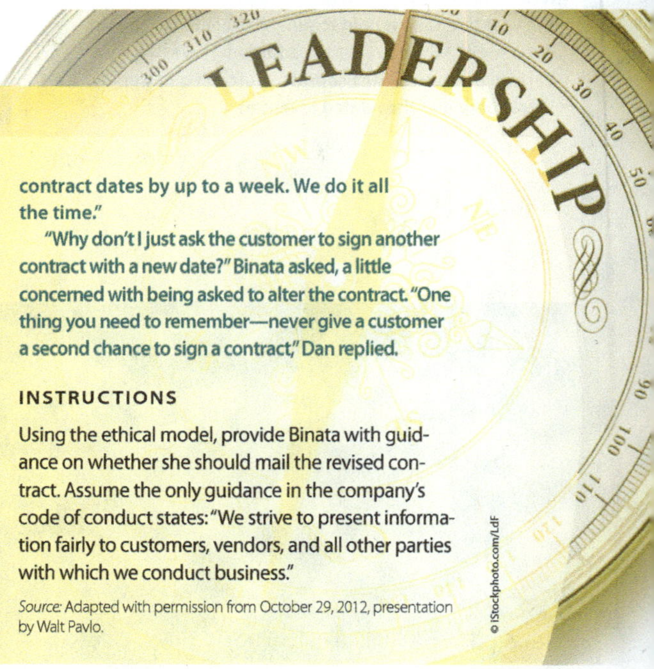

ETHICS IN ACTION

It's Just a Day or Two

Binata Barnes arrived for work on January 3 to find that MDK Industries had faxed a signed contract the day before. Binata had been working for months to land this contract. Excited that the deal was now official, she shared the news with Dan Smith, her supervisor.

"This is great! This contract will keep the plant working at full speed for months," Dan replied. "But for purposes of awarding annual bonuses, it needs to be included in last year's activity. None of us will get our bonuses without it."

"But what can we do? The contract is dated January 2," replied Binata. "Just change the date to December 30," Dan instructed. "We have an informal policy whereby we can adjust contract dates by up to a week. We do it all the time."

"Why don't I just ask the customer to sign another contract with a new date?" Binata asked, a little concerned with being asked to alter the contract. "One thing you need to remember—never give a customer a second chance to sign a contract," Dan replied.

INSTRUCTIONS

Using the ethical model, provide Binata with guidance on whether she should mail the revised contract. Assume the only guidance in the company's code of conduct states: "We strive to present information fairly to customers, vendors, and all other parties with which we conduct business."

Source: Adapted with permission from October 29, 2012, presentation by Walt Pavlo.

© iStockphoto.com/Ldf

ETHICS IN ACTION

Sample Solution

Knowingly transmitting information containing false representation is illegal. The action is considered wire fraud and can result in fines and up to 20 years in prison. Because the action is illegal, no evaluation of the statement in the company's code of conduct is necessary. You should advise Binata that she should not fax the revised contract. The fact that her supervisor stated that this practice is done regularly will not protect her from prosecution.

Source: Title 18 of the U.S. Code, Part I, Chapter 63, § 1343.

Make or Buy Decision LO1

	Make	Buy	Differential Analysis in Favor of Make
Direct materials	$ 35,000.00	—	$ 35,000.00
Direct labor	60,000.00	—	60,000.00
Variable overhead	20,000.00	—	20,000.00
Fixed overhead	25,000.00	$ 25,000.00	—
Purchase price	—	125,000.00	(125,000.00)
	$140,000.00	$150,000.00	$ (10,000.00)

Custom Cyclery Corporation has been purchasing 10,000 brake assemblies from an outside source at a cost of $12.50 per assembly. Since Custom Cyclery has excess capacity, it is considering making the brake assemblies in its own factory. No new machinery or equipment will need to be purchased. Custom Cyclery has idle machines and no other use for them.

Custom Cyclery's Accounting Department has estimated the costs associated with making 10,000 brake assemblies as shown above.

The variable overhead consists of indirect materials, indirect labor, and other expenses that are connected with making the brake assemblies. These costs will not exist if Custom Cyclery continues buying the assemblies. The fixed overhead consists of depreciation and other expenses that are allocated to each product. If Custom Cyclery continues to buy the assemblies, these costs will remain and will be allocated to other products manufactured.

The first step in the analysis is to determine relevant revenues and relevant costs. Direct materials, direct labor, and variable overhead costs are all relevant because they are different between the two options. Fixed overhead costs, however, are not relevant. Once the relevant costs have been determined, the costs are totaled.

As shown above, it will cost Custom Cyclery $140,000.00 to make 10,000 brake assemblies. It will cost Custom Cyclery $150,000.00 to buy 10,000 brake assemblies. Therefore, it should make the assemblies.

AVOIDABLE FIXED OVERHEAD

	Make	Buy	Differential Analysis in Favor of Make
Direct materials	$ 35,000.00	—	$ 35,000.00
Direct labor	60,000.00	—	60,000.00
Variable overhead	20,000.00	—	20,000.00
Fixed overhead	25,000.00	$ 10,000.00	15,000.00
Purchase price	—	125,000.00	(125,000.00)
	$140,000.00	$135,000.00	$ 5,000.00

Assume the same cost structure as above, but that only $10,000.00 of the fixed overhead will remain if the assemblies are purchased. Now, only $10,000.00 of fixed overhead is not relevant. The $15,000.00 of fixed overhead that can be avoided if Custom Cyclery buys the assemblies is a relevant cost. The differential analysis now shows that Custom Cyclery will save $5,000.00 by buying the assemblies from an outside source.

INPUT

- Explain that a decision is being made whether to continue buying brake assemblies from an outside source or to begin making them.
- Point out that variable overhead includes indirect materials, indirect labor, and other expenses associated with making the brake assemblies.
- Explain that variable overhead would not exist if the brake assemblies were purchased.
- Explain that relevant costs are different between the two options.
- Direct students to the illustration at the top of the page to point out direct materials, direct labor, and variable overhead as relevant costs.
- Explain that Custom Cyclery should make its own brake assemblies based on the differential analysis.

INPUT

- Point out that if the fixed overhead changes and all other costs remain the same, an analysis now determines that Custom Cyclery saves money by buying the assemblies from an outside source.
- Direct students to the illustration at the bottom of the page and compare it to the illustration at the top of the page.

Special Orders LO2

	Accept Special Order	Reject Special Order	Differential Analysis in Favor of Acceptance
Sales revenue	$110.00	—	$110.00
Direct materials	(60.00)	—	(60.00)
Direct labor	(35.00)	—	(35.00)
Variable overhead ($8.00 – $3.00)	(5.00)	—	(5.00)
Special emblem	(0.50)	—	(0.50)
Fixed costs	NR	NR	NR
Net increase	$ 9.50	$0.00	$ 9.50

Custom Cyclery was approached by a potential customer to make a special edition of a bicycle. The bicycle will have the retailer's name embossed on it. The retailer would like to buy 100 bicycles and will pay $110.00 for each bicycle. Custom Cyclery has ample excess capacity, and it can make 100 additional bicycles without affecting its normal production. Custom Cyclery calculates its per-unit cost to be $100.50, which includes $0.50 per unit for the cost of the special emblem. Excluded from the variable overhead costs are $1.00 for sales commissions and $2.00 for other selling expenses that will not have to be paid on this special order. The total fixed overhead costs for Custom Cyclery will remain the same whether the special order is accepted or rejected.

This particular model of bicycle usually sells for $150.00. However, the retailer is in a different region of the country, so the additional 100 bicycles will not impact Custom Cyclery's normal sales. Should Custom Cyclery accept this special order?

This special order decision can be analyzed on a per-unit basis or on a total revenue basis. The per-unit basis is used in the differential analysis shown above. Relevant revenue is $110.00 per unit. This is revenue that would not be received if the special order is rejected. Relevant costs include direct materials ($60.00), direct labor ($35.00), variable overhead ($5.00), and the special emblem ($0.50). Thus, Custom Cyclery will make an additional $9.50 per unit if it accepts the special order.

If this special order would affect normal sales for Custom Cyclery or if it had to decrease normal production in order to accept the special order, the differential analysis would have to include those relevant revenues and costs. Another potentially negative result of accepting the special order would be Custom Cyclery's normal customers learning about the special order and becoming upset that they are paying $150.00 for the same bicycle.

Discontinue a Segment LO3

Cartwright sells children's clothing and shoes. It is considering dropping its children's shoes because of disappointing results over the last few years. Financial data for the last year are as follows:

	Clothing	Shoes	Total Company
Sales	$200,000.00	$120,000.00	$320,000.00
Variable expenses	90,000.00	95,000.00	185,000.00
Contribution margin	$110,000.00	$ 25,000.00	$135,000.00
Fixed costs	48,000.00	32,000.00	80,000.00
Operating income	$ 62,000.00	$ (7,000.00)	$ 55,000.00

Further analysis reveals that the $32,000.00 of fixed costs for shoes includes $12,000.00 allocated for insurance, electricity, and taxes. If shoes are discontinued, these costs will remain and will all be allocated to clothing. The remaining $20,000.00 is the cost of salaries, which will be eliminated if the shoes are discontinued.

INPUT

- Remind students that relevant revenue and relevant costs must be considered in analyzing whether to accept a special order.
- Explain that the analysis illustrated is on a per-unit basis rather than a total revenue basis.
- Explain that other factors must be taken into consideration as well, such as how the special order may affect normal sales or customer relations should it become known that another retailer is selling the same bicycles for less.

INPUT

- Explain that differential analysis can also be used to determine if a product should be dropped from manufacturing.
- Point out that although a product may no longer be manufactured, certain fixed costs will remain, often meaning that it is not worth the effort of discontinuing the product, as in this case.
- Direct students to the illustrations on the page to explain the differential analysis.

DIFFERENTIATED INSTRUCTION

Interpersonal learners are people-oriented and learn best with cooperative learning groups or with a partner.
Gifted learners enjoy conducting further research on topics. Assign students to a partner. Each group should research private label manufacturers. Students should create a presentation for the class, explaining why a company would accept special orders. This presentation should also include a visual with examples of manufacturers that make the same product using different labels.

Cartwright management completes the following differential analysis:

	Keep Shoe Department	Drop Shoe Department	Differential Analysis in Favor of Keeping Shoe Department
Sales	$320,000.00	$200,000.00	$120,000.00
Variable expenses	185,000.00	90,000.00	95,000.00
Contribution margin	$135,000.00	$110,000.00	$ 25,000.00
Fixed costs	80,000.00	60,000.00	20,000.00
Operating income	$ 55,000.00	$ 50,000.00	$ 5,000.00

Since $12,000.00 of fixed costs will remain, it is not profitable for Cartwright to discontinue shoes. If it does, its operating income will decrease $5,000.00.

If the analysis indicated that it would be profitable for Cartwright to discontinue shoes, management would also have to consider other items. Will clothing sales be affected by discontinuing shoes? If Cartwright's customers desire the convenience of buying clothing and shoes in one stop, sales of clothing may actually be less than $200,000.00.

© iStockphoto.com/Norebbo

FINANCIAL LITERACY

Costs of Lost Productivity

Lowering direct labor costs is a necessity for thriving in any economic environment. Cross training, job sharing, and cutting the standard workweek are all efforts that companies are implementing to reduce labor costs.

Absenteeism costs billions of dollars per year due to wages paid to absent employees, to replacement workers, and to those who train the replacement workers. Longer production times, poor quality of goods caused by understaffing, safety issues, and employee error, as well as poor morale, add to the indirect and invisible costs of labor.

ACTIVITIES

1. An estimate of the cost of turnover for hourly employees is 25% of their annual salaries. Assume that you own a small clothing boutique. Calculate the cost of turnover for each of the following employees who leave your company. The yearly salary is based on the employee being paid for working 40 hours per week, 50 weeks per year.
   a. Anthony makes $10 per hour. Calculate the cost of turnover if Anthony leaves abruptly without giving notice.
   b. Shannon makes $20 per hour. Calculate the cost of turnover if Shannon leaves for another position in her field, after she gives a 2-week notice.
2. a. Clement earns $4,000 per month, based on working 220 days per year. He was absent 7 days this year, but he was paid because he used sick time. How much did his 7 absences cost the company in lost productivity?
   b. What did Clement's absences cost the company if it incurred an additional cost of 25% to replace him with another employee?

FINANCIAL LITERACY

Answers

1. a. $5,000.
   b. $10,000.
2. a. $1,527.27.
   b. $1,909.09 ($1,527.27 + $381.82*).

   *This amount represents the 25% additional cost for another employee to pick up Clement's lost productivity.

INPUT

- Explain joint products, split-off point, and joint costs as they relate to the lumber company example in the illustration.
- Point out the sunk costs in this example.
- Explain the differential analysis provided in the illustration at the bottom of the page.

Sell or Process Further LO4

Cruthers Corporation makes lumber. It gets timber from a saw mill, dries it, and cuts it into standard size boards. At that point, Cruthers can sell it to lumber yards or process it further into window frames. The window frames can be sold to a local window manufacturer.

The following costs have been compiled. These costs are based on the original purchase of 1,000 board feet of timber.

Item or Process	Number of Board Feet	Unit Cost or Selling Price
Purchase timber logs	1,000	$0.25
Kiln dry the logs	1,000	0.05
Cut to standard size	900	0.12
Sell as lumber	900	0.60
Process to window frames	500	0.60
Sell as window frames	500	2.00

Two or more products that are produced simultaneously with the same processes and costs and are inseparable up to a certain point are called **joint products**. The point where joint products are separable into identifiable products is called the **split-off point**. The costs of processing joint products to their split-off point are called **joint costs**.

For Cruthers, the lumber and the window frames are joint products from the time the logs are purchased, through the kiln-drying process and through the cutting process. The split-off point is when Cruthers must decide to sell the lumber or process it further into window frames. The joints costs are those associated with kiln-drying the lumber and cutting it into standard sizes. Since these joint costs are past costs that cannot be recovered by a future decision, they are also sunk costs. Since a sunk cost can never be a relevant cost, none of the joint costs in this example are relevant. Thus, differential analysis of the decision to sell the lumber or process it further begins at the split-off point. This analysis is shown below.

	Process Further	Sell at Split-Off Point	Differential Analysis in Favor of Processing Further
Revenue	$1,000.00	$540.00	$460.00
Cost to process further	300.00	—	300.00
Operating income	$ 700.00	$540.00	$160.00

If the lumber is processed further, it can be sold for $1,000.00 (500 board feet × $2.00). If the lumber is sold at the split-off point, it can be sold for $540.00 (900 board feet × $0.60). The cost to process the lumber into window frames is $300 (500 board feet × $0.60). There is no added cost to sell the lumber at the split-off point. Since the difference in revenue is greater than the additional processing costs, Cruthers should process the lumber into window frames. If the difference in revenue is less than the additional processing costs, Cruthers should sell the lumber at the split-off point.

FORMATIVE ASSESSMENT

- This is an ongoing process. Circulate around the classroom or lab, observing which students have difficulty with the assignments.
- Troubleshooting: Diagnose the kinds of problems students have with this section. Students may have difficulty understanding relevant costs and sunk costs.
- Assess student understanding by checking solutions to Independent Practice assignments and noting their answers to the Terms Review and Audit Your Understanding questions.

End of Lesson Review

LO1 Use differential analysis for make or buy decisions.

LO2 Use differential analysis for special order decisions.

LO3 Use differential analysis for discontinuing a segment decisions.

LO4 Use differential analysis for sell or process further decisions.

Terms Review

differential analysis
relevant revenues
relevant costs
sunk cost
joint products
split-off point
joint costs

Audit your understanding

1. What two features are necessary for a cost to be a relevant cost?
2. In a make or buy decision, how is an avoidable fixed cost treated?
3. Besides differential analysis, what other factors should a company consider when deciding whether to accept or reject a special order?
4. In a sell or process further decision, if the difference in revenue is less than the additional processing costs, what should the company do?

Work together 18-1

Determining relevant amounts

Forms are provided in the *Working Papers*. For each situation, list the amount of each item that is relevant and irrelevant. Your instructor will guide you through the following examples.

1. Bayfront Corporation is considering making a component part that it has been buying for $500,000.00 from an outside supplier. No new machinery will need to be purchased, and Bayfront has idle machines that have no other use. Costs to make the part include: direct materials, $125,000.00; direct labor, $150,000.00; and variable overhead, $75,000.00. In addition, total fixed overhead allocated to this part is $80,000.00. Variable overhead is directly related to making the part and will not exist if Bayfront continues to buy it. Fixed overhead includes costs that are allocated to each product made by Bayfront. If Bayfront continues to buy the part, these costs will remain and will be allocated to other products.
2. Carey Corporation sells canoe and paddleboard paddles. It is considering dropping its line of paddleboard paddles and has compiled the following data.

	Paddleboard Paddles	Canoe Paddles	Total Company
Sales	$420,000.00	$200,000.00	$620,000.00
Variable expenses	121,000.00	135,000.00	256,000.00
Contribution margin	$299,000.00	$ 65,000.00	$364,000.00
Fixed costs	130,000.00	70,000.00	200,000.00
Operating income	$169,000.00	$ (5,000.00)	$164,000.00

Further analysis shows that $15,000.00 of the fixed costs is allocated. If canoe paddles are discontinued, these costs will remain and be allocated to paddleboard paddles. The remaining $55,000.00 will be eliminated if canoe paddles are discontinued.

On your own 18-1

Determining relevant amounts

Forms are provided in the *Working Papers*. For each situation, list the amount of each item that is relevant and irrelevant. Work these problems independently.

1. Cosgrove Corporation sells safety glasses for $10.00 per pair. It is considering accepting a special order by a customer who offered to pay $7.00 per pair. It has ample excess capacity, and the special order will not affect normal sales. Cosgrove has determined that the variable costs for each pair of glasses are: direct materials, $2.00; direct labor, $2.50; and variable overhead, $3.50. Variable overhead includes $1.50 for selling expenses, which will not be incurred for this special order. At its normal level of production, fixed costs per unit are $0.75. These fixed costs will remain the same whether the order is accepted or not.
2. Deercreek Creamery gets milk from dairy farms and pasteurizes it. It can then sell it as whole milk or process it further into ice cream. Deercreek can sell whole milk for $3.00 per gallon. It can sell ice cream for $7.00 per gallon. The cost to pasteurize the milk is $1.50 per gallon. Processing it further into ice cream costs an additional $3.25 per gallon.

CHECK FOR UNDERSTANDING

Terms Review

- Call on students to define each term in the Terms Review. Definitions are given in the Glossary.

Audit Your Understanding

- Call on students to answer the Audit Your Understanding questions. Answers are given in Appendix D of the textbook.

GUIDED PRACTICE

Work Together

- Have students write the solution to the Work Together problem as you guide the class through the examples.
- Direct students to determine relevant amounts.

INDEPENDENT PRACTICE

On Your Own

- Assign the On Your Own problem to be worked independently.

Application Problem

- Assign Application Problem 18-1.1.
- Assign Application Problem 18-1.2.
- Assign Application Problem 18-1.3.
- Assign Application Problem 18-1.4.

Online Working Papers

- Students can access the Lesson 18-1 problems using this software.

Website

- Direct students to the C21 Accounting companion website for additional practice and review opportunities.

RETEACH

- Provide students with further examples of determining when to make or buy, when to manufacture a special order, when to discontinue a product, and when to sell or process the product further.
- Direct students to the differential analysis illustrations pertaining to the decision.
- Call on students to make a decision based on the above examples.

CLOSURE

- Ask students to summarize the differential analysis for make or buy decisions and special orders and for discontinuing a product and selling or processing further.

Essential Question

- If the net income of a business is increasing, why would a manager use differential analysis to make a decision? (*A business may be able to increase net income even more by analyzing decisions such as dropping a product, accepting additional business, or making and buying parts.*)

EXTENDED LEARNING

- Assign Accounting in the Real World on page 533.
- Assign Ethics in Action on page 534.
- Assign Financial Literacy on page 537.

LESSON

18-2

BRIDGE

- Point out that students already learned about compound interest in accounting classes. In this lesson, they will learn how to use compound interest to make decisions for the future.

TEACHING RESOURCES

- **Instructor's Resource CD/Website:**
  PowerPoint Slides
  Accounting Concepts
- **Working Papers:**
  Teacher's Edition of the Working Papers for Lesson 18-2
  Online Working Papers

ENGAGE

- Ask students if they have interest-bearing bank accounts. Ask students why someone would have money invested in an interest-bearing account.

PREVIEW

- Call on students to read the accounting terms and definitions introduced in this lesson: *time value of money, future value, compounding, present value, annuity, future value of an annuity,* and *present value of an annuity*.
- Point out the learning objectives for this lesson.
- Direct students to read the headings in this lesson and to examine the illustrations.

INPUT

- Explain that interest causes money to grow in value over time.
- Explain that businesses, like individuals, need to consider the time value of money when investing in assets.

WHY ACCOUNTING?

Answers

1. Answers will vary.
2. Answers will vary. At the time of publication, many companies were composting food waste. Several companies were expressing difficulties in getting rid of receipt paper, Styrofoam, and paper towels from the restrooms.

LESSON

18-2 Future and Present Value of Money

LO5 Calculate the future value and present value of an amount.
LO6 Calculate the future value and present value of an annuity.

Time Value of Money

Bank customers deposit their money in savings accounts and certificates of deposit to earn interest and increase their wealth. The expectation that invested money will increase over time is called the **time value of money**. Because of the time value of money, the promise of receiving $100.00 in three years is not worth $100.00 today. A bank customer would expect to deposit less than $100.00 today on the promise of receiving $100.00 in three years.

Like bank customers, managers must consider the time value of money when investing in plant assets. A business invests in plant assets, such as buildings, trucks, computers, and computer networks, to expand its operations and increase profits. When deciding whether to purchase a plant asset, managers should compare the asset's cost to the additional profits that will be earned in the future. If future profits exceed the cost, then management should purchase the asset.

When profits are earned is an important factor in an asset purchase decision. The value of a dollar earned several years from now should not be compared directly to the cost of the asset today. Managers must consider the time value of money when comparing future profits to today's costs.

WHY ACCOUNTING?

Selling Waste Products for a Profit?

Many manufacturing companies are finding new revenue sources in their waste products. Items that at one time cost money to be hauled away to a landfill are now finding new markets and are being sold. One of the original examples is used vegetable oil, a waste product of many restaurants and fast-food outlets. Instead of paying to have this oil disposed of in an environmentally safe way, the oil can be sold. One use for this oil is to fuel vehicles that have been adapted to run on vegetable oil. Other items that have a resale value include leather scrap, PVC pipe, and carpet.

Besides increasing net income, selling waste products is also environmentally friendly. Many companies are striving to move from "less waste" to "zero waste." Zero waste means that nothing is added to landfills. There are organizations that provide assistance to match sellers and buyers of commercial waste.

Manufacturing

CRITICAL THINKING

1. Use the Internet to find an organization that helps match sellers and buyers of waste products. Give two examples of waste products that are currently for sale on the site.
2. Investigate a company that has a goal of zero waste. Make a list of ways that the company disposes of its waste and any problems the company is encountering in actually achieving its zero waste policy.

Sources: www.recyclematch.com; www.tradingwaste.com.

© iStockphoto.com/AleksKo

Future Value of Money LO5

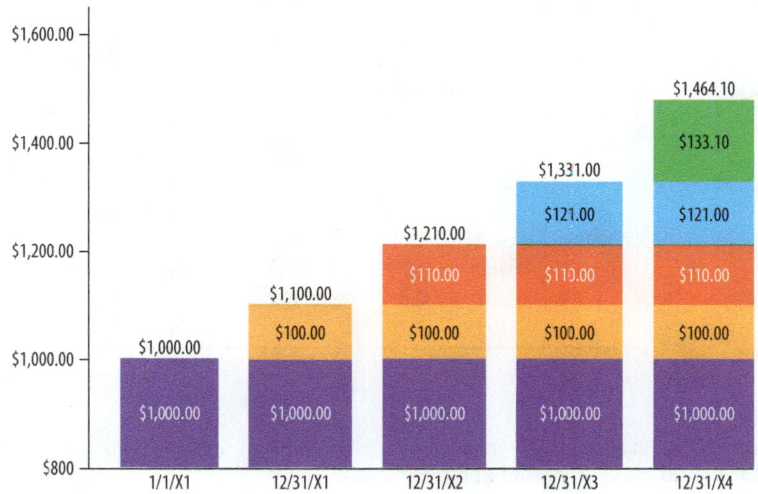

12/31/X1	12/31/X2	12/31/X3	12/31/X4
$1,000.00	$1,100.00	$1,210.00	$1,331.00
× 10%	× 10%	× 10%	× 10%
$ 100.00	$ 110.00	$ 121.00	$ 133.10

Individuals and businesses expect invested money to grow over time. The value of money invested today at some point in the future is called **future value**. The figure above shows how the value of a $1,000.00 investment on January 1, 20X1, at 10% annual interest will grow over time. The future value of $1,000.00 invested today at 10% interest is $1,464.10 in four years.

The interest earned each year is calculated by multiplying the current investment value by the interest rate. The calculation of interest earned in the third year is shown as follows:

Current Investment Value on 12/31/X2	×	Interest Rate	=	Interest Earned in 20X3
$1,210.00	×	10%	=	$121.00

Current Investment Value on 12/31/X2	+	Interest Earned in 20X3	=	Balance on 12/31/X3
$1,210.00	+	$121.00	=	$1,331.00

Each year, the interest earned increases the value of the investment. As the investment value increases, the amount of interest earned each year also increases. Interest earned in the fourth year, $133.10, is greater than the $121.00 interest earned in the third year. Earning interest on previously earned interest is called **compounding**. Compounding interest causes the annual interest earned to increase each year.

INPUT

- Explain that present value is basically the opposite of future value.
- Ask students to examine the figure as they say aloud "The present value of $1,464.10 at 10% interest for 4 years is $1,000.00."
- Use the math illustration to explain how each year's interest is calculated.
- Explain why the frequency of compounding interest affects the amount of interest.

MODEL

- Using the board, create a table with four columns: Year, Investment on 1/1/--, Interest Earned, and Investment on 12/31/--.
- Ask a student to show how interest is calculated in Year 1 for $3,000.00 invested at 8% interest.
- Ask individual students to complete the table for Years 2–4 (*Interest earned: $259.20, $279.40, $302.33*).
- Explain why interest earned increases each year. (*Interest is earned on larger amounts as interest accumulates.*)

INPUT

- Point out that tables can be used to calculate future values, which is helpful for calculating several years into the future.
- Explain that the number of periods and the periodic interest rate determine the future value factor.
- Discuss why the future value of $1,000.00 at 10% interest for 4 years is calculated to be $1,464.00 rather than $1,464.10. (*The difference in the calculation using the table is due to a rounding difference.*)

Future Value of $1					
	Interest Rate				
Period	4%	6%	8%	10%	12%
1	1.040	1.060	1.080	1.100	1.120
2	1.082	1.124	1.166	1.210	1.254
3	1.125	1.191	1.260	1.331	1.405
4	1.170	1.263	1.361	1.464	1.574
5	1.217	1.338	1.469	1.611	1.762
6	1.265	1.419	1.587	1.772	1.974
7	1.316	1.504	1.714	1.949	2.211
8	1.369	1.594	1.851	2.144	2.476
9	1.423	1.690	1.999	2.358	2.773
10	1.480	1.791	2.159	2.594	3.106
15	1.801	2.397	3.172	4.177	5.474
20	2.191	3.207	4.661	6.728	9.647

Rather than having to calculate the future value of an amount, tables can be used. This is especially helpful with calculations that go out more than a few years into the future. Notice that the above table is titled "Future Value of $1." The amounts in the tables are known as *future value factors*. This table can be used to determine the future value of any amount by multiplying the amount by the factor at the intersection of the appropriate interest rate and the number of compounding periods.

The formula to calculate the future value of $1,000.00 invested on January 1, 20X1, at 10% for four years is:

Current value	$1,000.00
Future value factor	× 1.464
Future value	$1,464.00

Using the future value of $1 table, the investment will grow to $1,464.00 by December 31, 20X4. The manual calculation, presented on the previous page, shows the future value of this investment to be $1,464.10. The $0.10 difference between the two calculations is due to the rounding of the table factors to three places after the decimal point.

fyi

A bank may advertise that its certificates of deposit earn "5% interest compounded annually." Each year, the bank calculates interest earned on 5% of the outstanding account balance and adds this amount to the account. The more often (daily, monthly, or quarterly) interest is compounded, the more quickly the account balance will grow. For example, a $1,000.00 investment at 10% interest compounded semiannually (twice each year) will grow to $1,628.90 in four years—$164.80 more than the $1,464.10 future value illustrated on the previous page.

Careers In Accounting

Deborah Gluzman

ENTERPRISE RESOURCE PLANNING PROJECT MANAGER

© lightwavemedia/Shutterstock.com

Deborah Gluzman works for an enterprise resource planning (ERP) consulting firm. ERP is an enterprise-wide system of integrating core business processes. It is achieved through the use of integrated software to manage the business.

As an ERP project manager, Ms. Gluzman works with a company through the entire process of ERP. She begins by developing an ERP plan for the business with which she is working. This involves gaining an understanding of the company's operations, such as production, processing, inventory management, human resources, sales, accounting, and customer support.

Once Ms. Gluzman acquires this information, she develops a proposed enterprise resource plan for the company. This plan will integrate all systems, so that data can be shared with other related functional areas. This usually includes a common database that is shared throughout the enterprise.

If the plan is accepted, the next step is to develop a plan for its implementation. This includes bringing the software onboard and providing the training necessary to operate and implement the software. The plan is then implemented under Ms. Gluzman's supervision. She sets deadlines, assigns responsibilities, and monitors the progress of the implementation to ensure that the plan is fully operational.

The project manager's work does not stop here, however. Ms. Gluzman also works with the company to analyze the ERP system. This includes evaluating and recommending changes to the system as the company's needs change.

Immediately out of college, Ms. Gluzman's first position with the company was as part of the implementation team. As she acquired more experience, she took on more supervisory positions. She now enjoys being a project manager and overseeing the work of the ERP team.

ERP project managers must have excellent communications skills as well as a basic understanding of a broad range of management areas, including technology, accounting, production management, human resources, and customer sales and support.

Salary Range: The average salary for an ERP project manager is $117,106. The range is from $90,000 to $143,000.

Qualifications: Most positions with ERP require a college degree in a related business area. Higher-level positions, such as project manager, also require work experience in enterprise resource planning.

Occupational Outlook: The growth for computer and information systems managers, including ERP project managers, is projected to average 10% to 19% for the period from 2010 to 2020.

Sources: www.onetonline.org; www.salary.com.

© iStockphoto.com/Mlenny

Careers In Accounting

Review the career of an enterprise resource planning project manager.

INPUT

- Explain that the present value table is used to calculate the present value for any amount. The number of periods and the periodic interest rate determine the present value factor.
- Discuss why the present value of $1,464.10 at 10% interest for 4 years is calculated to be $999.98 rather than $1,000.00. (*The decimal place accuracy of the present value table results in a rounding difference of 2 cents. A table with greater decimal place accuracy would yield exactly $1,000.00.*)

Present Value of Money

Present Value of $1					
	Interest Rate				
Period	4%	6%	8%	10%	12%
1	0.962	0.943	0.926	0.909	0.893
2	0.925	0.890	0.857	0.826	0.797
3	0.889	0.840	0.794	0.751	0.712
4	0.855	0.792	0.735	0.683	0.636
5	0.822	0.747	0.681	0.621	0.567
6	0.790	0.705	0.630	0.564	0.507
7	0.760	0.665	0.583	0.513	0.452
8	0.731	0.627	0.540	0.467	0.404
9	0.703	0.592	0.500	0.424	0.361
10	0.676	0.558	0.463	0.386	0.322
15	0.555	0.417	0.315	0.239	0.183
20	0.456	0.312	0.215	0.149	0.104

The current value of a future cash payment or receipt is called a **present value**. At 10% interest, $1,000.00 invested today will be worth $1,464.10 in four years. Therefore, $1,000.00 is the present value of $1,464.10 in four years at 10% interest.

Present value tables enable managers to calculate the present value of any future amount. The amounts in the tables are known as *present value factors*. The present value factor is determined by finding the intersection of the interest rate in the columns and the number of years in the rows. The calculation of the present value of $1,464.10 is shown in the next column.

Projected net cash flows	$1,464.10
Present value factor	× 0.683
Present value	$ 999.98

Again, the slight difference in the amounts is due to the present value factors in the table being rounded to three decimal places. Calculating the present value of $1,464.10 using a rounded present value factor results in a $0.02 rounding error. Such minor rounding errors are acceptable when managers are using present values to make business decisions.

© iStockphoto.com/KirbusEdvard

Future Value of an Annuity LO6

Future Value of an Annuity of $1					
	Interest Rate				
Period	4%	6%	8%	10%	12%
1	1.000	1.000	1.000	1.000	1.000
2	2.040	2.060	2.080	2.100	2.120
3	3.122	3.184	3.246	3.310	3.374
4	4.247	4.375	4.506	4.641	4.779
5	5.416	5.637	5.867	6.105	6.353
6	6.633	6.975	7.336	7.716	8.115
7	7.898	8.394	8.923	9.487	10.089
8	9.214	9.898	10.637	11.436	12.300
9	10.583	11.491	12.488	13.580	14.776
10	12.006	13.181	14.487	15.937	17.549
15	20.024	23.276	27.152	31.773	37.280
20	29.778	36.786	45.762	57.275	72.052

Some business transactions result in equal net cash flows each year. A series of equal cash flows is called an **annuity**. The future value of an equal series of investments over equal time periods at a given interest rate is called the **future value of an annuity**.

The future value of an annuity of $1 table shown above makes one very important assumption. It assumes that all payments are made at the end of each year. An example would be that a company knows that it will be receiving $1,000.00 at the end of each year, for four years, beginning at the end of the current year. On a timeline, the payments and investments would be:

If the company invests the money when it is received and earns 10% interest on it, how much will be in the investment account immediately after the fourth payment has been deposited?

Annual payment	$1,000.00
Future value factor	× 4.641
Future value	$4,641.00

The balance in the investment account immediately after the fourth payment will be $4,641.00.

INPUT

- Explain that an annuity is a series of equal payments where each amount is the same.
- Point out that a future value table can be used with factors to simplify the calculations.
- Explain that calculating the future value of equal payments made each year will allow a person to know the expected amount at the end of a period of time at a certain interest rate.

MODEL

- Demonstrate the calculation or refer students to the math illustration to calculate the future value of $1,000.00 payments made for four years at an interest rate of 10%.

DIFFERENTIATED INSTRUCTION

Logical/Mathematical learners enjoy reasoning and problem-solving activities. They enjoy learning through investigations. Provide students with additional data so that they can practice determining how much money they need to save annually at a particular interest rate for a certain number of years to have a specified amount for college, a down payment on a house, or a down payment on a car.

INPUT

- Explain that many individuals purchase annuities to provide a steady income for later in life. Determining the present value of an annuity allows an individual to determine if enough money has been invested to ensure the desired periodic income.
- Point out that two assumptions are made using the present value table—(1) the present value is calculated for the beginning of the current year, and (2) the payments will be made at the end of the current year and each following year.

MODEL

- Ask a student to come to the board and explain the process for calculating the present value of a $1,000.00 payment at the end of each year for five years at a 10% interest rate.
- Ask another student to come to the board and use the present value factor to calculate the same scenario.

TEACHING IDEA

Allow students to calculate the same amount for the same period of time using different interest rates. Discuss that the change in interest rate can have a significant impact on the required investment. You can demonstrate additional scenarios by showing the impact of different periods of time and/or different annual payments.

Present Value of an Annuity

Present Value of an Annuity of $1					
	Interest Rate				
Period	4%	6%	8%	10%	12%
1	0.962	0.943	0.926	0.909	0.893
2	1.886	1.833	1.783	1.736	1.690
3	2.775	2.673	2.577	2.487	2.402
4	3.630	3.465	3.312	3.170	3.037
5	4.452	4.212	3.993	3.791	3.605
6	5.242	4.917	4.623	4.355	4.111
7	6.002	5.582	5.206	4.868	4.564
8	6.733	6.210	5.747	5.335	4.968
9	7.435	6.802	6.247	5.759	5.328
10	8.111	7.360	6.710	6.145	5.650
15	11.118	9.712	8.559	7.606	6.811
20	13.590	11.470	9.818	8.514	7.469

An amount invested at a given interest rate that supports the payments of an annuity is called the **present value of an annuity**. Assume that a company wants to invest enough money at the beginning of the current year so that it earns enough interest to make a payment of $1,000.00 at the end of each year for the next five years.

The present value of an annuity of $1 table shown above makes two important assumptions. The present value is calculated for the beginning of the current year, and the payments will be made at the end of the current year and each following year. On a timeline, the payments and investment would be:

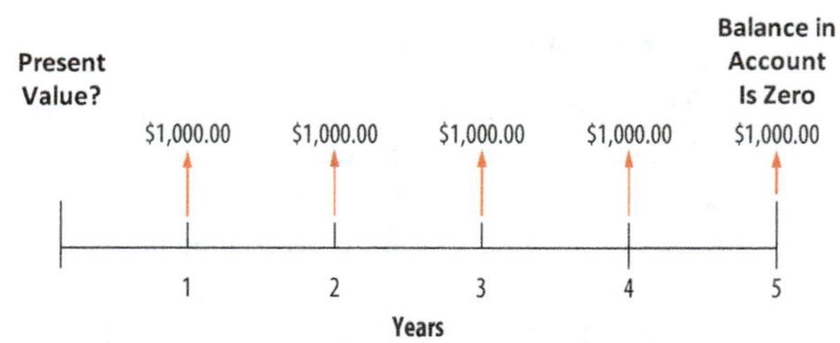

How much money does the company have to invest today (beginning of Year 1), at a 10% interest rate, to withdraw $1,000.00 at the end of each year for five years?

Annual payment	$1,000.00
Present value factor	× 3.791
Present value	$3,791.00

The company must invest $3,791.00 today.

FORMATIVE ASSESSMENT

- This is an ongoing process. Circulate around the classroom or lab, observing which students have difficulty with the assignments.
- Troubleshooting: Diagnose the kinds of problems students have with this lesson. Students may have difficulty (1) determining when to use the present value table versus the present value of an annuity table and (2) understanding the difference between when to use present value and future value.
- Assess student understanding by checking solutions to Independent Practice assignments and noting their answers to the Terms Review and Audit Your Understanding questions.

End of Lesson Review

LO5 Calculate the future value and present value of an amount.

LO6 Calculate the future value and present value of an annuity.

Terms Review

time value of money

future value

compounding

present value

annuity

future value of an annuity

present value of an annuity

Audit your understanding

1. Why does the amount of interest earned on an investment increase each year?
2. How is a present value factor determined?
3. When is the present value of $1 table used?

Work together 18-2

Calculating future and present values

Forms are provided in the *Working Papers*. Use the tables illustrated in this lesson. Your instructor will guide you through the following examples.

1. Calculate the future value of a one-time $3,000.00 investment in four years at 6%.
2. Calculate the present value of $20,000.00 received in five years at a 4% rate of return.
3. John's grandparents are going to put $1,000.00 in a savings account for John at the end of this year and each following year for a total of 20 deposits. If the savings account earns 8% per year, what will be the balance in the account immediately after the last deposit?
4. Jerry and Laurie Hoffman would like to deposit enough money today to allow their daughter to withdraw $5,000.00 at the end of each year for four years. The investment will earn 4% interest. How much do the Hoffmans have to invest today?

On your own 18-2

Calculating future and present values

Forms are provided in the *Working Papers*. Use the tables illustrated in this lesson. Work these problems independently.

1. Calculate the future value of a one-time $20,000.00 investment in five years at 10%.
2. Calculate the present value of $80,000.00 received in six years at a 6% rate of return.
3. The Greenstein family is hoping to take a family vacation in five years. They feel they can invest $3,000.00 per year at the end of this year and each of the next four years. If the investment earns 8% interest, how much will be in the account immediately after the last deposit?
4. Congratulations, you won the lottery! The lottery will be paid over 20 years, with a payment of $300,000.00 at the end of each year. You can invest each payment at 6%. What is the present value of the annuity payment?

CHECK FOR UNDERSTANDING

Terms Review

- Call on students to define each term in the Terms Review. Definitions are given in the Glossary.

Audit Your Understanding

- Call on students to answer the Audit Your Understanding questions. Answers are given in Appendix D of the textbook.

GUIDED PRACTICE

Work Together

- Have students write the solution to the Work Together problem as you guide the class through the examples.
- Direct students to calculate future and present values.

INDEPENDENT PRACTICE

On Your Own

- Assign the On Your Own problem to be worked independently.
- Use the Formative Assessment techniques to diagnose student understanding.

Application Problem

- Assign Application Problem 18-2.

Online Working Papers

- Students can access the Lesson 18-2 problems using this software.

RETEACH

- Instruct students to estimate when they would like to retire from working, how long they hope to live, and how much money they need each year to live when they are no longer working.
- Using a market rate of interest, instruct students to identify the amount of money they need to have invested prior to retiring.
- Call on students to explain their scenario and the steps for the calculations.

CLOSURE

- Ask students to develop a rule to decide which table to use for each business decision. (*One example is to use the present value of an annuity table when there are equal periodic payments; otherwise, use the present value table.*)
- Ask students to summarize what they learned in this lesson.

Essential Question

- Explain how learning about the time value of money might change how someone plans for the future. (*Answers might include choosing not to spend money today in favor of investing money for a future purchase or saving for college.*)

EXTENDED LEARNING

- Assign Why Accounting on page 540.
- Review Careers in Accounting on page 543.

LESSON
18-3

BRIDGE

- Point out that students have learned how to use differential analysis for short-term decisions. In this lesson, they will use the time value of money to make long-term decisions.

TEACHING RESOURCES

- **Instructor's Resource CD/Website:**
  PowerPoint Slides
  Accounting Concepts
- **Working Papers:**
  Teacher's Edition of the Working Papers for Lesson 18-3
  Online Working Papers

ENGAGE

- Explain that a business generally should not invest in assets that will not yield the desired rate of return. Instead, the business should continue searching for alternative investments that will yield the desired rate of return.

PREVIEW

- Call on students to read the accounting terms and definitions introduced in this lesson: *net cash flows* and *net present value*.
- Point out the learning objectives for this lesson.
- Direct students to read the headings in this lesson and to examine the illustrations.

MODEL

- Ask a student to read the third paragraph explaining the purchase of equipment and the net cash flow generated from this purchase.
- Point out that the present value of the net cash flow can be calculated using the single present value factor.
- Use the board or refer students to the illustration to calculate the present value of an annuity.
- Explain the meaning of the net present value and point out that the net present value is the amount used to determine if the decision to purchase the new equipment is financially rewarding.
- Use the board or refer students to the illustration to calculate the net present value.
- Explain that in this scenario, the $25,000 investment should be used differently to achieve the desired rate of return.

LESSON
18-3 Long-Term Management Decisions Using Net Present Value

LO7 Use net present value of an annuity to evaluate business decisions.
LO8 Use net present value of unequal cash flows to evaluate business decisions.
LO9 Use net present value to evaluate a lease or buy decision.

Calculating the Net Present Value of an Investment LO7

As a measure of the worth of an investment, managers typically focus on the cash receipts and cash payments connected with the investment. The difference between the cash receipts and cash payments is called the **net cash flows**.

Differential analysis, discussed earlier in this chapter, is commonly used in making short-term decisions. One shortcoming of differential analysis, however, is that it does not consider the time value of money. While the time value of money is not critical for short-term decisions, it should be considered when making long-term decisions.

Custom Cyclery Corporation is considering purchasing equipment for $25,000.00. The equipment will enable the company to generate net cash flows of $5,000.00 annually over the equipment's six-year useful life. Management expects assets to yield an 8% rate of return. Using the present value of an annuity of $1 table, the calculation of the present value of an annuity of $5,000 is shown below.

Annual net cash flows	$ 5,000.00
Present value factor	× 4.623
Present value of an annuity	$23,115.00

The difference between the present value of the cash flows of the investment and the amount of the investment is called the **net present value**. The net present value is the amount the business expects to earn above the desired rate of return on the investment. The net present value of the decision to purchase new equipment is calculated below.

Annual net cash flows	$ 5,000.00
Present value factor	× 4.623
Present value of an annuity	$ 23,115.00
Investment	(25,000.00)
Net present value	$ (1,885.00)

The net present value is a negative $1,885.00, and therefore, the investment fails to achieve the desired 8% rate of return.

Should management purchase the equipment? It may appear logical to purchase the equipment, since the net cash flows of $30,000 ($5,000.00 per year multiplied by 6 years) are greater than the cost of the equipment. However, effective managers will not purchase equipment that does not yield a positive net present value. Rather, they will continue to search for alternative uses of the $25,000.00 investment that will achieve the desired rate of return.

fyi
Managers may state that a future amount has been "discounted" to the present value.

Calculating the Net Present Value with an Unequal Net Cash Flow LO8

Year	Net Cash Flows		Present Value Factor		Present Value of Net Cash Flow
1	$ 500.00	×	0.926	=	$ 463.00
2	1,500.00	×	0.857	=	1,285.50
3	2,000.00	×	0.794	=	1,588.00
4	2,000.00	×	0.735	=	1,470.00
5	1,500.00	×	0.681	=	1,021.50
6	1,000.00	×	0.630	=	630.00
Present value of net cash flows					$ 6,458.00
Investment					(6,000.00)
Net present value					$ 458.00

Custom Cyclery Corporation is considering purchasing an assembly machine for $6,000.00. The expected net cash flows during the machine's six-year useful life are shown above. Management approves investments only if they earn an 8% rate of return. Since the cash flows are not equal, the present value of an annuity of $1 table cannot be used. Instead, each year's cash flow is discounted using present value factors for 8%.

For example, in Year 1, the first year the assembly machine is used, the net cash flow is estimated to be $500.00. The present value factor for this year is one period at 8%—0.926. The next net cash flow will be for two periods. The sum of the present values for each year is the total present value of the investment.

The investment in the assembly machine is expected to earn a net present value of $458.00. Custom Cyclery should invest in the machine because the net present value is positive. The discounted cash flows exceed the desired 8% rate of return.

© iStockphoto.com/Dan Bachman

THINK LIKE AN ACCOUNTANT

Evaluating Projects with the Internal Rate of Return

Power Contractors, Inc. (PCI), specializes in providing the cranes used in the construction of gas-fired power plants. PCI custom designs and builds each crane based on the needs of the customer and the physical constraints of the project, such as space restrictions, uneven terrain, and harsh weather. Because the cranes are only used at various stages of the project, PCI's contracts provide for unequal payments at specific dates. The amount of each payment is based on the time the crane is used and the complexity of the work at each state of construction. For example, PCI often receives 10% of the total contract price at the end of the second month when the foundation work is complete.

An alternative method for evaluating the profitability of a project is the internal rate of return. The method determines the rate of return of a series of cash flows that will yield a net present value of zero. PCI's management requires that projects earn a minimum internal rate of return of 10%.

OPEN THE SPREADSHEET TLA_CH18

The workbook contains the cost estimates and proposed payments of a contract proposal being submitted to a power company. Follow the steps on the Instructions tab to calculate the internal rate of return for the proposal. Answer these questions:

1. What are the rate of return and the total payments of the project as it is currently proposed?
2. After receiving the proposal, the power company is demanding a 3% reduction in the total project cost. Modify the proposal to increase the amount of early payments and reduce later payments, maintaining a minimum 10% rate of return. What are the rate of return and total payments of the revised project?
3. Compare the increase in the early stage payments relative to the later stage projects.

INPUT

- Point out that because the same amounts are not invested each year, the present value factor is used rather than the present value of an annuity factor.

MODEL

- Use the board or refer students to the illustration to calculate the net present value with unequal net cash flow.
- Point out that because the net present value is positive and exceeds the desired 8% rate of return, management would invest in this machine.

THINK LIKE AN ACCOUNTANT

Students are provided with a schedule of the payment dates and amounts of the initial proposal. After calculating the rate of return and total project payments, students copy and modify the schedule to determine payments that will yield PCI's minimum rate of return while reducing the total payments by 3%.

The activity reinforces the time value of money. Shifting contract payments to earlier dates means that PCI maintains its desired rate of return while it reduces the total payment amount.

Students may question the numbers adjacent to the Dates box in the Functions Arguments window. Dates are stored as serial numbers. The date 3/14/2014 is the 41,712th day since 1/1/1990. By storing dates as serial numbers, Excel can calculate the number of days between dates, as shown in column B.

Answers

1. Internal rate of return, 10.3%; total project payments, $1,750,000.
2. Solutions will vary.
3. Solutions will vary. A viable solution is to increase the first three payments by $100,000, $100,000, and $50,000, respectively, and to decrease the final three payments by $175,000, $60,000, and $70,000, respectively. These changes yield an internal rate of return of 10.1% and a revised project cost of $1,695,000.

INPUT

- Explain that before new machinery is acquired, an analysis must determine if leasing or buying is the better financial option.
- Ask a student to read aloud the paragraphs under the heading "Lease or Buy Decision."

MODEL

- Using the board or directing students to the illustration in the middle of the page, calculate the net cash flow for buying the machinery. Point out the tax savings due to bond interest and depreciation.
- Using the board or directing students to the illustration at the bottom of the page, calculate the present value of net cash flows for buying the machine.

Lease or Buy Decision LO9

Custom Cyclery would like to acquire a new machine which will increase net income $50,000 per year. It is considering buying or leasing the machine. Additional expenses for repairs and maintenance of the machine will average $3,000.00 per year.

If purchased, the price of the machine is $200,000.00. Custom Cyclery will pay $50,000.00 down and issue $150,000.00 of five-year, 10% bonds. The company will only use the machine for five years, although its useful life is 7 years. After five years, Custom Cyclery will sell the machine at its estimated value of $40,000.00.

Straight-line depreciation will be used to depreciate the machine. Custom Cyclery's tax rate is 30%, and it uses 6% in present value calculations.

If Custom Cyclery leases the machine, lease payments of $45,000.00 are due at the end of each of five years. In order to analyze this decision, Custom Cyclery will need to calculate the net present value of the cash flows connected with buying the machine and leasing the machine. The alternative with the higher positive (or lower negative) net present value of cash flows is the better choice.

CASH FLOWS FOR BUYING OPTION

Buy the machinery:

	Now	Years 1–5	Year 5
Down payment	$(50,000.00)		
Bond interest, net of tax savings		$(10,500.00)	
Tax savings due to depreciation		9,600.00	
Retirement of bonds			$(150,000.00)
Sale of asset			40,000.00
Net cash flows	$(50,000.00)	$ (900.00)	$ 110,000.00

The cash flows from the buying option are listed above. The down payment (–$50,000.00) must be paid when the machine is purchased. At the end of Years 1 through 5, Custom Cyclery will have cash flows connected with the payment of interest on the bonds (–$10,500.00) and with depreciation (+$9,600.00), which are explained more fully below. At the end of Year 5, Custom Cyclery will repay the bond (–$150,000.00) and sell the machine (+$40,000.00).

The additional net income and the additional repair and maintenance expenses will be generated whether the machine is bought or leased. Therefore, these costs are not relevant to the decision and are excluded from the calculation of net cash flows for both options.

The annual interest paid on the bond is $15,000.00 ($150,000.00 × 10%). Bond interest is a tax-deductible expense. The $15,000.00 interest payment will cause a tax savings of $4,500.00 ($15,000.00 × 30%). Therefore, the net cash flow from the interest payment is only $10,500.00 ($15,000.00 – $4,500.00).

Even though depreciation expense does not cause a cash flow, the tax savings as a result of depreciation does affect cash flows. Annual depreciation on the machine is $32,000.00 [($200,000.00 – $40,000.00) ÷ 5]. Depreciation expense of $32,000.00 per year saves Custom Cyclery $9,600.00 ($32,000.00 × 30%) in taxes each year. Therefore, the net cash flow effect from depreciation expense is a *positive (inflow)* of $9,600.00.

The net present value of the net cash flows connected with buying the machine is calculated as shown below.

Year	Net Cash Flows		Present Value of $1 Factor	Present Value of an Annuity Factor		Present Value of Net Cash Flow
0	$ (50,000.00)	×	1.000		=	$ (50,000.00)
1–5	(900.00)	×		4.212	=	(3,790.80)
5	(110,000.00)	×	0.747		=	(82,170.00)
Present value of net cash flows						$(135,960.80)

The $50,000.00 down payment, paid immediately, has a present value of $50,000.00. The net cash flows in Years 1 through 5 are equal payments, multiplied by the present value of an annuity factor of 4.212 (5 years, 6%). The cash flows connected with retiring the bonds and selling the machine is a single cash flow, multiplied by the present value of $1 factor of 0.747 (5 years, 6%). The present values are added together for a total of –$135,960.80 as the present value of the net cash flows for buying the machine.

DIFFERENTIATED INSTRUCTION

Auditory/Linguistic learners have highly developed auditory skills and often prefer to use spoken language as a means to remember information. Invite a financial manager who works for a car dealership to use the present value of net cash flow to explain scenarios of buying and leasing an automobile.

CASH FLOWS FOR LEASING OPTION

Lease the machinery:

	Now	Years 1–5	Year 5
Lease payment, net of tax		$(31,500.00)	
New cash flows	$—	$(31,500.00)	$—

There is only one cash flow connected with leasing the machine, the $45,000.00 annual lease payment. However, since the lease payment is a tax-deductible expense, it will cause a tax savings of $13,500.00 ($45,000.00 × 30%). Therefore, the net cash flow connected with the lease payment is $31,500.00 ($45,000.00 – $13,500.00).

The net present value of the net cash flows connected with leasing the machine is calculated as shown below.

Year	Net Cash Flows		Present Value Factor	Present Value of an Annuity Factor		Present Value of Net Cash Flow
1–5	$(31,500.00)	×		4.212	=	$(132,678.00)
Present value of net cash flows						$(132,678.00)

The net cash flows in Years 1 through 5 are equal payments, multiplied by the present value of an annuity factor of 4.212 (5 years, 6%). The present value of net cash flows for leasing the machine is –$132,678.00.

Since the present value of the net cash flows for leasing is a lower negative value than that for buying, Custom Cyclery should lease the machine.

© dwphotos/Shutterstock.com

INPUT

- Point out that only one cash flow is connected with the leasing option. Also remind students that lease payments are tax-deductible; therefore, the net cash flow is reduced by the amount of tax savings.

MODEL

- Direct students to the illustration or use the board to demonstrate how to calculate the present value of net cash flow for leasing the machinery.
- Point out that because leasing equates to a lower negative value, the company should lease rather than buy the machinery.

FORMATIVE ASSESSMENT

- This is an ongoing process. Circulate around the classroom or lab, observing which students have difficulty with the assignments.
- Troubleshooting: Diagnose the kinds of problems students have with this lesson. Students may have difficulty (1) remembering when to use the present value table rather than the present value of an annuity table and (2) remembering all of the steps necessary to calculate net cash flow for buying and leasing options.
- Assess student understanding by checking solutions to Independent Practice assignments and noting their answers to the Terms Review and Audit Your Understanding questions.

CHECK FOR UNDERSTANDING

Terms Review

- Call on students to define each term in the Terms Review. Definitions are given in the Glossary.

Audit Your Understanding

- Call on students to answer the Audit Your Understanding questions. Answers are given in Appendix D of the textbook.

GUIDED PRACTICE

Work Together

- Have students write the solution to the Work Together problem as you guide the class through the examples.
- Direct students to use net present value to make business decisions.

INDEPENDENT PRACTICE

On Your Own

- Assign the On Your Own problem to be worked independently.
- Use the Formative Assessment techniques to diagnose student understanding.

Application Problem

- Assign Application Problem 18-3.

Online Working Papers

- Students can access the Lesson 18-3 problems using this software.

RETEACH

- For additional practice, give students different assumptions to use with the sample data in the lesson.

CLOSURE

- Ask students to summarize calculating the net present value with equal and unequal net cash flow.
- Ask students to explain briefly the financial considerations for determining whether to lease or buy an asset.

Essential Question

- Why is net present value such an important evaluator when making an investment? (*It allows one to evaluate the financial implication to predict if today's investment will equate to the return expected in the future.*)

EXTENDED LEARNING

- Assign Think Like an Accountant on page 549.

End of Lesson Review

LO7 Use net present value of an annuity to evaluate business decisions.

LO8 Use net present value of unequal cash flows to evaluate business decisions.

LO9 Use net present value to evaluate a lease or buy decision.

Terms Review

net cash flows

net present value

Audit your understanding

1. Why is net present value used for long-term decisions?
2. If the cash flows from an investment are equal and occur at the end of each year, which present value table is used to determine a factor?
3. If the cash flows from an investment are unequal and occur at the end of each year, which present value table is used to determine a factor?
4. When using net present value to decide between investment options, which option is the better choice?

Work together 18-3

Using net present value to make business decisions

Forms are provided in the *Working Papers*. Your instructor will guide you through the following examples.

1. Robshaw Corporation is considering the purchase of equipment costing $30,000.00 that will have a six-year useful life. Projected net cash flows from the investment are shown below. Determine the net present value of the investment, assuming a rate of return of 10%. Should the company purchase the equipment?

Year	Cash Flows
1	$ 1,000.00
2	8,000.00
3	13,000.00
4	15,000.00
5	6,000.00
6	6,000.00

2. Spring Grove Corporation must replace a machine in its production facility. If purchased, the price of the machine is $150,000.00, which will be paid in cash. The machine will be used for 4 years, after which it will be sold for $20,000.00. Spring Grove uses straight-line depreciation, and its tax rate is 28%. If Spring Grove leases the machine, lease payments of $37,000.00 would be due at the end of each of four years. Spring Grove uses 4% in present value calculations. Should Spring Grove buy or lease the machine?

On your own 18-3

Using net present value to make business decisions

Forms are provided in the *Working Papers*. Work these problems independently.

1. Cedar Corporation is considering purchasing equipment for $38,000.00. The equipment will enable the company to generate net cash flows of $8,000.00 annually over the equipment's five-year useful life. Management expects assets to yield a 6% rate of return. Should the company purchase the equipment?
2. Cedar Corporation must replace a machine. If purchased, the price of the machine is $250,000.00, which will be paid in cash. The machine will be used for 5 years, after which it will be sold for $25,000.00. Cedar uses straight-line depreciation, and its tax rate is 30%. If Cedar leases the machine, lease payments of $37,000.00 would be due at the end of each of four years. Cedar uses 6% in present value calculations. Should Cedar buy or lease the machine?

Chapter Summary

Good decision making is critical for the success of a business. Some decisions have short-term effects, and some will affect the net income of the company for many years. Differential analysis helps simplify decision making by eliminating those revenues and expenses that are the same for all options being analyzed. Those revenues and costs that are different between options are said to be relevant to the decision and are included in the analysis.

In differential analysis, allocated fixed costs should be examined carefully. Some parts of allocated fixed costs are avoidable, meaning that they will go away if one of the options is chosen. Some parts of allocated fixed costs will remain, regardless of the decision made. Allocated fixed costs that will not go away will need to be allocated among the remaining units.

The time value of money should be considered when making long-term decisions. The timing of payments or receipts of cash are affected by the interest that can be earned. The value of an amount today is less than the value of an amount to be received three years in the future because money received today can be invested to grow to a higher amount in three years. The amount of the growth depends on the interest the investment can be expected to earn. Tables can assist in calculating present and future values.

Net present value calculations take into account the time value of money. The cash inflows and outflows of various investment options are determined, and the net cash flows are used to calculate the total net present value of the flows. The investment option with the higher positive (or lower negative) net present value is the better option.

The Power of Compounding

EXPLORE ACCOUNTING

Investing early in your life enables the power of compounding interest to increase your investment portfolio. Consider the example of two individuals: Sally Early and Jim Late. Sally began investing $1,000.00 every year, beginning at the age of 18. For many years, this was a struggle for her as she paid for college, started her career, established a home, and raised her children. Jim did not begin investing until he was 48, after his children were out of college. But Jim believed he could catch up by investing $4,000.00 annually.

By age 58, both Sally and Jim had invested $40,000 and were beginning to think about retirement. How well will their investments support their retirement? The graph compares how their investment portfolios grew over the 40 years.

At 8% interest, Sally's portfolio has grown to $279,781, whereas Jim's portfolio is only $62,581.95. Why is there such a significant difference? Because of the power of compounding, money earning 8% interest will double every 9 years. That means that Sally's first $1,000.00 investment at age 18 doubled to $2,000.00 by age 27, $4,000.00 by age 36, $8,000.00 by age 45, and $16,000.00 by age 54. The original $1,000.00 will reach $32,000.00 by age 63.

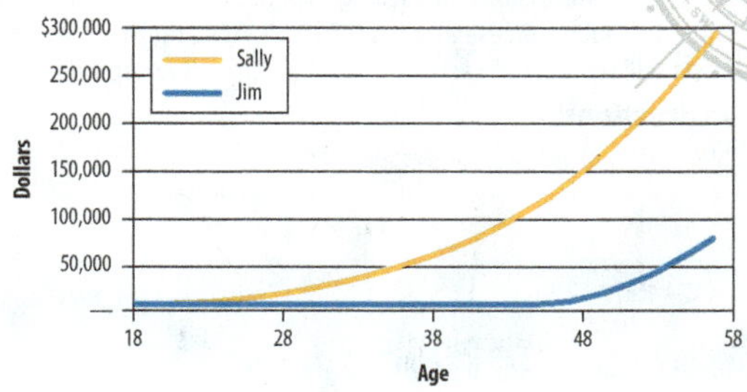

© iStockphoto.com/Makhnach_M

INSTRUCTIONS

Using an electronic spreadsheet, create a schedule to calculate the future value of annual investments. The headings and formulas for the first two years are shown below.

	A	B	C	D	E	F
1	Age	Investment	Balance on January 1	Interest Rate	Interest Earned	Balance on December 31
2	18	1,000.00	=+B2	0.06	=+C2*D2	=+B2+E2
3	=+A2+1	=+B2	=+B3+F2	=+D2	=+C3*D3	=+C3+E3

Copy the Year 2 formulas for the remaining years. Change the age in A2, annual investment in B2, and interest rate in D2 to develop a realistic plan that will guide you toward saving $1,000,000 for your retirement.

CLOSURE

- Review the Chapter Summary.
- Ask students to prepare a list of the new concepts introduced in this chapter.

Essential Questions

- How can people use differential analysis to make financial decisions as consumers? (*Examples might include comparing salary to cost of living in different geographic locations.*)
- How would someone use time value of money as a consumer? (*Examples might include saving for a future purchase, building wealth, or deciding the best use of monies received as gifts.*)

EXTENDED LEARNING

- Assign Explore Accounting on page 553.

EXPLORE ACCOUNTING

Answers

If students follow the instructions provided, their solutions should be nearly identical. The level of assistance required will depend on students' knowledge of electronic spreadsheets. Instruct students to print a solution containing Sally Early's annual payment and interest rate assumptions to ensure that their spreadsheets are accurate. Then instruct them to enter new assumptions for the annual payments and interest rate to develop their personal investment plan.

CHECK FIGURES

For complete solutions to Chapter 18 problems, see the Teacher's Edition of the Working Papers.

Application Problem 18-1.1

Variable overhead for Make, $45,000.00.

Application Problem 18-1.2

Variable overhead for Accept Special Order, $(7.50).

Application Problem 18-1.3

Fixed costs for Drop Men's Clothing Department, $72,500.00.

Apply Your Understanding

INSTRUCTIONS: Download problem instructions for Excel, QuickBooks, and Sage 50 from the textbook companion website at www.C21accounting.com.

18-1.1 Application Problem: Calculations for a make or buy decision LO1

Clarksville Corporation is considering making a component part that it has been buying for $220,000.00 from an outside supplier. No new machinery will need to be purchased, and Clarksville has idle machines that have no other use. Costs to make the part include: direct materials, $75,000.00; direct labor, $90,000.00; and variable overhead, $45,000.00. In addition, total fixed overhead costs for this part are $48,000. Variable overhead is directly related to making the part and will not exist if Clarksville continues to buy it. Fixed overhead includes $18,000.00 of costs that are directly related to buying the part. The remaining fixed costs are allocated to each product made by Clarksville. If Clarksville continues to buy the part, these costs will remain and will be allocated to other products.

Instructions:

Forms are provided in the *Working Papers*. Should Clarksville make the part or continue buying it?

18-1.2 Application Problem: Calculating relevant costs for a special order LO2

Worldwide Manufacturing, Inc., makes and sells suitcases. A particular model sells for $150.00. It is considering accepting a special order by a customer who offered to pay $125.00 per unit. Worldwide has determined that the variable costs for each suitcase are: direct materials, $40.00; direct labor, $45.00; and variable overhead, $10.00. Variable overhead includes $2.50 for commissions and selling expenses, which will not be incurred for this special order. A special emblem will be added to each suitcase at a cost of $0.25. At its normal level of production, fixed costs per unit are $38.00. These fixed costs will remain the same whether the order is accepted or not.

Instructions:

Should Worldwide accept the special order?

18-1.3 Application Problem: Calculating relevant costs for a decision to discontinue a segment LO3

Pierson, Inc., sells women's and men's clothing. It is considering dropping its line of men's clothing and has compiled the following data:

	Women's Clothing	Men's Clothing	Total Company
Sales	$210,000.00	$100,000.00	$310,000.00
Variable expenses	60,500.00	67,500.00	128,000.00
Contribution margin	$149,500.00	$ 32,500.00	$182,000.00
Fixed costs	65,000.00	35,000.00	100,000.00
Operating income	$ 84,500.00	$ (2,500.00)	$ 82,000.00

Further analysis shows that $7,500.00 of the fixed costs for men's clothing is allocated. If the Men's Clothing Department is discontinued, these costs will remain and be allocated to the Women's Clothing Department. The remaining $27,500.00 will be eliminated if the Men's Clothing Department is discontinued.

Instructions:

Should the department be discontinued?

18-1.4 Application Problem: Calculating relevant costs for a sell or process further decision LO4

Kato Cotton Corporation gets raw cotton and processes it into cotton material. It can sell the material or process it further into bed sheets. Kato can sell 100 yards of material for $300.00. It can use those 100 yards of material to make 40 bed sheets, which it can sell for a total of $800.00. The cost to process cotton into 100 yards of material is $200.00. Processing the material further into bed sheets costs an additional $550.00.

Instructions:

Should Kato sell the material or process it further?

18-2 Application Problem: Calculating future and present values LO5, 6

Forms are provided in the *Working Papers*. Use the tables illustrated in this lesson.

Instructions:

1. Calculate the future value of a one-time $5,000.00 investment in 10 years at 12%.
2. You won a contest and can choose between collecting $65,000.00 today or $100,000.00 five years from now. Current interest rates for a similar investment are 10%. Which option has the higher present value?
3. Sherry Greenstein is saving money for a down payment on a house. She can deposit $5,000.00 per year at the end of this year and each of the following 9 years. If her investment account earns 6% interest, how much will be in the account immediately after the last deposit?
4. You are selling a machine. You have received an offer to buy the machine and receive seven equal annual payments of $6,500.00 beginning one year from now. Assume an interest rate of 8%. What is the present value of this offer?

18-3 Application Problem: Using net present value to make business decisions LO7, 8, 9

Fireside Company is considering the purchase of several assets. You have been asked to analyze the following alternatives independently of each other. Forms are provided in the *Working Papers*.

Instructions:

1. Purchase installation equipment for $45,000.00. The equipment will enable the company to generate net cash flows of $9,000.00 annually over the equipment's six-year useful life. Management expects assets to yield a 4% rate of return. Should the company purchase the equipment?
2. Purchase a truck costing $21,000.00. The truck will have a five-year useful life. Projected net cash flows from the investment are shown below. Determine the net present value of the investment, assuming a rate of return of 4%. Should the company purchase the equipment?

Year	Cash Flows
1	$2,000.00
2	4,000.00
3	6,000.00
4	4,000.00
5	7,000.00

3. Fireside must replace a machine in its production facility. If purchased, the price of the machine is $400,000.00. Fireside will pay $5,000.00 down and issue $395,000.00 of five-year, 6% bonds. The machine will be used for five years, after which it will be sold for its estimated value of $275,000.00. Fireside uses straight-line depreciation, and its tax rate is 28%. If Fireside leases the machine, lease payments of $50,000.00 would be due at the end of each of five years. Fireside uses 4% in present value calculations. Should Fireside buy or lease the machine?

1. Calculate the net present value of each potential purchase.
2. Print the worksheet.

Application Problem 18-1.4

Revenue for Sell at Split-Off Point, $300.00.

Application Problem 18-2

1. Future value factor, 3.106.
2. Present value, $62,100.00.
4. Present value of an annuity factor, 5.206.

Application Problem 18-3

1. Net present value, $(2,178.00).
2. Present value of net cash flows, $20,132.00.
3. Present value of net cash flows for buying the machine, $(148,444.93).

INDEPENDENT PRACTICE

- Assign Mastery Problem 18-M for students as a culminating problem combining all new learning from the chapter.
- Assign Challenge Problem 18-C to accelerated students who work at a faster pace.
- Assign Study Guide 18.
- Students can access Online Working Papers to work end-of-chapter problems on the computer.
- Direct students to the C21 Accounting companion website for additional practice and review opportunities.

Mastery Problem 18-M

1. Present value of net cash flows for Abbott Industries, $113,632.00.

   Net present value for Costello Manufacturing, $6,540.00.

FORMATIVE ASSESSMENT

- Review solutions to the assigned problems in class, diagnosing trouble spots.

RETEACH

- Call on students to describe how they avoid the trouble spots diagnosed.
- Use reteaching suggestions from lesson plans as required.
- Assign Recycling Problem 18-R if needed.

Challenge Problem 18-C

Revenue for Process into Extra-Lean Ground Beef, $28.00.

Operating income for Process into Lean Ground Beef, $16.00.

21ST CENTURY SKILLS

Answers

1. Answers will vary.
2. Answers will vary.

EXTENDED LEARNING

- Assign 21st Century Skills on page 556.
- Assign Auditing for Errors on page 557.
- Assign Analyzing Home Depot's Financial Statements on page 557.

SUMMATIVE EVALUATION

- Chapter 18 Test
- Cognero for Chapter 18

18-M Mastery Problem: Calculating net present values LO5, 8

Clinton Company is evaluating the purchase of equipment from two vendors. Differences in the technology and labor requirements to operate the equipment of each vendor affect the projected net cash flows. The equipment purchased from Abbott Industries would cost $97,250.00 and is projected to generate total net cash flows of $168,000.00. The equipment from Costello Manufacturing would cost $135,200.00 and is projected to generate net cash flows totaling $235,000.00. The net cash flows for each year follow.

Year	Abbott Industries	Costello Manufacturing
1	$30,000.00	$10,000.00
2	28,000.00	20,000.00
3	26,000.00	30,000.00
4	24,000.00	40,000.00
5	22,000.00	50,000.00
6	20,000.00	60,000.00
7	18,000.00	25,000.00

Instructions:

1. Assuming that Clinton Company wants to earn a 12% rate of return, calculate the net present value of each equipment purchase.
2. Would you purchase the equipment and, if so, from which vendor?

1. Calculate the net present value of the equipment purchase from each company.
2. Print the worksheet.

18-C Challenge Problem: Calculating relevant costs for a multiple product sell or process further decision LO4

Lee Foods processes beef into ground beef. It can sell the regular ground beef or process it further into lean or extra-lean ground beef. Lee Foods can sell 10 pounds of regular ground beef for $15.00. The same amount of regular ground beef can be processed into 8 pounds of lean ground beef, which can be sold for $3.00 per pound or into 7 pounds of extra-lean ground beef, which can be sold for $4.00 per pound. The cost to process 10 pounds of regular ground beef into 8 pounds of lean ground beef is $1.00 per pound. The cost to process 10 pounds of regular ground beef into 7 pounds of extra-lean ground beef is $2.00 per pound.

Instructions:

Should Lee Foods sell regular ground beef, lean ground beef, or extra-lean ground beef?

21st Century Skills

Made in America Comeback

Theme: Financial, Economic, Business, Entrepreneurial Literacy, and Global Awareness

Skills: Information Literacy and Critical Thinking and Problem Solving

PARTNERSHIP FOR 21ST CENTURY SKILLS

For many years, the supply of low-cost labor has attracted American manufacturing jobs to China. An estimated 2.1 million such jobs have been displaced in the United States over the last 10 years. However, as China's middle class develops, wages and benefits are increasing at 15%–20% per year. Much of China's advantage is being eroded, resulting in an increase in direct labor costs.

COMMON CORE AND INTERDISCIPLINARY STUDIES

Extended learning features and activities present numerous opportunities to implement Common Core Standards through interdisciplinary studies. Practice is provided in the common core areas of English Language Arts & Literacy and Mathematical Practice. Many of these activities require short, critical-thinking and decision-making responses that apply reading, writing, speaking, listening, language, media and technology, and mathematical skills.

Since direct labor costs are only about 20% of the total manufacturing cost, the savings gained from outsourcing is minimal. In addition, direct labor in manufacturing is actually decreasing, due to automation. Once automation, transportation, and supply chain risks are considered, the savings gained from global relocation are causing American companies to rethink their decisions to manufacture overseas.

APPLICATION

1. American technology and innovative leadership should give U.S. companies the advantage in automation. Using the Internet, research companies that have brought manufacturing back to the United States. Cite the benefits.
2. Using the Internet, research technology manufacturing jobs. Write a report of your findings. Include names of companies, location, educational and/or skill requirements, and salaries.

Auditing for errors

Bachmann Corporation has the opportunity to purchase new machinery that will save the company $24,000.00 per year in manufacturing costs. The $124,000.00 of machinery is expected to be useful for 8 years, after which it could be sold for $5,000.00. The company requires an 8% return on investments. Eduardo Lopez, an accountant, prepared the following analysis and concluded that the company should purchase the equipment.

	Cash Flows	Present Value Factors	Present Values
Annual savings	$24,000.00	5.747	$137,928.00
Salvage value	5,000.00	0.540	2,700.00
Total present value			$140,628.00
Investment			(124,000.00)
Net present value			$ 16,628.00

Evaluate Eduardo's analysis to determine whether it is accurate. Did Eduardo make the correct decision?

Analyzing Home Depot's financial statements

Numerous accounting principles require companies to discount future cash flows when estimating amounts that are reported on financial statements. For example, the present value of a $10,000 account receivable expected to be collected in two years should be reported on the balance sheet as $8,570, assuming an 8% discount rate.

Accounting principles require companies to write down the value of plant assets if the fair value of the assets is less than the recorded book value. When establishing these principles, the Financial Accounting Standards Board (FASB) considered how present value should be applied to this situation. Home Depot presents its application of the FASB rules in the section "Impairment of Long-Lived Assets" of Note 1 on page B-13 in Appendix B of this text.

1. Does the FASB require Home Depot to discount future cash flows related to asset impairment? Support your answer.
2. Did Home Depot write down any plant assets during the period 2012 to 2013?

AUDITING FOR ERRORS

This activity provides a unique challenge. Having learned to expect errors, students must be confident enough in their auditing skills to express a conclusion that is contrary to their expectations.

Answer

Eduardo's analysis is correct. The company will earn a net present value of $16,628.00 and therefore should purchase the equipment.

ANALYZING HOME DEPOT'S FINANCIAL STATEMENTS

Answers

1. No, Home Depot's Note 1 states the following: "The assets of a store with indicators of impairment are evaluated by comparing its undiscounted cash flows with its carrying value."
2. Yes, Home Depot recorded impairments and lease obligations costs as well as store closings in 2012.

Chapter 19 Process Costing, Activity-Based Costing, and Product Pricing

Scope & Sequence

	New	Review/Enrich
Introduction		
Introduce the Chapter		
Lesson 19-1: Process Costing		
Comparing Job Order Costing and Process Costing	✓	
Calculating Equivalent Units	✓	
Journalizing the Transfer of Goods from One Department to the Next	✓	
Journalizing the Transfer of Goods to Finished Goods	✓	
Developing the Cost of Production Report	✓	
Lesson 19-2: Activity-Based Costing		
Issues with Allocating Overhead	✓	
Example of Traditional Overhead Allocation	✓	
Implementing Activity-Based Costing	✓	
Cost Pools and Cost Drivers	✓	
Allocating Overhead Costs Using Activity-Based Costing	✓	
Calculating Total Product Cost Using Activity-Based Costing	✓	
Comparison of Traditional and Activity-Based Methods of Allocating Overhead	✓	
Advantages and Disadvantages of Activity-Based Costing	✓	
Lesson 19-3: Product Pricing		
Cost-Based Product Pricing	✓	
Target Costing	✓	
Closure		

Enhancing Instruction

Features	Common Core Standards
• Accounting in the Real World: Wm. Wrigley Jr. Company	• ELAL—reading, media and technology, writing
• Ethics in Action: The Bad Pizza • Global Awareness: Repatriation of Profits Earned Abroad	• ELAL—reading • ELAL—reading
• Think Like an Accountant: Consolidating Corporate Information • Forensic Accounting: Vacations Prevent Lapping • Why Accounting?: College Marketing	• Mathematics • Mathematics • ELAL—reading
• Explore Accounting • 21st Century Skills • Analyzing Home Depot's Financial Statements	• ELAL—reading, writing • ELAL—reading, writing • Mathematics

ELAL = English Language Arts & Literacy

Calculator: © iStockphoto.com/picstodisc; Paper: © iStockphoto.com/Qingwa

Practice and Assessment

Technology & Media	Teaching Strategies	Guided Practice	Independent Practice	Reteach/Enrich
• Instructor's Resource CD/Website: PowerPoint Slides Accounting Concepts • Online Working Papers	• Logical/Mathematical Learners	• Terms Review • Audit Your Understanding • Work Together 19-1	• On Your Own 19-1 • Application Problem 19-1 • Formative Assessment, p. 565 • Online Working Papers	• Reteach, p. 566
• Instructor's Resource CD/Website: PowerPoint Slides Accounting Concepts • Online Working Papers	• Logical/Mathematical learners	• Terms Review • Audit Your Understanding • Work Together 19-2	• On Your Own 19-2 • Application Problem 19-2 • Formative Assessment, p. 572 • Online Working Papers	• Reteach, p. 573
• Instructor's Resource CD/Website: PowerPoint Slides Accounting Concepts • Online Working Papers	• Gifted Learners	• Terms Review • Audit Your Understanding • Work Together 19-3	• On Your Own 19-3 • Application Problem 19-3 • Formative Assessment, p. 575 • Online Working Papers	• Reteach, p. 576
• Online Working Papers	• Common Core and Interdisciplinary Studies		• Mastery Problem 19-M • Study Guide 19 • Chapter 19 Test • Cognero Chapter 19	• Challenge Problem 19-C • Reteach, p. 579 • Reinforcement Activity 4 • Recycling Problem 19-R

Introduce the Chapter

SET THE STAGE

GUIDING QUESTIONS

- Ask students to review the FIFO inventory method.
- Ask students to brainstorm different ways that a selling price could be determined for a product.
- Ask students how they would keep track of all the costs involved for manufacturing different products.
- Ask students to provide examples of when they might split the costs with someone else. Ask them to explain how they determine the individual costs and other considerations that might be made.
- Ask students to provide examples of services provided by the same provider that may vary in price due to different costs.
- Ask students what decisions management might make pertaining to costs.

PREVIEW CHAPTER OBJECTIVES

- Note that this chapter focuses on process costing for a manufacturer.
- Instruct a student to read each chapter objective aloud.

PREVIEW ACCOUNTING TERMS

- Read each term aloud to verify its pronunciation for students.
- Point out terms or parts of terms that should already be familiar to most students, such as *costs* and *pricing*.

Chapter 19 Process Costing, Activity-Based Costing, and Product Pricing

LEARNING OBJECTIVES

After studying Chapter 19, in addition to defining key terms, you will be able to:

LO1 Compare job order costing and process costing.

LO2 Calculate equivalent units of production.

LO3 Develop a cost of production report.

LO4 Journalize the transfer of costs in a process costing system.

LO5 Identify cost pools and cost drivers and calculate activity rates in activity-based costing.

LO6 Use activity-based costing to allocate overhead costs.

LO7 Use activity-based costing to calculate the total product cost.

LO8 Use cost-based pricing to calculate the price of a product.

LO9 Calculate the target cost of a product.

Calculator: © iStockphoto.com/picstodisc; Paper: © iStockphoto.com/Qingwa

© iStockphoto.com/Sportstock

Accounting In The Real World
Wm. Wrigley Jr. Company

Consumers young and old recognize many of the Wrigley brand of products: Juicy Fruit®, Wrigley's Spearmint®, Altoids®, Orbit®, Starburst®, Doublemint®, Skittles®, and Life Savers®. Fewer consumers know that Wrigley got its start in 1891 by selling soap. To encourage sales, Mr. Wrigley gave away baking powder to those merchants who carried Wrigley soap. Mr. Wrigley was very aware of his customers' preferences. When Wrigley baking powder became more popular than the soap line, Mr. Wrigley focused on selling baking powder and giving merchants free chewing gum for each can of baking powder they sold. As the Wrigley website states, "The rest is history."

Today, its products are sold in more than 180 countries and it has factories throughout the world. Wrigley is owned by Mars, Incorporated. Wrigley was the recipient of the 2013 *Vision for America* award from Keep America Beautiful, and Mars was named as one of the 100 Best Companies to Work For in the United States by *Fortune* magazine.

These two awards tie in to Wrigley's focus and principles, which focus on three areas: people, planet, and performance. It believes that it can grow its business while minimizing its footprint on the environment, respecting diversity, and encouraging inclusion.

CRITICAL THINKING

1. Visit the Wrigley website at www.wrigley.com and read about its three principles. Write a one- or two-sentence summary of its goals in each area.
2. In Chapter 17, two methods of measuring manufacturing costs were defined, job order costing and process costing. Which method would be more appropriate for Wrigley and why?

Source: www.wrigley.com.

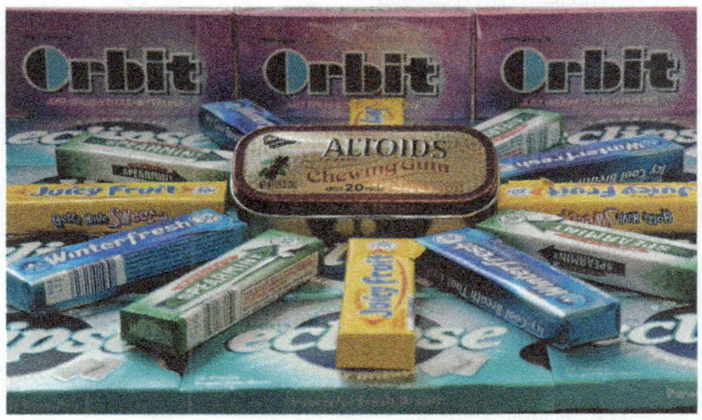

Background: © iStockphoto.com/Rovent; Real World: AP Photo/Brian Kersey

Key Terms

- equivalent units of production (EUP)
- conversion costs
- cost of production report
- activity-based costing (ABC)
- unit-level costs
- batch-level costs
- product-level costs
- facility-sustaining level costs
- cost pool
- cost driver
- activity rate
- cost-based pricing
- value-based pricing
- target costing

Accounting In The Real World

Answers

1. Answers will vary.
2. Process costing because Wrigley produces similar goods that flow continuously from one production process to another.

LESSON
19-1

BRIDGE

- Point out that students learned about using a job order costing system in Chapter 17. In this chapter, they will learn process costing.

TEACHING RESOURCES

- **Instructor's Resource CD/Website:**
  PowerPoint Slides
  Accounting Concepts
- **Working Papers:**
  Teacher's Edition of the Working Papers for Lesson 19-1
  Online Working Papers

ENGAGE

- Ask students to think of various products being manufactured in the same facility using the same equipment. How are costs calculated for the different products manufactured?

PREVIEW

- Call on students to read the accounting terms and definitions introduced in this lesson: *equivalent units of production (EUP)*, *conversion costs*, and *cost of production report*.
- Point out the learning objectives for this lesson.
- Direct students to read the headings in this lesson and to examine the illustrations.

INPUT

- Point out the difference between job order costing and process costing.

ETHICS IN ACTION

This activity requires students to use the guidance of a Q&A to determine if the action was ethical. Corporations often use the Q&A format to provide real-life examples that help to interpret the statements in the code.

Some students may agree with Devon's lack of action. It is reasonable to believe that Andy's family got sick from something other than eating the pizza. However, in its code, Pfizer clearly informs its employees that it is not their responsibility to make decisions on the value of any information regarding product quality. If every employee who obtains information about product quality elects not to report the information, the company loses a valuable source of information.

LESSON
19-1 Process Costing

LO1 Compare job order costing and process costing.
LO2 Calculate equivalent units of production.
LO3 Develop a cost of production report.
LO4 Journalize the transfer of costs in a process costing system.

Comparing Job Order Costing and Process Costing LO1

In Chapter 17, Custom Cyclery used a job order costing system to determine the cost of each bicycle produced. Job order costing is used when a company produces individual orders of different products in smaller quantities. In job order costing, the costs for each job are tracked and recorded.

Process costing is used when a single process with a continuous flow of inputs produces the same product. Process costing tracks the costs of the inputs added in each process or department of the facility. Costs are determined and recorded each period for all units produced in that period.

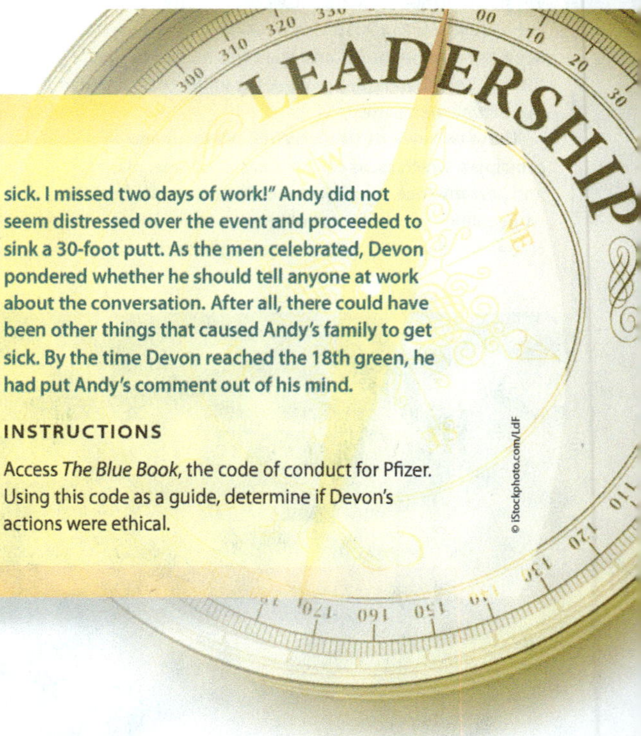

ETHICS IN ACTION

The Bad Pizza

Devon Stewart, an internal auditor for NBD Foods, loves to golf. Neither poor weather nor lack of a playing partner has ever kept Devon from his regular Friday afternoon round of golf. On one particular day, Devon was paired with three other men whom he had never met. As the men played, they shared information about their families and professions.

When Andy Foster, one of the golfers, learned that Devon worked for NBD Foods, he commented that his family used to love its frozen pizzas. "That was until a supreme pizza made the whole family sick. I missed two days of work!" Andy did not seem distressed over the event and proceeded to sink a 30-foot putt. As the men celebrated, Devon pondered whether he should tell anyone at work about the conversation. After all, there could have been other things that caused Andy's family to get sick. By the time Devon reached the 18th green, he had put Andy's comment out of his mind.

INSTRUCTIONS

Access *The Blue Book*, the code of conduct for Pfizer. Using this code as a guide, determine if Devon's actions were ethical.

© iStockphoto.com/LdF

See a suggested solution for this feature in the Instructional Strategies section at the front of this book.

Calculating Equivalent Units LO2

Financial statements must be prepared at the end of a fiscal period. [CONCEPT: Accounting Period Cycle] Preparing these statements can present unique challenges in a process accounting system. Premium Paints, a paint manufacturing company has two process departments, Mixing and Packaging. At Premium Paints, gallons of paint are continuously being produced. Therefore, not all processes will be complete at the end of a month. Gallons of unfinished paint will remain in the system at the end of the month. These units must be accounted for.

NO BEGINNING BALANCE IN WORK IN PROCESS

The data at the top of the next column are for the month of June for the Mixing Department at Premium Paints.

Units in beginning work in process	0
Units started this period	500,000
Units completed this period	495,000
Units in ending work in process (60% complete)	5,000

How should Premium Paints account for the 5,000 gallons of paint that are still in the Mixing Department at the end of the month? An estimate must be made of how complete these units are. An estimate of the amount of direct materials, direct labor, and overhead that have already been incurred on partially finished units, stated in terms of fully completed units, is called the **equivalent units of production** (EUP).

Premium Paints calculates EUP as shown:

		Equivalent Units of Production	
	Actual Units	Direct Materials	Conversion Costs
Beginning WIP	0		
Units started..........................	500,000		
Total units processed	500,000		
Beginning WIP	0	0	0
Units started and completed..............	495,000	495,000	495,000
Ending WIP (60% complete)..............	5,000	5,000	3,000
Units accounted for	500,000	500,000	498,000

At Premium Paints, all materials used to produce paint are added at the beginning of the process in the Mixing Department. Therefore, the 5,000 gallons of paint included in the ending work in process in the Mixing Department are 100% complete as to materials. However, these same 5,000 gallons are only 60% complete as to direct labor and overhead. The sum of the costs for direct labor and overhead are called **conversion costs**. At the end of the period, EUP must be calculated separately for direct materials and for conversion costs.

The EUP for direct materials is 5,000 units (5,000 units × 100%). The EUP for conversion cost is 3,000 units (5,000 units × 60%).

In the illustration, total units processed equals units accounted for. These two amounts must always be equal, which verifies that all units put into production are accounted for. In this example, the top calculation shows that 500,000 units must be accounted for. The bottom calculation accounts for the 500,000 units by showing that 495,000 units are complete and 5,000 are still in WIP.

BEGINNING BALANCE IN WORK IN PROCESS

In July, the 5,000 units of paint will be completed and more units will be introduced into production. Of the new units started during July, some will remain unfinished at the end of the month. On July 31, Premium Paints will have to calculate EUP again. The following data are for the month of July.

Units in beginning work in process (60% complete)	5,000
Units started this period	480,000
Units completed this period	475,000
Units in ending work in process (30% complete)	10,000

INPUT

- Explain the purpose of calculating equivalent units.
- Point out examples of products being manufactured that may not be complete at the end of a fiscal period.
- Explain how to calculate conversion costs and why they must be calculated.
- Direct students to the math illustration and explain why the ending WIP is the same as the actual units, yet the conversion costs are different.
- Remind students that total units processed must equal units accounted for.
- Explain that in the following month, the work that was not completed in the previous month will now be completed and that other work will remain unfinished at the end of the month.
- Direct students to the illustration to explain the calculations. Point out that ending WIP is 10,000 units, yet because it is only 30% complete, the equivalent units of conversion is 3,000.
- Also point out that with the beginning WIP of 5,000 units, no additional materials were added.

INPUT

- Explain that journal entries for a process costing system are similar to those for a job order costing system, with the exception of all costs flowing with the product to the next department.

MODEL

- Direct students to the illustration as you demonstrate journalizing the transfer of goods.
- Point out that the last department is Finished Goods.

The EUP for July is calculated as follows:

	Actual Units	Equivalent Units of Production: Direct Materials	Conversion Costs
Beginning WIP	5,000		
Units started	480,000		
Total units processed	485,000		
Beginning WIP (60% complete)	5,000	0	2,000
Units started and completed	470,000	470,000	470,000
Ending WIP (30% complete)	10,000	10,000	3,000
Units accounted for	485,000	480,000	475,000

The calculation of EUP with a beginning balance in WIP is more challenging. Since the 5,000 units in beginning WIP were 100% complete as to materials, no additional direct materials were added to those units. Therefore, EUP for direct materials is 0. However, conversion costs were added; therefore, an EUP must be calculated. Since the units were 60% complete at the end of June, only 40% (100% − 60%) of conversion costs were added in July to complete the units. The EUP for conversion costs is 2,000 units (5,000 × 40%).

The EUP for the ending WIP for July is calculated in the same manner as the ending WIP for June. The 10,000 units of paint are 100% complete as to materials, so the EUP for direct materials is 10,000 (10,000 units × 100%). These 10,000 units are only 30% complete as to conversion cost, so the EUP for conversion cost is 3,000 (10,000 × 30%). Note that the total units processed, 485,000, equals the units accounted for.

The EUP calculation for the Packaging Department is similar to the EUP calculation for the Mixing Department.

Journalizing the Transfer of Goods from One Department to the Next LO4

How costs are recorded in a Work in Process (WIP) account is different in job order costing and process costing. In job order costing, one WIP account is used. In process costing, a WIP account is used for each department or process. Premium Paints would have a Work in Process—Mixing account and a Work in Process—Packaging account.

GENERAL JOURNAL — PAGE 6

	DATE	ACCOUNT TITLE	DOC. NO.	POST. REF.	DEBIT	CREDIT	
22	30	*Work in Process—Packaging*	*M485*		*100 000 00*		22
23		*Work in Process—Mixing*				*100 000 00*	23
24							24
25							25

The journal entries for a process costing system are very similar to those for a job order costing system, with one exception. When goods are transferred to the next department, all costs from the former department flow with the product to the next department.

June 30. Recorded the transfer of goods from the Mixing Department to the Packaging Department, $100,000.00. M485.

Work in Process—Mixing is credited for $100,000.00 to decrease the account. Work in Process—Packaging is debited for $100,000.00 to increase the account. Notice that all costs incurred in the Mixing Department flow with the goods to the Packaging Department.

Journalizing the Transfer of Goods to Finished Goods

GENERAL JOURNAL — PAGE 6

	DATE		ACCOUNT TITLE	DOC. NO.	POST. REF.	DEBIT	CREDIT	
24		30	*Finished Goods*	*M486*		225 0 0 0 00		24
25			*Work in Process—Packaging*				225 0 0 0 00	25
26								26
27								27

At the end of a period, the cost of finished goods is transferred from the final department to the Finished Goods account.

Finished Goods is debited for the total costs of the units produced, $225,000.00. Work in Process—Packaging is credited for $225,000.00.

June 30. Recorded the transfer of finished goods out of the Packaging Department, $225,000.00. M486.

© iStockphoto.com/Lusky

GLOBAL AWARENESS

Repatriation of Profits Earned Abroad

"Repatriation," as it relates to money, is the act of converting foreign currency into the currency of one's own country. For example, when you change a foreign currency back into U.S. dollars, you are repatriating the currency.

Repatriation of profits is a similar concept. The profits earned by U.S. corporations in a foreign country would be subject to U.S. tax, just as though they were earned here.

Under U.S. tax law at the time of publication, profits earned by U.S. corporations in foreign countries are not subject to U.S. income taxes. The U.S. company must claim that these profits have been "permanently reinvested" in the foreign country. In addition to the tax effect, this action decreases domestic investment, which results in fewer American jobs. An additional negative effect is that the expenses incurred to earn these profits may be tax deductible. This means that a company can claim the expenses in order to lower its tax liability, but it does not have to claim the income related to those expenses, until the income is repatriated.

To encourage the repatriation of earnings, the U.S. Congress passed a one-time "holiday" for repatriated foreign profits. The law allowed foreign profits to be brought back to the United States at a much lower tax rate than that normally paid by U.S. corporations.

CRITICAL THINKING

1. If Congress was to declare another repatriation tax holiday, who would profit the most from it?
2. What behavior is encouraged by having a repatriation tax holiday?

Source: Center on Budget and Policy Priorities (www.cbpp.org).

GLOBAL AWARENESS

Answers

1. Those companies that kept the most earnings in foreign countries would benefit the most by bringing the earnings back to the United States at a much lower tax rate than those companies that repatriated their profits as the profits were earned.
2. The repatriation tax holiday encourages U.S. companies to keep their profits out of the United States permanently or temporarily until another holiday is allowed.

INPUT

- Explain the parts of a cost of production report.
- Explain that the cost of production report is completed for a process costing system.
- Point out that a per-unit cost must be calculated for each unit.
- Draw a timeline on the board showing the transfer of product.
- Explain that FIFO will be used as the method for determining the cost of production.

Developing the Cost of Production Report LO3

Premium Paints
Cost of Production Report—Mixing Department
For the Month Ended July 20--

		Equivalent Units of Production	
	Actual Units	**Direct Materials**	**Conversion Costs**
Beginning WIP	5,000		
Put into Production	480,000		
Total Units Processed	485,000		
Beginning WIP (60% complete)	5,000	0	2,000
Started and Completed	470,000	470,000	470,000
Ending WIP (30% complete)	10,000	10,000	3,000
Units Accounted For	485,000	480,000	475,000
COSTS OF PRODUCTION:			
Beginning WIP	$ 30,500.00	$ 20,000.00	$ 10,500.00
Current Period	3,582,500.00	1,920,000.00	1,662,500.00
Total Costs Incurred	$3,613,000.00	$1,940,000.00	$1,673,000.00
Cost per Unit	$ 7.50	$ 4.00	$ 3.50
Beginning WIP	$ 30,500.00	$ 20,000.00	$ 10,500.00
Cost to Complete Beg. WIP	7,000.00	0.00	7,000.00
Started and Completed	3,525,000.00	1,880,000.00	1,645,000.00
Cost Transferred to Packaging	$3,562,500.00		
Ending WIP	50,500.00	40,000.00	10,500.00
Costs Accounted For	$3,613,000.00	$1,940,000.00	$1,673,000.00

1 Calculate equivalent units of production.
2 Report production costs.
3 Calculate cost per unit.
4 Calculate cost to complete beginning WIP.
5 Calculate cost of units started and completed.
6 Calculate cost transferred to Packaging.
7 Calculate the cost of the units in ending WIP.
8 Calculate total cost allocated.

A report that shows unit information and cost information for a department using a process costing system is called a **cost of production report**. A cost of production report is completed by each department. The top section of the cost of production report shows actual units and EUP. Calculating EUP is the first section of the cost of production report for the month. The costs incurred in each department must also be calculated so that a per-unit cost can be assigned for each unit produced. The per-unit cost will be used in the journal entry to show the transfer of products from the Mixing Department to the Packaging Department and from the Packaging Department to Finished Goods.

The bottom section of the cost of production report explains the costs incurred by the department and the per-unit cost. The per-unit cost is used to allocate costs to completed units, which are transferred to the next department, and the units remaining in the ending WIP. Notice that the total costs incurred must equal the costs accounted for on this report.

The cost of production report can be prepared using the average cost method or the first-in, first-out (FIFO) method. The difference between the two methods is how the costs of the beginning inventory are treated. The average cost method averages the costs of the beginning inventory with the costs of the units put into production. The FIFO method keeps the costs of the beginning inventory separate from the costs of the units put into production. Only the FIFO method will be discussed here.

DIFFERENTIATED INSTRUCTION

Logical/Mathematical learners enjoy reasoning and problem-solving activities. They enjoy learning through investigations. Ask students to use the Internet and visit websites for three to five manufacturers. Ask students to identify the type of products manufactured and whether job order costing or a process costing method would be best for each company.

Completing the Cost of Production Report

1. Calculate equivalent units of production, as shown on the previous page.
2. Report and total the production costs. These costs are gathered by the Accounting Department. Premium Paints' production costs for July are Beginning WIP: Direct Materials, $20,000.00, and Conversion Costs, $10,500.00. Current period costs: Direct Materials, $1,920,000.00; Conversion Costs, $1,662,500.00.
3. In the FIFO method of preparing the cost of production report, the equivalent cost per unit for direct materials is calculated as:

$$\text{Cost per Unit, Direct Materials} = \frac{\text{Current Cost of Direct Materials}}{\text{Total Equivalent Units of Production}} = \frac{\$1{,}920{,}000.00}{480{,}000} = \$4.00$$

The cost per unit for conversion is calculated in the same manner:

$$\text{Cost per Unit, Conversion} = \frac{\text{Current Cost of Conversion}}{\text{Total Equivalent Units of Production}} = \frac{\$1{,}662{,}500.00}{475{,}000} = \$3.50$$

The total equivalent cost per unit is $7.50 ($4.00 + $3.50).

4. Steps 4 through 7 will allocate the total costs incurred to either cost transferred to packaging or to ending WIP. All costs must be allocated. The cost transferred to packaging consists of the costs of the beginning WIP units, the costs incurred to complete these units, and the cost of units started and completed this period. Calculate the cost to complete the beginning WIP. Since all the direct materials had already been entered into the ending WIP, the cost to complete these 5,000 units consists only of conversion costs. Completing the 5,000 units, which were 60% complete at the beginning of July, cost $7,000.00 (2,000 EUP × $3.50 cost per unit).
5. Calculate the cost of the units started and completed in July. The direct materials cost is calculated as:

   470,000 EUP × $4.00 direct materials cost per unit = $1,880,000.00.

   Conversion costs are calculated as:

   470,000 EUP × $3.50 conversion costs per unit = $1,645,000.00.
6. Add the totals for items from Steps 4 through 6 to determine the production costs for the units transferred to the Packaging Department. The total costs, $3,562,500.00, will be debited to WIP—Packaging and credited to WIP—Mixing to remove the costs from the Mixing Department and pass the costs on to the Packaging Department along with the physical units of product.
7. Calculate the cost of the units in the ending WIP. Direct materials cost is:

   10,000 EUP × $4.00 direct materials cost per unit = $40,000.00.

   Conversion costs are calculated as:

   3,000 EUP × $3.50 conversion costs per unit = $10,500.00.
8. Calculate the total cost allocated. This total must equal the total costs incurred, calculated in Step 2 above.

remember A cost of production report is completed by each department each period. The top section of the report shows actual units and equivalent units of production.

MODEL

- Direct students to the eight steps as you demonstrate the calculations.

FORMATIVE ASSESSMENT

- This is an ongoing process. Circulate around the classroom or lab, observing which students have difficulty with the assignments.
- Troubleshooting: Diagnose the kinds of problems students have with this section. Students may have difficulty remembering how to calculate the various parts of the cost of production report and how to journalize the transactions for process costing.
- Assess student understanding by checking solutions to Independent Practice assignments and noting their answers to the Terms Review and Audit Your Understanding questions.

CHECK FOR UNDERSTANDING

Terms Review

- Call on students to define each term in the Terms Review. Definitions are given in the Glossary.

Audit Your Understanding

- Call on students to answer the Audit Your Understanding questions. Answers are given in Appendix D of the textbook.

GUIDED PRACTICE

Work Together

- Have students write the solution to the Work Together problem as you guide the class through the examples.
- Direct students to calculate equivalent units of production and to complete journal entries in process costing.

INDEPENDENT PRACTICE

On Your Own

- Assign the On Your Own problem to be worked independently.
- Use the Formative Assessment techniques to diagnose student understanding.

Application Problem

- Assign Application Problem 19-1.

Online Working Papers

- Students can access the Lesson 19-1 problems using this software.

Website

- Direct students to the C21 Accounting companion website for additional practice and review opportunities throughout the chapter.

RETEACH

- Display a cost of production report and supply the data for actual units with no beginning WIP. Ask students to calculate the cost of production using FIFO. Ask students to complete another cost of production report with a beginning WIP amount supplied.
- Call on students to explain how to journalize the transfer of goods.

CLOSURE

- Ask students to describe the steps necessary to complete a cost of production report and explain why it should be prepared.

End of Lesson Review

LO1 Compare job order costing and process costing.

LO2 Calculate equivalent units of production.

LO3 Develop a cost of production report.

LO4 Journalize the transfer of costs in a process costing system.

Terms Review

equivalent units of production (EUP)

conversion costs

cost of production report

Audit your understanding

1. When is process costing used?
2. What is contained in the first section of the cost of production report?
3. What accounts are debited and credited to journalize the transfer of goods from the Processing Department to the Shipping Department?

Work together 19-1

Calculating equivalent units of production and completing journal entries in process costing

Schnieder Snacks, Inc., produces a variety of flavored potato chips. Schnieder uses a process costing system to record costs. On September 1, Schnieder had 10,000 units of potato chips in the Processing Department. The chips were 90% complete as to direct materials and 35% complete as to conversion costs. The following data were gathered on September 30:

Units started this period	560,000
Units completed this period	555,000
Units in ending work in process (50% complete as to direct materials and 25% complete as to conversion costs)	15,000

Partially completed forms and a blank general journal are provided in the *Working Papers*. Your instructor will guide you through the following examples.

1. Calculate equivalent units of production for the Processing Department for September.
2. Record the following transactions:
   a. Sept. 30. Recorded the transfer of goods from the Processing Department to the Packaging Department, $544,200.00. M666.
   b. Sept. 30. Recorded the transfer of finished goods out of the Packaging Department, $615,000.00. M667.

On your own 19-1

Calculating equivalent units of production and completing journal entries in process costing

Northstar Industries produces snack-size cupcakes. Northstar uses a process costing system to record costs. On March 1, Northstar had 90,000 units in the Mixing Department. The cupcakes were 40% complete as to direct materials and 30% complete as to conversion costs. The following data were gathered on March 31:

Units started this period	880,000
Units completed this period	870,000
Units in ending work in process (60% complete as to direct materials and 50% complete as to conversion costs)	100,000

Partially completed forms and a blank general journal are provided in the *Working Papers*. Work independently to complete the following problem.

1. Calculate equivalent units of production for the Mixing Department for March.
2. Record the following transactions:
   a. Mar. 31. Recorded the transfer of goods from the Mixing Department to the Baking Department, $850,000.00. M771.
   b. Mar. 31. Recorded the transfer of finished goods out of the Baking Department, $925,000.00. M772.

Essential Question

- Ask students to identify names of manufacturers that would likely use process costing. Explain. (*Names will vary. Most industries use mass production of similar products, such as pharmaceuticals, cereal, and beverages.*)

EXTENDED LEARNING

- Assign Accounting in the Real World on page 559.
- Assign Ethics in Action on page 560.
- Assign Global Awareness on page 563.

LESSON
19-2 Activity-Based Costing

LO5 Identify cost pools and cost drivers and calculate activity rates in activity-based costing.
LO6 Use activity-based costing to allocate overhead costs.
LO7 Use activity-based costing to calculate the total product cost.

Issues with Allocating Overhead

Both product costing and process costing methods use a predetermined overhead rate to allocate overhead costs. The predetermined overhead rate is commonly based on a cost element, such as direct labor hours, direct labor costs, or machine hours. These methods of allocating overhead costs are effective when there is a direct connection between the cost element and overhead costs.

Technology and manufacturing improvements may decrease the proportion of direct labor and materials used in production, while, at the same time, increase the proportion of indirect costs. This shift may decrease the effectiveness of using direct materials or direct labor to allocate overhead costs.

Using activity bases may be more effective for allocating factory overhead costs. Allocating factory overhead based on the level of major activities is called **activity-based costing (ABC)**.

THINK LIKE AN ACCOUNTANT

© iStockphoto.com/Dan Bachman

Consolidating Corporate Information

Superior, Inc., manufactures office furniture in six plants located in the southeast United States. Each line of furniture requires different raw materials, production equipment, and employee skills. Thus, each plant is divided into departments by the style of furniture produced. Not every plant produces every line of furniture.

Each completed item is inspected for quality. Any item having a flaw is returned to the department for repair, called *rework*. Most reworked items ultimately pass inspection. A small number with problems that cannot be easily corrected are sold as "seconds."

Superior's accounting system collects and reports the transactions for each plant by department. However, each plant manager is responsible for collecting the following production information on a daily basis:

- The number of units produced and sent to inspection.
- The number of units that passed inspection without rework.
- The number of units that passed inspection after rework.
- The number of units that failed inspection.

The plant managers enter this information in spreadsheets. The spreadsheets are printed and filed in a binder. Nothing is currently being done to combine the information into a single report. Superior's chief executive officer has asked the Accounting Department to assume the responsibility of collecting this information and providing upper management with a daily report.

OPEN THE SPREADSHEET TLA_CH19

The information from each of Superior's plants is stored in a file named by using the city where the plant is located. Follow the steps on the Instructions tab. Create a report that combines the information from each plant into a single report. Answer the following questions:

1. Which plant appears to be most effective in producing furniture in the Colonial line?
2. Which plant appears to be having problems producing furniture in the Victorian line?
3. Which furniture line has the highest rate of items that fail inspection?

LESSON
19-2

BRIDGE

- Point out that students have learned about using process costing to determine overhead costs. In this lesson, students will learn to use activity-based costing to allocate overhead costs and calculate the total product costs.

TEACHING RESOURCES

- **Instructor's Resource CD/Website:**
  PowerPoint Slides
  Accounting Concepts
- **Working Papers:**
  Teacher's Edition of the Working Papers for Lesson 19-2
  Online Working Papers

ENGAGE

- Ask students to summarize what is included in overhead costs.

PREVIEW

- Call on students to read the accounting terms and definitions introduced in this lesson: *activity-based costing (ABC)*, *unit-level costs*, *batch-level costs*, *product-level costs*, *facility-sustaining level costs*, *cost pool*, *cost driver*, and *activity rate*.
- Point out the learning objectives for this lesson.
- Direct students to read the headings in this lesson and to examine the illustrations.

INPUT

- Explain why activity-based costing may be more effective for allocating factory overhead costs.

TEACHING IDEA **To help explain activity-based costing, assume that four college students are going to split the costs of an apartment. Write the amount of rent on the board and costs for the Internet, groceries, utilities, and cable TV. Divide the total costs by four to determine the monthly costs per roommate. Then assume the following: one student will not be eating at the apartment, and another doesn't watch TV. Demonstrate the reallocation of costs based on activity used and determine the new monthly cost per roommate.**

THINK LIKE AN ACCOUNTANT

This activity requires students to use the Consolidation tool to prepare a summary of data from six spreadsheet files: Crossville, Dothan, Meridian, Natchez, Sumter, and Valdosta. Students use the summary to analyze production activity by product line and plant.

As an extended activity, instruct students to change an amount in any of the individual plant worksheets. The revision will be reflected in the summary report on the Analysis worksheet. This illustrates how daily reports can be obtained from each plant and be automatically reflected in the summary report.

Answers

1. Although Dothan had to rework 4 items, all 13 ultimately passed inspection.
2. Natchez had to rework 5 of 13 items, with 2 ultimately not passing inspection. Crossville also experienced problems. Crossville had to rework 20 of 32 items, with 2 ultimately not passing inspection.
3. The Early American line had 5 of 52 items, 9.6%, fail inspection.

INPUT

- Explain that with traditional overhead allocation, the predetermined rate per hour is multiplied by the number of hours the machine is in use to determine the overhead allocated for the product.
- Direct students to the illustration and explain the traditional overhead allocation.
- Point out that by using traditional overhead allocation, the per-unit cost may not be well defined, resulting in inaccurate costs and thus an inaccurate selling price.
- Explain that in the example provided, Midwest is losing sales to competitors that are pricing their products much lower than Midwest's.

INPUT

- Explain that when activity-based costing is used, the required activities must be identified.
- Direct students to the types of costs and ask a student to read the type and an example of each cost.

Example of Traditional Overhead Allocation

	Simple Product	Complex Product	Total Costs
Quantity	1,900	100	
Direct materials	$15,000.00	$12,000.00	$ 27,000.00
Direct labor	13,000.00	16,000.00	29,000.00
OH allocated on machine hours	47,500.00	2,500.00	50,000.00
Total cost	$75,500.00	$30,500.00	$106,000.00
Per-unit cost	$ 39.74	$ 305.00	

Assume that Midwest Manufacturing Company produces 1,900 units of Simple Product and 100 units of Complex Product. The factory overhead allocation is based on a predetermined rate of $50.00 per machine hour. Both products require 0.5 machine hour per unit. Therefore, Simple Product uses 950 machine hours and Complex Product uses 50 machine hours. The direct materials, direct labor, and allocated overhead costs are shown above. The total factory overhead costs for Midwest are $50,000.00. Simple Product is allocated $47,500.00 of overhead (950 machine hours × $50.00 per machine hour). Complex Product is allocated $2,500.00 of overhead (50 machine hours × $50.00 per machine hour). Using a traditional method of overhead allocation, Midwest's costs per unit for Simple Product and Complex Product are $39.74 and $305.00, respectively. Simple Product sells for $50.00 per unit, and Complex Product sells for $400.00 per unit.

Midwest has been losing business for Simple Product to its competitors, which are selling a similar product for $30.00 per unit. Midwest's sales of Complex Product are brisk.

Implementing Activity-Based Costing

If Midwest were to use activity-based costing, it would first need to identify the activities that are required to manufacture both products. An analysis of activities reveals that both products require the use of at least one machine. Each machine used requires a setup. Both products require at least one quality test. Complex Product also requires storage between production steps.

TYPES OF COSTS

Type of Cost	Examples of Costs
Unit-level	Electricity to run machines, indirect materials, machine and equipment depreciation, storage
Batch-level	Machine setup, ordering materials, quality testing
Product-level	Product design, consumer testing, inventory management, design changes
Facility-sustaining level	Building depreciation, factory supervisor's salary, property taxes, insurance

The costs associated with these activities can be classified into a hierarchy of costs: unit-level, batch-level, product-level, and facility-sustaining level.

Resources used on activities connected with each individual unit produced are called **unit-level costs**. Resources used on activities connected with a group of products are called **batch-level costs**. Resources used to support the entire product line are called **product-level costs**. Resources used to support the entire company and production process are called **facility-sustaining level costs**. Examples of each type of cost are given above.

remember

Activity-based costing is only used for allocating overhead costs. Direct materials costs and direct labor costs are treated in the same manner in activity-based costing and in traditional costing methods.

Cost Pools and Cost Drivers LO5

Cost Pool	Cost Driver
Machine setup	Number of machine setups
Machining	Machine hours
Quality testing	Number of tests performed
Storage	Number of times product is stored

A group of costs related to a specific activity is called a **cost pool**. The cost pools for Simple Product and Complex Product are machine setup, machining, quality testing, and storage. All the costs for each pool are gathered together under that pool. Midwest next needs to determine what item most closely affects the costs in the pool. The factor that affects the cost of an activity is called a **cost driver**. Midwest has found that the cost driver for machine setups is the number of machine setups each product requires. The cost driver for each cost pool is listed in the table above.

ACTIVITY RATES

	Total Activity Costs	Simple Product	Complex Product	Totals
Quantity		1,900	100	
Direct materials costs		$15,000.00	$12,000.00	$27,000.00
Direct labor costs		$13,000.00	$16,000.00	$29,000.00
Machine setups	$17,000.00	1	3	4
Machine hours	$5,000.00	950	50	1,000
Testing	$12,000.00	1	2	3
Storage	$16,000.00	0	4	4

The next step is to calculate the estimated total cost of each activity. As the above table illustrates, Manufacturing Company has estimated that the four machine setups will cost a total of $17,000.00. Using the data for each cost driver, Manufacturing will determine a price for each unit of activity, called an **activity rate**. The activity rate for the machine setup driver is calculated as:

$$\text{Activity Rate} = \frac{\text{Activity Cost}}{\text{Total Activity Useage}} = \frac{\$17{,}000.00}{4} = \$4{,}250.00 \text{ per setup}$$

Therefore, for each machine setup required by a product, that product will be allocated $4,250.00. An activity rate must be calculated for each cost driver. Midwest has calculated the following activity rate for each cost driver:

Cost Driver	Activity Rate
Machine setups	$4,250.00
Machine hours	$ 5.00
Quality testing	$4,000.00
Storage	$4,000.00

INPUT

- Explain the difference between a cost pool and a cost driver.
- Direct students to the illustration of activity rates.
- Point out that determining the activity rates requires more work than using traditional overhead allocation. However, more detailed data provide a more accurate measurement of costs.

MODEL

- Use the board or direct students to the illustration to demonstrate how to calculate the activity rate for each activity.

FORENSIC ACCOUNTING

The workbook contains a list of cash receipts. Students use functions and formulas to determine the number of days between transactions processed by each cash receipts clerk. The absence of a large gap indicates that a clerk did not take the required extended vacation. Although students may find it humorous that a vacation is an accounting control, today's auditors closely examine the vacation patterns of employees in management and accounting positions.

Solutions

1. Ten rows are identified.
2. See a suggested table for this question in the Instructional Strategies section at the front of this book.
3. Amanda Stillman did not take any extended vacation. Instead, she took 5 three-day weekends. In contrast, Jonas LaGrange worked for two weeks and Desha Davis took an extended vacation. This evidence indicates the possibility that lapping occurred.

FORENSIC ACCOUNTING

Vacations Prevent Lapping

One of the basic controls within an accounting system is the segregation of duties. The duties of having the authority to execute a transaction, the custody of the assets involved, and the responsibility for recording the transaction in the accounting records should be segregated.

Small businesses often find it difficult to segregate these duties. A lack of a sufficient number of staff in the accounting function often requires an individual to perform two or more of these duties. When this lack of segregation exists, other controls can help prevent or detect a fraud.

It may seem funny, but one such control requires employees in control positions to take extended vacations. The logic of this control is that another individual will need to perform the absent employee's duties. Many frauds require constant maintenance. Forcing another individual to perform an employee's duties, even for just two weeks, has a good chance of detecting fraudulent activities. Employees who know they will be unable to maintain a fraud are less likely to commit the fraud.

A fraud in the cash receipts and accounts receivable area that requires constant maintenance is known as *lapping*. This fraud involves the misuse of cash received from sales on account. The cash receipts clerk takes a check and deposits the check in his or her personal account. No entry is made in the customer's account in the accounts receivable ledger. When another check is received, the check is deposited in the company's account, but the first customer's account is credited in the accounts receivable ledger. As more checks are redirected to the clerk's account, the work required to maintain this fraud makes it impossible for the clerk to take an extended vacation.

ACTIVITY

Marshall Corporation provides services to companies involved in oil exploration. All sales are on account, and most customers use checks to submit their payments. Marshall employs two cash receipts clerks. The clerks are responsible for opening the mail, preparing the checks to be deposited, taking the deposits to the bank, and recording the transactions in the accounts receivable subsidiary ledger.

Amanda Stillman has worked for the company for over twenty years and handles payroll duties. Desha Davis has only worked for the company for two years. She is responsible for maintaining the company's extensive investment in plant assets. When either clerk takes an extended vacation, Jonas LaGrange, the accounts payable clerk, substitutes as a cash receipts clerk.

For the first time, Marshall Corporation has hired an accounting firm to perform an audit. Its accounting policy manual clearly states that all accounting personnel are required to take a two-week vacation. While reviewing accounting procedures with employees, a staff auditor learned that Jonas LaGrange had only substituted for Desha Davis. "Amanda has never asked me to substitute for her," he stated. "Maybe someone else took her place?"

In an earlier conversation, Amanda had stated that she did take an extended vacation. Given the inconsistency in the employees' stories, the staff auditor decided to analyze cash receipts records. The analysis would attempt to determine if there are any significant gaps in the dates that each cash receipts clerk processed a cash receipt. A large gap would indicate the clerk took the required extended vacation.

INSTRUCTIONS

Open the spreadsheet FA_CH19 and complete the steps on the Instructions tab. Provide answers to the following questions, supporting your answers.

1. How many rows of data have a large or unusual gap in days?
2. For each flagged row, complete a table with the following information: Date, User ID, Gap in Days, and Explanation. Use the transactions before and after each flagged row to explain the gap in days.
3. Does the evidence suggest either cash receipts clerk is involved in lapping?

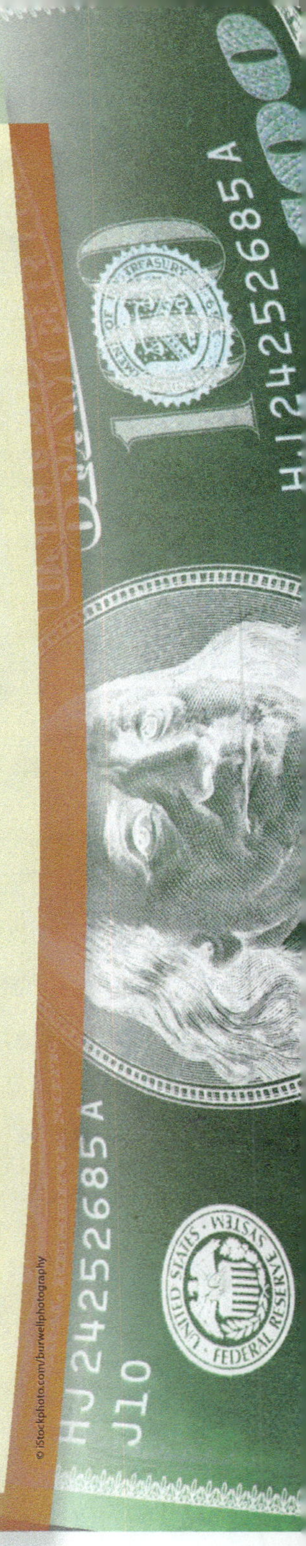

© iStockphoto.com/burwellphotography

Allocating Overhead Costs Using Activity-Based Costing LO6

Activity Pool	Simple Product	Complex Product	Total
Machine setups	$ 4,250.00	$12,750.00	$17,000.00
Machining	4,750.00	250.00	5,000.00
Testing	4,000.00	8,000.00	12,000.00
Storage	0.00	16,000.00	16,000.00
Overhead allocated	$13,000.00	$37,000.00	$50,000.00

Simple Product is allocated $4,250.00 of overhead cost for machine setups ($4,250.00 activity rate × 1 setup). Complex Product is allocated $12,750.00 of overhead cost for machine setups ($4,250.00 × 3 setups). Each activity pool is calculated in a similar manner. Simple Product is allocated $13,000.00 of total overhead, and Complex Product is allocated $37,000.00 of total overhead.

Calculating Total Product Cost Using Activity-Based Costing LO7

	Simple Product	Complex Product	Total Costs
Quantity	1,900	100	
Direct materials	$15,000.00	$12,000.00	$ 27,000.00
Direct labor	13,000.00	16,000.00	29,000.00
Overhead allocated	13,000.00	37,000.00	50,000.00
Total cost	$41,000.00	$65,000.00	$106,000.00
Per-unit cost	$ 21.58	$ 650.00	

The total cost of each product is the sum of the direct materials, direct labor, and allocated overhead for that product. The cost per unit for each product can also be calculated: for Simple Product, $21.58, and for Complex Product, $650.00.

Comparison of Traditional and Activity-Based Methods of Allocating Overhead

	Simple Product	Complex Product
Per-unit cost, traditional method	$39.74	$305.00
Per-unit cost, ABC method	21.58	650.00
Current selling price	50.00	400.00

When Midwest Manufacturing Company used the traditional method of overhead allocation, it overestimated its production costs for Simple Product and underestimated its production costs for Complex Product. This could be the reason that it has been losing sales of Simple Product to its competitors, who are charging $30.00 for a similar product. In addition, according to the ABC method, Midwest is selling each unit of Complex Product for less than its cost.

How does Midwest determine which costing method to use? It should use the method that more accurately reflects the actual cost of each product. This is determined by finding the method that most closely matches actual overhead costs with the activity that causes those costs.

fyi Activity-based costing works equally well in service businesses and in companies that sell products.

INPUT

- Direct students to the illustration at the top of the page as you continue to calculate the overhead costs for the activity pool.
- Once the overhead allocation is determined, demonstrate how to calculate the per-unit cost. Direct students to the second illustration on this page.
- Direct students to the table on this page that compares traditional and activity-based methods.
- Point out the differences in cost when activity-based costing and the traditional method are used.
- Explain managerial decisions that must be made based on the cost and the current selling price.
- Point out that the business must use the method that more accurately reflects the actual cost of the product.

DIFFERENTIATED INSTRUCTION

Logical/Mathematical learners enjoy reasoning and problem-solving activities. They enjoy being taught through investigations. Ask students to form groups of three. Ask each group to create a problem-solving scenario that involves activity-based costing. Examples might include a group of friends going out to eat at a restaurant.

INPUT

- Explain the advantages and disadvantages of activity-based costing, also called *ABC*.
- Point out that GAAP does not permit ABC to be used for external reporting. Explain that a company may use ABC for decision making, but must also use GAAP conformity for reporting.

Advantages and Disadvantages of Activity-Based Costing

Activity-based costing offers several advantages over other costing methods. One advantage is that once activities are identified and a cost for each activity is determined, the company can use this information to identify inefficient activities. A high-cost activity is a good candidate for reducing costs by simplifying the activity. Nonessential activities can be minimized or eliminated.

If there is a strong relationship between cost pools and cost drivers, ABC can ensure that the company is accurate in costing its products. It can eliminate the risk of charging too little or too much for its products because of inaccurate costing.

ABC can also be used effectively in service businesses, such as banking and health services. A service business uses ABC in order to determine what it should charge a customer for the service provided. In an online environment, the bank can determine the cost of providing a service online versus using bank personnel to perform the same activity.

A disadvantage of ABC is the initial cost and effort required to implement it. When identifying activities and cost pools, it is important to identify all major activities. However, a company that identifies too many cost pools may make the overall system cumbersome and inefficient. Many companies find it necessary to hire a consultant to implement an ABC system.

ABC does not conform to generally accepted accounting principles (GAAP). Therefore, it cannot be used for external reporting. If a company chooses to use ABC for internal decision-making purposes, it must also track costs by using a method that is in conformity with GAAP.

Not all product costs can be associated with activities. These costs usually relate to higher-order product-level costs and facility-sustaining level costs.

WHY ACCOUNTING?

College Marketing

Marketing is an important part of most business plans. Few industries have the luxury of not having to market to customers. This has not always been true in the marketing of colleges and universities.

In a time when there were more than enough students, a GI bill covering education costs for those serving in the military, and relatively low college costs, universities did not need to have efficient marketing programs to attract as many students as they could enroll. Times have changed.

Marketing is now considered a normal activity at most institutions of higher learning. College fairs, career fairs, and state fairs are just some of the places you can find colleges and universities marketing their programs. College viewbooks on social media and websites, campus tours, and alumni recruitment efforts are only a few of the ways colleges try to attract potential students.

How does a college develop a marketing plan and, more importantly, how does a college determine if the plan is effective? Any evaluation of a marketing plan should include the cost of the items within the plan, such as the cost of an actual campus tour versus a virtual tour, or the cost of a visit to a high school by a college recruiter versus a booth at a college fair.

CRITICAL THINKING

What are some of the costs that would be incurred to set up a booth at a college fair?

Source: http://buildingmarketingstrategies.wordpress.com/2009/05/20/this-just-in-from-the-university-of-california-marketing-isnt-a-dirty-word.

© iStockphoto.com/AleksKo

WHY ACCOUNTING?

Answers

Answers will vary but could include the registration fee for displaying at the college fair; transportation to the fair, including meals and lodging if there from out of town; the cost of the booth used to display the college materials; the salary of the person(s) representing the college at the fair; the brochures distributed at the fair and the cost of any swag handed out; the cost of notices sent out announcing the college's presence at the fair; and the cost of arranging (e.g., telephone calls) to have a display at the fair.

FORMATIVE ASSESSMENT

- This is an ongoing process. Circulate around the classroom or lab, observing which students have difficulty with the assignments.
- Troubleshooting: Diagnose the kinds of problems students have with this lesson. Students may have difficulty understanding cost pools and cost drivers.
- Assess student understanding by checking solutions to Independent Practice assignments and noting their answers to the Terms Review and Audit Your Understanding questions.

End of Lesson Review

LO5 Identify cost pools and cost drivers and calculate activity rates in activity-based costing.

LO6 Use activity-based costing to allocate overhead costs.

LO7 Use activity-based costing to calculate the total product cost.

Terms Review

activity-based costing (ABC)

unit-level costs

batch-level costs

product-level costs

facility-sustaining level costs

cost pool

cost driver

activity rate

Audit your understanding

1. Identify the four types of costs in an activity-based costing system.
2. Identify three possible cost drivers in a shipping department.
3. List two major disadvantages of activity-based costing.

Work together 19-2

Calculating activity rates and allocating costs

Wilkerson Corporation uses activity-based costing. It bases its activity rates on yearly estimates of cost and activity. The Materials Department has made the following estimates for the current year:

Activity Pool	Cost Driver	Estimated Cost	Estimated Activity
Preparing purchase orders	Number of purchase orders	$ 50,000.00	25,000 purchase orders
Receiving materials	Number of boxes received	100,000.00	100,000 boxes
Storage of materials	Cubic foot per day of storage	10,000.00	50,000 cubic foot storage days
Issuing materials to production	Number of materials requisitions	200,000.00	20,000 requisitions

Forms are provided in the *Working Papers*. Your instructor will guide you through the following examples.

1. Calculate the activity rate for each cost driver.
2. Allocate the materials handling costs for Job No. 455, which requires five purchase orders, 50 boxes of materials received, 100 cubic feet of storage for 25 days, and 3 materials requisitions.

On your own 19-2

Calculating activity rates and allocating costs

Medford Manufacturing uses activity-based costing. It bases its activity rates on yearly estimates of cost and activity. The Accounting Department has made the following estimates for the current year:

Activity Pool	Cost Driver	Estimated Cost	Estimated Activity
Machine setups	Number of machine setups	$600,000.00	10,000 machine setups
Machine processing	Number of machine hours	200,000.00	50,000 machine hours
Shipping of product	Number of boxes shipped	75,000.00	25,000 boxes shipped

Forms are provided in the *Working Papers*. Work independently to complete the following problem.

1. Calculate the activity rate for each cost driver.
2. Allocate the overhead production costs for Job No. 388, which requires 6 machine setups, 100 machine hours, and 15 boxes shipped.

EXTENDED LEARNING

- Assign Think Like an Accountant on page 567.
- Assign Forensic Accounting on page 570.
- Assign Why Accounting on page 572.

CHECK FOR UNDERSTANDING

Terms Review

- Call on students to define each term in the Terms Review. Definitions are given in the Glossary.

Audit Your Understanding

- Call on students to answer the Audit Your Understanding questions. Answers are given in Appendix D of the textbook.

GUIDED PRACTICE

Work Together

- Have students write the solution to the Work Together problem as you guide the class through the examples.
- Direct students to calculate activity rates and to allocate costs.

INDEPENDENT PRACTICE

On Your Own

- Assign the On Your Own problem to be worked independently.

Application Problem

- Assign Application Problem 19-2.

Online Working Papers

- Students can access the Lesson 19-2 problems using this software.

RETEACH

- Call on students to explain the difference between cost pools and cost drivers.
- Ask students to summarize the process for determining activity rates.
- Review the journal entries for factory overhead.

CLOSURE

- Ask students to summarize briefly the advantage of activity-based costing instead of traditional overhead allocation.

Essential Question

- As long as the costs are lower than the price, wouldn't it be a waste of time to implement ABC as a method of allocating overhead? Explain. (*No, because ABC identifies activities that cause costs and allows management to control these costs. Also, ABC allows management to make informed decisions about pricing in order to be profitable and competitive.*)

LESSON

19-3

BRIDGE

- Point out that students have learned how to calculate the cost of manufacturing a product. In this lesson, they will learn how to determine the price for a product.

TEACHING RESOURCES

- **Instructor's Resource CD/Website:**
  PowerPoint Slides
  Accounting Concepts
- **Working Papers:**
  Teacher's Edition of the Working Papers for Lesson 19-3
  Online Working Papers

ENGAGE

- Ask students to brainstorm how they would determine the price to charge for a product they manufactured.

PREVIEW

- Call on students to read the accounting terms and definitions introduced in this lesson: *cost-based pricing*, *value-based pricing*, and *target costing*.
- Point out the learning objectives for this lesson.
- Direct students to read the headings in this lesson and to examine the illustrations.

INPUT

- Explain that a variety of methods are used to set the price for a product or service.
- Point out that a common method of determining price is to add a fixed percentage or fixed sum to the cost of the product or service.
- Explain that another name for cost-based pricing is markup pricing.
- Direct students to the math illustration and demonstrate how to calculate the selling price using a 50% markup.

INPUT

- Explain the advantages and disadvantages of cost-based product pricing.
- Point out that the higher the markup, the greater the company profits.
- Direct students to the math illustration for gross profit margin as you explain the calculation.
- Point out that the markup will always be greater than the gross profit margin.

LESSON 19-3 Product Pricing

LO8 Use cost-based pricing to calculate the price of a product.
LO9 Calculate the target cost of a product.

Cost-Based Product Pricing LO8

The selling price of a product must be high enough to cover all of the costs of the product and administrative expenses of the company. The price must also provide an adequate profit for the capital invested in the company. Varieties of methods are used to set the price of a product or service. A method of establishing a price for a product or service in which a fixed percentage or a fixed sum is added to the cost of the product or service is called **cost-based pricing**. Cost-based pricing is also known as *markup pricing*.

In Chapter 17, Custom Cyclery tracked the total and per-unit cost to produce a model SFM bicycle. The bicycle had production costs of $101.00 per unit. Assuming that Custom Cyclery uses a 50% markup on its product, the selling price of model SFM is calculated as follows:

$$\begin{aligned}\text{Selling Price} &= \text{Total Cost of the Product} + (\text{Total Cost of the Product} \times \text{Percentage Markup})\\ &= \$101.00 + (\$101.00 \times 50\%)\\ &= \$151.50\end{aligned}$$

The total cost, $101.00, is multiplied by the percentage markup, 50%, to obtain the amount of the markup, $50.50. The markup is then added to the cost of the bicycle to obtain the selling price of the bicycle, $151.50.

ADVANTAGES AND DISADVANTAGES OF COST-BASED PRODUCT PRICING

An advantage of the cost-based method of product pricing is that it is easy to calculate and use. Software can calculate the selling price for each product. The markup can be set at any percentage desired by the company. The higher the markup, the greater the company profits.

The cost-based method of product pricing has several disadvantages. It focuses on the company and the company costs, instead of on the customer. It may lead to prices that are too high or too low. Perhaps the biggest disadvantage is that it provides no incentive to keep costs under control. This is especially true if software automatically tracks the cost of the product and calculates the selling price. Management must take measures to monitor costs and selling prices periodically. Finally, if the costs of the product change and the accounting software does not automatically calculate a new selling price, the profit margin on the product will change.

PERCENTAGE MARKUP VERSUS GROSS PROFIT MARGIN

Care should be taken not to confuse the percentage markup with the gross profit margin. The percentage markup will always be greater than the gross profit margin. As shown previously, if the cost of model SFM is $101.00 and the selling price is $151.50, the markup is 50%.

The gross profit margin on model SFM is 33.33%, calculated as shown below. Therefore, when the markup is 50%, the gross profit margin is only 33.33%.

$$\text{Gross Profit Margin} = \frac{\text{Gross Profit}}{\text{Selling Price}} = \frac{\$50.50}{\$151.50} = 33.33\%$$

DIFFERENTIATED INSTRUCTION

Gifted learners enjoy conducting further research on topics. Ask students to search the Internet for average markups in at least five industries. Students should prepare a visual aid in which to share their findings. **Tactile/Kinesthetic learners** learn best when learning involves movement. Ask students to interview three businesses about their pricing strategy and the reason they use the pricing method selected. Tell students to prepare a visual aid to share their findings with the class.

DIFFERENCES BETWEEN COST-BASED PRICING AND VALUE-BASED PRICING

A method of establishing a price for a product or service based on the value the product or service has to its customer is called **value-based pricing**. To use value-based pricing, the company must have a good understanding of its customers and the value the product or service gives to the customer. There is no formula for calculating a value-based price. Value-based pricing is effective in products or services that have emotional value, are in high demand and/or low supply, will increase efficiency or improve health, and where there is little or no competition for a product or service that is necessary. Artwork, pharmaceuticals, and new technology are some examples of industries that may use value-based pricing.

Value-based pricing focuses on the customer instead of the company or the company's costs. In the long term, value-based pricing always results in a higher-priced product than does cost-based pricing. This is because if the value of the product is less than the cost of the product, the company cannot generate a profit by producing and selling the product. Either the cost of the product must be decreased or the company will stop making the product.

Target Costing LO9

A method of establishing a price for a product or service, based on the price the customer is willing to pay and controlling the cost of the product so that the company still makes a profit, is called **target costing**. This method requires that management knows how much their customers are willing to pay for a product and the amount of profit the company requires.

Using the model SFM bicycle and assuming that customers are willing to pay $150.00 for the product and Custom Cyclery expects a 33.33% profit, the target cost of the bicycle is calculated as follows:

Target Cost per Unit	=	Desired Selling Price per Unit	–	Required Profit per Unit
	=	$150.00	–	$150.00 × 33.33%
$100.00	=	$150.00	–	$50.00

Target costing indicates that the model SFM bicycle can cost no more than $100.00. At a cost of $100.00, Custom Cyclery can sell the bicycle for $150.00 and earn a $50.00 profit per unit. Since the current cost of model SFM is $101.00, the company will have to investigate the production process and determine how to cut $1.00 off the cost of the bicycle.

Target costing focuses on the price customers are willing to pay and the cost of producing the product, so that the required profit can be achieved on each unit sold. Since this method focuses on a maximum selling price, company management realizes that the only way to increase profit margin is to lower the production costs. Target costing is especially helpful when products are in the design stages. The product developers estimate the selling price and the desired profit. The company can then determine if the product can be produced for the target cost. If the estimated cost of the product is higher than the target cost, design changes can be made more easily at this stage than after production actually begins.

fyi Value-based pricing can take advantage of emotional issues. How can one put a value on a drug that promises a cure for cancer?

remember The percentage markup on a product is not the same as the gross profit margin on the product.

INPUT

- Explain the difference between cost-based pricing and value-based pricing.
- Ask students to name products they have purchased knowing that they are paying for the value they place on the product. Explain.
- Point out that value-based pricing usually results in a higher-priced product than does cost-based pricing.
- Explain that if the value of the product becomes less than the cost, the company cannot generate a profit and will stop making the product.

INPUT

- Explain that target costing is a combination of determining what the customer will pay and controlling the cost so that the company still makes a profit.
- Direct students to the math illustration as you demonstrate how to calculate the target cost per unit to expect a 33.33% profit.
- Point out that because this method focuses on a maximum selling price, the only way to increase profit margin is to lower the production costs.
- Explain that companies often use this method in the design stages to determine what changes need to be made prior to production to make the desired profit.

FORMATIVE ASSESSMENT

- This is an ongoing process. Circulate around the classroom or lab, observing which students have difficulty with the assignments.
- Troubleshooting: Diagnose the kinds of problems students have with this lesson. Students may have difficulty remembering the differences in the pricing methods.
- Assess student understanding by checking solutions to Independent Practice assignments and noting their answers to the Terms Review and Audit Your Understanding questions.

CHECK FOR UNDERSTANDING

Terms Review

- Call on students to define each term in the Terms Review. Definitions are given in the Glossary.

Audit Your Understanding

- Call on students to answer the Audit Your Understanding questions. Answers are given in Appendix D of the textbook.

GUIDED PRACTICE

Work Together

- Have students write the solution to the Work Together problem as you guide the class through the examples.
- Direct students to calculate cost-based pricing and target costs.

INDEPENDENT PRACTICE

On Your Own

- Assign the On Your Own problem to be worked independently.
- Use the Formative Assessment techniques to diagnose student understanding.

Application Problem

- Assign Application Problem 19-3.

Online Working Papers

- Students can access the Lesson 19-3 problems using this software.

RETEACH

- Call on students to describe the pricing methods and the advantages and disadvantages of each.

CLOSURE

- Ask students to summarize briefly the examples of the different pricing methods.

Essential Question

- If you sold cell phones, which pricing method would you apply to your products? Explain. (*Students will have differing opinions, but most will probably say value-based pricing. Consumers are dependent on the latest technology and will usually pay a higher price to "stay connected."*)

End of Lesson Review

LO8 Use cost-based pricing to calculate the price of a product.

LO9 Calculate the target cost of a product.

Terms Review

cost-based pricing

value-based pricing

target costing

Audit your understanding

1 List four disadvantages of cost-based pricing.
2. Name four cases where value-based pricing is effective.
3. What is the formula for calculating target cost?

Work together 19-3

Calculating cost-based pricing and target costs

Holdger Manufacturing Company makes furniture. Your instructor will guide you through the following examples.

1. The costs and markups for several products are given in the *Working Papers*. For each item, calculate the following:
   a. Dollar amount of markup
   b. Selling price
   c. Profit margin
2. Holdger is in the process of designing an entertainment center. The company believes that the selling price cannot exceed $2,500.00, and it requires a profit of 40% per unit. What is the target cost for the entertainment center?

On your own 19-3

Calculating cost-based pricing and target costs

Unique Design Company makes jewelry and watches. Work independently to complete the following problem.

1. The costs and markups for several products are given in the *Working Papers*. For each item, calculate the following:
   a. Dollar amount of markup
   b. Selling price
   c. Profit margin
2. Unique Design is in the process of designing an anniversary pendant. The company believes that the selling price cannot exceed $1,800.00, and it requires a profit of 80% per unit. What is the target cost for the pendant?

Chapter Summary

Process costing is used when a company produces similar products in a continuous flow of inputs. Costs are recorded for each process for each financial period. Units produced are also measured so that a per-unit cost can be calculated. At the end of each fiscal period, some units of product are only partially completed. In order to include the cost of partially completed units, the company must calculate equivalent units of production for each process or department. The costs of totally and partially completed units are reported for each process or department in a cost of production report. A major difference between process costing and job order costing is that, in process costing, a separate work in process account is used for each process or department.

Activity-based costing is a method of allocating factory overhead costs based on the activities required to produce goods or provide a service. Cost pools and cost drivers are identified. An activity rate is calculated for each activity. This activity rate is used to calculate the overhead to be allocated. An activity-based costing system is expensive to establish, but it may allocate overhead costs more accurately than traditional overhead allocation methods.

A common method for calculating the price of a product is to base the price on the cost of the product. Typically, a specific percentage is used for each group of products. Cost-based pricing is easy to implement. Caution should be used to ensure that the price of a product changes as the costs of that product change. Target costing establishes the price for a product or service, based on the price the customer is willing to pay. It requires the company to control the cost of the product so that the company earns a specific level of profit. This method is most effective if used during the design stage of a product, when costs are more easily controlled.

Responsibility Centers

EXPLORE ACCOUNTING

Accountability is a term used in relation to organizations and people. It means that the person or organization must justify or be responsible for actions taken and decisions made. Assigning control of revenues, costs, and expenses to a specific manager is known as *responsibility accounting*. The unit of the business over which a manager has control is called a *responsibility center*. There are four kinds of responsibility centers: cost centers, revenue centers, profit centers, and investment centers.

A responsibility center in which the manager is only responsible for costs is called a *cost center*. The cost center manager is not responsible for revenues and, in many cases, does not provide a revenue-producing product or service. In most companies, the Accounting Department would be a cost center. It does not bring revenue into the company. Many production departments are also cost centers. Managers of a cost center are held accountable for the costs incurred in the department. Upper management may set quantity and price standards, which are used to evaluate the effectiveness of the cost center.

A responsibility center in which the manager is only responsible for revenues is called a *revenue center*. The revenue center manager is not responsible for costs. A revenue center is usually responsible for selling finished goods or services offered by a company. It may be able to set the selling price, and it is evaluated based on meeting sales goals set by upper management.

A responsibility center in which the manager is responsible for both costs and revenues is called a *profit center*. The profit center manager is not responsible for capital investments purchased by the company, but does have authority in decisions related to costs and revenues. Therefore, a profit center is both a cost center and a revenue center. The profit center manager may be evaluated based on such measures as gross margin, return on sales, and operating margin.

A responsibility center in which the manager is responsible for both the profits of the unit and the investments of the unit is called an *investment center*. In addition to those measures used to evaluate a profit center manager, the investment center manager may also be evaluated on profit margin and return on investments.

© iStockphoto.com/Makhnach_M

INSTRUCTIONS

Identify each of the following business units as a cost, revenue, profit, or investment center:

a. A corporation's subsidiary that is independent and whose manager makes decisions regarding capital investments.
b. Sales Department that is not responsible for costs.
c. Customer Service Department.
d. Bank branch that does not have the authority to make investment decisions.

CLOSURE

- Review the Chapter Summary.
- Ask students to prepare a list of the new concepts introduced in this chapter.

Essential Question

- Should managerial accounting information be provided to stockholders? Explain. (*Student answers may vary. Most will indicate that managerial accounting information should not be provided, as it is used internally for the purposes of planning, analyzing, and controlling the activities of the company.*)

EXPLORE ACCOUNTING

Answers

a. Investment center.
b. Revenue center.
c. Cost center.
d. Profit center.

EXTENDED LEARNING

- Assign Explore Accounting on page 577.

CHECK FIGURES

For complete solutions to Chapter 19 problems, see the Teacher's Edition of the Working Papers.

Application Problem 19-1

1. Equivalent Units of Production, Direct Materials, 320,000.
2. Second entry: Debit Finished Goods, $734,800.00.

Application Problem 19-2

1. Activity Rate, Storage, $0.20.
2. Allocated Costs, Moving, $150.00.

   Total Allocated Cost, $690.00.

Apply Your Understanding

INSTRUCTIONS: Download problem instructions for Excel, QuickBooks, and Sage 50 from the textbook companion website at www.C21accounting.com.

19-1 Application Problem: Calculating equivalent units of production and completing journal entries in process costing LO2, 3, 4

1. Calculate equivalent units of production to complete the worksheet.
2. Journalize transactions to the general journal.
3. Print the worksheets.

Jutko Corporation produces leather gloves. Jutko uses a process costing system to record costs. On December 1, Jutko had 15,000 gloves in the Cutting Department. The gloves were 80% complete as to direct materials and 40% complete as to conversion costs. The following data were gathered on December 30:

Units started this period	320,000
Units completed this period	325,000
Units in ending work in process (70% complete as to direct materials and 30% complete as to conversion costs)	10,000

Partially completed forms and a blank general journal are provided in the *Working Papers*.

Instructions:

1. Calculate equivalent units of production for the Cutting Department for December.
2. Record the following transactions:
   a. Dec. 31. Recorded the transfer of goods from the Cutting Department to the Stitching Department, $421,500.00. M524.
   b. Dec. 31. Recorded the transfer of finished goods out of the Stitching Department, $734,800.00. M525.

19-2 Application Problem: Calculating activity rates and allocating costs LO5, 6, 7

Regions Corporation uses activity-based costing. It bases its activity rates on yearly estimates of cost and activity. The Production Department has made the following estimates for the current year:

Activity Pool	Cost Driver	Estimated Cost	Estimated Activity
Cutting machine setups	Number of setups	$400,000.00	10,000 setups
Cutting machine usage	Machine minutes	500,000.00	125,000 minutes
Moving	Distance in feet	200,000.00	400,000 boxes
Storage	Cubic foot of storage	440,000.00	2,200,000 cubic feet
Assembly	Number of pieces in one unit	400,000.00	40,000 pieces

Forms are provided in the *Working Papers*.

Instructions:

1. Calculate the activity rate for each cost driver.
2. Allocate the materials handling costs for Job No. 220, which requires three machine setups, 50 minutes of machine usage, 300 feet of moving, 200 cubic feet of storage, and 18 pieces.

19-3 Application Problem: Calculating cost-based pricing and target costs LO8, 9

TravelRight Corporation makes suitcases. Your instructor will guide you through the following examples.

Instructions:

1. The costs and markups for several products are given in the *Working Papers*. For each item, calculate the following:
   a. Dollar amount of markup
   b. Selling price
   c. Profit margin
2. TravelRight is in the process of designing a protective computer case. The company believes that the selling price cannot exceed $150.00, and it requires a profit of 60% per unit. What is the target cost for the computer case?

19-M Mastery Problem: Calculating equivalent units of production and completing journal entries in process costing LO2, 4, 8, 9

Voeller Corporation produces ketchup. Voeller uses a process costing system to record costs. On October 1, Voeller had 18,000 bottles of ketchup in the Processing Department. The bottles were 100% complete as to direct materials and 30% complete as to conversion costs. The following data were gathered on October 31:

Units started this period	620,000
Units completed this period	618,000
Units in ending work in process (100% complete as to direct materials and 60% complete as to conversion costs)	20,000

Partially completed forms and a blank general journal are provided in the *Working Papers*.

Instructions:

1. Calculate equivalent units of production for the Processing Department for October.
2. Record the following transactions:
   a. Oct. 31. Recorded the transfer of goods from the Processing Department to the Bottling Department, $365,000.00. M357.
   b. Oct. 31. Recorded the transfer of goods out of the Bottling Department to the Packaging Department, $398,000. M358.
   c. Oct. 31. Recorded the transfer of finished goods out of the Packaging Department, $420,000. M359.
3. Using the cost information in Instruction 2c, assume that 560,000 bottles of ketchup were transferred to finished goods. If Voeller uses 20% as its percentage of markup, calculate the following per bottle:
   a. Cost
   b. Dollar amount of markup
   c. Selling price
   d. Profit margin
4. Voeller is in the process of developing a Cajun specialty sauce. The company believes that the selling price cannot exceed $3.00, and it requires a profit of 20% per unit. What is the target cost for the specialty sauce?

Sage 50 Accounting

1. Journalize and post transactions to the general journal.
2. Print the general journal and trial balance.

QB

1. Journalize and post transactions to the journal.
2. Print the journal and trial balance.

X

1. Calculate equivalent units of production to complete the worksheet.
2. Journalize transactions to the general journal.
3. Print the worksheets.

Application Problem 19-3

1. Carry-on: Dollar Markup, $16.50.
   32-inch: Profit Margin, 44.4%.
2. Target Cost, $60.00.

Mastery Problem 19-M

1. Equivalent Units of Production, Conversion Costs, 624,600.
2. First entry: Debit Work in Process—Bottling, $365,000.00.
3. Ketchup: Selling Price, $0.90.
4. Target Cost, $2.40.

INDEPENDENT PRACTICE

- Assign Mastery Problem 19-M for students as a culminating problem combining all new learning from the chapter.
- Assign Challenge Problem 19-C to accelerated students who work at a faster pace.
- Assign Study Guide 19.
- Students can access Online Working Papers to work end-of-chapter problems on the computer.
- Direct students to the C21 Accounting companion website for additional practice and review opportunities.

FORMATIVE ASSESSMENT

- Review solutions to the assigned problems in class, diagnosing trouble spots.

RETEACH

- Call on students to describe how they avoid the trouble spots diagnosed.
- Use reteaching suggestions from lesson plans as required.
- Assign Recycling Problem 19-R if needed.

EXTENDED LEARNING

- Assign 21st Century Skills on page 580.
- Assign Analyzing Home Depot's Financial Statements on page 581.

SUMMATIVE EVALUATION

- Chapter 19 Test
- Cognero for Chapter 19

Challenge Problem 19-C

1. X-rays: Activity Rate, $75.00.

   MRI—images: Activity Rate, $250.00.

2. a. Allocated Costs: CT scan, minutes, $3,000.00.

   Total allocated costs, $4,980.00.

2. b. MRI—images: Allocated Costs, $750.00.

   Total allocated costs, $4,125.00.

21ST CENTURY SKILLS

Answers

1. The customer probably values spending the holidays with friends or loved ones. The value of flying may be more convenient than driving, or the distance may be too far to allow the option of driving within the specified week of vacation. Emotions may be used to value this price.
2. Answers will vary. Accessibility, ease of receipt, timing, and customer service may be used to determine the value of the price.
3. Answers will vary but might include electronic devices or a coat. Value may include owning the latest technological devices, the brand, or the style.
4. Answers will vary but might include Nike, Under Armour, Coca-Cola, and other brands popular with students.

19-C Challenge Problem: Activity-based costing in a service business LO5, 6

Memorial Hospital uses activity-based costing. It bases its activity rates on yearly estimates of cost and activity. The Radiology Department has made the following estimates for the current year:

Activity Pool	Cost Driver	Estimated Cost	Estimated Activity
Patient intake processing	Number of intakes	$ 2,500,000.00	25,000 intakes
X-rays	Number of X-rays	750,000.00	10,000 X-rays
CT scan—scans	Number of scans	3,010,000.00	14,000 scans
CT scan—minutes	Length of scan, in minutes	25,000,000.00	250,000 minutes
MRI—images	Number of images	3,750,000.00	15,000 images
MRI—minutes	Length of test, in minutes	17,600,000.00	220,000 minutes

Forms are provided in the *Working Papers.*

Instructions:

1. Calculate the activity rate for each cost driver.
2. Allocate the costs for the following patients:
   a. Patient 03016598: One patient intake; 2 CT scans, total 30 minutes; 1 MRI image, total 15 minutes.
   b. Patient 10415423: One patient intake; 1 X-ray; 3 MRI images, total 40 minutes.

21st Century Skills

Think Like the Customer

PARTNERSHIP FOR 21ST CENTURY SKILLS

Theme: Financial, Economic, Business, and Entrepreneurial Literacy, and Global Awareness

Skills: Critical Thinking and Problem Solving

A common pricing mistake is setting prices simply by marking up costs. While it is easy to implement, this type of pricing does not take into consideration the amount that customers are willing to pay, nor does it evaluate the potential for additional profit. Prices should not be set too high for customers who cannot afford a needed product, or too low for customers willing to pay more for a product's benefits.

Value-based pricing is used in businesses that try to think like the customer to determine how much the products are worth to their customers. Who would be willing to buy? Why is this product unique? What is the next best alternative? Answering these questions can help assess the product's worth to the customer. Attributes that differentiate products include brand, quality, physical attributes, service, ease of purchase, style, and perhaps even timing. An amusement park that sets its umbrella prices when it looks like rain probably understands the value that a customer places on the product. A customer who prefers warm gloves from a department store instead of a thrift store probably values the brand or style more than the practicality of the gloves.

APPLICATION

1. The cost of airline tickets for the week of Thanksgiving is often 100% more than for a different week of November. Describe the value perceived from this pricing strategy.
2. Select a product of your choice. Research the price of the product from three different retailers. Explain the likely pricing strategy used by each of the retailers.
3. List three products that you have purchased recently, realizing that you likely paid a premium based on the value you placed on the product. Explain the value that you gained from purchasing each of these products.
4. List two examples of companies that likely use their brands to add value to price.

COMMON CORE AND INTERDISCIPLINARY STUDIES

Extended learning features and activities present numerous opportunities to implement Common Core Standards through interdisciplinary studies. Practice is provided in the common core areas of English Language Arts & Literacy and Mathematical Practice. Many of these activities require short, critical-thinking and decision-making responses that apply reading, writing, speaking, listening, language, media and technology, and mathematical skills.

Analyzing Home Depot's financial statements

Home Depot must determine a price for each item it sells. For the majority of items it sells, Home Depot will use a cost-based pricing method. This chapter identified the difference between gross profit margin and percentage markup.

INSTRUCTIONS

Use Home Depot's Consolidated Statements of Earnings on page B-6 of Appendix B to answer the following questions. Round answers to the nearest 0.0%.

1. Calculate Home Depot's gross profit margin for 2013, 2012, and 2011.
2. Calculate the percentage markup for Home Depot for 2013, 2012, and 2011.

ANALYZING HOME DEPOT'S FINANCIAL STATEMENTS

Answers

1. The formula for gross profit margin is Gross Profit Margin = Gross Profit ÷ Net Sales.

   Gross Profit Margin 2013 = \$25,842,000,000 ÷ \$74,754,000,000 = 34.6%.

   Gross Profit Margin 2012 = \$24,262,000,000 ÷ \$70,395,000,000 = 34.5%.

   Gross Profit Margin 2011 = \$23,304,000,000 ÷ \$67,997,000,000 = 34.3%.

2. The formula for markup is Cost + (Cost × Markup) = Selling Price.

   Markup 2013 = \$48,912,000,000 + (\$48,912,000,000 × X) = \$74,754,000,000 = 52.8%

   Markup 2012 = \$46,133,000,000 + (\$46,133,000,000 × X) = \$70,395,000,000 = 52.6%

   Markup 2011 = \$44,693,000,000 + (\$44,693,000,000 × X) = \$67,997,000,000 = 52.1%

Reinforcement Activity

BRIDGE

- Reinforcement Activity 4 begins after Chapter 19 and reinforces managerial and cost accounting concepts for a corporation.

TEACHING RESOURCES

- **Manual Accounting:**
  Working Papers for Reinforcement Activity 4
  Teacher's Edition of the Working Papers for Reinforcement Activity 4
  Online Working Papers
  Website for Audit Tests, Solutions, and Transparency Masters
- **Accounting Software:**
  QuickBooks, Excel, Sage 50, and Automated Accounting Online may be used to automate this Reinforcement Activity.

INPUT FOR AUTOMATING

- Direct students to read the Help screens for specific requirements for automating Reinforcement Activity 4.

Reinforcement Activity 4

Processing and Analyzing Cost Accounting Data for a Manufacturing Business

This activity reinforces selected learning from Chapters 17 through 19.

Alexandria Corporation

Alexandria Corporation manufactures custom plastic products. The company uses a job order cost accounting system to record manufacturing costs.

Part A: Recording Cost Accounting Activities

In Part A of this activity, Alexandria's daily cost accounting activities for one month will be recorded. Alexandria uses the chart of accounts shown on page 587. The journals and ledgers used by Alexandria are similar to those illustrated in Chapter 17. The job cost sheets, selected general ledger accounts, and other accounting records or forms are provided in the *Working Papers*.

The January 31 general ledger balances have been recorded. These balances are the result of posting completed during January. Note that Accounts Payable has a debit balance for this reason. Also, the balances of the payroll liability accounts are the amounts posted for sales and administrative salaries for January.

INSTRUCTIONS

1. **Calculate the factory overhead applied rate based on direct labor costs. The estimated annual factory overhead costs for the current year are $612,000.00. The estimated direct labor hours to be used during the current year are 34,000 hours at an estimated rate of $15.00 per hour.**
2. **Record the following transactions completed during January of the current year. Recording instructions, when necessary, are provided only for the first occurrence of each kind of transaction. Source documents are abbreviated as follows: check, C; memorandum, M; materials requisition, MR; purchase order, PO; sales invoice, S.**

   Transactions:

   Jan. 3. Opened a cost sheet for Job No. 232, with 250 C200 book racks ordered for stock. Date wanted, January 12.

   3. Issued direct materials to factory for Job No. 232, $10,200.00. MR750.
   Materials list:
   6,000 pounds of resin @ $0.40 per pound
   6,000 pounds of polymer @ $1.20 per pound
   187.5 ounces of dye @ $3.20 per ounce
   Record the direct materials in the materials ledger and the cost ledger.

   5. Opened a cost sheet for Job No. 233, with 200 P150 shelving units ordered for stock. Date wanted, January 17.

   5. Issued direct materials to factory for Job No. 233, $6,800.00. MR751.
   Materials list:
   4,000 pounds of resin @ $0.40 per pound
   4,000 pounds of polymer @ $1.20 per pound
   125 ounces of dye @ $3.20 per ounce

   5. Ordered 30,000 pounds of resin. PO520.
   Record the purchase order in the materials ledger only at this time, so that it is clear the materials have been ordered. Once the materials are received, the transaction will be journalized in the materials purchases journal.

   5. Ordered 20,000 pounds of polymer. PO521.

   7. Ordered 1,600 connectors. PO522.

   7. Issued direct materials to factory for Job No. 232, $2,500.00. MR752.
   Materials list:
   1,000 connectors @ $2.50 each

   7. Ordered 1,000 sets of hinges. PO523.

   7. Recorded weekly summary of time records to the cost ledger.
   Job No. 232: $6,600.00
   Job No. 233: 2,250.00

   7. Ordered 1,000 ounces of dye. PO524.

   10. Issued direct materials to factory for Job No. 233, $2,400.00. MR753.
   Materials list:
   800 connectors @ $2.50 each
   200 sets of metal glides @ $2.00 per set

   10. Ordered 300 sets of metal glides. PO525.

WINNING EDGE

Give students the *Winning Edge* by making competitive event prep part of their classroom materials throughout the year. Go to cengage.com/winningedge for a list of materials that prepare students for specific competitive events.

Jan. 10. Sold 100 C200 book racks to Office Mart. S323. Record only the cost in the finished goods ledger. Alexandria uses the first-in, first-out inventory method. Thus, the cost recorded first is the cost removed from inventory first when units are sold.

10. Ordered 1,000 fasteners. PO526.

10. Received at the materials stockroom 20,000 pounds of polymer @ $1.20 per pound. Materials were purchased on account from Palmdale Plastics, $24,000.00. PO521.
Record all receipts of materials in the materials ledger and materials purchases journal.

11. Completed Job No. 232. Interim summary of time records for Job No. 232, $2,775.00. When jobs are completed in the middle of a week, Alexandria makes a special interim summary of time records for these jobs. Therefore, direct labor costs will be complete. Apply factory overhead to job. Use the rate calculated in Instruction 1. Complete the cost sheet. Record the finished goods in the finished goods ledger.

12. Opened a cost sheet for Job No. 234, with 120 E400 inline skate boots ordered for stock. Date wanted, January 18.

12. Issued direct materials to factory for Job No. 234, $10,200.00. MR754.
Materials list:
6,000 pounds of resin @ $0.40 per pound
6,000 pounds of polymer @ $1.20 per pound
187.5 ounces of dye @ $3.20 per pound

12. Received at the materials stockroom 30,000 pounds of resin @ $0.40 per pound. Materials were purchased on account from Woodcrest, Inc., $12,000.00. PO520.

12. Received at the materials stockroom 1,600 connectors @ $2.50 each. Materials were purchased on account from Westmore Corporation, $4,000.00. PO522.

12. Received at the materials stockroom 300 sets of metal glides @ $2.00 per set. Materials were purchased on account from Smythe Company, $600.00. PO525.

14. Opened a cost sheet for Job No. 235, with 150 V110 benches ordered for stock. Date wanted, January 27.

Jan. 14. Issued direct materials to factory for Job No. 235, $4,080.00. MR755.
Materials list:
2,400 pounds of resin @ $0.40 per pound
2,400 pounds of polymer @ $1.20 per pound
75 ounces of dye @ $3.20 per ounce

14. Recorded weekly summary of time records to cost ledger.
Job No. 233: $3,750.00
Job No. 234: 3,600.00
Job No. 235: 450.00

14. Completed Job No. 233.

17. Paid cash for semimonthly factory payroll, $22,257.36 (direct labor, $19,425.00, and indirect labor, $7,935.00, less deductions: employee income tax, $3,009.60; social security tax, $1,696.32; Medicare, $396.72). C782.
Record the payroll entry in the cash payments journal. Post the general debit and general credit amounts.

17. Recorded employer factory payroll taxes, $3,734.64, for the semimonthly pay period ended January 15. Taxes owed are social security tax, $1,696.32; Medicare, $396.72; federal unemployment tax, $164.16; state unemployment tax, $1,477.44. M308.
Record the entry in the general journal. Post the amounts.

17. Sold 150 P150 shelving units to CompuFurnishings. S324.

18. Issued direct materials to factory for Job No. 234, $840.00. MR756.
Materials list:
240 sets of hinges @ $2.00 per set
240 fasteners @ $1.50 each

18. Opened a cost sheet for Job No. 236, with 200 B160 vertical bookcases ordered for stock. Date wanted, January 28.

18. Issued direct materials to factory for Job No. 236, $13,600.00. MR757.
Materials list:
8,000 pounds of resin @ $0.40 per pound
8,000 pounds of polymer @ $1.20 per pound
250 ounces of dye @ $3.20 per ounce

CHECK FIGURES

1. Factory Overhead Applied Rate, 120%.
2. Materials Ledger Card, Resin: Jan. 14 Balance, $11,840.00.
   Materials Ledger Card, Hinges: Jan. 24 Balance, $2,120.00.
   Cost Sheet, Job. No. 232: Cost per unit, $133.30.
   Cost Sheet, Job. No. 235: Total cost, $15,630.00.
   Finished Goods Ledger Card, Book Rack: Jan. 31 Balance, $13,330.00.
   Finished Goods Ledger Card, Bench: Jan. 27 Balance, $30,930.00.
3. Cost Sheet, Job. No. 238: Factory Overhead for January, $3,024.00.
4. Materials Purchases Journal: Total, $50,300.00.
5. Cash Payments Journal: General Debit Total, $59,430.00.
6. a. Credit Materials, $69,600.00.
   b. Debit Factory Overhead, $30,913.64.
7. Debit Factory Overhead, $123.36.
8. Debit Finished Goods, $146,363.00.
9. Credit Finished Goods, $122,275.00.
10. b. Work in Process: Ending Balance, $13,704.00.
11. Total Cost of Work Placed in Process, $160,067.00.
12. Total Labor Variance, $656.25 Unfavorable.
13. Buy: Total, $80,000.00.
14. Present value of an annuity, $33,120.00.
15. E400 Inline skate boot: Selling Price, $313.60.
    T120 Serving cart: Profit Margin, 33.3%.
16. Target Cost, $21.00.

Reinforcement Activity 4 (Cont.)

Processing and Analyzing Cost Accounting Data for a Manufacturing Business

Jan. 19. Completed Job No. 234. Interim summary of time record for Job No. 234, $3,600.00.

20. Sold 60 T120 serving carts to Office Mart. S325.

21. Issued direct materials to factory for Job No. 235, $1,650.00. MR758.

    Materials list:
    300 sets of metal glides @ $2.00 per set
    300 sets of hinges @ $2.00 per set
    300 fasteners @ $1.50 each

21. Received at the materials stockroom 1,000 ounces of dye @ $3.20 per ounce. Materials were purchased on account from Colton Dyes, $3,200.00. PO524.

21. Received at the materials stockroom 1,000 fasteners @ $1.50 each. Materials were purchased on account from Smythe Company, $1,500.00. PO526.

21. Ordered 300 sets of metal glides. PO527.

21. Posted weekly summary of time records to cost ledger.
    Job No. 235: $2,250.00
    Job No. 236: 4,500.00

24. Ordered 20,000 square feet of polymer. PO528.

24. Received at the materials stockroom 1,000 sets of hinges @ $2.00 per set. Materials were purchased on account from Smythe Company, $2,000.00. PO523.

25. Issued direct materials to factory for Job No. 236, $1,400.00. MR759.

    Materials list:
    400 sets of hinges @ $2.00 per set
    400 fasteners @ $1.50 each

25. Opened a cost sheet for Job No. 237, with 160 T120 serving carts ordered for stock. Date wanted, January 31.

25. Issued direct materials to factory for Job No. 237, $3,808.00. MR760.

    Materials list:
    2,240 pounds of resin @ $0.40 per pound
    2,240 pounds of polymer @ $1.20 per pound
    70 ounces of dye @ $3.20 per ounce

26. Sold 90 E400 inline skate boots to BizFurn. S326.

27. Completed Job No. 235. Interim summary of time records for Job No. 235, $1,800.00.

Jan. 27. Sold 200 V110 benches to CompuFurnishings. S327.

28. Issued direct materials to factory for Job No. 237, $1,600.00. MR761.

    Materials list:
    640 connectors @ $2.50 each

28. Opened a cost sheet for Job No. 238, with 200 C200 book racks ordered for stock. Date wanted, February 8.

28. Issued direct materials to factory for Job No. 238, $8,160.00. MR762.

    Materials list:
    4,800 pounds of resin @ $0.40 per pound
    4,800 pounds of polymer @ $1.20 per pound
    150 ounces dye @ $3.20 per ounce

28. Posted weekly summary of job-time records to cost ledger.
    Job No. 236: $4,500.00
    Job No. 237: 2,880.00
    Job No. 238: 1,260.00

28. Completed Job No. 236.

28. Sold 120 B160 bookcases to CompuFurnishings. S328.

31. Received at the materials stockroom 300 metal glides @ $2.00 per set. Materials were purchased on account from Smythe Company, $600.00. PO527.

31. Received at the materials stockroom indirect materials (bolts, screws, and nails). Materials were purchased on account from Greenleaf Manufacturing Supplies, $2,400.00. PO519. (Record indirect materials purchases only in the materials purchases journal.)

31. Posted summary of time records for January 31 to cost ledger.
    Job No. 237: $ 720.00
    Job No. 238: 1,260.00
    (Only Job No. 238 is still in process on January 31.)

31. Sold 200 C200 book racks to Straight Arrow, Inc., S329.

31. Paid cash for semimonthly factory payroll, $26,088.64 (direct labor, $22,770.00, and indirect labor, $9,300.00, less deductions: employee income tax, $3,528.00; social security tax, $1,988.34; Medicare tax, $465.02). C856.

Jan. 31. Recorded employer factory payroll taxes, $4,377.56, for the semimonthly pay period ended January 31. Taxes owed are social security tax, $1,988.34; Medicare tax, $465.02; federal unemployment tax, $192.42; state unemployment tax, $1,731.78. M345.

Completing Cost Records:

3. In the Summary column with the item description *Factory Overhead for January*, record the factory overhead for the job not completed on January 31 and the explanation of how it was calculated. Apply the factory overhead rate to the direct labor costs recorded on the cost sheet for work in process.
4. Total and rule the materials purchases journal. Post the total. Do not post the individual amounts. The abbreviation for the materials purchases journal is MP.
5. Prove and rule the cash payments journal. Do not post the total of the Cash Credit column.
6. Record the following entries. Continue using page 1 of the general journal. Use January 31 as the date. Post after journalizing each entry.
   a. Transfer the total of all direct materials requisitions to Work in Process and indirect materials to Factory Overhead. The total of all requisitions of direct materials issued during January is $67,238.00. The total of all requisitions of indirect materials issued is $2,362.00. M346.
   b. Close all individual manufacturing expense accounts to Factory Overhead. M347.
   c. Record the applied factory overhead to Work in Process (sum of factory overhead applied to cost sheets for the month). M348.
7. Continue using page 1 of the general journal. Journalize and post the entry to close the balance of the Factory Overhead account to Income Summary. M349.
8. Journalize and post the entry to transfer the total of all cost sheets completed from Work in Process to Finished Goods. M350.
9. Journalize and post the entry to transfer the cost of products sold from Finished Goods to Cost of Goods Sold. The total cost recorded on all sales invoices for January is $122,275.00. M351.
10. Prove the subsidiary ledgers as follows:
    a. Add the ending balances in the materials ledger. The ending balance of the indirect materials is $2,738.00. The total of the materials ledger must equal the ending balance of Materials in the general ledger.
    b. Add the costs recorded on all cost sheets in the cost ledger that have not been completed. This total must equal the ending balance of Work in Process in the general ledger.
    c. Add the ending balances in the finished goods ledger. This total must equal the ending balance of Finished Goods in the general ledger.
11. Prepare a statement of cost of goods manufactured for Alexandria for the month ended January 31 of the current year.

Part B: Analyzing Costs and Using Cost Data for Decision Making

12. Alexandria Corporation sets standards for both materials and labor for many of its products. These standards are analyzed annually. However, Alexandria spot-checks the standards each month, using specific job orders. The quantity standard for labor for the book racks on Job No. 232 is 2¼ hours per unit. The price standard for labor for the book racks is $15.50 per hour. Job No. 232 required 625 total labor hours. Using the data collected in Part A, calculate the following variances for Job No. 232 and summarize your findings:
    a. Total labor
    b. Labor price
    c. Labor quantity
13. Alexandria has been purchasing 30,000 connectors per year from an outside source at a cost of $2.50 each. Since Alexandria has excess capacity, it is considering making the connector in its own factory. No new machinery or equipment will need to be purchased. Alexandria has idle machines and no other use for them. Costs to make the part include direct materials, $25,500.00; direct labor, $24,000.00; and variable overhead, $23,500.00. In addition, the total fixed overhead allocated to the connectors is $5,000.00. Fixed overhead costs that

Reinforcement Activity 4 (Cont.)

Processing and Analyzing Cost Accounting Data for a Manufacturing Business

are allocated to each product will remain and will be allocated to other products. Variable overhead is related directly to making the connectors and will not exist if Alexandria continues to buy the connector. Using differential analysis, determine whether Alexandria should make the connectors or continue to buy them.

14. Alexandria is considering purchasing equipment for $35,000. The equipment will enable the company to generate net cash flows of $10,000.00 annually over the equipment's four-year useful life. Management expects assets to yield an 8% rate of return. Using the present value tables from Chapter 18, determine if Alexandria Corporation should purchase the equipment.

15. Alexandria uses cost-based pricing for all its products. Using the cost records from January and the form given in the *Working Papers*, calculate the following for each item:
    a. Dollar amount of markup
    b. Selling price
    c. Profit margin

16. Alexandria is in the process of designing a locker organizer. It believes that the selling price cannot exceed $30.00, and it requires a profit of 30% per unit. What is the target cost for the locker organizer?

17. Alexandria uses a job order costing system. How would its chart of accounts differ if it used a process costing system?

Alexandria Corporation Chart of Accounts

General Ledger

Balance Sheet Accounts

(1000) ASSETS

1100 Current Assets
1105 Cash
1110 Petty Cash
1115 Accounts Receivable
1120 Allowance for Uncollectible Accounts
1125 Materials
1130 Work in Process
1135 Finished Goods
1140 Supplies—Factory
1145 Supplies—Sales
1150 Supplies—Administrative
1155 Prepaid Insurance
1200 Plant Assets
1205 Factory Equipment
1210 Accumulated Depreciation—Factory Equipment
1215 Office Equipment
1220 Accumulated Depreciation—Office Equipment
1225 Store Equipment
1230 Accumulated Depreciation—Store Equipment
1235 Building
1240 Accumulated Depreciation—Building
1245 Land

(2000) LIABILITIES

2100 Current Liabilities
2105 Accounts Payable
2110 Employee Income Tax Payable
2115 Federal Income Tax Payable
2120 Social Security Tax Payable
2125 Medicare Tax Payable
2130 Unemployment Tax Payable—Federal
2135 Unemployment Tax Payable—State
2140 Dividends Payable
2200 Long-Term Liability
2205 Mortgage Payable

(3000) STOCKHOLDERS' EQUITY

3105 Capital Stock
3110 Retained Earnings
3115 Dividends
3120 Income Summary

Income Statement Accounts

(4000) OPERATING REVENUE

4105 Sales

(5000) COST OF SALES

5105 Cost of Goods Sold

(5500) MANUFACTURING COSTS

5505 Factory Overhead
5510 Depreciation Expense—Factory Equipment
5515 Depreciation Expense—Building
5520 Heat, Light, and Power Expense
5525 Insurance Expense—Factory
5530 Miscellaneous Expense—Factory
5535 Payroll Taxes Expense—Factory
5540 Property Tax Expense—Factory
5545 Supplies Expense—Factory

(6000) OPERATING EXPENSE

6100 Selling Expenses
6105 Advertising Expense
6110 Delivery Expense
6115 Depreciation Expense—Store Equipment
6120 Miscellaneous Expense—Sales
6125 Salary Expense—Sales
6130 Supplies Expense—Sales
6200 Administrative Expenses
6205 Depreciation Expense—Office Equipment
6210 Insurance Expense—Administrative
6215 Miscellaneous Expense—Administrative
6220 Payroll Taxes Expense—Administrative
6225 Property Tax Expense—Administrative
6230 Salary Expense—Administrative
6235 Supplies Expense—Administrative
6240 Uncollectible Accounts Expense
6245 Utilities Expense—Administrative

(7000) OTHER REVENUE

7105 Gain on Plant Assets
7110 Miscellaneous Revenue

(8000) OTHER EXPENSES

8105 Interest Expense
8110 Loss on Plant Assets

(9000) INCOME TAX

9105 Federal Income Tax Expense

587

Part 5 Internal Control and Other Organizational Structures

OVERVIEW

Chapter organization and content provide students with an expanded view of concepts related to internal control and other organizational structures.

- **Chapter 20** covers internal control.
- **Chapter 21** describes the organizational structure of a partnership.
- **Chapter 22** describes financial reporting for a partnership.
- **Chapter 23** describes budgeting and accounting for a not-for-profit organization.
- **Chapter 24** describes financial reporting for a not-for-profit organization.

ACCOUNTING SOFTWARE

For those instructors who want to integrate the accounting program fully, problems at the end of each chapter are flagged to show when files are provided for completing a problem using QuickBooks, Excel, or Sage 50. In addition, A Look at Accounting Software is provided at the end of Chapter 20. This feature is designed to show how the accounting procedures described in a chapter are handled in commercial accounting software.

Part 5 Internal Control and Other Organizational Structures

THE BUSINESS—

CASTILLO LIQUIDATORS, INC.

Castillo Liquidators is a retail merchandising business organized as a corporation. The business purchases discontinued and overstocked hardware for sale to homeowners. Jason Castillo got the idea for the company while working in his uncle's hardware store. He witnessed how the hardware store struggled to sell new models of power tools while it still had older models in stock. His idea was to encourage manufacturers to ask their customers to return discontinued items and allow him to sell them out of a low-cost warehouse.

© bikeriderlondon/Shutterstock.com

Chart of Accounts

CASTILLO LIQUIDATORS, INC.

GENERAL LEDGER

Balance Sheet Accounts

(1000) ASSETS

1100 Current Assets
1105 Cash
1110 Petty Cash
1115 Merchandise Inventory
1120 Supplies
1125 Prepaid Insurance

1200 Plant Assets
1205 Land
1210 Building
1215 Accumulated Depreciation—Building
1220 Office Equipment
1225 Accumulated Depreciation—Office Equipment
1230 Warehouse Equipment
1235 Accumulated Depreciation—Warehouse Equipment

(2000) LIABILITIES

2100 Current Liabilities
2105 Vouchers Payable
2110 Salaries Payable
2115 Employee Income Tax Payable
2120 Social Security Tax Payable
2125 Medicare Tax Payable
2130 Unemployment Tax Payable—Federal
2135 Unemployment Tax Payable—State

(3000) STOCKHOLDERS' EQUITY

3105 Capital Stock
3110 Retained Earnings
3115 Dividends
3120 Income Summary

Income Statement Accounts

(4000) OPERATING REVENUE

4105 Sales
4110 Sales Returns and Allowances

(5000) COST OF MERCHANDISE

5105 Purchases
5110 Purchases Discount
5115 Purchases Returns and Allowances

(6000) OPERATING EXPENSE

6105 Advertising Expense
6110 Depreciation Expense—Building
6115 Depreciation Expense—Office Equipment
6120 Depreciation Expense—Warehouse Equipment
6125 Insurance Expense
6130 Miscellaneous Expense
6135 Payroll Taxes Expense
6140 Property Tax Expense
6145 Salary Expense
6150 Supplies Expense

(7000) INCOME TAX

7105 Federal Income Tax Expense

The chart of accounts for Castillo Liquidators, Inc., is illustrated above for ready reference as you study Chapter 20 of this textbook.

Chart of Accounts

Castillo Liquidators is a retail merchandising business organized as a corporation. The business purchases discontinued and overstocked hardware for sale to owners. Jason Castillo got the idea for the company while working in his uncle's hardware store. He saw how the hardware store struggled to sell new models of power tools while it still had older models in stock. His idea was to encourage manufacturers to ask their customers to return discontinued items and allow him to sell them out of a low-cost warehouse.

- Emphasize that students should refer to this chart of accounts in Chapter 20.

Chapter 20

Internal Control

Scope & Sequence

	New	Review/Enrich
Introduction		
Introduce the Chapter		
Lesson 20-1: Internal Control Structure		
Controlling Accounting Systems	✓	
Laws and Regulations	✓	
Segregation of Duties	✓	
Lesson 20-2: Documenting Accounting Systems		
Documentation Methods	✓	
Documenting a Cash Receipts System	✓	
Performing a Risk Assessment	✓	
Lesson 20-3: Cash Payments Using a Voucher System		
A Voucher System	✓	
Verifying an Invoice	✓	
Journalizing a Voucher in a Voucher Register's Special Columns	✓	
Journalizing a Voucher in a Voucher Register's Special Columns	✓	
Proving, Ruling, and Posting a Voucher Register	✓	
Paying a Voucher	✓	
Journalizing Cash Payments in a Check Register	✓	
Maintaining Bank Columns in a Check Register	✓	
Lesson 20-4: Internal Controls in a Voucher System		
Narrative of a Voucher System	✓	
Flowchart of a Voucher System	✓	
Risk Assessment of Voucher Processing	✓	
Closure		

Enhancing Instruction

Features	Common Core Standards
Accounting in the Real World: PetSmart Inc.	• ELAL—reading
• Ethics in Action: Reporting Violations • Careers in Accounting: Partner in an Accounting Firm	• ELAL—reading, writing • ELAL—reading
• Why Accounting?: Clergy	• ELAL—reading, writing
• Financial Literacy: Stash the Cash • Think Like an Accountant: Documenting Cash Collections	• ELAL—reading, writing • Mathematics
• A Look at Accounting Software • Explore Accounting • 21st Century Skills • Analyzing Home Depot's Financial Statements	• ELAL—reading • ELAL—reading, writing • ELAL—media and technology, writing • Mathematics

ELAL = English Language Arts & Literacy

Calculator: © iStockphoto.com/picstodisc; Paper: © iStockphoto.com/Qingwa

Practice and Assessment

Technology & Media	Teaching Strategies	Guided Practice	Independent Practice	Reteach/Enrich
• Instructor's Resource CD/Website: PowerPoint Slides Accounting Concepts • Online Working Papers		• Terms Review • Audit Your Understanding • Work Together 20-1	• On Your Own 20-1 • Application Problem 20-1 • Formative Assessment, p. 595 • Online Working Papers	• Reteach, p. 596
• Instructor's Resource CD/Website: PowerPoint Slides Accounting Concepts • Online Working Papers	• Visual/Spatial Learners • Interpersonal Learners	• Terms Review • Audit Your Understanding • Work Together 20-2	• On Your Own 20-2 • Application Problem 20-2 • Formative Assessment, p. 599 • Online Working Papers	• Reteach, p. 600
• Instructor's Resource CD/Website: PowerPoint Slides Accounting Concepts • Online Working Papers • Transparency Masters: Voucher Register, Check Register	• Tactile/Kinesthetic Learners	• Terms Review • Audit Your Understanding • Work Together 20-3	• On Your Own 20-3 • Application Problem 20-3 • Formative Assessment, p. 606 • Online Working Papers • On Your Own 20-4	• Reteach, p. 607
• Instructor's Resource CD/Website: PowerPoint Slides Accounting Concepts • Online Working Papers	• Logical/Mathematical Learners	• Audit Your Understanding • Work Together 20-4	• Application Problem 20-4 • Formative Assessment, p. 610 • Online Working Papers	• Reteach, p. 611
• Online Working Papers			• Mastery Problem 20-M • Study Guide 20 • Chapter 20 Test • Cognero Chapter 20	• Challenge Problem 20-C • Reteach, p. 616 • Recycling Problem 20-R

Introduce the Chapter

SET THE STAGE

GUIDING QUESTIONS

- Ask students to think of other names for *fraud*.
- Ask students to give an example of an error in accounting. Ask them how this differs from fraud.
- Ask students if they ever worked for an employer who had controls in place to eliminate theft of assets.
- Ask students to identify different ways they could inform others of their internal control process.
- Ask students questions they might consider when evaluating risks involved in speeding, stealing, cheating, and losing money.
- Ask students to predict how a large company with locations worldwide would keep track of orders and payments.

PREVIEW CHAPTER OBJECTIVES

- Note that students will learn how to create and assess internal controls to avoid errors and fraud.
- Instruct a student to read each chapter objective aloud.

PREVIEW ACCOUNTING TERMS

- Read each term aloud to verify its pronunciation for students.
- Point out terms or parts of terms that should already be familiar to most students, such as *fraud*, *error*, *financial statement*, *invoice*, *purchase order*, and *check register*.

Chapter 20 Internal Control

LEARNING OBJECTIVES

After studying Chapter 20, in addition to defining key terms, you will be able to:

LO1 Explain the difference between an error and a fraud.

LO2 Describe how past events have affected the development of internal control and auditing standards.

LO3 Identify the tasks that should be segregated in an accounting system.

LO4 Use a flowchart to understand an accounting system.

LO5 Journalize data from vouchers in a voucher register.

LO6 Journalize voucher payment transactions in a check register.

LO7 Describe the key controls of a voucher system.

Calculator: © iStockphoto.com/picstodisc; Paper: © iStockphoto.com/Qingwa

© iStockphoto.com/AVAVA

Accounting In The Real World

PetSmart Inc.

Few businesses love their customers more than PetSmart. From grooming services, hotels, day camps, obedience schools, and adoption services, PetSmart is dedicated to the life-long care of its customers. Its stores carry over 10,000 items to cater to their health and happiness.

PetSmart also cares about its pet parents and vendors. The PetSmart *Code of Ethics and Business Conduct* provides its employees with guidance for ethical and legal conduct. In the purchase and sale of merchandise, legal conduct includes following the provisions of the Robinson-Patman Act. The act prohibits the sale of merchandise at different prices in a manner that reduces competition.

The act resulted from pricing practices that favored large chain stores. These stores were able to exert pressure on manufacturers to grant them discounted prices. Unable to earn the same discounts, smaller retailers were at a competitive disadvantage. The act makes it unlawful to knowingly give or receive certain favorable prices. Thus, whether buying merchandise from manufacturers or selling merchandise to pet parents, PetSmart must follow fair pricing practices.

PetSmart's code contains very specific guidance regarding the Robinson-Patman Act. PetSmart may match, but not beat, any competitor's lawful lower price. Quantity discounts may be offered, but only if most customers can buy enough to take advantage of the discount. The code prohibits the payment of a commission to a customer or a customer's representative.

CRITICAL THINKING

1. Select a merchandise item sold in PetSmart. Suggest a fair quantity a pet parent would have to purchase to obtain a discount. What advantage would PetSmart gain by offering the discount?
2. The PetSmart *Code of Ethics and Business Conduct* contains a section entitled "Predatory Pricing." Access the code and summarize its guidance.

Source: PetSmart *Code of Ethics and Business Conduct.*

Background: © iStockphoto.com/MichaelSvoboda, Real World: © iStockphoto.com/RiverNorthPhotography

Key Terms

- internal controls
- error
- fraud
- occupational fraud
- financial statement misstatement
- internal control structure
- control environment
- risk assessment
- control activities
- information and communication
- monitoring
- segregation of duties
- authority
- custody
- recording
- narrative
- flowchart
- voucher
- voucher system
- requisition
- purchase order
- receiving report
- invoice
- voucher register
- voucher check
- check register

Accounting In The Real World

Answers

1. Answers will vary. Students should identify a quantity that most customers would consider purchasing. PetSmart would benefit when the discount is less than the cost savings of selling large quantities.
2. Predatory pricing is the sale of merchandise at below cost. A business can use predatory pricing to gain or maintain a dominant market position. Some states make sales below cost unlawful, even when the business does not have a dominant market position. The code states that the company's Legal Department should be consulted prior to offering any merchandise below cost.

LESSON
20-1

BRIDGE

- Point out that students have learned about posting, bank reconciliations, petty cash, proving special journals, and the trial balance, all of which are internal controls. In this lesson, they will learn how and why an internal control structure must be implemented.

TEACHING RESOURCES

- **Instructor's Resource CD/Website:**
  PowerPoint Slides
  Accounting Concepts
- **Working Papers:**
  Teacher's Edition of the Working Papers for Lesson 20-1
  Online Working Papers

ENGAGE

- Ask students if they have heard of or read about an employee who committed fraud. Explain.
- Ask students what can happen to an employee who unknowingly reports inaccurate information on the financial statements.
- Ask students to describe some ways that fraud could be prevented when taking inventory or counting a cash drawer.

PREVIEW

- Call on students to read the accounting terms and definitions introduced in this lesson: *internal controls, error, fraud, occupational fraud, financial statement misstatement, internal control structure, control environment, risk assessment, control activities, information and communication, monitoring, segregation of duties, authority, custody,* and *recording.*
- Point out the learning objectives for this lesson.
- Direct students to read the headings in this lesson and to examine the illustrations.

INPUT

- Point out the internal controls already presented in this book.

LESSON
20-1 Internal Control Structure

LO1 Explain the difference between an error and a fraud.
LO2 Describe how past events have affected the development of internal control and auditing standards.
LO3 Identify the tasks that should be segregated in an accounting system.

Controlling Accounting Systems LO1

Accountants are responsible for designing accounting systems that produce accurate financial statements and other reports. Accountants are also responsible for ensuring that the assets of the business are secure and are used only as authorized by management.

Processes and procedures employed within a business to ensure that its operations are conducted ethically, accurately, and reliably are called **internal controls**. Consider the following internal controls presented in this textbook:

Posting. Writing the posting references in journals and ledgers helps to ensure that all transactions are posted.

Bank Reconciliation. The bank reconciliation helps to detect an incorrect posting of a check or deposit.

Petty Cash. A petty cash system helps to ensure that small cash payments are recorded in the accounting records on a timely basis.

Proving a Special Journal. Proving the totals of the debit and credit columns of a special journal helps to ensure that all transactions were journalized accurately.

Trial Balance. Comparing the totals of the debits and credits helps ensure that all transactions have been posted.

Note that the explanation of each procedure included the word *help*. Any one internal control rarely provides absolute assurance that a transaction is recorded accurately. For example, proving the cash payments journal would not detect a cash payment for $930.00 recorded as $390.00. Fortunately, a bank reconciliation would detect the error.

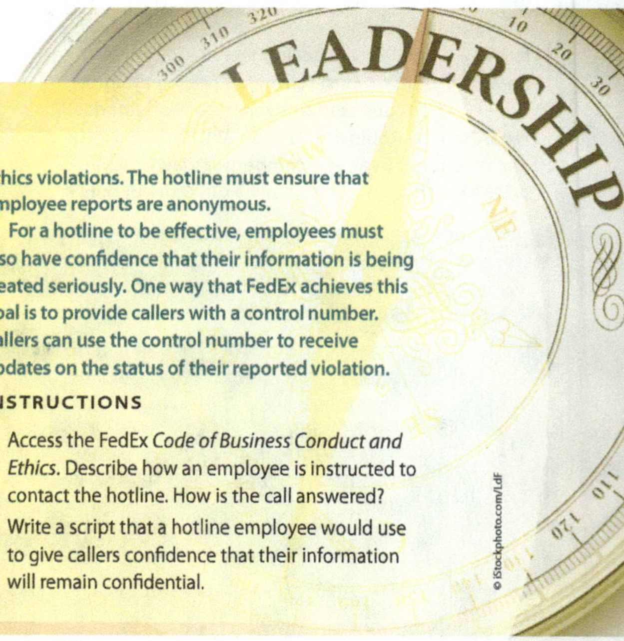

ETHICS IN ACTION

Reporting Violations

What should employees do when they witness another employee possibly violating a law or the company's code of conduct? A small business may direct its employees to discuss the matter with the owner or manager. Larger companies may instruct employees to report it to an ethics officer or a compliance department. Public companies are required to establish procedures for employees to report complaints regarding questionable accounting, internal accounting controls, or auditing matters. These companies must provide a phone number or "hotline" that allows an individual to provide confidential information regarding possible ethics violations. The hotline must ensure that employee reports are anonymous.

For a hotline to be effective, employees must also have confidence that their information is being treated seriously. One way that FedEx achieves this goal is to provide callers with a control number. Callers can use the control number to receive updates on the status of their reported violation.

INSTRUCTIONS

1. Access the FedEx *Code of Business Conduct and Ethics.* Describe how an employee is instructed to contact the hotline. How is the call answered?
2. Write a script that a hotline employee would use to give callers confidence that their information will remain confidential.

© iStockphoto.com/LdF

ETHICS IN ACTION

Suggested Solution

1. The FedEx Alert Line is available 24/7, toll free, anywhere in the world where permitted by local laws. Trained operators who are not FedEx employees answer the Alert Line. The operators forward the information to the appropriate level of FedEx management, which may include the Legal, Security, Human Resources, and Internal Audit departments.
2. "My name is [operator name]. Before you tell me anything, let me assure you that what you share with me today will remain confidential. Our system can't even track your phone number, so I have no idea where you are calling from. And I would suggest that you don't even say your name, where you work, or your position. May I call you [any name] for today? [Name], do you have any questions before we talk about why you called?"

TYPES OF FRAUD

Internal controls are usually effective in detecting an **error**, an unintentional mistake. They are less effective in detecting a **fraud**, the theft of assets by employees or the intentional misstatement of financial information.

Occupational fraud is the theft of assets by an employee. Occupational fraud is also referred to as *embezzlement* or *asset misappropriation*. Cash and inventory are common targets of occupational fraud. Employees can also use plant equipment for unauthorized uses. Occupational frauds are the most common form of business fraud. The amounts stolen can range from hundreds to millions of dollars.

Financial statement misstatement is the manipulation of amounts reported on a financial statement. Overstating revenues is the most common form of this kind of fraud. Although financial statement misstatement occurs with less frequency than occupational fraud, its impact is usually more damaging. An occupational fraud rarely causes a business to fail. In contrast, financial statement misstatement often results in a business failure, as in the case of Enron and WorldCom. Investors and creditors lost billions of dollars when these corporations failed.

Laws and Regulations LO2

For over one hundred years, a few notable accounting frauds have caused the accounting profession to re-evaluate its accounting and auditing rules. In some cases, the frauds involved individual companies, such as Enron and WorldCom. In others, the frauds involved many companies in a particular industry.

COMMITTEE OF SPONSORING ORGANIZATIONS

In 1985, five major financial and accounting organizations established the Committee of Sponsoring Organizations to study the factors that lead to fraudulent financial reporting. The organization was a reaction to a financial crisis in the savings and loan industry.

The commission's report broadened the accounting profession's perception of internal controls. The commission established a model that required accountants to consider more than internal control procedures. The **internal control structure** is a process designed to achieve effectiveness and efficiency of operations, reliability of financial reporting, and compliance with applicable laws and regulations. These control goals are best achieved by addressing each of the five components of the internal control structure.

Control Environment. The attitude and actions of management that indicate its commitment to strong internal controls and ethical standards are called the **control environment**. The control environment is often referred to as the *tone at the top*. Management must establish and enforce policies that ensure fair financial reporting and encourage employees to make ethical decisions. A corporation should have a code of conduct and regularly train its employees on how to make ethical decisions. Managers must follow the rules in the code of conduct if they expect their employees to follow the same rules.

Risk Assessment. The process of determining whether an error or fraud could occur is called **risk assessment**. A mistake in calculating employer payroll taxes could go undetected unless another employee verifies the amounts. Since cash is hard to trace and easy to use, it is most often the target of employees committing an occupational fraud. Recording false sales is the most effective way of increasing reported net income.

Control Activities. The policies and procedures designed to prevent or detect errors or fraud are called **control activities**. Verifying the work of an employee is a control activity. A point-of-sale system that prevents a salesclerk from changing sales prices without management approval is a control activity.

Information and Communication. The processes used to collect information about how the business is achieving its control goals are called **information and communication**. This information is generated at the operations level and reported to management. For example, the information technology staff should send management periodic reports on the number of hacking attempts on the company's website.

Monitoring. The process management uses to determine whether its policies are operating effectively is called **monitoring**. Management can employ internal auditors to observe procedures and collect information to ensure that policies are being followed.

SARBANES-OXLEY

Congress has generally allowed the accounting profession to develop standards to improve accounting and auditing rules. After Enron and WorldCom failed in the same year, Congress passed the Sarbanes-Oxley Act of 2002 (SOX). This act set higher standards for the development and auditing of internal control systems.

INPUT

- Explain the difference between an error and fraud.
- Explain the impact of financial statement misstatement.

INPUT

- Point out that the Committee of Sponsoring Organizations was started due to a financial crisis in the savings and loan industry.
- Explain the purpose of an internal control structure.
- Review the five components of the internal control structure.
- Explain that the Sarbanes-Oxley Act (SOX) is the first law that ensures that controls and financial reporting are in place.

INPUT

- Explain how segregation of duties is an important control activity.
- Read the three functions that should be segregated.
- Ask a student to read the italicized questions in the second column—questions that accountants should answer to help assess their risk of error or fraud.

SOX created the Public Company Accounting Oversight Board (PCAOB) with the power to set auditing standards. PCAOB standards apply to any business having publicly traded stocks or bonds. Unlike standards previously set by the accounting profession, PCAOB standards are law. Failure to adhere to PCAOB standards can result in penalties, including jail time.

SOX requires management to assess the quality of its internal controls. This process begins with the design of an effective internal control system. The business must also maintain comprehensive documentation of its system. Two methods of documenting an internal control system are presented later in the chapter.

Management must also document how it tests the effectiveness of its internal control system. This process enables the chief executive and chief financial officers to certify the internal controls of the business. These officers are personally responsible for the accuracy of their financial statements.

Segregation of Duties LO3

The most fundamental control activity is having one employee oversee or approve the work of another. This requires dividing the tasks of the accounting system among employees in different functions. This division of accounting tasks is called **segregation of duties**. For any single transaction, the following three functions should be segregated:

Authority is the ability of an employee to authorize a transaction. Authority would include:

- Selling merchandise.
- Requesting the purchase of merchandise.
- Accepting a customer's sales return.
- Authorizing the write-off of a customer account.
- Approving documents, such as invoices and checks.

Custody is the physical access to the assets involved in a transaction. Custody would include:

- Having access to merchandise.
- Having access to checks and petty cash funds.
- Receiving or shipping merchandise.

Recording is the entry of a transaction in the financial records. Recording would include:

- Journalizing a transaction in a journal.
- Entering a transaction in a computerized accounting system.

Segregation of duties requires that two or more employees be involved in every transaction. The risk of error or fraud increases when a single employee is given any two of these duties. The following situation illustrates a system common in small businesses.

> Mary works in a local yogurt shop. When a customer arrives, she prepares the requested item using the yogurt machines behind the counter. Mary gives the customer the yogurt and presses a cash register button for the type of item purchased. She asks the customer for the amount of the sale and makes any necessary change.
>
> At the end of the day, the owner arrives at the shop to count the money in the cash register. She compares the amount of cash with a sales record printed by the cash register. The amount of money on hand must equal the amount printed on the sales record. The owner has always been able to reconcile Mary's cash to the sales record.

Accountants begin their analysis by gaining an understanding of the system. Then they assess the risk of error or fraud by answering questions such as:

What business resources are at risk? Cash is a risky asset. Cash is difficult to trace and easy to convert to other goods or services. Although the yogurt is also at risk, it is more difficult for an employee to steal or use a large quantity of yogurt.

Could the cash from sales be incorrectly counted? The system ensures the proper accounting for every sale entered in the cash register. The cash collected is reconciled to sales according to the cash register.

Does Mary have motivation to perform a fraud? Most fraudsters steal assets because they already have a financial hardship. Accountants would need to talk with Mary, her coworkers, and the business owner to learn whether Mary is experiencing any financial problems.

How could Mary perform a fraud without the knowledge of the owner? Mary has both authority and custody functions. She has the authority to sell the yogurt and access to the yogurt machines and toppings. This lack of segregation of duties could enable several frauds, including:

1. Mary can give yogurt to her friends. She could dispense the yogurt as usual and then simply not enter the sale in the cash register.
2. Mary can sell yogurt to her friends at a reduced price. She could prepare a \$5.00 item but select a \$3.00 item in the cash register.
3. Mary can enter a lower-priced item in the cash register but ask the customer for the full price. She could serve a \$5.00 item but select a \$3.00 item in the cash register, pocketing the extra \$2.00.

Knowing the risks to the system, accountants can design control activities to prevent or detect any possible errors or frauds.

Careers In Accounting

Lisa Rodriguez

PARTNER IN AN ACCOUNTING FIRM

© Golden Pixels LLC/Shutterstock.com

Lisa Rodriguez is a partner in a regional accounting firm. She has been working for the same firm for over 20 years. Ms. Rodriguez started with the firm the summer before her last year in college. She started as an intern and was hired full-time after she graduated.

Ms. Rodriguez has followed a rather traditional career path to obtain her current position. She started as a junior accountant in the auditing area and earned her designation as a certified public accountant. She soon moved to senior accountant and to manager. Her promotions gave her more responsibility, and she supervised more people. She managed the audits of major customers and worked hard to bring in new business to the firm.

Ms. Rodriguez's duties shifted again when she was promoted to partner. She managed the local office of the firm and spent more time on administrative duties. As a partner, she is also expected to market the firm and its services.

When Ms. Rodriguez became a partner in the firm, she invested a rather large sum of money in the firm. In exchange for this investment, she shares in the profits of the firm. In addition, if the firm does well, the value of her ownership of the firm will increase.

Ms. Rodriguez worked very hard to achieve the position of partner. Most accountants in public accounting firms leave within three to five years to move into corporate accounting. Only a very small percentage of accountants rise to the level of partner. Ms. Rodriguez has always enjoyed public accounting and plans to stay with her firm for many more years.

Salary Range: The range in salary for a partner varies greatly, depending on the size and geographic location of the firm. The range can be from a few hundred thousand to several million dollars per year. The partner also gains from increases in the value of the firm.

Qualifications: Audit partners usually have at least a four-year accounting degree and have earned the designation "certified public accountant."

Occupational Outlook: As a career area, accounting is expected to experience above-average growth (over 20%) through 2018. Although only a very small percentage of accountants achieve the level of partner, the number of partners should grow as accounting positions grow.

Source: www.onetonline.org.

© iStockphoto.com/Mlenny

Careers In Accounting

Review a career as a partner in an accounting firm.

FORMATIVE ASSESSMENT

- This is an ongoing process. Circulate around the classroom or lab, observing which students have difficulty with the assignments.
- Troubleshooting: Diagnose the kinds of problems students have with this section. Students may have trouble distinguishing the difference between errors and fraud.
- Assess student understanding by checking solutions to Independent Practice assignments and noting their answers to the Terms Review and Audit Your Understanding questions.

CHECK FOR UNDERSTANDING

Terms Review

- Call on students to define each term in the Terms Review. Definitions are given in the Glossary.

Audit Your Understanding

- Call on students to answer the Audit Your Understanding questions. Answers are given in Appendix D.

GUIDED PRACTICE

Work Together

- Have students write the solution to the Work Together problem as you guide the class through the examples.
- Direct students to classify internal controls.

INDEPENDENT PRACTICE

On Your Own

- Assign the On Your Own problem to be worked independently.
- Use the Formative Assessment techniques to diagnose student understanding.

Application Problem

- Assign Application Problem 20-1.

Online Working Papers

- Students can access the Lesson 20-1 problems using this software.

RETEACH

- Ask students to name the internal controls presented previously in the textbook.
- Ask students to name the five components of the internal control structure.
- Ask students to describe the Sarbanes-Oxley Act and its impact on internal controls and financial reporting.
- Ask students to name the three functions that should be segregated.
- Review the questions to assess the risk of error or fraud.

CLOSURE

- Ask students to explain briefly the purpose of an internal control structure and how to create a structure to help eliminate errors or fraud.

End of Lesson Review

LO1 Explain the difference between an error and a fraud.

LO2 Describe how past events have affected the development of internal control and auditing standards.

LO3 Identify the tasks that should be segregated in an accounting system.

Terms Review

internal controls
error
fraud
occupational fraud
financial statement misstatement
internal control structure
control environment
risk assessment
control activities
information and communication
monitoring
segregation of duties
authority
custody
recording

Audit your understanding

1. What is the primary difference between an error and a fraud?
2. Which type of fraud is more likely to result in a business failure?
3. What component of the internal control structure is often referred to as the *tone at the top*?
4. What organization has the power to set auditing standards for publicly traded companies?
5. What is the first step accountants should perform when analyzing an accounting system?

Work together 20-1

Classify internal controls

Use the forms provided in the *Working Papers*. Your instructor will guide you through the following examples.

1. For each item, indicate the component of the internal control structure: control environment, risk assessment, control activities, information and communication, or monitoring. The first item is completed as an example.

Item	Description	Component of the Internal Control Structure
1	A manager approves an employee's time card.	Control activities

2. For each item, indicate whether the action is an authority, custody, or recording function. The first item is completed as an example.

Item	Description	Function
1	A department store clerk processes a customer sale.	Authority

On your own 20-1

Classify internal controls

Use the forms provided in the *Working Papers*. Complete this problem independently.

1. For each item, indicate the component of the internal control structure: control environment, risk assessment, control activities, information and communication, or monitoring.
2. For each item, indicate whether the action is an authority, custody, or recording function.

Essential Question

- When a person doesn't work all the hours they are supposed to work during the day, what internal controls could be put in place to eliminate this fraud? (*Fingerprint recognition programs could be implemented so the employee has to be recognized when arriving and departing work.*)

EXTENDED LEARNING

- Assign Accounting in the Real World on page 591.
- Assign Ethics in Action on page 592.
- Review Careers in Accounting on page 595.

LESSON

20-2 Documenting Accounting Systems

LO4 Use a flowchart to understand an accounting system.

Documentation Methods LO4

Effective internal controls begin with good documentation. Documenting the procedures of an accounting system forces a business to evaluate its processes and identify areas of weakness.

The simplest form of documentation to prepare is a written description of the system. A **narrative** is a written description of the flow of documents and information between employees, departments, and external parties. Although an effective tool for a simple system, a narrative can become confusing as the system becomes complex.

Many businesses also create diagrams of their accounting systems. A diagram that uses symbols and connecting lines to represent a process is called a **flowchart**. Flowcharting is a form of language. Understanding a foreign language requires an understanding of its words and their use in a sentence. In the same manner, flowcharting requires an understanding of the symbols and rules used. An explanation of three important components of a flowchart follows.

Segregated Functions. Dashed lines segregate the tasks of each primary employee, department, or external party.

Symbols. Each symbol represents an object, such as a document or process. Castillo Distributors also color-codes its symbols to assist the user in identifying like objects. For example, all documents are shaded in green. A solid line connects the symbols and represents the flow of information through the system.

Style. The flow of documents and information generally moves from the upper left to lower right corner of a flowchart.

Symbol	Description
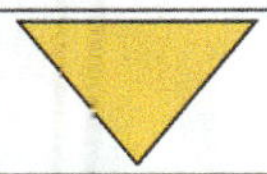	**Manual File.** A folder or file containing paper documents.
	**Document.** Any document, including time cards, sales invoices, and checks. A symbol may represent one document or many copies of the same document.
	**Process.** An accounting process, such as creating a form, comparing forms, journalizing a transaction, or signing a form.
	**Accounting Record.** Any accounting journal or ledger, such as a purchases journal, payroll register, or general ledger.
	**Terminate Process.** The beginning or end of a process. The symbol is often used to show a document being received from or sent to a department or external party not represented in the flowchart.
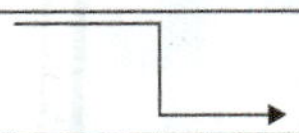	**Information Flow.** The transfer of information or the movement of a document between departments. The arrow indicates the direction of the transfer.
	**Control.** Identifies a key control to ensure that accounting transactions are recorded accurately. Numbers under the symbol identify each control.
	**Risk.** Identifies that a process is subject to the risk of error or fraud. Numbers under the symbol identify each risk.

A flowchart communicates a small segment of the internal control structure. A process may begin on one flowchart and continue on other flowcharts. Thus, even a small business could require 20 or more flowcharts to document a single system, such as sales and cash receipts. Inadequate segregation of duties is particularly visible when a process is documented in a flowchart.

LESSON

20-2

BRIDGE

- Point out that in previous lessons, students learned how to create an accounting system. In this lesson, they will create a flowchart to illustrate an accounting system.

TEACHING RESOURCES

- **Instructor's Resource CD/Website:**
  PowerPoint Slides
  Accounting Concepts
- **Working Papers:**
  Teacher's Edition of the Working Papers for Lesson 20-2
  Online Working Papers

ENGAGE

- Ask students to think of anything that involves steps or a process.
- Ask students to explain different methods of documenting the steps or process.

PREVIEW

- Call on students to read the accounting terms and definitions introduced in this lesson: *narrative* and *flowchart*.
- Point out the learning objective for this lesson.
- Direct students to read the headings in this lesson and to examine the illustrations.

INPUT

- Explain that documenting the procedures for an accounting system allows a business to evaluate its own processes and identify areas of weakness.
- Point out the symbols and rules used when flowcharting the accounting system.

INPUT

- Ask a student to read Castillo Distributors' narrative in the box at the top of the page.
- Direct students to the illustrated flowchart at the bottom of the page.
- Point out the symbols and segregated functions (dashed lines) in the flowchart.

Documenting a Cash Receipts System

Deposit of Cash Receipts by Mail

Mailroom. Customers submit payments in specially marked envelopes. A mailroom clerk opens each envelope, matches the amount of the check to the enclosed receipt, and endorses the check. The receipt is the bottom section of the invoice sent to the customer. The clerk prepares a two-part cash receipts report that includes the number and total dollar amount of checks received. The customer checks and a cash receipts report are sent to the cashier. The receipts are sent to accounts receivable. The original copy of the cash receipts report is sent to accounting.

Cashier. The cashier totals the checks and compares the total to the summary report. The clerk prepares a deposit slip and deposits the checks in the bank. The clerk forwards the validated deposit slip to accounting.

Accounting. An accounting clerk compares the amount on the validated deposit slip to the cash receipts report. The total of checks received is journalized in the cash receipts journal.

Castillo Distributors has always maintained narratives of its accounting systems. The narrative above describes Castillo's system for the deposit of cash received in the mail. After the passage of the Sarbanes-Oxley Act, the business elected to improve the quality of its documentation by preparing flowcharts of its accounting systems. The flowchart representing Castillo's system for the deposit of cash receipts by mail is shown below. Examples of flowchart components are highlighted.

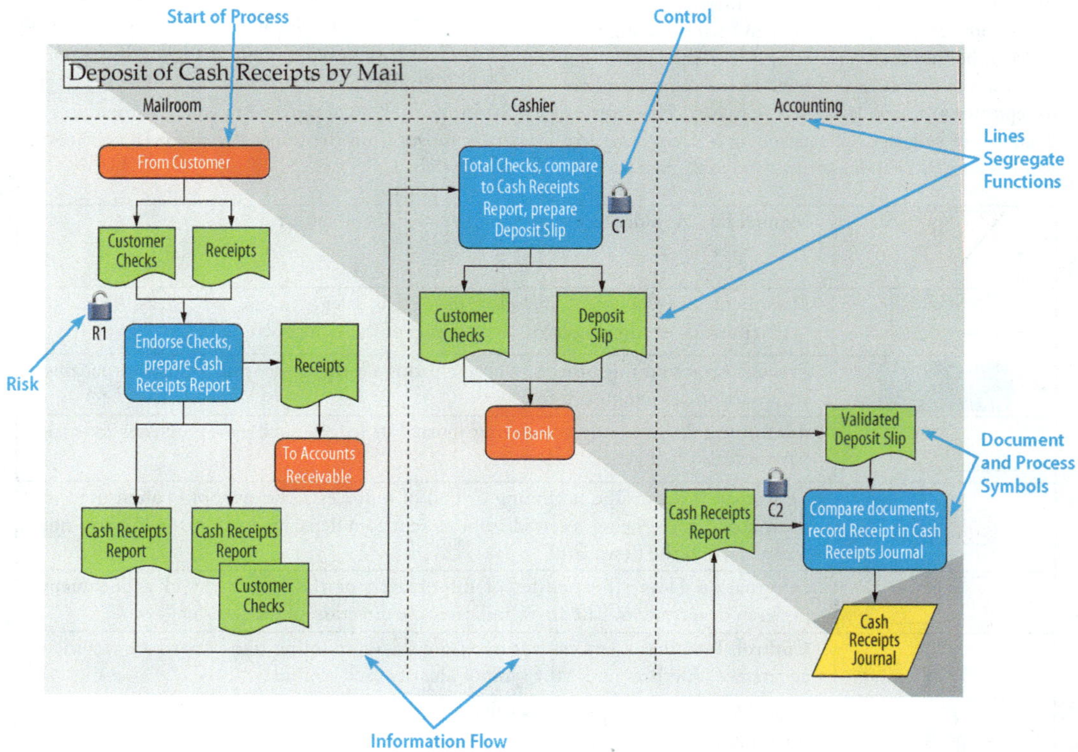

The flowchart shows the location of key risks and internal controls designed to protect the business against the risk of errors and fraud. Castillo has elected to highlight one risk and two key controls in this flowchart. These risks and controls are discussed on the next page.

DIFFERENTIATED INSTRUCTION

Visual/Spatial learners enjoy learning through drawing and physical imagery. Students can draw a flowchart illustrating a process. They should apply the symbols and rules presented in this lesson and create a heading to label the flowchart. The flowcharts can be displayed on posters throughout the room.

Interpersonal learners enjoy working with others to accomplish a goal. These students may enjoy working in pairs to create a flowchart.

Performing a Risk Assessment

Risk/Control Symbol	Risk Assessment	Control Activity
 R1	Any employee that has access to a check could steal the check, cash it, and take the proceeds. A mail clerk can steal a check before the cash receipts report is prepared.	Monthly statements (shown on another flowchart) are sent to customers. A customer not receiving credit for a check can be expected to alert the company.
 C1	The mailroom may deliver checks to the cashier that do not total to the amount on the cash receipts report.	The cashier totals the checks and compares the amount to the cash receipts report before preparing the bank deposit slip.
 C2	The cashier can steal a check, cash the check, and keep the proceeds.	An accounting clerk compares the validated deposit slip to the cash receipts report received directly from the mailroom. Any check stolen by the cashier would cause these amounts to differ.

A flowchart enables a business to identify risks and determine if adequate internal controls exist to prevent or detect an error or a fraud. A business should document how it identifies and evaluates key risks and controls.

Castillo recognizes that a mailroom clerk could steal a check. The risk is noted by the R1 symbol in the flowchart on the previous page. The analysis above indicates that Castillo has an internal control in place. Each month, the business sends statements to its customers. A stolen check would not have been credited to the customer's account. Castillo is assuming the customer will question why the check has been cashed but not credited to its account. When the customer contacts Castillo to question its statement, the theft of the check would be quickly detected.

Management must determine if this internal control is adequate. Other controls could be implemented to prevent or detect the fraud on a timelier basis. For example, a second employee could be present for the processing of the checks in the mailroom. Only management can decide whether reducing the risk of this fraud is offset by the added cost of the control. By noting this as a risk, Castillo is recognizing that its risk in this process needs to be corrected.

© iStockphoto.com/AlieksKo

WHY ACCOUNTING?

Clergy

Usually, people who consider a career as a religious leader do not do so because they like the area of business administration. They consider such a career because they feel called to support and promote the doctrine of their religion. While each individual may have plans for how to accomplish this mission, most of these plans require financial resources.

Being the leader of a religious organization is similar to running a corporation. Budgets must be developed, employees must be hired and trained, and financial reports must be prepared. When new facilities are required, the organization may have to hold a capital fund-raising campaign. Yet few religious training institutions offer courses in business administration or accounting as part of their curriculum.

Human Services

CRITICAL THINKING

Assume a religious organization is trying to balance its budget for next year. The executive committee, including the religious leaders, has determined that only four budget categories can be decreased. The four categories are (a) Building costs, (b) Training/Education of lay members, (c) Conferences/Seminars for religious leaders, and (d) Advertising (which includes publishing the date/time of scheduled classes and activities in local newspapers). For each category, list at least one negative aspect of decreasing the budgeted amount.

INPUT

- Ask students to look at the flowchart on page 598 and identify the one risk and two key controls by looking for the lock and unlocked symbols.
- Ask a student to read the risk assessment and control activity next to R1, C1, and C2 in the illustration at the top of page 599.
- Ask students to suggest solutions for the risk.

WHY ACCOUNTING?

Answers will vary, but could include the following:

a. Maintenance of the building might decrease, which would cause more to be spent in the future; less heat or less cooling might make members/visitors uncomfortable.

b. Training/Education is a major goal of some religious organizations. Decreasing this category could result in fewer educational opportunities for members. Some members might go to other similar organizations for these educational opportunities, and membership could drop.

c. Many religious organizations expect their leaders to attend continuing education conferences and seminars. Decreasing this category could result in dissatisfaction with the leader(s) and/or a leader's dissatisfaction with the organization.

d. When the organization advertises scheduled classes and activities, members and nonmembers learn of these activities and can attend them. Nonmembers who attend might eventually join the organization, which could lead to an increase in donations received. Decreasing this category could affect attendance at these activities.

FORMATIVE ASSESSMENT

- This is an ongoing process. Circulate around the classroom or lab, observing which students have difficulty with the assignments.
- Troubleshooting: Diagnose the kinds of problems students have with this lesson. Students may have difficulty remembering the symbols and rules for flowcharting.
- Assess student understanding by checking solutions to Independent Practice assignments and noting their answers to the Terms Review and Audit Your Understanding questions.

CHECK FOR UNDERSTANDING

Terms Review

- Call on students to define each term in the Terms Review. Definitions are given in the Glossary.

Audit Your Understanding

- Call on students to answer the Audit Your Understanding questions. Answers are given in Appendix D.

GUIDED PRACTICE

Work Together

- Have students write the solution to the Work Together problem as you guide the class through the examples.
- Direct students to prepare flowcharts.

INDEPENDENT PRACTICE

On Your Own

- Assign the On Your Own problem to be worked independently.
- Use the Formative Assessment techniques to diagnose student understanding.

Application Problem

- Assign Application Problem 20-2.

Online Working Papers

- Students can access the Lesson 20-2 problems using this software.

RETEACH

- Draw flowchart symbols on the board and ask students to explain what each symbol represents.
- Ask students to create a flowchart for a process in their personal life, using the symbols, segregated functions, and style from this lesson.

CLOSURE

- Ask students to describe two ways to document an accounting system.
- Ask students to explain the purpose of documenting accounting systems.

Essential Question

- Must changes be made to the flowchart if a risk or weak control activity exists? Explain. (*The flowchart does not have to be changed. However, it should identify risks or weak controls, and documentation should be provided to ensure controlling activities are in place.*)

End of Lesson Review

LO4 Use a flowchart to understand an accounting system.

Terms Review

narrative

flowchart

Audit your understanding

1. What is the simplest form of documentation of an accounting system?
2. Where is the beginning point of the processes presented in a flowchart?
3. What is indicated by a line with an arrow?
4. How does management decide whether to implement additional internal controls?

Work together 20-2

Preparing flowcharts

Use the forms provided in the *Working Papers*. For each statement, prepare a flowchart to represent the process described. Your instructor will guide you through the following examples.

a. An employee approves and signs a check by reviewing information on an invoice.
b. An employee posts sales return transactions from the general journal to the accounts receivable ledger.
c. A warehouse manager approves time cards and forwards the time cards to the Payroll Department.
d. A mailroom clerk receives customer checks, endorses the checks, and forwards the checks to the cashier. The cashier uses the checks to prepare a deposit slip.

On your own 20-2

Preparing flowcharts

Use the forms provided in the *Working Papers*. For each statement, prepare a flowchart to represent the process described. Work this problem independently.

a. An employee uses the accounts receivable ledger to prepare a schedule of accounts receivable.
b. An employee sorts a group of shipping orders in numerical order.
c. A credit manager prepares a receivables adjustment form. The accounting clerk uses the information on the form to journalize the write-off of an account receivable.
d. A sales representative prepares a sales order. The form is forwarded to a salesclerk, who prepares the sales invoice that is sent to the customer.

EXTENDED LEARNING

- Assign Why Accounting on page 599.

LESSON

20-3 Cash Payments Using a Voucher System

LO5 Journalize data from vouchers in a voucher register.
LO6 Journalize voucher payment transactions in a check register.

A Voucher System LO5

An accounting system includes procedures for recording and reporting accurate and up-to-date financial information. An accounting system should also include procedures to assist management in controlling a company's daily operations. Management is particularly concerned with procedures and records to control and protect assets. One asset that should be controlled and protected is cash. Cash is the asset most likely to be misused because its ownership is easily transferred. In addition, transactions generally affect the Cash account more often than other general ledger accounts. Many businesses, therefore, use specific cash control procedures.

Among the procedures used to control cash are storing it in a safe place, making bank deposits regularly, and approving all cash payments. Approving cash payments ensures that the goods or services were ordered, they have been received, and the amounts due are correct. In small businesses, the owner or manager usually approves cash payments. In large businesses, several persons may have authority to approve cash payments. A collection of documents used to authorize a cash payment is called a **voucher**. A set of procedures for controlling cash payments by preparing and approving vouchers before payments are made is called a **voucher system**.

FINANCIAL LITERACY

Stash the Cash

A bank or a credit union will provide a secure location for your cash. Both may offer checking and savings accounts, investment accounts, loans, and credit cards. However, their business structures set them apart.

An account holder at a credit union is called a *member*. Credit unions are not-for-profit organizations owned by their members. The members are usually a group formed by common interests, such as an employer or a geographic area. Credit unions have some advantages over banks. They often do not have advertising costs, typically pay higher interest rates on savings accounts, offer lower rates on loans, provide free checking accounts, and have fewer penalties like overdrafts and late payments.

A bank is a business formed to generate profits, which result from loaning money and earning interest off the loan. A bank offers some advantages over a credit union. Membership is not required, and banks typically offer more products, such as investing programs, and locations and ATMs that are more convenient.

© iStockphoto.com/Norebbo

ACTIVITIES

1. Make a list of three banks and three credit unions in your area. Provide the criteria for membership for the three credit unions.
2. Read the following and determine if the individual should select a credit union or a bank:
   a. Jeff recently accepted a position with a company whose employees are a part of the Engineering Society Credit Union. Jeff's job will require extensive travel.
   b. Julia is eligible to join Professionals Credit Union. She wants to begin saving for her first home, open a checking account, obtain a credit card, and obtain a mortgage in a few years.

LESSON 20-3

BRIDGE

- Point out that students previously learned about cash control systems such as checks and petty cash. In this lesson, they will learn to expand on specific cash controls.

TEACHING RESOURCES

- **Instructor's Resource CD/Website:**
  PowerPoint Slides
  Accounting Concepts
- **Working Papers:**
  Teacher's Edition of the Working Papers for Lesson 20-3
  Online Working Papers
- **Transparency Masters:**
  Voucher Register
  Check Register

ENGAGE

- Ask students to predict how an order process would take place for a small business with one location and three employees.
- Ask students to predict how an order process would take place for a large business operating globally with over 100 locations and thousands of employees.

PREVIEW

- Call on students to read the accounting terms and definitions introduced in this lesson: *voucher*, *voucher system*, *requisition*, *purchase order*, *receiving report*, *invoice*, *voucher register*, *voucher check*, and *check register*.
- Point out the learning objectives for this lesson.
- Direct students to read the headings in this lesson and to examine the illustrations.

INPUT

- Explain the purpose of a voucher and a voucher system.
- Point out the importance of a voucher system in a large business.

FINANCIAL LITERACY

Answers

1. Answers will vary.
2. a. Because Jeff's job requires extensive travel, his best choice is probably a bank so that he has access to many ATMs.
   b. Julia's best choice would be a credit union. Being a member of the credit union also places her in a better position for obtaining a mortgage because she will already be a member when she applies for the loan.

INPUT

- Explain the ordering process and the forms involved throughout the process.
- Point out other names used for an invoice (*statement, bill*).
- Explain the significance of a voucher stamp and accountability of initials in the process of handling transactions.

Verifying an Invoice

Invoice

Invoice #: 6482
Date: 7/24/--

Kelser Industries
1644 Sauget Industrial Pkwy
Centreville, IL 62207

Ship To:
Castillo Liquidators, Inc.
6277 Saginaw St.
Salem, OR 97302

DATE RECEIVED	7/26/--
MATERIAL RECEIVED	MCL
TERMS APPROVED	BAH
PRICES APPROVED	BAH
FIGURES CHECKED	BAH
VOUCHER NO.	721

Packed by	Shipping Method	Ship Date	Delivery Date	Terms	Payment Due
PLG	PHE-Ground	7/21/--	7/23/--	2/10, n/30 ✓	8/22/--

Qty	Item #	Description	Unit Price	Total
21 ✓	MAK-747-4 ✓	16-piece metric drill set ✓	$ 24.95 ✓	$ 523.95 ✓
13 ✓	CD-264-CL ✓	Cordless 18-volt drill ✓	$ 154.95 ✓	$ 2,014.35 ✓
			Total	$ 2,538.30 ✓

The best source for all your hand and power tool needs.

The process of ordering merchandise begins when an authorized employee submits a purchase request. A form requesting the purchase of merchandise is called a **requisition**. The requisition includes a description of the merchandise to be ordered, the quantity to be purchased, and the required delivery date. Requisitions generally require management approval.

An approved requisition is submitted to another employee, who is responsible for placing an order with the supplier that provides the best combination of quality and price. A form requesting that a vendor sell merchandise to a business is called a **purchase order**. The purchase order lists the number, description, quantity, and unit price of each item ordered. The vendor uses the purchase order to (1) approve the sale and (2) process the order. No transaction occurs until the customer receives the goods from the vendor. Thus, no journal entry is recorded when a purchase order is prepared or sent to the vendor.

When the order is received, the Receiving Department prepares a document to identify the qualities of the items received. A form that lists the item received from a vendor is called a **receiving report**.

The requisition, purchase order, and receiving report are submitted to an accounts payable clerk. A transaction is not recorded until the vendor submits an **invoice**, a form describing the goods or services sold, the quantity, the price, and the terms of sale. The accounts payable clerk compares the information on the invoice with the other documents to ensure that the business has only been invoiced for the goods it ordered and received.

A VOUCHER

The requisition, purchase order, receiving report, and invoice provide a historical account of the transaction. Together these documents comprise a voucher. The methods used to organize these documents vary. Some businesses prepare a prenumbered form that summarizes the information to be recorded in the accounting records. This form can be stapled with the documentation or assembled in a folder. Other businesses use the invoice as the cover document of the voucher. Castillo's accounts payable clerk stamps the invoice and records a voucher number. The other forms are stapled to the invoice.

The voucher stamp lists important steps required to verify the voucher. On the receiving report, Michael C. Langston identified the quantities of items received. His initials, MCL, are written in the stamp. Beth Ann Harris, the accounts payable clerk, signs her initials, BAH, on the tasks she performs. She also places check marks next to the items verified on the invoice. This process ensures that every step is performed. The voucher shows the employee responsible for each step in the verification process.

DIFFERENTIATED INSTRUCTION

Tactile/Kinesthetic learners learn best through physical activity and real objects. Ask students to collect samples of forms used in the voucher system. Allow students to create a visual or poster illustrating the voucher process, using the actual forms and labeling the steps.

Journalizing a Voucher in a Voucher Register's Special Columns

Date | Payee | Voucher Number | Voucher Amount

VOUCHER REGISTER — PAGE 15

	DATE	PAYEE	VCHR. NO.	PAID DATE	PAID CK. NO.	1 VOUCHERS PAYABLE CREDIT	2 PURCHASES DEBIT	3 SUPPLIES— SALES DEBIT	4 SUPPLIES— ADMIN. DEBIT	GENERAL ACCOUNT TITLE	GENERAL POST. REF.	5 GENERAL DEBIT	6 GENERAL CREDIT	
23	26	*Kelser Industries*	721			2 538 30	2 538 30							23
24														24

The voucher is recorded in the accounting records after it has been approved. A journal used to record vouchers is called a **voucher register**. A voucher register is similar to and replaces a purchases journal. The accounts payable clerk assigns sequential numbers to the vouchers. A missing voucher number shows that a voucher has not been recorded.

Castillo's voucher register has special columns for Vouchers Payable Credit, Purchases Debit, Supplies—Sales Debit, and Supplies—Administrative Debit. For accounts with no special amount columns, information is recorded in the General columns. Voucher 721 is recorded on line 23 of the voucher register.

July 26. Purchased merchandise on account from Kelser Industries, $2,538.30. Voucher No. 721.

The purchase of merchandise results in a debit to Purchases and a credit to Vouchers Payable. Similar to a purchases journal, a voucher register has special columns that are used to record this transaction. After a voucher is journalized, the voucher is filed in an unpaid vouchers file. The vouchers are placed in this file according to the expected payment date. Filing the vouchers by payment date makes it easier to determine which vouchers need to be paid each day. This method helps ensure payment of invoices within the discount period. To ensure the check will arrive at Kelser Industries by the 10th day, the accounts payable clerk files the voucher under the date on which it is to be paid, August 1. Payment of a voucher is described later in this lesson.

Purchases	
↑ 2,538.30	

Vouchers Payable	
	↑ 2,538.30

fyi Computerized accounting systems assign a sequential voucher number when a vendor invoice is entered.

© iStockphoto.com/jasantiso

INPUT

- Direct students to the illustration and describe a voucher register.
- Point out the special columns.
- Explain the vouchers file for unpaid vouchers and the significance of filing by the payment date.

MODEL

Analyze the transaction

- Draw two T accounts on the board.
- Read the transaction statements.
- Ask students to analyze the transactions. Complete the T accounts as the information is provided.

Record the transaction

- Use the voucher register transparency to illustrate the process for journalizing the two vouchers in a voucher register's special columns or direct students to the illustration in the book.

INPUT

- Explain that proving, ruling, and posting a voucher register is done the same as for other special journals.

THINK LIKE AN ACCOUNTANT

This activity allows students to apply their knowledge of flowcharting while gaining exposure to Excel's flowcharting tools. The activity resembles a common problem presented on the CPA examination. A flowchart of a business process is presented with many symbols lacking descriptions. CPA candidates are required to apply their knowledge of business processes and flowcharting to identify an appropriate description for each symbol. Unlike the CPA examination, this activity includes a narrative.

Answers

A. From customer
B. Remittance advice
C. Endorse checks
D. Check
E. Compares items, prepares remittance list
F. Remittance list
G. 1
H. 3
I. Remittance list (copy 1)
J. Remittance advice
K. Post receipts to customer accounts
L. Remittance file
M. Check
N. Deposit slip
O. From bank
P. 3
Q. Cash receipts journal
R. Daily deposits file

Journalizing a Voucher in a Voucher Register's Special Columns

Date — Payee — Voucher Number — Voucher Amount

VOUCHER REGISTER — PAGE 15

	DATE	PAYEE	VCHR. NO.	PAID DATE	PAID CK. NO.	1 VOUCHERS PAYABLE CREDIT	2 PURCHASES DEBIT	3 SUPPLIES—SALES DEBIT	4 SUPPLIES—ADMIN. DEBIT	GENERAL ACCOUNT TITLE	GENERAL POST. REF.	5 GENERAL DEBIT	6 GENERAL CREDIT	
23	26	Kelser Industries	721			2,538.30	2,538.30							23
24	28	Lakeland Company	722			145.00				Misc. Exp.—Sales	6220	145.00		24
25		Totals				21,943.36	16,281.10	1,510.68	1,814.58			2,615.85	278.85	25
26						(2105)	(5105)	(1145)	(1440)			(✔)	(✔)	26

Debit Amount and Account

Only two of the special journals illustrated in previous parts of this textbook contain General Debit and Credit columns—the cash receipts and cash payments journals. If no cash is involved, the transaction is recorded in a general journal.

July 28. Received an invoice for a sales miscellaneous expense from Lakeland Company, $145.00. Voucher No. 722.

Miscellaneous Expense—Sales	
↑ 145.00	

Vouchers Payable	
	↑ 145.00

A voucher register contains general columns that enable the business to record all transactions on account. Because no special column exists for miscellaneous expenses, this transaction is recorded in the General Debit column.

Proving, Ruling, and Posting a Voucher Register

The voucher register is proved, ruled, and posted, using the same steps as other special journals. Separate amounts recorded in the General Debit and General Credit columns of a voucher register are posted individually during the month. As each amount is posted, the account number is written in the Post. Ref. column of the voucher register.

At the end of each month, Castillo's voucher register is proved and ruled. The totals of special amount columns are posted to the general ledger accounts listed in the column headings. Totals of General Debit and General Credit amount columns are not posted.

THINK LIKE AN ACCOUNTANT

Documenting Cash Collections

Lancing Brick sells its products directly to contractors for the construction of both residential housing and commercial buildings. The company offers contractors 2/10, n/30 payment terms. Customers are sent an invoice on the same day the bricks are delivered to the construction site. A remittance advice and a pre-stamped envelope are included with the invoice. All of Lancing's customers pay their accounts by writing a check. A narrative describing the procedures for receiving customer payments is presented in the worksheet.

OPEN THE SPREADSHEET TLA_CH20

The worksheet contains an incomplete flowchart of Lancing's cash receipts procedures. Follow the steps on the Instructions tab to complete the flowchart.

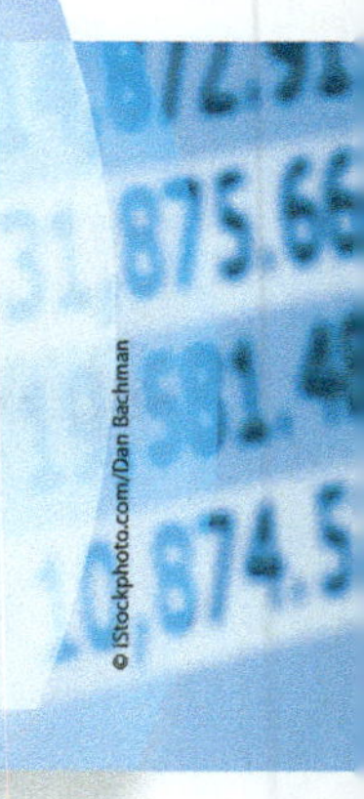

© iStockphoto.com/Dan Bachman

Paying a Voucher LO6

CASTILLO LIQUIDATORS, INC. DATE *8/1/20--* **No. 915**

PAYEE	*Kelser Industries*			
ACCOUNT	TITLE	VOUCHER	VENDOR INVOICE	AMOUNT
2105	*Purchases*	*721*	*6482*	*2,538.30*
5110	*Purchases Discount*			*50.77*

CASTILLO LIQUIDATORS, INC.
6277 Saginaw St.
Salem, OR 97302

FIRST AMERICAN BANK
101 S. Marion Street
Salem, OR 97302

No. 915

GENERAL ACCOUNT

DATE *8/1/20--* AMOUNT $ *2,487.53*

Two thousand four hundred eighty seven and 53/100 Dollars

FOR CLASSROOM USE ONLY

PAY TO THE ORDER OF *Kelser Industries*
1544 Sunset Industrial Pkwy
Centreville, IL 62207

Gerald C. Andrews

⑆0632603641⑆ 02⑈5643⑈64⑈ 0915

In a voucher system, a check cannot be issued without a properly authorized voucher. Castillo prepares a check for the amount of each voucher less any purchases discount. The check and voucher are presented to a person authorized to approve payment. A check with a detachable check stub, or *voucher*, that contains detailed information about the cash payment is called a **voucher check**. Castillo prepares voucher checks in duplicate.

On August 1, vouchers to be paid on that day are removed from the unpaid vouchers file. Included in this group is Voucher No. 721. Castillo's cash payments clerk prepares the voucher checks.

Castillo uses the detachable section of the voucher check to record details about the cash payment. On Check No. 915, the information includes the following items:

1. Castillo's voucher number, 721.
2. The vendor's invoice number, 6482.
3. The account debited and the amount of the invoice, $2,538.30.
4. The amount of the purchases discount, $50.77.
5. The net amount for which the check is written, $2,487.53.

The check signer, Gerald C. Andrews, verifies that the information on the check and on the voucher agrees and is accurate. After verification, he signs the check. The duplicate of the voucher check is attached to the voucher. The check signer cancels each voucher document to ensure the documents cannot be submitted for payment a second time. Documents are cancelled by using a stamp or a machine that punches holes spelling PAID or CANCELLED. The check is given or sent to the payee by the check signer.

The cancelled voucher is returned to the accounts payable clerk. Information about this payment is recorded in the voucher register. The date on which this voucher is paid, *8/1/--*, and the check number, *915*, are written in the Paid columns of the voucher register. The cancelled voucher is filed in the paid vouchers file according to the name of the vendor.

	DATE		PAYEE	VCHR. NO.	PAID		VOUCHERS PAYABLE CREDIT	
					DATE	CK. NO.		
23		26	Kelser Industries	721	8/1/--	915	2,538.30	23
24		28	Lakeland Company	722			145.00	24

INPUT

- Direct students to the illustration of the voucher check and explain its purpose compared with that of just a check.
- Point out the process for paying and recording the voucher check.

INPUT

- Point out that the check register in the voucher system replaces a cash payments journal.

MODEL

Analyze the transaction

- Draw three T accounts on the board.
- Read the transaction statement.
- Ask students to analyze the transaction. Complete the T accounts as the information is provided.

Record the transaction

- Direct students to the illustration of the check register or use the check register transparency to illustrate the process for journalizing checks in the check register and for maintaining the checking account balance.

Journalizing Checks in a Check Register

Date · Payee · Voucher Number · Purchases Discount

CHECK REGISTER — PAGE 21

	DATE		ACCOUNT TITLE	CK. NO.	VCHR. NO.	1 VOUCHERS PAYABLE DEBIT	2 PURCHASES DISCOUNT CREDIT	3 CASH CREDIT	4 BANK DEPOSITS	5 BANK BALANCE	
1	20-- Aug.	1	*Balance Forward*		✓					16 474 61	1
2		1	*Kelser Industries*	915	721	2 538 30	50 77	2 487 53		13 987 08	2
3		2	*Delwarth Corporation*	916	696	1 645 25		1 645 25		12 341 83	3
22		31	*Deposit*		✓				3 154 60	14 954 36	22
23			*Totals*			20 495 64	321 07	20 174 57			23
24						(2105)	(5110)	(1105)			24

Check Number · Voucher Amount · Check Amount · Updated Cash Balance

A journal used in a voucher system to record cash payments is called a **check register**. The check register is similar to and replaces a cash payments journal.

Castillo prepares a voucher for each approved cash payment. Therefore, each check is issued in payment of a voucher. Checks are recorded in the check register in the order they are written.

Castillo's check register has only three special amount columns: Vouchers Payable Debit, Purchases Discount Credit, and Cash Credit. Each check is recorded in a check register as a debit to the liability account, Vouchers Payable, and a credit to the asset account, Cash. If a discount is taken for prompt payment, the discount amount is recorded as a credit to the contra cost account, Purchases Discount.

Castillo's procedures for posting from its check register are the same as those previously described for special journals. However, no separate amounts are posted individually because the check register does not have a General Debit or General Credit column.

August 1. Paid cash to Kelser Industries, $2,487.53, covering Voucher No. 721 for $2,538.30, less 2% discount, $50.77. Check No. 915.

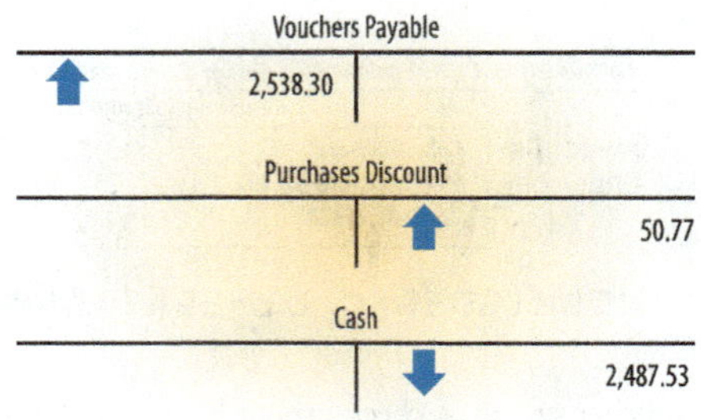

The liability account, Vouchers Payable, is debited for $2,538.30. The contra cost account, Purchases Discount, is credited for $50.77. Cash is credited for the net amount paid, $2,487.53. Castillo's procedures for posting from its check register are the same as those previously described for special journals. However, no separate amounts are posted individually because the check register does not have a General Debit or General Credit column.

Maintaining Bank Columns in a Check Register

Castillo uses a check register to maintain the checking account balance. The check register has two Bank columns, Deposits and Balance. The Bank Deposits column is used to record the amounts deposited in the checking account. The Bank Balance column shows the checking account balance after each check and each deposit are recorded in the check register.

A deposit in the checking account is shown on line 22 above. The Deposits column does not need to be totaled and posted because each cash receipt is recorded in the cash receipts journal and posted from that journal. At the end of each month, cash is proved by comparing the last amount in the Balance column of the check register with the balance in the general ledger cash account. The two Bank columns are used to summarize the status of the checking account balance. These two columns are neither ruled nor posted.

FORMATIVE ASSESSMENT

- This is an ongoing process. Circulate around the classroom or lab, observing which students have difficulty with the assignments.
- Troubleshooting: Diagnose the kinds of problems students have with this lesson. Students may have difficulty remembering the voucher system process or understanding why a voucher system is implemented.
- Assess student understanding by checking solutions to Independent Practice assignments and noting their answers to the Terms Review and Audit Your Understanding questions.

End of Lesson Review

LO5 Journalize data from vouchers in a voucher register.

LO6 Journalize voucher payment transactions in a check register.

Terms Review

voucher
voucher system
requisition
purchase order
receiving report
invoice
voucher register
voucher check
check register

Audit your understanding

1. In a voucher system, what general ledger account is used to record all amounts to be paid by check?
2. A voucher register is similar to and replaces what journal?
3. What account is debited for each check recorded in a check register?

Work together 20-3

Journalizing transactions in a voucher system

The following transactions of Kelley's Crafts were completed during July of the current year. A voucher register and check register are provided in the *Working Papers*. Your instructor will guide you through the following examples. Source documents are abbreviated as follows: voucher, V; check, C.

Transactions:

July 1. Purchased merchandise on account from Dickens Company, $754.60. V63.
3. Paid cash to LPG Industries, $1,635.00, covering V62. C121.
5. Bought sales supplies on account from College Supplies, $350.00. V64.
11. Paid cash to Dickens Company, $754.60, less 2% discount, covering V63. C122.
13. Paid cash to College Supplies, $350.00, less 2% discount, covering V64. C123.
16. Received an invoice from City Bagel for a miscellaneous expense, $65.00. V65.
24. Made a deposit in the checking account, $1,943.68.
29. Received an invoice for August rent from LaMure Development Co., $1,200.00. V66.

1. Record the bank balance brought forward on July 1, $8,265.66.
2. Journalize the transactions completed during July of the current year. Use page 7 of a voucher register and page 8 of a check register.
3. Prove and rule the voucher register.
4. Prove and rule the check register.

On your own 20-3

Journalizing transactions in a voucher system

The following transactions of Electronic Innovations were completed during September of the current year. A voucher register and check register are provided in the *Working Papers*. Work this problem independently. Source documents are abbreviated as follows: voucher, V; check, C.

Transactions:

Sept. 4. Received an invoice from James Peterson for a miscellaneous expense, $132.00. V124.
5. Paid cash to Danstin Corporation, $6,245.00, covering V123. C147.
9. Bought administrative supplies on account from Burrough Supplies, $234.00. V125.
14. Paid cash to James Peterson, $132.00, covering V124. C148.
16. Made a deposit in the checking account, $2,643.11.
18. Paid cash to Burrough Supplies, $234.00, less 2% discount, covering V125. C149.
25. Purchased merchandise on account from Clarmore Company, $1,375.75. V126.
26. Received an invoice for October rent from Office Properties, Inc., $1,400.00. V127.

1. Record the bank balance brought forward on September 1, $6,417.35.
2. Journalize the transactions completed during September of the current year. Use page 9 of a voucher register and page 11 of a check register.
3. Prove and rule the voucher register.
4. Prove and rule the check register.

CHECK FOR UNDERSTANDING

Terms Review

- Call on students to define each term in the Terms Review. Definitions are given in the Glossary.

Audit Your Understanding

- Call on students to answer the Audit Your Understanding questions. Answers are given in Appendix D.

GUIDED PRACTICE

Work Together

- Have students write the solution to the Work Together problem as you guide the class through the examples.
- Direct students to journalize transactions in a voucher system.

INDEPENDENT PRACTICE

On Your Own

- Assign the On Your Own problem to be worked independently.
- Use the Formative Assessment techniques to diagnose student understanding.

Application Problem

- Assign Application Problem 20-3.

Online Working Papers

- Students can access the Lesson 20-3 problems using this software.

RETEACH

- Ask students to explain the process of ordering merchandise from merchandise request to payment.
- Demonstrate journalizing a voucher in a voucher register.
- Demonstrate the payment of a voucher in the check register.

CLOSURE

- Ask students to describe briefly the voucher system process.

Essential Question

- Isn't a voucher system extra work for a small business owner? Explain the pros and cons of a voucher system for a small business. (*Additional steps may be necessary. However, a voucher system controls and protects assets, and the size of the company is indifferent unless the owner is the only employee.*)

EXTENDED LEARNING

- Assign Financial Literacy on page 601.
- Assign Think Like an Accountant on page 604.

LESSON

20-4

BRIDGE

- Point out that students learned about internal controls in a previous lesson. In this lesson, they will learn about controls of a voucher system.

TEACHING RESOURCES

- **Instructor's Resource CD/Website:**
  PowerPoint Slides
  Accounting Concepts
- **Working Papers:**
  Teacher's Edition of the Working Papers for Lesson 20-4
  Online Working Papers

ENGAGE

- Ask students what risks might exist in a voucher system.
- Ask students if a voucher system can prevent errors from occurring, because multiple steps typically involve different individuals.

PREVIEW

- Point out the learning objective for this lesson.
- Direct students to read the headings in this lesson and to examine the illustrations.

INPUT

- Ask a student to read the narrative describing Castillo Liquidators' voucher processing.
- Direct students to the flowchart illustrated at the top of page 609 as a visual of voucher processing for Castillo.
- Remind students of the meaning of the symbols used and direct students to the control symbols illustrated in the flowchart.

TEACHING IDEA **Types of risk can vary from business to business, but most businesses have some risks in common. Ask students to brainstorm other categories of risks besides financial.** ***(Examples might include operational, employee, safety, compliance, and environmental.)***

LESSON

20-4 Internal Controls in a Voucher System

LO7 Describe the key controls of a voucher system.

Narrative of a Voucher System LO7

Accounts Payable/Cash Payments System

Departments. Authorized managers may complete a requisition to request the purchase of goods and services. The requisition is forwarded to the Purchasing Department.

Purchasing. A purchasing employee identifies the best source for purchasing the good or service by (1) reviewing the price lists of approved vendors or (2) advertising requests for competitive bids. Upon approving a completed purchase order, a purchasing manager sends the purchase order to the selected vendor. Copies of the purchase order are also sent to the Receiving and Accounts Payable departments.

Receiving. Upon receiving goods, a Receiving Department employee matches the vendor's documentation with the purchase order to ensure the goods were ordered. The goods are counted and recorded on the purchase order copy, which serves as the receiving report. The receiving report is sent to the Accounts Payable Department.

Accounts Payable. When the vendor's invoice is received, the accounts payable clerk prepares a voucher. The documents are compared for consistency. The approved voucher is recorded in the voucher register and filed until its expected payment date. If the purchase is for services, no receiving report will exist. The invoice is sent to the appropriate manager for approval, providing support that the services were received.

Treasury. On the assigned date, approved vouchers are sent to the Treasury Department for payment. A treasury clerk prepares the check based on the information on the voucher. The check and voucher are forwarded to the check signer. After reviewing the documentation and signing the check, the signed check is sent to the vendor. The transaction is recorded in the check register. The voucher is cancelled and returned to the Accounts Payable Department.

Accounts Payable. The Accounts Payable Department records the check information in the voucher register. The cancelled vouchers are filed in the paid vouchers file according to the name of the vendor.

Accounting systems share common documents and processes. Most voucher systems will use requisitions and purchase orders. However, a business will modify a system to meet its individual needs. A business with a single location will have a different voucher system than a multinational corporation. The extent that a business has adopted computerized accounting systems will determine whether vouchers are in paper or electronic format.

Accountants must be able to understand the unique processes, forms, and controls of each system. Documentation is critical in helping accountants understand and evaluate accounting systems. Castillo Liquidators' accountants prepared the narrative above to document a segment of its voucher processing. A flowchart and a risk analysis of this system are presented on the following pages.

Flowchart of a Voucher System

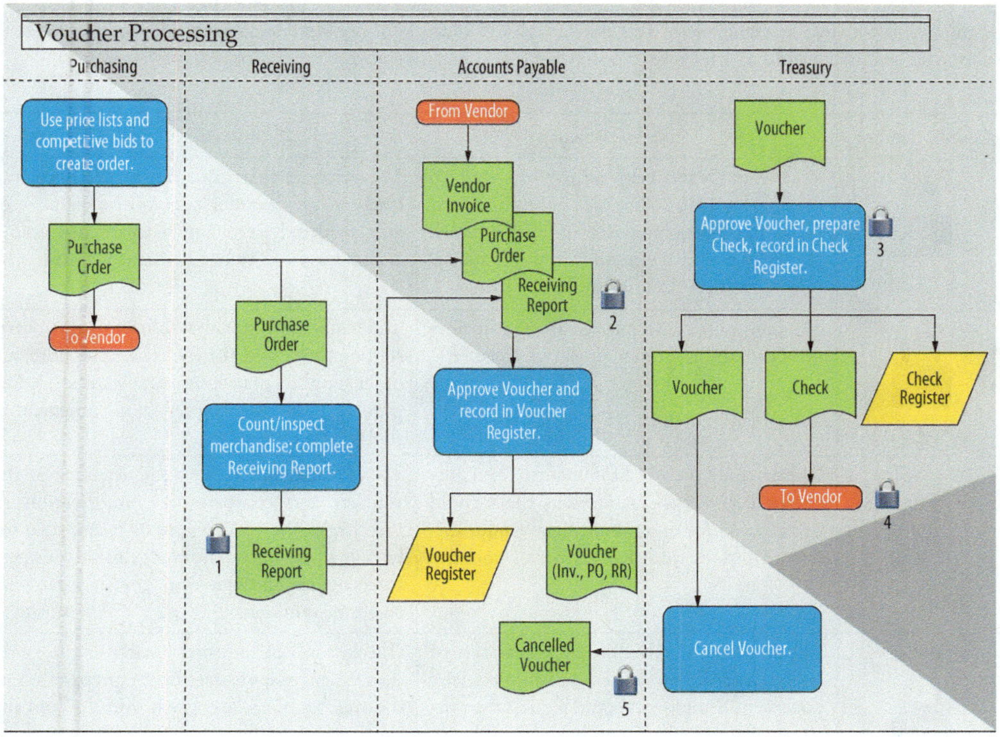

The flowchart representing a portion of Castillo's voucher processing is presented above. Two common flowchart writing styles are illustrated on this flowchart.

When multiple documents join together, a single flowchart symbol can be used to represent the documents. The flowchart illustrates how three documents—vendor invoice, purchase order, and receiving report—transform into a single document, a voucher. Castillo uses a stamp on the vendor invoice to document the verification of the voucher. The purchase order and receiving report are stapled to the invoice. Under the process in the Accounts Payable Department, the document *Voucher (Inv., PO, RR)* alerts the reader that the voucher consists of the three documents. Later in the flowchart, the documents are denoted only as *Voucher*.

A change in a document can be reflected by a change in the symbol label. Castillo's Treasury Department cancels the documents in the voucher. The document symbol entering the *Cancel Voucher* process is labeled *Voucher*. After the process, the document symbol label is changed to *Cancelled Voucher*. The change in the label reflects the change in the document.

Five key controls are identified on the flowchart. The controls are discussed on the next page.

DIFFERENTIATED INSTRUCTION

Logical/Mathematical learners enjoy reasoning and problem-solving activities. They like to create and enjoy working out strategies and using simulation. Ask students to imagine they are planning a concert for their school. Ask them to identify the featured guest, the date, and the location. Brainstorm at least ten risks associated with the concert, of which three should be financial.

INPUT

- Ask a student to read each of the five risk assessments and the accompanying internal control.

Risk Assessment of Voucher Processing

Castillo identified five key controls in this portion of its voucher processing system. The flowchart shows the location of key internal controls designed to protect the business against the risk of errors or fraud.

Control Symbol	Risk Assessment	Internal Control
1	Receiving Department employees need to make an accurate count of goods received. If the employees know the number ordered, they may simply check off that the goods are received without counting them.	The purchase order copy sent to the Receiving Department does not contain the quantity of goods ordered. Receiving Department employees are forced to count the items received.
2	The company could pay for an item it does not need, did not order, or did not receive.	The requisition (not shown on this flowchart) supports the need for the item. The purchase order supports that the company authorized its purchase. The receiving report documents that the items were received.
3	Checks could be issued for unauthorized purchases of goods and services. A check could be prepared for an amount or a vendor different from the information in the voucher.	The check signer reviews the accuracy of the voucher and compares this information to the check. The check signer is responsible for having an adequate knowledge of the business to recognize and question any unusual purchases or vendors.
4	Any employee involved in the preparation of any voucher document could submit a false document. Employees could request the purchase of unnecessary goods and services or purchase goods and services from a favored vendor.	Checks are not returned to any employee or department responsible for the preparation of the voucher. Checks are sent directly from the check signer to the vendor.
5	A document could be used to support multiple payments of a voucher.	The check signer cancels every document in the voucher before it is returned to Accounts Payable for filing. If the document was submitted to support another cash payment, the check signer should see the cancelled document when the vouchers are approved.

FORMATIVE ASSESSMENT

- This is an ongoing process. Circulate around the classroom or lab, observing which students have difficulty with the assignments.
- Troubleshooting: Diagnose the kinds of problems students have with this lesson. Students may have difficulty remembering the correct purpose of the symbols used in flowcharting.
- Assess student understanding by checking solutions to Independent Practice assignments and noting their answers to the Terms Review and Audit Your Understanding questions.

End of Lesson Review

LO7 Describe key controls of a voucher system.

Audit your understanding

1. Who prepares a requisition?
2. What happens to a check after it is signed by the check signer?
3. How does a business ensure that the Receiving Department counts the items received?
4. How does a business ensure that voucher documents are only used once to support a cash payment?

Work together 20-4

Performing a risk assessment

Perform a risk assessment of Glaston Company's voucher processing system. A portion of a flowchart documenting the system and a form are provided in the *Working Papers*. Use the control symbols on the form to mark the flowchart location of three significant risks. In the Internal Control column, describe how the system should be changed to prevent or detect errors or frauds. Your instructor will guide you through completing this problem.

On your own 20-4

Performing a risk assessment

Perform a risk assessment of Lamier Company's voucher processing system. A portion of a flowchart documenting the system and a form are provided in the *Working Papers*. Use the control symbols on the form to mark the flowchart location of four significant risks. In the Internal Control column, describe how the system should be changed to prevent or detect errors or frauds. Work this problem independently.

CHECK FOR UNDERSTANDING

Terms Review

- Call on students to define each term in the Terms Review. Definitions are given in the Glossary.

Audit Your Understanding

- Call on students to answer the Audit Your Understanding questions. Answers are given in Appendix D.

GUIDED PRACTICE

Work Together

- Have students write the solution to the Work Together problem as you guide the class through the examples.
- Direct students to perform a risk assessment.

INDEPENDENT PRACTICE

On Your Own

- Assign the On Your Own problem to be worked independently.
- Use the Formative Assessment techniques to diagnose student understanding.

Application Problem

- Assign Application Problem 20-4.

Online Working Papers

- Students can access the Lesson 20-4 problems using this software.

RETEACH

- Ask students to describe the symbols used for illustrating processes in a flowchart.

CLOSURE

- Ask students to describe briefly the key controls in a voucher system.

Essential Question

- Describe key controls that could be put in place when taking a test. (*Answers might include the following: Only the exact number of tests needed would be duplicated; tests could be locked up until needed; tests could be numbered and students assigned to a test number; two versions of the test could be provided, with students receiving alternating odd/even test numbers.*)

A Look at Accounting Software

To give students deeper insight into the type of control provided by assigning access privileges, ask each student to assign profiles to the user classifications mentioned in Step 3. Then conduct a class discussion in which students explain and defend the assignments they made for each position. There are no right or wrong choices in this exercise, but some would be better than others from a control perspective.

A discussion on the topic of passwords would also be of value. For example:

Why are longer passwords safer?

ANS: Each additional character greatly decreases the likelihood of a successful guess.

Why would capitalizing alphabetic characters within a word increase security?

ANS: Using capitals increases the number of guesses for each space in the password from 26 to 52 alphabetic characters.

Why is a mixture of alphabetic and numeric characters better than only alphabetic characters?

ANS: Combining the 10 numeric characters (0–9) with the 26 alphabetic characters increases the number of guesses for each space in the password to 36. Using capitalized alphabetic characters, the total is 62. The number can be further increased by adding symbols (e.g., * @ # &).

It is important to choose words that would only be familiar to the user. What are some strategies for selecting passwords?

ANS: Pet names, family names, hobbies, sports or entertainment figures, game characters, important dates, and geographic locations.

For Dabne Coulter, an easy password might be CoulterD. However, cou1t3r* would be better, and h@rr1sOn (Dabne's mother's maiden name) would be better still.

A Look at Accounting Software

Setting User Access Privileges

The principles you learned in this chapter related to internal controls are as important in a company using a computerized accounting system as in a manual accounting environment. To provide for internal control, automated accounting systems are designed to limit each user to specific types of access to the system. Defining and setting user access privileges are control activities. These settings determine which windows and reports users can open on their computers.

It is very important to understand that these system controls are only as good as the overall control system. For example, an employee might seek out a computer where another user with greater access privileges is logged in. That employee could then access and control the system in ways not allowed with his or her own login. Therefore, additional control measures need to be implemented and enforced.

Users who are logged on to the system might be required to put their computers in sleep mode if they will be out of sight of their computer for more than a few minutes. Sleep mode leaves the computer running but requires the user to log back in. Of course, if the employee had learned the password of the other user, the computer could still be accessed. Another control measure, then, would be to require that passwords be changed periodically.

Controlling user access to any automated system is a function of the system administrator. Generally, only a few highly trusted individuals are made system administrators, since they require complete access to the system. Administrators of a company's computerized accounting system would usually be under the direction of the chief financial officer, vice president of operations, or information systems director.

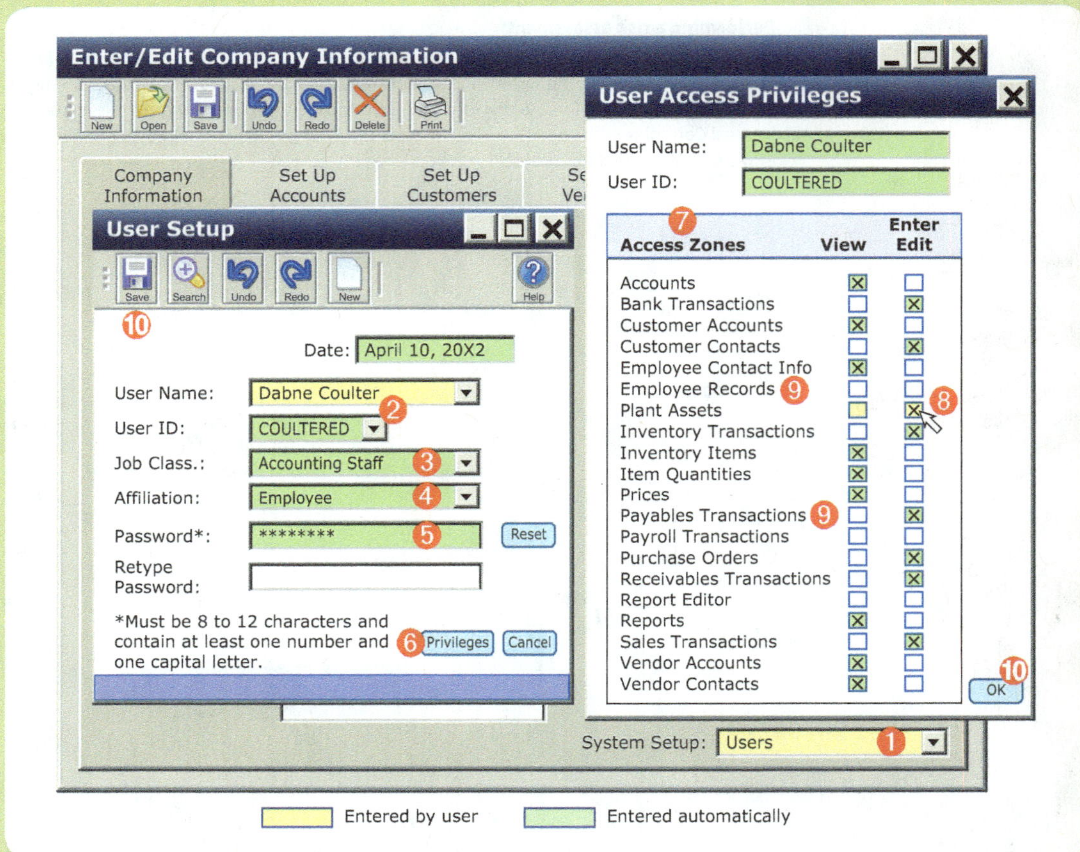

1. The system administrator has accessed the Company Information tab on the Enter/Edit Company Information window and selected **Users** in the System Setup field.
2. Information describing the user of an automated system is commonly called the **user profile.** The administrator has selected Dabne Coulter's user profile for editing. The User ID is an important feature for system control. Whenever users log on to the system, their User ID and the system date are attached to every entry they make. This feature makes it possible to hold users accountable for their entries and changes.
3. One part of the system control process is establishing user classifications and setting default access privileges for each class. Some classifications that might be listed would be Administrator, Accounting Manager, Executive Assistant—Sales, Sales Representative, Warehouse Manager, etc. These classifications define a user's level of authority and the type of access required to perform the user's job. Dabne Coulter's classification is Accounting Staff.
4. Not all users will be company employees. Outside users might include the company's CPA firm and external technical support staff. The Affiliation field identifies the user as an employee or an outside resource.
5. All users must enter a valid password to access the system. Longer passwords and those containing a variety of character types (alphabet, numbers, and symbols) increase the level of security because they make it more difficult for an unauthorized individual to guess the password. It is a common requirement that users change their passwords periodically. Occasionally, a user will forget a password or discover that it is no longer a secret. In that case, the administrator can reset the password.
6. The administrator clicked on the **Privileges** button to edit Dabne's access privileges. The system opened the User Access Privileges dialog box where privileges are set. The default profile for the Accounting Staff classification is displayed by the system. Users may be limited to only viewing certain types of information, they may be given the privilege of entering or editing data, or they may be prevented from accessing certain types of information.
7. When this system was originally set up, zones of access were established. Different types of data fields were linked to these zone labels. Access controls enable the system to limit the types of information users can view, enter, or change.
8. The administrator clicked on the second **check box** next to Plant Assets to change Dabne's access privilege from View to Enter Edit.
9. Note that neither check box for Employee Records or Payroll Transactions has been checked. Since Dabne has no payroll responsibilities, he should not have any access to employee records.
10. The administrator would click **OK** to close the dialog box and then click **Save** on the User Setup menu bar to keep the change.

CLOSURE

- Review the Chapter Summary.
- Ask students to prepare a list of the new concepts introduced in this chapter.

Essential Questions

- Why would internal controls be important in a computerized accounting system? (*A computerized accounting system often leaves more room for fraud, because transactions can easily be deleted or new ones created without having a paper trail or handwriting to compare.*)
- How are internal controls important in achieving goals? (*Internal controls are put in place to keep the business on track toward achieving profitability goals and the company mission.*)
- Why should small businesses care about internal controls? (*Any size business should be concerned about internal controls, as they are in place to protect the company assets and ensure accuracy in reporting.*)

EXTENDED LEARNING

- Review A Look at Accounting Software on pages 612 and 613.
- Assign Explore Accounting on page 614.

EXPLORE ACCOUNTING

Answers

Answers will vary depending on students' job and volunteer experience. For students who may be unable to identify a control activity, suggest they consider the control activities related to ticket sales at a school athletic (or artistic) event. Most schools segregate the duties of selling tickets and collecting them at the gate. Volunteer 1 sells prenumbered tickets. The fan must give the ticket to volunteer 2 at the gate. Volunteer 3 reconciles the money collected with the number of tickets sold. Several frauds can occur if two or more of the volunteers decide to collude.

1. Volunteer 1 can sell a limited number of fake tickets. Volunteer 2 would collude by not questioning fans presenting the fake tickets at the gate. The volunteers would pocket the proceeds from these ticket sales.
2. Volunteer 2 could take collected tickets and give them to volunteer 1 to be resold. The proceeds from the sales of these tickets would be pocketed by the two volunteers.
3. Volunteer 1 could take some of the ticket sale money. Volunteer 3 would overlook the theft and sign off that the correct amount of money was collected. The volunteers would split the stolen money.

Chapter Summary

Internal controls are a collection of procedures designed to reduce the risk of errors and fraud. An error is an unintentional mistake. In contrast, a fraud is the theft of assets or the intentional misstatement of financial statements.

Frauds during the early 1980s led to the creation of the Committee of Sponsoring Organizations (COSO) to study the factors that lead to fraudulent financial reporting. The result was an expanded view of the accounting profession's perception of internal controls. The internal control structure consists of the control environment, risk assessment, control activities, information and communication, and monitoring. Accountants use the internal control structure to guide their assessment of whether an accounting system is subject to error or fraud. One of the most basic internal controls is the segregation of the authority, custody, and recording functions of a transaction.

The frauds that caused the failures of Enron and WorldCom forced Congress to enact the Sarbanes-Oxley Act of 2002 (SOX). SOX created the Public Company Accounting Oversight Board (PCAOB) with the power to set auditing standards. SOX requires publicly held corporations to document their accounting systems and related internal controls.

Narratives and flowcharts are two common methods of documenting accounting systems. A flowchart is a collection of symbols and connecting lines that diagram the documents and the flow of information in an accounting system. A flowchart enables accountants to assess the risk that an error or fraud could occur.

A voucher system is an example of an accounting system with numerous control activities. A voucher is a group of documents that support a transaction. Approved vouchers are entered in a voucher register. When the assigned time to pay the voucher arrives, the documents are used to support the writing of a check. The check is recorded in a check register. Control activities help ensure that the business only pays authentic vendors for those items ordered and received.

EXPLORE ACCOUNTING Preventive and Detective Control Activities

© iStockphoto.com/Makhnach_M

Control activities are often classified as preventive, detective, and corrective. A preventive control prevents an error or fraud from occurring. A computer system that prevents an accounts receivable clerk from entering a sale is a preventive control. The system does not allow the clerk to access the window required to enter the sale. A detective control detects an error or fraud after it has occurred. A bank reconciliation is a detective control. A check incorrectly recorded in a cash payments journal or a check register should be detected by a bank reconciliation. A corrective control enables the business to correct the damage caused by an error or fraud. Insurance is the most common type of corrective control. Insurance covering key employees can reimburse a business for stolen assets.

Effective internal controls are designed to provide reasonable, but not absolute, assurance that errors and frauds are prevented or detected on a timely basis. There are many reasons why a well-designed control activity can fail. Most of the reasons involve people. Many control activities rely on one employee checking the work of another employee. For example, a payroll clerk totals the overtime hours reported on a time card. A manager performs the same process to ensure the amount of overtime hours is accurate. If the payroll clerk makes an error, the possibility exists that the manager will fail to detect the error. This chance increases if the manager is busy or not dedicated to performing control activities.

Suppose a salesclerk can only obtain sold merchandise by presenting a warehouse employee with a sales ticket. The sales ticket proves that the sale was recorded in the point-of-sale system. However, if the employees work together to commit a fraud, the control activity no longer exists. If the salesclerk can obtain merchandise without a sales ticket, the clerk and the warehouse employee can steal merchandise without being detected.

Two or more employees working together to commit a fraud is referred to as *collusion*. Most control activities are designed assuming that employees perform their assigned control activities. Knowing that collusion can occur, accountants must continually monitor the accounting systems to look for signs of fraudulent activities.

INSTRUCTIONS

Write a paragraph explaining a control activity that you have observed. Consider tasks you observed on a job or as a volunteer for a school or civic event. Describe how two individuals could collude to commit a fraud.

Apply Your Understanding

INSTRUCTIONS: Download problem instructions for Excel, QuickBooks, and Sage 50 from the textbook companion website at www.C21accounting.com.

20-1 Application Problem: Classify internal controls LO2, 3

Use the forms provided in the *Working Papers*.

Instructions:

1. For each item, indicate the component of the internal control structure: control environment, risk assessment, control activities, information and communication, or monitoring.
2. For each item, indicate whether the action is authority, custody, or recording function.

20-2 Application Problem: Preparing flowcharts LO4

Use the form provided in the *Working Papers*.

Instructions:

For each statement, prepare a flowchart to represent the process described.

a. A human resource manager approves an employee's vacation request form.

b. An employee journalizes a credit memorandum in the general ledger.

c. A warehouse employee records the quantity of items on a picking ticket and sends the form to the Shipping Department employee who compares the picking ticket with the number of items received from the warehouse.

d. A receptionist opens the mail and prepares a list of checks received. The list of checks is sent to an accounting clerk, who posts the total in a cash receipts journal.

20-3 Application Problem: Journalizing transactions in a voucher system LO5, 6

Sage 50 Accounting

1. Journalize and post transactions related to a voucher system to the general journal.
2. Journalize and post transactions related to a voucher system in the Write Checks window.
3. Print the general journal, cash disbursements journal, and the trial balance.

QB

1. Journalize and post transactions related to a voucher system to the journal.
2. Journalize and post transactions related to a voucher system in the Write Checks window.
3. Print the journal, check detail, and trial balance.

X

1. Journalize and post transactions related to a voucher system in the general journal.
2. Journalize and post transactions related to a voucher system in the cash payments journal.
3. Print the worksheets.

The following transactions of Marlon's Ceramics were completed during June of the current year. A voucher register and cash register are provided in the *Working Papers*. Source documents are abbreviated as follows: voucher, V; check, C.

Transactions:

June	4.	Paid cash to Baker Company, $3,670.00, covering V206. C234.
	6.	Purchased merchandise on account from Marsh Industries, $1,635.00. V208.
	10.	Received an invoice from Lynch Catering for a miscellaneous expense, $265.00. V209.
	11.	Paid cash to Marsh Industries, $1,635.00, less 2% discount, covering V208. C235.
	14.	Made a deposit in the checking account, $3,844.75.
	18.	Bought sales supplies on account from B&L Supplies, $450.00. V210.
	22.	Purchased merchandise on account from Abram Corp., $995.75. V211.
	26.	Paid cash to B&L Supplies, $450.00, less 2% discount, covering V210. C236.

Instructions:

1. Record the bank balance brought forward on June 1, $10,618.60.
2. Journalize the transactions completed during June of the current year. Use page 6 of a voucher register and page 9 of a check register.
3. Prove and rule the voucher register.
4. Prove and rule the check register.

CHECK FIGURES

For complete solutions to Chapter 20 problems, see the Teacher's Edition of the Working Papers.

Application Problem 20-1

1. Item 2, control activities.
   Item 4, control environment.
   Item 6, risk assessment.
   Item 8, monitoring.
2. Item 1, custody.
   Item 2, recording.
   Item 3, authority.
   Item 4, recording.

Application Problem 20-2

a. Three symbols: document, process, document.

b. Three symbols: document, process, accounting record.

c. Warehouse employee column: document, process; shipping department column: document, process.

Application Problem 20-3

Voucher register, Vouchers Payable Credit column total, $3,345.75.

Check register, Vouchers Payable Debit column total, $5,755.00.

Application Problem 20-4

Control symbol 1, risk assessment: The receiving report and purchase order are not forwarded to the Treasury Department. The check signer is not able to compare these documents to the vendor invoice.

Control symbol 2, risk assessment: Neither the treasury clerk nor the check signer perform any verification of the vendor invoice. No other department or individual is checking the work of the Accounts Payable Department.

Mastery Problem 20-M

Control symbol 1, risk assessment: The store manager does not send any order information to the bookkeeper. Thus, the bookkeeper has no information to verify the accuracy of the unit prices used on the vendor invoice.

Control symbol 2, risk assessment: The quantity of items reportedly shipped by the vendor appears on the vendor invoice. Store employees may be less motivated to make an authentic count of the items received.

Voucher register, Vouchers Payable Credit column total, $6,365.00.

Check register, Vouchers Payable Debit column total, $7,569.00.

INDEPENDENT PRACTICE

- Assign Mastery Problem 20-M for students as a culminating problem combining all new learning from the chapter.
- Assign Challenge Problem 20-C to accelerated students who work at a faster pace.
- Assign Study Guide 20.
- Students can access Online Working Papers to work end-of-chapter problems on the computer.
- Direct students to the C21 Accounting companion website for additional practice and review opportunities.

FORMATIVE ASSESSMENT

- Review solutions to the assigned problems in class, diagnosing trouble spots.

RETEACH

- Call on students to describe how they avoid the trouble spots diagnosed.
- Use reteaching suggestions from lesson plans as required.
- Assign Recycling Problem 20-R if needed.

20-4 Application Problem: Performing a risk assessment LO7

A portion of a flowchart documenting Quitman Company's voucher processing system and a form are provided in the *Working Papers*.

Instructions:

Perform a risk assessment of Quitman's voucher processing system. Use the control symbols on the form to mark the flowchart location of four significant risks. In the Internal Control column, describe how the system should be changed to prevent or detect errors or frauds.

20-M Mastery Problem: Analyzing a voucher system and journalizing transactions in a voucher system LO4, 5, 6, 7

Sage 50 Accounting

1. Journalize and post transactions related to a voucher system to the general journal.
2. Journalize and post transactions related to a voucher system in the Write Checks window.
3. Print the general journal, cash disbursements journal, and the trial balance.

QuickBooks

1. Journalize and post transactions related to a voucher system to the journal.
2. Journalize and post transactions related to a voucher system in the Write Checks window.
3. Print the journal, check detail and trial balance.

Excel

1. Journalize and post transactions related to a voucher system in the general journal.
2. Journalize and post transactions related to a voucher system in the cash payments journal.
3. Print the worksheets.

Avery Company is a small business that cannot employ the number of individuals required to separate adequately the duties in voucher processing. Its voucher processing is described in the following narrative.

Marcus Garran, store manager, is responsible for ordering the items required to maintain the store's merchandise inventory. He uses distributor websites to place the orders. When the merchandise arrives at the store, any available store employee is asked to receive the shipment. The employee compares the quantity of items received with the invoice included in the shipment and notes any differences. The goods are sent to the store floor and the invoice is sent to Patti Schmidt, the bookkeeper. She places the invoice in an Unpaid Invoices folder by the date the check should be written.

Each morning, Ms. Schmidt removes the invoices to be paid that day. She prepares a check for each invoice, attaches the check to the invoice, and records the checks in a cash payments journal. The documents are forwarded to Daniel Avery, the owner, for signing. He inspects the documents, signs the checks, and mails the checks to the vendors. A copy of the check is stapled to the invoice. The documents are returned to Ms. Schmidt for filing by vendor in the Paid Invoices file.

Instructions:

1. Prepare a flowchart of Avery Company's voucher system. Use a triangle ∇ to represent the Unpaid Invoices and Paid Invoices folders.
2. Identify four risks in the system. Complete the Risk Assessment and Internal Control columns of the form provided in the *Working Papers*. Use the control symbols on the form to mark the flowchart location of the risks.
3. Journalize the following transactions completed during August of the current year. Use page 8 of a voucher register and page 12 of a check register provided in the *Working Papers*.

Transactions:

Aug.	2.	Paid cash to O'Leary Company, $1,689.00, covering V613, no discount. C704.
	3.	Made a deposit in the checking account, $4,185.66.
	4.	Received an invoice from Kellogg Marketing for advertising, $3,500.00. V622.
	9.	Purchased merchandise on account from NTY Industries, $2,380.00. V623.
	12.	Paid cash to Kellogg Marketing, $3,500.00, less 2% discount, covering V622. C705.
	16.	Bought administrative supplies on account from Lakeland Supply, $485.00. V624.
	18.	Paid cash to NTY Industries, $2,380.00, less 1% discount, covering V623. C706.

4. Prove and rule the voucher register.
5. Prove and rule the check register.

COMMON CORE AND INTERDISCIPLINARY STUDIES

Extended learning features and activities present numerous opportunities to implement Common Core Standards through interdisciplinary studies. Practice is provided in the common core areas of English Language Arts & Literacy and Mathematical Practice. Many of these activities require short, critical-thinking and decision-making responses that apply reading, writing, speaking, listening, language, media and technology, and mathematical skills.

20-C Challenge Problem: Completing a flowchart LO4, 7

The Certified Public Accountant examination often requires candidates to complete a flowchart. The flowchart is complete with the exception of selected symbol descriptions. Candidates must use their knowledge of the accounting systems and flowchart symbols to describe the symbols. Candidates must also be able to assign a meaning to an unfamiliar symbol by understanding how that symbol is used elsewhere in the flowchart.

A flowchart for a portion of Velcar Corporation's sales processing system is shown below. Velcar uses a computerized accounting system.

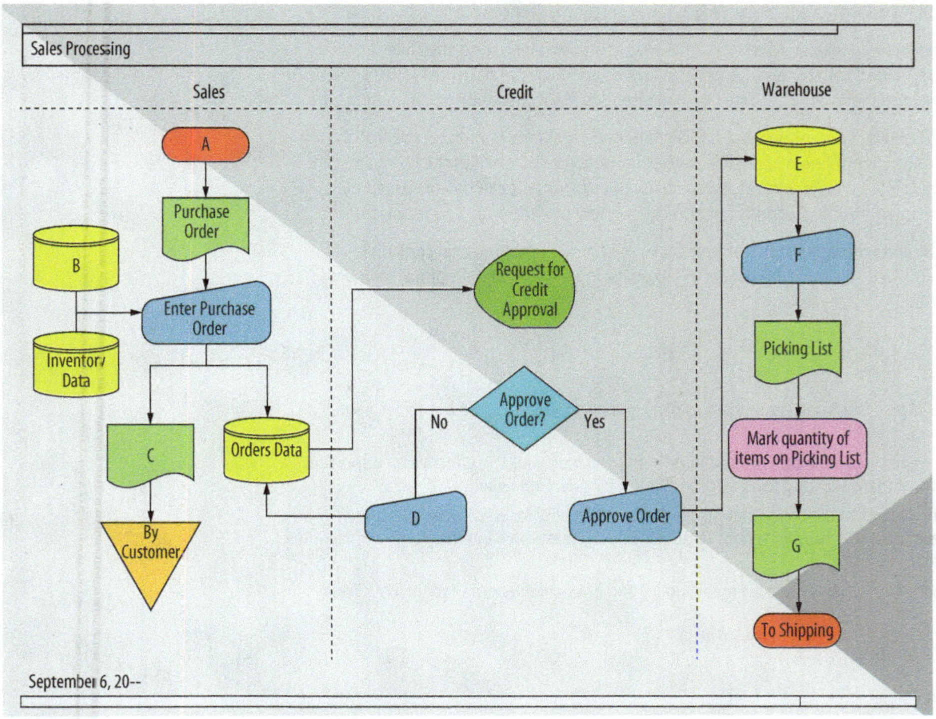

Instructions:

Complete the form provided in the *Working Papers*. The first item is completed as an example.

Symbol	Description
A	From customer

Challenge Problem 20-C

B, customer data.

D, cancel order.

F, print picking list.

EXTENDED LEARNING

- Assign 21st Century Skills on page 618.
- Assign Analyzing Home Depot's Financial Statements on page 619.

SUMMATIVE EVALUATION

- Chapter 20 Test
- Cognero for Chapter 20

21ST CENTURY SKILLS

Answers

1. a. Answers will vary.
   b. Internal control procedures might include password protection; training; and do's and don'ts for posting pictures, comments, blogs, and videos.
2. Both implement internal controls to minimize risk to the business.

21st Century Skills

Controls for Social Media

PARTNERSHIP FOR 21ST CENTURY SKILLS

Theme: Financial, Economic, Business, and Entrepreneurial Literacy

Skills: Creativity and Innovation, Critical Thinking and Problem Solving, Communication and Collaboration

Facebook has over 470 million users; Twitter, 74 million; and MySpace, 120 million. It comes as no surprise that social media is presenting new opportunities for conducting business.

Corporate blogs, fan pages on Facebook, and image- and video-sharing sites like Flickr and YouTube have helped companies find new customers and increase customer loyalty. These trends are also forcing internal auditors to evaluate risks associated with social media.

A lack of control over content poses a risk. Deciphering what information can be distributed to the public and identifying responsible parties for posting on behalf of the company can minimize the risk. Data leaks, viruses, and unfavorable comments can be consumed by millions of recipients within seconds and affect company performance and reputation.

Businesses should embrace the benefits of social media. However, internal controls must be established so employees know the expectation and the impact of not following procedures.

APPLICATION

1. Player's Choice, a new sporting goods company, has decided to jump on the social media bandwagon.
   a. Determine three examples of social media that you feel would be effective for a sporting goods company wanting to advertise products for sale. Explain why.
   b. Create a social media policy that focuses on user behavior for employees using (1) Facebook, (2) YouTube, and (3) Twitter. Include at least three internal control procedures for each.
2. Compare the similarities of a social media policy and a voucher system used for a business.

Analyzing Home Depot's financial statements

The financial statement frauds at Enron and WorldCom involved corporate officers at the highest levels. In response, Congress passed the Sarbanes-Oxley Act of 2002 in an effort to reduce the possibility of similar financial disasters. This act holds corporate officers more accountable for the accuracy of their corporation's financial statements. The new rules require select corporate officers to take personal responsibility for the accuracy of the financial statements.

INSTRUCTIONS

Refer to page B-3 in Appendix B to answer the following questions:

1. Who is responsible for the preparation of Home Depot's financial statements?
2. What three organizations have a role in the independent audit of Home Depot's financial statements?
3. Who is responsible for ensuring that the corporation has an adequate system of internal controls?
4. Which corporate officers are specifically mentioned as being involved in the corporation's evaluation of its internal control and signing the report?

ANALYZING HOME DEPOT'S FINANCIAL STATEMENTS

Answers

1. Management.
2. Audit Committee of the Board of Directors, the public accounting firm, and the internal auditors. The Audit Committee of the Board of Directors retains the independent registered public accounting firm, KPMG LLP, and reviews the activities of the independent registered public accounting firm and the internal auditors.
3. Management is responsible for establishing and maintaining adequate internal control over financial reporting.
4. Chief executive officer and chief financial officer.

Chapter 21

Organizational Structure of a Partnership

Scope & Sequence

	New	Review/Enrich
Introduction		
Introduce the Chapter		
Lesson 21-1: Forming a Partnership		
Organizing a Partnership		✓
Partnership Capital Accounts		✓
Partners' Initial Investments		✓
Journal Entries to Record Partners' Initial Investments		✓
Lesson 21-2: Admitting Partners to Existing Partnerships		
Admitting a Partner with No Change in Total Equity	✓	
Admitting a Partner with Equity Equal to New Partner's Investment	✓	
Admitting a Partner with Equity Greater than New Partner's Investment	✓	
Admitting a Partner When Goodwill Is Recognized	✓	
Equity Accounts after Goodwill Is Recognized	✓	
Closure		

Enhancing Instruction

Features	Common Core Standards
• Accounting in the Real World: PricewaterhouseCoopers, LLP	• ELAL—reading
• Ethics in Action: Serving as an Expert Witness • Global Awareness: Currency Manipulation • Think Like an Accountant: Improving Efficiency with Templates	• ELAL—reading • ELAL—reading, media and technology, writing • Mathematics
• Why Accounting?: Changing Services to Match the Times • Forensic Accounting: Improper Revenue Recognition	• ELAL—listening, speaking • Mathematics
• Explore Accounting • 21st Century Skills • Auditing for Errors • Analyzing Home Depot's Financial Statements	• ELAL—reading • ELAL—reading, writing • ELAL—reading, writing • Mathematics

ELAL = English Language Arts & Literacy

Calculator: © iStockphoto.com/picstodisc; Paper: © iStockphoto.com/Qingwa

Technology & Media	Teaching Strategies	Practice and Assessment: Guided Practice	Independent Practice	Reteach/Enrich
• Instructor's Resource CD/Website: PowerPoint Slides Accounting Concepts • Online Working Papers • Transparency Master: Cash Receipts Journal	• Visual/Spatial Learners	• Terms Review • Audit Your Understanding • Work Together 21-1	• On Your Own 21-1 • Application Problem 21-1 • Formative Assessment, p. 628 • Online Working Papers	• Reteach, p. 629
• Instructor's Resource CD/Website: PowerPoint Slides Accounting Concepts • Online Working Papers • Transparency Masters: Cash Receipts Journal, General Journal	• Verbal/Linguistic Learners	• Terms Review • Audit Your Understanding • Work Together 21-2	• On Your Own 21-2 • Application Problem 21-2 • Formative Assessment, p. 635 • Online Working Papers	• Reteach, p. 636
• Online Working Papers			• Mastery Problem 21-M • Study Guide 21 • Chapter 21 Test • Cognero Chapter 21	• Challenge Problem 21-C • Reteach, p. 640 • Recycling Problem 21-R

Introduce the Chapter

SET THE STAGE

GUIDING QUESTIONS

- Ask students to explain some of the reasons a business forms a partnership.
- Ask students how a partnership differs from a corporation.
- Ask students to identify businesses where the name of the partner may have helped the business gain public recognition.
- Ask students why an existing partnership might admit someone as a partner with equity greater than his or her investment.
- Ask students to predict how a business might increase its value other than by a new partner's investment.

PREVIEW CHAPTER OBJECTIVES

- Explain that most transactions for a partnership are similar to those for a corporation.
- Instruct a student to read each chapter objective aloud.

PREVIEW ACCOUNTING TERMS

- Read each term aloud to verify its pronunciation for students.
- Point out terms or parts of terms that should already be familiar to most students, such as *partnership agreement*, *balance sheet*, and *goodwill*.

Chapter 21 Organizational Structure of a Partnership

LEARNING OBJECTIVES

After studying Chapter 21, in addition to defining key terms, you will be able to:

LO1 Explain the organizational structure of a partnership.

LO2 Journalize transactions related to the formation of a partnership.

LO3 Journalize transactions to admit a new partner to an existing partnership.

Calculator: © iStockphoto.com/pickstodisc; Paper: © iStockphoto.com/Qingwa

© Pressmaster/Shutterstock.com

Accounting In The Real World

PricewaterhouseCoopers, LLP

PricewaterhouseCoopers (PwC) is one of the largest public accounting firms in the world. Like many public accounting firms, PwC earns a significant portion of its revenue by performing financial statement audits. Other services include preparing client tax returns, assisting clients with tax planning, and providing a wide range of business consulting services.

An accountant who conducts an audit is known as an auditor. A single auditor is capable of auditing a small business. However, a team of auditors is needed to audit larger businesses. These will have different levels of experience.

Public accounting firms tend to have very structured methods for promoting their professional staff. The method used by many accounting firms is described here. New college accounting graduates begin their careers as staff auditors. After three years of experience, staff auditors are promoted to senior auditors. Staff and senior auditors perform the majority of the procedures involved in an audit. Audit seniors are also responsible for supervising the staff auditors.

After the sixth year, an auditor is promoted to manager. Managers have primary responsibility for the audit and approve the work of the staff and senior auditors. Managers must possess a high level of competence in generally accepted accounting principles and auditing standards. To be promoted to partner, managers must also demonstrate the ability to recruit new clients. After 12 years of working with the firm, auditors may be admitted as partners in the firm.

Partners are responsible for the management of the firm and are ultimately responsible for the quality of all work performed by the accounting firm.

Only a very small percentage of individuals who begin their careers in public accounting ultimately become partners. Businesses recognize the skills developed by accountants in public accounting firms and actively recruit them for positions in their organizations. For this reason, most accountants leave public accounting for career opportunities in industry.

CRITICAL THINKING

1. What skills must a manager possess to be effective in recruiting new clients?
2. Why do you think a partnership is an attractive form of organization for a firm like PwC?

Background: © iStockphoto.com/TheOman; Real World: © Jeffrey Blackler/Alamy

Key Terms

- partnership agreement
- mutual agency
- fair market value balance sheet
- goodwill
- intangible asset

Accounting In The Real World

Answers

1. Answers will vary. Managers must have good communication skills. Managers must be able to listen to and appreciate the needs of potential clients. Managers must be able to articulate how the accounting firm will provide its services and bring value to potential clients by performing their audits. Without degrading the professional image of other accounting firms, managers must be able to support the reasons their accounting firm should be selected.
2. (a) Income of a partnership is reported on an individual partner's tax return and taxed accordingly. (b) Partners have limited liability for the actions of other partners, similar to the stockholders of a corporation. In a normal partnership, partners have unlimited liability, making them personally responsible for the partnership's debts.

INPUT

- Explain that Lamor Learning Center is a partnership that provides tutoring services to students.
- Direct students to the chart of accounts used by Lamor Learning Center. Remind students that they will reference these accounts for the next two chapters.

THE BUSINESS—

LAMOR LEARNING CENTER

Lamor Learning Center is a service business organized as a partnership. The business provides tutoring services to students of all ages and specializes in preparing candidates to excel on standardized tests.

© Goodluz/Shutterstock.com

Chart of Accounts

LAMOR LEARNING CENTER

Balance Sheet Accounts

(1000) ASSETS
- 1100 Current Assets
- 1105 Cash
- 1110 Petty Cash
- 1115 Accounts Receivable
- 1120 Allowance for Uncollectible Accounts
- 1125 Supplies—Educational
- 1130 Supplies—Office
- 1135 Prepaid Insurance
- 1200 Plant Assets
- 1205 Equipment
- 1210 Accumulated Depreciation—Equipment
- 1215 Car
- 1220 Accumulated Depreciation—Car

(2000) LIABILITIES
- 2100 Current Liabilities
- 2105 Accounts Payable

(3000) OWNERS' EQUITY
- 3105 LaDonna Alford, Capital
- 3110 LaDonna Alford, Drawing
- 3115 Morgan Colvin, Capital
- 3120 Morgan Colvin, Drawing
- 3125 Income Summary

(4000) OPERATING REVENUE
- 4105 Sales

(5000) OPERATING EXPENSES
- 5105 Advertising Expense
- 5110 Depreciation Expense—Equipment
- 5115 Depreciation Expense—Car
- 5120 Insurance Expense
- 5125 Miscellaneous Expense
- 5130 Rent Expense
- 5135 Supplies Expense—Educational
- 5140 Supplies Expense—Office
- 5145 Truck Expense
- 5150 Uncollectible Accounts Expense
- 5155 Utilities Expense

The chart of accounts for Lamor Learning Center is illustrated above for reference as you study Chapters 21 and 22 of this textbook.

LESSON

21-1 Forming a Partnership

LO1 Explain the organizational structure of a partnership.
LO2 Journalize transactions related to the formation of a partnership.

Organizing a Partnership LO1

A business in which two or more persons combine their assets and skills is known as a *partnership*. Each member of a partnership is known as a *partner*. Partnerships generally have only a few owners (partners), unlike a corporation that typically has many owners (stockholders). The partners' ownership is recorded in equity accounts for each of the partners. In contrast, a corporation records all stockholders' ownership in a single account. Except for recording owners' equity and income taxes, accounting procedures for a partnership are similar to those for a corporation.

A partnership has a limited life, unlike a corporation, which has an unlimited life. Any change in the number of partners terminates an existing partnership. When a new partner is admitted, the partners sign a new partnership agreement. The old partnership's accounting records are often continued for the new partnership. As a result, initial investment journal entries for all partners are not always needed. Journal entries are needed, however, to show clearly how the partners' equity has changed. One or both of the following journal entries may be needed:

1. To show how much the new partner invests.
2. To show how the new partner's admission affects existing partners' capital accounts.

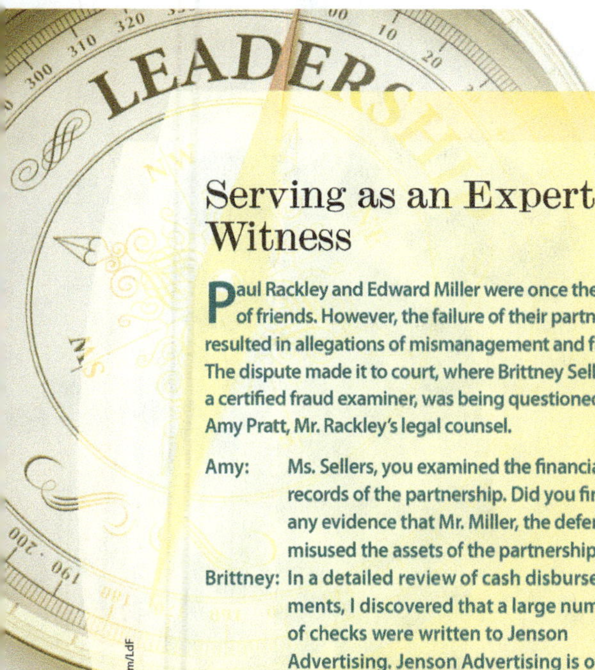

© iStockphoto.com/LdF

ETHICS IN ACTION

Serving as an Expert Witness

Paul Rackley and Edward Miller were once the best of friends. However, the failure of their partnership resulted in allegations of mismanagement and fraud. The dispute made it to court, where Brittney Sellers, a certified fraud examiner, was being questioned by Amy Pratt, Mr. Rackley's legal counsel.

Amy: Ms. Sellers, you examined the financial records of the partnership. Did you find any evidence that Mr. Miller, the defendant, misused the assets of the partnership?

Brittney: In a detailed review of cash disbursements, I discovered that a large number of checks were written to Jenson Advertising. Jenson Advertising is owned by Mr. Miller's sister, April Miller Jenson.

Amy: I assume these expenditures were for advertising?

Brittney: That was the purpose stated on the invoices. Specifically, the invoices were for Internet advertising on social media sites. However, I confirmed with those sites that no advertising contracts were ever signed with either the partnership or Jenson Advertising.

Amy: So you believe these checks were fraudulent?

Brittney: Jenson Advertising does not even maintain an office—only a post office box. This is a clear case of a shell company, a fictitious business set up for the sole purpose of committing a fraud.

Amy: Thank you, Ms. Sellers. No further questions.

INSTRUCTIONS

Access the *Code of Ethics* of the Association of Certified Fraud Examiners. Using this code as a guide, use the ethical model to help determine whether Brittney's testimony demonstrates ethical behavior.

LESSON

21-1

BRIDGE

- Review the accounting cycle that was presented for a corporation in Part 1. Point out the similarities and differences in accounting for a partnership and a corporation.
- Emphasize that the type of business—merchandising or service—is not attributable to the form of organization.

TEACHING RESOURCES

- **Instructor's Resource CD/Website:**
  PowerPoint Slides
  Accounting Concepts
- **Working Papers:**
  Teacher's Edition of the Working Papers for Lesson 21-1
  Online Working Papers
- **Transparency Master:**
  Cash Receipts Journal

ENGAGE

- Ask students to name some partnership businesses in the community.
- Ask students if they can identify any differences between the partnerships and corporations in their community.

PREVIEW

- Call on students to read the accounting terms and definitions introduced in this lesson: *partnership agreement, mutual agency,* and *fair market value balance sheet.*
- Point out the learning objectives for this lesson.
- Direct students to read the headings in this lesson and to examine the illustrations.

INPUT

- Point out the meaning of the limited life of a partnership.

ETHICS IN ACTION

Suggested Solution

1. Recognize that you are facing an ethical dilemma. Knowing that she is going to be questioned in court, Brittney should know about guidance in the *Code of Ethics.*
2. Identify the action. Brittney expressed an opinion based on her knowledge of the facts.
3. Analyze the action.

a. Is the action illegal? No. No law prohibits Brittney from expressing her opinion of facts presented in a court of law.

b. Does the action violate company or professional standards? Brittney's testimony violates the *Code of Ethics.* The code states, "No opinion shall be expressed regarding the guilt or innocence of any person or party." Her final sentence is a conclusion based on the evidence. Brittney should have limited her responses to the facts of her investigation.

INPUT

- Explain the purpose of a partnership agreement. Refer to the illustration on the following page.
- List and describe some of the stipulations that should be considered when preparing a partnership agreement.

TEACHING IDEA **Students can review a partnership agreement by obtaining a copy from a local business or by searching online.**

A partnership is created when two or more persons agree orally or in writing to start a business, using the partnership form of organization. As in other forms of business, a partnership's financial records are kept separate from those of the partners. [CONCEPT: Business Entity]

LaDonna Alford and Morgan Colvin agree to form a partnership called Lamor Learning Center. Prior to forming the partnership, Morgan owned a similar business and LaDonna was employed as a teacher.

Lamor Learning Center provides tutoring services and standardized test preparation classes. The business does not sell merchandise. For this reason, it does not need general ledger accounts for merchandise inventory, purchases, purchases discount, and purchases returns and allowances. Its clients cannot return a service and the business does not offer a sales discount. Thus, no sales returns and allowances or sales discount accounts are needed. The partners, who provide all the services to the clients, are not employees of the partnership. The Internal Revenue Service does not consider the money that partners receive from a partnership to be salaries. Therefore, until the growth of the business demands that it hire employees, the business does not need accounts for recording salaries and payroll taxes.

A written agreement setting forth the conditions under which a partnership is to operate is called a **partnership agreement**. A partnership agreement is also known as the *articles of partnership*. A partnership's life is limited to the length of time agreed on by the partners. A partnership is terminated by the partners' mutual agreement, death of a partner, withdrawal of one partner, or admission of a new partner.

Each partner can bind a partnership to any contract. The right of all partners to contract for a partnership is called **mutual agency**. Each partner is an agent of the partnership unless restricted by agreement.

Legally, a partnership agreement may be either written or oral. However, to avoid misunderstandings, a partnership agreement should be in writing. Some but not all states require that a partnership agreement be in writing. With an attorney's assistance, LaDonna and Morgan prepare their partnership agreement, shown on the next page.

INPUT

- Explain the meaning and importance of the term *mutual agency*. Emphasize the importance and impact this feature has to a partnership and its partners.
- Explain that the owners' equity division of a partnership's general ledger has two capital accounts for each partner.
- Explain that the two accounts are a capital account and a drawing account.
- Explain the purpose of each account.
- Explain how the accounts in the owners' equity section of a partnership differ from the accounts in the stockholders' equity section of a corporation.

Partnership Capital Accounts

The owners' equity division of a partnership's general ledger has two capital accounts for each partner.

1. An account in which to record a partner's equity includes the word *Capital* in the title. The two equity accounts in Lamor's general ledger are LaDonna Alford, Capital and Morgan Colvin, Capital.
2. An account in which the earnings taken out of the partnership during the fiscal period are recorded includes the word *Drawing* in the title. Assets taken out of a business for the owner's personal use are known as *withdrawals*. The two accounts in Lamor's general ledger used to record withdrawals are titled LaDonna Alford, Drawing and Morgan Colvin, Drawing.

Partners' withdrawals can be a cause of misunderstandings. For this reason, most partnership agreements include a statement controlling withdrawals. Lamor's partnership agreement has a controlling statement in Article VI of the partnership agreement.

© Alexander Image/Shutterstock.com

PARTNERSHIP AGREEMENT

THIS CONTRACT is made and entered into this 28th day of February 20--, by and between LaDonna Alford and Morgan Colvin of Plano, Texas.

WITNESSETH: That the said parties have this date formed a partnership to engage in and conduct a business under the following stipulations that are a part of this contract. The partnership will begin operation on March 1, 20--.

ARTICLE I: The business shall be conducted under the name of Lamor Learning Center, located initially at 1910 15th Street, Plano, TX 75023-5233.

ARTICLE II: The investment of each partner is: Morgan Colvin: Equity in a business located at 1910 15th Street, Plano, TX 75023-5233, and as shown in a fair market value balance sheet to be agreed upon by both partners prior to February 28, 20--. Total investment, $45,760.00. LaDonna Alford: Cash equal to the initial investment of Ms. Colvin. Total investment $22,800.00.

ARTICLE III: Both partners are to (a) participate in all general policy-making decisions, (b) devote full time and attention to the partnership business, and (c) engage in no other business enterprise without the written consent of the other partner. Ms. Colvin is to be general manager of the business's operations.

ARTICLE IV: Neither partner is to become a surety or bonding agent for anyone without the written consent of the other partner.

ARTICLE V: The partners' share in earnings and losses of the partnership are: Ms. Colvin: 5% interest on equity as of January 1 of each year; salary, $20,000.00 per year; remaining income or loss, 50%. Ms. Alford: 5% interest on equity as of January 1 of each year; salary, $15,000.00 per year; remaining income or loss, 50%.

ARTICLE VI: No partner is to withdraw assets in excess of the agreed-upon interest and salary without the other partner's written consent.

ARTICLE VII: All partnership transactions are to be recorded in accordance with standard and generally accepted accounting procedures and concepts. The partnership records are to be open at all times for inspection by either partner.

ARTICLE VIII: In case of either partner's death or legal disability, the equity of the partners is to be determined as of the time of the death or disability of the one partner. The continuing partner is to have first option to buy the deceased/disabled partner's equity at recorded book value.

ARTICLE IX: This partnership agreement is to continue indefinitely unless (a) terminated by the death of one partner, (b) terminated by giving the other partner written notice at least ninety (90) days prior to the termination date, or (c) terminated by written mutual agreement signed by both partners.

ARTICLE X: At the termination of this partnership agreement, the partnership's assets, after all liabilities are paid, will be distributed according to the balance in partners' capital accounts.

IN WITNESS WHEREOF, the parties to this contract have set their hands and seals on the date and year written.

Signed: *LaDonna Alford* (Seal) Date: February 28, 20--

Signed: *Morgan Colvin* (Seal) Date: February 28, 20--

DIFFERENTIATED INSTRUCTION

Visual/Spatial learners like to create mental images and learn by drawing. Ask students to draw a Venn diagram comparing and contrasting similarities of and differences between a partnership agreement they obtain and the example in the textbook.

GLOBAL AWARENESS

Answers

Answers will vary. At the time of publication, the WTO believes that its legal mandate on currency manipulation is questionable and therefore is calling on the countries involved (United States and China) to act rationally with regard to instituting tariffs.

GLOBAL AWARENESS

© iStockphoto.com/Lusky

Currency Manipulation

When the free market works correctly, foreign exchange rates can change almost daily. Many governments purchase or sell a currency on an exchange market with the intention of stabilizing the currency's exchange rate in the short run, which will help attract investors and free market trade. Usually, this action is not controversial.

In recent years, however, there has been some discussion about the ability of a government to manipulate foreign exchange rates to its country's advantage on a long-term basis. Currency manipulation, which is somewhat controversial, has been defined as:

> **"... when a government buys or sells foreign currency to push the exchange rate of its currency away from its equilibrium value or to prevent the exchange rate from moving toward its equilibrium value.[1]"**

Buying foreign currency tends to hold down the value of the domestic currency, which increases demand in the goods market as well as in the financial markets. This action has the opposite effect on the competing country's currency, which increases in value. In the long term, this action keeps the two currencies at those values artificially. The country whose currency is higher than it should be suffers from a deficit trade balance, which can cost that country jobs and hurt its economy.

The Articles of Agreement of the International Monetary Fund (IMF) prohibit the manipulation of currency values. However, the IMF has no procedures in place to stop or punish the country doing the manipulation. Also, it is difficult to prove the motive of a country that is buying foreign currency. Some think that the World Trade Organization (WTO) should respond to countries charged with currency manipulation. How can the United States counterbalance currency manipulation by other countries? One suggestion is to have Congress label the manipulation of currency as an illegal subsidy. Such action would allow duties to be placed on products shipped to the United States from that country. This would have the effect of increasing the price of those products, which would discourage their importation. This action is controversial, however, in that it could start a tariff war between the two countries.

CRITICAL THINKING

Search the Internet to find an article relating to the WTO and currency manipulation. Summarize any action taken by the WTO or proposed action rejected by this organization.

[1] "Combating Widespread Currency Manipulation," by Joseph E. Gagnon; Peterson Institute for International Economics, Policy Brief, Number PB12-19, July 2012. The equilibrium value of currency is the value at which the currency would remain without outside interference.

Partners' Initial Investments

Colvin Tutoring Center Fair Market Value Balance Sheet March 1, 20--			
ASSETS			
Current Assets:			
Cash		$18,268.40	
Accounts Receivable	$3,895.88		
Less Allowance for Uncollectible Accounts	120.00	3,775.88	
Supplies—Educational		4,380.00	
Supplies—Office		1,800.00	
Prepaid Insurance		235.00	
Total Current Assets			$28,459.28
Plant Assets:			
Equipment		$21,700.00	
Car		9,800.00	
Total Plant Assets			31,500.00
Total Assets			$59,959.28
LIABILITIES			
Accounts Payable			$14,199.28
OWNER'S EQUITY			
Morgan Colvin, Capital			45,760.00
Total Liabilities and Owner's Equity			$59,959.28

Morgan invests the assets of her existing business in the new partnership. According to Article II of the partnership agreement, she must provide financial information for her existing business.

Morgan's investment in the partnership includes cash and other assets, less liabilities, from her prior existing business. A balance sheet prepared in accordance with GAAP may not adequately report the value of the owner's contribution to the partnership. For example, although the book value of Morgan's car is $5,200.00, its market value is $9,800.00. She should be given credit for contributing $9,800.00 to the partnership.

A financial statement that presents the fair market value of a company's assets, liabilities, and owner's equity is called a **fair market value balance sheet**. The partners must agree on the current market value of the assets and liabilities being contributed. Some values, such as cash, accounts receivable, and accounts payable, are simple to verify with accounting records. Other values, such as inventory and plant assets, can be estimated using information available from independent sources. Finally, the partners must analyze available information and use judgment when agreeing on accounts, such as allowance for uncollectible accounts.

A copy of the fair market value balance sheet from Morgan's previous business, shown above, is attached to a receipt to provide needed details for the journal entry. [CONCEPT: Objective Evidence]

fyi The use of several individuals' names in the name of a business is often an indication of a partnership.

INPUT

- Explain that the initial investment to form a partnership may be cash or noncash assets.
- Note that the initial investment in the Lamor Learning Center partnership consists of the assets of Morgan Colvin's previous proprietorship business.
- Point out that a balance sheet prepared in accordance with GAAP may not reflect the fair market value of the owner's contribution.
- Direct students to the illustration and discuss the fair market value balance sheet.
- Remind students that there is no legal or accounting limit to the number of partners.

INPUT

- Explain that the journal entry consists of recording LaDonna Alford's cash investment and Morgan Colvin's assets from her previous proprietorship.
- Point out that liabilities and Allowance for Uncollectible Accounts are included.
- Explain that a separate journal entry is made for each partner's initial investment.
- Explain that the value of the noncash assets is recorded at a value agreed upon by the partners, not the book value of the assets in the previous business.
- Explain that each partner's capital account is credited for the net amount of the partner's initial investment to the partnership.

MODEL

- Draw T accounts on the board to analyze the transactions and record partners' initial investments.
- Use a transparency of a cash receipts journal to illustrate how to record partners' initial investments in a partnership.
- Direct students to the illustration as you describe each of the steps for recording partners' initial investments.

THINK LIKE AN ACCOUNTANT

Students download a template containing a sales invoice and make a variety of modifications. Encourage students to review the variety of templates available. Lead a classroom discussion on possible benefits and disadvantages to using a template versus creating an original worksheet.

Answers

1. Answers will vary.
2. Beginning with the line Net Income Before Taxes, the statement would have to be modified to reflect the fact that partnerships do not pay income taxes.

Journal Entries to Record Partners' Initial Investments LO2

Write Account Title | Debit Asset Amounts | Credit Liability and Owners' Equity Amounts | Debit Cash

CASH RECEIPTS JOURNAL — PAGE 1

	DATE		ACCOUNT TITLE	DOC. NO.	POST. REF.	GENERAL DEBIT (1)	GENERAL CREDIT (2)	ACCOUNTS RECEIVABLE CREDIT (3)	SALES CREDIT (4)	SALES TAX PAYABLE CREDIT (5)	SALES DISCOUNT DEBIT (6)	CASH DEBIT (7)	
1	20-- Mar.	1	LaDonna Alford, Capital	R1			22,880.00					22,880.00	1
2		1	Accounts Receivable	R2		3,895.88						18,268.40	2
3			Supplies—Educational			4,380.00							3
4			Supplies—Office			1,800.00							4
5			Prepaid Insurance			235.00							5
6			Equipment			21,700.00							6
7			Car			9,800.00							7
8			Allow. for Uncoll. Accounts				120.00						8
9			Accounts Payable				14,199.28						9
10			Morgan Colvin, Capital				45,760.00						10
11													11
12													12

The two partners agree on a value for all invested assets on the date the partnership begins, March 1. LaDonna's initial investment is cash of $22,880.00. Morgan's initial investment is $45,760.00, the agreed-upon value of her equity in her previous business, Colvin Tutoring Center.

A separate journal entry is made for each partner's initial investment as shown above.

March 1, 20--. Received cash from partner, LaDonna Alford, as an initial investment, $22,880.00. Receipt No. 1.

Cash is debited for $22,880.00. LaDonna Alford, Capital is credited for $22,880.00.

March 1, 20--. Accepted assets and liabilities of Morgan Colvin's existing business, Colvin Tutoring Center, as an initial investment, $45,760.00. Receipt No. 2.

All asset amounts on the balance sheet are debited. Allowance for Uncollectible Accounts and Accounts Payable are credited. Morgan Colvin, Capital is credited for the capital in her existing business, $45,760.00.

THINK LIKE AN ACCOUNTANT

Improving Efficiency with Templates

Sandra Evans and three of her close friends have started a small business that assists parents in planning and conducting birthday parties. Her friends are responsible for contacting potential clients and rendering the services. Sandra's responsibility is to handle the accounting duties.

The new partnership has very little capital and cannot afford to have custom source documents printed. Yet the partners want to present a professional image. Sandra has asked you to help her create these documents.

Excel contains templates for a wide variety of source documents that can be downloaded and modified. Use a template to create a sample invoice for Sandra's approval. Complete the invoice, using imaginary information about the company, the client, and the services provided.

OPEN THE SPREADSHEET TLA_CH21

The worksheet contains instructions for downloading a template containing a simple sales invoice. Follow the steps on the Instructions tab to modify the template. Answer these questions:

1. Select four other templates that Sandra might find useful in operating her new partnership. Draft an e-mail to Sandra that would explain why she should use each template.
2. Select the template "Income Statement" in the Records group. How would this income statement need to be modified to be used by a partnership?

© iStockphoto.com/Dan Bachman

FORMATIVE ASSESSMENT

- This is an ongoing process. Circulate around the classroom or lab, observing which students have difficulty with the assignments.
- Troubleshooting: Diagnose the kinds of problems students have with this section. Students may have trouble distinguishing the difference between partnership and corporation equities.
- Assess student understanding by checking solutions to Independent Practice assignments and noting their answers to the Terms Review and Audit Your Understanding questions.

End of Lesson Review

LO1 Explain the organizational structure of a partnership.

LO2 Journalize transactions related to the formation of a partnership.

Terms Review

partnership agreement

mutual agency

fair market value balance sheet

Audit your understanding

1. Why should a partnership agreement be in writing?
2. What happens to an existing partnership if a partner dies?
3. What does mutual agency mean?
4. Why is a balance sheet prepared in accordance with GAAP not appropriate to support a partner's contribution to a partnership?

Work together 21-1

Forming a partnership

A cash receipts journal is provided in the *Working Papers*. Your instructor will guide you through the following examples.

Ming Han and Keel Milner agree to form a partnership on May 1 of the current year. The partnership assumes the assets and liabilities of Keel's existing business. Ming invests cash equal to Keel's investment. Partners share equally in all changes in equity. The May 1 balance sheet for Keel's existing business is shown in the *Working Papers*. Source documents are abbreviated as follows: receipt, R.

Journalize the transactions in a cash receipts journal.

Transactions:

May 1. Received cash from partner, Ming Han, as an initial investment, $60,000.00. R1.

1. Accepted assets and liabilities of Keel Milner's existing business as an initial investment, $60,000.00. R2.

On your own 21-1

Forming a partnership

A cash receipts journal is provided in the *Working Papers*. Work independently to complete the following problem.

Willie Tribble and Janey Stapp agree to form a partnership on July 1 of the current year. The partnership assumes the assets and liabilities of Janey's existing business. Willie invests cash equal to Janey's investment. Partners share equally in all changes in equity. The July 1 balance sheet for Janey's existing business is shown in the *Working Papers*. Source documents are abbreviated as follows: receipt, R.

Journalize the transactions in a cash receipts journal.

Transactions:

July 1. Received cash from partner, Willie Tribble, as an initial investment, $38,000.00. R1.

1. Accepted assets and liabilities of Janey Stapp's existing business as an initial investment, $38,000.00. R2.

Essential Questions

- Many people equate the partnership agreement to a prenuptial agreement. Explain. (*They both are an agreement between two parties to help protect the assets of the individuals, should they part ways. The agreement clarifies financial rights and helps avoid arguments by clarifying the "what ifs".*)
- What are some questions that a businessperson should ask before admitting a new partner? (*Questions should help to determine if they share values and vision for the business; what skills and experiences they have that will add value; distractions they might experience; their financial condition.*)

CHECK FOR UNDERSTANDING

Terms Review

- Call on students to define each term in the Terms Review. Definitions are given in the Glossary.

Audit Your Understanding

- Call on students to answer the Audit Your Understanding questions. Answers are given in Appendix D.

GUIDED PRACTICE

Work Together

- Have students write the solution to the Work Together problem as you guide the class through the examples.
- Direct students to journalize the transactions in a cash receipts journal.

INDEPENDENT PRACTICE

On Your Own

- Assign the On Your Own problem to be worked independently.

Application Problem

- Assign Application Problem 21-1.

Online Working Papers

- Students can access the Lesson 21-1 problems using this software.

RETEACH

- Write on the board the initial investments to be made by two partners forming a new partnership, including one with noncash assets.
- Draw some T accounts on the board. Ask a student to analyze the initial investment entry for one of the partners.
- Ask a student to describe the correct journal entry for recording each partner's initial investment as you write the entry on a transparency of a cash receipts journal.

CLOSURE

- Ask students to summarize briefly the procedure for analyzing and journalizing partners' initial investments to form a partnership.

EXTENDED LEARNING

- Assign Accounting in the Real World on page 621.
- Assign Ethics in Action on page 623.
- Assign Global Awareness on page 626.
- Assign Think Like an Accountant on page 628.

LESSON
21-2

BRIDGE

- Point out that forming a partnership and journalizing the partners' initial investments were presented in the previous lesson.
- Explain that a new partner may be admitted to an existing partnership. When this occurs, a new partnership agreement must be written. Students will learn how to journalize the admission of a new partner.

TEACHING RESOURCES

- **Instructor's Resource CD/Website:**
  PowerPoint Slides
  Accounting Concepts
- **Working Papers:**
  Teacher's Edition of the Working Papers for Lesson 21-2
  Online Working Papers
- **Transparency Masters:**
  Cash Receipts Journal
  General Journal

ENGAGE

- Ask students why a new partnership agreement should be written every time a new partner is admitted to a partnership.
- Ask students why a new partner might be admitted to an existing partnership.

PREVIEW

- Call on students to read the accounting terms and definitions introduced in this lesson: *goodwill* and *intangible asset*.
- Point out the learning objective for this lesson.
- Direct students to read the headings in this lesson and to examine the illustrations.

INPUT

- Explain that partners might sell part of their equity to a new partner.
- Explain that the existing partners are selling part of their existing equity and that the cash received is a personal transaction.
- The only entry in the journal is the transfer of capital from the existing partners to the new partner.

LESSON
21-2 Admitting Partners to Existing Partnerships

LO3 Journalize transactions to admit a new partner to an existing partnership.

Admitting a Partner with No Change in Total Equity LO3

	Total Equity	×	Share of Equity	=	Mosley's Equity
Greenlee	$27,000.00				
Martin	27,000.00				
Total Equity	$54,000.00	×	1/3	=	$18,000.00

Determine New Partner's Equity

Calculate Total Equity

GENERAL JOURNAL — PAGE 4

	DATE		ACCOUNT TITLE	DOC. NO.	POST. REF.	DEBIT	CREDIT	
1	20-- Jan.	1	Joy Greenlee, Capital	M22		9 000 00		1
2			Dwaylon Martin, Capital			9 000 00		2
3			Jesse Mosley, Capital				18 000 00	3
4								4

Redistribute Capital

Joy Greenlee and Dwaylon Martin are partners in an existing business. The partners agree to admit Jesse Mosley as a new partner. However, the business does not need additional capital now. Therefore, Joy and Dwaylon agree to sell part of their existing equity to Jesse.

The existing partners each have $27,000.00 equity in the existing partnership. The three partners agree that Jesse is to pay $18,000.00 for a one-third equity in the new partnership. Joy and Dwaylon receive cash from Jesse for equity in the partnership. The partnership does not receive the cash from the sale of equity.

The two existing partners are each entitled to one-half of the price Jesse pays for one-third of the equity of the partnership. Therefore, Jesse pays $9,000.00 each to Joy and Dwaylon. Also, on the partnership's records, $18,000.00 of the existing equity is transferred to Jesse.

January 1, 20--. Journalized the personal sale of equity to a new partner, Jesse Mosley, for a one-third equity in the business, $18,000.00. Memorandum No. 22.

The receipt of cash, a personal transaction among Joy, Dwaylon, and Jesse, is not recorded on the partnership's records. However, the redistribution of capital is a partnership entry and is journalized.

remember

If partners agree to sell part of their existing equity to a new partner, the receipt of cash is a personal transaction that is not recorded on the partnership's records.

MODEL

- Use a transparency of a general journal to illustrate how to record the transfer of the existing partners' equity to the new partner.
- Direct students to the illustration as you calculate and journalize the new partner's equity in the partnership.

Admitting a Partner with Equity Equal to New Partner's Investment

	Total Equity	×	Share of Equity	=	Trackson's Equity
Jenkins	$30,000.00				
Lawson	30,000.00				
Trackson	20,000.00				
Total Equity	$80,000.00	×	1/4	=	$20,000.00

Calculate Total Equity

Determine New Partner's Equity

CASH RECEIPTS JOURNAL — PAGE 3

	DATE		ACCOUNT TITLE	DOC. NO.	POST. REF.	GENERAL DEBIT (1)	GENERAL CREDIT (2)	ACCOUNTS RECEIVABLE CREDIT (3)	SALES CREDIT (4)	SALES TAX PAYABLE CREDIT (5)	SALES DISCOUNT DEBIT (6)	CASH DEBIT (7)	
1	20-- Feb.	1	Rosean Trackson, Capital	R120			20 000 00					20 000 00	1
2													2
3													3

Record Additional Capital

Partnerships often seek to increase their total equity to allow the business to grow. Partnerships may seek to expand their current markets, move into new markets, or sell new types of merchandise. Additional capital gives partnerships added financial strength as the business grows.

John Jenkins and Natalia Lawson are partners in an existing partnership. Each partner's equity is $30,000.00, for a total equity of $60,000.00. The existing partners agree to admit Rosean Trackson as a partner with a one-fourth interest for a $20,000.00 cash investment. Rosean's equity is calculated as shown above. Rosean's investment does not change John's or Natalia's equity.

February 1, 20--. Received cash from new partner, Rosean Trackson, for a one-fourth equity in the business, $20,000.00. Receipt No. 120.

WHY ACCOUNTING?

Changing Services to Match the Times

The origin of the modern-day travel agency, which may be organized as a partnership, can be traced to the United Kingdom in the 19th century. Twenty years ago, the most common way to book an airline flight was to go through a travel agent, who had access to airline information. The agent could search for the lowest cost or best travel times for the customer and book the ticket. The agent would get a commission from the airlines for processing the booking.

The rise of the Internet changed drastically how flights are booked. Today, a traveler can search the Internet and actually book the ticket. If a travel agent does book a flight, the agency will often charge the traveler a fee for the service.

Travel agents still do most of the bookings for cruises and travel packages, which continue to pay commissions. To stay in business, the travel agent must be aware of how much time it takes to service each customer and the amount of commission to be earned on the sale. The source of such information is accurate accounting records.

© iStockphoto.com/Alekska

CRITICAL THINKING

Contact a travel agency by phone or via the Internet and determine what services the agency offers free and what services are offered for a fee. Ask the agent how the commission structure has changed in the last 10 years and what the implications of this change are for the profitability of the agency.

INPUT

- Explain that a partnership may seek an additional partner's investment to increase the assets available and expand the business.
- Explain that the existing partners and the potential new partner negotiate the amount of assets that will be invested by the new partner to buy a specific share of equity.
- Explain that negotiations may result in the new partner investing an amount equal to the share of partnership equity received.

MODEL

- Illustrate on the board how the new partner's equity is calculated.
- Use a transparency of a cash receipts journal to illustrate how to record the new partner's investment.
- Direct students to the illustration as you describe how to admit a partner with equity equal to the new partner's investment.

WHY ACCOUNTING?

Ask the class to list as many travel agencies as they can. Assign one agency to each student (or a small group of students). Tally the answers.

Answers

Answers will vary.

INPUT

- Explain that in an effort to attract a new partner, existing partners may agree to admit the new partner with a larger share of equity than the amount of investment.
- Explain that two journal entries will be required to record this kind of transaction: (1) receipt of cash and (2) redistribution of existing equity.
- Point out that the name of the business or individual can help gain public recognition.

MODEL

- Illustrate on the board how the new partner's equity is calculated.
- Use transparencies of a cash receipts journal and a general journal to illustrate how to record the new partner's investment and the redistribution of the existing partners' equity.
- Direct students to the illustration as you describe the steps needed to calculate the new partner's investment and admit the new partner with equity greater than the investment.

Admitting a Partner with Equity Greater than New Partner's Investment

	Total Equity	×	Share of Equity	=	Fant's Equity
Blette (Equity)	$ 42,000.00				
Campbell (Equity)	42,000.00				
Fant (Investment)	36,000.00				
Total Equity	$120,000.00	×	1/3	=	$40,000.00

Calculate Total Equity

Determine New Partner's Equity

CASH RECEIPTS JOURNAL — PAGE 7

	DATE		ACCOUNT TITLE	DOC. NO.	POST. REF.	1 GENERAL DEBIT	2 GENERAL CREDIT	3 ACCOUNTS RECEIVABLE CREDIT	4 SALES CREDIT	5 SALES TAX PAYABLE CREDIT	6 SALES DISCOUNT DEBIT	7 CASH DEBIT	
1	20-- May	1	Klaire Fant, Capital	R106			36 000 00					36 000 00	1
2													2
3													3

Record Additional Capital

GENERAL JOURNAL — PAGE 6

	DATE		ACCOUNT TITLE	DOC. NO.	POST. REF.	DEBIT	CREDIT	
1	20-- May	1	Kelsay Blette, Capital	M45		2 000 00		1
2			Marge Campbell			2 000 00		2
3			Klaire Fant, Capital				4 000 00	3
4								4

Redistribute Capital

Kelsay Blette and Marge Campbell both have equity of $42,000.00 in an existing partnership. The existing partners agree to admit Klaire Fant as a partner with a one-third interest for a $36,000.00 cash investment. Klaire's equity is calculated as shown above.

May 1, 20--. Received cash from new partner, Klaire Fant, for a one-third equity in the business, $36,000.00. Existing equity is redistributed as follows: from Kelsay Blette, $2,000.00; from Marge Campbell, $2,000.00. Receipt No. 106 and Memorandum No. 45.

Two journal entries are required to record this transaction. (1) The receipt of cash is recorded. (2) The redistribution of existing equity is recorded.

© Stuart Jenner/Shutterstock.com

Admitting a Partner When Goodwill Is Recognized

Yeatman's Contributed Equity	÷	Share of Equity	=	Total Agreed Value of Equity
$30,000.00	÷	1/3	=	$90,000.00

Estimate Total Partnership Equity

Total Agreed Value of Equity	−	Total Recorded Equity	=	Increase in Equity from Goodwill
$90,000.00	−	$80,000.00	=	$10,000.00

Calculate Goodwill

CASH RECEIPTS JOURNAL — PAGE 9

	DATE		ACCOUNT TITLE	DOC. NO.	POST. REF.	1 GENERAL DEBIT	2 GENERAL CREDIT	3 ACCOUNTS RECEIVABLE CREDIT	4 SALES CREDIT	5 SALES TAX PAYABLE CREDIT	6 SALES DISCOUNT DEBIT	7 CASH DEBIT	
1	20-- July	1	Marshall Yeatman, Capital	R344			30 000 00					30 000 00	1
2													2
3													3

Record Additional Capital

GENERAL JOURNAL — PAGE 7

	DATE		ACCOUNT TITLE	DOC. NO.	POST. REF.	DEBIT	CREDIT	
1	20-- July	1	Goodwill	M89		10 000 00		1
2			Kenya Norris, Capital				5 000 00	2
3			Tawanya Elrod, Capital				5 000 00	3
4								4

Record Goodwill and Redistribute Capital

The fair value of the assets may not be the best measure of the value of the business. The value of a business can also be valued based on the amount of revenue the business can generate. For example, the assets of a public accounting firm are relatively small, consisting primarily of office furniture and computers. The value of these assets is relatively small compared to the fees that the accountants earn by performing professional services. In this case, the transaction to admit a new partner needs to account for the full value of the business.

Kenya Norris and Tawanya Elrod are partners in an existing business. Each partner's equity is $25,000.00, for a total equity of $50,000.00. The existing partners agree to admit Marshall Yeatman as a partner with a one-third interest for a $30,000.00 cash investment. Based on the past revenue earned by the business, Marshall believes the total equity value is worth $90,000.00 after his investment.

The value of a business in excess of the total investment of owners is called **goodwill**. The partners agree that Marshall's willingness to pay $30,000.00 for a one-third interest is evidence that goodwill exists. The value of goodwill is calculated as shown above. The total recorded equity, $80,000.00, is the equity of the existing partners, $50,000.00, plus the amount to be contributed by Marshall, $30,000.00.

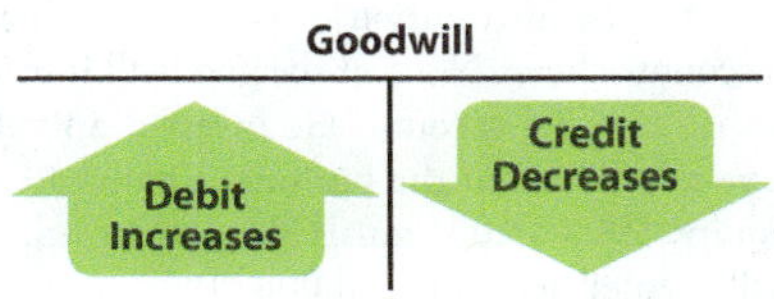

July 1, 20--. Received cash from new partner, Marshall Yeatman, for a one-third equity in the business, $30,000.00. Goodwill, $10,000.00, is distributed as follows: Kenya Norris, $5,000.00; Tawanya Elrod, $5,000.00. Receipt No. 344 and Memorandum No. 89.

Two journal entries are required for this transaction. (1) The receipt of cash is recorded. (2) The distribution of goodwill is recorded. The $10,000.00 amount of equity in excess of the total recorded investment of the three partners is the value of the goodwill.

INPUT

- Explain that in some cases, a partnership is so successful that a new partner is willing to invest a greater amount of assets than the share of equity received.
- Explain that the fact that a new partner is willing to pay a premium for a specified share of equity provides evidence that the partnership has earned goodwill.
- Explain that two journal entries will be required to record this kind of transaction: (1) receipt of cash from the new partner and (2) allocation of the goodwill to existing partners.

MODEL

- Illustrate on the board how the new partner's equity is calculated.
- Use transparencies of a cash receipts journal and a general journal to illustrate how to record the new partner's investment and the allocation of goodwill to the existing partners' equity.
- Direct students to the illustration as you describe how to admit a new partner when goodwill is recognized.

INPUT

- Point out that an asset that does not have physical substance is called an intangible asset.
- Explain that goodwill is considered an intangible asset.
- Explain that goodwill may be recorded only at the time of a change in ownership of the business when evidence of the value of goodwill is proven through the willingness of a new partner to invest a greater amount than the share of equity received.
- Direct students to the T accounts illustration and go over the effects on each equity account after goodwill is recognized.

Equity Accounts after Goodwill Is Recognized

Cash

Debit		Credit	
July 1 ↑	30,000.00		

Goodwill

Debit		Credit	
July 1 ↑	10,000.00		

Kenya Norris, Capital

Debit		Credit	
		Bal. ↑	25,000.00
		July 1	5,000.00
		(New Bal.	*30,000.00)*

Tawanya Elrod, Capital

Debit		Credit	
		Bal. ↑	25,000.00
		July 1	5,000.00
		(New Bal.	*30,000.00)*

Marshall Yeatman, Capital

Debit		Credit	
		July 1 ↑	30,000.00

	Recorded Equity	+	Share of Goodwill	=	New Equity
Norris	$25,000.00	+	$ 5,000.00	=	$30,000.00
Elrod	25,000.00	+	5,000.00	=	30,000.00
Yeatman	30,000.00	+	—	=	30,000.00
Totals	$80,000.00	+	$10,000.00	=	$90,000.00

The analysis of the investment of cash by Marshall Yeatman and the distribution of goodwill is shown in the T accounts above. None of the goodwill is recorded in Marshall's capital account. He invested $30,000.00 for a one-third share of the business. One-third of the total equity, $90,000.00, equals the current balance of Marshall's capital account, $30,000.00.

Goodwill may be recorded only at the time of a change in ownership of business. An ongoing business may be worth more than the equity value stated in the accounting records. However, goodwill may not be recorded without some evidence of its value. This evidence is provided by the willingness of an investor to pay a premium for an ownership interest in the business.

An asset that does not have physical substance is called an **intangible asset**. Unlike most other asset accounts, the amount of goodwill cannot be related to a physical asset, such as inventory, or to a legal right, such as accounts receivable. Therefore, the account Goodwill is located in a general ledger's Intangible Assets section.

© Geo Martinez/Shutterstock.com

DIFFERENTIATED INSTRUCTION

Verbal/Linguistic learners enjoy writing assignments and are good at creating imaginary worlds. Ask students to imagine that two friends want to add a partner to their personal training business so they can grow it. Ask students to write a letter to the two friends. Tell them that the letter should include at least five items they would consider prior to adding a new partner.

© iStockphoto.com/burwellphotography

FORENSIC ACCOUNTING

Improper Revenue Recognition

John Parchman has been trying to persuade his friend, Taylor Duke, to purchase his equity interest in Freshland Distributing, a business that operates in the food services industry. The business is organized as a partnership and currently has five other partners.

Every quarter, John sends Taylor a copy of Freshland's financial statements. The statements have shown a constant level of sales, despite the fact that the economy entered a recession a year ago. Taylor believes the business has the potential for significant growth, once the recession is over. After being courted by John for over a year, Taylor is about ready to make the investment.

At a New Year's social, Taylor was sharing his intent to purchase John's equity interest in Freshland. Marshall Edmonds, a CPA, was listening to Taylor explain how the business had maintained its sales despite the current state of the economy. Marshall jokingly interjected, "I hope they haven't been keeping the books open." Although Taylor seemed to ignore the comment, he was bothered by Marshall's facial expression, and he did not understand what was meant by "keeping the books open."

The first thing the next morning, Taylor was in Marshall's office seeking more information. "A few years ago," said Marshall, "I investigated a company that inflated its quarterly sales. The manager would record sales from the first few days of April, for example, as March sales. The first quarter's sales looked better than they should have. Of course, at the end of the next quarter, the manager had to do the same thing, just to keep sales from going down. To inflate that quarter's sales, even more July sales had to be recorded in June. After a few quarters, the fraud was totally out of control."

ACTIVITY

Taylor has obtained a data file of Freshland's sales and asked Marshall to search for fraud. Marshall has assigned you the task of analyzing the data to search for any "red flag" of improper revenue recognition. "This company's daily sales should be reasonably consistent," he stated. "Look for any sharp increase in daily sales at the end of a quarter, accompanied by a sharp decrease in daily sales right after the new quarter begins."

INSTRUCTIONS

Open the spreadsheet FA_CH21 and complete the steps on the Instructions tab. Provide answers to the following questions, supporting your answers.

1. Calculate the average daily sales.
2. Does the chart effectively provide evidence of a fraud?
3. Do the charts near the end of each quarter provide evidence of a fraud?

FORENSIC ACCOUNTING

The workbook contains a list of sales invoices. Students use a PivotChart to search for the red flag of improper revenue recognition.

Solutions

1. The average daily sales is \$14,610.86.
2. No. Although there is evidence of significant spikes in sales, there are too many columns and the columns are too thin to enable an accurate interpretation of the chart.
3. First quarter: There is a slight increase in sales during the two days of the first quarter, with a significant drop in sales for the first day of the second quarter. This fact by itself does not provide sufficient evidence of a fraud. These sales amounts could have easily resulted from other factors.

   Second quarter: Sales for the last three days of the second quarter are significantly above the daily average. At the same time, sales for the first three days of the third quarter are significantly below the daily average. These results suggest that some July sales could have been recorded in June.

   Third quarter: There is a dramatic shift in sales between the third and second quarters. Sales for the last day of September are over three times the daily average, whereas daily sales during the first five days of October range from approximately \$5,100 to \$8,400, well below the daily average. Combined with the evidence from the second quarter, these findings provide strong evidence of a fraud.

FORMATIVE ASSESSMENT

- This is an ongoing process. Circulate around the classroom or lab, observing which students have difficulty with the assignments.
- Troubleshooting: Diagnose the kinds of problems students have with this lesson. Students may have difficulty determining how partners' equities change when a new partner is admitted.
- Assess student understanding by checking solutions to Independent Practice assignments and noting their answers to the Terms Review and Audit Your Understanding questions.

CHECK FOR UNDERSTANDING

Terms Review

- Call on students to define each term in the Terms Review. Definitions are given in the Glossary.

Audit Your Understanding

- Call on students to answer the Audit Your Understanding questions. Answers are given in Appendix D.

GUIDED PRACTICE

Work Together

- Have students write the solution to the Work Together problem as you guide the class through the examples.
- Direct students to prepare appropriate journal entries to admit a new partner.

INDEPENDENT PRACTICE

On Your Own

- Assign the On Your Own problem to be worked independently.
- Use the Formative Assessment techniques to diagnose student understanding.

Application Problem

- Assign Application Problem 21-2.

Online Working Papers

- Students can access the Lesson 21-2 problems using this software.

RETEACH

- Write on the board some situations for admitting a new partner.
- Ask individual students to calculate the amount of equity that each partner should have after the new partner is admitted.

CLOSURE

- Ask students to summarize briefly the procedures for calculating and journalizing the admission of new partners to existing partnerships.

Essential Question

- What are some ways a business could increase goodwill? (*Examples could include methods of creating customer loyalty and reputation, such as the company becoming more environmentally responsible; and improved products.*)

End of Lesson Review

LO3 Journalize transactions to admit a new partner to an existing partnership.

Terms Review

goodwill

intangible asset

Audit your understanding

1. What happens to an existing partnership when a new partner is admitted?
2. When admitting a new partner, how is the new partner's equity calculated?
3. What accounts are debited and credited to record the distribution of goodwill when a new partner is admitted?

Work together 21-2

Admitting partners to existing partnerships

Four independent situations of an existing partnership admitting a new partner are given below. The partners share equally in all changes in equity. For each situation, prepare the appropriate journal entries to admit a new partner on June 1 of the current year. A cash receipts journal and a general journal are provided in the *Working Papers*. Source documents are abbreviated as follows: memorandum, M; receipt, R. Your instructor will guide you through the following examples.

1. Charles Fulton and Davis Stewart each have equity of $18,000.00. Each partner agrees to sell $6,000.00 of his equity to Moses Tate and to give Moses a one-third share of ownership. Moses is to pay the money directly to the two original partners. M42.
2. Kennedy Davies and Kelly Andrews each have equity of $60,000.00. Mason Wood will pay $60,000.00 cash to the partnership for a one-third equity in the business. R121.
3. Marie Henson and Bobby Edwards each have $40,000.00 of equity. Cindy Yates will pay the partnership $34,000.00 cash for a one-third share in the business. R135 and M38.
4. Tyrone Wegner and Brodie Thomas each have equity of $36,000.00. Sue Shinn will pay $42,000.00 cash to the partnership to purchase a one-third share in the partnership. R79 and M24.

On your own 21-2

Admitting partners to existing partnerships

Four independent situations of an existing partnership admitting a new partner are given below. The partners share equally in all changes in equity. For each situation, prepare the appropriate journal entries to admit a new partner on May 1 of the current year. A cash receipts journal and a general journal are provided in the *Working Papers*. Work independently to complete the following examples.

1. Churna Knox and Mack Daniels each have equity of $36,000.00. Each partner agrees to sell $12,000.00 in equity to Paola Diaz and to give her a one-third share of ownership. Paola is to pay the money directly to the two original partners. M52.
2. Barry Sales and Jeff Rhea each have $62,000.00 of equity. Murray Price will pay $62,000.00 to the partnership to purchase a one-third share in the partnership. R192.
3. Scott Polk and Erica Morgan each have equity of $40,000.00. Tiffany Macri will pay the partnership $34,000.00 for a one-third equity in the business. R160 and M44.
4. Avaline Laird and Ethel Howe each have $38,000.00 of equity. Shelly Harmon will pay $45,000.00 to the partnership for a one-third share in the business. R223 and M111.

EXTENDED LEARNING

- Assign Why Accounting on page 631.
- Assign Forensic Accounting on page 635.

Chapter Summary

A partnership is a business that is usually formed by a small group of individuals. Except for recording transactions involving owners' equity and income taxes, accounting procedures for a partnership are similar to those for a corporation. Each partner has two accounts: (1) a capital account to record contributions to the partnership and (2) a drawing account to record withdrawals. Partners are not employees of the partnership. Each partner's share of the income of the partnership is reported as income on that partner's individual tax return.

A written partnership agreement sets forth the conditions under which a partnership is to operate, including the addition or withdrawal of partners. A partnership's life is limited to the length of time agreed on by the partners and is terminated with any change in ownership. Unless limited by the partnership agreement, each partner has the authority to enter into transactions on behalf of the partnership.

A partner can contribute cash or other assets. The fair market value of assets contributed to a partnership should be determined and agreed upon by the partners. A fair market value balance sheet reports the value of an existing business's assets and liabilities that are contributed to the partnership.

The accounting for changes in the ownership of a partnership depends on (1) whether the new partner contributes assets to the partnership, (2) the amount contributed, and (3) the ownership percentage acquired. The addition of a new partner may require the recognition of goodwill when the amount of assets contributed exceeds the equity value of the partnership acquired. The goodwill increases the capital accounts of the existing partners.

Limited Liability Partnerships

EXPLORE ACCOUNTING

The organizational structure of a corporation differs from a partnership in four ways.

1. *Continuity of life.* A partnership ends upon the death or withdrawal of an owner. Stockholders of a corporation buy and sell stock without affecting the life of the corporation.
2. *Centralization of management.* A partnership generally is managed by one or more of its partners. A corporation generally is managed by professional managers employed by the stockholders.
3. *Limited liability.* All partners are liable for contracts and liabilities incurred by the partnership. Because a corporation is treated as a separate legal entity, stockholders are not liable for the contracts or liabilities of the corporation.
4. *Free transferability of interest.* Generally, a partnership ends if a partner dies or withdraws. In addition, other partners must agree before a partner can sell his/her interest to another person. Stockholders can buy and sell shares of a corporation without consulting other stockholders.

Most states allow a special kind of partnership, called a *limited liability partnership* and frequently referred to as an *LLP*. An LLP must file articles of organization with the state. The operating agreement is similar to a traditional partnership agreement. The LLP must be managed by the members or a group of managers who are elected by the members. To qualify to be taxed as a partnership, the partnership can have no more than two of the characteristics of a corporation. Most LLPs retain the two characteristics of centralization of management and limited liability.

The attractiveness of an LLP is twofold. (1) Partners can be taxed as a partnership (net income is reported on the individual partner's tax return). (2) Partners have limited liability for the actions of the partnership, much like stockholders of a corporation. For these reasons, many partnerships have changed to an LLP.

© iStockphoto.com/Makhnach_M

INSTRUCTIONS

1. Identify your state's process and requirements for registering to become an LLP.
2. After reading more about LLPs or interviewing local partners of an LLP, determine other advantages and disadvantages of an LLP.

CLOSURE

- Review the Chapter Summary.
- Ask students to prepare a list of the new concepts introduced in this chapter.

Essential Question

- Ask students if there should be a limit to the number of partners in a partnership. Explain. (*Some may feel that a large number of partners could limit profits once split among themselves. Also, there is more risk of liability for actions of other partners.*)

EXTENDED LEARNING

- Assign Explore Accounting on page 637.

EXPLORE ACCOUNTING

Answers

1. Answers will vary. Students should be able to obtain the answers from the website of the state's secretary of state office.
2. Answers will vary based on the experiences of the individuals interviewed.

CHECK FIGURES

For complete solutions to Chapter 21 problems, see the Teacher's Edition of the Working Papers.

Application Problem 21-1

Each partner's capital account is credited for $58,106.84.

Total Cash invested, $61,783.36.

Apply Your Understanding

INSTRUCTIONS: Download problem instructions for Excel, QuickBooks, and Sage 50 from the textbook companion website at www.C21accounting.com.

21-1 Application Problem: Forming a partnership LO2

Crystal Foote and Lillie Classen agree to form a partnership on May 1 of the current year. The partnership assumes the assets and liabilities of Lillie's existing business. Crystal invests cash equal to Lillie's investment. Partners share equally in all changes in equity. The May 1 fair market value balance sheet for Lillie's existing business is as follows. A cash receipts journal is given in the *Working Papers*.

Lil's Gifts
Fair Market Value Balance Sheet
May 1, 20--

ASSETS			
Current Assets:			
Cash		$ 3,676.52	
Accounts Receivable	$10,531.68		
Less Allowance for Uncollectible Accounts	4,400.00	6,131.68	
Inventory		32,150.00	
Supplies		830.00	
Total Current Assets			$42,788.20
Plant Assets:			
Equipment			24,800.00
Total Assets			$67,588.20
LIABILITIES			
Accounts Payable			$ 9,481.36
OWNER'S EQUITY			
Lillie Classen, Capital			58,106.84
Total Liabilities and Owner's Equity			$67,588.20

Instructions:

Journalize the transactions. Source documents are abbreviated as follows: receipt, R.

Transactions:

May 1. Received cash from partner, Crystal Foote, as an initial investment, $58,106.84. R1.
1. Accepted assets and liabilities of Lillie Classen's existing business as an initial investment, $58,106.84. R2.

AAONLINE

1. Go to www.cengage.com/login
2. Click on AA Online to access.
3. Go to the online assignment and follow the instructions.

21-2 Application Problem: Admitting a partner with no change in total equity LO3

Four independent situations are given below. The existing partners are Sadie Ryals and Shelly Perry. The new partner is Vergie Lowry. A general journal and cash receipts journal are given in the *Working Papers*. For each situation, prepare the appropriate journal entries to admit the new partner.

Instructions:

Journalize the transactions. Source documents are abbreviated as follows: memorandum, M; receipt, R.

Transactions:

1. Sadie Ryals and Shelly Perry have equity of $32,400.00 each in an existing partnership. On February 1 of the current year, the two partners agree to admit Vergie Lowry as a one-third partner. Each partner agrees to sell Vergie $21,600.00 in equity and to give her a one-third share of ownership. Vergie is to pay the money directly to the two original partners.

Feb. 1. Journalized personal sale of equity to new partner, Vergie Lowry, $21,600.00, distributed as follows: from Sadie Ryals, $10,800.00; from Shelly Perry, $10,800.00. M30.

2. Sadie Ryals and Shelly Perry have equity of $34,280.00 each in the partnership. Partners share equally in all changes in equity. On February 1 of the current year, the two partners agree to admit Vergie as a partner with a one-third share of the total equity.

Feb. 1. Received cash from new partner, Vergie Lowry, for a one-third equity in the business, $34,280.00. R222.

3. Sadie Ryals and Shelly Perry have equity of $24,250.00 each in an existing partnership. The partners share equally in all changes in equity. On February 1 of the current year, the existing partners agree to admit Vergie with a one-third share of the total equity.

Feb. 1. Received cash from new partner, Vergie Lowry, for a one-third equity in the business, $22,000.00. Existing equity is redistributed as follows: from Sadie Ryals, $750.00; from Shelly Perry, $750.00. R175 and M27.

4. Sadie Ryals and Shelly Perry each have $32,650.00 equity in an existing business. The partners share equally in all changes in equity. On February 1 of the current year, Vergie is admitted as a new partner with a one-third share of the total equity.

Feb. 1. Received cash from new partner, Vergie Lowry, for a one-third equity in the business, $40,000.00. Goodwill, $14,700.00, is distributed as follows: Sadie Ryals, $7,350.00; Shelly Perry, $7,350.00. R150 and M25.

Sage 50 Accounting

1. Journalize and post transactions related to admitting a new partner to the general journal.
2. Journalize and post transactions related to admitting a new partner in the Receipts window.
3. Print the general journal and cash receipts journal.

QB

1. Journalize and post transactions related to admitting a new partner to the journal.
2. Print the journal and the transaction detail by account report.

X

1. Journalize and post transactions related to admitting a new partner to the general journal.
2. Journalize and post transactions related to admitting a new partner to the cash receipts journal.
3. Print the worksheets.

Application Problem 21-2

1. Debit original partners' capital, $10,800.00 each.
2. Credit new partner's capital, $34,280.00.
3. Debit original partners' capital, $750.00 each.
4. Debit Goodwill, $14,700.00; credit partners' capital, $7,350.00 each.

Mastery Problem 21-M

General journal transactions:

Aug. 9, debit original partners' capital, $7,000.00 each.

Oct. 12, debit original partners' capital, $225.00 each.

Dec. 8, debit Goodwill, $16,000.00; credit partners' capital, $3,200.00 each.

INDEPENDENT PRACTICE

- Assign Mastery Problem 21-M for students as a culminating problem combining all new learning from the chapter.
- Assign Challenge Problem 21-C to accelerated students who work at a faster pace.
- Assign Study Guide 21.
- Students can access Online Working Papers to work end-of-chapter problems on the computer.
- Direct students to the C21 Accounting companion website for additional practice and review opportunities.

FORMATIVE ASSESSMENT

- Review solutions to the assigned problems in class, diagnosing trouble spots.

RETEACH

- Call on students to describe how they avoid the trouble spots diagnosed.
- Use reteaching suggestions from lesson plans as required.
- Assign Recycling Problem 21-R if needed.

EXTENDED LEARNING

- Assign 21st Century Skills on page 642.
- Assign Auditing for Errors on page 642.
- Assign Analyzing Home Depot's Financial Statements on page 643.

SUMMATIVE EVALUATION

- Chapter 21 Test
- Cognero for Chapter 21

21-M Mastery Problem: Forming and expanding a partnership LO2, 3

On May 1 of the current year, Tamra Hamby and Sharunda Massey form a partnership. The partners share equally in all changes in equity. The partnership assumes the assets and liabilities of Sharunda's existing business. Tamra invests cash equal to Sharunda's investment. A general journal and cash receipts journal are given in the *Working Papers*. The May 1 fair market value balance sheet for Sharunda's existing business is as follows.

Massey Specialty Shop
Fair Market Value Balance Sheet
May 1, 20--

ASSETS			
Current Assets:			
Cash		$ 5,028.26	
Accounts Receivable	$6,185.36		
Less Allowance for Uncollectible Accounts	1,000.00	5,185.36	
Inventory		24,100.00	
Supplies		1,050.00	
Total Current Assets			$35,363.62
Plant Assets:			
Equipment			12,600.00
Total Assets			$47,963.62
LIABILITIES			
Accounts Payable			$25,483.62
OWNER'S EQUITY			
Sharunda Massey, Capital			22,480.00
Total Liabilities and Owner's Equity			$47,963.62

Instructions:

Journalize the following transactions. Source documents are abbreviated as follows: memorandum, M; receipt, R.

Transactions:

May 1. Received cash from partner, Tamra Hamby, as an initial investment, $22,480.00. R1.
1. Accepted assets and liabilities of Sharunda Massey's existing business as an initial investment, $22,480.00. R2.
Aug. 9. Journalized personal sale of equity to new partner, Emma Laws, $14,000.00. Each existing partner has a current equity balance of $21,000.00. M8.
Oct. 3. Received cash from new partner, Antonio McKay, for a one-fourth equity in the business, $17,250.00. Each existing partner has a current equity balance of $17,250.00. R151.
12. Received cash from new partner, Luis Soto, for a one-fifth equity in the business, $21,300.00. Each existing partner has a current equity balance of $22,425.00. R158 and M42.
Dec. 8. Received cash from new partner, Octavia Ruffin, for a one-sixth equity in the business, $28,000.00. Goodwill is distributed evenly among the existing partners. Each existing partner has a current equity balance of $24,800.00. R184 and M48.

Sage 50 Accounting
1. Journalize and post transactions related to a partnership to the general journal.
2. Journalize and post transactions related to a partnership in the Receipts window.
3. Print the general journal and cash receipts journal.

QB
1. Journalize and post transactions related to a partnership to the journal.
2. Print the journal and the transaction detail by account report.

X
1. Journalize and post transactions related to a partnership to the general journal.
2. Journalize and post transactions related to a partnership to the cash receipts journal.
3. Print the worksheets.

AAONLINE
1. Go to www.cengage.com/login
2. Click on AA Online to access.
3. Go to the online assignment and follow the instructions.

21-C Challenge Problem: Expanding a partnership LO2, 3

College friends Dennis Brock, Joe Miller, and Kelly Mann operate a sporting goods store as a partnership. As a result of several transactions, the equity balances are as follows:

Dennis Brock	$40,000.00
Joe Miller	35,000.00
Kelly Mann	25,000.00

Partners share in all equity changes based on their relative equity balances.

Instructions:

Journalize the following transactions using the cash receipts journal and general journal provided in the *Working Papers*. Source documents are abbreviated as follows: memorandum, M; receipt, R.

Transactions:

Mar. 9. Received cash from new partner, Marilyn Pace, for a 10% equity ownership in the business, $15,000.00. R24 and M85. Each of the existing partners sold 10% of their equity to Ms. Pace. R215 and M35.

Aug. 14. Kelly Mann announced his desire to leave the partnership. Marilyn Pace purchased Kelly's equity interest for $32,000.00. M75.

Dec. 9. Danielle King closed her business and contributed inventory valued at $9,000.00 for a 5% equity ownership in the business. M92.

Sage 50 Accounting

1. Journalize and post transactions related to a partnership to the general journal.
2. Journalize and post transactions related to a partnership in the Receipts window.
3. Print the general journal and cash receipts journal.

QB

1. Journalize and post transactions related to a partnership to the journal.
2. Print the journal and the transaction detail by account report.

X

1. Journalize and post transactions related to a partnership to the general journal.
2. Journalize and post transactions related to a partnership to the cash receipts journal.
3. Print the worksheets.

Challenge Problem 21-C

General journal transactions:

Mar. 9, debit Goodwill, $35,000.00; credit partners' capital: Brock, $14,000.00; Miller, $12,250.00; Mann, $8,750.00.

Aug. 14, debit Mann capital and credit Pace capital, $33,750.00.

Dec. 9, credit King capital, $9,000.00.

Dec. 9, debit Goodwill, $21,000.00; credit partners' capital: Brock, $7,560.00; Miller, $6,615.00, Pace, $6,825.00.

COMMON CORE AND INTERDISCIPLINARY STUDIES

Extended learning features and activities present numerous opportunities to implement Common Core Standards through interdisciplinary studies. Practice is provided in the common core areas of English Language Arts & Literacy and Mathematical Practice. Many of these activities require short, critical-thinking and decision-making responses that apply reading, writing, speaking, listening, language, media and technology, and mathematical skills.

21ST CENTURY SKILLS

Answers

1. Many recalls are over one year old. Some include Coca-Cola, Toyota, and Tylenol. Most major recalls have resulted in an impairment of goodwill.
2. Posters or flyers will vary but should include names, photos, and the amount of goodwill impaired. Students may need assistance locating the annual report, or 10k. Encourage students to include goodwill impairments that have resulted due to a variety of reasons, such as recalls, executives, or competition.

AUDITING FOR ERRORS

Solution

Russell's $32,000 contribution for one-fourth equity indicates that the partnership is valued at $158,000 after the contribution ($42,000 × 3 + $32,000). Thus, each partner's equity account should reflect one-fourth, or $39,500 ($158,000 ÷ 4), interest in the partnership.

See the general journal entries in the solution in the Instructional Strategies section at the front of this book.

21st Century Skills

Causes and Consequences

PARTNERSHIP FOR 21ST CENTURY SKILLS

Theme: Financial, Economic, Business, and Entrepreneurial Literacy

Skills: Communication and Collaboration, Critical Thinking and Problem Solving, ICT Literacy, and Initiative and Self-Direction

When a company is acquired for a higher price than its book value, the excess is considered the value of the company and is recorded on the company's balance sheet under Goodwill. For example, a company's assets may be $1 million, but if someone is willing to pay $5 million for the company, the value of the company has increased $4 million due to goodwill.

Goodwill can be based on such factors as reputation, customer loyalty, products, executives, or ability to increase future revenue. However, if a company's reputation has suffered in any way, a company's value can be impaired and is noted on the balance sheet. Stock value could decrease, but a poor reputation could affect the company's bottom line for an extended period. Companies must work aggressively to protect the goodwill value that often takes years to build.

In 2005, Wendy's sales dropped after a woman claimed she found a human finger in her bowl of chili. She was later convicted of a fraud. Unfortunately, that same year, Wendy's goodwill was impaired $36.1 million, possibly due to this incident.

APPLICATION

1. Recalls over the years have impaired the goodwill of numerous companies. Using the Internet, find a famous recall that occurred one or more years ago. The websites of the Consumer Product Safety Commission (CPSC) and the Food and Drug Administration (FDA) list recalls. Research the company's balance sheet to find the impact on its goodwill, if any. Explain.
2. With a partner, create a poster or flyer highlighting at least four companies whose goodwill has been impaired. State the name of the company, include a photo representing a potential cause, and give the amount of goodwill impaired.

Auditing for errors

James Mangione, Carl Nelson, and Marris Trevathon are partners in an existing business. Each partner's equity is $42,000, for a total equity of $126,000. The partners agree to admit Kelly Russell as a partner with a one-fourth interest for contributing $32,000 of inventory. The firm's bookkeeper made the following entry in the partnership's general journal:

GENERAL JOURNAL — PAGE 7

	DATE		ACCOUNT TITLE	DOC. NO.	POST. REF.	DEBIT	CREDIT	
1	20-- July	1	*Inventory*	M23		32 000 00		1
2			*Goodwill*			10 000 00		2
3			*Kelly Russell, Capital*				42 000 00	3
4								4

What entry would you make to correct the bookkeeper's entry? Explain your answer.

Analyzing Home Depot's financial statements

Financial statements are interrelated and connected to one another. A change on one financial statement will have an impact on other financial statements. For example, if a corporation neglected to record a $10,000 cash payment for July rent, the cash amount reported on the balance sheet would be overstated. On the income statement, the net income would also be overstated, due to the $10,000 missing in the Rent Expense account. Since net income increases the retained earnings, the amount of retained earnings listed on the statement of stockholders' equity would be incorrect. Finally, since the amount of net income and year-end cash balance are reported on the statement of cash flows, that financial statement would be incorrect as well.

INSTRUCTIONS

Refer to Home Depot's financial statements shown on pages B-5 through B-9 in Appendix B of this textbook to answer the following questions:

1. Identify the amount of net income (earnings) reported on the Consolidated Statements of Earnings for the year ended February 3, 2013.
2. Locate the dollar amount in question 1 on Home Depot's Consolidated Statements of Stockholders' Equity. Identify the titles of the columns containing the amount.
3. Locate the dollar amount in question 1 on Home Depot's Consolidated Statements of Cash Flows. Identify the title of the section containing the amount.
4. Can you locate the dollar amount calculated in question 1 on Home Depot's Consolidated Balance Sheets? Explain.
5. List the financial statements that would be affected by a failure to account for a $100,000 purchase of equipment in the first month of the fiscal year.

ANALYZING HOME DEPOT'S FINANCIAL STATEMENTS

Answers

1. $4,535 million.
2. Retained Earnings and Stockholders' Equity.
3. Cash Flows from Operating Activities.
4. Net Earnings does not appear on the Consolidated Balance Sheets. That amount is reported on the statement as part of Retained Earnings.
5. All of the statements would be affected. Failure to record the equipment purchase would also result in the misstatement of depreciation expense and, as a result, net earnings. Net earnings are reported directly, or indirectly through Retained Earnings, on all of the statements.

Chapter 22

Financial Reporting for a Partnership

Scope & Sequence

	New	Review/Enrich
Introduction		
Introduce the Chapter		
Lesson 22-1: Distribution and Withdrawal of Partnership Earnings		
Distribution of Partnership Earnings	✓	
Distribution of Net Income Showing a Distribution Deficit	✓	
Withdrawal of Partnership Earnings	✓	
Withdrawal of Assets Other than Cash	✓	
Lesson 22-2: End-of-Period Work for a Partnership		
Income Statement		✓
Owners' Equity Statement		✓
Balance Sheet		✓
Adjusting and Closing Entries	✓	
Federal Income Taxes	✓	
Post-Closing Trial Balance	✓	
Lesson 22-3: Liquidation of a Partnership		
Recognizing a Gain on Realization in a Partnership Liquidation		✓
Recognizing a Loss on Realization in a Partnership Liquidation		✓
Liquidating Liabilities		✓
Account Balances After Liquidation of Noncash Assets and Liabilities		✓
Distributing a Gain or Loss on Realization to Partners		✓
Distributing Remaining Cash to Partners		✓
Closure		

Enhancing Instruction

Features	Common Core Standards
• Accounting in the Real World: PVR Partners, L.P.	• ELAL—reading
• Ethics in Action: The Client Is Not Always Right • Think Like an Accountant: Analyzing Partnership Distributions • Why Accounting?: Should We Buy Another Mill? • Financial Literacy: Signing Away the Future	• ELAL—reading • Mathematics • ELAL—reading • ELAL—reading, writing
• Careers in Accounting: Credit Analyst	• ELAL—reading
• Explore Accounting • 21st Century Skills • Analyzing Home Depot's Financial Statements	• ELAL—reading, writing • ELAL—reading, writing, media and technology, speaking • Mathematics

ELAL = English Language Arts & Literacy

Calculator: © iStockphoto.com/picstodisc; Paper: © iStockphoto.com/Qingwa

Practice and Assessment

Technology & Media	Teaching Strategies	Guided Practice	Independent Practice	Reteach/Enrich
• Instructor's Resource CD/Website: PowerPoint Slices Accounting Concepts • Online Working Papers • Transparency Masters: Cash Payments Journal, General Journal	• Tactile/Kinesthetic Learners • Auditory/Linguistic Learners	• Terms Review • Audit Your Understanding • Work Together 22-1	• On Your Own 22-1 • Application Problem 22-1 • Formative Assessment, p. 651 • Online Working Papers	• Reteach, p. 652
• Instructor's Resource CD/Website: PowerPoint Slides Accounting Concepts • Online Working Papers	• Visual/Spatial Learners	• Terms Review • Audit Your Understanding • Work Together 22-2	• On Your Own 22-2 • Application Problem 22-2 • Formative Assessment, p. 656 • Online Working Papers	• Reteach, p. 657
• Instructor's Resource CD/Website: PowerPoint Slides Accounting Concepts • Online Working Papers • Transparency Masters: Cash Receipts Journal, Cash Payments Journal, General Journal		• Terms Review • Audit Your Understanding • Work Together 22-3	• On Your Own 22-3 • Application Problem 22-3 • Formative Assessment, p. 662 • Online Working Papers	• Reteach, p. 663
• Online Working Papers			• Mastery Problem 22-M • Study Guide 22 • Chapter 22 Test • Cognero Chapter 22	• Challenge Problem 22-C • Reteach, p. 667 • Recycling Problem 22-R

Introduce the Chapter

SET THE STAGE

GUIDING QUESTIONS

- Ask students to explain the importance of financial statements to all types of businesses.
- Ask students to predict why a partnership does not incur a tax liability on its net income.
- Ask students why partners might want earnings distributed as salaries.
- Ask students why a partner might withdraw assets rather than cash from the business.

PREVIEW CHAPTER OBJECTIVES

- Explain that financial reporting for a partnership has many similarities to that of a corporation.
- Instruct a student to read each chapter objective aloud.

PREVIEW ACCOUNTING TERMS

- Read each term aloud to verify its pronunciation for students.
- Point out terms or parts of terms that should already be familiar to most students, such as *owners' equity statement*.

Chapter 22 Financial Reporting for a Partnership

LEARNING OBJECTIVES

After studying Chapter 22, in addition to defining key terms, you will be able to:

LO1 Calculate the distribution of partnership earnings.

LO2 Journalize entries for the withdrawal of partnership earnings.

LO3 Complete end-of-period work for a partnership.

LO4 Journalize entries for liquidating a partnership.

Calculator: © iStockphoto.com/picstodisc; Paper: © iStockphoto.com/Qingwa

© Monkey Business Images/Shutterstock.com

Background: © iStockphoto.com; Brusonik; Real World: © Photo Courtesy of PVR Partners L.P.

Accounting In The Real World

PVR Partners, L.P.

Believing that the demand for and the price of natural gas are increasing, an individual investor seeks to benefit from these trends by purchasing stock in a business that produces or distributes natural gas. After researching the income and dividend trends of several companies listed on the New York Stock Exchange (NYSE), the investor elects to purchase 300 shares of a stock with the ticker symbol PVR.

While collecting the documents required for filing a federal income tax return, the investor is surprised to open an envelope containing a Schedule K-1 from PVR Partners, L.P. Upon further examination, the investor learns that PVR is a partnership, not a corporation. The investor had disregarded the name of the company and assumed that only the stock of corporations is traded on a national exchange.

PVR Partners is a publicly traded limited partnership that owns and operates natural gas pipelines and processing plants and owns and manages coal properties. Although the business has operated since 1832, it has only been listed on the NYSE since 2001. A publicly traded limited partnership issues limited partnership units rather than stock. The units are traded on the exchange, just like the stock of a corporation.

A *limited partnership* is a form of business organization that has one general partner and can have many limited partners. The general partner manages the business and has the same rights and obligations of a typical partner. The general partner is personally responsible for the debts of the partnership. In contrast, limited partners are not personally liable for debts of the partnership. The financial loss of a limited partner is limited to the value of his or her investment.

The ability of a business to be a limited partnership is subject to individual state laws. The federal government taxes a limited partnership like other partnerships—the income of the partnership is distributed, or passes through, to its partners. For this reason, a partnership is often referred to as a *pass-through entity*. The partnership issues a Schedule K-1 that reports each partner's share of partnership net income. This amount must be reported as income on the partner's individual tax return.

CRITICAL THINKING

1. Why would a business elect to be organized as a limited partnership rather than a corporation?
2. Should the ticker symbols of limited liability partnerships denote that the business is not a corporation?

Source: www.pvrpartners.com.

Key Terms

- distribution deficit
- owners' equity statement
- liquidation of a partnership
- realization

Accounting In The Real World

Answers

1. The income of the limited partnership is only taxed once—on each partner's individual tax return. In contrast, the income of a corporation is taxed twice—the corporation pays income taxes on its earnings, and stockholders are taxed again when the earnings are distributed as dividends.
2. Answers will vary. Some students may devise a simple system to denote that a business is a limited partnership, such as including "-LP" after the ticker symbol. Other students may contend that investors who research their investment decisions will learn how the business is organized, in which country the business is headquartered, and other factors that might impact their investment decisions. These students will insist that this information is readily available to investors and no coding system should be required.

LESSON

22-1

BRIDGE

- Point out that students have learned how to distribute and withdraw earnings for a sole proprietorship. Explain that there are many similarities for a partnership.

TEACHING RESOURCES

- **Instructor's Resource CD/Website:**
  PowerPoint Slides
  Accounting Concepts
- **Working Papers:**
  Teacher's Edition of the Working Papers for Lesson 22-1
  Online Working Papers
- **Transparency Masters:**
  Cash Payments Journal
  General Journal

ENGAGE

- Explain that all earnings of a partnership must be distributed to the partners' capital accounts. The partners can then withdraw the earnings if cash is available in the partnership.
- Emphasize that there are two major differences between end-of-period work for a partnership and a corporation: (1) a corporation pays income tax on its net income; a partnership does not, and (2) a corporation maintains separate accounts for contributed and earned capital; partnerships maintain only one.

PREVIEW

- Call on a student to read the accounting term and definition introduced in this lesson: *distribution deficit*.
- Point out the learning objectives for this lesson.
- Direct students to read the headings in this lesson and to examine the illustrations.

INPUT

- Explain that partnership earnings are distributed to the partners based upon the partnership agreement.
- Explain that there are five commonly used methods for calculating the distribution of partnership earnings. One or more of the five methods listed may be used.

LESSON

22-1 Distribution and Withdrawal of Partnership Earnings

LO1 Calculate the distribution of partnership earnings.
LO2 Journalize entries for the withdrawal of partnership earnings.

Distribution of Partnership Earnings LO1

Most end-of-fiscal-period work is similar for corporations, proprietorships, and partnerships. Two major procedures are different. (1) A corporation calculates and pays income tax on its net income, but partnerships and proprietorships do not. (2) A corporation maintains separate accounts for contributed capital (Capital Stock) and earned capital (Retained Earnings). Partnerships and proprietorships combine contributed and earned capital in one account for each owner.

A corporation may distribute some, but usually not all, of its earnings to stockholders as dividends. Partnerships, like proprietorships, distribute all earnings of the business to the owners' capital accounts. The owners may then withdraw the earnings or leave them in the business.

All of the net income of a partnership is distributed to the partners. Five methods are commonly used for calculating the distribution of partnership earnings.

1. Fixed percentage.
2. Percentage of total equity.
3. Interest on equity.
4. Salaries.
5. Combination of methods.

ETHICS IN ACTION

The Client Is Not Always Right

For over ten years, Susan, a CPA, had prepared the tax returns for Oliver, an art dealer from Beverly Hills. Oliver often referred his clients to Susan and, thus, had been instrumental in building her tax practice.

While preparing Oliver's 2007 tax return, Susan noted a $1.3 million cash deposit that he had not reported. When questioned, Oliver told Susan that the money was from the sale of a painting from his collection. Relying on Oliver's response, Susan recorded the transaction on the proper tax form and filed the return.

Months later, IRS agents were at Susan's door, quizzing her about the transaction. Susan told the agents the details of her phone conversation with Oliver. She soon found herself testifying before a grand jury. Each time, Susan truthfully recounted her conversation with Oliver.

Unknown to Susan, Oliver had stolen money from the sale of a client's Picasso. However, in an attempt to avoid prosecution, Oliver was telling IRS agents a very different story. Oliver and his lawyer met with Susan and pressured her to change her story. Oliver even threatened legal action against Susan. Feeling trapped and wanting to satisfy an important client, Susan reluctantly signed a document stating that she *may have* misunderstood what Oliver told her.

That seemingly simple act would change her life. She had now recounted two different versions of the conversation to the IRS agents. In their eyes, she had lied. Federal law provides for up to 20 years in prison for making false statements to a government agency. Susan ultimately pled guilty and was sentenced to nine months in prison.

INSTRUCTIONS

Susan was placed in a position where she was forced to make an instant decision, a decision that violated her moral values. What could Susan have done to prepare herself better for this situation?

Source: Justin M. Paperny, *Ethics in Motion*, Encino, California: APS Publishing, 2010.

© iStockphoto.com/LdF

ETHICS IN ACTION

Suggested Solution

Susan might have benefited from periodic training in ethics and decision making. The objective of the training would have been to teach her a methodical approach to making important decisions. The training could (1) simulate similar situations to provide practice in handling ethical situations, (2) illustrate methods for taking control of interactions with people who are pushy and manipulative, and (3) demonstrate the negative outcomes of unethical decisions. Most importantly, the training should emphasize that business decisions must be made only after a thorough evaluation of all the facts and implications.

FIXED PERCENTAGE

	Total Net Income	×	Fixed Percentage	=	Share of Net Income
Derrick Bigham	$56,000.00	×	60%	=	$33,600.00
Ethan Ming	$56,000.00	×	40%	=	22,400.00
Total					$56,000.00

The basis on which a partnership's earnings are distributed is usually stated in the partnership agreement. If a partnership agreement does not indicate how to divide the earnings, most state laws stipulate that partners share the earnings equally. The law applies regardless of differences in the partners' investments, abilities, or time devoted to the business.

Derrick Bigham and Ethan Ming are partners. The partnership agreement states that Derrick is to receive 60% and Ethan is to receive 40% of the net income or net loss. The distribution of net income is calculated as shown above.

PERCENTAGE OF TOTAL EQUITY

	Partner's Equity	÷	Total Equity	=	Percentage of Total Equity
Derrick Bigham	$42,000.00	÷	$60,000.00	=	70.0%
Ethan Ming	18,000.00	÷	$60,000.00	=	30.0%
	$60,000.00				

	Total Net Income	×	Percentage of Total Equity	=	Share of Net Income
Derrick Bigham	$56,000.00	×	70.0%	=	$39,200.00
Ethan Ming	$56,000.00	×	30.0%	=	16,800.00
Total					$56,000.00

Partners often agree to use capital account balances on the first day of a fiscal year as the basis for calculating the distribution of partnership earnings. On January 1, Derrick's equity was $42,000.00, and Ethan's equity was $18,000.00. If Derrick and Ethan had agreed to use this method, referred to as the *percentage of total equity method*, each partner's share of net income would have been calculated as shown above.

fyi Limited partnerships include owners who have limited liability and limited operating responsibilities. Limited partnerships are sometimes formed for special projects, such as Broadway plays.

© iStockphoto.com/PhotoTalk

INPUT

- Explain that one of the most common methods for distributing partnership earnings is the fixed percentage method.
- Explain that if a partnership agreement does not specify how earnings are to be distributed, most states stipulate that partners share the earnings equally.

MODEL

- Direct students to the math illustration or use the board to demonstrate how to calculate partners' share of net income using the fixed percentage method.

INPUT

- Explain that the percentage of total equity is calculated in two steps: (1) calculate the percentage of each partner's equity to the total equity of the partnership and (2) multiply each partner's percentage times the total net income.
- Explain that partners often agree to use capital account balances on the first day of a fiscal year as the basis for calculating the equity percentage.

MODEL

- Direct students to the math illustration in the middle of the page and, using the board, demonstrate how to calculate each partner's share of net income using the percentage of total equity.

INPUT

- Explain that the interest on equity method is often used when partners invest different amount s in a partnership.
- Explain that partners often agree to use capital account balances on the first day of a fiscal year as the basis for this distribution. The partnership agreement should state the interest rate that is used.
- Explain that when this method is used, the remaining net income or net loss is distributed using another method.

MODEL

- Direct students to the math illustration at the top of the page and, using the board, demonstrate how to calculate each partner's share of net income using the interest on equity method.

INPUT

- Explain that salaries are often allowed when partners contribute different amounts of time to the partnership or bring different experiences to the partnership.
- Explain that the amount of net income distributed as salary should be stated in the partnership agreement.

INTEREST ON EQUITY

	Partner's Equity	×	Interest Rate	=	Interest on Equity
LaDonna Alford	$22,800.00	×	5%	=	$1,140.00
Morgan Colvin	$45,760.00	×	5%	=	$2,288.00

Interest on equity is often used as a method to distribute earnings when partners invest different amounts in a partnership. Partners often agree to use capital account balances on the first day of a fiscal year as the basis for this income distribution method. The partnership agreement states the interest rate.

Lamor Learning Center's partnership agreement, Article V, shown in Chapter 21, stipulates that each partner is to receive a 5% interest on equity. On January 1, LaDonna Alford's equity is $22,800.00, and Morgan Colvin's equity is $45,760.00. The interest on equity is calculated as shown above.

When the interest on equity method is used, the remaining net income or net loss is distributed using a combination of methods.

SALARIES

Salaries are often used as a method to distribute earnings when partners contribute different amounts of personal service or bring different prior experiences to a partnership. The amount of salary for each partner is stated in the partnership agreement.

Lamor's partnership agreement states that salaries are to be paid as follows: LaDonna Alford, $15,000.00; Morgan Colvin, $20,000.00. When salaries are used, the remaining net income or net loss is distributed using a combination of methods.

THINK LIKE AN ACCOUNTANT

Analyzing Partnership Distributions

Four friends from college own and operate Fun N' Sun, a water and amusement park. For years, the partners have distributed a portion of the partnership income as interest on each partner's equity. The partners initially agreed to use capital account balances on the first day of a fiscal year as the basis for calculating the interest on equity. The partnership agreement provides for an interest rate of 8% and states that partners cannot withdraw more than the balance in their equity accounts.

Over the years, two of the partners have become dissatisfied with the current method of distributing income. One of the other partners regularly withdraws capital soon after the start of the year. The partnership often has to borrow money to fund this withdrawal, causing the partnership to incur additional interest expense.

The partners have asked you to analyze the impact of a distribution method based on a partner's average capital balance. They have provided you with a list of all partner distributions for the prior year, as well as the beginning capital balances.

OPEN THE SPREADSHEET TLA_CH22

The workbook contains the withdrawal transactions and the January 1 capital balances. Follow the steps on the Instructions tab to create the formulas required to calculate the requested information. Answer these questions:

1. Describe the withdrawal patterns of each partner.
2. What would the distribution amounts have been if the prior year's interest were calculated on average equity?
3. Which distribution method do you believe is the most equitable? Support your answer.

© iStockphoto.com/Dan Bachman

THINK LIKE AN ACCOUNTANT

Students are provided a list of withdrawal transactions. Students create a PivotTable to calculate the monthly withdrawal amounts. This information is referenced in an AVERAGE function to calculate an average capital balance for each partner. Finally, students calculate the interest on equity using both the beginning and average capital balances.

The formulas that reference cells in the PivotTable yield a GETPIVOTDATA function. The function appears rather complex but closely resembles a VLOOKUP function. The function

=GETPIVOTDATA("Amount",$A$4,"Date",1, "Payee","Hanna Atwood")

looks up the *Amount* from the PivotTable beginning at *$A$4*, where the *Date* is equal to *1* (January is month 1) and the *Payee* is equal to *Hanna Atwood*. Students are given instructions for modifying the formula to enable it to be copied. Encourage students to explain the purpose of the absolute references entered in the formula. Their knowledge of using absolute references must be applied in the creation of other formulas.

Students are directed to display amounts to the nearest dollar. As a review, consider instructing students to calculate rounded amounts by adding the ROUND function to appropriate functions.

Solution

1. Kelly Willis and Lannie Spring make somewhat consistent withdrawals each month. Although Hanna Atwood does not make a withdrawal every month, her withdrawals are also somewhat consistent. In contrast, Jan Pitts made withdrawals only in January and March, early in the fiscal year. Jan also withdrew more than any other partner, significantly more than did Lannie Spring.
2. Atwood, $2,725; Pitts, $1,489; Willis, $2,694; Spring, $3,564.
3. Answers will vary. Students should note that the average capital differs significantly for Jan Pitts due to her early withdrawal of funds. The average method appears to yield amounts more consistent with each partner's continual investment in the partnership. However, the average method reduces the amount of interest on equity for each partner. As a result, the method leaves more partnership income to be distributed using other methods.

COMBINATION OF METHODS

	Interest on Equity	Salary	Distribution of Remaining Net Income or Net Loss
LaDonna Alford	5%	$5,000.00	50.0%
Morgan Colvin	5%	$3,000.00	50.0%

	LaDonna Alford	Morgan Colvin	Distribution
Total Net Income			$54,800.00
Interest on equity	$ 1,140.00	$ 2,288.00	
Salary	5,000.00	3,000.00	
Total	$ 6,140.00	$ 5,288.00	11,428.00
Remaining Net Income			$43,372.00
Distribution of Remaining Net Income	21,686.00	21,686.00	
Total Distribution	$27,826.00	$26,974.00	$54,800.00

A combination of income distribution methods may be used for distributing partnership earnings. Lamor's partnership agreement states the earnings distribution as shown above. Each partner receives 5% on her January 1 equity. Then each partner is given a salary. The amount of net income remaining, $43,372.00, is distributed using the fixed percentage method.

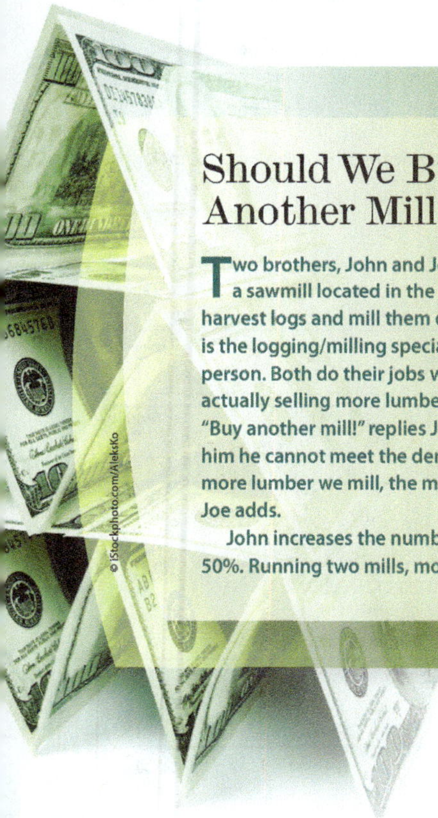

© iStockphoto.com/AleksKo

WHY ACCOUNTING?

Should We Buy Another Mill?

Two brothers, John and Joe, are partners in a sawmill located in the Northwest. They harvest logs and mill them down to lumber. John is the logging/milling specialist. Joe is the salesperson. Both do their jobs well. In fact, Joe is actually selling more lumber than John can mill. "Buy another mill!" replies Joe when John tells him he cannot meet the demand for orders. "The more lumber we mill, the more money we make!" Joe adds.

John increases the number of logs he cuts by 50%. Running two mills, more lumber is produced and sold. They are meeting the demand for lumber and cannot wait until they see the increased profits from the investment. However, when their accountant prepares year-end financial statements, the brothers are disappointed to learn that they had less net income this year than in the prior year.

Agriculture, Food & Natural Resources

CRITICAL THINKING

1. Name three possible reasons for the partnership's decrease in net income.
2. If Joe had taken an accounting class, how could it have helped him in this business decision?

INPUT

- Explain that when a combination of methods is used, the remaining net income or net loss is distributed using one or more additional methods.
- Explain that a combination of two or more of the previously described methods for distributing partnership net income may be used. When a combination of methods is used, generally the percentage of equity method is applied last to distribute any net income or net loss remaining after the distributions have been made by the other methods.

WHY ACCOUNTING?

Answers

1. Answers will vary. Possible answers include the new mill increased the fixed costs per period; the new mill increased variable costs per unit of lumber produced; the contribution margin per unit of lumber produced decreased; the new mill required more direct labor to operate; if money was borrowed to buy the mill, interest expense increased; if investments were sold to buy the mill, investment revenue was lost; even if the contribution margin remains the same, because production increased by only 50%, the contribution margin isn't enough to cover the increase in fixed costs.
2. Joe would have learned how to measure the additional variable and fixed costs associated with the new mill more accurately. He also could have used differential analysis to determine if buying a second mill was a good business decision.

DIFFERENTIATED INSTRUCTION

Tactile/Kinesthetic learners prefer to learn through movement. These students may enjoy going into the community to further explore partnerships. Instruct students to interview a partner from two different partnerships, asking the partner what stipulations were important to record in the agreement as well as which method of distribution of equity was used. Ask students to report their findings to the class.

Auditory/Linguistic learners have highly developed auditory skills and often use spoken language to remember information. Invite a partner in a partnership to speak to the class, explaining conditions of his or her partnership agreement and the method of distribution of income.

INPUT

- Explain that when salaries or interest on equity are stipulated, the amounts are allowed whether or not sufficient net income is available.
- Explain that if the net income is less than the total allowed, partners share in the resulting deficit according to the partnership agreement.
- Stress that a distribution deficit should not be confused with a net loss.

MODEL

- Use the board or direct students to the illustration on the page to demonstrate the distribution of net income showing a distribution deficit.

INPUT

- Explain that partners may take assets out of the partnership during the year. Assets taken out of a business for the owner's personal use are known as withdrawals.
- Explain that the partnership agreement usually limits the amount of assets that may be withdrawn.
- Emphasize that a partner's salary is designated as a method of distribution or as a withdrawal from the partner's equity, not an expense to the business.

MODEL

- Use a transparency or direct students to the illustration on the page to explain how to journalize the withdrawal of partnership earnings for personal use.

Distribution of Net Income Showing a Distribution Deficit

	Interest on Equity	Partner's Equity	Salary	Distribution of Remaining Net Income or Net Loss
Daniel Davis	10%	$60,000.00	$30,000.00	40.0%
Malorie Franks	10%	$14,000.00	$40,000.00	60.0%

	Daniel Davis	Malorie Franks	Distribution
Total net income			$74,600.00
Interest on equity	$ 6,000.00	$ 1,400.00	
Salary	30,000.00	40,000.00	
Total	$36,000.00	$41,400.00	77,400.00
Distribution deficit			$ (2,800.00)
Distribution of distribution deficit	(1,120.00)	(1,680.00)	
Total distribution	$34,880.00	$39,720.00	$74,600.00

Distribute the Distribution Deficit

Distribute Interest on Equity and Salaries

Calculate the Distribution Deficit

When salaries or interest on equity are stipulated, the amounts are allowed whether or not sufficient net income is available. D&F Landscaping's distributions of interest and salaries total $77,400.00, which is $2,800.00 more than the partnership's total net income of $74,600.00. A negative balance that remains after partner salaries and interest are subtracted from total income is called a **distribution deficit**. D&F Landscaping has a distribution deficit of $2,800.00 that is distributed to the partners by using the fixed percentage method.

A distribution deficit should not be confused with a net loss. A partnership with a net income can have a distribution deficit while calculating net income distributions. The distribution deficit simply reduces the amount of net income distributed to each partner.

Withdrawal of Partnership Earnings LO2

CASH PAYMENTS JOURNAL — PAGE 10

	DATE		ACCOUNT TITLE	CK. NO.	POST. REF.	1 GENERAL DEBIT	2 GENERAL CREDIT	3 ACCOUNTS PAYABLE DEBIT	4 PURCHASES DISCOUNT CREDIT	5 CASH CREDIT	
25	20-- June	28	LaDonna Alford, Drawing	123		1 000 00				1 000 00	25
26											26
27											27

A partner often needs a portion of the annual net income before the end of a fiscal year when the actual net income is known. Thus, during a fiscal year, partners take assets out of the partnership in anticipation of the net income for the year. Assets taken out of a business for the owner's personal use are known as *withdrawals*. Usually, the partnership agreement indicates limits on the amount of assets that may be withdrawn.

June 28, 20--. LaDonna Alford, partner, withdrew cash for personal use, $1,000.00. Check No. 123.

LaDonna Alford, Drawing	
1,000.00	

Cash	
	1,000.00

Withdrawal of Assets Other than Cash

GENERAL JOURNAL — PAGE 9

	DATE		ACCOUNT TITLE	DOC. NO.	POST. REF.	DEBIT	CREDIT	
1	20-- July	2	Morgan Colvin, Drawing	M33		150 00		1
2			Supplies—Office				150 00	2
3								3

A partner may elect to take partnership assets instead of cash. Assets such as office supplies withdrawn for personal use are not a business expense. This transaction reduces the partnership's office supplies inventory, and therefore, Supplies—Office is credited.

The withdrawal is a reduction of the partner's equity in the partnership. Rather than debiting Morgan Colvin's capital account, the transaction is debited to Morgan Colvin, Drawing. The accounting procedure of debiting withdrawals to a drawing account is consistent with accounting for a proprietorship.

July 2, 20--. Morgan Colvin, partner, withdrew office supplies for personal use, $150.00. Memorandum No. 33.

Morgan Colvin, Drawing	
150.00	

Supplies—Office	
	150.00

FINANCIAL LITERACY

Signing Away the Future

We have all heard stories about business partnerships failing. Unfortunately, it is estimated that over half of all business partnerships fail. At the same time, many business partnerships have thrived. Evan Williams and Biz Stone of Twitter, Ben Cohen and Jerry Greenfield of Ben & Jerry's, and William Procter and James Gamble of Procter & Gamble all discovered that planning and assessing potential risks are keys to preventing partnership pitfalls.

A planned exit strategy allows one of the partners to walk away from the partnership, which is an agreement not to pursue business from existing clients or compete against the existing business. Non-compete agreements usually include terms such as length of time and proximity. Some companies even require new employees to sign a non-compete agreement to protect the interests of the business.

© iStockphoto.com/Norebbo

ACTIVITIES

1. Jackson was employed as a salesperson for a uniform supply company. He obtained a job with another company that supplied rental equipment in addition to uniforms. After six months, Jackson's employer told him that they would have to let him go due to a non-compete agreement with his former employer. What could Jackson have done to avoid termination on this job? Explain.
2. Innovative industries such as Microsoft, Apple, and Google have recently been involved in some very public disputes to enforce non-compete agreements. Using the Internet, research examples of disputes involving non-compete agreements in innovative industries. Share with the class the name of the company, the name of the individual (if applicable), the problem, and the outcome.
3. Imara was required to sign a non-compete agreement for a term of one year after leaving her fast-food employer. She received an offer from another fast-food restaurant for more pay. Do you think the non-compete agreement will be enforced? Explain.

INPUT

- Explain that a partner may withdraw assets other than cash from the business. Such a transaction is recorded in a general journal.
- Explain that the asset withdrawn should be decreased by a credit entry to the asset account.

MODEL

- Prepare a transparency of a general journal to illustrate recording a partner's withdrawal of an asset other than cash or direct students to the illustration.

FINANCIAL LITERACY

Answers

1. Jackson could have taken a non-sales position with his new employer, or he could have taken a sales position with another company where he wouldn't be competing for the same customers as his former employer.
2. Answers will vary.
3. The non-compete agreement probably will not be enforced in this case, because Imara is not likely to be taking secret recipes or customers away from the former business.

FORMATIVE ASSESSMENT

- This is an ongoing process. Circulate around the classroom or lab, observing which students have difficulty with the assignments.
- Troubleshooting: Diagnose the kinds of problems students have with this section. Students may have trouble calculating the complete distribution of partnership net income. Students may also have difficulty distributing net income when interest on equity or salaries are used or when a distribution deficit occurs. Some students may have trouble determining which accounts to credit when a partner withdraws assets other than cash.
- Assess student understanding by checking solutions to Independent Practice assignments and noting their answers to the Term Review and Audit Your Understanding questions.

CHECK FOR UNDERSTANDING

Term Review

- Call on a student to define the term in the Term Review. A definition is given in the Glossary.

Audit Your Understanding

- Call on students to answer the Audit Your Understanding questions. Answers are given in Appendix D.

GUIDED PRACTICE

Work Together

- Have students write the solution to the Work Together problem as you guide the class through the examples.
- Direct students to calculate partnership earnings and to journalize partnership withdrawals.

INDEPENDENT PRACTICE

On Your Own

- Assign the On Your Own problem to be worked independently.
- Use the Formative Assessment techniques to diagnose student understanding.

Application Problem

- Assign Application Problem 22-1.

Online Working Papers

- Students can access the Lesson 22-1 problems using this software.

Website

- Direct students to the C21 Accounting companion website for additional practice and review opportunities throughout the chapter.

RETEACH

- Write on the board a partnership's net income and distribution methods to be used.
- Ask the class to calculate the distribution of net income using the methods provided.
- Ask a student to give the answer and describe how the calculation was performed.
- Repeat the process if some students need the review.

Essential Questions

- How would someone determine the fixed percentage if the partners' investments differed as well as the time devoted to the business? (*The total investment amount should be determined and each partner's investment should be divided into the total to determine the percentage of contribution. In addition, estimated work contribution could determine the percentage of total ownership as well.*)
- What are some reasons a partner with no financial investment still might receive a salary or fixed percentage in the distribution of earnings? (*The partner may be rewarded for contributing time, or a valuable name, or other assets to the business.*)

EXTENDED LEARNING

- Assign Accounting in the Real World on page 645.
- Assign Ethics in Action on page 646.
- Assign Think Like an Accountant on page 648.
- Assign Why Accounting on page 649.
- Assign Financial Literacy on page 651.

End of Lesson Review

LO1 Calculate the distribution of partnership earnings.

LO2 Journalize entries for the withdrawal of partnership earnings.

Term Review

distribution deficit

Audit your understanding

1. Where should the method of distributing partnership earnings be stated?
2. When does a distribution deficit occur?
3. What account is debited when a partner withdraws cash for personal use?
4. How is the accounting for owner withdrawals the same for partnerships and proprietorships?

Work together 22-1

Calculating partnership earnings and journalizing partnership withdrawals

Jen Turner and Lavenia Hogan are partners in a business. On January 1 of the current year, the partners' equities are Jen, $23,000.00, and Lavenia, $39,000.00. Forms are provided in the *Working Papers*. Your instructor will guide you through the following examples.

1. For each of the following independent cases, calculate how the net income of $50,000.00 will be distributed to the two partners.
   a. Each partner receives a share of net income based on a percentage of equity.
   b. Each partner receives 10% interest on equity and an equal share of remaining net income.
2. Calculate how net income of $40,000.00 will be distributed to the two partners. Jen receives 8% interest on equity and a salary of $18,000.00. Lavenia receives 8% interest on equity and a salary of $20,000.00. The partners share remaining net income, net loss, or distribution deficit as follows: Jen, 60% and Lavenia, 40%.
3. Record the following transactions in the appropriate journal.

Transactions:

July 20. Jen Turner, partner, withdrew cash for personal use, $750.00. Check No. 146.
23. Lavenia Hogan, partner, withdrew office supplies for personal use, $45.00. Memorandum No. 33.

On your own 22-1

Calculating partnership earnings and journalizing partnership withdrawals

Greg Judson and Pauline Malone are partners in a business. On January 1 of the current year, the partners' equities are Greg, $30,000.00, and Pauline, $18,000.00. Forms are provided in the *Working Papers*. Work independently to complete the following problem.

1. For each of the following independent cases, calculate how the net income of $60,000.00 will be distributed to the two partners.
   a. Each partner receives a share of net income based on a percentage of equity.
   b. Each partner receives 6% interest on equity and an equal share of remaining net income.
2. Calculate how net income of $70,000.00 will be distributed to the two partners. Greg receives 10% interest on equity and a salary of $34,000.00. Pauline receives 10% interest on equity and a salary of $42,000.00. The partners share remaining net income, net loss, or distribution deficit as follows: Greg, 65% and Pauline, 35%.
3. Record the following transactions in the appropriate journal.

Transactions:

Aug. 12. Greg Judson, partner, withdrew store supplies for personal use, $80.00. Memorandum No. 62.
15. Pauline Malone, partner, withdrew cash for personal use, $500.00. Check No. 206.

LESSON

22-2 End-of-Period Work for a Partnership

LO3 Complete end-of-period work for a partnership.

Income Statement LO3

Lamor Learning Center Income Statement For the Year Ended December 31, 20--			
			% of Sales*
Operating Revenue:			
Sales		$98,156.25	100.0
Operating Expenses:			
Advertising Expense	$ 2,185.00		2.2
Depreciation Expense—Equipment	5,460.00		5.6
Depreciation Expense—Car	4,800.00		4.9
Insurance Expenses	3,500.00		3.6
Miscellaneous Expense	6,153.50		6.3
Rent Expense	10,800.00		11.0
Supplies Expense—Educational	2,452.60		2.5
Supplies Expense—Office	1,984.80		2.0
Uncollectible Accounts Expense	2,405.00		2.5
Utilities Expense	3,615.35		3.7
Total Operating Expenses		43,356.25	44.2
Net Income		$54,800.00	55.8

*Rounded to the nearest 0.1%.

The end-of-period work for a partnership is similar to that for a proprietorship or a corporation. An unadjusted trial balance assists accountants in preparing adjusting entries. The adjusting entries are posted, and then an adjusted trial balance provides the amounts necessary for preparing the financial statements.

With one exception, Lamor Learning Center's income statement is the same as that of any small business that provides a service. Unlike a corporation, however, a partnership does not pay federal income taxes. As described later in this chapter, partnership net income is reported on the partners' personal tax returns. Thus, Lamor's income statement does not contain references to net income before federal income tax, federal income tax expense, or net income after federal income tax.

Lamor's income statement contains vertical analysis ratios for every amount. Each ratio is calculated by dividing each amount by sales. The partners use this information to determine if each amount is within its target range. Any ratios that are outside the target range should be investigated, and if necessary, corrective action should be taken.

LESSON

22-2

BRIDGE

- Point out that students have prepared an income statement and balance sheet for a merchandising business organized as a corporation. In this lesson, they will learn how to prepare these statements for a partnership.

TEACHING RESOURCES

- **Instructor's Resource CD/Website:**
  PowerPoint Slides
  Accounting Concepts
- **Working Papers:**
  Teacher's Edition of the Working Papers for Lesson 22-2
  Online Working Papers

ENGAGE

- Explain that, like a corporation, a partnership also prepares end-of-period statements.
- Point out that in this lesson, students will learn to prepare an owners' equity statement that is different from that of a corporation.

PREVIEW

- Call on a student to read the accounting term and definition introduced in this lesson: *owners' equity statement*.
- Point out the learning objective for this lesson.
- Direct students to read the headings in this lesson and to examine the illustrations.

INPUT

- Explain that after adjusting entries have been prepared and posted, an adjusted trial balance provides the amounts necessary to prepare the financial statements.
- Point out that a partnership, unlike a corporation, does not pay federal taxes because partnership net income is reported on the partners' personal tax returns.
- Explain that an income statement is used to report a partnership's financial progress during a period.
- Explain that an income statement of a partnership service business has two main sections: (1) revenue section and (2) expenses section.
- Explain how partners use the information provided from the vertical analysis ratios.

MODEL

- Direct students to the income statement shown in the illustration.
- Using several line items, divide each amount by total sales to demonstrate how the vertical analysis ratios are calculated.

INPUT

- Explain that the owners' equity represents the owners' share of the business.
- Explain that a successful business should continue to grow, as should owners' equity.
- Explain that the owners' equity statement summarizes the changes in owners' equity during a period.
- Explain that three factors are considered when calculating total owners' equity for each partner: (1) beginning capital, (2) share of net income or net loss, and (3) withdrawals.

MODEL

- Direct students to the illustration on the page while demonstrating on the board how to calculate total owners' equity.

Owners' Equity Statement

Lamor Learning Center
Owners' Equity Statement
For the Year Ended December 31, 20--

LaDonna Alford:			
Capital, January 1, 20--		$22,800.00	
Share of Net Income	$23,688.80		
Less Withdrawals	22,000.00		
Net Increase in Capital		1,688.80	
Capital, December 31, 20--			$24,488.80
Morgan Colvin:			
Capital, January 1, 20--		$45,760.00	
Share of Net Income	$31,111.20		
Less Withdrawals	24,500.00		
Net Increase in Capital		6,611.20	
Capital, December 31, 20--			52,371.20
Total Owners' Equity, December 31, 20--			$76,860.00

Partners' Distribution of Net Income

Beginning Capital Account Balance

Share of Net Income Less Withdrawals

Beginning Capital Plus Net Increase in Capital

Total of Partners' Withdrawals

Total Capital of All Partners

A corporation's equity is reported on a statement of stockholders' equity. A similar statement is prepared for a partnership. A financial statement that summarizes the changes in owners' equity during a fiscal period is called an **owners' equity statement**. This statement reports the changes in each partner's equity. The partner's share of net income, less any withdrawals, is added to the partner's beginning capital balance to calculate the partner's equity balance on the statement date.

© Stephen Coburn/Shutterstock.com

Balance Sheet

Lamor Learning Center Balance Sheet December 31, 20--		
OWNERS' EQUITY		
LaDonna Alford, Capital	$24,488.80	
Morgan Colvin, Capital	52,371.20	
Total Owners' Equity		76,860.00
Total Liabilities and Owners' Equity		$92,154.35

The asset and liability sections of a balance sheet are the same for a proprietorship, a partnership, and a corporation. The owners' equity section of a partnership's balance sheet, however, is different. On a partnership balance sheet, each partner's ending capital is reported under the heading Owners' Equity. Each partner's capital amount is obtained from the owners' equity statement.

Adjusting and Closing Entries

GENERAL JOURNAL PAGE 16

	DATE		ACCOUNT TITLE	DOC. NO.	POST. REF.	DEBIT	CREDIT		
1			*Closing Entries*					1	
23		31	*Income Summary*			54 800 00		23	Close Income Summary
24			*LaDonna Alford, Capital*				23 688 80	24	
25			*Morgan Colvin, Capital*				31 111 20	25	
26		31	*LaDonna Alford, Capital*			22 000 00		26	Close Drawing Accounts
27			*LaDonna Alford, Drawing*				22 000 00	27	
28		31	*Morgan Colvin, Capital*			24 500 00		28	
29			*Morgan Colvin, Drawing*				24 500 00	29	
30								30	
31								31	

The adjusting entries are similar for a proprietorship, a partnership, and a corporation. Only a corporation records federal income tax expenses.

The entries to close revenue and expense accounts are the same for all businesses. One entry closes all temporary accounts having a credit balance. A second entry closes all temporary accounts having a debit balance. Each closing entry results in a debit or a credit to Income Summary.

The entries to close Income Summary and temporary equity accounts are different for each form of organization. A partnership closes Income Summary to the partners' capital accounts. Each partner's drawing account is closed to the partner's capital account.

INPUT

- Explain that a balance sheet reports a partnership's financial condition on a specific date.
- Explain that on a corporate balance sheet, summarized information about capital stock is reported under the heading Stockholders' Equity. On a partnership balance sheet, each partner's ending capital is reported under the heading Owners' Equity.
- Explain that the owners' equity statement reports each partner's capital amount used for the balance sheet.

MODEL

- Direct students to the illustration of the balance sheet to review the format of the owners' equity section of the balance sheet.
- Emphasize that the only difference between a corporation balance sheet and a partnership balance sheet is the name and the way the owners' equity is reported.

INPUT

- Explain that the adjustments for revenue and expenses are the same for all businesses.
- Review that one entry closes all temporary accounts having a credit balance and that a second entry closes all temporary accounts having a debit balance. Each closing entry then results in a debit or credit to Income Summary.
- Explain that a partnership closes Income Summary to the partners' capital accounts and that each partner's drawing account is closed to the partner's capital account.
- Point out that no source document is necessary when journalizing adjusting entries.

DIFFERENTIATED INSTRUCTION

Visual/Spatial learners like to see what is being discussed. Ask students to create a sample balance sheet for each of the three forms of business ownership (sole proprietorship, partnership, and corporation). Ask students to prepare posters using a different font color to show the owners' equity portions of each statement. Display completed posters around the room.

INPUT

- Explain that the Internal Revenue Service classifies partners as self-employed persons whose salaries are not an expense of the partnership.
- Explain that although a partnership does not pay federal income tax on its net income, it does submit to the IRS a partnership tax return that reports the earnings distributed to each partner.
- Explain that partners include their share of the partnership net income or net loss on their personal income tax returns.

Federal Income Taxes

Lamor's distribution of net income includes salaries for each of the partners. However, the Internal Revenue Service does not consider partners to be employees of the partnership. The IRS classifies the partners as self-employed persons, whose salaries are not an expense of the partnership. Therefore, partners' salaries and withdrawals are considered the withdrawals of partnership equity, not expenses.

A partnership does not pay income tax on its earnings. However, a partnership does submit to the IRS a partnership tax return that reports the earnings distributed to each partner. This type of return is known as an *information return*. The partnership tax return is filed on Form 1065. Each partner receives a Schedule K-1 that reports the partner's capital balances and share of partnership net income. The partners include their respective share of the partnership net income or net loss on their personal income tax returns.

As self-employed persons, partners are entitled to old-age, survivors, disability, and hospitalization insurance benefits known collectively as social security and Medicare. Each partner personally pays a self-employment tax to qualify for social security and Medicare coverage. Therefore, the self-employment tax rate is double that of an employed individual's social security and Medicare tax rates. Thus, the same total amount of social security and Medicare taxes are paid for both self-employed persons and employees. The self-employment taxes are personal expenses of the partners, not of the partnership. Therefore, partners' self-employment social security and Medicare taxes are not recorded on partnership records. [CONCEPT: Business Entity]

INPUT

- Explain that after adjusting and closing entries have been posted, a partnership prepares a post-closing trial balance.
- Explain that a partnership post-closing trial balance is similar to that of a corporation, with the exception of the capital accounts.

Post-Closing Trial Balance

Lamor Learning Center
Post-Closing Trial Balance
December 31, 20--

Account Title	Debit	Credit
Cash	$ 8,568.45	
LaDonna Alford, Capital		24,488.80
Morgan Colvin, Capital		52,371.20
	$93,354.35	$93,354.35

After adjusting and closing entries have been posted, Lamor prepares a post-closing trial balance. Lamor's post-closing trial balance is similar to that of a corporation, with the exception of the partners' capital accounts.

© StockLite/Shutterstock.com

FORMATIVE ASSESSMENT

- This is an ongoing process. Circulate around the classroom or lab, observing which students have difficulty with the assignments.
- Troubleshooting: Diagnose the kinds of problems students have with this lesson. Students may have difficulty labeling the equity section of a partnership balance sheet, or they may need a reminder of how to complete closing entries.
- Assess student understanding by checking solutions to Independent Practice assignments and noting their answers to the Term Review and Audit Your Understanding questions.

End of Lesson Review

LO3 Complete end-of-period work for a partnership.

Term Review

owners' equity statement

Audit your understanding

1. Why does a partnership not record an adjusting entry for federal income taxes?
2. What is the purpose of the owners' equity statement?
3. Are partners taxed on their distributions or withdrawals? Explain.
4. How are social security and Medicare taxes paid on partners' distributions?

Work together 22-2

End-of-period work for a partnership

Jeffrey Lowe and Mona Ray are partners in a business. On January 1 of the current year, the partners' equities were Jeffrey, $46,000.00, and Mona, $34,000.00. The net income for the year is $70,000.00. Statement paper and a general journal are provided in the *Working Papers*. Your instructor will guide you through the following examples.

1. For the fiscal year ended December 31, 20--, prepare an owners' equity statement. Each partner is to receive 8% interest on January 1 equity. Also, partners' salaries are Jeffrey, $36,500.00, and Mona, $24,500.00. The remaining net income, net loss, or distribution deficit is shared equally. During the year, Jeffrey withdrew cash of $29,000.00 and Mona withdrew cash of $22,000.00.
2. Journalize the entries to close Income Summary and the owners' equity accounts.

On your own 22-2

End-of-period work for a partnership

Kim Peters and Mitzi West are partners in a business. On January 1 of the current year, the partners' equities were Kim, $63,000.00, and Mitzi, $15,000.00. The net income for the year is $89,000.00. Statement paper and a general journal are provided in the *Working Papers*. Work independently to complete the following problem.

1. For the fiscal year ended December 31, 20--, prepare an owners' equity statement. Each partner is to receive 10% interest on January 1 equity. Also, partners' salaries are Kim, $25,000.00, and Mitzi, $12,500.00. The remaining net income, net loss, or distribution deficit is shared 80% to Kim and 20% to Mitzi. During the year, Kim withdrew cash of $52,600.00 and Mitzi withdrew cash of $8,000.00.
2. Journalize the entries to close Income Summary and the owners' equity accounts.

CHECK FOR UNDERSTANDING

Term Review

- Call on a student to define the term in the Term Review. A definition is given in the Glossary.

Audit Your Understanding

- Call on students to answer the Audit Your Understanding questions. Answers are given in Appendix D.

GUIDED PRACTICE

Work Together

- Have students write the solution to the Work Together problem as you guide the class through the examples.
- Direct students to prepare end-of-period work for a partnership.

INDEPENDENT PRACTICE

On Your Own

- Assign the On Your Own problem to be worked independently.
- Use the Formative Assessment techniques to diagnose student understanding.

Application Problem

- Assign Application Problem 22-2.

Online Working Papers

- Students can access the Lesson 22-2 problems using this software.

RETEACH

- Use information from Recycling Problem 22-R and the board or transparencies to demonstrate how to prepare an income statement, an owners' equity statement, and a balance sheet.

CLOSURE

- Ask students to summarize briefly the procedures for preparing a distribution of net income statement and an owners' equity statement.

Essential Questions

- If rent expense and utilities expense are the greatest ratios on the income statement, what could be done to decrease these expenses? (*Other locations could be evaluated, or possibly a home office if applicable. Other sources for utilities could be considered, or an effort made to be more frugal with lights and temperature control.*)
- Are stipulations important to include in the partnership agreement for owner withdrawals? Explain. (*Limiting withdrawals is necessary. A business may not be able to operate effectively if an owner regularly withdraws cash.*)

LESSON

22-3

BRIDGE

- Point out that students have learned how to determine the book value of an asset. In this lesson, they will learn the importance of accounting for book value when an asset is liquidated.

TEACHING RESOURCES

- **Instructor's Resource CD/Website:**
  PowerPoint Slides
  Accounting Concepts
- **Working Papers:**
  Teacher's Edition of the Working Papers for Lesson 22-3
  Online Working Papers
- **Transparency Masters:**
  Cash Receipts Journal
  Cash Payments Journal
  General Journal

ENGAGE

- Ask students if they have seen an advertisement for a store's liquidation sale.
- Ask students why liabilities must be paid before remaining assets are distributed to partners.

PREVIEW

- Call on students to read the accounting terms and definitions introduced in this lesson: *liquidation of a partnership* and *realization*.
- Point out the learning objective for this lesson.
- Direct students to read the headings in this lesson and to examine the illustrations.

INPUT

- Explain that when a partnership is liquidated, the noncash assets are sold and the available cash is used to pay remaining partnership liabilities before remaining assets are distributed to the partners.
- Point out that when noncash assets are sold for more than the recorded book value, the amount in excess of the book value is recorded as a gain on realization. The account title is Gain or Loss on Realization.

LESSON

22-3 Liquidation of a Partnership

LO4 Journalize entries for liquidating a partnership.

Recognizing a Gain on Realization in a Partnership Liquidation LO4

Value of Asset Received	–	Book Value of Asset Sold		=	Gain on Realization
		Cost	$18,000.00		
		Acc. Depr.	12,000.00		
Cash $8,400.00	–	Book Value	$ 6,000.00	=	$2,400.00

CASH RECEIPTS JOURNAL — PAGE 14

	DATE		ACCOUNT TITLE	DOC. NO.	POST. REF.	1 GENERAL DEBIT	2 GENERAL CREDIT	3 ACCOUNTS RECEIVABLE CREDIT	4 SALES CREDIT	5 SALES TAX PAYABLE CREDIT	6 SALES DISCOUNT DEBIT	7 CASH DEBIT	
1	20-- Nov.	3	Accum. Depr.—Equipment	R845		12 000 00						8 400 00	1
2			Equipment				18 000 00						2
3			Gain or Loss on Realization				2 400 00						3
4													4
5													5

If a partnership elects or is forced to go out of business, its assets are distributed to the creditors and the partners. The process of paying a partnership's liabilities and distributing remaining assets to the partners is called **liquidation of a partnership**.

Cash received from the sale of assets during liquidation of a partnership is called **realization**. Typically, when a partnership is liquidated, the noncash assets are sold, and the available cash is used to pay the creditors. Any remaining cash is distributed to the partners according to each partner's total equity.

On November 1, Janice Rona and Ira Barnes began the process of liquidating their partnership. At that time, financial statements were prepared and adjusting and closing entries were journalized and posted.

Noncash assets might be sold for more than the recorded book value. When this happens, the amount received in excess of the book value is recorded as a gain on realization. The gain is recorded as a credit in an account titled Gain or Loss on Realization.

Gain or Loss on Realization	
Loss on Realization	Gain on Realization

November 3, 20--. Received cash from sale of equipment, $8,400.00; original cost, $18,000.00; total accumulated depreciation recorded to date, $12,000.00. Receipt No. 845.

remember In a partnership liquidation, remaining cash is distributed according to the balance in each partner's equity account—not according to the ratio by which they share income and losses.

MODEL

- Direct students to the illustration as you explain the amounts recorded in the noncash asset accounts. Explain that these are book values and not necessarily market values.
- Direct students to the T accounts illustrated to show account balances before liquidation and after equipment is sold.

The account balances before liquidation and the November 3 transaction to liquidate equipment are shown below. After the equipment is sold, the balance of the Equipment and Accumulated Depreciation—Equipment accounts are zero.

Cash

Beg. Bal.	5,000.00		
Nov. 3	8,400.00		
(New Bal.	*13,400.00)*		

Supplies

Beg. Bal.	1,000.00		

Equipment

Beg. Bal.	18,000.00	Nov. 3	18,000.00
(New Bal. zero)			

Accumulated Depreciation—Equipment

Nov. 3	12,000.00	Beg. Bal.	12,000.00
		(New Bal. zero)	

Accounts Payable

		Beg. Bal.	7,000.00

Janice Rona, Capital

		Beg. Bal.	3,000.00

Ira Barnes, Capital

		Beg. Bal.	2,000.00

Gain or Loss on Realization

		Nov. 3	2,400.00

Recognizing a Loss on Realization in a Partnership Liquidation

Value of Asset Received	–	**Book Value of Asset Sold**	=	**Loss on Realization**
Cash $800.00	–	Supplies $1,000.00	=	($200.00)

CASH RECEIPTS JOURNAL PAGE *14*

	DATE		ACCOUNT TITLE	DOC. NO.	POST. REF.	1 GENERAL DEBIT	2 GENERAL CREDIT	3 ACCOUNTS RECEIVABLE CREDIT	4 SALES CREDIT	5 SALES TAX PAYABLE CREDIT	6 SALES DISCOUNT DEBIT	7 CASH DEBIT	
4		6	*Gain or Loss on Realization*	*R846*		*200 00*						*800 00*	4
5			*Supplies*				*1 000 00*						5
6													6

Sometimes during liquidation, the sale of an asset brings in less cash than the recorded book value.

November 6, 20-- Received cash from sale of supplies, $800.00; balance of supplies account, $1,000.00. Receipt No. 846.

The supplies were sold for $200.00 less than the recorded value, resulting in a loss on realization. The loss is recorded as a debit to Gain or Loss on Realization.

Cash

Beg. Bal.	5,000.00		
Nov. 3	8,400.00		
Nov. 6	800.00		
(New Bal.	*14,200.00)*		

Supplies

Beg. Bal.	1,000.00	Nov. 6	1,000.00
(New Bal. zero)			

Gain or Loss on Realization

Nov. 6	200.00	Nov. 3	2,400.00
		(New Bal.	*2,200.00)*

INPUT

- Explain that sometimes during liquidation, the sale of an asset brings in less cash than the recorded book value.

MODEL

- Describe how to calculate the loss on realization, using the math illustration.
- Use the cash receipts journal transparency to show recording a loss on realization or direct students to the illustration.
- Point out that a loss on realization is a debit entry.
- Direct students to the T accounts illustrated to show account balances before liquidation and after supplies are sold for less than the recorded value.

Careers In Accounting

Review a career as a credit analyst.

Careers In Accounting

Emma Shoquist

CREDIT ANALYST

© wavebreakmedia/Shutterstock.com

Emma Shoquist is a credit analyst for a large bank with branches throughout the United States. In her role as credit analyst, she assists loan officers and other bank employees in granting loans to customers. Once a loan officer has met with the client and helped the client prepare the loan application, the application and all supporting documents are sent to Ms. Shoquist. She will analyze the application, credit bureau reports, financial statements, and other documentation. She will evaluate the client's financial position to determine the degree of risk the bank would take on by granting the loan. She will also compare the client's degree of risk with that of other companies in the same industry.

At times, Ms. Shoquist communicates with the client directly. For example, when Ms. Shoquist receives a credit bureau report that indicates the client is past due on several accounts, she will notify the client, who may disagree with the credit bureau report. She will work with the client to verify the accuracy of the report. Once she feels she has an accurate picture of the client, she will prepare a report for the loan committee, stating her appraisal of the creditworthiness of the application.

When Ms. Shoquist first started working at the bank, she evaluated loan applications primarily for individuals. As she acquired more experience, she moved to the commercial side of the bank, where she only analyzes credit applications for commercial loans.

Ms. Shoquist uses computers every day. Many of the reports she gathers are computer-generated. She also uses a spreadsheet program to calculate common accounting ratios when analyzing financial statements. She feels computers make her work more efficient and more accurate.

Ms. Shoquist likes working with her fellow employees and directly with clients. Her college personal communications classes prepared her to communicate ideas and findings in a clear manner. Her accounting classes taught her to evaluate financial statements. She feels that to be successful as a credit analyst, she must be comfortable making a decision—often involving hundreds of thousands of dollars.

Salary Range: In 2012, the median wage for a loan officer was $61,080.00.

Qualifications: Most jobs in the credit analyst field require a bachelor's degree. Course work and experience in finance and accounting are helpful.

Occupational Outlook: The growth for loan officer positions is projected to be faster than average (20% to 28%) for the period from 2010 to 2020.

Source: www.onetonline.org.

© iStockphoto.com/Mlenny

Liquidating Liabilities

CASH PAYMENTS JOURNAL — PAGE 18

	DATE		ACCOUNT TITLE	CK. NO.	POST. REF.	GENERAL DEBIT (1)	GENERAL CREDIT (2)	ACCOUNTS PAYABLE DEBIT (3)	PURCHASES DISCOUNT CREDIT (4)	CASH CREDIT (5)	
1	20-- Nov.	10	Hillside Supply	921				3 000 00		3 000 00	1
2		10	Mentory Industries	922				4 000 00		4 000 00	2
3											3

The partnership's available cash is used to pay creditors. The checks prepared to pay each creditor are recorded in the cash payments journal.

November 10, 20--. Paid cash to all creditors for the amounts owed, Check No. 921 to Hillside Supply for $3,000.00, and Check No. 922 to Mentory Industries for $4,000.00.

Cash

Debit		Credit	
Beg. Bal.	5,000.00	Nov. 10	3,000.00
Nov. 3	8,400.00	Nov. 10	4,000.00
Nov. 6	800.00		
(New Bal.	*7,200.00)*		

Accounts Payable

Debit		Credit	
Nov. 10	3,000.00	Beg. Bal.	7,000.00
Nov. 10	4,000.00	*(New Bal. zero)*	

Liquidating liabilities does not typically result in a gain or loss on liquidation. However, sometimes debtors are willing to settle their accounts for less than the recorded amount. In this case, a gain on liquidation would be recorded.

Account Balances After Liquidation of Noncash Assets and Liabilities

Cash

Debit		Credit	
Beg. Bal.	5,000.00	Nov. 10	3,000.00
Nov. 3	8,400.00	Nov. 10	4,000.00
Nov. 6	800.00		
(New Bal.	*7,200.00)*		

Accounts Payable

Debit		Credit	
Nov. 10	3,000.00	Beg. Bal.	7,000.00
Nov. 10	4,000.00	*(New Bal. zero)*	

Supplies

Debit		Credit	
Beg. Bal.	1,000.00	Nov. 6	1,000.00
(New Bal. zero)			

Janice Rona, Capital

Debit		Credit	
		Beg. Bal.	3,000.00

Equipment

Debit		Credit	
Beg. Bal.	18,000.00	Nov. 3	18,000.00
(New Bal. zero)			

Ira Barnes, Capital

Debit		Credit	
		Beg. Bal.	2,000.00

Accumulated Depreciation—Equipment

Debit		Credit	
Nov. 3	12,000.00	Beg. Bal.	12,000.00
(New Bal. zero)			

Gain or Loss on Realization

Debit		Credit	
Nov. 6	200.00	Nov. 3	2,400.00
		(New Bal.	*2,200.00)*

The transactions recorded for the sale of assets and the liquidation of liabilities are shown in the T accounts. When these transactions have been journalized and posted, the partnership has only four general ledger accounts with balances: Cash, Gain or Loss on Realization, and the two partners' capital accounts.

INPUT

- Explain that a partnership's available cash is used to pay creditors.

MODEL

- Use a transparency of a cash payments journal to show how to record a payment to creditors or direct students to the illustration.
- Describe the cash payments journal entry to record the payment of a liability.
- Direct students to the T accounts illustrated to show account balances before liquidation of liabilities and after payments.

INPUT

- Explain that after all noncash assets have been sold and liabilities paid, the balance in the account Gain or Loss on Realization must be distributed to the partners' equity accounts.

INPUT

- Explain that the balance in the account Gain or Loss on Realization is distributed to the partners' capital accounts in accordance with the partnership agreement.
- Explain that if a gain is distributed, Gain or Loss on Realization is debited to close the account. If a loss is distributed, Gain or Loss on Realization is credited.

MODEL

- Direct students to the board as you describe how to calculate each partner's share of a gain or loss.
- Use a general journal transparency or the illustration as you describe the entry to record each partner's share of gain or loss.

Distributing a Gain or Loss on Realization to Partners

	Balance of Gain or Loss on Realization	×	Equity Percentage	=	Share of Gain or Loss on Realization
Rona	$2,200.00	×	60%	=	$1,320.00
Barnes	$2,200.00	×	40%	=	880.00
Total					$2,200.00

GENERAL JOURNAL — PAGE 12

	DATE		ACCOUNT TITLE	DOC. NO.	POST. REF.	DEBIT	CREDIT	
9		15	*Gain or Loss on Realization*	*M211*		*2 200 00*		9
10			*Janice Rona, Capital*				*1 320 00*	10
11			*Ira Barnes, Capital*				*880 00*	11
12								12

When all creditors have been paid, the balance of Gain or Loss on Realization is distributed to the partners. A credit balance indicates a gain on realization. A debit balance indicates a loss. The distribution is based on the method of distributing net income or net loss as stated in the partnership agreement. The percentages for Janice Rona and Ira Barnes are 60.0% and 40.0%, respectively.

November 15, 20--. Recorded distribution of gain on realization: to Janice Rona, $1,320.00; to Ira Barnes, $880.00. Memorandum No. 211.

If a loss on realization is distributed to the partners, Gain or Loss on Realization is credited to close the account. Each partner's capital account is debited for the partner's share of the loss on realization.

INPUT

- Explain that the last step in liquidating the partnership is to distribute the remaining cash to the partners. At this point, the only accounts that have balances are the Cash account and the partners' capital accounts.
- Explain that the cash is distributed according to each partner's capital account balance, regardless of the method used to distribute net income or net loss.
- Explain that after this journal entry is posted, all of the accounts will have zero balances and the partnership is liquidated.

MODEL

- Use the cash payments journal transparency or the illustration on the page to show how to distribute the remaining cash to the partners.

Distributing Remaining Cash to Partners

CASH PAYMENTS JOURNAL — PAGE 18

	DATE		ACCOUNT TITLE	CK. NO.	POST. REF.	1 GENERAL DEBIT	2 GENERAL CREDIT	3 ACCOUNTS PAYABLE DEBIT	4 PURCHASES DISCOUNT CREDIT	5 CASH CREDIT	
3	20-- Nov.	17	*Janice Rona, Capital*	*923*		*4 320 00*				*4 320 00*	3
4		17	*Ira Barnes, Capital*	*924*		*2 880 00*				*2 880 00*	4
5											5

Any cash remaining after the partnership assets are sold and the liabilities are paid is distributed to the partners. The cash is distributed according to each partner's capital account balance, regardless of the method used to distribute net income or net loss.

November 17, 20--. Recorded the final distribution of remaining cash to partners: to Janice Rona, $4,320.00; to Ira Barnes, $2,880.00. Check Nos. 923 and 924.

After this entry is journalized and posted, all of the partnership's general ledger accounts will have zero balances. The partnership is liquidated.

FORMATIVE ASSESSMENT

- This is an ongoing process. Circulate around the classroom or lab, observing which students have difficulty with the assignments.
- Troubleshooting: Diagnose the kinds of problems students have with this lesson. Students may have trouble calculating the loss or gain on realization. Students may need to be reminded that the balance in the Gain or Loss on Realization account is distributed to the partners' capital accounts in accordance with the partnership agreement.
- Assess student understanding by checking solutions to Independent Practice assignments and noting their answers to the Terms Review and Audit Your Understanding questions.

End of Lesson Review

LO4 Journalize entries for liquidating a partnership.

Terms Review

liquidation of a partnership

realization

Audit your understanding

1. What accounting procedures must be completed before the partnership liquidation process begins?
2. What accounts are debited when distributing remaining cash to partners during liquidation?

Work together 22-3

Liquidation of a partnership

Mandi Stokes and Dustin Mann agreed to liquidate their partnership on March 15 of the current year. On that date, after financial statements were prepared and the closing entries were posted, the general ledger accounts had the balances shown in the *Working Papers*.

Journalize the transactions. A cash receipts journal, a cash payments journal, and a general journal are provided in the *Working Papers*. Source documents are abbreviated as follows: check, C; memorandum, M; receipt, R. Your instructor will guide you through the following examples.

Transactions:

Mar. 16. Received cash from sale of equipment, $5,000.00. R486.
17. Received cash from sale of supplies, $650.00. R487.
18. Paid cash on account to Daniel Supply, $450.00. C626.
19. Received cash from sale of truck, $12,500.00. R488.
20. Paid cash on account to PFG Consultants, $1,800.00. C627.
23. Distributed the balance of Gain or Loss on Realization to Mandi Stokes, 60%; to Dustin Mann, 40%. M211.
24. Distributed remaining cash to partners. C628 and C629.

On your own 22-3

Liquidation of a partnership

Petre Oakley and Jamal Beck agreed to liquidate their partnership on June 20 of the current year. On that date, after financial statements were prepared and the closing entries were posted, the general ledger accounts had the balances shown in the *Working Papers*.

Journalize the following transactions. A cash receipts journal, a cash payments journal, and a general journal are provided in the *Working Papers*. Source documents are abbreviated as follows: check, C; memorandum, M; receipt, R. Work independently to complete the following problem.

Transactions:

July 4. Received cash from sale of equipment, $8,000.00. R845.
5. Paid cash on account to N&T Supply Co., $445.00. C921.
8. Received cash from sale of supplies, $600.00. R846.
10. Paid cash on account to Ullman Associates, $430.00. C922.
12. Received cash from sale of truck, $10,500.00. R847.
14. Distributed the balance of Gain or Loss on Realization to Petre Oakley, 70%; to Jamal Beck, 30%. M292.
15. Distributed remaining cash to partners. C923 and C924.

CHECK FOR UNDERSTANDING

Terms Review

- Call on students to define each term in the Terms Review. Definitions are given in the Glossary.

Audit Your Understanding

- Call on students to answer the Audit Your Understanding questions. Answers are given in Appendix D.

GUIDED PRACTICE

Work Together

- Have students write the solution to the Work Together problem as you guide the class through the examples.
- Direct students to prepare transactions for liquidating a partnership.

INDEPENDENT PRACTICE

On Your Own

- Assign the On Your Own problem to be worked independently.
- Use the Formative Assessment techniques to diagnose student understanding.

Application Problem

- Assign Application Problem 22-3.

Online Working Papers

- Students can access the Lesson 22-3 problems using this software.

RETEACH

- Bring several inexpensive items to class to represent the fixed assets of a hypothetical partnership. Prepare a balance sheet for the partnership, assigning values to each item, recording an account payable for the real cost of the items, and making the class equal partners. Auction the items to the students, recording the gain or loss on realization for each transaction. Liquidate the partnership by distributing the available cash. Record each transaction on the board, using T accounts.

Essential Questions

- What are some quick methods for selling noncash assets? (*Selling them to a similar business or to employees.*)
- Why go to the trouble of liquidating a partnership if only one of the partners is leaving the partnership? Explain. (*Cash may not be available to distribute to the departing partner unless the partnership is liquidated.*)

EXTENDED LEARNING

- Review Careers in Accounting on page 660.

CLOSURE

- Ask students to summarize briefly the procedures for liquidating a partnership.

CLOSURE

- Review the Chapter Summary.
- Ask students to prepare a list of the new concepts introduced in this chapter.

Essential Question

- If net income is distributed evenly, why might each partner's tax liability be different? (*The tax liability of each individual is determined by the adjusted gross earnings, which could include additional sources of earnings aside from the partnership, as well as other deductions.*)

EXTENDED LEARNING

- Assign Explore Accounting on page 664.

EXPLORE ACCOUNTING

Answers

Answers will vary, and there is no single correct answer. Students should include reasons for their choices. Of the three methods, an appraisal method is least likely to be useful because the business is primarily a service business. The value of assets and liabilities may not give adequate value to the partnership. Students should be able to make a reasonable case for the other methods (comparable sales method and income capitalization method).

Chapter Summary

The end-of-period work is similar for proprietorships, partnerships, and corporations. The differences result from the structure of the owners' equity accounts and income tax policies. A partnership maintains a capital account and a drawing account for each partner. A partnership does not maintain a Retained Earnings account; rather, the net income retained in the partnership is included in the partners' capital accounts.

A partnership does not pay income tax on its net income, as does a corporation. The income of a partnership is reported on the partners' individual tax returns, regardless of the amount of income that is withdrawn by the partners.

Five methods are commonly used for calculating the distribution of partnership earnings. Distributions based on a fixed percentage, a percentage of total equity, interest on equity, and salaries are made first. These distributions do not depend on the amount of net income. The distributions are deducted from net income to determine the remaining net income to be distributed. If these distributions exceed the amount of net income, the remainder is called a distribution deficit. The remainder can be distributed to the partners by using a fixed percentage or a percentage of equity.

Two financial statements are unique to a partnership. The distribution of net income statement reports how the net income of a partnership is distributed to each partner. The owners' equity statement reports the changes in each partner's capital account over the fiscal period.

A partnership may elect or be forced to liquidate. After the assets of the business are sold and all liabilities are paid, any remaining cash is distributed to the partners, using the distribution method specified in the partnership agreement.

EXPLORE ACCOUNTING — Determining the Value of a Partnership

© iStockphoto.com/Makhnach_M

When a partnership decides to add another partner or an existing partner wants to withdraw, the value of a partnership must be determined. The book value of a partnership is not necessarily an equitable value to the new partner or the existing partners. Therefore, before admitting a new partner or retiring one, a current equitable value should be determined for the partnership. Three common methods used to value a partnership are (1) comparable sales, (2) appraisal, and (3) income capitalization.

Comparable sales method. **This method attempts to compare other comparable businesses that have been sold recently with the partnership business being valued. Factors to be considered in selecting comparable businesses are type, size, and location of the business. If a comparable business recently sold for $500,000.00, a sound basis for valuing the partnership is $500,000.00, regardless of the book value of the partnership.**

Appraisal method. **This method estimates the current fair market value of each of the assets and liabilities. A professional appraiser would be employed to determine the value of the assets and the liabilities of the business.**

Income capitalization method. **This method places most emphasis on the expected future earnings capacity of the business. The buyer of a share of a partnership probably is making the investment for the anticipated future earnings of the business. This method values the business based on those expected future earnings.**

INSTRUCTIONS

Assume that you are a doctor. You have been offered a one-quarter interest in a growing medical practice partnership located in a fast-growth area. Which method of valuing the existing partnership would you prefer? Explain the reason for your choice.

Apply Your Understanding

INSTRUCTIONS: Download problem instructions for Excel, QuickBooks, and Sage 50 from the textbook companion website at www.C21accounting.com.

22-1 Application Problem: Calculating partnership earnings and journalizing partnership withdrawals LO1, 2

Ann Marsh and Beth White are partners in a business. On December 31 of the current year, the partners' equities are Ann, $42,000.00, and Beth, $18,000.00. The net income for the year is $70,000.00. A form for calculating distribution of partners' earnings, a cash payments journal, and a general journal are provided in the *Working Papers*.

Instructions:

1. For each of the following independent cases, calculate how the $70,000.00 net income will be distributed to the two partners.
   a. Each partner receives a fixed percentage of 50% of net income.
   b. Each partner receives a percentage of net income based on the percentage of total equity.
   c. Each partner receives 6% interest on equity. The partners share remaining net income, net loss, or distribution deficit equally.
   d. Ann receives a salary of $30,000.00; Beth receives a salary of $35,000.00. The partners share remaining net income, net loss, or distribution deficit in a fixed percentage of Ann, 45%, and Beth, 55%.
   e. Ann is to receive 10% interest on equity and a salary of $32,000.00. Beth is to receive 12% interest on equity and a salary of $28,000.00. The partners share remaining net income, net loss, or distribution deficit equally.
   f. Ann and Beth are to receive salaries of $38,000.00 and $36,000.00, respectively. The partners share remaining net income, net loss, or distribution deficit equally.
2. Record the following transactions in the appropriate journal.

Transactions:

May 12. Ann Marsh, partner, withdrew store supplies for personal use, $120.00. Memorandum No. 92.
20. Beth White, partner, withdrew cash for personal use, $2,000.00. Check No. 433.

22-2 Application Problem: End-of-period work for a partnership LO3

Sherra Gray and Tynisha Banks are partners in Sherra's Home Health. The net income for the year is $48,000.00. On January 1 of the current year, the partners' equities were Sherra, $12,000.00, and Tynisha, $60,000.00. Source documents are abbreviated as follows: check, C; memorandum, M; receipt, R. Statement paper and a general journal are provided in the *Working Papers*.

Instructions:

1. Calculate the distribution of net income to the partners. Partners' salaries are Sherra, $25,000.00, and Tynisha, $15,000.00. Each partner is to receive 12% interest on her January 1 equity. The remaining net income, net loss, or distribution deficit is shared as follows: Sherra, 60%, and Tynisha, 40%.
2. Prepare an owners' equity statement. During the year, Sherra withdrew cash of $30,000.00 and Tynisha withdrew cash of $25,000.00.
3. Journalize the entries to close Income Summary and the owners' equity accounts.

CHECK FIGURES

For complete solutions to Chapter 22 problems, see the Teacher's Edition of the Working Papers.

Application Problem 22-1

1. a. Marsh, $35,000.00; White, $35,000.00.
   c. Marsh, $35,720.00; White, $34,280.00.
   e. Marsh, $38,020.00; White, $31,980.00.

Application Problem 22-2

1. Distribution deficit, $(640.00). Share of income: Gray, $26,056.00; Banks, $21,944.00.
2. Dec. 31 capital balances: Gray, $8,056.00; Banks, $56,944.00.
3. General journal debits: Income Summary, $48,000.00; Sherra Gray, Capital, $30,000.00; Tynisha Banks, Capital, $25,000.00.

Application Problem 22-3

Aug. 5, debit Gain or Loss on Realization, $400.00.

Aug. 7, debit Gain or Loss on Realization, $1,300.00.

Aug. 9, debit Gain or Loss on Realization, $150.00.

Aug. 12, credit Gain or Loss on Realization, $1,850.00.

22-3 Application Problem: Liquidating a partnership LO4

Janie Brooks and Duwanda Morris agreed to liquidate their partnership on July 22 of the current year. On that date, after financial statements were prepared and closing entries were posted, the general ledger accounts had the following balances:

Cash	$ 2,200.00
Supplies	600.00
Equipment	11,000.00
Accumulated Depreciation—Equipment	5,800.00
Truck	18,000.00
Accumulated Depreciation—Truck	13,200.00
Accounts Payable	650.00
Janie Brooks, Capital	6,150.00
Duwanda Morris, Capital	6,000.00

Instructions:

Journalize the following transactions. Source documents are abbreviated as follows: check, C; memorandum, M; receipt, R. A cash receipts journal, a cash payments journal, and a general journal are provided in the *Working Papers*.

Transactions:

Aug. 5. Received cash from sale of equipment, $4,800.00. R546.
7. Received cash from sale of truck, $3,500.00. R547.
8. Paid cash on account to Justin Enterprises, $650.00. C992.
9. Received cash from sale of supplies, $450.00. R548.
12. Distributed the balance of Gain or Loss on Realization to Janie Brooks, 35%; to Duwanda Morris, 65%. M198.
14. Distributed remaining cash to partners. C993 and C994.

Sage 50 Accounting

1. Journalize and post transactions related to liquidating a partnership to the cash receipts journal.
2. Journalize and post transactions related to liquidating a partnership to the cash disbursements journal.
3. Print the cash receipts journal, general journal, and cash disbursements journal.

QB

1. Journalize and post transactions related to liquidating a partnership to the journal.
2. Journalize and post transactions related to liquidating a partnership in the "Write Checks" window.
3. Print the journal, check detail, and trial balance.

X

1. Journalize and post transactions related to liquidating a partnership to the cash receipts journal.
2. Journalize and post transactions related to liquidating a partnership to the cash payments journal.
3. Print the cash receipts journal, general journal, and cash payments journal.

AAONLINE

1. Go to www.cengage.com/login
2. Click on AA Online to access.
3. Go to the online assignment and follow the instructions.

22-M Mastery Problem: Completing end-of-period work for a partnership LO1, 3

Marcie Davies and Dean Elmore are partners in Dean's Gym. On January 1 of the current year, the partners' equities were Marcie, $26,250.00, and Dean, $22,500.00. The net income for the year is $72,350.00. Statement paper and a general journal are provided in the *Working Papers*.

Instructions:

1. Calculate the distribution of net income to the partners. Each partner is to receive 10% interest on January 1 equity. Also, partners' salaries are Marcie, $35,000.00, and Dean, $22,000.00. The remaining net income, net loss, or distribution deficit is shared 68% to Marcie and 32% to Dean.
2. Prepare an owners' equity statement. During the year, Marcie withdrew cash of $32,600.00 and Dean withdrew cash of $25,300.00.
3. Journalize the entries to close Income Summary and the owners' equity accounts.

Sage 50 Accounting

1. Journalize and post transactions related to a partnership to the general journal.
2. Print the general journal.

QB

1. Journalize and post transactions related to a partnership to the journal.
2. Print the journal.

AA ONLINE

1. Go to www.cengage.com/login
2. Click on AA Online to access.
3. Go to the online assignment and follow the instructions.

22-C Challenge Problem: Completing end-of-period work for a partnership LO1, 3

Johan Cope and and Lou Newell are partners in C&N Plumbing. The partnership's adjusted trial balance for the year ended December 31 of the current year is provided in the *Working Papers*. Statement paper is provided in the *Working Papers*.

Instructions:

1. Prepare an income statement. Calculate and record the component percentages for the cost of merchandise sold, gross profit on operations, total operating expenses, and net income or net loss. Round percentage calculations to the nearest 0.1%. If there is a net loss, use a minus sign with the component percentage.
2. Calculate the distribution of net income to the partners. Each partner is to receive 10% interest on January 1 equity. The January 1 equity is Johan, $32,450.60, and Lou, $28,457.74. Also, partners' salaries are Johan, $25,000.00, and Lou, $36,000.00. The remaining net income, net loss, or distribution deficit is shared equally.
3. Prepare an owners' equity statement.
4. Prepare a balance sheet.

X (Excel)

1. Use the account information from the adjusted trial balance to prepare the required financial statements.
2. Print the worksheets.

Mastery Problem 22-M

1. Davies, $44,748.00; Elmore, $27,602.00.
2. Dec. 31 capital balances: Davies, $38,398.00; Elmore, $24,802.00.
3. General journal debits: Income Summary, $72,350.00; Marcie Davies, Capital, $32,600.00; Dean Elmore, Capital, $25,300.00.

Challenge Problem 22-C

1. Net income, $13,517.17, 20.9%.
2. Distribution deficit, $(53,573.66). Share of income: Copeland, $1,458.23; Newell, $12,058.94.
3. Dec. 31 capital balances: Copeland, $11,908.83; Newell, $22,316.68.
4. Total current assets, $21,222.81; total assets, $41,209.71.

INDEPENDENT PRACTICE

- Assign Mastery Problem 22-M for students as a culminating problem combining all new learning from the chapter.
- Assign Challenge Problem 22-C to accelerated students who work at a faster pace.
- Assign Study Guide 22.
- Students can access Online Working Papers to work end-of-chapter problems on the computer.
- Direct students to the C21 Accounting companion website for additional review opportunities.

FORMATIVE ASSESSMENT

- Review solutions to the assigned problems in class, diagnosing trouble spots.

RETEACH

- Call on students to describe how they avoid the trouble spots diagnosed.
- Use reteaching suggestions from lesson plans as required.
- Assign Recycling Problem 22-R if needed.

COMMON CORE AND INTERDISCIPLINARY STUDIES

Extended learning features and activities present numerous opportunities to implement Common Core Standards through interdisciplinary studies. Practice is provided in the common core areas of English Language Arts & Literacy and Mathematical Practice. Many of these activities require short, critical-thinking and decision-making responses that apply reading, writing, speaking, listening, language, media and technology, and mathematical skills.

EXTENDED LEARNING

- Assign 21st Century Skills on page 668.
- Assign Analyzing Home Depot's Financial Statements on page 669.

SUMMATIVE EVALUATION

- Chapter 22 Test
- Cognero for Chapter 22

21ST CENTURY SKILLS

Answers

1. Answers will vary but might include someone who has skills, qualities, or experiences that the student does not have. Also, students may mention that experience doing business or familiarity with the culture of the foreign country is beneficial.
2. Answers will vary. Some countries do not call U.S. partnerships by the same name and have different stipulations for establishing the partnership.
3. Answers will vary. The skit should include five important terms of the agreement and show how earnings are distributed. Both students should be engaged in the skit and should communicate clearly, and the skit should be informative.

21st Century Skills

Purposeful Partners

PARTNERSHIP FOR 21ST CENTURY SKILLS

Theme: Financial, Economic, Business, Entrepreneurial Literacy, and Global Awareness

Skills: Communication and Collaboration, Critical Thinking and Problem Solving, Creativity and Innovation

The selection process for finding a business partner should begin with asking why you want a partner. If you think finding someone who thinks just like you is like hitting the lottery, think again! A business partner should be someone who has skills that you do not have, so that you can expand as a team.

After finding that perfect partner whose skills and abilities complement your own, you can think about the legal agreement. Although business partnership agreements are not legally required, they are highly recommended. An example was shown in the previous chapter.

APPLICATION

1. Decide on a business that you would like to start in a foreign country. Explain the business and the country in which you would like to operate. Describe at least five qualities that you would seek in a business partner from that country. Explain why these qualities are important to you.
2. Using the Internet, research the requirements for forming a partnership in the country you selected. Draw a Venn diagram to compare and contrast establishing a partnership in this country and one in the United States.
3. With another classmate, write and perform a skit about your proposed partnership and its partners. Be sure to include the negotiation of at least five important terms in the partnership agreement and how partnership earnings will be distributed.

Analyzing Home Depot's financial statements

A corporation that does business in the United States must pay federal income taxes based on its net income. The amount of income tax varies from year to year, based on net income, corporate tax brackets, tax legislation, and changing tax regulations. The effective tax rate for a corporation can be calculated by dividing the "provision for income taxes" amount by the "earnings before provision for income taxes" amount. An awareness of the effective tax rate can help a corporation prepare budgets for future years.

INSTRUCTIONS

Refer to Home Depot's Consolidated Statements of Earnings on page B-6 of Appendix B in this textbook and complete the following items.

1. List the "provision for income taxes" amounts for each of the three years presented.
2. Calculate the effective tax rates for each of the three fiscal years.
3. Assume the management of Home Depot expects the corporation to earn $8,000 million before income taxes during the next fiscal year. What amount would you recommend be included in the budget for the provision for income taxes?

ANALYZING HOME DEPOT'S FINANCIAL STATEMENTS

Answers

1. 2012, $2,686 million; 2011, $2,185 million; 2010, $1,935 million.
2. 2012, $2,686 million ÷ $7,221 million = 37.2%.

   2011, $2,185 million ÷ $6,068 million = 36.0%.

   2010, $1,935 million ÷ $5,273 million = 36.7%.
3. Answers will vary. Using an average of the three effective tax rates yields a provision amount of $2,928 million ($8,000 × 36.6%). Some students may suggest that the latest fiscal year's effective tax rate of 37.2% most closely reflects current tax law and should be used in the computation. The tax provision using the 37.2% effective tax rate yields a provision amount of $2,976 million.

Chapter 23

Budgeting and Accounting for a Not-for-Profit Organization

Scope & Sequence

	New	Review/Enrich
Introduction		
Introduce the Chapter		
Lesson 23-1: Not-for-Profit Organizations		
Characteristics of Not-for-Profit Organizations	✓	
Characteristics of Governmental Organizations and Accounting Systems	✓	
Fund Accounting Balance Sheet	✓	
Difference Between Expenses and Expenditures	✓	
Financial Reporting Emphasis	✓	
Budgeting	✓	
Developing an Annual Governmental Operating Budget	✓	
Procedures to Prepare an Annual Operating Budget	✓	
Journalizing an Approved Annual Budget	✓	
Lesson 23-2: Journalizing Revenues		
Journalizing Current Property Tax Revenues	✓	
Collection of Current Property Taxes	✓	
Other Revenue	✓	
Accounting for Delinquent Property Taxes	✓	
Collection of Delinquent Property Taxes	✓	
Lesson 23-3: Journalizing Expenditures, Encumbrances, and Other Transactions		
Journalizing Expenditures	✓	
Journalizing Encumbrances	✓	
Journalizing Expenditures for Amounts Encumbered	✓	
Journalizing Expenditures Benefiting Future Periods	✓	
Journalize the Issuance of Liabilities	✓	
Journalize the Payment of Liabilities	✓	
Investing in Short-Term Investments	✓	
Receiving Cash from Short-Term Investments	✓	
Closure		

Enhancing Instruction

Features	Common Core Standards
• Accounting in the Real World: Amtrak	• ELAL—reading, writing
• Ethics in Action: Evaluating Auditor Independence • Why Accounting?: Charitable Giving Watchdogs • Forensic Accounting: Single Audits	• ELAL—reading • ELAL—reading, media and technology, writing • Mathematics
• Think Like an Accountant: Organizational Structure • Global Awareness: Foreign Currency Exchange Gains or Losses	• Mathematics • ELAL—reading, writing
• Explore Accounting • 21st Century Skills • Analyzing Home Depot's Financial Statements	• ELAL—reading, writing, media and technology • ELAL—reading, writing • ELAL—reading, writing

ELAL = English Language Arts & Literacy

Calculator: © iStockphoto.com/picstodisc; Paper: © iStockphoto.com/Qingwa

Practice and Assessment

Technology & Media	Teaching Strategies	Guided Practice	Independent Practice	Reteach/Enrich
• Instructor's Resource CD/Website: PowerPoint Slides Accounting Concepts • Online Working Papers • Transparency Master: Multicolumn Journal	• Tactile/Kinesthetic Learners • Auditory/Linguistic Learners	• Terms Review • Audit Your Understanding • Work Together 23-1	• On Your Own 23-1 • Application Problem 23-1 • Formative Assessment, p. 681 • Online Working Papers	• Reteach, p. 682
• Instructor's Resource CD/Website: PowerPoint Slides Accounting Concepts • Online Working Papers • Transparency Master: Multicolumn Journal	• Visual/Spatial Learners	• Term Review • Audit Your Understanding • Work Together 23-2	• On Your Own 23-2 • Application Problem 23-2 • Formative Assessment, p. 685 • Online Working Papers	• Reteach, p. 686
• Instructor's Resource CD/Website: PowerPoint Slides Accounting Concepts • Online Working Papers • Transparency Master: Multicolumn Journal	• Gifted Learners	• Terms Review • Audit Your Understanding • Work Together 23-3	• On Your Own 23-3 • Application Problem 23-3 • Formative Assessment, p. 692 • Online Working Papers	• Reteach, p. 693
• Online Working Papers			• Mastery Problem 23-M • Study Guide 23 • Chapter 23 Test • Cognero Chapter 23	• Challenge Problem 23-C • Reteach, p. 696 • Recycling Problem 23-R

Introduce the Chapter

SET THE STAGE

GUIDING QUESTIONS

- Ask students to identify not-for-profit organizations in their community or others with which they are familiar.
- Ask students to name services provided by the government that otherwise might be difficult for individuals to provide for themselves.
- Ask students to identify sources of revenue for a government.
- Ask students to predict how a government agency might keep track of spending for different divisions or departments.

PREVIEW CHAPTER OBJECTIVES

- Explain that budgeting and accounting for a not-for-profit organization are different from budgeting and accounting for a business that operates for a profit.
- Instruct a student to read each chapter objective aloud.

PREVIEW ACCOUNTING TERMS

- Read each term aloud to verify its pronunciation for students.
- Point out terms or parts of terms that should already be familiar to most students, such as *not-for-profit organization, expenditure, budget,* and *fixed assets*.

Chapter 23

Budgeting and Accounting for a Not-for-Profit Organization

LEARNING OBJECTIVES

After studying Chapter 23, in addition to defining key terms, you will be able to:

LO1 Describe the characteristics of not-for-profit organizations.

LO2 Describe the process used to develop an operating budget for a not-for-profit organization.

LO3 Journalize budget transactions for a not-for-profit organization.

LO4 Journalize revenues for a not-for-profit organization.

LO5 Journalize expenditures, encumbrances, and other transactions for a not-for-profit organization.

Calculator: © iStockphoto.com/picstodisc; Paper: © iStockphoto.com/Qingwa

Tetra Images/Getty Images

Accounting In The Real World

Amtrak

The transcontinental railway dramatically improved the ability to move people and goods between the East and West coasts. A dangerous trip that could require a year or more by covered wagon was reduced to a single week.

By the end of the nineteenth century, over 200,000 miles of track had been laid by thousands of railroads. Enduring several economic crises, these railroads provided the best method of transportation. However, the twentieth century ushered in two new methods of transportation—automobiles and airplanes—that provided stiff competition for the railroads. As more people and goods traveled by car, truck, and airplane, the traffic transported by the railroads steadily declined. Thousands of miles of track were abandoned as many railroads were forced to merge with other railroads or go bankrupt.

By 1970, it became clear that intercity passenger service would disappear unless the government intervened. Congress created the National Railroad Passenger Corporation, commonly known as Amtrak, to take over intercity passenger service from private railroads. Unlike most government agencies, Amtrak is a for-profit corporation. As a result, Amtrak issues an annual report that includes financial statements prepared using generally accepted accounting principles.

In recent years, Amtrak has seen steady increases in revenue and in the number of passengers served. Amtrak operates more than 300 daily intercity trains serving more than 500 destinations in 46 states, the District of Columbia, and Canada. Amtrak is aggressively pursuing high-speed trains in selected areas to attract new passengers. As major cities continue to become more populated, it is reasonable to predict that Amtrak will play a significant role in mass transportation.

Despite its recent financial and operational successes, Amtrak continues a history of net losses. As its sole stockholder, the U.S. Department of Transportation is frequently required to provide Amtrak with funds to continue operations.

CRITICAL THINKING

1. Obtain Amtrak's most recent annual report. Examine the statement of cash flows to identify the amount of funds received from the federal government.
2. Do taxpayers and society benefit from the government's annual subsidy of Amtrak's operations? Explain your answer.

Source: www.amtrak.com.

Background: © iStockphoto.com, moonlight365; Real World: © iStockphoto.com, EdStock

Key Terms

- not-for-profit organization
- fund
- expenditure
- statement of revenues, expenditures, and changes in fund balance
- fund equity
- operating budget
- appropriations
- tax levy
- encumbrance
- general fixed assets
- certificate of deposit

Accounting In The Real World

Answers

1. Answers will vary based on the year. The amounts appear as "Proceeds from federal paid-in capital" in the Financial Activities section of the statement of cash flows.
2. Answers will vary. Some students might cite the following benefits: (1) availability of low-cost transportation, (2) access to transportation in cities where car ownership is not practical, (3) ecologically friendly transportation, and (4) alleviation of highway congestion.

LESSON
23-1

BRIDGE

- Point out that students have learned accounting for businesses that are set up with a profit motive. This chapter will introduce students to the accounting for an organization that is not designed to make a profit, but to provide goods or services that otherwise might be unavailable to individuals.

TEACHING RESOURCES

- **Instructor's Resource CD/Website:**
  PowerPoint Slides
  Accounting Concepts
- **Working Papers:**
  Teacher's Edition of the Working Papers for Lesson 23-1
  Online Working Papers
- **Transparency Master:**
  Multicolumn Journal

ENGAGE

- Explain that the goal of most businesses is to make a profit. Not-for-profit organizations are not interested in making a profit for owners. These organizations focus on exercising control over expenditures and ensuring that spending does not exceed the budget. In this lesson, the development of an annual budget and the journal entry to record an approved operating budget will be presented.

PREVIEW

- Call on students to read the accounting terms and definitions introduced in this lesson: *not-for-profit organization; fund; expenditure; statement of revenues, expenditures, and changes in fund balance; fund equity; operating budget*; and *appropriations*.
- Point out the learning objectives for this lesson.
- Direct students to read the headings in this lesson and to examine the illustrations.

LESSON

23-1 Not-for-Profit Organizations

LO1 Describe the characteristics of not-for-profit organizations.
LO2 Describe the process used to develop an operating budget for a not-for-profit organization.
LO3 Journalize budget transactions for a not-for-profit organization.

Characteristics of Not-for-Profit Organizations LO1

The main objective of proprietorships, partnerships, and corporations is to earn a profit. Some organizations, however, are formed for purposes other than earning a profit. An organization providing goods or services with neither a conscious motive nor an expectation of earning a profit is called a **not-for-profit organization**. Not-for-profit organizations are also referred to as *non-profit organizations*. These organizations are formed to provide needed goods or services to a group of individuals without regard to earning a profit.

LEADERSHIP

ETHICS IN ACTION

Evaluating Auditor Independence

Teresa Stafford is a manager in the accounting firm of Turner & Avant. She has worked on the RBH Industries audit engagement since joining the firm seven years ago. RBH Industries is a family-owned business that processes wood products. Her younger brother Robbie, a junior accounting major at Macon University, has been offered a six-month internship with RBH Industries. Robbie is being recruited to work in the Tax Compliance Department. In the accounting profession, it is common for college interns to receive offers for full-time employment.

INSTRUCTIONS

Refer to the *Code of Professional Conduct* of the American Institute of Certified Public Accountants. Read Rule 101 related to independence and selected definitions in Rule 93. Can Teresa's accounting firm continue to perform the audit if her brother is hired as an intern? What if Robbie is hired for a full-time position?

© iStockphoto.com/LdF

ETHICS IN ACTION

Encourage students to share their conclusions. Some students will focus on the guidance in the code, which supports a conclusion that Robbie is not an immediate family member of Teresa and, therefore, there is no independence problem. Other students may focus on how Robbie and Teresa's relationship appears to impair independence. These students are likely to discuss how difficult it would be for Teresa to audit her brother.

See a suggested solution for this feature in the Instructional Strategies section at the front of this book.

TYPES OF NOT-FOR-PROFIT ORGANIZATIONS

Not-for-profit organizations may differ as to the types of goods or services they provide, their sources of revenues, or the procedures they use to select their leaders or managers. The major types of not-for-profit organizations are as follows.

1. Governmental, such as federal, state, county, city, town, and village.
2. Educational, such as elementary, secondary, and postsecondary schools.
3. Health, such as hospitals and nursing homes.
4. Charitable, such as United Way, United Fund, and American Red Cross.
5. Foundational, including trusts and corporations organized for charitable and educational purposes, such as the Carnegie Foundation and the Ford Foundation.
6. Religious, such as churches and other religious groups.

Since not-for-profit organizations have a common objective, they share many of the same needs for financial information. Thus, the accounting system and many of the financial reports are similar for all not-for-profit organizations. However, because of differences in goods or services provided, sources of revenues, or methods of leadership selection, their accounting procedures and reports are modified for the specific type of organization.

PURPOSE OF GOVERNMENTAL ORGANIZATIONS

All individuals are affected by or are members of one or more governmental organizations. Also, more individuals are employed by governmental organizations than any other type of not-for-profit organization. Therefore, Chapters 23 and 24 emphasize accounting for local governmental organizations.

A governmental organization's purpose is normally to provide needed goods or services that would be impossible for individuals to provide for themselves. For example, the federal government provides national defense for all citizens of the nation. Individual states and cities would find it difficult and very inefficient to provide for their own defense from foreign pressures. Similarly, cities provide police and fire protection that would be very expensive and inefficient for individuals to provide for themselves.

© iStockphoto.com/Aleksko

WHY ACCOUNTING?

Charitable Giving Watchdogs

Many not-for-profit organizations rely on contributions as their major source of revenue. Some organizations get most of their contributions from large corporations. Others rely on donations by individuals. Not-for-profit organizations are competing with each other for a limited number of donated dollars. In the United States, the total number of dollars donated each year remains relatively constant, even in years of economic downturn.

Each organization develops a plan for how it will raise money. Contributions can be obtained through grants, donations, fund-raising events, and online crowd-funding sites. Not all donated dollars go to the mission of the charitable organization. The organization incurs expenses for administrative salaries, maintaining an office, and fund-raising. What remains can be used to support the charity's mission, which could be hunger, animal rights, medical research, the arts, the environment, education, or youth programs.

Human Services

As a donor with limited dollars, you want to contribute to those organizations that operate most efficiently so that a high percentage of your donation actually supports the mission. It is important that not-for-profit organizations keep accurate records of donations and expenses. A variety of watchdog groups evaluate not-for-profit spending.

CRITICAL THINKING

1. Search the Internet for two charitable giving watchdog organizations. Summarize how each organization rates charitable organizations.
2. Choose which one of the two watchdog organizations you feel has a better evaluation method. Defend your choice in a short paragraph.

Source: www.charitynavigator.org.

INPUT

- Discuss the differences between a corporation and a governmental organization such as a city or county.

MODEL

- Ask students to develop a list of not-for-profit organizations.

WHY ACCOUNTING?

Answers

1. Answers will vary. At the time of publication, some watchdog groups were Charity Navigator, American Institute of Philanthropy (CharityWatch), Better Business Bureau Wise Giving Alliance, GiveWell, Philanthropedia, and GuideStar.
2. Answers will vary but should include a reason the watchdog organization was chosen.

INPUT

- Explain that measuring success in governmental organizations is difficult because profits are not the objective.
- Point out that leadership in governmental organizations changes frequently, affecting the goals of the organization.
- Explain the source of revenue for governmental organizations.
- Direct students to the chart comparing the characteristics of a governmental organization to a corporation.
- Stress the six accounting practices that are similar for businesses and governmental organizations.

Characteristics of Governmental Organizations and Accounting Systems

A governmental organization has several major characteristics that affect its accounting system. First, a government has no profit motive. A business's success can be measured by whether or not it earns a profit. A business that is inefficient, or not competitive, will not earn a profit. Without profits, a business will not be able to continue operations. However, since a governmental organization does not intend to earn a profit, success is much more difficult to measure. As long as money is available, a governmental organization can continue to operate, regardless of its efficiency or inefficiency.

Policy-making bodies of governmental organizations are generally elected by a popular vote of the group's members. Thus, the leadership depends on the political process and may change frequently. Policies and long-range goals may change when the leadership changes. These frequent changes make effective long-range planning difficult.

Revenues for governmental organizations are provided primarily by taxation on property, retail sales, or income. Organization members who have the greatest amount of property or income provide the greatest amount of revenues. However, the goods or services are normally provided to all members of the organization based on need. The amount that individuals pay is not related directly to the benefits they receive. Therefore, individuals have decreased incentive for ensuring that services are administered efficiently.

No direct relationship exists between who pays for and who receives the services provided by a governmental organization. Therefore, individuals generally support the organizational objective that is most advantageous to them. For example, some citizens of a city may give the construction of a library a high priority. Others who seldom use a library may give this project a low priority. Consequently, services provided by a governmental organization are usually determined through negotiation and compromise among the different interest groups. This procedure does not necessarily provide for the best services or the most efficiency.

The characteristics of governmental organizations have affected the development of governmental accounting systems. Therefore, numerous financial and legal regulations for determining the source and amount of revenues and for planning and executing expenditures of funds must be followed. These characteristics of a governmental organization compared to a corporation are summarized as follows:

Characteristic	Governmental Organization	Corporation
Profit motive	None	Maximize profits
Measure of success	Subjective evaluation of the quality of service provided	Earning a consistent profit indicates customer satisfaction with service
Ability to continue operations	Not dependent on effectiveness or efficiency—can continue as long as funding is available	Requires earning a consistent profit
Leadership	Changes frequently; elected by public or appointed by other government officials	Relatively stable; board of directors elected by stockholders
Effective long-term planning	Difficult due to frequent changes in leadership	Stable leadership in board of directors and management enables long-term planning
Objectives	Established through negotiation among both uses of services and taxpayers	Determined by management
Payment for services	Users of services rarely pay for service received	Customers pay for services or goods received
Source of funding	Taxes on property, retail sales, and/or income	Revenue from customers

Six accounting practices are similar for business and governmental organizations.

1. The accounting equation (assets equal liabilities plus equities) is applied.
2. An appropriate chart of accounts is prepared.
3. Transactions are analyzed into debit and credit elements.
4. Transactions are journalized and posted to ledgers.
5. Financial statements are prepared for each fiscal period.
6. Most of the same accounting concepts are applied.

The characteristics of governmental organizations and the conditions in which they operate create information and control requirements that differ from those of businesses. Because of these differences, governmental accounting and financial reporting differ in several ways from business accounting and financial reporting.

Fund Accounting Balance Sheet

Westburg General Fund	
ASSETS	
Cash	$425,000.00
Taxes Receivable	60,000.00
Total Assets	$485,000.00
LIABILITIES AND FUND EQUITY	
Liabilities:	
Accounts Payable	$ 45,000.00
Fund Equity:	
Fund Balance	440,000.00
Total Liabilities and Fund Equity	$485,000.00

Westburg Library Fund	
ASSETS	
Cash	$94,200.00
Late Fees Receivable	800.00
Total Assets	$95,000.00
LIABILITIES AND FUND EQUITY	
Liabilities:	
Accounts Payable	$ 6,000.00
Fund Equity:	
Fund Balance	89,000.00
Total Liabilities and Fund Equity	$95,000.00

The accounting system for a business includes a single accounting entity. That is, all accounts used to record accounting transactions for the entire business are part of a single set of accounts. Within this set of accounts, assets must equal liabilities plus equities. A governmental accounting entity with a set of accounts in which assets always equal liabilities plus equities is called a **fund**. A governmental unit, such as a city, may have several different funds.

A fund accounting system emphasizes strong controls on the use of funds. The amount in a fund can be spent only for the specified purpose of the fund. Different funds may be created for different purposes. For example, the town of Westburg has two funds: (1) a general fund and (2) a library fund. Balance sheets for the two funds are shown above.

The town of Westburg has total assets of $580,000.00 (general fund, $485,000.00, plus library fund, $95,000.00). However, the assets are accounted for separately. Assets in the library fund may be used only for library purposes. General fund assets may be used for other authorized town expenditures. Each fund is kept as a separate set of accounts.

The fund equity, similar to owners' equity for a business, is the net amount of assets available for use. For example, Westburg's library fund equity is $89,000.00 (assets, $95,000.00, less liabilities, $6,000.00). If $7,000.00 cash is spent for library salaries, total assets available for spending would be reduced to $88,000.00 ($95,000.00 less $7,000.00). The fund equity account, Fund Balance, would be reduced to $82,000.00 (assets, $88,000.00, less liabilities, $6,000.00). Total Liabilities and Fund Equity would be recalculated as $88,000.00. After this transaction, the governmental accounting equation, assets equal liabilities plus fund equity, is in balance.

Types of funds vary with the type of not-for-profit organization and the types of goods or services provided. A unique set of funds normally is used for each type of organization—federal government, state and local governments, hospitals, or schools.

MODIFIED ACCRUAL ACCOUNTING

Most businesses use accrual accounting so that revenue and expenses incurred during a fiscal period determine the resulting net income for the period. [CONCEPT: Matching Expenses with Revenue] Governmental organizations use modified accrual accounting. In modified accrual accounting, revenues are recorded in the accounting period in which they become measurable and available. For example, property taxes become measurable and available as soon as the amount is determined and tax statements are sent to property owners. However, sales taxes cannot be determined until sales are made. Thus, sales tax revenue is recognized when the taxes are received from merchants.

fyi As with the general fund, modified accrual accounting would be used for a library fund.

INPUT

- Ask students to compare and contrast the balance sheets in the illustration on this page.
- Point out that there is no "owners' or stockholders' equity" because profit is not the motive, nor are there any "owners." However, the fund equity is very similar.
- Explain the purpose of a fund.

MODEL

- Illustrate balance sheets from various funds of a local municipality. Point out that the various funds are accounted for individually.

INPUT

- Emphasize and discuss the differences between accrual and modified accrual accounting.

DIFFERENTIATED INSTRUCTION

Tactile/Kinesthetic learners prefer to learn through movement. These students may enjoy going into the community to explore. Ask students to attend a city council budget meeting or meet with a city manager, city clerk, city finance director, or a council member to discuss what occurs when the city budget is set.

Auditory/Linguistic learners have highly developed auditory skills and often use language as a means to remember information. A variation to the above activity might be to invite a member of the city government or a CPA who audits nonprofit organizations to speak to the class.

INPUT

- Review the differences and similarities between a corporation's and a governmental organization's financial statements.

MODEL

- Obtain samples of financial statements for a governmental agency. Compare and contrast these statements to sample financial statements for a business organization.

Difference Between Expenses and Expenditures

Cash disbursements and liabilities incurred for the cost of goods delivered or services rendered are called **expenditures**. In modified accrual accounting, expenditures are generally recognized when a liability is incurred. Therefore, governmental organizations record expenditures rather than expenses.

An important distinction is made between expenditures and expenses. Businesses emphasize matching expenses with revenue in each fiscal period. However, governmental accounting emphasizes determining and controlling revenues and expenditures during a fiscal period. For example, if a business buys a truck, Plant Asset or Truck is debited and Cash or Notes Payable is credited. No expense is incurred until the truck is used. If a governmental organization buys a truck out of its general fund, Expenditure is debited and Cash or Notes Payable is credited. The amount of money spent or the liability incurred is recorded, not the expense. Thus, expenditures are decreases in net financial resources. Emphasis is placed on the control of the net financial resources, not on matching expenses with revenue. Modified accrual accounting is used to measure the financial position and operating results of the general funds of governmental organizations.

Financial Reporting Emphasis

Both business and governmental organizations prepare financial statements at the end of a fiscal period. [CONCEPT: Accounting Period Cycle] However, because the organizations have different objectives, their charts of accounts and statements differ. The chart of accounts for Lindville appears on the next page.

The two most common financial statements prepared by businesses are the income statement and the balance sheet. Businesses prepare income statements to report the amount of net income earned during a fiscal period. Earning a net income is not an objective of governmental organizations. Rather, identifying and controlling the sources of revenues and the expenditure of funds are part of the control process. Therefore, government organizations prepare a different statement than do businesses. A statement that reports the sources of revenues and the expenditure of funds of a government organization is called a **statement of revenues, expenditures, and changes in fund balance**.

A business's balance sheet reports the assets, liabilities, and owners' equity of the business at the end of a fiscal period. A governmental organization's balance sheet (described in Chapter 24) also reports the current assets and liabilities of the organization at the end of a period. However, no specific ownership of a governmental organization exists. The amount of assets less liabilities of a governmental organization is called **fund equity**.

Budgeting

Both businesses and governmental organizations prepare budgets. The primary purpose of all budgets is planning and control. During a business's fiscal period, budgeted amounts are compared with actual amounts to provide information to management about the effectiveness of cost control. For a governmental organization, however, an approved budget becomes (1) a legal authorization to spend and (2) a legal limit on the amount that can be spent.

fyi The Governmental Accounting Standards Board (GASB) establishes generally accepted accounting principles for city and state government financial reporting.

THE BUSINESS—
TOWN OF LINDVILLE

The town of Lindville serves as the center of retail commerce for a three-county area. The town provides its residents with many basic services, such as police and fire protection. Located at the foothills of the Greystone Mountains, Lindville is the center of numerous recreational opportunities for residents and visitors.

© iStockphoto.com/DougSchneiderPhoto

Chart of Accounts
TOWN OF LINDVILLE GENERAL FUND

Balance Sheet Accounts

(1000) ASSETS
- 1010 Cash
- 1020 Taxes Receivable—Current
- 1030 Allowance for Uncollectible Taxes—Current
- 1040 Taxes Receivable—Delinquent
- 1050 Allowance for Uncollectible Taxes—Delinquent
- 1060 Interest Receivable
- 1070 Allowance for Uncollectible Interest
- 1080 Inventory of Supplies
- 1090 Investments—Short Term

(2000) LIABILITIES
- 2010 Accounts Payable
- 2020 Notes Payable

(3000) FUND EQUITY
- 3010 Unreserved Fund Balance
- 3020 Reserve for Encumbrances—Current Year
- 3030 Reserve for Encumbrances—Prior Year
- 3040 Reserve for Inventory of Supplies

Revenue and Expenditure Accounts

(4000) REVENUES
- 4010 Property Tax Revenue
- 4020 Interest Revenue
- 4030 Other Revenue

(5000) EXPENDITURES

5100 GENERAL GOVERNMENT
- 5110 Expenditure—Personnel, General Government
- 5120 Expenditure—Supplies, General Government
- 5130 Expenditure—Other Charges, General Government
- 5140 Expenditure—Capital Outlays, General Government

5200 PUBLIC SAFETY
- 5210 Expenditure—Personnel, Public Safety
- 5220 Expenditure—Supplies, Public Safety
- 5230 Expenditure—Other Charges, Public Safety
- 5240 Expenditure—Capital Outlays, Public Safety

5300 FIRE PROTECTION
- 5310 Expenditure—Personnel, Fire Protection
- 5320 Expenditure—Supplies, Fire Protection
- 5330 Expenditure—Other Charges, Fire Protection
- 5340 Expenditure—Capital Outlays, Fire Protection

5400 RECREATION
- 5410 Expenditure—Personnel, Recreation
- 5420 Expenditure—Supplies, Recreation
- 5430 Expenditure—Other Charges, Recreation
- 5440 Expenditure—Capital Outlays, Recreation

Budgetary Accounts

(6000) BUDGETARY
- 6010 Estimated Revenues
- 6020 Appropriations
- 6030 Budgetary Fund Balance

6100 GENERAL GOVERNMENT
- 6110 Encumbrance—Personnel, General Government
- 6120 Encumbrance—Supplies, General Government
- 6130 Encumbrance—Other Charges, General Government
- 6140 Encumbrance—Capital Outlays, General Government

6200 PUBLIC SAFETY
- 6210 Encumbrance—Personnel, Public Safety
- 6220 Encumbrance—Supplies, Public Safety
- 6230 Encumbrance—Other Charges, Public Safety
- 6240 Encumbrance—Capital Outlays, Public Safety

6300 FIRE PROTECTION
- 6310 Encumbrance—Personnel, Fire Protection
- 6320 Encumbrance—Supplies, Fire Protection
- 6330 Encumbrance—Other Charges, Fire Protection
- 6340 Encumbrance—Capital Outlays, Fire Protection

6400 RECREATION
- 6410 Encumbrance—Personnel, Recreation
- 6420 Encumbrance—Supplies, Recreation
- 6430 Encumbrance—Other Charges, Recreation
- 6440 Encumbrance—Capital Outlays, Recreation

The chart of accounts for Lindville is illustrated above for reference as you study Chapters 23 and 24 of this textbook.

INPUT

- Emphasize that students should refer to this chart of accounts throughout Chapters 23 and 24.
- Explain that this chart of accounts is for a general fund of a not-for-profit organization.
- Explain that this chart of account reflects the town of Lindville's use of a fund accounting system, which emphasizes strong controls on the use of funds.
- Stress that because the differences between a corporation and a governmental organization are significant, the differences in their respective charts of accounts will be significant.
- Explain that unlike a business corporation, a not-for-profit organization uses modified accrual accounting. This fact is reflected in the Expenditures section of the chart of accounts.
- Point out that charts of accounts are used to determine the classification of accounts and to identify which accounts are temporary and which are permanent.
- Stress that the chart of accounts is useful for completing automated accounting activities because account numbers are required for both data entry and file maintenance activities.

MODEL

- Ask students to compare and contrast the similarities and differences between this chart of accounts and the one in Part 1.
- Similarities: Assets, Liabilities, and Revenue. There are also many familiar accounts within divisions.
- Differences: Fund Equity, Expenditure, and Budgetary Accounts.

INPUT

- Explain the similarities and differences in the purpose and preparation of budgets for corporations and governmental organizations.

MODEL

- Discuss the illustration. Point out the major sections of the operating budget. Point out how the budgetary fund balance is calculated.

Developing an Annual Governmental Operating Budget LO2

Town of Lindville
Annual Operating Budget—General Fund
For Year Ended December 31, 20--

ESTIMATED REVENUES		
Property Tax	$1,675,000.00	
Interest	12,000.00	
Other	4,500.00	
Total Estimated Revenues		$1,691,500.00
ESTIMATED EXPENDITURES AND BUDGETARY FUND BALANCE		
General Government		
Personnel	$ 271,100.00	
Supplies	15,400.00	
Other Charges	114,400.00	
Capital Outlays	23,900.00	
Total General Government		$ 424,800.00
Public Safety		
Personnel	$ 597,500.00	
Supplies	28,800.00	
Other Charges	157,500.00	
Capital Outlays	96,000.00	
Total Public Safety		879,800.00
Fire Protection		
Personnel	$ 115,500.00	
Supplies	13,400.00	
Other Charges	50,200.00	
Capital Outlays	57,200.00	
Total Fire Protection		236,300.00
Recreation		
Personnel	$ 63,300.00	
Supplies	6,600.00	
Other Charges	28,900.00	
Capital Outlays	19,300.00	
Total Recreation		118,100.00
Total Estimated Expenditures		$1,659,000.00
Budgetary Fund Balance		32,500.00
Total Estimated Expenditures and Budgetary Fund Balance		$1,691,500.00

A plan of current expenditures and the proposed means of financing those expenditures is called an **operating budget**. A governmental fund's annual operating budget authorizes and provides the basis for controlling financial operations during a fiscal year. Since each governmental fund is a separate accounting entity, an operating budget is normally prepared to show the estimated revenues, estimated expenditures, and budgetary fund balance for each fund. The operating budget shown above was prepared for the general fund of the town of Lindville.

Lindville organizes revenue accounts by source of revenue. Expenditure accounts are organized by department and type of expenditure. Some organizations maintain subsidiary accounts for each of the general ledger accounts to provide more detail about the sources of revenues and types of expenditures. Because of its small size, Lindville maintains only the general ledger accounts listed in its chart of accounts.

© iStockphoto.com/burwellphotography

FORENSIC ACCOUNTING

Single Audits

A not-for-profit organization may receive funds from several agencies of the federal government. For example, a school district might receive funds from the Department of Education, the Department of Agriculture, and the National Science Foundation. An award of funds to an organization for a specified purpose is known as a *grant*. The organization and agency will sign a grant agreement, a legal document that identifies the purpose of the grant and how the funds must be spent. Every agency wants to ensure that its funds are used for only the intended purpose. Therefore, agencies may require the organization to be audited.

The Office of Management and Budget (OMB) has issued special rules for accountants auditing any organization that receives more than $500,000 of federal funds. These audits must be performed following the guidance of the Single Audit Act Amendments of 1996 and OMB Circular A-133, *Audits of States, Local Governments and Non-Profit Organizations*. An audit performed using this guidance is commonly known as a *single audit*.

Auditors aren't the only individuals who are involved in an audit. An organization's accounting staff must devote time to obtaining requested documents, preparing detailed schedules, and discussing issues with the auditors, all while performing their normal job responsibilities.

Prior to the issuance of OMB Circular A-133, an organization might be audited by every federal agency from which it received federal funds. Having to work with two or more auditors placed an unfair burden on the organization and its accounting staff. To solve the problem, the OMB allows the organization to have a single audit. Every federal agency must accept the results of the one audit.

A single audit expands the scope of tests performed by auditors in a normal financial statement audit. OMB Circular A-133 requires additional tests designed to ensure that the organization has complied with the regulations of the grants received from each of the funding agencies. For example, a grant may limit the types of expenses that can be paid with grant funds.

ACTIVITY

Farris & Talbot, a public accounting firm, is performing a single audit of a State Department of Education. One of the grants requires education counselors to travel to schools across the state to meet with special-needs students. The counselors are reimbursed after each trip for their expenses, including travel, lodging, and meals.

Farris & Talbot has designed an extensive list of audit tests to ensure the accuracy and appropriateness of counselor reimbursements. The first test is a Benford's Law test on reimbursement checks. Benford's Law states that select digits of numbers from a natural data set should match a specific frequency. For example, 30.1% of the first digit of each amount should begin with the number 1, whereas only 4.6% of the first digits of amounts should begin with the number 9. The law is based on the mathematics of logarithms and can be applied to most data sets. However, the law does not apply to data that has limits, such as test grades, or have significant digits, such as zip codes and phone numbers.

The auditors expect the frequency of the first digit of each check amount to follow percentages of Benford's Law. If the actual frequency of digits is significantly different, the auditors are alerted that some bias exists. Additional audit tests are required to determine if the bias is natural for the organization or the result of a fraud.

INSTRUCTIONS

Open the spreadsheet FA_CH23 and complete the steps on the Instructions tab.

1. Summarize the findings of the Benford's Law analysis.
2. Does the chart provide any evidence that a fraud has occurred?
3. What additional procedures in Excel could be performed to better understand the data?

FORENSIC ACCOUNTING

Students are provided with a list of over 1,200 checks and are instructed to perform a Benford's Law analysis. A more detailed description of Benford's Law can be obtained in Lesson 24-1 of the first-year textbook or in other sources.

Students use the LEFT and COUNTIF functions to identify the number of checks that begin with the digits 1 through 9. Selected cell references must be changed to absolute references. Students must create the formulas for calculating the percentage of each digit's count to the total number of checks. Entering the formula =F6/SUM($F$6:$N$6) at cell F7 enables the formula to be copied to create the formulas for the remaining digits.

Students discover a large number of checks beginning with the number 6. A further analysis of the check data could reveal that the minimum check amount is in the $60.00 range and the maximum is in the $600.00 range. As a result, it would appear that there is a natural bias that results in a higher number of 6-digit amounts than would be expected.

Solutions

1. Except for the digit 6, the actual frequency percentages closely follow the pattern of Benford's Law.
2. The chart clearly shows that more numbers begin with 6 than would be expected in an unbiased set of data. This result needs to be investigated to determine the nature of the bias. However, without additional evidence, there is not enough evidence to conclude that a fraud has occurred.
3. Possible answers:
   a. Determine the maximum and minimum check amounts.
   b. Analyze the reimbursements by month.
   c. Analyze the reimbursements by employee.

INPUT

- Discuss the procedures followed to prepare the annual operating budget.

MODEL

- Refer students to the illustration on page 678 and explain how an annual budget is prepared.

Procedures to Prepare an Annual Operating Budget

Some basic procedures are followed in preparing an annual governmental operating budget.

1. Departments of the governmental organization submit budget requests to the chief executive of the organization. Requests are based on an analysis of expenditures for the previous year and expected changes in expenditures for the coming year.
2. The chief executive reviews budget requests with department heads. When budget requests are acceptable to the chief executive, departmental requests are consolidated into a single budget request for the organization. The chief executive then submits the operating budget to the legislative body. The legislative body is a group of persons normally elected by the citizens/members of the organization and granted authority to make laws for the organization.
3. The legislative body approves the operating budget. The approved operating budget becomes an authorization to spend the amounts listed in the budget. Before the operating budget can be approved, revenues plus the available amount of fund equity must be at least as great as the expenditures. If the expenditures are more than the total of expected revenues and available fund equity, the expected sources of revenue must be increased or the expenditures decreased.

Lindville is a small town with a town manager and five town council members. The council members are elected to their positions. One member of the council serves as mayor. The council serves as the legislative body for Lindville. The council appoints the town manager who works full-time as chief executive of the town. Lindville has three department heads: Public Safety Director, Fire Protection Director, and Recreation Director. Because Lindville is small and most of its revenues come from property taxes, the accounting system contains only one fund—a general fund.

At the request of the town manager, Lindville's three department heads analyze the current year's expenditures and expected changes and then prepare budget requests for the next year. The town manager reviews the budget requests and prepares a single operating budget for Lindville's general fund for the next year. The operating budget is submitted to the town council.

The town council represents the interests of all the town's citizens. Thus, the council should evaluate the operating budget from at least four perspectives. (1) Are adequate services being provided? (2) Are the services desired by a majority of citizens? (3) Are the amounts requested sufficient to provide the desired level of services? (4) Does the city have the financial capacity to support the budget?

The approved operating budget determines the amount of revenues needed for the year. The town's tax rate necessary to provide the needed funds for the approved operating budget is then determined.

After completing its review, the Lindville council formally approves next year's governmental operating budget. The approval provides legal authorization for the town manager and the department heads to make expenditures for specified purposes. Authorizations to make expenditures for specific purposes are called **appropriations**. Lindville's approved operating budget has appropriations that authorize expenditures up to the amounts stated in the budget.

The tax rate is set at a rate that will raise at least enough revenue to cover the appropriations. Many governmental organizations restrict the amount that taxes can be increased. Public hearings may be required before taxes can be increased. A formal vote in an election may also be required. If a proposed operating budget exceeds the amount of taxes and other estimated revenue, the budget may need to be reduced to the level of available revenues.

© Dana Heinemann/Shutterstock.com

Journalizing an Approved Annual Budget LO3

JOURNAL — PAGE 1

	DATE		ACCOUNT TITLE	DOC. NO.	POST. REF.	GENERAL DEBIT (1)	GENERAL CREDIT (2)	CASH DEBIT (3)	CASH CREDIT (4)	
1	20-- Jan.	2	*Estimated Revenues*	M1		1691 5 0 0 00				1
2			*Appropriations*				1659 0 0 0 00			2
3			*Budgetary Fund Balance*				32 5 0 0 00			3
4										4

Estimated Revenues

Debit	Credit
Jan. 2 ↑ 1,691,500.00	

Appropriations

Debit	Credit
	Jan. 2 ↑ 1,659,000.00

Budgetary Fund Balance

Debit	Credit
	Jan. 2 ↑ 32,500.00

As an additional control measure, Lindville journalizes its approved operating budget as shown above. Budgetary accounts are for control purposes and are closed at the end of a fiscal period.

Governmental organizations, like businesses, record accounting transactions initially in a journal. Source documents are the basis for the journal entries. Governmental organizations may use a multicolumn journal, a general journal, or special journals adapted to the organization's needs. Lindville uses a multicolumn journal.

January 2. Recorded Lindville's approved operating budget: estimated revenues, $1,691,500.00; appropriations, $1,659,000.00; budgetary fund balance, $32,500.00. Memorandum No. 1.

Estimated Revenues is increased by a debit for the budgeted revenues, $1,691,500.00. Estimated Revenues has a normal debit balance, opposite the normal credit balance of an actual revenue account. Appropriations is increased by a credit for Lindville's budgeted expenditures, $1,659,000.00. Appropriations has a normal credit balance, opposite the normal debit balance of the actual expenditure accounts. Budgetary Fund Balance is increased by a credit, $32,500.00 (estimated revenues, $1,691,500.00, less appropriations, $1,659,000.00).

A separate revenue account will be credited as revenues are earned. Balances of the two accounts, Estimated Revenues and Revenues, can be reviewed to compare the amount of actual revenues earned and the amount of revenues estimated to be earned. If actual revenues are not as great as expected, expenditures may need to be reduced to avoid exceeding available funds. Recording the estimated revenues in the budgetary account Estimated Revenues provides this planning and control information.

Separate expenditure accounts will be debited as actual expenditures are made. Ensuring that expenditures do not exceed the appropriations (budgeted expenditures) is essential for governmental organizations. Periodically, the appropriations account balance can be compared with the total of expenditure account balances to avoid overspending appropriations. Appropriations less total expenditures is the amount still available for spending. Recording appropriations in the budgetary account Appropriations provides this additional control information. Each department also keeps records of its appropriated and expended amounts to ensure that no department exceeds its appropriation amounts.

If appropriations exceed estimated revenues, Budgetary Fund Balance is debited to make the total debits equal the total credits. However, most governmental organizations normally set their revenue sources slightly above appropriations to avoid exceeding appropriations.

INPUT

- Discuss the reason for journalizing a governmental organization's budget.
- Introduce the multicolumn journal used by Lindville. Refer to the illustration.

MODEL

- Use a multicolumn transparency to record the approved operating budget.

FORMATIVE ASSESSMENT

- This is an ongoing process. Circulate around the classroom or lab, observing which students have difficulty with the assignments.
- Troubleshooting: Diagnose the kinds of problems students have with this section. Students may have trouble remembering the entry for journalizing an approved annual operating budget.
- Assess student understanding by checking solutions to Independent Practice assignments and noting their answers to the Terms Review and Audit Your Understanding questions.

CHECK FOR UNDERSTANDING

Terms Review

- Call on students to define each term in the Terms Review. Definitions are given in the Glossary.

Audit Your Understanding

- Call on students to answer the Audit Your Understanding questions. Answers are given in Appendix D.

GUIDED PRACTICE

Work Together

- Have students write the solution to the Work Together problem as you guide the class through the examples.
- Direct students to journalize governmental operating budgets.

INDEPENDENT PRACTICE

On Your Own

- Assign the On Your Own problem to be worked independently.
- Use the Formative Assessment techniques to diagnose student understanding.

Application Problem

- Assign Application Problem 23-1.

Online Working Papers

- Students can access the Lesson 23-1 problems using this software.

Website

- Direct students to the C21 Accounting companion website for additional practice and review opportunities throughout the chapter.

RETEACH

- Instruct students to practice making the entry to journalize an approved annual operating budget. This can be done in groups of two students. One student develops a partial operating budget for a city, which includes the estimated revenue, appropriations, and budgetary fund balance. The other student records the journal entry.

Essential Questions

- Why is it important for citizens to vote for council members who reflect the citizens' preferences? (*Answers will vary. Students may realize that votes on spending could support mutual areas of interest.*)
- Why might a budget exceed appropriations? (*Examples might include adverse weather conditions that require additional personnel, supplies, or equipment, such as snow removal.*)

EXTENDED LEARNING

- Assign Accounting in the Real World on page 671.
- Assign Ethics in Action on page 672.
- Assign Why Accounting on page 673.
- Assign Forensic Accounting on page 679.

End of Lesson Review

LO1 Describe the characteristics of not-for-profit organizations.

LO2 Describe the process used to develop an operating budget for a not-for-profit organization.

LO3 Journalize budget transactions for a not-for-profit organization.

Terms Review

not-for-profit organization
fund
expenditure
statement of revenues, expenditures, and changes in fund balance
fund equity
operating budget
appropriations

Audit your understanding

1. How does a lack of a profit motive affect a governmental organization's measure of success and its ability to continue operations?
2. List the accounting practices that are similar for businesses and governmental organizations.
3. What is a fund?
4. What is the purpose of a governmental operating budget?
5. What accounts are debited and credited to journalize a governmental organization's approved operating budget?

Work together 23-1

Journalizing governmental operating budgets

The town of Lindforde approved its annual general fund operating budgets effective January 1 of the current year. A journal is provided in the *Working Papers*. Your instructor will guide you through the following example.

Journalize the entry to record the following operating budget for the town of Lindforde. The source document is Memorandum No. 1.

Estimated Revenues	Appropriations	Budgetary Fund Balance
$943,700.00	$936,800.00	$6,900.00

On your own 23-1

Journalizing governmental operating budgets

The town of Portsburg approved its annual general fund operating budgets effective January 1 of the current year. A journal is provided in the *Working Papers*. Work independently to complete the following problem.

Journalize the entry to record the following operating budget for the town of Portsburg. The source document is Memorandum No. 1.

Estimated Revenues	Appropriations	Budgetary Fund Balance
$1,987,300.00	$1,945,000.00	$42,300.00

LESSON

23-2 Journalizing Revenues

LO4 Journalize revenues for a not-for-profit organization.

Journalizing Current Property Tax Revenues LO4

JOURNAL PAGE 1

	DATE		ACCOUNT TITLE	DOC. NO.	POST. REF.	1 GENERAL DEBIT	2 GENERAL CREDIT	3 CASH DEBIT	4 CASH CREDIT	
4		2	*Taxes Receivable—Current*	M2		1699 0 0 0 00				4
5			*Allowance for Uncollectible Taxes—Current*				24 0 0 0 00			5
6			*Property Tax Revenue*				1675 0 0 0 00			6
7										7

Total Taxes Levied

Revenue Recognized from Tax Levy

Estimated Losses for Taxes Not Collected

Governmental fund revenues are recorded in the accounting period in which the revenues become measurable and available. Authorized action taken by a governmental organization to collect taxes by legal authority is called a **tax levy**. When tax rates have been set and tax amounts calculated, taxes are levied on all taxable property. Levied property taxes are considered measurable and available because they become a legal obligation of property owners. Therefore, when the levy is enacted, a journal entry to record property tax revenue is prepared, as shown above.

Although tax levies are legal obligations, some property owners do not pay their taxes. Legal action may eventually be taken against these property owners in an effort to collect the taxes. Even with these actions, a government generally does not collect all the taxes levied. On January 2, Lindville authorized its tax levy and sent out tax statements to property owners. Lindville estimated that $24,000.00 of property taxes will not be collected.

Taxes Receivable—Current is debited for the total tax levied, $1,699,000.00. This amount is the total of the tax statements sent to taxpayers. The contra asset account, Allowance for Uncollectible Taxes—Current, is credited for the estimated loss, $24,000.00. The credit to the revenue account Property Tax Revenue, $1,675,000.00, is the revenue presented on Lindville's annual operating budget for the general fund.

January 2. Recorded property tax levy: taxes receivable—current, $1,699,000.00; allowance for uncollectible taxes—current, $24,000.00; property tax revenue, $1,675,000.00. Memorandum No. 2.

Taxes Receivable—Current

Debit	Credit
Jan. 2 ↑ 1,699,000.00	

Allowance for Uncollectible Taxes—Current

Debit	Credit
	Jan. 2 ↑ 24,000.00

Property Tax Revenue

Debit	Credit
	Jan. 2 ↑ 1,675,000.00

LESSON 23-2

BRIDGE

- Point out that students have already learned how for-profit businesses generate revenues. In this lesson, students will learn how a city government might generate revenue.

TEACHING RESOURCES

- **Instructor's Resource CD/Website:** PowerPoint Slides; Accounting Concepts
- **Working Papers:** Teacher's Edition of the Working Papers for Lesson 23-2; Online Working Papers
- **Transparency Master:** Multicolumn Journal

ENGAGE

- Explain that city governments may collect a variety of revenues from its citizens. Explain that this section will describe how to record the collection of different revenues.
- Ask students to name different revenues that their local municipality collects from its citizens.

PREVIEW

- Call on a student to read the accounting term and definition introduced in this lesson: *tax levy*.
- Point out the learning objective for this lesson.
- Direct students to read the headings in this lesson and to examine the illustrations.

INPUT

- Direct students to the illustration. Discuss the necessity of having an allowance account for uncollectible taxes.
- Discuss journalizing property tax revenue before cash is received.

MODEL

- Draw three blank T accounts on the board.
- Read the transaction statement.
- Ask students to analyze the transaction by answering the following questions: Which accounts are affected? Are they increased or decreased? Are they debited or credited? Complete the T accounts as the information is provided.
- Use a transparency to illustrate how to record the transaction in a multicolumn journal.
- Record each item in the journal.

INPUT

- Direct students to the two illustrations on this page. Discuss the entry to record the collection of current property tax and the entry to record other revenue.

MODEL

- For each transaction, draw blank T accounts on the board.
- Read the transaction statement.
- Ask students to analyze the transaction by answering these questions: Which accounts are affected? Are they increased or decreased? Are they debited or credited? Complete the T accounts as the information is given.
- Use a transparency to illustrate how to record the two transactions in a multi-column journal.
- Record each transaction as shown.

Collection of Current Property Taxes

JOURNAL — PAGE 1

	DATE	ACCOUNT TITLE	DOC. NO.	POST. REF.	GENERAL DEBIT (1)	GENERAL CREDIT (2)	CASH DEBIT (3)	CASH CREDIT (4)	
7	10	Taxes Receivable—Current	R1			206 000 00	206 000 00		7
8									8
9									9

Tax collections reduce the amount of taxes to be received from taxpayers. Similar to a partnership or corporation, the receipt of cash from a receivable does not result in the recognition of revenue.

January 10. Received cash for current taxes receivable, $206,000.00. Receipt No. 1.

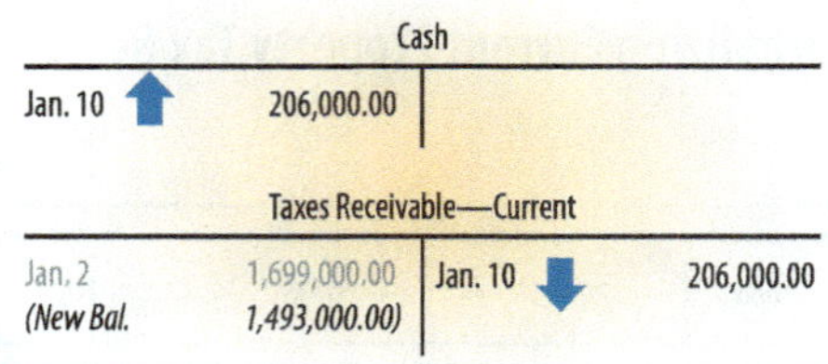

The outstanding balance of Taxes Receivable—Current is reduced by the amount of cash received.

Other Revenue

JOURNAL — PAGE 1

	DATE	ACCOUNT TITLE	DOC. NO.	POST. REF.	GENERAL DEBIT (1)	GENERAL CREDIT (2)	CASH DEBIT (3)	CASH CREDIT (4)	
8	12	Other Revenue	R2			1 25 00	1 25 00		8
9									9
10									10

Some revenues, such as fines, inspection charges, parking meter receipts, and penalties, are normally not known and, thus, are not measurable until cash is received. A journal entry to record such revenues, therefore, is generally made only when cash is received.

January 12. Received cash from a traffic fine, $125.00. Receipt No. 2.

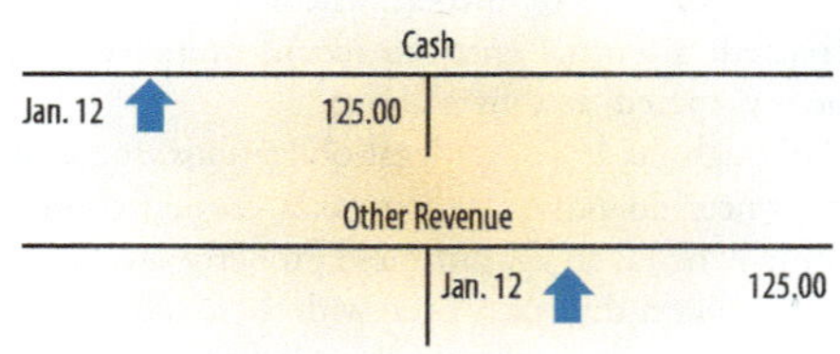

Unlike property taxes, no receivables account was established for this source of revenue. Therefore, Other Revenue is credited when the cash is collected.

remember Other Revenue is used to account for cash receipts that are not measurable until received.

DIFFERENTIATED INSTRUCTION

Visual/Spatial learners like to see what is being discussed. Ask students to create a poster-size balance sheet for a corporation and a fund accounting balance sheet for a governmental organization. Suggest that students use different colors to compare and contrast the differences.

Accounting for Delinquent Property Taxes

Establish Balances in Deliquent Receivable Accounts

JOURNAL — PAGE 5

	DATE		ACCOUNT TITLE	DOC. NO.	POST. REF.	GENERAL DEBIT (1)	GENERAL CREDIT (2)	CASH DEBIT (3)	CASH CREDIT (4)	
1	20-- Mar.	1	*Taxes Receivable—Delinquent*	*M15*		74 2 0 0 00				1
2			*Allowance for Uncollectible Taxes—Current*			24 0 0 0 00				2
3			*Taxes Receivable—Current*				74 2 0 0 00			3
4			*Allowance for Uncollectible Taxes—Delinquent*				24 0 0 0 00			4
15		20	*Taxes Receivable—Delinquent*	*R32*			5 0 0 0 00	5 0 0 0 00		15

Remove Balances in Current Receivable Accounts

Tax payments specify the date that property taxes are due and payable. Taxes not paid by the specified date are reclassified as delinquent. Lindville's property taxes are due on February 28. On March 1, taxes not paid are considered delinquent. On that date, a journal entry is made to transfer uncollected taxes from current to delinquent status as shown above.

Taxes that Lindville expects to collect are accounted for by using two accounts, Taxes Receivable—Current and Allowance for Uncollectible Taxes—Current. Delinquent taxes are accounted for using two accounts, Taxes Receivable—Delinquent and Allowance for Uncollectible Taxes—Delinquent. A journal entry transfers the balances of the two current accounts to the two delinquent accounts.

March 1. Recorded reclassification of current taxes receivable to delinquent status, $74,200.00, and the accompanying allowance for uncollectible accounts, $24,000.00. Memorandum No. 15.

Taxes Receivable—Delinquent

Debit		Credit	
Mar. 1 ↑	74,200.00		

Allowance for Uncollectible Taxes—Current

Debit		Credit	
Mar. 1 ↓	24,000.00	Jan. 2 *(New Bal. Zero)*	24,000.00

Taxes Receivable—Current

Debit		Credit	
Jan. 2 *(New Bal. zero)*	74,200.00	Mar. 1 ↓	74,200.00

Allowance for Uncollectible Taxes—Delinquent

Debit		Credit	
		Mar. 1 ↑	24,000.00

Collection of Delinquent Property Taxes

Although some taxes become delinquent, Lindville continues efforts to collect these taxes. Cash received for delinquent taxes reduces Taxes Receivable—Delinquent as shown in line 15 of the journal above.

March 20. Received cash for delinquent taxes receivable, $5,000.00. Receipt No. 32.

Cash

Debit		Credit	
Mar. 20 ↑	5,000.00		

Taxes Receivable—Delinquent

Debit		Credit	
		Mar. 20 ↓	5,000.00

INPUT

- Direct students to the illustration. Discuss the entry to record delinquent property taxes.
- Point out the T accounts at the bottom of the page and discuss what occurs when the delinquent property taxes are collected.

MODEL

- Draw four T accounts on the board.
- Read the transaction statement.
- Ask students to analyze the transaction by answering these questions: Which accounts are affected? Are they increased or decreased? Are they debited or credited? Complete the T accounts as the information is given.
- Use a transparency to illustrate how to record the transaction in a multicolumn journal.
- Record the transaction as shown.
- Repeat the same process for the collection of delinquent property taxes.

FORMATIVE ASSESSMENT

- This is an ongoing process. Circulate around the classroom or lab, observing which students have difficulty with the assignments.
- Troubleshooting: Diagnose the kinds of problems students have with this lesson. Students may have trouble remembering how to record delinquent property taxes.
- Assess student understanding by checking solutions to Independent Practice assignments and noting their answers to the Term Review and Audit Your Understanding questions.

CHECK FOR UNDERSTANDING

Term Review

- Call on a student to define the term in the Term Review. A definition is given in the Glossary.

Audit Your Understanding

- Call on students to answer the Audit Your Understanding questions. Answers are given in Appendix D.

GUIDED PRACTICE

Work Together

- Have students write the solution to the Work Together problem as you guide the class through the examples.
- Direct students to journalize governmental revenue transactions.

INDEPENDENT PRACTICE

On Your Own

- Assign the On Your Own problem to be worked independently.
- Use the Formative Assessment techniques to diagnose student understanding.

Application Problem

- Assign Application Problem 23-2.

Online Working Papers

- Students can access the Lesson 23-2 problems using this software.

RETEACH

- Make a transparency of a multicolumn journal. Ask a student to come forward and record the first line of the transaction for delinquent property taxes. Have a different student complete each line of the transparency.

CLOSURE

- Tell students to outline the steps to record each revenue transaction.

Essential Questions

- How long should a government agency attempt to collect on delinquent property taxes? (*A government agency will continue to collect and may use other enforcements besides imposing penalties. These may include placing liens on real estate, contacting financial institutions for monies from the taxpayer's account, and garnishing wages.*)
- What happens when property is sold but property taxes are delinquent? (*If taxes are delinquent, the property transfer cannot take place until the taxes are paid. On rare occasions, the new owner may be held accountable for the previous owner's delinquent taxes if measures are not taken before the property transfer.*)

End of Lesson Review

LO4 Journalize revenues for a not-for-profit organization.

Term Review

tax levy

Audit your understanding

1. When is the journal entry to record property tax revenue prepared?
2. What accounts are affected, and how, when a taxpayer pays current property taxes?
3. What accounts are affected, and how, when a taxpayer pays property taxes two months after the due date?

Work together 23-2

Journalizing governmental revenue transactions

Tomeville's town council recently approved the town's general fund operating budget for the current year. A journal is provided in the *Working Papers*. Source documents are abbreviated as follows: check, C; receipt, R; memorandum, M. Your instructor will guide you through the following examples.

Journalize the following transactions.

Transactions:

Jan. 2. Recorded property tax levy: taxes receivable—current, $2,723,000.00; allowance for uncollectible taxes—current, $30,000.00; property tax revenue, $2,693,000.00. M22.

15. Received cash from traffic fines, $1,488.00. R94. (Other Revenue)

Feb. 12. Received cash for current taxes receivable, $669,000.00. R103.

Mar. 1. Recorded reclassification of current taxes receivable to delinquent status, $89,200.00, and the accompanying allowance for uncollectible accounts, $30,000.00. M44.

13. Received cash for delinquent taxes receivable, $21,300.00. R137.

On your own 23-2

Journalizing governmental revenue transactions

Missville's town council recently approved the town's general fund operating budget for the current year. A journal is provided in the *Working Papers*. Source documents are abbreviated as follows: check, C; receipt, R; memorandum, M. Work independently to complete the following problem.

Journalize the following transactions.

Transactions:

Jan. 3. Recorded property tax levy: taxes receivable—current, $1,267,000.00; allowance for uncollectible taxes—current, $13,000.00; property tax revenue, $1,254,000.00. M15.

Feb. 2. Received cash for current taxes receivable, $948,200.00. R45.

14. Received cash from parking meter receipts, $1,060.00. R67. (Other Revenue)

Mar. 1. Recorded reclassification of current taxes receivable to delinquent status, $32,600.00, and the accompanying allowance for uncollectible accounts, $13,000.00. M34.

28. Received cash for delinquent taxes receivable, $16,920.00. R100.

LESSON

23-3 Journalizing Expenditures, Encumbrances, and Other Transactions

LO5 Journalize expenditures, encumbrances, and other transactions for a not-for-profit organization.

Journalizing Expenditures LO5

JOURNAL — PAGE 1

	DATE		ACCOUNT TITLE	DOC. NO.	POST. REF.	GENERAL DEBIT (1)	GENERAL CREDIT (2)	CASH DEBIT (3)	CASH CREDIT (4)	
10		14	*Expenditure—Supplies, Fire Protection*	C234		120 00			120 00	10
11										11
12										12

A primary objective of governmental accounting is to control the financial resources. Governmental accounting focuses on measuring changes in financial resources rather than determining net income. Therefore, in governmental accounting, expenditures rather than expenses are recorded. The use of two special accounting procedures enhances the control of expenditures.

1. Expenditures are classified into categories to assign specific responsibility for and to analyze the purpose of the expenditure. For example, Expenditure—Personnel, Fire Protection, is one of Lindville's expenditure accounts. Personnel indicates the type of expenditure (salaries for personnel). Fire Protection indicates the department for which the personnel expenditures were made.
2. Budgetary accounts are used to record estimated amounts of expenditures to protect against overspending the budgeted amounts. To accomplish this control procedure, encumbrance accounts are used. A commitment to pay for goods or services that have been ordered but not yet provided is called an **encumbrance**. When an order that will require a future expenditure is placed, a budgetary encumbrance account is debited for the estimated amount. This entry reduces the fund balance and ensures that commitments and expenditures will not be greater than the funds available.

Exact amounts of some expenditures are known as soon as the obligation is determined. For example, the amount and due date of payment for supplies is known when the department employee purchases the supplies at a local retailer. The entry to record the expenditure is shown above.

January 14. Paid cash for supplies in the Fire Department, $120.00. Check No. 234.

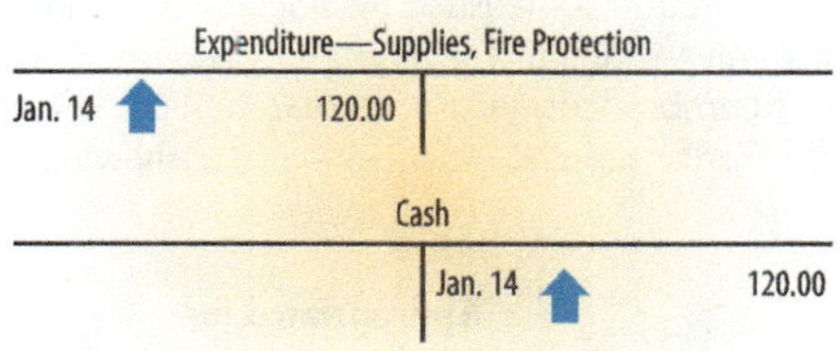

The major control of expenditures is achieved by holding department heads accountable for expenditures in their departments. Classification of expenditures is used to analyze major types of expenditures within each department. For Lindville, each department's expenditures are recorded in one of four classifications: personnel, supplies, other charges, or capital outlays. The other charges classification is used for all expenditures except salaries and related personnel expenditures, supplies expenditures, and capital outlays. Capital outlays is used for expenditures that will benefit future years.

LESSON

23-3

BRIDGE

- Point out that students have learned how to pay expenses for a for-profit business. In this lesson, they will learn how to order and pay for expenses for a not-for-profit organization.

TEACHING RESOURCES

- **Instructor's Resource CD/Website:** PowerPoint Slides; Accounting Concepts
- **Working Papers:** Teacher's Edition of the Working Papers for Lesson 23-3; Online Working Papers
- **Transparency Master:** Multicolumn Journal

ENGAGE

- Remind students that there are many differences between accounting for a not-for-profit organization and a for-profit organization.

PREVIEW

- Call on students to read the accounting terms and definitions introduced in this lesson: *encumbrance, general fixed assets*, and *certificate of deposit*.
- Point out the learning objective for this lesson.
- Direct students to read the headings in this lesson and to examine the illustrations.

INPUT

- Remind students that the primary objective of governmental accounting is to control financial resources, not to measure net income.
- Explain that an encumbrance reduces the fund balance and ensures that funds will be available when the bill must be paid.
- Direct students to the illustration to point out journalizing expenditures.

DIFFERENTIATED INSTRUCTION

Gifted learners enjoy conducting further research. Ask students to collect the operating budgets from three different government municipalities and select a medium in which to present the information and comparisons to the class.

INPUT

- Remind students that an encumbrance ensures that funds are available to pay a bill when it arrives. Therefore, an encumbrance is recorded when an amount can be estimated for an expenditure.
- Explain that this encumbrance will be removed when the exact amount of the transaction is known.
- Explain that the appropriated amount for a category, less the encumbrances and expenditures, equals the amount that can still be spent in that category. Refer to the math illustration.

MODEL

- Draw two blank T accounts on the board.
- Read the transaction statement.
- Ask students to analyze the transaction by answering these questions: Which accounts are affected? Are they increased or decreased? Are they debited or credited? Complete the T accounts as the information is given.
- Use a transparency to illustrate how to record the transaction in a multicolumn journal.
- Record each item in the journal.
- Ask a student to verify that debits equal credits for this transaction.

Journalizing Encumbrances

JOURNAL — PAGE 2

	DATE	ACCOUNT TITLE	DOC. NO.	POST. REF.	1 GENERAL DEBIT	2 GENERAL CREDIT	3 CASH DEBIT	4 CASH CREDIT	
4	16	*Encumbrance—Supplies, Fire Protection*	*M8*		480 00				4
5		*Reserve for Encumbrances—Current Year*				480 00			5
6									6

To avoid spending more resources than are available, encumbrance accounts are used. When goods or services are ordered that will be provided at a later date, an obligation for a future expenditure is made. Resources have not yet been used, but there is a promise to give up those resources when ordered goods or services are delivered. Encumbering resources is a way of setting aside the amount estimated to be needed to pay for the goods or services. When the goods or services are delivered, the estimated amount is removed from the encumbrance account and the exact amount of the expenditure is journalized in an expenditure account.

January 16. Encumbered estimated amount for supplies in Fire Protection Department, $480.00. Memorandum No. 8.

The budgetary account Encumbrance—Supplies, Fire Protection is increased by a debit for the amount of the order, $480.00. The fund equity account Reserve for Encumbrances—Current Year is increased by a credit for the supplies order, $480.00, as shown above.

Encumbrance—Supplies, Fire Protection	
Jan. 16 ↑ 480.00	

Reserve for Encumbrances—Current Year	
	Jan. 16 ↑ 480.00

This account serves as an offsetting account for the encumbrance account and shows that this amount of the fund equity is reserved for an encumbrance.

Expenditures plus encumbrances for a specific account equal the total commitment that has been made against the appropriated amount for that account. The appropriated amount less the encumbrances and expenditures equals the amount that can still be spent. For example, Lindville appropriated $13,400.00 for supplies for the Fire Protection Department. If expenditures are $120.00 and encumbrances are $480.00, then $12,800.00 is still available for fire protection supplies expenditures.

Appropriated for Supplies	–	Expenditures	–	Encumbrances	=	Amount Still Available
$13,400.00	–	$120.00	–	$480.00	=	$12,800.00

remember Governmental organizations record expenditures rather than expenses.

Journalizing Expenditures for Amounts Encumbered

JOURNAL — PAGE 2

	DATE		ACCOUNT TITLE	DOC. NO.	POST. REF.	GENERAL DEBIT (1)	GENERAL CREDIT (2)	CASH DEBIT (3)	CASH CREDIT (4)	
16		28	*Reserve for Encumbrances—Current Year*	*M19*		480 00				16
17			*Encumbrance—Supplies, Fire Protection*				480 00			17
18		28	*Expenditure—Supplies, Fire Protection*	*C246*		465 00			465 00	18

When goods or services that have been encumbered are received, two entries must be made.

1. The encumbrance entry is reversed to remove the estimated amount from the encumbrance and the reserve for encumbrance accounts.
2. The expenditure is recorded.

These entries are illustrated above.

January 28. Paid cash for Fire Protection Department supplies, $465.00, encumbered January 16 per Memorandum No. 8. Memorandum No. 19 and Check No. 246.

Effect of first entry

Reserve for Encumbrances—Current Year			
Jan. 28 ↓	480.00	Jan. 16 *(New Bal. zero)*	480.00

Encumbrance—Supplies, Fire Protection			
Jan. 16 *(New Bal. zero)*	480.00	Jan. 28 ↓	480.00

Effect of second entry

Expenditure—Supplies, Fire Protection			
Jan. 28 ↑	465.00		

Cash			
		Jan. 28 ↓	465.00

The first entry cancels the encumbrance entry by removing the estimated amount from the encumbrance and the reserve for encumbrance accounts. The encumbrance is no longer needed, since it is no longer outstanding. The encumbrance was for an estimated amount, $480.00.

The actual amount of an expenditure sometimes differs from the amount estimated when an order is placed. When the supplies were delivered, the actual cost was $465.00. Expenditure—Supplies, Fire Protection is debited for the actual cost of supplies, $465.00.

Journalizing Expenditures Benefiting Future Periods

JOURNAL — PAGE 5

	DATE		ACCOUNT TITLE	DOC. NO.	POST. REF.	GENERAL DEBIT (1)	GENERAL CREDIT (2)	CASH DEBIT (3)	CASH CREDIT (4)	
7		10	*Expenditure—Capital Outlays, Gen. Gov't.*	*C269*		290 00			290 00	7
8										8
9										9

Governmental organizations are formed to provide services that their members need, not to earn a profit. A business records the cost of property, such as a computer, as an asset. The business then depreciates the asset over its useful life. The depreciation expense is matched with revenue earned in each fiscal period. Since governmental organizations do not earn net income, they have no need for expense information. However, controlling the expenditure of funds is important. When money is spent for capital outlays, the amount is recorded as an

INPUT

- Remind students that once the goods or services encumbered are received, two entries must be made.
- The first entry reverses the encumbrance entry used to estimate the amount of the expenditure.
- The second entry records the actual expenditure.
- Refer to the illustration.

MODEL

- Draw four blank T accounts on the board.
- Read the transaction statement.
- Ask students to analyze the transaction by answering these questions: Which accounts are affected? Are they increased or decreased? Are they debited or credited? Complete the T accounts as the information is given.
- Use a transparency to illustrate how to record the transaction in a multicolumn journal.
- Record each item in the journal.
- Ask a student to verify that debits equal credits for this transaction.

INPUT

- Explain that when a governmental organization spends money for a capital outlay, the amount is recorded as an expenditure even though the item may benefit several accounting periods. Depreciation is not used for governmental units.

MODEL

- For each transaction, draw two blank T accounts on the board.
- Read each transaction statement.
- Ask students to analyze each transaction by answering these questions: Which accounts are affected? Are they increased or decreased? Are they debited or credited? Complete the T accounts as the information is given.
- Use a transparency to illustrate how to record the transaction in a multicolumn journal.
- Record each item in the journal.
- Ask a student to verify that debits equal credits for this transaction.

- Explain that the entry to record the issuance of a note payable for a governmental organization is similar to the entry to record the issuance of a note payable for a company.
- Explain that the account used for interest expense will connect the charge to a specific category of government.

MODEL

- For each transaction, draw two blank T accounts on the board.
- Read each transaction statement.
- Ask students to analyze each transaction by answering these questions: Which accounts are affected? Are they increased or decreased? Are they debited or credited? Complete the T accounts as the information is given.
- Use a transparency to illustrate how to record the transaction in a multicolumn journal.
- Record each item in the journal.
- Ask a student to verify that debits equal credits for this transaction.

expenditure in the period spent, even though the item may benefit several accounting periods.

On March 10, Lindville's General Government Department bought a new wireless router.

March 10. Paid cash for a wireless router for General Government Department, $290.00. Check No. 269.

Expenditure—Capital Outlays, General Government is increased by a debit for the cost of the computer, $290.00. Cash is decreased by a credit for the same amount, $290.00. The journal entry is shown on page 689.

Governmental properties that benefit future periods are called **general fixed assets**. Most governmental organizations keep a record of general fixed assets. This record helps to safeguard the government's ownership of the property. Lindville keeps a card file with information about each general fixed asset.

Journalize the Issuance of Liabilities

JOURNAL — PAGE 2

	DATE		ACCOUNT TITLE	DOC. NO.	POST. REF.	1 GENERAL DEBIT	2 GENERAL CREDIT	3 CASH DEBIT	4 CASH CREDIT	
1	20-- Jan.	15	Notes Payable	NP3			60 000 00	60 000 00		1
2										2
3										3

Governmental organizations may need to borrow cash for short periods until tax money is received. At other times, these organizations have cash to invest for short periods until the cash is needed to pay expenditures. Lindville sends tax statements to property owners on January 1 each year. Taxes can be paid between January 1 and February 28. Consequently, the town may need to borrow cash until taxes are received.

January 15. Issued a 30-day, 9% note, $60,000.00. Note Payable No. 3.

Cash is increased by a debit for the amount received, $60,000.00. Notes Payable is increased by a credit for the same amount, $60,000.00. The journal entry to record this transaction is shown above.

Journalize the Payment of Liabilities

JOURNAL — PAGE 4

	DATE		ACCOUNT TITLE	DOC. NO.	POST. REF.	1 GENERAL DEBIT	2 GENERAL CREDIT	3 CASH DEBIT	4 CASH CREDIT	
1	20-- Feb.	14	Notes Payable	C370		60 000 00			60 450 00	1
2			*Expenditure—Other Charges, Gen. Gov't.*			450 00				2
3										3

When Lindville's note payable is due on February 14, the amount of the note plus interest expense is paid to the bank. The bank uses a 360-day year when calculating interest.

February 14. Paid cash for the maturity value of NP3: principal, $60,000.00, plus interest, $450.00; total, $60,450.00. Check No. 370.

Notes Payable is decreased by a debit, $60,000.00. Expenditure—Other Charges, General Government is increased by a debit for the interest expense, $450.00. Cash is decreased by a credit for the total amount paid, $60,450.00. The journal entry is shown above.

Investing in Short-Term Investments

JOURNAL — PAGE 9

	DATE		ACCOUNT TITLE	DOC. NO.	POST. REF.	GENERAL DEBIT (1)	GENERAL CREDIT (2)	CASH DEBIT (3)	CASH CREDIT (4)	
1	20-- May	4	Investments—Short Term	C603		300 000 00			300 000 00	1
2										2
3										3

Most of Lindville's property taxes, the major portion of the town's revenue, are collected by March 1 each year. Cash that will not be needed for several months is placed in short-term investments. Interest on these investments provides additional revenue.

May 4. Paid cash for a 120-day, 2.5% certificate of deposit, $300,000.00. Check No. 603.

A document issued by a bank as evidence of money invested with the bank is called a **certificate of deposit**. The time and interest rate to be paid are included on the certificate.

Investments—Short Term is increased by a debit for the amount of the certificate, $300,000.00. Cash is decreased by a credit for the same amount, $300,000.00. The journal entry is shown above.

© iStockphoto.com/Dan Bachman

THINK LIKE AN ACCOUNTANT

Organizational Structure

Within the past year, Alexander County residents had suffered the loss of property and life as a result of a hurricane and two tornadoes. Unhappy with the timeliness and breadth of the response by federal agencies, the county supervisors decided to organize their own disaster response agency.

The job of organizing the Alexander County Taskforce (ACT) was assigned to Cerita Juarez and funded by a small grant from the county. Cerita assembled a group of individuals who would assume leadership roles. As ACT began operations, Cerita knew that ACT would need to seek significant financial support from local corporations.

Dennis Sparks, a CPA, accepted the role of development officer. Dennis would be responsible for obtaining ACT's financial support. His first task is to prepare a funding proposal to submit to corporations. The proposal needs to demonstrate that ACT is a legitimate organization deserving financial support. As a part of this proposal, Dennis decided to include a profile of each leader in the organization. At his request, Cerita prepared a document containing an alphabetical list of ACT leaders.

OPEN THE SPREADSHEET TLA_CH23

The workbook contains a description of the individuals who accepted ACT's leadership positions. Follow the steps on the Instructions tab to create a graphic image of ACT's organizational structure. Answer these questions:

1. How does an organizational chart help the corporations understand ACT's organizational structure?
2. What recommendation would you give Dennis to improve the organizational chart?

INPUT

- Remind students that the entry to record investing in a short-term investment is the same for a governmental organization as it is for a company.

MODEL

- For each transaction, draw blank T accounts on the board.
- Read each transaction statement.
- Ask students to analyze each transaction by answering these questions: Which accounts are affected? Are they increased or decreased? Are they debited or credited? Complete the T accounts as the information is given.
- Use a transparency to illustrate how to record each transaction in a multi-column journal.
- Record each item in the journal.
- Ask a student to verify that for this transaction, debits equal credits for this transaction.

THINK LIKE AN ACCOUNTANT

Accountants need to be able to communicate more than financial information. Accountants must possess good writing skills, which includes the use of technology to enhance how written information is presented.

The workbook contains a brief description of ACT's leaders. Students follow the instructions to complete an organizational chart using Excel's SmartArt tool. After creating the initial chart, students are challenged to identify alternative chart styles that could provide better information. Students using Excel 2010 or later versions should realize that using the "Name and Title Organizational Chart" design results in a graphic that shows additional important information. Some students may recognize that selected layouts enable pictures of the individuals to be added to the graphic. Students using Excel 2007 should recognize that each individual's position should be added in the box with the individual's name.

Solutions

1. Answers will vary. A chart clearly communicates (1) how ACT is organized into four departments and (2) the chain of command among the leaders.
2. Answers will vary. Selecting a design that includes the name and position of each individual provides more information than a design that includes only names.

INPUT

- Explain that the entry for receiving cash from short-term investments is the same for a governmental organization as it is for a company.

MODEL

- Draw three blank T accounts on the board.
- Read each transaction statement.
- Ask students to analyze the transaction by answering these questions: Which accounts are affected? Are they increased or decreased? Are they debited or credited? Complete the T accounts as the information is given.
- Use a transparency to illustrate how to record the transaction in a multicolumn journal.
- Record each item in the journal.
- Ask a student to verify that debits equal credits for this transaction.

GLOBAL AWARENESS

Answers

1. AmeriCom will realize a gain on the transaction.
2. Debit: Accounts Payable/ChinaCom $14,400.00.

   Credit: Gain or Loss on Foreign Currency Exchange $2,400.00.

   Credit: Cash $12,000.00.

Receiving Cash from Short-Term Investments

JOURNAL — PAGE 20

	DATE		ACCOUNT TITLE	DOC. NO.	POST. REF.	1 GENERAL DEBIT	2 GENERAL CREDIT	3 CASH DEBIT	4 CASH CREDIT	
1	20-- Sept.	1	*Investments—Short Term*	R172			300 000 00	302 500 00		1
2			*Interest Revenue*				2 500 00			2
3										3

When the certificate of deposit is due on September 1, cash is received for the original cost of the investment plus interest revenue earned.

September 1. Received cash for the maturity value of certificate of deposit due today: principal, $300,000.00, plus interest, $2,500.00; total, $302,500.00. Receipt No. 172.

Cash is increased by a debit for the cash received, $302,500.00. Investments—Short Term is decreased by a credit for the certificate of deposit's original cost, $300,000.00. Interest Revenue is increased by a credit for the interest earned, $2,500.00. The journal entry is shown above.

GLOBAL AWARENESS

Foreign Currency Exchange Gains or Losses

U.S. companies can purchase products from foreign suppliers. Even though a business purchases a product in a foreign country using foreign currency, that transaction will ultimately have to be presented in dollars by the U.S. firm. [CONCEPT: Unit of Measurement] Consequently, any changes in foreign exchange rates can have an impact on a firm's accounts payable and notes payable.

Assume that AmeriCom purchases computer cables from ChinaCom on account and agrees to pay a total of 120,000 yuan, the Chinese currency, in 60 days. At the time of the purchase, one yuan is equal to $0.12 American cents. Therefore, AmeriCom credits Accounts Payable for $14,400.00 (120,000 yuan × $0.12).

During the 60-day credit period, however, the exchange rate for the yuan rises to $0.14. Now it will cost AmeriCom $16,800.00 to purchase 120,000 yuan. Due to the 2-cent increase in the exchange rate, AmeriCom will spend an extra $2,400.00 through the currency exchange process. AmeriCom accounts for the loss on accounts payable with the entry below. The account Gain or Loss on Foreign Currency Exchange is classified as an other revenue account.

Account	Debit	Credit
Accounts Payable/ChinaCom	14,400.00	
Gain or Loss on Foreign Currency Exchange	2,400.00	
Cash		16,800.00

CRITICAL THINKING

1. Assume that instead of increasing during the 60-day credit period, the exchange rate for the yuan decreases to $0.10. Will AmeriCom realize a gain or a loss on the transaction?
2. Indicate the accounts and amounts debited and credited when AmeriCom records the payment.

© iStockphoto.com/Lusky

FORMATIVE ASSESSMENT

- This is an ongoing process. Circulate around the classroom or lab, observing which students have difficulty with the assignments.
- Troubleshooting: Diagnose the kinds of problems students have with this lesson. Students may not remember to reverse the original encumbrance when recording the exact amount of the expenditure.
- Assess student understanding by checking solutions to Independent Practice assignments and noting their answers to the Terms Review and Audit Your Understanding questions..

End of Lesson Review

LO5 Journalize expenditures, encumbrances, and other transactions for a not-for-profit organization.

Terms Review

encumbrance

general fixed assets

certificate of deposit

Audit your understanding

1. What is an encumbrance?
2. What two entries are required when goods or services that have been encumbered are received?
3. Why does a governmental organization not record depreciation expense?
4. What is a certificate of deposit?

Work together 23-3

Journalizing governmental encumbrances, expenditures, and other transactions

The town of Crystal Falls uses a general fund for all financial transactions. Expenditures are recorded by type of expenditure and by department. The four categories of expenditures are personnel, supplies, other charges, and capital outlays. Departments are General Government, Public Safety, Fire Protection, and Recreation.

A journal is provided in the *Working Papers*. Source documents are abbreviated as follows: memorandum, M; check, C; notes payable, NP. Your instructor will guide you through the following examples. Interest is calculated using a 360-day year.

Journalize the transactions completed during the current year.

Transactions:

Jan. 12. Paid cash for electrical service in Fire Protection Department, $692.00. C382.
17. Encumbered estimated amount for supplies for the Public Safety Department, $250.00. M18.
20. Issued a 30-day, 5% note, $120,000.00. NP5.
28. Paid cash for Public Safety Department supplies, $256.00, encumbered January 17 per M18. M22 and C397.
Feb. 7. Paid cash for printer for General Government Department, $625.00. C420. (Capital Outlays)
19. Paid cash for the maturity value of NP5: principal, $120,000.00, plus interest, $500.00; total, $120,500.00. C438.
Mar. 17. Paid cash for a 90-day, 3% certificate of deposit, $150,000.00. C467.
June 15. Received cash for the maturity value of certificate of deposit due today; principal, $150,000.00, plus interest, $1,125.00; total, $151,125.00. R212.

On your own 23-3

Journalizing governmental encumbrances, expenditures, and other transactions

The town of Emandale uses a general fund for all financial transactions. Expenditures are recorded by type of expenditure and by department. The four categories of expenditures are personnel, supplies, other charges, and capital outlays. Departments are General Government, Public Safety, Fire Protection, and Recreation.

A journal is provided in the *Working Papers*. Source documents are abbreviated as follows: memorandum, M; check, C; notes payable, NP. Work independently to complete the following problem. Interest is calculated using a 360-day year.

Journalize the transactions completed during the current year.

Transactions:

Jan. 10. Paid cash for consultant's services in Recreation Department, $332.00. C113. (Personnel)
15. Encumbered estimated amount for supplies in Fire Protection Department, $1,800.00. M12.
18. Issued a 30-day, 4% note, $45,000.00. NP3.
26. Paid cash for Fire Protection Department supplies, $1,726.00, encumbered January 15 per M12. M19 and C156.
Feb. 17. Paid cash for the maturity value of NP3: principal, $45,000.00, plus interest, $150.00; total, $45,150.00. C178.
Mar. 15. Paid cash for a 90-day, 3% certificate of deposit, $92,000.00. C210.
June 13. Received cash for the maturity value of certificate of deposit due today; principal, $92,000.00, plus interest, $690.00; total, $92,690.00. R97.

CHECK FOR UNDERSTANDING

Terms Review

- Call on students to define each term in the Terms Review. Definitions are given in the Glossary.

Audit Your Understanding

- Call on students to answer the Audit Your Understanding questions. Answers are given in Appendix D.

GUIDED PRACTICE

Work Together

- Have students write the solution to the Work Together problem as you guide the class through the examples.
- Direct students to journalize governmental encumbrances, expenditures, and other transactions.

INDEPENDENT PRACTICE

On Your Own

- Assign the On Your Own problem to be worked independently.
- Use the Formative Assessment techniques to diagnose student understanding.

Application Problem

- Assign Application Problem 23-3.

Online Working Papers

- Students can access the Lesson 23-3 problems using this software.

RETEACH

- Make a transparency of a multicolumn journal. Call on a student to come to the front of the room and record the first line of the entry to record the receipt of goods received that had been encumbered previously. Continue in this way until the entire entry is recorded on the transparency.

CLOSURE

- Ask each student to write a summary of what they remember about the entries used in governmental accounting to record transactions for encumbrances and expenditures.

Essential Questions

- If there are five "levels" of supervisors, which level would most likely determine the expenditures for the department? Explain. (*Usually the first-level manager, the department head, is responsible for determining expenditures, since he or she is more aware of the daily operational needs of the department.*)
- What procedures might be put in place if the actual expenditure amount exceeds the encumbered estimated amount? (*Answers might include holding the employee accountable for overspending, seeking emergency funds to cover the difference, or requiring additional approvals for payment.*)

EXTENDED LEARNING

- Assign Think Like an Accountant on page 691.
- Assign Global Awareness on page 692.

CLOSURE

- Review the Chapter Summary.
- Ask students to prepare a list of the new concepts introduced in this chapter.

Essential Questions

- What considerations should be made to avoid expenditures exceeding estimated encumbered amounts? (*Employee training should include implications and responsibility for not exceeding encumbered amounts.*)
- What are some creative ways that a government agency might increase revenue besides raising taxes? (*Revenue could be increased by renting facilities to groups during nonwork hours, offering classes for a fee, renting a booth at festivals, and advertising in publications.*)

EXTENDED LEARNING

- Assign Explore Accounting on page 694.

EXPLORE ACCOUNTING

Answers

Answers will vary according to the agency the student contacted. As an alternative to a written report, you may assign a group of students to prepare an electronic presentation or a video that describes job opportunities, requirements, and application procedures.

Chapter Summary

The goal of a not-for-profit organization is to provide goods or services rather than to earn a profit. Most government agencies are organized as not-for-profit organizations. A governmental organization has four major characteristics that affect the accounting system: (1) No profit motive exists. (2) Leadership is subject to frequent change. (3) Users of services do not necessarily pay for the services. (4) Conflicting pressures for differing objectives exist.

Government agencies use fund accounting systems. A governmental unit, such as a city, may have several different funds. The amount in a fund can be spent only for the specified purpose of the fund.

A governmental fund's annual operating budget authorizes and provides the basis for control of financial operations during a fiscal year. Appropriations are authorizations to make expenditures for specified purposes. As a control, the expected sources of revenues and appropriations are journalized in the fund's accounting system.

Accounting transactions are recorded using modified accrual accounting. Revenues are recorded in the accounting period in which they become measurable and available. To protect against overspending, government organizations use encumbrance accounts to record estimates of ordered goods or services not yet received. When the goods or services are received, the encumbrance is reversed and the actual cost is recorded as an expenditure. Governmental organizations record expenditures rather than expenses. Capital outlays, such as the purchase of equipment, are recorded as expenditures in the period when the liability is incurred.

EXPLORE ACCOUNTING — Accounting Opportunities in Not-for-Profit Organizations

© iStockphoto.com/Makhnach_M

When asked to think about accounting careers available in the not-for-profit sector, most people think about city, county, and state positions. Most often, these positions involve completing the accounting and reporting tasks required by these governmental agencies. However, there are other exciting and challenging accounting-related careers in the not-for-profit sector. These careers include working for the Federal Bureau of Investigation (FBI), the Internal Revenue Service (IRS), and/or insurance companies in an area called "forensic accounting."

Forensic accounting is the investigation of accounting records and reports when fraud and/or embezzlement is suspected. Forensic accountants may help investigate crimes such as extortion, fraud, and embezzlement.

FBI agents may use interview and research techniques to investigate crimes. Requirements for employment as an FBI agent working in the accounting field include a four-year accounting degree from an accredited school and at least three years of professional work experience. In addition, an agent must be a citizen of the United States between the ages of 23 and 36 and in good physical condition.

The IRS also employs accountants in various areas. Internal revenue agents are accountants who, by looking at the accounting records and the tax returns of a business, determine if the business owes taxes and, if so, how much. The IRS also employs accountants as special agents. A special agent investigates potential criminal violations of tax laws. Requirements for employment within the IRS vary, but most do include a four-year degree with some experience in the accounting field.

Insurance companies also hire accountants to assist in investigating cases involving suspected insurance fraud. States employ accountants to audit the accounting systems and financial statements of state and local agencies, school systems, and other government agencies.

INSTRUCTIONS

Access the employee recruitment section of a federal or state agency's Internet site. Search for detailed information on job opportunities, requirements, and application procedures. Report your findings in written form.

Apply Your Understanding

INSTRUCTIONS: Download problem instructions for Excel, QuickBooks, and Sage 50 from the textbook companion website at www.C21accounting.com.

23-1 Application Problem: Journalizing governmental operating budgets LO3

Three towns have approved their annual general fund operating budgets effective January 1 of the current year. A journal is provided in the *Working Papers*.

Instructions:

Journalize the entry to record the operating budgets for each of the three towns for the current year.

	Estimated Revenues	Appropriations	Budgetary Fund Balance
Westville	$1,831,000.00	$1,814,800.00	$16,200.00
Amberville	2,208,600.00	2,184,000.00	24,600.00
Smithburg	3,186,000.00	3,154,000.00	32,000.00

23-2 Application Problem: Journalizing governmental revenue transactions LO4

Milltown's town council recently approved the town's general fund operating budget for the current year. A journal is provided in the *Working Papers*.

Instructions:

Journalize the transactions for the current year.

Transactions:

Jan. 1. Recorded property tax levy: taxes receivable—current, $1,985,000.00; allowance for uncollectible taxes—current, $35,000.00; property tax revenue, $1,950,000.00. M99.
16. Received cash for current taxes receivable, $514,000.00. R155.
28. Received cash from traffic fines, $2,150.00. R164.
Feb. 23. Received cash for current taxes receivable, $725,000.00. R189.
Mar. 1. Recorded reclassification of current taxes receivable to delinquent status, $129,300.00, and the accompanying allowance for uncollectible accounts, $35,000.00. M128.
26. Received cash for delinquent taxes receivable, $45,300.00. R222.

CHECK FIGURES

For complete solutions to Chapter 23 problems, see the Teacher's Edition of the Working Papers.

Application Problem 23-1

Debit to Estimated Revenues:

Westville, $1,831,000.00.

Amberville, $2,208,600.00.

Smithburg, $3,186,000.00.

Application Problem 23-2

Column totals: General Debit, $2,149,300.00; General Credit, $3,435,750.00, Cash Debit, $1,286,450.00.

Application Problem 23-3

Column totals: General Debit, $261,770.00; General Credit, $223,181.67; Cash Debit, $150,041.67; Cash Credit, $188,630.00.

Mastery Problem 23-M

March 1 column totals: General Debit, $4,612,945.00; General Credit, $5,380,057.00, Cash Debit, $772,658.00; Cash Credit, $5,546.00.

May 10 column totals: General Debit, $609,014.00; General Credit, $164,485.67; Cash Debit, $162,216.67; Cash Credit, $606,745.00.

INDEPENDENT PRACTICE

- Assign Mastery Problem 23-M for students as a culminating problem combining all new learning from the chapter.
- Assign Challenge Problem 23-C to accelerated students who work at a faster pace.
- Assign Study Guide 23.
- Students can access Online Working Papers to work end-of-chapter problems on the computer.
- Direct students to the C21 Accounting companion website for additional practice and review opportunities.

FORMATIVE ASSESSMENT

- Review solutions to the assigned problems in class, diagnosing trouble spots.

RETEACH

- Call on students to describe how they avoid the trouble spots diagnosed.
- Use reteaching suggestions from lesson plans as required.
- Assign Recycling Problem 23-R if needed.

23-3 Application Problem: Journalizing governmental encumbrances, expenditures, and other transactions LO5

Sage 50 Accounting

1. Journalize and post transactions related to governmental encumbrances to the general journal.
2. Print the general journal and the trial balance.

QB Quick Books

1. Journalize and post transactions related to governmental encumbrances to the journal.
2. Print the journal and the trial balance.

Excel

1. Journalize and post transactions related to governmental encumbrances to the general journal.
2. Print the worksheet.

The town of Templeton uses a general fund for all financial transactions. Expenditures are recorded by type of expenditure and by department. The four categories of expenditures are personnel, supplies, other charges, and capital outlays. Departments are General Government, Public Safety, Fire Protection, and Recreation.

Instructions:

Journalize the transactions for the current year. Use page 1 of a journal. Interest is calculated using a 360-day year.

Transactions:

Jan.	6.	Paid cash for supplies in Public Safety Department, $625.00. C244.
	12.	Encumbered estimated amount for the purchase of a police car, $32,250.00. M44.
	22.	Issued a 30-day, 6% note, $125,000.00. NP12.
	25.	Encumbered estimated amount for supplies in the Fire Department, $4,320.00. M42.
Feb.	3.	Paid cash of $33,120.00 for the police car encumbered January 12 per M44. M55 and C320.
	21.	Paid cash for the maturity value of NP12: principal, $125,000.00, plus interest. C356.
	28.	Paid cash for a 30-day, 2% certificate of deposit, $25,000.00. C369.
Mar.	6.	Paid cash of $4,260.00 for supplies encumbered January 25 per M42. M67 and C406.
	30.	Received cash for the maturity value of certificate of deposit due today: principal, $25,000.00, plus interest. R334.

23-M Mastery Problem: Journalizing governmental transactions LO3, 4, 5

The town of Lanceburg uses a general fund for all financial transactions. Expenditures are recorded by type of expenditure and by department. The four categories of expenditures are personnel, supplies, other charges, and capital outlays. Departments are General Government, Public Safety, Fire Protection, and Recreation. Interest is calculated using a 360-day year.

Instructions:

Journalize the transactions for the current year.

Transactions:

Use page 1 of a journal.

Jan.	2.	Recorded current year's approved operating budget: estimated revenues, $2,200,000.00; appropriations, $2,162,000.00; budgetary fund balance, $38,000.00. M32.
	2.	Recorded current year's property tax levy: taxes receivable—current, $2,225,000.00; allowance for uncollectible taxes—current, $25,000.00; property tax revenue, $2,200,000.00. M33.
	14.	Received cash for current taxes receivable, $268,500.00. R95.
	22.	Paid cash for supplies in the General Government Department, $1,648.00. C198.
	24.	Issued a 45-day, 6% note, $500,000.00. NP6.
	30.	Encumbered estimated amount for supplies in the Fire Department, $3,415.00. M42.

COMMON CORE AND INTERDISCIPLINARY STUDIES

Extended learning features and activities present numerous opportunities to implement Common Core Standards through interdisciplinary studies. Practice is provided in the common core areas of English Language Arts & Literacy and Mathematical Practice. Many of these activities require short, critical-thinking and decision-making responses that apply reading, writing, speaking, listening, language, media and technology, and mathematical skills.

Feb. 2. Received cash from traffic fines, $4,158.00. R164. (Other Revenue)
6. Paid cash for car parts for the Police Department, $339.00. C226.
14. Paid cash for Fire Department supplies, $3,559.00, encumbered January 30 per M42. M50 and C240.
19. Encumbered estimated amount for equipment purchases by the Recreation Department, $2,269.00. M63.
Mar. 1. Recorded reclassification of current taxes receivable to delinquent status, $148,300.00, and the accompanying allowance for uncollectible accounts, $25,000.00. M80.

Use page 2 of a journal.

Mar. 10. Paid cash for the maturity value of NP6: principal, $500,000.00, plus interest. C255.
11. Paid cash for a 60-day, 2.5% certificate of deposit, $100,000.00. C278.
12. Paid cash for Recreation Department equipment, $2,315.00, encumbered February 19 per M63. M92 and C290.
16. Received cash for delinquent taxes receivable, $61,800.00. R223.
23. Paid cash for consultant's services in Public Safety Department, $680.00. C301. (Personnel)
May 10. Received cash for the maturity value of certificate of deposit due today: principal, $100,000.00, plus interest. R240.

Sage 50 Accounting

1. Journalize and post governmental transactions to the general journal.
2. Print the general journal and the trial balance.

QB

1. Journalize and post governmental transactions to the journal.
2. Print the journal and the trial balance.

X

1. Journalize and post governmental transactions to the general journal.
2. Print the worksheet.

23-C Challenge Problem: Determining the increase, decrease, and normal balance of accounts LO3, 4, 5

Instructions:

Complete a table to provide an easy reference tool to help new accounting clerks accurately record journal entries and calculate general ledger balances. For each account, enter "+" (for an increase) or "–" (for a decrease) in the appropriate Debit and Credit column to show the impact of a debit or credit to each account's balance. Enter Dr. or Cr. in the last column to indicate the normal balance for each account. Use the table in the *Working Papers* to complete this problem. The Cash account is provided as an example.

Account Title	Debit	Credit	Normal Balance
Cash	+	–	*Dr.*

Challenge Problem 23-C

Normal debit, 11 accounts (including Cash); normal credit, 11 accounts.

EXTENDED LEARNING

- Assign 21st Century Skills on page 698.
- Assign Analyzing Home Depot's Financial Statements on page 699.

SUMMATIVE EVALUATION

- Chapter 23 Test
- Cognero for Chapter 23

21ST CENTURY SKILLS

Answers

1. Answers will vary but might include long lunch lines, different ways of buying and making payments for school fees, lunches, and tickets to sporting events.
2. Answers will vary but might include new methods for accepting donations or distributions.

21st Century Skills

Nonprofits Benefit from Kaizen

Theme: Financial, Economic, Business, and Entrepreneurial Literacy

Skills: Communication and Collaboration, Critical Thinking and Problem Solving, Creativity and Innovation, Leadership and Responsibility

PARTNERSHIP FOR 21ST CENTURY SKILLS

Whether a CEO, an accountant, a software developer, or a musician, all workers need to find ways to improve processes in order to be successful and competitive. Improving processes means finding ways to minimize problems, eliminate waste and excess work, and increase productivity and performance.

Toyota is known for its continuous improvement, and the philosophy of kaizen is one of Toyota's core values and keys for success. *Kaizen* is a Japanese word that means *improvement* or *change for the best*. Kaizen in Toyota's organization means that all members of the organization are looking constantly for ways to improve operations.

Toyota recently took its kaizen philosophy to one of the country's largest anti-hunger nonprofit organizations, the Food Bank of New York City. Here, Toyota engineers found a solution to the problem of long lines for this soup kitchen. Guests would often find themselves waiting as long as 90 minutes. However, kaizen paid off. Toyota's focus on efficiency trimmed the wait time for dinner down to 18 minutes.

Source: www.nytimes.com/2013/07/27/nyregion/in-lieu-of-money-toyota-donates-efficiency-to-new-york-charity.html?ref=todayspaper

APPLICATION

1. Make a list of three processes that could be changed at your school. Look for ways to improve wait time or performance, or cut down on waste. Practice the kaizen philosophy by recommending a solution to improve each of the three processes. Share your answers with the class.
2. Visit a local charity and look for ways that processes could be improved to provide services more efficiently. Compose a letter to this organization explaining your recommendation and why it might improve its process to provide a better result.

Analyzing Home Depot's financial statements

Corporations seeking to expand into a new country often elect to purchase a similar business in the target country. Acquiring an existing business prevents the corporation from having to "start from scratch." The existing business already has the physical assets necessary to conduct business: merchandise, buildings, and equipment.

The intangible assets of the existing business are often the most valuable: an experienced management team, trained employees, and loyal customers. Thus, a corporation will often pay more than the value of the physical assets of the existing business. The price paid in excess of the physical assets purchased is recorded as goodwill and reported on the balance sheet. This amount is an estimate that represents the value of the intangible assets. As long as the benefit of these intangible assets is perceived to have value, the recorded balance in the goodwill account will not change.

INSTRUCTIONS

Refer to Home Depot's financial statements shown in Appendix B of this textbook to answer the following questions:

1. Identify the amount of goodwill for each year reported on the Consolidated Balance Sheets on page B-5.
2. Refer to the Goodwill and Other Intangible Assets section of Note 1 on page B-12. What term is used to describe a loss in the perceived value of goodwill?
3. Did Home Depot recognize any loss in the value of goodwill during fiscal 2012?
4. Refer to Note 2 on page B-14 to identify the reason for any loss in the value of goodwill.

ANALYZING HOME DEPOT'S FINANCIAL STATEMENTS

1. $1,170 million and $1,120 million as of February 3, 2013, and January 29, 2012, respectively.
2. Impairment.
3. Yes. Home Depot recorded a $97 million charge for the impairment of goodwill relating to its stores in China.
4. Home Depot closed its remaining big-box stores in China. Specifically,

   In fiscal 2012, the Company closed its remaining seven big box stores in China. As a result of the closings, the Company recorded a total charge of $145 million, net of tax, in fiscal 2012. Inventory markdown costs of $10 million are included in Cost of Sales, and $135 million of costs related to the impairment of Goodwill and other assets, lease terminations, severance and other charges are included in SG&A in the accompanying Consolidated Statements of Earnings.

Chapter 24

Financial Reporting for a Not-for-Profit Organization

Scope & Sequence

	New	Review/Enrich
Introduction		
Introduce the Chapter		
Lesson 24-1: Adjusting Entries for a General Fund		
Preparing Adjusting Entries	✓	
Preparing an Unadjusted Trial Balance	✓	
Adjustment for Inventory of Supplies	✓	
Adjustments for Interest Revenue and Reserve for Encumbrances	✓	
Lesson 24-2: Preparing Financial Statements for a Governmental Organization		
Statement of Revenues, Expenditures, and Changes in Fund Balance—Budget and Actual	✓	
Balance Sheet	✓	
Closing Entries	✓	
Preparing a Post-Closing Trial Balance	✓	
Comprehensive Annual Financial Report	✓	
Closure		

Enhancing Instruction

Features	Common Core Standards
• Accounting in the Real World: City of Tampa	• ELAL—reading
• Ethics in Action: Ethics in Government • Think Like an Accountant: Improving Your Efficiency	• ELAL— reading, writing • Mathematics
• Financial Literacy: Domino Effect in Detroit • Why Accounting?: Campaign Financing • Careers in Accounting: Municipal Treasurer	• ELAL—reading, writing • ELAL—reading, writing • ELAL—reading
• Explore Accounting • 21st Century Skills • Analyzing Home Depot's Financial Statements	• ELAL—reading, writing • Mathematics • ELAL—reading, writing

ELAL = English Language Arts & Literacy

Calculator: © iStockphoto.com/picstodisc; Paper: © iStockphoto.com/Qingwa

Practice and Assessment

Technology & Media	Teaching Strategies	Guided Practice	Independent Practice	Reteach/Enrich
• Instructor's Resource CD/Website: PowerPoint Slides Accounting Concepts • Online Working Papers • Transparency Master: Multicolumn Journal	• ESL Learners	• Audit Your Understanding • Work Together 24-1	• On Your Own 24-1 • Application Problem 24-1 • Formative Assessment, p. 705 • Online Working Papers	• Reteach, p. 706
• Instructor's Resource CD/Website: PowerPoint Slides Accounting Concepts • Online Working Papers • Transparency Masters: Statement of Revenues, Expenditures, and Changes in Fund Balance; Balance Sheet; Multicolumn Journal; Multicolumn Post-Closing Trial Balance	• Auditory/Linguistic Learners	• Terms Review • Audit Your Understanding • Work Together 24-2	• On Your Own 24-2 • Application Problem 24-2 • Formative Assessment, p. 713 • Online Working Papers	• Reteach, p. 714
• Online Working Papers			• Mastery Problem 24-M • Study Guide 24 • Chapter 24 Test • Cognero Chapter 24	• Challenge Problem 24-C • Reteach, p. 716 • Recycling Problem 24-R

Introduce the Chapter

SET THE STAGE

GUIDING QUESTIONS

- Ask students what differences they expect to find in the financial statements for not-for-profit organizations.
- Ask students how adjusting entries might be different for a governmental organization.

PREVIEW CHAPTER OBJECTIVES

- Explain that financial reporting for a not-for-profit organization is somewhat different from financial reporting for a corporation.
- Instruct a student to read each chapter objective aloud.

PREVIEW ACCOUNTING TERMS

- Read each term aloud to verify its pronunciation for students.
- Point out terms or parts of terms that should be familiar to most students, such as *annual financial report*, *government*, and *fund*.

Chapter 24 Financial Reporting for a Not-for-Profit Organization

LEARNING OBJECTIVES

After studying Chapter 24, in addition to defining key terms, you will be able to:

LO1 Prepare adjusting entries for a general fund.

LO2 Prepare financial statements for a general fund.

LO3 Prepare closing entries for a general fund.

LO4 Prepare a post-closing trial balance.

LO5 Describe the components of a comprehensive annual financial report.

Calculator: © iStockphoto.com/picstodisc; Paper: © iStockphoto.com/Qingwa

© Stephen Coburn/Shutterstock.com

Accounting In The Real World

City of Tampa

Background: © iStockphoto.com/DoxaDigital; Real World: © SeanPavonePhoto/Shutterstock.com

The city of Tampa was founded in 1855 and, with a population of over 345,000 residents, is the third most populous city in Florida. The city's total annual budget is in excess of $800 million.

Tampa uses numerous funds to account for the typical services provided by city government, such as police, fire rescue, parks and recreation, and roads. In fiscal 2012, over 70% of the city's revenue for these funds was obtained from taxes, contributions, grants, and investment income. The remaining revenue was collected from individuals and business for services and fees, such as building permits, traffic tickets, and court fees.

The accounting rules used are slightly different for funds that charge fees for providing services. Tampa accounts for its water utility, wastewater utility, solid waste system, parking facilities, and golf courses using these accounting rules. In fiscal 2012, these funds generated 96% of their revenue from charges for services.

With total assets in excess of $3 billion, Tampa must deal with the same economic challenges as the nation's largest corporations. Faced with the rising costs of health insurance and pension contributions, Tampa has been forced to decrease the number of city employees. Even with these cost-cutting measures, the city struggles to generate revenues to match its growing expenses. The city's financial statements provide its leaders with the information needed to make important decisions.

CRITICAL THINKING

1. If you were a city manager or a city council member, what suggestions might you recommend for increasing revenues?
2. If you were a city manager or a city council member, what suggestions might you recommend for decreasing expenditures? Remember, as a city council member, you need to keep in mind the best interests of your district's constituents.

Source: www.tampagov.net/dept_accounting.

Key Terms

- comprehensive annual financial report
- governmental fund
- proprietary fund
- fiduciary fund

Accounting In The Real World

Answers

1. Answers will vary. Recommendations might include increasing city fees for building permits and other city services, seeking new types of fees, selling surplus property and other assets, raising city hotel and restaurant taxes, and increasing penalties for traffic violations.
2. Answers will vary. Recommendations might include reducing the hours that libraries and other facilities are open, reducing the number of recreational offerings, reducing the level of street maintenance, closing select city parks and sports facilities, and postponing the construction of new parks and recreational facilities.

LESSON

24-1

BRIDGE

- Point out that students have learned how to record some transactions for a not-for-profit organization. This chapter will continue the accounting for not-for-profit organizations, focusing on financial reporting and end-of-period work.

TEACHING RESOURCES

- **Instructor's Resource CD/Website:**
  PowerPoint Slides
  Accounting Concepts
- **Working Papers:**
  Teacher's Edition of the Working Papers for Lesson 24-1
  Online Working Papers
- **Transparency Master:**
  Multicolumn Journal

ENGAGE

- Remind students that a governmental organization does not have the goal of making a profit. Therefore, the financial statements of a governmental organization are different from those for a company. However, both organizations prepare adjustments and financial statements.

PREVIEW

- Point out the learning objective for this lesson.
- Direct students to read the headings in this lesson and to examine the illustrations.

INPUT

- Ask a student to read the paragraphs on this page aloud.
- Discuss the purpose of the financial statements for not-for-profit organizations.

ETHICS IN ACTION

Most students will conclude that Jacob may accept the invitation if he feels confident he can present the information without bias toward a political party. However, students may question whether Jacob risks the chance that some attendees, and ultimately the media, may view his acceptance as self-serving. Some students may recommend that Jacob accept the speaking invitation but refuse the speaking honorarium.

LESSON

24-1 Adjusting Entries for a General Fund

LO1 Prepare adjusting entries for a general fund.

Preparing Adjusting Entries LO1

Both businesses and not-for-profit organizations prepare financial statements periodically to report the results of financial activities. [CONCEPT: Accounting Period Cycle] However, financial information for not-for-profit organizations differs from that needed for businesses. A business measures performance primarily through determining the amount of net income. Thus, the accounting records are designed to emphasize the measurement of net income, and the income statement reports the net income.

A not-for-profit organization's performance is measured primarily by the services provided and the efficiency with which resources are used. A not-for-profit organization does not prepare an income statement. Instead, it prepares a statement of revenues, expenditures, and changes in fund balance. A not-for-profit organization's financial statements are designed to provide information for the following purposes:

1. To make decisions about the use of resources.
2. To assess services provided and the ability to provide those services.
3. To assess management's financial accountability and performance.
4. To determine the assets, liabilities, and fund equity of the organization.

ETHICS IN ACTION

Ethics in Government

Jacob Estrada was a well-known history professor before entering the world of politics. What began with helping a friend get elected to a state office has evolved into serving as the chief of staff of the president of the United States.

It is now six months before the national elections. Jacob is extraordinarily busy organizing the president's reelection campaign, in addition to his normal duties as chief of staff. However, a phone call from a former colleague makes him cast aside all thoughts of his current duties.

Jacob has received a high honor—an invitation to be the keynote speaker at a national meeting of a prestigious association of historians. The requested topic is the origin of the two-party system. Jacob would be reimbursed for his travel expenses and receive a $10,000 honorarium. The meeting is scheduled for one month before the election, right in the middle of the most intense period of the campaign.

INSTRUCTIONS

Obtain the *Standards of Ethical Conduct for Employees of the Executive Branch*, issued by the U.S. Office of Government Ethics. Unlike the codes of conduct for corporations, these standards are "codified," meaning that the code is law. Using the ethical model, provide Jacob with guidance on whether he should accept the invitation.

© iStockphoto.com/LdF

See a suggested solution for this feature in the Instructional Strategies section at the front of this book.

Preparing an Unadjusted Trial Balance

Town of Lindville
Unadjusted Trial Balance
December 31, 20--

ACCOUNT TITLE	DEBIT	CREDIT
Cash	62,180.00	
Taxes Receivable—Current		
Allowance for Uncollectible Taxes—Current		
Taxes Receivable—Delinquent	21,660.00	
Allowance for Uncollectible Taxes—Delinquent		16,740.00
Interest Receivable		
Allowance for Uncollectible Interest		
Inventory of Supplies		
Accounts Payable		28,930.00
Notes Payable		
Unreserved Fund Balance		13,600.00
Reserve for Encumbrances—Current Year		2,190.00
Reserve for Encumbrances—Prior Year		
Reserve for Inventory of Supplies		
Property Tax Revenue		1675,000.00
Interest Revenue		10,860.00
Other Revenue		6,140.00
Expenditure—Personnel, General Government	273,200.00	
Expenditure—Supplies, General Government	14,900.00	
Expenditure—Other Charges, General Government	118,380.00	
Expenditure—Capital Outlays, General Government	22,950.00	
Expenditure—Personnel, Public Safety	598,650.00	
Expenditure—Supplies, Public Safety	28,790.00	
Expenditure—Other Charges, Public Safety	150,800.00	
Expenditure—Capital Outlays, Public Safety	99,350.00	
Expenditure—Personnel, Fire Protection	123,300.00	
Expenditure—Supplies, Fire Protection	14,200.00	
Expenditure—Other Charges, Fire Protection	51,350.00	
Expenditure—Capital Outlays, Fire Protection	53,950.00	
Expenditure—Personnel, Recreation	62,600.00	
Expenditure—Supplies, Recreation	7,050.00	
Expenditure—Other Charges, Recreation	26,480.00	
Expenditure—Capital Outlays, Recreation	21,480.00	
Estimated Revenues	1691,500.00	
Appropriations		1659,000.00
Budgetary Fund Balance		32,500.00
Encumbrance—Supplies, Public Safety	2,190.00	
Totals	3444,960.00	3444,960.00

General Ledger Accounts Other Than Encumbrances

Encumbrances Accounts with a Balance

Column Totals

The town of Lindville begins the process of preparing financial statements by creating an unadjusted trial balance.

The unadjusted trial balance provides accountants with the information needed to plan adjusting entries.

INPUT

- Stress that the unadjusted trial balance for a governmental organization begins with the same unadjusted trial balance as does a for-profit business.
- Review the definition of *encumbrances*: a commitment to pay for goods or services that have been ordered but not yet provided.
- Emphasize that only encumbrances accounts with balances are included in the unadjusted trial balance.

DIFFERENTIATED INSTRUCTION

ESL learners learn best by building engagement with others. Ask students to review the differences they learned about accounting for governmental organizations compared with for-profit businesses. Use Think/Pair/Share as an activity that allows for engagement with other learners. Allow students a few moments to "think" of their responses. They will "pair" with another student and "share" their response.

INPUT

- Point out that because governmental organizations report expenditures and not expenses, no adjustments are needed for expense accounts.
- Explain that supplies remaining at the end of the period need to be adjusted so that they will be reported as an asset.
- Remind students that when an expenditure is made, it is reported during that fiscal period, regardless of the purpose of the payment. In addition, an amount equal to the inventory of supplies is recorded in a restricted fund equity account. This amount is not available for spending.

MODEL

- To analyze the adjustment for supplies, draw two blank T accounts on the board.
- Direct students to the illustration as you show them how to record the supplies adjustment in the journal.
- Use a transparency of a multicolumn journal to demonstrate how to record the supplies adjustment.

THINK LIKE AN ACCOUNTANT

Students are provided with a financial statement similar to the one presented in the chapter. Students learn how to create a macro that is used to copy and paste the current month's financial information to update the year-to-date and prior month columns. The macro is stored in the workbook and assigned to an object.

Ensure that students are proficient at manually entering the commands before they record their macros. Although macros are not hard to record, mistakes made during the recording process can result in problems and cause students to become frustrated.

Solutions

1. Answers will vary. Possible answers include the following:
   - The task is performed with more efficiency.
   - The task is performed correctly.
   - The user is not required to perform repetitive, monotonous commands.
   - Other employees can use the worksheet without knowing the required commands.
2. Answers will vary. Students should identify a worksheet where a series of two or more commands are required to complete a single task. For example, the Chapter 21 Think Like an Accountant feature requires students to complete a sales invoice. To prepare the invoice for the next sale, the macro could print the invoice, delete data from the invoice, and increase the invoice number by one.

Adjustment for Inventory of Supplies

JOURNAL PAGE 20

	DATE		ACCOUNT TITLE	DOC. NO.	POST. REF.	GENERAL DEBIT (1)	GENERAL CREDIT (2)	CASH DEBIT (3)	CASH CREDIT (4)	
1			*Adjusting Entries*							1
2	20-- Dec.	31	*Inventory of Supplies*			2 750 00				2
3			*Reserve for Inventory of Supplies*				2 750 00			3
4										4

Some general ledger accounts for general funds need to be brought up to date before financial statements are prepared. However, since a general fund reports expenditures and not expenses, no adjustments are needed for expense accounts. The actual amounts that have been spent and recorded as expenditures are reported.

Lindville makes adjustments to three accounts: (1) Inventory of Supplies, (2) Interest Revenue, and (3) Reserve for Encumbrances—Current Year.

When supplies are bought, an expenditure account is debited. Some supplies may be unused at the end of a fiscal period. These unused supplies should be reported as an asset. [CONCEPT: Full Disclosure] Thus, an adjustment is made at the end of a period to record the remaining amount of supplies inventory as an asset. Expenditure accounts debited when supplies were bought are not adjusted. When an expenditure is made during a fiscal period, the expenditure is reported regardless of the purpose.

The total account balances of a general fund represent the equity of that fund. Thus, assets less liabilities equals total fund equity, which, unless reserved for a specified purpose, should represent resources that are available for appropriations and spending. The inventory of supplies, however, will be used by the organization. Therefore, this asset is not available for spending. To show that this asset, Inventory of Supplies, is not available for other uses, an equal amount of fund equity is reserved. Thus, the amount is credited to a restricted fund equity account titled Reserve for Inventory of Supplies.

Inventory of Supplies is increased by a debit for the amount of supplies on hand, $2,750.00. Reserve for Inventory of Supplies is increased by a credit for the same amount, $2,750.00.

Inventory of Supplies

Debit	Credit
↑ 2,750.00	

Reserve for Inventory of Supplies

Debit	Credit
	↑ 2,750.00

THINK LIKE AN ACCOUNTANT

Improving Your Efficiency

The accountant for the city of Grassville prepares a special monthly financial statement for the mayor. The financial statement shows year-to-date, prior month, and current month revenue and expenditures for the general fund. The accountant uses an Excel worksheet to create the financial statement.

Each month, the accountant must perform a series of repetitive tasks to prepare the worksheet for the next month. Having performed these tasks for many months, the accountant finally had enough. "I have more important things to do!" she exclaimed. So she decided it was time to automate the process. Rather than manually performing the command each month, she wants to run a macro to execute all the commands with a single click.

OPEN THE SPREADSHEET TLA_CH24

The workbook contains the financial statement. Follow the steps on the Instructions tab to create a macro to prepare the statement for entering the next month's financial results. Use the knowledge you gain to answer these questions:

1. What advantages are gained by storing a repetitive task in a macro?
2. Identify a workbook from this textbook or another source that contains a repetitive task that could be stored effectively as a macro.

© iStockphoto.com/Dan Bachman

Adjustments for Interest Revenue and Reserve for Encumbrances

JOURNAL — PAGE 20

	DATE		ACCOUNT TITLE	DOC. NO.	POST. REF.	GENERAL DEBIT (1)	GENERAL CREDIT (2)	CASH DEBIT (3)	CASH CREDIT (4)	
4		31	*Interest Receivable*			3 2 0 0 00				4
5			*Allowance for Uncollectible Interest*				1 2 8 0 00			5
6			*Interest Revenue*				1 9 2 0 00			6
7		31	*Reserve for Encumbrances—Current Year*			2 1 9 0 00				7
8			*Reserve for Encumbrances—Prior Year*				2 1 9 0 00			8
9										9
10										10
11										11
12										12

Since a general fund recognizes revenues when the revenues become measurable and available, an adjustment may be needed to record some revenues. Interest is assessed on all delinquent taxes. Interest on delinquent taxes becomes measurable and available when it is assessed. Thus, to bring the accounts up to date and record revenue earned but not collected at the end of the year, an adjustment is made.

Lindville's interest earned but not yet collected on December 31 is $3,200.00. Experience has shown that approximately 40% of this amount, $1,280.00 ($3,200.00 × 40%), will not be collected. Thus, the amount expected to be collected, $1,920.00 ($3,200.00 – $1,280.00), is recorded as revenue.

Interest Receivable	
↑ 3,200.00	

Allowance for Uncollectible Interest	
	↑ 1,280.00

Interest Revenue	
	↑ 1,920.00

At the end of a fiscal year, a governmental organization may have outstanding encumbrances—orders that have not yet been delivered. When goods are delivered that were encumbered against the preceding year's appropriations, the amount should not be recorded as an expenditure of the current period. Therefore, at the end of a period, the amount of encumbrances outstanding in the balance of Reserve for Encumbrances—Current Year should be reclassified to prior-year status. Then, when the prior year's orders arrive, they are debited to Reserve for Encumbrances—Prior Year, which prevents charging expenditures of one year to another year's appropriations.

Reserve for Encumbrances—Current Year	
↓ 2,190.00	2,190.00 *(New Bal. zero)*

Reserve for Encumbrances—Prior Year	
	↑ 2,190.00

Adjusting entries are posted to the general ledger. The adjusted balances are used to prepare an adjusted trial balance.

fyi Governments often issue bonds to pay for large construction projects, such as schools and highways. Investors are generally not required to pay federal income tax on the interest income on these bonds.

INPUT

- Explain that an adjustment must be made to bring the accounts related to delinquent taxes up to date. These include interest receivable, interest revenue, and allowance for uncollectible interest.
- Explain that outstanding encumbrances (orders that have not been delivered) should not be recorded as an expenditure in the period received. Therefore, an adjustment must be made to reclassify these encumbrances to the prior year.

MODEL

Record interest adjustment

- To analyze the adjustment for interest on delinquent taxes, draw three blank T accounts on the board.
- Direct students to the illustration as you show them how to journalize the interest adjustment.
- Use a transparency to demonstrate how to record the interest adjustment in a journal.

Record encumbrance adjustment

- To analyze the adjustment for Reserve for Encumbrances—Prior Year, draw two blank T accounts on the board.
- Direct students to the illustration as you demonstrate how to journalize the adjustment.
- Use a transparency to demonstrate how to record the adjustment in the journal.

FORMATIVE ASSESSMENT

- This is an ongoing process. Circulate around the classroom or lab, observing which students have difficulty with the assignments.
- Troubleshooting: Diagnose the kinds of problems students have with this section. Students may have trouble with adjusting entries.
- Assess student understanding by checking solutions to Independent Practice assignments and noting their answers to the Audit Your Understanding questions.

CHECK FOR UNDERSTANDING

Audit Your Understanding

- Call on students to answer the Audit Your Understanding questions. Answers are given in Appendix D.

GUIDED PRACTICE

Work Together

- Have students write the solution to the Work Together problem as you guide the class through the examples.
- Direct students to prepare adjusting entries for a general fund.

INDEPENDENT PRACTICE

On Your Own

- Assign the On Your Own problem to be worked independently.
- Use the Formative Assessment techniques to diagnose student understanding.

Application Problem

- Assign Application Problem 24-1.

Online Working Papers

- Students can access the Lesson 24-1 problems using this software.

Website

- Direct students to the C21 Accounting companion website for additional practice and review opportunities throughout the chapter.

RETEACH

- Ask students to practice recording the adjusting entries by pairing up and taking turns explaining each adjusting entry to his or her partner.

Essential Question

- What would be the danger in charging expenditures in the year the order is received rather than when it was encumbered? (*When funds are encumbered, they are already set aside so there would be no reason to wait for receipt. In addition, waiting could adversely affect the amounts budgeted.*)

EXTENDED LEARNING

- Assign Accounting in the Real World on page 701.
- Assign Ethics in Action on page 702.
- Assign Think Like an Accountant on page 704.

End of Lesson Review

LO1 Prepare adjusting entries for a general fund.

Audit your understanding

1. How do the measures of performance differ between businesses and not-for-profit organizations?
2. What accounts are not included on the unadjusted trial balance of a general fund?
3. What adjusting entries for expenses are made by a general fund?
4. In what account would a general fund record the amount of interest on delinquent taxes that it expects to collect?

Work together 24-1

Preparing adjusting entries for a general fund

The town of Kellerville uses a general fund. Adjustment information for December 31 is presented below. Analyze the adjustment information and prepare adjusting entries. A journal is provided in the *Working Papers*. Your instructor will guide you through the following examples.

Supplies inventory	$4,925.00
Interest revenue due but not collected	5,490.00

An estimated 30% of the interest revenue due will not be collected.
The reserve for encumbrances for the current year has a credit balance of $12,534.00.

On your own 24-1

Preparing adjusting entries for a general fund

The town of Harris City uses a general fund. Adjustment information for December 31 is presented below. Analyze the adjustment information and prepare adjusting entries. A journal is provided in the *Working Papers*. Work independently to complete the following problem.

Supplies inventory	$1,890.00
Interest revenue due but not collected	2,260.00

An estimated 40% of the interest revenue due will not be collected.
The reserve for encumbrances for the current year has a credit balance of $9,360.00.

LESSON

24-2 Preparing Financial Statements for a Governmental Organization

LO2 Prepare financial statements for a general fund.
LO3 Prepare closing entries for a general fund.
LO4 Prepare a post-closing trial balance.
LO5 Describe the components of a comprehensive annual financial report.

Statement of Revenues, Expenditures, and Changes in Fund Balance—Budget and Actual LO2

Town of Lindville General Fund
Statement of Revenues, Expenditures, and Changes in Fund Balance—Budget and Actual
For Year Ended December 31, 20--

	Budget	Actual	Variance—Favorable (Unfavorable)
Revenues:			
Property Tax Revenue	$1,675,000.00	$1,675,000.00	$ —
Interest Revenue	12,000.00	12,780.00	780.00
Other Revenue	4,500.00	6,140.00	1,640.00
Total Revenue	$1,691,500.00	$1,693,920.00	$ 2,420.00
Expenditures:			
General Government	$ 424,800.00	$ 429,430.00	$(4,630.00)
Public Safety	879,800.00	877,590.00	2,210.00
Fire Protection	236,300.00	242,800.00	(6,500.00)
Recreation	118,100.00	117,610.00	490.00
Total Expenditures	$1,659,000.00	$1,667,430.00	$(8,430.00)
Excess of Revenues Over Expenditures	$ 32,500.00	$ 26,490.00	$(6,010.00)
Less Outstanding Encumbrances, Dec. 31, 20--	—	2,190.00	(2,190.00)
Increase in Unreserved Fund Balance for Year	$ 32,500.00	$ 24,300.00	$(8,200.00)
Unreserved Fund Balance, Jan. 1, 20--	13,600.00	13,600.00	—
Unreserved Fund Balance, Dec. 31, 20--	$ 46,100.00	$ 37,900.00	$(8,200.00)

Revenues
Expenditures
Excess of Revenue Over Expenditures
Fund Balances
Change in Unreserved Fund Balance
Outstanding Encumbrances
Variances

Financial statements are prepared for each fund. [CONCEPT: Full Disclosure] Two of the financial statements that Lindville prepares for its general fund are (1) the statement of revenues, expenditures, and changes in fund balance—budget and actual and (2) the balance sheet.

Lindville's general fund statement of revenues, expenditures, and changes in fund balance—budget and actual for the fiscal year ended December 31 is shown above. This statement reports the amount of revenues earned and expenditures made for a fiscal period. The expenditures are listed by department. Departments are responsible for controlling expenditures through budgeting and appropriations of specific amounts for each department. Thus, to aid the control process, amounts actually spent are reported for each responsible department. The total expenditures for the whole fund are also shown on the statement.

LESSON
24-2

BRIDGE

- Point out that students have learned how to prepare an income statement and a balance sheet. In this lesson, they will learn how to prepare similar statements for a governmental organization.

TEACHING RESOURCES

- **Instructor's Resource CD/Website:**
  PowerPoint Slides
  Accounting Concepts
- **Working Papers:**
  Teacher's Edition of the Working Papers for Lesson 24-2
  Online Working Papers
- **Transparency Masters:**
  Statement of Revenues, Expenditures, and Changes in Fund Balance
  Balance Sheet
  Multicolumn Journal
  Multicolumn Post-Closing Trial Balance

ENGAGE

- Remind students that a governmental organization does not calculate net income; therefore, it does not prepare an income statement. However, a governmental organization is interested in ensuring that expenditures do not exceed the budgeted amounts. This section will present a new financial statement to accommodate these needs.

PREVIEW

- Call on students to read the accounting terms and definitions introduced in this lesson: *comprehensive annual financial report, governmental fund, proprietary fund,* and *fiduciary fund.*
- Point out the learning objectives for this lesson.
- Direct students to read the headings in this lesson and to examine the illustrations.

INPUT

- Explain that financial statements are prepared for each governmental fund or department.
- Present the statement of revenues, expenditures, and changes in fund balance—budget and actual and discuss how it is different from the income statement of a corporation.
- Describe the three sections and the three amount columns of the statement.
- Review the steps to complete the statement of revenues, expenditures, and changes in fund balance—budget and actual.
- Discuss how variances are calculated and which are favorable and unfavorable.

MODEL

- Use a blank transparency of the statement of revenues, expenditures, and changes in fund balance—budget and actual to illustrate how to complete the statement.
- Direct students to the illustration provided on this page as you use the steps given to complete the statement.

TEACHING IDEA **Instruct students to compare the statement of revenues, expenditures, and changes in fund balance—budget and actual in this chapter and the income statement for a corporation. List the differences and similarities on the board as students identify them.**

FINANCIAL LITERACY

Answers

1. Because the bankruptcy has been on your credit report for ten years, many creditors will consider you a high risk when you seek credit. This could affect your ability to buy or rent a home or a car or to obtain a credit card. Some employers run credit reports and frown on bankruptcies.
2. The U.S. Constitution states that bankruptcies are permitted in the United States. Our founding fathers must have wanted protection and relief for those under financial distress.

Any outstanding encumbrances for the current year are deducted from the excess of revenues over expenditures. Outstanding encumbrances are not deducted in figuring the excess of revenues over expenditures. However, funds will be required in the future when the goods for which the encumbrances were made are delivered. Therefore, the current year's encumbrances should be reported as a reduction in the current year's excess of revenues, rather than in the next year when the payment for goods is made. Because no amount is budgeted for the encumbrances, the amount shown in the Budget column is zero. The report concludes with an analysis of the change in the unreserved fund balance from the beginning to the end of the fiscal period.

The Variance column reports the difference between the budget and actual amounts for the item. For example, the variance for Other Revenue is $1,640.00 (actual, $6,140.00, less budget, $4,500.00). Variances are considered favorable if actual results are better than the amount budgeted for that item. When actual revenues are more than budgeted revenues, variances are favorable. When actual revenues are less than budgeted revenues, variances are unfavorable. When actual expenditures are less than budgeted expenditures, variances are favorable. When actual expenditures are more than budgeted expenditures, variances are unfavorable. A reserve for encumbrances variance has the same effect as an expenditure variance. Because encumbrances are not budgeted, any variance will be unfavorable, since an actual encumbrance will cause an increase. Unfavorable variances are indicated by placing the amounts in parentheses.

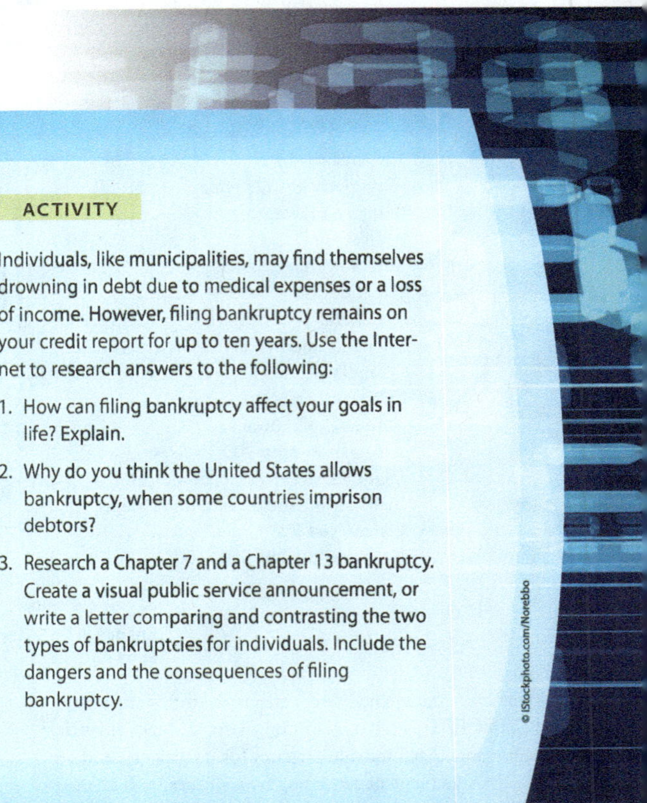

FINANCIAL LITERACY

Domino Effect in Detroit

At one time, Detroit was an industrial giant at the center of the automotive industry. It had a large population and a low unemployment rate. Over time, increased automotive competition greatly reduced the job opportunities. Many people were unemployed or on welfare. Others left for jobs in the suburbs, leaving Detroit starved for tax revenues. With fewer people paying taxes and city expenses on the rise, Detroit ran out of money to pay its creditors.

Detroit is not unlike San Bernardino, California, or Harrisburg, Pennsylvania. It just happens to be the largest municipality to file Chapter 9 bankruptcy. A Chapter 9 bankruptcy is a court proceeding that gives a municipality a fresh start while trying to arrange some form of repayment to its creditors.

ACTIVITY

Individuals, like municipalities, may find themselves drowning in debt due to medical expenses or a loss of income. However, filing bankruptcy remains on your credit report for up to ten years. Use the Internet to research answers to the following:

1. How can filing bankruptcy affect your goals in life? Explain.
2. Why do you think the United States allows bankruptcy, when some countries imprison debtors?
3. Research a Chapter 7 and a Chapter 13 bankruptcy. Create a visual public service announcement, or write a letter comparing and contrasting the two types of bankruptcies for individuals. Include the dangers and the consequences of filing bankruptcy.

© iStockphoto.com/Norebbo

3. Answers will vary. A Chapter 7 bankruptcy is a liquidation of assets, and financial burdens are dismissed. A Chapter 13 bankruptcy is a reorganization, with repayment in place for some creditors.

Balance Sheet

Town of Lindville General Fund Balance Sheet December 31, 20--		
ASSETS		
Cash		$62,180.00
Taxes Receivable—Delinquent	$21,660.00	
Less Allowance for Uncollectible Taxes—Delinquent	16,740.00	4,920.00
Interest Receivable	$ 3,200.00	
Less Allowance for Uncollectible Interest	1,280.00	1,920.00
Inventory of Supplies		2,750.00
Total Assets		$71,770.00
LIABILITIES AND FUND BALANCE		
Liabilities:		
Accounts Payable		$28,930.00
Fund Balance:		
Unreserved Fund Balance	$37,900.00	
Reserve for Encumbrances—Prior Year	2,190.00	
Reserve for Inventory of Supplies	2,750.00	
Total Fund Balance		42,840.00
Total Liabilities and Fund Balance		$71,770.00

A general fund balance sheet reports information about assets, liabilities, and fund equity for a specific date, usually the last day of a fiscal period. [CONCEPT: Full Disclosure] Assets and liabilities on a general fund balance sheet have characteristics similar to those on a corporation's balance sheet. However, a general fund does not have specific owners. Therefore, a general fund has no Owners' Equity section. Instead, the difference between assets and liabilities is reported as fund equity. Thus, unless restricted, fund equity represents the amount that is available for expenditures or encumbrances.

On December 31, Lindville's fund equity, consisting of three fund equity account balances, is $42,840.00. The **Unreserved Fund Balance**, $37,900.00, represents fund equity that has no restrictions (Total fund equity, $42,840.00, less **Reserve for Encumbrances—Prior Year**, $2,190.00, and less **Reserve for Inventory of Supplies**, $2,750.00). With proper authorization, Lindville may appropriate this amount for expenditures.

The other two fund equity account balances are reserved for specific purposes. The **Reserve for Encumbrances—Prior Year**, $2,190.00, is an amount of equity set aside for an encumbrance outstanding on December 31 of the prior year. Recording the payment for an order that was encumbered in a prior year closes the reserve for encumbrances account.

The **Reserve for Inventory of Supplies**, $2,750.00, represents the equity in the inventory of supplies. Although supplies are assets, they are available for use, not spending. Therefore, part of the fund equity is reserved for the amount of supplies on hand. This reserve avoids appropriating the amount of equity that is represented by the supplies.

On a general fund balance sheet, total assets must equal total liabilities and fund equity. Lindville's balance sheet has total assets of $71,770.00. The total of the liabilities and fund balance accounts is also $71,770.00.

INPUT

- Present the governmental fund balance sheet and discuss how it is different from the balance sheet of a corporation.
- Stress that because a governmental fund does not have specific owners, the balance sheet has no owners' equity section.
- The difference between assets and liabilities is reported as fund balance.
- Emphasize that total assets must equal total liabilities and fund balance.

MODEL

- Refer students to the illustration as you explain the balance sheet for a governmental organization.

INPUT

- Explain the four entries used to close the temporary and budgetary accounts of a governmental organization.
- Emphasize that the entry to close the budgetary accounts is the opposite of the original entry to record the operating budget.

MODEL

Record the closing entries

- Use a transparency to illustrate how to record the closing entries in a multicolumn journal.
- Record each entry in the journal.
- Ask a student to verify that debits equal credits for each adjusting entry.

Closing Entries LO3

JOURNAL PAGE 21

	Date		Account Title	Doc. No.	Post. Ref.	General Debit (1)	General Credit (2)	Cash Debit (3)	Cash Credit (4)	
1			*Closing Entries*							1
2	20-- Dec.	31	Property Tax Revenue			1,675,000.00				2
3			Interest Revenue			12,780.00				3
4			Other Revenue			6,140.00				4
5			Unreserved Fund Balance				1,693,920.00			5
6		31	Unreserved Fund Balance			1,667,430.00				6
7			Expend.—Personnel, Gen., Gov't.				273,200.00			7
8			Expend.—Supplies, Gen., Gov't.				14,900.00			8
9			Expend.—Other Chgs., Gen., Gov't.				118,380.00			9
10			Expend.—Cap. Outlays, Gen., Gov't.				22,950.00			10
11			Expend.—Personnel, Public Safety				598,650.00			11
12			Expend.—Supplies, Public Safety				28,790.00			12
13			Expend.—Other Chgs., Pub. Safety				150,800.00			13
14			Expend.—Cap. Outlays, Pub. Safety				99,350.00			14
15			Expend.—Personnel, Fire Protection				123,300.00			15
16			Expend.—Supplies, Fire Protection				14,200.00			16
17			Expend.—Other Chgs., Fire Protection				51,350.00			17
18			Expend.—Cap. Outlays, Fire Protection				53,950.00			18
19			Expend.—Personnel, Recreation				62,600.00			19
20			Expend.—Supplies, Recreation				7,050.00			20
21			Expend.—Other Chgs., Recreation				26,480.00			21
22			Expend.—Cap. Outlays, Recreation				21,480.00			22
23		31	Appropriations			1,659,000.00				23
24			Budgetary Fund Balance			32,500.00				24
25			Estimated Revenues				1,691,500.00			25
26		31	Unreserved Fund Balance			2,190.00				26
27			Encum.—Supplies, Public Safety				2,190.00			27

Information needed for the closing entries is obtained from the adjusted trial balance. Four closing entries are made:

1. Close all revenue accounts to the Unreserved Fund Balance account.
2. Close all expenditure accounts to the Unreserved Fund Balance account.
3. Close the budgetary accounts. At the beginning of the fiscal year, estimated revenues and appropriations were recorded based on the approved operating budget. At the end of the fiscal year, these budgetary accounts are closed. This entry is the opposite of the original entry to record the operating budget.
4. Close the outstanding encumbrance accounts to the Unreserved Fund Balance account. This entry reduces the Unreserved Fund Balance account by the amount of the outstanding encumbrance for supplies, public safety, $2,190.00. Reserve for Encumbrances—Prior Year is a fund equity account. This account balance now is the amount of total fund equity that is reserved for outstanding encumbrances.

After posting the closing entries, all temporary accounts have zero balances and are prepared for a new fiscal period. The difference between revenues and expenditures has been transferred to the Unreserved Fund Balance account. Fund equity amounts that are not available for appropriations are recorded in reserve accounts.

DIFFERENTIATED INSTRUCTION

Auditory/Linguistic learners express themselves through written words. Ask students to compose a letter or a poem explaining closing entries for a governmental organization.

Preparing a Post-Closing Trial Balance LO4

Town of Lindville General Fund Post-Closing Trial Balance December 31, 20--		
Cash	$62,180.00	
Taxes Receivable—Delinquent	21,660.00	
Allowance for Uncollectible Taxes—Delinquent		$16,740.00
Interest Receivable	3,200.00	
Allowance for Uncollectible Interest		1,280.00
Inventory of Supplies	2,750.00	
Accounts Payable		28,930.00
Unreserved Fund Balance		37,900.00
Reserve for Encumbrances—Prior Year		2,190.00
Reserve for Inventory of Supplies		2,750.00
	$89,790.00	$89,790.00

After all end-of-fiscal-period activities are complete, a post-closing trial balance is prepared to prove the equality of debits and credits in the account balances, as shown above. Because the debit and credit balance totals equal, the general ledger accounts are ready for the new fiscal period. [CONCEPT: Accounting Period Cycle]

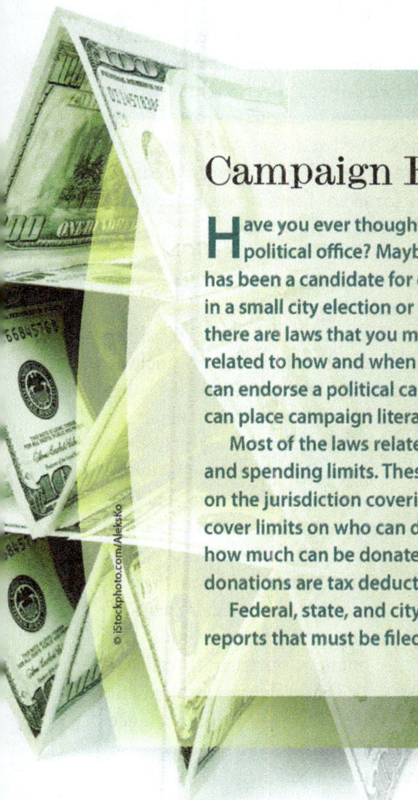

© iStockphoto.com/Aleksko

WHY ACCOUNTING?

Campaign Financing

Have you ever thought about running for a political office? Maybe you know someone who has been a candidate for election. Whether involved in a small city election or a large federal election, there are laws that you must follow. There are laws related to how and when you can campaign, who can endorse a political candidate, and where you can place campaign literature and signs.

Most of the laws relate to campaign donations and spending limits. These laws vary, depending on the jurisdiction covering the election. The laws cover limits on who can donate to the campaign, how much can be donated, and whether the donations are tax deductible.

Federal, state, and city laws also cover financial reports that must be filed. These reports require that the candidate or the campaign staff keep accurate financial records. The purpose of these records is to have full disclosure of who is supporting which candidate. Even in small city elections, the campaign treasurer may have to disclose the names and addresses of all donors, their places of employment, and the amounts of their donations.

Government & Public Administration

CRITICAL THINKING

1. Why is it important to have full disclosure of who is supporting a political candidate?
2. Research the laws of your local government. Is there a limit on the amount a contributor can donate? If so, what is the limit?

Source: www.fec.gov; www.completecampaigns.com.

INPUT

- Discuss the post-closing trial balance of a governmental organization.

MODEL

- Use a transparency to illustrate how to prepare a post-closing trial balance for a governmental organization.

WHY ACCOUNTING?

Answers

1. Answers will vary but may include the following: Voters may want to know who is supporting each candidate, who may have influence over the candidate by donating large amounts of money, and how broad the support of the candidate is.
2. Answers will vary. If the local government has a donation limit, the student should state the amount of the limit.

INPUT

- Point out the purpose of a comprehensive annual report.
- Explain the three types of funds reported in the CAFR.
- Explain the purpose of different names for government-wide financial statements.
- Direct students to the illustration to explain the relationship among the CAFR and the individual fund financial statements.

Comprehensive Annual Financial Report LO5

Comprehensive Annual Financial Report	Individual Fund Financial Statements		
	Governmental Funds	**Proprietary Funds**	**Fiduciary Funds**
Accrual	Modified Accrual	Accrual	Accrual
Statement of Activities	Statement of Revenues, Expenditures, and Changes in Fund Balance	Statement of Revenues, Expenses, and Changes in Fund Net Assets	Statement of Revenues, Expenses, and Changes in Fund Net Assets
Statement of Net Assets	Balance Sheet	Statement of Net Assets	Statement of Net Assets

Governmental accounting is governed by the Governmental Accounting Standards Board (GASB). The GASB was organized in 1984 to establish standards of financial accounting and reporting for governmental entities. The GASB's mission is "To establish and improve standards of state and local governmental accounting and financial reporting that will (1) result in useful information for users of financial reports, and (2) guide and educate the public, including issuers, auditors, and users of those financial reports."

Generally accepted accounting principles (GAAP) require that financial statements be prepared on a full accrual basis. This accounting method requires that plant assets be reported as assets and depreciated over the useful life of the assets. Amounts owed in future fiscal years are reported as liabilities. Users accustomed to GAAP financial statements may be confused over the lack of plant assets and long-term liabilities on the balance sheet of a general fund prepared on a modified accrual basis.

To address this confusion, the GASB requires state and local governments to prepare financial statements for each major fund as well as prepare combined financial statements. The detailed financial report of a governmental agency is called a **comprehensive annual financial report** (CAFR). The basic financial statements in the CAFR include (1) government-wide financial statements, (2) individual fund financial statements, and (3) notes to the financial statements.

Three types of funds are reported individually in the CAFR:

Governmental Funds: A fund that accounts for the tax-supported activities of a government agency is called a **governmental fund**. A government agency can establish a governmental fund to account for the revenues or expenditures of each special activity and project. All activities not accounted for in a special governmental fund are accounted for in a general fund. Individual financial statements of a governmental fund are accounted for on a modified accrual basis.

Proprietary Funds: A fund that accounts for the financial transactions of a government organization that operates as a for-profit enterprise is called a **proprietary fund**. Unlike a governmental fund, a proprietary fund earns most of its revenue from fees charged to individuals and businesses using its services. Examples of proprietary funds include water and sewer, sanitation, and power utilities. Individual financial statements of a proprietary fund are prepared on a full accrual basis.

Fiduciary Funds: A fund that reports assets held by a government agency to benefit a specific group of individuals is called a **fiduciary fund**. A common type of fiduciary fund is a pension plan for government employees. Financial statements of a fiduciary fund are prepared on a full accrual basis.

ADJUSTING FROM MODIFIED TO FULL ACCRUAL ACCOUNTING

The financial statements presented in this chapter do not report fixed assets and long-term liabilities. The individual financial statements of governmental funds, including the general fund, continue to be reported on a modified accrual basis. The fixed assets and long-term liabilities of a governmental fund are reported when the financial information for every fund is combined into the government-wide financial statements.

GASB standards have little impact on how cities and states record the daily accounting transactions of their governmental funds. However, fixed assets and long-term liabilities are not recorded in a general ledger. Rather, most cities and states record fixed assets (including accumulated depreciation and depreciation expense) and long-term liabilities (including interest expense) as reclassification entries. These entries only impact the trial balance used to prepare the government-wide financial statements and are not posted to general ledger accounts of the governmental funds.

To help readers understand the difference between statements, the GASB created slightly different names for government-wide financial statements. Instead of a balance sheet prepared for governmental funds, the similar government-wide financial statement is called a "statement of net assets." The equivalent of a statement of revenues, expenditures, and changes in fund balance prepared for governmental funds is called a "statement of activities" for a government-wide financial statement.

Careers In Accounting

Adwin Ballo

MUNICIPAL TREASURER

© iStockphoto.com/digitalskillet

Adwin Ballo is a city treasurer in a West Coast suburban municipality with a population of just over 25,000. As the treasurer, Mr. Ballo is responsible for all aspects of the city's cash. He oversees the collection of all property and business taxes, the primary source of revenue for the city. These receipts must be safeguarded while in the city's custody.

Since property taxes are paid once a year, Mr. Ballo must estimate the cash needs of the city and determine if there is enough cash available to pay current liabilities. If the supply of cash is insufficient, he must arrange for short-term borrowing to cover debt obligations. If excess cash exists, he must invest it, seeking as high an interest rate as possible for the level of risk the city is willing to take.

Long-term debt is also Mr. Ballo's responsibility. The city council authorizes the debt. Mr. Ballo leads the negotiations on the amount of debt, the interest, and the repayment plan, as well as oversees the actual repayment of the debt.

Mr. Ballo must have a firm understanding of fund accounting in order to ensure that all fund accounting policies are followed. He also oversees all payments made by the city, including payroll and related items, and he prepares a variety of budgets and monitors them throughout the year.

As a city treasurer, Mr. Ballo needs excellent management, communication, and leadership skills. In addition, he must have the ability to work with a broad range of people, including elected and appointed city officials, employees, community organizations, and the citizens of the community. One of the challenges of his position is that elected officials, such as the city council, can change with each election. Since the city council appoints many taskforce members, the taskforce leaders may change after each election. Mr. Ballo must be able to adjust to new city representatives and provide training on fund accounting systems and financial statements.

In the future, Mr. Ballo would like to be a city treasurer in a large city. He is hoping to earn the designation of Certified Public Finance Officer (CPFO), which is governed by the Government Finance Officers Association (GFOA). To obtain this certification, he must pass a series of five exams.

Salary Range: Salaries vary widely, depending on the size of the governmental unit. Salaries in midsize cities range from $110,000 to over $200,000.

Qualifications: A minimum of a bachelor's degree in accounting, finance, or a related field is required, as well as previous experience with fund accounting systems.

Occupational Outlook: The growth for treasurer positions is projected to be slower than average (3% to 9%) for the period from 2014 to 2020.

Source: www.onetonline.org.

© iStockphoto.com/Mlenny

Careers In Accounting

Review the career of a municipal treasurer.

FORMATIVE ASSESSMENT

- This is an ongoing process. Circulate around the classroom or lab, observing which students have difficulty with the assignments.
- Troubleshooting: Diagnose the kinds of problems students have with this lesson. Students may have trouble remembering to close the budgetary accounts by reversing the original entry that recorded the operating budget.
- Assess student understanding by checking solutions to Independent Practice assignments and noting their answers to the Terms Review and Audit Your Understanding questions.

CHECK FOR UNDERSTANDING

Terms Review

- Call on students to define each term in the Terms Review. Definitions are given in the Glossary.

Audit Your Understanding

- Call on students to answer the Audit Your Understanding questions. Answers are given in Appendix D.

GUIDED PRACTICE

Work Together

- Have students write the solution to the Work Together problem as you guide the class through the examples.
- Direct students to prepare financial statements for a governmental organization.

INDEPENDENT PRACTICE

On Your Own

- Assign the On Your Own problem to be worked independently.
- Use the Formative Assessment techniques to diagnose student understanding.

Application Problem

- Assign Application Problem 24-2.

Online Working Papers

- Students can access the Lesson 24-2 problems using this software.

RETEACH

- Ask students to use T accounts to analyze the closing entries presented in this lesson. Use the transparency to demonstrate how to journalize the closing entries for a governmental organization.

CLOSURE

- As a group, develop a summary of adjusting and closing entries for a governmental organization. Select a student to write the summary on the board as it is being developed by the group.

Essential Question

- Which account in a government agency is similar to Income Summary in a for-profit business? (*Unreserved Fund Balance*)

End of Lesson Review

LO2 Prepare financial statements for a general fund.

LO3 Prepare closing entries for a general fund.

LO4 Prepare a post-closing trial balance.

LO5 Describe the components of a comprehensive annual financial report.

Terms Review

comprehensive annual financial report
governmental fund
proprietary fund
fiduciary fund

Audit your understanding

1. Where is the prior-year fund balance on the statement of revenues, expenditures, and changes in fund balance—budget and actual obtained?
2. A city's expenditures are greater than its revenues. How will this difference be labeled on the statement of revenues, expenditures, and changes in fund balance?
3. When actual expenditures are more than budgeted expenditures, is the variance favorable or unfavorable?
4. Into what account are revenue and expenditure accounts closed?
5. Which of the following accounts will appear on a post-closing trial balance?

Appropriations	Reserve for Encumbrances—Prior Year
Property Tax Revenue	Taxes Receivable—Delinquent

6. What is the primary factor that determines whether a government organization is accounted for as a governmental fund or a proprietary fund?

Work together 24-2

Preparing financial statements for a governmental organization

The city of River Springs uses a general fund. The operating budget for the current year, an adjusted trial balance, and a journal are provided in the *Working Papers*. Your instructor will guide you through the following examples.

1. Prepare a statement of revenues, expenditures, and changes in fund balance—budget and actual for the year ended December 31 of the current year.
2. Prepare a balance sheet for December 31 of the current year.
3. Journalize the closing entries.
4. Prepare a post-closing trial balance.

On your own 24-2

Preparing financial statements for a governmental organization

The town of Parson uses a general fund. The operating budget for the current year, an adjusted trial balance, and a journal are provided in the *Working Papers*. Work independently to complete the following problem.

1. Prepare a statement of revenues, expenditures, and changes in fund balance—budget and actual for the year ended December 31 of the current year.
2. Prepare a balance sheet for December 31 of the current year.
3. Journalize the closing entries.
4. Prepare a post-closing trial balance.

EXTENDED LEARNING

- Assign Financial Literacy on page 708.
- Assign Why Accounting on page 711.
- Review Careers in Accounting on page 713.

Chapter Summary

Both businesses and not-for-profit organizations prepare financial statements periodically to report the results of financial activities. A business measures performance primarily through determining the amount of net income. In contrast, a not-for-profit organization's performance is measured primarily by the services provided and the efficiency with which resources are used.

The process of preparing financial statements is similar to that for a business. An unadjusted trial balance is prepared from all accounts in the general ledger, except for encumbrance accounts with a zero balance. Adjusting entries are made to record supplies on hand, to accrue interest revenue, and to reclassify current-year encumbrances as prior-year encumbrances. The adjusted trial balance provides the information required to prepare the financial statements.

The financial statements for a governmental fund include a statement of revenues, expenditures, and changes in fund balance. The assets, liabilities, and fund balance of a governmental fund are reported on a balance sheet.

Government agencies, such as city and state governments, typically have two types of funds. Governmental funds account for activities funded through taxes and grants that provide services, with little if any charge. Proprietary funds account for activities funded through fees paid by those individuals and businesses that use the services provided. Some cities and states may also have fiduciary funds to account for the assets held to benefit a specific group of individuals.

Government agencies are required to prepare a comprehensive annual financial report (CAFR) that includes financial statements for the combined funds as well as detailed reports for major funds. Financial statements for governmental funds are presented on a modified accrual basis. The financial statements for proprietary and fiduciary funds are presented on a full accrual basis.

Components of a Comprehensive Annual Financial Report

EXPLORE ACCOUNTING

Any individual or business seeking to relocate to a new city should first research the city's financial stability. The comprehensive annual financial report (CAFR) provides a wealth of information about the city. Many of the reports provide financial information in more detail than presented in the financial statements. Other reports contain nonfinancial information. A sample of questions that might be answered using a CAFR follows.

1. ***How likely is it that my taxes are going to increase?*** **A report presents the city's property tax rates for the past ten years.**
2. ***What would happen if a major employer closed?*** **A report presents the total property value and percent of the city's total taxes paid by the top ten taxpayers during the current year and ten years ago.**
3. ***Does the city do a good job in collecting its taxes?*** **A report shows, for the past ten years, the dollar amount and percent of taxes collected in the current and subsequent years.**
4. ***What major employers are located in the city?*** **A report shows the number of people employed by the top ten employers. The report includes the percentage of the county's workers employed by each employer.**
5. ***Are the city's residents financially stable?*** **A report shows the city's population and per capita personal income for the past ten years. The report also includes the unemployment rate for each year.**

INSTRUCTIONS

Prepare answers to the following questions:

1. Prepare three additional questions for which you would like to obtain the answers before moving to a new city.
2. Obtain a copy of the CAFR of a nearby city. Use the information in the Statistical section to obtain, for the current year, answers to the five questions just presented. Search the CAFR to determine if it contains the answers to your questions.

© iStockphoto.com/Makhnach_M

CLOSURE

- Review the Chapter Summary.
- Ask students to prepare a list of the new concepts introduced in this chapter.

Essential Questions

- What are some ways the following services could be provided to a community more efficiently: transportation, trash removal, and fire protection? (*Answers will vary, but might include outsourcing to independent companies or partnering with neighboring communities.*)
- What changes could be made to the statement of revenues, expenditures, and changes in fund balance—budget and actual so that continuous improvement can be measured? (*Answers will vary. Including comparative statements for multiple years and variances could help with measuring for improvements.*)
- What are some reasons for unfavorable budget variances? How could they be prevented? (*Reasons might include not budgeting properly, overspending, extenuating circumstances, or uncollected tax revenue. Preventions might include analyzing previous uncollectible tax percentage rates to estimate, and reviewing historical budgets more accurately.*)

EXTENDED LEARNING

- Assign Explore Accounting on page 715.

EXPLORE ACCOUNTING

Answers

1. Answers will vary.
2. Answers will vary.

CHECK FIGURES

For complete solutions to Chapter 24 problems, see the Teacher's Edition of the Working Papers.

Application Problem 24-1

Credit adjustments: Reserve for Inventory of Supplies, $1,648.00; Allowance for Uncollectible Interest, $247.50; Interest Revenue, $742.50; Reserve for Encumbrances—Prior Year, $2,950.00.

Application Problem 24-2

1. Increase (Decrease) in Unreserved Fund Balance for Year; Budget, $14,000.00; Actual, ($10,129.00); Variance, $(24,129.00).
2. Total Assets, $52,241.00; Unreserved Fund Balance, $20,451.00; Total Fund Balance, $28,061.00.
4. Post-Closing Trial Balance, column totals, $62,441.00.

Mastery Problem 24-M

1. Credit adjustments: Reserve for Inventory of Supplies, $2,590.00; Allowance for Uncollectible Interest, $432.00; Interest Revenue, $1,728.00; Reserve for Encumbrances—Prior Year, $5,250.00.
2. Increase in Unreserved Fund Balance for Year, Budget, $20,000.00, Actual, $42,985.00, Variance, $22,985.00.
3. Total Assets, $92,890.00; Unreserved Fund Balance, $69,135.00; Total Fund Balance, $77,905.00.
5. Post-Closing Trial Balance, column totals, $102,890.00.

Apply Your Understanding

INSTRUCTIONS: Download problem instructions for Excel, QuickBooks, and Sage 50 from the textbook companion website at www.C21accounting.com.

24-1 Application Problem: Preparing adjusting entries for a governmental organization LO1

The town of Ellieville uses a general fund. Adjustment information for December 31 is presented below.

Supplies inventory	$1,648.00
Interest revenue due but not collected	990.00

An estimated 25% of the interest revenue due will not be collected.
The reserve for encumbrances for the current year has a credit balance of $2,950.00.

Instructions:

Analyze the adjustment information and prepare adjusting entries. A journal is provided in the *Working Papers*.

24-2 Application Problem: Preparing financial statements for a governmental organization LO2, 3, 4

The city of Proffit Bluff uses a general fund. The operating budget for the current year, an adjusted trial balance, and a journal are provided in the *Working Papers*.

Instructions:

1. Prepare a statement of revenues, expenditures, and changes in fund balance—budget and actual for the year ended December 31 of the current year.
2. Prepare a balance sheet for December 31 of the current year.
3. Journalize the closing entries.
4. Prepare a post-closing trial balance.

Sage 50 Accounting

1. Journalize and post closing entries related to a governmental organization to the general journal.
2. Print the general journal and trial balance.

QB

1. Journalize and post closing entries related to a governmental organization to the journal.
2. Print the journal and trial balance.

Excel

1. Use the adjusted trial balance to prepare the required financial statements.
2. Print the worksheets.

24-M Mastery Problem: Completing the end-of-period work for a governmental organization LO1, 2, 3, 4

The city of Moserville uses a general fund. An operating budget for the current year, an adjusted trial balance, a journal, and forms are provided in the *Working Papers*. Save your work to complete Challenge Problem 24-C. The following adjustment information is available.

Adjustment Information, December 31

Supplies inventory	$2,590.00
Interest revenue due but not collected	2,160.00

An estimated 20% of the interest revenue due will not be collected.
The reserve for encumbrances for the current year has a credit balance of $5,250.00.

INDEPENDENT PRACTICE

- Assign Mastery Problem 24-M for students as a culminating problem combining all new learning from the chapter.
- Assign Challenge Problem 24-C to accelerated students who work at a faster pace.
- Assign Study Guide 24.
- Students can access Online Working Papers to work end-of-chapter problems on the computer.
- Direct students to the C21 Accounting companion website for additional practice and review opportunities.

FORMATIVE ASSESSMENT

- Review solutions to the assigned problems in class, diagnosing trouble spots.

RETEACH

- Call on students to describe how to avoid the trouble spots diagnosed.
- Use reteaching suggestions from lesson plans as required.
- Assign Recycling Problem 24-R if needed.

Instructions:

1. Analyze the adjustment information and record adjusting entries in the journal.
2. Prepare a statement of revenues, expenditures, and changes in fund balance—budget and actual for the year ended December 31 of the current year.
3. Prepare a balance sheet for December 31 of the current year.
4. Journalize the closing entries.
5. Prepare a post-closing trial balance.

Sage 50 Accounting

1. Journalize and post closing entries related to a governmental organization to the general journal.
2. Print the general journal and trial balance.

QB

1. Journalize and post closing entries related to a governmental organization to the journal.
2. Print the journal and trial balance.

X

1. Use the adjusted trial balance to prepare the required financial statements.
2. Print the worksheets.

24-C Challenge Problem: Completing the end-of-period work for a governmental organization LO5

To prepare its statement of net assets, the information presented in Moserville's general fund balance sheet must be modified to the full accrual basis. The city maintains separate records of its assets and long-term liabilities. Use the general journal in the *Working Papers* to prepare the reclassification entries necessary to modify the financial information to full accrual accounting. The impact on the fund balance should be reported as a single item, Invested in Capital Assets, Net of Related Debt, on the statement.

Adjustment Information, December 31

Land, at cost	$ 343,000.00
Buildings and equipment, at cost	1,637,000.00
Accumulated depreciation	521,000.00
Outstanding balance on a building mortgage	640,000.00

Instructions:

Use the balance sheet from Mastery Problem 24-M. A journal is provided in the *Working Papers*.

1. Record the reclassification entries in the journal.
2. Prepare a statement of net assets.

21st Century Skills

The True Cost of Credit

Theme: Financial, Economic, Business, and Entrepreneurial Literacy

Skill: Information Literacy

PARTNERSHIP FOR 21ST CENTURY SKILLS

In recent years, bankruptcy filings have increased, often due to indebtedness from credit card borrowing. Credit cards have increasingly become a more convenient method of payment; however, many people do not understand the impact of using credit cards. For example, some people do not pay their credit cards in full each month, or they are unaware of the long-term consequences of making low monthly payments.

Buying a car, tires, or a laptop all seem like great items to buy now and pay for later. Credit card companies advertise "low minimum payments" that appear to make the purchase affordable for most anyone. Before buying on credit, consider not only what you will pay on a monthly basis, but also the total cost. Understanding the true cost before making a credit card purchase may save money in the long run.

EXTENDED LEARNING

- Assign 21st Century Skills on page 717.
- Assign Analyzing Home Depot's Financial Statements on page 718.

SUMMATIVE EVALUATION

- Chapter 24 Test
- Cognero for Chapter 24

Challenge Problem 24-C

Credit entries: Accumulated Depreciation, $521,000; Invested in Capital Assets, Net of Related Debt, $1,459,000.00; Long-Term Liabilities, $640,000.00.

21ST CENTURY SKILLS

Answers

1. 333 months, or 27 years and 9 months.
2. 7 years, 8 months.
3. $8,396.48 vs. $4,656.00.
4. Answers may vary but could include making a down payment, making larger monthly payments, or finding a lower interest rate. Lauren needs to reconsider making a minimum payment because the laptop probably will not be functioning when she completes the payments.

COMMON CORE AND INTERDISCIPLINARY STUDIES

Extended learning features and activities present numerous opportunities to implement Common Core Standards through interdisciplinary studies. Practice is provided in the common core areas of English Language Arts & Literacy and Mathematical Practice. Many of these activities require short, critical-thinking and decision-making responses that apply reading, writing, speaking, listening, language, media and technology, and mathematical skills.

APPLICATION

Lauren would like to buy a high-performance laptop for her job. Her credit card allows her to make minimum payments equivalent to 2% of the balance. Using the Internet, go to www.bankrate.com or a comparable website with credit card calculators. Answer the following:

1. Use the card minimum payment calculator to determine how long it will take Lauren to pay off a laptop costing $2,500, with a credit card annual percentage rate (APR) of 18%, assuming she makes the minimum payment and does not purchase anything additional on her credit card.
2. Use the "How long will it take to pay off my credit card" calculator, or an equivalent, to determine how long it will take Lauren to pay off the laptop if she makes a $50-per-month payment.
3. Use a calculator to determine the total amount that Lauren will pay for the laptop that originally cost $2,500 if she makes the minimum monthly payment. Then, determine the total amount paid if she makes a $50-per-month payment.
4. Consider that the average lifetime of a laptop is five years. What advice would you give Lauren regarding the purchase of a laptop? What other considerations might be made if she must use her credit card?

Analyzing Home Depot's financial statements

Every publicly traded company is required to have an annual audit of its financial statements. Independent auditors—accountants from outside the company—examine how a company records transactions and prepares its financial statements. Auditors examine the records that support the financial records of a business to ensure that generally accepted accounting principles are followed. The auditors then issue an opinion that states whether the financial statements "present fairly, in all material respects, the consolidated financial position" of the company. The auditors' opinion gives external users confidence in the financial statement information. With this confidence, individuals and other companies are more likely to enter into business transactions with the company.

INSTRUCTIONS

Using Appendix B in this textbook, refer to Home Depot's Report of Independent Registered Public Accounting Firm on page B-4 to answer the following questions:

1. List the five financial statements that were audited by the independent public accounting firm.
2. Identify the fiscal periods examined by the independent public accounting firm.
3. State whether auditing standards require the independent public accounting firm to obtain "total and absolute" assurance that the financial statements are free of material misstatement.
4. State whether the independent public accounting firm examines every business transaction conducted by Home Depot.
5. Name the independent public accounting firm and which office is responsible for the audit of Home Depot's financial statements.

ANALYZING HOME DEPOT'S FINANCIAL STATEMENTS

Answers

1. Consolidated balance sheets and the consolidated statements of earnings, comprehensive income, stockholders' equity, and cash flows.
2. The three-year period ended February 3, 2013.
3. No, the auditors obtain "reasonable" assurance.
4. No. An audit includes examining, on a test basis, evidence supporting the amounts and disclosures in the financial statements.
5. KPMG LLP, the Atlanta, Georgia, office.

Appendix A

Accounting Concepts

Since 1973, the Financial Accounting Standards Board (FASB) has assumed responsibility for setting financial accounting standards known as *Generally Accepted Accounting Principles* (GAAP). One of the first tasks of the FASB was to establish a framework that describes the concepts underlying GAAP. That framework continues to guide the FASB's development of new standards.

In the United States, GAAP serves as a guide for reporting and interpreting accounting information. The accounting principles described in this textbook are based on the application of the concepts underlying GAAP. These concepts are described below and referenced throughout the textbook.

In 1973, the international financial community formed an organization with the ambitious goal of creating a universal set of accounting standards. Similar to the FASB, the International Accounting Standards Board (IASB) uses a framework to develop its standards, known as *International Financial Reporting Standards* (IFRS, pronounced ī'-fers).

The FASB and IASB are committed to merging GAAP and IFRS to achieve one universal set of accounting standards. At the time this textbook was written, the FASB and IASB were working to establish a common framework. That framework will provide the foundation for development of accounting standards to be used around the world.

ACCOUNTING PERIOD CYCLE

Changes in financial information are reported for a specific period of time in the form of financial statements.

Financial statements summarize the financial information that a business records. The time period for which financial statements are prepared depends on the needs of the business. An accounting period may be one month, three months, six months, or one year. An accounting period of one year is a fiscal year. Publicly held corporations must prepare fiscal year financial statements. For tax purposes, every business prepares financial statements at the end of each year.

BUSINESS ENTITY

Financial information is recorded and reported separately from the owner's personal financial information.

A business exists separately from its owners. A business's records must not be mixed with an owner's personal records and reports. For example, a business owner may buy insurance to protect the business and insurance to protect the owner's home. Only the insurance obtained for the business is recorded in the business' financial records. Insurance purchased for the owner's personal home is recorded in the owner's personal financial records. One bank account is used for the business and another for the owner.

CONSISTENT REPORTING

The same accounting principles must be followed in the same way in each accounting period.

Business decisions are based on the financial information reported on financial statements. Some decisions require a comparison of current financial statements with previous financial statements. If accounting information is recorded and reported differently each accounting period, comparisons from one accounting period to another may not be possible. If a business were to include $100,000 of supply purchases as a cost of merchandise sold in one period and as an operating expense in the next period, a user of this information could not adequately compare the two accounting periods. Therefore, unless a change is necessary to make information more easily understood, accounting information is reported in a consistent way every accounting period.

FULL DISCLOSURE

Financial statements contain all information necessary to understand a business's financial condition.

Owners, managers, lenders, and investors rely on financial statements to make informed decisions. All relevant financial information must be adequately and completely disclosed on financial statements.

Assume a business only reports total liabilities of $200,000 on its balance sheet. If that total includes $75,000 in current liabilities, then the balance sheet does not adequately disclose the nature of the liabilities. The critical information not disclosed is that $75,000 is due within the current fiscal year. Full disclosure requires an income statement, a balance sheet, a statement of owners' equity, a statement of cash flows, and the notes to the financial statements.

GOING CONCERN

Financial statements are prepared with the expectation that a business will remain in operation indefinitely.

New businesses are started with the expectation that they will be successful. Accounting records and financial statements are designed as though businesses will continue indefinitely. For example, a business buys store equipment for $80,000. After yearly depreciation is recorded and reported based on the expected life of the equipment, the equipment's book value (cost less accumulated depreciation) is $44,000. If the business ended operations and the equipment had to be sold, the amount received might be less or more than the $44,000. However, accounting records are maintained with the expectation that the business will remain in operation indefinitely and that the cost will be allocated over the useful life of the equipment. The equipment value, therefore, is $44,000 on the records regardless of what it may be worth when sold.

HISTORICAL COST

The actual amount paid for merchandise or other items bought is recorded.

The actual amount paid for an item in a business transaction may be different from its market value. For example, a business purchases a delivery truck that is advertised for sale at $28,500. The truck has a market value of $30,000. The business negotiated a purchase price of just $27,000. The amount recorded in accounting records for the delivery truck is the "historical" cost, $27,000—the actual amount paid.

MATCHING EXPENSES WITH REVENUE

The revenue from business activities and the expenses associated with earning that revenue are recorded in the same accounting period.

Business activities for an accounting period are summarized in financial statements. To adequately report how a business performed during an accounting period, all revenue earned as a result of business operations must be reported. Likewise, all expenses incurred in producing the revenue during the same accounting period must be reported. Matching expenses with revenue gives a true picture of business operations for an accounting period. The timing of when cash is exchanged does not impact when a transaction is recorded as either revenue or expense.

For example, in February, a business performs $50,000 of services and uses $5,000 of supplies that were purchased in the prior fiscal year. Matching expenses with revenue results in net income of $45,000. Including all required expenses gives readers of the financial statements a more complete picture of the financial condition of the business.

MATERIALITY

Business activities creating dollar amounts large enough to affect business decisions should be recorded and reported as separate items in accounting records and financial statements.

Business transactions are recorded in accounting records and reported in financial statements in dollar amounts. How the amounts are recorded and reported depends on the amount involved and the relative importance of the item in making business decisions. Dollar amounts that are large will generally be considered in making decisions about future operations. A separate accounting record is kept for items with dollar amounts large enough to be considered in making decisions about future operations. Dollar amounts that are small and not considered important in decision making may be combined with other amounts in the accounting records and financial statements.

NEUTRALITY

The process of making accounting estimates is free from bias.

Many accounting functions require a business to use estimates. These include the estimation of uncollectible accounts receivable and the assignment of a useful life and salvage value for a plant asset. A business must not set or alter these estimates to achieve some other goal, such as reducing net income to avoid income taxes. For example, a business could raise its estimate of uncollectible accounts receivable to reduce its operating income subject to income tax. However, in compliance with the neutrality principle, the book value of accounts receivable in the financial accounts must always be a reasonable and unbiased estimate of the money the business expects to collect in the future.

OBJECTIVE EVIDENCE

A source document is prepared for each transaction.

A source document is an original business paper indicating that a transaction did occur and that the amounts recorded in the accounting records are accurate and true. For example, a check is the original business paper for cash payments. The original business paper for purchases on account is the purchase invoice. When accounting information reported on the financial statements needs to be verified, an accountant will first check the accounting record. If the details of an entry need further checking, an accountant will then check the business papers as objective evidence that the transaction did occur as recorded.

Many transactions in modern computerized accounting systems are entered directly into the system. Although no paper document is ever prepared, an electronic version of the document is available in the system. The electronic record provides the same objective evidence of the transaction as would a paper record.

REALIZATION OF REVENUE

Revenue is recorded at the time goods or services are sold.

A business may sell goods or services or both. Cash may be received at the time of sale, or the business may agree to receive payment at a later date. Regardless of when cash is actually received, the sale amount is recorded in the accounting records at the time of sale. For example, merchandise is sold for $3,500. The business agrees to an initial payment of $500 with the remaining balance to be divided in four monthly payments of $750 each. The full $3,500 of revenue is recorded at the time of the sale even though $3,000 will be collected later.

UNIT OF MEASUREMENT

Business transactions are reported in numbers that have common values—that is, using a common unit of measurement.

All transactions are recorded in accounting records in terms of money. Useful nonfinancial information may also be recorded to describe the nature of a business transaction. If part of the information in the accounting records is financial and part is nonfinancial, the financial statements will not be clear. For example, if a business states its sales in number of units sold (nonfinancial) and its expenses in dollars (financial), net profit cannot be calculated. Instead, total expenses (financial) are subtracted from the money taken in through sales (financial) to determine net profit.

A-3

Appendix B

The Home Depot

FORM 10-K
(Annual Report)

for the Period Ending 02/03/2013

UNITED STATES
SECURITIES AND EXCHANGE COMMISSION
WASHINGTON, D.C. 20549

FORM 10-K

☒ **ANNUAL REPORT PURSUANT TO SECTION 13 OR 15(d) OF THE SECURITIES EXCHANGE ACT OF 1934**

For the fiscal year ended February 3, 2013

OR

☐ **TRANSITION REPORT PURSUANT TO SECTION 13 OR 15(d) OF THE SECURITIES EXCHANGE ACT OF 1934**

Commission File Number 1-8207

THE HOME DEPOT, INC.
(Exact name of registrant as specified in its charter)

DELAWARE
(State or other jurisdiction of incorporation or organization)

95-3261426
(I.R.S. Employer Identification No.)

2455 PACES FERRY ROAD, N.W., ATLANTA, GEORGIA 30339
(Address of principal executive offices) (Zip Code)

Registrant's Telephone Number, Including Area Code: **(770) 433-8211**

SECURITIES REGISTERED PURSUANT TO SECTION 12(b) OF THE ACT:

TITLE OF EACH CLASS	NAME OF EACH EXCHANGE ON WHICH REGISTERED
Common Stock, $0.05 Par Value Per Share	New York Stock Exchange

SECURITIES REGISTERED PURSUANT TO SECTION 12(g) OF THE ACT: **None**

Indicate by check mark if the Registrant is a well-known seasoned issuer, as defined in Rule 405 of the Securities Act. Yes ☒ No ☐

Indicate by check mark if the Registrant is not required to file reports pursuant to Section 13 or Section 15(d) of the Act. Yes ☐ No ☒

Indicate by check mark whether the Registrant (1) has filed all reports required to be filed by Section 13 or 15(d) of the Securities Exchange Act of 1934 during the preceding 12 months (or for such shorter period that the Registrant was required to file such reports), and (2) has been subject to such filing requirements for the past 90 days. Yes ☒ No ☐

Indicate by check mark whether the Registrant has submitted electronically and posted on its corporate Web site, if any, every Interactive Data File required to be submitted and posted pursuant to Rule 405 of Regulation S-T during the preceding 12 months (or for such shorter period that the Registrant was required to submit and post such files). Yes ☒ No ☐

Indicate by check mark if disclosure of delinquent filers pursuant to Item 405 of Regulation S-K is not contained herein, and will not be contained, to the best of Registrant's knowledge, in definitive proxy or information statements incorporated by reference in Part III of this Form 10-K or any amendment to this Form 10-K. ☐

Indicate by check mark whether the Registrant is a large accelerated filer, an accelerated filer, a non-accelerated filer, or a smaller reporting company. See the definitions of "large accelerated filer," "accelerated filer" and "smaller reporting company" in Rule 12b-2 of the Exchange Act. (Check one):

Large accelerated filer ☒	Accelerated filer ☐	Non-accelerated filer ☐ (Do not check if a smaller reporting company)	Smaller reporting company ☐

Indicate by check mark whether the Registrant is a shell company (as defined in Rule 12b-2 of the Exchange Act). Yes ☐ No ☒

The aggregate market value of the common stock of the Registrant held by non-affiliates of the Registrant on July 29, 2012 was $80.2 billion.

The number of shares outstanding of the Registrant's common stock as of March 11, 2013 was 1,485,517,485 shares.

DOCUMENTS INCORPORATED BY REFERENCE

Portions of the Registrant's proxy statement for the 2013 Annual Meeting of Shareholders are incorporated by reference in Part III of this Form 10-K to the extent described herein.

Item 8. Financial Statements and Supplementary Data.

Management's Responsibility for Financial Statements

The financial statements presented in this Annual Report have been prepared with integrity and objectivity and are the responsibility of the management of The Home Depot, Inc. These financial statements have been prepared in conformity with U.S. generally accepted accounting principles and properly reflect certain estimates and judgments based upon the best available information.

The financial statements of the Company have been audited by KPMG LLP, an independent registered public accounting firm. Their accompanying report is based upon an audit conducted in accordance with the standards of the Public Company Accounting Oversight Board (United States).

The Audit Committee of the Board of Directors, consisting solely of independent directors, meets five times a year with the independent registered public accounting firm, the internal auditors and representatives of management to discuss auditing and financial reporting matters. In addition, a telephonic meeting is held prior to each quarterly earnings release. The Audit Committee retains the independent registered public accounting firm and regularly reviews the internal accounting controls, the activities of the independent registered public accounting firm and internal auditors and the financial condition of the Company. Both the Company's independent registered public accounting firm and the internal auditors have free access to the Audit Committee.

Management's Report on Internal Control Over Financial Reporting

Our management is responsible for establishing and maintaining adequate internal control over financial reporting, as such term is defined in Rule 13a-15(f) promulgated under the Securities Exchange Act of 1934, as amended (the "Exchange Act"). Under the supervision and with the participation of our management, including our Chief Executive Officer and Chief Financial Officer, we conducted an evaluation of the effectiveness of our internal control over financial reporting as of February 3, 2013 based on the framework in *Internal Control – Integrated Framework* issued by the Committee of Sponsoring Organizations of the Treadway Commission (COSO). Based on our evaluation, our management concluded that our internal control over financial reporting was effective as of February 3, 2013 in providing reasonable assurance regarding the reliability of financial reporting and the preparation of financial statements for external purposes in accordance with U.S. generally accepted accounting principles. The effectiveness of our internal control over financial reporting as of February 3, 2013 has been audited by KPMG LLP, an independent registered public accounting firm, as stated in their report which is included on page 28 in this Form 10-K.

/s/ FRANCIS S. BLAKE	/s/ CAROL B. TOMÉ
Francis S. Blake **Chairman &** **Chief Executive Officer**	**Carol B. Tomé** **Chief Financial Officer &** **Executive Vice President – Corporate Services**

Report of Independent Registered Public Accounting Firm

The Board of Directors and Stockholders
The Home Depot, Inc.:

We have audited the accompanying Consolidated Balance Sheets of The Home Depot, Inc. and subsidiaries as of February 3, 2013 and January 29, 2012, and the related Consolidated Statements of Earnings, Comprehensive Income, Stockholders' Equity, and Cash Flows for each of the fiscal years in the three-year period ended February 3, 2013. These Consolidated Financial Statements are the responsibility of the Company's management. Our responsibility is to express an opinion on these Consolidated Financial Statements based on our audits.

We conducted our audits in accordance with the standards of the Public Company Accounting Oversight Board (United States). Those standards require that we plan and perform the audit to obtain reasonable assurance about whether the financial statements are free of material misstatement. An audit includes examining, on a test basis, evidence supporting the amounts and disclosures in the financial statements. An audit also includes assessing the accounting principles used and significant estimates made by management, as well as evaluating the overall financial statement presentation. We believe that our audits provide a reasonable basis for our opinion.

In our opinion, the Consolidated Financial Statements referred to above present fairly, in all material respects, the financial position of The Home Depot, Inc. and subsidiaries as of February 3, 2013 and January 29, 2012, and the results of their operations and their cash flows for each of the fiscal years in the three-year period ended February 3, 2013, in conformity with U.S. generally accepted accounting principles.

We also have audited, in accordance with the standards of the Public Company Accounting Oversight Board (United States), The Home Depot, Inc.'s internal control over financial reporting as of February 3, 2013, based on criteria established in *Internal Control – Integrated Framework* issued by the Committee of Sponsoring Organizations of the Treadway Commission (COSO), and our report dated March 28, 2013 expressed an unqualified opinion on the effectiveness of the Company's internal control over financial reporting.

/s/ KPMG LLP

Atlanta, Georgia
March 28, 2013

THE HOME DEPOT, INC. AND SUBSIDIARIES
CONSOLIDATED BALANCE SHEETS

amounts in millions, except share and per share data	February 3, 2013	January 29, 2012
ASSETS		
Current Assets:		
Cash and Cash Equivalents	**$ 2,494**	$ 1,987
Receivables, net	**1,395**	1,245
Merchandise Inventories	**10,710**	10,325
Other Current Assets	**773**	963
Total Current Assets	**15,372**	14,520
Property and Equipment, at cost	**38,491**	38,975
Less Accumulated Depreciation and Amortization	**14,422**	14,527
Net Property and Equipment	**24,069**	24,448
Notes Receivable	**140**	135
Goodwill	**1,170**	1,120
Other Assets	**333**	295
Total Assets	**$ 41,084**	$ 40,518
LIABILITIES AND STOCKHOLDERS' EQUITY		
Current Liabilities:		
Accounts Payable	**$ 5,376**	$ 4,856
Accrued Salaries and Related Expenses	**1,414**	1,372
Sales Taxes Payable	**472**	391
Deferred Revenue	**1,270**	1,147
Income Taxes Payable	**22**	23
Current Installments of Long-Term Debt	**1,321**	30
Other Accrued Expenses	**1,587**	1,557
Total Current Liabilities	**11,462**	9,376
Long-Term Debt, excluding current installments	**9,475**	10,758
Other Long-Term Liabilities	**2,051**	2,146
Deferred Income Taxes	**319**	340
Total Liabilities	**23,307**	22,620
STOCKHOLDERS' EQUITY		
Common Stock, par value $0.05; authorized: 10 billion shares; issued: 1.754 billion shares at February 3, 2013 and 1.733 billion shares at January 29, 2012; outstanding: 1.484 billion shares at February 3, 2013 and 1.537 billion shares at January 29, 2012	**88**	87
Paid-In Capital	**7,948**	6,966
Retained Earnings	**20,038**	17,246
Accumulated Other Comprehensive Income	**397**	293
Treasury Stock, at cost, 270 million shares at February 3, 2013 and 196 million shares at January 29, 2012	**(10,694)**	(6,694)
Total Stockholders' Equity	**17,777**	17,898
Total Liabilities and Stockholders' Equity	**$ 41,084**	$ 40,518

See accompanying Notes to Consolidated Financial Statements.

THE HOME DEPOT, INC. AND SUBSIDIARIES
CONSOLIDATED STATEMENTS OF EARNINGS

amounts in millions, except per share data	Fiscal Year Ended[(1)] February 3, 2013	January 29, 2012	January 30, 2011
NET SALES	**$ 74,754**	$ 70,395	$ 67,997
Cost of Sales	**48,912**	46,133	44,693
GROSS PROFIT	**25,842**	24,262	23,304
Operating Expenses:			
Selling, General and Administrative	**16,508**	16,028	15,849
Depreciation and Amortization	**1,568**	1,573	1,616
Total Operating Expenses	**18,076**	17,601	17,465
OPERATING INCOME	**7,766**	6,661	5,839
Interest and Other (Income) Expense:			
Interest and Investment Income	**(20)**	(13)	(15)
Interest Expense	**632**	606	530
Other	**(67)**	—	51
Interest and Other, net	**545**	593	566
EARNINGS BEFORE PROVISION FOR INCOME TAXES	**7,221**	6,068	5,273
Provision for Income Taxes	**2,686**	2,185	1,935
NET EARNINGS	**$ 4,535**	$ 3,883	$ 3,338
Weighted Average Common Shares	**1,499**	1,562	1,648
BASIC EARNINGS PER SHARE	**$ 3.03**	$ 2.49	$ 2.03
Diluted Weighted Average Common Shares	**1,511**	1,570	1,658
DILUTED EARNINGS PER SHARE	**$ 3.00**	$ 2.47	$ 2.01

(1) Fiscal year ended February 3, 2013 includes 53 weeks. Fiscal years ended January 29, 2012 and January 30, 2011 include 52 weeks.

See accompanying Notes to Consolidated Financial Statements.

THE HOME DEPOT, INC. AND SUBSIDIARIES
CONSOLIDATED STATEMENTS OF COMPREHENSIVE INCOME

amounts in millions	Fiscal Year Ended[(1)]		
	February 3, 2013	**January 29, 2012**	**January 30, 2011**
Net Earnings	**$ 4,535**	$ 3,883	$ 3,338
Other Comprehensive Income (Loss):			
Foreign Currency Translation Adjustments	**100**	(143)	206
Cash Flow Hedges, net of tax	**5**	5	(116)
Other	**(1)**	(14)	(7)
Total Other Comprehensive Income (Loss)	**104**	(152)	83
COMPREHENSIVE INCOME	**$ 4,639**	$ 3,731	$ 3,421

(1) Fiscal year ended February 3, 2013 includes 53 weeks. Fiscal years ended January 29, 2012 and January 30, 2011 include 52 weeks.

See accompanying Notes to Consolidated Financial Statements.

THE HOME DEPOT, INC. AND SUBSIDIARIES
CONSOLIDATED STATEMENTS OF STOCKHOLDERS' EQUITY

amounts in millions, except per share data	Common Stock Shares	Common Stock Amount	Paid-In Capital	Retained Earnings	Accumulated Other Comprehensive Income (Loss)	Treasury Stock Shares	Treasury Stock Amount	Stockholders' Equity
Balance, January 31, 2010	**1,716**	**$ 86**	**$ 6,304**	**$ 13,226**	**$ 362**	**(18)**	**$ (585)**	**$ 19,393**
Net Earnings	—	—	—	3,338	—	—	—	3,338
Shares Issued Under Employee Stock Plans	6	—	42	—	—	—	—	42
Tax Effect of Stock-Based Compensation	—	—	2	—	—	—	—	2
Foreign Currency Translation Adjustments	—	—	—	—	206	—	—	206
Cash Flow Hedges, net of tax	—	—	—	—	(116)	—	—	(116)
Stock Options, Awards and Amortization of Restricted Stock	—	—	214	—	—	—	—	214
Repurchases of Common Stock	—	—	—	—	—	(81)	(2,608)	(2,608)
Cash Dividends ($0.945 per share)	—	—	—	(1,569)	—	—	—	(1,569)
Other	—	—	(6)	—	(7)	—	—	(13)
Balance, January 30, 2011	**1,722**	**$ 86**	**$ 6,556**	**$ 14,995**	**$ 445**	**(99)**	**$ (3,193)**	**$ 18,889**
Net Earnings	—	—	—	3,883	—	—	—	3,883
Shares Issued Under Employee Stock Plans	11	1	196	—	—	—	—	197
Tax Effect of Stock-Based Compensation	—	—	(2)	—	—	—	—	(2)
Foreign Currency Translation Adjustments	—	—	—	—	(143)	—	—	(143)
Cash Flow Hedges, net of tax	—	—	—	—	5	—	—	5
Stock Options, Awards and Amortization of Restricted Stock	—	—	215	—	—	—	—	215
Repurchases of Common Stock	—	—	—	—	—	(97)	(3,501)	(3,501)
Cash Dividends ($1.04 per share)	—	—	—	(1,632)	—	—	—	(1,632)
Other	—	—	1	—	(14)	—	—	(13)
Balance, January 29, 2012	**1,733**	**$ 87**	**$ 6,966**	**$ 17,246**	**$ 293**	**(196)**	**$ (6,694)**	**$ 17,898**
Net Earnings	—	—	—	4,535	—	—	—	4,535
Shares Issued Under Employee Stock Plans	21	1	678	—	—	—	—	679
Tax Effect of Stock-Based Compensation	—	—	82	—	—	—	—	82
Foreign Currency Translation Adjustments	—	—	—	—	100	—	—	100
Cash Flow Hedges, net of tax	—	—	—	—	5	—	—	5
Stock Options, Awards and Amortization of Restricted Stock	—	—	218	—	—	—	—	218
Repurchases of Common Stock	—	—	—	—	—	(74)	(4,000)	(4,000)
Cash Dividends ($1.16 per share)	—	—	—	(1,743)	—	—	—	(1,743)
Other	—	—	4	—	(1)	—	—	3
Balance, February 3, 2013	**1,754**	**$ 88**	**$ 7,948**	**$ 20,038**	**$ 397**	**(270)**	**$ (10,694)**	**$ 17,777**

See accompanying Notes to Consolidated Financial Statements.

THE HOME DEPOT, INC. AND SUBSIDIARIES
CONSOLIDATED STATEMENTS OF CASH FLOWS

amounts in millions	Fiscal Year Ended[1] February 3, 2013	January 29, 2012	January 30, 2011
CASH FLOWS FROM OPERATING ACTIVITIES:			
Net Earnings	**$ 4,535**	$ 3,883	$ 3,338
Reconciliation of Net Earnings to Net Cash Provided by Operating Activities:			
Depreciation and Amortization	**1,684**	1,682	1,718
Stock-Based Compensation Expense	**218**	215	214
Goodwill Impairment	**97**	—	—
Changes in Assets and Liabilities, net of the effects of acquisitions and disposition:			
Receivables, net	**(143)**	(170)	(102)
Merchandise Inventories	**(350)**	256	(355)
Other Current Assets	**93**	159	12
Accounts Payable and Accrued Expenses	**698**	422	(133)
Deferred Revenue	**121**	(29)	10
Income Taxes Payable	**87**	14	(85)
Deferred Income Taxes	**107**	170	104
Other Long-Term Liabilities	**(180)**	(2)	(61)
Other	**8**	51	(75)
Net Cash Provided by Operating Activities	**6,975**	6,651	4,585
CASH FLOWS FROM INVESTING ACTIVITIES:			
Capital Expenditures, net of $98, $25 and $62 of non-cash capital expenditures in fiscal 2012, 2011 and 2010, respectively	**(1,312)**	(1,221)	(1,096)
Proceeds from Sale of Business, net	**—**	101	—
Payments for Businesses Acquired, net	**(170)**	(65)	—
Proceeds from Sales of Property and Equipment	**50**	56	84
Net Cash Used in Investing Activities	**(1,432)**	(1,129)	(1,012)
CASH FLOWS FROM FINANCING ACTIVITIES:			
Proceeds from Long-Term Borrowings, net of discount	**—**	1,994	998
Repayments of Long-Term Debt	**(32)**	(1,028)	(1,029)
Repurchases of Common Stock	**(3,984)**	(3,470)	(2,608)
Proceeds from Sales of Common Stock	**784**	306	104
Cash Dividends Paid to Stockholders	**(1,743)**	(1,632)	(1,569)
Other Financing Activities	**(59)**	(218)	(347)
Net Cash Used in Financing Activities	**(5,034)**	(4,048)	(4,451)
Change in Cash and Cash Equivalents	**509**	1,474	(878)
Effect of Exchange Rate Changes on Cash and Cash Equivalents	**(2)**	(32)	2
Cash and Cash Equivalents at Beginning of Year	**1,987**	545	1,421
Cash and Cash Equivalents at End of Year	**$ 2,494**	$ 1,987	$ 545
SUPPLEMENTAL DISCLOSURE OF CASH PAYMENTS MADE FOR:			
Interest, net of interest capitalized	**$ 617**	$ 580	$ 579
Income Taxes	**$ 2,482**	$ 1,865	$ 2,067

(1) Fiscal year ended February 3, 2013 includes 53 weeks. Fiscal years ended January 29, 2012 and January 30, 2011 include 52 weeks.

See accompanying Notes to Consolidated Financial Statements.

NOTES TO CONSOLIDATED FINANCIAL STATEMENTS

1. SUMMARY OF SIGNIFICANT ACCOUNTING POLICIES

Business, Consolidation and Presentation

The Home Depot, Inc. and its subsidiaries (the "Company") operate The Home Depot stores, which are full-service, warehouse-style stores averaging approximately 104,000 square feet of enclosed space, with approximately 24,000 additional square feet of outside garden area. The stores stock approximately 30,000 to 40,000 different kinds of building materials, home improvement supplies and lawn and garden products that are sold to do-it-yourself customers, do-it-for-me customers and professional customers. The Company also offers over 600,000 products through its Home Depot and Home Decorators Collection websites. At the end of fiscal 2012, the Company was operating 2,256 The Home Depot stores, which included 1,976 stores in the United States, including the Commonwealth of Puerto Rico and the territories of the U.S. Virgin Islands and Guam ("U.S."), 180 stores in Canada and 100 stores in Mexico. The Consolidated Financial Statements include the accounts of the Company and its wholly-owned subsidiaries. All significant intercompany transactions have been eliminated in consolidation.

Fiscal Year

The Company's fiscal year is a 52- or 53-week period ending on the Sunday nearest to January 31. The fiscal year ended February 3, 2013 ("fiscal 2012") includes 53 weeks and fiscal years ended January 29, 2012 ("fiscal 2011") and January 30, 2011 ("fiscal 2010") include 52 weeks.

Use of Estimates

Management of the Company has made a number of estimates and assumptions relating to the reporting of assets and liabilities, the disclosure of contingent assets and liabilities, and reported amounts of revenues and expenses in preparing these financial statements in conformity with U.S. generally accepted accounting principles. Actual results could differ from these estimates.

Fair Value of Financial Instruments

The carrying amounts of Cash and Cash Equivalents, Receivables and Accounts Payable approximate fair value due to the short-term maturities of these financial instruments. The fair value of the Company's Long-Term Debt is discussed in Note 11.

Cash Equivalents

The Company considers all highly liquid investments purchased with original maturities of three months or less to be cash equivalents. The Company's cash equivalents are carried at fair market value and consist primarily of money market funds.

Accounts Receivable

The Company has an agreement with a third-party service provider who directly extends credit to customers, manages the Company's private label credit card program and owns the related receivables. The Company evaluated the third-party entities holding the receivables under the program and concluded that they should not be consolidated by the Company. The agreement with the third-party service provider expires in 2018, with the Company having the option, but no obligation, to purchase the receivables at the end of the agreement. The deferred interest charges incurred by the Company for its deferred financing programs offered to its customers are included in Cost of Sales. The interchange fees charged to the Company for the customers' use of the cards and any profit sharing with the third-party service provider are included in Selling, General and Administrative expenses ("SG&A"). The sum of the three is referred to by the Company as "the cost of credit" of the private label credit card program.

In addition, certain subsidiaries of the Company extend credit directly to customers in the ordinary course of business. The receivables due from customers were $42 million and $45 million as of February 3, 2013 and January 29, 2012, respectively. The Company's valuation reserve related to accounts receivable was not material to the Consolidated Financial Statements of the Company as of the end of fiscal 2012 or 2011.

Merchandise Inventories

The majority of the Company's Merchandise Inventories are stated at the lower of cost (first-in, first-out) or market, as determined by the retail inventory method. As the inventory retail value is adjusted regularly to reflect market conditions, the inventory valued using the retail method approximates the lower of cost or market. Certain subsidiaries, including retail operations in Canada and Mexico, and distribution centers, record Merchandise Inventories at the lower of cost or market, as determined by a cost method. These Merchandise Inventories represent approximately 24% of the total Merchandise Inventories balance. The Company evaluates the inventory valued using a cost method at the end of each quarter to ensure that it is carried at the lower of cost or market. The valuation allowance for Merchandise Inventories valued under a cost method was not material to the Consolidated Financial Statements of the Company as of the end of fiscal 2012 or 2011.

Independent physical inventory counts or cycle counts are taken on a regular basis in each store and distribution center to ensure that amounts reflected in the accompanying Consolidated Financial Statements for Merchandise Inventories are properly stated. During the period between physical inventory counts in stores, the Company accrues for estimated losses related to shrink on a store-by-store basis based on historical shrink results and current trends in the business. Shrink (or in the case of excess inventory, "swell") is the difference between the recorded amount of inventory and the physical inventory. Shrink may occur due to theft, loss, inaccurate records for the receipt of inventory or deterioration of goods, among other things.

Income Taxes

Income taxes are accounted for under the asset and liability method. The Company provides for federal, state and foreign income taxes currently payable, as well as for those deferred due to timing differences between reporting income and expenses for financial statement purposes versus tax purposes. Deferred tax assets and liabilities are recognized for the future tax consequences attributable to temporary differences between the financial statement carrying amounts of existing assets and liabilities and their respective tax bases. Deferred tax assets and liabilities are measured using enacted income tax rates expected to apply to taxable income in the years in which those temporary differences are expected to be recovered or settled. The effect of a change in income tax rates is recognized as income or expense in the period that includes the enactment date.

The Company recognizes the effect of income tax positions only if those positions are more likely than not of being sustained. Recognized income tax positions are measured at the largest amount that is greater than 50% likely of being realized. Changes in recognition or measurement are reflected in the period in which the change in judgment occurs.

The Company and its eligible subsidiaries file a consolidated U.S. federal income tax return. Non-U.S. subsidiaries and certain U.S. subsidiaries, which are consolidated for financial reporting purposes, are not eligible to be included in the Company's consolidated U.S. federal income tax return. Separate provisions for income taxes have been determined for these entities. The Company intends to reinvest substantially all of the unremitted earnings of its non-U.S. subsidiaries and postpone their remittance indefinitely. Accordingly, no provision for U.S. income taxes for these non-U.S. subsidiaries was recorded in the accompanying Consolidated Statements of Earnings.

Depreciation and Amortization

The Company's Buildings, Furniture, Fixtures and Equipment are recorded at cost and depreciated using the straight-line method over the estimated useful lives of the assets. Leasehold Improvements are amortized using the straight-line method over the original term of the lease or the useful life of the improvement, whichever is shorter. The Company's Property and Equipment is depreciated using the following estimated useful lives:

	Life
Buildings	5 – 45 years
Furniture, Fixtures and Equipment	2 – 20 years
Leasehold Improvements	5 – 45 years

Capitalized Software Costs

The Company capitalizes certain costs related to the acquisition and development of software and amortizes these costs using the straight-line method over the estimated useful life of the software, which is three to six years. These costs are included in Furniture, Fixtures and Equipment as discussed further in Note 4. Certain development costs not meeting the criteria for capitalization are expensed as incurred.

Revenues

The Company recognizes revenue, net of estimated returns and sales tax, at the time the customer takes possession of merchandise or receives services. The liability for sales returns is estimated based on historical return levels. When the Company receives payment from customers before the customer has taken possession of the merchandise or the service has been performed, the amount received is recorded as Deferred Revenue in the accompanying Consolidated Balance Sheets until the sale or service is complete. The Company also records Deferred Revenue for the sale of gift cards and recognizes this revenue upon the redemption of gift cards in Net Sales. Gift card breakage income is recognized based upon historical redemption patterns and represents the balance of gift cards for which the Company believes the likelihood of redemption by the customer is remote. During fiscal 2012, 2011 and 2010, the Company recognized $33 million, $42 million and $46 million, respectively, of gift card breakage income. This income is included in the accompanying Consolidated Statements of Earnings as a reduction in SG&A.

Services Revenue

Net Sales include services revenue generated through a variety of installation, home maintenance and professional service programs. In these programs, the customer selects and purchases material for a project, and the Company provides or arranges professional installation. These programs are offered through the Company's stores and in-home sales programs. Under certain programs, when the Company provides or arranges the installation of a project and the subcontractor provides material as part of the installation, both the material and labor are included in services revenue. The Company recognizes this revenue when the service for the customer is complete.

All payments received prior to the completion of services are recorded in Deferred Revenue in the accompanying Consolidated Balance Sheets. Services revenue was $3.2 billion, $2.9 billion and $2.7 billion for fiscal 2012, 2011 and 2010, respectively.

Self-Insurance

The Company is self-insured for certain losses related to general liability (including products liability), workers' compensation, employee group medical and automobile claims. The expected ultimate cost for claims incurred as of the balance sheet date is not discounted and is recognized as a liability. The expected ultimate cost of claims is estimated based upon analysis of historical data and actuarial estimates.

Prepaid Advertising

Television and radio advertising production costs, along with media placement costs, are expensed when the advertisement first appears. Amounts included in Other Current Assets in the accompanying Consolidated Balance Sheets relating to prepayments of production costs for print and broadcast advertising as well as sponsorship promotions were not material at the end of fiscal 2012 and 2011.

Vendor Allowances

Vendor allowances primarily consist of volume rebates that are earned as a result of attaining certain purchase levels and advertising co-op allowances for the promotion of vendors' products that are typically based on guaranteed minimum amounts with additional amounts being earned for attaining certain purchase levels. These vendor allowances are accrued as earned, with those allowances received as a result of attaining certain purchase levels accrued over the incentive period based on estimates of purchases.

Volume rebates and certain advertising co-op allowances earned are initially recorded as a reduction in Merchandise Inventories and a subsequent reduction in Cost of Sales when the related product is sold. Certain advertising co-op allowances that are reimbursements of specific, incremental and identifiable costs incurred to promote vendors' products are recorded as an offset against advertising expense. In fiscal 2012, 2011 and 2010, gross advertising expense was $831 million, $846 million and $864 million, respectively, and is included in SG&A. Specific, incremental and identifiable advertising co-op allowances were $85 million, $94 million and $90 million for fiscal 2012, 2011 and 2010, respectively, and are recorded as an offset to advertising expense in SG&A.

Cost of Sales

Cost of Sales includes the actual cost of merchandise sold and services performed, the cost of transportation of merchandise from vendors to the Company's stores, locations or customers, the operating cost of the Company's sourcing and distribution network and the cost of deferred interest programs offered through the Company's private label credit card program.

The cost of handling and shipping merchandise from the Company's stores, locations or distribution centers to the customer is classified as SG&A. The cost of shipping and handling, including internal costs and payments to third parties, classified as SG&A was $435 million, $430 million and $410 million in fiscal 2012, 2011 and 2010, respectively.

Impairment of Long-Lived Assets

The Company evaluates its long-lived assets each quarter for indicators of potential impairment. Indicators of impairment include current period losses combined with a history of losses, management's decision to relocate or close a store or other location before the end of its previously estimated useful life or when changes in other circumstances indicate the carrying amount of an asset may not be recoverable. The evaluation for long-lived assets is performed at the lowest level of identifiable cash flows, which is generally the individual store level.

The assets of a store with indicators of impairment are evaluated by comparing its undiscounted cash flows with its carrying value. The estimate of cash flows includes management's assumptions of cash inflows and outflows directly resulting from the use of those assets in operations, including gross margin on Net Sales, payroll and related items, occupancy costs, insurance allocations and other costs to operate a store. If the carrying value is greater than the undiscounted cash flows, an impairment loss is recognized for the difference between the carrying value and the estimated fair market value. Impairment losses are recorded as a component of SG&A in the accompanying Consolidated Statements of Earnings. When a leased location closes, the Company also recognizes in SG&A the net present value of future lease obligations less estimated sublease income. The Company recorded impairments and lease obligation costs on closings and relocations in the ordinary course of business, as well as for the closing of seven stores in China in fiscal 2012, which were not material to the Consolidated Financial Statements in fiscal 2012, 2011 or 2010.

Goodwill and Other Intangible Assets

Goodwill represents the excess of purchase price over the fair value of net assets acquired. The Company does not amortize goodwill but does assess the recoverability of goodwill in the third quarter of each fiscal year, or more often if indicators warrant, by determining whether the fair value of each reporting unit supports its carrying value. The Company assesses qualitative factors to determine whether it is more likely than not that the fair value of each reporting unit is less than its carrying amount as a basis for determining whether it is necessary to complete quantitative impairment assessments. During fiscal 2012, for all reporting units other than the China reporting unit, the Company used qualitative factors to determine that its goodwill balances for each reporting unit were not impaired. For the China reporting unit, the Company recorded a charge of $97 million to impair all of the goodwill associated with that reporting unit in fiscal 2012. Impairment charges related to the remaining goodwill were not material for fiscal 2012, 2011 or 2010.

The Company amortizes the cost of other intangible assets over their estimated useful lives, which range up to ten years, unless such lives are deemed indefinite. Intangible assets with indefinite lives are tested in the third quarter of each fiscal year for impairment, or more often if indicators warrant. Impairment charges related to other intangible assets were not material for fiscal 2012, 2011 or 2010.

Stock-Based Compensation

The per share weighted average fair value of stock options granted during fiscal 2012, 2011 and 2010 was $9.86, $7.42 and $6.70, respectively. The fair value of these options was determined at the date of grant using the Black-Scholes option-pricing model with the following assumptions:

	Fiscal Year Ended		
	February 3, 2013	**January 29, 2012**	**January 30, 2011**
Risk-free interest rate	**1.2%**	2.0%	3.1%
Assumed volatility	**27.0%**	27.3%	26.4%
Assumed dividend yield	**2.3%**	2.7%	2.9%
Assumed lives of options	**5 years**	5 years	5 years

Derivatives

The Company uses derivative financial instruments from time to time in the management of its interest rate exposure on long-term debt and its exposure on foreign currency fluctuations. The Company accounts for its derivative financial instruments in accordance with the Financial Accounting Standards Board Accounting Standards Codification ("FASB ASC") Subtopic 815-10. The fair value of the Company's derivative financial instruments is discussed in Note 11.

Comprehensive Income

Comprehensive Income includes Net Earnings adjusted for certain gains and losses that are excluded from Net Earnings under U.S. generally accepted accounting principles. Adjustments to Net Earnings and Accumulated Other Comprehensive Income consist primarily of foreign currency translation adjustments.

Foreign Currency Translation

Assets and liabilities denominated in a foreign currency are translated into U.S. dollars at the current rate of exchange on the last day of the reporting period. Revenues and expenses are generally translated using average exchange rates for the period and equity transactions are translated using the actual rate on the day of the transaction.

Segment Information

The Company operates within a single reportable segment primarily within North America. Net Sales for the Company outside the U.S. were $8.4 billion, $8.0 billion and $7.5 billion for fiscal 2012, 2011 and 2010, respectively. Long-lived assets outside the U.S. totaled $3.1 billion and $3.1 billion as of February 3, 2013 and January 29, 2012, respectively.

Reclassifications

Certain amounts in prior fiscal years have been reclassified to conform with the presentation adopted in the current fiscal year.

2. CHINA STORE CLOSINGS

In fiscal 2012, the Company closed its remaining seven big box stores in China. As a result of the closings, the Company recorded a total charge of $145 million, net of tax, in fiscal 2012. Inventory markdown costs of $10 million are included in Cost of Sales, and $135 million of costs related to the impairment of Goodwill and other assets, lease terminations, severance and other charges are included in SG&A in the accompanying Consolidated Statements of Earnings.

3. DEBT GUARANTEE

In connection with the sale of HD Supply, Inc. on August 30, 2007, the Company guaranteed a $1.0 billion senior secured amortizing term loan of HD Supply. The original expiration date of the guarantee was August 30, 2012. In March 2010, the Company amended the guarantee to extend the expiration date to April 1, 2014. The fair value of the guarantee at August 30, 2007 was $16 million and was recorded as a liability of the Company in Other Long-Term Liabilities. The extension of the guarantee increased the fair value of the guarantee to $67 million, resulting in a $51 million charge to Interest and Other, net, for fiscal 2010. In April 2012, the term loan guarantee was terminated. As a result, the Company reversed its $67 million liability related to the guarantee, resulting in a $67 million pretax benefit to Interest and Other, net, for fiscal 2012.

Five-Year Summary of Financial and Operating Results
The Home Depot, Inc. and Subsidiaries

amounts in millions, except where noted	2012[1]	2011	2010	2009	2008
STATEMENT OF EARNINGS DATA[2]					
Net sales	**$ 74,754**	$ 70,395	$ 67,997	$ 66,176	$ 71,288
Net sales increase (decrease) (%)	**6.2**	3.5	2.8	(7.2)	(7.8)
Earnings before provision for income taxes	**7,221**	6,068	5,273	3,982	3,590
Net earnings	**4,535**	3,883	3,338	2,620	2,312
Net earnings increase (decrease) (%)	**16.8**	16.3	27.4	13.3	(45.1)
Diluted earnings per share ($)	**3.00**	2.47	2.01	1.55	1.37
Diluted earnings per share increase (decrease) (%)	**21.5**	22.9	29.7	13.1	(39.6)
Diluted weighted average number of common shares	**1,511**	1,570	1,658	1,692	1,686
Gross margin – % of sales	**34.6**	34.5	34.3	33.9	33.7
Total operating expenses – % of sales	**24.2**	25.0	25.7	26.6	27.5
Interest and other, net – % of sales	**0.7**	0.8	0.8	1.2	1.1
Earnings before provision for income taxes – % of sales	**9.7**	8.6	7.8	6.0	5.0
Net earnings – % of sales	**6.1**	5.5	4.9	4.0	3.2
BALANCE SHEET DATA AND FINANCIAL RATIOS[2]					
Total assets	**$ 41,084**	$ 40,518	$ 40,125	$ 40,877	$ 41,164
Working capital	**3,910**	5,144	3,357	3,537	2,209
Merchandise inventories	**10,710**	10,325	10,625	10,188	10,673
Net property and equipment	**24,069**	24,448	25,060	25,550	26,234
Long-term debt	**9,475**	10,758	8,707	8,662	9,667
Stockholders' equity	**17,777**	17,898	18,889	19,393	17,777
Book value per share ($)	**11.97**	11.64	11.64	11.42	10.48
Long-term debt-to-equity (%)	**53.3**	60.1	46.1	44.7	54.4
Total debt-to-equity (%)	**60.7**	60.3	51.6	49.9	64.3
Current ratio	**1.34:1**	1.55:1	1.33:1	1.34:1	1.20:1
Inventory turnover	**4.5x**	4.3x	4.1x	4.1x	4.0x
Return on invested capital (%)	**17.0**	14.9	12.8	10.7	9.5
STATEMENT OF CASH FLOWS DATA					
Depreciation and amortization	**$ 1,684**	$ 1,682	$ 1,718	$ 1,806	$ 1,902
Capital expenditures	**1,312**	1,221	1,096	966	1,847
Cash dividends per share ($)	**1.160**	1.040	0.945	0.900	0.900
STORE DATA					
Number of stores	**2,256**	2,252	2,248	2,244	2,274
Square footage at fiscal year-end	**235**	235	235	235	238
Increase (decrease) in square footage (%)	**—**	—	—	(1.3)	1.3
Average square footage per store (in thousands)	**104**	104	105	105	105
STORE SALES AND OTHER DATA					
Comparable store sales increase (decrease) (%)[3]	**4.6**	3.4	2.9	(6.6)	(8.7)
Weighted average weekly sales per operating store (in thousands)	**$ 627**	$ 601	$ 581	$ 563	$ 601
Weighted average sales per square foot ($)	**319**	299	289	279	298
Number of customer transactions	**1,364**	1,318	1,306	1,274	1,272
Average ticket ($)	**54.89**	53.28	51.93	51.76	55.61
Number of associates at fiscal year-end (in thousands)[2]	**340**	331	321	317	322

(1) Fiscal year 2012 includes 53 weeks; all other fiscal years reported include 52 weeks.
(2) Continuing operations only.
(3) Includes Net Sales at locations open greater than 12 months, including relocated and remodeled stores and excluding closed stores. Retail stores become comparable on the Monday following their 365th day of operation. Comparable store sales is intended only as supplemental information and is not a substitute for Net Sales or Net Earnings presented in accordance with generally accepted accounting principles. Net Sales for the 53rd week of fiscal 2012 are not included in comparable store sales results for fiscal 2012.

Appendix C

Recycling Problems

1-R Recycling Problem: Journalizing departmental purchases and cash payments
LO3, 4, 5, 6, 7, 8

Boardtown Station has two departments: Antiques and Trophies. Post the following transactions when journalized: (1) transactions impacting the accounts payable subsidiary ledger, (2) transactions recorded in the general journal, and (3) cash payments entered in a general amount column of the cash payments journal. Journals and partial general and accounts payable ledgers are given in the *Recycling Problems Working Papers*. Source documents are abbreviated as follows: check, C; debit memorandum, DM; purchase invoice, P.

Instructions:

1. Journalize the transactions completed during October of the current year. Use page 10 of a purchases journal, page 10 of a general journal, and page 16 of a cash payments journal. Post the items that are to be posted individually.
2. Prove and rule the purchases journal. Post the totals.
3. Prove and rule the cash payments journal. Post the totals.

Transactions:

Oct. 1. Wrote Check No. 810 to Davis Properties for rent, $2,450.00.
3. Gave John Platte a $324.60 check for making various repairs (miscellaneous expense). C811.
5. Purchased $2,514.62 of trophy parts from Paton Trophy Supply. P624.
9. Issued a check to Mountain Electric Department for last month's utility bill, $425.00. C812.
10. Returned defective trophy parts to Paton Trophy Supply, $68.50, from P624. DM51.
11. Wrote Check No. 813 to Paton Trophy Supply for the unpaid balance of purchase invoice 567, less items returned on debit memo 51, less 2% discount.
12. Purchased on account from Lampkin Supply various parts to restore antiques, $784.22. P625.
14. Purchased a printer toner cartridge from Davis Office Source, $65.25. C814.
16. Received a shipment of trophy parts on account from Ulman Import, $1,874.90, with 1/10, n/30 payment terms. P626.
21. Purchased an antique dining room set from Gail Mason, $930.00. C815.
22. Received a shipment of antiques from Abernathy Furniture, $4,258.80. P627.
24. Sent a check to Ulman Import for purchase invoice 626, less a 1% discount. C816.
28. Returned a $1,308.00 china cabinet purchased on October 22 to Abernathy Furniture. DM52.
29. Team Sports closed and sold its inventory at auction. Won the bid for trophy supplies, $275.00. C817.
31. Paid cash to replenish the petty cash fund for (1) an advertisement promoting soccer team trophies, $25.00; (2) snacks for office workers, $16.95 (miscellaneous expense); and (3) pens and memo pads, $18.26. C818.

Recycling Problem 1-R

Purchases Journal totals: $9,432.54; $5,043.02; $4,389.52.

General Journal: Two entries dated Aug. 10 and Aug. 28.

Cash Payments Journal totals: $4,530.06; $4,321.02; $18.75; $48.92; $8,783.41.

August 31 balance in Accounts Payable: $11,751.64.

2-R Recycling Problem: Journalizing departmental sales, sales returns and allowances, and cash receipts LO2, 3, 4, 5

The sales journal, cash receipts journal, general journal, and partial accounts receivable ledger and partial general ledger for K&D Flooring are provided in the *Recycling Problems Working Papers*. K&D Flooring has two departments: Carpet and Tile. The company offers credit terms of 2/10, n/30.

Instructions:

1. Journalize the transactions completed during August of the current year. Use page 8 of a sales journal, page 10 of a general journal, and page 12 of a cash receipts journal. The sales tax rate is 6%. Assume sales tax was paid on all cash and credit card sales. Use the transaction dates to determine the sales discounts. Post transactions impacting the accounts receivable subsidiary ledger and transactions in the general journal when journalized. Source documents are abbreviated as follows: credit memorandum, CM; receipt, R; sales invoice, S; terminal summary, TS.
2. Prove and rule the sales journal. Post the totals to the general ledger.
3. Prove and rule the cash receipts journal. Post the totals to the general ledger.

Transactions:

Aug. 2. Trevethan Construction purchased $2,489.00 of carpet on account, plus sales tax. S638.
3. Received a check from Delton Apartments for tile it purchased on July 5, $4,407.48. R711.
6. Received a partial payment of $1,500.00 from Trevethan Constructions for tile purchased on June 26. R712.
7. Sold tile on account to Carlson Properties, $3,128.00, plus sales tax. S639.
9. Recorded cash and credit card sales: carpet, $6,224.80; tile, $8,148.61; plus sales tax. TS34.
12. Granted credit to Carlson Properties for tile returned, $352.00, from S639. CM42.
15. Delivered $4,158.00 of carpet to LaFlore Medical, on account, plus sales tax. S640.
16. Carlson Properties sent a check in full payment of its August 7 purchase, less the tile returned on August 12. R713.
18. Cash and credit card sales for the past two weeks are carpet, $7,195.62; tile, $5,189.14; plus sales tax. TS35.
19. LaFlore Medical returned $295.00 of carpet purchased on August 15. CM43.
22. Completed a sale of tile on account to Delton Apartments, $1,950.00, plus sales tax. S641.
23. Received full payment from LaFlore Medical for carpet purchased on August 15, less the carpet returned on August 19. R714.
29. Received the remaining amount due on Trevethan Construction's August 1 outstanding balance. R715.

Recycling Problem 2-R

Sales Journal totals: $12,428.50; $703.50; $6,647.00; $5,078.00.

General Journal: Two return entries dated Aug. 12 and Aug. 19.

Cash Receipts Journal totals: $13,385.50; $1,605.49; $13,420.42; $13,337.75; $81.90; $147.00; $41,520.26.

August 31 balance in Accounts Receivable: $15,305.27.

3-R Recycling Problem: Completing payroll records, journalizing payment of a payroll, and journalizing payroll taxes LO2, 3, 4, 5

Boardroom Designs installs electronic presentation and sound systems. The company is organized based on the two categories of customers it serves: Commercial and Education. A partial payroll register for the pay period ended July 8, 20--, a blank earnings record form, page 10 of a cash payments journal, and page 7 of a general journal are provided in the *Recycling Problems Working Papers*. Use the appropriate withholding tax tables shown in Chapter 3 to determine the federal income tax. Deductions for all employees are 2% of total earnings for state income tax, 6.2% for social security tax, and 1.45% for Medicare tax.

Instructions:

1. Prepare a commissions record for Cheryl T. Turner (employee number 11), Commercial Department manager, for June of the current year. Ms. Turner's biweekly salary of $1,200.00 is assigned to the Commercial Department. She also receives a monthly commission of 15% of net sales to commercial customers and 10% of net sales to education customers. Commissions for the previous month are paid in the first pay period of the current month. Accounting records for the month ended June 30 of the current year are as follows:

	Commercial	Education
Sales on account	$7,154.05	—
Cash and credit card sales	245.15	$215.68
Sales discounts	113.04	24.85
Sales returns and allowances	62.58	84.19

2. Prepare the payroll register entries for the following two employees:
   a. On line 5: Cheryl T. Turner, Commercial Department manager, single, one allowance, regular salary $1,000.00 per pay period. Use the commission calculated in part 1. Her medical insurance premium is $60.00 and retirement plan contribution is $150.00.
   b. On line 6: Rick C. Wray, employee number 12, educational installation specialist, married, and three allowances. He worked 84 hours during the pay period, with 4 of those hours being overtime hours. Mr. Wray earns $20.00 per hour. His health insurance premium is $100.00 and retirement plan contribution is $75.00.
3. Complete the payroll register by totaling each amount column.
4. Prepare Ms. Turner's earnings record for the first pay period of the quarter ended June 30, 20--. Accumulated earnings for the quarter ended June 30, 20--, are $24,895.90.
5. Calculate departmental payroll taxes for the pay period ended July 8. No employees have earned more than the social security tax base. Unemployment taxes are due on the following earnings for this period: Commercial, $1,520.00, and Education, $1,720.00.
6. Journalize the following transactions for June of the current year.

Transactions:

July	9.	Paid the July 8 payroll. Check No. 762.
	9.	Recorded employer's payroll taxes for the pay period ended July 8. Memorandum No. 51.
	15.	Made a deposit using the EFTPS for employee and employer payroll taxes for the June pay periods: employee federal income tax withholding, $1,342.00; social security tax, $2,358.94; and Medicare tax, $551.68. Memorandum No. 53.
	29.	Paid state unemployment tax for the quarter ended June 30, $432.85. (No payment of federal unemployment tax is required for the most recent quarter.) Check No. 779.

Recycling Problem 3-R

Cheryl T. Turner commissions: Commercial, $1,083.54; Education, $10.66.

Payroll Register totals: Overtime, $207.00; Commission, $1,957.30; Commercial, $4,958.75; Education, $3,446.55.

Departmental Total Payroll Taxes: Commercial, $473.59; Education, $370.30; Administrative, $90.50.

July 9 Cash Payments Journal: Cash Credit, $6,700.03.

4-R Recycling Problem: Completing end-of-period work for a departmentalized merchandising business LO2, 3, 4, 6, 7, 8, 9

L&K Exteriors is a merchandising business that specializes in doors and windows. The company uses a calendar fiscal year. An adjusted trial balance as of December 31, general journals, selected general ledger accounts, and statement paper are provided in the *Recycling Problems Working Papers*. Round percentage calculations to the nearest 0.1%. The adjustment information for December 31 follows.

Estimate of uncollectible accounts	$ 3,150.00
Ending merchandise inventory—doors	134,180.00
Ending merchandise inventory—windows	103,140.00
Supplies on hand	650.00
Value of prepaid insurance	800.00
Depreciation expense—office equipment	5,500.00
Depreciation expense—store equipment	6,200.00

Instructions:

1. Record the adjusting entries on page 20 of a general journal.
2. Post the adjusting entries to the general ledger accounts.
3. Enter the adjusted general account balances on the adjusted trial balance.
4. Calculate federal income tax expense using the tax table presented in the chapter. Prepare and post the adjusting entry for federal income tax expense.
5. Complete the adjusted trial balance.
6. Prepare a departmental margin statement for each department. Calculate vertical analysis ratios for cost of merchandise sold, gross profit, total direct expenses, and departmental margin.
7. Prepare the income statement, statement of stockholders' equity, and balance sheet. There were 78,000 shares of $1.00 par value stock issued as of January 1. There were 2,000 shares issued during the current year. Calculate and record the vertical analysis ratios for each amount in the fourth column of the income statement and third column of the balance sheet.
8. Use the following information to complete the statement of cash flows. L&K Exteriors began the fiscal year with a cash balance of $4,558.29.

Cash received from:	
Issuance of stock	$ 2,000.00
Sale of equipment	4,620.00
Sales to customers	650,102.03
Cash payments for:	
Dividends	$ 20,000.00
Income taxes	21,152.25
Insurance	7,800.00
Inventory purchases	271,252.81
Other operating expenses	45,484.35
Purchase of equipment	29,530.00
Rent	16,800.00
Salaries and wages	220,043.63

9. Journalize the closing entries. Use page 21 of a general journal.

Recycling Problem 4-R

Net Income: $70,625.04, 10.8%.

Total Stockholders' Equity, $268,366.97.

Total Assets, $302,867.77.

Net cash provided by operating activities, $67,568.99.

Closing entry to close Income Summary to Retained Earnings: debit Income Summary—General, credit Retained Earnings, $70,625.04.

5-R Recycling Problem: Costing and financial analysis of merchandise inventory

LO3, 4, 5, 6

On December 31 of the current year, Hinshaw, Inc., took a physical inventory. Units in the December 31 inventory and the market prices are shown below.

Stock Item	Quantity of Units on Hand	Market Price
AC-23	37	$52.25
XT-67	107	8.85
HP-435	26	12.30

Instructions:

1. Calculate the inventory costs using the FIFO, LIFO, and weighted-average inventory costing methods. Use the form in the *Recycling Problems Working Papers*.
2. Hinshaw uses the LIFO inventory costing method to determine the cost of inventory. In the form, use the ending inventory quantities and the market prices given at the beginning of the problem to determine the cost of each inventory item using the lower of cost or market. Total the Lower of Cost or Market column. Use the form in the *Recycling Problems Working Papers*.
3. Calculate the corporation's estimated ending inventory using the gross profit method of estimating inventory. The corporation's records show the following on December 31 of the current year.

Item	Cost	Retail
Beginning inventory, January 1	$ 72,160.00	$139,250.00
Net purchases for year	195,150.00	376,180.00
Net sales for year	—	406,840.00
Gross profit percentage	48.2%	

4. Calculate the corporation's estimated ending inventory using the retail method of estimating inventory. Round the percentage to the nearest 0.1%.
5. Use the information and the estimated inventory calculated using the gross profit method. Calculate the corporation's inventory turnover ratio. Round the ratio to two decimal places.
6. Calculate the corporation's days' sales in inventory. Round the amount to the nearest day.

Recycling Problem 5-R

Stock item AC-23, cost of ending inventory: FIFO, $1,930.80; LIFO, $1,877.35; weighted-average, $1,916.60.

Estimated ending inventory: gross profit method, $56,566.88; retail method, $56,358.21.

Inventory turnover ratio, 3.27.

6-R Recycling Problem: Journalizing entries for uncollectible accounts—allowance method; calculating and journalizing the adjusting entry for uncollectible accounts expense LO2, 3, 4, 5

Townsend, Inc., uses the allowance method of recording uncollectible accounts expense. The following information was obtained from Townsend's records for the current year:

	January 1	December 31
Accounts receivable	$72,184.68	$ 79,118.47
Allowance for doubtful accounts	4,918.25	6,047.49
Net sales on account	—	944,807.15

A general journal and cash receipts journal are provided in the *Recycling Problems Working Papers.*

Instructions:

1. Journalize the selected transactions that were completed during the current year. Use page 1 of a general journal and page 1 of a cash receipts journal. Source documents are abbreviated as follows: memorandum, M; receipt, R.
2. Journalize the adjusting entry for uncollectible accounts expense on December 31 of the current year. Townsend estimates that the amount of uncollectible accounts expense is equal to 1.5% of its net sales of $1,018,844.00.
3. Compute the accounts receivable turnover and days' sales in accounts receivable.

Transactions:

Feb. 15. Received a letter from Alford Company stating that the company was closing effective February 14 and would be unable to pay its account. The Alford account has a balance of $3,482.00. M233.

Mar. 6. Received a $3,514.50 check from Dudley Corp. The account was written off as uncollectible in the prior fiscal period. M249 and R678.

May 30. A collection letter to Hughes, Inc., was returned and marked "unable to deliver." Write off the company's $2,266.00 account as uncollectible. M298.

July 22. Received an e-mail from an employee of Phyfer Supply stating that $85.00 of merchandise was damaged during shipment. Since Phyfer has never claimed damaged merchandise in the past, Townsend's collection manager approved writing off the amount. M305.

Oct. 29. Received a $1,000.00 check from Alford Company's law firm. The attached letter states that a lawsuit against Alford's owners provided adequate funds to make partial payments on outstanding debts of the company. M344 and R821.

Recycling Problem 6-R

Accounts credited on general journal, Accounts Receivable: Feb. 15, May 30, July 22.

Uncollectible Accounts Expense, $15,283.26.

Accounts Receivable Turnover Ratio, 13.5.

7-R Recycling Problem: Recording entries for plant assets LO1, 2, 3, 4, 7

Betterson, Inc., uses the straight-line method of calculating depreciation expense. The plant asset records, depreciation schedules, and journals for Betterson are given in the *Recycling Problems Working Papers*.

Instructions:

1. Journalize the transactions for 20X3 and 20X6. Journalize an entry for additional depreciation expense if needed. Use page 4 of a general journal, page 8 of a cash receipts journal, and page 5 of a cash payments journal. Source documents are abbreviated as follows: check, C; memorandum, M; receipt, R.
2. Make needed notations on plant asset records 166 and 412.
3. Prepare double declining-balance and MACRS depreciation schedules for a $3,600.00 copy machine purchased on January 4 of the current year. (Refer to the MACRS table in the chapter.) The machine has an estimated salvage value of $600.00 and a useful life of seven years. Round the double declining-balance depreciation rate to two decimal places.
4. Betterson has elected to begin using IFRS to depreciate plant assets. On September 22, 20X7, Betterson purchased a warehouse for $480,000.00, paying $50,000.00 down and signing a note with the seller for the remainder. The warehouse is structurally sound but requires significant repairs to the roof. The warehouse has an appraised value of $500,000.00, of which 10% is attributed to the land, 60% to the structure, 10% to the electrical systems, 15% to the roof, and 5% to the parking lot. Determine the cost assigned to each item.

Transactions:

June 29, 20X3.	Paid cash, $2,400.00, and traded in an old office desk, plant asset no. 166, for a new desk; serial no. 53-B256-235, plant asset no. 412. The new desk has been assigned a five-year useful life and has an estimated salvage value of $1,000.00. M116 and C345.
Oct. 6, 20X6.	Sold an office desk, plant asset no. 412, to an employee for $1,200.00. M401 and R877.
Nov. 9, 20X6.	Purchased a warehouse from Ulmann Industries. The $420,000.00 purchase price includes the warehouse building and five acres of land. The building and land together were appraised for $450,000.00, with $405,000.00 assigned to the building. Betterson paid $100,000.00 down and financed the remainder, signing a note with First National Bank. C915.

Recycling Problem 7-R

Oct. 6 loss on plant assets, $692.50.

Office desk, plant asset no. 412: 20X3 depreciation, $255.00.

Copy machine, year 2 annual depreciation: double declining-balance, $734.67; MACRS, $881.64.

Warehouse assigned costs: land, $48,000.00; structure, $288,000.00.

8-R Recycling Problem: Journalizing notes payable transactions and adjusting and reversing entries LO1, 2, 4, 5

Tiffin, Inc., completed the following transactions during the current year. Tiffin initially records supplies and insurance as expenses, records advertising as a prepaid expense, and maintains a liability account for estimated warranty expenses. Source documents are abbreviated as follows: check, C; memorandum, M; receipt, R.

Instructions:

1. Journalize the following transactions in a cash receipts journal.

Transactions:

July	20.	Agreed to a 180-day, 6% note with Bank of Commerce for $30,000.00. R332.
Aug.	12.	Received $20,000.00 from First National Bank, signing a 150-day, 7% note. R362.
Nov.	15.	Signed an $18,000.00, 90-day, 7% note with First Commerce Bank. R411.
Dec.	4.	Drew $4,500.00 from its First National Bank line of credit. The bank deposited the funds directly to its checking account. R498.

2. Use the following information to journalize adjusting entries for prepaid expenses and accrued expenses on December 31 of the current year. Include the adjusting entry for the accrued interest on the outstanding notes payable listed above.

Supplies inventory	$ 695.00
Value of prepaid insurance	5,000.00
Advertising used	24,000.00
Additional federal income tax	3,750.00

3. Journalize the appropriate reversing entries on January 1 of the next year.
4. Calculate the maturity date for each note payable and the total amount of interest due at the maturity date.
5. Journalize the following transactions on a cash payments journal. For the payment of each note payable, use the maturity dates calculated in the prior step.

Transactions:

Jan.		Paid the maturity value of the First National Bank note, plus interest. C641.
	14.	Wrote a check to Vance Company for a repair performed on a Tiffin item under warranty, $125.90. C649.
		Paid the maturity value of the Bank of Commerce note, plus interest. C658.
	31.	Paid $2,000.00 plus $136.75 interest on its line of credit. C664.
		Wrote Check No. 672 to pay off the First Commerce Bank note, plus interest.

Recycling Problem 8-R

Cash payments journal, Interest Expense debits: Jan. 9, $575.34; Jan. 16, $887.67; Feb. 13, $310.68.

Adjusting entries credits: Supplies Expense, $695.00; Insurance Expense, $5,000.00; Prepaid Advertising, $24,000.00; Interest Payable, $1,508.38; Federal Income Tax Payable, $3,750.00.

9-R Recycling Problem: Journalizing unearned revenue, accrued revenue, and gift card and installment note receivable transactions LO1, 2, 3, 4, 6, 7

Acker Supply completed the following transactions during December of the current year. Acker records unearned items initially as revenue. The company uses the accounts Gift Cards Outstanding and Breakage Revenue to account for gift card transactions. The sales tax rate is 6.0%. A cash receipts journal, general journals, and amortization schedules for installment notes are provided in the *Recycling Problems Working Papers*.

Instructions:

1. Journalize the following transactions on page 15 of a cash receipts journal and page 14 of a general journal.

Transactions:

Dec. 16. Sold $2,600.00 of merchandise to Marc Latham, receiving a $356.00 down payment and accepting a $2,400.00, 36-month, 9% installment note receivable for the balance. NR144.
18. Received cash for the sale of gift cards, $7,750.00. R664.
19. Customers redeemed gift cards for the sale of merchandise, $842.60, plus sales taxes. M103.
20. Received cash for Bobbie Tabb's December payment on her installment note, $121.00. R669.
28. Received cash for the sale of gift cards, $495.00. R675.
29. Received cash for Shawn Nick's December payment on his installment note, $195.57. R681.
30. Customers redeemed gift cards for the sale of merchandise, $4,820.40, plus sales taxes. M106.
31. Sold $3,680.00 of merchandise to Rocky Holman, receiving a $900.80 down payment and accepting a 36-month, 10% installment note receivable for the $3,000.00 balance. NR145.

2. Use the following information to record adjusting entries on December 31 of the current year. Use page 15 of a general journal.
   a. On November 1, Acker Supply received $3,000.00 from Donald James for special display space within the store. The payment represents a $1,000.00 monthly fee for November, December, and January. Acker Supply initially records this type of revenue as rental revenue.
   b. Acker Supply periodically loans money to employees. The company has two notes outstanding to employees on December 31.

Note No.	Interest Rate	Term	Principal	Date
E12	6.0%	180 days	$24,000.00	September 13
E16	6.5%	90 days	$16,000.00	October 16

   c. Acker Supply estimates that $3,200.00 of gift cards will never be redeemed.

3. On December 31, Acker Supply has $148,948.25 of installment notes receivable outstanding. Of that amount, $46,184.50 is expected to be collected during the next fiscal period. Record the reclassification entry using page 16 of a general journal.
4. Journalize any adjusting or reclassification entries that should be reversed. Use page 17 of a general journal.

Recycling Problem 9-R

Dec. 19 debit: Gift Cards Outstanding, $893.16.

Dec. 28 credit: Gift Cards Outstanding, $495.00.

Dec. 29 credit: Notes Receivable, $149.28; Interest Income, $46.29.

Adjusting entries credits: Unearned Rent, $1,000.00; Interest Income, $646.58; Breakage Revenue, $3,200.00.

Reclassification entry debit: Current Portion of Notes Receivable, $46,184.50.

Reversing entries credits: Rent Income, $1,000.00; Interest Receivable, $646.58; Current Portion of Notes Receivable, $46,184.50.

Recycling Problem 10-R

Credit to Paid-In Capital in Excess of Par Value—Preferred: Mar. 18, $400.00.

Credit to Paid-In Capital in Excess of Par Value—Common: Mar. 25, $4,500.00.

10-R Recycling Problem: Journalizing stock transactions LO4, 5

Steven Maynard and Kerry Petty are starting a business and have elected to organize the business as a corporation. The new corporation received its charter on January 4 of the current year. The corporation is authorized to issue 300,000 shares of $1.00 par-value common stock and 200,000 shares of 4%, $100.00 par-value preferred stock.

Instructions:

Journalize the following transactions. Page 1 of a general journal and page 1 of a cash receipts journal are provided in the *Recycling Problems Working Papers*. Source documents are abbreviated as follows: memorandum, M; receipt, R.

Transactions:

Jan. 6. Received cash from Steven Maynard for 30,000 shares of common stock at par value. R1.
7. Received cash from Kerry Petty for 25,000 shares of common stock at par value. R2.
12. Received cash from Lambert Financial for 500 shares of preferred stock at par value. R3.
Feb. 4. Received equipment from Steven Maynard at an agreed-upon value of $42,600.00 in exchange for 40,000 shares of common stock. M8.
Mar. 18. Received cash from Equity Investors for 200 shares of preferred stock at $102.00 per share. R33.
25. Received cash from Kerry Perry for 15,000 shares of common stock at $1.30 per share. R42.

11-R Recycling Problem: Journalizing dividend, treasury stock, and investment transactions LO1, 2, 3, 4, 5

Pitado Corporation has 50,000 shares of $1.00 par-value common stock and 900 shares of 6%, $50.00 par-value preferred stock outstanding.

Instructions:

Journalize each transaction completed during the current year. Page 7 of a general journal, page 8 of a cash receipts journal, and page 9 of a cash payments journal are provided in the *Recycling Problems Working Papers*. Source documents are abbreviated as follows: check, C; memorandum, M; receipt, R.

Transactions:

July	1.	The board of directors declared a quarterly cash dividend of $4,000.00, payable on July 21. M42.
	19.	Purchased 400 shares of Rush Corporation for $26.00 per share. C260.
	21.	Paid the July 1 dividend. C266.
Aug.	9.	The board of directors declared a 2% stock dividend on common stock. An independent appraisal service has estimated that the common stock has a market value of $9.50 on August 9. M58.
	18.	Paid cash to Anita Ratliff for 2,500 shares of the corporation's common stock at $9.85 per share. C289.
	31.	Issued the August 9 stock dividend. M63.
Sept.	3.	Received a $0.27 per share cash dividend from Rush Corporation. R239.
	5.	Received cash from Claudine Ray for 2,000 shares of treasury stock at $10.00 per share. R241.
	12.	Sold all of its shares of Rush Corporation for $27.30 per share. R249.

Recycling Problem 11-R

General journal debits: July 1, Dividends—Common, $3,325.00; Aug. 9, Stock Dividends, $9,500.00.

General journal credits: July 1, Dividends Payable, $4,000.00; Aug. 9, Stock Dividends Distributable, $1,000.00.

Cash receipts journal credits: Sept. 3, Dividend Revenue, $108.00; Sept. 5, Paid-In Capital from Sale of Treasury Stock, $300.00; Sept. 12, Gain on Sale of Investments, $520.00.

Recycling Problem 12-R

Cash receipts journal: June 1, Discount on Bonds Payable, debit $4,422.27.

Cash payments journal debits: Apr. 27, Interest Expense, $15,765.88; May 1, Loss on Redemption of Bonds, $15,980.83.

Cash payments journal credit: July 1, Discount on Bonds Payable, $606.71.

12-R Recycling Problem: Journalizing bond transactions LO2, 3, 4, 5, 6

TA Post Corporation has the following bonds outstanding as of January 1:

- 8%, 10-year, $1,000 face-value bonds, $400,000.00, issued at a 7.8% effective interest rate, callable at 105%.
- 7%, 10-year, $5,000 face-value bonds, $600,000.00, issued at a 7.3% effective interest rate.

The corporation accrued interest income and interest expense when preparing its December 31 financial statements. These accruals were reversed at the start of the current fiscal year.

Instructions:

Journalize each transaction completed during the current year. Page 3 of a cash receipts journal and page 4 of a cash payments journal are provided in the *Recycling Problems Working Papers*. Source documents are abbreviated as follows: check, C; receipt, R.

Transactions:

Apr. 1. Purchased ten of Ray Corporation's 6.75% $5,000.00 face-value bonds at $4,982.07 each, resulting in a yield of 6.80%. C663.

27. Paid cash to trustee for the semiannual interest payment on the $400,000.00 bond issue, which has a carrying value of $404,253.29. C689.

May 1. Paid cash to trustee to call the $400,000.00 bond issue. C715.

June 1. Received cash for 300 ten-year, 6.0%, $1,000.00 face-value bonds, issued to yield 6.2%, $295,577.73. R258.

July 1. Paid cash to trustee for the semiannual interest payment on the $600,000.00 bond issue, which has a carrying value of $591,964.60. C734.

Oct. 1. Received the semiannual interest payment on its Ray Corporation bonds. R332.

1. Sold its investment in Ray Corporation bonds for $4,924.15 per bond. R333.

13-R Recycling Problem: Analyzing financial statements LO1, 2, 3, 4, 5

Information taken from Quest Corporation's financial statements is provided in the *Recycling Problems Working Papers*.

Instructions:

Calculate the following ratios and measures for the current year and the prior year. Round percentage calculations to the nearest 0.1%, dollar amounts to the nearest $0.01, and ratios to the nearest tenth. Use the results to determine whether the trend between the prior year and the current year appears to be favorable, unfavorable, or neutral. Give reasons for your responses.

1. Working capital
2. Current ratio
3. Quick ratio
4. Debt ratio
5. Equity ratio
6. Common equity per share
7. Interest coverage ratio
8. Gross margin
9. Operating margin
10. Rate earned on average total assets
11. Rate earned on average stockholders' equity
12. Free cash flow
13. Accounts receivable turnover ratio
14. Days' sales in accounts receivable
15. Inventory turnover ratio
16. Days' sales in inventory
17. Earnings per share
18. Price-earnings ratio
19. Dividend yield

Recycling Problem 13-R

1. Working capital, prior year, $571,260.00
4. Debt ratio, current year, 44.7%
7. EBIT, current year, $107,860.00
10. Average assets, prior year, $914,380.00
16. Days' sales in inventory, prior year, 107
17. Earnings per share, current year, $10.45

Recycling Problem 14-R

1. Net income is a source of cash.

2e. An increase in Merchandise Inventory is a use of cash.

An increase in Accounts Payable is a source of cash.

3d. An increase in Equipment is a use of cash.

4d. A decrease in Mortgage Payable is a use of cash.

6. Cash provided by operating activities, $130,660.00.

8. Cash balance, end of period, $139,760.00.

14-R Recycling Problem: Preparing a statement of cash flows LO1, 2, 3

Use the abbreviated comparative financial statements for New Brighton Corporation in the *Recycling Problems Working Papers*.

Instructions:

1. Review the comparative income statement and identify the amounts of net income (or net loss) and depreciation expense for the 20X2 period. Indicate if each item represents a source of cash or a use of cash.
2. Analyze the comparative balance sheet and complete the following steps:
   a. Prepare a list of noncash current assets and current liabilities.
   b. Write the balances for 20X2 and 20X1.
   c. Classify each account as a current asset or a current liability.
   d. Write the amount of increase or decrease from 20X1.
   e. Indicate if the increase or decrease represents a source of cash or a use of cash.
3. Analyze the comparative balance sheet and complete the following steps:
   a. Prepare a list of long-term assets.
   b. Write the balances for 20X2 and 20X1.
   c. Write the amount of increase or decrease from 20X1.
   d. Indicate if the increase or decrease represents a source of cash or a use of cash.
4. Reexamine the comparative balance sheet and complete the following steps:
   a. Prepare a list of long-term liabilities.
   b. Write the balances for 20X2 and 20X1.
   c. Write the amount of increase or decrease from 20X1.
   d. Indicate if the increase or decrease represents a source of cash or a use of cash.
5. Review the comparative statement of stockholders' equity and (1) identify the amounts of any additional stock issued or cash dividends paid and (2) indicate if each item represents a source of cash or a use of cash.
6. Prepare the operating, investing, and financing activities sections of the 20X2 statement of cash flows, using the indirect method.
7. Enter the cash balance at the beginning of the year as shown on the comparative balance sheet.
8. Compute the cash balance for the end of the period to complete the statement of cash flows.
9. Verify the accuracy of the statement of cash flows by comparing the statement's ending cash balance with the cash balance listed for 20X2 on New Brighton's comparative balance sheet.
10. Calculate the following ratios:
    a. Operating cash flow ratio
    b. Cash flow margin ratio
11. Assume that for 20X1, New Brighton Corporation's operating cash flow ratio was 0.28 and its cash flow margin ratio was 0.05. Compare the two-year trend for each calculation and write a short summary of each trend.

15-R Recycling Problem: Preparing a budgeted income statement and a cash budget with supporting budget schedules LO1, 2, 3, 4, 5, 6, 7, 8, 9

On December 31, 20X2, the accounting records of XYZ Corporation show the following unit sales for 20X2.

1st quarter	41,200 units	3rd quarter	45,800 units
2nd quarter	43,000 units	4th quarter	70,000 units

The following are additional actual amounts for the 4th quarter of 20X2.

Sales (70,000 units @ $5.20)	$364,000
Purchases (58,800 units @ $2.80)	$164,640
Ending inventory	24,700 units

Management has established a unit sales goal of 240,000 units for 20X3 and 50,000 units for the first quarter of 20X4. The sales manager, after reviewing price trends and checking with the company's merchandise suppliers, projects that the unit cost of merchandise will stay at the 20X2 price, $2.80 per unit, through 20X3. Because of stable costs, the company will be able to keep its unit sales price at $5.20 through 20X3.

After considering the time required to reorder merchandise, the sales manager requests that 50.0% of each quarter's unit sales be available in the prior quarter's ending inventory.

Expenses are projected as shown below. Except where noted, percentages are based on quarterly projected net sales. For these items, calculate each quarter's amount by multiplying the percentage times that quarter's net sales. Calculate the annual total by adding the four quarterly amounts. When a dollar amount is given, the total amount should be divided equally among the four quarters.

Interest expense for each quarter is projected to be $900.00.

Federal income taxes are calculated using the tax rate table shown in this chapter. Equal quarterly income tax payments are based on the projected annual federal income tax expense.

Additional information is as follows:

a. The balance of cash on hand on January 1, 20X3, is $45,080.00.

b. In each quarter, cash sales are 20.0% and collections of accounts receivable are 25.0% of the projected net sales for the current quarter. Collections from the preceding quarter's net sales are 54.5% of that quarter. Uncollectible accounts expense is 0.5% of net sales.

Selling Expenses		Administrative Expenses	
Advertising Expense	1.2%	Depreciation Expense—Office Equipment	$2,880
Delivery Expense	0.7%	Insurance Expense	$7,280
Depreciation Expense—Delivery Equipment	$8,400	Miscellaneous Expense—Administrative	$4,800
Depreciation Expense—Store Equipment	$3,600	Payroll Taxes Expense	12.0% of salaries
Miscellaneous Expense—Sales	0.2%	Rent Expense	$13,280
Salary Expense—Sales	5.4%	Salary Expense—Administrative	$52,000
Supplies Expense—Sales	0.8%	Supplies Expense—Administrative	$3,600
		Uncollectible Accounts Expense	0.5%
		Utilities Expense	1.5%

c. In each quarter, cash payments for cash purchases are 10.0% and for accounts payable 50.0% of the purchases for the current quarter. Cash payments for purchases of the preceding quarter are 40.0% of that quarter.

d. In the first quarter, $24,000 will be borrowed on a promissory note and equipment costing $35,000 will be purchased for cash. In each quarter, dividends of $30,000 will be paid in cash. In the fourth quarter, the promissory note plus interest will be paid in cash, $25,920.

Instructions:

Prepare the following budget schedules for the year ended December 31, 20X3. Round percentage amounts to the nearest 0.1%, unit amounts to the nearest 100 units, and dollar amounts to the nearest $10.

1. Prepare a sales budget schedule (Schedule 1).
2. Prepare a purchases budget schedule (Schedule 2).
3. Prepare a selling expenses budget schedule (Schedule 3).
4. Prepare an administrative expenses budget schedule (Schedule 4).
5. Prepare an other revenue and expenses budget schedule (Schedule 5).
6. Prepare a budgeted income statement.
7. Prepare a cash receipts budget schedule (Schedule A).
8. Prepare a cash payments budget schedule (Schedule B).
9. Prepare a cash budget.

Recycling Problem 15-R

Projected unit sales, 20X3 3rd quarter, 55,000.

Net Sales, 4th quarter, $436,800.

Ending inventory, 2nd quarter, 27,500.

Purchases, 1st quarter, 50,500.

Total selling expenses, annual budget, $115,580.

Total administrative expenses, 4th quarter, $34,080.

Interest expense, annual budget, $3,600.

Net income before federal income tax, annual budget, $333,720.

Net income after federal income tax, 4th quarter, $99,020.

Total cash receipts, 1st quarter, $337,980.

Total payments from purchases, 2nd quarter, $146.100.

Total cash payments 3rd quarter, $286,480.

Ending cash balance, 4th quarter, $95,610.

16-R Recycling Problem: Calculating breakeven and the sales required for a desired income LO2, 3, 4, 5, 6

A blank income statement for North Country Kayaks is included in the *Recycling Problems Working Papers*.

Instructions:

1. Use the following information to prepare North Country Kayaks' income statement reporting contribution margin.

Net Sales (units)	180
Sales Price (per unit)	$375.00
Cost of Merchandise Sold (per unit)	$230.00
Selling Expenses:	
Sales Commission (per unit)	$12.50
Delivery Cost (per unit)	$7.50
Other Variable Selling Expenses (per unit)	$9.10
Other Fixed Selling Expenses	$3,225.00
Administrative Expense:	
Rent Expense	$600.00
Insurance Expense	$225.00
Other Variable Administrative Expenses (per unit)	$3.40
Other Fixed Administrative Expenses	$7,950.00

2. Calculate the contribution margin per unit.
3. Use the income statement to calculate the breakeven point in sales dollars and in unit sales for May. (Round to the next whole number of units.)
4. Assume that North Country Kayaks wants a net income of $12,000.00 for June. Calculate the amount of sales dollars and unit sales needed to achieve this net income. (Round to the next whole number of units.)

Recycling Problem 16-R

1. Contribution margin, $20,250.00.
2. Contribution margin per unit, $112.50.
3. Breakeven point in sales dollars, $40,000.00.
4. Breakeven point in sales dollars, $80,000.00.

17-R Recycling Problem: Preparing cost records and journalizing entries that summarize cost records at the end of a fiscal period LO2, 3, 4, 5, 6, 7, 8

Hammond Corporation manufactures televisions. The company records manufacturing costs by job number and uses a factory overhead applied rate to charge overhead costs to its products.

Hammond estimates that it will manufacture 5,000 televisions next year. For this amount of production, total factory overhead is estimated to be $396,000.00. Estimated direct labor costs for next year are $440,000.00.

The following information is taken from the records of Hammond on November 30 of the current year.

a. The total factory payroll for the month according to the payroll register is $308,000.00, distributed as follows.

Work in Process	$229,040.00	Employee Income Tax Payable	$33,880.00
Factory Overhead	78,960.00	Social Security Tax Payable	19,096.00
Cash	250,558.00	Medicare Tax Payable	4,466.00

b. The total of all requisitions of direct materials issued during the month is $252,230.00. The total of all requisitions of indirect materials issued during the month is $20,170.00.

c. Manufacturing expense accounts and their balances for the month are as follows:

Depreciation Expense—Factory Equipment	$5,770.24	Miscellaneous Expense—Factory	$13,780.48
Depreciation Expense—Building	2,822.40	Payroll Taxes Expense—Factory	43,736.00
Heat, Light and Power Expense	9,055.20	Property Tax Expense—Factory	6,088.32
Insurance Expense—Factory	1,505.28	Supplies Expense—Factory	18,063.36

d. The total of all cost sheets completed during the month is $628,880.00.

e. The total of costs recorded on all sales invoices for the month is $654,052.00.

Instructions:

1. Calculate Hammond's factory overhead applied rate for next year as a percentage of direct labor cost.
2. On November 3, Hammond began work on Job No. 317. The order is for 30 No. C32 televisions for stock; date wanted is November 13. Open a cost sheet for Job No. 317 and record the following items.

Transactions:

Nov. 3. Direct materials, $1,984.00. Materials Requisition No. 551.
3. Direct labor, $240.00. Daily summary of job-time records.
4. Direct labor, $360.00. Daily summary of job-time records.
5. Direct materials, $682.00. Materials Requisition No. 557.
5. Direct labor, $272.00. Daily summary of job-time records.
6. Direct labor, $252.00. Daily summary of job-time records.
7. Direct labor, $420.00. Daily summary of job-time records.
10. Direct materials, $514.00. Materials Requisition No. 565.
10. Direct labor, $396.00. Daily summary of job-time records.
11. Direct labor, $372.00. Daily summary of job-time records.
12. Direct labor, $328.00. Daily summary of job-time records.

3. Complete the cost sheet, recording factory overhead at the rate calculated in part (1).
4. Prepare a finished goods ledger card for Stock No. C32 televisions. Minimum quantity is set at 10. Inventory location is Sec. R.
5. Record on the finished goods ledger card the beginning balance on November 1. The November 1 balance of C32 televisions is 20 units at a unit cost of $267.00. Hammond uses the first-in, first-out method to record inventory costs.
6. Record the following transactions on the finished goods ledger card for C32 televisions.

Transactions:

Nov. 5. Sold 8 C32 televisions. Sales Invoice No. 446.
12. Received 30 C32 televisions. Record cost from cost sheet for Job No. 317.
18. Sold 20 C32 televisions. Sales Invoice No. 465.

7. Journalize the factory payroll entry on page 10 of a cash payments journal. C725.
8. Journalize the following entries on page 5 of a general journal.
   a. An entry to transfer the total of all direct materials requisitions to Work in Process and indirect materials to Factory Overhead. M323.
   b. An entry to close all individual manufacturing expense accounts to Factory Overhead. M324.
   c. An entry to record applied factory overhead to Work in Process. M325.
9. Continue using page 5 of the general journal. Journalize the entry to close the balance of the Factory Overhead account to Income Summary. M326.
10. Journalize the entry to transfer the total of all cost sheets completed from Work in Process to Finished Goods. M327.
11. Journalize the entry to transfer the cost of products sold from Finished Goods to Cost of Goods Sold. M328.

Recycling Problem 17-R

1. Factory overhead applied rate, 90%.
3. Factory overhead, $2,376.00.
   Total cost, $8,196.00.
6. Balance on November 18: 22 units at $273.20.
7. Debit Cash, $250,558.00.

8a. Credit Materials, $272,400.00.

8b. Debit Factory Overhead, $100,821.28.

8c. Credit Factory Overhead, $206,136.00.

9. Credit Income Summary, $6,184.72.
10. Debit Finished Goods, $628,880.00.
11. Credit Finished Goods, $654,052.00.

Recycling Problem 18-R

Total cost to make, $667,000.00.

18-R Recycling Problem: Calculations for a make or buy decision LO1

McCure Company is considering making a component part that it has been buying for $640,000.00 from an outside supplier. No new machinery will need to be purchased, and McCure has idle machines that have no other use. Costs to make the part include direct materials, $225,000.00; direct labor, $300,000.00; and variable overhead, $82,000.00. In addition, total fixed overhead costs for this part are $60,000.00. Variable overhead is directly related to making the part and will not exist if McCure continues to buy it. Fixed overhead includes $20,000.00 of costs that are directly related to buying the part. The remaining fixed costs are allocated to each product made by McCure. If McCure continues to buy the part, these costs will remain and will be allocated to other products.

Instructions:

Forms are provided in the *Recycling Problems Working Papers*. Should McCure make the part or continue buying it?

19-R Recycling Problem: Calculating cost-based pricing and target costs LO8, 9

Light Master Company makes a variety of lighting products. The costs and markups for several of its products are given in the *Recycling Problems Working Papers.*

Instructions:

1. For each item, calculate the following:
   a. Dollar amount of markup
   b. Selling price
   c. Profit margin (round to the nearest 0.1%)
2. Light Master is in the process of designing a ceiling light. It believes that the selling price cannot exceed $80.00, and it requires a profit of 70% per unit. What is the target cost for the ceiling light?

Recycling Problem 19-R

1a. Dollar markup, floor lamp, $28.50.

1c. Profit margin, track lighting, 47.4%.

2. Target cost, $24.00.

Recycling Problem 20-R

Control symbol 1, risk assessment: There is no evidence that the accounting assistant verifies the accuracy of the vendor invoice. The company may pay for items not ordered or received. The quantity and unit prices on the invoice may be different from those on the purchase order and receiving report.

Control symbol 2, internal control: The unpaid invoices should be filed in chronological order by the expected payment date. Requiring the cashier to look through all the invoices increases the chance of missing a payment and losing any purchases discount.

Voucher register, Vouchers Payable Credit column total, $6,264.00.

Check register, Vouchers Payable Debit column total, $9,048.00.

20-R Recycling Problem: Analyzing a voucher system and journalizing transactions in a voucher system LO4, 5, 6, 7

A portion of Lester Company's voucher processing system is described in the following narrative.

Jamal Burke, the accounting assistant, opens the mail and records all vendor invoices in the voucher register. He stamps each invoice and writes the voucher number, account number, and target payment date in the spaces provided. He then files the invoices in an Unpaid Invoices folder by the vendor's name.

Every day, Donna Ervin, the cashier, removes the invoices to be paid that day from the Unpaid Invoices folder. She prepares a check for each invoice and records the checks in a cash payments journal. The check is forwarded to the owner, John Lester, for signing. He returns the signed checks to Donna Ervin to be mailed to the vendors. She attaches the check copy to the invoice and files the invoice by vendor in the Paid Invoices file.

Instructions:

1. Prepare a flowchart of Lester Company's voucher system.
2. Identify five risks in the system. Complete the Risk Assessment and Internal Control columns of the form provided in the *Recycling Problems Working Papers*. Use the control symbols on the form to mark the flowchart location of the risks.
3. Journalize the following transactions completed during July of the current year. Use page 7 of a voucher register and page 8 of a check register provided in the *Recycling Problems Working Papers*.

Transactions:

July 6. Paid cash to Marshall Company, $3,159.00, covering V583, less 2% discount. C622.
8. Received an invoice from Roark Consulting for computer services, $4,200.00. V591.
12. Purchased merchandise on account from Dash Manufacturing, $1,689.00. V592.
14. Made a deposit in the checking account, $6,990.58.
16. Paid cash to Roark Consulting, $4,200.00, less 1% discount, covering V591. C623.
22. Bought sales supplies on account from Sanders Company, $375.00. V593.
30. Paid cash to Dash Manufacturing, $1,689.00, no discount, covering V592. C624.

4. Prove and rule the voucher register.
5. Prove and rule the check register.

21-R Recycling Problem: Forming and expanding a partnership LO2, 3

On March 1 of the current year, Donald Kleban and Luke Rice form a partnership. The partners share equally in all changes in equity. The partnership assumes the assets and liabilities of Luke's existing business. Donald invests cash equal to Luke's investment. A general journal and cash receipts journal are given in the *Recycling Problems Working Papers*. The March 1 fair market value balance sheet for Luke's existing business is as follows.

Vintage Auto Parts
Fair Market Value Balance Sheet
May 1, 20--

ASSETS			
Current Assets:			
Cash		$16,483.05	
Accounts Receivable	$13,684.05		
Less Allowance for Uncollectible Accounts	750.00	12,934.05	
Inventory		55,184.15	
Supplies		2,180.00	
Total Current Assets			$ 86,781.25
Plant Assets:			
Equipment			35,000.00
Total Assets			$121,781.25
LIABILITIES			
Accounts Payable			$ 16,481.25
OWNER'S EQUITY			
Luke Rice, Capital			105,300.00
Total Liabilities and Owner's Equity			$121,781.25

Instructions:

Journalize the following transactions. Source documents are abbreviated as follows: memorandum, M; receipt, R.

Transactions:

Mar. 1. Received cash from partner, Donald Kleban, as an initial investment, $105,300.00. R1.
1. Accepted assets and liabilities of Luke Rice's existing business as an initial investment, $105,300.00. R2.
June 16. Received cash from a new partner, Sid Parvin, for a one-third equity in the business, $99,000.00. Each of the existing partners has equity of $99,000.00. Existing equity is redistributed evenly among the existing partners. R124.
July 22. Journalized the personal sale of one-fourth equity in the partnership to a new partner, Kenji Maye. Each partner agreed to sell an equal share of his equity. Mr. Maye paid $25,800.00 directly to each of the existing partners. M33.
Aug. 30. Received cash from new partner, Vance Turner, for a one-fifth equity in the business, $85,000.00. Each of the existing partners has equity of $88,200.00. Changes in equity are redistributed evenly among the existing partners. R160 and M45.
Dec. 13. Received cash from new partner, Freddie Nowell, for a one-sixth equity in the business, $98,000.00. Each of the existing partners has equity of $90,000.00. Changes in equity are redistributed evenly among the existing partners. R201 and M69.

Recycling Problem 21-R

General journal transactions:

July 22, debit original partners' capital, $25,800.00 each.

Aug. 30, debit existing partners' capital, $640.00 each.

Dec. 13, debit Goodwill, $40,000.00; credit partners' capital, $8,000.00 each.

Cash receipts journal debits: Aug. 30, Vance Turner, Capital, $85,000.00; Dec. 13, Freddie Nowell, Capital, $98,000.00.

Recycling Problem 22-R

Share of Net Income: Pharr, \$35,988.16; Rogers, \$26,311.84.

Dec. 31 capital balances: Pharr, \$26,868.16; Rogers, \$32,161.84.

General journal debits: Income Summary, \$62,300.00; Shellie Pharr, Capital, \$33,600.00; Geneva Rogers, Capital, \$22,800.00.

22-R Recycling Problem: Completing end-of-period work for a partnership LO1, 3

Shellie Pharr and Geneva Rogers are partners in Pheva Interiors. On January 1 of the current year, the partners' equities were Shellie, \$24,480.00, and Geneva, \$28,650.00. The net income for the year is \$62,300.00. Statement paper and a general journal are provided in the *Recycling Problems Working Papers*.

Instructions:

1. Calculate the distribution of net income to the partners. Each partner is to receive 8% interest on January 1 equity. Also, partners' salaries are Shellie, \$28,000.00, and Geneva, \$20,000.00. The remaining net income, net loss, or distribution deficit is shared 60% to Shellie and 40% to Geneva.
2. Prepare an owners' equity statement. During the year, Shellie withdrew cash of \$33,600.00 and Geneva withdrew cash of \$22,800.00.
3. Journalize the entries to close Income Summary and the owners' equity accounts.

23-R Recycling Problem: Journalizing governmental transactions LO3, 4, 5

The town of Lanceburg uses a general fund for all financial transactions. Expenditures are recorded by type of expenditure and by department. The four categories of expenditures are personnel, supplies, other charges, and capital outlays. Departments are General Government, Public Safety, Fire Protection, and Recreation.

Instructions:

Journalize the following transactions for the current year.

Transactions:

Use page 1 of a journal.

Jan. 2. Recorded current year's approved operating budget: estimated revenues, $3,205,000.00; appropriations, $3,160,000.00; budgetary fund balance, $45,000.00. M1.

2. Recorded current year's property tax levy: taxes receivable—current, $3,243,000.00; allowance for uncollectible taxes—current, $38,000.00; property tax revenue, $3,205,000.00. M2.

8. Paid cash for supplies in the General Government Department, $3,598.00. C24.

22. Issued a 60-day, 6% note, $600,000.00. NP1.

24. Received cash for current taxes receivable, $548,000.00. R33.

Feb. 3. Encumbered estimated amount for supplies in the Recreation Department, $6,228.00. M18.

5. Received cash from traffic fines, $4,158.00. R61.

11. Paid cash for fire truck parts, $11,605.00. C84.

16. Encumbered estimated amount for equipment purchases by the Recreation Department, $3,309.00. M28.

21. Paid cash for Recreation Department supplies, $6,228.00, encumbered February 3 per M18. M30 and C100.

Mar. 1. Recorded reclassification of current taxes receivable to delinquent status, $184,300.00, and the accompanying allowance for uncollectible accounts, $32,600.00. M35.

Use page 2 of a journal.

Mar. 6. Paid cash for the maturity value of NP1: principal, $600,000.00, plus interest. The bank uses a 360-day year when calculating interest. C115.

8. Paid cash for Recreation Department equipment, $3,309.00, encumbered February 16 per M28. M40 and C120.

9. Received cash for delinquent taxes receivable, $39,800.00. R109.

14. Paid cash for a 60-day, 2.5% certificate of deposit, $75,000.00. C155.

19. Paid cash for supplies for the Public Safety Department, $1,115.00. C168.

May 13. Received cash for the maturity value of certificate of deposit due today: principal, $75,000.00, plus interest. The bank uses a 360-day year when calculating interest. R130.

Recycling Problem 23-R

March 1 column totals: General Debit, $6,702,096.00; General Credit, $7,832,823.00; Cash Debit, $1,152,158.00; Cash Credit, $21,431.00.

May 13 column totals: General Debit, $688,733.00; General Credit, $118,421.50; Cash Debit, $115,112.50; Cash Credit, $685,424.00.

C-23

Recycling Problem 24-R

Credit adjustments: Reserve for Inventory of Supplies, $3,650.00; Allowance for Uncollectible Interest, $1,278.00; Interest Revenue, $2,982.00; Reserve for Encumbrances—Prior Year, $6,950.00.

Increase in Unreserved Fund Balance for Year: Budget, $86,000.00; Actual, $50,932.00; Variance, ($35,068.00).

Total Assets, $110,894.00; Unreserved Fund Balance, $82,312.00; Total Fund Balance, $92,912.00.

Post-Closing Trial Balance, column totals, $123,572.00.

24-R Recycling Problem: Completing the end-of-period work for a governmental organization LO1, 2, 3

The city of Glennville uses a general fund. An operating budget for the current year, an adjusted trial balance, a journal, and forms are provided in the *Recycling Problems Working Papers*. The following adjustment information is available.

Adjustment Information, December 31	
Supplies inventory	$3,650.00
Interest revenue due but not collected	4,260.00

An estimated 30% of the interest revenue due will not be collected. The reserve for encumbrances for the current year has a credit balance of $6,950.00.

Instructions:

1. Analyze the adjustment information and record adjusting entries on journal page 30.
2. Prepare a statement of revenues, expenditures, and changes in fund balance—budget and actual for the year ended December 31 of the current year.
3. Prepare a balance sheet for December 31 of the current year.
4. Journalize the closing entries on journal page 31.
5. Prepare a post-closing trial balance.

Appendix D

Answers to Audit Your Understanding

Chapter 1, Lesson 1-1, page 6

1. Assets = Liabilities + Owners' Equity.
2. An asset account has a normal debit balance; a revenue account has a normal credit balance.
3. (a) A separate numeric listing is provided for each ledger division. (b) A predesigned arrangement of numbers is provided within each ledger division. (c) Account number digits are spaced to allow the addition of new accounts.

Chapter 1, Lesson 1-2, page 13

1. Purchases—Grills is debited; Accounts Payable is credited.
2. Accounts Payable is debited; Purchases Returns and Allowances—Furniture is credited.

Chapter 1, Lesson 1-3, page 20

1. Accounts Payable is debited; Cash and Purchases Discount—Furniture are credited.
2. In the General Debit and Credit columns of the cash payments journal.
3. To ensure that all expenses are recorded during the fiscal period in which they occurred.

Chapter 2, Lesson 2-1, page 38

1. Information such as departmental gross profit from operations can help business managers decide if each department is earning an appropriate profit.
2. A tax-exempt customer is not required to pay sales tax. Examples include federal, state, and local government agencies; not-for-profit educational institutions; and certain religious and charitable organizations.
3. An invoice.
4. Sales are recorded at the time of sale, regardless of when payment is received.
5. A credit memorandum is issued by a vendor to show the amount deducted from the customer's account for returns and allowances.

Chapter 2, Lesson 2-2, page 47

1. To encourage early payment.
2. A 2% sales discount may be deducted if sales on account are paid within 10 days of the invoice date. All sales on account must be paid within 30 days of the invoice date.
3. None. A sales discount only reduces the amount due from the customer.
4. Both cash sales and credit card sales result in an immediate increase in the bank account balance.
5. Individual amounts in the Accounts Receivable Credit column are posted in individual customer accounts on the same date that the transaction is recorded in the cash receipts journal. This procedure keeps the customer accounts up to date. The total of the Accounts Receivable column is posted to the controlling account in the general ledger at the end of the period.

Chapter 3, Lesson 3-1, page 64

1. Federal income tax, social security tax, and Medicare tax.
2. By consulting withholding tax tables provided by the Internal Revenue Service.
3. Total Earnings − Total Deductions = Net Pay.
4. Total earnings for the pay period.

Chapter 3, Lesson 3-2, page 76

1. Cash.
2. a. Employer social security tax.
   b. Employer Medicare tax.
   c. Federal unemployment tax.
   d. State unemployment tax.
3. Using the Electronic Federal Tax Payment System (EFTPS).

Chapter 4, Lesson 4-1, page 96

1. Schedule of accounts receivable and schedule of accounts payable.
2. To bring certain general ledger accounts up to date.

3. Subtract the total of the income statement accounts having a debit balance, except for Federal Income Tax Expense, from the total of the income statement accounts having a credit balance. Include any debit or credit balances of income summary accounts.

Chapter 4, Lesson 4-2, page 108

1. a. Each manager is assigned responsibility for those revenues, costs, and expenses for which the manager can make decisions and affect the outcome.
   b. The revenues, costs, and expenses must be readily identifiable with the manager's unit.
2. Revenue, cost of merchandise sold, and direct expenses.
3. By dividing the amount on each line by the amount of departmental net sales.

Chapter 4, Lesson 4-3, page 112

1. Account titles and balances are obtained from the adjusted trial balance.
2. Totals are obtained from the departmental margin statements.
3. The totals of capital stock and retained earnings are obtained from the statement of stockholders' equity.

Chapter 4, Lesson 4-4, page 117

1. To update general ledger accounts at the end of a fiscal year.
2. a. Income statement accounts having credit balances.
   b. Income statement accounts having debit balances.
   c. The Income Summary account.
   d. The Dividends account.
3. To prove the equality of the debits and credits in the general ledger after all closing entries have been posted.
4. Asset, liability, and owners' equity accounts.

Chapter 5, Lesson 5-1, page 144

1. a. Cost of the beginning merchandise inventory.
   b. Cost of the net purchases added to the inventory during the fiscal year.
2. Understated.
3. a. By physically counting the items.
   b. By keeping a continuous record showing the number purchased and sold for each item.

Chapter 5, Lesson 5-2, page 151

1. The last-in, first-out (LIFO) method.
2. The first-in, first-out (FIFO) method.
3. To qualify to use the LIFO method for tax reporting, a business must also use LIFO for its preparation of financial statements using GAAP. Since IFRS do not allow LIFO for preparing financial statements, a business may be unable to use LIFO for its tax reporting.
4. The LIFO method.
5. a. The cost of the inventory using the FIFO, LIFO, or weighted-average method.
   b. The current market price of the inventory.

Chapter 5, Lesson 5-3, page 159

1. That a continuing relationship exists between gross profit and net sales.
2. Separate records of both cost and retail prices for net purchases, net sales, and the beginning merchandise inventory.
3. An inventory ratio of 5.0 means the business sold its average merchandise inventory 5 times during the current year.
4. On average, each item in merchandise inventory is sold 60 days after it is purchased.

Chapter 6, Lesson 6-1, page 174

1. When a customer's account is believed to be uncollectible, it should be written off because it is no longer an asset of the business.
2. Uncollectible Accounts Expense is debited; Accounts Receivable is credited. The customer's account in the accounts receivable ledger is also credited.
3. The account is reopened to provide a complete history of the customer's credit activities.

Chapter 6, Lesson 6-2, page 178

1. a. Percentage of sales method.
   b. Percentage of accounts receivable method.
2. Net sales times the percentage expected to be uncollectible equals the estimated uncollectible accounts expense.
3. a. Compute an estimate for each age group by multiplying the amount of each group by the percentage estimate.
   b. Compute the total of the uncollectible estimates for all age groups.
   c. Subtract the current credit balance or add the current debit balance to the balance of Allowance for Uncollectible Accounts to determine the addition to the account.
4. The direct write-off method can be used when the difference between the accounts receivable reported on the balance sheet, using the two methods, is immaterial.

Chapter 6, Lesson 6-3, page 186

1. Net sales on account divided by average book value of accounts receivable equals accounts receivable turnover ratio.
2. Customers are taking about 60 days to pay their accounts. The business needs to encourage prompter payment in order to reduce the number of days to receive payment to 30 days.

D-2

3. Business can be lost as some customers may buy from competitors with less restrictive credit terms.

Chapter 7, Lesson 7-1, page 198

1. All costs necessary to get the plant asset ready for its intended use are included in the cost of a plant asset.
2. The cost is allocated to individual plant assets based on their appraised values.
3. Components of the plant asset having different useful lives are assigned a cost and recorded in different plant asset accounts.
4. a. General information completed when the asset is purchased.
   b. Disposal section completed when the asset is discarded, sold, or traded.
   c. Section to record annual depreciation expense.
5. The assessed value of the property is multiplied by the millage rate of the governmental unit.

Chapter 7, Lesson 7-2, page 205

1. Matching Expenses with Revenue.
2. Because of its permanent nature, depreciation is not recorded for land.
3. Original cost, estimated salvage value, and estimated useful life.
4. The cost of the elevator should be added to the historical cost of the building. The addition adds to the value of the building.
5. A calendar month.

Chapter 7, Lesson 7-3, page 211

1. The date, type, and amount of disposal.
2. Depreciation Expense will be debited and Accumulated Depreciation will be credited to bring the accounts up to date before the disposal.
3. Cash received minus the book value of the asset sold.
4. Cash plus the book value of the store equipment traded equals the book value of the new store equipment.

Chapter 7, Lesson 7-4, page 218

1. Declining-balance and MACRS.
2. The amount of use the asset receives, measured in hours, units, weight, or volume.
3. The five-year property class includes cars, general-purpose trucks, computers, manufacturing equipment, and office machinery. The seven-year property class includes office furniture and fixtures.
4. Tons of material mined times the depletion rate equals annual depletion expense. The depletion rate is calculated by dividing the estimated total value of the mineral resource by the estimated number of tons of the mineral to be recovered.

Chapter 8, Lesson 8-1, page 236

1. Reporting interest expense as Other Expense enables the comparison of operating income between companies in the same industry.
2. Interest on a line of credit is typically calculated daily because the principal amount and interest range can change during a month.
3. 7.2 % [Interest: $9,800.00 – $9,629.05 = $170.95; implied interest rate: $170.95 ÷ $9,629.05 ÷ (90 ÷ 365) = 7.2%].

Chapter 8, Lesson 8-2, page 242

1. Matching Expenses with Revenue.
2. To record the amount of supplies used during the period as an expense.
3. If an adjusting entry creates a balance in an asset or liability account, the adjusting entry is reversed.
4. The balance of the prepaid expense and related expense accounts should be the same, regardless of the procedure used.
5. Similarities:
   - The ending balances in the asset and related expense accounts are identical.
   - The closing entries are identical.

   Differences:
   - The amounts of the adjusting entries are different.
   - The debit and credit accounts of the adjusting entries are reversed.
   - Only the procedure that initially debits prepaid expenses to an expense account requires a reversing entry.

Chapter 8, Lesson 8-3, page 248

1. a. Determine the amounts of the accrual.
   b. Record the expense accounts.
   c. Record the liability accounts.
2. Accountants generally reverse an adjusting entry that creates a balance in a liability account.
3. In the fiscal period in which the item is sold.
4. Similarities: With each sale on account, there is a chance that the business will incur warranty costs and that the customer will not pay its account. An estimate of these expenses is recorded in the same fiscal period as the sale.
   Differences: Allowance for Uncollectible Accounts has a related asset account and is reported on the balance sheet as a contra asset account. Accrued Warranty Payable does not have a related asset and is reported as a liability on the balance sheet.

Chapter 9, Lesson 9-1, page 264

1. Deferred revenue.
2. As a current liability.
3. If an adjusting entry creates a balance in an asset or liability account, the adjusting entry is normally reversed.
4. In the Other Revenue section.

Chapter 9, Lesson 9-2, page 270

1. Virtual gift cards, unlike plastic gift cards, enable the retailer to collect the name and contact information of the cardholder and track the unused card balance.
2. The Credit CARD Act does not allow the retailer to charge fees on unredeemed cards for 12 months. Unredeemed cards cannot be canceled until five years after the date of issuance.
3. A sale is recorded when a customer pays for merchandise using a gift card.
4. Other Revenue.
5. The notes to the financial statements include the policies for how and when breakage revenue is recognized, the amount of unredeemed cards, and how gift-card-related accounts are presented on the financial statements.

Chapter 9, Lesson 9-3, page 274

1. At the time of sale.
2. Beginning balance, interest, principal, and ending balance.
3. The monthly payment does not change, the interest decreases, and the principal increases.
4. The total principal payments expected to be collected during the next fiscal period.

Chapter 10, Lesson 10-1, page 294

1. A board of directors determines corporate policies and selects corporate officers to supervise the day-to-day management of the corporation.
2. Common and preferred.
3. a. To vote at stockholders' meetings, unless an exception is made for holders of a particular kind of stock.
   b. To share in a corporation's earnings.
   c. To share in the distribution of the assets of the corporation if it ceases operations and sells all its assets.
4. A single summary general ledger capital account is used for each kind of stock issued.
5. The earnings of a corporation may be subject to federal and state income taxes. When the earnings of the corporation are distributed to the stockholders, individual stockholders may also have to pay income taxes on the dividends.
6. The earnings of an LLC are divided among its members. The earnings are only taxed on the members' personal tax returns.

Chapter 10, Lesson 10-2, page 303

1. By selling stock to investors or borrowing money.
2. No. Only publicly held corporations are required to file their financial statements with the Securities and Exchange Commission.
3. By issuing preferred stock that does not offer voting rights.
4. An investor willing to accept a dividend rate lower than that offered by the preferred stock will pay more than the par value. An investor demanding a dividend rate higher than that offered by the preferred stock will pay less than the par value.
5. The conversion option enables the corporation to issue the stock with a lower dividend rate. Convertible preferred stock gives the stockholder the ability to share in the income of the corporation through an increase in the market price of the common stock.
6. Stockholders should convert their stock if they believe the market price of the common stock will increase by more than 6% per year, less the effect of any dividends paid on common stock.

Chapter 11, Lesson 11-1, page 318

1. The board of directors.
2. When a board of directors declares a dividend, the corporation is obligated to pay it.
3. No transaction is recorded on the date of record.
4. Ex-dividend.
5. Credit.
6. a. The stockholders do not receive anything of value. The transaction increases the number of shares outstanding. Each stockholder retains his or her share of the corporation.
   b. The stock dividend transfers amounts among equity accounts. The market price per share of the stock will decline.

Chapter 11, Lesson 11-2, page 325

1. Debit.
2. A corporation believes that its stock is undervalued by the stock market.
3. The net income of the corporation is divided among fewer shares.
4. Dividends are not paid on treasury stock.

Chapter 11, Lesson 11-3, page 330

1. To earn a return on its cash assets until the cash is required for reinvesting in the business, paying a dividend, or reducing liabilities.

2. As a Current Asset.
3. As an Other Revenue account.
4. As an Other Revenue account.

Chapter 12, Lesson 12-1, page 342

1. a. Additional capital becomes part of a corporation's permanent capital.
   b. Dividends do not have to be paid to stockholders unless the earnings are sufficient.
2. Stockholders' equity is not spread over additional shares of stock.
3. Interest must be paid on the loan, which decreases the net income, and the loan principal must be repaid.
4. Principal, maturity value, and par value.
5. a. The stated interest rate is often a rounded percentage.
   b. Market interest rates change daily.

Chapter 12, Lesson 12-2, page 346

1. Carrying Value × Effective Interest Rate × Time as Fraction of a Year.
2. The effective interest rate has no impact on the amount of semiannual interest payments.
3. The amount of interest expense increases.
4. The carrying value decreases.

Chapter 12, Lesson 12-3, page 350

1. Term bonds mature on the same date, while serial bonds are portions of a bond issue that mature on different dates.
2. If market interest rates fall, the corporation can be relieved of the burden of paying higher-than-market interest rates.
3. $5,000.00/25 = $200.00.
4. GAAP, $600,000.00; IFRS, $585,000.00.

Chapter 12, Lesson 12-4, page 355

1. Mutual funds and pension plans.
2. Unlike the issuing corporation, the institutional investor does not record the discount or premium in a separate account.
3. Carrying value of the bonds multiplied by the effective interest rate, multiplied by time as a fraction of a year.
4. The total face value of the bonds.
5. As Other Revenue or Other Expense.

Chapter 13, Lesson 13-1, page 368

1. Working capital, current ratio, and quick ratio.
2. To ensure that a reasonable balance between stockholders' capital and borrowed capital is maintained.
3. Total liabilities divided by total assets equals the debt ratio.

Chapter 13, Lesson 13-2, page 378

1. Income from operations divided by net sales.
2. How well a business is using its assets to earn net income.
3. How much net income the stockholders' investment is earning.

Chapter 13, Lesson 13-3, page 385

1. The amount of net income earned on one share of common stock during a fiscal period.
2. Market price per share divided by earnings per share.
3. Dividend yield will increase.

Chapter 13, Lesson 13-4, page 391

1. Generally accepted accounting principles (GAAP).
2. Tax laws developed by Congress.
3. Permanent differences and temporary differences.
4. All changes in equity for the period except changes caused by owner investments and owner distributions.

Chapter 14, Lesson 14-1, page 402

1. The actual cash outflow occurred in a prior fiscal period when the asset was bought.
2. A company did not replace all the supplies it used during the year. Therefore, cash was saved by not spending it on replacement supplies.
3. A company bought more merchandise inventory than it sold. Therefore, more cash was used to buy inventory than was shown on the income statement for cost of merchandise sold. The company has more cash tied up in inventory than it did at the end of the previous period.
4. Net income (net loss).

Chapter 14, Lesson 14-2, page 411

1. By analyzing the changes in long-term assets (plant assets) on the comparative balance sheet.
2. The increase in accumulated depreciation matches the depreciation expense that was recorded on the income statement. The effect on cash flows due to depreciation expense was already accounted for under operating activities.
3. By examining the changes in long-term liabilities on the balance sheet and reviewing the statement of stockholders' equity.
4. If the cash balance, end of period, shown on the statement of cash flows equals the current year's cash balance reported on the comparative balance sheet.

Chapter 15, Lesson 15-1, page 432

1. Identifying company goals.
2. Budgeted income statement and cash budget.
3. One year.
4. They help establish targets to work toward in the coming year and help coordinate the efforts of all areas toward a common direction.

Chapter 15, Lesson 15-2, page 439

1. Past records, company plans, sales and selling expenses budgets, and discussions with other managers.
2. Interest income, interest expense, and gains or losses on the sale of plant assets.
3. Management must adjust the supporting budgets by either increasing revenue or decreasing expenses.

Chapter 15, Lesson 15-3, page 447

1. Good cash management requires the planning and controlling of cash so that cash will be available to meet obligations when due.
2. Quarterly cash sales, quarterly collections on account from customers, and cash to be received quarterly from other sources.
3. Quarterly cash payments for accounts payable or notes payable; each selling, administrative, and other expense item; equipment purchases; cash dividends; and investments.
4. The reasons for the decrease should be determined and action should be taken to correct the problem.

Chapter 15, Lesson 15-4, page 452

1. It helps managers identify areas that need to be reviewed, allows managers to make changes that will correct negative effects on net income for the year, and provides the opportunity to revise the budget if necessary.
2. A performance report compares actual amounts with projected amounts for the same period. A comparative income statement compares actual amounts of one period with actual amounts of a prior period.
3. Learning and growth, internal business, customer service, and financial.
4. Determine how the outcomes will be measured, set target goals, and develop an initiative to help ensure that the objectives are met.

Chapter 16, Lesson 16-1, page 468

1. The line would be sloping because the total variable costs will increase as the number of units increase.
2. Gross profit is determined by subtracting only the cost of merchandise sold from net sales. Contribution margin is determined by subtracting all variable costs from net sales.

Chapter 16, Lesson 16-2, page 474

1. In sales dollars and unit sales.
2. A net income for the company.
3. A net loss for the company.
4. By using the contribution margin per unit.
5. Prepare an income statement using the breakeven point numbers. If the breakeven point is accurate, net income will be zero.

Chapter 16, Lesson 16-3, page 479

1. They intersect.
2. Total variable costs will increase.
3. Total fixed costs will remain the same.
4. Total fixed costs plus planned net income.

Chapter 17, Lesson 17-1, page 495

1. a. Direct materials.
   b. Direct labor.
   c. Factory overhead.
2. Work in process.
3. To keep a record of all charges for direct materials, direct labor, and factory overhead for each specific job.
4. To authorize transfer of items from the storeroom to the factory.

Chapter 17, Lesson 17-2, page 507

1. Overapplied overhead.
2. Applied factory overhead is only an estimate used to assign factory overhead to jobs. The amount of actual factory overhead is determined at the end of the period. It consists of the actual costs for indirect labor, indirect materials, and other factory expenses.

Chapter 17, Lesson 17-3, page 512

1. Overapplied overhead is subtracted from the cost of goods sold.
2. Current Assets.

Chapter 17, Lesson 17-4, page 519

1. Total Materials Variance = Actual Cost – Standard Cost.
2. Favorable.
3. Answers will vary. Some examples: Spending less on materials may require more labor hours in rework, and spending more on materials may allow the use of less experienced workers.

Chapter 18, Lesson 18-1, page 534

1. A relevant cost must be a future cost, and it must differ between alternatives.
2. As a relevant cost.

3. If the special order will affect sales for the product and if normal customers will be upset by the discounted price of the special order.
4. Sell the product at the split-off point.

Chapter 18, Lesson 18-2, page 540

1. Compounding interest causes the annual interest earned to increase each year.
2. The present value factor is determined by finding the intersection of the interest rate in the columns and the number of years in the rows in a present value table.
3. When the problem is to determine the present value of an amount to be received in the future.

Chapter 18, Lesson 18-3, page 548

1. Net present value takes into account the time value of money.
2. Present value of an annuity of $1.
3. Present value of $1.
4. The option with the higher positive (or lower negative) net present value.

Chapter 19, Lesson 19-1, page 560

1. When a single process with a continuous flow of inputs produces the same product.
2. The actual units processed and the equivalent units of production.
3. Debit Work in Process—Shipping; credit Work in Process—Processing.

Chapter 19, Lesson 19-2, page 567

1. Unit-level, batch-level, product-level, and facility-sustaining level.
2. Number of orders shipped, weight of shipment, number of products in the shipment that need special packaging, distance order is shipped, and number of cartons in the shipment.
3. Activity-based costing requires initial cost and effort to implement, and it does not conform to GAAP.

Chapter 19, Lesson 19-3, page 574

1. Cost-based pricing focuses on company costs instead of the customer; it may lead to prices that are too high or too low; it provides no incentive to contain costs; and if the cost of the product changes and the price is not changed, the profit margin will change.
2. When products or services have emotional value, are in high demand/low supply, will increase efficiency or improve health, and there is little or no competition for a product or service that is necessary.
3. Target cost equals desired selling price per unit minus required profit per unit.

Chapter 20, Lesson 20-1, page 592

1. Intent. An error is unintentional, whereas a fraud is intentional.
2. Financial statement misstatement.
3. Control environment.
4. Public Company Accounting Oversight Board (PCAOB).
5. Gain an understanding of the system.

Chapter 20, Lesson 20-2, page 597

1. A written description or narrative.
2. Upper left corner of the page.
3. The transfer of information or the movement of a document.
4. If the added cost of the control is offset by the benefit of reducing the risk of fraud.

Chapter 20, Lesson 20-3, page 601

1. Vouchers Payable.
2. Purchases journal.
3. Vouchers Payable.

Chapter 20, Lesson 20-4, page 608

1. Authorized managers.
2. The check is sent to the vendor.
3. The purchase order copy sent to the Receiving Department does not contain the quantity of goods ordered.
4. The documents are cancelled by the check signer.

Chapter 21, Lesson 21-1, page 623

1. To avoid misunderstandings. Some states require that partnership agreements be in writing.
2. The existing partnership is terminated.
3. The right of all partners to contract for a partnership.
4. A balance sheet may not report adequately the value of the owner's contribution to the partnership. Assets such as inventory and plant assets should be valued at their current market value.

Chapter 21, Lesson 21-2, page 630

1. The existing partnership is terminated.
2. Total equity (including the investment by the new partner) multiplied by the new partner's share of equity equals the new partner's equity.
3. Goodwill is debited; the existing partners' capital accounts are credited.

Chapter 22, Lesson 22-1, page 646

1. In the partnership agreement.
2. When the amount of guaranteed distributions exceeds the amount of net income available for distribution.
3. The partner's drawing account.
4. Withdrawals are debited to a drawing account.

Chapter 22, Lesson 22-2, page 653

1. Because a partnership does not pay federal income tax.
2. The statement reports the changes in each partner's equity.
3. Partners are personally taxed on their share of partnership net income. In contrast, withdrawals are considered the withdrawals of partnership equity and are not subject to income taxes.
4. Each partner personally pays both the employee and employer portion of social security and Medicare taxes on his or her share of partnership net income.

Chapter 22, Lesson 22-3, page 658

1. Noncash assets are sold, and available cash is used to pay the creditors.
2. The partners' capital accounts.

Chapter 23, Lesson 23-1, page 672

1. A governmental organization must use a subjective evaluation of the quality of the service provided. Its ability to continue operations is not dependent on its effectiveness or efficiency as long as funding is available.
2. a. The accounting equation is applied.
   b. An appropriate chart of accounts is prepared.
   c. Transactions are analyzed into debit and credit elements.
   d. Transactions are journalized and posted to ledgers.
   e. Financial statements are prepared for each fiscal period.
   f. Most of the same accounting concepts are applied.
3. A fund is a governmental accounting entity with a set of accounts in which assets always equal liabilities plus equities.
4. The governmental operating budget is used to authorize and provide the basis for control of financial operations during a fiscal year.
5. Estimated Revenues is debited; Appropriations and Budgetary Fund Balance are credited.

Chapter 23, Lesson 23-2, page 683

1. When property taxes are levied.
2. Cash is debited; Taxes Receivable—Current is credited.
3. Cash is debited; Taxes Receivable—Delinquent is credited.

Chapter 23, Lesson 23-3, page 687

1. A commitment to pay for goods or services that have been ordered but not yet provided.
2. a. The encumbrance entry is reversed to remove the estimated amount from the encumbrance and the reserve for encumbrance accounts.
   b. The expenditure is recorded.
3. Because the organization does not earn a net income, it has no need for expense information. Expenditures rather than expenses are recorded. The primary objective is to control financial resources rather than determine net income.
4. A certificate of deposit (or CD) is a document with the maturity date and interest to be paid by a bank and is issued as evidence of money invested with the bank.

Chapter 24, Lesson 24-1, page 702

1. A business measures performance primarily through determining the amount of net income. A not-for-profit organization's performance is measured primarily by the services provided and the efficiency with which resources are used.
2. Encumbrance accounts with zero balances.
3. None. A governmental fund has expenditures rather than expenses.
4. Interest Revenue.

Chapter 24, Lesson 24-2, page 707

1. The prior year's balance sheet.
2. Excess of expenditures over revenues.
3. Unfavorable.
4. Unreserved Fund Balance.
5. Reserve for Encumbrances—Prior Year and Taxes Receivable—Delinquent.
6. Whether the government organization obtains most of its revenue from fees charged to individuals and businesses using its services.

Glossary

A

Account A record that summarizes all the transactions pertaining to a single item in the accounting equation. (p. 9)

Accounting cycle The series of accounting activities included in recording financial information for a fiscal period. (p. 121)

Accounting equation An equation showing the relationship among assets, liabilities, and owners' equity. (p. 7)

Accounts receivable turnover ratio The number of times the average amount of accounts receivable is collected during a specified period. (p. 186)

Accrued expenses Expenses incurred in one fiscal period, but not paid until a later fiscal period. (p. 248)

Accrued revenue Revenue earned in one fiscal period but not received until a later fiscal period. (p. 267)

Activity rate The price for each unit of activity, determined by Manufacturing. (p. 569)

Activity-based costing (ABC) Allocating factory overhead based on the level of major activities. (p. 567)

Adjusted trial balance A trial balance prepared after adjusting entries are posted. (p. 103)

Adjusting entries Journal entries recorded to update general ledger accounts at the end of a fiscal period. (p. 98)

Administrative expenses budget A statement that shows the projected expenses for all operating expenses not directly related to selling operations. (p. 441)

Aging accounts receivable Analyzing accounts receivable according to when they are due. (p. 180)

Allowance method Crediting the estimated value of uncollectible accounts to a contra account. (p. 178)

Amortization schedule A schedule of the periodic payments on a note. (p. 275)

Annuity A series of equal cash flows. (p. 545)

Applied overhead The estimated amount of factory overhead recorded on cost sheets. (p. 507)

Appropriations Authorizations to make expenditures for specific purposes. (p. 680)

Articles of incorporation A legal document that identifies basic characteristics of a corporation, which is a part of the application submitted to a state to become a corporation. (p. 294)

Assessed value The value of an asset determined by tax authorities for the purpose of calculating taxes. (p. 203)

Asset Anything of value that is owned. (p. 7)

Authority The ability of an employee to authorize a transaction. (p. 594)

Automatic check deposit Depositing payroll checks directly to an employee's checking or savings account. (p. 76)

B

Balance sheet A financial statement that reports assets, liabilities, and owners' equity on a specific date. (p. 114)

Balanced scorecard A planning and measurement system developed by R. S. Kaplan and D. P. Norton to use multiple performance measures to ensure that a company's vision and strategy are reflected in its goals and activities. (p. 453)

Batch-level costs Resources used on activities connected with a group of products. (p. 568)

Board of directors A group of persons elected by the stockholders to govern a corporation. (p. 295)

Bond A long-term promise to pay a specified amount on a specified date and to pay interest at stated intervals. (p. 342)

Bond amortization Reducing the amount of a bond discount or premium over time. (p. 347)

Bond issue All bonds representing the total amount of a loan. (p. 342)

Book value The difference between an asset's account balance and its related contra account balance. (p. 178)

Book value of a plant asset The original cost of a plant asset minus accumulated depreciation. (p. 206)

Breakage The value of unredeemed gift cards. (p. 272)

Breakeven point The amount of sales at which net sales is equal to total costs. (p. 474)

Budget A financial road map used by individuals and companies as a guide for spending and saving. (p. 432)

Budget period The length of time covered by a budget. (p. 433)

Budgeted income statement A statement that reports a company's projected sales, costs, expenses, and net income. (p. 443)

Budgeting Planning the financial operations of a business. (p. 432)

Buyback A program approved by a board of directors authorizing the corporation to repurchase its stock. (p. 325)

C

Call option The right of a corporation to repurchase its security for a specified price. (p. 350)

Callable bond A bond that can be called before its maturity date. (p. 350)

Capital expenditures Purchases of plant assets used in the operation of a business. (p. 383)

Capital stock The total shares of ownership in a corporation. (p. 113)

Carrying value The face value of a bond adjusted for any unamortized discount or premium. (p. 347)

Cash budget A statement that shows for each month or quarter a projection of a company's beginning cash balance, cash receipts, cash payments, and ending cash balance. (p. 450)

Cash discount A deduction that a vendor allows on the invoice amount to encourage prompt payment. (p. 20)

Cash equivalents Short-term, liquid investments that are readily convertible to cash and which mature in three months or less. (p. 371)

Cash flow The cash receipts and cash payments of a company. (p. 115)

Cash payments budget A statement that reports projected cash payments for a budget period. (p. 449)

Cash receipts budget A statement that reports projected cash receipts for a budget period. (p. 447)

Certificate of deposit A document issued by a bank as evidence of money invested with the bank. (p. 691)

Charter The legal right for a business to conduct operations as a corporation. (p. 295)

Check register A journal used in a voucher system to record cash payments. (p. 606)

Closing entries Journal entries used to prepare temporary accounts for a new fiscal period. (p. 117)

Common equity per share The amount of common stockholders' equity belonging to a single share of common stock. (p. 376)

Common stock Stock that does not give stockholders any special preferences. (p. 296)

Comparative financial statements Financial statements that provide information for multiple fiscal periods. (p. 368)

Compounding Earning interest on previously earned interest. (p. 541)

Comprehensive annual financial report The detailed financial report of a governmental agency. (p. 712)

Comprehensive income All changes in equity for the period, except changes caused by owner investments and owner distributions. (p. 392)

Consignee The person or business that receives goods on consignment. (p. 146)

Consignment Goods that are given to a business to sell but for which title remains with the vendor. (p. 146)

Consignor The person or business that gives goods on consignment. (p. 146)

Contra account An account that reduces a related account on a financial statement. (p. 18)

Contribution margin Income determined by subtracting all variable costs from net sales. (p. 471)

Control activities The policies and procedures designed to prevent or detect errors or fraud. (p. 593)

Control environment The attitude and actions of management that indicate its commitment to strong internal controls and ethical standards. (p. 593)

Controlling account An account in a general ledger that summarizes all accounts in a subsidiary ledger. (p. 11)

Conversion costs The sum of the costs for direct labor and overhead. (p. 561)

Conversion option The ability of a security to be traded for a specified number of shares of another security. (p. 307)

Conversion price The par or stated value of the preferred stock divided by the conversion ratio. (p. 307)

Conversion ratio The number of shares of common stock received when a security is converted. (p. 307)

Convertible preferred stock Preferred stock that can be exchanged for a specified number of common shares. (p. 307)

Corporation An organization with the legal rights of a person which many persons or other corporations may own. (p. 294)

Cost driver The factor that affects the cost of an activity. (p. 569)

Cost ledger A ledger containing all cost sheets for products in the process of being manufactured. (p. 497)

Cost of production report A report that shows unit information and cost information for a department using a process costing system. (p. 564)

Cost pool A group of costs related to a specific activity. (p. 569)

Cost-based pricing A method of establishing a price for a product or service in which a fixed percentage or a fixed sum is added to the cost of the product or service. Also known as *markup pricing*. (p. 574)

Credit memorandum A form prepared by the vendor showing the amount deducted for sales returns and allowances. (p. 43)

Current assets Cash and other assets expected to be exchanged for cash or consumed within a year. (p. 198)

Current liabilities Liabilities that are due within a short time, usually a year. (p. 237)

Current ratio A ratio that measures the relationship of current assets to current liabilities. (p. 374)

Custody The physical access to the assets involved in a transaction. (p. 594)

G-2

D

Date of a note The day a note is issued. (p. 236)

Date of declaration The date on which a board of directors votes to distribute a dividend. (p. 318)

Date of payment The date on which dividends are actually to be paid to stockholders. (p. 318)

Date of record The date that determines which stockholders are to receive dividends. (p. 318)

Days' sales in accounts receivable The average period of time to collect an account receivable. (p. 186)

Days' sales in inventory The time needed to sell an average amount of merchandise inventory. (p. 161)

Debit memorandum A form prepared by the customer showing the price deduction taken by the customer for a return or an allowance. (p. 18)

Debt financing Obtaining capital by borrowing money for a period of time. (p. 236)

Debt ratio Total liabilities divided by total assets. (p. 375)

Declaring a dividend Action by a board of directors to distribute corporate earnings to stockholders. (p. 318)

Declining-balance method of depreciation A type of accelerated depreciation that multiplies the book value of an asset by a constant depreciation rate to determine annual depreciation. (p. 218)

Deflation The rate at which the price for goods and services decreases over time. (p. 155)

Departmental accounting system An accounting system showing accounting information for two or more departments. (p. 13)

Departmental margin The revenue earned by a department less its cost of merchandise sold and less its direct expenses. (p. 109)

Departmental margin statement A statement that reports departmental margin for a specific department. (p. 109)

Depletion The decrease in the value of a plant asset because of the removal of a natural resource. (p. 222)

Depreciation expense The portion of a plant asset's cost that is transferred to an expense account in each fiscal period during that asset's useful life. (p. 102)

Differential analysis Analyzing only the differences between the revenues and expenses resulting from each of two options. (p. 534)

Direct expense An operating expense identifiable with and chargeable to the operation of a specific department. (p. 108)

Direct labor Salaries of factory workers who make a product. (p. 496)

Direct materials Materials that are of significant value in the cost of a finished product and that become an identifiable part of the product. (p. 496)

Direct method Listing cash flows from operating activities as cash receipts and cash payments. (p. 403)

Direct write-off method Recording uncollectible accounts expense only when an amount is actually known to be uncollectible. (p. 175)

Distribution deficit A negative balance that remains after partner salaries and interest are subtracted from total income. (p. 650)

Dividend yield The relationship between dividends per share and market price per share. (p. 389)

Dividends Earnings distributed to stockholders. (p. 113)

Double taxation The taxation of earnings when earned by a corporation and again when dividends are received by stockholders. (p. 298)

Double-entry accounting The recording of debit and credit parts of a transaction. (p. 8)

E

Earnings per share (EPS) Net income after federal income tax divided by the number of outstanding shares of stock. (p. 387)

EBIT Earnings before interest expense and taxes. (p. 376)

Effective interest rate The market interest rate at the time bonds are issued. (p. 346)

Electronic funds transfer (EFT) A computerized cash payments system that transfers funds without the use of checks, currency, or other paper documents. (p. 76)

Employee earnings record A business form used to record details of an employee's earnings and deductions. (p. 73)

Encumbrance A commitment to pay for goods or services that have been ordered but not yet provided. (p. 687)

Equities Financial rights to the assets of a business. (p. 7)

Equity ratio The ratio found by dividing stockholders' equity by total assets. (p. 375)

Equivalent units of production (EUP) An estimate of the amount of direct materials, direct labor, and overhead that have already been incurred on partially finished units, stated in terms of fully completed units. (p. 561)

Error An unintentional mistake. (p. 593)

Expenditures Cash disbursements and liabilities incurred for the cost of goods delivered or services rendered. (p. 676)

F

Face value The amount to be paid to a bondholder at the bond maturity date. (p. 343)

Facility-sustaining level costs Resources used to support the entire company and production process. (p. 568)

Factory overhead All expenses other than direct materials and direct labor that apply to making products. (p. 496)

Fair market value balance sheet A financial statement that presents the fair market value of a company's assets, liabilities, and owner's equity. (p. 627)

Fiduciary fund A fund that reports assets held by a government agency to benefit a specific group of individuals. (p. 712)

File maintenance The procedure for arranging accounts in a general ledger, assigning account numbers, and keeping records current. (p. 11)

Financial ratio A comparison between two components of financial information. (p. 110)

Financial statement misstatement The manipulation of amounts reported on a financial statement. (p. 593)

Financing activities Cash receipts and payments involving debt or equity transactions. (p. 115)

Finished goods Manufactured products that are fully completed. (p. 496)

Finished goods ledger A ledger containing records of all finished goods on hand. This ledger is similar to a materials ledger. (p. 497)

First-in, first-out inventory costing method Using the price of merchandise purchased first to calculate the cost of merchandise sold first. (p. 151)

Fiscal period The length of time for which a business summarizes its financial information and reports its financial performance. (p. 96)

Fiscal year A fiscal period consisting of 12 consecutive months. (p. 96)

Fixed costs Costs that remain constant regardless of a change in business activity. (p. 470)

Flowchart A diagram that uses symbols and connecting lines to represent a process. (p. 597)

Fraud The theft of assets by employees or the intentional misstatement of financial information. (p. 593)

Free cash flow A measure equal to cash flows from operations less cash used for capital expenditures. (p. 383)

Fund A governmental accounting entity with a set of accounts in which assets always equal liabilities plus equities. (p. 675)

Fund equity The amount of assets less liabilities of a governmental organization. (p. 676)

Future value The value of money invested today at some point in the future. (p. 541)

Future value of an annuity The future value of an equal series of investments over equal time periods at a given interest rate. (p. 545)

G

General fixed assets Governmental properties that benefit future periods. (p. 690)

General ledger A ledger that contains all accounts needed to prepare financial statements. (p. 11)

Generally accepted accounting principles The standards and rules that accountants follow while recording and reporting financial activities. (p. 151)

Goodwill The value of a business in excess of the total investment of owners. (p. 633)

Governmental fund A fund that accounts for the tax-supported activities of a government agency. (p. 712)

Gross margin Gross profit as a percent of net sales. (p. 378)

Gross profit The operating revenue remaining after cost of merchandise sold has been deducted. (p. 109)

Gross profit method of estimating inventory Estimating inventory by using the previous year's percentage of gross profit on operations. (p. 159)

H

Half-year convention A method that recognizes one half of a year's depreciation in the year of acquisition. (p. 207)

I

Income statement A financial statement showing the revenue and expenses for a fiscal period. (p. 112)

Indirect expense An operating expense chargeable to overall business operations and not identifiable with a specific department. (p. 108)

Indirect labor Salaries paid to factory workers who are not actually making products. (p. 496)

Indirect materials Materials used in the completion of a product that are of insignificant value to justify accounting for separately. (p. 496)

Indirect method Listing cash flows from operating activities by starting with net income and adjusting for noncash items. (p. 403)

Inflation The rate at which the price for goods and services increases over time. (p. 154)

Information and communication The processes used to collect information about how the business is achieving its control goals. (p. 593)

Initial public offering The initial issue of a security on a public exchange. Also called *IPO*. (p. 303)

Installment note A note resulting from a sale that requires monthly payments of principal and interest. (p. 274)

Institutional investors Organizations that manage the investments of individual investors. (p. 355)

Intangible asset An asset that does not have physical substance. (p. 634)

Interest An amount paid for the use of money for a period of time. (p. 236)

Interest coverage ratio The number of times a company can cover its interest expense with its earnings. (p. 376)

Interest expense Interest accrued on borrowed funds. (p. 239)

Interest rate The percentage of the principal that is due for the use of the funds secured by a note. (p. 236)

Interest-bearing note A note having a stated interest rate. (p. 239)

Internal control structure A process designed to achieve effectiveness and efficiency of operations, reliability of financial reporting, and compliance with applicable laws and regulations. (p. 593)

Internal controls Processes and procedures employed within a business to ensure that its operations are conducted ethically, accurately, and reliably. (p. 592)

International financial reporting standards A set of accounting standards being adopted across the world. (p. 156)

Inventory record A form used during a physical inventory to record information about each item of merchandise on hand. (p. 148)

Inventory turnover ratio The number of times the average amount of merchandise inventory is sold during a specific period of time. (p. 161)

Investing activities Cash receipts and cash payments involving the sale or purchase of assets used to earn revenue over a period of time. (p. 115)

Invoice A form describing the goods or services sold, the quantity, the price, and the terms of sale. (p. 602)

J

Job order costing Measuring the manufacturing costs of a specific order or batch as it goes through the production process. (p. 497)

Joint costs The costs of processing joint products to their split-off point. (p. 538)

Joint products Two or more products that are produced simultaneously with the same processes and costs and are inseparable up to a certain point. (p. 538)

Journal A form for recording transactions in chronological order. (p. 8)

L

Labor price standard The estimated cost per hour of direct labor. Also referred to as the *labor rate standard*. (p. 519)

Labor price variance The difference between the actual price paid for labor and the labor price standard at the actual quantity used. (p. 523)

Labor quantity standard The estimated amount of direct labor needed to produce one unit of output. Also referred to as the *labor efficiency standard*. (p. 519)

Labor quantity variance The difference between the actual quantity of labor used in production and the standard quantity of labor for that level of production at the standard price. (p. 523)

Last-in, first-out inventory costing method Using the price of merchandise purchased last to calculate the cost of merchandise sold first. (p. 152)

Ledger A group of accounts. (p. 11)

Liability An amount owed by a business. (p. 7)

Limited liability corporation A type of corporation that does not pay taxes on its earnings. The earnings are divided among its members and are only taxed on the members' personal tax returns, thus eliminating the disadvantage of double taxation. Also called *LLC*. (p. 298)

Line of credit A bank loan agreement that provides immediate short-term access to cash. (p. 240)

Liquidation of a partnership The process of paying a partnership's liabilities and distributing remaining assets to the partners. (p. 658)

Lower of cost or market inventory costing method Using the lower of cost or market price to calculate the cost of the ending merchandise inventory. (p. 157)

M

Marginal tax rate The tax rate associated with a tax bracket. (p. 104)

Market value of a share of stock The price at which a share of stock may be sold on the stock market at any given time. (p. 388)

Materials ledger A ledger containing all records of materials. (p. 497)

Materials price standard The estimated cost per unit of direct materials. (p. 519)

Materials price variance The difference between the actual price paid for materials and the materials price standard at the actual quantity purchased and used. (p. 521)

Materials quantity standard The estimated amount of direct materials to be used per unit of output. (p. 519)

Materials quantity variance The difference between the actual quantity of materials purchased and used in production and the standard quantity of materials for that level of production at the standard price. (p. 521)

Maturity date The date on which the principal of a note is due to be repaid. (p. 236)

Maturity value The amount that is due on the maturity date of a note. (p. 239)

Merchandising business A business that purchases and sells goods. (p. 13)

Millage rate The tax rate used to calculate property taxes. (p. 203)

Modified Accelerated Cost Recovery System (MACRS) A depreciation method required by the Internal Revenue Service to be used for income tax calculation purposes for most plant assets. (p. 220)

Modified half-year convention A method that recognizes a full year's depreciation if the asset is acquired in the first half of the year. (p. 207)

Monitoring The process management uses to determine whether its policies are operating effectively. (p. 593)

Mutual agency The right of all partners to contract for a partnership. (p. 624)

N

Narrative A written description of the flow of documents and information between employees, departments, and external parties. (p. 597)

Net cash flows The difference between the cash receipts and cash payments. (p. 548)

Net present value The difference between the present value of the cash flows of the investment and the amount of the investment. (p. 548)

Net realizable value See *book value*.

Noninterest-bearing note A note that deducts interest from the face value of the note. (p. 239)

No-par-value stock A share of stock that has no authorized value printed on the stock certificate. (p. 297)

Notes payable Promissory notes signed by a business and given to a creditor. (p. 236)

Not-for-profit organization An organization providing goods or services with neither a conscious motive nor an expectation of earning a profit. Also referred to as *nonprofit organizations*. (p. 672)

O

Occupational fraud The theft of business assets by an employee. It is also referred to as *embezzlement* or *asset misappropriation*. (p. 593)

Operating activities The cash receipts and payments necessary to operate a business on a day-to-day basis. (p. 115)

Operating budget A plan of current expenditures and the proposed means of financing those expenditures. (p. 678)

Operating margin Income from operations as a percent of net sales. (p. 379)

Other revenue and expenses budget A statement that shows budgeted revenue and expenses from activities other than normal operations. (p. 442)

Overapplied overhead The amount by which applied factory overhead is more than actual factory overhead. (p. 510)

Owners' equity The amount remaining after the value of all liabilities is subtracted from the value of all assets. (p. 7)

Owners' equity statement A financial statement that summarizes the changes in owners' equity during a fiscal period. (p. 654)

P

Par value A value assigned to a share of stock and printed on the stock certificate. (p. 296)

Partnership A business in which two or more persons combine their assets and skills. (p. 298)

Partnership agreement A written agreement setting forth the conditions under which a partnership is to operate. Also known as the *articles of partnership*. (p. 624)

Par-value stock A share of stock that has par value. (p. 296)

Pay period The number of days or weeks of work covered by an employee's paycheck. (p. 64)

Payroll The total amount earned by all employees for a pay period. (p. 64)

Payroll register An accounting form that summarizes the earnings, deductions, and net pay of all employees for one pay period. (p. 68)

Payroll taxes Taxes based on the payroll of a business. (p. 64)

Performance report A report showing a comparison of projected and actual amounts for a specific period. (p. 453)

Permanent difference A difference between net income and taxable income only for that year that is never balanced out in a future year. (p. 391)

Personal property All property not classified as real property. (p. 203)

Petty cash An amount of cash kept on hand and used for making small payments. (p. 25)

Plant asset record An accounting form on which a business records information about each plant asset. (p. 203)

Plant assets Physical assets that will be used for a number of years in the operation of a business. (p. 102)

Point-of-sale (POS) terminal A specialized computer used to collect, store, and report all the information about a sales transaction. (p. 49)

Post-closing trial balance A trial balance prepared after the closing entries are posted. (p. 120)

Posting Transferring transaction information from a journal entry to a ledger account. (p. 15)

Preferred stock A class of stock that gives preferred shareholders preference over common shareholders in dividends along with other rights. (p. 296)

Prepaid expense Cash paid for an expense in one fiscal period that is not used until a later period. (p. 242)

Present value The current value of a future cash payment or receipt. (p. 544)

Present value of an annuity An amount invested at a given interest rate that supports the payments of an annuity. (p. 546)

Price-earnings ratio The relationship between the market value per share and earnings per share of a stock. (p. 388)

Prime interest rate The interest rate charged to a bank's most creditworthy customers. (p. 240)

Principal The original amount of a note. (p. 236)

Privately held corporation A corporation owned by a small number of individuals. (p. 303)

Process costing Measuring the manufacturing costs of similar goods as they flow continuously from one production process to another. (p. 497)

Product-level costs Resources used to support the entire product line. (p. 568)

Promissory note A written and signed promise to pay a sum of money at a specified time. (p. 236)

Proprietary fund A fund that accounts for the financial transactions of a government organization that operates as a for-profit enterprise. (p. 712)

Proprietorship A business owned by one person. (p. 298)

Publicly held corporation A corporation having its stock traded on public exchanges. (p. 303)

Purchase order A form requesting that a vendor sell merchandise to a business. (p. 602)

Purchases budget A statement that shows the projected amount of purchases that will be required during a budget period. (p. 437)

Purchases discount When a company that has purchased merchandise on account takes a cash discount. (p. 20)

Q

Quick assets Cash and other current assets that can be converted quickly into cash. (p. 374)

Quick ratio A ratio that measures the relationship of quick assets to current liabilities. (p. 374)

R

Rate earned on average stockholders' equity The relationship between net income and average stockholders' equity. (p. 382)

Rate earned on average total assets The relationship between net income and average total assets. (p. 381)

Real property Land and anything attached to it; also called *real estate.* (p. 203)

Realization Cash received from the sale of assets during liquidation of a partnership. (p. 658)

Receiving report A form that lists the item received from a vendor. (p. 602)

Reclassification entry An entry that transfers account balances between accounts on one financial statement. (p. 276)

Recording The entry of a transaction in the financial records. (p. 594)

Registration statement The document submitted to the SEC for permission to sell a security on a public exchange. (p. 303)

Relevant costs Costs that are different between two options. (p. 534)

Relevant revenue Revenues that are different between two options. (p. 534)

Requisition A form requesting the purchase of merchandise. (p. 602)

Responsibility accounting Assigning control of revenues, costs, and expenses to a specific manager. (p. 108)

Responsibility statements Financial statements reporting revenue, costs, and direct expenses under a specific department's control. (p. 109)

Retail method of estimating inventory Estimating inventory by using a percentage based on both cost and retail prices. (p. 160)

Retained earnings An amount earned by a corporation and not yet distributed to stockholders. (p. 113)

Retiring a bond issue Paying the amounts owed to bondholders for a bond issue. (p. 350)

Reversing entry An entry made at the beginning of one fiscal period to reverse an adjusting entry made in the previous fiscal period. (p. 244)

Risk assessment The process of determining whether an error or fraud could occur. (p. 593)

S

Salary A fixed annual sum of money divided among equal pay periods. (p. 64)

Sales budget A statement that shows the projected net sales for a budget period. (p. 436)

Sales discount A cash discount on a sale taken by the customer. (p. 47)

Sales mix The relative distribution of sales among various products. (p. 485)

Salvage value The amount that will be received for an asset at the time of its disposal. (p. 205)

Schedule of accounts payable A listing of vendor accounts, account balances, and the total amount due all vendors. Some businesses call this listing an accounts payable trial balance. (p. 97)

Schedule of accounts receivable A listing of customer accounts, account balances, and total amount due from all customers. (p. 97)

Segregation of duties Dividing the tasks of the accounting system among employees in different functions. (p. 594)

Selling expenses budget A statement that shows projected expenditures related directly to the selling operations. (p. 439)

Serial bonds Portions of a bond issue that mature on different dates. (p. 350)

Share of stock A unit of ownership in a corporation. (p. 294)

Source document A business paper from which information is obtained for a journal entry. (p. 7)

Special journal A journal used to record only one kind of transaction. (p. 8)

Split-off point The point where joint products are separable into identifiable products. (p. 538)

Standard An estimated amount of direct materials or direct labor, usually in price or quantity, established for each unit produced. (p. 519)

Standard costing system A system of setting standards for each cost of production. (p. 519)

Stated interest rate The rate of interest used to calculate periodic interest payments on a bond. (p. 343)

Stated-value stock No-par-value stock that is assigned a value by a corporation. Stated-value stock is similar to par-value stock except that the value is not printed on the stock certificates. (p. 297)

Statement of cash flows A financial statement that summarizes cash receipts and cash payments resulting from business activities during a fiscal period. (p. 115)

Statement of cost of goods manufactured A statement showing details about the cost of finished goods. (p. 515)

Statement of revenues, expenditures, and changes in fund balance A statement that reports the sources of revenues and the expenditure of funds of a government organization. (p. 676)

Statement of stockholders' equity A financial statement that shows changes in a corporation's ownership for a fiscal period. (p. 113)

Stock certificate Written evidence of the number of shares that each stockholder owns in a corporation. (p. 296)

Stock dividend The payment of a dividend with the stock of the corporation. (p. 321)

Stock ledger A file of stock records for all merchandise on hand. (p. 147)

Stock record A form used to show the type of merchandise, quantity received, quantity sold, and balance on hand. (p. 147)

G-7

Stockholder The owner of one or more shares of stock. (p. 294)

Stockholders' equity The owners' equity in a corporation. (p. 7)

Straight-line method of depreciation Recording an equal amount of depreciation expense for a plant asset in each year of its useful life. (p. 206)

Subsidiary ledger A ledger that is summarized in a single general ledger account. (p. 11)

Sunk cost A cost that occurred in the past and cannot be recovered by a future decision. (p. 534)

T

Target costing A method of establishing a price for a product or service, based on the price the customer is willing to pay and controlling the cost of the product so that the company still makes a profit. (p. 575)

Tax base The maximum amount of earnings on which a tax is calculated. (p. 65)

Tax bracket Each tax rate and taxable income amount on one line of a tax table. (p. 104)

Tax levy Authorized action taken by a governmental organization to collect taxes by legal authority. (p. 683)

Temporary difference A difference between net income and taxable income for more than one period that reverses out over the entire period. (p. 391)

Term bonds Bonds that all mature on the same date. (p. 350)

Terminal summary The report that summarizes the cash and credit card sales of a point-of-sale terminal. (p. 49)

Time value of money The expectation that invested money will increase over time. (p. 540)

Total costs All costs for a specific period of time. (p. 469)

Total labor variance The difference between the actual cost of labor and the expected standard cost of labor. (p. 522)

Total materials variance The difference between the actual cost of materials and the expected standard cost of materials. (p. 520)

Treasury stock A corporation's own stock that has been issued and reacquired. (p. 325)

Trial balance A proof of the equality of debits and credits in a general ledger. (p. 98)

U

Unadjusted trial balance A trial balance prepared before adjusting entries are posted. (p. 98)

Uncollectible accounts Accounts receivable that cannot be collected. (p. 174)

Underapplied overhead The amount by which applied factory overhead is less than actual factory overhead. (p. 510)

Unearned revenue Cash received for goods or services which have not been provided. (p. 264)

Unit cost An amount spent for one unit of a specific product or service. (p. 469)

Unit-level costs Resources used on activities connected with each individual unit produced. (p. 568)

Units-of-production method of depreciation Calculating the estimated annual depreciation expense based on the amount of production expected from a plant asset. (p. 219)

V

Value-based pricing A method of establishing a price for a product or service based on the value the product or service has to its customer. (p. 575)

Variable costs Costs that change in direct proportion to a change in the number of units. (p. 470)

Vertical analysis Reporting an amount on a financial statement as a percentage of another item on the same financial statement. (p. 110)

Voucher A collection of documents used to authorize a cash payment. (p. 601)

Voucher check A check with a detachable check stub, or *voucher*, that contains detailed information about the cash payment. (p. 605)

Voucher register A journal used to record vouchers. (p. 603)

Voucher system A set of procedures for controlling cash payments by preparing and approving vouchers before payments are made. (p. 601)

W

Wage The amount paid to an employee for every hour worked. (p. 64)

Weighted-average inventory costing method Using the average cost of the beginning inventory plus merchandise purchased during a fiscal period to calculate the cost of merchandise sold. (p. 153)

Withholding allowance A deduction from total earnings for each person legally supported by a taxpayer, including the employee. (p. 65)

Work in process Products that are being manufactured but are not yet complete. (p. 496)

Work sheet A columnar accounting form used to summarize the general ledger information needed for preparing financial statements. (p. 106)

Working capital The amount of total current assets less total current liabilities. (p. 373)

Writing off an account Canceling the balance of a customer account because the customer does not pay. (p. 174)

Glosario

A

Account *Cuenta* Un registro que da un resumen de toda la información que pertenece a un solo artículo en la ecuación de contabilidad. (p. 9)

Accounting cycle *Ciclo contable* La serie de actividades de contabilidad que se incluyen en el registro de la información financiera en un período fiscal. (p. 121)

Accounting equation *Ecuación de contabilidad* Una ecuación que muestra la relación entre activos, pasivos y capital propio. (p. 7)

Accounts receivable turnover ratio *Índice de rotación de cuentas por cobrar* El número de veces que la cantidad promedia de cuentas por cobrar se recibe durante un período específico. (p. 186)

Accrued expenses *Gastos acumulados* Los gastos incurridos durante un período fiscal, pero pagados en otro período fiscal posterior. (p. 248)

Accrued revenue *Ingreso acumulado* Ingresos ganados en un período fiscal, pero no recibido hasta un período fiscal posterior. (p. 267)

Activity rate *Tarifa de actividad* El precio de cada unidad de actividad. (p. 569)

Activity-based costing (ABC) *Determinación de costo por actividad (costeo ABC)* Asignar los gastos generales de la fábrica basados en el nivel de actividades mayores. (p. 567)

Adjusted trial balance *Balance de comprobación ajustado* Un balance de comprobación después de registrarse los asientos de ajuste. (p. 103)

Adjusting entries *Asientos de ajuste* Asientos registrados para poner al corriente las cuentas del libro mayor al final de un período fiscal. (p. 98)

Administrative expenses budget *Presupuesto de gastos administrativos* Una declaración que muestra la proyección de los gastos de todos los gastos operativos que no están directamente relacionados con las operaciones de ventas. (p. 441)

Aging accounts receivable *Antigüedad de cuentas por cobrar* Analizar las cuentas por cobrar de acuerdo a cuando se deben de pagar. (p. 180)

Allowance method *Método de concesión* Acreditar el valor estimado de las cuentas incobrables a una contra cuenta. (p. 178)

Amortization schedule *Plan de amortización* Un plan de los pagos regulares de un pagaré. (p. 275)

Annuity *Anualidad* Una serie de flujos de efectivo equitativos. (p. 545)

Applied overhead *Gastos fijos aplicados* La cantidad estimada de gastos fijos mostrada en las hojas de gastos. (p. 507)

Appropriations *Distribución de recursos* Autorizaciones para hacer gastos para propósitos específicos. (p. 680)

Articles of incorporation *Acta constitutiva de una sociedad* Un documento legal que identifica las características básicas de una corporación, el cual es parte de la solicitud sometida al estado para volverse una corporación. (p. 294)

Assessed value *Valor fiscal* El valor de un activo determinado por las autoridades de impuestos para calcular los impuestos. (p. 203)

Asset *Activo* Cualquier cosa de valor que se posee. (p. 7)

Authority *Autoridad* La habilidad de un empleado de autorizar una transacción. (p. 594)

Automatic check deposit *Depósito automático* Depositar los cheques de nómina de un empleado directamente a su cuenta de cheques o de ahorros. (p. 76)

B

Balance sheet *Balance general* Un estado financiero que informa sobre los activos, las obligaciones y el capital propio en una fecha específica. (p. 114)

Balanced scorecard *Cuadro de Mando Integral* Un sistema de medición y planeación desarrollado por R. S. Kaplan y D. P. Norton de utilizar varias medidas de desempeño para asegurar que la visión y estrategia de una compañía estén reflejadas en sus metas y actividades. (p. 453)

Batch-level costs *Costos a nivel de lote* Los recursos utilizados en las actividades relacionadas con un grupo de productos. (p. 568)

Board of directors *Consejo directivo* Un grupo de personas elegidas por los accionistas para dirigir una corporación. (p. 295)

Bond amortization *Amortización de bono* Reducir la cantidad de descuento o prima de un bono con el paso del tiempo. (p. 347)

Bond *Bono* Una promesa de largo plazo de pagar una cantidad específica en una fecha específica y de pagar interés a intervalos estipulados. (p. 342)

Bond issue *Emisión de bonos* Todos los bonos que representan la cantidad total de un préstamo. (p. 342)

Book value *Valor contable* La diferencia entre el saldo de cuenta de un activo y el saldo de su contra cuenta relacionada. (p. 178)

Book value of a plant asset *Valor contable de un activo fijo* El costo original de un activo fijo menos la depreciación acumulada. (p. 206)

Breakage *Tarjetas no redimidas* El valor de las tarjetas de regalo sin redimir. (p. 272)

Breakeven point *Punto de equilibrio* La cantidad de ventas en la cual las ventas netas igualan el gasto total. (p. 474)

Budget *Presupuesto* Una guía financiera utilizada por los individuos y compañías como una guía de gastos y ahorros. (p. 432)

Budget period *Período presupuestario* El plazo de tiempo cubierto por un presupuesto. (p. 433)

Budgeted income statement *Declaración de ingresos presupuestado* Una declaración que informa las proyecciones de las ventas, gastos, costos, e ingresos netos de una compañía. (p. 443)

Budgeting *Preparación del presupuesto* La planeación de las operaciones financieras de un negocio. (p. 432)

Buyback *Recompra* Un programa aprobado por el consejo directivo que autoriza a la compañía de readquirir sus acciones. (p. 325)

C

Call option *Opción de compra* El derecho de una corporación de readquirir sus valores bursátiles a un precio especificado. (p. 350)

Callable bond *Bono rescatable* Un bono que puede ser rescatado antes de su fecha de vencimiento. (p. 350)

Capital expenditures *Gastos de capital* Las compras de activos fijos utilizados en la operación de un negocio. (p. 383)

Capital stock *Capital social* El número total de acciones de propiedad en una corporación. (p. 113)

Carrying value *Valor contable* El valor nominal de un bono ajustado por cualquier descuento o prima no amortizado. (p. 347)

Cash budget *Presupuesto de efectivo* Un informe que muestra por mes o trimestre una proyección del balance inicial, recibos, pagos, y balance final de efectivo de una compañía. (p. 450)

Cash discount *Descuento de efectivo* Un descuento que un vendedor permite en una factura para motivar un pago rápido. (p. 20)

Cash equivalents *Equivalentes de caja* Inversiones disponibles de corto plazo que se pueden convertir rápidamente en efectivo y que se vencen en tres meses o menos. (p. 371)

Cash flow *Flujo de caja* Los recibos y pagos de efectivo de una compañía. (p. 115)

Cash payments budget *Presupuesto de pagos en efectivo* Un informe que muestra la proyección de pagos en efectivo de un período presupuestario. (p. 449)

Cash receipts budget *Presupuesto de recibos en efectivo* Un informe que muestra la proyección de recibos en efectivo de un período presupuestario. (p. 447)

Certificate of deposit *Certificado de depósito* Un documento emitido por un banco como evidencia del dinero invertido con el banco. (p. 691)

Charter *Acta constitutiva* El derecho legal para que un negocio lleve a cabo sus operaciones como una corporación. (p. 295)

Check register *registro de cheque* Un diario que se utiliza en un sistema de comprobantes para registrar pagos en efectivo. (p. 606)

Closing entries *Asientos de cierre* Los asientos en el diario que se usan para preparar cuentas temporales para un período fiscal nuevo. (p. 117)

Common equity per share *Capital ordinario por acción* La cantidad de capital propio de un accionista común que pertenece a una sola unidad de acción común. (p. 376)

Common stock *Acción ordinaria* Acciones que no dan preferencia especial a los accionistas. (p. 296)

Comparative financial statements *Estados financieros comparativos* Informes financieros que proveen información de múltiples períodos fiscales. (p. 368)

Compounding *Intereses compuestos* Ganar intereses sobre los intereses previamente ganados. (p. 541)

Comprehensive annual financial report *Informe financiero anual completo* El informe financiero detallado de una agencia gubernamental. (p. 712)

Comprehensive income *Ingreso total* Todos los cambios de capital por el período, con la excepción de los cambios causados por las inversiones y distribuciones del dueño. (p. 392)

Consignee *Consignatario* La persona o negocio que recibe bienes a consignación. (p. 146)

Consignment *Consignación* Los bienes que se otorgan a un negocio para vender pero que la titularidad permanece con el vendedor. (p. 146)

Consignor *Consignador* La persona o negocio que otorga bienes a consignación. (p. 146)

Contra account *Contra cuenta* Cuenta que reduce una cuenta relacionada en un estado financiero. (p. 18)

Contribution margin *Margen de contribución* Los ingresos determinados al restar todos los gastos variables de las ventas netas. (p. 471)

Control activities *Actividades de control* Las pólizas y procedimientos diseñados para prevenir o detectar errores o fraude. (p. 593)

Control environment *Ambiente de control* Las acciones y actitudes de la gerencia que indica su compromiso a los controles firmes internos y estándares de ética. (p. 593)

Controlling account *Cuenta de control* Una cuenta en el libro mayor general que da un resumen de todas las cuentas de un libro mayor auxiliar. (p. 11)

Conversion costs *Costos de conversión* La suma de los gastos fijos y los gastos de mano de obra directa. (p. 561)

Conversion option *Opción de conversión* La habilidad de poder intercambiar un valor bursátil por un número específico de acciones de otro valor bursátil. (p. 307)

Conversion price *Precio de conversión* El valor nominal de una acción preferida dividida por el índice de conversión. (p. 307)

Conversion ratio *Índice de conversión* El número de acciones comunes recibidas cuando un valor es convertido. (p. 307)

Convertible preferred stock *Acción preferente convertible* Acciones preferentes que se pueden intercambiar por un número específico de acciones comunes. (p. 307)

Corporation *Corporación* Una organización con los derechos legales de una persona y de la cual varias personas u otras corporaciones son dueñas. (p. 294)

Cost driver *Origen del costo* El factor que afecta el costo de una actividad. (p. 569)

Cost ledger *Libro mayor de costos* Un libro mayor que contiene todas las hojas de costos de los productos que están en el proceso de fabricación. (p. 497)

Cost of production report *Informe sobre el costo de producción* Un informe que muestra la información de unidades y costos de un departamento que utiliza un proceso de sistema de *costeo.* (p. 564)

Cost pool *Agrupación de costos* Un grupo de costos relacionados con una actividad específica. (p. 569)

Cost-based pricing *Fijación de precios según costo* Un método para establecer el precio de un producto o servicio en el cual se añade un porcentaje fijo o una cantidad fija al costo del producto o servicio. (p. 574)

Credit memorandum *Memorándum de crédito* Un documento preparado por el vendedor que muestra la cantidad deducida por las devoluciones de ventas y concesiones. (p. 43)

Current assets *Activos actuales* El efectivo y otros activos que se espera que se intercamb en por efectivo o que se consuman dentro de un año. (p. 198)

Current liabilities *Obligaciones actuales* Las obligaciones que se deben dentro de un corto plazo, generalmente dentro de año. (p. 237)

Current ratio *Índice actual* Un índice que mide la relación actual de los activos actuales con las obligaciones actuales. (p. 374)

Custody *Custodia* El acceso físico a los activos involucrados en una transacción. (p. 594)

D

Date of a note *Fecha del pagaré* El día que un pagaré es emitido. (p. 236)

Date of declaration *Fecha de declaración* La fecha en la que el consejo directivo vota para distribuir un dividendo. (p. 318)

Date of payment *Fecha de pago* La fecha actual en la cual se pagan dividendos a los accionistas. (p. 318)

Date of record *Fecha de registro* La fecha que determina cuales accionistas recibirán dividendos. (p. 318)

Days' sales in accounts receivable *Días promedio de Cuentas por cobrar* El período de tiempo promedio para cobrar una cuenta por cobrar. (p. 186)

Days' sales in inventory *Días promedio en inventario* El tiempo necesario para vender una cantidad promedia de mercancía en inventario. (p. 161)

Debit memorandum *Memorándum de débito* Un documento preparado por el cliente que muestra la deducción de precio tomada por el cliente por una devolución o concesión. (p. 18)

Debt financing *Financiamiento de deuda* Obteniendo capital al pedir prestado por un período de tiempo. (p. 236)

Debt ratio *Índice de deuda* El total de las obligaciones dividido por el total de los activos. (p. 375)

Declaring a dividend *Declaración de dividendos* La acción tomada por el consejo directivo para distribuir las ganancias de la corporación a los accionistas. (p. 318)

Declining-balance method of depreciation *Método de depreciación de saldo decreciente* Un tipo de depreciación acelerada que multiplica el valor contable de un activo por un índice de depreciación constante para determinar su depreciación. (p. 218)

Deflation *Deflación* El índice al cual el precio de bienes y servicios disminuye con el paso del tiempo. (p. 155)

Departmental accounting system *Sistema de contabilidad departamental* Un sistema de contabilidad que muestra la información contable de dos o más departamentos. (p. 13)

Departmental margin *Margen departamental* Los ingresos de un departamento menos sus gastos directos y de la mercancía vendida. (p. 109)

Departmental margin statement *Informe del margen departamental* Un informe que muestra el margen departamental de un departamento específico. (p. 109)

Depletion *Agotamiento* La depreciación en valor de un activo fijo debido a la extracción de un recurso natural. (p. 222)

Depreciation expense *Gasto de depreciación* La porción del costo de un activo fijo que es transferida a una cuenta de gastos cada período fiscal durante la vida útil de ese activo. (p. 102)

Differential analysis *Análisis diferencial* Analizar solamente las diferencias entre los ingresos y los gastos que resultan de cada uno de dos opciones. (p. 534)

Direct expense *Gasto directo* Un gasto operativo que se identifica y es cobrable a la operación de un departamento específico. (p. 108)

Direct labor *Mano de obra directa* Los salarios de los obreros de la fábrica quienes hacen un producto. (p. 496)

Direct materials *Materia prima directa* Los materiales que son de valor significativo en el costo de un producto terminado y los cuales se vuelven una parte identificable del producto. (p. 496)

Direct method *Método directo* Una lista de flujos de caja de las actividades operativas tales como los recibos y pagos de efectivo. (p. 403)

Direct write-off method *Método de pérdida directa* Registrar los gastos de cuentas incobrables solamente cuando en verdad se sabe que una cantidad es incobrable. (p. 175)

Distribution deficit *Déficit distributivo* Un balance negativo que queda después de que los sueldos de los socios y el interés son descontados del ingreso total. (p. 650)

Dividend yield *Rendimiento de dividendo* La relación entre los dividendos por acción y el precio del mercado de cada acción. (p. 389)

Dividends *Dividendos* Las ganancias que se distribuyen a los accionistas. (p. 113)

Double taxation *Tributación doble* La imposición de impuestos sobre las ganancias de una corporación y nuevamente cuando los dividendos son recibidos por los accionistas. (p. 298)

Double-entry accounting *Contabilidad de partida doble* El registro de las partes de débito y crédito de una transacción. (p. 8)

E

Earnings per share (EPS) *Ganancia por acción (GPA)* Ganancias netas después del impuesto fiscal dividido por la cantidad pendiente de acciones. (p. 387)

EBIT *BAII* Beneficios antes de intereses e impuestos. (p. 376)

Effective interest rate *Tasa de interés vigente* La tasa de interés de mercado cuando los bonos son emitidos. (p. 346)

Electronic funds transfer (EFT) *Transferencia electrónica de fondos (TEF)* Un sistema computarizado de pagos de efectivo, el cual transfiere fondos sin el uso de cheques, moneda, u otro documento de papel. (p. 76)

Employee earnings record *Registro de ganancias de los empleados* Un documento de negocios que registra todos los detalles de las ganancias y deducciones de un empleado. (p. 73)

Encumbrance *Gravamen* El compromiso de pagar por los bienes o servicios que han sido ordenados pero que todavía no han sido proveídos. (p. 687)

Equities *Derechos de propiedad* Los derechos financieros a los activos de un negocio. (p. 70)

Equity ratio *Proporción de capital* La proporción que es el resultado de dividir el capital de un accionista por el total de activos. (p. 375)

Equivalent units of production (EUP) *Unidades equivalentes de producción* Una estimación de la cantidad de materia prima directa, la mano de obra directa, y los gastos fijos que ya han sido incurridos en las unidades parcialmente terminadas, declarados en términos de unidades ya completadas. (p. 561)

Error *Error* Una equivocación no intencional. (p. 593)

Expenditures *Gastos* La distribución de efectivo y las obligaciones incurridas por el costo de los bienes entregados o los servicios otorgados. (p. 676)

F

Face value *Valor nominal* La cantidad a ser pagada a un obligacionista en la fecha de vencimiento del bono. (p. 343)

Facility-sustaining level costs *Gastos de producción y mantenimiento* Los recursos utilizados para el sustentamiento de la compañía y el proceso de producción. (p. 568)

Factory overhead *Gastos fijos de fábrica* Todos los gastos aparte de la materia prima y mano de obra directa que aplican para fabricar productos. (p. 496)

Fair market value balance sheet *Estado de cuenta del valor justo de mercado* Una declaración financiera que presenta el valor justo de mercado de los activos, obligaciones, y el capital social de una compañía. (p. 627)

Fiduciary fund *Fondo fiduciario* Un fondo que informa sobre los activos de una agencia gubernamental para el beneficio de un grupo específico de individuos. (p. 712)

File maintenance *Mantenimiento de archivos* El procedimiento de ordenar cuentas en un libro mayor general, asignando números de cuenta y manteniendo los registros al corriente. (p. 11)

Financial ratio *Proporción financiera* Una comparación entre dos componentes de información financiera. (p. 110)

Financial statement misstatement *Declaración falsa del estado de cuenta* La manipulación de las cantidades reportadas en un estado de cuenta financiero. (p. 593)

Financing activities *Actividades financieras* Recibos y pagos de efectivo que involucran transacciones de deuda o patrimonio neto. (p. 115)

Finished goods *Bienes terminados* Los productos fabricados que están completamente terminados. (p. 496)

Finished goods ledger *Libro mayor de bienes terminados* Un libro mayor que contiene los registros de todos los bienes terminados a la mano. Este libro mayor es similar a un libro mayor de materiales. (p. 497)

First-in, first-out inventory costing method *Método de costos de inventario de primero en entrar, primero en salir* Utilizando el precio de la mercancía comprada primero para calcular el costo de la mercancía que se vende primero. (p. 151)

Fiscal period *Período fiscal* El plazo de tiempo en el cual un negocio da un resumen de su información financiera y reporta su desempeño financiero. (p. 96)

Fiscal year *Año fiscal* Un período fiscal que consiste de doce meses consecutivos. (p. 96)

Fixed costs *Gastos fijos* Los gastos que permanecen constantes independientes de un cambio en las actividades de negocio. (p. 470)

Flowchart *Diagrama de flujo* Un diagrama que utiliza símbolos y conexiones para representar un proceso. (p. 597)

Fraud *Fraude* El robo de activos por empleados o la declaración falsa intencional de la información financiera. (p. 593)

Free cash flow *Flujo libre de caja* Una medida igual a los flujos de efectivo de las operaciones menos el efectivo utilizado en los gastos de capital. (p. 383)

Fund *Fondo* Una entidad contable gubernamental con una colección de cuentas en las cuales los activos siempre igualan las obligaciones más los valores. (p. 675)

Fund equity *Capital de fondo* La cantidad de activos menos las obligaciones de una organización gubernamental. (p. 676)

Future value *Valor futuro* El valor futuro del dinero que es invertido hoy en día. (p. 541)

Future value of an annuity *Valor futuro de una anualidad* El valor futuro de una serie de inversiones iguales sobre plazos de tiempo iguales a una tasa de interés determinada. (p. 545)

G

General fixed assets *Activos fijos generales* Propiedades gubernamentales que benefician a períodos futuros. (p. 690)

General ledger *Libro mayor general* Un libro mayor que contiene todas las cuentas necesarias para preparar estados financieros. (p. 11)

Generally accepted accounting principles *Principios de Contabilidad Generalmente Aceptados* Los estándares y normas que los contadores siguen mientras que registran y reportan actividades financieras. (p. 151)

Goodwill *Fondo de comercio* El valor de un negocio en exceso de la inversión total de los dueños. (p. 633)

Governmental fund *Fondo gubernamental* Un fondo que justifica las actividades de una agencia gubernamental financiadas por impuestos. (p. 712)

Gross margin *Margen bruto* Ganancia bruta como un porcentaje de ventas netas. (p. 378)

Gross profit *Ganancia bruta* El ingreso operativo restante después de deducir el costo de la mercancía vendida. (p. 109)

Gross profit method of estimating inventory *Método de ganancia bruta para estimar un inventario* Estimando del inventario mediante el uso de los porcentajes de ganancia bruta de operaciones en años anteriores. (p. 159)

H

Half-year convention *Convención de medio año* Un método que reconoce medio año de la depreciación anual en el año en que se adquiere. (p. 207)

I

Income statement *Estado de ingresos* Un estado financiero que muestra los gastos e ingresos durante un período fiscal. (p. 112)

Indirect expense *Gasto indirecto* Un gasto operativo facturable a las operaciones en general del negocio y que no se identifica con un departamento específico. (p. 108)

Indirect labor *Mano de obra indirect* Los salarios pagados a los obreros de la fábrica que no están haciendo los productos. (p. 496

Indirect materials *Materia prima indirecta* Los materiales utilizados para completar un producto que tienen un valor insignificante para justificarlos por separado. (p. 496)

Indirect method *Método indirecto* Hacer una lista de flujos de efectivo de las actividades operativas comenzando con los ingresos netos y ajustando por los artículos no monetarios. (p. 403)

Inflation *Inflación* El índice al cual el precio de bienes y servicios aumenta con el paso del tiempo. (p. 154)

Information and communication *Información y comunicación* El proceso utilizado para recolectar información sobre como el negocio está logrando sus metas de control. (p. 593)

Initial public offering *Oferta pública inicial* La emisión inicial de valores para el mercado público. También llamado *IPO*. (p. 303)

Installment note *Pagaré a plazos* Un pagaré que resulta de una venta y que requiere de pagos mensuales de principal e interés. (p. 274)

Institutional investors *Inversionistas institucionales* Organizaciones que administran las inversiones de los inversionistas individuales. (p. 355)

Intangible asset *Activo intangible* Un activo que no tiene forma física. (p. 634)

Interest *Interés* Una cantidad que se paga por el uso de dinero durante un período de tiempo. (p. 236)

Interest coverage ratio *Índice de cobertura de intereses* El número de veces que una compañía puede cubrir sus gastos de interés con las ganancias. (p. 376)

Interest expense *Gastos de interés* El interés que se acumula en dinero que se ha tomado prestado. (p. 239)

Interest rate *Tasa de interés* El porcentaje del capital que se debe por el uso de los fondos garantizados por un pagaré. (p. 236)

Interest-bearing note *Pagaré con intereses* Un pagaré con una tasa de interés estipulado. (p. 239)

Internal control structure *Estructura de control interno* Un proceso diseñado para lograr operaciones eficientes y efectivas, la confiabilidad de informes financieros, y el cumplimiento con las leyes y regulaciones aplicables. (p. 593)

Internal controls *Controles internos* Los procesos y procedimientos utilizados dentro de un negocio para asegurar que sus operaciones son manejadas con ética, precisión, y confiabilidad. (p. 592)

International financial reporting standards *Normas Internacionales de Información Financiera (NIIF)* Un conjunto de normas de contabilidad adoptadas por todo el mundo. (p. 156)

Inventory record *Registro de inventario* Un formulario que se usa durante un inventario físico para registrar información acerca de cada artículo de mercancía a la mano. (p. 148)

Inventory turnover ratio *Índice de rotación de inventario* El número de veces que la cantidad promedia de mercancía en inventario es vendida durante un período de tiempo específico. (p. 161)

Investing activities *Actividades de inversión* Recibos y pagos de efectivo que involucran la venta o compra de activos utilizados para generar ingresos sobre un período de tiempo. (p. 115)

Invoice *Factura* Un formulario que describe los bienes o servicios vendidos, la cantidad, el precio, y los términos de venta. (p. 602)

J

Job order costing *Costeo por orden de fabricación* Calculando el costo de fabricación de una orden o lote en específico mientras pasa por el proceso de producción. (p. 497)

Joint costs *Costos conjuntos* El costo de fabricar productos conjuntos hasta su punto de separación. (p. 538)

Joint products *Productos conjuntos* Dos o más productos que son fabricados simultáneamente con los mismos procesos y costos y que son inseparables hasta cierto punto. (p. 538)

Journal *Diario* Un formulario para registrar transacciones en orden cronológico. (p. 80)

G-13

L

Labor price standard *Precio estándar de mano de obra* El costo estimado por hora de mano de obra directa. También se le refiere como el *estándar de la tarifa laboral.* (p. 519)

Labor price variance *Variación en el precio de mano de obra* La diferencia entre el precio actual pagado por la mano de obra y el precio estándar de mano de obra en la cantidad utilizada actualmente. (p. 523)

Labor quantity standard *Cantidad estándar de mano de obra* La cantidad estimada de mano de obra directa necesaria para fabricar una unidad de producción. También referido como el *estándar de productividad de mano de obra.* (p. 519)

Labor quantity variance *Variación en la cantidad de mano de obra* La diferencia entre la cantidad actual de mano de obra utilizada durante la fabricación y la cantidad estándar de mano de obra por el nivel de producción al precio estándar. (p. 523)

Last-in, first-out inventory costing method *Método de inventario de costos del último en entrar, primero en salir* Se usa el precio de la mercancía que se compra al último para calcular el costo de la mercancía que se vende primero. (p. 152)

Ledger *Libro mayor* Un grupo de cuentas. (p. 11)

Liability *Obligación* Una cantidad que debe un negocio. (p. 7)

Limited liability corporation *Corporación con responsabilidad legal limitada* El tipo de corporación que no paga impuestos sobre sus ganancias. Las ganancias son divididas entre sus miembros y solamente son sujetas a impuestos en las declaraciones de impuestos personales de los miembros, así eliminando la desventaja de tributación doble. También conocido como *LLC.* (p. 298)

Line of credit *Línea de crédito* Un acuerdo de préstamo bancario que provee acceso inmediato de corto plazo a efectivo. (p. 240)

Liquidation of a partnership *Disolución de una sociedad* El proceso de pagar las obligaciones de la sociedad y distribuir los activos restantes entre los socios. (p. 658)

Lower of cost or market inventory costing method *Método de inventario de costo de mercado del menor costo* Utilizando el más bajo del costo o del valor de mercado para calcular el costo del inventario final de mercancías. (p. 157)

M

Marginal tax rate *Índice de impuestos marginal* El índice de impuestos asociado con una tabla de impuestos. (p. 104)

Market value of a share of stock *Valor de mercado de una unidad de acción* El precio al cual una acción pude ser vendida en la bolsa de valores en cualquier momento. (p. 388)

Materials ledger *Libro mayor de materiales* Un libro mayor que contiene todos los registros de los materiales. (p. 497)

Materials price standard *Precio estándar de materia prima* El costo estimado de cada unidad de materia prima directa. (p. 519)

Materials price variance *Variación en precio de material* La diferencia entre el precio actual pagado por materiales y el precio estándar de materiales en la cantidad comprada y utilizada actualmente. (p. 521)

Materials quantity standard *Calidad de material estándar* El costo estimado de materia prima directa utilizada por cada unidad producida. (p. 519)

Materials quantity variance *Variación en la calidad de material* La diferencia entre la cantidad actual de materiales comprados y utilizados durante la fabricación y la cantidad estándar de materiales por el nivel de producción al precio estándar. (p. 521)

Maturity date *Fecha de vencimiento* La fecha en la cual el capital de un pagaré se debe pagar. (p. 236)

Maturity value *Valor de vencimiento* La cantidad que se debe en la fecha de vencimiento de un pagaré. (p. 239)

Merchandising business *Negocio mercantil* Un negocio que compra y revende bienes. (p. 13)

Millage rate *Tasa de la milésima* La tasa de impuestos utilizada para calcular los impuestos de propiedad. (p. 203)

Modified Accelerated Cost Recovery System (MACRS) *Sistema Modificado de Recuperación Acelerada de Costo (MACRS)* Un método de depreciación requerida por el Servicio de Impuestos Internos que se utiliza para el propósito de calcular los impuestos sobre los ingresos de la mayoría de los activos fijos. (p. 220)

Modified half-year convention *Convención de medio año modificado* Un método que reconoce la depreciación de un año completo si el activo se adquiere en la primera mitad del año. (p. 207)

Monitoring *Monitorear* El proceso que utiliza la gerencia para determinar si sus políticas están funcionando eficazmente. (p. 593)

Mutual agency *Agencia mutualista* El derecho de todos los socios de solicitar una sociedad. (p. 624)

N

Narrative *Narrativa* Una descripción por escrito de la circulación de documentos e información entre empleados, departamentos, y personas exteriores. (p. 597)

Net cash flows *Flujo de caja neto* La diferencia entre los recibos y pagos de efectivo. (p. 548)

Net present value *Valor actual neto* La diferencia entre el valor actual de los flujos de efectivo de la inversión y la cantidad de la inversión. (p. 548)

Net realizable value *Valor neto realizable* Véase *Valor contable.*

Noninterest-bearing note *Pagaré sin intereses* Un pagaré que resta el interés del valor nominal del pagaré. (p. 239)

No-par-value stock *Acción sin valor nominal* Una acción que no indica un valor autorizado en el certificado de acciones. (p. 297)

Notes payable *Pagarés pendientes* Pagarés firmados por un negocio y otorgados a un acreedor. (p. 236)

Not-for-profit organization *Organización sin fines de lucro* Una organización que provee bienes o servicios sin ningún motivo deliberado o alguna expectativa de generar una ganancia. (p. 672)

G-14

O

Occupational fraud *Fraude ocupacional* El robo de activos del negocio por parte de un empleado. También se le refiere como *desfalco* o *apropiación indebida de activos.* (p. 593)

Operating activities *Actividades operativas* Los recibos de efectivo y pagos necesarios para operar un negocio día a día. (p. 115)

Operating budget *Presupuesto operativo* Un plan de gastos actuales y los recursos sugeridos para financiar esos gastos. (p. 678)

Operating margin *Margen operativo* Los ingresos operativos como un porcentaje de las ventas netas. (p. 379)

Other revenue and expenses budget *Presupuesto de otros gastos e ingresos* Una declaración que muestra los ingresos y gastos presupuestados de las actividades que no son parte de las operaciones normales. (p. 442)

Overapplied overhead *Gastos fijos sobre aplicados* La cantidad por la cual los gastos fijos de fábrica son más que los gastos fijos actuales de fábrica. (p. 510)

Owners' equity *Capital propio* La cantidad que queda después que el valor de las obligaciones es restada del valor de los activos. (p. 7)

Owners' equity statement *Estado de cuenta de capital propio* Un estado financiero que resume los cambios en el capital propio durante un período fiscal. (p. 654)

P

Par value *Valor nominal* Un valor asignado a una acción e impreso en el certificado de acciones. (p. 296)

Partnership *Sociedad* Un negocio en el cual dos o más personas combinan sus activos y sus habilidades. (p. 296)

Partnership agreement *Convenio de sociedad* Un acuerdo por escrito que establece las condiciones bajo las cuales opera una sociedad. También conocido como *los artículos de sociedad.* (p. 624)

Par-value stock *Acción con valor nominal* Una unidad de acción que tiene valor nominal. (p. 298)

Pay period *Período de pago* El número de días o semanas laborales cubiertas en un cheque de nómina del empleado. (p. 64)

Payroll *Nómina* La cantidad total que ganan todos los empleados durante un período de pago. (p. 64)

Payroll register *Registro de nomina* Un formulario de contabilidad que resume las ganancias, deducciones, y pago neto de todos los empleados por un período de pago. (p. 68)

Payroll taxes *Impuestos de nómina* Impuestos basados en la nómina de un negocio. (p. 64)

Performance report *Informe de desempeño* Un informe que muestra la comparación de las cantidades proyectadas y las actuales de un período específico. (p. 453)

Permanent difference *Diferencia permanente* Una diferencia entre los ingresos netos y los ingresos sujetos a impuestos solamente por aquel año que no es balanceado en un año futuro. (p. 391)

Personal property *Propiedad personal* Toda la propiedad no clasificada como propiedad inmueble. (p. 203)

Petty cash *Caja chica* Una cantidad de efectivo que se tiene a la mano y se usa para hacer pagos menores. (p. 25)

Plant asset record *Registro de activo fijo* Un formulario de contabilidad en el cual se registra la información de cada activo fijo de un negocio. (p. 203)

Plant assets *Activos fijos* Activos físicos que se usarán durante un número de años en la operación de un negocio. (p. 102)

Point-of-sale (POS) terminal *Terminal de punto de venta* Un computadora especializada que se usa para recolectar, guardar, y reportar toda la información de una transacción de venta. (p. 49)

Post-closing trial balance *Balance de comprobación posterior al cierre* Un balance de comprobación preparado después de pasar los asientos de cierre. (p. 120)

Posting *Pasar asientos* Transferir información de las transacciones de un asiento diario a una cuenta del libro mayor. (p. 15)

Preferred stock *Acción preferente* Un tipo de acción que les da preferencia a los accionistas privilegiados sobre los accionistas comunes en cuanto a los dividendos y otros derechos. (p. 296)

Prepaid expense *Gasto pre pagado* Efectivo pagado por un gasto en un período fiscal el cual no es utilizado hasta otro período después. (p. 242)

Present value *Valor actual* El valor actual de un pago o recibo de efectivo en el futuro. (p. 544)

Present value of an annuity *Valor actual de una anualidad* La cantidad invertida a una tasa de interés determinada que sustenta los pagos de una anualidad. (p. 546)

Price-earnings ratio *Índice de ganancias sobre precio* La relación entre el valor de mercado por acción y las ganancias por acción de una inversión. (p. 388)

Prime interest rate *Tase de interés preferencial* La tasa de interés que se les cobra a los clientes más dignos de crédito de un banco. (p. 240)

Principal *Principal* La cantidad original de una pagaré. (p. 236)

Privately held corporation *Corporación privada* Una corporación de la cual son dueños un pequeño número de individuos. (p. 303)

Process costing *Costeo del proceso* Calculando el costo de fabricación de bienes similares mientras se mueven continuamente de un proceso de fabricación a otra. (p. 497)

Product-level costs *Costo al nivel de producto* Los recursos utilizados para sustentar toda la línea de fabricación. (p. 568)

Promissory note *Pagaré* Una promesa por escrito y firmado para pagar una suma de dinero a una fecha específica. (p. 236)

Proprietary fund *Fondo propietario* Un fondo que justifica las transacciones financieras de una agencia gubernamental la cual opera como una empresa con fines de lucro. (p. 712)

Proprietorship *Empresa de propietario único* Un negocio cuyo dueño es una sola persona. (p. 298)

Publicly held corporation *Corporación públicamente comercializada* Una corporación cuyas acciones son cotizadas en las bolsas de valores. (p. 303)

Purchase order *Orden de compra* Un documento que solicita que un proveedor le venda mercancía a un negocio. (p. 602)

Purchases budget *Presupuesto de compras* Una declaración que muestra la cantidad de compras proyectadas que serán requeridas durante el período presupuestado. (p. 437)

Purchases discount *Descuento de compras* Cuando una compañía que compra mercancía a cuenta toma un descuento de efectivo. (p. 20)

Q

Quick assets *Activos realizables* Efectivo y otros activos actuales que se pueden convertir rápidamente en efectivo. (p. 374)

Quick ratio *Índice de realización* Un índice que mide la relación de los activos realizables a las responsabilidades actuales. (p. 374)

R

Rate earned on average stockholders' equity *Índice ganado sobre el promedio de capital del accionista* La relación entre los ingresos netos y el promedio del capital del accionista. (p. 382)

Rate earned on average total assets *Índice ganado sobre el promedio del total de activos* La relación entre los ingresos netos y el promedio del total de activos. (p. 381)

Real property *Propiedad de inmuebles* Terreno y cualquier cosa unida al terreno; también llamado *bienes raíces*. (p. 203)

Realization *Ganancia* Efectivo recibido de la venta de activos durante la disolución de una sociedad. (p. 658)

Receiving report *Informe de recibido* Un formulario que muestra los artículos recibidos de un proveedor. (p. 602)

Reclassification entry *Asiento de reclasificación* Un asiento que transfiere saldos entre cuentas en un solo informe financiero. (p. 276)

Recording *asentar* El asiento de una transacción en los registros financieros. (p. 594)

Registration statement *Declaración de registro* El documento presentado a la SEC para obtener permiso de vender valores en la bolsa de valores. (p. 303)

Relevant costs *Costos relevantes* Los costos que son diferentes entre dos opciones. (p. 534)

Relevant revenues *Ingresos relevantes* Los ingresos que son diferentes entre dos opciones. (p. 534)

Requisition *Requisición* Un documento solicitando la compra de mercancía. (p. 602)

Responsibility accounting *Contabilidad por áreas de responsabilidad* La asignación de control de ingresos, costos, y gastos a un gerente en particular. (p. 108)

Responsibility statements *Declaraciones por áreas de responsabilidad* Declaraciones financieras que informan sobre los ingresos, costos, y gastos directos que están bajo el control de un departamento en particular. (p. 109)

Retail method of estimating inventory *Método ventas al detalle para estimar inventario* La estimación de inventario utilizando un porcentaje basado en costos y precios minoristas. (p. 160)

Retained earnings *Ganancias retenidas* Una cantidad que gana una corporación y aún no ha sido distribuida entre los accionistas. (p. 113)

Retiring a bond issue *Retirar la emisión de un bono* El pago de la cantidad adeudada al tenedor de bonos por la emisión de un bono. (p. 350)

Reversing entry *Asiento revertido* Un asiento hecho al principio de un período fiscal para revertir un asiento de ajuste hecho en el período fiscal anterior. (p. 244)

Risk assessment *Evaluación de riesgo* El proceso de determinar si pudiera ocurrir un error o fraude. (p. 593)

S

Salary *Sueldo* Una suma fija de dinero dividida igualmente entre los períodos de pago. (p. 64)

Sales budget *Presupuesto de ventas* Una declaración que muestra las ventas netas proyectadas durante el período presupuestado. (p. 436)

Sales discount *Descuento de venta* Un descuento en el precio de una venta por el cliente. (p. 47)

Sales mix *Ventas mixtas* La distribución relativa de ventas entre varios productos. (p. 485)

Salvage value *Valor de recuperación* La cantidad que será recibida por un activo al tiempo de su eliminación. (p. 205)

Schedule of accounts payable *Plan de cuentas por pagar* Una lista de cuentas de proveedores, saldos de las cuentas, y la cantidad total que se debe a todos los proveedores. A esto algunos negocios le llaman balance de comprobación de cuentas por pagar. (p. 97)

Schedule of accounts receivable *Plan de cuentas por cobrar* Una lista de cuentas de clientes, saldos de las cuentas y la cantidad total que deben todos los clientes. (p. 97)

Segregation of duties *División de responsabilidades* La división de tareas del sistema de contabilidad entre empleados con diferentes funciones. (p. 594)

Selling expenses budget *Presupuesto de los gastos de ventas* Una declaración que muestra las proyecciones de gastos directamente relacionados con las operaciones de ventas. (p. 439)

Serial bonds *Bonos de vencimiento escalonado* Porciones de una emisión de bonos que se vencen en fechas diferentes. (p. 350)

Share of stock *Unidad de acción* Una unidad de titularidad en una corporación. (p. 294)

Source document *Documento original* Un documento de negocios del cual se obtiene información para asentar en un diario. (p. 7)

Special journal *Diario especial* Un diario que se usa para registrar solamente un tipo de transacción. (p. 8)

Split-off point *Punto de separación* El punto en el cual los productos conjuntos son separables en productos identificables. (p. 538)

Standard *Estándar* Una cantidad estimada por lo general en precio o cantidad de materia prima directa o mano de obra directa, establecida por cada unidad fabricada. (p. 519)

Standard costing system *Sistema de costeo estándar* Un sistema de establecer estándares por cada unidad de producción. (p. 519)

Stated interest rate *Tasa de interés especificada* La tasa de interés que se usa para calcular los pagos de interés periódicos de un bono. (p. 343)

Stated-value stock *Acción de valor contable* Acciones sin valor nominal a las cuales una corporación les asigna un valor. Una acción de valor contable es similar a una acción de valor nominal con la excepción de que el valor no está indicado en los certificados. (p. 297)

Statement of cash flows *Declaración de flujo de efectivo* Un estado financiero que resume os recibos y pagos de efectivo que resultan de las actividades de negocios durante un período fiscal. (p. 115)

Statement of cost of goods manufactured *Declaración del costo de bienes fabricados* Una declaración que muestra los detalles sobre el costo de bienes terminados (p. 515)

Statement of revenues, expenditures, and changes in fund balance *Declaración de ingresos, gastos, y cambios en el balance de fondos* Una declaración que informa las fuentes de ingresos y los gastos de los fondos de una agencia gubernamental. (p. 676)

Statement of stockholders' equity *Estado financiero del capital de accionistas* Un estado financiero que muestra los cambios en la titularidad de una corporación durante un período fiscal. (p. 113)

Stock certificate *Certificado de acciones* Evidencia por escrito del número de acciones que tiene cada accionista en una corporación. (p. 296)

Stock dividend *Dividendo en acciones* El pago de dividendos con acciones de la compañía. (p. 321)

Stock ledger *Libro mayor de inventario* Un archivo para el registro del inventario de la mercancía a la mano. (p. 147)

Stock record *Registro de existencias* Un documento que se usa para mostrar la clase de mercancía, cantidad recibida, cantidad vendida y cantidad a la mano. (p. 147)

Stockholder *Accionista* Dueño de una o más acciones en una corporación. (p. 294)

Stockholders' equity *Capital del accionista* El capital propio de un dueño en una corporación. (p. 7)

Straight-line method of depreciation *Método de depreciación de línea directa* El registro de una cantidad igual de gasto de depreciación para un activo fijo en cada año de su vida útil. (p. 206)

Subsidiary ledger *Libro mayor auxiliar* Un libro mayor que esta resumida en una sola cuenta del libro mayor general. (p. 11)

Sunk cost *Costo hundido* Un gasto que ocurrió en el pasado y no se puede recuperar con una decisión en el futuro. (p. 534)

T

Target costing *Costeo objetivo* Un método de establecer un precio por un producto o servicio basado en el precio que el consumidor está dispuesto a pagar, y controlar el precio de los productos para que la compañía todavía pueda generar una ganancia. (p. 575)

Tax base *Base de impuestos* La cantidad máxima de ganancias sobre la cual se calculan los impuestos. (p. 65)

Tax bracket *Escala contributiva* Cada índice de impuestos e ingresos sujetos a impuestos en una sola línea de una tabla de impuestos. (p. 104)

Tax levy *Recaudación de impuestos* La acción autorizada por una agencia de gobierno para cobrar impuestos por medio de una autoridad legal. (p. 683)

Temporary difference *Diferencia temporal* Una diferencia entre los ingresos netos y los ingresos sujetos a impuestos por más de un período, la cual se equilibra con el paso completo del período. (p. 391)

Term bonds *Bonos a plazo* Bonos que se vencen en la misma fecha. (p. 350)

Terminal summary *Resumen de terminal* El informe que resume las ventas en efectivo y de crédito de una terminal de punto de venta. (p. 49)

Time value of money *Valor del dinero con el tiempo* La expectativa de que el dinero invertido crecerá con el paso del tiempo. (p. 540)

Total costs *Gasto total* Todos los gastos de un período de tiempo específico. (p. 469)

Total labor variance *Variación de mano de obra total* La diferencia entre el costo actual de mano de obra y el costo estándar anticipado de mano de obra. (p. 522)

Total materials variance *Variación del material total* La diferencia entre el costo actual de materiales y el costo estándar anticipado de materiales. (p. 520)

Treasury stock *Acciones de tesorería* Las acciones propias de una corporación que han sido emitidas y readquiridas. (p. 325)

Trial balance *Balance de comprobación* Una prueba de la igualdad de débitos y créditos en el libro mayor general. (p. 98)

U

Unadjusted trial balance *Balance de comprobación no ajustado*Un balance de comprobación antes de que los asientos de ajuste sean registrados. (p. 98)

Uncollectible accounts *Cuentas incobrables* Cuentas por cobrar que no pueden ser cobradas. (p. 174)

Underapplied overhead *Ajuste de gastos fijos* La cantidad por la cual los gastos fijos de fábrica es menor que los gastos fijos actuales de fábrica. (p. 510)

Unearned revenue *Ingreso no ganados* Efectivo recibido por bienes y servicios que aún no han sido proveídos. (p. 264)

Unit cost *Costo por unidad* La cantidad gastada por una unidad de un producto o servicio específico. (p. 469)

Unit-level costs *Costos a nivel de unidad* Los recursos utilizados en las actividades relacionadas con cada unidad individual fabricada. (p. 568)

Units-of-production method of depreciation *Método de depreciación por unidades de fabricación* Calculando el gasto estimado de la depreciación anual basado en la cantidad de producción anticipada de un activo fijo. (p. 219)

V

Value-based pricing *Fijación de precios según valor* Un método para establecer el precio de un producto o servicio basado en el valor que tiene el producto o servicio para el consumidor. (p. 575)

Variable costs *Costos variables* Los costos que cambian en proporción directa con un cambio en el número de unidades. (p. 470)

Vertical analysis *Análisis vertical* Reportar una cantidad en un estado financiero como un porcentaje de otro artículo en el mismo estado financiero. (p. 110)

Voucher *Comprobante* Una colección de documentos utilizados para autorizar un pago. (p. 601)

Voucher check *Comprobante de cheque* Un cheque que tiene un talón desprendible, o comprobante, que contiene información detallada sobre el pago de efectivo. (p. 605)

Voucher register *Registro de comprobantes* Un libro mayor utilizado para registrar comprobantes. (p. 603)

Voucher system *Sistema de comprobantes* Un conjunto de procedimientos para controlar pagos de efectivo al preparar y aprobar comprobantes antes de que se realicen los pagos. (p. 601)

W

Wage *Salario* La cantidad que se le paga a un empleado por cada hora laboral. (p. 64)

Weighted-average inventory costing method *Método de inventario de costo promedio* Utilizando el costo promedio del inventario inicial más las mercancías compradas durante un período fiscal para calcular el costo de la mercancía vendida. (p. 153)

Withholding allowance *Deducción en la retención de impuestos* Una deducción del ingreso total por cada persona legalmente mantenida por el contribuyente, incluyendo al empleado. (p. 65)

Work in process *Trabajo en proceso* Productos que están en el proceso de fabricación que todavía no han sido terminados. (p. 496)

Work sheet *Hoja de trabajo* Un formulario de contabilidad que contiene columnas que se usa para resumir la información del libro general mayor que es necesario para preparar estados financieros. (p. 106)

Working capital *Capital de trabajo* La cantidad del total de los activos actuales menos el total de las obligaciones actuales. (p. 373)

Writing off an account *Anulación de una cuenta* Cancelar el saldo de la cuenta de un cliente por incumplimiento de pago. (p. 174)

Index

A

B

C

E

F

G

H

I

I-6

L

M

N

I-8

I-9

S

T

I-10

Features Index

21st Century Skills

A Look at Accounting Software

Accounting In The Real World

Careers In Accounting

ETHICS IN ACTION

EXPLORE ACCOUNTING

FINANCIAL LITERACY

FORENSIC ACCOUNTING

GLOBAL AWARENESS

THINK LIKE AN ACCOUNTANT

I-13

WHY ACCOUNTING?

I-14